Collins *Gem*

Spanish
Dictionary

Spanish▸English English▸Spanish

Grijalbo

Collins Gem

An Imprint of HarperCollinsPublishers

sixth edition 2004

© William Collins Sons & Co. Ltd. 1982, 1989
© HarperCollins Publishers 1993, 1998, 2001, 2004

HarperCollins Publishers
Westerhill Road, Bishopbriggs, Glasgow G64 2QT
Great Britain

www.collinsdictionaries.com

Collins Gem® and Bank of English® are registered
trademarks of HarperCollins Publishers Limited

ISBN 0-00-712625-5

Grupo Editorial Random House Mondadori, S.L.
Travessera de Gràcia 47-49, 08021 Barcelona

www.diccionarioscollins.com

ISBN 84-253-3823-9

A catalogue record for this book is available from the British Library

Typeset by Thomas Callan

Printed by Legoprint S.P.A.

ÍNDICE

CONTENTS

general editor/dirección general
Michela Clari

contributors/colaboradores
José Martín Galera, Wendy Lee, José María Ruiz Vaca

editorial coordination/coordinación editorial
Joyce Littlejohn, Marianne Davidson, Maree Airlie

series editor/colección dirigida por
Lorna Sinclair Knight

Introducción

Estamos muy satisfechos de que hayas decidido comprar este diccionario y esperamos que lo disfrutes y que te sirva de gran ayuda ya sea en el colegio, en el trabajo, en tus vacaciones o en casa.

Esta introducción pretende darte algunas indicaciones para ayudarte a sacar el mayor provecho de este diccionario; no sólo de su extenso vocabulario, sino de toda la información que te proporciona cada entrada. Esta te ayudará a leer y comprender – y también a comunicarte y a expresarte – en inglés moderno. Este diccionario comienza con una lista de abreviaturas utilizadas en el texto y con una ilustración de los sonidos representados por los símbolos fonéticos. Al final del diccionario encontrarás una tabla de los verbos irregulares del inglés, y para terminar, una sección sobre el uso de los números y de las expresiones de tiempo.

El manejo de tu diccionario

La amplia información que te ofrece este diccionario aparece presentada en distintas tipografías, con caracteres de diversos tamaños y con distintos símbolos, abreviaturas y paréntesis. Los apartados siguientes explican las reglas y símbolos utilizados.

Entradas

Las palabras que consultas en el diccionario – las "entradas" – aparecen ordenadas alfabéticamente y en **caracteres gruesos** para una identificación más rápida. Las dos palabras que ocupan el margen superior de cada página indican la primera y la última entrada de la página en cuestión.

La información sobre el uso o la forma de determinadas entradas aparece entre paréntesis, detrás de la transcripción fonética, y generalmente en forma abreviada y en cursiva (p. ej.: (*fam*), (*COM*)). En algunos casos se ha considerado oportuno agrupar palabras de una misma familia (**nación**, ❏ **nacionalismo**; **accept**, ❏ **acceptance**) bajo una misma entrada en caracteres gruesos.

Las expresiones de uso corriente en las que aparece una entrada se dan en negrita (p. ej.: **hurry**: [...] **to be in a ~**).

Símbolos fonéticos

La transcripción fonética de cada entrada inglesa (que indica su pronunciación) aparece entre corchetes, inmediatamente después de la entrada (p. ej. **knead** [ni:d]). En la página xiii encontrarás una lista de los símbolos fonéticos utilizados en este diccionario.

Traducciones

Las traducciones de las entradas aparecen en caracteres normales, y en los casos en los que existen significados o usos diferentes, éstos aparecen separados mediante un punto y coma. A menudo encontrarás también otras palabras en cursiva y entre paréntesis antes de las traducciones. Estas sugieren contextos en los que la entrada podría aparecer (p. ej.: **rough** (*voice*) o (*weather*)) o proporcionan sinónimos (p. ej.: **rough** (*violent*)).

Palabras clave

Particular relevancia reciben ciertas palabras inglesas y españolas que han sido consideradas palabras "clave" en cada lengua. Estas pueden, por ejemplo, ser de utilización muy corriente o tener distintos usos (**de, haber; get, that**). La combinación de rombos y números te permitirá distinguir las diferentes categorías gramaticales y los diferentes significados. Las indicaciones en cursiva y entre paréntesis proporcionan además importante información adicional.

Información gramatical

Las categorías gramaticales aparecen en forma abreviada y en cursiva después de la transcripción fonética de cada entrada (*vt, adv, conj*). También se indican la forma femenina y los plurales irregulares de los sustantivos del inglés (**child, -ren**).

Introduction

We are delighted that you have decided to buy this dictionary and hope you will enjoy and benefit from using it at school, at home, on holiday or at work.

This introduction gives you a few tips on how to get the most out of your dictionary – not simply from its comprehensive wordlist but also from the information provided in each entry. This will help you to read and understand modern Spanish, as well as communicate and express yourself in the language.

This dictionary begins by listing the abbreviations used in the text and illustrating the sounds shown by the phonetic symbols. You will also find Spanish verb tables, followed by a final section on numbers and time expressions.

Using your dictionary

A wealth of information is presented in the dictionary, using various typefaces, sizes of type, symbols, abbreviations and brackets. The various conventions and symbols used are explained in the following sections.

Headwords

The words you look up in a dictionary – "headwords" – are listed alphabetically. They are printed in **bold type** for rapid identification. The two headwords appearing at the top of each page indicate the first and last word dealt with on the page in question.

Information about the usage or form of certain headwords is given in brackets after the phonetic spelling. This usually appears in abbreviated form and in italics (e.g. (*fam*), (*COMM*)).

Where appropriate, words related to headwords are grouped in the same entry (**nación**, ▢ **nacionalismo; accept**, ▢ **acceptance**) and preceded by a white box. Common expressions in which the headword appears are shown in a different bold roman type (e.g. **cola**: [...] **hacer ~**).

Phonetic spellings

The phonetic spelling of each headword (indicating its pronunciation) is given in square brackets immediately after the headword (e.g. **cohete** [ko'ete]). A list of these symbols is given on page xi.

Translations

Headword translations are given in ordinary type and, where more than one meaning or usage exists, these are separated by a semi-colon. You will often find other words in italics in brackets before the translations. These offer suggested contexts in which the headword might appear (e.g. **grande** (*de tamaño*)) or provide synonyms (e.g. **grande** (*alto*) o (*distinguido*)).

The gender of the translation also appears in *italics* immediately following the key element of the translation, except where this is a regular masculine singular noun ending in "o", or a regular feminine noun ending in "a".

"Key" words

Special status is given to certain Spanish and English words which are considered as "key" words in each language. They may, for example, occur very frequently or have several types of usage (e.g. **de**, **haber**; **get**, **that**). A combination of lozenges and numbers helps you to distinguish different parts of speech and different meanings. Further helpful information is provided in brackets and italics.

Grammatical information

Parts of speech are given in abbreviated form in italics after the phonetic spellings of headwords (e.g. *vt*, *adv*, *conj*).

Genders of Spanish nouns are indicated as follows: *nm* for a masculine and *nf* for a feminine noun. Feminine and irregular plural forms of nouns are also shown (**irlandés**, **esa**; **luz**, (*pl* **luces**)).

Abreviaturas		Abbreviations
abreviatura	*ab(b)r*	abbreviation
adjetivo, locución adjetiva	*adj*	adjective, adjectival phrase
administración	*ADMIN*	administration
adverbio, locución adverbial	*adv*	adverb, adverbial phrase
agricultura	*AGR*	agriculture
anatomía	*ANAT*	anatomy
Argentina	*ARG*	Argentina
arquitectura	*ARQ, ARCH*	architecture
el automóvil	*AUT(O)*	the motor car and motoring
aviación, viajes aéreos	*AVIAC, AVIAT*	flying, air travel
biología	*BIO(L)*	biology
botánica, flores	*BOT*	botany
inglés británico	*BRIT*	British English
Centroamérica	*CAm*	Central America
química	*CHEM*	chemistry
comercio, finanzas, banca	*COM(M)*	commerce, finance, banking
informática	*COMPUT*	computing
conjunción	*conj*	conjunction
construcción	*CONSTR*	building
compuesto	*cpd*	compound element
Cono Sur	*CS*	Southern Cone
cocina	*CULIN*	cookery
economía	*ECON*	economics
eletricidad, electrónica	*ELEC*	electricity, electronics
enseñanza, sistema escolar y universitario	*ESCOL*	schooling, schools and universities
España	*ESP*	Spain
especialmente	*esp*	especially
exclamación, interjección	*excl*	exclamation, interjection
femenino	*f*	feminine
lengua familiar (! vulgar)	*fam(!)*	colloquial usage (! particularly offensive)
ferrocarril	*FERRO*	railways
uso figurado	*fig*	figurative use

viii

fotografía	FOTO	photography
(verbo inglés) del cual la	fus	(phrasal verb) where
partícula es inseparable		the particle is inseparable
generalmente	gen	generally
geografía, geología	GEO	geography, geology
geometría	GEOM	geometry
historia	HIST	history
uso familiar (! vulgar)	inf(!)	colloquial usage
		(! particularly offensive)
infinitivo	infin	infinitive
informática	INFORM	computing
invariable	inv	invariable
irregular	irreg	irregular
lo jurídico	JUR	law
América Latina	LAm	Latin America
gramática, lingüística	LING	grammar, linguistics
masculino	m	masculine
matemáticas	MAT(H)	mathematics
masculino/femenino	m/f	masculine/feminine
medicina	MED	medicine
México	MÉX, MEX	Mexico
lo militar, ejército	MIL	military matters
música	MÚS, MUS	music
substantivo, nombre	n	noun
navegación, náutica	NÁUT, NAUT	sailing, navigation
sustantivo numérico	num	numeral noun
complemento	obj	(grammatical) object
	o.s.	oneself
peyorativo	pey, pej	derogatory, pejorative
fotografía	PHOT	photography
fisiología	PHYSIOL	physiology
plural	pl	plural
política	POL	politics
participio de pasado	pp	past participle
preposición	prep	preposition
pronombre	pron	pronoun
psicología, psiquiatría	PSICO, PSYCH	psychology, psychiatry
tiempo pasado	pt	past tense

química	QUÍM	chemistry
ferrocarril	RAIL	railways
religión	REL	religion
Río de la Plata	RPI	River Plate
	sb	somebody
Cono Sur	SC	Southern Cone
enseñanza, sistema escolar y universitario	SCOL	schooling, schools and universities
singular	sg	singular
España	SP	Spain
	sth	something
sujeto	su(bj)	(grammatical) subject
subjuntivo	subjun	subjunctive
tauromaquia	TAUR	bullfighting
también	tb	also
técnica, tecnología	TEC(H)	technical term, technology
telecomunicaciones	TELEC,TEL	telecommunications
imprenta, tipografía	TIP,TYP	typography, printing
televisión	TV	television
universidad	UNIV	university
inglés norteamericano	US	American English
verbo	vb	verb
verbo intransitivo	vi	intransitive verb
verbo pronominal	vr	reflexive verb
verbo transitivo	vt	transitive verb
zoología	ZOOL	zoology
marca registrada	®	registered trademark
indica un equivalente cultural	≈	introduces a cultural equivalent

Spanish Pronunciation

VOWELS

a	[a]	p**a**ta	not as long as **a** in f**a**r. When followed by a consonant in the same syllable (i.e. in a closed syllable), as in am**a**nte, the **a** is short, as in b**a**t
e	[e]	m**e**	like **e** in th**e**y. In a closed syllable, as in g**e**nte, the **e** is short as in p**e**t
i	[i]	p**i**no	as in m**ea**n or mach**i**ne
o	[o]	l**o**	as in l**o**cal. In a closed syllable, as in c**o**ntrol, the **o** is short as in c**o**t
u	[u]	l**u**nes	as in r**u**le. It is silent after **q**, and in **gue**, **gui**, unless marked **güe**, **güi** e.g. antig**ü**edad, when it is pronounced like **w** in **w**olf

SEMIVOWELS

i, y	[j]	b**i**en h**i**elo **y**unta	pronounced like **y** in **y**es
u	[w]	h**u**evo f**u**ento antig**ü**edad	unstressed **u** between consonant and vowel is pronounced like **w** in **w**ell. See notes on **u** above.

DIPHTHONGS

ai, ay	[ai]	b**ai**le	as **i** in r**i**de
au	[au]	**au**to	as **ou** in sh**ou**t
ei, ey	[ei]	b**uey**	as **ey** in gr**ey**
eu	[eu]	d**eu**da	both elements pronounced independently [e] + [u]
oi, oy	[oi]	h**oy**	as **oy** in t**oy**

CONSONANTS

b	[b, β]	**b**oda **b**omba la**b**or	see notes on **v** below
c	[k]	**c**aja	**c** before **a**, **o** or **u** is pronounced as in **c**at
ce, ci	[θi, θe]	**c**ero **c**ielo	**c** before **e** or **i** is pronounced as in **th**in

xi

ch	[tʃ]	**ch**iste	**ch** is pronounced as **ch** in **ch**air
d	[d, ð]	**d**anés	at the beginning of a phrase or after **l** or **n**, **d** is pronounced as in English. In any other position it is pronounced like **th** in **the**
		ciu**d**ad	
g	[g, ɣ]	**g**afas	**g** before **a**, **o** or **u** is pronounced as in **g**ap, if at the beginning of a phrase or after **n**. In other positions the sound is softened
		pa**g**a	
ge, gi	[xe, xi]	**g**ente	**g** before **e** or **i** is pronounced similar to **ch** in Scottish lo**ch**
		girar	
h		**h**aber	**h** is always silent in Spanish
j	[x]	**j**ugar	**j** is pronounced similar to **ch** in Scottish lo**ch**
ll	[ʎ]	ta**ll**e	**ll** is pronounced like the **lli** in mi**lli**on
ñ	[ɲ]	ni**ñ**o	**ñ** is pronounced like the **ni** in o**ni**on
q	[k]	**q**ue	**q** is pronounced as **k** in **k**ing
r, rr	[r, rr]	quita**r**	**r** is always pronounced in Spanish, unlike the silent **r** in dance**r**. **rr** is trilled, like a Scottish **r**
		ga**rr**a	
s	[s]	quizá**s**	**s** is usually pronounced as in pa**ss**, but before **b**, **d**, **g**, **l**, **m** or **n** it is pronounced as in ro**s**e
		i**s**la	
v	[b, β]	**v**ía	**v** is pronounced something like **b**. At the beginning of a phrase or after **m** or **n** it is pronounced as **b** in **b**oy. In any other position the sound is softened
z	[θ]	tena**z**	**z** is pronounced as **th** in **th**in

f, k, l, m, n, p, t and **x** are pronounced as in English.

STRESS

The rules of stress in Spanish are as follows:

(a) when a word ends in a vowel or in **n** or **s**, the second last syllable is stressed: pa**ta**ta, pa**ta**tas, **co**me, **co**men

(b) when a word ends in a consonant other than **n** or **s**, the stress falls on the last syllable: pa**red**, ha**blar**

(c) when the rules set out in (a) and (b) are not applied, an acute accent appears over the stressed vowel: co**mún**, geogra**fía**, in**glés**

In the phonetic transcription, the symbol ['] precedes the syllable on which the stress falls.

La pronunciación inglesa

VOCALES

	Ejemplo inglés	Explicación
[ɑː]	father	Entre *a* de p*a*dre y *o* de n*o*che
[ʌ]	but, come	*a* muy breve
[æ]	man, cat	Con los labios en la posición de *e* en p*e*na y luego se pronuncia el sonido *a* parecido a la *a* de c*a*rro
[ə]	father, ago	Vocal neutra parecida a una *e* u *o* casi muda
[əː]	bird, heard	Entre *e* abierta, y *o* cerrada, sonido alargado
[ɛ]	get, bed	Como en p*e*rro
[ɪ]	it, big	Más breve que en s*i*
[iː]	tea, see	Como en f*í*no
[ɔ]	hot, wash	Como en t*o*rre
[ɔː]	saw, all	Como en p*o*r
[u]	put, book	Sonido breve, más cerrado que b*u*rro
[uː]	too, you	Sonido largo, como en *u*no

DIPTONGOS

	Ejemplo inglés	Explicación
[aɪ]	fly, high	Como en fr*ai*le
[au]	how, house	Como en p*au*sa
[ɛə]	there, bear	Casi como en v*ea*, pero el sonido *a* se mezcla con el indistinto [ə]
[eɪ]	day, obey	*e* cerrada seguida por una *i* débil
[ɪə]	here, hear	Como en man*ía*, mezclándose el sonido *a* con el indistinto [ə]
[əu]	go, note	[ə] seguido por una breve *u*
[ɔɪ]	boy, oil	Como en v*oy*
[uə]	poor, sure	*u* bastante larga más el sonido indistinto [ə]

CONSONANTES

	Ejemplo inglés	Explicación
[b]	**b**ig, lo**bb**y	Como en tum**b**an
[d]	men**d**ed	Como en con**d**e, an**d**ar
[g]	**g**o, **g**et, bi**g**	Como en **g**rande, **g**ol
[dʒ]	**g**in, **j**udge	Como en la **ll** andaluza y en **G**eneralitat (catalán)
[ŋ]	si**ng**	Como en ví**n**culo
[h]	**h**ouse, **h**e	Como la jota hispanoamericana
[j]	**y**oung, **y**es	Como en **y**a
[k]	**c**ome, mo**ck**	Como en **c**aña, Es**c**ocia
[r]	**r**ed, t**r**ead	Se pronuncia con la punta de la lengua hacia atrás y sin hacerla vibrar
[s]	**s**and, ye**s**	Como en ca**s**a, **s**e**s**ión
[z]	ro**s**e, **z**ebra	Como en de**s**de, mi**s**mo
[ʃ]	**sh**e, ma**ch**ine	Como en **ch**ambre (francés), ro**x**o (portugués)
[tʃ]	**ch**in, ri**ch**	Como en **ch**ocolate
[v]	**v**alley	Como en **f**, pero se retiran los dientes superiores vibrándolos contra el labio inferior
[w]	**w**ater, **wh**ich	Como la **u** de h**u**evo, p**u**ede
[ʒ]	vi**s**ion	Como en **j**ournal (francés)
[θ]	**th**ink, my**th**	Como en re**c**eta, **z**apato
[ð]	**th**is, **th**e	Como en habla**d**o, verda**d**

f, l, m, n, p, t iguales que en español

El signo [*] indica que la r final escrita apenas se pronuncia en inglés británico cuando la palabra siguiente empieza con vocal. El signo ['] indica la sílaba acentuada.

Spanish Verb Tables

1 Gerund 2 Imperative 3 Present 4 Preterite 5 Future 6 Present subjunctive 7 Imperfect subjunctive 8 Past participle 9 Imperfect *Etc* indicates that the irregular root is used for all persons of the tense, *e.g.* **oír:** 6 oiga, oigas, oigamos, oigáis, oigan

agradecer 3 agradezco 6 agradezca etc

aprobar 2 aprueba 3 apruebo, apruebas, aprueba, aprueban 6 apruebe, apruebes, apruebe, aprueben

atravesar 2 atraviesa 3 atravieso, atraviesas, atraviesa, atraviesan 6 atraviese, atravieses, atraviese, atraviesen

caber 3 quepo 4 cupe, cupiste, cupo, cupimos, cupisteis, cupieron 5 cabré etc 6 quepa etc 7 cupiera etc

caer 1 cayendo 3 caigo 4 cayó, cayeron 6 caiga etc 7 cayera etc

cerrar 2 cierra 3 cierro, cierras, cierra, cierran 6 cierre, cierres, cierre, cierren

COMER 1 comiendo 2 come, comed 3 como, comes, come, comemos, coméis, comen 4 comí, comiste, comió, comimos, comisteis, comieron 5 comeré, comerás, comerá, comeremos, comeréis, comerán 6 coma, comas, coma, comamos, comáis, coman 7 comiera, comieras, comiera, comiéramos, comierais, comieran 8 comido 9 comía, comías, comía, comíamos, comíais, comían

conocer 3 conozco 6 conozca etc

contar 2 cuenta 3 cuento, cuentas, cuenta, cuentan 6 cuente, cuentes, cuente, cuenten

dar 3 doy 4 di, diste, dio, dimos, disteis, dieron 7 diera etc

decir 2 di 3 digo 4 dije, dijiste, dijo, dijimos, dijisteis, dijeron 5 diré etc 6 diga etc 7 dijera etc 8 dicho

despertar 2 despierta 3 despierto, despiertas, despierta, despiertan 6 despierte, despiertes, despierte, despierten

divertir 1 divirtiendo 2 divierte 3 divierto, diviertes, divierte, divierten 4 divirtió, divirtieron 6 divierta, diviertas, divierta, divirtamos, divirtáis, diviertan 7 divirtiera etc

dormir 1 durmiendo 2 duerme 3 duermo, duermes, duerme, duermen 4 durmió, durmieron 6 duerma, duermas, duerma, durmamos, durmáis, duerman 7 durmiera etc

empezar 2 empieza 3 empiezo, empiezas, empieza, empiezan 4 empecé 6 empiece, empieces, empiece, empecemos, empecéis, empiecen

entender 2 entiende 3 entiendo, entiendes, entiende, entienden 6 entienda, entiendas, entienda, entiendan

ESTAR 2 está 3 estoy, estás, está, están 4 estuve, estuviste, estuvo, estuvimos, estuvisteis, estuvieron 6 esté, estés, esté, estén 7 estuviera etc

HABER 3 he, has, ha, hemos, han hube, hubiste, hubo, hubimos, hubisteis, hubieron 5 habré etc 6 haya etc 7 hubiera etc

HABLAR 1 hablando 2 habla, hablad 3 hablo, hablas, habla, hablamos, habláis, hablan 4 hablé, hablaste, habló, hablamos, hablasteis, hablaron 5 hablaré, hablarás, hablará, hablaremos, hablaréis, hablarán 6 hable, hables, hable, hablemos, habléis, hablen 7 hablara, hablaras, hablara, habláramos, hablarais, hablaran 8 hablado 9 hablaba, hablabas, hablaba, hablábamos, hablabais, hablaban

hacer 2 haz 3 hago 4 hice, hiciste, hizo, hicimos, hicisteis, hicieron 5 haré etc 6 haga etc 7 hiciera etc 8 hecho

instruir 1 instruyendo 2 instruye 3 instruyo, instruyes, instruye, instruyen 4 instruyó, instruyeron 6 instruya etc 7 instruyera etc

ir 1 yendo 2 ve 3 voy, vas, va, vamos, vais, van 4 fui, fuiste, fue, fuimos, fuisteis, fueron 6 vaya, vayas, vaya, vayamos, vayáis, vayan 7 fuera etc 9 iba, ibas, iba, íbamos, ibais, iban

jugar 2 juega 3 juego, juegas, juega, juegan 4 jugué 6 juegue etc

leer 1 leyendo 4 leyó, leyeron 7 leyera etc

morir 1 muriendo 2 muere 3 muero, mueres, muere, mueren 4 murió, murieron 6 muera, mueras, muera, muramos, muráis, mueran 7 muriera etc 8 muerto

mover 2 mueve 3 muevo, mueves, mueve, mueven 6 mueva, muevas, mueva, muevan

negar 2 niega 3 niego, niegas, niega, niegan 4 negué 6 niegue, niegues, niegue, neguemos, neguéis, nieguen

ofrecer 3 ofrezco 6 ofrezca etc

oír 1 oyendo 2 oye 3 oigo, oyes, oye, oyen 4 oyó, oyeron 6 oiga etc 7 oyera etc

oler 2 huele 3 huelo, hueles, huele, huelen 6 huela, huelas, huela, huelan

parecer 3 parezco 6 parezca etc

pedir 1 pidiendo 2 pide 3 pido, pides, pide, piden 4 pidió, pidieron 6 pida etc 7 pidiera etc

pensar 2 piensa 3 pienso, piensas, piensa, piensan 6 piense, pienses, piense, piensen

perder 2 pierde 3 pierdo, pierdes, pierde, pierden 6 pierda, pierdas, pierda, pierdan

poder 1 pudiendo 2 puede 3 puedo, puedes, puede, pueden 4 pude, pudiste, pudo, pudimos, pudisteis, pudieron 5 podré etc 6 pueda, puedas, pueda, puedan 7 pudiera etc

poner 2 pon 3 pongo 4 puse, pusiste, puso, pusimos, pusisteis, pusieron 5 pondré etc 6 ponga etc 7 pusiera etc 8 puesto

preferir 1 prefiriendo 2 prefiere 3 prefiero, prefieres, prefiere, prefieren 4 prefirió, prefirieron 6 prefiera, prefieras, prefiera, prefiramos, prefiráis, prefieran 7 prefiriera etc

querer 2 quiere 3 quiero, quieres, quiere, quieren 4 quise, quisiste,
quiso, quisimos, quisisteis, quisieron 5 querré etc 6 quiera,
quieras, quiera, quieran 7 quisiera etc

reír 2 ríe 3 río, ríes, ríe, ríen 4 reí, rieron 6 ría, rías, ría, riamos, riáis,
rían 7 riera etc

repetir 1 repitiendo 2 repite 3 repito, repites, repite, repiten
4 repitió, repitieron 6 repita etc 7 repitiera etc

rogar 2 ruega 3 ruego, ruegas, ruega, ruegan 4 rogué 6 ruegue,
ruegues, ruegue, roguemos, roguéis, rueguen

saber 3 sé 4 supe, supiste, supo, supimos, supisteis, supieron
5 sabré etc 6 sepa etc 7 supiera etc

salir 2 sal 3 salgo 5 saldré etc 6 salga etc

seguir 1 siguiendo 2 sigue 3 sigo, sigues, sigue, siguen 4 siguió,
siguieron 6 siga etc 7 siguiera etc

sentar 2 sienta 3 siento, sientas, sienta, sientan 6 siente, sientes,
siente, sienten

sentir 1 sintiendo 2 siente 3 siento, sientes, siente, sienten 4 sintió,
sintieron 6 sienta, sientas, sienta, sintamos, sintáis, sientan 7 sintiera etc

SER 2 sé 3 soy, eres, es, somos, sois, son 4 fui, fuiste, fue, fuimos,
fuisteis, fueron 6 sea etc 7 fuera etc 9 era, eras, era, éramos, erais,
eran

servir 1 sirviendo 2 sirve 3 sirvo, sirves, sirve, sirven 4 sirvió,
sirvieron 6 sirva etc 7 sirviera etc

soñar 2 sueña 3 sueño, sueñas, sueña, sueñan 6 sueñe, sueñes,
sueñe, sueñen

tener 2 ten 3 tengo, tienes, tiene, tienen 4 tuve, tuviste, tuvo,
tuvimos, tuvisteis, tuvieron 5 tendré etc 6 tenga etc 7 tuviera etc

traer 1 trayendo 3 traigo 4 traje, trajiste, trajo, trajimos, trajisteis,
trajeron 6 traiga etc 7 trajera etc

valer 2 val 3 valgo 5 valdré etc 6 valga etc

venir 2 ven 3 vengo, vienes, viene, vienen 4 vine, viniste, vino,
vinimos, vinisteis, vinieron 5 vendré etc 6 venga etc 7 viniera etc

ver 3 veo 6 vea etc 8 visto 9 veía etc

vestir 1 vistiendo 2 viste 3 visto, vistes, viste, visten 4 vistió, vistieron 6
vista etc 7 vistiera etc

VIVIR 1 viviendo 2 vive, vivid 3 vivo, vives, vive, vivimos, vivís, viven 4 viví,
viviste, vivió, vivimos, vivisteis, vivieron 5 viviré, vivirás, vivirá, viviremos,
viviréis, vivirán 6 viva, vivas, viva, vivamos, viváis, vivan
7 viviera, vivieras, viviera, viviéramos, vivierais, vivieran 8 vivido
9 vivía, vivías, vivía, vivíamos, vivíais, vivían

volver 2 vuelve 3 vuelvo, vuelves, vuelve, vuelven 6 vuelva, vuelvas,
vuelva, vuelvan 8 vuelto

Verbos irregulares en inglés

presente	pasado	participio de pasado	presente	pasado	participio de pasado
arise	arose	arisen	**creep**	crept	crept
awake	awoke	awoken	**cut**	cut	cut
be (am, is, are; being)	was, were	been	**deal**	dealt	dealt
			dig	dug	dug
			do (does)	did	done
bear	bore	born(e)	**draw**	drew	drawn
beat	beat	beaten	**dream**	dreamed, dreamt	dreamed, dreamt
become	became	become			
begin	began	begun	**drink**	drank	drunk
bend	bent	bent	**drive**	drove	driven
bet	bet, betted	bet, betted	**dwell**	dwelt	dwelt
			eat	ate	eaten
bid *(at auction, cards)*	bid	bid	**fall**	fell	fallen
			feed	fed	fed
			feel	felt	felt
bid *(say)*	bade	bidden	**fight**	fought	fought
bind	bound	bound	**find**	found	found
bite	bit	bitten	**flee**	fled	fled
bleed	bled	bled	**fling**	flung	flung
blow	blew	blown	**fly**	flew	flown
break	broke	broken	**forbid**	forbad(e)	forbidden
breed	bred	bred	**forecast**	forecast	forecast
bring	brought	brought	**forget**	forgot	forgotten
build	built	built	**forgive**	forgave	forgiven
burn	burnt, burned	burnt, burned	**forsake**	forsook	forsaken
burst	burst	burst	**freeze**	froze	frozen
buy	bought	bought	**get**	got	got, (US) gotten
can	could	(been able)			
			give	gave	given
			go (goes)	went	gone
cast	cast	cast	**grind**	ground	ground
catch	caught	caught	**grow**	grew	grown
choose	chose	chosen	**hang**	hung	hung
cling	clung	clung	**hang** *(execute)*	hanged	hanged
come	came	come			
cost	cost	cost	**have**	had	had
cost *(work out price of)*	costed	costed	**hear**	heard	heard
			hide	hid	hidden

presente	pasado	participio de pasado	presente	pasado	participio de pasado
hit	hit	hit	**say**	said	said
hold	held	held	**see**	saw	seen
hurt	hurt	hurt	**seek**	sought	sought
keep	kept	kept	**sell**	sold	sold
kneel	knelt, kneeled	knelt, kneeled	**send**	sent	sent
			set	set	set
know	knew	known	**sew**	sewed	sewn
lay	laid	laid	**shake**	shook	shaken
lead	led	led	**shear**	sheared	shorn, sheared
lean	leant, leaned	leant, leaned			
			shed	shed	shed
leap	leapt, leaped	leapt, leaped	**shine**	shone	shone
			shoot	shot	shot
learn	learnt, learned	learnt, learned	**show**	showed	shown
			shrink	shrank	shrunk
leave	left	left	**shut**	shut	shut
lend	lent	lent	**sing**	sang	sung
let	let	let	**sink**	sank	sunk
lie (lying)	lay	lain	**sit**	sat	sat
light	lit, lighted	lit, lighted	**slay**	slew	slain
			sleep	slept	slept
lose	lost	lost	**slide**	slid	slid
make	made	made	**sling**	slung	slung
may	might	—	**slit**	slit	slit
mean	meant	meant	**smell**	smelt, smelled	smelt, smelled
meet	met	met			
mistake	mistook	mistaken	**sow**	sowed	sown, sowed
mow	mowed	mown, mowed			
must	(had to)	(had to)	**speak**	spoke	spoken
pay	paid	paid	**speed**	sped, speeded	sped, speeded
put	put	put			
quit	quit, quitted	quit, quitted	**spell**	spelt, spelled	spelt, spelled
read	read	read	**spend**	spent	spent
rid	rid	rid	**spill**	spilt, spilled	spilt, spilled
ride	rode	ridden	**spin**	spun	spun
ring	rang	rung	**spit**	spat	spat
rise	rose	risen	**spoil**	spoiled, spoilt	spoiled, spoilt
run	ran	run			
saw	sawed	sawed, sawn	**spread**	spread	spread
			spring	sprang	sprung

presente	pasado	participio de pasado	presente	pasado	participio de pasado
stand	stood	stood	**think**	thought	thought
steal	stole	stolen	**throw**	threw	thrown
stick	stuck	stuck	**thrust**	thrust	thrust
sting	stung	stung	**tread**	trod	trodden
stink	stank	stunk	**wake**	woke, waked	woken, waked
stride	strode	stridden			
strike	struck	struck	**wear**	wore	worn
strive	strove	striven	**weave**	wove	woven
swear	swore	sworn	**weave** (wind)	weaved	weaved
sweep	swept	swept			
swell	swelled	swollen, swelled	**wed**	wedded, wed	wedded, wed
swim	swam	swum			
swing	swung	swung	**weep**	wept	wept
take	took	taken	**win**	won	won
teach	taught	taught	**wind**	wound	wound
tear	tore	torn	**wring**	wrung	wrung
tell	told	told	**write**	wrote	written

ESPAÑOL - INGLÉS
SPANISH - ENGLISH

A, a

a

PALABRA CLAVE

[a] (a + el = al) prep

1 (dirección) to; **fueron a Madrid/Grecia** they went to Madrid/Greece; **me voy a casa** I'm going home

2 (distancia): **está a 15 km de aquí** it's 15 kms from here

3 (posición): **estar a la mesa** to be at table; **al lado de** next to, beside; ver tb **puerta**

4 (tiempo): **a las 10/a medianoche** at 10/midnight; **a la mañana siguiente** the following morning; **a los pocos días** after a few days; **estamos a 9 de julio** it's the ninth of July; **a los 24 años** at the age of 24; **al año/a la semana** a year/week later

5 (manera): **a la francesa** the French way; **a caballo** on horseback; **a oscuras** in the dark

6 (medio, instrumento): **a lápiz** in pencil; **a mano** by hand; **cocina a gas** gas stove

7 (razón): **a 30 céntimos el kilo** at 30 cents a kilo, **a más de 50 km/h** at more than 50 kms per hour

8 (dativo): **se lo di a él** I gave it to him; **vi al policía** I saw the policeman; **se lo compré a él** I bought it from him

9 (tras ciertos verbos): **voy a verle** I'm going to see him; **empezó a trabajar** he started working o to work

10 (+ infin): **al verlo, lo reconocí inmediatamente** when I saw him I recognized him at once; **el camino a recorrer** the distance we etc have to travel; **¡a callar!** keep quiet!; **¡a comer!** let's eat!

abad, esa [a'βaδ, 'δesa] nm/f abbot/abbess □ **abadía** nf abbey

abajo [a'βaxo] adv (situación) (down) below, underneath; (en edificio) downstairs; (dirección) down, downwards; **el piso de ~** the downstairs flat; **la parte de ~** the lower part; **¡~ el gobierno!** down with the government!; **cuesta/río ~** downhill/downstream; **de arriba ~** from top to bottom; **el ~ firmante** the undersigned; **más ~** lower o further down

abalanzarse [aβalan'θarse] vr: **~ sobre** o **contra** to throw o.s. at

abanderado, -a [aβande'raδo] nm/f (portaestandarte) standard bearer; (de un movimiento) champion, leader; (MÉX: linier) linesman, assistant referee

abandonado, -a [aβando'naδo, a] adj derelict; (desatendido) abandoned; (desierto) deserted; (descuidado) neglected

abandonar [aβando'nar] vt to leave; (persona) to abandon, desert; (cosa) to abandon, leave behind; (descuidar) to neglect; (renunciar a) to give up; (INFORM) to quit; **abandonarse** vr: **abandonarse a** to abandon o.s. to □ **abandono** nm (acto) desertion, abandonment; (estado) abandon, neglect; (renuncia) withdrawal, retirement; **ganar por abandono** to win by default

abanico [aβa'niko] nm fan; (NÁUT) derrick

abarcar [aβar'kar] vt to include, embrace; (LAm: acaparar) to monopolize

abarrotado, -a [aβarro'taðo, a] adj packed

abarrotar [aβarro'tar] vt (local, estadio, teatro) to fill, pack

abarrotero, -a [aβarro'tero, a] (MÉX) nm/f grocer ❑ **abarrotes** (MÉX) nmpl groceries; **tienda de abarrotes** (MÉX, CAm) grocery store

abastecer [aβaste'θer] vt: ~ **(de)** to supply (with) ❑ **abastecimiento** nm supply

abasto [a'βasto] nm supply; **no dar** ~ to be unable to cope with

abatible [aβa'tiβle] adj: **asiento** ~ tip-up seat; (AUTO) reclining seat

abatido, -a [aβa'tiðo, a] adj dejected, downcast

abatir [aβa'tir] vt (muro) to demolish; (pájaro) to shoot o bring down; (fig) to depress

abdicar [aβði'kar] vi to abdicate

abdomen [aβ'ðomen] nm abdomen ❑ **abdominales** nmpl (tb: **ejercicios abdominales**) sit-ups

abecedario [aβeθe'ðarjo] nm alphabet

abedul [aβe'ðul] nm birch

abeja [a'βexa] nf bee

abejorro [aβe'xorro] nm bumblebee

abertura [aβer'tura] nf = **apertura**

abeto [a'βeto] nm fir

abierto, -a [a'βjerto, a] pp de **abrir** ♦ adj open

abismal [aβis'mal] adj (fig) vast, enormous

abismo [a'βismo] nm abyss

ablandar [aβlan'dar] vt to soften; **ablandarse** vr to get softer

abocado, -a [aβo'kaðo, a] adj (vino) smooth, pleasant

abochornar [aβot∫or'nar] vt to embarrass

abofetear [aβofete'ar] vt to slap (in the face)

abogado, -a [aβo'ɣaðo, a] nm/f lawyer; (notario) solicitor; (en tribunal) barrister (BRIT), attorney (US) ▶ **abogado defensor** defence lawyer o (US) attorney

abogar [aβo'ɣar] vi: ~ **por** to plead for; (fig) to advocate

abolir [aβo'lir] vt to abolish; (cancelar) to cancel

abolladura [aβoʎa'ðura] nf dent

abollar [aβo'ʎar] vt to dent

abombarse [aβom'barse] (LAm) vr to go bad

abominable [aβomi'naβle] adj abominable

abonado, -a [aβo'naðo, a] adj (deuda) paid(-up) ♦ nm/f subscriber

abonar [aβo'nar] vt (deuda) to settle; (terreno) to fertilize; (idea) to endorse; **abonarse** vr to subscribe ❑ **abono** nm payment; fertilizer; subscription

abordar [aβor'ðar] vt (barco) to board; (asunto) to broach

aborigen [aβo'rixen] nmf aborigine

aborrecer [aβorre'θer] vt to hate, loathe

abortar [aβor'tar] vi (malparir) to have a miscarriage; (deliberadamente) to have an abortion ❑ **aborto** nm miscarriage; abortion

abovedado, -a [aβoβe'ðaðo, a] adj vaulted, domed

abrasar [aβra'sar] vt to burn (up); (AGR) to dry up, parch

abrazar [aβra'θar] vt to embrace, hug

abrazo [a'βraθo] nm embrace, hug; **un** ~ (en carta) with best wishes

abrebotellas [aβreβo'teʎas] nm inv bottle opener

abrecartas [aβre'kartas] nm inv letter opener

abrelatas [aβre'latas] nm inv tin (BRIT) o can opener

abreviatura [aβreβja'tura] nf abbreviation

abridor [aβri'ðor] nm bottle opener; (de latas) tin (BRIT) o can opener

abrigador, -a (MÉX) adj warm

abrigar [aβri'ɣar] vt (proteger) to shelter; (ropa) to keep warm; (fig) to cherish

abrigo [a'βriɣo] nm (prenda) coat, overcoat; (lugar protegido) shelter

abril [a'βril] nm April

abrillantador nm polish

abrillantar [aβriʎan'tar] vt to polish

abrir [a'βrir] vt to open (up) ♦ vi to open; **abrirse** vr to open (up); (extenderse) to open out; (cielo) to clear; **abrirse paso** to find o force a way through

abrochar [aβro'tʃar] vt (con botones) to button (up); (zapato, con broche) to do up

abrupto, -a [a'βrupto, a] adj abrupt; (empinado) steep

absoluto, -a [aβso'luto, a] adj absolute; **en ~** adv not at all

absolver [aβsol'βer] vt to absolve; (JUR) to pardon; (: acusado) to acquit

absorbente [aβsor'βente] adj absorbent; (interesante) absorbing

absorber [aβsor'βer] vt to absorb; (embeber) to soak up

absorción [aβsor'θjon] nf absorption; (COM) takeover

abstemio, -a [aβs'temjo, a] adj teetotal

abstención [aβsten'θjon] nf abstention

abstenerse [aβste'nerse] vr: **~ (de)** to abstain o refrain (from)

abstinencia [aβsti'nenθja] nf abstinence; (ayuno) fasting

abstracto, -a [aβs'trakto, a] adj abstract

abstraer [aβstra'er] vt to abstract; **abstraerse** vr to be o become absorbed

abstraído, -a [aβstra'iðo, a] adj absent-minded

absuelto [aβ'swelto] pp de **absolver**

absurdo, -a [aβ'surðo, a] adj absurd

abuchear [aβutʃe'ar] vt to boo

abuelo, -a [a'βwelo, a] nm/f grandfather(-mother); **abuelos** nmpl grandparents

abultado, -a [aβul'taðo, a] adj bulky

abultar [aβul'tar] vi to be bulky

abundancia [aβun'danθja] nf: **una ~ de** plenty of □ **abundante** adj abundant, plentiful

abundar [aβun'dar] vi to abound, be plentiful

aburrido, -a [aβu'rriðo, a] adj (hastiado) bored; (que aburre) boring □ **aburrimiento** nm boredom, tedium

aburrir [aβu'rrir] vt to bore; **aburrirse** vr to be bored, get bored

abusado, -a (MÉX: fam) [aβu'saðo, a] adj (astuto) sharp, cunning ♦ excl: **¡~!** (inv) look out!, careful!

abusar [aβu'sar] vi to go too far; **~ de** to abuse

abusivo, -a [aβu'siβo, a] adj (precio) exorbitant

abuso [a'βuso] nm abuse

acá [a'ka] adv (lugar) here

acabado, -a [aka'βaðo, a] adj finished, complete; (perfecto) perfect; (agotado) worn out; (fig) masterly ♦ nm finish

acabar [aka'βar] vt (llevar a su fin) to finish, complete; (consumir) to use up; (rematar) to finish off ♦ vi to finish, end; **acabarse** vr to finish, stop; (terminarse) to be over; (agotarse) to run out; **~ con** to put an end to; **~ de llegar** to have just arrived; **~ por hacer** to end (up) by doing; **¡se acabó!** it's all over!; (¡basta!) that's enough!

acabóse [aka'βose] nm: **esto es el ~ this** is the last straw

academia [aka'ðemja] nf academy □ **académico, -a** adj academic

acalorado, -a [akalo'raðo, a] adj (discusión) heated

acampar [akam'par] vi to camp

acantilado [akanti'laðo] nm cliff

acaparar [akapa'rar] vt to monopolize; (acumular) to hoard

acariciar [akari'θjar] vt to caress; (esperanza) to cherish

acarrear [akarre'ar] vt to transport; (fig) to cause, result in

acaso [a'kaso] adv perhaps, maybe; (por) si ~ (just) in case

acatar [aka'tar] vt to respect; (ley) obey

acatarrarse [akata'rrarse] vr to catch a cold

acceder [akθe'ðer] vi: ~ a (petición etc) to agree to; (tener acceso a) to have access to; (INFORM) to access

accesible [akθe'siβle] adj accessible

acceso [ak'θeso] nm access, entry; (camino) access, approach; (MED) attack, fit

accesorio, -a [akθe'sorjo, a] adj, nm accessory

accidentado, -a [akθiðen'taðo, a] adj uneven; (montañoso) hilly; (azaroso) eventful ♦ nm/f accident victim

accidental [akθiðen'tal] adj accidental

accidente [akθi'ðente] nm accident; **accidentes** nmpl (de terreno) unevenness sg ▸ **accidente laboral/de trabajo** o **de tráfico** industrial/road o traffic accident

acción [ak'θjon] nf action; (acto) action, act; (COM) share; (JUR) action, lawsuit ▫ **accionar** vt to work, operate; (INFORM) to drive

accionista [akθjo'nista] nmf shareholder, stockholder

acebo [a'θeβo] nm holly; (árbol) holly tree

acechar [aθe'tʃar] vt to spy on; (aguardar) to lie in wait for ▫ **acecho** nm: **estar al acecho (de)** to lie in wait (for)

aceite [a'θeite] nm oil ▸ **aceite de girasol/oliva** olive/sunflower oil

▫ **aceitera** nf oilcan ▫ **aceitoso, -a** adj oily

aceituna [aθei'tuna] nf olive ▸ **aceituna rellena** stuffed olive

acelerador [aθelera'ðor] nm accelerator

acelerar [aθele'rar] vt to accelerate

acelga [a'θelɣa] nf chard, beet

acento [a'θento] nm accent; (acentuación) stress

acentuar [aθen'twar] vt to accent; to stress; (fig) to accentuate

acepción [aθep'θjon] nf meaning

aceptable [aθep'taβle] adj acceptable

aceptación [aθepta'θjon] nf acceptance; (aprobación) approval

aceptar [aθep'tar] vt to accept; (aprobar) to approve; ~ **hacer algo** o agree to do sth

acequia [a'θekja] nf irrigation ditch

acera [a'θera] nf pavement (BRIT), sidewalk (US)

acerca [a'θerka]: ~ **de** prep about, concerning

acercar [aθer'kar] vt to bring o move nearer o closer; **acercarse** vr to approach, come near

acero [a'θero] nm steel

acérrimo, -a [a'θerrimo, a] adj (partidario) staunch; (enemigo) bitter

acertado, -a [aθer'taðo, a] adj correct; (apropiado) apt; (sensato) sensible

acertar [aθer'tar] vt (blanco) to hit; (solución) to get right; (adivinar) to guess ♦ vi to get it right, be right; ~ **a** to manage to; ~ **con** to happen o hit upon

acertijo [aθer'tixo] nm riddle, puzzle

achacar [atʃa'kar] vt to attribute

achacoso, -a [atʃa'koso, a] adj sickly

achicar [atʃi'kar] vt to reduce; (NÁUT) to bale out

achicharrar [atʃitʃa'rrar] vt to scorch, burn

achichincle [MÉX: fam] nmf minion

achicoria [atʃi'korja] nf chicory

achuras [RPI] nfpl offal sg

acicate [aθi'kate] nm spur

acidez [aθi'ðeθ] nf acidity

ácido, -a [a'θiðo, a] adj sour, acid ♦ nm acid

acierto etc [a'θjerto] vb ver **acertar** ♦ nm success; (buen paso) wise move; (solución) solution; (habilidad) skill, ability

acitronar [MÉX: fam] vt to brown

aclamar [akla'mar] vt to acclaim; (aplaudir) to applaud

aclaración [aklara'θjon] nf clarification, explanation

aclarar [akla'rar] vt to clarify, explain; (ropa) to rinse ♦ vi to clear up; **aclararse** vr (explicarse) to understand; **aclararse la garganta** to clear one's throat

aclimatación [aklimata'θjon] nf acclimatization

aclimatar [aklima'tar] vt to acclimatize; **aclimatarse** vr to become acclimatized

acné [ak'ne] nm acne

acobardar [akoβar'ðar] vt to intimidate

acogedor, a [akoxe'ðor, a] adj welcoming; (hospitalario) hospitable

acoger [ako'xer] vt to welcome; (abrigar) to shelter

acogida [ako'xiða] nf reception; refuge

acomedido, -a [MÉX] adj helpful, obliging

acometer [akome'ter] vt to attack; (emprender) to undertake □ **acometida** nf attack, assault

acomodado, -a [akomo'ðaðo, a] adj (persona) well-to-do

acomodador, a [akomoða'ðor, a] nm/f usher(ette)

acomodar [akomo'ðar] vt to adjust; (alojar) to accommodate; **acomodarse** vr to conform; (instalarse) to install o.s.; (adaptarse) to adapt; **acomodarse (a)** to adapt (to)

acompañar [akompa'ɲar] vt to accompany; (documentos) to enclose

acondicionar [akondiθjo'nar] vt to arrange, prepare; (pelo) to condition

aconsejar [akonse'xar] vt to advise, counsel; ~ **a algn hacer** o **que haga algo** to advise sb to do sth

acontecer [akonte'θer] vi to happen, occur □ **acontecimiento** nm event

acopio [a'kopjo] nm store, stock

acoplar [ako'plar] vt to fit; (ELEC) to connect; (vagones) to couple

acorazado, -a [akora'θaðo, a] adj armour-plated, armoured ♦ nm battleship

acordar [akor'ðar] vt (resolver) to agree, resolve; (recordar) to remind; **acordarse** vr to agree; ~ **hacer algo** to agree to do sth; ~ **hacer algo** to remember (sth) □ **acorde** adj (MÚS) harmonious; **acorde con** (medidas etc) in keeping with ♦ nm chord

acordeón [akorðe'on] nm accordion

acordonado, -a [akorðo'naðo, a] adj (calle) cordoned-off

acorralar [akorra'lar] vt to round up, corral

acortar [akor'tar] vt to shorten; (duración) to cut short; (cantidad) to reduce; **acortarse** vr to become shorter

acosar [ako'sar] vt to pursue relentlessly; (fig) to hound, pester □ **acoso** nm harassment ▶ **acoso sexual** sexual harassment

acostar [akos'tar] vt (en cama) to put to bed; (en suelo) to lay down; **acostarse** vr to go to bed; to lie down; **acostarse con algn** to sleep with sb

acostumbrado, -a [akostum'braðo, a] adj usual; ~ **a** used to

acostumbrar [akostum'brar] vt: ~ **a algn a algo** to get sb used to sth ♦ vi: **(a) hacer** o to be in the habit of doing; **acostumbrarse** vr: **acostumbrarse a** to get used to

acotación [akota'θjon] nf marginal note; (GEO) elevation mark; (de limite) boundary mark; (TEATRO) stage direction

acotamiento (MÉX) nm hard shoulder (BRIT), berm (US)

acre ['akre] adj (olor) acrid; (fig) biting ♦ nm acre

acreditar [akreði'tar] vt (garantizar) to vouch for, guarantee; (autorizar) to authorize; (dar prueba de) to prove; (COM: abonar) to credit; (embajador) to accredit

acreedor, a [akree'ðor, a] nm/f creditor

acribillar [akriβi'ʎar] vt: ~ a balazos to riddle with bullets

acróbata [a'kroβata] nmf acrobat

acta ['akta] nf certificate; (de comisión) minutes pl, record ► **acta de matrimonio/nacimiento** (MÉX) marriage/birth certificate ► **acta notarial** affidavit

actitud [akti'tuð] nf attitude; (postura) posture

activar [akti'βar] vt to activate; (acelerar) to speed up

actividad [aktiβi'ðað] nf activity

activo, -a [ak'tiβo, a] adj active; (vivo) lively ♦ nm (COM) assets pl

acto ['akto] nm act, action; (ceremonia) ceremony; (TEATRO) act; **en el ~** immediately

actor [ak'tor] nm actor; (JUR) plaintiff ♦ adj: **parte actora** prosecution

actriz [ak'triθ] nf actress

actuación [aktwa'θjon] nf action; (comportamiento) conduct, behaviour; (JUR) proceedings pl; (desempeño) performance

actual [ak'twal] adj present(-day), current ▢ **actualidad** nf present; **actualidades** nfpl (noticias) news sg; **en la actualidad** at present; (hoy día) nowadays ▢ **actualizar** [aktwali'θar] vt to update, modernize

▢ **actualmente** [aktwal'mente] adv at present; (hoy día) nowadays

⚠ No confundir **actual** con la palabra inglesa actual.

⚠ No confundir **actualmente** con la palabra inglesa actually.

actuar [ak'twar] vi (obrar) to work, operate; (actor) to act, perform ♦ vt to work, operate; ~ **de** to act as

acuarela [akwa'rela] nf watercolour

acuario [a'kwarjo] nm aquarium; (ASTROLOGÍA): **A~** Aquarius

acuático, -a [a'kwatiko, a] adj aquatic

acudir [aku'ðir] vi (asistir) to attend; (ir) to go; ~ **a** (fig) to turn to; ~ **a una cita** to keep an appointment; ~ **en ayuda de** to go to the aid of

acuerdo etc [a'kwerðo] vb ver **acordar** ♦ nm agreement; **¡de ~!** agreed!; **de ~ con** (persona) in agreement with; (acción, documento) in accordance with; **estar de ~** to be agreed, agree

acumular [akumu'lar] vt to accumulate, collect

acuñar [aku'ɲar] vt (moneda) to mint; (frase) to coin

acupuntura [akupun'tura] nf acupuncture

acurrucarse [akurru'karse] vr to crouch; (ovillarse) to curl up

acusación [akusa'θjon] nf accusation

acusar [aku'sar] vt to accuse; (revelar) to reveal; (denunciar) to denounce

acuse [a'kuse] nm: ~ **de recibo** acknowledgement of receipt

acústica [a'kustika] nf acoustics pl

acústico, -a [a'kustiko, a] adj acoustic

adaptación [aðapta'θjon] nf adaptation

adaptador [aðapta'ðor] nm (ELEC) adapter, adaptor ► **adaptador universal** universal adapter o adaptor

adaptar [aðap'tar] vt to adapt; (acomodar) to fit

adecuado, -a [aðe'kwaðo, a] *adj* (*apto*) suitable; (*oportuno*) appropriate

a. de J.C. *abr* (= *antes de Jesucristo*) B.C.

adelantado, -a [aðelan'taðo, a] *adj* advanced; (*reloj*) fast; **pagar por ~** to pay in advance

adelantamiento [aðelanta'mjento] *nm* (*AUTO*) overtaking

adelantar [aðelan'tar] *vt* to move forward; (*avanzar*) to advance; (*acelerar*) to speed up; (*AUTO*) to overtake ♦ *vi* to go forward, advance; **adelantarse** *vr* to go forward, advance

adelante [aðe'lante] *adv* forward(s), ahead ♦ *excl* come in!; **de hoy en ~** from now on; **más ~** later on; (*más allá*) further on

adelanto [aðe'lanto] *nm* advance; (*mejora*) improvement; (*progreso*) progress

adelgazar [aðelɣa'θar] *vt* to thin (down) ♦ *vi* to get thin; (*con régimen*) to slim down, lose weight

ademán [aðe'man] *nm* gesture; **ademanes** *nmpl* manners

además [aðe'mas] *adv* besides; (*por otra parte*) moreover; (*también*) also; **~ de** besides, in addition to

adentrarse [aðen'trarse] *vr*: **~ en** to go into, get inside; (*penetrar*) to penetrate (into)

adentro [a'ðentro] *adv* inside, in; **mar ~** out at sea; **tierra ~** inland

adepto, -a [a'ðepto, a] *nm/f* supporter

aderezar [aðere'θar] *vt* (*ensalada*) to dress; (*comida*) to season □ **aderezo** *nm* dressing, seasoning

adeudar [aðeu'ðar] *vt* to owe

adherirse [aðe'rirse] *vr*: **~ a** to adhere to; (*partido*) to join

adhesión [aðe'sjon] *nf* adhesion; (*fig*) adherence

adicción [aðik'θjon] *nf* addiction

adición [aði'θjon] *nf* addition

adicto, -a [a'ðikto, a] *adj*: **~ a** addicted to; (*dedicado*) devoted to ♦ *nm/f*

supporter, follower; (*toxicómano*) addict

adiestrar [aðjes'trar] *vt* to train, teach; (*conducir*) to guide, lead

adinerado, -a [aðine'raðo, a] *adj* wealthy

adiós [a'ðjos] *excl* (*para despedirse*) goodbye!, cheerio!; (*al pasar*) hello!

aditivo [aði'tiβo] *nm* additive

adivinanza [aðiβi'nanθa] *nf* riddle

adivinar [aðiβi'nar] *vt* to prophesy; (*conjeturar*) to guess □ **adivino, -a** *nm/f* fortune-teller

adj *abr* (= *adjunto*) encl

adjetivo [aðxe'tiβo] *nm* adjective

adjudicar [aðxuði'kar] *vt* to award; **adjudicarse algo** to appropriate sth

adjuntar [aðxun'tar] *vt* to attach, enclose □ **adjunto, -a** *adj* attached, enclosed ♦ *nm/f* assistant

administración [aðministra'θjon] *nf* administration; (*dirección*) management □ **administrador, a** *nm/f* administrator, manager(ess)

administrar [aðminis'trar] *vt* to administer □ **administrativo, -a** *adj* administrative

admirable [aðmi'raβle] *adj* admirable

admiración [aðmira'θjon] *nf* admiration; (*asombro*) wonder; (*LING*) exclamation mark

admirar [aðmi'rar] *vt* to admire; (*extrañar*) to surprise

admisible [aðmi'siβle] *adj* admissible

admisión [aðmi'sjon] *nf* admission; (*reconocimiento*) acceptance

admitir [aðmi'tir] *vt* to admit, (*aceptar*) to accept

adobar [aðo'βar] *vt* (*CULIN*) to season

adobe [a'ðoβe] *nm* adobe, sun-dried brick

adolecer [aðole'θer] *vi*: **~ de** to suffer from

adolescente [aðoles'θente] nmf adolescent, teenager

adonde [a'ðonde] conj (to) where

adónde [a'ðonde] adv = **dónde**

adopción [aðop'θjon] nf adoption

adoptar [aðop'tar] vt to adopt

adoptivo, -a [aðop'tiβo, a] adj (padres) adoptive; (hijo) adopted

adoquín [aðo'kin] nm paving stone

adorar [aðo'rar] vt to adore

adornar [aðor'nar] vt to adorn

adorno [a'ðorno] nm ornament; (decoración) decoration

adosado, -a [aðo'saðo, a] adj: **casa adosada** semi-detached house

adosar (MÉX) [aðo'sar] vt (adjuntar) to attach, enclose (with a letter)

adquiero etc vb ver **adquirir**

adquirir [aðki'rir] vt to acquire, obtain

adquisición [aðkisi'θjon] nf acquisition

adrede [a'ðreðe] adv on purpose

aduana [a'ðwana] nf customs pl

aduanero, -a [aðwa'nero, a] adj customs cpd ♦ nm/f customs officer

adueñarse [aðwe'narse] vr: **~ de** to take possession of

adular [aðu'lar] vt to flatter

adulterar [aðulte'rar] vt to adulterate

adulterio [aðul'terjo] nm adultery

adúltero, -a [a'ðultero, a] adj adulterous ♦ nm/f adulterer/ adulteress

adulto, -a [a'ðulto, a] adj, nm/f adult

adverbio [að'βerβjo] nm adverb

adversario, -a [aðβer'sarjo, a] nm/f adversary

adversidad [aðβersi'ðað] nf adversity; (contratiempo) setback

adverso, -a [að'βerso, a] adj adverse

advertencia [aðβer'tenθja] nf warning; (prefacio) preface, foreword

advertir [aðβer'tir] vt to notice; (avisar): **~ a algn de** to warn sb about o of

Adviento [að'βjento] nm Advent

advierto etc vb ver **advertir**

aéreo, -a [a'ereo, a] adj aerial

aerobic [ae'roβik] nm aerobics
□ **aerobics** (MÉX) nmpl aerobics sg

aeromozo, -a [aero'moθo, a] (LAm) nm/f air steward(ess)

aeronáutica [aero'nautika] nf aeronautics sg

aeronave [aero'naβe] nm spaceship

aeroplano [aero'plano] nm aeroplane

aeropuerto [aero'pwerto] nm airport

aerosol [aero'sol] nm aerosol

afamado, -a [afa'maðo, a] adj famous

afán [a'fan] nm hard work; (deseo) desire

afanador, a (MÉX) nm/f (de limpieza) cleaner

afanar [afa'nar] vt to harass; (fam) to pinch

afear [afe'ar] vt to disfigure

afección [afek'θjon] nf (MED) disease

afectado, -a [afek'taðo, a] adj affected

afectar [afek'tar] vt to affect

afectísimo, -a [afek'tisimo, a] adj affectionate; **suyo ~** yours truly

afectivo, -a [afek'tiβo, a] adj (problema etc) emotional

afecto [a'fekto] nm affection; **tenerle ~ a algn** to be fond of sb

afectuoso, -a [afek'twoso, a] adj affectionate

afeitar [afei'tar] vt to shave; **afeitarse** vr to shave

afeminado, -a [afemi'naðo, a] adj effeminate

Afganistán [afɣanis'tan] nm Afghanistan

afianzar [afjan'θar] vt to strengthen; to secure; **afianzarse** vr to become established

afiche [a'fitʃe] (RPl) nm poster

afición [afi'θjon] nf fondness, liking; **la ~** the fans pl; **pinto por ~** I paint as a hobby □ **aficionado, -a** adj keen, enthusiastic; (no profesional) amateur

♦ *nm/f* enthusiast, fan; amateur; **ser aficionado a algo** to be very keen on o fond of sth

aficionar [afiθjo'nar] *vt*: ~ **a algn a algo** to make sb like sth; **aficionarse** *vr*: **aficionarse a algo** to grow fond of sth

afilado, -a [afi'laðo, a] *adj* sharp

afilar [afi'lar] *vt* to sharpen

afiliarse [afi'ljarse] *vr* to affiliate

afín [a'fin] *adj (parecido)* similar; *(conexo)* related

afinar [afi'nar] *vt (TEC)* to refine; *(MÚS)* to tune ♦ *vi (tocar)* to play in tune; *(cantar)* to sing in tune

afincarse [afin'karse] *vr* to settle

afinidad [afini'ðað] *nf* affinity; *(parentesco)* relationship; **por ~** by marriage

afirmación [afirma'θjon] *nf* affirmation

afirmar [afir'mar] *vt* to affirm, state ▫ **afirmativo, -a** *adj* affirmative

afligir [afli'xir] *vt* to afflict; *(apenar)* to distress

aflojar [aflo'xar] *vt* to slacken; *(desatar)* to loosen, undo; *(relajar)* to relax ♦ *vi* to drop; *(bajar)* to go down; **aflojarse** *vr* to relax

afluente [aflu'ente] *adj* flowing ♦ *nm* tributary

afmo, -a *abr* (= *afectísimo(a) suyo(a)*) Yours

afónico, -a [a'foniko, a] *adj*: **estar ~** to have a sore throat; to have lost one's voice

aforo [a'foro] *nm (de teatro etc)* capacity

afortunado, -a [afortu'naðo, a] *adj* fortunate, lucky

África ['afrika] *nf* Africa ▶ **África del Sur** South Africa ▫ **africano, -a** *adj, nm/f* African

afrontar [afron'tar] *vt* to confront; *(poner cara a cara)* to bring face to face

afrutado, -a *adj* fruity

after *(PL* **afters)** *nm* after-hours club ▫ **afterhours** [after'aurs] *nm inv* = **after**

afuera [a'fwera] *adv* out, outside; **afueras** *nfpl* outskirts

agachar [aɣa'tʃar] *vt* to bend, bow; **agacharse** *vr* to stoop, bend

agalla [a'ɣaʎa] *nf (ZOOL)* gill; **tener agallas** *(fam)* to have guts

agarradera [aɣarra'ðera] *(MÉX) nf* handle

agarrado, -a [aɣa'rraðo, a] *adj* mean, stingy

agarrar [aɣa'rrar] *vt* to grasp, grab; *(LAm: tomar)* to take, catch; *(recoger)* to pick up ♦ *vi (planta)* to take root; **agarrarse** *vr* to hold on (tightly)

agencia [a'xenθja] *nf* agency ▶ **agencia de viajes** travel agency ▶ **agencia inmobiliaria** estate *(BRIT)* o real estate *(US)* agent's (office)

agenciarse [axen'θjarse] *vr* to obtain, procure

agenda [a'xenda] *nf* diary; ~ **electronica** PDA

⚠ No confundir **agenda** con la palabra inglesa *agenda*.

agente [a'xente] *nmf* agent; *(tb:* **~ de policía)** policeman/policewoman ▶ **agente de seguros** insurance agent ▶ **agente de tránsito** *(MÉX)* traffic cop ▶ **agente inmobiliario** estate agent *(BRIT)*, realtor *(US)*

ágil [a'xil] *adj* agile, nimble ▫ **agilidad** *nf* agility, nimbleness

agilizar [axili'θar] *vt (trámites)* to speed up

agiotista *(MÉX) nmf (usurero)* usurer

agitación [axita'θjon] *nf (de mano etc)* shaking, waving; *(de líquido etc)* stirring; *(fig)* agitation

agitado, -a [axi'taðo, a] *adj* hectic; *(viaje)* bumpy

agitar [axi'tar] *vt* to wave, shake; *(líquido)* to stir; *(fig)* to stir up, excite;

agitarse *vr* to get excited; (*inquietarse*) to get worried o upset

aglomeración [aɣlomeraˈθjon] *nf* agglomeration ► **aglomeración de gente/tráfico** mass of people/traffic jam

agnóstico, -a [aɣˈnostiko, a] *adj, nm/f* agnostic

agobiar [aɣoˈβjar] *vt* to weigh down; (*oprimir*) to oppress; (*cargar*) to burden

agolparse [aɣolˈparse] *vr* to crowd together

agonía [aɣoˈnia] *nf* death throes *pl*; (*fig*) agony, anguish

agonizante [aɣoniˈθante] *adj* dying

agonizar [aɣoniˈθar] *vi* to be dying

agosto [aˈɣosto] *nm* August

agotado, -a [aɣoˈtaðo, a] *adj* (*persona*) exhausted; (*libros*) out of print; (*acabado*) finished; (*COM*) sold out
❏ **agotador, a** [aɣotaˈðor, a] *adj* exhausting

agotamiento [aɣotaˈmjento] *nm* exhaustion

agotar [aɣoˈtar] *vt* to exhaust; (*consumir*) to drain; (*recursos*) to use up, deplete; **agotarse** *vr* to be exhausted; (*acabarse*) to run out; (*libro*) to go out of print

agraciado, -a [aɣraˈθjaðo, a] *adj* (*atractivo*) attractive; (*en sorteo etc*) lucky

agradable [aɣraˈðaβle] *adj* pleasant, nice

agradar [aɣraˈðar] *vt*: **él me agrada** I like him

agradecer [aɣraðeˈθer] *vt* to thank; (*favor etc*) to be grateful for
❏ **agradecido, -a** *adj* grateful; **¡muy agradecido!** thanks a lot!
❏ **agradecimiento** *nm* thanks *pl*; gratitude

agradezco *etc vb ver* **agradecer**

agrado [aˈɣraðo] *nm*: **ser de tu** *etc* ~ to be to your *etc* liking

agrandar [aɣranˈdar] *vt* to enlarge; (*fig*) to exaggerate; **agrandarse** *vr* to get bigger

agrario, -a [aˈɣrarjo, a] *adj* agrarian, land *cpd*; (*política*) agricultural, farming

agravante [aɣraˈβante] *adj* aggravating ♦ *nm*: **con el ~ de que ...** with the further difficulty that ...

agravar [aɣraˈβar] *vt* (*pesar sobre*) to make heavier; (*irritar*) to aggravate; **agravarse** *vr* to worsen, get worse

agraviar [aɣraˈβjar] *vt* to offend; (*ser injusto con*) to wrong

agredir [aɣreˈðir] *vt* to attack

agregado, -a [aɣreˈɣaðo, a] *nm/f*: **A~** ≈ teacher (*who is not head of department*) ♦ *nm* aggregate; (*persona*) attaché

agregar [aɣreˈɣar] *vt* to gather; (*añadir*) to add; (*persona*) to appoint

agresión [aɣreˈsjon] *nf* aggression

agresivo, -a [aɣreˈsiβo, a] *adj* aggressive

agriar [aˈɣrjar] *vt* to (turn) sour

agrícola [aˈɣrikola] *adj* farming *cpd*, agricultural

agricultor, a [aɣrikulˈtor, a] *nm/f* farmer

agricultura [aɣrikulˈtura] *nf* agriculture, farming

agridulce [aɣriˈðulθe] *adj* bittersweet; (*CULIN*) sweet and sour

agrietarse [aɣrjeˈtarse] *vr* to crack; (*piel*) to chap

agrio, -a [ˈaɣrjo, a] *adj* bitter

agrupación [aɣrupaˈθjon] *nf* group; (*acto*) grouping

agrupar [aɣruˈpar] *vt* to group

agua [ˈaɣwa] *nf* water; (*NÁUT*) wake; (*ARQ*) slope of a roof; **aguas** *nfpl* (*de piedra*) water *sg*, sparkle *sg*; (*MED*) water *sg*, urine *sg*; (*NÁUT*) waters ► **agua bendita/destilada/potable** holy/distilled/drinking water ► **agua caliente** hot water ► **agua corriente**

running water ► **agua de colonia** eau de cologne ► **agua mineral (con/sin gas)** (sparkling/still) mineral water ► **agua oxigenada** hydrogen peroxide ► **aguas abajo/arriba** downstream/upstream ► **aguas jurisdiccionales** territorial waters

aguacate [aɣwa'kate] nm avocado (pear)

aguacero [aɣwa'θero] nm (heavy) shower, downpour

aguado, -a [a'ɣwaðo, a] adj watery, watered down

aguafiestas [aɣwa'fjestas] nmf inv spoilsport, killjoy

aguamiel (MEX) [aɣwa'mjel] nf fermented maguey o agave juice

aguanieve [aɣwa'njeβe] nf sleet

aguantar [aɣwan'tar] vt to bear, put up with; (sostener) to hold up ♦ vi to last; **aguantarse** vr to restrain o.s. □ **aguante** nm (paciencia) patience; (resistencia) endurance

aguar [a'ɣwar] vt to water down

aguardar [aɣwar'ðar] vt to wait for

aguardiente [aɣwar'ðjente] nm brandy, liquor

aguarrás [aɣwa'rras] nm turpentine

aguaviva (RPL) [aɣwa'βiβa] nf jellyfish

agudeza [aɣu'ðeθa] nf sharpness; (ingenio) wit

agudo, -a [a'ɣuðo, a] adj sharp; (voz) high-pitched, piercing; (dolor, enfermedad) acute

agüero [a'ɣwero] nm: **buen/mal ~** good/bad omen

aguijón [aɣi'xon] nm sting; (fig) spur

águila [a'ɣila] nf eagle; (fig) genius

aguileño, -a [aɣi'leɲo, a] adj (nariz) aquiline; (rostro) sharp-featured

aguinaldo [aɣi'naldo] nm Christmas box

aguja [a'ɣuxa] nf needle; (de reloj) hand; (ARQ) spire; (TEC) firing-pin; **agujas** nfpl (ZOOL) ribs; (FERRO) points

agujerear [aɣuxere'ar] vt to make holes in

agujero [aɣu'xero] nm hole

agujetas [aɣu'xetas] nfpl stitch sg; (rigidez) stiffness sg

ahí [a'i] adv there; **de ahí que** so that, with the result that; **ahí llega** here he comes; **por ahí** that way; (allá) over there; **200 o por ahí** 200 or so

ahijado, -a [ai'xaðo, a] nm/f godson/ daughter

ahogar [ao'ɣar] vt to drown; (asfixiar) to suffocate, smother; (fuego) to put out; **ahogarse** vr (en el agua) to drown; (por asfixia) to suffocate

ahogo [a'oɣo] nm breathlessness; (fig) financial difficulty

ahondar [aon'dar] vt to deepen, make deeper; (fig) to study thoroughly ♦ vi: **~ en** to study thoroughly

ahora [a'ora] adv now; (hace poco) a moment ago, just now; (dentro de poco) in a moment; **~ voy** I'm coming; **~ mismo** right now; **~ bien** now then; **por ~** for the present

ahorcar [aor'kar] vt to hang

ahorita [ao'rita] (fam) adv (LAm: en este momento) right now; (MÉX: hace poco) just now; (: dentro de poco) in a minute

ahorrar [ao'rrar] vt (dinero) to save; (esfuerzos) to save, avoid □ **ahorro** nm (acto) saving; **ahorros** nmpl (dinero) savings

ahuecar [awe'kar] vt to hollow (out); (voz) to deepen; **ahuecarse** vr to give o.s. airs

ahumar [au'mar] vt to smoke, cure, (llenar de humo) to fill with smoke ♦ vi to smoke; **ahumarse** vr to fill with smoke

ahuyentar [aujen'tar] vt to drive off, frighten off; (fig) to dispel

aire ['aire] nm air; (viento) wind; (corriente) draught; (MÚS) tune; **al ~ libre** in the open air ► **aire acondicionado** air conditioning

❏ **airear** vt to air; **airearse** vr (persona) to go out for a breath of fresh air
❏ **airoso, -a** adj windy; draughty; (fig) graceful

aislado, -a [ais'laðo, a] adj isolated; (incomunicado) cut-off; (ELEC) insulated

aislar [ais'lar] vt to isolate; (ELEC) to insulate

ajardinado, -a [axarði'naðo, a] adj landscaped

ajedrez [axe'ðreθ] nm chess

ajeno, -a [a'xeno, a] adj (que pertenece a otro) somebody else's; **~ a** foreign to

ajetreado, -a [axetre'aðo, a] adj busy

ajetreo [axe'treo] nm bustle

ají [a'xi] (CS) nm chil(l)i, red pepper; (salsa) chil(l)i sauce

ajillo [a'xiʎo] nm: **gambas al ~** garlic prawns

ajo ['axo] nm garlic

ajuar [a'xwar] nm household furnishings pl; (de novia) trousseau; (de niño) layette

ajustado, -a [axus'taðo, a] adj (tornillo) tight; (cálculo) right; (ropa) tight(-fitting); (resultado) close

ajustar [axus'tar] vt (adaptar) to adjust; (encajar) to fit; (TEC) to engage; (IMPRENTA) to make up; (apretar) to tighten; (concertar) to agree (on); (reconciliar) to reconcile; (cuentas, deudas) to settle ♦ vi to fit; **ajustarse** vr: **ajustarse a** (precio etc) to be in keeping with, fit in with; **~ las cuentas a algn** to get even with sb

ajuste [a'xuste] nm adjustment; (COSTURA) fitting; (acuerdo) compromise; (de cuenta) settlement

al [al] (= a + el); ver **a**

ala ['ala] nf wing; (de sombrero) brim; winger ❏ **ala delta** nf hang-glider

alabanza [ala'βanθa] nf praise

alabar [ala'βar] vt to praise

alacena [ala'θena] nf kitchen cupboard (BRIT) o closet (US)

alacrán [ala'kran] nm scorpion

alambrada [alam'braða] nf wire fence; (red) wire netting

alambre [a'lambre] nm wire
▶ **alambre de púas** barbed wire

alameda [ala'meða] nf (plantío) poplar grove; (lugar de paseo) avenue, boulevard

álamo ['alamo] nm poplar

alarde [a'larðe] nm show, display; **hacer ~ de** to boast of

alargador [alarɣa'ðor] nm (ELEC) extension lead

alargar [alar'ɣar] vt to lengthen, extend; (paso) to hasten; (brazo) to stretch out; (cuerda) to pay out; (conversación) to spin out; **alargarse** vr to get longer

alarma [a'larma] nf alarm ▶ **alarma de incendios** fire alarm ❏ **alarmar** vt to alarm; **alarmarse** vr to get alarmed ❏ **alarmante** [alar'mante] adj alarming

alba ['alβa] nf dawn

albahaca [al'βaka] nf basil

Albania [al'βanja] nf Albania

albañil [alβa'ɲil] nm bricklayer; (cantero) mason

albarán [alβa'ran] nm (COM) delivery note, invoice

albaricoque [alβari'koke] nm apricot

albedrío [alβe'ðrio] nm: **libre ~** free will

alberca [al'βerka] nf reservoir; (MÉX: piscina) swimming pool

albergar [alβer'ɣar] vt to shelter

albergue etc [al'βerɣe] vb ver **albergar** ♦ nm shelter, refuge ▶ **albergue juvenil** youth hostel

albóndiga [al'βondiɣa] nf meatball

albornoz [alβor'noθ] nm (de los árabes) burnous; (para el baño) bathrobe

alborotar [alβoro'tar] vi to make a row ♦ vt to agitate, stir up; **alborotarse** vr to get excited; (mar) to get rough
❏ **alboroto** nm row, uproar

álbum [ˈalβum] (pl **álbums, álbumes**) nm album ▶ **álbum de recortes** scrapbook

albur (MÉX) nm (juego de palabras) pun; (doble sentido) double entendre

alcachofa [alkaˈtʃofa] nf artichoke

alcalde, -esa [alˈkalde, esa] nm/f mayor(ess)

alcaldía [alkalˈdia] nf mayoralty; (lugar) mayor's office

alcance etc [alˈkanθe] vb ver **alcanzar**
♦ nm reach; (COM) adverse balance; **al ~ de algn** available to sb

alcancía (LAm) nf [al (para ahorrar) money box; (para colectas) collection box

alcantarilla [alkantaˈriʎa] nf (de aguas cloacales) sewer; (en la calle) gutter

alcanzar [alkanˈθar] vt (algo: con la mano, el pie) to reach; (alguien: en el camino etc) to catch up (with); (autobús) to catch; (bala) to hit, strike
♦ vi (ser suficiente) to be enough; **~ a hacer** to manage to do

alcaparra [alkaˈparra] nf caper

alcayata [alkaˈjata] nf hook

alcázar [alˈkaθar] nm fortress; (NÁUT) quarter-deck

alcoba [alˈkoβa] nf bedroom

alcohol [alˈkol] nm alcohol ▶ **alcohol metílico** methylated spirits pl (BRIT), wood alcohol (US) ❏ **alcohólico, -a** adj, nm/f alcoholic ❏ **alcoholímetro** [alkoˈlimetro] nm Breathalyser® (BRIT), drunkometer (US) ❏ **alcoholismo** [alkoˈlismo] nm alcoholism

alcornoque [alkorˈnoke] nm cork tree; (fam) idiot

aldea [alˈdea] nf village ❏ **aldeano, -a** adj village cpd ♦ nm/f villager

aleación [aleaˈθjon] nf alloy

aleatorio, -a [aleaˈtorjo, a] adj random

aleccionar [alekθjoˈnar] vt to instruct; (adiestrar) to train

alegar [aleˈɣar] vt to claim; (JUR) to plead ♦ vi (LAm: discutir) to argue

alegoría [aleɣoˈria] nf allegory

alegrar [aleˈɣrar] vt (causar alegría) to cheer (up); (fuego) to poke; (fiesta) to liven up; **alegrarse** vr (fam) to get merry or tight; **alegrarse de** to be glad about

alegre [aˈleɣre] adj happy, cheerful; (fam) merry, tight; (chiste) risqué, blue ❏ **alegría** nf happiness; merriment

alejar [aleˈxar] vt to remove; (fig) to estrange; **alejarse** vr to move away

alemán, -ana [aleˈman, ana] adj, nm/f German ♦ nm (LING) German

Alemania [aleˈmanja] nf Germany

alentador, a [alentaˈðor, a] adj encouraging

alentar [alenˈtar] vt to encourage

alergia [aˈlerxja] nf allergy

alero [aˈlero] nm (de tejado) eaves pl; (guardabarros) mudguard

alerta [aˈlerta] adj, nm alert

aleta [aˈleta] nf (de pez) fin; (ala) wing; (de foca, DEPORTE) flipper; (AUTO) mudguard

aletear [aleteˈar] vi to flutter

alevín [aleˈβin] nm fry, young fish

alevosía [aleβoˈsia] nf treachery

alfabeto [alfaˈβeto] nm alphabet

alfalfa [alˈfalfa] nf alfalfa, lucerne

alfarería [alfareˈria] nf pottery; (tienda) pottery shop ❏ **alfarero, -a** nm/f potter

alféizar [alˈfeiθar] nm window-sill

alférez [alˈfereθ] nm (MIL) second lieutenant; (NÁUT) ensign

alfil [alˈfil] nm (AJEDREZ) bishop

alfiler [alfiˈler] nm pin; (broche) clip

alfombra [alˈfombra] nf carpet; (más pequeña) rug ❏ **alfombrilla** nf rug, mat; (INFORM) mouse mat o pad

alforja [alˈforxa] nf saddlebag

algas [ˈalɣas] nfpl seaweed

álgebra [ˈalxeβra] nf algebra

algo [ˈalɣo] pron something; anything ♦ adv somewhat, rather; **¿~ más?**

anything else?; (*en tienda*) is that all?; **por ~ será** there must be some reason for it

algodón [alɣo'ðon] *nm* cotton; (*planta*) cotton plant ▶ **algodón de azúcar** candy floss (BRIT), cotton candy (US) ▶ **algodón hidrófilo** cotton wool (BRIT), absorbent cotton (US)

alguien ['alɣjen] *pron* someone, somebody; (*en frases interrogativas*) anyone, anybody

alguno, -a [al'ɣuno, a] *adj* (*delante de nm*): **algún** some; (*después de n*): **no tiene talento ~** he has no talent, he doesn't have any talent ♦ *pron* (*alguien*) someone, somebody; **algún que otro libro** some book or other; **algún día iré** I'll one go o some day; **sin interés** ~ without the slightest interest; ~ **que otro** an occasional one; **algunos piensan** some (people) think

alhaja [a'laxa] *nf* jewel; (*tesoro*) precious object, treasure

alhelí [ale'li] *nm* wallflower, stock

aliado, -a [a'ljaðo, a] *adj* allied

alianza [a'ljanθa] *nf* alliance; (*anillo*) wedding ring

aliar [a'ljar] *vt* to ally; **aliarse** *vr* to form an alliance

alias ['aljas] *adv* alias

alicatado (*ESP*) *nm* tiling

alicates [ali'kates] *nmpl* pliers

aliciente [ali'θjente] *nm* incentive; (*atracción*) attraction

alienación [aljena'θjon] *nf* alienation

aliento [a'ljento] *nm* breath; (*respiración*) breathing; **sin ~** breathless

aligerar [alixe'rar] *vt* to lighten; (*reducir*) to shorten; (*aliviar*) to alleviate; (*mitigar*) to ease; (*paso*) to quicken

alijo [a'lixo] *nm* consignment

alimaña [ali'maɲa] *nf* pest

alimentación [alimenta'θjon] *nf* (*comida*) food; (*acción*) feeding; (*tienda*) grocer's (shop)

alimentar [alimen'tar] *vt* to feed; (*nutrir*) to nourish; **alimentarse** *vr* to feed

alimenticio, -a [alimen'tiθjo, a] *adj* food *cpd*; (*nutritivo*) nourishing, nutritious

alimento [ali'mento] *nm* food; (*nutrición*) nourishment

alineación [alinea'θjon] *nf* alignment; (*DEPORTE*) line-up

alinear [aline'ar] *vt* to align; (*DEPORTE*) to select, pick

aliñar [ali'ɲar] *vt* (*CULIN*) to season ❑ **aliño** *nm* (*CULIN*) dressing

alioli [ali'oli] *nm* garlic mayonnaise

alisar [ali'sar] *vt* to smooth

alistarse [alis'tarse] *vr* to enlist; (*inscribirse*) to enrol

aliviar [ali'βjar] *vt* (*carga*) to lighten; (*persona*) to relieve; (*dolor*) to relieve, alleviate

alivio [a'liβjo] *nm* alleviation, relief

aljibe [al'xiβe] *nm* cistern

allá [a'ʎa] *adv* (*lugar*) there; (*por ahí*) over there; (*tiempo*) then; **allá abajo** down there; **más allá** further on; **más allá de** beyond; **¡allá tú!** that's your problem!; **¡allá voy!** I'm coming!

allanamiento [aʎana'mjento] *nm* (*LAm: de policía*) raid ▶ **allanamiento de morada** burglary

allanar [aʎa'nar] *vt* to flatten, level (out); (*igualar*) to smooth (out); (*fig*) to subdue; (*JUR*) to burgle, break into

allegado, -a [aʎe'ɣaðo, a] *adj* near, close ♦ *nm/f* relation

allí [a'ʎi] *adv* there; **allí mismo** right there; **por allí** over there; (*por ese camino*) that way

alma ['alma] *nf* soul; (*persona*) person

almacén [alma'θen] *nm* (*depósito*) warehouse, store; (*MIL*) magazine; (*CS: de comestibles*) grocer's (shop);

grandes almacenes department store *sg* ▶ **almacenaje** *nm* storage

almacenar [almaθe'nar] *vt* to store, put in storage; (*proveerse*) to stock up with

almanaque [alma'nake] *nm* almanac

almeja [al'mexa] *nf* clam

almendra [al'mendra] *nf* almond ❏ **almendro** *nm* almond tree

almíbar [al'miβar] *nm* syrup

almidón [almi'ðon] *nm* starch

almirante [almi'rante] *nm* admiral

almohada [almo'aða] *nf* pillow; (*funda*) pillowcase ❏ **almohadilla** *nf* cushion; (*para alfileres*) pincushion; (*TEC*) pad

almohadón [almoa'ðon] *nm* large pillow; bolster

almorranas [almo'rranas] *nfpl* piles, haemorrhoids

almorzar [almor'θar] *vt*: ~ **una tortilla** to have an omelette for lunch ♦ *vi* to (have) lunch

almuerzo *etc* [al'mwerθo] *vb ver* **almorzar** ♦ *nm* lunch

alocado, -a [alo'kaðo, a] *adj* crazy

alojamiento [aloxa'mjento] *nm* lodging(s) *pl*; (*viviendas*) housing

alojar [alo'xar] *vt* to lodge; **alojarse** *vr* to lodge, stay

alondra [a'londra] *nf* lark, skylark

alpargata [alpar'ɣata] *nf* rope-soled sandal, espadrille

Alpes ['alpes] *nmpl*: **los ~** the Alps

alpinismo [alpi'nismo] *nm* mountaineering, climbing ❏ **alpinista** *nmf* mountaineer, climber

alpiste [al'piste] *nm* birdseed

alquilar [alki'lar] *vt* (*propietario*: *inmuebles*) to let, rent (out); (: *coche*) to hire out; (: *TV*) to rent (out); (*alquilador*: *inmuebles*, *TV*) to rent; (: *coche*) to hire, **"se alquila casa"** "house to let (*BRIT*) or for rent (*US*)"

alquiler [alki'ler] *nm* renting; letting; hiring; (*arriendo*) rent; hire charge; **de ~**

for hire ▶ **alquiler de automóviles** *o* **coches** car hire

alquimia [al'kimja] *nf* alchemy

alquitrán [alki'tran] *nm* tar

alrededor [alreðe'ðor] *adv* around, about; ~ **de** around, about; **mirar a su** ~ to look (round) about one ❏ **alrededores** *nmpl* surroundings

alta ['alta] *nf* (certificate of) discharge

altar [al'tar] *nm* altar

altavoz [alta'βoθ] *nm* loudspeaker; (*amplificador*) amplifier

alteración [altera'θjon] *nf* alteration; (*alboroto*) disturbance

alterar [alte'rar] *vt* to alter; to disturb; **alterarse** *vr* (*persona*) to get upset

altercado [alter'kaðo] *nm* argument

alternar [alter'nar] *vt* to alternate ♦ *vi* to alternate; (*turnar*) to take turns; **alternarse** *vr* to alternate; to take turns; ~ **con** to mix with ❏ **alternativa** *nf* alternative; (*elección*) choice ❏ **alternativo, -a** *adj* alternative; (*alterno*) alternating ❏ **alterno, -a** *adj* alternate; (*ELEC*) alternating

Alteza [al'teθa] *nf* (*tratamiento*) Highness

altibajos [alti'βaxos] *nmpl* ups and downs

altiplano [alti'plano] *nm* = **altiplanicie**

altisonante [altiso'nante] *adj* high-flown, high-sounding

altitud [alti'tuð] *nf* height; (*AVIAC, GEO*) altitude

altivo, -a [al'tiβo, a] *adj* haughty, arrogant

alto, -a ['alto, a] *adj* high; (*persona*) tall; (*sonido*) high, sharp; (*noble*) high, lofty ♦ *nm* halt; (*MÚS*) alto; (*GEO*) hill ♦ *adv* (*de sitio*) high; (*de sonido*) loudly ♦ *excl* halt!; **la pared tiene 2 metros de** ~ the wall is 2 metres high; **en alta mar** on the high seas; **en voz alta** in a loud voice; **las altas horas de la noche** the

small o wee hours; **en lo ~ de** at the top of; **pasar por ~** to overlook
❏ **altoparlante** [altopar'lante] (*LAm*) *nm* loudspeaker

altura [al'tura] *nf* height; (*NÁUT*) depth; (*GEO*) latitude; **la pared tiene 1.80 de ~** the wall is 1 metre 80cm high; **a estas alturas** at this stage; **a estas alturas del año** at this time of the year

alubia [a'luβja] *nf* bean

alucinación [aluθina'θjon] *nf* hallucination

alucinar [aluθi'nar] *vi* to hallucinate ♦ *vt* to deceive; (*fascinar*) to fascinate

alud [a'luð] *nm* avalanche; (*fig*) flood

aludir [alu'ðir] *vi*: ~ **a** to allude to; **darse por aludido** to take the hint

alumbrado [alum'braðo] *nm* lighting

alumbrar [alum'brar] *vt* to light (up) ♦ *vi* (*MED*) to give birth

aluminio [alu'minjo] *nm* aluminium (*BRIT*), aluminum (*US*)

alumno, -a [a'lumno, a] *nm/f* pupil, student

alusión [alu'sjon] *nf* allusion

alusivo, -a [alu'siβo, a] *adj* allusive

aluvión [alu'βjon] *nm* alluvium; (*fig*) flood

alverja [al'βerxa] (*LAm*) *nf* pea

alza ['alθa] *nf* rise; (*MIL*) sight

alzamiento [alθa'mjento] *nm* (*rebelión*) rising

alzar [al'θar] *vt* to lift (up); (*precio, muro*) to raise; (*cuello de abrigo*) to turn up; (*AGR*) to gather in; (*IMPRENTA*) to gather; **alzarse** *vr* to get up, rise; (*rebelarse*) to revolt; (*COM*) to go fraudulently bankrupt; (*JUR*) to appeal

ama ['ama] *nf* lady of the house; (*dueña*) owner; (*institutriz*) governess; (*madre adoptiva*) foster mother ► **ama de casa** housewife ► **ama de llaves** housekeeper

amabilidad [amaβili'ðað] *nf* kindness; (*simpatía*) niceness ❏ **amable** *adj*

kind; nice; **es usted muy amable** that's very kind of you

amaestrado, -a [amaes'traðo, a] *adj* (*animal: en circo etc*) performing

amaestrar [amaes'trar] *vt* to train

amago [a'mayo] *nm* threat; (*gesto*) threatening gesture; (*MED*) symptom

amainar [amai'nar] *vi* (*viento*) to die down

amamantar [amaman'tar] *vt* to suckle, nurse

amanecer [amane'θer] *vi* to dawn ♦ *nm* dawn; ~ **afiebrado** to wake up with a fever

amanerado, -a [amane'raðo, a] *adj* affected

amante [a'mante] *adj*: ~ **de** fond of ♦ *nmf* lover

amapola [ama'pola] *nf* poppy

amar [a'mar] *vt* to love

amargado, -a [amar'γaðo, a] *adj* bitter

amargar [amar'γar] *vt* to make bitter; (*fig*) to embitter; **amargarse** *vr* to become embittered

amargo, -a [a'maryo, a] *adj* bitter

amarillento, -a [amari'ʎento, a] *adj* yellowish; (*tez*) sallow ❏ **amarillo, -a** *adj, nm* yellow

amarrado, -a [a'maraðo, a] (*MÉX: fam*) *adj* mean, stingy

amarrar [ama'rrar] *vt* to moor; (*sujetar*) to tie up

amarras [a'marras] *nfpl*: **soltar ~** to set sail

amasar [ama'sar] *vt* (*masa*) to knead; (*mezclar*) to mix, prepare; (*confeccionar*) to concoct

amateur [ama'ter] *nmf* amateur

amazona [ama'θona] *nf* horsewoman ❏ **Amazonas** *nm*: **el Amazonas** the Amazon

ámbar ['ambar] *nm* amber

ambición [ambi'θjon] *nf* ambition ❏ **ambicionar** *vt* to aspire to ❏ **ambicioso, -a** *adj* ambitious

ambidextro, -a [ambiˈðekstro, a] *adj* ambidextrous

ambientación [ambjentaˈθjon] *nf* (*CINE, TEATRO etc*) setting; (*RADIO*) sound effects

ambiente [amˈbjente] *nm* atmosphere; (*medio*) environment

ambigüedad [ambiɣweˈðað] *nf* ambiguity ☐ **ambiguo, -a** *adj* ambiguous

ámbito [ˈambito] *nm* (*campo*) field; (*fig*) scope

ambos, -as [ˈambos, as] *adj pl, pron pl* both

ambulancia [ambuˈlanθja] *nf* ambulance

ambulante [ambuˈlante] *adj* travelling *cpd*, itinerant

ambulatorio [ambulaˈtorjo] *nm* state health-service clinic

amén [aˈmen] *excl* amen; **~ de** besides

amenaza [ameˈnaθa] *nf* threat ☐ **amenazar** [amenaˈθar] *vt* to threaten ♦ *vi*: **amenazar con hacer** to threaten to do

ameno, -a [aˈmeno, a] *adj* pleasant

América [aˈmerika] *nf* America ▶ **América Central/Latina** Central/Latin America ▶ **América del Norte/del Sur** North/South America ☐ **americana** *nf* coat, jacket; *ver tb* **americano** ☐ **americano, -a** *adj, nm/f* American

ametralladora [ametraʎaˈðora] *nf* machine gun

amigable [amiˈɣaβle] *adj* friendly

amígdala [aˈmiɣðala] *nf* tonsil ☐ **amigdalitis** *nf* tonsillitis

amigo, -a [aˈmiɣo, a] *adj* friendly ♦ *nm/f* friend, (*amante*) lover; **ser ~ de algo** to be fond of sth; **ser muy amigos** to be close friends

aminorar [aminoˈrar] *vt* to diminish; (*reducir*) to reduce; **~ la marcha** to slow down

amistad [amisˈtað] *nf* friendship; **amistades** *nfpl* (*amigos*) friends ☐ **amistoso, -a** *adj* friendly

amnesia [amˈnesja] *nf* amnesia

amnistía [amnisˈtia] *nf* amnesty

amo [ˈamo] *nm* owner; (*jefe*) boss

amolar (*MÉX: fam*) [amoˈlar] *vt* to ruin, damage

amoldar [amolˈdar] *vt* to mould; (*adaptar*) to adapt

amonestación [amonestaˈθjon] *nf* warning; **amonestaciones** *nfpl* (*REL*) marriage banns

amonestar [amonesˈtar] *vt* to warn; (*REL*) to publish the banns of

amontonar [amontoˈnar] *vt* to collect, pile up; **amontonarse** *vr* to crowd together; (*acumularse*) to pile up

amor [aˈmor] *nm* love; (*amante*) lover; **hacer el ~** to make love ▶ **amor propio** self-respect

amoratado, -a [amoraˈtaðo, a] *adj* purple

amordazar [amorðaˈθar] *vt* to muzzle; (*fig*) to gag

amorfo, -a [aˈmorfo, a] *adj* amorphous, shapeless

amoroso, -a [amoˈroso, a] *adj* affectionate, loving

amortiguador [amortiɣwaˈðor] *nm* shock absorber; (*parachoques*) bumper; **amortiguadores** *nmpl* (*AUTO*) suspension *sg*

amortiguar [amortiˈɣwar] *vt* to deaden; (*ruido*) to muffle; (*color*) to soften

amotinar [amotiˈnar] *vt* to stir up, incite (to riot); **amotinarse** *vr* to mutiny

amparar [ampaˈrar] *vt* to protect; **ampararse** *vr* to seek protection; (*de la lluvia etc*) to shelter ☐ **amparo** *nm* help, protection; **al amparo de** under the protection of

amperio [amˈperjo] *nm* ampère, amp

ampliación [ampljaˈθjon] *nf* enlargement; (*extensión*) extension

ampliar [am'pljar] vt to enlarge; to extend

amplificador [amplifika'ðor] nm amplifier

amplificar [amplifi'kar] vt to amplify

amplio, -a ['ampljo, a] adj spacious; (de falda etc) full; (extenso) extensive; (ancho) wide □ **amplitud** nf spaciousness; extent; (fig) amplitude

ampolla [am'poʎa] nf blister; (MED) ampoule

amputar [ampu'tar] vt to cut off, amputate

amueblar [amwe'βlar] vt to furnish

anales [a'nales] nmpl annals

analfabetismo [analfaβe'tismo] nm illiteracy □ **analfabeto, -a** adj, nm/f illiterate

analgésico [anal'xesiko] nm painkiller, analgesic

análisis [a'nalisis] nm inv analysis

analista [ana'lista] nmf (gen) analyst

analizar [anali'θar] vt to analyse

analógico, -a [ana'loxiko, a] adj (INFORM) analog; (reloj) analogue (BRIT), analog (US)

análogo, -a [a'naloɣo, a] adj analogous, similar

ananá [ana'na] nm (RPl) pineapple

anarquía [anar'kia] nf anarchy □ **anarquista** nmf anarchist

anatomía [anato'mia] nf anatomy

anca ['anka] nf rump, haunch; **ancas** nfpl (fam) behind sg

ancho, -a ['antʃo, a] adj wide; (falda) full; (fig) liberal ♦ nm width; (FERRO) gauge; **ponerse ~** to get conceited; **estar a sus anchas** to be at one's ease

anchoa [an'tʃoa] nf anchovy

anchura [an'tʃura] nf width; (extensión) wideness

anciano, -a [an'θjano, a] adj old, aged ♦ nm/f old man/woman; elder

ancla ['ankla] nf anchor

Andalucía [andalu'θia] nf Andalusia □ **andaluz, -a** adj, nm/f Andalusian

andamio [an'damjo] nm scaffold(ing)

andar [an'dar] vt to go, cover, travel ♦ vi to go, walk, travel; (funcionar) to go, work; (estar) to be ♦ nm walk, gait, pace; **andarse** vr to go away; **~ a pie/a caballo/en bicicleta** to go on foot/on horseback/by bicycle; **~ haciendo algo** to be doing sth; **¡anda!** (sorpresa) go on!; **anda por o en los 40** he's about 40

andén [an'den] nm (FERRO) platform; (NÁUT) quayside; (CAm: de la calle) pavement (BRIT), sidewalk (US)

Andes ['andes] nmpl: **los ~** the Andes

andinismo (LAm) [andi'nismo] nm mountaineering, climbing

Andorra [an'dorra] nf Andorra

andrajoso, -a [andra'xoso, a] adj ragged

anduve etc [an'duβe] vb ver **andar**

anécdota [a'nekðota] nf anecdote, story

anegar [ane'ɣar] vt to flood; (ahogar) to drown

anemia [a'nemja] nf anaemia

anestesia [anes'tesja] nf (sustancia) anaesthetic; (proceso) anaesthesia ▶ **anestesia general/local** general/local anaesthetic

anexar [anek'sar] vt to annex; (documento) to attach □ **anexión** nf annexation □ **anexo, -a** adj attached ♦ nm annexe

anfibio, -a [an'fiβjo, a] adj amphibious ♦ nm amphibian

anfiteatro [anfite'atro] nm amphitheatre; (TEATRO) dress circle

anfitrión, -ona [anfi'trjon, ona] nm/f host(ess)

ánfora nf (cántaro) amphora; (MÉX POL) ballot box

ángel ['anxel] nm angel ▶ **ángel de la guarda** guardian angel

angina [an'xina] nf (MED) inflammation of the throat; tonsillitis ▸ **angina de pecho** angina

anglicano, -a [angli'kano, a] adj, nm/f Anglican

anglosajón, -ona [anglosa'xon, ona] adj Anglo-Saxon

anguila [an'gila] nf eel

angula [an'gula] nf elver, baby eel

ángulo ['angulo] nm angle; (esquina) corner; (curva) bend

angustia [an'gustja] nf anguish

anhelar [ane'lar] vt to be eager for; (desear) to long for, desire ♦ vi to pant, gasp □ **anhelo** nm eagerness; desire

anidar [ani'ðar] vi to nest

anillo [a'niʎo] nm ring ▸ **anillo de boda/compromiso** wedding/ engagement ring

animación [anima'θjon] nf liveliness; (vitalidad) life; (actividad) activity; bustle

animado, -a [ani'maðo, a] adj lively; (vivaz) animated □ **animador, a** nm/f (TV) host(ess), compère; (DEPORTE) cheerleader

animal [ani'mal] adj animal; (fig) stupid ♦ nm animal; (fig) fool; (bestia) brute

animar [ani'mar] vt (BIO) to animate, give life to; (fig) to liven up, brighten up, cheer up; (estimular) to stimulate; **animarse** vr to cheer up; to feel encouraged; (decidirse) to make up one's mind

ánimo ['animo] nm (alma) soul; (mente) mind; (valentía) courage ♦ excl cheer up!

animoso, -a [ani'moso, a] adj brave; (vivo) lively

aniquilar [aniki'lar] vt to annihilate, destroy

anís [a'nis] nm aniseed; (licor) anisette

aniversario [aniβer'sarjo] nm anniversary

anoche [a'notʃe] adv last night; **antes de ~** the night before last

anochecer [anotʃe'θer] vi to get dark ♦ nm nightfall, dark; **al ~** at nightfall

anodino, -a [ano'ðino, a] adj dull, anodyne

anomalía [anoma'lia] nf anomaly

anonadado, -a [anona'ðaðo, a] adj: **estar ~** to be overwhelmed o amazed

anonimato [anoni'mato] nm anonymity

anónimo, -a [a'nonimo, a] adj anonymous; (COM) limited ♦ nm (carta anónima) anonymous letter; (: maliciosa) poison-pen letter

anormal [anor'mal] adj abnormal

anotación [anota'θjon] nf note; annotation

anotar [ano'tar] vt to note down; (comentar) to annotate

ansia ['ansja] nf anxiety; (añoranza) yearning □ **ansiar** vt to long for

ansiedad [ansje'ðað] nf anxiety

ansioso, -a [an'sjoso, a] adj anxious; (anhelante) eager; **~ de** o **por algo** greedy for sth

antaño [an'taɲo] adv long ago, formerly

Antártico [an'tartiko] nm: **el ~** the Antarctic

ante ['ante] prep before, in the presence of; (problema etc) faced with ♦ nm (piel) suede; **~ todo** above all

anteanoche [antea'notʃe] adv the night before last

anteayer [antea'jer] adv the day before yesterday

antebrazo [ante'βraθo] nm forearm

antecedente [anteθe'ðente] adj previous ♦ nm antecedent; **antecedentes** nmpl (historial) record sg ▸ **antecedentes penales** criminal record

anteceder [anteθe'ðer] vt to precede, go before

antecesor, a [anteθe'sor, a] nm/f predecessor

antelación [antela'θjon] *nf:* **con ~** in advance

antemano [ante'mano]: **de ~** *adv* beforehand, in advance

antena [an'tena] *nf* antenna; *(de televisión etc)* aerial ▶ **antena parabólica** satellite dish

antenoche (*LAm*) *adv* the night before last

anteojo [ante'oxo] *nm* eyeglass; **anteojos** *nmpl* (*LAm: gafas*) glasses, spectacles

antepasados [antepa'saðos] *nmpl* ancestors

anteponer [antepo'ner] *vt* to place in front; *(fig)* to prefer

anterior [ante'rjor] *adj* preceding, previous ◻ **anterioridad** *nf:* **con anterioridad a** prior to, before

antes ['antes] *adv (con prioridad)* before ♦ *prep:* **~ de** before ♦ *conj:* **~ de ir/de que te vayas** before going/before you go; **~ bien** (but) rather; **dos días ~** two days before o previously; **no quiso venir ~** she didn't want to come any earlier; **tomo el avión ~ que el barco** I take the plane rather than the boat; **~ de o que nada** (*en el tiempo*) first of all; *(indicando preferencia)* above all; **~ que yo** before me; **lo ~ posible** as soon as possible; **cuanto ~ mejor** the sooner the better

antibalas [anti'βalas] *adj inv:* **chaleco ~** bullet-proof jacket

antibiótico [anti'βjotiko] *nm* antibiotic

anticipación [antiθipa'θjon] *nf* anticipation; **con 10 minutos de ~** 10 minutes early

anticipado, -a [antiθi'paðo, a] *adj* (*pago*) advance; **por ~** in advance

anticipar [antiθi'par] *vt* to anticipate; *(adelantar)* to bring forward; *(COM)* to advance; **anticiparse** *vr:* **anticiparse a su época** to be ahead of one's time

anticipo [anti'θipo] *nm* (*COM*) advance

anticonceptivo, -a [antikonθep'tiβo, a] *adj, nm* contraceptive

anticongelante [antikonxe'lante] *nm* antifreeze

anticuado, -a [anti'kwaðo, a] *adj* out-of-date, old-fashioned; *(desusado)* obsolete

anticuario [anti'kwarjo] *nm* antique dealer

anticuerpo [anti'kwerpo] *nm* (*MED*) antibody

antidepresivo [antiðepre'siβo] *nm* antidepressant

antídoto [an'tiðoto] *nm* antidote

antiestético, -a [anties'tetiko, a] *adj* unsightly

antifaz [anti'faθ] *nm* mask; *(velo)* veil

antiglobalización *nf* anti-globalization ◻ **antiglobalizador, a** *adj* anti-globalization *cpd*

antiguamente [antiɣwa'mente] *adv* formerly; *(hace mucho tiempo)* long ago

antigüedad [antiɣwe'ðað] *nf* antiquity; *(artículo)* antique; *(rango)* seniority

antiguo, -a [an'tiɣwo, a] *adj* old, ancient; *(que fue)* former

Antillas [an'tiʎas] *nfpl:* **las ~** the West Indies

antílope [an'tilope] *nm* antelope

antinatural [antinatu'ral] *adj* unnatural

antipatía [antipa'tia] *nf* antipathy, dislike ◻ **antipático, -a** *adj* disagreeable, unpleasant

antirrobo [anti'rroβo] *adj inv* (*alarma etc*) anti-theft

antisemita [antise'mita] *adj* anti-Semitic ♦ *nmf* anti-Semite

antiséptico, -a [anti'septiko, a] *adj* antiseptic ♦ *nm* antiseptic

antojarse [anto'xarse] *vr* (*desear*): **se me antoja comprarlo** I have a mind to buy it; (*pensar*): **se me antoja que ...** I have a feeling that ...

antojitos (MÉX) nmpl snacks, nibbles

antojo [an'toxo] nm caprice, whim; (rosa) birthmark; (lunar) mole

antología [antolo'xia] nf anthology

antorcha [an'tortʃa] nf torch

antro ['antro] nm cavern

antropología [antropolo'xia] nf anthropology

anual [a'nwal] adj annual

anuario [a'nwarjo] nm yearbook

anulación [anula'θjon] nf annulment; (cancelación) cancellation

anular [anu'lar] vt (contrato) to annul, cancel; (ley) to revoke, repeal; (suscripción) to cancel ♦ nm ring finger

anunciar [anun'θjar] vt to announce; (proclamar) to proclaim; (COM) to advertise

anuncio [a'nunθjo] nm announcement; (señal) sign; (COM) advertisement; (cartel) poster

anzuelo [an'θwelo] nm hook; (para pescar) fish hook

añadidura [aɲaði'ðura] nf addition, extra; **por ~** besides, in addition

añadir [aɲa'ðir] vt to add

añejo, -a [a'ɲexo, a] adj old; (vino) mellow

añicos [a'ɲikos] nmpl: **hacer ~** to smash, shatter

año ['aɲo] nm year; **¡Feliz A~ Nuevo!** Happy New Year!; **tener 15 años** to be 15 (years old); **los años 90** the nineties; **el ~ que viene** next year ♦ **año bisiesto/escolar/fiscal/sabático** leap/school/tax/sabbatical year

añoranza [aɲo'ranθa] nf nostalgia; (anhelo) longing

apa (MÉX) excl goodness me!, good gracious!

apabullar [apaβu'ʎar] vt to crush, squash

apacible [apa'θiβle] adj gentle, mild

apaciguar [apaθi'ɣwar] vt to pacify, calm (down)

apadrinar [apaðri'nar] vt to sponsor, support; (REL) to be godfather to

apagado, -a [apa'ɣaðo, a] adj (volcán) extinct; (color) dull; (voz) quiet; (sonido) muted, muffled; (persona: apático) listless; **estar ~** (fuego, luz) to be out; (RADIO, TV etc) to be off

apagar [apa'ɣar] vt to put out; (ELEC, RADIO, TV) to turn off; (sonido) to silence, muffle; (sed) to quench

apagón [apa'ɣon] nm blackout; power cut

apalabrar [apala'βrar] vt to agree to; (contratar) to engage

apalear [apale'ar] vt to beat, thrash

apantallar (MÉX) vt to impress

apañar [apa'nar] vt to pick up; (asir) to take hold of, grasp; (reparar) to mend, patch up; **apañarse** vr to manage, get along

apapachar (MÉX: fam) [apapa'tʃar] vt to cuddle, hug

aparador [apara'ðor] nm sideboard; (MÉX: escaparate) shop window

aparato [apa'rato] nm apparatus; (máquina) machine; (doméstico) appliance; (boato) ostentation
▶ **aparato digestivo** (ANAT) digestive system ❑ **aparatoso, -a** adj showy, ostentatious

aparcamiento [aparka'mjento] nm car park (BRIT), parking lot (US)

aparcar [apar'kar] vt, vi to park

aparear [apare'ar] vt (objetos) to pair, match; (animales) to mate; **aparearse** vr to make a pair; to mate

aparecer [apare'θer] vi to appear; **aparecerse** vr to appear

aparejador, a [aparexa'ðor, a] nm/f (ARQ) master builder

aparejo [apa'rexo] nm harness; rigging; (de poleas) block and tackle

aparentar [aparen'tar] vt (edad) to look; (fingir): **~ tristeza** to pretend to be sad

aparente [apaˈrente] *adj* apparent; (*adecuado*) suitable

aparezco *etc vb ver* **aparecer**

aparición [apariˈθjon] *nf* appearance; (*de libro*) publication; (*espectro*) apparition

apariencia [apaˈrjenθja] *nf* (outward) appearance; **en ~** outwardly, seemingly

apartado, -a [aparˈtaðo, a] *adj* separate; (*lejano*) remote ♦ *nm* (*tipográfico*) paragraph ▸ **apartado de correos** (*ESP*) post office box ▸ **apartado postal** (*LAm*) post office box

apartamento [apartaˈmento] *nm* apartment, flat (*BRIT*)

apartar [aparˈtar] *vt* to separate; (*quitar*) to remove; **apartarse** *vr* to separate, part; (*irse*) to move away; to keep away

aparte [aˈparte] *adv* (*separadamente*) separately; (*además*) besides ♦ *nm* aside; (*tipográfico*) new paragraph

apasionado, -a [apasjoˈnaðo, a] *adj* passionate

apasionar [apasjoˈnar] *vt* to excite; **le apasiona el fútbol** she's crazy about football; **apasionarse** *vr* to get excited

apatía [apaˈtia] *nf* apathy

apático, -a [aˈpatiko, a] *adj* apathetic

Apdo *abr* (= *Apartado (de Correos)*) PO Box

apeadero [apeaˈðero] *nm* halt, stop, stopping place

apearse [apeˈarse] *vr* (*jinete*) to dismount; (*bajarse*) to get down o out; (*AUTO, FERRO*) to get off o out

apechugar [apetʃuˈɣar] *vr*: **~ con algo** to face up to sth

apegarse [apeˈɣarse] *vr*: **~ a** to become attached to ▫ **apego** *nm* attachment, devotion

apelar [apeˈlar] *vi* to appeal; **~ a** (*fig*) to resort to

apellidar [apeʎiˈðar] *vt* to call, name; **apellidarse** *vr*: **se apellida Pérez** her (sur)name's Pérez

apellido [apeˈʎiðo] *nm* surname

apenar [apeˈnar] *vt* to grieve, trouble; (*LAm: avergonzar*) to embarrass; **apenarse** *vr* to grieve; (*LAm: avergonzarse*) to be embarrassed

apenas [aˈpenas] *adv* scarcely, hardly ♦ *conj* as soon as, no sooner

apéndice [aˈpendiθe] *nm* appendix ▫ **apendicitis** *nf* appendicitis

aperitivo [aperiˈtiβo] *nm* (*bebida*) aperitif; (*comida*) appetizer

apertura [aperˈtura] *nf* opening; (*POL*) liberalization

apestar [apesˈtar] *vt* to infect ♦ *vi*: **~ (a)** to stink (of)

apetecer [apeteˈθer] *vt*: **¿te apetece un café?** do you fancy a (cup of) coffee? ▫ **apetecible** *adj* desirable; (*comida*) appetizing

apetito [apeˈtito] *nm* appetite ▫ **apetitoso, -a** *adj* appetizing; (*fig*) tempting

apiadarse [apjaˈðarse] *vr*: **~ de** to take pity on

ápice [ˈapiθe] *nm* whit, iota

apilar [apiˈlar] *vt* to pile o heap up

apiñarse [apiˈɲarse] *vr* to crowd o press together

apio [ˈapjo] *nm* celery

apisonadora [apisonaˈðora] *nf* steamroller

aplacar [aplaˈkar] *vt* to placate

aplastante [aplasˈtante] *adj* overwhelming; (*lógica*) compelling

aplastar [aplasˈtar] *vt* to squash (flat); (*fig*) to crush

aplaudir [aplauˈðir] *vt* to applaud

aplauso [aˈplauso] *nm* applause; (*fig*) approval, acclaim

aplazamiento [aplaθa'mjento] nm postponement

aplazar [apla'θar] vt to postpone, defer

aplicación [aplika'θjon] nf application; (esfuerzo) effort

aplicado, -a [apli'kaðo, a] adj diligent, hard-working

aplicar [apli'kar] vt (ejecutar) to apply; **aplicarse** vr to apply o.s.

aplique etc [a'plike] vb ver **aplicar** ♦ nm wall light

aplomo [a'plomo] nm aplomb, self-assurance

apodar [apo'ðar] vt to nickname

apoderado [apoðe'raðo] nm agent, representative

apoderarse [apoðe'rarse] vr: ~ **de** to take possession of

apodo [a'poðo] nm nickname

apogeo [apo'xeo] nm peak, summit

apoquinar [apoki'nar] (fam) vt to fork out, cough up

aporrear [aporre'ar] vt to beat (up)

aportar [apor'tar] vt to contribute ♦ vi to reach port; **aportarse** vr (LAm: llegar) to arrive, come

aposta [a'posta] adv deliberately, on purpose

apostar [apos'tar] vt to bet, stake; (tropas etc) to station, post ♦ vi to bet

apóstol [a'postol] nm apostle

apóstrofo [a'postrofo] nm apostrophe

apoyar [apo'jar] vt to lean, rest; (fig) to support, back; **apoyarse** vr: **apoyarse en** to lean on ▫ **apoyo** nm (gen) support; backing, help

apreciable [apre'θjaβle] adj considerable; (fig) esteemed

apreciar [apre'θjar] vt to evaluate, assess; (COM) to appreciate, value; (persona) to respect; (tamaño) to gauge, assess; (detalles) to notice

aprecio [a'preθjo] nm valuation, estimate; (fig) appreciation

aprehender [apreen'der] vt to apprehend, detain

apremio [a'premjo] nm urgency

aprender [apren'der] vt, vi to learn; ~ **algo de memoria** to learn sth (off) by heart

aprendiz, a [apren'diθ, a] nm/f apprentice; (principiante) learner ▫ **aprendizaje** nm apprenticeship

aprensión [apren'sjon] nm apprehension, fear ▫ **aprensivo, -a** adj apprehensive

apresar [apre'sar] vt to seize; (capturar) to capture

apresurado, -a [apresu'raðo, a] adj hurried, hasty

apresurar [apresu'rar] vt to hurry, accelerate; **apresurarse** vr to hurry, make haste

apretado, -a [apre'taðo, a] adj tight; (escritura) cramped

apretar [apre'tar] vt to squeeze; (TEC) to tighten; (presionar) to press together, pack ♦ vi to be too tight

apretón [apre'ton] nm squeeze ▸ **apretón de manos** handshake

aprieto [a'prjeto] nm squeeze; (dificultad) difficulty; **estar en un** ~ to be in a fix

aprisa [a'prisa] adv quickly, hurriedly

aprisionar [aprisjo'nar] vt to imprison

aprobación [aproβa'θjon] nf approval

aprobar [apro'βar] vt to approve (of); (examen, materia) to pass ♦ vi to pass

apropiado, -a [apro'pjaðo, a] adj suitable

apropiarse [apro'pjarse] vr: ~ **de** to appropriate

aprovechado, -a [aproβe'tʃaðo, a] adj industrious, hard-working; (económico) thrifty; (pey) unscrupulous

aprovechar [aproβe'tʃar] vt to use; (explotar) to exploit; (experiencia) to profit from; (oferta, oportunidad) to take advantage of ♦ vi to progress, improve; **aprovecharse** vr:

aprovecharse de to make use of; to take advantage of; **¡que aproveche!** enjoy your meal!

aproximación [aproksima'θjon] *nf* approximation; (*de lotería*) consolation prize

aproximar [aproksi'mar] *vt* to bring nearer; **aproximarse** *vr* to come near, approach

apruebo *etc vb ver* **aprobar**

aptitud [apti'tuð] *nf* aptitude

apto, -a ['apto, a] *adj* suitable

apuesta [a'pwesta] *nf* bet, wager

apuesto, -a [a'pwesto, a] *adj* neat, elegant

apuntar [apun'tar] *vt* (*con arma*) to aim at; (*con dedo*) to point a o to; (*anotar*) to note (down); (*TEATRO*) to prompt; **apuntarse** *vr* (*DEPORTE: tanto, victoria*) to score; (*ESCOL*) to enrol

⚠ No confundir **apuntar** con la palabra inglesa **appoint**.

apunte [a'punte] *nm* note

apuñalar [apuɲa'lar] *vt* to stab

apurado, -a [apu'raðo, a] *adj* needy; (*difícil*) difficult; (*peligroso*) dangerous; (*LAm: con prisa*) hurried, rushed

apurar [apu'rar] *vt* (*agotar*) to drain; (*recursos*) to use up; (*molestar*) to annoy; **apurarse** *vr* (*preocuparse*) to worry; (*LAm: darse prisa*) to hurry

apuro [a'puro] *nm* (*aprieto*) fix, jam; (*escasez*) want, hardship; (*vergüenza*) embarrassment; (*LAm: prisa*) haste, urgency

aquejado, -a [ake'xaðo, a] *adj*: ~ **de** (*MED*) afflicted by

aquel, aquella [a'kel, a'keʎa] *pron* that (one); **aquéllos(as)** those (ones)

aquel, aquella [a'kel, a'keʎa] *adj* that; **aquellos(as)** those

aquello [a'keʎo] *pron* that, that business

aquí [a'ki] *adv* (*lugar*) here; (*tiempo*) now; **aquí arriba** up here; **aquí mismo**

right here; **aquí yace** here lies; **de aquí a siete días** a week from now

ara ['ara] *nf*: **en aras de** for the sake of

árabe ['araβe] *adj, nmf* Arab ♦ *nm* (*LING*) Arabic

Arabia [a'raβja] *nf* Arabia ▶ **Arabia Saudí** o **Saudita** Saudi Arabia

arado [a'raðo] *nm* plough

Aragón [ara'yon] *nm* Aragon ❏ **aragonés, -esa** *adj, nm/f* Aragonese

arancel [aran'θel] *nm* tariff, duty

arandela [aran'dela] *nf* (*TEC*) washer

araña [a'raɲa] *nf* (*ZOOL*) spider; (*lámpara*) chandelier

arañar [ara'ɲar] *vt* to scratch

arañazo [ara'ɲaθo] *nm* scratch

arbitrar [arβi'trar] *vt* to arbitrate in; (*DEPORTE*) to referee ♦ *vi* to arbitrate

arbitrario, -a [arβi'trarjo, a] *adj* arbitrary

árbitro ['arβitro] *nm* arbitrator; (*DEPORTE*) referee; (*TENIS*) umpire

árbol ['arβol] *nm* (*BOT*) tree; (*NÁUT*) mast; (*TEC*) axle, shaft ▶ **árbol de Navidad** Christmas tree

arboleda [arβo'leða] *nf* grove, plantation

arbusto [ar'βusto] *nm* bush, shrub

arca ['arka] *nf* chest, box

arcada [ar'kaða] *nf* arcade; (*de puente*) arch, span; **arcadas** *nfpl* (*náuseas*) retching *sg*

arcaico, -a [ar'kaiko, a] *adj* archaic

arce ['arθe] *nm* maple tree

arcén [ar'θen] *nm* (*de autopista*) hard shoulder; (*de carretera*) verge

archipiélago [artʃi'pjelaɣo] *nm* archipelago

archivador [artʃiβa'ðor] *nm* filing cabinet

archivar [artʃi'βar] *vt* to file (away) ❏ **archivo** *nm* file, archive(s) *pl* ▶ **archivo adjunto** (*INFORM*) attachment ▶ **archivo de seguridad** (*INFORM*) backup file

arcilla [ar'θiʎa] *nf* clay

arco ['arko] *nm* arch; (*MAT*) arc; (*MIL, MÚS*) bow ▶ **arco iris** rainbow

arder [ar'ðer] *vi* to burn; **estar que arde** (*persona*) to fume

ardid [ar'ðið] *nm* ploy, trick

ardiente [ar'ðjente] *adj* burning, ardent

ardilla [ar'ðiʎa] *nf* squirrel

ardor [ar'ðor] *nm* (*calor*) heat; (*fig*) ardour ▶ **ardor de estómago** heartburn

arduo, -a ['arðwo, a] *adj* arduous

área ['area] *nf* area; (*DEPORTE*) penalty area

arena [a'rena] *nf* sand; (*de una lucha*) arena ▶ **arenas movedizas** quicksand *sg* ▶ **arenal** [are'nal] *nm* (*terreno arenoso*) sandy spot

arenisca [are'niska] *nf* sandstone; (*cascajo*) grit

arenoso, -a [are'noso, a] *adj* sandy

arenque [a'renke] *nm* herring

arete (*MÉX*) [a'rete] *nm* earring

Argel [ar'xel] *n* Algiers ❑ **Argelia** *nf* Algeria ❑ **argelino, -a** *adj, nm/f* Algerian

Argentina [arxen'tina] *nf* (*tb:* **la ~**) Argentina

argentino, -a [arxen'tino, a] *adj* Argentinian; (*de plata*) silvery ♦ *nm/f* Argentinian

argolla [ar'ɣoʎa] *nf* (large) ring

argot [ar'ɣo] (*pl* **argots**) *nm* slang

argucia [ar'ɣuθja] *nf* subtlety, sophistry

argumentar [arɣumen'tar] *vt, vi* to argue

argumento [arɣu'mento] *nm* argument; (*razonamiento*) reasoning; (*de novela etc*) plot; (*CINE, TV*) storyline

aria ['arja] *nf* aria

aridez [ari'ðeθ] *nf* aridity, dryness

árido, -a ['ariðo, a] *adj* arid, dry

Aries ['arjes] *nm* Aries

arisco, -a [a'risko, a] *adj* surly; (*insociable*) unsociable

aristócrata [aris'tokrata] *nmf* aristocrat

arma ['arma] *nf* arm; **armas** *nfpl* arms ▶ **arma blanca** blade, knife ▶ **arma de doble filo** double-edged sword ▶ **arma de fuego** firearm

armada [ar'maða] *nf* armada; (*flota*) fleet

armadillo [arma'ðiʎo] *nm* armadillo

armado, -a [ar'maðo, a] *adj* armed; (*TEC*) reinforced

armadura [arma'ðura] *nf* (*MIL*) armour; (*TEC*) framework; (*ZOOL*) skeleton; (*FÍSICA*) armature

armamento [arma'mento] *nm* armament; (*NÁUT*) fitting-out

armar [ar'mar] *vt* (*soldado*) to arm; (*máquina*) to assemble; (*navío*) to fit out; **armarla, ~ un lío** to start a row, kick up a fuss

armario [ar'marjo] *nm* wardrobe; (*de cocina, baño*) cupboard ▶ **armario empotrado** built-in cupboard

armatoste [arma'toste] *nm* (*mueble*) monstrosity; (*máquina*) contraption

armazón [arma'θon] *nf o m* body, chassis; (*de mueble etc*) frame; (*ARQ*) skeleton

armiño [ar'miɲo] *nm* stoat; (*piel*) ermine

armisticio [armis'tiθjo] *nm* armistice

armonía [armo'nia] *nf* harmony

armónica [ar'monika] *nf* harmonica

armonizar [armoni'θar] *vt* to harmonize; (*diferencias*) to reconcile

aro ['aro] *nm* ring; (*tejo*) quoit; (*CS: pendiente*) earring

aroma [a'roma] *nm* aroma, scent ❑ **aromaterapia** *nf* aromatherapy ❑ **aromático, -a** [aro'matiko, a] *adj* aromatic

arpa ['arpa] *nf* harp

arpía [ar'pia] *nf* shrew

arpón [ar'pon] nm harpoon

arqueología [arkeolo'xia] nf archaeology ▫ **arqueólogo, -a** nm/f archaeologist

arquetipo [arke'tipo] nm archetype

arquitecto [arki'tekto] nm architect ▫ **arquitectura** nf architecture

arrabal [arra'βal] nm poor suburb, slum; **arrabales** nmpl (afueras) outskirts

arraigar [arrai'ɣar] vt to establish ♦ vi to take root

arrancar [arran'kar] vt (sacar) to extract, pull out; (arrebatar) to snatch (away); (INFORM) to boot; (fig) to extract ♦ vi (AUTO, máquina) to start; (ponerse en marcha) to get going; ~ **de** to stem from

arranque etc [a'rranke] vb ver **arrancar** ♦ nm sudden start; (AUTO) start; (fig) fit, outburst

arrasar [arra'sar] vt (aplanar) to level, flatten; (destruir) to demolish

arrastrar [arras'trar] vt to drag (along); (fig) to drag down, degrade; (agua, viento) to carry away ♦ vi to drag, trail on the ground; **arrastrarse** vr to crawl; (fig) to grovel; **llevar algo arrastrado** to drag sth along

arrear [arre'ar] vt to drive on, urge on ♦ vi to hurry along

arrebatar [arreβa'tar] vt to snatch (away), seize; (fig) to captivate

arrebato [arre'βato] nm fit of rage, fury; (éxtasis) rapture

arrecife [arre'θife] nm reef

arreglado, -a [arre'ɣlaðo, a] adj (ordenado) neat, orderly; (moderado) moderate, reasonable

arreglar [arre'ɣlar] vt (poner orden) to tidy up; (algo roto) to fix, repair; (problema) to solve; **arreglarse** vr to reach an understanding; **arreglárselas** (fam) to get by, manage

arreglo [a'rreɣlo] nm settlement; (orden) order; (acuerdo) agreement; (MÚS) arrangement, setting

arremangar [arreman'gar] vt to roll up, turn up; **arremangarse** vr to roll up one's sleeves

arremeter [arreme'ter] vi: ~ **contra** to attack, rush at

arrendamiento [arrenda'mjento] nm letting; (alquilar) hiring; (contrato) lease; (alquiler) rent ▫ **arrendar** vt to let, lease; to rent ▫ **arrendatario, -a** nm/f tenant

arreos [a'rreos] nmpl (de caballo) harness sg, trappings

arrepentimiento [arrepenti'mjento] nm regret, repentance

arrepentirse [arrepen'tirse] vr to repent; ~ **de** to regret

arresto [a'rresto] nm arrest; (MIL) detention; (audacia) boldness, daring ▶ **arresto domiciliario** house arrest

arriar [a'rrjar] vt (velas) to haul down; (bandera) to lower, strike; (cable) to pay out

arriba

PALABRA CLAVE

[a'rriβa] adv

1 (posición) above; **desde arriba** from above; **arriba de todo** at the very top, right on top; **Juan está arriba** Juan is upstairs; **lo arriba mencionado** the aforementioned

2 (dirección): **calle arriba** up the street

3: **de arriba abajo** from top to bottom; **mirar a algn de arriba abajo** to look sb up and down

4: **para arriba**: **de 50 euros para arriba** from 50 euros up(wards)

♦ adj: **de arriba**: **el piso de arriba** the upstairs (BRIT) flat o apartment; **la parte de arriba** the top o upper part

♦ prep: **arriba de** (LAm: por encima de)

above; **arriba de 200 dólares** more than 200 dollars
♦ *excl*: **¡arriba!** up!; **¡manos arriba!** hands up!; **¡arriba España!** long live Spain!

arribar [arri'βar] *vi* to put into port; (*llegar*) to arrive

arriendo *etc* [a'rrjendo] *vb ver* **arrendar** ♦ *nm* = **arrendamiento**

arriesgado, -a [arrjes'yaðo, a] *adj* (*peligroso*) risky; (*audaz*) bold, daring

arriesgar [arrjes'yar] *vt* to risk; (*poner en peligro*) to endanger; **arriesgarse** *vr* to take a risk

arrimar [arri'mar] *vt* (*acercar*) to bring close; (*poner de lado*) to set aside; **arrimarse** *vr* to come close o closer; **arrimarse a** to lean on

arrinconar [arrinko'nar] *vt* (*colocar*) to put in a corner; (*enemigo*) to corner; (*fig*) to put on one side; (*abandonar*) to push aside

arrodillarse [arroði'ʎarse] *vr* to kneel (down)

arrogante [arro'yante] *adj* arrogant

arrojar [arro'xar] *vt* to throw, hurl; (*humo*) to emit, give out; (*COM*) to yield, produce; **arrojarse** *vr* to throw o hurl o.s.

arrojo [a'rroxo] *nm* daring

arrollador, a [arroʎa'ðor, a] *adj* overwhelming

arrollar [arro'ʎar] *vt* (*AUTO etc*) to run over, knock down; (*DEPORTE*) to crush

arropar [arro'par] *vt* to cover, wrap up; **arroparse** *vr* to wrap o.s. up

arroyo [a'rrojo] *nm* stream; (*de la calle*) gutter

arroz [a'rroθ] *nm* rice ▶ **arroz con leche** rice pudding

arruga [a'rruya] *nf* (*de cara*) wrinkle; (*de vestido*) crease ❑ **arrugar** [arru'yar] *vt* to wrinkle; to crease; **arrugarse** *vr* to get creased

arruinar [arrwi'nar] *vt* to ruin, wreck; **arruinarse** *vr* to be ruined, go bankrupt

arsenal [arse'nal] *nm* naval dockyard; (*MIL*) arsenal

arte ['arte] (*gen m en sg y siempre f en pl*) *nm* art; (*maña*) skill, guile; **artes** *nfpl* (*bellas artes*) arts

artefacto [arte'fakto] *nm* appliance

arteria [ar'terja] *nf* artery

artesanía [artesa'nia] *nf* craftsmanship; (*artículos*) handicrafts *pl* ❑ **artesano, -a** *nm/f* artisan, craftsman(-woman)

ártico, -a ['artiko, a] *adj* Arctic ♦ *nm*: **el Ártico** the Arctic

articulación [artikula'θjon] *nf* articulation; (*MED, TEC*) joint

artículo [ar'tikulo] *nm* article; (*cosa*) thing, article; **artículos** *nmpl* (*COM*) goods ▶ **artículos de escritorio** stationery

artífice [ar'tifiθe] *nmf* (*fig*) architect

artificial [artifi'θjal] *adj* artificial

artillería [artiʎe'ria] *nf* artillery

artilugio [arti'luxjo] *nm* gadget

artimaña [arti'maɲa] *nf* trap, snare; (*astucia*) cunning

artista [ar'tista] *nmf* (*pintor*) artist, painter; (*TEATRO*) artist, artiste ▶ **artista de cine** film actor/actress ❑ **artístico, -a** *adj* artistic

artritis [ar'tritis] *nf* arthritis

arveja [ar'βexa] *nf* (*LAm*) pea

arzobispo [arθo'βispo] *nm* archbishop

as [as] *nm* ace

asa ['asa] *nf* handle; (*fig*) lever

asado [a'saðo] *nm* roast (meat); (*LAm: barbacoa*) barbecue

ASADO

Traditional Latin American barbecues, especially in the River Plate area, are celebrated in the open air around a large grill which is used to grill mainly beef and various kinds of spicy pork sausage. They are usually very common during the summer and can go on for several days. The head cook is nearly always a man.

asador [asa'ðor] nm spit

asadura [asa'ðura] nf entrails pl, offal

asalariado, -a [asala'rjaðo, a] adj paid, salaried ♦ nm/f wage earner

asaltar [asal'tar] vt to attack, assault; (fig) to assail ▫ **asalto** nm attack, assault; (DEPORTE) round

asamblea [asam'blea] nf assembly; (reunión) meeting

asar [a'sar] vt to roast

ascendencia [asθen'denθja] nf ancestry; (LAm: influencia) ascendancy; **de ~ francesa** of French origin

ascender [asθen'der] vi (subir) to ascend, rise; (ser promovido) to gain promotion ♦ vt to promote; **~ a** to amount to ▫ **ascendiente** nm influence ♦ nmf ancestor

ascensión [asθen'sjon] nf ascent; (REL): **la A~** the Ascension

ascenso [as'θenso] nm ascent; (promoción) promotion

ascensor [asθen'sor] nm lift (BRIT), elevator (US)

asco ['asko] nm: **¡qué ~!** how revolting o disgusting; **el ajo me da ~** I hate o loathe garlic; **estar hecho un ~** to be filthy

ascua ['askwa] nf ember

aseado, -a [ase'aðo, a] adj clean; (arreglado) tidy; (pulcro) smart

asear [ase'ar] vt to clean, wash; to tidy (up)

asediar [ase'ðjar] vt (MIL) to besiege, lay siege to; (fig) to chase, pester ▫ **asedio** nm siege; (COM) run

asegurado, -a [aseɣu'raðo, a] adj insured

asegurador, a [aseɣura'ðor, a] nm/f insurer

asegurar [aseɣu'rar] vt (consolidar) to secure, fasten; (dar garantía de) to guarantee; (preservar) to safeguard; (afirmar, dar por cierto) to assure, affirm; (tranquilizar) to reassure; (tomar un seguro) to insure; **asegurarse** vr to assure o.s., make sure

asemejarse [aseme'xarse] vr to be alike; **~ a** to be like, resemble

asentado, -a [asen'taðo, a] adj established, settled

asentar [asen'tar] vt (sentar) to seat, sit down; (poner) to place, establish; (alisar) to level, smooth down o out; (anotar) to note down ♦ vi to be suitable, suit

asentir [asen'tir] vi to assent, agree; **~ con la cabeza** to nod (one's head)

aseo [a'seo] nm cleanliness; **aseos** nmpl (servicios) toilet sg (BRIT), cloakroom sg (BRIT), restroom sg (US)

aséptico, -a [a'septiko, a] adj germ-free, free from infection

asequible [ase'kiβle] adj (precio) reasonable; (meta) attainable; (persona) approachable

asesinar [asesi'nar] vt to murder; (POL) to assassinate ▫ **asesinato** nm murder; assassination

asesino, -a [ase'sino, a] nm/f murderer, killer; (POL) assassin

asesor, a [ase'sor, a] nm/f adviser, consultant ▫ **asesorar** [aseso'rar] vt (JUR) to advise, give legal advice to; (COM) to act as consultant to; **asesorarse** vr: **asesorarse con** o **de** to take advice from, consult ▫ **asesoría** nf (cargo) consultancy; (oficina) consultant's office

asestar [ases'tar] vt (golpe) to deal, strike

asfalto [as'falto] nm asphalt

asfixia [as'fiksja] nf asphyxia, suffocation ◘ **asfixiar** [asfik'sjar] vt to asphyxiate, suffocate; **asfixiarse** vr to be asphyxiated, suffocate

así [a'si] adv (de esta manera) in this way, like this, thus; (aunque) although; (tan pronto como) as soon as; **así que** so; **así como** as well as; **así y todo** even so; **¿no es así?** isn't it?, didn't you? etc; **así de grande** this big

Asia ['asja] nf Asia ◘ **asiático, -a** adj, nm/f Asian, Asiatic

asiduo, -a [a'siðwo, a] adj assiduous; (frecuente) frequent ◆ nm/f regular (customer)

asiento [a'sjento] nm (mueble) seat, chair; (de coche, en tribunal etc) seat; (localidad) seat, place; (fundamento) site ▶ **asiento delantero/trasero** front/back seat

asignación [asiɣna'θjon] nf (atribución) assignment; (reparto) allocation; (sueldo) salary ▶ **asignación (semanal)** pocket money

asignar [asiɣ'nar] vt to assign, allocate

asignatura [asiɣna'tura] nf subject; course

asilo [a'silo] nm (refugio) asylum, refuge; (establecimiento) home, institution ▶ **asilo político** political asylum

asimilar [asimi'lar] vt to assimilate

asimismo [asi'mismo] adv in the same way, likewise

asistencia [asis'tenθja] nf audience; (MED) attendance; (ayuda) assistance ▶ **asistencia en carretera** roadside assistance ◘ **asistente** nmf assistant; **los asistentes** those present ▶ **asistente social** social worker

asistido, -a [asis'tiðo, a] adj: ~ **por ordenador** computer-assisted

asistir [asis'tir] vt to assist, help ◆ vi: ~ **a** to attend, be present at

asma ['asma] nf asthma

asno ['asno] nm donkey; (fig) ass

asociación [asoθja'θjon] nf association; (COM) partnership ◘ **asociado, -a** adj associate ◆ nm/f associate; (COM) partner

asociar [aso'θjar] vt to associate

asomar [aso'mar] vt to show, stick out ◆ vi to appear; **asomarse** vr to appear, show up; ~ **la cabeza por la ventana** to put one's head out of the window

asombrar [asom'brar] vt to amaze, astonish; **asombrarse** vr (sorprenderse) to be amazed; (asustarse) to get a fright ◘ **asombro** nm amazement, astonishment; (susto) fright ◘ **asombroso, -a** adj astonishing, amazing

asomo [a'somo] nm hint, sign

aspa ['aspa] nf (cruz) cross; (de molino) sail; **en** ~ X-shaped

aspaviento [aspa'βjento] nm exaggerated display of feeling; (fam) fuss

aspecto [as'pekto] nm (apariencia) look, appearance; (fig) aspect

áspero, -a ['aspero, a] adj rough; bitter; sour; harsh

aspersión [asper'sjon] nf sprinkling

aspiración [aspira'θjon] nf breath, inhalation; (MÚS) short pause; **aspiraciones** nfpl (ambiciones) aspirations

aspirador [aspira'ðor] nm = **aspiradora**

aspiradora [aspira'ðora] nf vacuum cleaner, Hoover®

aspirante [aspi'rante] nmf (candidato) candidate; (DEPORTE) contender

aspirar [aspi'rar] vt to breathe in ◆ vi: ~ **a** to aspire to

aspirina [aspi'rina] nf aspirin

asqueroso, -a [aske'roso, a] adj disgusting, sickening

asta ['asta] *nf* lance; (*arpón*) spear; (*mango*) shaft, handle; (*ZOOL*) horn; **a media ~** at half mast

asterisco [aste'risko] *nm* asterisk

astilla [as'tiʎa] *nf* splinter; (*pedacito*) chip; **astillas** *nfpl* (*leña*) firewood *sg*

astillero [asti'ʎero] *nm* shipyard

astro ['astro] *nm* star

astrología [astrolo'xia] *nf* astrology ❑ **astrólogo, -a** *nm/f* astrologer

astronauta [astro'nauta] *nmf* astronaut

astronomía [astrono'mia] *nf* astronomy

astucia [as'tuθja] *nf* astuteness; (*ardid*) clever trick

asturiano, -a [astu'rjano, a] *adj, nm/f* Asturian

astuto, -a [as'tuto, a] *adj* astute; (*taimado*) cunning

asumir [asu'mir] *vt* to assume

asunción [asun'θjon] *nf* assumption; (*REL*): **A~** Assumption

asunto [a'sunto] *nm* (*tema*) matter, subject; (*negocio*) business

asustar [asus'tar] *vt* to frighten; **asustarse** *vr* to be (o become) frightened

atacar [ata'kar] *vt* to attack

atadura [ata'ðura] *nf* bond, tie

atajar [ata'xar] *vt* (*enfermedad, mal*) to stop ♦ *vi* (*persona*) to take a short cut

atajo [a'taxo] *nm* short cut

atañer [ata'ɲer] *vi* ~ **a** to concern

ataque *etc* [a'take] *vb ver* **atacar** ♦ *nm* attack ▶ **ataque cardíaco** heart attack

atar [a'tar] *vt* to tie, tie up

atarantado, -a [MÉX] *adj* (*aturdido*) dazed

atardecer [atarðe'θer] *vi* to get dark ♦ *nm* evening; (*crepúsculo*) dusk

atareado, -a [atare'aðo, a] *adj* busy

atascar [atas'kar] *vt* to clog up; (*obstruir*) to jam; (*fig*) to hinder;

atascarse *vr* to stall; (*cañería*) to get blocked up ❑ **atasco** *nm* obstruction; (*AUTO*) traffic jam

ataúd [ata'uð] *nm* coffin

ataviar [ata'βjar] *vt* to deck, array

atemorizar [atemori'θar] *vt* to frighten, scare

Atenas [a'tenas] *n* Athens

atención [aten'θjon] *nf* attention; (*bondad*) kindness ♦ *excl* (be) careful!, look out!

atender [aten'der] *vt* to attend to, look after; (*TEL*) to answer ♦ *vi* to pay attention

atenerse [ate'nerse] *vr*: ~ **a** to abide by, adhere to

atentado [aten'taðo] *nm* crime, illegal act; (*asalto*) assault; ~ **contra la vida de algn** attempt on sb's life

atentamente [atenta'mente] *adv*: **Le saluda ~** Yours faithfully

atentar [aten'tar] *vi*: ~ **a** o **contra** to commit an outrage against

atento, -a [a'tento, a] *adj* attentive, observant; (*cortés*) polite, thoughtful; **estar ~ a** (*explicación*) to pay attention to

atenuar [ate'nwar] *vt* (*disminuir*) to lessen, minimize

ateo, -a [a'teo, a] *adj* atheistic ♦ *nm/f* atheist

aterrador, a [aterra'ðor, a] *adj* frightening

aterrizaje [aterri'θaxe] *nm* landing ▶ **aterrizaje forzoso** emergency o forced landing

aterrizar [aterri'θar] *vi* to land

aterrorizar [aterrori'θar] *vt* to terrify

atesorar [ateso'rar] *vt* to hoard

atestar [ates'tar] *vt* to pack, stuff; (*JUR*) to attest, testify to

atestiguar [atesti'ɣwar] *vt* to testify to, bear witness to

atiborrar [atiβo'rrar] *vt* to fill, stuff; **atiborrarse** *vr* to stuff o.s.

ático ['atiko] nm (desván) attic; (apartamento) penthouse

atinado, -a [ati'naðo, a] adj (sensato) wise; (correcto) right, correct

atinar [ati'nar] vi (al disparar): ~ **al blanco** to hit the target; (fig) to be right

atizar [ati'θar] vt (fuego; (horno etc) to stoke; (fig) to stir up, rouse

atlántico, -a [at'lantiko, a] adj Atlantic ♦ nm: **el (océano) A~** the Atlantic (Ocean)

atlas ['atlas] nm atlas

atleta [at'leta] nm athlete ▢ **atlético, -a** adj athletic ▢ **atletismo** nm athletics sg

atmósfera [at'mosfera] nf atmosphere

atolladero [atoʎa'ðero] nm (fig) jam, fix

atómico, -a [a'tomiko, a] adj atomic

átomo ['atomo] nm atom

atónito, -a [a'tonito, a] adj astonished, amazed

atontado, -a [aton'taðo, a] adj stunned; (bobo) silly, daft

atormentar [atormen'tar] vt to torture; (molestar) to torment; (acosar) to plague, harass

atornillar [atorni'ʎar] vt to screw on o down

atosigar [atosi'ɣar] vt to harass, pester

atracador, a [atraka'ðor, a] nm/f robber

atracar [atra'kar] vt (NÁUT) to moor; (robar) to hold up, rob ♦ vi to moor; **atracarse** vr: **atracarse (de)** to stuff o.s. (with)

atracción [atrak'θjon] nf attraction

atraco [a'trako] nm holdup, robbery

atracón [atra'kon] nm: **darse o pegarse un ~ (de)** (fam) to stuff o.s. (with)

atractivo, -a [atrak'tiβo, a] adj attractive ♦ nm appeal

atraer [atra'er] vt to attract

atragantarse [atraɣan'tarse] vr: ~ **(con)** to choke (on); **se me ha**

atragantado el chico I can't stand the boy

atrancar [atran'kar] vt (puerta) to bar, bolt

atrapar [atra'par] vt to trap; (resfriado etc) to catch

atrás [a'tras] adv (movimiento) back(-wards); (lugar) behind; (tiempo) previously; **ir hacia** ~ to go back(wards), to go to the rear; **estar** ~ to be behind o at the back

atrasado, -a [atra'saðo, a] adj slow; (pago) overdue, late; (país) backward

atrasar [atra'sar] vi to be slow; **atrasarse** vr to remain behind; (tren) to be o run late ▢ **atraso** nm slowness; lateness, delay; (de país) backwardness; **atrasos** nmpl (COM) arrears

atravesar [atraβe'sar] vt (cruzar) to cross (over); (traspasar) to pierce; to go through; (poner al través) to lay o put across; **atravesarse** vr to come in between; (intervenir) to interfere

atravieso etc vb ver **atravesar**

atreverse [atre'βerse] vr to dare; (insolentarse) to be insolent ▢ **atrevido, -a** adj daring; insolent ▢ **atrevimiento** nm daring; insolence

atribución [atriβu'θjon] nf attribution; **atribuciones** nfpl (POL) powers; (ADMIN) responsibilities

atribuir [atriβu'ir] vt to attribute; (funciones) to confer

atributo [atri'βuto] nm attribute

atril [a'tril] nm (para libro) lectern; (MÚS) music stand

atropellar [atrope'ʎar] vt (derribar) to knock over o down; (empujar) to push (aside); (AUTO) to run over, run down; (agraviar) to insult ▢ **atropello** nm (AUTO) accident; (empujón) push; (agravio) wrong; (atrocidad) outrage

atroz [a'troθ] adj atrocious, awful

ATS nmf abr (= Ayudante Técnico Sanitario) nurse

atuendo [a'twendo] *nm* attire

atún [a'tun] *nm* tuna

aturdir [atur'ðir] *vt* to stun; *(de ruido)* to deafen; *(fig)* to dumbfound, bewilder

audacia [au'ðaθja] *nf* boldness, audacity ❏ **audaz** *adj* bold, audacious

audición [auði'θjon] *nf* hearing; *(TEATRO)* audition

audiencia [au'ðjenθja] *nf* audience; *(JUR: tribunal)* court

audífono [au'ðifono] *nm (para sordos)* hearing aid

auditor [auði'tor] *nm (JUR)* judge advocate; *(COM)* auditor

auditorio [auði'torjo] *nm* audience; *(sala)* auditorium

auge ['auxe] *nm* boom; *(climax)* climax

augurar [auɣu'rar] *vt* to predict; *(presagiar)* to portend

augurio [au'ɣurjo] *nm* omen

aula ['aula] *nf* classroom; *(en universidad etc)* lecture room

aullar [au'ʎar] *vi* to howl, yell

aullido [au'ʎiðo] *nm* howl, yell

aumentar [aumen'tar] *vt* to increase; *(precios)* to put up; *(producción)* to step up; *(con microscopio, anteojos)* to magnify ♦ *vi* to increase, be on the increase; **aumentarse** *vr* to increase, be on the increase ❏ **aumento** *nm* increase; rise

aun [a'un] *adv* even; ~ **así** even so; ~ **más** even *o* yet more

aún [a'un] *adv*: ~ **está aquí** he's still here; ~ **no lo sabemos** we don't know yet; ¿**no ha venido** ~? hasn't she come yet?

aunque [a'unke] *conj* though, although, even though

aúpa [a'upa] *excl* come on!

auricular [auriku'lar] *nm (TEL)* receiver; **auriculares** *nmpl (cascos)* headphones

aurora [au'rora] *nf* dawn

ausencia [au'senθja] *nf* absence

ausentarse [ausen'tarse] *vr* to go away; *(por poco tiempo)* to go out

ausente [au'sente] *adj* absent

austero, -a [aus'tero, a] *adj* austere

austral [aus'tral] *adj* southern ♦ *nm* monetary unit of Argentina

Australia [aus'tralja] *nf* Australia ❏ **australiano, -a** *adj, nm/f* Australian

Austria ['austrja] *nf* Austria ❏ **austríaco, -a** *adj, nm/f* Austrian

auténtico, -a [au'tentiko, a] *adj* authentic

auto ['auto] *nm (JUR)* edict, decree; *(: orden)* writ; *(AUTO)* car; **autos** *nmpl (JUR)* proceedings; *(: acta)* court record *sg*

autoadhesivo [autoaðe'siβo] *adj* self-adhesive; *(sobre)* self-sealing

autobiografía [autoβjoɣra'fia] *nf* autobiography

autobomba *(RPI) nm* fire engine

autobronceador [autoβronθea'ðor] *adj* self-tanning

autobús [auto'βus] *nm* bus ► **autobús de línea** long-distance coach

autocar [auto'kar] *nm* coach *(BRIT)*, *(passenger)* bus *(US)*

autóctono, -a [au'toktono, a] *adj* native, indigenous

autodefensa [autoðe'fensa] *nf* self-defence

autodidacta [autoði'ðakta] *adj* self-taught

autoescuela [autoes'kwela] *(ESP) nf* driving school

autógrafo [au'toɣrafo] *nm* autograph

autómata [au'tomata] *nm* automaton

automático, -a [auto'matiko, a] *adj* automatic ♦ *nm* press stud

automóvil [auto'moβil] *nm (motor)* car *(BRIT)*, automobile *(US)* ❏ **automovilismo** *nm (actividad)* motoring; *(DEPORTE)* motor racing ❏ **automovilista** *nmf* motorist, driver

autonomía [autono'mia] nf autonomy ▪ **autonómico, a** adj (POL) autonomous

autopista [auto'pista] nf motorway (BRIT), freeway (US) ▸ **autopista de cuota** (ESP) o **peaje** (MÉX) toll (BRIT) o turnpike (US) road

autopsia [au'topsja] nf autopsy, postmortem

autor, a [au'tor, a] nm/f author

autoridad [autori'ðað] nf authority ▪ **autoritario, -a** adj authoritarian

autorización [autoriθa'θjon] nf authorization ▪ **autorizado, -a** adj authorized; (aprobado) approved

autorizar [autori'θar] vt to authorize; (aprobar) to approve

autoservicio [autoser'βiθjo] nm (tienda) self-service shop (BRIT) o store (US); (restaurante) self-service restaurant

autostop [auto'stop] nm hitch-hiking; **hacer ~** to hitch-hike ▪ **autostopista** nmf hitch-hiker

autovía [auto'βia] nf ≈ A-road (BRIT), dual carriageway (BRIT), ≈ state highway (US)

auxiliar [auksi'ljar] vt to help ♦ nmf assistant ▪ **auxilio** nm assistance, help; **primeros auxilios** first aid sg

Av abr (= Avenida) Av(e)

aval [a'βal] nm guarantee; (persona) guarantor

avalancha [βa'lantʃa] nf avalanche

avance [a'βanθe] nm advance; (pago) advance payment; (CINE) trailer

avanzar [aβan'θar] vt, vi to advance

avaricia [aβa'riθja] nf avarice, greed ▪ **avaricioso, -a** adj avaricious, greedy

avaro, -a [a'βaro, a] adj miserly, mean ♦ nm/f miser

Avda abr (= Avenida) Av(e)

AVE ['aβe] nm abr (= Alta Velocidad Española) ≈ bullet train

ave ['aβe] nf bird ▸ **ave de rapiña** bird of prey

avecinarse [aβeθi'narse] vr (tormenta: fig) to be on the way

avellana [aβe'ʎana] nf hazelnut ▪ **avellano** nm hazel tree

avemaría [aβema'ria] nm Hail Mary, Ave Maria

avena [a'βena] nf oats pl

avenida [aβe'niða] nf (calle) avenue

aventajar [aβenta'xar] vt (sobrepasar) to surpass, outstrip

aventón [MÉX: fam] [aβen'ton] nm ride; **dar ~ a algn** to give sb a ride

aventura [aβen'tura] nf adventure ▪ **aventurero, -a** adj adventurous

avergonzar [aβeryon'θar] vt to shame; (desconcertar) to embarrass; **avergonzarse** vr to be ashamed; to be embarrassed

avería [aβe'ria] nf (TEC) breakdown, fault

averiado, -a [aβe'rjaðo, a] adj broken down; "~" "out of order"

averiguar [aβeri'ɣwar] vt to investigate; (descubrir) to find out, ascertain

avestruz [aβes'truθ] nm ostrich

aviación [aβja'θjon] nf aviation; (fuerzas aéreas) air force

aviador, a [aβja'ðor, a] nm/f aviator, airman(-woman)

ávido, -a [a'βiðo, a] adj avid, eager

avinagrado, -a [aβina'ɣraðo, a] adj sour, acid

avión [a'βjon] nm aeroplane; (ave) martin ▸ **avión de reacción** jet (plane)

avioneta [aβjo'neta] nf light aircraft

avisar [aβi'sar] vt (advertir) to warn, notify; (informar) to tell; (aconsejar) to advise, counsel ▪ **aviso** nm warning; (noticia) notice

avispa [a'βispa] nf wasp

avispado, -a [aβis'paðo, a] *adj* sharp, clever

avivar [aβi'βar] *vt* to strengthen, intensify

axila [ak'sila] *nf* armpit

ay [ai] *excl* (*dolor*) owl!, ouch!; (*aflicción*) oh!, oh dear!; **¡ay de mí!** poor me!

ayer [a'jer] *adv, nm* yesterday; **antes de ~** the day before yesterday; **~ mismo** only yesterday

ayote [a'jote] (*CAm*) *nm* pumpkin

ayuda [a'juða] *nf* help, assistance ♦ *nm* page ❑ **ayudante** *nm* assistant, helper; (*ESCOL*) assistant; (*MIL*) adjutant ❑ **ayudar** [aju'ðar] *vt* to help, assist

ayunar [aju'nar] *vi* to fast ❑ **ayunas** *nfpl*: **estar en ayunas** to be fasting ❑ **ayuno** *nm* fast; fasting

ayuntamiento [ajunta'mjento] *nm* (*consejo*) town *o* city council; (*edificio*) town *o* city hall

azafata [aθa'fata] *nf* air stewardess

azafrán [aθa'fran] *nm* saffron

azahar [aθa'ar] *nm* orange/lemon blossom

azar [a'θar] *nm* (*casualidad*) chance, fate; (*desgracia*) misfortune, accident; **por ~** by chance; **al ~** at random

Azores [a'θores] *nfpl*: **las ~** the Azores

azotar [aθo'tar] *vt* to whip, beat; (*pegar*) to spank ❑ **azote** *nm* (*látigo*) whip; (*latigazo*) lash, stroke; (*en las nalgas*) spank; (*calamidad*) calamity

azotea [aθo'tea] *nf* flat roof

azteca [aθ'teka] *adj, nmf* Aztec

azúcar [a'θukar] *nm* sugar ❑ **azucarado, -a** *adj* sugary, sweet

azucarero, -a [aθuka'rero, a] *adj* sugar *cpd* ♦ *nm* sugar bowl

azucena [aθu'θena] *nf* white lily

azufre [a'θufre] *nm* sulphur

azul [a'θul] *adj, nm* blue ► **azul celeste/ marino** sky/navy blue

azulejo [aθu'lexo] *nm* tile

azuzar [aθu'θar] *vt* to incite, egg on

B, b

B.A. *abr* (= *Buenos Aires*) B.A.

baba ['baβa] *nf* spittle, saliva ❑ **babear** *vi* to drool, slaver

babero [ba'βero] *nm* bib

babor [ba'βor] *nm* port (side)

babosada (*MEX, CAm: fam*) *nf* drivel ❑ **baboso, -a** [ba'βoso, a] (*LAm: fam*) *adj* silly

baca ['baka] *nf* (*AUTO*) luggage *o* roof rack

bacalao [baka'lao] *nm* cod(fish)

bache ['batʃe] *nm* pothole, rut; (*fig*) bad patch

bachillerato [batʃiʎe'rato] *nm* higher secondary school course

bacinica (*LAm*) *nf* [baθi'nika] potty

bacteria [bak'terja] *nf* bacterium, germ

Bahama [ba'ama]: **las (Islas)** *nfpl* the Bahamas

bahía [ba'ia] *nf* bay

bailar [bai'lar] *vt, vi* to dance ❑ **bailarín, -ina** *nm/f* (*ballet*) dancer ❑ **baile** *nm* dance; (*formal*) ball

baja ['baxa] *nf* drop, fall; (*MIL*) casualty; **dar de ~** (*soldado*) to discharge; (*empleado*) to dismiss

bajada [ba'xaða] *nf* descent; (*camino*) slope; (*de aguas*) ebb

bajar [ba'xar] *vi* to go down, come down; (*temperatura, precios*) to drop, fall ♦ *vt* (*cabeza*) to bow; (*escalera*) to go down, come down; (*precio, voz*) to lower; (*llevar abajo*) to take down; **bajarse** *vr* (*de coche*) to get out; (*de autobús, tren*) to get off; **bajarse algo de Internet** to download sth from the Internet; **~ de** (*coche*) to get out of; (*autobús, tren*) to get off

bajío [ba'xio] (*LAm*) *nm* lowlands *pl*

bajo, -a ['baxo] *adj* (*mueble, número, precio*) low; (*piso*) ground; (*de estatura*) small, short; (*color*) pale; (*sonido*) faint,

bajón soft, low; (voz: en tono) deep; (metal base; (humilde) low, humble ♦ adv (hablar) softly, quietly; (volar) low ♦ prep under, below, underneath ♦ nm (MÚS) bass; **~ la lluvia** in the rain

bajón [ba'xon] nm fall, drop

bakalao [baka'lao] (ESP: fam) nm rave (music)

bala ['bala] nf bullet

balacear (MÉX, CAm) vt to shoot

balance [ba'lanθe] nm (COM) balance; (: libro) balance sheet; (: cuenta general) stocktaking

balancear [balanθe'ar] vt to balance ♦ vi to swing (to and fro); (vacilar) to hesitate; **balancearse** vr to swing (to and fro), to hesitate

balanza [ba'lanθa] nf scales pl, balance ▶ **balanza comercial** balance of trade ▶ **balanza de pagos** balance of payments

balaustrada [balaus'traða] nf balustrade; (pasamanos) banisters pl

balazo [ba'laθo] nm (golpe) shot; (herida) bullet wound

balbucear [balβuθe'ar] vi, vt to stammer, stutter

balcón [bal'kon] nm balcony

balde ['balde] nm bucket, pail; **de ~** (for) free, for nothing; **en ~** in vain

baldosa [bal'dosa] nf (azulejo) floor tile; (grande) flagstone ❑ **baldosín** nm (small) tile

Baleares [bale'ares] nfpl: **las (Islas) ~** the Balearic Islands

balero (LAm) nm (juguete) cup-and-ball toy

baliza [ba'liθa] nf (AVIAC) beacon; (NÁUT) buoy

ballena [ba'ʎena] nf whale

ballet [ba'le] (pl **ballets**) nm ballet

balneario [balne'arjo] nm spa; (CS: en la costa) seaside resort

balón [ba'lon] nm ball

baloncesto [balon'θesto] nm basketball

balonmano [balon'mano] nm handball

balsa ['balsa] nf raft; (BOT) balsa wood

bálsamo ['balsamo] nm balsam, balm

baluarte [ba'lwarte] nm bastion, bulwark

bambú [bam'bu] nm bamboo

banana [ba'nana] (LAm) nf banana ❑ **banano** nm (LAm: árbol) banana tree; (CAm: fruta) banana

banca ['banka] nf (COM) banking

bancario, -a [ban'karjo, a] adj banking cpd, bank cpd

bancarrota [banka'rrota] nf bankruptcy; **hacer ~** to go bankrupt

banco ['banko] nm bench; (ESCOL) desk; (COM) bank; (GEO) stratum ▶ **banco de arena** sandbank ▶ **banco de crédito** credit bank ▶ **banco de datos** databank

banda ['banda] nf band; (pandilla) gang; (NÁUT) side, edge ▶ **banda sonora** soundtrack

bandada [ban'daða] nf (de pájaros) flock; (de peces) shoal

bandazo [ban'daθo] nm: **dar bandazos** to sway from side to side

bandeja [ban'dexa] nf tray

bandera [ban'dera] nf flag

banderilla [bande'riʎa] nf banderilla

bandido [ban'diðo] nm bandit

bando ['bando] nm (edicto) edict, proclamation; (facción) faction; **bandos** nmpl (REL) banns

bandolera [bando'lera] nf: **llevar en ~** to wear across one's chest

banquero [ban'kero] nm banker

banqueta [ban'keta] nf stool; (MÉX: en calle) pavement (BRIT), sidewalk (US)

banquete [ban'kete] nm banquet; (para convidados) formal dinner ▶ **banquete de boda(s)** wedding reception

banquillo [banˈkiʎo] nm (JUR) dock, prisoner's bench; (banco) bench; (para los pies) footstool

banquina (RPI) nf hard shoulder (BRIT), berm (US)

bañadera (RPI) nf bathtub

bañador [baɲaˈðor] (ESP) nm swimming costume (BRIT), bathing suit (US)

bañar [baˈɲar] vt to bath, bathe; (objeto) to dip; (de barniz) to coat; **bañarse** vr (en el mar) to bathe, swim; (en la bañera) to have a bath

bañera [baˈɲera] (ESP) nf bath(tub)

bañero, -a [baˈɲero, a] (CS) nm/f lifeguard

bañista [baˈɲista] nmf bather

baño [ˈbaɲo] nm (en bañera) bath; (en río) dip, swim; (cuarto) bathroom; (bañera) bath(tub); (capa) coating; **darse** o **tomar un ~** (en bañera) to have o take a bath; (en mar, piscina) to have a swim ▶ **baño María** bain-marie

bar [bar] nm bar

barahúnda [baraˈunda] nf uproar, hubbub

baraja [baˈraxa] nf pack (of cards) ❑ **barajar** vt (naipes) to shuffle; (fig) to jumble up

baranda [baˈranda] nf = **barandilla**

barandilla [baranˈdiʎa] nf rail, railing

barata (MÉX) nf (bargain) sale

baratillo [baraˈtiʎo] nm (tienda) junkshop; (subasta) bargain sale; (conjunto de cosas) secondhand goods pl

barato, -a [baˈrato, a] adj cheap ♦ adv cheap, cheaply

barba [ˈbarβa] nf (mentón) chin; (pelo) beard

barbacoa [barβaˈkoa] nf (parrilla) barbecue; (carne) barbecued meat

barbaridad [barβariˈðað] nf barbarity; (acto) barbarism; (atrocidad) outrage; **una ~** (fam) loads; **¡qué ~!** (fam) how awful!

barbarie [barˈβarje] nf barbarism, savagery; (crueldad) barbarity

bárbaro, -a [ˈbarβaro, a] adj barbarous, cruel; (grosero) rough, uncouth ♦ nm/f barbarian ♦ adv: **lo pasamos ~** (fam) we had a great time; **¡qué ~!** (fam) how marvellous!; **un éxito ~** (fam) a terrific success; **es un tipo ~** (fam) he's a great bloke

barbero [barˈβero] nm barber, hairdresser

barbilla [barˈβiʎa] nf chin, tip of the chin

barbudo, -a [barˈβuðo, a] adj bearded

barca [ˈbarka] nf (small) boat ❑ **barcaza** nf barge

Barcelona [barθeˈlona] n Barcelona

barco [ˈbarko] nm boat; (grande) ship ▶ **barco de carga/pesca** cargo/ fishing boat ▶ **barco de vela** sailing ship

barda [ˈbarða] (MÉX) nf (de madera) fence

baremo [baˈremo] nm (MAT: fig) scale

barítono [baˈritono] nm baritone

barman [ˈbarman] nm barman

barniz [barˈniθ] nm varnish; (en loza) glaze; (fig) veneer ❑ **barnizar** vt to varnish; (loza) to glaze

barómetro [baˈrometro] nm barometer

barquillo [barˈkiʎo] nm cone, cornet

barra [ˈbarra] nf bar, rod; (de un bar, café) bar; (de pan) French stick; (palanca) lever ▶ **barra de labios** lipstick ▶ **barra libre** free bar

barraca [baˈrraka] nf hut, cabin

barranco [baˈrranko] nm ravine; (fig) difficulty

barrena [baˈrrena] nf drill

barrer [baˈrrer] vt to sweep; (quitar) to sweep away

barrera [baˈrrera] nf barrier

barriada [baˈrrjaða] nf quarter, district

barricada [barriˈkaða] nf barricade

barrida [baˈrriða] nf sweep, sweeping

barriga [ba'rriɣa] nf belly; (panza) paunch ▸ **barrigón, -ona** adj potbellied ◻ **barrigudo, -a** adj potbellied

barril [ba'rril] nm barrel, cask

barrio ['barrjo] nm (vecindad) area, neighborhood (US); (en afueras) suburb ▸ **barrio chino** (ESP) red-light district

barro ['barro] nm (lodo) mud; (objetos) earthenware; (MED) pimple

barroco, -a [ba'rroko, a] adj, nm baroque

barrote [ba'rrote] nm (de ventana) bar

bartola [bar'tola] nf: **tirarse o tumbarse a la ~** to take it easy, be lazy

bártulos ['bartulos] nmpl things, belongings

barullo [ba'ruʎo] nm row, uproar

basar [ba'sar] vt to base; **basarse** vr: **basarse en** to be based on

báscula ['baskula] nf (platform) scales

base ['base] nf base; a ~ **de** on the basis of; (mediante) by means of ▸ **base de datos** (INFORM) database

básico, -a ['basiko, a] adj basic

basílica [ba'silika] nf basilica

básquetbol (LAm) nm basketball

---

bastante

PALABRA CLAVE

[bas'tante] adj

1 (suficiente) enough; **bastante dinero** enough o sufficient money; **bastantes libros** enough books

2 (valor intensivo): **bastante gente** quite a lot of people; **tener bastante calor** to be rather hot

♦ adv: **bastante bueno/malo** quite good/rather bad; **bastante rico** pretty rich; **(lo) bastante inteligente (como) para hacer algo** clever enough o sufficiently clever to do sth

---

bastar [bas'tar] vi to be enough o sufficient; **bastarse** vr to be self-sufficient; ~ **para** to be enough to; **¡basta!** (that's) enough!

bastardo, -a [bas'tarðo, a] adj, nm/f bastard

bastidor [basti'ðor] nm frame; (de coche) chassis; (TEATRO) wing; **entre bastidores** (fig) behind the scenes

basto, -a ['basto, a] adj coarse, rough ◻ **bastos** nmpl (NAIPES) ≈ clubs

bastón [bas'ton] nm stick, staff; (para pasear) walking stick

bastoncillo [baston'θiʎo] nm cotton bud

basura [ba'sura] nf rubbish (BRIT), garbage (US) ♦ adj: **comida/televisión** ~ junk food/TV

basurero [basu'rero] nm (hombre) dustman (BRIT), garbage man (US); (lugar) dump; (cubo) (rubbish) bin (BRIT), trash can (US)

bata ['bata] nf (gen) dressing gown; (cubretodo) smock, overall; (MED, TEC etc) lab(oratory) coat

batalla [ba'taʎa] nf battle; **de** ~ (fig) for everyday use ▸ **batalla campal** pitched battle

batallón [bata'ʎon] nm battalion

batata [ba'tata] nf sweet potato

batería [bate'ria] nf battery; (MÚS) drums ▸ **batería de cocina** kitchen utensils

batido, -a [ba'tiðo, a] adj (camino) beaten, well-trodden ♦ nm (CULIN: de leche) milk shake

batidora [bati'ðora] nf beater, mixer ▸ **batidora eléctrica** food mixer, blender

batir [ba'tir] vt to beat, strike; (vencer) to beat, defeat; (revolver) to beat, mix; **batirse** vr to fight; ~ **palmas** to applaud

batuta [ba'tuta] nf baton; **llevar la** ~ (fig) to be the boss, be in charge

baúl [ba'ul] nm trunk; (AUTO) boot (BRIT), trunk (US)

bautismo [bau'tismo] nm baptism, christening

bautizar [bauti'θar] vt to baptize, christen; (fam: diluir) to water down ❏ **bautizo** nm baptism, christening

bayeta [ba'jeta] nf floorcloth

baza ['baθa] nf trick; **meter ~** to butt in

bazar [ba'θar] nm bazaar

bazofia [ba'θofja] nf trash

be nf name of the letter B ▶ **be chica/grande** (MÉX) V/B ▶ **be larga** (LAm) B

beato, -a [be'ato, a] adj blessed; (piadoso) pious

bebé [be'βe] (pl **~s**) nm baby

bebedero [MÉX, CS] [beβe'ðero, a] nm drinking fountain

bebedor, a [beβe'ðor, a] adj hard-drinking

beber [be'βer] vt, vi to drink

bebida [be'βiða] nf drink ❏ **bebido, -a** adj drunk

beca ['beka] nf grant, scholarship ❏ **becario, -a** [be'karjo, a] nm/f scholarship holder, grant holder

bedel [be'ðel] nm (ESCOL) janitor; (UNIV) porter

béisbol ['beisβol] nm baseball

Belén [be'len] nm Bethlehem ❏ **belén** nm (de Navidad) nativity scene, crib

belga ['belɣa] adj, nmf Belgian

Bélgica ['belxika] nf Belgium

bélico, -a [be'liko, a] adj (actitud) warlike

belleza [be'ʎeθa] nf beauty

bello, -a ['beʎo, a] adj beautiful, lovely; **Bellas Artes Fine Art**

bellota [be'ʎota] nf acorn

bemol [be'mol] nm (MÚS) flat; **esto tiene bemoles** (fam) this is a tough one

bencina [ben'θina] nf (QUIM) benzine

bendecir [bende'θir] vt to bless

bendición [bendi'θjon] nf blessing

bendito, -a [ben'dito, a] pp de **bendecir** ♦ adj holy; (afortunado) lucky; (feliz) happy; (sencillo) simple ♦ nm/f simple soul

beneficencia [benefi'θenθja] nf charity

beneficiario, -a [benefi'θjarjo, a] nm/f beneficiary

beneficio [bene'fiθjo] nm (bien) benefit, advantage; (ganancia) profit, gain; **a ~ de algn** in aid of sb ❏ **beneficioso, -a** adj beneficial

benéfico, -a [be'nefiko, a] adj charitable

beneplácito [bene'plaθito] nm approval, consent

benévolo, -a [be'neβolo, a] adj benevolent, kind

benigno, -a [be'niɣno, a] adj kind; (suave) mild; (MED: tumor) benign, non-malignant

berberecho [berβe'retʃo] nm (ZOOL, CULIN) cockle

berenjena [beren'xena] nf aubergine (BRIT), eggplant (US)

Berlín [ber'lin] n Berlin

berlinesa [RPI] nf doughnut, donut (US)

bermudas [ber'muðas] nfpl Bermuda shorts

berrido [be'rriðo] nm bellow(ing)

berrinche [be'rrintʃe] (fam) nm temper, tantrum

berro ['berro] nm watercress

berza ['berθa] nf cabbage

besamel [besa'mel] nf (CULIN) white sauce, bechamel sauce

besar [be'sar] vt to kiss; (fig: tocar) to graze; **besarse** vr to kiss (one another) ❏ **beso** nm kiss

bestia ['bestja] nf beast, animal; (fig) idiot ▶ **bestia de carga** beast of burden ❏ **bestial** [bes'tjal] adj bestial; (fam) terrific ❏ **bestialidad** nf bestiality; (fam) stupidity

besugo [be'suɣo] nm sea bream; (fam) idiot

besuquear [besuke'ar] vt to cover with kisses; **besuquearse** vr to kiss and cuddle

betabel (MÉX) nm beetroot (BRIT), beet (US)

betún [be'tun] nm shoe polish; (QUÍM) bitumen

biberón [biβe'ron] nm feeding bottle

Biblia ['biβlja] nf Bible

bibliografía [biβljoɣra'fia] nf bibliography

biblioteca [biβljo'teka] nf library; (mueble) bookshelves ▶ **biblioteca de consulta** reference library ❏ **bibliotecario, -a** nm/f librarian

bicarbonato [bikarβo'nato] nm bicarbonate

bicho ['bitʃo] nm (animal) small animal; (sabandija) bug, insect; (TAUR) bull

bici ['biθi] (fam) nf bike ❏ **bicicleta** [biθi'kleta] nf bicycle, cycle; **ir en bicicleta** to cycle

bidé [bi'ðe] (pl ~s) nm bidet

bidón [bi'ðon] nm (de aceite) drum; (de gasolina) can

bien

PALABRA CLAVE

[bjen] nm

1 (bienestar) good; **te lo digo por tu bien** I'm telling you for your own good; **el bien y el mal** good and evil

2 (posesión): **bienes** goods; **bienes de consumo** consumer goods; **bienes inmuebles o raíces/bienes muebles** real estate sg/personal property sg

♦ adv

1 (de manera satisfactoria, correcta etc) well; **trabaja/come bien** she works/eats well; **contestó bien** he answered correctly; **me siento bien** I feel fine; **no me siento bien** I don't feel very well; **se está bien aquí** it's nice here

2 (frases): **hiciste bien en llamarme** you were right to call me

3 (valor intensivo) very; **un cuarto bien caliente** a nice warm room; **bien se ve que ...** it's quite clear that ...

4: **estar bien**: **estoy muy bien aquí** I feel very happy here; **está bien que vengan** it's all right for them to come; **¡está bien! lo haré** oh all right, I'll do it

5 (de buena gana): **yo bien que iría pero ...** I'd gladly go but ...

♦ excl: **¡bien!** (aprobación) O.K.!; **¡muy bien!** well done!

♦ adj inv (matiz despectivo): **gente bien** posh people

♦ conj

1: **bien ... bien**: **bien en coche bien en tren** either by car or by train

2 (LAm): **no bien**: **no bien llegue te llamaré** as soon as I arrive I'll call you

3: **si bien** even though; ver tb **más**

bienal [bje'nal] adj biennial

bienestar [bjenes'tar] nm well-being, welfare

bienvenida [bjembe'niða] nf welcome; **dar la ~ a algn** to welcome sb

bienvenido [bjembe'niðo] excl welcome!

bife ['bife] (CS) nm steak

bifurcación [bifurka'θjon] nf fork

bígamo, -a ['biɣamo, a] adj bigamous ♦ nm/f bigamist

bigote [bi'ɣote] nm moustache ❏ **bigotudo, -a** adj with a big moustache

bikini [bi'kini] nm bikini; (CULIN) toasted ham and cheese sandwich

bilingüe [bi'lingwe] adj bilingual

billar [bi'ʎar] nm billiards sg; **billares** nmpl (lugar) billiard hall; (sala de *juegos)* amusement arcade ▶ **billar americano** pool

billete [bi'ʎete] *nm* ticket; *(de banco)* (bank)note *(BRIT)*, bill *(US)*; *(carta)* note; **~ de 20 libras** £20 note ▶ **billete de ida y vuelta** *(BRIT)* return *(BRIT)* o round-trip *(US)* ticket ▶ **billete sencillo** o **de ida** single *(BRIT)* o one-way *(US)* ticket

billetera [biʎe'tera] *nf* wallet

billón [bi'ʎon] *nm* billion

bimensual [bimen'swal] *adj* twice monthly

bingo ['bingo] *nm* bingo

biodegradable [bioðeɣra'ðaβle] *adj* biodegradable

biografía [bioɣra'fia] *nf* biography

biología [biolo'xia] *nf* biology
❏ **biológico, -a** *adj* biological; *(cultivo, producto)* organic ▶ **biólogo, -a** *nm/f* biologist

biombo ['bjombo] *nm* (folding) screen

bioterrorismo *nm* bioterrorism

biquini [bi'kini] *nm* o *(RPI)* f bikini

birlar [bir'lar] *(fam)* vt to pinch

Birmania [bir'manja] *nf* Burma

birome *(RPI)* *nf* ballpoint (pen)

birria ['birrja] *nf*: **ser una ~** *(película, libro)* to be rubbish

bis [bis] *excl* encore!

bisabuelo, -a [bisa'βwelo, a] *nm/f* great-grandfather(-mother)

bisagra [bi'saɣra] *nf* hinge

bisiesto [bi'sjesto] *adj*: **año ~** leap year

bisnieto, -a [bis'njeto, a] *nm/f* great-grandson/daughter

bisonte [bi'sonte] *nm* bison

bisté [bis'te] *nm* = **bistec**

bistec [bis'tek] *nm* steak

bisturí [bistu'ri] *nm* scalpel

bisutería [bisute'ria] *nf* imitation o costume jewellery

bit [bit] *nm (INFORM)* bit

bizco, -a ['biθko, a] *adj* cross-eyed

bizcocho [biθ'kotʃo] *nm (CULIN)* sponge cake

blanca ['blanka] *nf (MÚS)* minim; **estar sin ~** *(ESP: fam)* to be broke; *ver tb* **blanco**

blanco, -a ['blanko, a] *adj* white ♦ *nm/f* white man/woman, white ♦ *nm (color)* white; *(en texto)* blank; *(MIL, fig)* target; **en ~** blank; **noche en ~** sleepless night

blandir [blan'dir] *vt* to brandish

blando, -a ['blando, a] *adj* soft; *(tierno)* tender, gentle; *(carácter)* mild; *(fam)* cowardly

blanqueador *(MÉX)* *nm* bleach

blanquear [blanke'ar] *vt* to whiten; *(fachada)* to whitewash; *(paño)* to bleach ♦ *vi* to turn white

blanquillo *(MÉX, CAm)* *nm* egg

blasfemar [blasfe'mar] *vi* to blaspheme, curse

bledo ['bleðo] *nm*: **me importa un ~** I couldn't care less

blindado, -a [blin'daðo, a] *adj (MIL)* armour-plated; *(antibala)* bullet-proof; **coche** *(LAm)* o **carro** *(ESP)* **~** armoured car

bloc [blok] *(pl* **blocs**) *nm* writing pad

blof *(MÉX)* *nm* bluff ❏ **blofear** *(MÉX)* *vi* to bluff

bloque ['bloke] *nm* block; *(POL)* bloc

bloquear [bloke'ar] *vt* to blockade ❏ **bloqueo** *nm* blockade; *(COM)* freezing, blocking ▶ **bloqueo mental** mental block

blusa ['blusa] *nf* blouse

bobada [bo'βaða] *nf* foolish action; foolish statement; **decir bobadas** to talk nonsense

bobina [bo'βina] *nf (TEC)* bobbin; *(FOTO)* spool; *(ELEC)* coil

bobo, -a ['boβo, a] *adj (tonto)* daft, silly; *(cándido)* naive ♦ *nm/f* fool, idiot ♦ *nm (TEATRO)* clown, funny man

boca ['boka] *nf* mouth; *(de crustáceo)* pincer; *(de cañón)* muzzle; *(entrada)* mouth, entrance; **bocas** *nfpl (de río)* mouth *sg*; **~ abajo/arriba** face down/up; **se me hace la ~ agua** my mouth is

bocacalle ► **boca de incendios** watering ► **boca del estómago** pit of the stomach ► **boca de metro** underground (BRIT) o subway (US) entrance

bocacalle [boka'kaʎe] nf (entrance to a) street; **la primera ~** the first turning o street

bocadillo [boka'ðiʎo] nm sandwich

bocado [bo'kaðo] nm mouthful, bite; (de caballo) bridle

bocajarro [boka'xarro]: **a ~** adv (disparar) point-blank

bocanada [boka'naða] nf (de vino) mouthful, swallow; (de aire) gust, puff

bocata [bo'kata] (fam) nm sandwich

bocazas [bo'kaθas] (fam) nm inv bigmouth

boceto [bo'θeto] nm sketch, outline

bochorno [bo'tʃorno] nm (vergüenza) embarrassment; (calor): **hace ~** it's very muggy

bocina [bo'θina] nf (MÚS) trumpet; (AUTO) horn; (para hablar) megaphone

boda [boða] nf (tb: **bodas**) wedding, marriage; (fiesta) wedding reception ► **bodas de oro/plata** golden/silver wedding sg

bodega [bo'ðeɣa] nf (de vino) (wine) cellar; (depósito) storeroom; (de barco) hold

bodegón [boðe'ɣon] nm (ARTE) still life

bofetada [bofe'taða] nf slap (in the face)

boga [boɣa] nf: **en ~** (fig) in vogue

Bogotá [boɣo'ta] n Bogotá

bohemio, -a [bo'emjo, a] adj, nm/f Bohemian

bohío (CAm) nm shack, hut

boicot [boi'kot] (pl **boicots**) nm boycott ❏ **boicotear** vt to boycott

bóiler (MÉX) nm boiler

boina ['boina] nf beret

bola ['bola] nf ball; (canica) marble; (NAIPES) (grand) slam; (betún) shoe polish; (mentira) tale, story; **bolas** (fpl) (LAm: caza) bolas sg ► **bola de billar** billiard ball ► **bola de nieve** snowball

boleadoras [bolea'ðoras] nfpl bolas sg

bolear (MÉX) vt (zapatos) to polish, shine

bolera [bo'lera] nf skittle o bowling alley

bolero, -a (MÉX) [bo'lero] nm/f (limpiabotas) shoeshine boy/girl

boleta [bo'leta] (LAm) nf (de voto) ticket; (CS: recibo) receipt ► **boleta de calificaciones** (MÉX) report card

boletería [bolete'ria] (LAm) nf ticket office

boletín [bole'tin] nm bulletin; (periódico) journal, review ► **boletín de noticias** news bulletin

boleto [bo'leto] nm (LAm) ticket ► **boleto de ida y vuelta** (LAm) round trip ticket ► **boleto redondo** (MÉX) round trip ticket

boli ['boli] (fam) nm Biro®

bolígrafo [bo'liɣrafo] nm ball-point pen, Biro®

bolilla (RPl) nf topic

bolillo [bo'liʎo] nm (bread) roll

bolita (CS) nf marble

bolívar [bo'liβar] nm monetary unit of Venezuela

Bolivia [bo'liβja] nf Bolivia ❏ **boliviano, -a** adj, nm/f Bolivian

bollería [boʎe'ria] nf cakes pl and pastries pl

bollo ['boʎo] nm (pan) roll; (bulto) bump, lump; (abolladura) dent

bolo ['bolo] nm skittle; (píldora) (large) pill; (juego de) **bolos** nmpl skittles sg

bolsa ['bolsa] nf (para llevar algo) bag; (MÉX, CAm: bolsillo) pocket; (MÉX: de mujer) handbag; (ANAT) cavity, sac; (COM) stock exchange; (MINERÍA) pocket; **de ~** pocket cpd ► **bolsa de agua caliente** hot water bottle ► **bolsa de aire** air pocket ► **bolsa de dormir** (MÉX, RPl) sleeping bag

▶ **bolsa de la compra** shopping bag
▶ **bolsa de papel/plástico** paper/
plastic bag

bolsear (*MÉX, CAm*) vt: ~ **a algn** to pick
sb's pocket

bolsillo [bol'siʎo] nm pocket; (*cartera*)
purse; **de** ~ pocket(-size)

bolso ['bolso] nm (*bolsa*) bag; (*de mujer*)
handbag

bomba ['bomba] nf (*MIL*) bomb; (*TEC*)
pump ♦ adj (*fam*): **noticia** ~ bombshell
♦ adv (*fam*): **pasarlo** ~ to have a great
time ▶ **bomba atómica/de efecto
retardado/de humo** atomic/time/
smoke bomb

bombacha (*RPI*) nf panties pl

bombardear [bombarðe'ar] vt to
bombard; (*MIL*) to bomb
□ **bombardeo** nm bombardment;
bombing

bombazo (*MÉX*) nm (*explosión*)
explosion; (*fam: notición*) bombshell;
(: *éxito*) smash hit

bombear [bombe'ar] vt (*agua*) to
pump (out o up)

bombero [bom'bero] nm fireman

bombilla [bom'biʎa] (*ESP*) nf (*light*)
bulb

bombita (*RPI*) nf (*light*) bulb

bombo ['bombo] nm (*MÚS*) bass drum;
(*TEC*) drum

bombón [bom'bon] nm chocolate;
(*MÉX: de caramelo*) marshmallow

bombona [bom'bona] (*ESP*) nf (*de
butano, oxígeno*) cylinder

bonachón, -ona [bona'tʃon, ona] adj
good-natured, easy-going

bonanza [bo'nanθa] nf (*NÁUT*) fair
weather; (*fig*) bonanza; (*MINERÍA*) rich
pocket o vein

bondad [bon'dað] nf goodness,
kindness; **tenga la** ~ **de** (please) be
good enough to

bonito, -a [bo'nito, a] adj pretty;
(*agradable*) nice ♦ nm (*atún*) tuna (fish)

bono ['bono] nm voucher; (*FINANZAS*)
bond

bonobús [bono'βus] (*ESP*) nm bus pass

bonoloto [bono'loto] nf state-run
weekly lottery

boquerón [boke'ron] nm (*pez*) (kind of)
anchovy; (*agujero*) large hole

boquete [bo'kete] nm gap, hole

boquiabierto, -a [bokia'βjerto, a] adj:
quedarse ~ to be amazed o
flabbergasted

boquilla [bo'kiʎa] nf (*para riego*)
nozzle; (*para cigarro*) cigarette holder;
(*MÚS*) mouthpiece

borbotón [borβo'ton] nm: **salir a
borbotones** to gush out

borda ['borða] nf (*NÁUT*) (ship's) rail;
tirar algo/caerse por la ~ to throw sth/
fall overboard

bordado [bor'ðaðo] nm embroidery

bordar [bor'ðar] vt to embroider

borde ['borðe] nm edge, border; (*de
camino etc*) side; (*en la costura*) hem; **al
~ de** (*fig*) on the verge o brink of; **ser** ~
(*ESP: fam*) to be rude □ **bordear** vt to
border

bordillo [bor'ðiʎo] nm kerb (*BRIT*), curb
(*US*)

bordo ['borðo] nm (*NÁUT*) side; **a** ~ on
board

borlote (*MÉX*) nm row, uproar

borrachera [borra'tʃera] nf (*ebriedad*)
drunkenness; (*orgía*) spree, binge

borracho, -a [bo'rratʃo, a] adj drunk
♦ nm/f (*habitual*) drunkard, drunk;
(*temporal*) drunk, drunk man/woman

borrador [borra'ðor] nm (*escritura*) first
draft, rough sketch; (*goma*) rubber
(*BRIT*), eraser

borrar [bo'rrar] vt to erase, rub out

borrasca [bo'rraska] nf storm

borrego, -a [bo'rreɣo, a] nm/f (*ZOOL:
joven*) (yearling) lamb; (*adulto*) sheep
♦ nm (*MÉX: fam*) false rumour

borrico, -a [bo'rriko, a] nm/f donkey;
she-donkey; (*fig*) stupid man/woman

borrón [bo'rron] nm (mancha) stain

borroso, -a [bo'rroso, a] adj vague, unclear; (escritura) illegible

bosque ['boske] nm wood; (grande) forest

bostezar [boste'θar] vi to yawn
❏ **bostezo** nm yawn

bota ['bota] nf (calzado) boot; (para vino) leather wine bottle ▸ **botas de agua** o **goma** Wellingtons

botana (MÉX) nf snack, appetizer

botánica [bo'tanika] nf (ciencia) botany; ver tb **botánico**

botánico, -a [bo'taniko, a] adj botanical ♦ nm/f botanist

botar [bo'tar] vt to throw, hurl; (NÁUT) to launch; (LAm: echar) to throw out ♦ vi (ESP: saltar) to bounce

bote ['bote] nm (salto) bounce; (golpe) thrust; (ESP: envase) tin, can; (embarcación) boat; (MÉX, CAm: pey: cárcel) jail; **de ~ en ~** packed, jammed full ▸ **bote de la basura** (MÉX) dustbin (BRIT), trashcan (US) ▸ **bote salvavidas** lifeboat

botella [bo'teʎa] nf bottle ❏ **botellín** nm small bottle ❏ **botellón** (ESP: fam) outdoor drinking session

botijo [bo'tixo] nm (earthenware) jug

botín [bo'tin] nm (calzado) half boot; (polaina) spat; (MIL) booty

botiquín [boti'kin] nm (armario) medicine cabinet; (portátil) first-aid kit

botón [bo'ton] nm button; (BOT) bud

botones [bo'tones] nm inv bellboy (BRIT), bellhop (US)

bóveda ['boβeða] nf (ARQ) vault

boxeador [boksea'ðor] nm boxer

boxeo [bok'seo] nm boxing

boya ['boja] nf (NÁUT) buoy; (de caña) float

boyante [bo'jante] adj prosperous

bozal [bo'θal] nm (para caballos) halter; (de perro) muzzle

bragas ['braɣas] nfpl (de mujer) panties, knickers (BRIT)

bragueta [bra'ɣeta] nf fly, flies pl

braille [breil] nm braille

brasa ['brasa] nf live o hot coal

brasero [bra'sero] nm brazier

brasier (MÉX) nm bra

Brasil [bra'sil] nm (tb: **el ~**) Brazil
❏ **brasileño, -a** adj, nm/f Brazilian

brassier (MÉX) nm ver **brasier**

bravo, -a ['braβo, a] adj (valiente) brave; (feroz) ferocious; (salvaje) wild; (mar etc) rough, stormy ♦ excl bravo!
❏ **bravura** nf bravery; ferocity

braza ['braθa] nf fathom; **nadar a ~** to swim breast-stroke

brazalete [braθa'lete] nm (pulsera) bracelet; (banda) armband

brazo ['braθo] nm arm; (ZOOL) foreleg; (BOT) limb, branch; **luchar a ~ partido** to fight hand-to-hand; **ir cogidos del ~** to walk arm in arm

brebaje [bre'βaxe] nm potion

brecha ['bretʃa] nf (hoyo, vacío) gap, opening; (MIL: fig) breach

brega ['breɣa] nf (lucha) struggle; (trabajo) hard work

breva ['breβa] nf early fig

breve ['breβe] adj short, brief ♦ nf (MÚS) breve; **en ~** (pronto) shortly, before long ❏ **brevedad** nf brevity, shortness

bribón, -ona [bri'βon, ona] adj idle, lazy ♦ nm/f (pícaro) rascal, rogue

bricolaje [briko'laxe] nm do-it-yourself, DIY

brida ['briða] nf bridle, rein; (TEC) clamp

bridge [britʃ] nm bridge

brigada [bri'ɣaða] nf (de unidad) brigade; (de trabajadores) squad, gang ♦ nm ≈ staff-sergeant, sergeant-major

brillante [bri'ʎante] adj brilliant ♦ nm diamond

brillar [bri'ʎar] vi to shine; (joyas) to sparkle

brillo ['briʎo] nm shine; (brillantez) brilliance; (fig) splendour; **sacar ~ a** to polish

brincar [brin'kar] vi to skip about, hop about, jump about

brinco ['brinko] nm jump, leap

brindar [brin'dar] vi: **~ a o por** to drink (a toast) to ♦ vt to offer, present

brindis ['brindis] nm inv toast

brío ['brio] nm spirit, dash

brisa ['brisa] nf breeze

británico, -a [bri'taniko, a] adj British ♦ nm/f Briton, British person

brizna ['briθna] nf (de hierba, paja) blade; (de tabaco) leaf

broca ['broka] nf (TEC) drill, bit

brocha ['brotʃa] nf (large) paintbrush ▶ **brocha de afeitar** shaving brush

broche ['brotʃe] nm brooch

broma ['broma] nf joke; **de o en ~** in fun, as a joke ▶ **broma pesada** practical joke ▶ **bromear** vi to joke

bromista [bro'mista] adj fond of joking ♦ nmf joker, wag

bronca ['bronka] nf row; **echar una ~ a algn** to tick sb off

bronce ['bronθe] nm bronze ❑ **bronceado, -a** adj bronze; (por el sol) tanned ♦ nm (sun)tan; (TEC) bronzing

bronceador [bronθea'ðor] nm suntan lotion

broncearse [bronθe'arse] vr to get a suntan

bronquio ['bronkjo] nm (ANAT) bronchial tube

bronquitis [bron'kitis] nf inv bronchitis

brotar [bro'tar] vi (BOT) to sprout; (aguas) to gush (forth); (MED) to break out

brote ['brote] nm (BOT) shoot; (MED, fig) outbreak

bruces ['bruθes]: **de ~** adv: **caer o dar de ~** to fall headlong, fall flat

bruja ['bruxa] nf witch ❑ **brujería** nf witchcraft

brujo ['bruxo] nm wizard, magician

brújula ['bruxula] nf compass

bruma ['bruma] nf mist

brusco, -a ['brusko, a] adj (súbito) sudden; (áspero) brusque

Bruselas [bru'selas] n Brussels

brutal [bru'tal] adj brutal ❑ **brutalidad** [brutali'ðað] nf brutality

bruto, -a ['bruto, a] adj (idiota) stupid; (bestial) brutish; (peso) gross; **en ~** raw, unworked

Bs.As. abr (= Buenos Aires) B.A.

bucal [bu'kal] adj oral; **por vía ~** orally

bucear [buθe'ar] vi to dive ♦ vt to explore ❑ **buceo** nm diving

bucle ['bukle] nm curl

budismo [bu'ðismo] nm Buddhism

buen [bwen] adj V **bueno**

buenamente [bwena'mente] adv (fácilmente) easily; (voluntariamente) willingly

buenaventura [bwenaβen'tura] nf (suerte) good luck; (adivinación) fortune

buenmozo (MÉX) adj handsome

bueno, -a

PALABRA CLAVE

['bweno, a] (antes de nmsg: **buen**) adj

1 (excelente etc) good; **es un libro bueno, es un buen libro** it's a good book; **hace bueno, hace buen tiempo** the weather is fine, it is fine; **el bueno de Paco** good old Paco; **fue muy bueno conmigo** he was very nice o kind to me

2 (apropiado): **ser bueno para** to be good for; **creo que vamos por buen camino** I think we're on the right track

3 (irónico): **le di un buen rapapolvo** I gave him a good o real ticking off;

¡buen conductor estás hecho! some o a fine driver you are!; **¡estaría bueno que ...!** a fine thing it would be if ...!

d (atractivo, sabroso): **está bueno este bizcocho** this sponge is delicious; **Carmen está muy buena** Carmen is gorgeous

e (saludos): **¡buen día!**, **¡buenos días!** (good) morning!; **¡buenas (tardes)!** (good) afternoon!; (más tarde) (good) evening!; **¡buenas noches!** good night!

f (otras locuciones): **estar de buenas** to be in a good mood; **por las buenas o por las malas** by hook or by crook; **de buenas a primeras** all of a sudden ♦ excl: **¡bueno!** all right!; **bueno, ¿y qué?** well, so what?

Buenos Aires [bweno'saires] nm Buenos Aires

buey [bwei] nm ox

búfalo ['bufalo] nm buffalo

bufanda [bu'fanda] nf scarf

bufete [bu'fete] nm (despacho de abogado) lawyer's office

bufón [bu'fon] nm clown

buhardilla [buar'ðiʎa] nf attic

búho ['buo] nm owl; (fig) hermit, recluse

buitre ['bwitre] nm vulture

bujía [bu'xia] nf (vela) candle; (ELEC) candle (power); (AUTO) spark plug

bula ['bula] nf (papal) bull

bulbo ['bulβo] nm bulb

bulevar [bule'βar] nm boulevard

Bulgaria [bul'ɣarja] nf Bulgaria ❑ **búlgaro, -a** adj, nm/f Bulgarian

bulla ['buʎa] nf (ruido) uproar; (de gente) crowd

bullicio [bu'ʎiθjo] nm (ruido) uproar; (movimiento) bustle

bulto ['bulto] nm (paquete) package; (fardo) bundle; (tamaño) size,

bulkiness; (MED) swelling, lump; (silueta) vague shape

buñuelo [bu'nwelo] nm ≈ doughnut (BRIT), ≈ donut (US); (fruta de sartén) fritter

buque [buke] nm ship, vessel ▶ **buque de guerra** warship

burbuja [bur'βuxa] nf bubble

burdel [bur'ðel] nm brothel

burgués, -esa [bur'ɣes, esa] adj middle-class, bourgeois ❑ **burguesía** nf middle class, bourgeoisie

burla ['burla] nf (mofa) gibe; (broma) joke; (engaño) trick ❑ **burlar** [bur'lar] vt (engañar) to deceive ♦ vi to joke; **burlarse** vr to joke; **burlarse de** to make fun of

burlón, -ona [bur'lon, ona] adj mocking

buró (MÉX) [bu'ro] nm bedside table

burocracia [buro'kraθja] nf civil service

burrada [bu'rraða] nf: **decir o soltar burradas** to talk nonsense; **hacer burradas** to act stupid; **una ~** (ESP: mucho) a hell of a lot

burro, -a [burro, -a] nm/f donkey/she-donkey; (fig) ass, idiot

bursátil [bur'satil] adj stock-exchange cpd

bus [bus] nm bus

busca ['buska] nf search, hunt ♦ nm (TEL) bleeper; **en ~ de** in search of

buscador [buska'ðor] nm (INTERNET) search engine

buscar [bus'kar] vt to look for, search for, seek ♦ vi to look, search, seek; **se busca secretaria** secretary wanted

busque etc ['buske] vb ver **buscar**

búsqueda ['buskeða] nf = **busca**

busto ['busto] nm (ANAT, ARTE) bust

butaca [bu'taka] nf armchair; (de cine, teatro) stall, seat

butano [bu'tano] nm butane (gas)

buzo [buθo] nm diver

buzón [bu'θon] nm (en puerta) letter box; (en calle) pillar box

C, c

C. abr = **centígrado**; (= **compañía**) Co.

C/ abr (= **calle**) St

cabal [ka'βal] adj (exacto) exact; (correcto) right, proper; (acabado) finished, complete ▫ **cabales** nmpl: **no está en sus cabales** she isn't in her right mind

cábalas ['kaβalas] nfpl: **hacer ~** to guess

cabalgar [kaβal'ɣar] vi, vt to ride

cabalgata [kaβal'ɣata] nf procession

caballa [ka'βaʎa] nf mackerel

caballería [kaβaʎe'ria] nf mount; (MIL) cavalry

caballero [kaβa'ʎero] nm gentleman; (de la orden de caballería) knight; (trato directo) sir

caballete [kaβa'ʎete] nm (ARTE) easel; (TEC) trestle

caballito [kaβa'ʎito] nm (caballo pequeño) small horse, pony; **caballitos** nmpl (en verbena) roundabout, merrygo-round

caballo [ka'βaʎo] nm horse; (AJEDREZ) knight; (NAIPES) queen; **ir en ~** to ride ▶ **caballo de carreras** racehorse ▶ **caballo de fuerza** o **vapor** horsepower

cabaña [ka'βaɲa] nf (casita) hut, cabin

cabecear [kaβeθe'ar] vt, vi to nod

cabecera [kaβe'θera] nf head; (IMPRENTA) headline

cabecilla [kaβe'θiʎa] nm ringleader

cabellera [kaβe'ʎera] nf (head of) hair; (de cometa) tail

cabello [ka'βeʎo] nm (tb: **cabellos**) hair ▶ **cabello de ángel** confectionery and pastry filling made of pumpkin and syrup

caber [ka'βer] vi (entrar) to fit, lie, go; **caben 3 más** there's room for 3 more

cabestrillo [kaβes'triʎo] nm sling

cabeza [ka'βeθa] nf head; (POL) chief, leader ▶ **cabeza de ajo** bulb of garlic ▶ **cabeza de familia** head of the household ▶ **cabeza rapada** skinhead ▫ **cabezada** nf (golpe) butt; **dar cabezadas** to nod off ▫ **cabezón, -ona** adj (vino) heady; (fam: persona) pig-headed

cabida [ka'βiða] nf space

cabina [ka'βina] nf cabin; (de avión) cockpit; (de camión) cab ▶ **cabina telefónica** telephone (BRIT) box o booth

cabizbajo, -a [kaβiθ'βaxo, a] adj crestfallen, dejected

cable ['kaβle] nm cable

cabo ['kaβo] nm (de objeto) end, extremity; (MIL) corporal; (NÁUT) rope, cable; (GEO) cape; **al ~ de 3 días** after 3 days; **llevar a ~** to carry out

cabra ['kaβra] nf goat

cabré etc [ka'βre] vb ver **caber**

cabrear [kaβre'ar] (fam) vt to bug; **cabrearse** vr (enfadarse) to fly off the handle

cabrito [ka'βrito] nm kid

cabrón [ka'βron] nm cuckold; (fam!) bastard (!)

caca ['kaka] (fam) nf pooh

cacahuete [kaka'wete] (ESP) nm peanut

cacao [ka'kao] nm cocoa; (BOT) cacao

cacarear [kakare'ar] vi (persona) to boast; (gallina) to crow

cacería [kaθe'ria] nf hunt

cacarizo, -a [MÉX] adj pockmarked

cacerola [kaθe'rola] nf pan, saucepan

cachalote [katʃa'lote] nm (ZOOL) sperm whale

cacharro [ka'tʃarro] nm earthenware pot; **cacharros** nmpl pots and pans

cachear [katʃe'ar] vt to search, frisk

cachemir [katʃe'mir] nm cashmere

cachetada [LAm: fam] nf (bofetada) slap

cachete [ka'tʃete] nm (ANAT) cheek; (ESP: bofetada) slap (in the face)

cachivache [katʃi'βatʃe] nm (trasto) piece of junk; **cachivaches** nmpl junk sg

cacho ['katʃo] nm (small) bit; (LAm: cuerno) horn

cachondeo [katʃon'deo] (ESP: fam) nm farce, joke

cachondo, -a [ka'tʃondo, a] adj (ZOOL) on heat; (fam: sexualmente) randy; (: gracioso) funny

cachorro, -a [ka'tʃorro, a] nm/f (perro) pup, puppy; (león) cub

cachucha [ka'tʃutʃa] (MÉX: fam) nf cap

cacique [ka'θike] nm chief, local ruler; (POL) local party boss

cactus ['kaktus] nm inv cactus

cada ['kaða] adj inv each; (antes de número) every; ~ **día** each day, every day; ~ **dos días** every other day; ~ **uno/a** each one, every one; ~ **vez más/menos** more and more/less and less; ~ **vez que ...** whenever, every time (that) ...; **uno de** ~ **diez** one out of every ten

cadáver [ka'ðaβer] nm (dead) body, corpse

cadena [ka'ðena] nf chain; (TV) channel; **trabajo en** ~ assembly line work ► **cadena montañosa** mountain range ► **cadena perpetua** (JUR) life imprisonment

cadera [ka'ðera] nf hip

cadete [ka'ðete] nm cadet

caducar [kaðu'kar] vi to expire ❏ **caduco, -a** adj expired; (persona) very old

caer [ka'er] vi to fall (down); **caerse** vr to fall (down); **me cae bien/mal** I get on well with him/I can't stand him; ~ **en la cuenta** to realize; **dejar** ~ to drop; **su cumpleaños cae en viernes** her birthday falls on a Friday

café [ka'fe] (pl ~s) nm (bebida, planta) coffee; (lugar) café ♦ adj (MÉX: color) brown, tan ► **café con leche** white

coffee ► **café negro** (LAm) black coffee ► **café solo** (ESP) black coffee

cafetera [kafe'tera] nf coffee pot

cafetería [kafete'ria] nf (gen) café

cafetero, -a [kafe'tero, a] adj coffee cpd; **ser muy** ~ to be a coffee addict

cafishio [ka'fiʃjo] (CS) nm pimp

cagar [ka'ɣar] (fam!) vt to bungle, mess up ♦ vi to have a shit (!)

caída [ka'iða] nf fall; (declive) slope; (disminución) fall, drop

caído, -a [ka'iðo, a] adj drooping

caiga etc ['kaiɣa] vb ver **caer**

caimán [kai'man] nm alligator

caja ['kaxa] nf box; (para reloj) case; (de ascensor) shaft; (COM) cashbox; (donde se hacen los pagos) cashdesk; (: en supermercado) checkout, till ► **caja de ahorros** savings bank ► **caja de cambios** gearbox ► **caja de fusibles** fuse box ► **caja fuerte** o **de caudales** safe, strongbox

cajero, -a [ka'xero, a] nm/f cashier ► **cajero automático** cash dispenser

cajetilla [kaxe'tiʎa] nf (de cigarrillos) packet

cajón [ka'xon] nm big box; (de mueble) drawer

cajuela [ka'xwela] (MÉX) nf (AUTO) boot (BRIT), trunk (US)

cal [kal] nf lime

cala ['kala] nf (GEO) cove, inlet; (de barco) hold

calabacín [kalaβa'θin] nm (BOT) baby marrow; (: más pequeño) courgette (BRIT), zucchini (US)

calabacita [kalaβa'θita] (MÉX) nf courgette (BRIT), zucchini (US)

calabaza [kala'βaθa] nf (BOT) pumpkin

calabozo [kala'βoθo] nm (cárcel) prison; (celda) cell

calada [ka'laða] (ESP) nf (de cigarrillo) puff

calado, -a [ka'laðo, a] adj (prenda) lace cpd ♦ nm (NÁUT) draught

calamar [kala'mar] nm squid no pl

calambre [ka'lambre] nm (ELEC) shock

calar [ka'lar] vt (penetrar) to soak, drench; (penetrar) to pierce, penetrate; (comprender) to see through; (vela) to lower; **calarse** vr (AUTO) to stall; **calarse las gafas** to stick one's glasses on

calavera [kala'βera] nf skull

calcar [kal'kar] vt (reproducir) to trace; (imitar) to copy

calcetín [kalθe'tin] nm sock

calcio ['kalθjo] nm calcium

calcomanía [kalkoma'nia] nf transfer

calculador, a [kalkula'ðor, a] adj (persona) calculating □ **calculadora** [kalkula'ðora] nf calculator

calcular [kalku'lar] vt (MAT) to calculate, compute; ~ **que** ... to reckon that ...

caldera [kal'dera] nf boiler

calderilla [kalde'riʎa] nf (moneda) small change

caldo ['kaldo] nm stock; (consomé) consommé

calefacción [kalefak'θjon] nf heating ► **calefacción central** central heating

calefón (RPI) nm boiler

calendario [kalen'darjo] nm calendar

calentador [kalenta'ðor] nm heater

calentamiento [kalenta'mjento] nm (DEPORTE) warm-up

calentar [kalen'tar] vt to heat (up); **calentarse** vr to heat up, warm up; (fig: discusión etc) to get heated

calentón (RPI: fam) adj (sexualmente) horny, randy (BRIT)

calentura [kalen'tura] nf (MED) fever, (high) temperature

calesita (RPI) nf merry-go-round, carousel

calibre [ka'liβre] nm (de cañón) calibre, bore; (diámetro) diameter; (fig) calibre

calidad [kali'ðað] nf quality; **de ~** quality cpd; **en ~ de** in the capacity of, as

cálido, -a ['kaliðo, a] adj hot; (fig) warm

caliente etc [ka'ljente] vb ver **calentar** ♦ adj hot; (fig) fiery; (disputa) heated; (fam: cachondo) randy

calificación [kalifika'θjon] nf qualification; (de alumno) grade, mark

calificado, -a (LAm) adj (competente) qualified; (obrero) skilled

calificar [kalifi'kar] vt to qualify; (alumno) to grade, mark; ~ **de** to describe as

calima [ka'lima] nf (cerca del mar) mist

cáliz ['kaliθ] nm chalice

caliza [ka'liθa] nf limestone

callado, -a [ka'ʎaðo, a] adj quiet

callar [ka'ʎar] vt (asunto delicado) to keep quiet about, say nothing about; (persona, opinión) to silence ♦ vi to keep quiet, be silent; **callarse** vr to keep quiet, be silent; **¡cállate!** be quiet!, shut up!

calle ['kaʎe] nf street; (DEPORTE) lane; ~ **arriba/abajo** up/down the street ► **calle de sentido único** one-way street ► **calle mayor** (ESP) high (BRIT) o main (US) street ► **calle peatonal** pedestrianized o pedestrian street ► **calle principal** (LAm) high (BRIT) o main (US) street □ **callejear** vi to wander (about) the streets □ **callejero, -a** adj street cpd ♦ nm street map □ **callejón** nm alley, passage ► **callejón sin salida** cul-de-sac □ **callejuela** nf side-street, alley

callista [ka'ʎista] nmf chiropodist

callo [ka'ʎo] nm callus; (en el pie) corn; **callos** nmpl (CULIN) tripe sg

calma ['kalma] nf calm

calmante [kal'mante] nm sedative, tranquillizer

calmar [kal'mar] vt to calm, calm down ♦ vi (tempestad) to abate; (mente etc) to become calm

calor [ka'lor] *nm* heat; (*agradable*) warmth; **hace ~** it's hot; **tener ~** to be hot

caloría [kalo'ria] *nf* calorie

calumnia [ka'lumnja] *nf* calumny, slander

caluroso, -a [kalu'roso, a] *adj* hot; (*sin exceso*) warm; (*fig*) enthusiastic

calva ['kalβa] *nf* bald patch; (*en bosque*) clearing

calvario [kal'βarjo] *nm* stations *pl* of the cross

calvicie [kal'βiθje] *nf* baldness

calvo, -a ['kalβo, a] *adj* bald; (*terreno*) bare, barren; (*tejido*) threadbare

calza ['kalθa] *nf* wedge, chock

calzada [kal'θaða] *nf* roadway, highway

calzado, -a [kal'θaðo, a] *adj* shod ♦ *nm* footwear

calzador [kalθa'ðor] *nm* shoehorn

calzar [kal'θar] *vt* (*zapatos etc*) to wear; (*mueble*) to put a wedge under; **calzarse** *vr*: **calzarse los zapatos** to put on one's shoes; **¿qué (número) calza?** what size do you take?

calzón [kal'θon] *nm, nm* (*ESP: pantalón corto*) shorts; (*LAm: ropa interior: de hombre*) underpants, pants (*BRIT*), shorts (*US*); (: *de mujer*) panties, knickers (*BRIT*)

calzoncillos [kalθon'θiʎos] *nmpl* underpants

cama ['kama] *nf* bed; **hacer la ~** to make the bed ▸ **cama individual/de matrimonio** single/double bed

camaleón [kamale'on] *nm* chameleon

cámara ['kamara] *nf* chamber; (*habitación*) room; (*sala*) hall; (*CINE*) cine camera; (*fotográfica*) camera
▸ **cámara de aire** (*ESP*) inner tube
▸ **cámara de comercio** chamber of commerce ▸ **cámara de gas** gas chamber ▸ **cámara digital** digital camera ▸ **cámara frigorífica** cold-storage room

camarada [kama'raða] *nm* comrade, companion

camarera [kama'rera] *nf* (*en restaurante*) waitress; (*en casa, hotel*) maid

camarero [kama'rero] *nm* waiter

camarógrafo, -a (*LAm*) *nm/f* cameraman/camerawoman

camarón [kama'ron] *nm* shrimp

camarote [kama'rote] *nm* cabin

cambiable [kam'bjaβle] *adj* (*variable*) changeable, variable; (*intercambiable*) interchangeable

cambiante [kam'bjante] *adj* variable

cambiar [kam'bjar] *vt* to change; (*dinero*) to exchange ♦ *vi* to change; **cambiarse** *vr* (*mudarse*) to move; (*de ropa*) to change; ~ **de idea** o **opinión** to change one's mind; **cambiarse de ropa** to change (one's clothes)

cambio ['kambjo] *nm* change; (*trueque*) exchange; (*COM*) rate of exchange; (*oficina*) bureau de change; (*dinero menudo*) small change; **a ~ de** in return o exchange for; **en ~** on the other hand; (*en lugar de*) instead ▸ **cambio de divisas** foreign exchange ▸ **cambio de marchas** o **velocidades** gear lever

camelar [kame'lar] *vt* to sweet-talk

camello [ka'meʎo] *nm* camel; (*fam: traficante*) pusher

camerino [kame'rino] *nm* dressing room

camilla [ka'miʎa] *nf* (*MED*) stretcher

caminar [kami'nar] *vi* (*marchar*) to walk, go ♦ *vt* (*recorrer*) to cover, travel

caminata [kami'nata] *nf* long walk; (*por el campo*) hike

camino [ka'mino] *nm* way, road; (*sendero*) track; **a medio ~** halfway (there); **en el ~** on the way, en route; **~ de** on the way to ▸ **Camino de**

Santiago Way of St James ► **camino particular** private road

CAMINO DE SANTIAGO

The **Camino de Santiago** is a medieval pilgrim route stretching from the Pyrenees to Santiago de Compostela in north-west Spain, where tradition has it the body of the Apostle James is buried. Nowadays it is a popular tourist route as well as a religious one.

camión [ka'mjon] nm lorry (BRIT), truck (US); (MÉX: autobús) bus ► **camión cisterna** tanker ► **camión de la basura** dustcart, refuse lorry ► **camión de mudanzas** removal (BRIT) o moving (US) van ❑ **camionero, -a** nm/f lorry o truck driver

camioneta [kamjo'neta] nf van, light truck

camisa [ka'misa] nf shirt; (BOT) skin ► **camisa de fuerza** straitjacket

camiseta [kami'seta] nf (prenda) tee-shirt; (: ropa interior) vest; (de deportista) top

camisón [kami'son] nm nightdress, nightgown

camorra [ka'morra] nf: **buscar ~** to look for trouble

camote nm (MÉX, CS: batata) sweet potato, yam; (MÉX: bulbo) tuber, bulb; (CS: fam: enamoramiento) crush

campamento [kampa'mento] nm camp

campana [kam'pana] nf bell ❑ **campanada** nf peal ❑ **campanario** nm belfry

campanilla [kampa'niʎa] nf small bell

campaña [kam'paɲa] nf (MIL, POL) campaign ► **campaña electoral** election campaign

campechano, -a [kampe'tʃano, a] adj (franco) open

campeón, -ona [kampe'on, ona] nm/f champion ❑ **campeonato** nm championship

cámper (LAm) nm o f caravan (BRIT), trailer (US)

campera (RPI) nf anorak

campesino, -a [kampe'sino, a] adj country cpd, rural; (gente) peasant cpd ♦ nm/f countryman/woman; (agricultor) farmer

campestre [kam'pestre] adj country cpd, rural

camping ['kampin] nm (pl **campings**) nm camping; (lugar) campsite; ir o **estar de ~** to go camping

campo ['kampo] nm (fuera de la ciudad) country, countryside; (AGR, ELEC) field; (de fútbol) pitch; (de golf) course; (MIL) camp ► **campo de batalla** battlefield ► **campo de concentración** concentration camp ► **campo de deportes** sports ground, playing field ► **campo visual** field of vision, visual field

camuflaje [kamu'flaxe] nm camouflage

cana ['kana] nf white o grey hair; **tener canas** to be going grey

Canadá [kana'ða] nm Canada ❑ **canadiense** adj, nmf Canadian ♦ nf fur-lined jacket

canal [ka'nal] nm canal; (GEO) channel, strait; (de televisión) channel; (de tejado) gutter ► **canal de Panamá** Panama Canal

canaleta (LAm) nf (de tejado) gutter

canalizar [kanali'θar] vt to channel

canalla [ka'naʎa] nf rabble, mob ♦ nm swine

canapé [kana'pe] (pl **~s**) nm sofa, settee; (CULIN) canapé

Canarias [ka'narjas] nfpl (tb: **las Islas ~**) the Canary Islands, the Canaries

canario, -a [ka'narjo, a] adj, nm/f (native) of the Canary Isles ♦ nm (ZOOL) canary

canasta [ka'nasta] nf (round) basket

canasto [ka'nasto] nm large basket

cancela [kan'θela] nf gate

cancelación [kanθela'θjon] nf cancellation

cancelar [kanθe'lar] vt to cancel; (una deuda) to write off

cáncer ['kanθer] nm (MED) cancer; **C~** (ASTROLOGÍA) Cancer

cancha [kantʃa] nf (de baloncesto) court; (LAm: campo) pitch ▸ **cancha de tenis** (LAm) tennis court

canciller [kanθi'ʎer] nm chancellor

canción [kan'θjon] nf song ▸ **canción de cuna** lullaby

candado [kan'daðo] nm padlock

candente [kan'dente] adj red-hot; (fig: tema) burning

candidato, -a [kandi'ðato, a] nm/f candidate

cándido, -a ['kandiðo, a] adj simple; naive

⚠ No confundir **cándido** con la palabra inglesa candid.

candil [kan'dil] nm oil lamp ❑ **candilejas** nfpl (TEATRO) footlights

canela [ka'nela] nf cinnamon

canelones [kane'lones] nmpl cannelloni

cangrejo [kaŋ'grexo] nm crab

canguro [kaŋ'guro] nm kangaroo; **hacer de ~** to babysit

caníbal [ka'niβal] adj, nmf cannibal

canica [ka'nika] nf marble

canijo, -a [ka'nixo, a] adj frail, sickly

canilla [ka'niʎa] nf (RPl) tap (BRIT), faucet (US)

canjear [kanxe'ar] vt to exchange

canoa [ka'noa] nf canoe

canon ['kanon] nm canon; (pensión) rent; (COM) tax

canonizar [kanoni'θar] vt to canonize

canoso, -a [ka'noso, a] adj grey-haired

cansado, -a [kan'saðo, a] adj tired, weary; (tedioso) tedious, boring

cansancio [kan'sanθjo] nm tiredness, fatigue

cansar [kan'sar] vt (fatigar) to tire, tire out; (aburrir) to bore; (fastidiar) to bother; **cansarse** vr to tire, get tired; (aburrirse) to get bored

cantábrico, -a [kan'taβriko, a] adj Cantabrian; **mar C~** Bay of Biscay

cantante [kan'tante] adj singing ♦ nmf singer

cantar [kan'tar] vt to sing ♦ vi to sing; (insecto) to chirp ♦ nm (acción) singing; (canción) song; (poema) poem

cántaro ['kantaro] nm pitcher, jug; **llover a cántaros** to rain cats and dogs

cante ['kante] nm (MÚS) Andalusian folk song ▸ **cante jondo** flamenco singing

cantera [kan'tera] nf quarry

cantero (RPl) nm (arriate) border

cantidad [kanti'ðað] nf quantity, amount; **~ de** lots of

cantimplora [kantim'plora] nf (frasco) water bottle, canteen

cantina [kan'tina] nf canteen; (de estación) buffet; (LAm: bar) bar

cantinero, -a [kanti'nero, a] (MÉX) nm barman/barmaid, bartender (US)

canto ['kanto] nm singing; (canción) song; (borde) edge, rim; (de cuchillo) back ▸ **canto rodado** boulder

cantor, -a [kan'tor, a] nm/f singer

canturrear [kanturre'ar] vi to sing softly

canuto [ka'nuto] nm (tubo) small tube; (fam: droga) joint

caña ['kaɲa] nf (BOT: tallo) stem, stalk; (carrizo) reed; (vaso) tumbler; (de cerveza) glass of beer; (ANAT) shinbone ▸ **caña de azúcar** sugar cane ▸ **caña de pescar** fishing rod

cañada [ka'ɲaða] nf (entre dos montañas) gully, ravine; (camino) cattle track

cáñamo ['kaɲamo] nm hemp

cañería [kaɲeˈria] *nf* (*tubo*) pipe

caño [ˈkaɲo] *nm* (*tubo*) tube, pipe; (*de albañal*) sewer; (*MÚS*) pipe; (*de fuente*) jet

cañón [kaˈɲon] *nm* (*MIL*) cannon; (*de fusil*) barrel; (*GEO*) canyon, gorge

caoba [kaˈoβa] *nf* mahogany

caos [ˈkaos] *nm* chaos

capa [ˈkapa] *nf* cloak, cape; (*GEO*) layer, stratum ► **capa de ozono** ozone layer

capacidad [kapaθiˈðað] *nf* (*medida*) capacity; (*aptitud*) capacity, ability

caparazón [kaparaˈθon] *nm* shell

capataz [kapaˈtaθ] *nm* foreman

capaz [kaˈpaθ] *adj* able, capable; (*amplio*) capacious, roomy

capellán [kapeˈʎan] *nm* chaplain; (*sacerdote*) priest

capicúa [kapiˈkua] *adj inv* (*número, fecha*) reversible

capilla [kaˈpiʎa] *nf* chapel

capital [kapiˈtal] *adj* capital ♦ *nm* (*COM*) capital ♦ *nf* (*ciudad*) capital ► **capital social** share o authorized capital

capitalismo [kapitaˈlismo] *nm* capitalism ❑ **capitalista** *adj, nmf* capitalist

capitán [kapiˈtan] *nm* captain

capítulo [kaˈpitulo] *nm* chapter

capó [kaˈpo] *nm* (*AUTO*) bonnet

capón [kaˈpon] *nm* (*gallo*) capon

capota [kaˈpota] *nf* (*de mujer*) bonnet; (*AUTO*) hood (*BRIT*), top (*US*)

capote [kaˈpote] *nm* (*abrigo: de militar*) greatcoat; (*de torero*) cloak

capricho [kaˈpritʃo] *nm* whim, caprice ❑ **caprichoso, -a** *adj* capricious

Capricornio [kapriˈkornjo] *nm* Capricorn

cápsula [ˈkapsula] *nf* capsule

captar [kapˈtar] *vt* (*comprender*) to understand; (*RADIO*) to pick up; (*atención, apoyo*) to attract

captura [kapˈtura] *nf* capture; (*JUR*) arrest ❑ **capturar** *vt* to capture; to arrest

capucha [kaˈputʃa] *nf* hood, cowl

capuchón [kapuˈtʃon] *nm* (*de bolígrafo*) cap

capullo [kaˈpuʎo] *nm* (*BOT*) bud; (*ZOOL*) cocoon; (*fam*) idiot

caqui [ˈkaki] *nm* khaki

cara [ˈkara] *nf* (*ANAT: de moneda*) face; (*de disco*) side; (*descaro*) boldness; ~ **a** facing; **de** ~ **opposite**, facing; **dar la** ~ to face the consequences; **¿** ~ **o cruz?** heads or tails?; **¡qué** ~ **(más dura)!** what a nerve!

Caracas [kaˈrakas] *n* Caracas

caracol [karaˈkol] *nm* (*ZOOL*) snail; (*concha*) (sea) shell

carácter [kaˈrakter] (*pl* **caracteres**) *nm* character; **tener buen/mal** ~ to be good natured/bad tempered

característica [karakteˈristika] *nf* characteristic

característico, -a [karakteˈristiko, a] *adj* characteristic

caracterizar [karakteriˈθar] *vt* to characterize, typify

caradura [karaˈðura] *nmf*: **es un** ~ he's got a nerve

carajillo [karaˈxiʎo] *nm* coffee with a dash of brandy

carajo [kaˈraxo] (*fam!*) *nm*: **¡** ~ **!** shit! (*!*)

caramba [kaˈramba] *excl* good gracious!

caramelo [karaˈmelo] *nm* (*dulce*) sweet; (*azúcar fundida*) caramel

caravana [karaˈβana] *nf* caravan; (*fig*) group; (*AUTO*) tailback

carbón [karˈβon] *nm* coal; **papel** ~ carbon paper

carbono [karˈβono] *nm* carbon

carburador [karβuraˈðor] *nm* carburettor

carburante [karβuˈrante] *nm* (*para motor*) fuel

carcajada [karka'xaða] nf (loud) laugh, guffaw

cárcel ['karθel] nf prison, jail; (TEC) clamp

carcoma [kar'koma] nf woodworm

cardar [kar'ðar] vt (pelo) to backcomb

cardenal [karðe'nal] nm (REL) cardinal; (MED) bruise

cardíaco, -a [kar'ðiako, a] adj cardiac, heart cpd

cardinal [karði'nal] adj cardinal

cardo ['karðo] nm thistle

carecer [kare'θer] vi: ~ **de** to lack, be in need of

carencia [ka'renθja] nf lack; (escasez) shortage; (MED) deficiency

careta [ka'reta] nf mask

carga ['karɣa] nf (peso, ELEC) load; (de barco) cargo, freight; (MIL) charge; (responsabilidad) duty, obligation

cargado, -a [kar'ɣaðo, a] adj loaded; (ELEC) live; (café, té) strong; (cielo) overcast

cargamento [karɣa'mento] nm (acción) loading; (mercancías) load, cargo

cargar [kar'ɣar] vt (barco, arma) to load; (ELEC) to charge; (COM: algo en cuenta) to charge; (INFORM) to load ♦ vi (MIL) to charge; (AUTO) to load (up); ~ **con** to pick up, carry away; (peso: fig) to shoulder, bear; **cargarse** vr (fam: estropear) to break; (matar) to bump off

cargo ['karɣo] nm (puesto) post, office; (responsabilidad) duty, obligation; (JUR) charge; **hacerse ~ de** to take charge of o responsibility for

carguero [kar'ɣero] nm freighter, cargo boat; (avión) freight plane

Caribe [ka'riβe] nm: **el ~** the Caribbean; **del ~** Caribbean ▸ **caribeño, -a** [kari'βeɲo, a] adj Caribbean

caricatura [karika'tura] nf caricature

caricia [ka'riθja] nf caress

caridad [kari'ðað] nf charity

caries ['karjes] nf inv tooth decay

cariño [ka'riɲo] nm affection, love; (caricia) caress; (en carta) love ...; **tener ~ a** to be fond of □ **cariñoso, -a** adj affectionate

carisma [ka'risma] nm charisma

caritativo, -a [karita'tiβo, a] adj charitable

cariz [ka'riθ] nm: **tener** o **tomar buen/ mal ~** to look good/bad

carmín [kar'min] nm lipstick

carnal [kar'nal] adj carnal; **primo ~** first cousin

carnaval [karna'βal] nm carnival

carne ['karne] nf flesh; (CULIN) meat; **se me pone la ~ de gallina sólo verlo** I get the creeps just seeing it ▸ **carne de cerdo/cordero/ternera/vaca** pork/lamb/veal/beef ▸ **carne de gallina** (fig) gooseflesh ▸ **carne molida** (LAm) mince (BRIT), ground meat ▸ **carne picada** (ESP, RPI) mince (BRIT), ground meat

carné [kar'ne] (ESP) (pl ~s) nm: **carné de conducir** driving licence (BRIT), driver's license (US); **carné de identidad** identity card; **carné de socio** membership card

carnero [kar'nero] nm sheep, ram; (carne) mutton

carnet [kar'ne] (ESP) (pl carnets) nm = **carné**

carnicería [karniθe'ria] nf butcher's (shop); (fig: matanza) carnage, slaughter

carnicero, -a [karni'θero, a] adj carnivorous ♦ nm/f butcher; (carnívoro) carnivore

carnívoro, -a [kar'niβoro, a] adj carnivorous

caro, -a ['karo, a] adj dear; (COM) dear, expensive ♦ adv dear, dearly

carpa ['karpa] nf (pez) carp; (de circo) big top; (LAm: tienda de campaña) tent

carpeta [kar'peta] nf folder, file
▶ **carpeta de anillas** ring binder

carpintería [karpinte'ria] nf carpentry, joinery □ **carpintero** nm carpenter

carraspear [karraspe'ar] vi to clear one's throat

carraspera [karras'pera] nf hoarseness

carrera [ka'rrera] nf (acción) run(ning); (espacio recorrido) run; (competición) race; (trayecto) course; (profesión) career; (licenciatura) degree; **a la ~** (at) full speed ▶ **carrera de obstáculos** (DEPORTE) steeplechase

carrete [ka'rrete] nm reel, spool; (TEC) coil

carretera [karre'tera] nf (main) road, highway ▶ **carretera de circunvalación** ring road ▶ **carretera nacional** ≈ A road (BRIT), ≈ state highway (US)

carretilla [karre'tiʎa] nf trolley; (AGR) (wheel)barrow

carril [ka'rril] nm furrow; (de autopista) lane; (FERRO) rail ▶ **carril-bici** cycle lane

carrito [ka'rrito] nm trolley

carro ['karro] nm cart, wagon; (MIL) tank; (LAm: coche) car ▶ **carro patrulla** (LAm) patrol o panda (BRIT) car

carrocería [karroθe'ria] nf bodywork, coachwork

carroña [ka'rroɲa] nf carrion no pl

carroza [ka'rroθa] nf (carruaje) coach

carrusel [karru'sel] nm merry-go-round, roundabout

carta ['karta] nf letter; (CULIN) menu; (naipe) card; (mapa) map; (JUR) document ▶ **carta certificada/urgente** registered/special-delivery letter

cartabón [karta'βon] nm set square

cartel [kar'tel] nm (anuncio) poster, placard; (ESCOL) wall chart; (COM) cartel □ **cartelera** nf hoarding, billboard; (en periódico etc) entertainments guide; **"en cartelera"** "showing"

cartera [kar'tera] nf (de bolsillo) wallet; (de colegial, cobrador) satchel; (de señora) handbag; (para documentos) briefcase; (COM) portfolio; **ocupa la ~ de Agricultura** she is Minister of Agriculture

carterista [karte'rista] nmf pickpocket

cartero [kar'tero] nm postman

cartilla [kar'tiʎa] nf primer, first reading book ▶ **cartilla de ahorros** savings book

cartón [kar'ton] nm cardboard
▶ **cartón piedra** papier-mâché

cartucho [kar'tutʃo] nm (MIL) cartridge

cartulina [kartu'lina] nf card

casa ['kasa] nf house; (hogar) home; (COM) firm, company; **en ~** at home ▶ **casa consistorial** town hall ▶ **casa de campo** country house ▶ **casa de huéspedes** boarding house ▶ **casa de socorro** first aid post ▶ **casa rodante** (CS) caravan (BRIT), trailer (US)

casado, -a [ka'saðo, a] adj married ♦ nm/f married man/woman

casar [ka'sar] vt to marry; (JUR) to quash, annul; **casarse** vr to marry, get married

cascabel [kaska'βel] nm (small) bell

cascada [kas'kaða] nf waterfall

cascanueces [kaska'nweθes] nm inv nutcrackers pl

cascar [kas'kar] vt to crack, split, break (open); **cascarse** vr to crack, split, break (open)

cáscara ['kaskara] nf (de huevo, fruta seca) shell; (de fruta) skin; (de limón) peel

casco ['kasko] nm (de bombero, soldado) helmet; (NÁUT: de barco) hull; (ZOOL: de caballo) hoof; (botella) empty bottle; (de ciudad): **el ~ antiguo** the old part; **el ~ urbano** the town centre; **los cascos azules** the UN peace-keeping force, the blue berets

cascote [kas'kote] nm rubble

caserío [kase'rio] (ESP) nm farmhouse; (casa) country mansion

casero, -a [ka'sero, a] adj (pan etc) home-made ♦ nm/f (propietario) landlord/lady; **ser muy ~** to be home-loving; **"comida casera"** "home cooking"

caseta [ka'seta] nf hut; (para bañista) cubicle; (de feria) stall

casete [ka'sete] nm o f = **cassette**

casi ['kasi] adv almost, nearly; **~ nada** hardly anything; **~ nunca** hardly ever, almost never; **~ te caes** you almost fell

casilla [ka'siʎa] nf (casita) hut, cabin; (AJEDREZ) square; (para cartas) pigeonhole ▸ **casilla de correo** (CS) P.O. Box ▸ **casillero** nm (para cartas) pigeonholes pl

casino [ka'sino] nm club; (de juego) casino

caso ['kaso] nm case; **en ~ de** in case of; **en ~ de que ...** in case ...; **el ~ es que ...** the fact is that ...; **en ese/todo ~** in that/ any case; **hacer ~ a** to pay attention to; **venir al ~** to be relevant

caspa ['kaspa] nf dandruff

cassette [ka'sete] nf o m = **casete**

castaña [kas'taɲa] nf chestnut

castaño, -a [kas'taɲo, a] adj chestnut(-coloured), brown ♦ nm chestnut tree

castañuelas [kasta'ɲwelas] nfpl castanets

castellano, -a [kaste'ʎano, a] adj, nm/f Castilian ♦ nm (LING) Castilian, Spanish

castigar [kasti'ɣar] vt to punish; (DEPORTE) to penalize ▸ **castigo** nm punishment; (DEPORTE) penalty

Castilla [kas'tiʎa] nf Castile

castillo [kas'tiʎo] nm castle

castizo, -a [kas'tiθo, a] adj (LING) pure

casto, -a ['kasto, a] adj chaste, pure

castor [kas'tor] nm beaver

castrar [kas'trar] vt to castrate

casual [ka'swal] adj chance, accidental ▸ **casualidad** nf chance, accident; (combinación de circunstancias) coincidence; **da la casualidad de que ... ** it (just) so happens that ...; **¡qué casualidad!** what a coincidence!

⚠ No confundir **casual** con la palabra inglesa casual.

cataclismo [kata'klismo] nm cataclysm

catador, a [kata'ðor, a] nm/f wine taster

catalán, -ana [kata'lan, ana] adj, nm/f Catalan ♦ nm (LING) Catalan

catalizador [kataliθa'ðor] nm catalyst; (AUTO) catalytic convertor

catalogar [katalo'ɣar] vt to catalogue; **~ a algn (de)** (fig) to categorize sb (as)

catálogo [ka'taloɣo] nm catalogue

Cataluña [kata'luɲa] nf Catalonia

catar [ka'tar] vt to taste, sample

catarata [kata'rata] nf (GEO) waterfall; (MED) cataract

catarro [ka'tarro] nm catarrh; (constipado) cold

catástrofe [ka'tastrofe] nf catastrophe

catear [kate'ar] (fam) vt (examen, alumno) to fail

cátedra ['kateðra] nf (UNIV) chair, professorship

catedral [kate'ðral] nf cathedral

catedrático, -a [kate'ðratiko, a] nm/f professor

categoría [kateɣoˈria] nf category; (rango) rank, standing; (calidad) quality; **de ~** (hotel) top-class

cateto, -a [kaˈteto, a] (ESP: pey) nm/f peasant

catolicismo [katoliˈθismo] nm Catholicism

católico, -a [kaˈtoliko, a] adj, nm/f Catholic

catorce [kaˈtorθe] num fourteen

cauce [ˈkauθe] nm (de río) riverbed; (fig) channel

caucho [ˈkautʃo] (ESP) nm rubber

caudal [kauˈðal] nm (de río) volume, flow; (fortuna) wealth; (abundancia) abundance

caudillo [kauˈðiʎo] nm leader, chief

causa [ˈkausa] nf cause; (razón) reason; (JUR) lawsuit, case; **a ~ de** because of ❑ **causar** [kauˈsar] vt to cause

cautela [kauˈtela] nf caution, cautiousness ❑ **cauteloso, -a** adj cautious, wary

cautivar [kautiˈβar] vt to capture; (atraer) to captivate

cautiverio [kautiˈβerjo] nm captivity

cautividad [kautiβiˈðað] nf = **cautiverio**

cautivo, -a [kauˈtiβo, a] adj, nm/f captive

cauto, -a [ˈkauto, a] adj cautious, careful

cava [ˈkaβa] nm champagne-type wine

cavar [kaˈβar] vt to dig

caverna [kaˈβerna] nf cave, cavern

cavidad [kaβiˈðað] nf cavity

cavilar [kaβiˈlar] vt to ponder

cayendo etc [kaˈjendo] vb ver **caer**

caza [ˈkaθa] nf (acción: gen) hunting; (: con fusil) shooting; (una caza) hunt, chase; (de animales) game ♦ nm (AVIAC) fighter; **ir de ~** to go hunting ♦ **caza mayor** game hunting ❑ **cazador, a** [kaθaˈðor, a] nm/f hunter ❑ **cazadora**

nf jacket ❑ **cazar** [kaˈθar] vt to hunt; (perseguir) to chase; (prender) to catch

cazo [ˈkaθo] nm saucepan

cazuela [kaˈθwela] nf (vasija) pan; (guisado) casserole

CD nm abr (= compact disc) CD

CD-ROM nm abr CD-ROM

CE nf abr (= Comunidad Europea) EC

cebada [θeˈβaða] nf barley

cebar [θeˈβar] vt (animal) to fatten (up); (anzuelo) to bait; (MIL, TEC) to prime

cebo [ˈθeβo] nm (para animales) feed, food; (para peces, fig) bait; (de arma) charge

cebolla [θeˈβoʎa] nf onion ❑ **cebolleta** nf spring onion

cebra [ˈθeβra] nf zebra

cecear [θeθeˈar] vi to lisp

ceder [θeˈðer] vt to hand over, give up, part with ♦ vi (renunciar) to give in, yield; (disminuir) to diminish, decline; (romperse) to give way

cedro [ˈθeðro] nm cedar

cédula [ˈθeðula] nf certificate, document ▶ **cédula de identidad** (LAm) identity card ▶ **cédula electoral** (LAm) ballot

cegar [θeˈɣar] vt to blind; (tubería etc) to block up, stop up ♦ vi to go blind; **cegarse vr: cegarse (de)** to be blinded (by)

ceguera [θeˈɣera] nf blindness

ceja [ˈθexa] nf eyebrow

cejar [θeˈxar] vi (fig) to back down

celador, a [θelaˈðor, a] nm/f (de edificio) watchman; (de museo etc) attendant

celda [ˈθelda] nf cell

celebración [θeleβraˈθjon] nf celebration

celebrar [θeleˈβrar] vt to celebrate; (alabar) to praise ♦ vi to be glad; **celebrarse** vr to occur, take place

célebre [ˈθeleβre] adj famous

celebridad [θeleβri'ðað] *nf* fame; (*persona*) celebrity

celeste [θe'leste] *adj* (*azul*) sky-blue

celestial [θeles'tjal] *adj* celestial, heavenly

celo¹ ['θelo] *nm* zeal; (*REL*) fervour; (*ZOOL*): **en ~** on heat; **celos** *nmpl* jealousy *sg*; **dar celos a algn** to make sb jealous; **tener celos** to be jealous

celo®² ['θelo] *nm* Sellotape®

celofán [θelo'fan] *nm* cellophane

celoso, -a [θe'loso, a] *adj* jealous; (*trabajador*) zealous

celta ['θelta] *adj* ♦ *nmf* Celt

célula ['θelula] *nf* cell

celulitis [θelu'litis] *nf* cellulite

cementerio [θemen'terjo] *nm* cemetery, graveyard

cemento [θe'mento] *nm* cement; (*hormigón*) concrete; (*LAm: cola*) glue

cena ['θena] *nf* evening meal, dinner
❑ **cenar** [θe'nar] *vt* to have for dinner
♦ *vi* to have dinner

cenicero [θeni'θero] *nm* ashtray

ceniza [θe'niθa] *nf* ash, ashes *pl*

censo ['θenso] *nm* census ► **censo electoral** electoral roll

censura [θen'sura] *nf* (*POL*) censorship
❑ **censurar** [θensu'rar] *vt* (*idea*) to censure; (*cortar: película*) to censor

centella [θen'teʎa] *nf* spark

centenar [θente'nar] *nm* hundred

centenario, -a [θente'narjo, a] *adj* centenary; hundred-year-old ♦ *nm* centenary

centeno [θen'teno] *nm* (*BOT*) rye

centésimo, -a [θen'tesimo, a] *adj* hundredth

centígrado [θen'tiɣraðo] *adj* centigrade

centímetro [θen'timetro] *nm* centimetre (*BRIT*), centimeter (*US*)

céntimo [θen'timo] *nm* cent

centinela [θenti'nela] *nm* sentry, guard

centollo [θen'toʎo] *nm* spider crab

central [θen'tral] *adj* central ♦ *nf* head office; (*TEC*) plant; (*TEL*) exchange
► **central eléctrica** power station
► **central nuclear** nuclear power station ► **central telefónica** telephone exchange

centralita [θentra'lita] *nf* switchboard

centralizar [θentrali'θar] *vt* to centralize

centrar [θen'trar] *vt* to centre

céntrico, -a ['θentriko, a] *adj* central

centrifugar [θentrifu'ɣar] *vt* to spin-dry

centro ['θentro] *nm* centre ► **centro comercial** shopping centre ► **centro de atención al cliente** call centre ► **centro de salud** health centre ► **centro escolar** school ► **centro juvenil** youth club ► **centro turístico** (*lugar muy visitado*) tourist centre ► **centro urbano** urban area, city

centroamericano, -a [θentroameri'kano, a] *adj, nm/f* Central American

ceñido, -a [θe'ɲiðo, a] *adj* (*chaqueta, pantalón*) tight(-fitting)

ceñir [θe'ɲir] *vt* (*rodear*) to encircle, surround; (*ajustar*) to fit (tightly)

ceño ['θeɲo] *nm* frown, scowl; **fruncir el ~** to frown, knit one's brow

cepillar [θepi'ʎar] *vt* to brush; (*madera*) to plane (down)

cepillo [θe'piʎo] *nm* brush; (*para madera*) plane ► **cepillo de dientes** toothbrush

cera ['θera] *nf* wax

cerámica [θe'ramika] *nf* pottery; (*arte*) ceramics

cerca ['θerka] *nf* fence ♦ *adv* near, nearby, close; **~ de** near, close to

cercanías [θerka'nias] *nfpl* (*afueras*) outskirts, suburbs

cercano, -a [θer'kano, a] *adj* close, near

cercar [θer'kar] *vt* to fence in; (*rodear*) to surround

cerco ['θerko] *nm* (AGR) enclosure; (*LAm: valla*) fence; (*MIL*) siege

cerdo, -a ['θerðo, a] *nm/f* pig/sow

cereal [θere'al] *nm* cereal; **cereales** *nmpl* cereals, grain *sg*

cerebro [θe'reβro] *nm* brain; (*fig*) brains *pl*

ceremonia [θere'monja] *nf* ceremony
❑ **ceremonioso, -a** *adj* ceremonious

cereza [θe'reθa] *nf* cherry

cerilla [θe'riʎa] *nf* (*fósforo*) match

cerillo (MÉX) [θe'riʎo] *nm* match

cero ['θero] *nm* nothing, zero

cerquillo (CAm, RPl) *nm* fringe (BRIT), bangs *pl* (US)

cerrado, -a [θe'rraðo, a] *adj* closed, shut; (*con llave*) locked; (*tiempo*) cloudy, overcast; (*curva*) sharp; (*acento*) thick, broad

cerradura [θerra'ðura] *nf* (*acción*) closing; (*mecanismo*) lock

cerrajero [θerra'xero] *nm* locksmith

cerrar [θe'rrar] *vt* to close, shut; (*paso, carretera*) to close; (*grifo*) to turn off; (*cuenta, negocio*) to close ♦ *vi* to close, shut; (*noche*) to come down; **cerrarse** *vr* to close, shut; **~ con llave** to lock; **~ un trato** to strike a bargain

cerro ['θerro] *nm* hill

cerrojo [θe'rroxo] *nm* (*herramienta*) bolt; (*de puerta*) latch

certamen [θer'tamen] *nm* competition, contest

certero, -a [θer'tero, a] *adj* (*gen*) accurate

certeza [θer'teθa] *nf* certainty

certidumbre [θerti'ðumbre] *nf* = **certeza**

certificado, -a [θertifi'kaðo, a] *adj* (*carta, paquete*) registered; (*aprobado*) certified ♦ *nm* certificate
▶ **certificado médico** medical certificate

certificar [θertifi'kar] *vt* (*asegurar, atestar*) to certify

cervatillo [θerβa'tiʎo] *nm* fawn

cervecería [θerβeθe'ria] *nf* (*fábrica*) brewery; (*bar*) public house, pub

cerveza [θer'βeθa] *nf* beer

cesar [θe'sar] *vi* to cease, stop, ♦ *vt* (*funcionario*) to remove from office

cesárea [θe'sarea] *nf* (MED) Caesarean operation o section

cese ['θese] *nm* (*de trabajo*) dismissal; (*de pago*) suspension

césped ['θespeð] *nm* grass, lawn

cesta ['θesta] *nf* basket

cesto ['θesto] *nm* (large) basket, hamper

cfr *abr* (= *confróntese*) cf.

chabacano, -a [tʃaβa'kano, a] *adj* vulgar, coarse

chabola [tʃa'βola] (*ESP*) *nf* shack
▶ **barrio de chabolas** shanty town

chacal [tʃa'kal] *nm* jackal

chacha [tʃatʃa] (*fam*) *nf* maid

cháchara [tʃatʃara] *nf* chatter; **estar de ~** to chatter away

chacra ['tʃakra] (*CS*) *nf* smallholding

chafa (MÉX: *fam*) *adj* useless, dud

chafar [tʃa'far] *vt* (*aplastar*) to crush; (*plan etc*) to ruin

chal [tʃal] *nm* shawl

chalado, -a [tʃa'laðo, a] (*fam*) *adj* crazy

chalé [tʃa'le] (*pl* **~s**) *nm* villa, ≈ detached house

chaleco [tʃa'leko] *nm* waistcoat, vest (US) ▶ **chaleco salvavidas** life jacket

chalet [tʃa'le] (*pl* **chalets**) *nm* = **chalé**

chamaco, -a (MÉX) [tʃa'mako, a] *nm/f* (*niño*) kid

chambear (MÉX: *fam*) *vi* to earn one's living

champán [tʃam'pan] *nm* champagne

champiñón [tʃampi'ɲon] *nm* mushroom

champú [tʃam'pu] (*pl* **~es**, **~s**) *nm* shampoo

chamuscar [tʃamus'kar] vt to scorch, sear, singe

chance ['tʃanθe] (LAm) nm chance

chancho, -a ['tʃantʃo, a] (LAm) nm/f pig

chanchullo [tʃan'tʃuʎo] (fam) nm fiddle

chandal [tʃan'dal] nm tracksuit

chantaje [tʃan'taxe] nm blackmail

chapa ['tʃapa] nf (de metal) plate, sheet; (de madera) board, panel; (RPI AUTO) number (BRIT) o license (US) plate
  ❑ **chapado, -a** adj: **chapado en oro** gold-plated

chaparrón [tʃapa'rron] nm downpour, cloudburst

chaperón (MÉX) nm: **hacer de ~** to play gooseberry □ **chaperona** (LAm) nf: **hacer de chaperona** to play gooseberry

chapopote (MÉX) [tʃapo'pote] nm tar

chapulín (MÉX, CAm) [tʃapu'lin] nm grasshopper

chapurrear [tʃapurre'ar] vt (idioma) to speak badly

chapuza [tʃa'puθa] nf botched job

chapuzón [tʃapu'θon] nm: **darse un ~** to go for a dip

chaqueta [tʃa'keta] nf jacket

chaquetón [tʃake'ton] nm long jacket

charca ['tʃarka] nf pond, pool

charco ['tʃarko] nm pool, puddle

charcutería [tʃarkute'ria] nf (tienda) shop selling chiefly pork meat products; (productos) cooked pork meats pl

charla ['tʃarla] nf talk, chat; (conferencia) lecture □ **charlar** [tʃar'lar] vi to talk, chat □ **charlatán, -ana** [tʃarla'tan, ana] nm/f (hablador) chatterbox; (estafador) trickster

charol [tʃa'rol] nm varnish; (cuero) patent leather

charola (MÉX) [tʃa'rola] nf tray

charro (MÉX) ['tʃarro, a] nm typical Mexican

chasco ['tʃasko] nm (desengaño) disappointment

chasis ['tʃasis] nm inv chassis

chasquido [tʃas'kiðo] nm crack; click

chat (INTERNET) nm chat room

chatarra [tʃa'tarra] nf scrap (metal)

chato, -a [a'tʃato, a] adj flat; (nariz) snub

chaucha (RPI) ['tʃautʃa] nf runner (BRIT) o pole (US) bean

chaval, -a [tʃa'βal, a] (ESP) nm/f kid, lad/ lass

chavo, -a (MÉX: fam) ['tʃaβo] nm/f guy/ girl

checar (MÉX) vt: **~ tarjeta** (al entrar) to clock in o on; (al salir) to clock off o out

checo, -a ['tʃeko, a] adj, nm/f Czech ♦ nm (LING) Czech

checoslovaco, -a [tʃekoslo'βako, a] adj, nm/f Czech, Czechoslovak

Checoslovaquia [tʃekoslo'βakja] nf (HIST) Czechoslovakia

cheque ['tʃeke] nm cheque (BRIT), check (US); **cobrar un ~** to cash a cheque ▸ **cheque al portador** cheque payable to bearer ▸ **cheque de viaje** traveller's cheque (BRIT), traveler's check (US) ▸ **cheque en blanco** blank cheque

chequeo [tʃe'keo] nm (MED) check-up; (AUTO) service

chequera [tʃe'kera] (LAm) nf chequebook (BRIT), checkbook (US)

chévere (LAm: fam) ['tʃeβere] adj great

chícharo [tʃi'tʃaro] (MÉX, CAm) nm pea

chichón [tʃi'tʃon] nm bump, lump

chicle ['tʃikle] nm chewing gum

chico, -a ['tʃiko, a] adj small, little ♦ nm/ f (niño) child; (muchacho) boy/girl

chiflado, -a [tʃi'flaðo, a] adj crazy

chiflar [tʃi'flar] vt to hiss, boo

chilango, -a (MÉX) adj of o from Mexico City

Chile ['tʃile] nm Chile □ **chileno, -a** adj, nm/f Chilean

chile ['tʃile] nm chilli pepper

chillar [tʃiˈʎar] vi (persona) to yell, scream; (animal salvaje) to howl; (cerdo) to squeal

chillido [tʃiˈʎiðo] nm (de persona) yell, scream; (de animal) howl

chimenea [tʃimeˈnea] nf chimney; (hogar) fireplace

China [ˈtʃina] nf (tb: **la ~**) China

chinche [ˈtʃintʃe] nf (insecto) (bed)bug; (TEC) drawing pin (BRIT), thumbtack (US) ♦ nmf nuisance, pest

chincheta [tʃinˈtʃeta] nf drawing pin (BRIT), thumbtack (US)

chingada [MÉX: fam!] [tʃinˈɡaða] nf: **hijo de la ~** bastard

chino, -a [ˈtʃino, a] adj, nm/f Chinese ♦ nm (LING) Chinese

chipirón [tʃipiˈron] nm (ZOOL, CULIN) squid

Chipre [ˈtʃipre] nf Cyprus ❏ **chipriota** adj, nmf Cypriot

chiquillo, -a [tʃiˈkiʎo, a] nm/f (fam) kid

chirimoya [tʃiriˈmoja] nf custard apple

chiringuito [tʃirinˈɣito] nm small open-air bar

chiripa [tʃiˈripa] nf fluke

chirriar [tʃiˈrrjar] vi to creak, squeak

chirrido [tʃiˈrriðo] nm creak(ing), squeak(ing)

chisme [ˈtʃisme] nm (habladurías) piece of gossip; (fam: objeto) thingummyjig

chismoso, -a [tʃisˈmoso, a] adj gossiping ♦ nm/f gossip

chispa [ˈtʃispa] nf spark; (fig) sparkle; (ingenio) wit; (fam) drunkenness

chispear [tʃispeˈar] vi (lloviznar) to drizzle

chiste [ˈtʃiste] nm joke, funny story

chistoso, -a [tʃisˈtoso, a] adj funny, amusing

chivo, -a [ˈtʃiβo, a] nm/f (billy-/nanny-) goat ► **chivo expiatorio** scapegoat

chocante [tʃoˈkante] adj startling; (extraño) odd; (ofensivo) shocking

chocar [tʃoˈkar] vi (coches etc) to collide, crash ♦ vt to shock; (sorprender) to startle; **~ con** to collide with; (fig) to run into, run up against; **¡chócala!** (fam) put it there!

chochear [tʃotʃeˈar] vi to be senile

chocho, -a [ˈtʃotʃo, a] adj doddering, senile; (fig) soft, doting

choclo (CS) [ˈtʃoklo] nm (grano) sweet corn; (mazorca) corn on the cob

chocolate [tʃokoˈlate] adj, nm chocolate ❏ **chocolatina** nf chocolate

chofer [tʃoˈfer] nm = **chófer**

chófer [ˈtʃofer] nm driver

chollo [ˈtʃoʎo] (ESP: fam) nm bargain, snip

choque etc [ˈtʃoke] vb ver **chocar** ♦ nm (impacto) impact; (golpe) jolt; (AUTO) crash; (fig) conflict ► **choque frontal** head-on collision

chorizo [tʃoˈriθo] nm hard pork sausage, (type of) salami

chorrada [tʃoˈrraða] (ESP: fam) nf: **¡es una ~!** that's crap! (!); **decir chorradas** to talk crap (!)

chorrear [tʃorreˈar] vi to gush (out), spout (out); (gotear) to drip, trickle

chorro [ˈtʃorro] nm jet; (fig) stream

choza [ˈtʃoθa] nf hut, shack

chubasco [tʃuˈβasko] nm squall

chubasquero [tʃuβasˈkero] nm lightweight raincoat

chuchería [tʃutʃeˈria] nf trinket

chuleta [tʃuˈleta] nf chop, cutlet

chulo [ˈtʃulo] nm (de prostituta) pimp

chupaleta [MÉX] nf lollipop

chupar [tʃuˈpar] vt to suck; (absorber) to absorb; **chuparse** vr to grow thin

chupete [tʃuˈpete] (ESP, CS) nm dummy (BRIT), pacifier (US)

chupetín (RPl) nm lollipop

chupito [tʃuˈpito] (fam) nm shot

chupón [tʃu'pon] nm (piruleta) lollipop; (LAm: chupete) dummy (BRIT), pacifier (US)

churro ['tʃurro] nm (type of) fritter

chusma ['tʃusma] nf rabble, mob

chutar [tʃu'tar] vi to shoot (at goal)

Cía abr (= compañía) Co.

cianuro [θja'nuro] nm cyanide

cibercafé [θiβerka'fe] nm cybercafé

ciberterrorista nmf cyberterrorist

cicatriz [θika'triθ] nf scar ❏ **cicatrizarse** vr to heal (up), form a scar

ciclismo [θi'klismo] nm cycling

ciclista [θi'klista] adj cycle cpd ♦ nmf cyclist

ciclo ['θiklo] nm cycle ❏ **cicloturismo** nm touring by bicycle

ciclón [θi'klon] nm cyclone

ciego, -a ['θjeɣo, a] adj blind ♦ nm/f blind man/woman

cielo ['θjelo] nm sky; (REL) heaven; ¡cielos! good heavens!

ciempiés [θjem'pjes] nm inv centipede

cien [θjen] num ver **ciento**

ciencia [θjenθja] nf science; **ciencias** nfpl (ESCOL) science sg ❏ **ciencia-ficción** nf science fiction

científico, -a [θjen'tifiko, a] adj scientific ♦ nm/f scientist

ciento ['θjento] num hundred; **pagar al 10 por ~** to pay at 10 per cent; ver tb **cien**

cierre etc ['θjerre] vb ver **cerrar** ♦ nm closing, shutting; (con llave) locking; (LAm: cremallera) zip (fastener)

cierro etc vb ver **cerrar**

cierto, -a ['θjerto, a] adj sure, certain; (un tal) a certain; (correcto) right, correct; **por ~** by the way; **~ hombre** a certain man; **ciertas personas** certain o some people; **sí, es ~** yes, that's correct

ciervo ['θjerβo] nm deer; (macho) stag

cifra ['θifra] nf number; (secreta) code ❏ **cifrar** vt to code, write in code

cigala [θi'ɣala] nf Norway lobster

cigarra [θi'ɣarra] nf cicada

cigarrillo [θiɣa'rriλo] nm cigarette

cigarro [θi'ɣarro] nm cigarette; (puro) cigar

cigüeña [θi'ɣweɲa] nf stork

cilíndrico, -a [θi'lindriko, a] adj cylindrical

cilindro [θi'lindro] nm cylinder

cima ['θima] nf (de montaña) top, peak; (de árbol) top; (fig) height

cimentar [θimen'tar] vt to lay the foundations of; (fig: fundar) to found

cimiento [θi'mjento] nm foundation

cincel [θin'θel] nm chisel

cinco ['θinko] num five

cincuenta [θin'kwenta] num fifty

cine ['θine] nm cinema ❏ **cinematográfico, -a** [θinemato'ɣrafiko, a] adj cine-, film cpd

cínico, -a ['θiniko, a] adj cynical ♦ nm/f cynic

cinismo [θi'nismo] nm cynicism

cinta ['θinta] nf band, strip; (de tela) ribbon; (película) reel; (de máquina de escribir) ribbon ▶ **cinta adhesiva/ aislante** sticky/insulating tape ▶ **cinta de vídeo** videotape ▶ **cinta magnetofónica** tape ▶ **cinta métrica** tape measure

cintura [θin'tura] nf waist

cinturón [θintu'ron] nm belt ▶ **cinturón de seguridad** safety belt

ciprés [θi'pres] nm cypress (tree)

circo ['θirko] nm circus

circuito [θir'kwito] nm circuit

circulación [θirkula'θjon] nf circulation; (AUTO) traffic

circular [θirku'lar] adj, nf circular ♦ vi, to circulate ♦ vi (AUTO) to drive; "**circule por la derecha**" "keep (to the) right"

círculo ['θirkulo] nm circle ► **círculo vicioso** vicious circle

circunferencia [θirkunfe'renθja] nf circumference

circunstancia [θirkuns'tanθja] nf circumstance

cirio ['θirjo] nm (wax) candle

ciruela [θi'rwela] nf plum ► **ciruela pasa** prune

cirugía [θiru'xia] nf surgery ► **cirugía estética** o **plástica** plastic surgery

cirujano [θiru'xano] nm surgeon

cisne ['θisne] nm swan

cisterna [θis'terna] nf cistern, tank

cita ['θita] nf appointment, meeting; (de novios) date; (referencia) quotation

citación [θita'θjon] nf (JUR) summons sg

citar [θi'tar] vt (gen) to make an appointment with; (JUR) to summons; (un autor, texto) to quote; **citarse** vr: **se citaron en el cine** they arranged to meet at the cinema

cítricos ['θitrikos] nmpl citrus fruit's

ciudad [θju'ðað] nf town; (más grande) city □ **ciudadano, -a** nm/f citizen

cívico, -a [θi'βiko, a] adj civic

civil [θi'βil] adj civil ♦ nm (guardia) policeman □ **civilización** [θiβiliθa'θjon] nf civilization □ **civilizar** [θiβili'θar] vt to civilize

cizaña [θi'θaɲa] nf (fig) discord

cl. abr (= centilitro) cl.

clamor [kla'mor] nm clamour, protest

clandestino, -a [klandes'tino, a] adj clandestine; (POL) underground

clara ['klara] nf (de huevo) egg white

claraboya [klara'βoja] nf skylight

clarear [klare'ar] vi (el día) to dawn; (el cielo) to clear up, brighten up; **clarearse** vr to be transparent

claridad [klari'ðað] nf (de día) brightness; (de estilo) clarity

clarificar [klarifi'kar] vt to clarify

clarinete [klari'nete] nm clarinet

claro, -a ['klaro, a] adj clear; (luminoso) bright; (color) light; (evidente) clear, evident; (poco espeso) thin ♦ nm (en bosque) clearing ♦ adv clearly ♦ excl: **¡~ que sí!** of course!; **¡~ que no!** of course not!

clase ['klase] nf class; **dar ~(s)** to teach ► **clase alta/media/obrera** upper/middle/working class ► **clases particulares** private lessons o tuition sg

clásico, -a ['klasiko, a] adj classical

clasificación [klasifika'θjon] nf classification; (DEPORTE) league (table)

clasificar [klasifi'kar] vt to classify

claustro ['klaustro] nm cloister

cláusula ['klausula] nf clause

clausura [klau'sura] nf closing, closure

clavar [kla'βar] vt (clavo) to hammer in; (cuchillo) to stick, thrust

clave ['klaβe] nf key; (MÚS) key ► **clave de acceso** password ► **clave lada** (MÉX) dialling (BRIT) o area (US) code

clavel [kla'βel] nm carnation

clavícula [kla'βikula] nf collar bone

clavija [kla'βixa] nf peg, dowel, pin; (ELEC) plug

clavo ['klaβo] nm (de metal) nail; (BOT) clove

claxon ['klakson] (pl **claxons**) nm horn

clérigo ['kleriγo] nm priest

clero ['klero] nm clergy

clicar vi (INTERNET) to click; **~ en el icono** to click on an icon; **~ dos veces** to double-click

cliché [kli'tʃe] nm cliché; (FOTO) negative

cliente, -a ['kljente, a] nm/f client, customer □ **clientela** [kljen'tela] nf clientele, customers pl

clima ['klima] nm climate □ **climatizado, -a** [klimati'θaðo, a] adj air-conditioned

clímax ['klimaks] nm inv climax

clínica ['klinika] nf clinic; (particular) private hospital

clip [klip] (pl **clips**) nm paper clip

clítoris ['klitoris] nm inv (ANAT) clitoris

cloaca [klo'aka] nf sewer

cloro ['kloro] nm chlorine

clóset (MÉX) nm cupboard

club [klub] (pl **clubs** o **clubes**) nm club
▶ **club nocturno** night club

cm abr (= centímetro, centímetros) cm

coágulo [ko'aɣulo] nm clot

coalición [koali'θjon] nf coalition

coartada [koar'taða] nf alibi

coartar [koar'tar] vt to limit, restrict

coba ['koβa] nf: **dar ~ a algn** (adular) to suck up to sb

cobarde [ko'βarðe] adj cowardly ♦ nm coward □ **cobardía** nf cowardice

cobaya [ko'βaja] nf guinea pig

cobertizo [koβer'tiθo] nm shelter

cobertura [koβer'tura] nf cover; **estar fuera de ~** to be out of range; **no tengo ~** I'm out of range

cobija [ko'βixa] (LAm) nf blanket □ **cobijar** [koβi'xar] vt (cubrir) to cover; (proteger) to shelter □ **cobijo** nm shelter

cobra ['koβra] nf cobra

cobrador, a [koβra'ðor, a] nm/f (de autobús) conductor/conductress; (de impuestos, gas) collector

cobrar [ko'βrar] vt (cheque) to cash; (sueldo) to collect, draw; (objeto) to recover; (precio) to charge; (deuda) to collect ♦ vi to be paid; **cóbrese al entregar** cash on delivery; **¿me cobra, por favor?** how much do I owe you?, can I have the bill, please?

cobre ['koβre] nm copper; **cobres** nmpl (MÚS) brass instruments

cobro ['koβro] nm (de cheque) cashing; **presentar al ~** to cash

cocaína [koka'ina] nf cocaine

cocción [kok'θjon] nf (CULIN) cooking; (en agua) boiling

cocer [ko'θer] vt, vi to cook; (en agua) to boil; (en horno) to bake

coche ['kotʃe] nm (AUTO) car (BRIT), automobile (US); (de tren, de caballos) coach, carriage; (para niños) pram (BRIT), baby carriage (US); **ir en ~** to drive ▶ **coche celular** police van
▶ **coche de bomberos** fire engine
▶ **coche de carreras** racing car
▶ **coche fúnebre** hearse □ **coche-cama** (pl **coches-cama**) nm (FERRO) sleeping car, sleeper

cochera [ko'tʃera] nf garage; (de autobuses, trenes) depot

coche restaurante (pl **coches restaurante**) nm (FERRO) dining car, diner

cochinillo [kotʃi'niʎo] nm (CULIN) suckling pig, sucking pig

cochino, -a [ko'tʃino, a] adj filthy, dirty ♦ nm/f pig

cocido [ko'θiðo] nm stew

cocina [ko'θina] nf kitchen; (aparato) cooker, stove; (acto) cookery ▶ **cocina eléctrica/de gas** electric/gas cooker
▶ **cocina francesa** French cuisine □ **cocinar** vt, vi to cook

cocinero, -a [koθi'nero, a] nm/f cook

coco ['koko] nm coconut

cocodrilo [koko'ðrilo] nm crocodile

cocotero [koko'tero] nm coconut palm

cóctel ['koktel] nm cocktail ▶ **cóctel molotov** petrol bomb, Molotov cocktail

codazo [ko'ðaθo] nm: **dar un ~ a algn** to nudge sb

codicia [ko'ðiθja] nf greed □ **codiciar** vt to covet

código ['koðiɣo] nm code ▶ **código civil** common law ▶ **código de barras** bar code ▶ **código de circulación** highway code ▶ **código de la zona** (LAm) dialling (BRIT) o area (US) code ▶ **código postal** postcode

codillo [ko'ðiʎo] nm (ZOOL) knee; (TEC) elbow (joint)

codo ['koðo] nm (ANAT, de tubo) elbow; (ZOOL) knee

codorniz [koðor'niθ] nf quail

coexistir [koe(k)sis'tir] vi to coexist

cofradía [kofra'ðia] nf brotherhood, fraternity

cofre ['kofre] nm (de joyas) case; (de dinero) chest

coger [ko'xer] (ESP) vt to take (hold of); (objeto caído) to pick up; (frutas) to pick, harvest; (resfriado, ladrón, pelota) to catch ♦ vi: **~ por el buen camino** to take the right road; **cogerse** vr (el dedo) to catch; **cogerse a algo** to get hold of sth

cogollo [ko'ɣoλo] nm (de lechuga) heart

cogote [ko'ɣote] nm back o nape of the neck

cohabitar [koaβi'tar] vi to live together, cohabit

coherente [koe'rente] adj coherent

cohesión [koe'sjon] nm cohesion

cohete [ko'ete] nm rocket

cohibido, -a [koi'βiðo, a] adj (PSICO) inhibited; (tímido) shy

coincidencia [koinθi'ðenθja] nf coincidence

coincidir [koinθi'ðir] vi (en idea) to coincide, agree; (en lugar) to coincide

coito ['koito] nm intercourse, coitus

coja etc vb ver **coger**

cojear [koxe'ar] vi (persona) to limp, hobble; (mueble) to wobble, rock

cojera [ko'xera] nf limp

cojín [ko'xin] nm cushion

cojo, -a etc ['koxo, a] vb ver **coger** ♦ adj (que no puede andar) lame, crippled; (mueble) wobbly ♦ nm/f lame person, cripple

cojón [ko'xon] (fam!) nm: **¡cojones!** shit! (f) ☐ **cojonudo, -a** (fam) adj great, fantastic

col [kol] nf cabbage ▶ **coles de Bruselas** Brussels sprouts

cola ['kola] nf tail; (de gente) queue; (lugar) end, last place; (para pegar) glue, gum; **hacer ~** to queue (up)

colaborador, a [kolaβora'ðor, a] nm/f collaborator

colaborar [kolaβo'rar] vi to collaborate

colada [ko'laða] (ESP) nf: **hacer la ~** to do the washing

colador [kola'ðor] nm (para líquidos) strainer; (para verduras etc) colander

colapso [ko'lapso] nm collapse

colar [ko'lar] vt (líquido) to strain off; (metal) to cast ♦ vi to ooze, seep (through); **colarse** vr to jump the queue; **colarse en** to get into without paying; (fiesta) to gatecrash

colcha ['koltʃa] nf bedspread

colchón [kol'tʃon] nm mattress
▶ **colchón inflable** air bed o mattress

colchoneta [koltʃo'neta] nf (en gimnasio) mat; (de playa) air bed

colección [kolek'θjon] nf collection
☐ **coleccionar** vt to collect
☐ **coleccionista** nmf collector

colecta [ko'lekta] nf collection

colectivo, -a [kolek'tiβo, a] adj collective, joint ♦ nm (ARG: autobús) (small) bus

colega [ko'leɣa] nmf colleague; (ESP: amigo) mate

colegial, a [kole'xjal, a] nm/f schoolboy(-girl)

colegio [ko'lexjo] nm college; (escuela) school; (de abogados etc) association
▶ **colegio electoral** polling station
▶ **colegio mayor** (ESP) hall of residence

COLEGIO

A **colegio** is normally a private primary or secondary school. In the state system it means a primary school although these are also called **escuelas**. State secondary schools are called **institutos**.

cólera ['kolera] nf (ira) anger; (MED) cholera

colesterol [koleste'rol] nm cholesterol

coleta [ko'leta] nf pigtail

colgante [kol'ɣante] adj hanging ♦ nm (joya) pendant

colgar [kol'ɣar] vt to hang (up); (ropa) to hang out ♦ vi to hang; (TEL) to hang up

cólico ['koliko] nm colic

coliflor [koli'flor] nf cauliflower

colilla [ko'liʎa] nf cigarette end, butt

colina [ko'lina] nf hill

colisión [koli'sjon] nf collision
  ► **colisión frontal** head-on crash

collar [ko'ʎar] nm necklace; (de perro) collar

colmar [kol'mar] vt to fill to the brim; (fig) to fulfil, realize

colmena [kol'mena] nf beehive

colmillo [kol'miʎo] nm (diente) eye tooth; (de elefante) tusk; (de perro) fang

colmo ['kolmo] nm: **¡es el ~!** it's the limit!

colocación [koloka'θjon] nf (acto) placing; (empleo) job, position

colocar [kolo'kar] vt to place, put, position; (dinero) to invest; (poner en empleo) to find a job for; **colocarse** vr to get a job

Colombia [ko'lombja] nf Colombia
  □ **colombiano, -a** adj, nm/f Colombian

colonia [ko'lonja] nf colony; (agua de colonia) cologne; (MÉX: de casas) residential area ► **colonia proletaria** (MÉX) shantytown

colonización [koloniθa'θjon] nf colonization □ **colonizador, a** [koloniθa'ðor, a] adj colonizing ♦ nm/f colonist, settler

colonizar [koloni'θar] vt to colonize

coloquio [ko'lokjo] nm conversation; (congreso) conference

color [ko'lor] nm colour

colorado, -a [kolo'raðo, a] adj (rojo) red; (MÉX: chiste) smutty, rude

colorante [kolo'rante] nm colouring

colorear [kolore'ar] vt to colour

colorete [kolo'rete] nm blusher

colorido [kolo'riðo] nm colouring

columna [ko'lumna] nf column; (pilar) pillar; (apoyo) support; (tb: ~ **vertebral**) spine, spinal column; (fig) backbone

columpiar [kolum'pjar] vt to swing; **columpiarse** vr to swing □ **columpio** nm swing

coma ['koma] nf comma ♦ nm (MED) coma

comadre [ko'maðre] nf (madrina) godmother; (chismosa) gossip
  □ **comadrona** nf midwife

comal (MÉX, CAm) nm griddle

comandante [koman'dante] nm commandant

comarca [ko'marka] nf region

comba ['komba] (ESP) nf (cuerda) skipping rope; **saltar a la ~** to skip

combate [kom'bate] nm fight

combatir [komba'tir] vt to fight, combat

combinación [kombina'θjon] nf combination; (QUÍM) compound; (prenda) slip

combinar [kombi'nar] vt to combine

combustible [kombus'tiβle] nm fuel

comedia [ko'meðja] nf comedy; (TEATRO) play, drama ► **comediante** [kome'ðjante] nmf (comic) actor/ actress

comedido, -a [kome'ðiðo, a] adj moderate

comedor, a [kome'ðor, a] nm (habitación) dining room; (cantina) canteen

comensal [komen'sal] nmf fellow guest (o diner)

comentar [komen'tar] vt to comment on □ **comentario** [komen'tarjo] nm comment, remark; *(literario)* commentary; **comentarios** nmpl *(chismes)* gossip sg ❑ **comentarista** [komenta'rista] nmf commentator

comenzar [komen'θar] vt, vi to begin, start; **~ a hacer algo** to begin o start doing sth

comer [ko'mer] vt to eat; *(DAMAS, AJEDREZ)* to take, capture ♦ vi to eat; *(ESP, MÉX: almorzar)* to have lunch; **comerse** vr to eat up

comercial [komer'θjal] adj commercial; *(relativo al negocio)* business cpd ❑ **comercializar** vt *(producto)* to market; *(pey)* to commercialize

comerciante [komer'θjante] nmf trader, merchant

comerciar [komer'θjar] vi to trade, do business

comercio [ko'merθjo] nm commerce, trade; *(tienda)* shop, store; *(negocio)* business; *(fig)* dealings pl ▶ **comercio electrónico** e-commerce ▶ **comercio exterior/interior** foreign/domestic trade

comestible [komes'tiβle] adj eatable, edible ❑ **comestibles** nmpl food sg, foodstuffs

cometa [ko'meta] nm comet ♦ nf kite

cometer [kome'ter] vt to commit

cometido [kome'tiðo] nm task, assignment

cómic ['komik] nm comic

comicios [ko'miθjos] nmpl elections

cómico, -a ['komiko, a] adj comic(al) ♦ nm/f comedian

comida [ko'miða] nf *(alimento)* food; *(almuerzo, cena)* meal; *(de mediodía)* lunch ▶ **comida basura** junk food ▶ **comida chatarra** *(MÉX)* junk food

comidilla [komi'ðiʎa] nf: **ser la ~ del barrio** o **pueblo** to be the talk of the town

comienzo etc [ko'mjenθo] vb ver **comenzar** ♦ nm beginning, start

comillas [ko'miʎas] nfpl quotation marks

comilona [komi'lona] *(fam)* nf blowout

comino [ko'mino] nm: **(no) me importa un ~** I don't give a damn

comisaría [komisa'ria] nf *(de policía)* police station; *(MIL)* commissariat

comisario [komi'sarjo] nm *(MIL etc)* commissary; *(POL)* commissar

comisión [komi'sjon] nf commission ▶ **Comisiones Obreras** *(ESP)* Communist trade union

comité [komi'te] *(pl ~s)* nm committee

comitiva [komi'tiβa] nf retinue

como ['komo] adv as; *(tal)*: like; *(aproximadamente)* about, approximately ♦ conj *(ya que, puesto que)* as, since; **¡~ no!** of course!; **~ no lo haga hoy** unless he does it today; **~ si** as if; **es tan alto ~ ancho** it is as high as it is wide

cómo ['komo] adv how?, why? ♦ excl what?, I beg your pardon? ♦ nm: **el ~ y el porqué** the whys and wherefores

cómoda ['komoða] nf chest of drawers

comodidad [komoði'ðað] nf comfort

comodín [komo'ðin] nm joker

cómodo, -a ['komoðo, a] adj comfortable; *(práctico, de fácil uso)* convenient

compact *(pl* **compacts)** nm *(tb:* **~ disc)** compact disk player

compacto, -a [kom'pakto, a] adj compact

compadecer [kompaðe'θer] vt to pity, be sorry for; **compadecerse** vr: **compadecerse de** to pity, to o feel sorry for

compadre [kom'paðre] nm *(padrino)* godfather; *(amigo)* friend, pal

compañero, -a [kompa'ɲero, a] nm/f companion; *(novio)* boy/girlfriend ▶ **compañero de clase** classmate

compañía [kompa'ɲia] nf company; **hacer ~ a algn** to keep sb company

comparación [kompara'θjon] nf comparison; **en ~ con** in comparison with

comparar [kompa'rar] vt to compare

comparecer [kompare'θer] vi to appear (in court)

comparsa [kom'parsa] nmf (TEATRO) extra

compartimiento [komparti'mjento] nm (FERRO) compartment

compartir [kompar'tir] vt to share; (dinero, comida etc) to divide (up), share (out)

compás [kom'pas] nm (MÚS) beat, rhythm; (MAT) compasses pl; (NÁUT etc) compass

compasión [kompa'sjon] nf compassion, pity

compasivo, -a [kompa'siβo, a] adj compassionate

compatible [kompa'tiβle] adj compatible

compatriota [kompa'trjota] nmf compatriot, fellow countryman/woman

compenetrarse [kompene'trarse] vr to be in tune

compensación [kompensa'θjon] nf compensation

compensar [kompen'sar] vt to compensate

competencia [kompe'tenθja] nf (incumbencia) domain, field; (JUR, habilidad) competence; (rivalidad) competition

competente [kompe'tente] adj competent

competición [kompeti'θjon] nf competition

competir [kompe'tir] vi to compete

compinche (LAm) [kom'pintʃe] nmf mate, buddy (US)

complacer [kompla'θer] vt to please; **complacerse** vr to be pleased

complaciente [kompla'θjente] adj kind, obliging, helpful

complejo, -a [kom'plexo, a] adj, nm complex

complementario, -a [komplemen'tarjo, a] adj complementary

completar [komple'tar] vt to complete

completo, -a [kom'pleto, a] adj complete; (perfecto) perfect; (lleno) full ♦ nm full complement

complicado, -a [kompli'kaðo, a] adj complicated; **estar ~ en** to be mixed up in

cómplice ['kompliθe] nmf accomplice

complot [kom'plo(t)] (pl **complots**) nm plot

componer [kompo'ner] vt (MÚS, LITERATURA, IMPRENTA) to compose; (algo roto) to mend, repair; (arreglar) to arrange; **componerse** vr: **componerse de** to consist of

comportamiento [komporta'mjento] nm behaviour, conduct

comportarse [kompor'tarse] vr to behave

composición [komposi'θjon] nf composition

compositor, a [komposi'tor, a] nm/f composer

compostura [kompos'tura] nf (actitud) composure

compra ['kompra] nf purchase; **hacer la ~** to do the shopping; **ir de compras** to go shopping □ **comprador, a** nm/f buyer, purchaser □ **comprar** [kom'prar] vt to buy, purchase

comprender [kompren'der] vt to understand; (incluir) to comprise, include

comprensión [kompren'sjon] nf understanding □ **comprensivo, -a** adj (actitud) understanding

compresa [kom'presa] nf (para mujer) sanitary towel (BRIT) o napkin (US)

comprimido, -a [kompri'miðo, a] adj compressed ♦ nm (MED) pill, tablet

comprimir [kompri'mir] vt to compress

comprobante [kompro'βante] nm proof; (COM) voucher ▶ **comprobante de compra** proof of purchase

comprobar [kompro'βar] vt to check; (probar) to prove; (TEC) to check, test

comprometer [komprome'ter] vt to compromise; (poner en peligro) to endanger; **comprometerse** vr (involucrarse) to get involved

compromiso [kompro'miso] nm (obligación) obligation; (cometido) commitment; (convenio) agreement; (apuro) awkward situation

compuesto, -a [kom'pwesto, a] adj: ~ **de** composed of, made up of ♦ nm compound

computadora (LAm) [kompu'taðora] nf computer ▶ **computadora central** mainframe (computer) ▶ **computadora personal** personal computer

cómputo ['komputo] nm calculation

comulgar [komul'γar] vi to receive communion

común [ko'mun] adj common ♦ nm: **el ~ the community**

comunicación [komunika'θjon] nf communication; (informe) report

comunicado [komuni'kaðo] nm announcement ▶ **comunicado de prensa** press release

comunicar [komuni'kar] vt, vi to communicate; **comunicarse** vr to communicate; **está comunicando** (TEL) the line's engaged (BRIT) o busy (US) ▫ **comunicativo, -a** adj communicative

comunidad [komuni'ðað] nf community ▶ **comunidad autónoma** (ESP) autonomous region ▶ **Comunidad (Económica) Europea** European (Economic) Community ▶ **comunidad de vecinos** residents' association

comunión [komu'njon] nf communion

comunismo [komu'nismo] nm communism ▫ **comunista** adj, nmf communist

con

PALABRA CLAVE

[kon] prep

1 (medio, compañía) with; **comer con cuchara** to eat with a spoon; **pasear con algn** to go for a walk with sb

2 (a pesar de): **con todo, merece nuestros respetos** all the same, he deserves our respect

3 (para con): **es muy bueno para con los niños** he's very good with the children

4 (+ infin): **con llegar a las seis estará bien** if you come by six it will be fine

♦ conj: **con que: será suficiente con que le escribas** it will be sufficient if you write to her

concebir [konθe'βir] vt, vi to conceive

conceder [konθe'ðer] vt to concede

concejal, a [konθe'xal, a] nm/f town councillor

concentración [konθentra'θjon] nf concentration

concentrar [konθen'trar] vt to concentrate; **concentrarse** vr to concentrate

concepto [kon'θepto] nm concept

concernir [konθer'nir] vi to concern; **en lo que concierne a ...** as far as ... is concerned; **en lo que a mí concierne** as far as I'm concerned

concertar [konθer'tar] vt (MÚS) to harmonize; (acordar: precio) to agree; (: tratado) to conclude; (trato) to arrange, fix up; (combinar: esfuerzos) to coordinate ♦ vi to harmonize, be in tune

concesión [konθe'sjon] nf concession

concesionario [konθesjo'narjo] nm (licensed) dealer, agent

concha ['kontʃa] nf shell

conciencia [kon'θjenθja] nf conscience; **tomar ~ de** to become aware of; **tener la ~ tranquila** to have a clear conscience

concienciar [konθjen'θjar] vt to make aware; **concienciarse** vr to become aware

concienzudo, -a [konθjen'θuðo, a] adj conscientious

concierto etc [kon'θjerto] vb ver **concertar ♦** nm concert; (obra) concerto

conciliar [konθi'ljar] vt to reconcile; **~ el sueño** to get to sleep

concilio [kon'θiljo] nm council

conciso, -a [kon'θiso, a] adj concise

concluir [konklu'ir] vt, vi to conclude; **concluirse** vr to conclude

conclusión [konklu'sjon] nf conclusion

concordar [konkor'ðar] vt to reconcile ♦ vi to agree, tally

concordia [kon'korðja] nf harmony

concretar [konkre'tar] vt to make concrete, make more specific; **concretarse** vr to become more definite

concreto, -a [kon'kreto, a] adj, nm (LAm: hormigón) concrete; **en ~** (en resumen) to sum up; (específicamente) specifically; **no hay nada en ~** there's nothing definite

concurrido, -a [konku'rriðo, a] adj (calle) busy; (local, reunión) crowded

concursante [konkur'sante] nmf competitor

concurso [kon'kurso] nm (de público) crowd; (ESCOL, DEPORTE, competencia) competition; (ayuda) help, cooperation

condal [kon'dal] adj: **la Ciudad C~** Barcelona

conde ['konde] nm count

condecoración [kondekora'θjon] nf (MIL) medal

condena [kon'dena] nf sentence
❑ **condenación** [kondena'θjon] nf condemnation; (REL) damnation
❑ **condenar** [konde'nar] vt to condemn; (JUR) to convict; **condenarse** vr (REL) to be damned

condesa [kon'desa] nf countess

condición [kondi'θjon] nf condition; **a ~ de que ...** on condition that ...
❑ **condicional** adj conditional

condimento [kondi'mento] nm seasoning

condominio (LAm) [kondo'minjo] nm condominium

condón [kon'don] nm condom

conducir [kondu'θir] vt to take, convey; (AUTO) to drive ♦ vi to drive; (fig) to lead; **conducirse** vr to behave

conducta [kon'dukta] nf conduct, behaviour

conducto [kon'dukto] nm pipe, tube; (fig) channel

conductor, a [konduk'tor, a] adj leading, guiding ♦ nm (FÍSICA) conductor; (de vehículo) driver

conduje etc [kon'duxe] vb ver **conducir**

conduzco etc vb ver **conducir**

conectado, -a [konek'taðo, a] adj (INFORM) on-line

conectar [konek'tar] vt to connect (up); (enchufar) plug in

conejillo [kone'xiʎo] nm: **~ de Indias** guinea pig

conejo [ko'nexo] nm rabbit

conexión [konek'sjon] nf connection

confección [konfe(k)'θjon] nf preparation; (industria) clothing industry

confeccionar [konfekθjo'nar] vt to make (up)

conferencia [konfe'renθja] nf conference; (lección) lecture; (ESP TEL) call ▶ **conferencia de prensa** press conference

conferir [konfe'rir] vt to award

confesar [konfe'sar] vt to confess, admit

confesión [konfe'sjon] nf confession

confesionario [konfesjo'narjo] nm confessional

confeti [kon'feti] nm confetti

confiado, -a [kon'fjaðo, a] adj (crédulo) trusting; (seguro) confident

confianza [kon'fjanθa] nf trust; (seguridad) confidence; (familiaridad) intimacy, familiarity

confiar [kon'fjar] vt to entrust ♦ vi to trust; **~ en algn** to trust sb; **~ en que** ... to hope that ...

confidencial [konfiðen'θjal] adj confidential

confidente [konfi'ðente] nmf confidant/e; (policial) informer

configurar [konfiɣu'rar] vt to shape, form

confín [kon'fin] nm limit; **confines** nmpl confines, limits

confirmar [konfir'mar] vt to confirm

confiscar [konfis'kar] vt to confiscate

confite [kon'fite] nm sweet (BRIT), candy (US) □ **confitería** [konfite'ria] nf (tienda) confectioner's (shop)

confitura [konfi'tura] nf jam

conflictivo, -a [konflik'tiβo, a] adj (asunto, propuesta) controversial; (país, situación) troubled

conflicto [kon'flikto] nm conflict; (fig) clash

confluir [konflu'ir] vi (ríos) to meet; (gente) to gather

conformar [konfor'mar] vt to shape, fashion ♦ vi to agree; **conformarse** vr to conform; (resignarse) to resign o.s.; **conformarse con algo** to be happy with sth

conforme [kon'forme] adj (correspondiente): **~ con** in line with; (de acuerdo): **estar conformes (con algo)**

to be in agreement (with sth) ♦ adv as ♦ excl agreed! ♦ prep: **~ a** in accordance with; **quedarse ~ (con algo)** to be satisfied (with sth)

confortable [konfor'taβle] adj comfortable

confortar [konfor'tar] vt to comfort

confrontar [konfron'tar] vt to confront; (dos personas) to bring face to face; (cotejar) to compare

confundir [konfun'dir] vt (equivocar) to mistake, confuse; (turbar) to confuse; **confundirse** vr (turbarse) to get confused; (equivocarse) to make a mistake; (mezclarse) to mix

confusión [konfu'sjon] nf confusion

confuso, -a [kon'fuso, a] adj confused

congelado, -a [konxe'laðo, a] adj frozen □ **congelados** nmpl frozen food(s) □ **congelador** nm (aparato) freezer, deep freeze

congelar [konxe'lar] vt to freeze; **congelarse** vr (sangre, grasa) to congeal

congeniar [konxe'njar] vi to get on (BRIT) o along (US) well

congestión [konxes'tjon] nf congestion

congestionar [konxestjo'nar] vt to congest

congraciarse [kongra'θjarse] vr to ingratiate o.s.

congratular [kongratu'lar] vt to congratulate

congregar [kongre'ɣar] vt to gather together; **congregarse** vr to gather together

congresista [kongre'sista] nmf delegate, congressman/woman

congreso [kon'greso] nm congress

conjetura [konxe'tura] nf guess □ **conjeturar** vt to guess

conjugar [konxu'ɣar] vt to combine, fit together; (LING) to conjugate

conjunción [konxun'θjon] nf conjunction

conjunto, -a [kon'xunto, a] *adj* joint, united ♦ *nm* whole; (*MÚS*) band; **en ~** as a whole

conmemoración [konmemora'θjon] *nf* commemoration

conmemorar [konmemo'rar] *vt* to commemorate

conmigo [kon'miɣo] *pron* with me

conmoción [konmo'θjon] *nf* shock; (*fig*) upheaval ► **conmoción cerebral** (*MED*) concussion

conmovedor, -a [konmoβe'ðor, a] *adj* touching, moving; (*emocionante*) exciting

conmover [konmo'βer] *vt* to shake, disturb; (*fig*) to move

conmutador [konmuta'ðor] *nm* switch; (*LAm: centralita*) switchboard; (: *central*) telephone exchange

cono ['kono] *nm* cone ► **Cono Sur** Southern Cone

conocedor, a [konoθe'ðor, a] *adj* expert, knowledgeable ♦ *nm/f* expert

conocer [kono'θer] *vt* to know; (*por primera vez*) to meet, get to know; (*entender*) to know about; (*reconocer*) to recognize; **conocerse** *vr* (*una persona*) to know o.s.; (*dos personas*) to (get to) know each other; **~ a algn de vista** to know sb by sight

conocido, -a [kono'θiðo, a] *adj* (well-)known ♦ *nm/f* acquaintance

conocimiento [konoθi'mjento] *nm* knowledge; (*MED*) consciousness; **conocimientos** *nmpl* (*saber*) knowledge *sg*

conozco *etc vb ver* **conocer**

conque ['konke] *conj* and so, then

conquista [kon'kista] *nf* conquest ❑ **conquistador, a** *adj* conquering ♦ *nm* conqueror ❑ **conquistar** [konkis'tar] *vt* to conquer

consagrar [konsa'ɣrar] *vt* (*REL*) to consecrate; (*fig*) to devote

consciente [kons'θjente] *adj* conscious

consecución [konseku'θjon] *nf* acquisition; (*de fin*) attainment

consecuencia [konse'kwenθja] *nf* consequence, outcome; (*coherencia*) consistency

consecuente [konse'kwente] *adj* consistent

consecutivo, -a [konseku'tiβo, a] *adj* consecutive

conseguir [konse'ɣir] *vt* to get, obtain; (*objetivo*) to attain

consejero, -a [konse'xero, a] *nm/f* adviser, consultant; (*POL*) councillor

consejo [kon'sexo] *nm* advice; (*POL*) council ► **consejo de administración** (*COM*) board of directors ► **consejo de guerra** court martial ► **consejo de ministros** cabinet meeting

consenso [kon'senso] *nm* consensus

consentimiento [konsenti'mjento] *nm* consent

consentir [konsen'tir] *vt* (*permitir, tolerar*) to consent to; (*mimar*) to pamper, spoil; (*aguantar*) to put up with ♦ *vi* to agree, consent; **~ que algn haga algo** to allow sb to do sth

conserje [kon'serxe] *nm* caretaker; (*portero*) porter

conservación [konserβa'θjon] *nf* conservation; (*de alimentos, vida*) preservation

conservador, a [konserβa'ðor, a] *adj* (*POL*) conservative ♦ *nm/f* conservative

conservante [konser'βante] *nm* preservative

conservar [konser'βar] *vt* to conserve, keep; (*alimentos, vida*) to preserve; **conservarse** *vr* to survive

conservas [kon'serβas] *nfpl* canned food(s) *pl*

conservatorio [konserβa'torjo] *nm* (*MÚS*) conservatoire, conservatory

considerable [konside'raβle] *adj* considerable

consideración [konsiðeɾa'θjon] nf
consideration; (*estimación*) respect

considerado, -a [konsiðe'raðo, a] adj
(*atento*) considerate; (*respetado*)
respected

considerar [konsiðe'rar] vt to consider

consigna [kon'siɣna] nf (*orden*) order,
instruction; (*para equipajes*) left-
luggage office

consigo etc [kon'siɣo] vb ver
conseguir ♦ pron (m) with him; (f)
with her; (Vd) with you; (*reflexivo*) with
o.s.

consiguiendo etc [konsi'ɣjendo] vb
ver **conseguir**

consiguiente [konsi'ɣjente] adj
consequent; **por ~** and so, therefore,
consequently

consistente [konsis'tente] adj
consistent; (*sólido*) solid, firm; (*válido*)
sound

consistir [konsis'tir] vi: **~ en**
(*componerse de*) to consist of

consola [kon'sola] nf (*mueble*) console
table; (*de videojuegos*) console

consolación [konsola'θjon] nf
consolation

consolar [konso'lar] vt to console

consolidar [konsoli'ðar] vt to
consolidate

consomé [konso'me] (pl **~s**) nm
consommé, clear soup

consonante [konso'nante] adj
consonant, harmonious ♦ nf
consonant

consorcio [kon'sorθjo] nm consortium

conspiración [konspira'θjon] nf
conspiracy

conspirar [konspi'rar] vi to conspire

constancia [kons'tanθja] nf
constancy; **dejar ~ de** to put on record

constante [kons'tante] adj, nf constant

constar [kons'tar] vi (*evidenciarse*) to be
clear o evident; **~ de** to consist of

constipado, -a [konsti'paðo, a] adj:
estar ~ to have a cold ♦ nm cold

⚠ No confundir **constipado** con la
palabra inglesa *constipated*.

constitución [konstitu'θjon] nf
constitution

constituir [konstitu'ir] vt (*formar*,
componer) to constitute, make up;
(*fundar, erigir, ordenar*) to constitute,
establish

construcción [konstruk'θjon] nf
construction, building

constructor, a [konstruk'tor, a] nm/f
builder

construir [konstru'ir] vt to build,
construct

construyendo etc [konstru'jendo] vb
ver **construir**

consuelo [kon'swelo] nm consolation,
solace

cónsul ['konsul] nm consul
❑ **consulado** nm consulate

consulta [kon'sulta] nf consultation;
(*MED*): **horas de ~** surgery hours
❑ **consultar** [konsul'tar] vt to consult;
consultar algo con algn to discuss sth
with sb ❑ **consultorio** [konsul'torjo]
nm (*MED*) surgery

consumición [konsumi'θjon] nf
consumption; (*bebida*) drink; (*comida*)
food ▶ **consumición mínima** cover
charge

consumidor, a [konsumi'ðor, a] nm/f
consumer

consumir [konsu'mir] vt to consume;
consumirse vr to be consumed;
(*persona*) to waste away

consumismo [konsu'mismo] nm
consumerism

consumo [kon'sumo] nm
consumption

contabilidad [kontaβili'ðað] nf
accounting, book-keeping; (*profesión*)
accountancy ❑ **contable** nmf
accountant

contacto [kon'takto] nm contact; (AUTO) ignition; **estar/ponerse en ~ con algn** to be/to get in touch with sb

contado, -a [kon'taðo, a] adj; **contados** (escasos) numbered, scarce, few ♦ nm: **pagar al ~** to pay (in) cash

contador [konta'ðor] nm (ESP: aparato) meter ♦ nmf (LAm COM) accountant

contagiar [konta'xjar] vt (enfermedad) to pass on, transmit; (persona) to infect; **contagiarse** vr to become infected

contagio [kon'taxjo] nm infection ❏ **contagioso, -a** adj infectious; (fig) catching

contaminación [kontamina'θjon] nf contamination; (polución) pollution

contaminar [kontami'nar] vt to contaminate; (aire, agua) to pollute

contante [kon'tante] adj: **dinero ~ (y sonante)** cash

contar [kon'tar] vt (páginas, dinero) to count; (anécdota, chiste etc) to tell ♦ vi to count; **~ con** to rely on, count on

contemplar [kontem'plar] vt to contemplate; (mirar) to look at

contemporáneo, -a [kontempo'raneo, a] adj, nm/f contemporary

contenedor [kontene'ðor] nm container

contener [konte'ner] vt to contain, hold; (retener) to hold back, contain; **contenerse** vr to control o restrain o.s.

contenido, -a [konte'niðo, a] adj (moderado) restrained; (risa etc) suppressed ♦ nm contents pl, content

contentar [konten'tar] vt (satisfacer) to satisfy; (complacer) to please; **contentarse** vr to be satisfied

contento, -a [kon'tento, a] adj (alegre) pleased; (feliz) happy

contestación [kontesta'θjon] nf answer, reply

contestador [kontesta'ðor] nm (tb: ~ automático) answering machine

contestar [kontes'tar] vt to answer, reply; (JUR) to corroborate, confirm

⚠ No confundir **contestar** con la palabra inglesa contest.

contexto [kon'te(k)sto] nm context

contigo [kon'tiɣo] pron with you

contiguo, -a [kon'tiɣwo, a] adj adjacent, adjoining

continente [konti'nente] adj, nm continent

continuación [kontinwa'θjon] nf continuation; **a ~** then, next

continuar [konti'nwar] vt to continue, go on with ♦ vi to continue, go on; **~ hablando** to continue talking o to talk

continuidad [kontinwi'ðað] nf continuity

continuo, -a [kon'tinwo, a] adj (sin interrupción) continuous; (acción perseverante) continual

contorno [kon'torno] nm outline; (GEO) contour; **contornos** nmpl neighbourhood sg, surrounding area sg

contra ['kontra] prep, adv against ♦ nm inv con ♦ nf: **la C~** (de Nicaragua) the Contras pl

contraataque [kontraa'take] nm counter-attack

contrabajo [kontra'βaxo] nm double bass

contrabandista [kontraβan'dista] nmf smuggler

contrabando [kontra'βando] nm (acción) smuggling; (mercancías) contraband

contracción [kontrak'θjon] nf contraction

contracorriente [kontrako'rrjente] nf cross-current

contradecir [kontraðe'θir] vt to contradict

contradicción [kontraðik'θjon] nf contradiction

contradictorio, -a [kontraðik'torjo, a] *adj* contradictory

contraer [kontra'er] *vt* to contract; (*limitar*) to restrict; **contraerse** *vr* to contract; (*limitarse*) to limit o.s.

contraluz [kontra'luθ] *nm* view against the light

contrapartida [kontrapar'tiða] *nf*: **como ~ (de)** in return (for)

contrapelo [kontra'pelo]: **a ~** *adv* the wrong way

contrapeso [kontra'peso] *nm* counterweight

contraportada [kontrapor'taða] *nf* (*de revista*) back cover

contraproducente [kontraproðu'θente] *adj* counterproductive

contrario, -a [kon'trarjo, a] *adj* contrary; (*persona*) opposed; (*sentido, lado*) opposite ♦ *nm/f* enemy, adversary; (DEPORTE) opponent; **al o por el ~** on the contrary; **de lo ~** otherwise

contrarreloj [kontrarre'lo] *nf* (*tb*: **prueba ~**) time trial

contrarrestar [kontrarres'tar] *vt* to counteract

contrasentido [kontrasen'tiðo] *nm* (*contradicción*) contradiction

contraseña [kontra'seɲa] *nf* (INFORM) password

contrastar [kontras'tar] *vt, vi* to contrast

contraste [kon'traste] *nm* contrast

contratar [kontra'tar] *vt* (*firmar un acuerdo para*) to contract for; (*empleados, obreros*) to hire, engage

contratiempo [kontra'tjempo] *nm* setback

contratista [kontra'tista] *nmf* contractor

contrato [kon'trato] *nm* contract

contraventana [kontraβen'tana] *nf* shutter

contribución [kontriβu'θjon] *nf* (*municipal etc*) tax; (*ayuda*) contribution

contribuir [kontriβu'ir] *vt, vi* to contribute; (COM) to pay (in taxes)

contribuyente [kontriβu'jente] *nmf* (COM) taxpayer; (*que ayuda*) contributor

contrincante [kontrin'kante] *nmf* opponent

control [kon'trol] *nm* control; (*inspección*) inspection, check ▶ **control de pasaportes** passport inspection ❑ **controlador, a** *nm/f* controller ▶ **controlador aéreo** air-traffic controller ❑ **controlar** [kontro'lar] *vt* to control; (*inspeccionar*) to inspect, check

contundente [kontun'dente] *adj* (*instrumento*) blunt; (*argumento, derrota*) overwhelming

contusión [kontu'sjon] *nf* bruise

convalecencia [kombale'θenθja] *nf* convalescence

convalecer [kombale'θer] *vi* to convalesce, get better

convalidar [kombali'ðar] *vt* (*título*) to recognize

convencer [komben'θer] *vt* to convince; **~ a algn (de o para hacer algo)** to persuade sb (to do sth)

convención [komben'θjon] *nf* convention

conveniente [kombe'njente] *adj* suitable; (*útil*) useful

convenio [kom'benjo] *nm* agreement, treaty

convenir [kombe'nir] *vi* (*estar de acuerdo*) to agree; (*venir bien*) to suit, be suitable

⚠ No confundir **convenir** con la palabra inglesa *convene*.

convento [kom'bento] *nm* convent

convenza *etc* [kom'benθa] *vb ver* **convencer**

convergir [komber'xir] vi =
converger

conversación [kombersa'θjon] nf
conversation

conversar [komber'sar] vi to talk,
converse

conversión [komber'sjon] nf
conversion

convertir [komber'tir] vt to convert

convidar [kombi'ðar] vt to invite; ~ a
algn a una cerveza to buy sb a beer

convincente [kombin'θente] adj
convincing

convite [kom'bite] nm invitation;
(banquete) banquet

convivencia [kombi'βenθja] nf
coexistence, living together

convivir [kombi'βir] vi to live together

convocar [kombo'kar] vt to summon,
call (together)

convocatoria [komboka'torja] nf (de
oposiciones, elecciones) notice; (de
huelga) call

cónyuge ['konjuxe] nmf spouse

coñac [ko'na(k)] (pl coñacs) nm cognac,
brandy

coño ['kono] (fam!) excl (enfado) shit! (!);
(sorpresa) bloody hell! (!)

cool [kul] adj cool

cooperación [koopera'θjon] nf
cooperation

cooperar [koope'rar] vi to cooperate

cooperativa [koopera'tiβa] nf
cooperative

coordinadora [koorðina'ðora] nf
(comité) coordinating committee

coordinar [koorði'nar] vt to
coordinate

copa ['kopa] nf cup; (vaso) glass;
(bebida): **tomar una ~** (to have a) drink;
(de árbol) top; (de sombrero) crown;
copas nfpl (NAIPES) = hearts

copia ['kopja] nf copy ▸ **copia de
respaldo** o **seguridad** (INFORM) backup copy ❏ **copiar** vt to copy

copla ['kopla] nf verse; (canción)
(popular) song

copo ['kopo] nm: ~ **de nieve** snowflake;
copos de maíz cornflakes

coqueta [ko'keta] adj flirtatious,
coquettish ❏ **coquetear** vi to flirt

coraje [ko'raxe] nm courage; (ánimo)
spirit; (ira) anger

coral [ko'ral] adj choral ♦ nf (MÚS) choir
♦ nm (ZOOL) coral

coraza [ko'raθa] nf (armadura) armour;
(blindaje) armour-plating

corazón [kora'θon] nm heart

corazonada [koraθo'naða] nf impulse;
(presentimiento) hunch

corbata [kor'βata] nf tie

corchete [kor'tʃete] nm catch, clasp

corcho ['kortʃo] nm cork; (PESCA) float

cordel [kor'ðel] nm cord, line

cordero [kor'ðero] nm lamb

cordial [kor'ðjal] adj cordial

cordillera [korði'ʎera] nf range (of
mountains)

Córdoba ['korðoβa] n Cordova

cordón [kor'ðon] nm (cuerda) cord,
string; (de zapatos) lace; (MIL etc)
cordon ▸ **cordón umbilical** umbilical
cord

cordura [kor'ðura] nf: **con ~** (obrar,
hablar) sensibly

corneta [kor'neta] nf bugle

cornisa [kor'nisa] nf (ARQ) cornice

coro ['koro] nm chorus; (conjunto de
cantores) choir

corona [ko'rona] nf crown; (de flores)
garland

coronel [koro'nel] nm colonel

coronilla [koro'niʎa] nf (ANAT) crown
(of the head)

corporal [korpo'ral] adj corporal,
bodily

corpulento, -a [korpu'lento, a] adj
(persona) heavily-built

corral [ko'rral] nm farmyard

correa [ko'rrea] nf strap; (cinturón) belt; (de perro) lead, leash ▶ **correa del ventilador** (AUTO) fan belt

corrección [korrek'θjon] nf correction; (reprensión) rebuke ❑ **correccional** nm reformatory

correcto, -a [ko'rrekto, a] adj correct; (persona) well-mannered

corredizo, -a [korre'ðiθo, a] adj (puerta etc) sliding

corredor, a [korre'ðor, a] nm (pasillo) corridor; (balcón corrido) gallery; (COM) agent, broker ♦ nm/f (DEPORTE) runner

corregir [korre'xir] vt (error) to correct; **corregirse** vr to reform

correo [ko'rreo] nm post, mail; (persona) courier; **Correos** nmpl (ESP) Post Office sg ▶ **correo aéreo** airmail ▶ **correo basura** (INFORM) spam ▶ **correo electrónico** e-mail, electronic mail ▶ **correo web** webmail

correr [ko'rrer] vt to run; (cortinas) to draw; (cerrojo) to shoot ♦ vi to run; (líquido) to run, flow; **correrse** vr to slide, move; (colores) to run

correspondencia [korrespon'denθja] nf correspondence; (FERRO) connection

corresponder [korrespon'der] vi to correspond; (convenir) to be suitable; (pertenecer) to belong; (concernir) to concern; **corresponderse** vr (por escrito) to correspond; (amarse) to love one another

correspondiente [korrespon'djente] adj corresponding

corresponsal [korrespon'sal] nmf correspondent

corrida [ko'rriða] nf (de toros) bullfight

corrido, -a [ko'rriðo, a] adj (avergonzado) abashed; **un kilo ~** a good kilo

corriente [ko'rrjente] adj (agua) running; (dinero etc) current; (común) ordinary, normal ♦ nf current ♦ nm

current month; **estar al ~ de** to be informed about ▶ **corriente eléctrica** electric current

corrija etc [ko'rrixa] vb ver **corregir**

corro ['korro] nm ring, circle (of people)

corromper [korrom'per] vt (madera) to rot; (fig) to corrupt

corrosivo, -a [korro'siβo, a] adj corrosive

corrupción [korrup'θjon] nf rot, decay; (fig) corruption

corsé [kor'se] nm corset

cortacésped [korta'θespeð] nm lawn mower

cortado, -a [kor'taðo, a] adj (gen) cut; (leche) sour; (tímido) shy; (avergonzado) embarrassed ♦ nm coffee (with a little milk)

cortar [kor'tar] vt to cut; (suministro) to cut off; (un pasaje) to cut out ♦ vi to cut; **cortarse** vr (avergonzarse) to become embarrassed; (leche) to turn, curdle; **cortarse el pelo** to have one's hair cut

cortauñas [korta'uɲas] nm inv nail clippers pl

corte ['korte] nm cut, cutting; (de tela) piece, length ♦ nf: **las Cortes** the Spanish Parliament ▶ **corte de luz** power cut ▶ **corte y confección** dressmaking

cortejo [kor'texo] nm entourage ▶ **cortejo fúnebre** funeral procession

cortés [kor'tes] adj courteous, polite

cortesía [korte'sia] nf courtesy

corteza [kor'teθa] nf (de árbol) bark; (de pan) crust

cortijo [kor'tixo] nm (ESP) farm, farmhouse

cortina [kor'tina] nf curtain

corto, -a ['korto, a] adj (breve) short; (tímido) bashful; **~ de luces** not very bright; **~ de vista** short-sighted; **estar ~ de fondos** to be short of funds ❑ **cortocircuito** nm short circuit ❑ **cortometraje** nm (CINE) short

cosa ['kosa] nf thing; **~ de** about; **eso es ~ mía** that's my business

coscorrón [kosko'rron] nm bump on the head

cosecha [ko'setʃa] nf (AGR) harvest; (de vino) vintage ► **cosechar** [kose'tʃar] vt to harvest, gather (in)

coser [ko'ser] vt to sew

cosmético, -a [kos'metiko, a] adj, nm cosmetic

cosquillas [kos'kiʎas] nfpl: **hacer ~** to tickle; **tener ~** to be ticklish

costa ['kosta] nf (GEO) coast; **a toda ~** at all costs ► **Costa Brava** Costa Brava ► **Costa Cantábrica** Cantabrian Coast ► **Costa del Sol** Costa del Sol

costado [kos'taðo] nm side

costanera (CS) [kosta'nera] nf promenade, sea front

costar [kos'tar] vt (valer) to cost; **me cuesta hablarle** I find it hard to talk to him

Costa Rica [kosta'rika] nf Costa Rica ❏ **costarricense** adj, nmf Costa Rican ❏ **costarriqueño, -a** adj, nm/f Costa Rican

coste ['koste] nm = **costo**

costear [koste'ar] vt to pay for

costero, -a [kos'tero, a] adj (pueblecito, camino) coastal

costilla [kos'tiʎa] nf rib; (CULIN) cutlet

costo ['kosto] nm cost, price ► **costo de (la) vida** cost of living ❏ **costoso, -a** adj costly, expensive

costra ['kostra] nf (corteza) crust; (MED) scab

costumbre [kos'tumbre] nf custom, habit

costura [kos'tura] nf sewing, needlework; (zurcido) seam

costurera [kostu'rera] nf dressmaker

costurero [kostu'rero] nm sewing box o case

cotidiano, -a [koti'ðjano, a] adj daily, day to day

cotilla [ko'tiʎa] (ESP: fam) nmf gossip ❏ **cotillear** (ESP) vi to gossip ❏ **cotilleo** (ESP) nm gossip(ing)

cotizar [koti'θar] vt (COM) to quote, price; **cotizarse** vr: **cotizarse a** to sell at, fetch; (BOLSA) to stand at, be quoted at

coto ['koto] nm (terreno cercado) enclosure; (de caza) reserve

cotorra [ko'torra] nf parrot

coyote [ko'jote] nm coyote, prairie wolf

coz [koθ] nf kick

crack nm (droga) crack

cráneo ['kraneo] nm skull, cranium

cráter ['krater] nm crater

crayón (MÉX, RPl) nm crayon, chalk

creación [krea'θjon] nf creation

creador, a [krea'ðor, a] adj creative ♦ nm/f creator

crear [kre'ar] vt to create, make

crecer [kre'θer] vi to grow; (precio) to rise

creces ['kreθes]: **con ~** adv amply, fully

crecido, -a [kre'θiðo, a] adj (persona, planta) full-grown; (cantidad) large

crecimiento [kreθi'mjento] nm growth; (aumento) increase

credencial [kreðen'θjal] nf (LAm: tarjeta) card; **credenciales** nfpl credentials ► **credencial de socio** (LAm) membership card

crédito ['kreðito] nm credit

credo ['kreðo] nm creed

creencia [kre'enθja] nf belief

creer [kre'er] vt, vi to think, believe; **creerse** vr to believe o.s. (to be); **~ en** to believe in; **creo que sí/no** I think/don't think so; **¡ya lo creo!** I should think so!

creído, -a [kre'iðo, a] adj (engreído) conceited

crema ['krema] nf cream ► **crema batida** (LAm) whipped cream ► **crema pastelera** (confectioner's) custard

cremallera [krema'ʎera] nf zip (fastener)

crepe (*ESP*) *nf* pancake

cresta ['kresta] *nf* (*GEO, ZOOL*) crest

creyendo *etc* [kre'jendo] *vb ver* **creer**

creyente [kre'jente] *nmf* believer

creyó *etc* [kre'jo] *vb ver* **creer**

crezco *etc vb ver* **crecer**

cría *etc* ['kria] *vb ver* **criar ♦** *nf* (*de animales*) rearing, breeding; (*animal*) young; *ver tb* **crío**

criadero [kria'ðero] *nm* (*ZOOL*) breeding place

criado, -a [kri'aðo, a] *nm* servant ♦ *nf* servant, maid

criador [kria'ðor] *nm* breeder

crianza [kri'anθa] *nf* rearing, breeding; (*fig*) breeding

criar [kri'ar] *vt* (*educar*) to bring up; (*producir*) to grow, produce; (*animales*) to breed

criatura [kria'tura] *nf* creature; (*niño*) baby, (small) child

cribar [kri'βar] *vt* to sieve

crimen ['krimen] *nm* crime

criminal [krimi'nal] *adj, nmf* criminal

crines *nfpl* mane

crío, -a ['krio, a] (*fam*) *nm/f* (*niño*) kid

crisis ['krisis] *nf inv* crisis ▶ **crisis nerviosa** nervous breakdown

crisma (*ESP*) *nm inv* Christmas card

cristal [kris'tal] *nm* crystal; (*de ventana*) glass, pane; (*lente*) lens ❏ **cristalino, -a** *adj* crystalline; (*fig*) clear ♦ *nm* lens (of the eye)

cristianismo [kristja'nismo] *nm* Christianity

cristiano, -a [kris'tjano, a] *adj, nm/f* Christian

Cristo ['kristo] *nm* Christ; (*crucifijo*) crucifix

criterio [kri'terjo] *nm* criterion; (*juicio*) judgement

crítica [kri'tika] *nf* criticism; *ver tb* **crítico**

criticar [kriti'kar] *vt* to criticize

crítico, -a ['kritiko, a] *adj* critical ♦ *nm/f* critic

Croacia [kro'aθja] *nf* Croatia

cromo ['kromo] *nm* chrome

crónica ['kronika] *nf* chronicle, account

crónico, -a ['kroniko, a] *adj* chronic

cronómetro [kro'nometro] *nm* stopwatch

croqueta [kro'keta] *nf* croquette

cruce *etc* [kru'θe] *vb ver* **cruzar ♦** *nm* (*para peatones*) crossing; (*de carreteras*) crossroads

crucero [kru'θero] *nm* (*viaje*) cruise

crucificar [kruθifi'kar] *vt* to crucify

crucifijo [kruθi'fixo] *nm* crucifix

crucigrama [kruθi'ɣrama] *nm* crossword (puzzle)

cruda (*MÉX, CAm: fam*) *nf* hangover

crudo, -a ['kruðo, a] *adj* raw; (*no maduro*) unripe; (*petróleo*) crude; (*rudo, cruel*) cruel ♦ *nm* crude (oil)

cruel [krwel] *adj* cruel ❏ **crueldad** *nf* cruelty

crujiente [kru'xjente] *adj* (*galleta etc*) crunchy

crujir [kru'xir] *vi* (*madera etc*) to creak; (*dedos*) to crack; (*dientes*) to grind; (*nieve, arena*) to crunch

cruz [kruθ] *nf* cross; (*de moneda*) tails *sg* ▶ **cruz gamada** swastika

cruzada [kru'θaða] *nf* crusade

cruzado, -a [kru'θaðo, a] *adj* crossed ♦ *nm* crusader

cruzar [kru'θar] *vt* to cross; **cruzarse** *vr* (*líneas etc*) to cross; (*personas*) to pass each other

Cruz Roja *nf* Red Cross

cuaderno [kwa'ðerno] *nm* notebook; (*de escuela*) exercise book; (*NÁUT*) logbook

cuadra ['kwaðra] *nf* (*caballeriza*) stable; (*LAm: entre calles*) block

cuadrado, -a [kwa'ðraðo, a] *adj* square ♦ *nm* (*MAT*) square

cuadrar [kwa'ðrar] vt to square ♦ vi: ~ **con** to square with, tally with; **cuadrarse** vr (soldado) to stand to attention

cuadrilátero [kwaðri'latero] nm (DEPORTE) boxing ring; (GEOM) quadrilateral

cuadrilla [kwa'ðriʎa] nf party, group

cuadro ['kwaðro] nm square; (ARTE) painting; (TEATRO) scene; (diagrama) chart; (DEPORTE, MED) team; **tela a cuadros** checked (BRIT) o chequered (US) material

cuajar [kwa'xar] vt (leche) to curdle; (sangre) to congeal; (CULIN) to set; **cuajarse** vr to curdle; to congeal; to set; (llenarse) to fill up

cuajo ['kwaxo] nm: **de ~** (arrancar) by the roots; (cortar) completely

cual [kwal] adv like, as ♦ pron: **el** etc ~ which; (persona sujeto) who; (: objeto) whom ♦ adj such as; **cada** ~ each one; **déjalo tal** ~ leave it just as it is

cuál [kwal] pron interr which (one)

cualesquier, a [kwales'kjer,a] pl de **cualquier(a)**

cualidad [kwali'ðað] nf quality

cualquier [kwal'kjer] adj ver **cualquiera**

cualquiera [kwal'kjera] (pl **cualesquiera**) adj (delante de nm y f **cualquier**) any ♦ pron anybody; **un coche ~ servirá** any car will do; **no es un hombre ~** he isn't just anybody; **cualquier día/libro** any day/book; **eso ~ lo sabe hacer** anybody can do that; **es un ~** he's a nobody

cuando ['kwando] adv when; (aún si) if, even if ♦ conj (puesto que) since ♦ prep: **yo, ~ niño ...** when I was a child ...; ~ **no sea así** even if it is not so; ~ **más** at (the) most; ~ **menos** at least; ~ **no** if not, otherwise; **de ~ en ~** from time to time

cuándo ['kwando] adv when; **¿desde ~?** since when?

cuantía [kwan'tia] nf (importe: de pérdidas, deuda, daños) extent

['kwanto, a] adj

1 (todo): **tiene todo cuanto desea** he's got everything he wants; **le daremos cuantos ejemplares necesite** we'll give him as many copies as o all the copies he needs; **cuantos hombres la ven** all the men who see her

2: **unos cuantos: había unos cuantos periodistas** there were a few journalists

3 (+ más): **cuanto más vino bebes peor te sentirás** the more wine you drink the worse you'll feel

♦ pron: **tiene cuanto desea** he has everything he wants; **tome cuanto/ cuantos quiera** take as much/many as you want

♦ adv: **en cuanto: en cuanto profesor** as a teacher; **en cuanto a mí** as for me; ver tb **antes**

♦ conj

1: **cuanto más gana menos gasta** the more he earns the less he spends; **cuanto más joven más confiado** the younger you are the more trusting you are

2: **en cuanto: en cuanto llegue/ llegué** as soon as I arrive/arrived

cuánto, -a ['kwanto, a] adj (exclamación) what a lot of; (interr: sg) how much?; (: pl) how many? ♦ pron, adv how: (: interr: sg) how much?; (: pl) how many?; **¡cuánta gente!** what a lot of people!; **¿~ cuesta?** how much does it cost?; **¿a cuántos estamos?** what's the date?

cuarenta [kwa'renta] num forty

cuarentena [kwaren'tena] *nf*
quarantine

cuaresma [kwa'resma] *nf* Lent

cuarta ['kwarta] *nf* (MAT) quarter,
fourth; (*palmo*) span

cuartel [kwar'tel] *nm* (MIL) barracks *pl*
▶ **cuartel de bomberos** (RPI) fire
station ▶ **cuartel general**
headquarters *pl*

cuarteto [kwar'teto] *nm* quartet

cuarto, -a ['kwarto, a] *adj* fourth ♦ *nm*
(MAT) quarter, fourth; (*habitación*)
room ▶ **cuarto de baño** bathroom
▶ **cuarto de estar** living room
▶ **cuarto de hora** quarter (of an) hour
▶ **cuarto de kilo** quarter kilo
▶ **cuartos de final** quarter finals

cuatro ['kwatro] *num* four

Cuba ['kuβa] *nf* Cuba

cuba ['kuβa] *nf* cask, barrel

cubano, -a [ku'βano, a] *adj, nm/f*
Cuban

cubata [ku'βata] *nm* (*fam*) large drink
(*of rum and coke etc*)

cubeta (ESP, MÉX) [ku'βeta] *nf* (*balde*)
bucket, tub

cúbico, -a ['kuβiko, a] *adj* cubic

cubierta [ku'βjerta] *nf* cover, covering;
(*neumático*) tyre; (NÁUT) deck

cubierto, -a [ku'βjerto, a] *pp de* **cubrir**
♦ *adj* covered ♦ *nm* cover; (*lugar en la
mesa*) place; **cubiertos** *nmpl* cutlery *sg*;
a ~ under cover

cubilete [kuβi'lete] *nm* (*en juegos*) cup

cubito [ku'βito] *nm* (*tb:* **~ de hielo**) ice-
cube

cubo ['kuβo] *nm* (MAT) cube; (ESP: *balde*)
bucket, tub; (TEC) drum ▶ **cubo de (la)
basura** dustbin (BRIT), trash can (US)

cubrir [ku'βrir] *vt* to cover; **cubrirse** *vr*
(*cielo*) to become overcast

cucaracha [kuka'ratʃa] *nf* cockroach

cuchara [ku'tʃara] *nf* spoon; (TEC)
scoop ❑ **cucharada** *nf* spoonful
❑ **cucharadita** *nf* teaspoonful

cucharilla [kutʃa'riʎa] *nf* teaspoon

cucharón [kutʃa'ron] *nm* ladle

cuchilla [ku'tʃiʎa] *nf* (*large*) knife; (*de
arma blanca*) blade ▶ **cuchilla de
afeitar** razor blade

cuchillo [ku'tʃiʎo] *nm* knife

cuchitril [kutʃi'tril] *nm* hovel

cuclillas [ku'kliʎas] *nfpl*: **en ~** squatting

cuco, -a ['kuko, a] *adj* pretty; (*astuto*)
sharp ♦ *nm* cuckoo

cucurucho [kuku'rutʃo] *nm* cornet

cueca *nf* Chilean national dance

cuello ['kweʎo] *nm* (ANAT) neck; (*de
vestido, camisa*) collar

cuenca ['kwenka] *nf* (ANAT) eye socket;
(GEO) bowl, deep valley

cuenco ['kwenko] *nm* bowl

cuenta *etc* ['kwenta] *vb ver* **contar** ♦ *nf*
(*cálculo*) count, counting; (*en café,
restaurante*) bill (BRIT), check (US);
(COM) account; (*de collar*) bead; **a fin de
cuentas** in the end; **caer en la ~** to
catch on; **darse ~ de** to realize; **tener
en ~** to bear in mind; **echar cuentas** to
take stock ▶ **cuenta atrás**
countdown ▶ **cuenta corriente/de
ahorros** current/savings account
▶ **cuenta de correo (electrónica)**
(INFORM) email account
❑ **cuentakilómetros** *nm inv*
= milometer; (*de velocidad*)
speedometer

cuento *etc* ['kwento] *vb ver* **contar**
♦ *nm* story ▶ **cuento chino** tall story
▶ **cuento de hadas** a fairy tale

cuerda ['kwerða] *nf* rope; (*fina*) string;
(*de reloj*) spring; **dar ~ a un reloj** to
wind up a clock ▶ **cuerda floja**
tightrope ▶ **cuerdas vocales** vocal
cords

cuerdo, -a ['kwerðo, a] *adj* sane;
(*prudente*) wise, sensible

cuerno ['kwerno] *nm* horn

cuero ['kwero] *nm* leather; **en cueros**
stark naked ▶ **cuero cabelludo** scalp

cuerpo ['kwerpo] *nm* body

cuervo ['kwerβo] *nm* crow

cuesta etc ['kwesta] vb ver **costar** ♦ nf slope; (en camino etc) hill; ~ **arriba/ abajo** uphill/downhill; **a cuestas** on one's back

cueste etc vb ver **costar**

cuestión [kwes'tjon] nf matter, question, issue

cuete adj (MÉX: fam) drunk ♦ nm (LAm: cohete) rocket; (MÉX, RPl: fam: embriaguez) drunkenness; (MÉX CULIN) steak

cueva ['kweβa] nf cave

cuidado [kwi'ðaðo] nm care, carefulness; (preocupación) care, worry ♦ excl careful!, look out!; **eso me tiene sin ~** I'm not worried about that

cuidadoso, -a [kwiða'ðoso, a] adj careful; (preocupado) anxious

cuidar [kwi'ðar] vt (MED) to care for; (ocuparse de) to take care of, look after ♦ vi: ~ **de** to take care of, look after; **cuidarse** vr to look after o.s.; **cuidarse de hacer algo** to take care to do sth

culata [ku'lata] nf (de fusil) butt

culebra [ku'leβra] nf snake

culebrón [kule'βron] (fam) nm (TV) soap(opera)

culo ['kulo] nm bottom, backside; (de vaso, botella) bottom

culpa ['kulpa] nf fault; (JUR) guilt; **por ~ de** because of; **echar la ~ a algn** to blame sb for sth; **tener la ~ (de)** to be to blame (for) ❑ **culpable** adj guilty ♦ nmf culprit ❑ **culpar** [kul'par] vt to blame; (acusar) to accuse

cultivar [kulti'βar] vt to cultivate

cultivo [kul'tiβo] nm (acto) cultivation; (plantas) crop

culto, -a ['kulto, a] adj (que tiene cultura) cultured, educated ♦ nm (homenaje) worship; (religión) cult

cultura [kul'tura] nf culture

culturismo [kultu'rismo] nm body-building

cumbia nf popular Colombian dance

cumbre ['kumbre] nf summit, top

cumpleaños [kumple'aɲos] nm inv birthday

cumplido, -a [kum'pliðo, a] adj (abundante) plentiful; (cortés) courteous ♦ nm compliment; **visita de ~** courtesy call

cumplidor, a [kumpli'ðor, a] adj reliable

cumplimiento [kumpli'mjento] nm (de un deber) fulfilment; (acabamiento) completion

cumplir [kum'plir] vt (orden) to carry out, obey; (promesa) to carry out, fulfil; (condena) to serve ♦ vi: ~ **con** (deber) to carry out, fulfil; **cumplirse** vr (plazo) to expire; **hoy cumple dieciocho años** he is eighteen today

cuna ['kuna] nf cradle, cot

cundir [kun'dir] vi (noticia, rumor, pánico) to spread; (rendir) to go a long way

cuneta [ku'neta] nf ditch

cuña ['kuɲa] nf wedge

cuñado, -a [ku'ɲaðo, a] nm/f brother-/sister-in-law

cuota ['kwota] nf (parte proporcional) share; (cotización) fee, dues pl

cupe etc vb ver **caber**

cupiera etc [ku'pjera] vb ver **caber**

cupo ['kupo] vb ver **caber** ♦ nm quota

cupón [ku'pon] nm coupon

cúpula ['kupula] nf dome

cura ['kura] nf (curación) cure; (método curativo) treatment ♦ nm priest

curación [kura'θjon] nf cure; (acción) curing

curandero, -a [kuran'dero, a] nm/f quack

curar [ku'rar] vt (MED: herida) to treat, dress; (: enfermo) to cure; (CULIN) to cure, salt; (cuero) to tan; **curarse** vr to get well, recover

curiosear [kurjose'ar] vt to glance at, look over ♦ vi to look round, wander round; (explorar) to poke about

curiosidad [kurjosi'ðað] nf curiosity

curioso, -a [ku'rjoso, a] adj curious
♦ nm/f bystander, onlooker

curita (LAm) [ku'rita] nf (sticking)
plaster (BRIT), Bandaid® (US)

currante [ku'rrante] (ESP: fam) nmf
worker

currar [ku'rrar] (ESP: fam) vi to work

currículo [ku'rrikulo] = **curriculum**

curriculum [ku'rrikulum] nm
curriculum vitae

cursi ['kursi] (fam) adj affected

cursillo [kur'siʎo] nm short course

cursiva [kur'siβa] nf italics pl

curso ['kurso] nm course; **en ~** (año)
current; (proceso) going on, under way

cursor [kur'sor] nm (INFORM) cursor

curul (MÉX) nm (escaño) seat

curva ['kurβa] nf curve, bend

custodia [kus'toðja] nf safekeeping;
custody

cutis ['kutis] nm inv skin, complexion

cutre ['kutre] (ESP: fam) adj (lugar)
grotty

cuyo, -a ['kujo, a] pron (de quien)
whose; (de que) whose, of which; **en ~
caso** in which case

C.V. abr (= caballos de vapor) H.P.

D, d

D. abr (= Don) Esq

dado, -a ['daðo, a] pp de **dar** ♦ nm die;
dados nmpl dice; **~ que** given that

daltónico, -a [dal'toniko, a] adj
colour-blind

dama ['dama] nf (gen) lady; (AJEDREZ)
queen; **damas** nfpl (juego) draughts sg
▶ **dama de honor** bridesmaid

damasco (RPl) [da'masko] nm apricot

danés, -esa [da'nes, esa] adj Danish
♦ nm/f Dane

dañar [da'ɲar] vt (objeto) to damage;
(persona) to hurt; **dañarse** vr (objeto) to
get damaged

dañino, -a [da'ɲino, a] adj harmful

daño ['daɲo] nm (objeto) damage;
(persona) harm, injury; **daños y
perjuicios** (JUR) damages; **hacer ~ a** to
damage; (persona) to hurt, injure;
hacerse ~ to hurt o.s.

dar

PALABRA CLAVE

['dar] vt

1 (gen) to give; (obra de teatro) to put
on; (film) to show; (fiesta) to hold; **dar
algo a algn** to give sb sth o sth to sb;
dar de beber a algn to give sb a drink

2 (producir: intereses) to yield; (fruta)
to produce

3 (locuciones + n): **da gusto
escucharle** it's a pleasure to listen to
him; ver tb **paseo**

4 (+ n: = perífrasis de verbo): **me da
asco** it sickens me

5 (considerar): **dar algo por
descontado/entendido** to take sth for
granted/as read; **dar algo por
concluido** to consider sth finished

6 (hora): **el reloj dio las 6** the clock
struck 6 (o'clock)

7: **me da lo mismo** it's all the same to
me; ver tb **igual**; **más**

♦ vi

1: **dar con**: **dimos con él dos horas
más tarde** we came across him two
hours later; **al final di con la solución**
I eventually came up with the answer

2: **dar en** (blanco, suelo): to hit; **el sol
me da en la cara** the sun is shining
(right) on my face

3: **dar de sí** (zapatos etc) to stretch,
give

♦ **darse** vr

1: **darse por vencido** to give up
2 (*ocurrir*): **se han dado muchos casos** there have been a lot of cases
3: **darse a: se ha dado a la bebida** he's taken to drinking
4: **se me dan bien/mal las ciencias** I'm good/bad at science
5: **dárselas de: se las da de experto** he fancies himself o poses as an expert

dardo ['darðo] *nm* dart

dátil ['datil] *nm* date

dato ['dato] *nm* fact, piece of information ▶ **datos personales** personal details

dcha. *abr* (= *derecha*) r.h.

d. de C. *abr* (= *después de Cristo*) A.D.

de

PALABRA CLAVE

[de] (*de + el = del*) *prep*
1 (*posesión*): of; **la casa de Isabel/mis padres** Isabel's/my parents' house; **es de ellos** it's theirs
2 (*origen, distancia, con números*) from; **soy de Gijón** I'm from Gijón; **de 8 a 20** from 8 to 20; **salir del cine** to go out of o leave the cinema; **de 2 en 2** 2 by 2, o at a time
3 (*valor descriptivo*): **una copa de vino** a glass of wine; **la mesa de la cocina** the kitchen table; **un billete de 10 euros** a 10 euro note; **un niño de tres años** a three-year-old (child); **una máquina de coser** a sewing machine; **ir vestido de gris** to be dressed in grey; **la niña del vestido azul** the girl in the blue dress; **trabaja de profesora** she works as a teacher; **de lado** sideways; **de atrás/delante** rear/front
4 (*hora, tiempo*): **a las 8 de la mañana** at 8 o'clock in the morning; **de día/**

noche by day/night; **de hoy en ocho días** a week from now; **de niño era gordo** as a child he was fat
5 (*comparaciones*): **más/menos de cien personas** more/less than a hundred people; **el más caro de la tienda** the most expensive in the shop; **menos/más de lo pensado** less/more than expected
6 (*causa*): **del calor** from the heat
7 (*tema*) about; **clases de inglés** English classes; **¿sabes algo de él?** do you know anything about him?; **un libro de física** a physics book
8 (*adj + de + infin*): **fácil de entender** easy to understand
9 (*oraciones pasivas*): **fue respetado de todos** he was loved by all
10 (*condicional + infin*) if; **de ser posible** if possible; **de no terminarlo hoy** if I *etc* don't finish it today

dé [de] *vb ver* **dar**

debajo [de'βaxo] *adv* underneath; **~ de** below, under; **por ~ de** beneath

debate [de'βate] *nm* debate ❑ **debatir** *vt* to debate

deber [de'βer] *nm* duty ♦ *vt* to owe ♦ *vi*: **debe (de)** it must, it should; **deberes** *nmpl* (*ESCOL*) homework; **deberse** *vr*: **deberse a** to be owing o due to; **debo hacerlo** I must do it; **debe de ir** he should go

debido, -a [de'βiðo, a] *adj* proper, just; **~ a** due to, because of

débil ['deβil] *adj* (*persona, carácter*) weak; (*luz*) dim ❑ **debilidad** *nf* weakness; dimness

debilitar [deβili'tar] *vt* to weaken; **debilitarse** *vr* to grow weak

débito ['deβito] *nm* debit ▶ **débito bancario** (*LAm*) direct debit (*BRIT*) o billing (*US*)

debutar [deβu'tar] *vi* to make one's debut

década ['dekaða] *nf* decade

decadencia [deka'ðenθja] *nf* (*estado*) decadence; (*proceso*) decline, decay

decaído, -a [deka'iðo, a] *adj*: **estar ~** (*abatido*) to be down

decano, -a [de'kano, a] *nm/f* (*de universidad etc*) dean

decena [de'θena] *nf*: **una ~** ten (or so)

decente [de'θente] *adj* decent

decepción [deθep'θjon] *nf* disappointment

⚠ No confundir **decepción** con la palabra inglesa *deception*.

decepcionar [deθepθjo'nar] *vt* to disappoint

decidir [deθi'ðir] *vt, vi* to decide; **decidirse** *vr*: **decidirse a** to make up one's mind to

décimo, -a ['deθimo, a] *adj* tenth ♦ *nm* tenth

decir [de'θir] *vt* to say; (*contar*) to tell; (*hablar*) to speak ♦ *nm* saying; **decirse** *vr*: **se dice que** it is said that; **es ~** that is (to say); **~ para sí** to say to o.s.; **querer ~** to mean; **¡dígame!** (*TEL*) hello!; (*en tienda*) can I help you?

decisión [deθi'sjon] *nf* (*resolución*) decision; (*firmeza*) decisiveness

decisivo, -a [deθi'siβo, a] *adj* decisive

declaración [deklara'θjon] *nf* (*manifestación*) statement; (*de amor*) declaration ▶ **declaración fiscal** o **de la renta** income-tax return

declarar [dekla'rar] *vt* to declare; (*JUR*) to testify; **declararse** *vr* to propose

decoración [dekora'θjon] *nf* decoration

decorado [deko'raðo] *nm* (*CINE, TEATRO*) scenery, set

decorar [deko'rar] *vt* to decorate ❏ **decorativo, -a** *adj* ornamental, decorative

decreto [de'kreto] *nm* decree

dedal [de'ðal] *nm* thimble

dedicación [deðika'θjon] *nf* dedication

dedicar [deði'kar] *vt* (*libro*) to dedicate; (*tiempo, dinero*) to devote; (*palabras: decir, consagrar*) to dedicate, devote ❏ **dedicatoria** *nf* (*de libro*) dedication

dedo ['deðo] *nm* finger; **hacer ~** (*fam*) to hitch (a lift) ▶ **dedo anular** ring finger ▶ **dedo corazón** middle finger ▶ **dedo (del pie)** toe ▶ **dedo gordo** (*de la mano*) thumb; (*del pie*) big toe ▶ **dedo índice** index finger ▶ **dedo meñique** little finger ▶ **dedo pulgar** thumb

deducción [deðuk'θjon] *nf* deduction

deducir [deðu'θir] *vt* (*concluir*) to deduce, infer; (*COM*) to deduct

defecto [de'fekto] *nm* defect, flaw ❏ **defectuoso, -a** *adj* defective, faulty

defender [defen'der] *vt* to defend; **defenderse** *vr* (*desenvolverse*) to get by

defensa [de'fensa] *nf* defence ♦ *nm* (*DEPORTE*) defender, back. ❏ **defensivo, -a** *adj* defensive; **a la defensiva** on the defensive

defensor, a [defen'sor, a] *adj* defending ♦ *nm/f* (*abogado defensor*) defending counsel; (*protector*) protector

deficiencia [defi'θjenθja] *nf* deficiency

deficiente [defi'θjente] *adj* (*defectuoso*) defective; **~ en** lacking o deficient in; **ser un ~ mental** to be mentally handicapped

déficit ['defiθit] (*pl* **déficits**) *nm* deficit

definición [defini'θjon] *nf* definition

definir [defi'nir] *vt* (*determinar*) to determine, establish; (*decidir*) to define; (*aclarar*) to clarify ❏ **definitivo, -a** *adj* definitive; **en definitiva** definitively; (*en resumen*) in short

deformación [deforma'θjon] nf (alteración) deformation; (RADIO etc) distortion

deformar [defor'mar] vt (gen) to deform; **deformarse** vr to become deformed ❑ **deforme** adj (informe) deformed; (feo) ugly; (malhecho) misshapen

defraudar [defrau'ðar] vt (decepcionar) to disappoint; (estafar) to defraud

defunción [defun'θjon] nf death, demise

degenerar [dexene'rar] vi to degenerate

degradar [deɣra'ðar] vt to debase, degrade; **degradarse** vr to demean o.s.

degustación [deɣusta'θjon] nf sampling, tasting

dejar [de'xar] vt to leave; (permitir) to allow, let; (abandonar) to abandon, forsake; (beneficios) to produce, yield ♦ vi: ~ **de** (parar) to stop; (no hacer) to fail to; ~ **a un lado** to leave o set aside; ~ **entrar/salir** to let in/out; ~ **pasar** to let through

del [del] (=**de** + **el**) ver **de**

delantal [delan'tal] nm apron

delante [de'lante] adv in front; (enfrente) opposite; (adelante) ahead; ~ **de** in front of, before

delantera [delan'tera] nf (de vestido, casa etc) front part; (DEPORTE) forward line; **llevar la ~ (a algn)** to be ahead (of sb)

delantero, -a [delan'tero, a] adj front ♦ nm (DEPORTE) forward, striker

delatar [dela'tar] vt to inform on o against, betray ❑ **delator, a** nm/f informer

delegación [deleɣa'θjon] nf (acción, delegados) delegation; (COM: oficina, delegados) office, branch ▶ **delegación de policía** (MÉX) police station

delegado, -a [dele'ɣaðo, a] nm/f delegate; (COM) agent

delegar [dele'ɣar] vt to delegate

deletrear [deletre'ar] vt to spell (out)

delfín [del'fin] nm dolphin

delgado, -a [del'ɣaðo, a] adj thin; (persona) slim, thin; (tela etc) light, delicate

deliberar [deliβe'rar] vt to debate, discuss

delicadeza [delika'ðeθa] nf (gen) delicacy; (refinamiento, sutileza) refinement

delicado, -a [deli'kaðo, a] adj (gen) delicate; (sensible) sensitive; (quisquilloso) touchy

delicia [de'liθja] nf delight

delicioso, -a [deli'θjoso, a] adj (gracioso) delightful; (exquisito) delicious

delimitar [delimi'tar] vt (función, responsabilidades) to define

delincuencia [delin'kwenθja] nf delinquency ❑ **delincuente** nmf delinquent; (criminal) criminal

delineante [deline'ante] nmf draughtsman/woman

delirante [deli'rante] adj delirious

delirar [deli'rar] vi to be delirious, rave

delirio [de'lirjo] nm (MED) delirium; (palabras insensatas) ravings pl

delito [de'lito] nm (gen) crime; (infracción) offence

delta ['delta] nm delta

demacrado, -a [dema'kraðo, a] adj: **estar ~** to look pale and drawn, be wasted away

demanda [de'manda] nf (pedido, COM) demand; (petición) request; (JUR) action, lawsuit ❑ **demandar** [deman'dar] vt (gen) to demand; (JUR) to sue, file a lawsuit against

demás [de'mas] adj: **los ~ niños** the other o remaining children ♦ pron: **los/las ~** the others, the rest (of them); **lo ~** the rest (of it)

demasía [dema'sia] nf (exceso) excess, surplus; **comer en ~** to eat to excess

demasiado, -a [dema'sjaðo, a] adj: ~ **vino** too much wine ♦ adv (antes de adj, adv) too; **demasiados libros** too many books; ¡**esto es ~!** that's the limit!; **hace ~ calor** it's too hot; ~ **despacio** too slowly; **demasiados** too many

demencia [de'menθja] nf (locura) madness

democracia [demo'kraθja] nf democracy

demócrata [de'mokrata] nmf democrat □ **democrático, -a** adj democratic

demoler [demo'ler] vt to demolish □ **demolición** nf demolition

demonio [de'monjo] nm devil, demon; ¡**demonios!** hell!, damn!; ¿**cómo demonios?** how the hell?

demora ['demora] nf delay

demos ['demos] vb ver **dar**

demostración [demostra'θjon] nf (MAT) proof; (de afecto) show, display

demostrar [demos'trar] vt (probar) to prove; (mostrar) to show; (manifestar) to demonstrate

den [den] vb ver **dar**

denegar [dene'ɣar] vt (rechazar) to refuse; (JUR) to reject

denominación [denomina'θjon] nf (acto) naming ► **Denominación de Origen** see note

densidad [densi'ðað] nf density; (fig) thickness

denso, -a ['denso, a] adj dense; (espeso, pastoso) thick; (fig) heavy

dentadura [denta'ðura] nf (set of) teeth pl ► **dentadura postiza** false teeth pl

dentera [den'tera] nf (grima): **dar ~ a algn** to set sb's teeth on edge

dentífrico, -a [den'tifriko, a] adj dental ♦ nm toothpaste

dentista [den'tista] nmf dentist

dentro ['dentro] adv inside ♦ prep: ~ **de** in, inside, within; **por ~** (on the) inside; **mirar por ~** to look inside; ~ **de tres meses** within three months

denuncia [de'nunθja] nf (delación) denunciation; (acusación) accusation; (de accidente) report □ **denunciar** vt to report; (delatar) to inform on o against

departamento [departa'mento] nm sección administrativa, department, section; (LAm: apartamento) flat (BRIT), apartment

depender [depen'der] vi: ~ **de** to depend on; **depende** it (all) depends

dependienta [depen'djenta] nf saleswoman, shop assistant

dependiente [depen'djente] adj dependent ♦ nm salesman, shop assistant

depilar [depi'lar] vt (con cera) to wax; (cejas) to pluck

deportar [depor'tar] vt to deport

deporte [de'porte] nm sport; **hacer ~** to play sports □ **deportista** adj sports cpd ♦ nmf sportsman/woman □ **deportivo, -a** adj (club, periódico) sports cpd ♦ nm sports car

depositar [deposi'tar] vt (dinero) to deposit; (mercancías) to put away, store; **depositarse** vr to settle

depósito [de'posito] nm (gen) deposit; (almacén) warehouse, store; (de agua, gasolina etc) tank ► **depósito de cadáveres** mortuary

depredador, a [depreða'ðor, a] *adj* predatory ♦ *nm* predator

depresión [depre'sjon] *nf* depression
▶ **depresión nerviosa** nervous breakdown

deprimido, -a [depri'miðo, a] *adj* depressed

deprimir [depri'mir] *vt* to depress; **deprimirse** *vr* (*persona*) to become depressed

deprisa [de'prisa] *adv* quickly, hurriedly

depurar [depu'rar] *vt* to purify; (*purgar*) to purge

derecha [de'retʃa] *nf* right(-hand) side; (*POL*) right; **a la ~** (*estar*) on the right; (*torcer etc*) (to the) right

derecho, -a [de'retʃo, a] *adj* right, right-hand ♦ *nm* (*privilegio*) right; (*lado*) right(-hand) side; (*leyes*) law ♦ *adv* straight, directly; **derechos** *nmpl* (*de aduana*) duty *sg*; (*de autor*) royalties; **tener ~ a** to have a right to ▶ **derechos de autor** royalties

deriva [de'riβa] *nf*: **ir** *o* **estar a la ~** to drift, be adrift

derivado [deri'βaðo] *nm* (*COM*) by-product

derivar [deri'βar] *vt* to derive; (*desviar*) to direct ♦ *vi* to derive, be derived; (*NÁUT*) to drift; **derivarse** *vr* to derive, be derived; to drift

derramamiento [derrama'mjento] *nm* (*dispersión*) spilling ▶ **derramamiento de sangre** bloodshed

derramar [derra'mar] *vt* to spill; (*verter*) to pour out; (*esparcir*) to scatter; **derramarse** *vr* to pour out

derrame [de'rrame] *nm* (*de líquido*) spilling; (*de sangre*) shedding; (*de tubo etc*) overflow; (*pérdida*) leakage ▶ **derrame cerebral** brain haemorrhage

derredor [derre'ðor] *adv*: **al** *o* **en ~ de** around, about

derretir [derre'tir] *vt* (*gen*) to melt; (*nieve*) to thaw; **derretirse** *vr* to melt

derribar [derri'βar] *vt* to knock down; (*construcción*) to demolish; (*persona, gobierno, político*) to bring down

derrocar [derro'kar] *vt* (*gobierno*) to bring down, overthrow

derrochar [derro'tʃar] *vt* to squander ❑ **derroche** *nm* (*despilfarro*) waste, squandering

derrota [de'rrota] *nf* (*NÁUT*) course; (*MIL, DEPORTE etc*) defeat, rout ❑ **derrotar** *vt* (*gen*) to defeat ❑ **derrotero** *nm* (*rumbo*) course

derrumbar [derrum'bar] *vt* (*edificio*) to knock down; **derrumbarse** *vr* to collapse

des *etc* [des] *vb ver* **dar**

desabrochar [desaβro'tʃar] *vt* (*botones, broches*) to undo, unfasten; **desabrocharse** *vr* (*ropa etc*) to come undone

desacato [desa'kato] *nm* (*falta de respeto*) disrespect; (*JUR*) contempt

desacertado, -a [desaθer'taðo, a] *adj* (*equivocado*) mistaken; (*inoportuno*) unwise

desacierto [desa'θjerto] *nm* mistake, error

desaconsejar [desakonse'xar] *vt* to advise against

desacreditar [desakreði'tar] *vt* (*desprestigiar*) to discredit, bring into disrepute; (*denigrar*) to run down

desacuerdo [desa'kwerðo] *nm* disagreement, discord

desafiar [desa'fjar] *vt* (*retar*) to challenge; (*enfrentarse a*) to defy

desafilado, -a [desafi'laðo, a] *adj* blunt

desafinado, -a [desafi'naðo, a] *adj*: **estar ~** to be out of tune

desafinar [desafi'nar] *vi* (*al cantar*) to be *o* sing out of tune

desafío etc [desa'fio] vb ver **desafiar**
♦ nm (reto) challenge; (combate) duel;
(resistencia) defiance

desafortunado, -a [desafortu'naðo,
a] adj (desgraciado) unfortunate,
unlucky

desagradable [desaɣra'ðaβle] adj
(fastidioso, enojoso) unpleasant;
(irritante) disagreeable

desagradar [desaɣra'ðar] vi (disgustar)
to displease; (molestar) to bother

desagradecido, -a [desaɣraðe'θiðo,
a] adj ungrateful

desagrado [desa'ɣraðo] nm (disgusto)
displeasure; (contrariedad)
dissatisfaction

desagüe [des'aɣwe] nm (de un líquido)
drainage; (cañería) drainpipe; (salida)
outlet, drain

desahogar [desao'ɣar] vt (aliviar) to
ease, relieve; (ira) to vent;
desahogarse vr (relajarse) to relax;
(desfogarse) to let off steam

desahogo [desa'oɣo] nm (alivio) relief;
(comodidad) comfort, ease

desahuciar [desau'θjar] vt (enfermo) to
give up hope for; (inquilino) to evict

desairar [desai'rar] vt (menospreciar) to
slight, snub

desalentador, a [desalenta'ðor, a] adj
discouraging

desaliño [desa'liɲo] nm slovenliness

desalmado, -a [desal'maðo, a] adj
(cruel) cruel, heartless

desalojar [desalo'xar] vt (expulsar,
echar) to eject; (abandonar) to move
out of ♦ vi to move out

desamor [desa'mor] nm (frialdad)
indifference; (odio) dislike

desamparado, -a [desampa'raðo, a]
adj (persona) helpless; (lugar: expuesto)
exposed; (desierto) deserted

desangrar [desaŋ'grar] vt to bleed; (fig:
persona) to bleed dry; **desangrarse** vr
to lose a lot of blood

desanimado, -a [desani'maðo, a] adj
(persona) downhearted; (espectáculo,
fiesta) dull

desanimar [desani'mar] vt (desalentar)
to discourage; (deprimir) to depress;
desanimarse vr to lose heart

desapacible [desapa'θiβle] adj (gen)
unpleasant

desaparecer [desapare'θer] vi (gen) to
disappear; (el sol, el luz) to vanish
❏ **desaparecido, -a** adj missing
❏ **desaparición** nf disappearance

desapercibido, -a [desaperθi'βiðo, a]
adj (desprevenido) unprepared; **pasar ~**
to go unnoticed

desaprensivo, -a [desapren'siβo, a]
adj unscrupulous

desaprobar [desapro'βar] vt (reprobar)
to disapprove of; (condenar) to
condemn; (no consentir) to reject

desaprovechado, -a
[desaproβe'tʃaðo, a] adj (oportunidad,
tiempo) wasted; (estudiante) slack

desaprovechar [desaproβe'tʃar] vt to
waste

desarmador (MÉX) [desarma'ðor] nm
screwdriver

desarmar [desar'mar] vt (MIL, fig) to
disarm; (TEC) to take apart, dismantle
❏ **desarme** nm disarmament

desarraigar [desarrai'ɣar] vt to uproot
❏ **desarraigo** nm uprooting

desarreglar [desarre'ɣlar] vt
(desordenar) to disarrange; (trastocar)
to upset, disturb

desarrollar [desarro'ʎar] vt (gen) to
develop; **desarrollarse** vr to develop;
(ocurrir) to take place; (FOTO) to
develop ❏ **desarrollo** nm
development

desarticular [desartiku'lar] vt (hueso)
to dislocate; (objeto) to take apart; (fig)
to break up

desasosegar [desasose'ɣar] vt
(inquietar) to disturb, make uneasy

desasosiego etc [desaso'sjeɣo] vb ver **desasosegar ♦** nm (intranquilidad) uneasiness, restlessness; (ansiedad) anxiety

desastre [de'sastre] nm disaster
❏ **desastroso, -a** adj disastrous

desatar [desa'tar] vt (nudo) to untie; (paquete) to undo; (separar) to detach; **desatarse** vr (zapatos) to come untied; (tormenta) to break

desatascar [desatas'kar] vt (cañería) to unblock, clear

desatender [desaten'der] vt (no prestar atención a) to disregard; (abandonar) to neglect

desatino [desa'tino] nm (idiotez) foolishness, folly; (error) blunder

desatornillar [desatorni'ʎar] vt to unscrew

desatrancar [desatran'kar] vt (puerta) to unbolt; (cañería) to clear, unblock

desautorizado, -a [desautori'θaðo, a] adj unauthorized

desautorizar [desautori'θar] vt (oficial) to deprive of authority; (informe) to deny

desayunar [desaju'nar] vi to have breakfast ♦ vt to have for breakfast
❏ **desayuno** nm breakfast

desazón [desa'θon] nf anxiety

desbarajuste [desβara'xuste] nm confusion, disorder

desbaratar [desβara'tar] vt (deshacer, destruir) to ruin

desbloquear [desβloke'ar] vt (negociaciones, tráfico) to get going again; (COM: cuenta) to unfreeze

desbordar [desβor'ðar] vt (sobrepasar) to go beyond; (exceder) to exceed; **desbordarse** vr (río) to overflow; (entusiasmo) to erupt

descabellado, -a [deskaβe'ʎaðo, a] adj (disparatado) wild, crazy

descafeinado, -a [deskafei'naðo, a] adj decaffeinated ♦ nm decaffeinated coffee

descalabro [deska'laβro] nm blow; (desgracia) misfortune

descalificar [deskalifi'kar] vt to disqualify; (desacreditar) to discredit

descalzar [deskal'θar] vt (zapato) to take off ♦ **descalzo, -a** adj barefoot(ed)

descambiar [deskam'bjar] vt to exchange

descaminado, -a [deskami'naðo, a] adj (equivocado) on the wrong road; (fig) misguided

descampado [deskam'paðo] nm open space

descansado, -a [deskan'saðo, a] adj (gen) rested; (que tranquiliza) restful

descansar [deskan'sar] vt (gen) to rest ♦ vi to rest, have a rest; (echarse) to lie down

descansillo [deskan'siʎo] nm (de escalera) landing

descanso [des'kanso] nm (reposo) rest; (alivio) relief; (pausa) break; (DEPORTE) interval, half time

descapotable [deskapo'taβle] nm (tb: coche ~) convertible

descarado, -a [deska'raðo, a] adj shameless; (insolente) cheeky

descarga [des'karɣa] nf (ARQ, ELEC, MIL) discharge; (NÁUT) unloading
❏ **descargar** [deskar'ɣar] vt to unload; (golpe) to let fly; **descargarse** vr to unburden o.s.; **descargarse algo de Internet** to download sth from the Internet

descaro [des'karo] nm nerve

descarriar [deska'rrjar] vt (descaminar) to misdirect; (fig) to lead astray; **descarriarse** vr (perderse) to lose one's way; (separarse) to stray; (pervertirse) to err, go astray

descarrilamiento [deskarrila'mjento] nm (de tren) derailment

descarrilar [deskarri'lar] vi to be derailed

descartar [deskar'tar] vt (rechazar) to reject; (eliminar) to rule out; **descartarse** vr (NAIPES) to discard; **descartarse de** to shirk

descendencia [desθen'denθja] nf (origen) origin, descent; (hijos) offspring

descender [desθen'der] vt (bajar: escalera) to go down ♦ vi to descend; (temperatura, nivel) to fall, drop; **~ de** to be descended from

descendiente [desθen'djente] nmf descendant

descenso [des'θenso] nm descent; (de temperatura) drop

descifrar [desθi'frar] vt to decipher; (mensaje) to decode

descolgar [deskol'ɣar] vt (bajar) to take down; (teléfono) to pick up; **descolgarse** vr to let o.s. down

descolorido, -a [deskolo'riðo, a] adj faded; (pálido) pale

descompasado, -a [deskompa'saðo, a] adj (sin proporción) out of all proportion; (excesivo) excessive

descomponer [deskompo'ner] vt (desordenar) to disarrange, disturb; (TEC) to put out of order; (dividir) to break down (into parts); (fig) to provoke; **descomponerse** vr (corromperse) to rot, decompose; (LAm TEC) to break down

descomposición [deskomposi'θjon] nf (de un objeto) breakdown; (de fruta etc) decomposition
▶ **descomposición de vientre** (ESP) stomach upset, diarrhoea

descompostura [deskompos'tura] nf (MÉX: avería) breakdown, fault; (LAm: diarrea) diarrhoea

descompuesto, -a [deskom'pwesto, a] adj (corrompido) decomposed; (roto) broken

desconcertado, -a [deskonθer'taðo, a] adj disconcerted, bewildered

desconcertar [deskonθer'tar] vt (confundir) to baffle; (incomodar) to upset, put out; **desconcertarse** vr (turbarse) to be upset

desconchado, -a [deskon'tʃaðo, a] adj (pintura) peeling

desconcierto etc [deskon'θjerto] vb ver **desconcertar** ♦ nm (gen) disorder; (desorientación) uncertainty; (inquietud) uneasiness

desconectar [deskonek'tar] vt to disconnect

desconfianza [deskon'fjanθa] nf distrust

desconfiar [deskon'fjar] vi to be distrustful; **~ de** to distrust, suspect

descongelar [deskonxe'lar] vt to defrost; (COM, POL) to unfreeze

descongestionar [deskonxestjo'nar] vt (cabeza, tráfico) to clear

desconocer [deskono'θer] vt (ignorar) not to know, to be ignorant of

desconocido, -a [deskono'θiðo, a] adj unknown ♦ nm/f stranger

desconocimiento [deskonoθi'mjento] nm falta de conocimientos, ignorance

desconsiderado, -a [deskonsiðe'raðo, a] adj inconsiderate; (insensible) thoughtless

desconsuelo etc [deskon'swelo] vb ver **desconsolar** ♦ nm (tristeza) distress; (desesperación) despair

descontado, -a [deskon'taðo, a] adj: **dar por ~ (que)** to take (it) for granted (that)

descontar [deskon'tar] vt (deducir) to take away, deduct; (rebajar) to discount

descontento, -a [deskon'tento, a] adj dissatisfied ♦ nm dissatisfaction, discontent

descorchar [deskor'tʃar] vt to uncork

descorrer [desko'rrer] vt (cortinas, cerrojo) to draw back

descortés [deskor'tes] adj (mal educado) discourteous; (grosero) rude

descoser [desko'ser] vt to unstitch; **descoserse** vr to come apart (at the seams)

descosido, -a [desko'siðo, a] adj (COSTURA) unstitched

descreído, -a [deskre'iðo, a] adj (incrédulo) incredulous; (falto de fe) unbelieving

descremado, -a [deskre'maðo, a] adj skimmed

describir [deskri'βir] vt to describe ❑ **descripción** [deskrip'θjon] nf description

descrito [des'krito] pp de **describir**

descuartizar [deskwarti'θar] vt (animal) to cut up

descubierto, -a [desku'βjerto, a] pp de **descubrir** ♦ adj uncovered, bare; (persona) bareheaded ♦ nm (bancario) overdraft; **al ~** in the open

descubrimiento [deskuβri'mjento] nm (hallazgo) discovery; (revelación) revelation

descubrir [desku'βrir] vt to discover, find; (inaugurar) to unveil; (vislumbrar) to detect; (revelar) to reveal, show; (destapar) to uncover; **descubrirse** vr to reveal o.s.; (quitarse sombrero) to take off one's hat; (confesar) to confess

descuento etc [des'kwento] vb ver **descontar** ♦ nm discount

descuidado, -a [deskwi'ðaðo, a] adj (sin cuidado) careless; (desordenado) untidy; (olvidadizo) forgetful; (dejado) neglected; (desprevenido) unprepared

descuidar [deskwi'ðar] vt (dejar) to neglect; (olvidar) to overlook; **descuidarse** vr (distraerse) to be careless; (abandonarse) to let o.s. go; (desprevenirse) to drop one's guard; **¡descuida!** don't worry! ❑ **descuido** nm (dejadez) carelessness; (olvido) negligence

desde

PALABRA CLAVE

['desðe] prep

1 (lugar) from; **desde Burgos hasta mi casa hay 30 km** it's 30 km from Burgos to my house

2 (posición): **hablaba desde el balcón** she was speaking from the balcony

3 (tiempo: + adv, n): **desde ahora** from now on; **desde la boda** since the wedding; **desde niño** since I etc was a child; **desde 3 años atrás** since 3 years ago

4 (tiempo: + vb, fecha) since; for; **nos conocemos desde 1992/desde hace 20 años** we've known each other since 1992/for 20 years; **no le veo desde 1997/desde hace 5 años** I haven't seen him since 1997/for 5 years

5 (gama): **desde los más lujosos hasta los más económicos** from the most luxurious to the most reasonably priced

6: **desde luego (que no)** of course (not)

♦ conj: **desde que: desde que recuerdo** for as long as I can remember; **desde que llegó no ha salido** he hasn't been out since he arrived

desdén [des'ðen] nm scorn

desdeñar [desðe'nar] vt (despreciar) to scorn

desdicha [des'ðitʃa] nf (desgracia) misfortune; (infelicidad) unhappiness ❑ **desdichado, -a** adj (sin suerte) unlucky; (infeliz) unhappy

desear [dese'ar] vt to want, desire; for

desechar [dese'tʃar] vt (basura) to throw out o away; (ideas) to reject, discard ❑ **desechos** nmpl rubbish sg, waste sg

desembalar [desemba'lar] vt to unpack

desembarazar [desembara'θar] vt (desocupar) to clear; (desenredar) to free; **desembarazarse** vr: **desembarazarse de** to free o.s. of, get rid of

desembarcar [desembar'kar] vt (mercancías etc) to unload ♦ vi to disembark

desembocadura [desemboka'ðura] nf (de río) mouth; (de calle) opening

desembocar [desembo'kar] vi (río) to flow into; (fig) to result in

desembolso [desem'bolso] nm payment

desembrollar [desembro'ʎar] vt (madeja) to unravel; (asunto, malentendido) to sort out

desemejanza [deseme'xanθa] nf dissimilarity

desempaquetar [desempake'tar] vt (regalo) to unwrap; (mercancía) to unpack

desempate [desem'pate] nm (FÚTBOL) replay, play-off; (TENIS) tie-break(er)

desempeñar [desempe'ɲar] vt (cargo) to hold; (papel) to perform; (lo empeñado) to redeem; **~ un papel** (fig) to play (a role)

desempleado, -a [desemple'aðo, a] nm/f unemployed person ❑ **desempleo** nm unemployment

desencadenar [desenkaðe'nar] vt to unchain; (ira) to unleash; **desencadenarse** vr to break loose; (tormenta) to burst; (guerra) to break out

'esencajar [desenka'xar] vt (hueso) to 'islocate; (mecanismo, pieza) to 'sconnect, disengage

desencanto [desen'kanto] nm disillusionment

desenchufar [desentʃu'far] vt to unplug

desenfadado, -a [desenfa'ðaðo, a] adj (desenvuelto) uninhibited; (descarado) forward ❑ **desenfado** nm (libertad) freedom; (comportamiento) free and easy manner; (descaro) forwardness

desenfocado, -a [desenfo'kaðo, a] adj (FOTO) out of focus

desenfreno [desen'freno] nm wildness; (de las pasiones) lack of self-control

desenganchar [desengan'tʃar] vt (gen) to unhook; (FERRO) to uncouple

desengañar [desenga'ɲar] vt to disillusion; **desengañarse** vr to become disillusioned ❑ **desengaño** nm disillusionment; (decepción) disappointment

desenlace [desen'laθe] nm outcome

desenmascarar [desenmaska'rar] vt to unmask

desenredar [desenre'ðar] vt (pelo) to untangle; (problema) to sort out

desenroscar [desenros'kar] vt to unscrew

desentenderse [desenten'derse] vr: **~ de** to pretend not to know about; (apartarse) to have nothing to do with

desenterrar [desente'rrar] vt to exhume; (tesoro, fig) to unearth, dig up

desentonar [desento'nar] vi (MÚS) to sing (o play) out of tune; (color) to clash

desentrañar [desentra'ɲar] vt (misterio) to unravel

desenvoltura [desenβol'tura] nf ease

desenvolver [desenβol'βer] vt (paquete) to unwrap; (fig) to develop; **desenvolverse** vr (desarrollarse) to unfold, develop; (arreglárselas) to cope

deseo [de'seo] nm desire, wish ❑ **deseoso, -a** adj: **estar deseoso de** to be anxious to

desequilibrado, -a [desekili'βraðo, a] *adj* unbalanced

desertar [deser'tar] *vi* to desert

desértico, -a [de'sertiko, a] *adj* desert *cpd*

desesperación [desespera'θjon] *nf* (*impaciencia*) desperation, despair; (*irritación*) fury

desesperar [desespe'rar] *vt* to drive to despair; (*exasperar*) to drive to distraction ♦ *vi*: ~ **de** to despair of; **desesperarse** *vr* to despair, lose hope

desestabilizar [desestaβili'θar] *vt* to destabilize

desestimar [desesti'mar] *vt* (*menospreciar*) to have a low opinion of; (*rechazar*) to reject

desfachatez [desfatʃa'teθ] *nf* (*insolencia*) impudence; (*descaro*) rudeness

desfalco [des'falko] *nm* embezzlement

desfallecer [desfaʎe'θer] *vi* (*perder las fuerzas*) to become weak; (*desvanecerse*) to faint

desfasado, -a [desfa'saðo, a] *adj* (*anticuado*) old-fashioned ♦ **desfase** *nm* (*diferencia*) gap

desfavorable [desfaβo'raβle] *adj* unfavourable

desfigurar [desfiɣu'rar] *vt* (*cara*) to disfigure; (*cuerpo*) to deform

desfiladero [desfila'ðero] *nm* gorge

desfilar [desfi'lar] *vi* to parade
❏ **desfile** *nm* procession ▸ **desfile de modelos** fashion show

desgana [des'ɣana] *nf* (*falta de apetito*) loss of appetite; (*apatía*) unwillingness
❏ **desganado, -a** *adj*: **estar desganado** (*sin apetito*) to have no appetite; (*sin entusiasmo*) to have lost interest

desgarrar [desɣa'rrar] *vt* to tear (up); (*fig*) to shatter ♦ **desgarro** *nm* (*en tela*) tear; (*aflicción*) grief

desgastar [desɣas'tar] *vt* (*deteriorar*) to wear away o down; (*estropear*) to spoil;

desgastarse *vr* to get worn out
❏ **desgaste** *nm* wear (and tear)

desglosar [desɣlo'sar] *vt* (*factura*) to break down

desgracia [des'ɣraθja] *nf* misfortune; (*accidente*) accident; (*vergüenza*) disgrace; (*contratiempo*) setback; **por ~** unfortunately ❏ **desgraciado, -a** [desɣra'θjaðo, a] *adj* (*sin suerte*) unlucky, unfortunate; (*miserable*) wretched; (*infeliz*) miserable

desgravar [desɣra'βar] *vt* (*impuestos*) to reduce the tax o duty on

desguace (*ESP*) [des'ɣwaθe] *nm* junkyard

deshabitado, -a [desaβi'taðo, a] *adj* uninhabited

deshacer [desa'θer] *vt* (*casa*) to break up; (*TEC*) to take apart; (*enemigo*) to defeat; (*diluir*) to melt; (*contrato*) to break; (*intriga*) to solve; **deshacerse** *vr* (*disolverse*) to melt; (*despedazarse*) to come apart o undone; **deshacerse de** to get rid of; **deshacerse en lágrimas** to burst into tears

deshecho, -a [des'etʃo, a] *adj* undone; (*roto*) smashed; (*persona*): **estar ~** to be shattered

desheredar [desere'ðar] *vt* to disinherit

deshidratar [desiðra'tar] *vt* to dehydrate

deshielo [des'jelo] *nm* thaw

deshonesto, -a [deso'nesto, a] *adj* indecent

deshonra [des'onra] *nf* (*deshonor*) dishonour; (*vergüenza*) shame

deshora [des'ora]: **a ~** *adv* at the wrong time

deshuesadero (*MÉX*) *nm* junkyard

deshuesar [deswe'sar] *vt* (*carne*) to bone; (*fruta*) to stone

desierto, -a [de'sjerto, a] *adj* (*casa, calle, negocio*) deserted ♦ *nm* desert

designar [desiɣ'nar] *vt* (*nombrar*) to designate; (*indicar*) to fix

desigual [desiɣ'wal] *adj* (*terreno*) uneven; (*lucha etc*) unequal

desilusión [desilu'sjon] *nf* disillusionment; (*decepción*) disappointment □ **desilusionar** *vt* to disillusion; to disappoint; **desilusionarse** *vr* to become disillusioned

desinfectar [desinfek'tar] *vt* to disinfect

desinflar [desin'flar] *vt* to deflate

desintegración [desinteɣra'θjon] *nf* disintegration

desinterés [desinte'res] *nm* (*desgana*) lack of interest; (*altruismo*) unselfishness

desintoxicarse [desintoksi'karse] *vr* (*drogadicto*) to undergo detoxification

desistir [desis'tir] *vi* (*renunciar*) to stop, desist

desleal [desle'al] *adj* (*infiel*) disloyal; (*COM: competencia*) unfair □ **deslealtad** *nf* disloyalty

desligar [desli'ɣar] *vt* (*desatar*) to untie, undo; (*separar*) to separate; **desligarse** *vr* (*de un compromiso*) to extricate o.s.

desliz [des'liθ] *nm* (*fig*) lapse □ **deslizar** *vt* to slip, slide

deslumbrar [deslum'brar] *vt* to dazzle

desmadrarse [desma'ðrarse] (*fam*) *vr* (*descontrolarse*) to run wild; (*divertirse*) to let one's hair down □ **desmadre** (*fam*) *nm* (*desorganización*) chaos; (*jaleo*) commotion

desmán [des'man] *nm* (*exceso*) outrage; (*abuso de poder*) abuse

desmantelar [desmante'lar] *vt* (*deshacer*) to dismantle; (*casa*) to strip

desmaquillador [desmaki'λa'ðor] *nm* make-up remover

desmayar [desma'jar] *vi* to lose heart; **desmayarse** *vr* (*MED*) to faint □ **desmayo** *nm* (*MED: acto*) faint; (*: estado*) unconsciousness

desmemoriado, -a [desmemo'rjaðo, a] *adj* forgetful

desmentir [desmen'tir] *vt* (*contradecir*) to contradict; (*refutar*) to deny

desmenuzar [desmenu'θar] *vt* (*deshacer*) to crumble; (*carne*) to chop; (*examinar*) to examine closely

desmesurado, -a [desmesu'raðo, a] *adj* disproportionate

desmontable [desmon'taβle] *adj* (*que se quita: pieza*) detachable; (*plegable*) collapsible, folding

desmontar [desmon'tar] *vt* (*deshacer*) to dismantle; (*tierra*) to level ♦ *vi* to dismount

desmoralizar [desmorali'θar] *vt* to demoralize

desmoronar [desmoro'nar] *vt* to wear away, erode; **desmoronarse** *vr* (*edificio, dique*) to collapse; (*economía*) to decline

desnatado, -a [desna'taðo, a] *adj* skimmed

desnivel [desni'βel] *nm* (*de terreno*) unevenness

desnudar [desnu'ðar] *vt* (*desvestir*) to undress; (*despojar*) to strip; **desnudarse** *vr* (*desvestirse*) to get undressed □ **desnudo, -a** *adj* naked ♦ *nm/f* nude; **desnudo de** devoid o bereft of

desnutrición [desnutri'θjon] *nf* malnutrition □ **desnutrido, -a** *adj* undernourished

desobedecer [desoβeðe'θer] *vt, vi* to disobey □ **desobediencia** *nf* disobedience

desocupado, -a [desoku'paðo, a] *adj* at leisure; (*desempleado*) unemployed; (*deshabitado*) empty, vacant

desodorante [desoðo'rante] *nm* deodorant

desolación [desola'θjon] *nf* (*de lugar*) desolation; (*fig*) grief

desolar [deso'lar] *vt* to ruin, lay waste

desorbitado, -a [desorβi'taðo, a] *adj* (*excesivo: ambición*) boundless; (*deseos*) excessive; (*: precio*) exorbitant

desorden [des'orðen] nm confusion; (político) disorder, unrest

desorganización [desorɣaniθa'θjon] nf (de persona) disorganization; (en empresa, oficina) disorder, chaos

desorientar [desorjen'tar] vt (extraviar) to mislead; (confundir, desconcertar) to confuse; **desorientarse** vr (perderse) to lose one's way

despabilado, -a [despaβi'laðo, a] adj (despierto) wide-awake; (fig) alert, sharp

despachar [despa'tʃar] vt (negocio) to do, complete; (enviar) to send, dispatch; (vender) to sell, deal in; (billete) to issue; (mandar ir) to send away

despacho [des'patʃo] nm (oficina) office; (de paquetes) dispatch; (venta) sale; (comunicación) message

despacio [des'paθjo] adv slowly

desparpajo [despar'paxo] nm self-confidence; (pey) nerve

desparramar [desparra'mar] vt (esparcir) to scatter; (líquido) to spill

despecho [des'petʃo] nm spite

despectivo, -a [despek'tiβo, a] adj (despreciativo) derogatory; (LING) pejorative

despedida [despe'ðiða] nf (adiós) farewell; (de obrero) sacking

despedir [despe'ðir] vt (visita) to see off, show out; (empleado) to dismiss; (inquilino) to evict; (objeto) to hurl; (olor etc) to give out o off; **despedirse** vr: **despedirse de** to say goodbye to

despegar [despe'ɣar] vt to unstick ♦ vi (avión) to take off; **despegarse** vr to come loose, come unstuck ❑ **despego** nm detachment

despegue etc [des'peɣe] vb ver **despegar** ♦ nm takeoff

despeinado, -a [despei'naðo, a] adj dishevelled, unkempt

despejado, -a [despe'xaðo, a] adj (lugar) clear, free; (cielo) clear; (persona) wide-awake, bright

despejar [despe'xar] vt (gen) to clear; (misterio) to clear up ♦ vi (el tiempo) to clear; **despejarse** vr (tiempo, cielo) to clear (up); (misterio) to become clearer; (cabeza) to clear

despensa [des'pensa] nf larder

despeñarse [despe'narse] vr to hurl o.s. down; (coche) to tumble over

desperdicio [desper'ðiθjo] nm (despilfarro) squandering; **desperdicios** nmpl (basura) rubbish sg (BRIT), garbage sg (US); (residuos) waste sg

desperezarse [despere'θarse] vr to stretch

desperfecto [desper'fekto] nm (deterioro) slight damage; (defecto) flaw, imperfection

despertador [desperta'ðor] nm alarm clock

despertar [desper'tar] nm awakening ♦ vt (persona) to wake up; (recuerdos) to revive; (sentimiento) to arouse ♦ vi to awaken, wake up; **despertarse** vr to awaken, wake up

despido etc [des'piðo] vb ver **despedir** ♦ nm dismissal, sacking

despierto, -a etc [des'pjerto, a] vb ver **despertar** ♦ adj awake; (fig) sharp, alert

despilfarro [despil'farro] nm (derroche) squandering; (lujo desmedido) extravagance

despistar [despis'tar] vt to throw off the track o scent; (confundir) to mislead, confuse; **despistarse** vr to take the wrong road; (confundirse) to become confused

despiste [des'piste] nm absent-mindedness; **un ~** a mistake o slip

desplazamiento [desplaθa'mjento] nm displacement

desplazar [despla'θar] vt to move; (NÁUT) to displace; (INFORM) to scroll; (fig) to oust; **desplazarse** vr (persona) to travel

desplegar [desple'ɣar] vt (tela, papel) to unfold, open out; (bandera) to unfurl □ **despliegue** etc [des'pleɣe] vb ver **desplegar** ♦ nm display

desplomarse [desplo'marse] vr (edificio, gobierno, persona) to collapse

desplumar [desplu'mar] vt (ave) to pluck; (fam: estafar) to fleece

despoblado, -a [despo'βlaðo, a] adj (sin habitantes) uninhabited

despojar [despo'xar] vt (alguien: de sus bienes) to divest of, deprive of; (casa) to strip, leave bare; (alguien: de su cargo) to strip of

despojo [des'poxo] nm (acto) plundering; (objetos) plunder, loot; **despojos** nmpl (de ave, res) offal sg

desposado, -a [despo'saðo, a] adj, nm/f newly-wed

despreciar [despre'θjar] vt (desdeñar) to despise, scorn; (afrentar) to slight □ **desprecio** nm scorn, contempt; slight

desprender [despren'der] vt (broche) to unfasten; (olor) to give off; **desprenderse** vr (botón: caerse) to fall off; (broche) to come unfastened; (olor, perfume) to be given off; **desprenderse de algo que ...** to draw from sth that ...

desprendimiento [desprendi'mjento] nm (gen) loosening; (generosidad) disinterestedness; (de tierra, rocas) landslide ▶ **desprendimiento de retina** detachment of the retina

despreocupado, -a [despreoku'paðo, a] adj (sin preocupación) unworried, nonchalant; (negligente) careless

despreocuparse [despreoku'parse] vr not to worry; ~ **de** to have no interest in

desprestigiar [despresti'xjar] vt (criticar) to run down; (desacreditar) to discredit

desprevenido, -a [despreβe'niðo, a] adj (no preparado) unprepared, unready

desproporcionado, -a [desproporθjo'naðo, a] adj disproportionate, out of proportion

desprovisto, -a [despro'βisto, a] adj: ~ **de** devoid of

después [des'pwes] adv afterwards, later; (próximo paso) next; ~ **de comer** after lunch; **un año** ~ a year later; ~ **se debatió el tema** next the matter was discussed; ~ **de corregido el texto** after the text had been corrected; ~ **de todo** after all

desquiciado, -a [deski'θjaðo, a] adj deranged

destacar [desta'kar] vt to emphasize, point up; (MIL) to detach, detail ♦ vi (resaltarse) to stand out; (persona) to be outstanding o exceptional; **destacarse** vr to stand out; to be outstanding o exceptional

destajo [des'taxo] nm: **trabajar a** ~ to do piecework

destapar [desta'par] vt (botella) to open; (cacerola) to take the lid off; (descubrir) to uncover; **destaparse** vr (revelarse) to reveal one's true character

destartalado, -a [destarta'laðo, a] adj (desordenado) untidy; (ruinoso) tumbledown

destello [des'teʎo] nm (de estrella) twinkle; (de faro) signal light

destemplado, -a [destem'plaðo, a] adj (MÚS) out of tune; (voz) harsh; (MED) out of sorts; (tiempo) unpleasant, nasty

desteñir [deste'ɲir] vt to fade ♦ vi to fade; **desteñirse** vr to fade; **esta tela no destiñe** this fabric will not run

desternillarse [desterni'ʎarse] vr: ~ **de risa** to split one's sides laughing

desterrar [deste'rrar] vt (exiliar) to exile; (fig) to banish, dismiss

destiempo [des'tjempo]: **a ~** adv out of turn

destierro etc [des'tjerro] vb ver **desterrar** ♦ nm exile

destilar [desti'lar] vt to distil ❏ **destilería** nf distillery

destinar [desti'nar] vt (funcionario) to appoint, assign; (fondos): **~ (a)** to set aside (for)

destinatario, -a [destina'tarjo, a] nm/f addressee

destino [des'tino] nm (suerte) destiny; (de avión, viajero) destination; **con ~ a Londres** (barco) (bound) for London; (avión, carta) to London

destituir [destitu'ir] vt to dismiss

destornillador [destorniʎa'ðor] nm screwdriver

destornillar [destorni'ʎar] vt (tornillo) to unscrew; **destornillarse** vr to unscrew

destreza [des'treθa] nf (habilidad) skill; (maña) dexterity

destrozar [destro'θar] vt (romper) to smash, break (up); (estropear) to ruin; (nervios) to shatter

destrozo [des'troθo] nm (acción) destruction; (desastre) smashing; **destrozos** nmpl (pedazos) pieces; (daños) havoc sg

destrucción [destruk'θjon] nf destruction

destruir [destru'ir] vt to destroy

desuso [des'uso] nm disuse; **caer en ~** to become obsolete

desvalijar [desvali'xar] vt (persona) to rob; (casa, tienda) to burgle; (coche) to break into

desván [des'ßan] nm attic

desvanecer [desßane'θer] vt (disipar) to dispel; (borrar) to blot out; **desvanecerse** vr (humo etc) to vanish, disappear; (color) to fade; (recuerdo,

sonido) to fade away; (MED) to pass out; (duda) to be dispelled

desvariar [desßa'rjar] vi (enfermo) to be delirious

desvelar [desße'lar] vt to keep awake; **desvelarse** vr (no poder dormir) to stay awake; (preocuparse) to be vigilant o watchful

desventaja [desßen'taxa] nf disadvantage

desvergonzado, -a [desßerɣon'θaðo, a] adj shameless

desvestir [desßes'tir] vt to undress; **desvestirse** vr to undress

desviación [desßja'θjon] nf deviation; (AUTO) diversion, detour

desviar [des'ßjar] vt to turn aside; (río) to alter the course of; (navío) to divert, re-route; (conversación) to sidetrack; **desviarse** vr (apartarse del camino) to turn aside; (: barco) to go off course

desvío etc [des'ßio] vb ver **desviar** ♦ nm (desviación) detour, diversion; (fig) indifference

desvivirse [desßi'ßirse] vr: **~ por** (anhelar) to long for, crave for; (hacer lo posible por) to do one's utmost for

detallar [deta'ʎar] vt to detail

detalle [de'taʎe] nm detail; (gesto) gesture, token; **al ~** in detail; (COM) retail

detallista [deta'ʎista] nmf (COM) retailer

detective [detek'tiße] nmf detective ▶ **detective privado** private detective

detener [dete'ner] vt (gen) to stop; (JUR) to arrest; (objeto) to keep; **detenerse** vr to stop; (demorarse): **detenerse en** to delay over, linger over

detenidamente [deteniða'mente] adv (minuciosamente) carefully; (extensamente) at great length

detenido, -a [dete'niðo, a] adj (arrestado) under arrest ♦ nm/f person under arrest, prisoner

detenimiento [deteni'mjento] nm:
con ~ thoroughly; (observar,
considerar) carefully

detergente [deter'xente] nm
detergent

deteriorar [deterjo'rar] vt to spoil,
damage; **deteriorarse** vr to
deteriorate ☐ **deterioro** nm
deterioration

determinación [determina'θjon] nf
(empeño) determination; (decisión)
decision ☐ **determinado, -a** adj
specific

determinar [determi'nar] vt (plazo) to
fix; (precio) to settle; **determinarse** vr
to decide

detestar [detes'tar] vt to detest

detractor, a [detrak'tor, a] nm/f
slanderer, libeller

detrás [de'tras] adv (tb: por ~) behind;
(atrás) at the back; ~ **de** behind

detrimento [detri'mento] nm: **en ~ de**
to the detriment of

deuda ['deuða] nf debt ▶ **deuda
exterior/pública** foreign/national
debt

devaluación [deβalwa'θjon] nf
devaluation

devastar [deβas'tar] vt (destruir) to
devastate

deveras (MÉX) nf inv: **un amigo de (a) ~**
a true o real friend

devoción [deβo'θjon] nf devotion

devolución [deβolu'θjon] nf (reenvío)
return, sending back; (reembolso)
repayment; (JUR) devolution

devolver [deβol'βer] vt to return; (lo
extraviado, lo prestado) to give back;
(carta al correo) to send back; (COM) to
repay, refund ◆ vi (vomitar) to be sick

devorar [deβo'rar] vt to devour

devoto, -a [de'βoto, a] adj devout
◆ nm/f admirer

devuelto [de'βwelto] pp de **devolver**

devuelva etc [de'βwelβa] vb ver
devolver

di etc [di] vb ver **dar; decir**

día ['dia] nm day; **¿qué ~ es?** what's the
date?; **estar/poner al ~** to be/keep up
to date; **el ~ de hoy/de mañana** today/
tomorrow; **al ~ siguiente** (on) the
following day; **vivir al ~** to live from
hand to mouth; **de ~** by day, in
daylight; **en pleno ~** in full daylight
▶ **Día de la Independencia**
Independence Day ▶ **Día de los
Muertos** (MÉX) All Souls' Day ▶ **Día de
Reyes** Epiphany ▶ **día feriado** (LAm)
holiday ▶ **día festivo** (ESP) holiday
▶ **día lectivo** teaching day ▶ **día
libre** day off

diabetes [dja'βetes] nf diabetes

diablo ['djaβlo] nm devil ☐ **diablura** nf
prank

diadema [dja'ðema] nf tiara

diafragma [dja'fraɣma] nm
diaphragm

diagnóstico [djaɣ'nostiko] nm =
diagnosis

diagonal [djaɣo'nal] adj diagonal

diagrama [dja'ɣrama] nm diagram

dial [djal] nm dial

dialecto [dja'lekto] nm dialect

dialogar [djalo'ɣar] vi: ~ **con** (POL) to
hold talks with

diálogo ['djaloɣo] nm dialogue

diamante [dja'mante] nm diamond

diana ['djana] nf (MIL) reveille; (de
blanco) centre, bull's-eye

diapositiva [djaposi'tiβa] nf (FOTO)
slide, transparency

diario, -a ['djarjo, a] adj daily ◆ nm
newspaper; **a ~** daily; **de ~** everyday

diarrea [dja'rrea] nf diarrhoea

dibujar [diβu'xar] vt to draw, sketch
☐ **dibujo** nm drawing ▶ **dibujos
animados** cartoons

diccionario [dikθjo'narjo] nm
dictionary

dice etc vb ver **decir**

dicho, -a ['ditʃo, a] pp de **decir** ♦ adj: en dichos países in the aforementioned countries ♦ nm saying

dichoso, -a [di'tʃoso, a] adj happy

diciembre [di'θjembre] nm December

dictado [dik'taðo] nm dictation

dictador [dikta'ðor] nm dictator
❏ **dictadura** nf dictatorship

dictar [dik'tar] vt (carta) to dictate; (JUR: sentencia) to pronounce; (decreto) to issue; (LAm: clase) to give

didáctico, -a [di'ðaktiko, a] adj educational

diecinueve [djeθi'nweβe] num nineteen

dieciocho [djeθi'otʃo] num eighteen

dieciséis [djeθi'seis] num sixteen

diecisiete [djeθi'sjete] num seventeen

diente ['djente] nm (ANAT, TEC) tooth; (ZOOL) fang; (: de elefante) tusk; (de ajo) clove

diera etc ['djera] vb ver **dar**

diesel ['disel] adj: **motor ~** diesel engine

diestro, -a ['djestro, a] adj (derecho) right; (hábil) skilful

dieta ['djeta] nf diet; **estar a ~** to be on a diet

diez [djeθ] num ten

diferencia [dife'renθja] nf difference; **a ~ de** unlike ❏ **diferenciar** vt to differentiate between ♦ vi to differ; **diferenciarse** vr to differ, be different; (distinguirse) to distinguish o.s.

diferente [dife'rente] adj different

diferido [dife'riðo] nm: **en ~** (TV etc) recorded

difícil [di'fiθil] adj difficult

dificultad [difikul'taθ] nf difficulty; (problema) trouble

dificultar [difikul'tar] vt (complicar) to complicate, make difficult; (estorbar) to obstruct

difundir [difun'dir] vt (calor, luz) to diffuse; (RADIO, TV) to broadcast; **~ una**

noticia to spread a piece of news; **difundirse** vr to spread (out)

difunto, -a [di'funto, a] adj dead, deceased ♦ nm/f deceased (person)

difusión [difu'sjon] nf (RADIO, TV) broadcasting

diga etc ['diɣa] vb ver **decir**

digerir [dixe'rir] vt to digest; (fig) to absorb ❏ **digestión** nf digestion ❏ **digestivo, -a** adj digestive

digital [dixi'tal] adj digital

dignarse [diɣ'narse] vr to deign to

dignidad [diɣni'ðað] nf dignity

digno, -a ['diɣno, a] adj worthy

digo etc vb ver **decir**

dije etc ['dixe] vb ver **decir**

dilatar [dila'tar] vt (cuerpo) to dilate; (prolongar) to prolong

dilema [di'lema] nm dilemma

diluir [dilu'ir] vt to dilute

diluvio [di'luβjo] nm deluge, flood

dimensión [dimen'sjon] nf dimension

diminuto, -a [dimi'nuto, a] adj tiny, diminutive

dimitir [dimi'tir] vi to resign

dimos ['dimos] vb ver **dar**

Dinamarca [dina'marka] nf Denmark

dinámico, -a [di'namiko, a] adj dynamic

dinamita [dina'mita] nf dynamite

dínamo [dinamo] nf dynamo

dineral [dine'ral] nm large sum of money, fortune

dinero [di'nero] nm money ▶ **dinero en efectivo** o **metálico** cash ▶ **dinero suelto** (loose) change

dlo [djo] vb ver **dar**

dios [djos] nm god; **¡D~ mío!** (oh,) my God!; **¡por D~!** for heaven's sake! ❏ **diosa** ['djosa] nf goddess

diploma [di'ploma] nm diploma

diplomacia [diplo'maθja] nf diplomacy; (fig) tact

diplomado, -a [diplo'maðo, a] adj qualified

diplomático, -a [diplo'matiko, a] *adj* diplomatic ♦ *nm/f* diplomat

diputación [diputa'θjon] *nf* (*tb*: ~ **provincial**) ≈ county council

diputado, -a [dipu'taðo, a] *nm/f* delegate; (*POL*) ≈ member of parliament (*BRIT*), ≈ representative (*US*)

dique ['dike] *nm* dyke

diré *etc* [di're] *vb ver* **decir**

dirección [direk'θjon] *nf* direction; (*señas*) address; (*AUTO*) steering; (*gerencia*) management; (*POL*) leadership ▶ **dirección única/prohibida** one-way street/no entry

direccional (*MÉX*) *nf* (*AUTO*) indicator

directa [di'rekta] *nf* (*AUTO*) top gear

directiva [direk'tiβa] *nf* (*tb*: **junta ~**) board of directors

directo, -a [di'rekto, a] *adj* direct; (*RADIO, TV*) live; **transmitir en ~** to broadcast live

director, a [direk'tor, a] *adj* leading ♦ *nm/f* director; (*ESCOL*) head(teacher) (*BRIT*), principal (*US*); (*gerente*) manager/ess; (*PRENSA*) editor ▶ **director de cine** film director ▶ **director general** managing director

directorio (*MÉX*) [direk'torjo] *nm* (*telefónico*) phone book

dirigente [diri'xente] *nm/f* (*POL*) leader

dirigir [diri'xir] *vt* to direct; (*carta*) to address; (*obra de teatro, film*) to direct; (*MÚS*) to conduct; (*negocio*) to manage; **dirigirse** *vr*: **dirigirse a** to go towards, make one's way towards; (*hablar con*) to speak to

dirija *etc* [di'rixa] *vb ver* **dirigir**

disciplina [disθi'plina] *nf* discipline

discípulo, -a [disθi'pulo, a] *nm/f* disciple

Discman® *nm* Discman®

disco ['disko] *nm* disc; (*DEPORTE*) discus; (*TEL*) dial; (*AUTO*: *semáforo*) light; (*MÚS*) record ▶ **disco compacto/de larga duración** compact disc/long-playing record ▶ **disco de freno** brake disc ▶ **disco flexible/duro** o **rígido** (*INFORM*) floppy/hard disk

disconforme [diskon'forme] *adj* differing; **estar ~ (con)** to be in disagreement (with)

discordia [dis'korðja] *nf* discord

discoteca [disko'teka] *nf* disco(theque)

discreción [diskre'θjon] *nf* discretion; (*reserva*) prudence; **comer a ~** to eat as much as one wishes

discreto, -a [dis'kreto, a] *adj* discreet

discriminación [diskrimina'θjon] *nf* discrimination

disculpa [dis'kulpa] *nf* excuse; (*pedir perdón*) apology; **pedir disculpas a/por** to apologize to/for ▫ **disculpar** *vt* to excuse, pardon; **disculparse** *vr* to excuse o.s., to apologize

discurso [dis'kurso] *nm* speech

discusión [disku'sjon] *nf* (*diálogo*) discussion; (*riña*) argument

discutir [disku'tir] *vt* (*debatir*) to discuss; (*pelear*) to argue about; (*contradecir*) to argue against ♦ *vi* (*debatir*) to discuss; (*pelearse*) to argue

disecar [dise'kar] *vt* (*conservar*: *animal*) to stuff; (: *planta*) to dry

diseñar [dise'ɲar] *vt, vi* to design

diseño [di'seɲo] *nm* design

disfraz [dis'fraθ] *nm* (*máscara*) disguise; (*excusa*) pretext ▫ **disfrazar** *vt* to disguise; **disfrazarse** *vr*: **disfrazarse de** to disguise o.s. as

disfrutar [disfru'tar] *vt* to enjoy ♦ *vi* to enjoy o.s.; **~ de** to enjoy, possess

disgustar [disɣus'tar] *vt* (*no gustar*) to displease; (*contrariar, enojar*) to annoy, upset; **disgustarse** *vr* (*enfadarse*) to get upset; (*dos personas*) to fall out

⚠ No confundir **disgustar** con la palabra inglesa *disgust*.

disgusto [dis'yusto] *nm* (*contrariedad*) annoyance; (*tristeza*) grief; (*riña*) quarrel

disimular [disimu'lar] *vt* (*ocultar*) to hide, conceal ♦ *vi* to dissemble

dislocarse [dislo'karse] *vr* (*articulación*) to sprain, dislocate

disminución [disminu'θjon] *nf* decrease, reduction

disminuido, -a [disminu'iðo, a] *nm/f*: ~ **mental/físico** mentally/physically handicapped person

disminuir [disminu'ir] *vt* to decrease, diminish

disolver [disol'βer] *vt* (*gen*) to dissolve; **disolverse** *vr* to dissolve; (*COM*) to go into liquidation

dispar [dis'par] *adj* different

disparar [dispa'rar] *vt, vi* to shoot, fire

disparate [dispa'rate] *nm* (*tontería*) foolish remark; (*error*) blunder; **decir disparates** to talk nonsense

disparo [dis'paro] *nm* shot

dispersar [disper'sar] *vt* to disperse; **dispersarse** *vr* to scatter

disponer [dispo'ner] *vt* (*arreglar*) to arrange; (*ordenar*) to put in order; (*preparar*) to prepare, get ready ♦ *vi*: ~ **de** to have, own; **disponerse** *vr*: **disponerse a** o **para hacer** to prepare to do

disponible [dispo'niβle] *adj* available

disposición [disposi'θjon] *nf* arrangement, disposition; (*voluntad*) willingness; (*INFORM*) layout; **a su ~ at** your service

dispositivo [disposi'tiβo] *nm* device, mechanism

dispuesto, -a [dis'pwesto, a] *pp de* **disponer** ♦ *adj* (*arreglado*) arranged; (*preparado*) disposed

disputar [dispu'tar] *vt* (*carrera*) to compete in

disquete [dis'kete] *nm* floppy disk, diskette

distancia [dis'tanθja] *nf* distance

❏ **distanciar** [distan'θjar] *vt* to space out; **distanciarse** *vr* to become estranged ❏ **distante** [dis'tante] *adj* distant

diste ['diste] *vb ver* **dar**

disteis ['disteis] *vb ver* **dar**

distinción [distin'θjon] *nf* distinction; (*elegancia*) elegance; (*honor*) honour

distinguido, -a [distin'giðo, a] *adj* distinguished

distinguir [distin'gir] *vt* to distinguish; (*escoger*) to single out; **distinguirse** *vr* to be distinguished

distintivo [distin'tiβo] *nm* badge; (*fig*) characteristic

distinto, -a [dis'tinto, a] *adj* different; (*claro*) clear

distracción [distrak'θjon] *nf* distraction; (*pasatiempo*) hobby, pastime; (*olvido*) absent-mindedness, distraction

distraer [distra'er] *vt* (*atención*) to distract; (*divertir*) to amuse; (*fondos*) to embezzle; **distraerse** *vr* (*entretenerse*) to amuse o.s.; (*perder la concentración*) to allow one's attention to wander

distraído, -a [distra'iðo, a] *adj* (*gen*) absent-minded; (*entretenido*) amusing

distribuidor, a [distriβui'ðor, a] *nm/f* distributor ❏ **distribuidora** *nf* (*COM*) dealer, agent; (*CINE*) distributor

distribuir [distriβu'ir] *vt* to distribute

distrito [dis'trito] *nm* (*sector, territorio*) region; (*barrio*) district ▶ **Distrito Federal** (*MÉX*) Federal District ▶ **distrito postal** postal district

disturbio [dis'turβjo] *nm* disturbance; (*desorden*) riot

disuadir [diswa'ðir] *vt* to dissuade

disuelto [di'swelto] *pp de* **disolver**

DIU *nm abr* (= *dispositivo intrauterino*) IUD

diurno, -a ['djurno, a] *adj* day *cpd*

divagar [diβa'yar] *vi* (*desviarse*) to digress

diván [di'βan] nm divan

diversidad [diβersi'ðað] nf diversity, variety

diversión [diβer'sjon] nf (gen) entertainment; (actividad) hobby, pastime

diverso, -a [di'βerso, a] adj diverse; **diversos libros** several books ❑ **diversos** nmpl sundries

divertido, -a [diβer'tiðo, a] adj (chiste) amusing; (fiesta etc) enjoyable

divertir [diβer'tir] vt (entretener, recrear) to amuse; **divertirse** vr (pasarlo bien) to have a good time; (distraerse) to amuse o.s.

dividendos [diβi'ðendos] nmpl (COM) dividends

dividir [diβi'ðir] vt (gen) to divide; (distribuir) to distribute, share out

divierta etc [di'βjerta] vb ver **divertir**

divino, -a [di'βino, a] adj divine

divirtiendo etc [diβir'tjendo] vb ver **divertir**

divisa [di'βisa] nf (emblema) emblem, badge; **divisas** nfpl foreign exchange sg

divisar [diβi'sar] vt to make out, distinguish

división [diβi'sjon] nf (gen) division; (de partido) split; (de país) partition

divorciar [diβorθ'jar] vt to divorce; **divorciarse** vr to get divorced ❑ **divorcio** nm divorce

divulgar [diβul'ɣar] vt (ideas) to spread; (secreto) to divulge

DNI (ESP) nm abr (= Documento Nacional de Identidad) national identity card

---

DNI

The **Documento Nacional de Identidad** is a Spanish ID card which must be carried at all times and produced on request for the police. It contains the holder's photo, fingerprints and personal details. It is also known as the **DNI** or "carnet de identidad".

Dña. abr (= doña) Mrs

do [do] nm (MÚS) do, C

dobladillo [doβla'ðiʎo] nm (de vestido) hem; (de pantalón: vuelta) turn-up (BRIT), cuff (US)

doblar [do'βlar] vt to double; (papel) to fold; (caño) to bend; (la esquina) to turn, go round; (film) to dub ♦ vi to turn; (campana) to toll; **doblarse** vr (plegarse) to fold (up), crease; (encorvarse) to bend; **~ a la derecha/izquierda** to turn right/left

doble ['doβle] adj double; (de dos aspectos) dual; (fig) two-faced ♦ nm double ♦ nmf (TEATRO) double, stand-in; **dobles** nmpl (DEPORTE) doubles sg; **con ~ sentido** with a double meaning

doce ['doθe] num twelve ❑ **docena** nf dozen

docente [do'θente] adj: **centro/personal ~** teaching establishment/staff

dócil ['doθil] adj (pasivo) docile; (obediente) obedient

doctor, a [dok'tor, a] nm/f doctor

doctorado [dokto'raðo] nm doctorate

doctrina [dok'trina] nf doctrine, teaching

documentación [dokumenta'θjon] nf documentation, papers pl

documental [dokumen'tal] adj, nm documentary

documento [doku'mento] nm (certificado) document ▶ **documento adjunto** (INFORM) attachment ▶ **documento nacional de identidad** identity card

dólar ['dolar] nm dollar

doler [do'ler] vt, vi to hurt; (fig) to grieve; **dolerse** vr (de su situación) to grieve, feel sorry; (de las desgracias ajenas) to sympathize; **me duele el brazo** my arm hurts

dolor [do'lor] nm pain; (fig) grief, sorrow ▶ **dolor de cabeza/**

estómago/muelas headache/
stomachache/toothache

domar [do'mar] vt to tame

domesticar [domesti'kar] vt = **domar**

doméstico, -a [do'mestiko, a] adj
(vida, servicio) home; (tareas)
household; (animal) tame, pet

domicilio [domi'θiljo] nm home;
servicio a ~ home delivery service; **sin
~ fijo** of no fixed abode ▸ **domicilio
particular** private residence

dominante [domi'nahte] adj
dominant; (persona) domineering

dominar [domi'nar] vt (gen) to
dominate; (idiomas) to be fluent in ♦ vi
to dominate, prevail

domingo [do'mingo] nm Sunday
▸ **Domingo de Ramos/
Resurrección** Palm/Easter Sunday

dominio [do'minjo] nm (tierras)
domain; (autoridad) power, authority;
(de las pasiones) grip, hold; (de idiomas)
command

don [don] nm (talento) gift; **~ Juan
Gómez** Mr Juan Gómez, Juan Gómez
Esq (BRIT)

DON/DOÑA

The term **don/doña** often abbreviated
to **D./Dña** is placed before the first
name as a mark of respect to an older
or more senior person - eg Don Diego,
Doña Inés. Although becoming rarer
in Spain it is still used with names and
surnames on official documents and
formal correspondence - eg "Sr. D.
Pedro Rodríguez Hernández", "Sra.
Dña. Inés Rodríguez Hernández".

---

dona [MÉX] nf doughnut, donut (US)

donar [do'nar] vt to donate

donativo [dona'tiβo] nm donation

donde ['donde] adv where ♦ prep: **el
coche está allí ~ el farol** the car is over
there by the lamppost o where the
lamppost is; **en ~** where, in which

dónde ['donde] adv where?; **¿a ~ vas?**
where are you going (to)?; **¿de ~
vienes?** where have you been?; **¿por
~?** where?, whereabouts?

dondequiera [donde'kjera] adv
anywhere; **por ~** everywhere, all over
the place ♦ conj: **~ que** wherever

donut® (ESP) nm doughnut, donut (US)

doña [doɲa] nf: **~ Alicia** Alicia; **~
Victoria Benito** Mrs Victoria Benito

dorado, -a [do'raðo, a] adj (color)
golden; (TEC) gilt

dormir [dor'mir] vt: **~ la siesta** to have
an afternoon nap ♦ vi to sleep;
dormirse vr to fall asleep

dormitorio [dormi'torjo] nm
bedroom

dorsal [dor'sal] nm (DEPORTE) number

dorso ['dorso] nm (de mano) back; (de
hoja) other side

dos [dos] num two

dosis ['dosis] nf inv dose, dosage

dotado, -a [do'taðo, a] adj gifted; **~ de**
endowed with

dotar [do'tar] vt to endow □ **dote** nf
dowry; **dotes** nfpl (talentos) gifts

doy [doj] vb ver **dar**

drama ['drama] nm drama
□ **dramaturgo** [drama'turɣo] nm
dramatist, playwright

drástico, -a [a'drastiko, a] adj drastic

drenaje [dre'naxe] nm drainage

droga ['droɣa] nf drug □ **drogadicto,
-a** [droɣa'ðikto, a] nm/f drug addict

droguería [droɣe'ria] nf hardware
shop (BRIT) o store (US)

ducha ['dutʃa] nf (baño) shower; (MED)
douche; **ducharse** vr to take a shower

duda ['duða] nf doubt; **no cabe ~** there
is no doubt about it □ **dudar** vt, vi to
doubt □ **dudoso, -a** [du'ðoso, a] adj
(incierto) hesitant; (sospechoso)
doubtful

duela etc vb ver **doler**

duelo ['dwelo] vb ver **doler** ♦ nm (combate) duel; (luto) mourning

duende ['dwende] nm imp, goblin

dueño, -a ['dweɲo, a] nm/f (propietario) owner; (de pensión, taberna) landlord/lady; (empresario) employer

duermo etc vb ver **dormir**

dulce ['dulθe] adj sweet ♦ adv gently, softly ♦ nm sweet

dulcería (LAm) nf confectioner's (shop)

dulzura [dul'θura] nf sweetness; (ternura) gentleness

dúo ['duo] nm duet

duplicar [dupli'kar] vt (hacer el doble de) to duplicate

duque ['duke] nm duke ❏ **duquesa** nf duchess

duración [dura'θjon] nf (de película, disco etc) length; (de pila etc) life; (curso: de acontecimientos etc) duration

duradero, -a [dura'ðero, a] adj (tela etc) hard-wearing; (fe, paz) lasting

durante [du'rante] prep during

durar [du'rar] vi to last; (recuerdo) to remain

durazno [du'raθno] (LAm) nm (fruta) peach; (árbol) peach tree

durex ['dureks] (MÉX, ARG) nm (tira adhesiva) Sellotape® (BRIT), Scotch tape® (US)

dureza [du'reθa] nf (calidad) hardness

duro, -a ['duro, a] adj hard; (carácter) tough ♦ adv hard ♦ nm (moneda) five-peseta coin o piece

DVD nm abr (= disco de vídeo digital) DVD

E, e

E abr (= este) E

e [e] conj and

ébano ['eβano] nm ebony

ebrio, -a ['eβrjo, a] adj drunk

ebullición [eβuʎi'θjon] nf boiling

echar [e'tʃar] vt to throw; (agua, vino) to pour (out); (empleado: despedir) to fire, sack; (hojas) to sprout; (cartas) to post; (humo) to emit, give out ♦ vi: ~ a correr to run off; **echarse** vr to lie down; ~ **llave a** to lock (up); ~ **abajo** (gobierno) to overthrow; (edificio) to demolish; ~ **mano a** to lay hands on; ~ **una mano a algn** (ayudar) to give sb a hand; ~ **de menos** to miss; **echarse atrás** (fig) to back out

eclesiástico, -a [ekle'sjastiko, a] adj ecclesiastical

eco ['eko] nm echo; **tener ~** to catch on

ecología [ekolo'ɣia] nf ecology ❏ **ecológico, -a** adj (producto, método) environmentally-friendly; (agricultura) organic ❏ **ecologista** adj ecological, environmental ♦ nmf environmentalist

economía [ekono'mia] nf (sistema) economy; (carrera) economics

económico, -a [eko'nomiko, a] adj (barato) cheap, economical; (ahorrativo) thrifty; (COM: año etc) financial; (: situación) economic

economista [ekono'mista] nmf economist

Ecuador [ekwa'ðor] nm Ecuador ❏ **ecuador** nm (GEO) equator

ecuatoriano, -a [ekwato'rjano, a] adj, nm/f Ecuadorian

ecuestre [e'kwestre] adj equestrian

edad [e'ðað] nf age; **¿qué ~ tienes?** how old are you?; **tiene ocho años de ~** he's eight (years old); **de ~ mediana/avanzada** middle-aged/advanced in years; **la E~ Media** the Middle Ages

edición [eði'θjon] nf (acto) publication; (ejemplar) edition

edificar [eðifi'kar] vt, vi to build

edificio [eði'fiθjo] nm building; (fig) edifice, structure

Edimburgo [eðim'burɣo] nm Edinburgh

editar [eði'tar] vt (*publicar*) to publish; (*preparar textos*) to edit

editor, a [eði'tor, a] nm/f (*que publica*) publisher; (*redactor*) editor ♦ adj publishing cpd ❑ **editorial** adj editorial ♦ nm leading article, editorial; **casa editorial** publisher

edredón [eðre'ðon] nm duvet

educación [eðuka'θjon] nf education; (*crianza*) upbringing; (*modales*) (good) manners pl

educado, -a [eðu'kaðo, a] adj: **bien/ mal ~** well/badly behaved

educar [eðu'kar] vt to educate; (*criar*) to bring up; (*voz*) to train

EE. UU. nmpl abr (= Estados Unidos) US(A)

efectivamente [efectiβa'mente] adv (*como respuesta*) exactly, precisely; (*verdaderamente*) really; (*de hecho*) in fact

efectivo, -a [efek'tiβo, a] adj effective; (*real*) actual, real ♦ nm: **pagar en ~** to pay (in) cash; **hacer ~ un cheque** to cash a cheque

efecto [e'fekto] nm effect, result; **efectos** nmpl (*efectos personales*) effects; (*bienes*) goods; (*COM*) assets; **en ~** in fact; (*respuesta*) exactly, indeed ▶ **efecto invernadero** greenhouse effect ▶ **efectos especiales/ secundarios/sonoros** special/side/ sound effects

efectuar [efek'twar] vt to carry out; (*viaje*) to make

eficacia [efi'kaθja] nf (*de persona*) efficiency; (*de medicamento etc*) effectiveness

eficaz [efi'kaθ] adj (*persona*) efficient; (*acción*) effective

eficiente [efi'θjente] adj efficient

egipcio, -a [e'xipθjo, a] adj, nm/f Egyptian

Egipto [e'xipto] nm Egypt

egoísmo [eɣo'ismo] nm egoism

egoísta [eɣo'ista] adj egoistical, selfish ♦ nmf egoist

Eire ['eire] nm Eire

ej. abr (= ejemplo) eg

eje ['exe] nm (GEO, MAT) axis; (*de rueda*) axle; (*de máquina*) shaft, spindle

ejecución [exeku'θjon] nf execution; (*cumplimiento*) fulfilment; (*MÚS*) performance; (*JUR: embargo de deudor*) attachment

ejecutar [exeku'tar] vt to execute, carry out; (*matar*) to execute; (*cumplir*) to fulfil; (*MÚS*) to perform; (*JUR: embargar*) to attach, distrain (on)

ejecutivo, -a [exeku'tiβo, a] adj executive; **el (poder) ~** the executive (power)

ejemplar [exem'plar] adj exemplary ♦ nm example; (ZOOL) specimen; (*de libro*) copy; (*de periódico*) number, issue

ejemplo [e'xemplo] nm example; **por ~** for example

ejercer [exer'θer] vt to exercise; (*influencia*) to exert; (*un oficio*) to practise ♦ vi (*practicar*) to practise; **~ (de)** to practise (as)

ejercicio [exer'θiθjo] nm exercise; (*período*) tenure; **hacer ~** to take exercise ▶ **ejercicio comercial** financial year

ejército [e'xerθito] nm army; **entrar en el ~** to join the army, join up ▶ **ejército del aire/de tierra** Air Force/Army

ejote [e'xote] (MÉX) nm green bean

el

PALABRA CLAVE

[el] (f **la**, pl **los, las**, neutro **lo**) art def

1 **el libro/la mesa/los estudiantes** the book/table/students

2 (*con n abstracto: no se traduce*): **el amor/la juventud** love/youth

3 (*posesión: se traduce a menudo por adj posesivo*): **romperse el brazo** to break one's arm; **levantó la mano** he put his hand up; **se puso el sombrero** she put her hat on

4 (*valor descriptivo*): **tener la boca grande/los ojos azules** to have a big mouth/blue eyes

5 (*con días*) on; **me iré el viernes** I'll leave on Friday; **los domingos suelo ir a nadar** on Sundays I generally go swimming

6 (*lo +adj*): **lo difícil/caro** what is difficult/expensive; (*cuán*): **no se da cuenta de lo pesado que es** he doesn't realise how boring he is

♦ *pron demos*

1: **mi libro y el de usted** my book and yours; **las de Pepe son mejores** Pepe's are better; **no la(s) blanca(s) sino la(s) gris(es)** not the white one(s) but the grey one(s)

2: **lo de: lo de ayer** what happened yesterday; **lo de las facturas** that business about the invoices

♦ *pron relativo*

1 (*indef*): **el que: el (los) que quiera(n) que se vaya(n)** anyone who wants to can leave; **llévese el que más le guste** take the one you like best

2 (*def*): **el que: el que compré ayer** the one I bought yesterday; **los que se van** those who leave

3: **lo que: lo que pienso yo/más me gusta** what I think/like most

♦ *conj*: **el que: el que lo diga** the fact that he says so; **el que sea tan vago me molesta** his being so lazy bothers me

♦ *excl*: **¡el susto que me diste!** what a fright you gave me!

♦ *pron personal*

1 (*persona: m*) him; (*: f*) her; (*: pl*)

them; **lo/las veo** I can see him/them

2 (*animal, cosa: sg*) it; (*: pl*) them; **lo (o la) veo** I can see it; **los (o las) veo** I can see them

3 (*como sustituto de frase*): **lo: no lo sabía** I didn't know; **ya lo entiendo** I understand now

él [el] *pron* (*persona*) he; (*cosa*) it; (*después de prep: persona*) him; (*: cosa*) it; **de él** his

elaborar [elaβo'rar] *vt* (*producto*) to make, manufacture; (*preparar*) to prepare; (*madera, metal etc*) to work; (*proyecto etc*) to work on *o* out

elástico, -a [e'lastiko, a] *adj* elastic; (*flexible*) flexible ♦ *nm* elastic; (*un elástico*) elastic band

elección [elek'θjon] *nf* election; (*selección*) choice, selection

▶ **elecciones generales** general election *sg*

electorado [elekto'raðo] *nm* electorate, voters *pl*

electricidad [elektriθi'ðað] *nf* electricity

electricista [elektri'θista] *nmf* electrician

eléctrico, -a [e'lektriko, a] *adj* electric

electro... [elektro] *prefijo* electro... ❏ **electrocardiograma** *nm* electrocardiogram ❏ **electrocutar** *vt* to electrocute ❏ **electrodo** *nm* electrode ❏ **electrodomésticos** *nmpl* (electrical) household appliances

electrónica [elek'tronika] *nf* electronics *sg*

electrónico, -a [elek'troniko, a] *adj* electronic

elefante [ele'fante] *nm* elephant

elegancia [ele'ɣanθja] *nf* elegance, grace; (*estilo*) stylishness

elegante [ele'ɣante] *adj* elegant, graceful; (*estiloso*) stylish, fashionable

elegir [ele'xir] vt (escoger) to choose, select; (optar) to opt for; (presidente) to elect

elemental [elemen'tal] adj (claro, obvio) elementary; (fundamental) elemental, fundamental

elemento [ele'mento] nm element; (fig) ingredient; **elementos** nmpl elements, rudiments

elepé [ele'pe] (pl ~s) nm L.P.

elevación [eleβa'θjon] nf elevation; (acto) raising, lifting; (de precios) rise; (GEO etc) height, altitude

elevar [ele'βar] vt to raise, lift (up); (precio) to put up; **elevarse** vr (edificio) to rise; (precios) to go up

eligiendo etc [eli'xjenðo] vb ver **elegir**

elija etc [e'lixa] vb ver **elegir**

eliminar [elimi'nar] vt to eliminate, remove

eliminatoria [elimina'torja] nf heat, preliminary (round)

élite ['elite] nf elite

ella ['eλa] pron (persona) she; (cosa) it; (después de prep: persona) her; (: cosa) it; **de ~** hers

ellas ['eλas] pron (personas y cosas) they; (después de prep) them; **de ~** theirs

ello ['eλo] pron it

ellos ['eλos] pron they; (después de prep) them; **de ~** theirs

elogiar [elo'xjar] vt to praise ▢ **elogio** nm praise

elote [e'lote] (MÉX) nm corn on the cob

eludir [elu'ðir] vt to avoid

email [i'mel] nm email; (dirección) email address; **mandar un ~ a** algn to email sb, send sb an email

embajada [emba'xaða] nf embassy

embajador, a [embaxa'ðor, a] nm/f ambassador/ambassadress

embalar [emba'lar] vt to parcel, wrap (up); **embalarse** vr to go fast

embalse [em'balse] nm (presa) dam; (lago) reservoir

embarazada [embara'θaða] adj pregnant ♦ nf pregnant woman

⚠ No confundir **embarazada** con la palabra inglesa *embarrassed*.

embarazo [emba'raθo] nm (de mujer) pregnancy; (impedimento) obstacle, obstruction; (timidez) embarrassment ▢ **embarazoso, -a** adj awkward, embarrassing

embarcación [embarka'θjon] nf (barco) boat, craft; (acto) embarkation, boarding

embarcadero [embarka'ðero] nm pier, landing stage

embarcar [embar'kar] vt (cargamento) to ship, stow; (persona) to embark, put on board; **embarcarse** vr to embark, go on board

embargar [embar'ɣar] vt (JUR) to seize, impound

embargo [em'barɣo] nm (JUR) seizure; (COM, POL) embargo

embargue etc [em'barɣe] vb ver **embargar**

embarque etc [em'barke] vb ver **embarcar** ♦ nm shipment, loading

embellecer [embeλe'θer] vt to embellish, beautify

embestida [embes'tiða] nf attack, onslaught; (carga) charge

embestir [embes'tir] vt to attack, assault; to charge, attack ♦ vi to attack

emblema [em'blema] nm emblem

embobado, -a [embo'βaðo, a] adj (atontado) stunned, fascinated

embolia [em'bolja] nf (MED) clot

émbolo ['embolo] nm (AUTO) piston

emborrachar [emborra't͡ʃar] vt to make drunk, intoxicate; **emborracharse** vr to get drunk

emboscada [embos'kaða] nf ambush

embotar [embo'tar] vt to blunt, dull

embotellamiento [emboteλa'mjento] nm (AUTO) traffic jam

embotellar [embote'ʎar] *vt* to bottle

embrague [em'braɣe] *nm* (*tb*: **pedal de ~**) clutch

embrión [em'brjon] *nm* embryo

embrollo [em'broʎo] *nm* (*enredo*) muddle, confusion; (*aprieto*) fix, jam

embrujado, -a [embru'xaðo, a] *adj* bewitched; **casa embrujada** haunted house

embrutecer [embrute'θer] *vt* (*atontar*) to stupefy

embudo [em'buðo] *nm* funnel

embuste [em'buste] *nm* (*mentira*) lie □ **embustero, -a** *adj* lying, deceitful ♦ *nm/f* (*mentiroso*) liar

embutido [embu'tiðo] *nm* (*CULIN*) sausage; (*TEC*) inlay

emergencia [emer'xenθja] *nf* emergency; (*surgimiento*) emergence

emerger [emer'xer] *vi* to emerge, appear

emigración [emiɣra'θjon] *nf* emigration; (*de pájaros*) migration

emigrar [emi'ɣrar] *vi* (*personas*) to emigrate; (*pájaros*) to migrate

eminente [emi'nente] *adj* eminent, distinguished; (*elevado*) high

emisión [emi'sjon] *nf* (*acto*) emission; (*COM etc*) issue; (*RADIO, TV*: *acto*) broadcasting; (: *programa*) broadcast, programme (*BRIT*), program (*US*)

emisora [emi'sora] *nf* radio o broadcasting station

emitir [emi'tir] *vt* (*olor etc*) to emit, give off; (*moneda etc*) to issue; (*opinión*) to express; (*RADIO*) to broadcast

emoción [emo'θjon] *nf* emotion; (*excitación*) excitement; (*sentimiento*) feeling

emocionante [emoθjo'nante] *adj* exciting, thrilling

emocionar [emoθjo'nar] *vt* (*excitar*) to excite, thrill; (*conmover*) to move, touch; (*impresionar*) to impress

emoticón, **emoticono** *nm* smiley

emotivo, -a [emo'tiβo, a] *adj* emotional

empacho [em'patʃo] *nm* (*MED*) indigestion; (*fig*) embarrassment

empalagoso, -a [empala'ɣoso, a] *adj* cloying; (*fig*) tiresome

empalmar [empal'mar] *vt* to join, connect ♦ *vi* (*dos caminos*) to meet, join □ **empalme** *nm* joint, connection; junction; (*de trenes*) connection

empanada [empa'naða] *nf* pie, pasty

empañarse [empa'narse] *vr* (*cristales etc*) to steam up

empapar [empa'par] *vt* (*mojar*) to soak, saturate; (*absorber*) to soak up, absorb; **empaparse** *vr*: **empaparse de** to soak up

empapelar [empape'lar] *vt* (*paredes*) to paper

empaquetar [empake'tar] *vt* to pack, parcel up

empastar [empas'tar] *vt* (*embadurnar*) to paste; (*diente*) to fill

empaste [em'paste] *nm* (*de diente*) filling

empatar [empa'tar] *vi* to draw, tie; **empataron a dos** they drew two-all □ **empate** *nm* draw, tie

empecé *etc* [empe'θe] *vb ver* **empezar**

empedernido, -a [empeðer'niðo, a] *adj* hard, heartless; (*fumador*) inveterate

empeine [em'peine] *nm* (*de pie*, *zapato*) instep

empeñado, -a [empe'naðo, a] *adj* (*persona*) determined; (*objeto*) pawned

empeñar [empe'nar] *vt* (*objeto*) to pawn, pledge; (*persona*) to compel; **empeñarse** *vr* (*endeudarse*) to get into debt; **empeñarse en** to be set on, be determined to

empeño [em'peno] *nm* (*determinación, insistencia*) determination, insistence; **casa de empeños** pawnshop

empeorar [empeo'rar] vt to make worse, worsen ♦ vi to get worse, deteriorate

empezar [empe'θar] vt, vi to begin, start

empiece etc [em'pjeθe] vb ver **empezar**

empiezo etc [em'pjeθo] vb ver **empezar**

emplasto [em'plasto] nm (MED) plaster

emplazar [empla'θar] vt (ubicar) to site, locate; (JUR) to summons; (convocar) to summon

empleado, -a [emple'aðo, a] nm/f (gen) employee; (de banco etc) clerk

emplear [emple'ar] vt (usar) to use, employ; (dar trabajo a) to employ; **emplearse** vr (conseguir trabajo) to be employed; (ocuparse) to occupy o.s.

empleo [em'pleo] nm (puesto) job; (puestos: colectivamente) employment; (uso) use, employment

empollar [empo'ʎar] (ESP: fam) vt, vi to swot (up) ❑ **empollón, -ona** (ESP: fam) nm/f swot

emporio [em'porjo] (LAm) nm (gran almacén) department store

empotrado, -a [empo'traðo, a] adj (armario etc) built-in

emprender [empren'der] vt (empezar) to begin, embark on; (acometer) to tackle, take on ❑ **empresa** [em'presa] nf (de espíritu etc) enterprise; (COM) company, firm ❑ **empresariales** nfpl business studies ❑ **empresario, -a** nm/f (COM) businessman(-woman)

empujar [empu'xar] vt to push, shove

empujón [empu'xon] nm push, shove

empuñar [empu'ɲar] vt (asir) to grasp, take (firm) hold of

en

PALABRA CLAVE

[en] prep

1 (posición) in; (: sobre) on; **está en el cajón** it's in the drawer; **en**

Argentina/La Paz in Argentina/La Paz; **en la oficina/el colegio** at the office/school; **está en el suelo/quinto piso** it's on the floor/the fifth floor

2 (dirección) into; **entró en el aula** she went into the classroom; **meter algo en el bolso** to put sth into one's bag

3 (tiempo) in; on; **en 1605/3 semanas/invierno** in 1605/3 weeks/winter; **en (el mes de) enero** in (the month of) January; **en aquella ocasión/época** on that occasion/at that time

4 (precio) for; **lo vendió en 20 dólares** he sold it for 20 dollars

5 (diferencia) by; **reducir/aumentar en una tercera parte/un 20 por ciento** to reduce/increase by a third/ 20 per cent

6 (manera): **en avión/autobús** by plane/bus; **escrito en inglés** written in English

7 (después de vb que indica gastar etc) on; **han cobrado demasiado en dietas** they've charged too much to expenses; **se le va la mitad del sueldo en comida** he spends half his salary on food

8 (tema, ocupación): **experto en la materia** expert on the subject; **trabaja en la construcción** he works in the building industry

9 (adj + en + infin): **lento en reaccionar** slow to react

enaguas [e'naɣwas] nfpl petticoat sg, underskirt sg

enajenación [enaxena'θjon] nf (PSICO: tb: ~ **mental**) mental derangement

enamorado, -a [enamo'raðo, a] adj in love ♦ nm/f lover; **estar ~ (de)** to be in love (with)

enamorar [enamo'rar] *vt* to win the love of; **enamorarse** *vr*: **enamorarse de algn** to fall in love with sb

enano, -a [e'nano, a] *adj* tiny ♦ *nm/f* dwarf

encabezamiento [enkaβeθa'mjento] *nm* (*de carta*) heading; (*de periódico*) headline

encabezar [enkaβe'θar] *vt* (*movimiento, revolución*) to lead, head; (*lista*) to head, be at the top of; (*carta*) to put a heading to

encadenar [enkaðe'nar] *vt* to chain (together); (*poner grilletes a*) to shackle

encajar [enka'xar] *vt* (*ajustar*): ~ **(en)** to fit (into); (*fam: golpe*) to take ♦ *vi* to fit (well); (*fig: corresponder a*) to match

encaje [en'kaxe] *nm* (*labor*) lace

encallar [enka'ʎar] *vi* (*NÁUT*) to run aground

encaminar [enkami'nar] *vt* to direct, send

encantado, -a [enkan'taðo, a] *adj* (*hechizado*) bewitched; (*muy contento*) delighted; **¡~!** how do you do, pleased to meet you

encantador, a [enkanta'ðor, a] *adj* charming, lovely ♦ *nm/f* magician, enchanter/enchantress

encantar [enkan'tar] *vt* (*agradar*) to charm, delight; (*hechizar*) to bewitch, cast a spell on; **me encanta eso** I love that ☐ **encanto** *nm* (*hechizo*) spell, charm; (*fig*) charm, delight

encarcelar [enkarθe'lar] *vt* to imprison, jail

encarecer [enkare'θer] *vt* to put up the price of; **encarecerse** *vr* to get dearer

encargado, -a [enkar'ɣaðo, a] *adj* in charge ♦ *nm/f* agent, representative; (*responsable*) person in charge

encargar [enkar'ɣar] *vt* to entrust; (*recomendar*) to urge, recommend; **encargarse** *vr*: **encargarse de** to look after, take charge of; ~ **algo a algn** to

put sb in charge of sth; ~ **a algn que haga algo** to ask sb to do sth

encargo [en'karɣo] *nm* (*tarea*) assignment, job; (*responsabilidad*) responsibility; (*COM*) order

encariñarse [enkari'narse] *vr*: ~ **con** to grow fond of, get attached to

encarnación [enkarna'θjon] *nf* incarnation, embodiment

encarrilar [enkarri'lar] *vt* (*tren*) to put back on the rails; (*fig*) to correct, put on the right track

encasillar [enkasi'ʎar] *vt* (*fig*) to pigeonhole; (*actor*) to typecast

encendedor [enθende'ðor] *nm* lighter

encender [enθen'der] *vt* (*con fuego*) to light; (*luz, radio*) to put on, switch on; (*avivar: pasión*) to inflame; **encenderse** *vr* to catch fire; (*excitarse*) to get excited; (*de cólera*) to flare up; (*el rostro*) to blush

encendido [enθen'diðo] *nm* (*AUTO*) ignition

encerado [enθe'raðo] *nm* (*ESCOL*) blackboard

encerrar [enθe'rrar] *vt* (*confinar*) to shut in, shut up; (*comprender, incluir*) to include, contain

encharcado, -a [entʃar'kaðo, a] *adj* (*terreno*) flooded

encharcarse [entʃar'karse] *vr* to get flooded

enchufado, -a [entʃu'faðo, a] (*fam*) *nm/f* well-connected person

enchufar [entʃu'far] *vt* (*ELEC*) to plug in; (*TEC*) to connect, fit together ☐ **enchufe** *nm* (*ELEC: clavija*) plug; (*: toma*) socket; (*dos tubos*) joint, connection; (*fam: influencia*) contact, connection; (*: puesto*) cushy job

encía [en'θia] *nf* gum

encienda *etc* [en'θjenda] *vb ver* **encender**

encierro *etc* [en'θjerro] *vb ver* **encerrar** ♦ *nm* shutting in, shutting up; (*calabozo*) prison

encima [en'θima] adv (sobre) above, over; (además) besides; ~ **de** (en) on, on top of; (sobre) above, over; (además de) besides, on top of; **por ~ de** besides, on top of; **¿llevas dinero ~?** have you (got) any money on you?; **se me vino ~** it took me by surprise

encina [en'θina] nf holm oak

encinta [en'θinta] adj pregnant

enclenque [en'klenke] adj weak, sickly

encoger [enko'xer] vt to shrink, contract; **encogerse** vr to shrink, contract; (fig) to cringe; **encogerse de hombros** to shrug one's shoulders

encomendar [enkomen'dar] vt to entrust, commend; **encomendarse** vr: **encomendarse a** to put one's trust in

encomienda etc [enko'mjenda] vb ver **encomendar ♦** nf (encargo) charge, commission; (elogio) tribute
▶ **encomienda postal** (LAm) package

encontrar [enkon'trar] vt (hallar) to find; (inesperadamente) to meet, run into; **encontrarse** vr to meet (each other); (situarse) to be (situated); **encontrarse con** to meet; **encontrarse bien (de salud)** to feel well

encrucijada [enkruθi'xaða] nf crossroads sg

encuadernación [enkwaðerna'θjon] nf binding

encuadrar [enkwa'ðrar] vt (retrato) to frame; (ajustar) to fit, insert; (contener) to contain

encubrir [enku'βrir] vt (ocultar) to hide, conceal; (criminal) to harbour, shelter

encuentro etc [en'kwentro] vb ver **encontrar ♦** nm (de personas) meeting; (AUTO etc) collision, crash; (DEPORTE) match, game; (MIL) encounter

encuerado, -a [MÉX] [enkwe'raðo, a] adj nude, naked

encuesta [en'kwesta] nf inquiry, investigation; (sondeo) (public) opinion poll

encumbrar [enkum'brar] vt to exalt

endeble [en'deβle] adj (persona) weak; (argumento, excusa, persona) weak

endemoniado, -a [endemo'njaðo, a] adj possessed (of the devil); (travieso) devilish

enderezar [endere'θar] vt (poner derecho) to straighten (out); (: verticalmente) to set upright; (situación) to straighten o sort out; (dirigir) to direct; **enderezarse** vr (persona sentada) to straighten up

endeudarse [endeu'ðarse] vr to get into debt

endiablado, -a [endja'βlaðo, a] adj devilish, diabolical; (travieso) mischievous

endilgar [endil'ɣar] (fam) vt: **endilgarle algo a algn** to lumber sb with sth

endiñar [endi'ɲar] (ESP: fam) vt (bofetón) to land, belt

endosar [endo'sar] vt (cheque etc) to endorse

endulzar [endul'θar] vt to sweeten; (suavizar) to soften

endurecer [endure'θer] vt to harden; **endurecerse** vr to harden, grow hard

enema [e'nema] nm (MED) enema

enemigo, -a [ene'miɣo, a] adj enemy, hostile ♦ nm/f enemy

enemistad [enemis'tað] nf enmity

enemistar [enemis'tar] vt to make enemies of, cause a rift between; **enemistarse** vr to become enemies; (amigos) to fall out

energía [ener'xia] nf (vigor) energy, drive; (empuje) push; (TEC, ELEC) energy, power ▶ **energía eólica** wind power
▶ **energía solar** solar energy o power

enérgico, -a [e'nerxiko, a] adj (gen) energetic; (voz, modales) forceful

energúmeno, -a [ener'yumeno, a] (fam) nm/f (fig) madman(-woman)

enero [e'nero] nm January

enfadado, -a [enfa'ðaðo, a] adj angry, annoyed

enfadar [enfa'ðar] vt to anger, annoy; **enfadarse** vr to get angry o annoyed

enfado [en'faðo] nm (enojo) anger, annoyance; (disgusto) trouble, bother

énfasis ['enfasis] nm emphasis, stress

enfático, -a [en'fatiko, a] adj emphatic

enfermar [enfer'mar] vt to make ill ♦ vi to fall ill, be taken ill

enfermedad [enferme'ðað] nf illness
▶ **enfermedad venérea** venereal disease

enfermera [enfer'mera] nf nurse

enfermería [enferme'ria] nf infirmary; (de colegio etc) sick bay

enfermero [enfer'mero] nm (male) nurse

enfermizo, -a [enfer'miθo, a] adj (persona) sickly, unhealthy; (fig) unhealthy

enfermo, -a [en'fermo, a] adj ill, sick ♦ nm/f invalid, sick person; (en hospital) patient; **caer** o **ponerse ~** to fall ill

enfocar [enfo'kar] vt (foto etc) to focus; (problema etc) to approach

enfoque etc [en'foke] vb ver **enfocar**
♦ nm focus

enfrentar [enfren'tar] vt (peligro) to face (up to), confront; (oponer) to bring face to face; **enfrentarse** vr (dos personas) to face o confront each other; (DEPORTE: dos equipos) to meet; **enfrentarse a** o **con** to face up to, confront

enfrente [en'frente] adv opposite; **la casa de ~** the house opposite, the house across the street; **~ de** opposite, facing

enfriamiento [enfria'mjento] nm chilling, refrigeration; (MED) cold, chill

enfriar [enfri'ar] vt (alimentos) to cool, chill; (algo caliente) to cool down;

enfriarse vr to cool down; (MED) to catch a chill; (amistad) to cool

enfurecer [enfure'θer] vt to enrage, madden; **enfurecerse** vr to become furious, fly into a rage; (mar) to get rough

enganchar [engan'tʃar] vt to hook; (dos vagones) to hitch up; (TEC) to couple, connect; (MIL) to recruit; **engancharse** vr (MIL) to enlist, join up

enganche [en'gantʃe] nm hook; (ESP TEC) coupling, connection; (acto) hooking (up); (MIL) recruitment, enlistment; (MÉX) depósito) deposit

engañar [enga'ɲar] vt to deceive; (estafar) to cheat, swindle; **engañarse** vr (equivocarse) to be wrong; (disimular la verdad) to deceive o.s.

engaño [en'gaɲo] nm deceit; (estafa) trick, swindle; (error) mistake, misunderstanding; (ilusión) delusion ❏ **engañoso, -a** adj (tramposo) crooked; (mentiroso) dishonest, deceitful; (aspecto) deceptive; (consejo) misleading

engatusar [engatu'sar] (fam) vt to coax

engendro [en'xendro] nm (BIO) foetus; (fig) monstrosity

englobar [englo'βar] vt to include, comprise

engordar [engor'ðar] vt to fatten ♦ vi to get fat, put on weight

engorroso, -a [engo'rroso, a] adj bothersome, trying

engranaje [engra'naxe] nm (AUTO) gear

engrasar [engra'sar] vt (TEC: poner grasa) to grease; (: lubricar) to lubricate, oil; (manchar) to make greasy

engreído, -a [engre'iðo, a] adj vain, conceited

enhebrar [ene'βrar] vt to thread

enhorabuena [enora'βwena] excl ¡~! congratulations! ♦ nf: **dar la ~ a** to congratulate

enigma [e'niɣma] nm enigma; (problema) puzzle; (misterio) mystery

enjambre [en'xambre] nm swarm

enjaular [enxau'lar] vt to put in a cage; (fam) to jail, lock up

enjuagar [enxwa'ɣar] vt (ropa) to rinse (out)

enjuague etc [en'xwaɣe] vb ver **enjuagar ♦** nm (MED) mouthwash; (de ropa) rinse, rinsing

enlace [en'laθe] nm link, connection; (relación) relationship; (tb: ~ **matrimonial**) marriage; (de carretera, trenes) connection ▶ **enlace sindical** shop steward

enlatado, -a [enla'taðo, a] adj (alimentos, productos) tinned, canned

enlazar [enla'θar] vt (unir con lazos) to bind together; (atar) to tie; (conectar) to link, connect; (LAm: caballo) to lasso

enloquecer [enloke'θer] vt to drive mad ♦ vi to go mad

enmarañar [enmara'ɲar] vt (enredar) to tangle (up), entangle; (complicar) to complicate; (confundir) to confuse

enmarcar [enmar'kar] vt (cuadro) to frame

enmascarar [enmaska'rar] vt to mask; **enmascararse** vr to put on a mask

enmendar [enmen'dar] vt to emend, correct; (constitución etc) to amend; (comportamiento) to reform; **enmendarse** vr to reform, mend one's ways ❏ **enmienda** nf correction; amendment; reform

enmudecer [enmuðe'θer] vi (perder el habla) to fall silent; (guardar silencio) to remain silent

ennoblecer [ennoβle'θer] vt to ennoble

enojado, -a [LAm] [eno'xaðo, a] adj angry

enojar [eno'xar] vt (encolerizar) to anger; (disgustar) to annoy, upset; **enojarse** vr to get angry; to get annoyed

enojo [e'noxo] nm (cólera) anger; (irritación) annoyance

enorme [e'norme] adj enormous, huge; (fig) monstrous

enredadera [enreða'ðera] nf (BOT) creeper, climbing plant

enredar [enre'ðar] vt (cables, hilos etc) to tangle (up), entangle; (situación) to complicate, confuse; (meter cizaña) to sow discord among o between; (implicar) to embroil, implicate; **enredarse** vr to get entangled, get tangled (up); (situación) to get complicated; (persona) to get embroiled; (LAm: fam) to meddle

enredo [en'reðo] nm (maraña) tangle; (confusión) mix-up, confusion; (intriga) intrigue

enriquecer [enrike'θer] vt to make rich, enrich; **enriquecerse** vr to get rich

enrojecer [enroxe'θer] vt to redden ♦ vi (persona) to blush; **enrojecerse** vr to blush

enrollar [enro'ʎar] vt to roll (up), wind (up)

ensalada [ensa'laða] nf salad ❏ **ensaladilla (rusa)** nf Russian salad

ensanchar [ensan'tʃar] vt (hacer más ancho) to widen; (agrandar) to enlarge, expand; (COSTURA) to let out; **ensancharse** vr to get wider, expand

ensayar [ensa'jar] vt to test, try (out); (TEATRO) to rehearse

ensayo [en'sajo] nm test, trial; (QUÍM) experiment; (TEATRO) rehearsal; (DEPORTE) try; (ESCOL, LITERATURA) essay

enseguida [ense'ɣiða] adv at once, right away

ensenada [ense'naða] nf inlet, cove

enseñanza [ense'ɲanθa] nf (educación) education; (acción) teaching; (doctrina) teaching, doctrine ▶ **enseñanza (de) primaria/secundaria** elementary/secondary education

enseñar [ense'nar] vt (educar) to teach; (mostrar, señalar) to show

enseres [en'seres] nmpl belongings

ensuciar [ensu'θjar] vt (manchar) to dirty, soil; (fig) to defile; **ensuciarse** vr to get dirty; (bebé) to dirty one's nappy

entablar [enta'βlar] vt (recubrir) to board (up); (AJEDREZ, DAMAS) to set up; (conversación) to strike up; (JUR) to draw ♦ vi to draw

ente ['ente] nm (organización) body, organization; (fam: persona) odd character

entender [enten'der] vt (comprender) to understand; (darse cuenta) to realize ♦ vi to understand; (creer) to think, believe; **entenderse** vr (comprenderse) to be understood; (ponerse de acuerdo) to agree, reach an agreement; **~ de** to know all about; **~ algo de** to know a little about; **~ en** to deal with, have to do with; **~ mal** to misunderstand; **entenderse con algn** (llevarse bien) to get on o along with sb; **entenderse mal** (dos personas) to get on badly

entendido, -a [enten'diðo, a] adj (comprendido) understood; (hábil) skilled; (inteligente) knowledgeable ♦ nm/f (experto) expert ♦ excl agreed! ☐ **entendimiento** nm (comprensión) understanding; (inteligencia) mind, intellect; (juicio) judgement

enterado, -a [ente'raðo, a] adj well-informed; **estar ~ de** to know about, be aware of

enteramente [entera'mente] adv entirely, completely

enterar [ente'rar] vt (informar) to inform, tell; **enterarse** vr to find out, get to know

enterito [ente'rito] nm boiler suit (BRIT), overalls (US)

entero, -a [en'tero, a] adj (total) whole, entire; (fig: honesto) honest; (: firme) firm, resolute ♦ nm (COM: punto) point

enterrar [ente'rrar] vt to bury

entidad [enti'ðað] nf (empresa) firm, company; (organismo) body; (sociedad) society; (FILOSOFÍA) entity

entiendo etc vb ver **entender**

entierro [en'tjerro] nm (acción) burial; (funeral) funeral

entonación [entona'θjon] nf (LING) intonation

entonar [ento'nar] vt (canción) to intone; (colores) to tone; (MED) to tone up ♦ vi to be in tune

entonces [en'tonθes] adv then, at that time; **desde ~** since then; **en aquel ~** at that time; **(pues) ~** and so

entornar [entor'nar] vt (puerta, ventana) to half-close, leave ajar; (los ojos) to screw up

entorpecer [entorpe'θer] vt (entendimiento) to dull; (impedir) to obstruct, hinder; (: tránsito) to slow down, delay

entrada [en'traða] nf (acción) entry, access; (sitio) entrance, way in; (INFORM) input; (COM) receipts pl, takings pl; (CULIN) starter; (DEPORTE) innings sg; (TEATRO) house, audience; (billete) ticket; **entradas y salidas** (COM) income and expenditure; **de ~** from the outset ▸ **entrada de aire** (TEC) air intake o inlet

entrado, -a [en'traðo, a] adj: **~ en años** elderly; **una vez ~ el verano** in the summer(time), when summer comes

entramparse [entram'parse] vr to get into debt

entrante [en'trante] adj next, coming; **mes/año ~** next month/year ☐ **entrantes** nmpl starters

entraña [en'traɲa] nf (fig: centro) heart, core; (raíz) root; **entrañas** nfpl (ANAT) entrails; (fig) heart sg ☐ **entrañable** adj close, intimate ☐ **entrañar** vt to entail

entrar [en'trar] vt (introducir) to bring in; (INFORM) to input ♦ vi (meterse) to go in, come in, enter; (comenzar): **~**

diciendo to begin by saying; **hacer ~** to show in; **me entró sed/sueño** I started to feel thirsty/sleepy; **no me entra** I can't get the hang of it

entre ['entre] prep (dos) between; (más de dos) among(st)

entreabrir [entrea'βrir] vt to half-open, open halfway

entrecejo [entre'θexo] nm: **fruncir el ~** to frown

entredicho [entre'ðitʃo] nm (JUR) injunction; **poner en ~** to cast doubt on; **estar en ~** to be in doubt

entrega [en'treɣa] nf (de mercancías) delivery; (de novela etc) instalment ❑ **entregar** [entre'ɣar] vt (dar) to hand (over), deliver; **entregarse** vr (rendirse) to surrender, give in, submit; (dedicarse) to devote o.s.

entremeses [entre'meses] nmpl hors d'œuvres

entremeter [entreme'ter] vt to insert, put in; **entremeterse** vr to meddle, interfere ❑ **entremetido, -a** adj meddling, interfering

entremezclar [entremeθ'klar] vt to intermingle; **entremezclarse** vr to intermingle

entrenador, a [entrena'ðor, a] nm/f trainer, coach

entrenarse [entre'narse] vr to train

entrepierna [entre'pjerna] nf crotch

entresuelo [entre'swelo] nm mezzanine

entretanto [entre'tanto] adv meanwhile, meantime

entretecho (CS) [entre'tetʃo] nm attic

entretejer [entrete'xer] vt to interweave

entretener [entrete'ner] vt (divertir) to entertain, amuse; (detener) to hold up, delay; **entretenerse** vr (divertirse) to amuse o.s.; (retrasarse) to delay, linger ❑ **entretenido, -a** adj entertaining, amusing ❑ **entretenimiento** nm entertainment, amusement

entrever [entre'βer] vt to glimpse, catch a glimpse of

entrevista [entre'βista] nf interview ❑ **entrevistar** vt to interview; **entrevistarse** vr to have an interview

entristecer [entriste'θer] vt to sadden, grieve; **entristecerse** vr to grow sad

entrometerse [entrome'terse] vr: ~ **(en)** to interfere (in o with)

entumecer [entume'θer] vt to numb, benumb; **entumecerse** vr (por el frío) to go o become numb

enturbiar [entur'βjar] vt (el agua) to make cloudy; (fig) to confuse; **enturbiarse** vr (oscurecerse) to become cloudy; (fig) to get confused, become obscure

entusiasmar [entusjas'mar] vt to excite, fill with enthusiasm; (gustar mucho) to delight; **entusiasmarse** vr: **entusiasmarse o con o por** to get enthusiastic o excited about

entusiasmo [entu'sjasmo] nm enthusiasm; (excitación) excitement

entusiasta [entu'sjasta] adj enthusiastic ♦ nm/f enthusiast

enumerar [enume'rar] vt to enumerate

envainar [embai'nar] vt to sheathe

envalentonar [embalento'nar] vt to give courage to; **envalentonarse** vr (pey: jactarse) to boast, brag

envasar [emba'sar] vt (empaquetar) to pack, wrap; (enfrascar) to bottle; (enlatar) to can; (embolsar) to pocket

envase [em'base] nm (en paquete) packing, wrapping; (en botella) bottling; (en lata) canning; (recipiente) container; (paquete) package; (botella) bottle; (lata) tin (BRIT), can

envejecer [embexe'θer] vt to make old, age ♦ vi (volverse viejo) to grow old; (parecer viejo) to age

envenenar [embene'nar] vt to poison; (fig) to embitter

envergadura [emberɣaˈðura] nf (fig) scope, compass

enviar [emˈbjar] vt to send; ~ **un mensaje a algn** (por movil) to text sb, to send sb a text message

enviciarse [embiˈθjarse] vr: ~ **(con)** to get addicted (to)

envidia [emˈbiðja] nf envy; **tener ~ a** to envy, be jealous of ❏ **envidiar** vt to envy

envío [emˈbio] nm (acción) sending; (de mercancías) consignment; (de dinero) remittance

enviudar [embjuˈðar] vi to be widowed

envoltura [embolˈtura] nf (cobertura) cover; (embalaje) wrapper, wrapping ❏ **envoltorio** nm package

envolver [embolˈβer] vt to wrap (up); (cubrir) to cover; (enemigo) to surround; (implicar) to involve, implicate

envuelto [emˈbwelto] pp de **envolver**

enyesar [enjeˈsar] vt (pared) to plaster; (MED) to put in plaster

enzarzarse [enθarˈθarse] vr: ~ **en** (pelea) to get mixed up in; (disputa) to get involved in

épica [ˈepika] nf epic

epidemia [epiˈðemja] nf epidemic

epilepsia [epiˈlepsja] nf epilepsy

episodio [epiˈsoðjo] nm episode

época [ˈepoka] nf period, time; (HIST) age, epoch; **hacer época** to be epoch-making

equilibrar [ekiliˈβrar] vt to balance ❏ **equilibrio** nm balance, equilibrium; **mantener/perder el equilibrio** to keep/lose one's balance ❏ **equilibrista** nmf (funámbulo) tightrope walker; (acróbata) acrobat

equipaje [ekiˈpaxe] nm luggage; (avíos) hacer el ~ to pack ▶ **equipaje de mano** hand luggage

equipar [ekiˈpar] vt (proveer) to equip

equipararse [ekipaˈrarse] vr: ~ **con** to be on a level with

equipo [eˈkipo] nm (conjunto de cosas) equipment; (DEPORTE) team; (de obreros) shift

equis [ˈekis] nf inv (the letter) X

equitación [ekitaˈθjon] nf horse riding

equivalente [ekiβaˈlente] adj, nm equivalent

equivaler [ekiβaˈler] vi to be equivalent o equal

equivocación [ekiβokaˈθjon] nf mistake, error

equivocado, -a [ekiβoˈkaðo, a] adj wrong, mistaken

equivocarse [ekiβoˈkarse] vr to be wrong, make a mistake; ~ **de camino** to take the wrong road

era [ˈera] vb ver **ser** ✦ nf era, age

erais vb ver **ser**

éramos [ˈeramos] vb ver **ser**

eran [ˈeran] vb ver **ser**

eras [ˈeras] vb ver **ser**

erección [erekˈθjon] nf erection

eres vb ver **ser**

erigir [eriˈxir] vt to erect, build; **erigirse** vr: **erigirse en** to set o.s. up as

erizo [eˈriθo] nm (ZOOL) hedgehog ▶ **erizo de mar** sea-urchin

ermita [erˈmita] nf hermitage ❏ **ermitaño, -a** [ermiˈtaɲo, a] nm/f hermit

erosión [eroˈsjon] nf erosion

erosionar [erosjoˈnar] vt to erode

erótico, -a [eˈrotiko, a] adj erotic ❏ **erotismo** nm eroticism

errante [eˈrrante] adj wandering, errant

erróneo, -a [eˈrroneo, a] adj (equivocado) wrong, mistaken

error [eˈrror] nm error, mistake; (INFORM) bug ▶ **error de imprenta** misprint

eructar [erukˈtar] vt to belch, burp

erudito, -a [eru'ðito, a] *adj* erudite, learned

erupción [erup'θjon] *nf* eruption; (MED) rash

es [es] *vb ver* **ser**

esa ['esa] (*pl* **esas**) *adj demos ver* **ese**

ésa ['esa] (*pl* **ésas**) *pron ver* **ése**

esbelto, -a [es'βelto, a] *adj* slim, slender

esbozo [es'βoθo] *nm* sketch, outline

escabeche [eska'βetʃe] *nm* brine; (*de aceitunas etc*) pickle; **en ~** pickled

escabullirse [eskaβu'ʎirse] *vr* to slip away, to clear out

escafandra [eska'fandra] *nf* (*buzo*) diving suit; (*escafandra espacial*) space suit

escala [es'kala] *nf* (*proporción*, MÚS) scale; (*de mano*) ladder; (AVIAC) stopover; **hacer ~ en** to stop o call in at

escalafón [eskala'fon] *nm* (*escala de salarios*) salary scale, wage scale

escalar [eska'lar] *vt* to climb, scale

escalera [eska'lera] *nf* stairs *pl*, staircase; (*escala*) ladder; (NAIPES) run
  ▶ **escalera de caracol** spiral staircase
  ▶ **escalera de incendios** fire escape
  ▶ **escalera mecánica** escalator

escalfar [eskal'far] *vt* (*huevos*) to poach

escalinata [eskali'nata] *nf* staircase

escalofriante [eskalo'frjante] *adj* chilling

escalofrío [eskalo'frio] *nm* (MED) chill; **escalofríos** *nmpl* (*fig*) shivers

escalón [eska'lon] *nm* step, stair; (*de escalera*) rung

escalope [eska'lope] *nm* (CULIN) escalope

escama [es'kama] *nf* (*de pez, serpiente*) scale; (*de jabón*) flake; (*fig*) resentment

escampar [eskam'par] *vb impers* to stop raining

escandalizar [eskandali'θar] *vt* to scandalize, shock; **escandalizarse** *vr* to be shocked; (*ofenderse*) to be offended

escándalo [es'kandalo] *nm* scandal; (*alboroto, tumulto*) row, uproar
  ❏ **escandaloso, -a** *adj* scandalous, shocking

escandinavo, -a [eskandi'naβo, a] *adj, nm/f* Scandinavian

escaño [es'kaɲo] *nm* bench; (POL) seat

escapar [eska'par] *vi* (*gen*) to escape, run away; (DEPORTE) to break away; **escaparse** *vr* to escape, get away; (*agua, gas*) to leak (out)

escaparate [eskapa'rate] *nm* shop window

escape [es'kape] *nm* (*de agua, gas*) leak; (*de motor*) exhaust

escarabajo [eskara'βaxo] *nm* beetle

escaramuza [eskara'muθa] *nf* skirmish

escarbar [eskar'βar] *vt* (*tierra*) to scratch

escarceos [eskar'θeos] *nmpl*: **en mis ~ con la política ...** in my dealings with politics ... ▶ **escarceos amorosos** love affairs

escarcha [es'kartʃa] *nf* frost

escarchado, -a [eskar'tʃaðo, a] *adj* (CULIN: *fruta*) crystallized

escarlatina [eskarla'tina] *nf* scarlet fever

escarmentar [eskarmen'tar] *vt* to punish severely ♦ *vi* to learn one's lesson

escarmiento *etc* [eskar'mjento] *vb ver* **escarmentar** ♦ *nm* (*ejemplo*) lesson; (*castigo*) punishment

escarola [eska'rola] *nf* endive

escarpado, -a [eskar'paðo, a] *adj* (*pendiente*) sheer, steep; (*rocas*) craggy

escasear [eskase'ar] *vi* to be scarce

escasez [eska'seθ] *nf* (*falta*) shortage, scarcity; (*pobreza*) poverty

escaso, -a [es'kaso, a] *adj* (*poco*) scarce; (*raro*) rare; (*ralo*) thin, sparse; (*limitado*) limited

escatimar [eskati'mar] *vt* to skimp (on), to be sparing with

escayola [eska'jola] *nf* plaster

escena [es'θena] nf scene □ **escenario** [esθe'narjo] nm (TEATRO) stage; (CINE) set; (fig) scene □ **escenografía** nf set design

⚠ No confundir **escenario** con la palabra inglesa *scenery*.

escéptico, -a [es'θeptiko, a] adj sceptical ♦ nm/f sceptic

esclarecer [esklare'θer] vt (misterio, problema) to shed light on

esclavitud [esklaβi'tuð] nf slavery

esclavizar [esklaβi'θar] vt to enslave

esclavo, -a [es'klaβo, a] nm/f slave

escoba [es'koβa] nf broom □ **escobilla** nf brush

escocer [esko'θer] vi to burn, sting; **escocerse** vr to chafe, get chafed

escocés, -esa [esko'θes, esa] adj Scottish ♦ nm/f Scotsman(-woman), Scot

Escocia [es'koθja] nf Scotland

escoger [esko'xer] vt to choose, pick, select □ **escogido, -a** adj chosen, selected

escolar [esko'lar] adj school cpd ♦ nmf schoolboy(-girl), pupil

escollo [es'koʎo] nm (obstáculo) pitfall

escolta [es'kolta] nf escort □ **escoltar** vt to escort

escombros [es'kombros] nmpl (basura) rubbish sg; (restos) debris sg

esconder [eskon'der] vt to hide, conceal; **esconderse** vr to hide □ **escondidas** (LAm) nfpl: **a escondidas** secretly □ **escondite** nm hiding place; (ESP: juego) hide-and-seek □ **escondrijo** nm hiding place, hideout

escopeta [esko'peta] nf shotgun

escoria [es'korja] nf (de alto horno) slag; (fig) scum, dregs pl

Escorpio [es'korpjo] nm Scorpio

escorpión [eskor'pjon] nm scorpion

escotado, -a [esko'taðo, a] adj low-cut

escote [es'kote] nm (de vestido) low neck; **pagar a ~** to share the expenses

escotilla [esko'tiʎa] nf (NÁUT) hatch(way)

escozor [esko'θor] nm (dolor) sting(ing)

escribir [eskri'βir] vt, vi to write; **~ a máquina** to type; **¿cómo se escribe?** how do you spell it?

escrito, -a [es'krito, a] pp de **escribir** ♦ nm (documento) document; (manuscrito) text, manuscript; **por ~** in writing

escritor, a [eskri'tor, a] nm/f writer

escritorio [eskri'torjo] nm desk

escritura [eskri'tura] nf (acción) writing; (caligrafía) (hand)writing; (JUR: documento) deed

escrúpulo [es'krupulo] nm scruple; (minuciosidad) scrupulousness □ **escrupuloso, -a** adj scrupulous

escrutinio [eskru'tinjo] nm (examen atento) scrutiny; (POL: recuento de votos) count(ing)

escuadra [es'kwaðra] nf (MIL etc) squad; (NÁUT) squadron; (flota: de coches etc) fleet □ **escuadrilla** nf (de aviones) squadron; (LAm: de obreros) gang

escuadrón [eskwa'ðron] nm squadron

escuálido, -a [es'kwaliðo, a] adj skinny, scraggy; (sucio) squalid

escuchar [esku'tʃar] vt to listen to ♦ vi to listen

escudo [es'kuðo] nm shield

escuela [es'kwela] nf school ▶ **escuela de artes y oficios** (ESP) = technical college ▶ **escuela de choferes** (LAm) driving school ▶ **escuela de manejo** (MÉX) driving school

escueto, -a [es'kweto, a] adj plain; (estilo) simple

escuincle, -a [es'kwinkle, a] (MÉX: fam) nm/f kid

esculpir [eskul'pir] vt to sculpt; (grabar) to engrave; (tallar) to carve □ **escultor, a** nm/f sculptor(-tress) □ **escultura** nf sculpture

escupidera [eskupi'ðera] nf spittoon

escupir [esku'pir] vt, vi to spit (out)

escurreplatos [eskurre'platos] (ESP) nm inv draining board (BRIT), drainboard (US)

escurridero (LAm) nm draining board (BRIT), drainboard (US)

escurridizo, -a [eskurri'ðiθo, a] adj slippery

escurridor [eskurri'ðor] nm colander

escurrir [esku'rrir] vt (ropa) to wring out; (verduras, platos) to drain ♦ vi (líquidos) to drip; **escurrirse** vr (secarse) to drain; (resbalarse) to slip, slide; (escaparse) to slip away

ese¹ ['ese] (f **esa**, pl **esos, esas**) adj demos (sg) that; (pl) those

ése² ['ese] (f **ésa**, pl **ésos, ésas**) pron (sg) that (one); (pl) those (ones); **ése ... éste ...** the former ... the latter ...; **no me vengas con ésas** don't give me any more of that nonsense

esencia [e'senθja] nf essence ❑ **esencial** adj essential

esfera [es'fera] nf sphere; (de reloj) face ❑ **esférico, -a** adj spherical

esforzarse [esfor'θarse] vr to exert o.s., make an effort

esfuerzo etc [es'fwerθo] vb ver **esforzarse** ♦ nm effort

esfumarse [esfu'marse] vr (apoyo, esperanzas) to fade away

esgrima [es'ɣrima] nf fencing

esguince [es'ɣinθe] nm (MED) sprain

eslabón [esla'βon] nm link

eslip [ez'lip] nm pants pl (BRIT), briefs pl

eslovaco, -a [eslo'βako, a] adj, nm/f Slovak, Slovakian ♦ nm (LING) Slovak, Slovakian

Eslovaquia [eslo'βakja] nf Slovakia

esmalte [es'malte] nm enamel ▶ **esmalte de uñas** nail varnish o polish

esmeralda [esme'ralda] nf emerald

esmerarse [esme'rarse] vr (aplicarse) to take great pains, exercise great care; (afanarse) to work hard

esmero [es'mero] nm (great) care

esnob [es'nob] (pl **esnobs**) adj (persona) snobbish ♦ nmf snob

eso ['eso] pron that, that thing o matter; **~ de su coche** that business about his car; **~ de al cine** all that about going to the cinema; **a ~ de las cinco** at about five o'clock; **en ~** thereupon, at that point; **~ es** that's it; **¡~ sí que es vida!** now that is really living!; **por ~ te lo dije** that's why I told you; **y ~ que llovía** in spite of the fact that it was raining

esos ['esos] adj demos ver **ese**

ésos ['esos] pron ver **ése**

espabilar etc [espaβi'lar] = **despabilar** etc

espacial [espa'θjal] adj (del espacio) space cpd

espaciar [espa'θjar] vt to space (out)

espacio [es'paθjo] nm space; (MÚS) interval; (RADIO, TV) programme (BRIT), program (US); **el ~ space ▶ espacio aéreo/exterior** air/outer space ❑ **espacioso, -a** adj spacious, roomy

espada [es'paða] nf sword; **espadas** nfpl (NAIPES) spades

espaguetis [espa'ɣetis] nmpl spaghetti sg

espalda [es'palda] nf (gen) back; **espaldas** nfpl (hombros) shoulders; **a espaldas de algn** behind sb's back; **estar de espaldas** to have one's back turned; **tenderse de espaldas** to lie (down) on one's back; **volver la ~ a algn** to cold-shoulder sb

espantajo [espan'taxo] nm = **espantapájaros**

espantapájaros [espanta'paxaros] nm inv scarecrow

espantar [espan'tar] vt (asustar) to frighten, scare; (ahuyentar) to frighten off; (asombrar) to horrify, appal;

espantarse vr to get frightened o scared; to be appalled

espanto [es'panto] nm (susto) fright; (terror) terror; (asombro) astonishment ▫ **espantoso, -a** adj frightening; terrifying; astonishing

España [es'paŋa] nf Spain ▫ **español, a** adj Spanish ♦ nm/f Spaniard ♦ nm (LING) Spanish

esparadrapo [espara'ðrapo] nm (sticking) plaster (BRIT), adhesive tape (US)

esparcir [espar'θir] vt to spread; (diseminar) to scatter; **esparcirse** vr to spread (out), to scatter; (divertirse) to enjoy o.s.

espárrago [es'parraɣo] nm asparagus

esparto [es'parto] nm esparto (grass)

espasmo [es'pasmo] nm spasm

espátula [es'patula] nf spatula

especia [es'peθja] nf spice

especial [espe'θjal] adj special ▫ **especialidad** nf speciality (BRIT), specialty (US)

especie [es'peθje] nf (BIO) species; (clase) kind, sort; **en ~** in kind

especificar [espeθifi'kar] vt to specify ▫ **específico, -a** adj specific

espécimen [es'peθimen] (pl **especímenes**) nm specimen

espectáculo [espek'takulo] nm (gen) spectacle; (TEATRO etc) show

espectador, a [espekta'ðor, a] nm/f spectator

especular [espeku'lar] vt, vi to speculate

espejismo [espe'xismo] nm mirage

espejo [es'pexo] nm mirror ▶ **espejo retrovisor** rear-view mirror

espeluznante [espeluθ'nante] adj horrifying, hair-raising

espera [es'pera] nf (pausa, intervalo) wait; (JUR: plazo) respite; **en ~ de** waiting for; (con esperanza) expecting

esperanza [espe'ranθa] nf (confianza) hope; (expectativa) expectation; **hay pocas esperanzas de que venga** there is little prospect of his coming ▶ **esperanza de vida** life expectancy

esperar [espe'rar] vt (aguardar) to wait for; (tener expectativa de) to expect; (desear) to hope for ♦ vi to wait; to expect; to hope; **hacer ~ a algn** to keep sb waiting; **~ un bebé** to be expecting (a baby)

esperma [es'perma] nf sperm

espeso, -a [es'peso, a] adj thick ▫ **espesor** nm thickness

espía [es'pia] nmf spy ▫ **espiar** vt (observar) to spy on

espiga [es'piɣa] nf (BOT: de trigo etc) ear

espigón [espi'ɣon] nm (BOT) ear; (NÁUT) breakwater

espina [es'pina] nf thorn; (de pez) bone ▶ **espina dorsal** (ANAT) spine

espinaca [espi'naka] nf spinach

espinazo [espi'naθo] nm (ANAT) spine, backbone

espinilla [espi'niʎa] nf (ANAT: tibia) shin(bone); (grano) blackhead

espinoso, -a [espi'noso, a] adj (planta) thorny, prickly; (asunto) difficult

espionaje [espjo'naxe] nm spying, espionage

espiral [espi'ral] adj, nf spiral

espirar [espi'rar] vt to breathe out, exhale

espiritista [espiri'tista] adj, nmf spiritualist

espíritu [es'piritu] nm spirit ▶ **Espíritu Santo** Holy Ghost o Spirit ▫ **espiritual** adj spiritual

espléndido, -a [es'plendiðo, a] adj (magnífico) magnificent, splendid; (generoso) generous

esplendor [esplen'dor] nm splendour

espolvorear [espolβore'ar] vt to dust, sprinkle

esponja [es'ponxa] nf sponge; (fig) sponger ▫ **esponjoso, -a** adj spongy

espontaneidad [espontanei'ðað] *nf* spontaneity ❑ **espontáneo, -a** *adj* spontaneous

esposa [es'posa] *nf* wife; **esposas** *nfpl* handcuffs ❑ **esposar** *vt* to handcuff

esposo [es'poso] *nm* husband

espray [es'prai] *nm* spray

espuela [es'pwela] *nf* spur

espuma [es'puma] *nf* foam; (*de cerveza*) froth, head; (*de jabón*) lather
▶ **espuma de afeitar** shaving foam
❑ **espumadera** *nf* (*utensilio*) skimmer
❑ **espumoso, -a** *adj* frothy, foamy; (*vino*) sparkling

esqueleto [eske'leto] *nm* skeleton

esquema [es'kema] *nm* (*diagrama*) diagram; (*dibujo*) plan; (*FILOSOFÍA*) schema

esquí [es'ki] (*pl* ~**s**) *nm* (*objeto*) ski; (*DEPORTE*) skiing ▶ **esquí acuático** water-skiing ❑ **esquiar** *vi* to ski

esquilar [eski'lar] *vt* to shear

esquimal [eski'mal] *adj, nmf* Eskimo

esquina [es'kina] *nf* corner
❑ **esquinazo** [eski'naθo] *nm*: **dar esquinazo a algn** to give sb the slip

esquirol [eski'rol] (*ESP*) *nm* strikebreaker, scab

esquivar [eski'βar] *vt* to avoid

esta ['esta] *adj demos ver* **este²**

está [es'ta] *vb ver* **estar**

ésta ['esta] *pron ver* **éste**

estabilidad [estaβili'ðað] *nf* stability ❑ **estable** *adj* stable

establecer [estaβle'θer] *vt* to establish; **establecerse** *vr* to establish o.s.; (*echar raíces*) to settle (down) ❑ **establecimiento** *nm* establishment

establo [es'taβlo] *nm* (*AGR*) stable

estaca [es'taka] *nf* stake, post; (*de tienda de campaña*) peg

estacada [esta'kaða] *nf* (*cerca*) fence, fencing; (*palenque*) stockade

estación [esta'θjon] *nf* station; (*del año*) season ▶ **estación balnearia** seaside resort ▶ **estación de autobuses** bus station ▶ **estación de servicio** service station

estacionamiento [estaθjona'mjento] *nm* (*AUTO*) parking; (*MIL*) stationing

estacionar [estaθjo'nar] *vt* (*AUTO*) to park; (*MIL*) to station

estadía (*LAm*) [esta'ðia] *nf* stay

estadio [esta'ðjo] *nm* (*fase*) stage, phase; (*DEPORTE*) stadium

estadista [esta'ðista] *nm* (*POL*) statesman; (*MAT*) statistician

estadística [esta'ðistika] *nf* figure, statistic; (*ciencia*) statistics *sg*

estado [es'taðo] *nm* (*POL: condición*) state; **estar en** ~ to be pregnant
▶ **estado civil** marital status
▶ **estado de ánimo** state of mind
▶ **estado de cuenta** bank statement
▶ **estado de sitio** state of siege
▶ **estado mayor** staff ▶ **Estados Unidos** United States (of America)

estadounidense [estaðouni'ðense] *adj* United States *cpd*, American ♦ *nmf* American

estafa [es'tafa] *nf* swindle, trick ❑ **estafar** *vt* to swindle, defraud

estáis *vb ver* **estar**

estallar [esta'ʎar] *vi* to burst; (*bomba*) to explode, go off; (*epidemia, guerra, rebelión*) to break out; ~ **en llanto** to burst into tears ❑ **estallido** *nm* explosion; (*fig*) outbreak

estampa [es'tampa] *nf* print, engraving ❑ **estampado, -a** [estam'paðo, a] *adj* printed ♦ *nm* (*impresión: acción*) printing; (*: efecto*) print; (*marca*) stamping ❑ **estampar** [estam'par] *vt* (*imprimir*) to print; (*marcar*) to stamp; (*metal*) to engrave; (*poner sello en*) to stamp; (*fig*) to stamp, imprint

estampida [estam'piða] *nf* stampede

estampido [estam'piðo] *nm* bang, report

estampilla (*LAm*) [estam'piʎa] *nf* (postage) stamp

están [es'tan] *vb ver* **estar**

estancado, -a [estaŋ'kaðo, a] *adj* stagnant

estancar [estaŋ'kar] *vt* (*aguas*) to hold up, hold back; (*COM*) to monopolize; (*fig*) to block, hold up; **estancarse** *vr* to stagnate

estancia [es'tanθja] *nf* (*ESP, MÉX: permanencia*) stay; (*sala*) room; (*RPl: de ganado*) ranch ❏ **estanciero** (*RPl*) *nm* farmer, rancher

estanco, -a [es'tanko, a] *adj* watertight ♦ *nm* tobacconist's (shop), cigar store (*US*)

ESTANCO

Cigarettes, tobacco, postage stamps and official forms are all sold under state monopoly in shops called **estancos**. Although tobacco can also be bought in bars and quioscos they are generally more expensive.

estándar [es'tandar] *adj, nm* standard

estandarte [estan'darte] *nm* banner, standard

estanque [es'tanke] *nm* (*lago*) pool, pond; (*AGR*) reservoir

estanquero, -a [estaŋ'kero, a] *nm/f* tobacconist

estante [es'tante] *nm* (*armario*) rack, stand; (*biblioteca*) bookcase; (*anaquel*) shelf ❏ **estantería** *nf* shelving, shelves *pl*

estar

PALABRA CLAVE

[es'tar] *vi*

1 (*posición*) to be; **está en la plaza** it's in the square; **¿está Juan?** is Juan in?; **estamos a 30 km de Junín** we're 30

kms from Junín

2 (+ *adj: estado*) to be; **estar enfermo** to be ill; **está muy elegante** he's looking very smart; **¿cómo estás?** how are you keeping?

3 (+ *gerundio*) to be; **estoy leyendo** I'm reading

4 (*uso pasivo*): **está condenado a muerte** he's been condemned to death; **está envasado en ...** it's packed in ...

5 (*con fechas*): **¿a cuántos estamos?** what's the date today?; **estamos a 5 de mayo** it's the 5th of May

6 (*locuciones*): **¿estamos?** (*¿de acuerdo?*) okay?; (*¿listo?*) ready?

7: **estar de: estar de vacaciones/ viaje** to be on holiday/away o on a trip; **está de camarero** he's working as a waiter

8: **estar para: está para salir** he's about to leave; **no estoy para bromas** I'm not in the mood for jokes

9: **estar por** (*propuesta etc*) to be in favour of; (*persona etc*) to support, side with; **está por limpiar** it still has to be cleaned

10: **estar sin: estar sin dinero** to have no money; **está sin terminar** it isn't finished yet

♦ **estarse** *vr*: **se estuvo en la cama toda la tarde** he stayed in bed all afternoon

estas ['estas] *adj demos ver* **este²**

éstas ['estas] *pron ver* **éste**

estatal [esta'tal] *adj* state *cpd*

estático, -a [es'tatiko, a] *adj* static

estatua [es'tatwa] *nf* statue

estatura [esta'tura] *nf* stature, height

este¹ ['este] *nm* east

este² ['este] (*f* **esta**, *pl* **estos, estas**) *adj demos* (*sg*) this; (*pl*) these

esté etc [es'te] vb ver **estar**

éste ['este] (f **ésta**, pl **éstos, éstas**) pron (sg) this (one); (pl) these (ones); **ése ... éste ...** the former ... the latter ...

estén etc [es'ten] vb ver **estar**

estepa [es'tepa] nf (GEO) steppe

estera [es'tera] nf mat(ting)

estéreo [es'tereo] adj inv, nm stereo □ **estereotipo** nm stereotype

estéril [es'teril] adj sterile, barren; (fig) vain, futile □ **esterilizar** vt to sterilize

esterlina [ester'lina] adj: **libra ~** pound sterling

estés etc [es'tes] vb ver **estar**

estética [es'tetika] nf aesthetics sg

estético, -a [es'tetiko, a] adj aesthetic

estiércol [es'tjerkol] nm dung, manure

estigma [es'tiɣma] nm stigma

estilo [es'tilo] nm style; (TEC) stylus; (NATACIÓN) stroke; **algo por el ~** something along those lines

estima [es'tima] nf esteem, respect □ **estimación** [estima'θjon] nf (evaluación) estimation; (aprecio, afecto) esteem, regard □ **estimar** [esti'mar] vt (evaluar) to estimate; (valorar) to value; (apreciar) to esteem, respect; (pensar, considerar) to think, reckon

estimulante [estimu'lante] adj stimulating ♦ nm stimulant

estimular [estimu'lar] vt to stimulate; (excitar) to excite

estímulo [es'timulo] nm stimulus; (ánimo) encouragement

estirar [esti'rar] vt to stretch; (dinero, suma etc) to stretch out; **estirarse** vr to stretch

estirón [esti'ron] nm pull, tug; (crecimiento) spurt, sudden growth; **dar** o **pegar un ~** (fam: niño) to shoot up (inf)

estirpe [es'tirpe] nf stock, lineage

estival [esti'βal] adj summer cpd

esto ['esto] pron this, this thing o matter; **~ de la boda** this business about the wedding

Estocolmo [esto'kolmo] nm Stockholm

estofado [esto'faðo] nm stew

estómago [es'tomaɣo] nm stomach; **tener ~** to be thick-skinned

estorbar [estor'βar] vt to hinder, obstruct; (molestar) to bother, disturb ♦ vi to be in the way □ **estorbo** nm (molestia) bother, nuisance; (obstáculo) hindrance, obstacle

estornudar [estornu'ðar] vi to sneeze

estos ['estos] adj demos ver **este²**

éstos ['estos] pron ver **éste**

estoy [es'toi] vb ver **estar**

estrado [es'traðo] nm platform

estrafalario, -a [estrafa'larjo, a] adj odd, eccentric

estrago [es'traɣo] nm ruin, destruction; **hacer estragos en** to wreak havoc among

estragón [estra'ɣon] nm tarragon

estrambótico, -a [estram'botiko, a] adj (persona) eccentric; (peinado, ropa) outlandish

estrangular [estrangu'lar] vt (persona) to strangle; (MED) to strangulate

estratagema [estrata'xema] nf (MIL) stratagem; (astucia) cunning

estrategia [estra'texja] nf strategy □ **estratégico, -a** adj strategic

estrato [es'trato] nm stratum, layer

estrechar [estre'tʃar] vt (reducir) to narrow; (COSTURA) to take in; (abrazar) to hug, embrace; **estrecharse** vr (reducirse) to narrow, grow narrow; (abrazarse) to embrace; **~ la mano** to shake hands

estrechez [estre'tʃeθ] nf narrowness; (de ropa) tightness; **estrecheces** nfpl (dificultades económicas) financial difficulties

estrecho, -a [es'tretʃo, a] adj narrow; (apretado) tight; (íntimo) close, intimate; (*miserable*) mean ♦ *nm* strait; ~ **de miras** narrow-minded

estrella [es'treʎa] *nf* star ► **estrella de mar** (*ZOOL*) starfish ► **estrella fugaz** shooting star

estrellar [estre'ʎar] *vt* (*hacer añicos*) to smash (to pieces); (*huevos*) to fry; **estrellarse** *vr* to smash; (*chocarse*) to crash; (*fracasar*) to fail

estremecer [estreme'θer] *vt* to shake; **estremecerse** *vr* to shake, tremble

estrenar [estre'nar] *vt* (*vestido*) to wear for the first time; (*casa*) to move into; (*película, obra de teatro*) to première; **estrenarse** *vr* (*persona*) to make one's début □ **estreno** (*CINE etc*) première

estreñido, -a [estre'ɲiðo, a] *adj* constipated

estreñimiento [estreɲi'mjento] *nm* constipation

estrepitoso, -a [estrepi'toso, a] *adj* noisy; (*fiesta*) rowdy

estría [es'tria] *nf* groove

estribar [estri'βar] *vi*: ~ **en** to lie on

estribillo [estri'βiʎo] *nm* (*LITERATURA*) refrain; (*MÚS*) chorus

estribo [es'triβo] *nm* (*de jinete*) stirrup; (*de coche, tren*) step; (*de puente*) support; (*GEO*) spur; **perder los estribos** to fly off the handle

estribor [estri'βor] *nm* (*NÁUT*) starboard

estricto, -a [es'trikto, a] *adj* (*riguroso*) strict; (*severo*) severe

estridente [estri'ðente] *adj* (*color*) loud; (*voz*) raucous

estropajo [estro'paxo] *nm* scourer

estropear [estrope'ar] *vt* to spoil; (*dañar*) to damage; **estropearse** *vr* (*objeto*) to get damaged; (*persona, piel*) to be ruined

estructura [estruk'tura] *nf* structure

estrujar [estru'xar] *vt* (*apretar*) to squeeze; (*aplastar*) to crush; (*fig*) to drain, bleed

estuario [es'twarjo] *nm* estuary

estuche [es'tutʃe] *nm* box, case

estudiante [estu'ðjante] *nmf* student □ **estudiantil** *adj* student *cpd*

estudiar [estu'ðjar] *vt* to study

estudio [es'tuðjo] *nm* study; (*CINE, ARTE, RADIO*) studio; **estudios** *nmpl* studies; (*erudición*) learning *sg* □ **estudioso, -a** *adj* studious

estufa [es'tufa] *nf* heater, fire

estupefaciente [estupefa'θjente] *nm* drug, narcotic

estupefacto, -a [estupe'fakto, a] *adj* speechless, thunderstruck

estupendo, -a [estu'pendo, a] *adj* wonderful, terrific; (*fam*) great; ¡~! that's great!, fantastic!

estupidez [estupi'ðeθ] *nf* (*torpeza*) stupidity; (*acto*) stupid thing (to do)

estúpido, -a [es'tupiðo, a] *adj* stupid, silly

estuve *etc* [es'tuβe] *vb ver* **estar**

ETA ['eta] (*ESP*) *nf abr* (= *Euskadi ta Askatasuna*) ETA

etapa [e'tapa] *nf* (*de viaje*) stage; (*DEPORTE*) leg; (*parada*) stopping place; (*fase*) stage, phase

etarra [e'tarra] *nmf* member of ETA

etc. *abr* (= *etcétera*) etc

etcétera [et'θetera] *adv* etcetera

eternidad [eterni'ðað] *nf* eternity □ **eterno, -a** *adj* eternal, everlasting

ética ['etika] *nf* ethics *pl*

ético, -a [l, a] *adj* ethical

etiqueta [eti'keta] *nf* (*modales*) etiquette; (*rótulo*) label, tag

Eucaristía [eukaris'tia] *nf* Eucharist

euforia [eu'forja] *nf* euphoria

euro ['euro] *nm* (*moneda*) euro

eurodiputado, -a [euroðipu'taðo, a] *nm/f* Euro MP, MEP

Europa [eu'ropa] *nf* Europe □ **europeo, -a** *adj, nm/f* European

Euskadi [eus'kaði] *nm* the Basque Country *o* Provinces *pl*

euskera [eus'kera] *nm* (*LING*) Basque

evacuación [eβakwa'θjon] nf
evacuation

evacuar [eβa'kwar] vt to evacuate

evadir [eβa'ðir] vt to evade, avoid;
evadirse vr to escape

evaluar [eβa'lwar] vt to evaluate

evangelio [eβaŋ'xeljo] nm gospel

evaporar [eβapo'rar] vt to evaporate;
evaporarse vr to vanish

evasión [eβa'sjon] nf escape, flight;
(fig) evasion ▶ **evasión de capitales**
flight of capital

evasiva [eβa'siβa] nf (pretexto) excuse

evento [e'βento] nm event

eventual [eβen'twal] adj possible,
conditional (upon circumstances);
(trabajador) casual, temporary

> ⚠ No confundir **eventual** con la
> palabra inglesa *eventual*.

evidencia [eβi'ðenθja] nf evidence,
proof

evidente [eβi'ðente] adj obvious, clear,
evident

evitar [eβi'tar] vt (evadir) to avoid;
(impedir) to prevent; ~ **hacer algo** to
avoid doing sth

evocar [eβo'kar] vt to evoke, call forth

evolución [eβolu'θjon] nf (desarrollo)
evolution, development; (cambio)
change; (MIL) manoeuvre
❏ **evolucionar** vi to evolve; to
manoeuvre

ex [eks] adj ex-; **el ex ministro** the
former minister, the ex-minister

exactitud [eksakti'tuð] nf exactness;
(precisión) accuracy; (puntualidad)
punctuality ❏ **exacto, -a** adj exact;
accurate; punctual; **¡exacto!** exactly!

exageración [eksaxera'θjon] nf
exaggeration

exagerar [eksaxe'rar] vt, vi to
exaggerate

exaltar [eksal'tar] vt to exalt, glorify;
exaltarse vr (excitarse) to get excited o
worked up

examen [ek'samen] nm examination
▶ **examen de conducir** driving test
▶ **examen de ingreso** entrance
examination

examinar [eksami'nar] vt to examine;
examinarse vr to be examined, take an
examination

excavadora [ekskaβa'ðora] nf
excavator

excavar [ekska'βar] vt to excavate

excedencia [eksθe'ðenθja] nf: **estar en**
~ to be on leave; **pedir** o **solicitar la** ~
to ask for leave

excedente [eksθe'ðente] adj, nm
excess, surplus

exceder [eksθe'ðer] vt to exceed,
surpass; **excederse** vr (extralimitarse)
to go too far

excelencia [eksθe'lenθja] nf
excellence; **su E~** his Excellency
❏ **excelente** adj excellent

excéntrico, -a [eks'θentriko, a] adj,
nm/f eccentric

excepción [eksθep'θjon] nf exception;
a ~ **de** with the exception of, except
for ❏ **excepcional** adj exceptional

excepto [eks'θepto] adv excepting,
except (for)

exceptuar [eksθep'twar] vt to except,
exclude

excesivo, -a [eksθe'siβo, a] adj
excessive

exceso [eks'θeso] nm (gen) excess;
(COM) surplus ▶ **exceso de equipaje/
peso** excess luggage/weight
▶ **exceso de velocidad** speeding

excitado, -a [eksθi'taðo, a] adj excited;
(emociones) aroused

excitar [eksθi'tar] vt to excite; (incitar)
to urge; **excitarse** vr to get excited

exclamación [eksklama'θjon] nf
exclamation

exclamar [ekskla'mar] vi to exclaim

excluir [eksklu'ir] vt to exclude; (dejar
fuera) to shut out; (descartar) to reject

exclusiva [eksklu'siβa] nf (PRENSA) exclusive, scoop; (COM) sole right

exclusivo, -a [eksklu'siβo, a] adj exclusive; **derecho ~** sole o exclusive right

Excmo. abr = **excelentísimo**

excomulgar [ekskomul'ɣar] vt (REL) to excommunicate

excomunión [ekskomu'njon] nf excommunication

excursión [ekskur'sjon] nf excursion, outing ▢ **excursionista** nmf (turista) sightseer

excusa [eks'kusa] nf excuse; (disculpa) apology ▢ **excusar** [eksku'sar] vt to excuse

exhaustivo, -a [eksaus'tiβo, a] adj (análisis) thorough; (estudio) exhaustive

exhausto, -a [ek'sausto, a] adj exhausted

exhibición [eksiβi'θjon] nf exhibition, display, show

exhibir [eksi'βir] vt to exhibit, display, show

exigencia [eksi'xenθja] nf demand, requirement ▢ **exigente** adj demanding

exigir [eksi'xir] vt (gen) to demand, require; **~ el pago** to demand payment

exiliado, -a [eksi'ljaðo, a] adj exiled ♦ nm/f exile

exilio [ek'siljo] nm exile

eximir [eksi'mir] vt to exempt

existencia [eksis'tenθja] nf existence; **existencias** nfpl stock(s) pl

existir [eksis'tir] vi to exist, be

éxito ['eksito] nm (triunfo) success; (MÚS etc) hit; **tener éxito** to be successful

⚠ No confundir **éxito** con la palabra inglesa exit.

exorbitante [eksorβi'tante] adj (precio) exorbitant; (cantidad) excessive

exótico, -a [ek'sotiko, a] adj exotic

expandir [ekspan'dir] vt to expand

expansión [ekspan'sjon] nf expansion

expansivo, -a [ekspan'siβo, a] adj: **onda expansiva** shock wave

expatriarse [ekspa'trjarse] vr to emigrate; (POL) to go into exile

expectativa [ekspekta'tiβa] nf (espera) expectation; (perspectiva) prospect

expedición [ekspeði'θjon] nf (excursión) expedition

expediente [ekspe'ðjente] nm expedient; (JUR: procedimiento) action, proceedings pl; (: papeles) dossier, file, record

expedir [ekspe'ðir] vt (despachar) to send, forward; (pasaporte) to issue

expensas [eks'pensas] nfpl: **a ~ de** at the expense of

experiencia [ekspe'rjenθja] nf experience

experimentado, -a [eksperimen'taðo, a] adj experienced

experimentar [eksperimen'tar] vt (en laboratorio) to experiment with; (probar) to test, try out; (notar, observar) to experience; (deterioro, pérdida) to suffer ▢ **experimento** nm experiment

experto, -a [eks'perto, a] adj expert, skilled ♦ nm/f expert

expirar [ekspi'rar] vi to expire

explanada [ekspla'naða] nf (llano) plain

explayarse [ekspla'jarse] vr (en discurso) to speak at length; **~ con algn** to confide in sb

explicación [eksplika'θjon] nf explanation

explicar [ekspli'kar] vt to explain; **explicarse** vr to explain (o.s.)

explícito, -a [eks'pliθito, a] adj explicit

explique etc [eks'plike] vb ver **explicar**

explorador, a [eksplora'ðor, a] nm/f (pionero) explorer; (MIL) scout ♦ nm (MED) probe; (TEC) (radar) scanner

explorar [eksplo'rar] vt to explore; (MED) to probe; (radar) to scan

explosión [eksplo'sjon] nf explosion
❏ **explosivo, -a** adj explosive

explotación [eksplota'θjon] nf exploitation; (de planta etc) running

explotar [eksplo'tar] vt to exploit to run, operate ♦ vi to explode

exponer [ekspo'ner] vt to expose; (cuadro) to display; (vida) to risk; (idea) to explain; **exponerse** vr: **exponerse a (hacer) algo** to run the risk of (doing) sth

exportación [eksporta'θjon] nf (acción) export; (mercancías) exports pl

exportar [ekspor'tar] vt to export

exposición [eksposi'θjon] nf (gen) exposure; (de arte) show, exhibition; (explicación) explanation; (declaración) account, statement

expresamente [espresa'mente] adv (decir) clearly; (a propósito) expressly

expresar [ekspre'sar] vt to express
❏ **expresión** nf expression

expresivo, -a [ekspre'siβo, a] adj (persona, gesto, palabras) expressive; (cariñoso) affectionate

expreso, -a [eks'preso, a] pp de **expresar** ♦ adj (explícito) express; (claro) specific, clear; (tren) fast ♦ adv: **enviar ~** to send by express (delivery)

express [eks'pres] (LAm) adv: **enviar algo ~** to send sth special delivery

exprimidor [eksprimi'ðor] nm squeezer

exprimir [ekspri'mir] vt (fruta) to squeeze; (zumo) to squeeze out

expuesto, -a [eks'pwesto, a] pp de **exponer** ♦ adj exposed; (cuadro etc) on show, on display

expulsar [ekspul'sar] vt (echar) to eject, throw out; (alumno) to expel; (despedir) to sack, fire; (DEPORTE) to send off
❏ **expulsión** nf expulsion; sending-off

exquisito, -a [ekski'sito, a] adj exquisite; (comida) delicious

éxtasis ['ekstasis] nm ecstasy

extender [eksten'der] vt to extend; (los brazos) to stretch out, hold out; (mapa, tela) to spread (out), open (out); (mantequilla) to spread; (certificado) to issue; (cheque, recibo) to make out; (documento) to draw up; **extenderse** vr (gen) to extend; (persona: en el suelo) to stretch out; (epidemia) to spread
❏ **extendido, -a** adj (abierto) spread out, open; (brazos) outstretched; (costumbre) widespread

extensión [eksten'sjon] nf (de terreno, mar) expanse, stretch; (de tiempo) length, duration; (TEL) extension; **en toda la ~ de la palabra** in every sense of the word

extenso, -a [eks'tenso, a] adj extensive

exterior [ekste'rjor] adj (de fuera) external; (afuera) outside, exterior; (apariencia) outward; (deuda, relaciones) foreign ♦ nm (gen) exterior, outside; (aspecto) outward appearance; (DEPORTE) wing(er); (países extranjeros) abroad; **en el ~** abroad; **al ~** outwardly, on the surface

exterminar [ekstermi'nar] vt to exterminate

externo, -a [eks'terno, a] adj (exterior) external, outside; (superficial) outward ♦ nm/f day pupil

extinguir [ekstin'gir] vt (fuego) to extinguish, put out; (raza, población) to wipe out; **extinguirse** vr (fuego) to go out; (BIO) to die out, become extinct

extintor [ekstin'tor] nm (fire) extinguisher

extirpar [ekstir'par] vt (MED) to remove (surgically)

extra ['ekstra] adj inv (tiempo) extra; (chocolate, vino) good-quality ♦ nmf extra ♦ nm extra; (bono) bonus

extracción [ekstrak'θjon] nf extraction; (en lotería) draw

extracto [eks'trakto] nm extract

extradición [ekstraði'θjon] nf
extradition

extraer [ekstra'er] vt to extract, take
out

extraescolar [ekstraesko'lar] adj:
actividad ~ extracurricular activity

extranjero, -a [ekstran'xero, a] adj
foreign ♦ nm/f foreigner ♦ nm foreign
countries pl; **en el ~** abroad

⚠ No confundir **extranjero** con la
palabra inglesa *stranger*.

extrañar [ekstra'nar] vt (sorprender) to
find strange o odd; (echar de menos) to
miss; **extrañarse** vr (sorprenderse) to be
amazed, be surprised; **me extraña** I'm
surprised

extraño, -a [eks'trano, á] adj
(extranjero) foreign; (raro,
sorprendente) strange, odd

extraordinario, -a [ekstraorði'narjo,
a] adj extraordinary; (edición, número)
special ♦ nm (de periódico) special
edition; **horas extraordinarias**
overtime sg

extrarradio [ekstra'rraðjo] nm
suburbs

extravagante [ekstraβa'ɣante] adj
(excéntrico) eccentric; (estrafalario)
outlandish

extraviado, -a [ekstra'βjaðo, a] adj
lost, missing

extraviar [ekstra'βjar] vt (persona:
desorientar) to mislead, misdirect;
(perder) to lose, misplace; **extraviarse**
vr to lose one's way, get lost

extremar [ekstre'mar] vt to carry to
extremes

extremaunción [ekstremaun'θjon] nf
extreme unction

extremidad [ekstremi'ðað] nf (punta)
extremity; **extremidades** nfpl (ANAT)
extremities

extremo, -a [eks'tremo, á] adj
extreme; (último) last ♦ nm end; (límite,

grado sumo) extreme; **en último ~** as a
last resort

extrovertido, -a [ekstroβer'tiðo, a]
adj, nm/f extrovert

exuberante [eksuβe'rante] adj
exuberant; (fig) luxuriant, lush

eyacular [ejaku'lar] vt, vi to ejaculate

F, f

fa nm (MÚS) fa, F

fabada [fa'βaða] nf bean and sausage
stew

fábrica [fa'βrika] nf factory; **marca de ~**
trademark; **precio de ~** factory price

⚠ No confundir **fábrica** con la
palabra inglesa *fabric*.

fabricación [faβrika'θjon] nf
(manufactura) manufacture;
(producción) production; **de ~ casera**
home-made ▸ **fabricación en serie**
mass production

fabricante [faβri'kante] nmf
manufacturer

fabricar [faβri'kar] vt (manufacturar) to
manufacture, make; (construir) to
build; (cuento) to fabricate, devise

fábula [ˈfaβula] nf (cuento) fable;
(chisme) rumour; (mentira) fib

fabuloso, -a [faβuˈloso, a] adj
(oportunidad, tiempo) fabulous, great

facción [fak'θjon] nf (POL) faction;
facciones nfpl (de rostro) features

faceta [fa'θeta] nf facet

facha [ˈfatʃa] (fam) nf (aspecto) look;
(cara) face

fachada [fa'tʃaða] nf (ARQ) façade, front

fácil [ˈfaθil] adj (simple) easy; (probable)
likely

facilidad [faθili'ðað] nf (capacidad)
ease; (sencillez) simplicity; (de palabra)
fluency; **facilidades** nfpl facilities

▶ **facilidades de pago** credit facilities

facilitar [faθili'tar] vt (hacer fácil) to make easy; (proporcionar) to provide

factor [fak'tor] nm factor

factura [fak'tura] nf (cuenta) bill ❏ **facturación** nf (de equipaje) check-in ❏ **facturar** vt (COM) to invoice, charge for; (equipaje) to check in

facultad [fakul'tað] nf (aptitud, ESCOL etc) faculty; (poder) power

faena [fa'ena] nf (trabajo) work; (quehacer) task, job

faisán [fai'san] nm pheasant

faja ['faxa] nf (para la cintura) sash; (de mujer) corset; (de tierra) strip

fajo ['faxo] nm (de papeles) bundle; (de billetes) wad

falda ['falda] nf (prenda de vestir) skirt ▶ **falda pantalón** culottes pl, split skirt

falla ['faʎa] nf (defecto) fault ▶ **falla humana** (LAm) human error

fallar [fa'ʎar] vt (JUR) to pronounce sentence on ♦ vi (memoria) to fail; (motor) to miss

Fallas nfpl Valencian celebration of the feast of St Joseph

FALLAS

In the week of 19 March (the feast of San José), Valencia honours its patron saint with a spectacular fiesta called **Las Fallas**. The **Fallas** are huge papier-mâché, cardboard and wooden sculptures which are built by competing teams throughout the year. They depict politicians and well-known public figures and are thrown onto bonfires and set alight once a jury has judged them - only the best sculpture escapes the flames.

---

fallecer [faʎe'θer] vi to pass away, die ❏ **fallecimiento** nm decease, demise

fallido, -a [fa'ʎiðo, a] adj (gen) frustrated, unsuccessful

fallo ['faʎo] nm (JUR) verdict, ruling; (fracaso) failure ▶ **fallo cardíaco** heart failure ▶ **fallo humano** (ESP) human error

falsificar [falsifi'kar] vt (firma etc) to forge; (moneda) to counterfeit

falso, -a ['falso, a] adj false; (documento, moneda etc) fake; **en ~** falsely

falta ['falta] nf (defecto) fault, flaw; (privación) lack, want; (ausencia) absence; (carencia) shortage; (equivocación) mistake; (DEPORTE) foul; **echar en ~** to miss; **hacer ~ hacer algo** to be necessary to do sth; **me hace ~ una pluma** I need a pen ▶ **falta de educación** bad manners pl ▶ **falta de ortografía** spelling mistake

faltar [fal'tar] vi (escasear) to be lacking, be wanting; (ausentarse) to be absent, be missing; **faltan 2 horas para llegar** there are 2 hours to go till arrival; **~ al respeto a algn** to be disrespectful to sb; **¡no faltaba más!** (no hay de qué) don't mention it

fama ['fama] nf (renombre) fame; (reputación) reputation

familia [fa'milja] nf family ▶ **familia numerosa** large family ▶ **familia política** in-laws pl ❏ **familiar** [fami'ljar] adj relativo a la familia, family cpd; (conocido, informal) familiar ♦ nm relative, relation

famoso, -a [fa'moso, a] adj (renombrado) famous

fan [fan] (pl **fans**) nmf fan

fanático, -a [fa'natiko, a] adj fanatical ♦ nm/f fanatic; (CINE, DEPORTE) fan

fanfarrón, -ona [fanfa'rron, ona] adj boastful

fango ['fango] nm mud

fantasía [fanta'sia] nf fantasy, imagination; **joyas de ~** imitation jewellery sg

fantasma [fan'tasma] nm (espectro) ghost, apparition; (fanfarrón) show-off

fantástico, -a [fan'tastiko, a] adj fantastic

farmacéutico, -a [farma'θeutiko, a] adj pharmaceutical ♦ nm/f chemist (BRIT), pharmacist

farmacia [far'maθja] nf chemist's (shop) (BRIT), pharmacy ▸ **farmacia de guardia** all-night chemist

fármaco ['farmako] nm drug

faro ['faro] nm (NÁUT: torre) lighthouse; (AUTO) headlamp ▸ **faros antiniebla** fog lamps ▸ **faros delanteros/ traseros** headlights/rear lights

farol [fa'rol] nm lantern, lamp

farola [fa'rola] nf street lamp (BRIT) o light (US)

farra [LAm: fam] ['farra] nf party; **ir de ~** to go on a binge

farsa ['farsa] nf (gen) farce ☐ **farsante** [far'sante] nmf fraud, fake

fascículo [fas'θikulo] nm (de revista) part, instalment

fascinar [fasθi'nar] vt (gen) to fascinate

fascismo [fas'θismo] nm fascism ☐ **fascista** adj, nmf fascist

fase ['fase] nf phase

fashion adj (fam) trendy

fastidiar [fasti'ðjar] vt (molestar) to annoy, bother; (estropear) to spoil; **fastidiarse** vr: **¡que se fastidie!** (fam) he'll just have to put up with it!

fastidio [fas'tiðjo] nm (molestia) annoyance ☐ **fastidioso, -a** adj (molesto) annoying

fatal [fa'tal] adj (gen) fatal; (desgraciado) ill-fated; (fam: malo, pésimo) awful ☐ **fatalidad** nf (destino) fate; (mala suerte) misfortune

fatiga [fa'tiɣa] nf (cansancio) fatigue, weariness ☐ **fatigar** [fati'ɣar] vt to tire, weary ☐ **fatigoso, -a** [fati'ɣoso, a] adj (cansador) tiring

fauna ['fauna] nf fauna

favor [fa'βor] nm favour; **estar a ~ de** to be in favour of; **haga el ~ de ...** would you be so good as to ...; kindly ...; **por ~** please ☐ **favorable** adj favourable

favorecer [faβore'θer] vt to favour; (vestido etc) to become, flatter; **este peinado le favorece** this hairstyle suits him

favorito, -a [faβo'rito, a] adj, nm/f favourite

fax [faks] nm inv fax; **mandar por ~** to fax

fe [fe] nf (REL) faith; (documento) certificate; **actuar con buena/mala fe** to act in good/bad faith

febrero [fe'βrero] nm February

fecha ['fetʃa] nf date; **con ~ adelantada** postdated; **en ~ próxima** soon; **hasta la ~** to date, so far; **poner ~** to date ▸ **fecha de caducidad** (de producto alimenticio) expiry date ▸ **fecha de nacimiento** date of birth ▸ **fecha límite** o **tope** deadline

fecundo, -a [fe'kundo, a] adj (fértil) fertile; (fig) prolific; (productivo) productive

federación [feðera'θjon] nf federation

felicidad [feliθi'ðað] nf happiness; **¡felicidades!** (deseos) best wishes, congratulations!; (en cumpleaños) happy birthday!

felicitación [feliθita'θjon] nf (tarjeta) greeting(s) card

felicitar [feliθi'tar] vt to congratulate

feliz [fe'liθ] adj happy

felpudo [fel'puðo] nm doormat

femenino, -a [feme'nino, a] adj, nm feminine

feminista [femi'nista] adj, nmf feminist

fenómeno [fe'nomeno] nm phenomenon; (fig) freak, accident ♦ adj great ♦ excl great!, marvellous! ☐ **fenomenal** adj = **fenómeno**

feo, -a ['feo, a] adj (gen) ugly; (desagradable) bad, nasty

féretro ['feretro] nm (ataúd) coffin; (sarcófago) bier

feria ['ferja] nf (gen) fair; (descanso) holiday, rest day; (MÉX: cambio) small o loose change; (CS: mercado) village market

feriado (LAm) nm holiday

fermentar [fermen'tar] vi to ferment

feroz [fe'roθ] adj (cruel) cruel; (salvaje) fierce

férreo, -a ['ferreo, a] adj iron

ferretería [ferrete'ria] nf (tienda) ironmonger's (shop) (BRIT), hardware store (US)

ferrocarril [ferroka'rril] nm railway

ferroviario, -a [ferro'βjarjo, a] adj rail cpd

ferry (pl **ferrys** o **ferries**) nm ferry

fértil ['fertil] adj (productivo) fertile; (rico) rich ❏ **fertilidad** nf (gen) fertility; (productividad) fruitfulness

fervor [fer'βor] nm fervour

festejar [feste'xar] vt (celebrar) to celebrate

festejo [fes'texo] nm celebration; **festejos** nmpl (fiestas) festivals

festín [fes'tin] nm feast, banquet

festival [festi'βal] nm festival

festividad [festiβi'ðað] nf festivity

festivo, -a [fes'tiβo, a] adj (de fiesta) festive; (CINE, LITERATURA) humorous; **día ~** holiday

feto ['feto] nm foetus

fiable ['fjaβle] adj (persona) trustworthy; (máquina) reliable

fiambre ['fjambre] nm cold meat

fiambrera [fjam'brera] nf (para almuerzo) lunch box

fianza [fian'θa] nf surety; (JUR): **libertad bajo ~** release on bail

fiar [fi'ar] vt (salir garante de) to guarantee; (vender a crédito) to sell on credit ♦ vi to trust; **fiarse** vr to trust (in),

rely on; **~ a** (secreto) to confide (to); **fiarse de algn** to rely on sb

fibra ['fiβra] nf fibre ▸ **fibra óptica** optical fibre

ficción [fik'θjon] nf fiction

ficha ['fitʃa] nf (TEL) token; (en juegos) counter, marker; (tarjeta) (index) card ❏ **fichaje** nm (DEPORTE) signing ❏ **fichar** vt (archivar) to file, index; (DEPORTE) to sign; **estar fichado** to have a record ❏ **fichero** nm box file; (INFORM) file

ficticio, -a [fik'tiθjo, a] adj (imaginario) fictitious; (falso) fabricated

fidelidad [fiðeli'ðað] nf (lealtad) fidelity, loyalty; **alta ~** high fidelity, hi-fi

fideos [fi'ðeos] nmpl noodles

fiebre ['fjeβre] nf (MED) fever; (fig) fever, excitement; **tener ~** to have a temperature ▸ **fiebre aftosa** foot-and-mouth disease

fiel [fjel] adj (leal) faithful, loyal; (fiable) reliable; (exacto) accurate, faithful ♦ nm: **los fieles** the faithful

fieltro ['fjeltro] nm felt

fiera ['fjera] nf (animal feroz) wild animal o beast; (fig) dragon; ver tb **fiero**

fiero, -a ['fjero, a] adj (cruel) cruel; (feroz) fierce; (duro) harsh

fierro (LAm) ['fjerro] nm (hierro) iron

fiesta ['fjesta] nf party; (de pueblo) festival; (vacaciones: tb: **fiestas**) holiday sg ▸ **fiesta mayor** annual festival ▸ **fiesta patria** (LAm) independence day

figura 132 **flama**

figura [fi'γura] nf (gen) figure; (forma, imagen) shape, form; (NAIPES) face card

figurar [fiγu'rar] vt (representar) to represent; (fingir) to figure ♦ vi to figure; **figurarse** vr (imaginarse) to imagine; (suponer) to suppose

fijador [fixa'ðor] nm (FOTO etc) fixative; (de pelo) gel

fijar [fi'xar] vt (gen) to fix; (estampilla) to affix, stick (on); **fijarse** vr: **fijarse en** to notice

fijo, -a ['fixo, a] adj (gen) fixed; (firme) firm; (permanente) permanent ♦ adv: **mirar ~** to stare

fila ['fila] nf row; (MIL) rank; **ponerse en ~** to line up, get into line ▶ **fila india** single file

filatelia [fila'telja] nf philately, stamp collecting

filete [fi'lete] nm (de carne) fillet steak; (de pescado) fillet

filiación [filja'θjon] nf (POL) affiliation

filial [fi'ljal] adj filial ♦ nf subsidiary

Filipinas [fili'pinas] nfpl: **las (Islas) ~** the Philippines ▢ **filipino, -a** adj, nm/f Philippine

filmar [fil'mar] vt to film, shoot

filo ['filo] nm (gen) edge; **sacar ~ a** to sharpen; **al ~ del mediodía** at about midday; **de doble ~** double-edged

filología [filolo'γia] nf philology ▶ **filología inglesa** (UNIV) English Studies

filón [fi'lon] nm (MINERÍA) vein, lode; (fig) goldmine

filosofía [filoso'fia] nf philosophy ▢ **filósofo, -a** nm/f philosopher

filtrar [fil'trar] vt, vi to filter, strain; **filtrarse** vr to filter ▢ **filtro** nm (TEC, utensilio) filter

fin [fin] nm end; (objetivo) aim, purpose; **al ~ y al cabo** when all's said and done; **a ~ de** in order to; **por ~** finally; **en ~** in short ▶ **fin de semana** weekend

final [fi'nal] adj final ♦ nm end, conclusion ♦ nf final; **al ~** in the end; **a**

finales de at the end of ▢ **finalidad** nf (propósito) purpose, intention ▢ **finalista** nmf finalist ▢ **finalizar** vt to end, finish; (INFORM) to log out o off ♦ vi to end, come to an end

financiar [finan'θjar] vt to finance ▢ **financiero, -a** adj financial ♦ nm/f financier

finca ['finka] nf (casa de campo) country house; (ESP: bien inmueble) property, land; (LAm: granja) farm

finde nm abr (fam: fin de semana) weekend

fingir [fin'xir] vt (simular) to simulate, feign ♦ vi (aparentar) to pretend

finlandés, -esa [finlan'des, esa] adj Finnish ♦ nm/f Finn ♦ nm (LING) Finnish

Finlandia [fin'landja] nf Finland

fino, -a ['fino, a] adj fine; (delgado) slender; (de buenas maneras) polite, refined; (jerez) fino, dry

firma ['firma] nf signature; (COM) firm, company

firmamento [firma'mento] nm firmament

firmar [fir'mar] vt to sign

firme ['firme] adj firm; (estable) stable; (sólido) solid; (constante) steady; (decidido) resolute ♦ nm road (surface) ▢ **firmeza** nf firmness; (constancia) steadiness; (solidez) solidity

fiscal [fis'kal] adj fiscal ♦ nmf public prosecutor; **año ~** tax o fiscal year

fisgonear [fisγone'ar] vt to poke one's nose into ♦ vi to pry, spy

física ['fisika] nf physics sg; ver tb **físico**

físico, -a ['fisiko, a] adj physical ♦ nm physique ♦ nm/f physicist

fisura [fi'sura] nf crack; (MED) fracture

flác(c)ido, -a [fla(k)θiðo, a] adj flabby

flaco, -a ['flako, a] adj (muy delgado) skinny, thin; (débil) weak, feeble

flagrante [fla'γrante] adj flagrant

flama (MÉX) nf flame ▢ **flamable** (MÉX) adj flammable

flamante [fla'mante] *(fam) adj* brilliant; *(nuevo)* brand-new

flamenco, -a [fla'menko, a] *adj (de Flandes)* Flemish; *(baile, música)* flamenco ♦ *nm (baile, música)* flamenco; *(ZOOL)* flamingo

flamingo (MÉX) *nm* flamingo

flan [flan] *nm* creme caramel

⚠ No confundir **flan** con la palabra inglesa *flan*.

flash [flaʃ] *(pl ∼ o flashes) nm (FOTO)* flash

flauta ['flauta] *nf (MÚS)* flute

flecha ['fletʃa] *nf* arrow

flechazo [fle'tʃaθo] *nm* love at first sight

fleco ['fleko] *nm* fringe

flema ['flema] *nm* phlegm

flequillo [fle'kiʎo] *nm (pelo)* fringe

flexible [flek'siβle] *adj* flexible

flexión [flek'sjon] *nf* press-up

flexo ['flekso] *nm* adjustable table-lamp

flirtear [flirte'ar] *vi* to flirt

flojera [flo'xera] (LAm: fam) *nf*: **me da ∼** I can't be bothered

flojo, -a [floxo, a] *adj (gen)* loose; *(sin fuerzas)* limp; *(débil)* weak

flor [flor] *nf* flower; **a ∼ de** on the surface of ❏ **flora** *nf* flora ❏ **florecer** *vi (BOT)* to flower, bloom; *(fig)* to flourish ❏ **floreciente** (LAm) *adj* flourishing ❏ **florero** *nm* vase ❏ **floristería** *nf* florist's (shop)

flota ['flota] *nf* fleet

flotador [flota'ðor] *nm (gen)* float; *(para nadar)* rubber ring

flotar [flo'tar] *vi (gen)* to float ❏ **flote** *nm*: **a flote** afloat; **salir a flote** *(fig)* to get back on one's feet

fluidez [flui'ðeθ] *nf* fluidity; *(fig)* fluency

fluido, -a [flu'iðo, a] *adj, nm* fluid

fluir [flu'ir] *vi* to flow

flujo ['fluxo] *nm* flow ▸ **flujo y reflujo** ebb and flow

flúor ['fluor] *nm* fluoride

fluorescente [flwores'θente] *adj* fluorescent ♦ *nm* fluorescent light

fluvial [fluβi'al] *adj (navegación, cuenca)* fluvial, river cpd

fobia ['foβja] *nf* phobia ▸ **fobia a las alturas** fear of heights

foca ['foka] *nf* seal

foco ['foko] *nm* focus; *(ELEC)* floodlight; *(MÉX: bombilla)* (light) bulb

fofo, -a ['fofo, a] *adj* soft, spongy; *(carnes)* flabby

fogata [fo'yata] *nf* bonfire

fogón [fo'yon] *nm (de cocina)* ring, burner

folio ['foljo] *nm* folio, page

follaje [fo'ʎaxe] *nm* foliage

folleto [fo'ʎeto] *nm (POL)* pamphlet

follón [fo'ʎon] *(ESP: fam) nm (lío)* mess; *(conmoción)* fuss; **armar un ∼** to kick up a row

fomentar [fomen'tar] *vt (MED)* to foment

fonda ['fonda] *nf* inn

fondo ['fondo] *nm (de mar)* bottom; *(de coche, sala)* back; *(reserva)* fund; **fondos** *nmpl* (COM) funds, resources; **una investigación a ∼** a thorough investigation; **en el ∼** at bottom, deep down

fonobuzón [fonoβu'θon] *nm* voice mail

fontanería [fontane'ria] *nf* plumbing ❏ **fontanero, -a** *nm/f* plumber

footing ['futin] *nm* jogging; **hacer ∼** to jog, go jogging

forastero, -a [foras'tero, a] *nm/f* stranger

forcejear [forθexe'ar] *vi (luchar)* to struggle

forense [fo'rense] *nmf* pathologist

forma ['forma] nf (figura) form, shape; (MED) fitness; (método) way, means; **las formas** the conventions; **estar en ~** to be fit; **de ~ que ...** so that ...; **de todas formas** in any case

formación [forma'θjon] nf (gen) formation; (educación) education ▶ **formación profesional** vocational training

formal [for'mal] adj (gen) formal; (fig: serio) serious; (: de fiar) reliable □ **formalidad** nf formality; seriousness □ **formalizar** vt (JUR) to formalize; (situación) to put in order, regularize; **formalizarse** vr (situación) to be put in order, be regularized

formar [for'mar] vt (componer) to form, shape; (constituir) to make up, constitute; (ESCOL) to train, educate; **formarse** vr (ESCOL) to be trained, educated; (cobrar forma) to form, take form; (desarrollarse) to develop

formatear [formate'ar] vt to format

formato [for'mato] nm format

formidable [formi'ðaβle] adj (temible) formidable; (estupendo) tremendous

fórmula ['formula] nf formula

formulario [formu'larjo] nm form

fornido, -a [for'niðo, a] adj well-built

foro ['foro] nm (POL, INFORM etc) forum

forrar [fo'rrar] vt (abrigo) to line; (libro) to cover □ **forro** nm (de cuaderno) cover; (COSTURA) lining; (de sillón) upholstery; **forro polar** fleece

fortalecer [fortale'θer] vt to strengthen

fortaleza [forta'leθa] nf (MIL) fortress, stronghold; (fuerza) strength; (determinación) resolution

fortuito, -a [for'twito, a] adj accidental

fortuna [for'tuna] nf (suerte) fortune, (good) luck; (riqueza) fortune, wealth

forzar [for'θar] vt (puerta) to force (open); (compeler) to compel

forzoso, -a [for'θoso, a] adj necessary

fosa ['fosa] nf (sepultura) grave; (en tierra) pit ▶ **fosas nasales** nostrils

fósforo ['fosforo] nm (QUÍM) phosphorus; (cerilla) match

fósil ['fosil] nm fossil

foso ['foso] nm ditch; (TEATRO) pit; (AUTO) inspection pit

foto ['foto] nf photo, snap(shot); **sacar una ~** to take a photo o picture ▶ **foto (de) carné** passport(-size) photo

fotocopia [foto'kopja] nf photocopy □ **fotocopiadora** nf photocopier □ **fotocopiar** vt to photocopy

fotografía [fotoɣra'fia] nf (ARTE) photography; (una fotografía) photograph □ **fotografiar** vt to photograph

fotógrafo, -a [fo'toɣrafo, a] nm/f photographer

fotomatón [fotoma'ton] nm photo booth

FP (ESP) nf abr (= Formación Profesional) vocational courses for 14- to 18-year-olds

fracasar [fraka'sar] vi (gen) to fail

fracaso [fra'kaso] nm failure

fracción [frak'θjon] nf fraction

fractura [frak'tura] nf fracture, break

fragancia [fra'ɣanθja] nf (olor) fragrance, perfume

frágil ['fraxil] adj (débil) fragile; (COM) breakable

fragmento [fraɣ'mento] nm (pedazo) fragment

fraile ['fraile] nm (REL) friar; (: monje) monk

frambuesa [fram'bwesa] nf raspberry

francés, -esa [fran'θes, esa] adj French ♦ nm/f Frenchman(-woman) ♦ nm (LING) French

Francia ['franθja] nf France

franco, -a ['franko, a] adj (cándido) frank, open; (COM: exento) free ♦ nm (moneda) franc

francotirador, a [frankotira'ðor, a] nm/f sniper

franela [fra'nela] *nf* flannel

franja ['franxa] *nf* fringe

franquear [franke'ar] *vt* (*camino*) to clear; (*carta, paquete postal*) to frank, stamp; (*obstáculo*) to overcome

franqueo [fran'keo] *nm* postage

franqueza [fran'keθa] *nf* (*candor*) frankness

frasco ['frasko] *nm* bottle, flask

frase ['frase] *nf* sentence ▸ **frase hecha** set phrase; (*pey*) stock phrase

fraterno, -a [fra'terno, a] *adj* brotherly, fraternal

fraude ['frauðe] *nm* (*cualidad*) dishonesty; (*acto*) fraud

frazada [fra'saða] (*LAm*) *nf* blanket

frecuencia [fre'kwenθja] *nf* frequency; **con ~** frequently, often

frecuentar [frekwen'tar] *vt* to frequent

frecuente [fre'kwente] *adj* (*gen*) frequent

fregadero [freɣa'ðero] *nm* (kitchen) sink

fregar [fre'ɣar] *vt* (*frotar*) to scrub; (*platos*) to wash (up); (*LAm: fam: fastidiar*) to annoy; (: *malograr*) to screw up

fregona [fre'ɣona] *nf* mop

freír [fre'ir] *vt* to fry

frenar [fre'nar] *vt* to brake; (*fig*) to check

frenazo [fre'naθo] *nm*: **dar un ~** to brake sharply

frenesí [frene'si] *nm* frenzy

freno ['freno] *nm* (*TEC, AUTO*) brake; (*de cabalgadura*) bit; (*fig*) check ▸ **freno de mano** handbrake

frente ['frente] *nm* (*ARQ, POL*) front; (*de objeto*) front part ♦ *nf* forehead, brow; **~ a** in front of; (*en situación opuesta de*) opposite; **al ~ de** (*fig*) at the head of; **chocar de ~** to crash head-on; **hacer ~ a** to face up to

fresa ['fresa] (*ESP*) *nf* strawberry

fresco, -a ['fresko, a] *adj* (*nuevo*) fresh; (*frío*) cool; (*descarado*) cheeky ♦ *nm* (*aire*) fresh air; (*ARTE*) fresco; (*LAm: jugo*) fruit drink ♦ *nm/f* (*fam*): **ser un ~** to have a nerve; **tomar el ~** to get some fresh air □ **frescura** *nf* freshness; (*descaro*) cheek, nerve

frialdad [frial'dað] *nf* (*gen*) coldness; (*indiferencia*) indifference

frigidez [frixi'ðeθ] *nf* frigidity

frigorífico [friɣo'rifiko] *nm* refrigerator

frijol [fri'xol] *nm* kidney bean

frío, -a etc ['frio, a] *vb ver* **freír** ♦ *adj* cold; (*indiferente*) indifferent ♦ *nm* cold; indifference; **hace ~** it's cold; **tener ~** to be cold

frito, -a ['frito, a] *adj* fried; **me trae ~ ese hombre** I'm sick and tired of that man □ **fritos** *nmpl* fried food

frívolo, -a ['friβolo, a] *adj* frivolous

frontal [fron'tal] *adj* frontal; **choque ~** head-on collision

frontera [fron'tera] *nf* frontier □ **fronterizo, -a** *adj* frontier *cpd*; (*contiguo*) bordering

frontón [fron'ton] *nm* (*DEPORTE: cancha*) pelota court; (: *juego*) pelota

frotar [fro'tar] *vt* to rub; **frotarse** *vr*: **frotarse las manos** to rub one's hands

fructífero, -a [fruk'tifero, a] *adj* fruitful

fruncir [frun'θir] *vt* to pucker; (*COSTURA*) to pleat; **~ el ceño** to knit one's brow

frustrar [frus'trar] *vt* to frustrate

fruta ['fruta] *nf* fruit □ **frutería** *nf* fruit shop □ **frutero, -a** *adj* fruit *cpd* ♦ *nm/f* fruiterer ♦ *nm* fruit bowl

frutilla [fru'tiʎa] (*CS*) *nf* strawberry

fruto ['fruto] *nm* fruit; (*fig: resultado*) result; (: *beneficio*) benefit ▸ **frutos secos** nuts and dried fruit *pl*

fucsia ['fuksja] *nf* fuchsia

fue ['fwe] *vb ver* **ser**; **ir**

fuego ['fweɣo] nm (gen) fire; **a ~ lento** on a low heat; **¿tienes ~?** have you (got) a light? ▸ **fuego amigo** friendly fire ▸ **fuegos artificiales** fireworks

fuente ['fwente] nf fountain; (manantial: fig) spring; (origen) source; (plato) large dish

fuera etc ['fwera] vb ver **ser**; **ir** ♦ adv out(side); (en otra parte) away; (excepto, salvo) except, save ♦ prep: **~ de** outside; (fig) besides; **~ de sí** beside o.s.; **por ~** (on) the outside

fuera-borda [fwera'βorða] nm speedboat

fuerte ['fwerte] adj strong; (golpe) hard; (ruido) loud; (comida) rich; (lluvia) heavy; (dolor) intense ♦ adv strongly; hard; loud(ly)

fuerza etc ['fwerθa] vb ver **forzar** ♦ nf (fortaleza) strength; (TEC, ELEC) power; (coacción) force; (MIL, POL) force; **a ~ de** by dint of; **cobrar fuerzas** to recover one's strength; **tener fuerzas para** to have the strength to; **a la ~** forcibly, by force; **por ~** of necessity ▸ **fuerza de voluntad** willpower ▸ **fuerzas aéreas** air force sg ▸ **fuerzas armadas** armed forces

fuga ['fuɣa] nf (huida) flight, escape; (de gas etc) leak

fugarse [fu'ɣarse] vr to flee, escape

fugaz [fu'ɣaθ] adj fleeting

fugitivo, a [fuxi'tiβo, a] adj, nm/f fugitive

fui [fwi] vb ver **ser**; **ir**

fulano, -a [fu'lano, a] nm/f so-and-so, what's-his-name/what's-her-name

fulminante [fulmi'nante] adj (fig: mirada) fierce; (MED: enfermedad, ataque) sudden; (fam: éxito, golpe) sudden

fumador, a [fuma'ðor, a] nm/f smoker

fumar [fu'mar] vt, vi to smoke; **~ en pipa** to smoke a pipe

función [fun'θjon] nf function; (en trabajo) duties pl; (espectáculo) show;

entrar en funciones to take up one's duties

funcionar [funθjo'nar] vi (gen) to function; (máquina) to work; **"no funciona"** "out of order"

funcionario, -a [funθjo'narjo, a] nm/f civil servant

funda ['funda] nf (gen) cover; (de almohada) pillowcase

fundación [funda'θjon] nf foundation

fundamental [fundamen'tal] adj fundamental, basic

fundamento [funda'mento] nm (base) foundation

fundar [fun'dar] vt to found; **fundarse** vr: **fundarse en** to be founded on

fundición [fundi'θjon] nf fusing; (fábrica) foundry

fundir [fun'dir] vt (gen) to fuse; (metal) to smelt, melt down; (nieve etc) to melt; (COM) to merge; (estatua) to cast; **fundirse** vr (colores etc) to merge, blend; (unirse) to fuse together; (ELEC: fusible, lámpara etc) to fuse, blow; (nieve etc) to melt

fúnebre [fune'βre] adj funeral cpd, funereal

funeral [fune'ral] nm funeral ❑ **funeraria** nf undertaker's

funicular [funiku'lar] nm (tren) funicular; (teleférico) cable car

furgón [fur'ɣon] nm wagon ❑ **furgoneta** nf (AUTO, COM) (transit) van (BRIT), pick-up (truck) (US)

furia ['furja] nf (ira) fury; (violencia) violence ❑ **furioso, -a** adj (iracundo) furious; (violento) violent

furtivo, -a [fur'tiβo, a] adj furtive ♦ nm poacher

fusible [fu'siβle] nm fuse

fusil [fu'sil] nm rifle ❑ **fusilar** vt to shoot

fusión [fu'sjon] nf (gen) melting; (unión) fusion; (COM) merger

fútbol ['futβol] nm football (BRIT), soccer (US) ▸ **fútbol americano**

American football (*BRIT*), football (*US*)
▶ **fútbol sala** indoor football (*BRIT*) o
soccer (*US*) □ **futbolín** *nm* table
football □ **futbolista** *nmf* footballer

futuro, -a [fu'turo, a] *adj, nm* future

G, g

gabardina [gaβar'ðina] *nf* raincoat,
gabardine
gabinete [gaβi'nete] *nm* (*POL*) cabinet;
(*estudio*) study; (*de abogados etc*) office
gachas ['gatʃas] *nfpl* porridge *sg*
gafas ['gafas] *nfpl* glasses ▶ **gafas de
sol** sunglasses
gafe ['gafe] (*ESP*) *nmf* jinx
gaita ['gaita] *nf* bagpipes *pl*
gajes ['gaxes] *nmpl*: **~ del oficio**
occupational hazards
gajo ['gaxo] *nm* (*de naranja*) segment
gala ['gala] *nf* (*traje de etiqueta*) full
dress; **galas** *nfpl* (*ropa*) finery *sg*; **estar
de ~** to be in one's best clothes; **hacer
~ de** to display
galápago [ga'lapaɣo] *nm* (*ZOOL*) turtle
galardón [galar'ðon] *nm* award, prize
galaxia [ga'laksja] *nf* galaxy
galera [ga'lera] *nf* (*nave*) galley; (*carro*)
wagon; (*IMPRENTA*) galley
galería [gale'ria] *nf* (*gen*) gallery;
(*balcón*) veranda(h); (*pasillo*) corridor
▶ **galería comercial** shopping mall
Gales ['gales] *nm* (*tb*: **País de ~**) Wales
□ **galés, -esa** *adj* Welsh ♦ *nm/f*
Welshman(-woman) ♦ *nm* (*LING*) Welsh
galgo, -a ['galɣo, a] *nm/f* greyhound
gallego, -a [ga'ʎeɣo, a] *adj, nm/f*
Galician
galleta [ga'ʎeta] *nf* biscuit (*BRIT*),
cookie (*US*)
gallina [ga'ʎina] *nf* hen ♦ *nmf* (*fam:
cobarde*) chicken □ **gallinero** *nm*
henhouse; (*TEATRO*) top gallery

gallo ['gaʎo] *nm* cock, rooster
galopar [galo'par] *vi* to gallop
gama ['gama] *nf* (*fig*) range
gamba ['gamba] *nf* prawn (*BRIT*),
shrimp (*US*)
gamberro, -a [gam'berro, a] (*ESP*) *nm/f*
hooligan, lout
gamuza [ga'muθa] *nf* chamois
gana ['gana] *nf* (*deseo*) desire, wish;
(*apetito*) appetite; (*voluntad*) will;
(*añoranza*) longing; **de buena ~**
willingly; **de mala ~** reluctantly; **me da
ganas de** I feel like, I want to; **no me da
la ~** I don't feel like it; **tener ganas de**
to feel like
ganadería [ganaðe'ria] *nf* (*ganado*)
livestock; (*ganado vacuno*) cattle *pl*;
(*cría, comercio*) cattle raising
ganadero, -a [gana'ðero, a] *nm/f*
(*hacendado*) rancher
ganado [ga'naðo] *nm* livestock
▶ **ganado porcino** pigs *pl*
ganador, a [gana'ðor, a] *adj* winning
♦ *nm/f* winner
ganancia [ga'nanθja] *nf* (*lo ganado*)
gain; (*aumento*) increase; (*beneficio*)
profit; **ganancias** *nfpl* (*ingresos*)
earnings; (*beneficios*) profit *sg*,
winnings
ganar [ga'nar] *vt* (*obtener*) to get,
obtain; (*sacar ventaja*) to gain; (*salario
etc*) to earn; (*DEPORTE, premio*) to win;
(*derrotar a*) to beat; (*alcanzar*) to reach
♦ *vi* (*DEPORTE*) to win; **ganarse** *vr*:
ganarse la vida to earn one's living
ganchillo [gan'tʃiʎo] *nm* crochet
gancho ['gantʃo] *nm* (*gen*) hook;
(*colgador*) hanger
gandul, a [gan'dul, a] *adj, nm/f* good-
for-nothing, layabout
ganga ['ganga] *nf* bargain
gangrena [gan'grena] *nf* gangrene
ganso, -a ['ganso, a] *nm/f* (*ZOOL*) goose;
(*fam*) idiot
ganzúa [gan'θua] *nf* skeleton key

garabato [gara'βato] nm (escritura) scrawl, scribble

garaje [ga'raxe] nm garage

garantía [garan'tia] nf guarantee

garantizar [garanti'θar] vt to guarantee

garbanzo [gar'βanθo] nm chickpea (BRIT), garbanzo (US)

garfio ['garfjo] nm grappling iron

garganta [gar'ganta] nf (ANAT) throat; (de botella) neck ❏ **gargantilla** nf necklace

gárgaras ['garɣaras] nfpl: **hacer ~** to gargle

gargarear (LAm) vi to gargle

garita [ga'rita] nf cabin, hut; (MIL) sentry box

garra ['garra] nf (de gato, TEC) claw; (de ave) talon; (fam: mano) hand, paw

garrafa [ga'rrafa] nf carafe, decanter

garrapata [garra'pata] nf tick

gas [gas] nm **gas ► gases lacrimógenos** tear gas sg

gasa ['gasa] nf gauze

gaseosa [gase'osa] nf lemonade

gaseoso, -a [gase'oso, a] adj gassy, fizzy

gasoil [ga'soil] nm diesel (oil)

gasóleo [ga'soleo] nm = **gasoil**

gasolina [gaso'lina] nf petrol (BRIT), gas(oline) (US) ❏ **gasolinera** nf petrol (BRIT) o gas (US) station

gastado, -a [gas'taðo, a] adj (dinero) spent; (ropa) worn out; (usado: frase etc) trite

gastar [gas'tar] vt (dinero, tiempo) to spend; (fuerzas) to use up; (desperdiciar) to waste; (llevar) to wear; **gastarse** vr to wear out; (estropearse) to waste; **~ en** to spend on; **~ bromas** to crack jokes; **¿qué número gastas?** what size (shoe) do you take?

gasto ['gasto] nm (desembolso) expenditure, spending; (consumo, uso)

use; **gastos** nmpl (desembolsos) expenses; (cargos) charges, costs

gastronomía [gastrono'mia] nf gastronomy

gatear [gate'ar] vi (andar a gatas) to go on all fours

gatillo [ga'tiʎo] nm (de arma de fuego) trigger; (de dentista) forceps

gato, -a ['gato, a] nm/f cat ♦ nm (TEC) jack; **andar a gatas** to go on all fours

gaucho ['gautʃo] nm gaucho

GAUCHO

Gauchos are the herdsmen or riders of the Southern Cone plains. Although popularly associated with Argentine folklore, **gauchos** belong equally to the cattle-raising areas of Southern Brazil and Uruguay. **Gauchos'** traditions and clothing reflect their mixed ancestry and cultural roots. Their baggy trousers are Arabic in origin, while the horse and guitar are inherited from the Spanish conquistadors; the poncho, maté and **boleadoras** (strips of leather weighted at either end with stones) form part of the Indian tradition.

---

gaviota [ga'βjota] nf seagull

gay [ge] adj inv, nm gay, homosexual

gazpacho [gaθ'patʃo] nm gazpacho

gel [xel] nm: **~ de baño/ducha** bath/shower gel

gelatina [xela'tina] nf jelly; (polvos etc) gelatine

gema ['xema] nf gem

gemelo, -a [xe'melo, a] adj, nm/f twin; **gemelos** nmpl (de camisa) cufflinks; (prismáticos) field glasses, binoculars

gemido [xe'miðo] nm (quejido) moan, groan; (aullido) howl

Géminis ['xeminis] nm Gemini

gemir [xe'mir] vi (quejarse) to moan, groan; (aullar) to howl

generación [xenera'θjon] nf generation

general [xene'ral] adj general ♦ nm general; **por lo** o **en ~** in general ❑ **Generalitat** nf Catalan parliament ❑ **generalizar** vt to generalize; **generalizarse** vr to become generalized, spread

generar [xene'rar] vt to generate

género ['xenero] nm (clase) kind, sort; (tipo) type; (BIO) genus; (LING) gender; (COM) material ▶ **género humano** human race

generosidad [xenerosi'ðað] nf generosity ❑ **generoso, -a** adj generous

genial [xe'njal] adj inspired; (idea) brilliant; (estupendo) wonderful

genio ['xenjo] nm (carácter) nature, disposition; (humor) temper; (facultad creadora) genius; **de mal ~** bad-tempered

genital [xeni'tal] adj genital ❑ **genitales** nmpl genitals

gente ['xente] nf (personas) people pl; (parientes) relatives pl

gentil [xen'til] adj (elegante) graceful; (encantador) charming

⚠ No confundir **gentil** con la palabra inglesa *gentle*.

genuino, -a [xe'nwino, a] adj genuine

geografía [xeoɣra'fia] nf geography

geología [xeolo'xia] nf geology

geometría [xeome'tria] nf geometry

gerente [xe'rente] nmf (supervisor) manager; (jefe) director

geriatría [xeria'tria] nf (MED) geriatrics sg

germen ['xermen] nm germ

gesticular [xestiku'lar] vi to gesticulate; (hacer muecas) to grimace ❑ **gesticulación** nf gesticulation; (mueca) grimace

gestión [xes'tjon] nf management; (diligencia, acción) negotiation

gesto ['xesto] nm (mueca) grimace; (ademán) gesture

Gibraltar [xiβral'tar] nm Gibraltar ❑ **gibraltareño, -a** adj, nm/f Gibraltarian

gigante [xi'ɣante] adj, nmf giant ❑ **gigantesco, -a** adj gigantic

gilipollas [xili'poʎas] (fam) adj inv daft ♦ nmf inv wally

gimnasia [xim'nasja] nf gymnastics pl ❑ **gimnasio** nm gymnasium ❑ **gimnasta** nmf gymnast

ginebra [xi'neβra] nf gin

ginecólogo, -a [xine'koloɣo, a] nm/f gynaecologist

gira ['xira] nf tour, trip

girar [xi'rar] vt (dar la vuelta) to turn (around); (: rápidamente) to spin; (COM: giro postal) to draw; (: letra de cambio) to issue ♦ vi to turn (round); (rápido) to spin

girasol [xira'sol] nm sunflower

giratorio, -a [xira'torjo, a] adj revolving

giro ['xiro] nm (movimiento) turn, revolution; (LING) expression; (COM) draft ▶ **giro bancario/postal** bank draft/money order

gis [xis] (MÉX) nm chalk

gitano, -a [xi'tano, a] adj, nm/f gypsy

glacial [gla'θjal] adj icy, freezing

glaciar [gla'θjar] nm glacier

glándula ['glandula] nf gland

global [glo'βal] adj global ❑ **globalización** nf globalization

globo ['gloβo] nm (esfera) globe, sphere; (aerostato, juguete) balloon

glóbulo ['gloβulo] nm globule; (ANAT) corpuscle

gloria ['glorja] nf glory

glorieta [glo'rjeta] nf (de jardín) bower, arbour; (plazoleta) roundabout (BRIT), traffic circle (US)

glorioso, -a [glo'rjoso, a] adj glorious

glotón, -ona [glo'ton, ona] *adj* gluttonous, greedy ♦ *nm/f* glutton

glucosa [glu'kosa] *nf* glucose

gobernador, a [goβerna'ðor, a] *adj* governing ♦ *nm/f* governor
❏ **gobernante** *adj* governing

gobernar [goβer'nar] *vt* (*dirigir*) to guide, direct; (*POL*) to rule, govern ♦ *vi* to govern; (*NÁUT*) to steer

gobierno *etc* [go'βjerno] *vb ver* **gobernar** ♦ *nm* (*POL*) government; (*dirección*) guidance, direction; (*NÁUT*) steering

goce *etc* [ˈgoθe] *vb ver* **gozar** ♦ *nm* enjoyment

gol [gol] *nm* goal

golf [golf] *nm* golf

golfa [ˈgolfa] (*fam!*) *nf* (*mujer*) slut, whore

golfo, -a [ˈgolfo, a] *nm* (*GEO*) gulf ♦ *nm/f* (*fam: niño*) urchin; (*gamberro*) lout

golondrina [golon'drina] *nf* swallow

golosina [golo'sina] *nf* (*dulce*) sweet ❏ **goloso, -a** *adj* sweet-toothed

golpe [ˈgolpe] *nm* blow; (*de puño*) punch; (*de mano*) smack; (*de remo*) stroke; (*fig: choque*) clash; **no dar ~** to be bone idle; **de un ~** with one blow; **de ~** suddenly ♦ **golpe (de estado)** coup (d'état) ❏ **golpear** *vt*, *vi* to strike, knock; (*asestar*) to beat; (*de puño*) to punch; (*golpetear*) to tap

goma [ˈgoma] *nf* (*caucho*) rubber; (*elástico*) elastic; (*una goma*) elastic band ▶ **goma de borrar** eraser, rubber (*BRIT*) ▶ **goma espuma** foam rubber

gomina [go'mina] *nf* hair gel

gomita (*RPl*) [go'mita] *nf* rubber band

gordo, -a [ˈgorðo, a] *adj* (*gen*) fat; (*persona*) enormous; **el (premio) ~** (*en lotería*) first prize

gorila [go'rila] *nm* gorilla

gorra [ˈgorra] *nf* cap; (*de bebé*) bonnet; (*militar*) bearskin; **entrar de ~** (*fam*) to gatecrash; **ir de ~** to sponge

gorrión [go'rrjon] *nm* sparrow

gorro [ˈgorro] *nm* (*gen*) cap; (*de bebé, mujer*) bonnet

gorrón, -ona [go'rron, ona] *nm/f* scrounger ❏ **gorronear** (*fam*) *vi* to scrounge

gota [ˈgota] *nf* (*gen*) drop; (*de sudor*) bead; (*MED*) gout ❏ **gotear** *vi* to drip; (*lloviznar*) to drizzle ❏ **gotera** *nf* leak

gozar [go'θar] *vi* to enjoy o.s.; ~ **de** (*disfrutar*) to enjoy; (*poseer*) to possess

gr. *abr* (= *gramo, gramos*) g

grabación [graβa'θjon] *nf* recording

grabado [gra'βaðo] *nm* print, engraving

grabadora [graβa'ðora] *nf* tape-recorder

grabar [gra'βar] *vt* to engrave; (*discos, cintas*) to record

gracia [ˈgraθja] *nf* (*encanto*) grace, gracefulness; (*humor*) humour, wit; **¡(muchas) gracias!** thanks (very much)!; **gracias a** thanks to; **dar las gracias a algn por algo** to thank sb for sth; **tener ~** (*chiste etc*) to be funny; **no me hace ~** I am not keen ❏ **gracioso, -a** *adj* (*divertido*) funny, amusing; (*cómico*) comical ♦ *nm/f* (*TEATRO*) comic character

grada [ˈgraða] *nf* (*de escalera*) step; (*de anfiteatro*) tier, row; **gradas** *nfpl* (*DEPORTE: de estadio*) terraces

grado [ˈgraðo] *nm* degree; (*de aceite, vino*) grade; (*grada*) step; (*MIL*) rank; **de buen ~** willingly ▶ **grado centígrado/Fahrenheit** degree centigrade/Fahrenheit

graduación [graðwa'θjon] *nf* (*del alcohol*) proof, strength; (*ESCOL*) graduation; (*MIL*) rank

gradual [gra'ðwal] *adj* gradual

graduar [gra'ðwar] *vt* (*gen*) to graduate; (*MIL*) to commission; **graduarse** *vr* to graduate; **graduarse la vista** to have one's eyes tested

gráfica [ˈgrafika] *nf* graph

gráfico, -a ['grafiko, a] *adj* graphic
♦ *nm* diagram; **gráficos** *nmpl* (*INFORM*) graphics

grajo ['graxo] *nm* rook

gramática [gra'matika] *nf* grammar

gramo ['gramo] *nm* gramme (*BRIT*), gram (*US*)

gran [gran] *adj ver* **grande**

grana ['grana] *nf* (*color, tela*) scarlet

granada [gra'naða] *nf* pomegranate; (*MIL*) grenade

granate [gra'nate] *adj* deep red

Gran Bretaña [-bre'taɲa] *nf* Great Britain

grande ['grande] (*antes de nmsg* **gran**) *adj* (*de tamaño*) big, large; (*alto*) tall; (*distinguido*) great; (*impresionante*) grand ♦ *nm* grandee

granel [gra'nel]: **a ~** *adv* (*COM*) in bulk

granero [gra'nero] *nm* granary, barn

granito [gra'nito] *nm* (*AGR*) small grain; (*roca*) granite

granizado [grani'θaðo] *nm* iced drink

granizar [grani'θar] *vi* to hail
❏ **granizo** *nm* hail

granja ['granxa] *nf* (*gen*) farm
❏ **granjero, -a** *nm/f* farmer

grano ['grano] *nm* grain; (*semilla*) seed; (*de café*) bean; (*MED*) pimple, spot

granuja [gra'nuxa] *nmf* rogue; (*golfillo*) urchin

grapa ['grapa] *nf* staple; (*TEC*) clamp
❏ **grapadora** *nf* stapler

grasa ['grasa] *nf* (*gen*) grease; (*de cocinar*) fat, lard; (*sebo*) suet; (*mugre*) filth ❏ **grasiento, -a** *adj* greasy; (*de aceite*) oily ❏ **graso, -a** *adj* (*leche, queso, carne*) fatty; (*pelo, piel*) greasy

gratinar [grati'nar] *vt* to cook au gratin

gratis ['gratis] *adv* free

grato, -a ['grato, a] *adj* (*agradable*) pleasant, agreeable

gratuito, -a [gra'twito, a] *adj* (*gratis*) free; (*sin razón*) gratuitous

grave ['graβe] *adj* heavy; (*serio*) grave, serious ♦ **gravedad** *nf* gravity

Grecia ['greθja] *nf* Greece

gremio ['gremjo] *nm* trade, industry

griego, -a ['grjeɣo, a] *adj, nm/f* Greek

grieta ['grjeta] *nf* crack

grifo ['grifo] (*ESP*) *nm* tap (*BRIT*), faucet (*US*)

grillo ['griʎo] *nm* (*ZOOL*) cricket

gripa (*MÉX*) ['gripa] *nf* flu, influenza

gripe ['gripe] *nf* flu, influenza

gris [gris] *adj* (*color*) grey

gritar [gri'tar] *vt, vi* to shout, yell
❏ **grito** *nm* shout, yell; (*de horror*) scream

grosella [gro'seʎa] *nf* (red)currant

grosero, -a [gro'sero, a] *adj* (*poco cortés*) rude, bad-mannered; (*ordinario*) vulgar, crude

grosor [gro'sor] *nm* thickness

grúa ['grua] *nf* (*TEC*) crane; (*de petróleo*) derrick

grueso, -a ['grweso, a] *adj* thick; (*persona*) stout ♦ *nm* bulk; **el ~ de** the bulk of

grulla ['gruʎa] *nf* crane

grumo ['grumo] *nm* clot, lump

gruñido [gru'ɲiðo] *nm* grunt; (*de persona*) grumble

gruñir [gru'ɲir] *vi* (*animal*) to growl; (*persona*) to grumble

grupo ['grupo] *nm* group; (*TEC*) unit, set
▸ **grupo de presión** pressure group
▸ **grupo sanguíneo** blood group

gruta ['gruta] *nf* grotto

guacho, -a (*CS*) ['gwatʃo, a] *nm/f* homeless child

guajolote (*MÉX*) [gwaxo'lote] *nm* turkey

guante ['gwante] *nm* glove ▸ **guantes de goma** rubber gloves ❏ **guantera** *nf* glove compartment

guapo, -a ['gwapo, a] *adj* good-looking, attractive; (*elegante*) smart

guarda ['gwarða] *nmf* (*persona*) guard, keeper ♦ *nf* (*acto*) guarding; (*custodia*) custody ► **guarda jurado** (armed) security guard ► **guardabarros** nm inv mudguard (BRIT), fender (US) ❑ **guardabosques** nm inv gamekeeper ❑ **guardacostas** nm inv coastguard vessel ♦ nmf guardian, protector ❑ **guardaespaldas** nmf inv bodyguard ❑ **guardameta** nmf goalkeeper ❑ **guardar** vt (gen) to keep; (vigilar) to guard, watch over; (dinero: ahorrar) to save; **guardarse** vr (preservarse) to protect o.s.; (evitar) to avoid; **guardar cama** to stay in bed ❑ **guardarropa** nm (armario) wardrobe; (en establecimiento público) cloakroom

guardería [gwarðe'ria] nf nursery

guardia ['gwarðja] nf (MIL) guard; (cuidado) care, custody ♦ nmf guard; (policía) policeman(-woman); **estar de ~** to be on guard; **montar de ~** to mount guard ► **Guardia Civil** Civil Guard

guardián, -ana [gwar'ðjan, ana] nm/f (gen) guardian, keeper

guarida [gwa'riða] nf (de animal) den, lair; (refugio) refuge

guarnición [gwarni'θjon] nf (de vestimenta) trimming; (de piedra) mount; (CULIN) garnish; (arneses) harness; (MIL) garrison

guarro, -a ['gwarro, a] nm/f pig

guasa ['gwasa] nf joke ❑ **guasón, -ona** [gwa'son, ona] adj (bromista) joking ♦ nm/f wit, joker

Guatemala [gwate'mala] nf Guatemala

guay [gwai] (fam) adj super, great

güero, -a [MÉX] ['gwero, a] adj blond(e)

guerra ['gerra] nf war; **dar ~** to annoy ► **guerra civil** civil war ► **guerra fría** cold war ❑ **guerrero, -a** adj fighting; (carácter) warlike ♦ nm/f warrior

guerrilla [ge'rriʎa] nf guerrilla warfare; (tropas) guerrilla band o group

guía etc ['gia] vb ver **guiar** ♦ nmf (persona) guide; (nf: libro) guidebook

► **guía telefónica** telephone directory ► **guía turística** tourist guide

guiar [gi'ar] vt to guide, direct; (AUTO) to steer; **guiarse** vr: **guiarse por** to be guided by

guinda ['ginda] nf morello cherry

guindilla [gin'diʎa] nf chilli pepper

guiñar [gi'ɲar] vt to wink

guión [gi'on] nm (LING) hyphen, dash; (CINE) script ❑ **guionista** nmf scriptwriter

guiri ['giri] (ESP: fam, pey) nmf foreigner

guirnalda [gir'nalda] nf garland

guisado [gi'saðo] nm stew

guisante [gi'sante] nm pea

guisar [gi'sar] vt, vi to cook ❑ **guiso** nm cooked dish

guitarra [gi'tarra] nf guitar

gula ['gula] nf gluttony, greed

gusano [gu'sano] nm worm; (lombriz) earthworm

gustar [gus'tar] vt to taste, sample ♦ vi to please, be pleasing; **~ de algo** to like o enjoy sth; **me gustan las uvas** I like grapes; **le gusta nadar** she likes o enjoys swimming

gusto ['gusto] nm (sentido, sabor) taste; (placer) pleasure; **tiene ~ a menta** it tastes of mint; **tener buen ~** to have good taste; **coger el o tomar ~ a algo** to take a liking to sth; **sentirse a ~** to feel at ease; **mucho ~ (en conocerle)** pleased to meet you; **el ~ es mío** the pleasure is mine; **con ~** willingly, gladly

H, h

ha [a] vb ver **haber**

haba ['aβa] nf bean

Habana [a'βana] nf: **la ~** Havana

habano [a'βano] nm Havana cigar

habéis vb ver **haber**

haber

PALABRA CLAVE

[aˈβer] *vb aux*

1 (*tiempos compuestos*) to have; **había comido** I had eaten; **antes/después de haberlo visto** before seeing/after seeing *o* having seen it

2: **¡haberlo dicho antes!** you should have said so before!

3: **haber de, he de hacerlo** I have to do it; **ha de llegar mañana** it should arrive tomorrow

♦ *vb impers*

1 (*existencia: sg*) there is; (*: pl*) there are; **hay un hermano/dos hermanos** there is one brother/there are two brothers; **¿cuánto hay de aquí a Sucre?** how far is it from here to Sucre?

2 (*obligación*): **hay que hacer algo** something must be done; **hay que apuntarlo para acordarse** you have to write it down to remember

3: **¡hay que ver!** well I never!

4: **¡no hay de *o* por** (*LAm*) **qué!** don't mention it!, not at all!

5: **¿qué hay?** (*¿qué pasa?*) what's up?, what's the matter?; (*¿qué tal?*) how's it going?

♦ *vt*: **he aquí unas sugerencias** here are some suggestions; **no hay cintas blancas pero sí las hay rojas** there aren't any white ribbons but there are some red ones

♦ *nm* (*en cuenta*) credit side; **haberes** *nmpl* assets; **¿cuánto tengo en mi haber?** how much do I have in my account?; **tiene varias novelas en su haber** he has several novels to his credit

♦ **haberse** *vr*: **habérselas con algn** to have it out with sb

habichuela [aβiˈtʃwela] *nf* kidney bean

hábil [ˈaβil] *adj* (*listo*) clever, smart; (*capaz*) fit, capable; (*experto*) expert; **día ~** working day ◻ **habilidad** *nf* skill, ability

habitación [aβitaˈθjon] *nf* (*cuarto*) room; (*BIO: morada*) habitat
▸ **habitación doble *o* de matrimonio** double room
▸ **habitación individual *o* sencilla** single room

habitante [aβiˈtante] *nmf* inhabitant

habitar [aβiˈtar] *vt* (*residir en*) to inhabit; (*ocupar*) to occupy ♦ *vi* to live

hábito [ˈaβito] *nm* habit

habitual [aβiˈtwal] *adj* usual

habituar [aβiˈtwar] *vt* to accustom; **habituarse** *vr*: **habituarse a** to get used to

habla [ˈaβla] *nf* (*capacidad de hablar*) speech; (*idioma*) language; (*dialecto*) dialect; **perder el ~** to become speechless; **de ~ francesa** French-speaking; **estar al ~** to be in contact; (*TEL*) to be on the line; **¡González al ~!** (*TEL*) González speaking!

hablador, a [aβlaˈðor, a] *adj* talkative ♦ *nm/f* chatterbox

habladuría [aβlaðuˈria] *nf* rumour; **habladurías** *nfpl* gossip *sg*

hablante [aˈβlante] *adj* speaking ♦ *nmf* speaker

hablar [aˈβlar] *vt* to speak, talk ♦ *vi* to speak; **hablarse** *vr* to speak to each other; **~ con** to speak to; **~ de** to speak of *o* about; **¡ni ~!** it's out of the question!; **"se habla inglés"** "English spoken here"

habré *etc* [aˈβre] *vb ver* **haber**

hacendado (*LAm*) [aθenˈdaðo] *nm* rancher, farmer

hacendoso, -a [aθenˈdoso, a] *adj* industrious

hacer

PALABRA CLAVE

[a'θer] vt

1 (fabricar, producir) to make; (construir) to build; **hacer una película/un ruido** to make a film/noise; **el guisado lo hice yo** I made o cooked the stew

2 (ejecutar: trabajo etc) to do; **hacer la colada** to do the washing; **hacer la comida** to do the cooking; **¿qué haces?** what are you doing?; **hacer el malo** o **el papel del malo** (TEATRO) to play the villain

3 (estudios, algunos deportes) to do; **hacer español/económicas** to do o study Spanish/economics; **hacer yoga/gimnasia** to do yoga/go to gym

4 (transformar, incidir en): **esto lo hará más difícil** this will make it more difficult; **salir te hará sentir mejor** going out will make you feel better

5 (cálculo): **2 y 2 hacen 4** 2 and 2 make 4; **éste hace 100** this one makes 100

6 (+ sub): **esto hará que ganemos** this will make us win; **harás que no quiera venir** you'll stop him wanting to come

7 (como sustituto de vb) to do; **él bebió y yo hice lo mismo** he drank and I did likewise

8: **no hace más que criticar** all he does is criticize

♦ vb semi-aux (directo): **hacer** +infin: **les hice venir** I made o had them come; **hacer trabajar a los demás** to get others to work

♦ vi

1: **haz como que no lo sabes** act as if you don't know

2 (ser apropiado): **si os hace** if it's alright with you

3: **hacer de: hacer de Otelo** to play Othello

♦ vb impers

1: **hace calor/frío** it's hot/cold; ver tb **bueno; sol; tiempo**

2 (tiempo): **hace 3 años** 3 years ago; **hace un mes que voy/no voy** I've been going/I haven't been for a month

3: **¿cómo has hecho para llegar tan rápido?** how did you manage to get here so quickly?

♦ hacerse vr

1 (volverse) to become; **se hicieron amigos** they became friends

2 (acostumbrarse): **hacerse a** to get used to

3: **se hace con huevos y leche** it's made out of eggs and milk; **eso no se hace** that's not done

4 (obtener): **hacerse de** o **con algo** to get hold of sth

5 (fingirse): **hacerse el sueco** to turn a deaf ear

hacha ['atʃa] nf axe; (antorcha) torch

hachís [a'tʃis] nm hashish

hacia ['aθja] prep (en dirección de) towards; (cerca de) near; (actitud) towards; **~ adelante/atrás** forwards/backwards; **~ arriba/abajo** up(wards)/down(wards); **~ mediodía/las cinco** about noon/five

hacienda [a'θjenda] nf (propiedad) property; (finca) farm; (LAm: rancho) ranch; **(Ministerio de) H~** Exchequer (BRIT), Treasury Department (US) ▶ **hacienda pública** public finance

hada ['aða] nf fairy

hago etc vb ver **hacer**

Haití [ai'ti] nm Haiti

halagar [ala'ɣar] vt to flatter

halago [a'laɣo] nm flattery

halcón [al'kon] nm falcon, hawk

hallar [a'ʎar] vt (gen) to find; (descubrir) to discover; (toparse con) to run into; **hallarse** vr to be (situated)

halterofilia [altero'filja] nf weightlifting

hamaca [a'maka] nf hammock

hambre ['ambre] nf hunger; (plaga) famine; (deseo) longing; **tener ~** to be hungry; **¡me muero de ~!** I'm starving!; ❑ **hambriento, -a** adj hungry, starving

hamburguesa [ambur'ɣesa] nf hamburger ❑ **hamburguesería** nf burger bar

han [an] vb ver **haber**

harapos [a'rapos] nmpl rags

haré [a're] vb ver **hacer**

harina [a'rina] nf flour ▸ **harina de maíz** cornflour (BRIT), cornstarch (US) ▸ **harina de trigo** wheat flour

hartar [ar'tar] vt to satiate, glut; (fig) to tire, sicken; **hartarse** vr (de comida) to fill o.s., gorge o.s.; (cansarse): **hartarse (de)** to get fed up (with) ❑ **harto, -a** adj (lleno) full; (cansado) fed up ♦ adv (bastante) enough; (muy) very; **estar harto de hacer algo/de algn** to be fed up of doing sth/with sb

has [as] vb ver **haber**

hasta ['asta] adv even ♦ prep (alcanzando a) as far as; up to; down to; (de tiempo: a tal hora) till, until; (antes de) before ♦ conj: **~ que ...** until; **~ luego/el sábado** see you soon/on Saturday; **~ ahora** (al despedirse) see you in a minute; **~ pronto** see you soon

hay [ai] vb ver **haber**

Haya ['aja] nf: **la ~** The Hague

haya etc ['aja] vb ver **haber** ♦ nf beech tree

haz [aθ] vb ver **hacer** ♦ nm (de luz) beam

hazaña [a'θaɲa] nf feat, exploit

hazmerreír [aθmerre'ir] nm inv laughing stock

he [e] vb ver **haber**

hebilla [e'βiʎa] nf buckle, clasp

hebra ['eβra] nf thread; (BOT: fibra) fibre, grain

hebreo, -a [e'βreo, a] adj, nm/f Hebrew ♦ nm (LING) Hebrew

hechizar [etʃi'θar] vt to cast a spell on, bewitch

hechizo [e'tʃiθo] nm witchcraft, magic; (acto de magia) spell, charm

hecho, -a [e'tʃo, a] pp de **hacer** ♦ adj (carne) done; (COSTURA) ready-to-wear ♦ nm deed, act; (dato) fact; (cuestión) matter; (suceso) event ♦ excl agreed!, done!; **de ~** in fact, as a matter of fact; **el ~ es que ...** the fact is that ...; **¡bien ~!** well done!

hechura [e'tʃura] nf (forma) form, shape; (de persona) build

hectárea [ek'tarea] nf hectare

helada [e'laða] nf frost

heladera [ela'ðera] nf (LAm) (refrigerador) refrigerator

helado, -a [e'laðo, a] adj frozen; (glacial) icy; (fig) chilly, cold ♦ nm ice cream

helar [e'lar] vt to freeze, ice (up); (dejar atónito) to amaze; (desalentar) to discourage ♦ vi to freeze; **helarse** vr to freeze

helecho [e'letʃo] nm fern

hélice [e'liθe] nf (TEC) propeller

helicóptero [eli'koptero] nm helicopter

hembra ['embra] nf (BOT, ZOOL) female; (mujer) woman; (TEC) nut

hemorragia [emo'rraxja] nf haemorrhage

hemorroides [emo'rroiðes] nfpl haemorrhoids, piles

hemos ['emos] vb ver **haber**

heno ['eno] nm hay

heredar [ere'ðar] *vt* to inherit
☐ **heredero, -a** *nm/f* heir(ess)

hereje [e'rexe] *nmf* heretic

herencia [e'renθja] *nf* inheritance

herida [e'riða] *nf* wound, injury; *ver tb* **herido**

herido, -a [e'riðo, a] *adj* injured, wounded ♦ *nm/f* casualty

herir [e'rir] *vt* to wound, injure; *(fig)* to offend

hermanastro, -a [erma'nastro, a] *nm/f* stepbrother/sister

hermandad [erman'daθ] *nf* brotherhood

hermano, -a [er'mano, a] *nm/f* brother/sister ► **hermano(-a) gemelo(-a)** twin brother/sister ► **hermano(-a) político(-a)** brother-in-law/sister-in-law

hermético, -a [er'metiko, a] *adj* hermetic; *(fig)* watertight

hermoso, -a [er'moso, a] *adj* beautiful, lovely; *(estupendo)* splendid; *(guapo)* handsome ☐ **hermosura** *nf* beauty

hernia ['ernja] *nf* hernia ► **hernia discal** slipped disc

héroe ['eroe] *nm* hero

heroína [ero'ina] *nf (mujer)* heroine; *(droga)* heroin

herradura [erra'ðura] *nf* horseshoe

herramienta [erra'mjenta] *nf* tool

herrero [e'rrero] *nm* blacksmith

hervidero [erβi'ðero] *nm (fig)* swarm; *(POL etc)* hotbed

hervir [er'βir] *vi* to boil; *(burbujear)* to bubble; **~ a fuego lento** to simmer ☐ **hervor** *nm* boiling; *(fig)* ardour, fervour

heterosexual [eterosek'swal] *adj* heterosexual

hice *etc vb ver* **hacer**

hidratante [iðra'tante] *adj:* **crema ~** moisturizing cream, moisturizer ☐ **hidratar** *vt (piel)* to moisturize ☐ **hidrato** *nm* hydrate ► **hidratos de carbono** carbohydrates

hidráulico, -a [i'ðrauliko, a] *adj* hydraulic

hidro... [iðro] *prefijo* hydro..., water-... ☐ **hidroeléctrico, -a** *adj* hydroelectric ☐ **hidrógeno** *nm* hydrogen

hiedra ['jeðra] *nf* ivy

hiel [jel] *nf* gall, bile; *(fig)* bitterness

hiela *etc vb ver* **helar**

hielo ['jelo] *nm (gen)* ice; *(escarcha)* frost; *(fig)* coldness, reserve

hiena ['jena] *nf* hyena

hierba ['jerβa] *nf (pasto)* grass; *(CULIN, MED: planta)* herb; **mala ~** weed; *(fig)* evil influence ☐ **hierbabuena** *nf* mint

hierro ['jerro] *nm (metal)* iron; *(objeto)* iron object

hígado [i'yaðo] *nm* liver

higiene [i'xjene] *nf* hygiene ☐ **higiénico, -a** *adj* hygienic

higo ['iyo] *nm* fig ► **higo seco** dried fig ☐ **higuera** *nf* fig tree

hijastro, -a [i'xastro, a] *nm/f* stepson/daughter

hijo, -a [i'xo, a] *nm/f* son/daughter, child; **hijos** *nmpl* children, sons and daughters ► **hijo adoptivo** adopted child ► **hijo de papá/mamá** daddy's/mummy's boy ► **hijo de puta** *(fam!)* bastard *(!)*, son of a bitch *(!)* ► **hijo/a político/a** son-/daughter-in-law

hilera [i'lera] *nf* row, file

hilo ['ilo] *nm* thread; *(BOT)* fibre; *(metal)* wire; *(de agua)* trickle, thin stream

hilvanar [ilβa'nar] *vt (COSTURA)* to tack *(BRIT)*, baste *(US)*; *(fig)* to do hurriedly

himno ['imno] *nm* hymn ► **himno nacional** national anthem

hincapié [inka'pje] *nm:* **hacer hincapié en** to emphasize

hincar [in'kar] *vt* to drive (in), thrust (in)

hincha ['intʃa] *(fam) nmf* fan

hinchado, -a [in'tʃaðo, a] *adj (gen)* swollen; *(persona)* pompous

hinchar [in'tʃar] *vt* (*gen*) to swell; (*inflar*) to blow up, inflate; (*fig*) to exaggerate; **hincharse** *vr* (*inflarse*) to swell up; (*fam: de comer*) to stuff o.s. □ **hinchazón** *nf* (*MED*) swelling; (*altivez*) arrogance

hinojo [i'noxo] *nm* fennel

hipermercado [ipɛrmɛr'kaðo] *nm* hypermarket, superstore

hípico, -a [i'ipiko, a] *adj* horse *cpd*

hipnotismo [ipno'tismo] *nm* hypnotism □ **hipnotizar** *vt* to hypnotize

hipo ['ipo] *nm* hiccups *pl*

hipocresía [ipokre'sia] *nf* hypocrisy □ **hipócrita** *adj* hypocritical ♦ *nmf* hypocrite

hipódromo [i'poðromo] *nm* racetrack

hipopótamo [ipo'potamo] *nm* hippopotamus

hipoteca [ipo'teka] *nf* mortgage

hipótesis [i'potesis] *nf inv* hypothesis

hispánico, -a [is'paniko, a] *adj* Hispanic

hispano, -a [is'pano, a] *adj* Hispanic, Spanish, Hispano- ♦ *nm/f* Spaniard □ **Hispanoamérica** *nf* Latin America □ **hispanoamericano, -a** *adj, nm/f* Latin American

histeria [is'terja] *nf* hysteria

historia [is'torja] *nf* history; (*cuento*) story, tale; **historias** *nfpl* (*chismes*) gossip *sg*; **dejarse de historias** to come to the point; **pasar a la ~** to go down in history □ **historiador, a** *nm/f* historian □ **historial** *nm* (*profesional*) curriculum vitae, C.V.; (*MED*) case history □ **histórico, -a** *adj* historical; (*memorable*) historic

historieta [isto'rjeta] *nf* tale, anecdote; (*dibujos*) comic strip

hito ['ito] *nm* (*fig*) landmark

hizo ['iθo] *vb ver* **hacer**

hocico [o'θiko] *nm* snout

hockey ['xokei] *nm* hockey ► **hockey sobre hielo/patines** ice/roller hockey

hogar [o'ɣar] *nm* fireplace, hearth; (*casa*) home; (*vida familiar*) home life □ **hogareño, -a** *adj* home *cpd*; (*persona*) home-loving

hoguera [o'ɣera] *nf* (*gen*) bonfire

hoja ['oxa] *nf* (*gen*) leaf; (*de flor*) petal; (*de papel*) sheet; (*página*) page ► **hoja de afeitar** (*LAm*) razor blade ► **hoja electrónica** o **de cálculo** spreadsheet ► **hoja informativa** leaflet, handout

hojalata [oxa'lata] *nf* tin(plate)

hojaldre [o'xaldre] *nm* (*CULIN*) puff pastry

hojear [oxe'ar] *vt* to leaf through, turn the pages of

hojuela (*MEX*) *nf* flake

hola ['ola] *excl* hello!

holá (*RPl*) *excl* hello!

Holanda [o'landa] *nf* Holland □ **holandés, -esa** *adj* Dutch ♦, *nm/f* Dutchman(-woman) ♦ *nm* (*LING*) Dutch

holgado, -a [ol'ɣaðo, a] *adj* (*ropa*) loose, baggy; (*rico*) comfortable

holgar [ol'ɣar] *vi* (*descansar*) to rest; (*sobrar*) to be superfluous

holgazán, -ana [olɣa'θan, ana] *adj* idle, lazy ♦ *nm/f* loafer

hollín [o'λin] *nm* soot

hombre ['ombre] *nm* (*gen*) man; (*raza humana*): **el ~** man(kind) ♦ *excl*: **¡sí ~!** (*claro*) of course!; (*para énfasis*) man, old boy ► **hombre de negocios** businessman ► **hombre de pro** honest man ► **hombre-rana** frogman

hombrera [om'brera] *nf* shoulder strap

hombro ['ombro] *nm* shoulder

homenaje [ome'naxe] *nm* (*gen*) homage; (*tributo*) tribute

homicida [omi'θiða] *adj* homicidal ♦ *nmf* murderer □ **homicidio** *nm* murder, homicide

homologar [omolo'ðar] *vt* (*COM: productos, tamaños*) to standardize

homólogo, -a [o'moloɣo, a] nmf/f: **su**
etc **~** his etc counterpart o opposite
number

homosexual [omosek'swal] adj, nmf
homosexual

honda (CS) ['onda] nf catapult

hondo, -a ['ondo, a] adj deep; **lo ~** the
depth(s) pl, the bottom
❏ **hondonada** nf hollow, depression;
(cañón) ravine

Honduras [on'duras] nf Honduras

hondureño, -a [ondu'reɲo, a] adj, nm/
f Honduran

honestidad [onesti'ðað] nf purity,
chastity; (decencia) decency
❏ **honesto, -a** adj chaste; decent;
honest; (justo) just

hongo ['ongo] nm (BOT: gen) fungus;
(: comestible) mushroom; (: venenoso)
toadstool

honor [o'nor] nm (gen) honour; **en ~ a
la verdad** to be fair ❏ **honorable** adj
honourable

honorario, -a [ono'rarjo, a] adj
honorary ❏ **honorarios** nmpl fees

honra ['onra] nf (gen) honour;
(renombre) good name ❏ **honradez**
nf honesty; (de persona) integrity
❏ **honrado, -a** adj honest, upright
❏ **honrar** [on'rar] vt to honour

hora ['ora] nf (una hora) hour; (tiempo)
time; **¿qué ~ es?** what time is it? **¿a
qué ~?** at what time? **media ~** half an
hour; **a la ~ de recreo** at playtime; **a
primera ~** first thing (in the morning);
a última ~ at the last moment; **a altas
horas** in the small hours; **¡a buena ~!**
about time too!; **pedir ~** to make an
appointment; **dar la ~** to strike the
hour ▶ **horas de oficina/trabajo**
office/working hours ▶ **horas de
visita** visiting times ▶ **horas extras** o
extraordinarias overtime sg ▶ **horas
pico** (LAm) rush o peak hours ▶ **horas
punta** (ESP) rush hours

horario, -a [o'rarjo, a] adj hourly, hour
cpd ♦ nm timetable ▶ **horario
comercial** business hours pl

horca ['orka] nf gallows sg

horcajadas [orka'xaðas]: **a ~** adv
astride

horchata [or'tʃata] nf cold drink made
from tiger nuts and water, tiger nut milk

horizontal [oriθon'tal] adj horizontal

horizonte [ori'θonte] nm horizon

horma ['orma] nf mould

hormiga [or'miɣa] nf ant; **hormigas**
nfpl (MED) pins and needles

hormigón [ormi'ɣon] nm concrete
▶ **hormigón armado/pretensado**
reinforced/prestressed concrete

hormigonera nf cement mixer

hormigueo [ormi'ɣeo] nm (comezón)
itch

hormona [or'mona] nf hormone

hornillo [or'niʎo] nm (cocina) portable
stove ▶ **hornillo de gas** gas ring

horno ['orno] nm (CULIN) oven; (TEC)
furnace; **alto ~** blast furnace

horóscopo [o'roskopo] nm horoscope

horquilla [or'kiʎa] nf hairpin; (AGR)
pitchfork

horrendo, -a [o'rrendo, a] adj
horrendous, frightful

horrible [o'rriβle] adj horrible, dreadful

horripilante [orripi'lante] adj hair-
raising, horrifying

horror [o'rror] nm horror, dread;
(atrocidad) atrocity; **¡qué ~!** (fam) how
awful! ❏ **horrorizar** vt to horrify,
frighten; **horrorizarse** vr to be
horrified ❏ **horroroso, -a** adj
horrifying, ghastly

hortaliza [orta'liθa] nf vegetable

hortelano, -a [orte'lano, a] nm/f
(market) gardener

hortera [or'tera] (fam) adj tacky

hospedar [ospe'ðar] vt to put up;
hospedarse vr to stay, lodge

hospital [ospi'tal] nm hospital

hospitalario, -a [ospita'larjo, a] *adj*
(*acogedor*) hospitable
❏ **hospitalidad** *nf* hospitality

hostal [os'tal] *nm* small hotel

hostelería [ostele'ria] *nf* hotel
business o trade

hostia ['ostja] *nf* (*REL*) host, consecrated
wafer; (*fam!: golpe*) whack, punch
♦ *excl* (*fam!*) **¡~(s)!** damn!

hostil [os'til] *adj* hostile

hotdog (*LAm*) *nm* hotdog

hotel [o'tel] *nm* hotel ❏ **hotelero, -a**
adj hotel *cpd* ♦ *nm/f* hotelier

HOTEL

In Spain you can choose from the
following categories of
accommodation, in descending order
of quality and price: **hotel** (from 5
stars to 1), **hostal**, **pensión**, **casa de
huéspedes**, **fonda**. The State also runs
luxury hotels called **paradores**, which
are usually sited in places of particular
historical interest and are often
historic buildings themselves.

---

hoy [oi] *adv* (*este día*) today; (*la
actualidad*) now(adays) ♦ *nm* present
time; **~ (en) día** now(adays)

hoyo ['ojo] *nm* hole, pit

hoz [oθ] *nf* sickle

hube *etc* ['uβe] *vb ver* **haber**

hucha ['utʃa] *nf* money box

hueco, -a ['weko, a] *adj* (*vacío*) hollow,
empty; (*resonante*) booming ♦ *nm*
hollow, cavity

huelga *etc* ['welɣa] *vb ver* **holgar** ♦ *nf*
strike; **declararse en ~** to go on strike,
come out on strike ▶ **huelga de
hambre** hunger strike ▶ **huelga
general** general strike

huelguista [wel'ɣista] *nmf* striker

huella ['weʎa] *nf* (*pisada*) tread; (*marca
del paso*) footprint, footstep; (: *de
animal, máquina*) track ▶ **huella
dactilar** fingerprint

huelo *etc vb ver* **oler**

huérfano, -a ['werfano, a] *adj*
orphan(ed) ♦ *nm/f* orphan

huerta ['werta] *nf* market garden; (*en
Murcia y Valencia*) irrigated region

huerto ['werto] *nm* kitchen garden; (*de
árboles frutales*) orchard

hueso ['weso] *nm* (*ANAT*) bone; (*de fruta*)
stone

huésped ['wespeð] *nmf* guest

hueva ['weβa] *nf* roe

huevera [we'βera] *nf* eggcup

huevo ['weβo] *nm* egg ▶ **huevo a la
copa** (*CS*) soft-boiled egg ▶ **huevo
duro/escalfado** hard-boiled/
poached egg ▶ **huevo estrellado**
(*LAm*) fried egg ▶ **huevo frito** (*ESP*)
fried egg ▶ **huevo pasado por agua**
soft-boiled egg ▶ **huevos revueltos**
scrambled eggs ▶ **huevo tibio** (*MÉX*)
soft-boiled egg

huida [u'iða] *nf* escape, flight

huir [u'ir] *vi* (*escapar*) to flee, escape;
(*evitar*) to avoid

hule ['ule] *nm* oilskin; (*MÉX: goma*)
rubber

hulera (*MÉX*) *nf* catapult

humanidad [umani'ðað] *nf* (*género
humano*) man(kind); (*cualidad*)
humanity

humanitario, -a [umani'tarjo, a] *adj*
humanitarian

humano, -a [u'mano, a] *adj* (*gen*)
human; (*humanitario*) humane ♦ *nm*
human; **ser ~** human being

humareda [uma'reða] *nf* cloud of
smoke

humedad [ume'ðað] *nf* (*de clima*)
humidity; (*de pared etc*) dampness; **a
prueba de ~** damp-proof
❏ **humedecer** *vt* to moisten, wet;
humedecerse *vr* to get wet

húmedo, -a [u'meðo, a] *adj* (*mojado*)
damp, wet; (*tiempo etc*) humid

humilde [u'milde] *adj* humble, modest

humillación [umiˈʎaˈθjon] nf humiliation □ **humillante** adj humiliating

humillar [umiˈʎar] vt to humiliate

humo [ˈumo] nm (de fuego) smoke; (gas nocivo) fumes pl; (vapor) steam, vapour; **humos** nmpl (fig) conceit sg

humor [uˈmor] nm (disposición) mood, temper; (lo que divierte) humour; **de buen/mal** ~ in a good/bad mood □ **humorista** nmf comic □ **humorístico, -a** adj funny, humorous

hundimiento [undiˈmjento] nm (gen) sinking; (colapso) collapse

hundir [unˈdir] vt to sink; (edificio, plan) to ruin, destroy; **hundirse** vr to sink, collapse

húngaro, -a [ˈungaro, a] adj, nm/f Hungarian

Hungría [unˈgria] nf Hungary

huracán [uraˈkan] nm hurricane

huraño, -a [uˈraɲo, a] adj (antisocial) unsociable

hurgar [urˈɣar] vt to poke, jab; (remover) to stir (up); **hurgarse** vr: **hurgarse (las narices)** to pick one's nose

hurón, -ona [uˈron, ona] nm (ZOOL) ferret

hurtadillas [urtaˈðiʎas]: **a ~** adv stealthily, on the sly

hurtar [urˈtar] vt to steal □ **hurto** nm theft, stealing

husmear [usmeˈar] vt (oler) to sniff out, scent; (fam) to pry into

huyo etc vb ver **huir**

I, i

iba etc ['iβa] vb ver **ir**

ibérico, -a [iˈβeriko, a] adj Iberian

iberoamericano, -a [iβeroameriˈkano, a] adj, nm/f Latin American

Ibiza [iˈβiθa] nf Ibiza

iceberg [iˈθeβer] nm iceberg

icono [iˈkono] nm ikon, icon

ida [ˈiða] nf going, departure; ~ **y vuelta** round trip, return

idea [iˈðea] nf idea; **no tengo la menor ~** I haven't a clue

ideal [iðeˈal] adj, nm ideal □ **idealista** nmf idealist □ **idealizar** vt to idealize

ídem [ˈiðem] pron ditto

idéntico, -a [iˈðentiko, a] adj identical

identidad [iðentiˈðað] nf identity

identificación [iðentifikaˈθjon] nf identification

identificar [iðentifiˈkar] vt to identify; **identificarse** vr: **identificarse con** to identify with

ideología [iðeoloˈxia] nf ideology

idilio [iˈðiljo] nm love-affair

idioma [iˈðjoma] nm (gen) language

> ⚠ No confundir **idioma** con la palabra inglesa idiom.

idiota [iˈðjota] adj idiotic ♦ nmf idiot

ídolo [ˈiðolo] nm (tb fig) idol

idóneo, -a [iˈðoneo, a] adj suitable

iglesia [iˈɣlesja] nf church

ignorante [iɣnoˈrante] adj ignorant, uninformed ♦ nmf ignoramus

ignorar [iɣnoˈrar] vt not to know, be ignorant of; (no hacer caso a) to ignore

igual [iˈɣwal] adj (gen) equal; (similar) like, similar; (mismo) (the) same; (constante) constant; (temperatura) even ♦ nmf equal; ~ **que** like, the same as; **me da** o **es** ~ I don't care; **son iguales** they're the same; **al ~ que** (prep, conj) like, just like

igualar [iɣwaˈlar] vt (gen) to equalize, make equal; (allanar, nivelar) to level (off), even (out); **igualarse** vr (platos de balanza) to balance out

igualdad [iɣwal'daθ] *nf* equality; (*similaridad*) sameness; (*uniformidad*) uniformity

igualmente [iɣwal'mente] *adv* equally; (*también*) also, likewise ♦ *excl* the same to you!

ilegal [ile'ɣal] *adj* illegal

ilegítimo, -a [ile'xitimo, a] *adj* illegitimate

ileso, -a [i'leso, a] *adj* unhurt

ilimitado, -a [ilimi'taðo, a] *adj* unlimited

iluminación [ilumina'θjon] *nf* illumination; (*alumbrado*) lighting

iluminar [ilumi'nar] *vt* to illuminate, light (up); (*fig*) to enlighten

ilusión [ilu'sjon] *nf* illusion; (*quimera*) delusion; (*esperanza*) hope; **hacerse ilusiones** to build up one's hopes
❏ **ilusionado, -a** *adj* excited
❏ **ilusionar** *vi*: **le ilusiona ir de vacaciones** he's looking forward to going on holiday; **ilusionarse** *vr*: **ilusionarse (con)** to get excited (about)

iluso, -a [i'luso, a] *adj* easily deceived ♦ *nm/f* dreamer

ilustración [ilustra'θjon] *nf* illustration; (*saber*) learning, erudition; **la I~** the Enlightenment ❏ **ilustrado, -a** *adj* illustrated; learned

ilustrar [ilus'trar] *vt* to illustrate; (*instruir*) to instruct; (*explicar*) to explain, make clear

ilustre [i'lustre] *adj* famous, illustrious

imagen [i'maxen] *nf* (*gen*) image; (*dibujo*) picture

imaginación [imaxina'θjon] *nf* imagination

imaginar [imaxi'nar] *vt* (*gen*) to imagine; (*idear*) to think up; (*suponer*) to suppose; **imaginarse** *vr* to imagine ❏ **imaginario, -a** *adj* imaginary ❏ **imaginativo, -a** *adj* imaginative

imán [i'man] *nm* magnet

imbécil [im'beθil] *nmf* imbecile, idiot

imitación [imita'θjon] *nf* imitation; **de ~** imitation *cpd*

imitar [imi'tar] *vt* to imitate; (*parodiar, remedar*) to mimic, ape

impaciente [impa'θjente] *adj* impatient; (*nervioso*) anxious

impacto [im'pakto] *nm* impact

impar [im'par] *adj* odd

imparcial [impar'θjal] *adj* impartial, fair

impecable [impe'kaβle] *adj* impeccable

impedimento [impeðiˈmento] *nm* impediment, obstacle

impedir [impe'ðir] *vt* (*obstruir*) to impede, obstruct; (*estorbar*) to prevent; **~ a algn hacer** *o* **que algn haga algo** to prevent sb (from) doing sth, stop sb doing sth

imperativo, -a [impera'tiβo, a] *adj* (*urgente, LING*) imperative

imperdible [imper'ðiβle] *nm* safety pin

imperdonable [imperðo'naβle] *adj* unforgivable, inexcusable

imperfecto, -a [imper'fekto, a] *adj* imperfect

imperio [im'perjo] *nm* empire; (*autoridad*) rule, authority; (*fig*) pride, haughtiness

impermeable [imperme'aβle] *adj* waterproof ♦ *nm* raincoat, mac (*BRIT*)

impersonal [imperso'nal] *adj* impersonal

impertinente [imperti'nente] *adj* impertinent

ímpetu ['impetu] *nm* (*impulso*) impetus, impulse; (*impetuosidad*) impetuosity; (*violencia*) violence

implantar [implan'tar] *vt* to introduce

implemento (*LAm*) *nm* tool, implement

implicar [impli'kar] *vt* to involve; (*entrañar*) to imply

implícito, -a [im'pliθito, a] *adj* (*tácito*) implicit; (*sobreentendido*) implied

imponente [impo'nente] *adj* (*impresionante*) impressive, imposing; (*solemne*) grand

imponer [impo'ner] *vt* (*gen*) to impose; (*exigir*) to exact; **imponerse** *vr* to assert o.s.; (*prevalecer*) to prevail □ **imponible** *adj* (COM) taxable

impopular [impopu'lar] *adj* unpopular

importación [importa'θjon] *nf* (*acto*) importing; (*mercancías*) imports *pl*

importancia [impor'tanθja] *nf* importance; (*valor*) value, significance; (*extensión*) size, magnitude; **no tiene ~** it's nothing □ **importante** *adj* important; valuable, significant

importar [impor'tar] *vt* (*del extranjero*) to import; (*costar*) to amount to ♦ *vi* to be important, matter; **me importa un rábano** I couldn't care less; **no importa** it doesn't matter; **¿le importa que fume?** do you mind if I smoke?

importe [im'porte] *nm* (*total*) amount; (*valor*) value

imposible [impo'siβle] *adj* (*gen*) impossible; (*insoportable*) unbearable, intolerable

imposición [imposi'θjon] *nf* imposition; (COM: *impuesto*) tax; (: *inversión*) deposit

impostor, a [impos'tor, a] *nm/f* impostor

impotencia [impo'tenθja] *nf* impotence □ **impotente** *adj* impotent

impreciso, -a [impre'θiso, a] *adj* imprecise, vague

impregnar [impreɣ'nar] *vt* to impregnate; **impregnarse** *vr* to become impregnated

imprenta [im'prenta] *nf* (*acto*) printing; (*aparato*) press; (*casa*) printer's; (*letra*) print

imprescindible [impresθin'diβle] *adj* essential, vital

impresión [impre'sjon] *nf* (*gen*) impression; (IMPRENTA) printing; (*edición*) edition; (FOTO) print; (*marca*) imprint ▸ **impresión digital** fingerprint

impresionante [impresjo'nante] *adj* impressive; (*tremendo*) tremendous; (*maravilloso*) great, marvellous

impresionar [impresjo'nar] *vt* (*conmover*) to move; (*afectar*) to impress, strike; (*película fotográfica*) to expose; **impresionarse** *vr* to be impressed; (*conmoverse*) to be moved

impreso, -a [im'preso, a] *pp de* **imprimir** ♦ *adj* printed □ **impresos** *nmpl* printed matter □ **impresora** *nf* printer

imprevisto, -a [impre'βisto, a] *adj* (*gen*) unforeseen; (*inesperado*) unexpected

imprimir [impri'mir] *vt* to imprint, impress, stamp; (*textos*) to print; (INFORM) to output, print out

improbable [impro'βaβle] *adj* improbable; (*inverosímil*) unlikely

impropio, -a [im'propjo, a] *adj* improper

improvisado, -a [improβi'saðo, a] *adj* improvised

improvisar [improβi'sar] *vt* to improvise

improviso, -a [impro'βiso, a] *adj*: **de ~** unexpectedly, suddenly

imprudencia [impru'ðenθja] *nf* imprudence; (*indiscreción*) indiscretion; (*descuido*) carelessness □ **imprudente** *adj* unwise, imprudent; (*indiscreto*) indiscreet

impuesto, -a [im'pwesto, a] *adj* imposed ♦ *nm* tax ▸ **impuesto al valor agregado** o **añadido** (*LAm*) value added tax (BRIT), ≈ sales tax (US) ▸ **impuesto sobre el valor añadido** (*ESP*) value added tax (BRIT), ≈ sales tax (US)

impulsar [impul'sar] vt to drive; (promover) to promote, stimulate

impulsivo, -a [impul'siβo, a] adj impulsive ► **impulso** nm impulse; (fuerza, empuje) thrust, drive; (fig: sentimiento) urge, impulse

impureza [impu'reθa] nf impurity ▢ **impuro, -a** adj impure

inaccesible [inakθe'siβle] adj inaccessible

inaceptable [inaθep'taβle] adj unacceptable

inactivo, -a [inak'tiβo, a] adj inactive

inadecuado, -a [inaðe'kwaðo, a] adj (insuficiente) inadequate; (inapto) unsuitable

inadvertido, -a [inaðβer'tiðo, a] adj (no visto) unnoticed

inaguantable [inaɣwan'taβle] adj unbearable

inanimado, -a [inani'maðo, a] adj inanimate

inaudito, -a [inau'ðito, a] adj unheard-of

inauguración [inauɣura'θjon] nf inauguration; opening

inaugurar [inauɣu'rar] vt to inaugurate; (exposición) to open

inca ['inka] nmf Inca

incalculable [inkalku'laβle] adj incalculable

incandescente [inkandes'θente] adj incandescent

incansable [inkan'saβle] adj tireless, untiring

incapacidad [inkapaθi'ðað] nf incapacity; (incompetencia) incompetence ► **incapacidad física/mental** physical/mental disability

incapacitar [inkapaθi'tar] vt (inhabilitar) to incapacitate, render unfit; (descalificar) to disqualify

incapaz [inka'paθ] adj incapable

incautarse [inkau'tarse] vr: ~ **de** to seize, confiscate

incauto, -a [in'kauto, a] adj (imprudente) incautious, unwary

incendiar [inθen'djar] vt to set fire to; (fig) to inflame ▢ **incendiarse** vr to catch fire ▢ **incendiario, -a** adj incendiary

incendio [in'θendjo] nm fire

incentivo [inθen'tiβo] nm incentive

incertidumbre [inθerti'ðumbre] nf (inseguridad) uncertainty; (duda) doubt

incesante [inθe'sante] adj incessant

incesto [in'θesto] nm incest

incidencia [inθi'ðenθja] nf (MAT) incidence

incidente [inθi'ðente] nm incident

incidir [inθi'ðir] vi (influir) to influence; (afectar) to affect

incienso [in'θjenso] nm incense

incierto, -a [in'θjerto, a] adj uncertain

incineración [inθinera'θjon] nf incineration; (de cadáveres) cremation

incinerar [inθine'rar] vt to burn; (cadáveres) to cremate

incisión [inθi'sjon] nf incision

incisivo, -a [inθi'siβo, a] adj sharp, cutting; (fig) incisive

incitar [inθi'tar] vt to incite, rouse

inclemencia [inkle'menθja] nf (severidad) harshness, severity; (del tiempo) inclemency

inclinación [inklina'θjon] nf (gen) inclination; (de terras) slope, incline; (de cabeza) nod, bow; (fig) leaning, bent

inclinar [inkli'nar] vt to incline; (cabeza) to nod, bow ♦ vi to lean, slope; **inclinarse** vr to bow; (encorvarse) to stoop; **inclinarse a** (parecerse a) to take after, resemble; **inclinarse ante** to bow down to; **me inclino a pensar que ...** I'm inclined to think that ...

incluir [inklu'ir] vt to include; (incorporar) to incorporate; (meter) to enclose

inclusive [inklu'siβe] *adv* inclusive
♦ *prep* including

incluso [in'kluso] *adv* even

incógnita [in'koɣnita] *nf* (MAT)
unknown quantity

incógnito [in'koɣnito] *nm*: **de ~**
incognito

incoherente [inkoe'rente] *adj*
incoherent

incoloro, -a [inko'loro, a] *adj*
colourless

incomodar [inkomo'ðar] *vt* to
inconvenience; (*molestar*) to bother,
trouble; (*fastidiar*) to annoy

incomodidad [inkomoði'ðað] *nf*
inconvenience; (*fastidio, enojo*)
annoyance; (*de vivienda*) discomfort

incómodo, -a [in'komoðo, a] *adj*
(*inconfortable*) uncomfortable;
(*molesto*) annoying; (*inconveniente*)
inconvenient

incomparable [inkompa'raβle] *adj*
incomparable

incompatible [inkompa'tiβle] *adj*
incompatible

incompetente [inkompe'tente] *adj*
incompetent

incompleto, -a [inkom'pleto, a] *adj*
incomplete, unfinished

incomprensible [inkompren'siβle]
adj incomprehensible

incomunicado, -a [inkomuni'kaðo,
a] *adj* (*aislado*) cut off, isolated;
(*confinado*) in solitary confinement

incondicional [inkondiθjo'nal] *adj*
unconditional; (*apoyo*) wholehearted;
(*partidario*) staunch

inconfundible [inkonfun'diβle] *adj*
unmistakable

incongruente [inkon'grwente] *adj*
incongruous

inconsciente [inkons'θjente] *adj*
unconscious; thoughtless

inconsecuente [inkonse'kwente] *adj*
inconsistent

inconstante [inkons'tante] *adj*
inconstant

incontable [inkon'taβle] *adj*
countless, innumerable

inconveniencia [inkombe'njenθja] *nf*
unsuitability, inappropriateness;
(*descortesía*) impoliteness
❑ **inconveniente** *adj* unsuitable;
impolite ♦ *nm* obstacle; (*desventaja*)
disadvantage; **el inconveniente es
que ...** the trouble is that ...

incordiar [inkor'ðjar] (*fam*) *vt* to bug,
annoy

incorporar [inkorpo'rar] *vt* to
incorporate; **incorporarse** *vr* to sit up;
incorporarse a to join

incorrecto, -a [inko'rrekto, a] *adj* (*gen*)
incorrect, wrong; (*comportamiento*)
bad-mannered

incorregible [inkorre'xiβle] *adj*
incorrigible

incrédulo, -a [in'kreðulo, a] *adj*
incredulous, unbelieving; sceptical

increíble [inkre'iβle] *adj* incredible

incremento [inkre'mento] *nm*
increment; (*aumento*) rise, increase

increpar [inkre'par] *vt* to reprimand

incruento, -a [in'krwento, a] *adj*
bloodless

incrustar [inkrus'tar] *vt* to incrust;
(*piedras: en joya*) to inlay

incubar [inku'βar] *vt* to incubate

inculcar [inkul'kar] *vt* to inculcate

inculto, -a [in'kulto, a] *adj* (*persona*)
uneducated; (*grosero*) uncouth ♦ *nm/f*
ignoramus

incumplimiento [inkumpli'mjento]
nm non-fulfilment
▶ **incumplimiento de contrato**
breach of contract

incurrir [inku'rrir] *vi*: **~ en** to incur;
(*crimen*) to commit

indagar [inda'ɣar] *vt* to investigate; to
search; (*averiguar*) to ascertain

indecente [inde'θente] *adj* indecent,
improper; (*lascivo*) obscene

indeciso, -a [inde'θiso, a] *adj (por decidir)* undecided; *(vacilante)* hesitant

indefenso, -a [inde'fenso, a] *adj* defenceless

indefinido, -a [indefi'niðo, a] *adj* indefinite; *(vago)* vague, undefined

indemne [in'demne] *adj (objeto)* undamaged; *(persona)* unharmed, unhurt

indemnizar [indemni'θar] *vt* to indemnify; *(compensar)* to compensate

independencia [independen'θja] *nf* independence

independiente [independ'djente] *adj (libre)* independent; *(autónomo)* self-sufficient

indeterminado, -a [indetermi'naðo, a] *adj (indefinido)* indefinite; *(desconocido)* indeterminate

India ['indja] *nf:* **la ~** India

indicación [indika'θjon] *nf* indication; *(señal)* sign; *(sugerencia)* suggestion, hint

indicado, -a [indi'kaðo, a] *adj (momento, método)* right; *(tratamiento)* appropriate; *(solución)* likely

indicador [indika'ðor] *nm* indicator; *(TEC)* gauge, meter

indicar [indi'kar] *vt (mostrar)* to indicate, show; *(termómetro etc)* to read, register; *(señalar)* to point to

índice ['indiθe] *nm* index; *(catálogo)* catalogue; *(ANAT)* index finger, forefinger ▶ **índice de materias** table of contents

indicio [in'diθjo] *nm* indication, sign; *(en pesquisa etc)* clue

indiferencia [indife'renθja] *nf* indifference; *(apatía)* apathy ❑ **indiferente** *adj* indifferent

indígena [in'dixena] *adj* indigenous, native ♦ *nmf* native

indigestión [indixes'tjon] *nf* indigestion

indigesto, -a [indi'xesto, a] *adj (alimento)* indigestible; *(fig)* turgid

indignación [indiɣna'θjon] *nf* indignation

indignar [indiɣ'nar] *vt* to anger, make indignant; **indignarse** *vr:* **indignarse por** to get indignant about

indigno, -a [in'diɣno, a] *adj (despreciable)* low, contemptible; *(inmerecido)* unworthy

indio, -a ['indjo, a] *adj, nm/f* Indian

indirecta [indi'rekta] *nf* insinuation, innuendo; *(sugerencia)* hint

indirecto, -a [indi'rekto, a] *adj* indirect

indiscreción [indiskre'θjon] *nf (imprudencia)* indiscretion; *(irreflexión)* tactlessness; *(acto)* gaffe, faux pas

indiscreto, -a [indis'kreto, a] *adj* indiscreet

indiscutible [indisku'tiβle] *adj* indisputable, unquestionable

indispensable [indispen'saβle] *adj* indispensable, essential

indispuesto, -a [indis'pwesto, a] *adj (enfermo)* unwell, indisposed

indistinto, -a [indis'tinto, a] *adj* indistinct; *(vago)* vague

individual [indiβi'ðwal] *adj* individual; *(habitación)* single ♦ *nm (DEPORTE)* singles *sg*

individuo, -a [indi'βiðwo, a] *adj, nm* individual

índole ['indole] *nf (naturaleza)* nature; *(clase)* sort, kind

inducir [indu'θir] *vt (persuadir)* to induce; *(inferir)* to infer; *(persuadir)* to persuade

indudable [indu'ðaβle] *adj* undoubted; *(incuestionable)* unquestionable

indultar [indul'tar] *vt (perdonar)* to pardon, reprieve; *(librar de pago)* to exempt ❑ **indulto** *nm* pardon; exemption

industria [in'dustrja] *nf* industry; *(habilidad)* skill ❑ **industrial** *adj* industrial ♦ *nm* industrialist

inédito, -a [ine'ðito, a] adj (texto) unpublished; (nuevo) new

ineficaz [inefi'kaθ] adj (inútil) ineffective; (ineficiente) inefficient

ineludible [inelu'ðiβle] adj inescapable, unavoidable

ineptitud [inepti'tuð] nf ineptitude, incompetence □ **inepto, -a** adj inept, incompetent

inequívoco, -a [ine'kiβoko, a] adj unequivocal; (inconfundible) unmistakable

inercia [in'erθja] nf inertia; (pasividad) passivity

inerte [in'erte] adj inert; (inmóvil) motionless

inesperado, -a [inespe'raðo, a] adj unexpected, unforeseen

inestable [ines'taβle] adj unstable

inevitable [ineβi'taβle] adj inevitable

inexacto, -a [inek'sakto, a] adj inaccurate; (falso) untrue

inexperto, -a [inek'sperto, a] adj (novato) inexperienced

infalible [infa'liβle] adj infallible; (plan) foolproof

infame [in'fame] adj infamous; (horrible) dreadful □ **infamia** nf infamy; (deshonra) disgrace

infancia [in'fanθja] nf infancy, childhood

infantería [infante'ria] nf infantry

infantil [infan'til] adj (pueril, aniñado) infantile; (cándido) childlike; (literatura, ropa etc) children's

infarto [in'farto] nm (tb: ~ de miocardio) heart attack

infatigable [infati'γaβle] adj tireless, untiring

infección [infek'θjon] nf infection □ **infeccioso, -a** adj infectious

infectar [infek'tar] vt to infect; **infectarse** vr to become infected

infeliz [infe'liθ] adj unhappy, wretched ♦ nmf wretch

inferior [infe'rjor] adj inferior; (situación) lower ♦ nmf inferior, subordinate

inferir [infe'rir] vt (deducir) to infer, deduce; (causar) to cause

infidelidad [infiðeli'ðað] nf (gen) infidelity, unfaithfulness

infiel [in'fjel] adj unfaithful, disloyal; (erróneo) inaccurate ♦ nmf infidel, unbeliever

infierno [in'fjerno] nm hell

infiltrarse [infil'trarse] vr: ~ en to infiltrate in(to); (persona) to work one's way in(to)

ínfimo, -a ['infimo, a] adj (más bajo) lowest; (despreciable) vile, mean

infinidad [infini'ðað] nf infinity; (abundancia) great quantity

infinito, -a [infi'nito, a] adj, nm infinite

inflación [infla'θjon] nf (hinchazón) swelling; (monetaria) inflation; (fig) conceit

inflamable adj flammable

inflamar [infla'mar] vt (MED: fig) to inflame; **inflamarse** vr to catch fire; to become inflamed

inflar [in'flar] vt (hinchar) to inflate, blow up; (fig) to exaggerate; **inflarse** vr to swell (up); (fig) to get conceited

inflexible [inflek'siβle] adj inflexible; (fig) unbending

influencia [influ'enθja] nf influence

influir [influ'ir] vt to influence

influjo [in'fluxo] nm influence

influya etc vb ver **influir**

influyente [influ'jente] adj influential

información [informa'θjon] nf information; (noticias) news sg; (JUR) inquiry; **I~** (oficina) Information Office; (mostrador) Information Desk; (TEL) Directory Enquiries

informal [infor'mal] adj (gen) informal

informar [infor'mar] vt (gen) to inform; (revelar) to reveal, make known ♦ vi (JUR) to plead; (denunciar) to inform; (dar cuenta de) to report on;

informarse vr to find out; **informarse de** to inquire into

informática [infor'matika] nf computer science, information technology

informe [in'forme] adj shapeless ♦ nm report

infracción [infrak'θjon] nf infraction, infringement

infravalorar [infrabalo'rar] vt to undervalue, underestimate

infringir [infrin'xir] vt to infringe, contravene

infundado, -a [infun'daðo, a] adj groundless, unfounded

infundir [infun'dir] vt to infuse, instil

infusión [infu'sjon] nf infusion
▶ **infusión de manzanilla** camomile tea

ingeniería [inxenje'ria] nf engineering ▶ **ingeniería genética** genetic engineering ❑ **ingeniero, -a** [inxe'njero, a] nm/f engineer ▶ **ingeniero civil** o **de caminos** civil engineer

ingenio [in'xenjo] nm (talento) talent; (agudeza) wit; (habilidad) ingenuity, inventiveness ▶ **ingenio azucarero** (LAm) sugar refinery ❑ **ingenioso, -a** [inxe'njoso, a] adj ingenious, clever; (divertido) witty ❑ **ingenuo, -a** adj ingenuous

ingerir [inxe'rir] vt to ingest; (tragar) to swallow; (consumir) to consume

Inglaterra [ingla'terra] nf England

ingle ['ingle] nf groin

inglés, -esa [in'gles, esa] adj English ♦ nm/f Englishman(-woman) ♦ nm (LING) English

ingrato, -a [in'grato, a] adj (gen) ungrateful

ingrediente [ingre'ðjente] nm ingredient

ingresar [ingre'sar] vt (dinero) to deposit ♦ vi to come in; **~ en el hospital** to go into hospital

ingreso [in'greso] nm (entrada) entry; (en hospital etc) admission; **ingresos** nmpl (dinero) income sg; (COM) takings pl

inhabitable [inaβi'taβle] adj uninhabitable

inhalar [ina'lar] vt to inhale

inhibir [ini'βir] vt to inhibit

inhóspito, -a [i'nospito, a] adj (región, paisaje) inhospitable

inhumano, -a [inu'mano, a] adj inhuman

inicial [ini'θjal] adj, nf initial

iniciar [ini'θjar] vt (persona) to initiate; (empezar) to begin, commence; (conversación) to start up

iniciativa [iniθja'tiβa] nf initiative
▶ **iniciativa privada** private enterprise

ininterrumpido, -a [ininterrum'piðo, a] adj uninterrupted

injertar [inxer'tar] vt to graft ❑ **injerto** nm graft

injuria [in'xurja] nf (agravio, ofensa) offence; (insulto) insult

> ⚠ No confundir **injuria** con la palabra inglesa **injury**.

injusticia [inxus'tiθja] nf injustice

injusto, -a [in'xusto, a] adj unjust, unfair

inmadurez [inmaðu'reθ] nf immaturity

inmediaciones [inmeðja'θjones] nfpl neighbourhood sg, environs

inmediato, -a [inme'ðjato, a] adj immediate; (contiguo) adjoining; (rápido) prompt; (próximo) neighbouring, next; **de ~** immediately

inmejorable [inmexo'raβle] adj unsurpassable; (precio) unbeatable

inmenso, -a [in'menso, a] adj immense, huge

inmigración [inmiɣra'θjon] nf immigration

inmobiliaria [inmoβi'ljarja] nf estate agency

inmolar [inmo'lar] vt to immolate, sacrifice

inmoral [inmo'ral] adj immoral

inmortal [inmor'tal] adj immortal
□ **inmortalizar** vt to immortalize

inmóvil [in'moβil] adj immobile

inmueble [in'mweβle] adj: **bienes inmuebles** real estate, landed property ♦ nm property

inmundo, -a [in'mundo, a] adj filthy

inmune [in'mune] adj: ~ **(a)** (MED) immune (to)

inmunidad [inmuni'ðað] nf immunity

inmutarse [inmu'tarse] vr to turn pale; **no se inmutó** he didn't turn a hair

innato, -a [in'nato, a] adj innate

innecesario, -a [inneθe'sarjo, a] adj unnecessary

innovación [innoβa'θjon] nf innovation

innovar [inno'βar] vt to introduce

inocencia [ino'θenθja] nf innocence

inocentada [inoθen'taða] nf practical joke

inocente [ino'θente] adj (ingenuo) naive, innocent; (inculpable) innocent; (sin malicia) harmless ♦ nmf simpleton; **el día de los (Santos) Inocentes** ≈ April Fools' Day

DÍA DE LOS (SANTOS) INOCENTES

The 28th December, el **día de los (Santos) Inocentes**, is when the Church commemorates the story of Herod's slaughter of the innocent children of Judaea. On this day Spaniards play **inocentadas** (practical jokes) on each other, much like our April Fool's Day pranks.

inodoro [ino'ðoro] nm toilet, lavatory (BRIT)

inofensivo, -a [inofen'siβo, a] adj inoffensive, harmless

inolvidable [inolβi'ðaβle] adj unforgettable

inoportuno, -a [inopor'tuno, a] adj untimely; (molesto) inconvenient

inoxidable [inoksi'ðaβle] adj: **acero ~** stainless steel

inquietar [inkje'tar] vt to worry, trouble; **inquietarse** vr to worry, get upset □ **inquieto, -a** adj anxious, worried □ **inquietud** nf anxiety, worry

inquilino, -a [inki'lino, a] nm/f tenant

insaciable [insa'θjaβle] adj insatiable

inscribir [inskri'βir] vt to inscribe; ~ **a algn en** (lista) to put sb on; (censo) to register sb on

inscripción [inskrip'θjon] nf inscription; (ESCOL etc) enrolment; (en censo) registration

insecticida [insekti'θiða] nm insecticide

insecto [in'sekto] nm insect

inseguridad [inseɣuri'ðað] nf insecurity ▶ **inseguridad ciudadana** lack of safety in the streets

inseguro, -a [inse'ɣuro, a] adj insecure; (inconstante) unsteady; (incierto) uncertain

insensato, -a [insen'sato, a] adj foolish, stupid

insensible [insen'siβle] adj (gen) insensitive; (movimiento) imperceptible; (sin sentido) numb

insertar [inser'tar] vt to insert

inservible [inser'βiβle] adj useless

insignia [in'siɣnja] nf (señal distintiva) badge; (estandarte) flag

insignificante [insiɣnifi'kante] adj insignificant

insinuar [insi'nwar] vt to insinuate, imply

insípido, -a [in'sipiðo, a] adj insipid

insistir [insis'tir] vi to insist; ~ **en algo** to insist on sth; (enfatizar) to stress sth

insolación [insola'θjon] nf (MED) sunstroke

insolente [inso'lente] *adj* insolent

insólito, -a [in'solito, a] *adj* unusual

insoluble [inso'luβle] *adj* insoluble

insomnio [in'somnjo] *nm* insomnia

insonorizado, -a [insonori'θaðo, a] *adj (cuarto etc)* soundproof

insoportable [insopor'taβle] *adj* unbearable

inspección [inspek'θjon] *nf* inspection, check ☐ **inspeccionar** *vt (examinar)* to inspect, examine; *(controlar)* to check

inspector, a [inspek'tor, a] *nm/f* inspector

inspiración [inspira'θjon] *nf* inspiration

inspirar [inspi'rar] *vt* to inspire; *(MED)* to inhale; **inspirarse** *vr*: **inspirarse en** to be inspired by

instalación [instala'θjon] *nf (equipo)* fittings *pl*, equipment ▶ **instalación eléctrica** wiring

instalar [insta'lar] *vt (establecer)* to instal; *(erguir)* to set up, erect; **instalarse** *vr* to establish o.s.; *(en una vivienda)* to move into

instancia [ins'tanθja] *nf (JUR)* petition; *(ruego)* request; **en última ~** as a last resort

instantáneo, -a [instan'taneo, a] *adj* instantaneous; **café ~** instant coffee

instante [ins'tante] *nm* instant, moment; **al ~** right now

instar [ins'tar] *vt* to press, urge

instaurar [instau'rar] *vt (costumbre)* to establish; *(normas, sistema)* to bring in, introduce; *(gobierno)* to instal

instigar [insti'γar] *vt* to instigate

instinto [ins'tinto] *nm* instinct; **por ~** instinctively

institución [institu'θjon] *nf* institution, establishment

instituir [institu'ir] *vt* to establish; *(fundar)* to found ☐ **instituto** *nm (gen)* institute; *(ESP ESCOL)*

≈ comprehensive *(BRIT)* o high *(US)* school

institutriz [institu'triθ] *nf* governess

instrucción [instruk'θjon] *nf* instruction

instruir [instru'ir] *vt (gen)* to instruct; *(enseñar)* to teach, educate

instrumento [instru'mento] *nm (gen)* instrument; *(herramienta)* tool, implement

insubordinarse [insuβorði'narse] *vr* to rebel

insuficiente [insufi'θjente] *adj (gen)* insufficient; *(ESCOL: calificación)* unsatisfactory

insular [insu'lar] *adj* insular

insultar [insul'tar] *vt* to insult ☐ **insulto** *nm* insult

insuperable [insupe'raβle] *adj (excelente)* unsurpassable; *(problema etc)* insurmountable

insurrección [insurrek'θjon] *nf* insurrection, rebellion

intachable [inta'tʃaβle] *adj* irreproachable

intacto, -a [in'takto, a] *adj* intact

integral [inte'γral] *adj* integral; *(completo)* complete; **pan ~** wholemeal *(BRIT)* o wholewheat *(US)* bread

integrar [inte'γrar] *vt* to make up, compose; *(MAT: fig)* to integrate

integridad [inteγri'ðað] *nf* wholeness; *(carácter)* integrity ☐ **íntegro, -a** *adj* whole, entire; *(honrado)* honest

intelectual [intelek'twal] *adj, nmf* intellectual

inteligencia [inteli'xenθja] *nf* intelligence; *(ingenio)* ability ☐ **inteligente** *adj* intelligent

intemperie [intem'perje] *nf*: **a la ~** out in the open, exposed to the elements

intención [inten'θjon] *nf (gen)* intention, purpose; **con segundas intenciones** maliciously; **con ~** deliberately

intencionado, -a [intenθjo'naðo, a] *adj* deliberate; **mal ~** ill-disposed, hostile

intensidad [intensi'ðað] *nf* (*gen*) intensity; (*ELEC, TEC*) strength; **llover con ~** to rain hard

intenso, -a [in'tenso, a] *adj* intense; (*sentimiento*) profound, deep

intentar [inten'tar] *vt* (*tratar*) to try, attempt ☐ **intento** *nm* attempt

interactivo, -a [interak'tiβo, a] *adj* (*INFORM*) interactive

intercalar [interka'lar] *vt* to insert

intercambio [inter'kambjo] *nm* exchange, swap

interceder [interθe'ðer] *vi* to intercede

interceptar [interθep'tar] *vt* to intercept

interés [inte'res] *nm* (*gen*) interest; (*parte*) share, part; (*pey*) self-interest ▸ **intereses creados** vested interests

interesado, -a [intere'saðo, a] *adj* interested; (*prejuiciado*) prejudiced; (*pey*) mercenary, self-seeking

interesante [intere'sante] *adj* interesting

interesar [intere'sar] *vt, vi* to interest, be of interest to; **interesarse** *vr*: **interesarse en o por** to take an interest in

interferir [interfe'rir] *vt* to interfere with; (*TEL*) to jam ♦ *vi* to interfere

interfón (*MÉX*) *nm* entry phone

interino, -a [inte'rino, a] *adj* temporary ♦ *nm/f* temporary holder of a post; (*MED*) locum; (*ESCOL*) supply teacher

interior [inte'rjor] *adj* inner, inside; (*COM*) domestic, internal ♦ *nm* interior, inside; (*fig*) soul, mind; **Ministerio del I~** ≈ Home Office (*BRIT*), ≈ Department of the Interior (*US*) ☐ **interiorista** (*ESP*) *nmf* interior designer

interjección [interxek'θjon] *nf* interjection

interlocutor, a [interloku'tor, a] *nm/f* speaker

intermedio, -a [inter'meðjo, a] *adj* intermediate ♦ *nm* interval

interminable [intermi'naβle] *adj* endless

intermitente [intermi'tente] *adj* intermittent ♦ *nm* (*AUTO*) indicator

internacional [internaθjo'nal] *adj* international

internado [inter'naðo] *nm* boarding school

internar [inter'nar] *vt* to intern; (*en un manicomio*) to commit; **internarse** *vr* (*penetrar*) to penetrate

Internet, internet [inter'net] *nm o f* Internet

interno, -a [in'terno, a] *adj* internal, interior; (*POL etc*) domestic ♦ *nm/f* (*alumno*) boarder

interponer [interpo'ner] *vt* to interpose, put in; **interponerse** *vr* to intervene

interpretación [interpreta'θjon] *nf* interpretation

interpretar [interpre'tar] *vt* to interpret; (*TEATRO, MÚS*) to perform, play ☐ **intérprete** *nmf* (*LING*) interpreter, translator; (*MÚS, TEATRO*) performer, artist(e)

interrogación [interroγa'θjon] *nf* interrogation; (*LING: tb*: **signo de ~**) question mark

interrogar [interro'γar] *vt* to interrogate, question

interrumpir [interrum'pir] *vt* to interrupt

interrupción [interrup'θjon] *nf* interruption

interruptor [interrup'tor] *nm* (*ELEC*) switch

intersección [intersek'θjon] *nf* intersection

interurbano, -a [interur'βano, a] *adj*: **llamada interurbana** long-distance call

intervalo [inter'βalo] *nm* interval; (*descanso*) break

intervenir [interβe'nir] *vt* (*controlar*) to control, supervise; (*MED*) to operate on ♦ *vi* (*participar*) to take part, participate; (*mediar*) to intervene

interventor, a [interβen'tor, a] *nm/f* inspector; (*COM*) auditor

intestino [intes'tino] *nm* (*MED*) intestine

intimar [inti'mar] *vi* to become friendly

intimidad [intimi'ðað] *nf* intimacy; (*familiaridad*) familiarity; (*vida privada*) private life; (*JUR*) privacy

íntimo, -a [ˈintimo, a] *adj* intimate

intolerable [intoleˈraβle] *adj* intolerable, unbearable

intoxicación [intoksika'θjon] *nf* poisoning ► **intoxicación alimenticia** food poisoning

intranet [intra'net] *nf* intranet

intranquilo, -a [intran'kilo, a] *adj* worried

intransitable [intransi'taβle] *adj* impassable

intrépido, -a [in'trepiðo, a] *adj* intrepid

intriga [in'triɣa] *nf* intrigue; (*plan*) plot ❑ **intrigar** *vt, vi* to intrigue

intrínseco, -a [in'trinseko, a] *adj* intrinsic

introducción [introðuk'θjon] *nf* introduction

introducir [introðu'θir] *vt* (*gen*) to introduce; (*moneda etc*) to insert; (*INFORM*) to input, enter

intromisión [intromi'sjon] *nf* interference, meddling

introvertido, -a [introβer'tiðo, a] *adj, nm/f* introvert

intruso, -a [in'truso, a] *adj* intrusive ♦ *nm/f* intruder

intuición [intwi'θjon] *nf* intuition

inundación [inunda'θjon] *nf* flood(ing) ❑ **inundar** *vt* to flood; (*fig*) to swamp, inundate

inusitado, -a [inusi'taðo, a] *adj* unusual, rare

inútil [in'util] *adj* useless; (*esfuerzo*) vain, fruitless

inutilizar [inutili'θar] *vt* to make o render useless

invadir [imba'ðir] *vt* to invade

inválido, -a [im'baliðo, a] *adj* invalid ♦ *nm/f* invalid

invasión [imba'sjon] *nf* invasion

invasor, a [imba'sor, a] *adj* invading ♦ *nm/f* invader

invención [imben'θjon] *nf* invention

inventar [imben'tar] *vt* to invent

inventario [imben'tarjo] *nm* inventory

invento [im'bento] *nm* invention

inventor, a [im'bentor, a] *nm/f* inventor

invernadero [imberna'ðero] *nm* greenhouse

inverosímil [imbero'simil] *adj* implausible

inversión [imber'sjon] *nf* (*COM*) investment

inverso, -a [im'berso, a] *adj* inverse, opposite; **en el orden ~** in reverse order; **a la inversa** inversely, the other way round

inversor, a [imber'sor, a] *nm/f* (*COM*) investor

invertir [imber'tir] *vt* (*COM*) to invest; (*volcar*) to turn upside down; (*tiempo etc*) to spend

investigación [imbestiɣa'θjon] *nf* investigation; (*ESCOL*) research ► **investigación y desarrollo** research and development

investigar [imbesti'ɣar] *vt* to investigate; (*ESCOL*) to do research into

invierno [im'bjerno] *nm* winter

invisible [imbi'siβle] *adj* invisible

invitado, -a [imbi'taðo, a] *nm/f* guest

invitar [imbi'tar] vt to invite; (incitar) to entice; (pagar) to buy, pay for

invocar [imbo'kar] vt to invoke, call on

involucrar [imbolu'krar] vt: ~ **en** to involve in; **involucrarse** vr (persona): ~ **en** to get mixed up in

involuntario, -a [imbolun'tarjo, a] adj (movimiento, gesto) involuntary; (error) unintentional

inyección [injek'θjon] nf injection

inyectar [injek'tar] vt to inject

ir
PALABRA CLAVE

[ir] vi

1 to go; (a pie) to walk; (viajar) to travel; **ir caminando** to walk; **fui en tren** I went o travelled by train; **¡(ahora) voy!** (I'm just) coming!

2: ir a por: (ir a) **por el médico** to fetch the doctor

3 (progresar: persona, cosa) to go; **el trabajo va muy bien** work is going very well; **¿cómo te va?** how are things going?; **me va muy bien** I'm getting on very well; **le fue fatal** it went awfully badly for him

4 (funcionar): **el coche no va muy bien** the car isn't running very well

5 **te va estupendo ese color** that colour suits you fantastically well

6 (locuciones): **¿vino?** — **¡que va!** did he come? — of course not!; **vamos, no llores** come on, don't cry; **¡vaya coche!** what a car!, that's some car!

7: no vaya a ser: tienes que correr, no vaya a ser que pierdas el tren you'll have to run so as not to miss the train

8 (+ pp): **iba vestido muy bien** he was very well dressed

9: ni me etc **va ni me** etc **viene** I etc don't care

♦ vb aux

1: ir a: voy/iba a hacerlo hoy I am/ was going to do it today

2 (+ gerundio): **iba anocheciendo** it was getting dark; **todo se me iba aclarando** everything was gradually becoming clearer to me

3 (+ pp: = pasivo): **van vendidos 300 ejemplares** 300 copies have been sold so far

♦ **irse** vr

1: ¿por dónde se va al zoológico? which is the way to the zoo?

2 (marcharse) to leave; **ya se habrán ido** they must already have left o gone

ira ['ira] nf anger, rage

Irak [i'rak] nm = **Iraq**

Irán [i'ran] nm Iran ❑ **iraní** adj, nmf Iranian

Iraq [i'rak] nm Iraq ❑ **iraquí** adj, nmf Iraqi

iris ['iris] nm inv (tb: **arco ~**) rainbow; (ANAT) iris

Irlanda [ir'landa] nf Ireland ❑ **irlandés, -esa** adj Irish ♦ nm/f Irishman(-woman); **los irlandeses** the Irish

ironía [iro'nia] nf irony ❑ **irónico, -a** adj ironic(al)

IRPF nm abr (= Impuesto sobre la Renta de las Personas Físicas) (personal) income tax

irreal [irre'al] adj unreal

irregular [irreɣu'lar] adj (gen) irregular; (situación) abnormal

irremediable [irremeðjaβle] adj irremediable; (vicio) incurable

irreparable [irrepa'raβle] adj (daños) irreparable; (pérdida) irrecoverable

irrespetuoso, -a [irrespe'twoso, a] adj disrespectful

irresponsable [irrespon'saβle] adj irresponsible

irreversible [irreβer'sible] *adj* irreversible

irrigar [irri'ɣar] *vt* to irrigate

irrisorio, -a [irri'sorjo, a] *adj* derisory, ridiculous

irritar [irri'tar] *vt* to irritate, annoy

irrupción [irrup'θjon] *nf* irruption; (*invasión*) invasion

isla ['isla] *nf* island

islandés, -esa [islan'des, esa] *adj* Icelandic ♦ *nm/f* Icelander

Islandia [is'landja] *nf* Iceland

isleño, -a [is'leɲo, a] *adj* island *cpd* ♦ *nm/f* islander

Israel [isra'el] *nm* Israel ❏ **israelí** *adj*, *nmf* Israeli

istmo ['istmo] *nm* isthmus

Italia [i'talja] *nf* Italy ❏ **italiano, -a** *adj*, *nm/f* Italian

itinerario [itine'rarjo] *nm* itinerary, route

ITV (*ESP*) *nf abr* (= *Inspección técnica de vehículos*) roadworthiness test, ≈ MOT (*BRIT*)

IVA ['iβa] *nm abr* (= *impuesto sobre el valor añadido*) VAT

izar [i'θar] *vt* to hoist

izdo, -a *abr* (= *izquierdo, a*) l

izquierda [iθ'kjerða] *nf* left; (*POL*) left (wing); **a la ~** (*estar*) on the left; (*torcer etc*) (to the) left

izquierdo, -a [iθ'kjerðo, a] *adj* left

J, j

jabalí [xaβa'li] *nm* wild boar

jabalina [xaβa'lina] *nf* javelin

jabón [xa'βon] *nm* soap

jaca ['xaka] *nf* pony

jacal (*MÉX*) [xa'kal] *nm* shack

jacinto [xa'θinto] *nm* hyacinth

jactarse [xak'tarse] *vr* to boast, brag

jadear [xaðe'ar] *vi* to pant, gasp for breath

jaguar [xa'ɣwar] *nm* jaguar

jaiba (*LAm*) ['xaiβa] *nf* crab

jalar (*LAm*) [xa'lar] *vt* to pull

jalea [xa'lea] *nf* jelly

jaleo [xa'leo] *nm* racket, uproar; **armar un ~** to kick up a racket

jalón [xa'lon] (*LAm*) *nm* tug

jamás [xa'mas] *adv* never

jamón [xa'mon] *nm* ham ► **jamón dulce** o **de York** cooked ham ► **jamón serrano** cured ham

Japón [xa'pon] *nm* Japan ❏ **japonés, -esa** *adj, nm/f* Japanese ♦ *nm* (*LING*) Japanese

jaque ['xake] *nm* (*AJEDREZ*) check ► **jaque mate** checkmate

jaqueca [xa'keka] *nf* (very bad) headache, migraine

jarabe [xa'raβe] *nm* syrup

jardín [xar'ðin] *nm* garden ► **jardín infantil** o **de infancia** nursery (school) ❏ **jardinería** *nf* gardening ❏ **jardinero, -a** *nm/f* gardener

jarra ['xarra] *nf* jar; (*jarro*) jug

jarro ['xarro] *nm* jug

jarrón [xa'rron] *nm* vase

jaula ['xaula] *nf* cage

jauría [xau'ria] *nf* pack of hounds

jazmín [xaθ'min] *nm* jasmine

J.C. *abr* (= *Jesucristo*) J.C.

jeans [jins, dʒins] (*LAm*) *nmpl* jeans, denims; **unos ~** a pair of jeans

jefatura [xefa'tura] *nf* (*tb*: **~ de policía**) police headquarters *sg*

jefe, -a ['xefe, a] *nm/f* (*gen*) chief, head; (*patrón*) boss ► **jefe de cocina** chef ► **jefe de estación** stationmaster ► **jefe de Estado** head of state ► **jefe de estudios** (*ESCOL*) director of studies ► **jefe de gobierno** head of government

jengibre [xen'xiβre] *nm* ginger

jeque ['xeke] *nm* sheik

jerárquico, -a [xe'rarkiko, a] adj hierarchic(al)

jerez [xe'reθ] nm sherry

jerga ['xerɣa] nf jargon

jeringa [xe'ringa] nf syringe; (LAm: molestia) annoyance, bother □ **jeringuilla** nf syringe

jeroglífico [xero'ɣlifiko] nm hieroglyphic

jersey [xer'sei] (pl **jerseys**) nm jersey, pullover, jumper

Jerusalén [xerusa'len] n Jerusalem

Jesucristo [xesu'kristo] nm Jesus Christ

jesuita [xe'swita] adj, nm Jesuit

Jesús [xe'sus] nm Jesus; **¡~!** good heavens!; (al estornudar) bless you!

jinete [xi'nete] nmf horseman(-woman), rider

jipijapa [xipi'xapa] (LAm) nm straw hat

jirafa [xi'rafa] nf giraffe

jirón [xi'ron] nm rag, shred

jitomate (MÉX) [xito'mate] nm tomato

joder [xo'ðer] (fam!) vt, vi to fuck (!)

jogging ['joyin] (RPl) nm tracksuit (BRIT), sweat suit (US)

jornada [xor'naða] nf (viaje de un día) day's journey; (camino o viaje entero) journey; (día de trabajo) working day

jornal [xor'nal] nm (day's) wage □ **jornalero** nm (day) labourer

joroba [xo'roβa] nf hump, hunched back □ **jorobado, -a** adj hunchbacked ♦ nm/f hunchback

jota ['xota] nf (the letter) J; (danza) Aragonese dance; **no saber ni ~** to have no idea

joven ['xoβen] (pl **jóvenes**) adj young ♦ nm young man, youth ♦ nf young woman, girl

joya ['xoja] nf jewel, gem; (fig: persona) gem ► **joyas de fantasía** costume or imitation jewellery □ **joyería** nf (joyas) jewellery; (tienda) jeweller's

(shop) □ **joyero** nm (persona) jeweller; (caja) jewel case

juanete [xwa'nete] nm (del pie) bunion

jubilación [xuβila'θjon] nf (retiro) retirement

jubilado, -a [xuβi'laðo, a] adj retired ♦ nm/f pensioner (BRIT), senior citizen

jubilar [xuβi'lar] vt to pension off, retire; (fam) to discard; **jubilarse** vr to retire

júbilo ['xuβilo] nm joy, rejoicing □ **jubiloso, -a** adj jubilant

judía [xu'ðia] (ESP) nf (CULIN) bean ► **judía blanca/verde** haricot/French bean; ver tb **judío**

judicial [xuði'θjal] adj judicial

judío, -a [xu'ðio, a] adj Jewish ♦ nm/f Jew(ess)

judo ['juðo] nm judo

juego etc ['xweɣo] vb ver **jugar** ♦ nm (gen) play; (pasatiempo, partido) game; (en casino) gambling; (conjunto) set; **fuera de ~** (DEPORTE: persona) offside; (: pelota) out of play ► **juego de palabras** pun, play on words ► **Juegos Olímpicos** Olympic Games

juerga ['xwerɣa] (ESP: fam) nf binge; (fiesta) party; **ir de ~** to go out on a binge

jueves ['xweβes] nm inv Thursday

juez [xweθ] nmf judge ► **juez de instrucción** examining magistrate ► **juez de línea** linesman ► **juez de salida** starter

jugada [xu'ɣaða] nf play; **buena ~** good move o shot or stroke etc

jugador, a [xuɣa'ðor, a] nm/f player; (en casino) gambler

jugar [xu'ɣar] vt, vi to play; (en casino) to gamble; (apostar) to bet; **~ al fútbol** to play football

juglar [xu'ɣlar] nm minstrel

jugo ['xuɣo] nm (BOT) juice; (fig) essence, substance ► **jugo de naranja** (LAm) orange juice

❑ **jugoso, -a** adj juicy; (fig) substantial, important

juguete [xu'ɣete] nm toy ❑ **juguetear** vi to play ❑ **juguetería** nf toyshop

juguetón, -ona [xuɣe'ton, ona] adj playful

juicio ['xwiθjo] nm judgement; (razón) sanity, reason; (opinión) opinion

julio ['xuljo] nm July

jumper ['dʒumper] nm (LAm) pinafore dress (BRIT), jumper (US)

junco ['xunko] nm rush, reed

jungla ['xungla] nf jungle

junio ['xunjo] nm June

junta ['xunta] nf (asamblea) meeting, assembly; (comité, consejo) council, committee; (COM, FINANZAS) board; (TEC) joint ♦ **junta directiva** board of directors

juntar [xun'tar] vt to join, unite; (maquinaria) to assemble, put together; (dinero) to collect; **juntarse** vr to join, meet; (reunirse: personas) to meet, assemble; (arrimarse) to approach, draw closer; **juntarse con algn** to join sb

junto, -a ['xunto, a] adj joined; (unido) united; (anexo) near, close; (contiguo, próximo) next, adjacent ♦ adv: **todo ~** all at once; **juntos** together; **~ a** near (to), next to; **~ con** (together) with

jurado [xu'raðo] nm (JUR: individuo) juror; (: grupo) jury; (de concurso: grupo) panel (of judges); (: individuo) member of a panel

juramento [xura'mento] nm oath; (maldición) oath, curse; **prestar ~** to take the oath; **tomar ~ a** to swear in, administer the oath

jurar [xu'rar] vt, vi to swear; **~ en falso** to commit perjury; **tenérsela jurada a algn** to have it in for sb

jurídico, -a [xu'riðiko, a] adj legal

jurisdicción [xurisðik'θjon] nf (poder, autoridad) jurisdiction; (territorio) district

justamente [xusta'mente] adv justly, fairly; (precisamente) just, exactly

justicia [xus'tiθja] nf justice; (equidad) fairness, justice

justificación [xustifika'θjon] nf justification ❑ **justificar** vt to justify

justo, -a ['xusto, a] adj (equitativo) just, fair, right; (preciso) exact, correct; (ajustado) tight ♦ adv (precisamente) exactly, precisely; (LAm: apenas a tiempo) just in time

juvenil [xuβe'nil] adj youthful

juventud [xuβen'tuð] nf (adolescencia) youth; (jóvenes) young people pl

juzgado [xuθ'ɣaðo] nm tribunal; (JUR) court

juzgar [xuθ'ɣar] vt to judge; **a ~ por ...** to judge by ..., judging by ...

K, k

kárate ['karate] nm karate

kg abr (= kilogramo) kg

kilo ['kilo] nm kilo ❑ **kilogramo** nm kilogramme ❑ **kilometraje** nm distance in kilometres, = mileage ❑ **kilómetro** nm kilometre ❑ **kilovatio** nm kilowatt

kiosco ['kjosko] nm = **quiosco**

kleenex® nm paper handkerchief, tissue

Kosovo [ko'soβo] nm Kosovo

km abr (= kilómetro) km

kv abr (= kilovatio) kw

L, l

l abr (= litro) l

la [la] art def the ♦ pron her; (Ud.) you; (cosa) it ♦ nm (MÚS) la; **la del sombrero rojo** the girl in the red hat; ver tb **el**

laberinto [laβe'rinto] nm labyrinth

labio ['laβjo] nm lip

labor [la'βor] nf labour; (AGR) farm work; (tarea) job, task; (COSTURA) needlework ► **labores domésticas** o **del hogar** household chores □ **laborable** adj (AGR) workable; **día laborable** working day □ **laboral** adj (accidente) at work; (jornada) working

laboratorio [laβora'torjo] nm laboratory

laborista [laβo'rista] adj: **Partido L~** Labour Party

labrador, a [laβra'ðor, a] adj farming cpd ♦ nm/f farmer

labranza [la'βranθa] nf (AGR) cultivation

labrar [la'βrar] vt (gen) to work; (madera etc) to carve; (fig) to cause, bring about

laca ['laka] nf lacquer

lacio, -a ['laθjo, a] adj (pelo) straight

lacón [la'kon] nm shoulder of pork

lactancia [lak'tanθja] nf lactation

lácteo, -a ['lakteo, a] adj: **productos lácteos** dairy products

ladear [laðe'ar] vt to tip, tilt ♦ vi to tilt; **ladearse** vr to lean

ladera [la'ðera] nf slope

lado ['laðo] nm (gen) side; (fig) protection; (MIL) flank; **al ~ de** beside; **poner de ~** to put on its side; **poner a un ~** to put to one side; **por todos lados** on all sides, all round (BRIT)

ladrar [la'ðrar] vi to bark □ **ladrido** nm bark, barking

ladrillo [la'ðriʎo] nm (gen) brick; (azulejo) tile

ladrón, -ona [la'ðron, ona] nm/f thief

lagartija [layar'tixa] nf (ZOOL) (small) lizard

lagarto [la'yarto] nm (ZOOL) lizard

lago ['layo] nm lake

lágrima ['layrima] nf tear

laguna [la'yuna] nf (lago) lagoon; (hueco) gap

lamentable [lamen'taβle] adj lamentable, regrettable; (miserable) pitiful

lamentar [lamen'tar] vt (sentir) to regret; (deplorar) to lament; **lamentarse** vr to lament; **lo lamento mucho** I'm very sorry

lamer [la'mer] vt to lick

lámina ['lamina] nf (plancha delgada) sheet; (para estampar, estampa) plate

lámpara ['lampara] nf lamp ► **lámpara de alcohol/gas** spirit/gas lamp ► **lámpara de pie** standard lamp

lana ['lana] nf wool

lancha ['lantʃa] nf launch ► **lancha motora** motorboat, speedboat

langosta [lan'gosta] nf (crustáceo) lobster; (: de río) crayfish □ **langostino** nm Dublin Bay prawn

lanza ['lanθa] nf (arma) lance, spear

lanzamiento [lanθa'mjento] nm (gen) throwing; (NÁUT, COM) launch, launching ► **lanzamiento de peso** putting the shot

lanzar [lan'θar] vt (gen) to throw; (DEPORTE: pelota) to bowl; (NÁUT, COM) to launch; (JUR) to evict; **lanzarse** vr to throw o.s.

lapa ['lapa] nf limpet

lapicero [lapi'θero] (CAm) nm (bolígrafo) ballpoint pen, Biro®

lápida ['lapiða] nf stone ► **lápida mortuoria** headstone

lápiz ['lapiθ] nm pencil ► **lápiz de color** coloured pencil ► **lápiz de labios** lipstick ► **lápiz de ojos** eyebrow pencil

largar [lar'yar] vt (soltar) to release; (aflojar) to loosen; (lanzar) to launch; (fam) to let fly; (velas) to unfurl; (LAm: lanzar) to throw; **largarse** vr (fam) to beat it; **largarse a** (CS: empezar) to start to

largo, -a ['laryo, a] adj (longitud) long; (tiempo) lengthy; (fig) generous ♦ nm

length; (MÚS) largo; **dos años largos**
two long years; **tiene 9 metros de ~** it
is 9 metres long; **a la larga** in the long
run; **a lo ~ de** along; (tiempo) all
through, throughout
❑ **largometraje** nm feature film

⚠ No confundir **largo** con la palabra
inglesa **large**.

laringe [la'rinxe] nf larynx
❑ **laringitis** nf laryngitis

las [las] art def the ♦ pron them; **~ que
cantan** the o women o girls who
sing; ver tb **el**

lasaña [la'saɲa] nf lasagne, lasagna

láser ['laser] nm laser

lástima ['lastima] nf (pena) pity; **dar ~**
to be pitiful; **es una ~** it's a pity
that ...; **¡qué ~!** what a pity!; **está hecha
una ~** she looks pitiful

lastimar [lasti'mar] vt (herir) to wound;
(ofender) to offend; **lastimarse** vr to
hurt o.s.

lata ['lata] nf (metal) tin; (caja) tin (BRIT),
can; (fam) nuisance; **en ~** tinned (BRIT),
canned; **dar la ~** to be a nuisance

latente [la'tente] adj latent

lateral [late'ral] adj side cpd, lateral
♦ nm (TEATRO) wings

latido [la'tiðo] nm (de corazón) beat

latifundio [lati'fundjo] nm large
estate

latigazo [lati'ɣaθo] nm (golpe) lash;
(sonido) crack

látigo ['latiɣo] nm whip

latín [la'tin] nm Latin

latino, -a [la'tino, a] adj Latin
❑ **latinoamericano, -a** adj, nm/f
Latin-American

latir [la'tir] vi (corazón, pulso) to beat

latitud [lati'tuð] nf (GEO) latitude

latón [la'ton] nm brass

laurel [lau'rel] nm (BOT) laurel; (CULIN)
bay

lava ['laβa] nf lava

lavabo [la'βaβo] nm (pila) washbasin;
(tb: **lavabos**) toilet

lavado [la'βaðo] nm washing; (de ropa)
laundry; (ARTE) wash ▶ **lavado de
cerebro** brainwashing ▶ **lavado en
seco** dry-cleaning

lavadora [laβa'ðora] nf washing
machine

lavanda [la'βanda] nf lavender

lavandería [laβande'ria] nf laundry;
(automática) launderette

lavaplatos [laβa'platos] nm inv
dishwasher

lavar [la'βar] vt to wash; (borrar) to wipe
away; **lavarse** vr to wash o.s.; **lavarse
las manos** to wash one's hands;
lavarse los dientes to brush one's
teeth; **~ y marcar** (pelo) to shampoo
and set; **~ en seco** to dry-clean; **~ los
platos** to wash the dishes

lavarropas (RPI) nm inv washing
machine

lavavajillas [laβaβa'xiʎas] nm inv
dishwasher

laxante [lak'sante] nm laxative

lazarillo [laθa'riʎo] nm (tb: **perro ~**)
guide dog

lazo ['laθo] nm knot; (lazada) bow; (para
animales) lasso; (trampa) snare;
(vínculo) tie

le [le] pron (directo) him (o her); (: usted)
you; (indirecto) to him (o her o it);
(: usted) to you

leal [le'al] adj loyal ❑ **lealtad** nf loyalty

lección [lek'θjon] nf lesson

leche ['letʃe] nf milk; **tiene mala ~** (fam!)
he's a swine (!) ▶ **leche condensada**
condensed milk ▶ **leche desnatada**
skimmed milk

lecho ['letʃo] nm (cama: de río) bed;
(GEO) layer

lechón [le'tʃon] nm sucking (BRIT) o
suckling (US) pig

lechoso, -a [le'tʃoso, a] adj milky

lechuga [le'tʃuɣa] nf lettuce

lechuza [le'tʃuθa] nf owl

lector, a [lek'tor, a] *nm/f* reader ♦ *nm*: ~ **de discos compactos** CD player

lectura [lek'tura] *nf* reading

leer [le'er] *vt* to read

legado [le'ɣaðo] *nm* (*don*) bequest; (*herencia*) legacy; (*enviado*) legate

legajo [le'ɣaxo] *nm* file

legal [le'ɣal] *adj* (*gen*) legal; (*persona*) trustworthy □ **legalizar** [leɣali'θar] *vt* to legalize; (*documento*) to authenticate

legaña [le'ɣaɲa] *nf* sleep (*in eyes*)

legión [le'xjon] *nf* legion □ **legionario, -a** *adj* legionary ♦ *nm* legionnaire

legislación [lexisla'θjon] *nf* legislation

legislar [lexis'lar] *vi* to legislate

legislatura [lexisla'tura] *nf* (*POL*) period of office

legítimo, -a [le'xitimo, a] *adj* (*genuino*) authentic; (*legal*) legitimate

legua ['leɣwa] *nf* league

legumbres [le'ɣumbres] *nfpl* pulses

leído, -a [le'iðo, a] *adj* well-read

lejanía [lexa'nia] *nf* distance □ **lejano, -a** *adj* far-off; (*en el tiempo*) distant; (*fig*) remote

lejía [le'xia] *nf* bleach

lejos ['lexos] *adv* far, far away; **a lo ~** in the distance; **de** o **desde ~** from afar; ~ **de** far from

lema ['lema] *nm* motto; (*POL*) slogan

lencería [lenθe'ria] *nf* linen, drapery

lengua ['leŋgwa] *nf* tongue; (*LING*) language; **morderse la ~** to hold one's tongue

lenguado [leŋ'gwaðo] *nm* sole

lenguaje [leŋ'gwaxe] *nm* language ► **lenguaje de programación** program(m)ing language

lengüeta [leŋ'gweta] *nf* (*ANAT*) epiglottis; (*zapatos*) tongue; (*MÚS*) reed

lente ['lente] *nf* lens; (*lupa*) magnifying glass □ **lentes** *nfpl* lenses ♦ *nmpl* (*LAm: gafas*) glasses ► **lentes**

bifocales/de sol (*LAm*) bifocals/ sunglasses ► **lentes de contacto** contact lenses

lenteja [len'texa] *nf* lentil □ **lentejuela** *nf* sequin

lentilla [len'tiʎa] *nf* contact lens

lentitud [lenti'tuð] *nf* slowness; **con ~** slowly

lento, -a ['lento, a] *adj* slow

leña ['leɲa] *nf* firewood □ **leñador, a** *nm/f* woodcutter

leño ['leɲo] *nm* (*trozo de árbol*) log; (*madero*) timber; (*fig*) blockhead

Leo ['leo] *nm* Leo

león [le'on] *nm* lion ► **león marino** sea lion

leopardo [leo'parðo] *nm* leopard

leotardos [leo'tarðos] *nmpl* tights

lepra ['lepra] *nf* leprosy □ **leproso, -a** *nm/f* leper

les [les] *pron* (*directo*) them; (: *ustedes*) you; (*indirecto*) to them; (: *ustedes*) you

lesbiana [les'βjana] *adj, nf* lesbian

lesión [le'sjon] *nf* wound, lesion; (*DEPORTE*) injury □ **lesionado, -a** *adj* injured ♦ *nm/f* injured person

letal [le'tal] *adj* lethal

letanía [leta'nia] *nf* litany

letra ['letra] *nf* letter; (*escritura*) handwriting; (*MÚS*) lyrics *pl* ► **letra de cambio** bill of exchange ► **letra de imprenta** print □ **letrado, -a** *adj* learned ♦ *nm/f* lawyer □ **letrero** *nm* (*cartel*) sign; (*etiqueta*) label

letrina [le'trina] *nf* latrine

leucemia [leu'θemja] *nf* leukaemia

levadura [leβa'ðura] *nf* (*para el pan*) yeast; (*de cerveza*) brewer's yeast

levantar [leβan'tar] *vt* (*gen*) to raise; (*del suelo*) to pick up; (*hacia arriba*) to lift (up); (*plan*) to make, draw up; (*mesa*) to clear; (*campamento*) to strike; (*fig*) to cheer up, hearten; **levantarse** *vr* to get up; (*enderezarse*) to straighten up; (*rebelarse*) to rebel; **~ el ánimo** to cheer up

levante [le'βante] *nm* east coast; **el L~** region of Spain extending from Castellón to Murcia

levar [le'βar] *vt* to weigh

leve ['leβe] *adj* light; (*fig*) trivial

levita [le'βita] *nf* frock coat

léxico ['leksiko] *nm* (*vocabulario*) vocabulary

ley [lei] *nf* (*gen*) law; (*metal*) standard

leyenda [le'jenda] *nf* legend

leyó *etc vb ver* **leer**

liar [li'ar] *vt* to tie (up); (*unir*) to bind; (*envolver*) to wrap (up); (*enredar*) to confuse; (*cigarrillo*) to roll; **liarse** *vr* (*fam*) to get involved; **liarse a palos** to get involved in a fight

Líbano ['liβano] *nm*: **el ~** the Lebanon

libélula [li'βelula] *nf* dragonfly

liberación [liβera'θjon] *nf* liberation; (*de la cárcel*) release

liberal [liβe'ral] *adj*, *nmf* liberal

liberar [liβe'rar] *vt* to liberate

libertad [liβer'tað] *nf* liberty, freedom
  ▶ **libertad bajo fianza** bail
  ▶ **libertad bajo palabra** parole
  ▶ **libertad condicional** probation
  ▶ **libertad de culto/de prensa/de comercio** freedom of worship/of the press/of trade

libertar [liβer'tar] *vt* (*preso*) to set free; (*de una obligación*) to release; (*eximir*) to exempt

libertino, -a [liβer'tino, a] *adj* permissive ♦ *nm/f* permissive person

libra ['liβra] *nf* pound; **L~** (*ASTROLOGÍA*) Libra ▶ **libra esterlina** pound sterling

libramiento (*MÉX*) [liβra'mjento] *nm* ring road (*BRIT*), beltway (*US*)

librar [li'βrar] *vt* (*de peligro*) to save; (*batalla*) to wage, fight; (*de impuestos*) to exempt; (*cheque*) to make out; (*JUR*) to exempt; **librarse** *vr*: **librarse de** to escape from, free o.s. from

libre ['liβre] *adj* free; (*lugar*) unoccupied; (*asiento*) vacant; (*de deudas*) free of debts; **~ de impuestos** free of tax; **tiro ~** free kick; **los 100 metros libres** the 100 metres freestyle (race); **al aire ~** in the open air

librería [liβre'ria] *nf* (*tienda*) bookshop ❏ **librero, -a** *nm/f* bookseller

⚠ No confundir **librería** con la palabra inglesa *library*.

libreta [li'βreta] *nf* notebook

libro ['liβro] *nm* book ▶ **libro de bolsillo** paperback ▶ **libro de texto** textbook ▶ **libro electrónico** e-book

Lic. *abr* = **licenciado, a**

licencia [li'θenθja] *nf* (*gen*) licence; (*permiso*) permission ▶ **licencia de caza** game licence ▶ **licencia por enfermedad** (*MÉX*, *RPI*) sick leave ❏ **licenciado, -a** *adj* licensed ♦ *nm/f* graduate ❏ **licenciar** *vt* (*empleado*) to dismiss; (*permitir*) to permit, allow; (*soldado*) to discharge; (*estudiante*) to confer a degree upon; **licenciarse** *vr*: **licenciarse en Derecho** to graduate in law

lícito, -a ['liθito, a] *adj* (*legal*) lawful; (*justo*) fair, just; (*permisible*) permissible

licor [li'kor] *nm* spirits *pl* (*BRIT*), liquor (*US*); (*de frutas etc*) liqueur

licuadora [likwa'ðora] *nf* blender

líder ['liðer] *nmf* leader ❏ **liderato** *nm* leadership ❏ **liderazgo** *nm* leadership

lidia ['liðja] *nf* bullfighting; (*una lidia*) bullfight; **toros de ~** fighting bulls ❏ **lidiar** *vt*, *vi* to fight

liebre ['ljeβre] *nf* hare

lienzo ['ljenθo] *nm* linen; (*ARTE*) canvas; (*ARQ*) wall

liga ['liɣa] *nf* (*de medias*) garter, suspender; (*LAm: goma*) rubber band; (*confederación*) league

ligadura [liɣa'ðura] *nf* bond, tie; (*MED*, *MÚS*) ligature

ligamento [liɣa'mento] nm ligament

ligar [li'ɣar] vt (atar) to tie; (unir) to join; (MED) to bind up; (MÚS) to slur ♦ vi to mix, blend; (fam): **(él) liga mucho** he pulls a lot of women; **ligarse** vr to commit o.s.

ligero, -a [li'xero, a] adj (de peso) light; (tela) thin; (rápido) swift, quick; (ágil) agile, nimble; (de importancia) slight; (de carácter) flippant, superficial ♦ adv: **a la ligera** superficially

liguero [li'ɣero] nm suspender (BRIT) o garter (US) belt

lija ['lixa] nf (ZOOL) dogfish; (tb: **papel de** ~) sandpaper

lila ['lila] nf lilac

lima ['lima] nf file; (BOT) lime ► **lima de uñas** nailfile ❑ **limar** vt to file

limitación [limita'θjon] nf limitation, limit

limitar [limi'tar] vt to limit; (reducir) to reduce, cut down ♦ vi: ~ **con** to border on; **limitarse** vr: **limitarse a** to limit o.s. to

límite ['limite] nm (gen) limit; (fin) end; (frontera) border ► **límite de velocidad** speed limit

limítrofe [li'mitrofe] adj neighbouring

limón [li'mon] nm lemon ♦ adj: **amarillo** ~ lemon-yellow ❑ **limonada** nf lemonade

limosna [li'mosna] nf alms pl; **vivir de** ~ to live on charity

limpiaparabrisas (MÉX) [limpja'ðor] nm = **limpiaparabrisas**

limpiaparabrisas [limpjapara'βrisas] nm inv windscreen (BRIT) o windshield (US) wiper

limpiar [lim'pjar] vt to clean; (con trapo) to wipe; (quitar) to wipe away; (zapatos) to shine, polish; (fig) to clean up

limpieza [lim'pjeθa] nf (estado) cleanliness; (acto) cleaning; (: de las calles) cleansing; (: de zapatos) polishing; (habilidad) skill; (fig: POLICÍA)

clean-up; (pureza) purity; (MIL): **operación de** ~ mopping-up operation ► **limpieza en seco** dry cleaning

limpio, -a ['limpjo, a] adj clean; (moralmente) pure; (COM) clear, net; (fam) honest ♦ adv: **jugar** ~ to play fair; **pasar a** (LAm) o **en** (ESP) ~ to make a clean copy of

lince ['linθe] nm lynx

linchar [lin'tʃar] vt to lynch

lindar [lin'dar] vi to adjoin; ~ **con** to border on

lindo, -a ['lindo, a] adj pretty, lovely ♦ adv: **nos divertimos de lo** ~ we had a marvellous time; **canta muy** ~ (LAm) he sings beautifully

línea ['linea] nf (gen) line; **en** ~ (INFORM) on line ► **línea aérea** airline ► **línea de meta** goal line; (en carrera) finishing line ► **línea discontinua** (AUTO) broken line ► **línea recta** straight line

lingote [lin'ɡote] nm ingot

lingüista [lin'ɡwista] nmf linguist ❑ **lingüística** nf linguistics sg

lino ['lino] nm linen; (BOT) flax

linterna [lin'terna] nf torch (BRIT), flashlight (US)

lío ['lio] nm bundle; (fam) fuss; (desorden) muddle, mess; **armar un** ~ to make a fuss

liquen ['liken] nm lichen

liquidación [likiða'θjon] nf liquidation; **venta de** ~ clearance sale

liquidar [liki'ðar] vt (mercancías) to liquidate; (deudas) to pay off; (empresa) to wind up

líquido, -a ['likiðo, a] adj liquid; (ganancia) net ♦ nm liquid ► **líquido imponible** net taxable income

lira ['lira] nf (MÚS) lyre; (moneda) lira

lírico, -a ['liriko, a] adj lyrical

lirio ['lirjo] nm (BOT) iris

lirón [li'ron] nm (ZOOL) dormouse; (fig) sleepyhead

Lisboa [lis'βoa] n Lisbon

lisiar [li'sjar] vt to maim

liso, -a ['liso, a] adj (terreno) flat; (cabello) straight; (superficie) even; (tela) plain

lista ['lista] nf list; (de alumnos) school register; (de libros) catalogue; (de platos) menu; (de precios) price list; **pasar ~** to call the roll; **tela de listas** striped material ▶ **lista de espera** waiting list ▶ **lista de precios** price list □ **listín** nm (tb: **listín telefónico o de teléfonos**) telephone directory

listo, -a ['listo, a] adj (perspicaz) smart, clever; (preparado) ready

listón [lis'ton] nm (de madera, metal) strip

litera [li'tera] nf (en barco, tren) berth; (en dormitorio) bunk, bunk bed

literal [lite'ral] adj literal

literario, -a [lite'rarjo, a] adj literary

literato, -a [lite'rato, a] adj literary ♦ nm/f writer

literatura [litera'tura] nf literature

litigio [li'tixjo] nm (JUR) lawsuit; (fig): **en ~ con** in dispute with

litografía [litoɣra'fia] nf lithography; (una litografía) lithograph

litoral [lito'ral] adj coastal ♦ nm coast, seaboard

litro ['litro] nm litre

lívido, -a ['liβiðo, a] adj livid

llaga ['ʎaɣa] nf wound

llama ['ʎama] nf flame; (ZOOL) llama

llamada [ʎa'maða] nf call ▶ **llamada a cobro revertido** reverse-charge (BRIT) o collect (US) call ▶ **llamada al orden** call to order ▶ **llamada de atención** warning ▶ **llamada local** (LAm) local call ▶ **llamada metropolitana** (ESP) local call ▶ **llamada por cobrar** (MÉX) reverse-charge (BRIT) o collect (US) call

llamamiento [ʎama'mjento] nm call

llamar [ʎa'mar] vt to call; (atención) to attract ♦ vi (por teléfono) to telephone;

(a la puerta) to knock (o ring); (por señas) to beckon; (MIL) to call up; **llamarse** vr to be called, be named; **¿cómo se llama (usted)?** what's your name?

llamativo, -a [ʎama'tiβo, a] adj showy; (color) loud

llano, -a ['ʎano, a] adj (superficie) flat; (persona) straightforward; (estilo) clear ♦ nm plain, flat ground

llanta ['ʎanta] nf (ESP) (wheel) rim ▶ **llanta (de goma)** (LAm: neumático) tyre; (: cámara) inner (tube) ▶ **llanta de repuesto** (LAm) spare tyre

llanto ['ʎanto] nm weeping

llanura [ʎa'nura] nf plain

llave ['ʎaβe] nf key; (del agua) tap; (MECÁNICA) spanner; (de la luz) switch; (MÚS) key; **echar la ~ a** to lock up ▶ **llave de contacto** (ESP AUTO) ignition key ▶ **llave de encendido** (LAm AUTO) ignition key ▶ **llave de paso** stopcock ▶ **llave inglesa** monkey wrench ▶ **llave maestra** master key □ **llavero** nm keyring

llegada [ʎe'ɣaða] nf arrival

llegar [ʎe'ɣar] vi to arrive; (alcanzar) to reach; (bastar) to be enough; **llegarse** vr: **llegarse a** to approach; **~ a** to manage to, succeed in; **~ a saber** to find out; **~ a ser** to become; **~ a las manos de** to come into the hands of

llenar [ʎe'nar] vt to fill; (espacio) to cover; (formulario) to fill in o up; (fig) to heap

lleno, -a ['ʎeno, a] adj full, filled; (repleto) full up ♦ nm (TEATRO) full house; **dar de ~ contra un muro** to hit a wall head-on

llevadero, -a [ʎeβa'ðero, a] adj bearable, tolerable

llevar [ʎe'βar] vt to take; (ropa) to wear; (cargar) to carry; (quitar) to take away; (en coche) to drive; (transportar) to transport; (traer: dinero) to carry; (conducir) to lead; (MAT) to carry ♦ vi (suj: camino etc): **~ a** to lead to; **llevarse** vt to carry off, take away; **llevamos dos días aquí** we have been here for two days; **él me lleva 2 años** he's 2 years older than me; **~ los libros** (COM) to keep the books; **llevarse bien** to get on well (together)

llorar [ʎoˈɾar] vt, vi to cry, weep; **~ de risa** to cry with laughter

llorón, -ona [ʎoˈɾon, ona] adj tearful ♦ nm/f cry-baby

lloroso, -a [ʎoˈɾoso, a] adj (gen) weeping, tearful; (triste) sad, sorrowful

llover [ʎoˈβer] vi to rain

llovizna [ʎoˈβiθna] nf drizzle
❑ **lloviznar** vi to drizzle

llueve etc [ˈʎweβe] vb ver **llover**

lluvia [ˈʎuβja] nf rain ► **lluvia radioactiva** (radioactive) fallout
❑ **lluvioso, -a** adj rainy

lo [lo] art def: **lo bello** the beautiful, what is beautiful, that which is beautiful ♦ pron (persona) him; (cosa) it; **lo que sea** whatever; ver tb **el**

loable [loˈaβle] adj praiseworthy

lobo [ˈloβo] nm wolf ► **lobo de mar** (fig) sea dog

lóbulo [ˈloβulo] nm lobe

local [loˈkal] adj local ♦ nm place, site; (oficinas) premises pl ❑ **localidad** nf (barrio) locality; (lugar) location; (TEATRO) seat, ticket ❑ **localizar** vt (ubicar) to locate, find; (restringir) to localize; (situar) to place

loción [loˈθjon] nf lotion

loco, -a [ˈloko, a] adj mad ♦ nm/f lunatic, mad person; **estar ~ con o por algo/por algn** to be mad about sth/sb

locomotora [lokomoˈtora] nf engine, locomotive

locuaz [loˈkwaθ] adj loquacious

locución [lokuˈθjon] nf expression

locura [loˈkura] nf madness; (acto) crazy act

locutor, a [lokuˈtor, a] nm/f (RADIO) announcer; (comentarista) commentator; (TV) newsreader

locutorio [lokuˈtorjo] nm (en telefónica) telephone booth

lodo [ˈloðo] nm mud

lógica [ˈloxika] nf logic

lógico, -a [ˈloxiko, a] adj logical

login nm login

logística [loˈxistika] nf logistics sg

logotipo [loɣoˈtipo] nm logo

logrado, -a [loˈɣraðo, a] adj (interpretación, reproducción) polished, excellent

lograr [loˈɣrar] vt to achieve; (obtener) to get, obtain; **~ hacer** to manage to do; **~ que algn venga** to manage to get sb to come

logro [ˈloɣro] nm achievement, success

lóker (LAm) nm locker

loma [ˈloma] nf hillock (BRIT), small hill

lombriz [lomˈbriθ] nf worm

lomo [ˈlomo] nm (de animal) back; (CULIN: de cerdo) pork loin; (: de vaca) rib steak; (de libro) spine

lona [ˈlona] nf canvas

loncha [ˈlontʃa] nf = **lonja**

lonchería (LAm) [lontʃeˈria] nf snack bar, diner (US)

Londres [ˈlondres] n London

longaniza [lonɡaˈniθa] nf pork sausage

longitud [lonxiˈtuð] nf length; (GEO) longitude; **tener 3 metros de ~** to be 3 metres long ► **longitud de onda** wavelength

lonja [ˈlonxa] nf slice; (de tocino) rasher ► **lonja de pescado** fish market

loro [ˈloro] nm parrot

los [los] art def the ♦ pron them; (ustedes) you; **mis libros y ~ tuyos** my books and yours; ver tb **el**

losa [ˈlosa] nf stone

lote [ˈlote] nm portion; (COM) lot

lotería [lote'ria] nf lottery; (juego) lotto

loza ['loθa] nf crockery
lubina [lu'βina] nf sea bass
lubricante [luβri'kante] nm lubricant
lubricar [luβri'kar] vt to lubricate
lucha ['lutʃa] nf fight, struggle ▶ **lucha de clases** class struggle ▶ **lucha libre** wrestling ❑ **luchar** vi to fight
lúcido, -a ['luθiðo, a] adj (persona) lucid; (mente) logical; (idea) crystal-clear
luciérnaga [lu'θjernaɣa] nf glow-worm
lucir [lu'θir] vt to illuminate, light (up); (ostentar) to show off ♦ vi (brillar) to shine; **lucirse** vr (irónico) to make a fool of o.s.
lucro ['lukro] nm profit, gain
lúdico, -a ['luðiko, a] adj (aspecto, actividad) play cpd
luego ['lweɣo] adv (después) next; (más tarde) later, afterwards
lugar [lu'ɣar] nm place; (sitio) spot; en primer ~ in the first place, firstly; **en de** instead of; **hacer ~** to make room; **fuera de ~** out of place; **sin ~ a dudas** without doubt, undoubtedly; **dar ~ a** to give rise to; **tener ~** to take place; **yo en su ~** if I were him ▶ **lugar común** commonplace
lúgubre ['luɣuβre] adj mournful
lujo ['luxo] nm luxury; (fig) profusion, abundance; **de ~** luxury cpd, de luxe ❑ **lujoso, -a** adj luxurious

lujuria [lu'xurja] nf lust
lumbre ['lumbre] nf fire; (para cigarrillo) light
luminoso, -a [lumi'noso, a] adj luminous, shining
luna ['luna] nf moon; (de un espejo) glass; (de gafas) lens; (fig) crescent; **estar en la ~** to have one's head in the clouds ▶ **luna de miel** honeymoon ▶ **luna llena/nueva** full/new moon
lunar [lu'nar] adj lunar ♦ nm (ANAT) mole; **tela de lunares** spotted material
lunes ['lunes] nm inv Monday
lupa ['lupa] nf magnifying glass
lustre ['lustre] nm polish; (fig) lustre; **dar ~ a** to polish
luto ['luto] nm mourning; **llevar el o vestirse de ~** to be in mourning
Luxemburgo [luksem'burɣo] nm Luxembourg
luz [luθ] (pl **luces**) nf light; **dar a ~ un niño** to give birth to a child; **sacar a la ~** to bring to light; **dar o encender** (LAm) o **prender** (ESP)/**apagar la ~** to switch the light on/off; **tener pocas luces** to be dim o stupid; **traje de luces** bullfighter's costume ▶ **luces de tráfico** traffic lights ▶ **luz de freno** brake light ▶ **luz roja/verde** red/green light

M, m

m abr (= metro) m; (= minuto) m
macana [MÉX] [ma'kana] nf truncheon (BRIT), billy club (US)
macarrones [maka'rrones] nmpl macaroni sg
macedonia [maθe'ðonja] nf (tb: ~ de frutas) fruit salad
maceta [ma'θeta] nf (de flores) pot of flowers; (para plantas) flowerpot
machacar [matʃa'kar] vt to crush, pound ♦ vi (insistir) to go on, keep on

machete [maˈtʃete] *nm* machete, (large) knife

machetear (*MÉX*) *vt* to swot (*BRIT*), grind away (*US*)

machismo [maˈtʃismo] *nm* male chauvinism ◻ **machista** *adj, nm* sexist

macho [ˈmatʃo] *adj* male; (*fig*) virile ♦ *nm* male; (*fig*) he-man

macizo, -a [maˈθiθo, a] *adj* (*grande*) massive; (*fuerte, sólido*) solid ♦ *nm* mass, chunk

madeja [maˈðexa] *nf* (*de lana*) skein, hank; (*de pelo*) mass, mop

madera [maˈðera] *nf* wood; (*fig*) nature, character; **una ~** a piece of wood

madrastra [maˈðrastra] *nf* stepmother

madre [ˈmaðre] *adj* mother *cpd* ♦ *nf* mother; (*de vino etc*) dregs *pl* ▶ **madre política/soltera** mother-in-law/ unmarried mother

Madrid [maˈðrið] *n* Madrid

madriguera [maðriˈɣera] *nf* burrow

madrileño, -a [maðriˈleɲo, a] *adj* of o from Madrid ♦ *nm/f* native of Madrid

madrina [maˈðrina] *nf* godmother; (*ARQ*) prop, shore; (*TEC*) brace; (*de boda*) bridesmaid

madrugada [maðruˈɣaða] *nf* early morning; (*alba*) dawn, daybreak

madrugador, a [maðruɣaˈðor, a] *adj* early-rising

madrugar [maðruˈɣar] *vi* to get up early; (*fig*) to get ahead

madurar [maðuˈrar] *vt, vi* (*fruta*) to ripen; (*fig*) to mature ◻ **madurez** *nf* ripeness; maturity ◻ **maduro, -a** *adj* ripe; mature

maestra [maˈestra] *nf ver* **maestro**

maestría [maesˈtria] *nf* mastery; (*habilidad*) skill, expertise

maestro, -a [maˈestro, a] *adj* masterly; (*principal*) main ♦ *nm/f* master/ mistress; (*profesor*) teacher ♦ *nm* (*autoridad*) authority; (*MÚS*) maestro; (*experto*) master ▶ **maestro albañil** master mason

magdalena [maɣðaˈlena] *nf* fairy cake

magia [ˈmaxja] *nf* magic ◻ **mágico, -a** *adj* magic(al) ♦ *nm/f* magician

magisterio [maxisˈterjo] *nm* (*enseñanza*) teaching; (*profesión*) teaching profession; (*maestros*) teachers *pl*

magistrado [maxisˈtraðo] *nm* magistrate

magistral [maxisˈtral] *adj* magisterial; (*fig*) masterly

magnate [maɣˈnate] *nm* magnate, tycoon

magnético, -a [maɣˈnetiko, a] *adj* magnetic

magnetofón [maɣnetoˈfon] *nm* tape recorder

magnetófono [maɣneˈtofono] *nm* = **magnetofón**

magnífico, -a [maɣˈnifiko, a] *adj* splendid, magnificent

magnitud [maɣniˈtuð] *nf* magnitude

mago, -a [ˈmaɣo, a] *nm/f* magician; **los Reyes Magos** the Three Wise Men

magro, -a [ˈmaɣro, a] *adj* (*carne*) lean

mahonesa [mao̯ˈnesa] *nf* mayonnaise

maître [ˈmetre] *nm* head waiter

maíz [maˈiθ] *nm* maize (*BRIT*), corn (*US*); sweet corn

majestad [maxesˈtað] *nf* majesty

majo, -a [ˈmaxo, a] *adj* nice; (*guapo*) attractive, good-looking; (*elegante*) smart

mal [mal] *adv* badly; (*equivocadamente*) wrongly ♦ *adj* = **malo** ♦ *nm* evil; (*desgracia*) misfortune; (*daño*) harm, damage; (*MED*) illness; **~ que bien** rightly or wrongly; **ir de ~ en peor** to get worse and worse

malabarista [malaβaˈrista] *nmf* juggler

malaria [maˈlarja] *nf* malaria

malcriado, -a [malˈkrjaðo, a] *adj* spoiled

maldad [malˈdað] *nf* evil, wickedness

maldecir [malde'θir] vt to curse

maldición [maldi'θjon] nf curse

maldito, -a [mal'dito, a] adj (condenado) damned; (perverso) wicked; **¡~ sea!** damn it!

malecón (LAm) [male'kon] nm sea front, promenade

maleducado, -a [maleðu'kaðo, a] adj bad-mannered, rude

malentendido [malenten'diðo] nm misunderstanding

malestar [males'tar] nm (gen) discomfort; (fig: inquietud) uneasiness; (POL) unrest

maleta [ma'leta] nf case, suitcase; (AUTO) boot (BRIT), trunk (US); **hacer las maletas** to pack ▸ **maletero** nm (AUTO) boot (BRIT), trunk (US) ▢ **maletín** nm small case, bag

maleza [ma'leθa] nf (malas hierbas) weeds pl; (arbustos) thicket

malgastar [malɣas'tar] vt (tiempo, dinero) to waste; (salud) to ruin

malhechor, a [male'tʃor, a] nm/f delinquent

malhumorado, -a [malumo'raðo, a] adj bad-tempered

malicia [ma'liθja] nf (maldad) wickedness; (astucia) slyness, guile; (mala intención) malice, spite; (carácter travieso) mischievousness

maligno, -a [ma'liɣno, a] adj evil; (malévolo) malicious; (MED) malignant

malla ['maʎa] nf mesh; (de baño) swimsuit; (de ballet, gimnasia) leotard; **mallas** nfpl tights ▸ **malla de alambre** wire mesh

Mallorca [ma'ʎorka] nf Majorca

malo, -a ['malo, a] adj bad, false ♦ nm/f villain; **estar ~** to be ill

malograr [malo'ɣrar] vt to spoil; (plan) to upset; (ocasión) to waste

malparado, -a [malpa'raðo, a] adj: **salir ~** to come off badly

malpensado, -a [malpen'saðo, a] adj nasty

malteada [malte'aða] (LAm) nf milkshake

maltratar [maltra'tar] vt to ill-treat, mistreat

malvado, -a [mal'βaðo, a] adj evil, villainous

Malvinas [mal'βinas] nfpl (tb: **Islas ~**) Falklands, Falkland Islands

mama ['mama] nf (de animal) teat; (de mujer) breast

mamá [ma'ma] (pl **~s** (fam)) nf mum, mummy

mamar [ma'mar] vt, vi to suck

mamarracho [mama'rratʃo] nm sight, mess

mameluco (RPl) [mame'luko] nm dungarees pl (BRIT), overalls pl (US)

mamífero [ma'mifero] nm mammal

mampara [mam'para] nf (entre habitaciones) partition; (biombo) screen

mampostería [mamposte'ria] nf masonry

manada [ma'naða] nf (ZOOL) herd; (: de leones) pride; (: de lobos) pack

manantial [manan'tjal] nm spring

mancha ['mantʃa] nf stain, mark; (ZOOL) patch ▸ **manchar** vt (gen) to stain, mark; (ensuciar) to soil, dirty

manchego, -a [man'tʃeɣo, a] adj of o from La Mancha

manco, -a ['manko, a] adj (de un brazo) one-armed; (de una mano) one-handed; (fig) defective, faulty

mancuernas (MÉX) [man'kwernas] nfpl cufflinks

mandado (LAm) [man'daðo] nm errand

mandamiento [manda'mjento] nm (orden) order, command; (REL) commandment

mandar [man'dar] vt (ordenar) to order; (dirigir) to lead, command; (enviar) to send; (pedir) to order, ask for ♦ vi to be in charge; (pey) to be bossy; **¿mande?** (MÉX: ¿cómo dice?) pardon?, excuse me?; **~ hacer un traje** to have a suit made

mandarina [manda'rina] (*ESP*) *nf* tangerine, mandarin (orange)

mandato [man'dato] *nm* (*orden*) order; (*POL: periodo*) term of office; (: *territorio*) mandate

mandíbula [man'diβula] *nf* jaw

mandil [man'dil] *nm* apron

mando ['mando] *nm* (*MIL*) command; (*de país*) rule; (*el primer lugar*) lead; (*POL*) term of office; (*TEC*) control; **~ a la izquierda** left-hand drive ▶ **mando a distancia** remote control

mandón, -ona [man'don, ona] *adj* bossy, domineering

manejar [mane'xar] *vt* to manage; (*máquina*) to work, operate; (*caballo etc*) to handle; (*casa*) to run, manage; (*LAm AUTO*) to drive; **manejarse** *vr* (*comportarse*) to act, behave; (*arreglárselas*) to manage ❑ **manejo** *nm* (*de bicicleta*) handling; (*de negocio*) management, running; (*LAm AUTO*) driving; (*facilidad de trato*) ease, confidence; **manejos** *nmpl* (*intrigas*) intrigues

manera [ma'nera] *nf* way, manner, fashion; **maneras** *nfpl* (*modales*) manners; **su ~ de ser** the way he is; (*aire*) his manner; **de ninguna ~** no way, by no means; **de otra ~** otherwise; **de todas maneras** at any rate; **no hay ~ de persuadirle** there's no way of convincing him

manga ['manga] *nf* (*de camisa*) sleeve; (*de riego*) hose

mango ['mango] *nm* handle; (*BOT*) mango

manguera [man'gera] *nf* hose

maní (*LAm*) [ma'ni] *nm* peanut

manía [ma'nia] *nf* (*MED*) mania; (*fig: moda*) rage, craze; (*disgusto*) dislike; (*malicia*) spite; **coger ~ a algn** to take a dislike to sb; **tener ~ a algn** to dislike

sb ❑ **maníaco, -a** *adj* maniac(al)
♦ *nm/f* maniac

maniático, -a [ma'njatiko, a] *adj* maniac(al) ♦ *nm/f* maniac

manicomio [mani'komjo] *nm* mental hospital (*BRIT*), insane asylum (*US*)

manifestación [manifesta'θjon] *nf* (*declaración*) statement, declaration; (*de emoción*) show, display; (*POL: desfile*) demonstration; (: *concentración*) mass meeting

manifestar [manifes'tar] *vt* to show, manifest; (*declarar*) to state, declare ❑ **manifiesto, -a** *adj* clear, manifest
♦ *nm* manifesto

manillar [mani'ʎar] *nm* handlebars *pl*

maniobra [ma'njoβra] *nf* manœuvre; **maniobras** *nfpl* (*MIL*) manœuvres ❑ **maniobrar** *vt* to manœuvre

manipulación [manipula'θjon] *nf* manipulation

manipular [manipu'lar] *vt* to manipulate; (*manejar*) to handle

maniquí [mani'ki] *nm* dummy ♦ *nmf* model

manivela [mani'βela] *nf* crank

manjar [man'xar] *nm* (tasty) dish

mano ['mano] *nf* hand; (*ZOOL*) foot, paw; (*de pintura*) coat; (*serie*) lot, series; **a ~** by hand; **a ~ derecha/izquierda** on the right(-hand side)/left(-hand side); **de primera ~** (at) first hand; **de segunda ~** (at) second hand; **robo a ~ armada** armed robbery; **estrechar la ~ a algn** to shake sb's hand ▶ **mano de obra** labour, manpower

manojo [ma'noxo] *nm* handful, bunch; (*de llaves*) bunch

manopla [ma'nopla] *nf* mitten

manosear [manose'ar] *vt* (*tocar*) to handle, touch; (*desordenar*) to mess up, rumple; (*insistir en*) to overwork; (*LAm: acariciar*) to caress, fondle

manotazo [mano'taθo] *nm* slap, smack

mansalva [man'salβa]: **a ~** *adv* indiscriminately

mansión [man'sjon] *nf* mansion

manso, -a ['manso, a] *adj* gentle, mild; *(animal)* tame

manta ['manta] *(ESP) nf* blanket

manteca [man'teka] *nf* fat; *(CS: mantequilla)* butter ▶ **manteca de cerdo** lard ❑ **mantecado** [mante'kaðo] *(ESP) nm* Christmas sweet made from flour, almonds and lard

mantel [man'tel] *nm* tablecloth

mantendré *etc* [manten'dre] *vb ver* **mantener**

mantener [mante'ner] *vt* to support, maintain; *(alimentar)* to sustain; *(conservar)* to keep; *(TEC)* to maintain, service; **mantenerse** *vr (seguir de pie)* to be still standing; *(no ceder)* to hold one's ground; *(subsistir)* to sustain o.s., keep going ❑ **mantenimiento** *nm* maintenance; sustenance; *(sustento)* support

mantequilla [mante'kiʎa] *nf* butter

mantilla [man'tiʎa] *nf* mantilla; **mantillas** *nfpl (de bebé)* baby clothes

manto ['manto] *nm (capa)* cloak; *(de ceremonia)* robe, gown

mantuve *etc* [man'tuβe] *vb ver* **mantener**

manual [ma'nwal] *adj* manual ♦ *nm* manual, handbook

manuscrito, -a [manus'krito, a] *adj* handwritten ♦ *nm* manuscript

manutención [manuten'θjon] *nf* maintenance; *(sustento)* support

manzana [man'θana] *nf* apple; *(ARQ)* block (of houses)

manzanilla [manθa'niʎa] *nf (planta)* camomile; *(infusión)* camomile tea

manzano [man'θano] *nm* apple tree

maña ['maɲa] *nf (gen)* skill, dexterity; *(pey)* guile; *(destreza)* trick, knack

mañana [ma'ɲana] *adv* tomorrow ♦ *nm* future ♦ *nf* morning; **de o por la ~** in the morning; **¡hasta ~!** see you

tomorrow!; **~ por la ~** tomorrow morning

mapa ['mapa] *nm* map

maple *(LAm) nm* maple

maqueta [ma'keta] *nf (scale)* model

maquiladora *(MÉX)* [makila'ðora] *nf (COM)* bonded assembly plant

maquillaje [maki'ʎaxe] *nm* make-up; *(acto)* making up

maquillar [maki'ʎar] *vt* to make up; **maquillarse** *vr* to put on (some) make-up

máquina ['makina] *nf* machine; *(de tren)* locomotive, engine; *(FOTO)* camera; *(fig)* machinery; **~ a** *typewritten* ▶ **máquina de coser** sewing machine ▶ **máquina de escribir** typewriter ▶ **máquina fotográfica** camera

maquinaria [maki'narja] *nf (máquinas)* machinery; *(mecanismo)* mechanism, works *pl*

maquinilla [maki'niʎa] *(ESP) nf (tb: ~ de afeitar)* razor

maquinista [maki'nista] *nmf (de tren)* engine driver; *(TEC)* operator; *(NÁUT)* engineer

mar [mar] *nm o f* sea; **~ adentro** out at sea; **en alta ~** on the high seas; **la ~ de** *(fam)* lots of ▶ **el Mar Negro/Báltico** the Black/Baltic Sea

maraña [ma'raɲa] *nf (maleza)* thicket; *(confusión)* tangle

maravilla [mara'βiʎa] *nf* marvel, wonder; *(BOT)* marigold ❑ **maravillar** *vt* to astonish, amaze; **maravillarse** *vr* to be astonished, be amazed ❑ **maravilloso, -a** *adj* wonderful, marvellous

marca ['marka] *nf (gen)* mark; *(sello)* stamp; *(COM)* make, brand; **de ~** excellent, outstanding ▶ **marca de fábrica** trademark ▶ **marca registrada** registered trademark

marcado, -a [mar'kaðo, a] *adj* marked, strong

marcador [marka'ðor] nm (DEPORTE) scoreboard; (: persona) scorer

marcapasos [marka'pasos] nm inv pacemaker

marcar [mar'kar] vt (gen) to mark; (número de teléfono) to dial; (gol) to score; (números) to record, keep a tally of; (pelo) to set ♦ vi (DEPORTE) to score; (TEL) to dial

marcha ['martʃa] nf march; (TEC) running, working; (AUTO) gear; (velocidad) speed; (fig) progress; (dirección) course; **poner en ~** to put into gear; (fig) to set in motion, get going; **dar ~ atrás** to reverse, put into reverse; **estar en ~** to be under way, be in motion □ **marchar** [mar'tʃar] vi (ir) to go; (funcionar) to work, go; **marcharse** vr to go (away), leave

marchitar [martʃi'tar] vt to wither, dry up; **marchitarse** vr (BOT) to wither; (fig) to fade away □ **marchito, -a** adj withered, faded; (fig) in decline

marciano, -a [mar'θjano, a] adj, nm/f Martian

marco ['marko] nm frame; (moneda) mark; (fig) framework

marea [ma'rea] nf tide ▶ **marea negra** oil slick

marear [mare'ar] vt (fig) to annoy, upset; (MED): **~ a algn** to make sb feel sick; **marearse** vr (tener náuseas) to feel sick; (desvanecerse) to feel faint; (aturdirse) to feel dizzy; (fam: emborracharse) to get tipsy

maremoto [mare'moto] nm tidal wave

mareo [ma'reo] nm (náusea) sick feeling; (en viaje) travel sickness; (aturdimiento) dizziness; (fam: lata) nuisance

marfil [mar'fil] nm ivory

margarina [marɣa'rina] nf margarine

margarita [marɣa'rita] nf (BOT) daisy; (TIP) daisywheel

margen ['marxen] nm (borde) edge, border; (fig) margin, space ♦ vt (de río

etc) bank; **dar ~ para** to give an opportunity for; **mantenerse al ~** to keep out (of things)

marginar [marxi'nar] vt (socialmente) to marginalize, ostracize

mariachi [ma'rjatʃi] nm (persona) mariachi musician; (grupo) mariachi band

---

MARIACHI

Mariachi music is the musical style most characteristic of Mexico. From the state of Jalisco in the 19th century, this music spread rapidly throughout the country, until each region had its own particular style of the Mariachi "sound". A Mariachi band can be made up of several singers, up to eight violins, two trumpets, guitars, a "vihuela" (an old form of guitar), and a harp. The dance associated with this music is called the "zapateado".

---

marica [ma'rika] (fam) nm sissy

maricón [mari'kon] (fam) nm queer

marido [ma'riðo] nm husband

marihuana [mari'wana] nf marijuana, cannabis

marina [ma'rina] nf navy ▶ **marina mercante** merchant navy

marinero, -a [mari'nero, a] adj sea cpd ♦ nm sailor, seaman

marino, -a [ma'rino, a] adj sea cpd, marine ♦ nm sailor

marioneta [marjo'neta] nf puppet

mariposa [mari'posa] nf butterfly

mariquita [mari'kita] nf ladybird (BRIT), ladybug (US)

marisco [ma'risko] (ESP) nm shellfish inv, seafood □ **mariscos** (LAm) nmpl = **marisco**

marítimo, -a [ma'ritimo, a] adj sea cpd, maritime

mármol [ˈmarmol] nm marble

marqués, -esa [mar'kes, esa] nm/f marquis/marchioness

marrón [ma'rron] *adj* brown

marroquí [marro'ki] *adj, nmf*
Moroccan ♦ *nm* Morocco (leather)

Marruecos [ma'rrwekos] *nm* Morocco

martes ['martes] *nm inv* Tuesday; **~ y
trece** ≈ Friday 13th

MARTES Y TRECE

According to Spanish superstition
Tuesday is an unlucky day, even more
so if it falls on the 13th of the month.

martillo [mar'tiʎo] *nm* hammer

mártir ['martir] *nmf* martyr
❑ **martirio** *nm* martyrdom; (*fig*)
torture, torment

marxismo [mark'sismo] *nm* Marxism

marzo ['marθo] *nm* March

más

PALABRA CLAVE

[mas] *adj, adv*

1: **más (que** o **de)** (*compar*) more
(than), ...+ er (than); **más grande/
inteligente** bigger/more intelligent;
trabaja más (que yo) he works more
(than me); *ver tb* **cada**

2 (*superl*): **el más** the most, ...+ est; **el
más grande/inteligente (de)** the
biggest/most intelligent (in)

3 (*negativo*): **no tengo más dinero** I
haven't got any more money; **no
viene más por aquí** he doesn't come
round here any more

4 (*adicional*): **no le veo más solución
que ...** I see no other solution than to
...; **¿quién más?** anybody else?

5 (+ *adj*: *valor intensivo*): **¡qué perro
más sucio!** what a filthy dog!; **¡es más
tonto!** he's so stupid!

6 (*locuciones*): **más o menos** more or
less; **los más** most people; **es más**
furthermore; **más bien** rather; **¡qué
más da!** what does it matter!; *ver tb*

no

7: **por más: por más que te
esfuerces** no matter how hard you
try; **por más que quisiera ...** much as
I should like to

8: **de más: veo que aquí estoy de
más** I can see I'm not needed here;
tenemos uno de más we've got one
extra

♦ *prep*: **2 más 2 son 4** 2 and 2
are 4 o plus 2 are 4

♦ *nm inv*: **este trabajo tiene sus más y
sus menos** this job's got its good
points and its bad points

mas [mas] *conj* but

masa ['masa] *nf* (*mezcla*) dough;
(*volumen*) volume, mass; (*FÍSICA*) mass;
en ~ en masse; **las masas** (*POL*) the
masses

masacre [ma'sakre] *nf* massacre

masaje [ma'saxe] *nm* massage

máscara ['maskara] *nf* mask
► **máscara antigás/de oxígeno** gas/
oxygen mask ❑ **mascarilla** *nf* (*de
belleza, MED*) mask

masculino, -a [masku'lino, a] *adj*
masculine; (*BIO*) male

masía [ma'sia] *nf* farmhouse

masivo, -a [ma'siβo, a] *adj* mass *cpd*

masoquista [maso'kista] *nmf*
masochist

máster (*ESP*) ['master] *nm* master

masticar [masti'kar] *vt* to chew

mástil ['mastil] *nm* (*de navío*) mast; (*de
guitarra*) neck

mastín [mas'tin] *nm* mastiff

masturbarse [mastur'βarse] *vr* to
masturbate

mata ['mata] *nf* (*arbusto*) bush, shrub;
(*de hierba*) tuft

matadero [mata'ðero] *nm*
slaughterhouse, abattoir

matamoscas [mata'moskas] nm inv (pala) fly swat

matanza [ma'tanθa] nf slaughter

matar [ma'tar] vt, vi to kill; **matarse** vr (suicidarse) to kill o.s., commit suicide; (morir) to be o get killed; ~ **el hambre** to stave off hunger

matasellos [mata'seʎos] nm inv postmark

mate ['mate] adj matt ♦ nm (en ajedrez) (check)mate; (LAm: hierba) maté; (: vasija) gourd

matemáticas [mate'matikas] nfpl mathematics □ **matemático, -a** adj mathematical ♦ nm/f mathematician

materia [ma'terja] nf (gen) matter; (TEC) material; (ESCOL) subject; **en ~ de** on the subject of ▶ **materia prima** raw material □ **material** adj material ♦ nm material; (TEC) equipment □ **materialista** adj materialist(ic) □ **materialmente** adv materially; (fig) absolutely

maternal [mater'nal] adj motherly, maternal

maternidad [materni'ðað] nf motherhood, maternity □ **materno, -a** adj maternal; (lengua) mother cpd

matinal [mati'nal] adj morning cpd

matiz [ma'tiθ] nm shade □ **matizar** vt (variar) to vary; (ARTE) to blend; **matizar de** to tinge with

matón [ma'ton] nm bully

matorral [mato'rral] nm thicket

matrícula [ma'trikula] nf (registro) register; (AUTO) registration number; (: placa) number plate ▶ **matrícula de honor** (UNIV) top marks in a subject at university with the right to free registration the following year □ **matricular** vt to register, enrol

matrimonio [matri'monjo] nm (pareja) (married) couple; (unión) marriage

matriz [ma'triθ] nf (ANAT) womb; (TEC) mould

matrona [ma'trona] nf (persona de edad) matron; (comadrona) midwife

matufia [RPI: fam] nf put-up job

maullar [mau'ʎar] vi to mew, miaow

maxilar [maksi'lar] nm jaw(bone)

máxima ['maksima] nf maxim

máximo, -a ['maksimo, a] adj maximum; (más alto) highest; (más grande) greatest ♦ nm maximum; **como ~** at most

mayo ['majo] nm May

mayonesa [majo'nesa] nf mayonnaise

mayor [ma'jor] adj main, chief; (adulto) adult; (de edad avanzada) elderly; (MÚS) major; (compar: de tamaño) bigger; (: de edad) older; (superl: de tamaño) biggest; (: de edad) oldest ♦ nm (adulto) adult; **mayores** nmpl (antepasados) ancestors; **al por ~** wholesale ▶ **mayor de edad** adult

mayoral [majo'ral] nm foreman

mayordomo [major'ðomo] nm butler

mayoría [majo'ria] nf majority, greater part

mayorista [majo'rista] nmf wholesaler

mayoritario, -a [majori'tarjo, a] adj majority cpd

mayúscula [ma'juskula] nf capital letter

mazapán [maθa'pan] nm marzipan

mazo ['maθo] nm (martillo) mallet; (de flores) bunch; (DEPORTE) bat

me [me] pron (directo) me; (indirecto) (to) me; (reflexivo) (to) myself; **¡dámelo!** give it to me!

mear [me'ar] (fam) vi to pee, piss (!)

mecánica [me'kanika] nf (ESCOL) mechanics sg; (mecanismo) mechanism; ver tb **mecánico**

mecánico, -a [me'kaniko, a] adj mechanical ♦ nm/f mechanic

mecanismo [meka'nismo] nm mechanism; (marcha) gear

mecanografía [mekanoɣɾaˈfia] nf typewriting ◻ **mecanógrafo, -a** nm/f typist

mecate [meˈkate] (MÉX, CAm) nm rope

mecedora [meθeˈðoɾa] nf rocking chair

mecer [meˈθeɾ] vt (cuna) to rock; **mecerse** vr to rock; (rama) to sway

mecha [ˈmetʃa] nf (de vela) wick; (de bomba) fuse

mechero [meˈtʃeɾo] nm (cigarette) lighter

mechón [meˈtʃon] nm (gen) tuft; (de pelo) lock

medalla [meˈðaʎa] nf medal

media [ˈmeðja] nf stocking; (LAm: calcetín) sock; (promedio) average

mediado, -a [meˈðjaðo, a] adj half-full; (trabajo) half-completed; **a mediados de** in the middle of, halfway through

mediano, -a [meˈðjano, a] adj (regular) medium, average; (mediocre) mediocre

medianoche [meðjaˈnotʃe] nf midnight

mediante [meˈðjante] adv by (means of), through

mediar [meˈðjaɾ] vi (interceder) to mediate, intervene

medicamento [meðikaˈmento] nm medicine, drug

medicina [meðiˈθina] nf medicine

médico, -a [ˈmeðiko, a] adj medical ♦ nm/f doctor

medida [meˈðiða] nf measure; (medición) measurement; (prudencia) moderation, prudence; **en cierta/gran** ~ up to a point/to a great extent; **un traje a la** ~ a made-to-measure suit; ~ **de cuello** collar size; **a** ~ **de** in proportion to; (de acuerdo con) in keeping with; **a** ~ **que** (conforme) as ◻ **medidor** (LAm) nm meter

medio, -a [ˈmeðjo, a] adj half (a); (punto) mid, middle; (promedio) average ♦ adv half ♦ nm (centro)

middle, centre; (promedio) average; (método) means, way; (ambiente) environment; **medios** nmpl means, resources; ~ **litro** half a litre; **las tres y media** half past three; **a** ~ **terminar** half finished; **pagar a medias** to share the cost ► **medio ambiente** environment ► **medio de transporte** means of transport ► **Medio Oriente** Middle East ► **medios de comunicación** media ◻ **medioambiental** adj (política, efectos) environmental

mediocre [meˈðjokɾe] adj mediocre

mediodía [meðjoˈðia] nm midday, noon

medir [meˈðiɾ] vt, vi (gen) to measure

meditar [meðiˈtaɾ] vt to ponder, think over, meditate on; (planear) to think out

mediterráneo, -a [meðiteˈrraneo, a] adj Mediterranean ♦ nm: **el M~** the Mediterranean

médula [ˈmeðula] nf (ANAT) marrow ► **médula espinal** spinal cord

medusa [meˈðusa] (ESP) nf jellyfish

megáfono [meˈɣafono] nm megaphone

mejilla [meˈxiʎa] nf cheek

mejillón [mexiˈʎon] nm mussel

mejor [meˈxoɾ] adj, adv (compar) better; (superl) best; **a lo** ~ probably; (quizá) maybe; ~ **dicho** rather; **tanto** ~ so much the better ◻ **mejora** [meˈxoɾa] nf improvement ◻ **mejorar** vt to improve, make better ♦ vi to improve, get better; **mejorarse** vr to improve, get better

melancólico, -a [melanˈkoliko, a] adj (triste) sad, melancholy; (soñador) dreamy

melena [meˈlena] nf (de persona) long hair; (ZOOL) mane

mellizo, -a [meˈʎiθo, a] adj, nm/f twin

melocotón [melokoˈton] (ESP) nm peach

melodía [melo'ðia] nf melody, tune

melodrama [melo'ðrama] nm melodrama ❑ **melodramático, -a** adj melodramatic

melón [me'lon] nm melon

membrete [mem'brete] nm letterhead

membrillo [mem'briʎo] nm quince; **(carne de) ~** quince jelly

memoria [me'morja] nf (gen) memory; **memorias** nfpl (de autor) memoirs ❑ **memorizar** vt to memorize

menaje [me'naxe] nm (tb: **artículos de ~**) household items

mencionar [menθjo'nar] vt to mention

mendigo, -a [men'diɣo, a] nm/f beggar

menear [mene'ar] vt to move; **menearse** vr to shake; (balancearse) to sway; (moverse) to move; (fig) to get a move on

menestra [me'nestra] nf (tb: **~ de verduras**) vegetable stew

menopausia [meno'pausja] nf menopause

menor [me'nor] adj (más pequeño: compar) smaller; (: superl) smallest; (más joven: compar) younger; (: superl) youngest; (MÚS) minor ♦ nmf (joven) young person, juvenile; **no tengo la ~ idea** I haven't the faintest idea; **al por ~** retail ▸ **menor de edad** person under age

Menorca [me'norka] nf Minorca

menos

PALABRA CLAVE

[menos] adj

1: menos (que o de) (compar: cantidad) less (than); (: número) fewer (than); **con menos entusiasmo** with less enthusiasm; **menos gente** fewer people; ver tb **cada**

2 (superl): **es el que menos culpa tiene** he is the least to blame

♦ adv

1 (compar): **menos (que o de)** less (than); **me gusta menos que el otro** I like it less than the other one

2 (superl): **es el menos listo (de su clase)** he's the least bright in his class; **de todas ellas es la que menos me agrada** out of all of them she's the one I like least

3 (locuciones): **no quiero verle y menos visitarle** I don't want to see him, let alone visit him; **tenemos siete de menos** we're seven short; **(por) lo menos** at (the very) least; **¡menos mal!** thank goodness!

♦ prep except; (cifras) minus; **todos menos él** everyone except (for) him; **5 menos 2** 5 minus 2

♦ conj: **a menos que: a menos que venga mañana** unless he comes tomorrow

menospreciar [menospre'θjar] vt to underrate, undervalue; (despreciar) to scorn, despise

mensaje [men'saxe] nm message; **enviar un ~ a algn** (por móvil) to text sb, send sb a text message ▸ **mensaje de texto** nm text message ❑ **mensajero, -a** nm/f messenger

menso, -a ['menso, a] (MÉX: fam) adj stupid

menstruación [menstrua'θjon] nf menstruation

mensual [men'swal] adj monthly; **100 euros mensuales** 100 euros a month ❑ **mensualidad** nf (salario) monthly salary; (COM) monthly payment, monthly instalment

menta ['menta] nf mint

mental [men'tal] adj mental ❑ **mentalidad** nf mentality ❑ **mentalizar** vt (sensibilizar) to make aware; (convencer) to convince; (padres) to prepare (mentally); **mentalizarse** vr (concienciarse) to become aware; **mentalizarse (de)** to get used to the idea (of); **mentalizarse de que ...** (convencerse) to get it into one's head that ...

mente ['mente] nf mind

mentir [men'tir] vi to lie ❏ **mentira** [men'tira] nf (una mentira) lie; (acto) lying; (invención) fiction; **parece mentira que ...** it seems incredible that ..., I can't believe that ... ❏ **mentiroso, -a** [menti'roso, a] adj lying ♦ nm/f liar

menú [me'nu] (pl ~s) nm menu ▶ **menú del día** set menu ▶ **menú turístico** tourist menu

menudencias (LAm) nfpl giblets

menudo, -a [me'nuðo, a] adj (pequeño) small, tiny; (sin importancia) petty, insignificant; ¡~ negocio! (fam) some deal!; **a ~** often, frequently

meñique [me'ɲike] nm little finger

mercadillo (ESP) nm flea market

mercado [mer'kaðo] nm market ▶ **mercado de pulgas** (LAm) flea market

mercancía [merkan'θia] nf commodity; **mercancías** nfpl goods, merchandise sg

mercenario, -a [merθe'narjo, a] adj, nm mercenary

mercería [merθe'ria] nf haberdashery (BRIT), notions pl (US); (tienda) haberdasher's (BRIT), notions store (US)

mercurio [mer'kurjo] nm mercury

merecer [mere'θer] vt to deserve, merit ♦ vi to be deserving, be worthy; **merece la pena** it's worthwhile ❏ **merecido, -a** [mere'θiðo, a] adj (well) deserved; **llevar su merecido** to get one's deserts

merendar [meren'dar] vt to have for tea ♦ vi to have tea; (en el campo) to have a picnic ❏ **merendero** nm open-air cafe

merengue [me'renge] nm meringue

meridiano [meri'ðjano] nm (GEO) meridian

merienda [me'rjenda] nf (light) tea, afternoon snack; (de campo) picnic

mérito ['merito] nm merit; (valor) worth, value

merluza [mer'luθa] nf hake

mermelada [merme'laða] nf jam

mero, -a ['mero, a] adj mere; (MÉX, CAm: fam) very

merodear [meroðe'ar] vi: ~ **por** to prowl about

mes [mes] nm month

mesa ['mesa] nf table; (de trabajo) desk; (GEO) plateau; **poner/quitar la ~** to lay/ clear the table ▶ **mesa electoral** officials in charge of a polling station ▶ **mesa redonda** (reunión) round table ❏ **mesero, -a** [me'sero, a] (LAm) nm/f waiter/waitress

meseta [me'seta] nf (GEO) plateau, tableland

mesilla [me'siʎa] nf (tb: ~ **de noche**) bedside table

mesón [me'son] nm inn

mestizo, -a [mes'tiθo, a] adj half-caste, of mixed race ♦ nm/f half-caste

meta ['meta] nf goal; (de carrera) finish

metabolismo [metaβo'lismo] nm metabolism

metáfora [me'tafora] nf metaphor

metal [me'tal] nm (materia) metal; (MÚS) brass ❏ **metálico, -a** adj metallic; (de metal) metal ♦ nm (dinero contante) cash

meteorología nf meteorology

meter [me'ter] vt (colocar) to put, place; (introducir) to put in, insert; (involucrar) to involve; (causar) to make, cause; **meterse** vr: **meterse en** to go into, enter; (fig) to interfere, meddle in; **meterse a escritor** to become a writer; **meterse con uno** to provoke sb, pick a quarrel with sb

meticuloso, -a [metiku'loso, a] adj meticulous, thorough

metódico, -a [me'toðiko, a] adj methodical

método ['metoðo] nm method

metralleta [metra'ʎeta] nf sub-machine-gun

métrico, -a ['metriko, a] adj metric

metro ['metro] nm metre; (tren) underground (BRIT), subway (US)

mexicano, -a [mexi'kano, a] adj, nm/f Mexican

México ['mexiko] nm Mexico; **Ciudad de ~** Mexico City

mezcla ['meθkla] nf mixture ☐ **mezcladora** (MÉX) nf (tb: **mezcladora de cemento**) cement mixer ☐ **mezclar** vt to mix (up); **mezclarvt** to mix, mingle; **mezclarse en** to get mixed up in, get involved in

mezquino, -a [meθ'kino, a] adj mean

mezquita [meθ'kita] nf mosque

mg. abr (= miligramo) mg

mi [mi] adj pos my ♦ nm (MÚS) E

mí [mi] pron me; myself

mía ['mia] pron ver **mío**

michelín [mitʃe'lin] (fam) nm (de grasa) spare tyre

microbio [mi'kroβjo] nm microbe

micrófono [mi'krofono] nm microphone

microondas [mikro'ondas] nm inv (tb: **horno ~**) microwave (oven)

microscopio [mikro'skopjo] nm microscope

miedo ['mjeðo] nm fear; (nerviosismo) apprehension, nervousness; **tener ~** to be afraid; **de ~** wonderful, marvellous; **hace un frío de ~** (fam) it's terribly cold ☐ **miedoso, -a** adj fearful, timid

miel [mjel] nf honey

miembro ['mjembro] nm limb; (socio) member ▶ **miembro viril** penis

mientras ['mjentras] conj while; (duración) as long as ♦ adv meanwhile; **~ tanto** meanwhile

miércoles ['mjerkoles] nm inv Wednesday

mierda ['mjerða] (fam!) nf shit (!)

miga ['miɣa] nf crumb; (fig: meollo) essence; **hacer buenas migas** (fam) to get on well

mil [mil] num thousand; **dos ~ libras** two thousand pounds

milagro [mi'laɣro] nm miracle ☐ **milagroso, -a** adj miraculous

milésima [mi'lesima] nf (de segundo) thousandth

mili ['mili] (ESP: fam) nf: **hacer la ~** to do one's military service

milímetro [mi'limetro] nm millimetre

militante [mili'tante] adj militant

militar [mili'tar] adj military ♦ nmf soldier ♦ vi (MIL) to serve; (en un partido) to be a member

milla ['miʎa] nf mile

millar [mi'ʎar] nm thousand

millón [mi'ʎon] num million ☐ **millonario, -a** nm/f millionaire

milusos (MÉX) nm inv odd-job man

mimar [mi'mar] vt to spoil, pamper

mimbre ['mimbre] nm wicker

mímica ['mimika] nf (para comunicarse) sign language; (imitación) mimicry

mimo ['mimo] nm (caricia) caress; (de niño) spoiling; (TEATRO) mime; (: actor) mime artist

mina ['mina] nf mine

mineral [mine'ral] adj mineral ♦ nm (GEO) mineral; (mena) ore

minero, -a [mi'nero, a] adj mining cpd ♦ nm/f miner

miniatura [minja'tura] adj inv, nf miniature

minidisco [mini'disko] nm MiniDisc®

minifalda [mini'falda] nf miniskirt

mínimo, -a ['minimo, a] adj, nm minimum

minino, -a [mi'nino, a] (fam) nm/f puss, pussy

ministerio [minis'terjo] nm Ministry ▶ **Ministerio de Hacienda/de Asuntos Exteriores** Treasury (BRIT),

Treasury Department (US)/Foreign Office (BRIT), State Department (US)

ministro, -a [mi'nistro, a] nm/f minister

minoría [mino'ria] nf minority

minúscula [mi'nuskula] nf small letter

minúsculo, -a [mi'nuskulo, a] adj tiny, minute

minusválido, -a [minus'βalido, a] adj (physically) handicapped ♦ nm/f (physically) handicapped person

minuta [mi'nuta] nf (de comida) menu

minutero [minu'tero] nm minute hand

minuto [mi'nuto] nm minute

mío, -a ['mio, a] pron: **el ~/la mía** mine; **un amigo ~** a friend of mine; **lo ~** what is mine

miope [mi'ope] adj short-sighted

mira ['mira] nf (de arma) sight(s) (pl); (fig) aim, intention

mirada [mi'raða] nf look, glance; (expresión) look, expression; **clavar la ~ en** to stare at; **echar una ~ a** to glance at

mirado, -a [mi'raðo, a] adj (sensato) sensible; (considerado) considerate; **bien/mal ~** (estimado) well/not well thought of; **bien ~ ...** all things considered ...

mirador [mira'ðor] nm viewpoint, vantage point

mirar [mi'rar] vt to look at; (observar) to watch; (considerar) to consider, think over; (vigilar, cuidar) to watch, look after ♦ vi to look; to face; **mirarse** vr (dos personas) to look at each other; **~ bien/mal** to think highly of/have a poor opinion of; **mirarse al espejo** to look at o.s. in the mirror

mirilla [mi'riʎa] nf spyhole, peephole

mirlo ['mirlo] nm blackbird

misa ['misa] nf mass

miserable [mise'raβle] adj (avaro) mean, stingy; (nimio) miserable, paltry;

(lugar) squalid; (fam) vile, despicable ♦ nmf (malvado) rogue

miseria [mi'serja] nf (pobreza) poverty; (tacañería) meanness, stinginess; (condiciones) squalor; **una ~** a pittance

misericordia [miseri'korðja] nf (compasión) compassion, pity; (piedad) mercy

misil [mi'sil] nm missile

misión [mi'sjon] nf mission
   ❏ **misionero, -a** nm/f missionary

mismo, -a [mi'smo, a] adj (semejante) same; (después de pron) -self; (para énfasis) very ♦ adv: **aquí/hoy ~** right here/this very day; **ahora ~** right now ♦ conj: **lo ~ que** just like o as; **el ~ traje** the same suit; **en ese ~ momento** at that very moment; **vino el ~ ministro** the minister himself came; **yo ~ lo vi** I saw it myself; **lo ~** the same (thing); **da lo ~** it's all the same; **quedamos en las mismas** we're no further forward; **por lo ~** for the same reason

misterio [mis'terjo] nm mystery
   ❏ **misterioso, -a** adj mysterious

mitad [mi'tað] nf (medio) half; (centro) middle; **a ~ de precio** (a) half-price; **en o a ~ del camino** halfway along the road; **cortar por la ~** to cut through the middle

mitin ['mitin] (pl **mítines**) nm meeting

mito ['mito] nm myth

mixto, -a ['miksto, a] adj mixed

ml. abr (= mililitro) ml

mm. abr (= milímetro) mm

mobiliario [moβi'ljarjo] nm furniture

mochila [mo'tʃila] nf rucksack (BRIT), back-pack

moco ['moko] nm mucus; **mocos** nmpl (fam) snot; **limpiarse los mocos de la nariz** (fam) to wipe one's nose

moda ['moða] nf fashion; (estilo) style; **a la o de** in fashion, fashionable; **pasado de ~** out of fashion

modales [mo'ðales] nmpl manners

modelar [moðe'lar] vt to model

modelo [mo'ðelo] *adj inv, nmf* model

módem ['moðem] *nm* (INFORM) modem

moderado, -a [moðe'raðo, a] *adj* moderate

moderar [moðe'rar] *vt* to moderate; (*violencia*) to restrain, control; (*velocidad*) to reduce; **moderarse** *vr* to restrain o.s., control o.s.

modernizar [moðerni'θar] *vt* to modernize

moderno, -a [mo'ðerno, a] *adj* modern; (*actual*) present-day

modestia [mo'ðestja] *nf* modesty ❏ **modesto, -a** *adj* modest

modificar [moðifi'kar] *vt* to modify

modisto, -a [mo'ðisto, a] *nm/f* (*diseñador*) couturier, designer; (*que confecciona*) dressmaker

modo ['moðo] *nm* way, manner; (MÚS) mode; **modos** *nmpl* manners; **de ningún ~** in no way; **de todos modos** at any rate ▸ **modo de empleo** directions *pl* (for use)

mofarse [mo'farse] *vr*: **~ de** to mock, scoff at

mofle (MÉX, CAm) *nm* silencer (BRIT), muffler (US)

mogollón [moɣo'ʎon] (ESP: fam) *adv* a hell of a lot

moho ['moo] *nm* mould, mildew; (*en metal*) rust

mojar [mo'xar] *vt* to wet; (*humedecer*) to damp(en), moisten; (*calar*) to soak; **mojarse** *vr* to get wet

molcajete (MÉX) [molka'xete] *nm* mortar

molde ['molde] *nm* mould; (COSTURA) pattern; (*fig*) model ❏ **moldeado** *nm* soft perm ❏ **moldear** *vt* to mould

mole ['mole] *nf* mass, bulk; (*edificio*) pile

moler [mo'ler] *vt* to grind, crush

molestar [moles'tar] *vt* to bother; (*fastidiar*) to annoy; (*incomodar*) to inconvenience, put out ♦ *vi* to be a nuisance; **molestarse** *vr* to bother; (*incomodarse*) to go to trouble;

(*ofenderse*) to take offence; **¿(no) te molesta si ...?** do you mind if ...?

> ⚠ No confundir **molestar** con la palabra inglesa *molest*.

molestia [mo'lestja] *nf* bother, trouble; (*incomodidad*) inconvenience; (MED) discomfort; **es una ~** it's a nuisance ❏ **molesto, -a** *adj* (*que fastidia*) annoying; (*incómodo*) inconvenient; (*inquieto*) uncomfortable, ill at ease; (*enfadado*) annoyed

molido, -a [mo'liðo, a] *adj*: **estar ~** (*fig*) to be exhausted o dead beat

molinillo [moli'niʎo] *nm* hand mill ▸ **molinillo de café** coffee grinder

molino [mo'lino] *nm* (*edificio*) mill; (*máquina*) grinder

momentáneo, -a [momen'taneo, a] *adj* momentary

momento [mo'mento] *nm* moment; **de ~** at o for the moment

momia ['momja] *nf* mummy

monarca [mo'narka] *nmf* monarch, ruler ❏ **monarquía** *nf* monarchy

monasterio [monas'terjo] *nm* monastery

mondar [mon'dar] *vt* to peel; **mondarse** *vr* (ESP): **mondarse de risa** (*fam*) to split one's sides laughing

mondongo (LAm) *nm* tripe

moneda [mo'neða] *nf* (*tipo de dinero*) currency, money; (*pieza*) coin; **una ~ de 2 euros** a 2 euro piece ❏ **monedero** *nm* purse

monitor, a [moni'tor, a] *nm/f* instructor, coach ♦ *nm* (TV) set; (INFORM) monitor

monja ['monxa] *nf* nun

monje ['monxe] *nm* monk

mono, -a ['mono, a] *adj* (*bonito*) lovely, pretty; (*gracioso*) nice, charming ♦ *nm/ f* monkey, ape ♦ *nm* dungarees *pl*; (*overoles*) overalls *pl*

monopatín [monopa'tin] *nm* skateboard

monopolio [mono'poljo] *nm* monopoly ❑ **monopolizar** *vt* to monopolize

monótono, -a [mo'notono, a] *adj* monotonous

monstruo ['monstrwo] *nm* monster ♦ *adj inv* fantastic ❑ **monstruoso, -a** *adj* monstrous

montaje [mon'taxe] *nm* assembly; (TEATRO) décor; (CINE) montage

montaña [mon'taɲa] *nf* (monte) mountain; (sierra) mountains *pl*, mountainous area ▶ **montaña rusa** roller coaster ❑ **montañero, -a** *nm/f* mountaineer ❑ **montañismo** *nm* mountaineering

montar [mon'tar] *vt* (subir a) to mount, get on; (TEC) to assemble, put together; (negocio) to set up; (arma) to cock; (colocar) to lift on to; (CULIN) to beat ♦ *vi* to mount, get on; (sobresalir) to overlap; ~ **en bicicleta** to ride a bicycle; ~ **en cólera** to get angry; ~ **a caballo** to ride, go horseriding

monte [monte] *nm* (montaña) mountain; (bosque) woodland; (área sin cultivar) wild area, wild country ▶ **monte de piedad** pawnshop

montón [mon'ton] *nm* heap, pile; (fig): **un ~ de** heaps o lots of

monumento [monu'mento] *nm* monument

moño ['moɲo] *nm* bun

moqueta [mo'keta] *nf* fitted carpet

mora ['mora] *nf* blackberry; *ver tb* **moro**

morado, -a [mo'raðo, a] *adj* purple, violet ♦ *nm* bruise

moral [mo'ral] *adj* moral ♦ *nf* (ética) ethics *pl*; (moralidad) morals *pl*, morality; (ánimo) morale

moraleja [mora'lexa] *nf* moral

morboso, -a [mor'βoso, a] *adj* morbid

morcilla [mor'θiʎa] *nf* blood sausage, ≈ black pudding (BRIT)

mordaza [mor'ðaθa] *nf* (para la boca) gag; (TEC) clamp

morder [mor'ðer] *vt* to bite; (fig: consumir) to eat away, eat into ❑ **mordisco** *nm* bite

moreno, -a [mo'reno, a] *adj* (color) (dark) brown; (de tez) dark; (de pelo moreno) dark-haired; (negro) black

morfina [mor'fina] *nf* morphine

moribundo, -a [mori'βundo, a] *adj* dying

morir [mo'rir] *vi* to die; (fuego) to die down; (luz) to go out; **morirse** *vr* to die; (fig) to be dying; **murió en un accidente** he was killed in an accident; **morirse por algo** to be dying for sth

moro, -a ['moro, a] *adj* Moorish ♦ *nm/f* Moor

moroso, -a [mo'roso, a] *nm/f* bad debtor, defaulter

morralla [mo'raʎa] (MÉX) *nf* (cambio) small o loose change

morro ['moro] *nm* (ZOOL) snout, nose; (AUTO, AVIAC) nose

morsa ['morsa] *nf* walrus

mortadela [morta'ðela] *nf* mortadella

mortal [mor'tal] *adj* mortal; (golpe) deadly ❑ **mortalidad** *nf* mortality

mortero [mor'tero] *nm* mortar

mosca ['moska] *nf* fly

Moscú [mos'ku] *n* Moscow

mosquearse [moske'arse] (fam) *vr* (enojarse) to get cross; (ofenderse) to take offence

mosquitero [moski'tero] *nm* mosquito net

mosquito [mos'kito] *nm* mosquito

mostaza [mos'taθa] *nf* mustard

mosto ['mosto] *nm* (unfermented) grape juice

mostrador [mostra'ðor] *nm* (de tienda) counter; (de café) bar

mostrar [mos'trar] *vt* to show; (exhibir) to display, exhibit; (explicar) to explain; **mostrarse** *vr*: **mostrarse amable** to be kind; to prove to be kind; **no se muestra muy inteligente** he doesn't seem (to be) very intelligent

mota ['mota] nf speck, tiny piece; (en diseño) dot

mote ['mote] nm nickname

motín [mo'tin] nm (del pueblo) revolt, rising; (del ejército) mutiny

motivar [moti'βar] vt (causar) to cause, motivate; (explicar) to explain, justify
❏ **motivo** nm motive, reason

moto ['moto] (fam) nf = **motocicleta**

motocicleta [motoθi'kleta] nf motorbike (BRIT), motorcycle

motoneta (CS) [moto'neta] nf scooter

motor, ~ra [mo'tor] nm motor, engine
▶ **motor a chorro** o **de reacción/de explosión** jet engine/internal combustion engine

motora [mo'tora] nf motorboat

movedizo, -a [moβe'ðiθo, a] adj ver **arena**

mover [mo'βer] vt to move; (cabeza) to shake; (accionar) to drive; (fig) to cause, provoke; **moverse** vr to move; (fig) to get a move on

móvil ['moβil] adj mobile; (pieza de máquina) moving; (mueble) movable
♦ nm motive

movimiento [moβi'mjento] nm movement; (TEC) motion; (actividad) activity

mozo, -a ['moθo, a] adj (joven) young
♦ nm/f youth, young man/girl; (CS: mesero) waiter/waitress

MP3 nm MP3; **reproductor (de) ~** MP3 player

mucama (RPl) [mu'kama] nf maid

muchacho, -a [mu'tʃatʃo, a] nm/f (niño) boy/girl; (criado) servant; (criada) maid

muchedumbre [mutʃe'ðumbre] nf crowd

mucho, -a

PALABRA CLAVE

['mutʃo, a] adj

1 (cantidad) a lot of, much; (número) lots of, a lot of, many; **mucho dinero** a lot of money; **hace mucho calor** it's very hot; **muchas amigas** lots o a lot of friends

2 (sg: grande): **ésta es mucha casa para él** this house is much too big for him

♦ pron: **tengo mucho que hacer** I've got a lot to do; **muchos dicen que ...** a lot of people say that ...; ver tb **tener**

♦ adv

1: **me gusta mucho** I like it a lot; **lo siento mucho** I'm very sorry; **come mucho** he eats a lot; **¿te vas a quedar mucho?** are you going to be staying long?

2 (respuesta) very; **¿estás cansado?**
— **¡mucho!** are you tired? — very!

3 (locuciones): **como mucho** at (the) most; **con mucho** by far the best; **ni mucho menos: no es rico ni mucho menos** he's far from being rich

4: **por mucho que: por mucho que lo creas** no matter how o however much you believe her

muda ['muða] nf change of clothes

mudanza [mu'ðanθa] nf (de casa) move

mudar [mu'ðar] vt to change; (ZOOL) to shed ♦ vi to change; **mudarse** vr (ropa) to change; **mudarse de casa** to move house

mudo, -a ['muðo, a] adj dumb; (callado, CINE) silent

mueble ['mweβle] nm piece of furniture; **muebles** nmpl furniture sg

mueca ['mweka] nf face, grimace; **hacer muecas a** to make faces at

muela ['mwela] nf back tooth ▶ **muela del juicio** wisdom tooth

muelle ['mweʎe] nm spring; (NÁUT) wharf; (malecón) quay

muero etc vb ver **morir**

muerte ['mwerte] nf death; (homicidio) murder; **dar ~ a** to kill

muerto, -a ['mwerto, a] pp de **morir**
♦ adj dead ♦ nm/f dead man/woman; (difunto) deceased; (cadáver) corpse; **estar ~ de cansancio** to be dead tired
► **Día de los Muertos** (MÉX) All Souls' Day

DÍA DE LOS MUERTOS

All Souls' Day (or "Day of the Dead") in Mexico coincides with All Saints' Day, which is celebrated in the Catholic countries of Latin America on November 1st and 2nd. All Souls' Day is actually a celebration which begins in the evening of October 31st and continues until November 2nd. It is a combination of the Catholic tradition of honouring the Christian saints and martyrs, and the ancient Mexican or Aztec traditions, in which death was not something sinister. For this reason all the dead are honoured by bringing offerings of food, flowers and candles to the cemetery.

---

muestra ['mwestra] nf (señal) indication, sign; (demostración) demonstration; (prueba) proof; (estadística) sample; (modelo) model, pattern; (testimonio) token

muestro etc vb ver **mostrar**

muevo etc vb ver **mover**

mugir [mu'xir] vi (vaca) to moo

mugre ['muɣre] nf dirt, filth

mujer [mu'xer] nf woman; (esposa) wife ❑ **mujeriego** nm womanizer

mula ['mula] nf mule

muleta [mu'leta] nf (para andar) crutch; (TAUR) stick with red cape attached

multa ['multa] nf fine; **poner una ~ a** to fine ❑ **multar** vt to fine

multicines [multi'θines] nmpl multiscreen cinema sg

multinacional [multinaθjo'nal] nf multinational

múltiple ['multiple] adj multiple; (pl) many, numerous

multiplicar [multipli'kar] vt (MAT) to multiply; (fig) to increase; **multiplicarse** vr (BIO) to multiply; (fig) to be everywhere at once

multitud [multi'tuð] nf (muchedumbre) crowd; **~ de** lots of

mundial [mun'djal] adj world-wide, universal; (guerra, récord) world cpd

mundo ['mundo] nm world; **todo el ~** everybody; **tener ~** to be experienced, know one's way around

munición [muni'θjon] nf ammunition

municipal [muniθi'pal] adj municipal, local

municipio [muni'θipjo] nm (ayuntamiento) town council, corporation; (territorio administrativo) town, municipality

muñeca [mu'neka] nf (ANAT) wrist; (juguete) doll

muñeco [mu'neko] nm (figura) figure; (marioneta) puppet; (fig) puppet, pawn

mural [mu'ral] adj mural, wall cpd ♦ nm mural

muralla [mu'raʎa] nf (city) wall(s) (pl)

murciélago [mur'θjelaɣo] nm bat

murmullo [mur'muʎo] nm murmur(ing); (cuchicheo) whispering

murmurar [murmu'rar] vi to murmur, whisper; (cotillear) to gossip

muro ['muro] nm wall

muscular [musku'lar] adj muscular

músculo ['muskulo] nm muscle

museo [mu'seo] nm museum ► **museo de arte** art gallery

musgo ['musɣo] nm moss

música ['musika] nf music; ver tb **músico**

músico, -a ['musiko, a] adj musical
♦ nm/f musician

muslo ['muslo] nm thigh

musulmán, -ana [musul'man, ana] nm/f Moslem

mutación [muta'θjon] nf (BIO) mutation; (cambio) (sudden) change

mutilar [muti'lar] vt to mutilate; (a una persona) to maim

mutuo, -a ['mutwo, a] adj mutual

muy [mwi] adv very; (demasiado) too; M~ Señor mío Dear Sir; ~ de noche very late at night; eso es ~ de él that's just like him

N, n

N abr (= norte) N

nabo ['naβo] nm turnip

nacer [na'θer] vi to be born; (de huevo) to hatch; (vegetal) to sprout; (río) to rise; nací en Barcelona I was born in Barcelona □ **nacido, -a** adj born; **recién nacido** newborn □ **nacimiento** nm birth; (de Navidad) Nativity; (de río) source

nación [na'θjon] nf nation □ **nacional** adj national □ **nacionalismo** nm nationalism

nada ['naða] pron nothing ♦ adv not at all, in no way; **no decir** ~ to say nothing, not to say anything; ~ **más** nothing else; **de** ~ don't mention it

nadador, a [naða'ðor, a] nm/f swimmer

nadar [na'ðar] vi to swim

nadie ['naðje] pron nobody, no-one; ~ **habló** nobody spoke; **no había** ~ there was nobody there, there wasn't anybody there

nado ['naðo]: **a** ~ adv: **pasar a** ~ to swim across

nafta ['nafta] (RPl) nf petrol (BRIT), gas (US)

naipe ['naipe] nm (playing) card; **naipes** nmpl cards

nalgas ['nalɣas] nfpl buttocks

nalguear (MÉX, CAm) vt to spank

nana ['nana] (ESP) nf lullaby

naranja [na'ranxa] adj inv, nf orange; **media** ~ (fam) better half □ **naranjada** nf orangeade □ **naranjo** nm orange tree

narciso [nar'θiso] nm narcissus

narcótico, -a [nar'kotiko, a] adj, nm narcotic □ **narcotizar** vt to drug □ **narcotráfico** nm drug trafficking o running

nariz [na'riθ] nf nose ▶ **nariz chata/respingona** snub/turned-up nose

narración [narra'θjon] nf narration

narrar [na'rrar] vt to narrate, recount □ **narrativa** nf narrative

nata ['nata] nf cream ▶ **nata montada** whipped cream

natación [nata'θjon] nf swimming

natal [na'tal] adj: **ciudad** ~ home town □ **natalidad** nf birth rate

natillas [na'tiʎas] nfpl custard sg

nativo, -a [na'tiβo, a] adj, nm/f native

natural [natu'ral] adj natural; (fruta etc) fresh ♦ nmf native ♦ nm (disposición) nature

naturaleza [natura'leθa] nf nature; (género) species, kind ▶ **naturaleza muerta** still life

naturalmente [natural'mente] adv (de modo natural) in a natural way; ¡~! of course!

naufragar [naufra'ɣar] vi to sink □ **naufragio** nm shipwreck

nauseabundo, -a [nausea'βundo, a] adj nauseating, sickening

náuseas ['nauseas] nfpl nausea sg; **me da** ~ it makes me feel sick

náutico, -a ['nautiko, a] adj nautical

navaja [na'βaxa] nf knife; (de barbero, peluquero) razor

naval [na'βal] adj naval

Navarra [na'βarra] n Navarre

nave ['naβe] nf (barco) ship, vessel; (ARQ) nave ► **nave espacial** spaceship ► **nave industrial** factory premises pl

navegador nm (INFORM) browser

navegante [naβe'ɣante] nmf navigator

navegar [naβe'ɣar] vi (barco) to sail; (avión) to fly; ~ **por Internet** to surf the Net

Navidad [naβi'ðað] nf Christmas; **Navidades** nfpl Christmas time; **¡Feliz ~!** Merry Christmas! ❏ **navideño, -a** adj Christmas cpd

nazca etc vb ver **nacer**

nazi ['naθi] adj, nmf Nazi

NE abr (= nor(d)este) NE

neblina [ne'βlina] nf mist

necesario, -a [neθe'sarjo, a] adj necessary

neceser [neθe'ser] nm toilet bag; (bolsa grande) holdall

necesidad [neθesi'ðað] nf need; (lo inevitable) necessity; (miseria) poverty; **en caso de ~** in case of need o emergency; **hacer sus necesidades** to relieve o.s.

necesitado, -a [neθesi'taðo, a] adj needy, poor; **~ de** in need of

necesitar [neθesi'tar] vt to need, require

necio, -a ['neθjo, a] adj foolish

nectarina [nekta'rina] nf nectarine

nefasto, -a [ne'fasto, a] adj ill-fated, unlucky

negación [neɣa'θjon] nf negation; (rechazo) refusal, denial

negar [ne'ɣar] vt (renegar, rechazar) to refuse; (prohibir) to refuse, deny; (desmentir) to deny; **negarse** vr: **negarse a** to refuse to

negativa [neɣa'tiβa] nf negative; (rechazo) refusal, denial

negativo, -a [neɣa'tiβo, a] adj, nm negative

negociante [neɣo'θjante] nmf businessman/woman

negociar [neɣo'θjar] vt, vi to negotiate; **~ en** to deal o trade in

negocio [ne'ɣoθjo] nm (COM) business; (asunto) affair, business; (operación comercial) deal, transaction; (lugar) place of business; **los negocios** business sg; **hacer ~** to do business

negra ['neɣra] nf (MÚS) crotchet; ver tb **negro**

negro, -a ['neɣro, a] adj black; (suerte) awful ♦ nm black ♦ nm/f black man/woman

nene, -a ['nene, a] nm/f baby, small child

neón [ne'on] nm: **luces/lámpara de ~** neon lights/lamp

neoyorquino, -a [neojor'kino, a] adj (of) New York

nervio ['nerβjo] nm nerve ❏ **nerviosismo** nm nervousness, nerves pl ❏ **nervioso, -a** adj nervous

neto, -a ['neto, a] adj net

neumático, -a [neu'matiko, a] adj pneumatic ♦ nm (ESP) tyre (BRIT), tire (US) ► **neumático de recambio** spare tyre

neurólogo, -a [neu'roloɣo, a] nm/f neurologist

neurona [neu'rona] nf nerve cell

neutral [neu'tral] adj neutral ❏ **neutralizar** vt to neutralize; (contrarrestar) to counteract

neutro, -a ['neutro, a] adj (BIO, LING) neuter

neutrón [neu'tron] nm neutron

nevada [ne'βaða] nf snowstorm; (caída de nieve) snowfall

nevar [ne'βar] vi to snow

nevera [ne'βera] nf (ESP) refrigerator (BRIT), icebox (US)

nevería [neβe'ria] (MÉX) nf ice-cream parlour

nexo ['nekso] nm link, connection

ni [ni] conj nor, neither; (tb: **ni siquiera**) not ... even; **ni aunque que** not even if;

ni blanco ni negro neither white nor black

Nicaragua [nika'raɣwa] *nf* Nicaragua ❏ **nicaragüense** *adj, nmf* Nicaraguan

nicho ['nitʃo] *nm* niche

nicotina [niko'tina] *nf* nicotine

nido ['niðo] *nm* nest

niebla ['njeβla] *nf* fog; *(neblina)* mist

niego *etc* ['njeɣo] *vb ver* **negar**

nieto, -a ['njeto, a] *nm/f* grandson/ daughter; **nietos** *nmpl* grandchildren

nieve *etc* ['njeβe] *vb ver* **nevar** ♦ *nf* snow; *(MÉX: helado)* icecream

NIF *nm abr* (= *Número de Identificación Fiscal*) personal identification number used for financial and tax purposes

ninfa ['ninfa] *nf* nymph

ningún [nin'ɡun] *adj ver* **ninguno**

ninguno, -a [nin'ɡuno, a] *(delante de nm* **ningún***) adj no* ♦ *pron (nadie)* nobody; *(ni uno)* none, not one; *(ni uno ni otro)* neither; **de ninguna manera** by no means, not at all

niña ['niɲa] *nf (ANAT)* pupil; *ver tb* **niño**

niñera [ni'ɲera] *nf* nursemaid, nanny

niñez [ni'ɲeθ] *nf* childhood; *(infancia)* infancy

niño, -a ['niɲo, a] *adj (joven)* young; *(inmaduro)* immature ♦ *nm/f* child, boy/girl

nipón, -ona [ni'pon, ona] *adj, nm/f* Japanese

níquel ['nikel] *nm* nickel

níspero ['nispero] *nm* medlar

nítido, -a ['nitiðo, a] *adj* clear; sharp

nitrato [ni'trato] *nm* nitrate

nitrógeno [ni'troxeno] *nm* nitrogen

nivel [ni'βel] *nm (GEO)* level; *(norma)* level, standard; *(altura)* height ♦ **nivel de aceite** oil level ♦ **nivel de aire** spirit level ♦ **nivel de vida** standard of living ❏ **nivelar** *vt* to level out; *(fig)* to even up; *(COM)* to balance

no [no] *adv* no; not; *(con verbo)* not ♦ *excl* no!; **no tengo nada** I don't have

anything, I have nothing; **no es el mío** it's not mine; **ahora no** not now; **¿no lo sabes?** don't you know?; **no mucho** not much; **no bien termine, lo entregaré** as soon as I finish, I'll hand it over; **no más, ayer no más** just yesterday; **¡pase no más!** come in!; **¡a que no lo sabes!** I bet you don't know!; **¡cómo no!** of course!; **la no intervención** non-intervention

noble ['noβle] *adj, nmf* noble ❏ **nobleza** *nf* nobility

noche ['notʃe] *nf* night, night-time; *(la tarde)* evening; **de ~, por la ~** at night; **es de ~** it's dark ▶ **Noche de San Juan** see note

NOCHE DE SAN JUAN

The **Noche de San Juan** on the 24th June is a **fiesta** coinciding with the summer solstice and which has taken the place of other ancient pagan festivals. Traditionally fire plays a major part in these festivities with celebrations and dancing taking place around bonfires in towns and villages across the country.

nochebuena [notʃe'βwena] *nf* Christmas Eve

NOCHEBUENA

Traditional Christmas celebrations in Spanish-speaking countries mainly take place on the night of **Nochebuena**, Christmas Eve. Families gather together for a large meal and the more religiously inclined attend Midnight Mass. While presents are traditionally given by **los Reyes Magos** on the 6th January, more and more people are exchanging gifts on Christmas Eve.

nochevieja [notʃe'βjexa] *nf* New Year's Eve

nocivo, -a [no'θiβo, a] *adj* harmful

noctámbulo, -a [nok'tambulo, a] *nm/f* sleepwalker

nocturno, -a [nok'turno, a] *adj (de la noche)* nocturnal, night *cpd*; *(de la tarde)* evening *cpd* ♦ *nm* nocturne

nogal [no'ɣal] *nm* walnut tree

nómada ['nomaða] *adj* nomadic ♦ *nmf* nomad

nombrar [nom'brar] *vt (designar)* to name; *(mencionar)* to mention; *(dar puesto a)* to appoint

nombre ['nombre] *nm* name; *(sustantivo)* noun; ~ **y apellidos** name in full; **poner ~ a** to call, name
▶ **nombre común/propio** common/ proper noun ● **nombre de pila/de soltera** Christian/maiden name

nómina ['nomina] *nf (lista)* payroll; *(hoja)* payslip

nominal [nomi'nal] *adj* nominal

nominar [nomi'nar] *vt* to nominate

nominativo, -a [nomina'tiβo, a] *adj (COM)*: **cheque ~ a X** cheque made out to X

nordeste [nor'ðeste] *adj* north-east, north-eastern, north-easterly ♦ *nm* north-east

nórdico, -a ['norðiko, a] *adj* Nordic

noreste [no'reste] *adj, nm* = **nordeste**

noria ['norja] *nf (AGR)* waterwheel; *(de carnaval)* big *(BRIT)* or Ferris *(US)* wheel

norma ['norma] *nf* rule (of thumb)

normal [nor'mal] *adj (corriente)* normal; *(habitual)* usual, natural ❑ **normalizarse** *vr* to return to normal ❑ **normalmente** *adv* normally

normativa [norma'tiβa] *nf (set of)* rules *pl*, regulations *pl*

noroeste [noro'este] *adj* north-west, north-western, north-westerly ♦ *nm* north-west

norte ['norte] *adj* north, northern, northerly ♦ *nm* north; *(fig)* guide

norteamericano, -a [norteameri'kano, a] *adj, nm/f* (North) American

Noruega [no'rweɣa] *nf* Norway

noruego, -a [no'rweɣo, a] *adj, nm/f* Norwegian

nos [nos] *pron (directo)* us; *(indirecto)* us; to us; for us; from us; *(reflexivo)* (to) ourselves; *(reciproco)* (to) each other; ~ **levantamos a las 7** we get up at 7

nosotros, -as [no'sotros, as] *pron (sujeto)* we; *(después de prep)* us

nostalgia [nos'talxja] *nf* nostalgia

nota ['nota] *nf* note; *(ESCOL)* mark

notable [no'taβle] *adj* notable; *(ESCOL)* outstanding

notar [no'tar] *vt* to notice, note; **notarse** *vr* to be obvious; **se nota que** ... one observes that ...

notario [no'tarjo] *nm* notary

noticia [no'tiθja] *nf (información)* piece of news; **las noticias** the news *sg*; **tener noticias de algn** to hear from sb

⚠ No confundir **noticia** con la palabra inglesa *notice*.

noticiero [noti'θjero] *(LAm) nm* news bulletin

notificar [notifi'kar] *vt* to notify, inform

notorio, -a [no'torjo, a] *adj (público)* well-known; *(evidente)* obvious

novato, -a [no'βato, a] *adj* inexperienced ♦ *nm/f* beginner, novice

novecientos, -as [noβe'θjentos, as] *num* nine hundred

novedad [noβe'ðað] *nf (calidad de nuevo)* newness; *(noticia)* piece of news; *(cambio)* change, (new) development

novel [no'βel] *adj* new; *(inexperto)* inexperienced ♦ *nmf* beginner

novela [no'βela] *nf* novel

noveno, -a [no'βeno, a] *adj* ninth

noventa [no'βenta] *num* ninety

novia ['noβja] nf ver **novio**

novicio, -a [no'βiθjo, a] nm/f novice

noviembre [no'βjembre] nm November

novillada [noβi'ʎaða] nf (TAUR) bullfight with young bulls ❑ **novillero** nm novice bullfighter ❑ **novillo** nm young bull, bullock; **hacer novillos** (fam) to play truant

novio, -a ['noβjo, a] nm/f boyfriend/ girlfriend; (prometido) fiancé/fiancée; (recién casado) bridegroom/bride; **los novios** the newly-weds

nube ['nuβe] nf cloud

nublado, -a [nu'βlaðo, a] adj cloudy; **nublarse** vr to grow dark

nubosidad [nuβosi'ðað] nf cloudiness; **había mucha ~** it was very cloudy

nuca ['nuka] nf nape of the neck

nuclear [nukle'ar] adj nuclear

núcleo ['nukleo] nm (centro) core; (FÍSICA) nucleus ▸ **núcleo urbano** city centre

nudillo [nu'ðiʎo] nm knuckle

nudista [nu'ðista] adj nudist

nudo ['nuðo] nm knot; (de carreteras) junction

nuera ['nwera] nf daughter-in-law

nuestro, -a ['nwestro, a] adj pos our ♦ pron ours; **~ padre** our father; **un amigo ~** a friend of ours; **es el ~** it's ours

Nueva York [-'jɔrk] n New York

Nueva Zelanda [-θe'landa] nf New Zealand

nueve ['nweβe] num nine

nuevo, -a ['nweβo, a] adj (gen) new; **de ~** again

nuez [nweθ] nf walnut; (ANAT) Adam's apple ▸ **nuez moscada** nutmeg

nulo, -a ['nulo, a] adj (inepto, torpe) useless; (inválido) (null and) void; (DEPORTE) drawn, tied

núm. abr (= número) no.

numerar [nume'rar] vt to number

número ['numero] nm (gen) number; (tamaño: de zapato) size; (ejemplar: de diario) number, issue; **sin ~** numberless, unnumbered ▸ **número atrasado** back number ▸ **número de matrícula/teléfono** registration/ telephone number ▸ **número impar/ par** odd/even number ▸ **número romano** Roman numeral

numeroso, -a [nume'roso, a] adj numerous

nunca ['nunka] adv (jamás) never; **~ lo pensé** I never thought it; **no viene ~** he never comes; **~ más** never again; **más que ~** more than ever

nupcias ['nupθjas] nfpl wedding sg, nuptials

nutria ['nutrja] nf otter

nutrición [nutri'θjon] nf nutrition

nutrir [nu'trir] vt (alimentar) to nourish; (dar de comer) to feed; (fig) to strengthen ❑ **nutritivo, -a** adj nourishing, nutritious

nylon [ni'lon] nm nylon

Ñ, ñ

ñango, -a (MÉX) adj puny

ñapa (LAm) ['napa] nf extra

ñata (LAm: fam) nf nose; ver tb **ñato**

ñato, -a ['nato, a] (LAm) adj snub-nosed

ñoñería [none'ria] nf insipidness

ñoño, -a ['nono, a] adj (fam: tonto) silly, stupid; (soso) insipid; (persona) spineless; (ESP: película, novela) sentimental

O, o

O abr (= oeste) W

o [o] conj or

oasis [o'asis] nm inv oasis

obcecarse [oβθe'karse] *vr* to get o become stubborn

obedecer [oβeðe'θer] *vt* to obey ☐ **obediente** *adj* obedient

obertura [oβer'tura] *nf* overture

obeso, -a [o'βeso, a] *adj* obese

obispo [o'βispo] *nm* bishop

obituario (*LAm*) *nm* obituary

objetar [oβxe'tar] *vt, vi* to object

objetivo, -a [oβxe'tiβo, a] *adj, nm* objective

objeto [oβ'xeto] *nm* (*cosa*) object; (*fin*) aim

objetor, a [oβxe'tor, a] *nm/f* objector

obligación [oβliɣa'θjon] *nf* obligation; (*COM*) bond

obligar [oβli'ɣar] *vt* to force; **obligarse** *vr* to bind o.s. ☐ **obligatorio, -a** *adj* compulsory, obligatory

oboe [o'βoe] *nm* oboe

obra ['oβra] *nf* work; (*ARQ*) construction, building; (*TEATRO*) play; **por ~ de** thanks to (the efforts of) ▶ **obra maestra** masterpiece ▶ **obras públicas** public works ☐ **obrar** *vt* to work; (*tener efecto*) to have an effect on ♦ *vi* to act, behave; (*tener efecto*) to have an effect; **la carta obra en su poder** the letter is in his/her possession

obrero, -a [o'βrero, a] *adj* (*clase*) working; (*movimiento*) labour *cpd* ♦ *nm/f* (*gen*) worker; (*sin oficio*) labourer

obsceno, -a [oβs'θeno, a] *adj* obscene

obscu... = **oscu...**

obsequiar [oβse'kjar] *vt* (*ofrecer*) to present with; (*agasajar*) to make a fuss of, lavish attention on ☐ **obsequio** *nm* (*regalo*) gift; (*cortesía*) courtesy, attention

observación [oβserβa'θjon] *nf* observation; (*reflexión*) remark

observador, a [oβserβa'ðor, a] *nm/f* observer

observar [oβser'βar] *vt* to observe; (*anotar*) to notice; **observarse** *vr* to keep to, observe

obsesión [oβse'sjon] *nf* obsession ☐ **obsesivo, -a** *adj* obsessive

obstáculo [oβs'takulo] *nm* obstacle; (*impedimento*) hindrance, drawback

obstante [oβs'tante]: **no ~** *adv* nevertheless

obstinado, -a [oβsti'naðo, a] *adj* obstinate, stubborn

obstinarse [oβsti'narse] *vr* to be obstinate; **~ en** to persist in

obstruir [oβstru'ir] *vt* to obstruct

obtener [oβte'ner] *vt* (*gen*) to obtain; (*premio*) to win

obturador [oβtura'ðor] *nm* (*FOTO*) shutter

obvio, -a ['oββjo, a] *adj* obvious

oca ['oka] *nf* (*animal*) goose, (*juego*) ≈ snakes and ladders

ocasión [oka'sjon] *nf* (*oportunidad*) opportunity, chance; (*momento*) occasion, time; (*causa*) cause; **de ~** secondhand ☐ **ocasionar** *vt* to cause

ocaso [o'kaso] *nm* (*fig*) decline

occidente [okθi'ðente] *nm* west

OCDE *nf abr* (= *Organización de Cooperación y Desarrollo Económico*) OECD

océano [o'θeano] *nm* ocean ▶ **Océano Índico** Indian Ocean

ochenta [o'tʃenta] *num* eighty

ocho ['otʃo] *num* eight; **dentro de ~ días** within a week

ocio ['oθjo] *nm* (*tiempo*) leisure; (*pey*) idleness

octavilla [okta'βiʎa] *nf* leaflet, pamphlet

octavo, -a [ok'taβo, a] *adj* eighth

octubre [ok'tuβre] *nm* October

oculista [oku'lista] *nmf* oculist

ocultar [okul'tar] *vt* (*esconder*) to hide; (*callar*) to conceal ☐ **oculto, -a** *adj* hidden; (*fig*) secret

ocupación [okupa'θjon] *nf* occupation

ocupado, -a [oku'paðo, a] *adj* (*persona*) busy; (*plaza*) occupied, taken; (*teléfono*) engaged □ **ocupar** *vt* (*gen*) to occupy; **ocuparse** *vr*: **ocuparse de** o **en** (*gen*) to concern o.s. with; (*cuidar*) to look after

ocurrencia [oku'rrenθja] *nf* (*idea*) bright idea

ocurrir [oku'rrir] *vi* to happen; **ocurrirse** *vr*: **se me ocurrió que ...** it occurred to me that ...

odiar [o'ðjar] *vt* to hate □ **odio** *nm* hate, hatred □ **odioso, -a** *adj* (*gen*) hateful; (*malo*) nasty

odontólogo, -a [oðon'toloɣo, a] *nm/f* dentist, dental surgeon

oeste [o'este] *nm* west; **una película del ~** a western

ofender [ofen'der] *vt* (*agraviar*) to offend; (*insultar*) to insult; **ofenderse** *vr* to take offence □ **ofensa** *nf* offence □ **ofensiva** *nf* offensive □ **ofensivo, -a** *adj* offensive

oferta [o'ferta] *nf* offer; (*propuesta*) proposal; **la ~ y la demanda** supply and demand; **artículos en ~** goods on offer

oficial [ofi'θjal] *adj* official ♦ *nm* (MIL) officer

oficina [ofi'θina] *nf* office ▶ **oficina de correos** post office ▶ **oficina de información** information bureau ▶ **oficina de turismo** tourist office □ **oficinista** *nmf* clerk

oficio [o'fiθjo] *nm* (*profesión*) profession; (*puesto*) post; (REL) service; **ser del ~** to be an old hand; **tener mucho ~** to have a lot of experience ▶ **oficio de difuntos** funeral service

ofimática [ofi'matika] *nf* office automation

ofrecer [ofre'θer] *vt* (*dar*) to offer; (*proponer*) to propose; **ofrecerse** *vr* (*persona*) to offer o.s., volunteer; (*situación*) to present itself; **¿qué se le**

ofrece?, ¿se le ofrece algo? what can I do for you?, can I get you anything?

ofrecimiento [ofreθi'mjento] *nm* offer

oftalmólogo, -a [oftal'moloɣo, a] *nm/f* ophthalmologist

oída [o'iða] *nf*: **de oídas** by hearsay

oído [o'iðo] *nm* (ANAT) ear; (*sentido*) hearing

oigo *etc vb ver* **oír**

oír [o'ir] *vt* (*gen*) to hear; (*atender a*) to listen to; **¡oiga!** listen!; **~ misa** to attend mass

OIT *nf abr* (= *Organización Internacional del Trabajo*) ILO

ojal [o'xal] *nm* buttonhole

ojalá [oxa'la] *excl* if only (it were so!), some hope! ♦ *conj* if only ...!, would that ...!; **ojalá (que) venga hoy** I hope he comes today

ojeada [oxe'aða] *nf* glance

ojera [o'xera] *nf*: **tener ojeras** to have bags under one's eyes

ojo [o'xo] *nm* eye; (*de puente*) span; (*de cerradura*) keyhole ♦ *excl* careful!; **tener ~ para** to have an eye for ▶ **ojo de buey** porthole

okey [o'kei] (*Lam*) *excl* O.K.

okupa [o'kupa] (ESP: *fam*) *nmf* squatter

ola ['ola] *nf* wave

olé [o'le] *excl* bravo!, olé!

oleada [ole'aða] *nf* big wave, swell; (*fig*) wave

oleaje [ole'axe] *nm* swell

óleo ['oleo] *nm* oil □ **oleoducto** *nm* (oil) pipeline

oler [o'ler] *vt* (*gen*) to smell; (*inquirir*) to pry into; (*fig: sospechar*) to sniff out ♦ *vi* to smell; **~ a** to smell of

olfatear [olfate'ar] *vt* to smell; (*inquirir*) to pry into □ **olfato** *nm* sense of smell

olimpiada [olim'pjaða] *nf*: **las Olimpiadas** the Olympics □ **olímpico, -a** [o'limpiko, a] *adj* Olympic

oliva [o'liβa] *nf (aceituna)* olive; **aceite de ~** olive oil □ **olivo** *nm* olive tree

olla ['oʎa] *nf* pan; *(comida)* stew ► **olla exprés** *o* **a presión** *(ESP)* pressure cooker ► **olla podrida** *type of Spanish stew*

olmo ['olmo] *nm* elm (tree)

olor [o'lor] *nm* smell □ **oloroso, -a** *adj* scented

olvidar [olβi'ðar] *vt* to forget; *(omitir)* to omit; **olvidarse** *vr (fig)* to forget o.s.; **se me olvidó** I forgot

olvido [ol'βiðo] *nm* oblivion; *(despiste)* forgetfulness

ombligo [om'bliɣo] *nm* navel

omelette *(LAm) nf* omelet(te)

omisión [omi'sjon] *nf (abstención)* omission; *(descuido)* neglect

omiso, -a [o'miso, a] *adj:* **hacer caso ~ de** to ignore, pass over

omitir [omi'tir] *vt* to omit

omnipotente [omnipo'tente] *adj* omnipotent

omóplato [o'moplato] *nm* shoulder blade

OMS *nf abr (= Organización Mundial de la Salud)* WHO

once ['onθe] *num* eleven □ **onces** *(CS) nfpl* tea break *sg*

onda ['onda] *nf* wave ► **onda corta/larga/media** short/long/medium wave □ **ondear** *vt, vi* to wave; *(tener ondas)* to be wavy; *(agua)* to ripple

ondulación [ondula'θjon] *nf* undulation □ **ondulado, -a** *adj* wavy

ONG *nf abr (= organización no gubernamental)* NGO

ONU ['onu] *nf abr (= Organización de las Naciones Unidas)* UNO

opaco, -a [o'pako, a] *adj* opaque

opción [op'θjon] *nf (gen)* option; *(derecho)* right, option

OPEP ['opep] *nf abr (= Organización de Países Exportadores de Petróleo)* OPEC

ópera ['opera] *nf* opera ► **ópera bufa** *o* **cómica** comic opera

operación [opera'θjon] *nf (gen)* operation; *(COM)* transaction, deal

operador, a [opera'ðor, a] *nm/f* operator; *(CINE: de proyección)* projectionist; *(: de rodaje)* cameraman

operar [ope'rar] *vt (producir)* to produce, bring about; *(MED)* to operate on ♦ *vi (COM)* to operate, deal; **operarse** *vr* to occur; *(MED)* to have an operation

opereta [ope'reta] *nf* operetta

opinar [opi'nar] *vt* to think ♦ *vi* to give one's opinion □ **opinión** *(creencia)* belief; *(criterio)* opinion

opio ['opjo] *nm* opium

oponer [opo'ner] *vt (resistencia)* to put up, offer; **oponerse** *vr (objetar)* to object; *(estar frente a frente)* to be opposed; *(dos personas)* to oppose each other; **~ A a B** to set A against B; **me opongo a pensar que ...** I refuse to believe *o* think that ...

oportunidad [oportuni'ðað] *nf (ocasión)* opportunity; *(posibilidad)* chance

oportuno, -a [opor'tuno, a] *adj (en su tiempo)* opportune, timely; *(respuesta)* suitable; **en el momento ~** at the right moment

oposición [oposi'θjon] *nf* opposition; **oposiciones** *nfpl (ESCOL)* public examinations

opositor, a [oposi'tor, a] *nm/f (adversario)* opponent; *(candidato):* **~ (a)** candidate (for)

opresión [opre'sjon] *nf* oppression □ **opresor, a** *nm/f* oppressor

oprimir [opri'mir] *vt* to squeeze; *(fig)* to oppress

optar [op'tar] *vi (elegir)* to choose; **~ por** to opt for □ **optativo, -a** *adj* optional

óptico, -a [optiko, a] *adj* optic(al) ♦ *nm/f* optician □ **óptica** *nf* optician's (shop); **desde esta óptica** from this point of view

optimismo [opti'mismo] *nm* optimism ❏ **optimista** *nmf* optimist

opuesto, -a [o'pwesto, a] *adj* (*contrario*) opposite; (*antagónico*) opposing

oración [ora'θjon] *nf* (REL) prayer; (LING) sentence

orador, a [ora'ðor, a] *nm/f* (*conferenciante*) speaker, orator

oral [o'ral] *adj* oral

orangután [orangu'tan] *nm* orangutan

orar [o'rar] *vi* to pray

oratoria [ora'torja] *nf* oratory

órbita [or'βita] *nf* orbit

orden ['orðen] *nm* (*gen*) order ♦ *nf* (*gen*) order; (INFORM) command; **en ~ de prioridad** in order of priority ▶ **orden del día** agenda

ordenado, -a [orðe'naðo, a] *adj* (*metódico*) methodical; (*arreglado*) orderly

ordenador [orðena'ðor] *nm* computer ▶ **ordenador central** mainframe computer

ordenar [orðe'nar] *vt* (*mandar*) to order; (*poner orden*) to put in order, arrange; **ordenarse** *vr* (REL) to be ordained

ordeñar [orðe'ɲar] *vt* to milk

ordinario, -a [orði'narjo, a] *adj* (*común*) ordinary, usual; (*vulgar*) vulgar, common

orégano [o'reɣano] *nm* oregano

oreja [o'rexa] *nf* ear; (MECÁNICA) lug, flange

orfanato [orfa'nato] *nm* orphanage

orfebrería [orfeβre'ria] *nf* gold/silver work

orgánico, -a [or'ɣaniko, a] *adj* organic

organismo [orɣa'nismo] *nm* (BIO) organism; (POL) organization

organización [orɣaniθa'θjon] *nf* organization ❏ **organizar** *vt* to organize

órgano ['orɣano] *nm* organ

orgasmo [or'ɣasmo] *nm* orgasm

orgía [or'xia] *nf* orgy

orgullo [or'ɣuʎo] *nm* pride ❏ **orgulloso, -a** *adj* (*gen*) proud; (*altanero*) haughty

orientación [orjenta'θjon] *nf* (*posición*) position; (*dirección*) direction

oriental [orjen'tal] *adj* eastern; (*del Lejano Oriente*) oriental

orientar [orjen'tar] *vt* (*situar*) to orientate; (*señalar*) to point; (*dirigir*) to direct; (*guiar*) to guide; **orientarse** *vr* to get one's bearings

oriente [or'jente] *nm* east; **el O~ Medio** the Middle East; **el Próximo/Extremo O~** the Near/Far East

origen [o'rixen] *nm* origin

original [orixi'nal] *adj* (*nuevo*) original; (*extraño*) odd, strange ❏ **originalidad** *nf* originality

originar [orixi'nar] *vt* to start, cause; **originarse** *vr* to originate ❏ **originario, -a** *adj* original; **originario de** native of

orilla [o'riʎa] *nf* (*borde*) border; (*de río*) bank; (*de bosque, tela*) edge; (*de mar*) shore

orina [o'rina] *nf* urine ❏ **orinal** *nm* (chamber) pot ❏ **orinar** *vi* to urinate; **orinarse** *vr* to wet o.s.

oro ['oro] *nm* gold; **oros** *nmpl* (NAIPES) hearts

orquesta [or'kesta] *nf* orchestra ▶ **orquesta sinfónica** symphony orchestra

orquídea [or'kiðea] *nf* orchid

ortiga [or'tiɣa] *nf* nettle

ortodoxo, -a [orto'ðokso, a] *adj* orthodox

ortografía [ortoɣra'fia] *nf* spelling

ortopedia [orto'peðja] nf orthopaedics sg □ **ortopédico, -a** adj orthopaedic

oruga [o'ruɣa] nf caterpillar

orzuelo [or'θwelo] nm stye

os [os] pron (gen) you; (a vosotros) to you

osa ['osa] nf (she-)bear ▸ **Osa Mayor/ Menor** Great/Little Bear

osadía [osa'ðia] nf daring

osar [o'sar] vi to dare

oscilación [osθila'θjon] nf (movimiento) oscillation; (fluctuación) fluctuation

oscilar [osθi'lar] vi to oscillate; to fluctuate

oscurecer [oskure'θer] vt to darken ♦ vi to grow dark; **oscurecerse** vr to grow o get dark

oscuridad [oskuri'ðað] nf obscurity; (tinieblas) darkness

oscuro, -a [os'kuro, a] adj dark; (fig) obscure; **a oscuras** in the dark

óseo, -a ['oseo, a] adj bone cpd

oso ['oso] nm bear ▸ **oso de peluche** teddy bear ▸ **oso hormiguero** anteater

ostentar [osten'tar] vt (gen) to show; (pey) to flaunt, show off; (poseer) to have, possess

ostión (MÉX) nm = **ostra**

ostra ['ostra] nf oyster

OTAN ['otan] nf abr (= Organización del Tratado del Atlántico Norte) NATO

otitis [o'titis] nf earache

otoñal [oto'ɲal] adj autumnal

otoño [o'toɲo] nm autumn

otorgar [otor'ɣar] vt (conceder) to concede; (dar) to grant

otorrino, -a [oto'rrino, a], **otorrinolaringólogo, a** [otorrinolarin'goloɣo, a] nm/f ear, nose and throat specialist

otro, -a

PALABRA CLAVE

['otro, a] adj

1 (distinto: sg) another; (: pl) other; **con otros amigos** with other o different friends

2 (adicional): **tráigame otro café (más), por favor** can I have another coffee please; **otros diez días más** another ten days

♦ pron

1: **el otro** the other one; **(los) otros** (the) others; **de otro** somebody else's; **que lo haga otro** let somebody else do it

2 (recíproco): **se odian (la) una a (la) otra** they hate one another o each other

3: **otro tanto: comer otro tanto** to eat the same o as much again; **recibió una decena de telegramas y otras tantas llamadas** he got about ten telegrams and as many calls

ovación [oβa'θjon] nf ovation

oval [o'βal] adj oval □ **ovalado, -a** adj oval □ **óvalo** nm oval

ovario [o'βarjo] nm ovary

oveja [o'βexa] nf sheep

overol [oβe'rol] (LAm) nm overalls pl

ovillo [o'βiʎo] nm (de lana) ball of wool

OVNI ['oβni] nm abr (= objeto volante no identificado) UFO

ovulación [oβula'θjon] nf ovulation □ **óvulo** nm ovum

oxidación [oksiða'θjon] nf rusting

oxidar [oksi'ðar] vt to rust; **oxidarse** vr to go rusty

óxido ['oksiðo] nm oxide

oxigenado, -a [oksixe'naðo, a] adj (QUÍM) oxygenated; (pelo) bleached

oxígeno [ok'sixeno] nm oxygen

oyente [o'jente] nmf listener

oyes etc vb ver **oír**

ozono [o'θono] nm ozone

P, p

pabellón [paβe'ʎon] nm bell tent; (ARQ) pavilion; (de hospital etc) block, section; (bandera) flag

pacer [pa'θer] vi to graze

paciencia [pa'θjenθja] nf patience

paciente [pa'θjente] adj, nmf patient

pacificación [paθifika'θjon] nf pacification

pacífico, -a [pa'θifiko, a] adj (persona) peaceable; (existencia) peaceful; **el (Océano) P~** the Pacific (Ocean)

pacifista [paθi'fista] nmf pacifist

pacotilla [pako'tiʎa] nf: **de ~** (actor, escritor) third-rate

pactar [pak'tar] vt to agree to o on ♦ vi to come to an agreement

pacto ['pakto] nm (tratado) pact; (acuerdo) agreement

padecer [paðe'θer] vt (sufrir) to suffer; (soportar) to endure, put up with
□ **padecimiento** nm suffering

padrastro [pa'ðrastro] nm stepfather

padre ['paðre] nm father ♦ adj (fam): **un éxito ~** a tremendous success; **padres** nmpl parents ▶ **padre político** father-in-law

padrino [pa'ðrino] nm (REL) godfather; (tb: **~ de boda**) best man; (fig) sponsor, patron; **padrinos** nmpl godparents

padrón [pa'ðron] nm (censo) census, roll

padrote (MÉX: fam) [pa'ðrote] nm pimp

paella [pa'eʎa] nf paella, dish of rice with meat, shellfish etc

paga ['paɣa] nf (pago) payment; (sueldo) pay, wages pl

pagano, -a [pa'ɣano, a] adj, nm/f pagan, heathen

pagar [pa'ɣar] vt to pay; (las compras, crimen) to pay for; (fig: favor) to repay ♦ vi to pay; **~ al contado/a plazos** to pay (in) cash/in instalments

pagaré [paɣa're] nm I.O.U.

página ['paxina] nf page ▶ **página de inicio** (INFORM) home page ▶ **página web** (INFORM) web page

pago ['paɣo] nm (dinero) payment; **en ~ de** in return for ▶ **pago anticipado/a cuenta/contra reembolso/en especie** advance payment/payment on account/cash on delivery/payment in kind

pág(s). abr (= página(s)) p(p).

pague etc ['paɣe] vb ver **pagar**

país [pa'is] nm (gen) country; (región) land; **los Países Bajos** the Low Countries; **el P~ Vasco** the Basque Country

paisaje [pai'saxe] nm landscape, scenery

paisano, -a [pai'sano, a] adj of the same country ♦ nm/f (compatriota) fellow countryman/woman; **vestir de ~** (soldado) to be in civvies; (guardia) to be in plain clothes

paja ['paxa] nf straw; (fig) rubbish (BRIT), trash (US)

pajarita [paxa'rita] nf (corbata) bow tie

pájaro ['paxaro] nm bird ▶ **pájaro carpintero** woodpecker

pajita [pa'xita] nf (drinking) straw

pala ['pala] nf spade, shovel; (raqueta etc) bat; (: de tenis) racquet; (CULIN) slice ▶ **pala mecánica** power shovel

palabra [pa'laβra] nf word; (facultad) (power of) speech; (derecho de hablar) right to speak; **tomar la ~** (en mitin) to take the floor

palabrota [pala'βrota] nf swearword

palacio [pa'laθjo] nm palace; (mansión) mansion, large house ▶ **palacio de justicia** courthouse ▶ **palacio municipal** town o city hall

paladar [pala'ðar] nm palate
□ **paladear** vt to taste

palanca [pa'lanka] nf lever; (fig) pull, influence

palangana [palan'gana] nf washbasin

palco ['palko] nm box

Palestina [pales'tina] nf Palestine
❏ **palestino, -a** nm/f Palestinian

paleta [pa'leta] nf (de pintor) palette; (de albañil) trowel; (de ping-pong) bat; (MÉX, CAm: helado) ice lolly (BRIT), Popsicle® (US)

palidecer [paliðe'θer] vi to turn pale
❏ **palidez** nf paleness ❏ **pálido, -a** adj pale

palillo [pa'liʎo] nm (mondadientes) toothpick; (para comer) chopstick

palito [RPI] nm (helado) ice lolly (BRIT), Popsicle® (US)

paliza [pa'liθa] nf beating, thrashing

palma ['palma] nf (ANAT) palm; (árbol) palm tree; **batir** o **dar palmas** to clap, applaud ❏ **palmada** nf slap; **palmadas** nfpl clapping sg, applause sg

palmar [pal'mar] (fam) vi (tb: **palmarla**) to die, kick the bucket

palmear [palme'ar] vi to clap

palmera [pal'mera] nf (BOT) palm tree

palmo ['palmo] nm (medida) span; (fig) small amount; **~ a ~** inch by inch

palo ['palo] nm stick; (poste) post; (de tienda de campaña) pole; (mango) handle, shaft; (golpe) blow, hit; (de golf) club; (de béisbol) bat; (NÁUT) mast; (NAIPES) suit

paloma [pa'loma] nf dove, pigeon

palomitas [palo'mitas] nfpl popcorn sg

palpar [pal'par] vt to touch, feel

palpitar [palpi'tar] vi to palpitate; (latir) to beat

palta ['palta] (CS) nf avocado

paludismo [palu'ðismo] nm malaria

pamela [pa'mela] nf picture hat, sun hat

pampa ['pampa] nf pampas, prairie

pan [pan] nm bread; (una barra) loaf ▶ **pan integral** wholemeal (BRIT) o wholewheat (US) bread ▶ **pan rallado** breadcrumbs pl ▶ **pan tostado** (MÉX: tostada) toast

pana ['pana] nf corduroy

panadería [panaðe'ria] nf baker's (shop) ❏ **panadero, -a** nm/f baker

Panamá [pana'ma] nm Panama
❏ **panameño, -a** adj Panamanian

pancarta [pan'karta] nf placard, banner

panceta (ESP, RPI) nf bacon

pancho (RPI) ['pantʃo] nm hot dog

pancito [pan'θito] nm (bread) roll

panda ['panda] nm (ZOOL) panda

pandereta [pande'reta] nf tambourine

pandilla [pan'diʎa] nf set, group; (de criminales) gang; (pey: camarilla) clique

panecillo [pane'θiʎo] (ESP) nm (bread) roll

panel [pa'nel] nm panel ▶ **panel solar** solar panel

panfleto [pan'fleto] nm pamphlet

pánico ['paniko] nm panic

panorama [pano'rama] nm panorama; (vista) view

panqueque (LAm) nm pancake

pantalla [pan'taʎa] nf (de cine) screen; (de lámpara) lampshade

pantalón [panta'lon] nm trousers; **pantalones** nmpl trousers; **pantalones cortos** shorts

pantano [pan'tano] nm (ciénaga) marsh, swamp; (depósito: de agua) reservoir; (fig) jam, difficulty

panteón [pante'on] nm (monumento) pantheon

pantera [pan'tera] nf panther

pantimedias (MÉX) nfpl = **pantis**

pantis ['pantis] nmpl tights (BRIT), pantyhose (US)

pantomima [panto'mima] nf pantomime

pantorrilla [panto'rriʎa] nf calf (of the leg)

pants (MÉX) nmpl tracksuit (BRIT), sweat suit (US)

pantufla [pan'tufla] nf slipper

panty(s) ['panti(s)] *nm(pl)* tights (BRIT), pantyhose (US)

panza ['panθa] *nf* belly, paunch

pañal [pa'ɲal] *nm* nappy (BRIT), diaper (US); **pañales** *nmpl (fig)* early stages, infancy *sg*

paño ['paɲo] *nm (tela)* cloth; *(pedazo de tela)* (piece of) cloth; *(trapo)* duster, rag ▸ **paños menores** underclothes

pañuelo [pa'ɲwelo] *nm* handkerchief, hanky; *(fam: para la cabeza)* (head)scarf

papa ['papa] *nm*: **el P~** the Pope ♦ *nf* *(LAm: patata)* potato ▸ **papas fritas** *(LAm)* French fries, chips (BRIT); *(de bolsa)* crisps (BRIT), potato chips (US)

papá [pa'pa] *(fam)* dad(dy), pa (US)

papada [pa'paða] *nf* double chin

papagayo [papa'ɣajo] *nm* parrot

papalote [MÉX, CAm] [papa'lote] *nm* kite

papanatas [papa'natas] *(fam) nm inv* simpleton

papaya [pa'paja] *nf* papaya

papear [pape'ar] *(fam) vt, vi* to scoff

papel [pa'pel] *nm* paper; *(hoja de papel)* sheet of paper; *(TEATRO: fig)* role ▸ **papel de aluminio** aluminium (BRIT) *o* aluminum (US) foil ▸ **papel de arroz/envolver/fumar** rice/wrapping/cigarette paper ▸ **papel de estaño** *o* **plata** tinfoil ▸ **papel de lija** sandpaper ▸ **papel higiénico** toilet paper ▸ **papel moneda** paper money ▸ **papel secante** blotting paper

papeleo [pape'leo] *nm* red tape

papelera [pape'lera] *nf* wastepaper basket; *(en la calle)* litter bin ▸ **papelera (de reciclaje)** *(INFORM)* wastebasket

papelería [papele'ria] *nf* stationer's (shop)

papeleta [pape'leta] *(ESP) nf (POL)* ballot paper

paperas [pa'peras] *nfpl* mumps *sg*

papilla [pa'piʎa] *nf (de bebé)* baby food

paquete [pa'kete] *nm (de cigarrillos etc)* packet; (CORREOS etc) parcel

par [par] *adj (igual)* like, equal; (MAT) even ♦ *nm* equal; *(de guantes)* pair; *(de veces)* couple; (POL) peer; (GOLF, COM) par; **abrir de ~ en ~** to open wide

para ['para] *prep* for; **no es ~ comer** it's not for eating; **decir ~ sí** to say to o.s.; **¿~ qué lo quieres?** what do you want it for?; **se casaron ~ separarse otra vez** they married only to separate again; **lo tendré ~ mañana** I'll have it (for) tomorrow; **ir ~ casa** to go home, head for home; **~ profesor es muy estúpido** he's very stupid for a teacher; **¿quién es usted ~ gritar así?** who are you to shout like that?; **tengo bastante ~ vivir** I have enough to live on; *ver tb* **con**

parabién [para'βjen] *nm* congratulations *pl*

parábola [pa'raβola] *nf* parable; (MAT) parabola □ **parabólica** *nf (tb: antena parabólica)* satellite dish

parabrisas [para'βrisas] *nm inv* windscreen (BRIT), windshield (US)

paracaídas [paraka'iðas] *nm inv* parachute □ **paracaidista** *nmf* parachutist; (MIL) paratrooper

parachoques [para'tʃokes] *nm inv* (AUTO) bumper; (MECÁNICA etc) shock absorber

parada [pa'raða] *nf* stop; *(acto)* stopping; *(de industria)* shutdown, stoppage; *(lugar)* stopping place ▸ **parada de autobús** bus stop ▸ **parada de taxis** taxi stand *o* rank (BRIT)

paradero [para'ðero] *nm* stopping-place; *(situación)* whereabouts

parado, -a [pa'raðo, a] *adj (persona)* motionless, standing still; *(fábrica)* closed, at a standstill; *(coche)* stopped; *(LAm: de pie)* standing (up); *(ESP: sin empleo)* unemployed, idle

paradoja [para'ðoxa] *nf* paradox

parador [para'ðor] nm parador, state-run hotel

paragolpes (RPl) nm inv (AUTO) bumper, fender (US)

paraguas [pa'raɣwas] nm inv umbrella

Paraguay [para'ɣwai] nm Paraguay
❑ **paraguayo, -a** adj, nm/f Paraguayan

paraíso [para'iso] nm paradise, heaven

paraje [pa'raxe] nm place, spot

paralelo, -a [para'lelo, a] adj parallel

parálisis [pa'ralisis] nf inv paralysis
❑ **paralítico, -a** adj, nm/f paralytic

paralizar [parali'θar] vt to paralyse; **paralizarse** vr to become paralysed; (fig) to come to a standstill

páramo ['paramo] nm bleak plateau

paranoico, -a [para'noiko, a] nm/f paranoiac

parapente [para'pente] nm (deporte) paragliding; (aparato) paraglider

parapléjico, -a [para'plexiko, a] adj, nm/f paraplegic

parar [pa'rar] vt to stop; (golpe) to ward off ♦ vi to stop; **pararse** vr to stop; (LAm: ponerse de pie) to stand up; **ha parado de llover** it has stopped raining; **van a ir a ~ a comisaría** they're going to end up in the police station; **pararse en** to pay attention to

pararrayos [para'rrajos] nm inv lightning conductor

parásito, -a [pa'rasito, a] nm/f parasite

parcela [par'θela] nf plot, piece of ground

parche ['partʃe] nm (gen) patch

parchís [par'tʃis] nm ludo

parcial [par'θjal] adj (pago) part-; (eclipse) partial; (JUR) prejudiced, biased; (POL) partisan

parecer [pare'θer] nm (opinión) opinion, view; (aspecto) looks pl ♦ vi (tener apariencia) to seem, look; (asemejarse) to look o seem like; (aparecer, llegar) to appear; **parecerse** vr to look alike, resemble each other; **al** ~ apparently; **según parece** evidently, apparently; **parecerse a** to look like, resemble; **me parece que** I think (that), it seems to me that

parecido, -a [pare'θiðo, a] adj similar ♦ nm similarity, likeness, resemblance; **bien** ~ good-looking, nice-looking

pared [pa'reð] nf wall

pareja [pa'rexa] nf (par) pair; (dos personas) couple; (otro: de un par) other one (of a pair); (persona) partner

parentesco [paren'tesko] nm relationship

paréntesis [pa'rentesis] nm inv parenthesis; (en escrito) bracket

parezco etc vb ver **parecer**

pariente [pa'rjente] nmf relative, relation

⚠ No confundir **pariente** con la palabra inglesa parent.

parir [pa'rir] vt to give birth to ♦ vi (mujer) to give birth, have a baby

París [pa'ris] n Paris

parka (LAm) nf anorak

parking ['parkin] nm car park (BRIT), parking lot (US)

parlamentar [parlamen'tar] vi to parley

parlamentario, -a [parlamen'tarjo, a] adj parliamentary ♦ nm/f member of parliament

parlamento [parla'mento] nm parliament

parlanchín, -ina [parlan'tʃin, ina] adj indiscreet ♦ nm/f chatterbox

parlar [par'lar] vi to chatter (away)

paro ['paro] nm (huelga) stoppage (of work), strike; (ESP: desempleo) unemployment; (: subsidio) unemployment benefit; **estar en ~** (ESP) to be unemployed ► **paro cardíaco** cardiac arrest

parodia [pa'roðja] nf parody
❑ **parodiar** vt to parody

parpadear [parpaðe'ar] vi (ojos) to blink; (luz) to flicker

párpado ['parpaðo] nm eyelid

parque ['parke] nm (lugar verde) park; (MÉX: munición) ammunition ▶ **parque de atracciones** fairground ▶ **parque de bomberos** (ESP) fire station ▶ **parque infantil/temático/zoológico** playground/theme park/zoo

parqué [par'ke] nm parquet (flooring)

parquímetro [par'kimetro] nm parking meter

parra ['parra] nf (grape)vine

párrafo ['parrafo] nm paragraph; **echar un ~** (fam) to have a chat

parranda [pa'rranda] nf (fam) spree, binge

parrilla [pa'rriʎa] nf (CULIN) grill; (de coche) grille; (carne a la) ~ barbecue ▫ **parrillada** nf barbecue

párroco ['parroko] nm parish priest

parroquia [pa'rrokja] nf parish; (iglesia) parish church; (COM) clientele, customers pl ▫ **parroquiano, -a** nm/f parishioner; client, customer

parte ['parte] nm message; (informe) report ♦ nf part; (lado, cara) side; (de reparto) share; (JUR) party; **en alguna ~ de Europa** somewhere in Europe; **en o por todas partes** everywhere; **en gran ~** to a large extent; **la mayor ~ de los españoles** most Spaniards; **de un tiempo a esta ~** for some time past; **de ~ de algn** on sb's behalf; **¿de ~ de quién?** (TEL) who is speaking?; **por ~ de** on the part of; **yo por mi ~** I for my part; **por otra ~** on the other hand; **dar ~ a** to inform; **tomar ~** to take part ▶ **parte meteorológico** weather forecast o report

participación [partiθipa'θjon] nf (acto) participation, taking part; (parte, COM) share; (de lotería) shared prize; (aviso) notice, notification

participante [partiθi'pante] nmf participant

participar [partiθi'par] vt to notify, inform ♦ vi to take part, participate

partícipe [par'tiθipe] nmf participant

particular [partiku'lar] adj (especial) particular, special; (individual, personal) private, personal ♦ nm (punto, asunto) particular, point; (individuo) individual; **tiene coche** ~ he has a car of his own

partida [par'tiða] nf (salida) departure; (COM) entry, item; (juego) game; (grupo de personas) band, group; **mala ~** dirty trick ▶ **partida de nacimiento/matrimonio/defunción** (ESP) birth/marriage/death certificate

partidario, -a [parti'ðarjo, a] adj partisan ♦ nm/f supporter, follower

partido [par'tiðo] nm (POL) party; (DEPORTE) game, match; **sacar ~ de** to profit o benefit from; **tomar ~** to take sides

partir [par'tir] vt (dividir) to split, divide; (compartir, distribuir) to share (out), distribute; (romper) to break open, split open; (rebanada) to cut (off) ♦ vi (ponerse en camino) to set off o out; (comenzar) to start (off o out); **partirse** vr to crack o split o break (in two etc); **a ~ de** (starting) from

partitura [parti'tura] nf (MÚS) score

parto ['parto] nm birth; (fig) product, creation; **estar de ~** to be in labour

parvulario (ESP) [parβu'larjo] nm nursery school, kindergarten

pasa ['pasa] nf raisin ▶ **pasa de Corinto** currant

pasacintas (LAm) nm cassette player

pasada [pa'saða] nf passing; passage; **de ~** in passing, incidentally; **una mala ~** a dirty trick

pasadizo [pasa'ðiθo] nm (pasillo) passage, corridor; (callejuela) alley

pasado, -a [pa'saðo, a] adj past; (malo: comida, fruta) bad; (muy cocido) overdone; (anticuado) out of date

♦ *nm* past; **~ mañana** the day after tomorrow; **el mes ~** last month

pasador [pasa'ðor] *nm* (*cerrojo*) bolt; (*de pelo*) hair slide; (*horquilla*) grip

pasaje [pa'saxe] *nm* passage; (*pago de viaje*) fare; (*los pasajeros*) passengers *pl*; (*pasillo*) passageway

pasajero, -a [pasa'xero, a] *adj* passing; (*situación, estado*) temporary; (*amor, enfermedad*) brief ♦ *nm/f* passenger

pasamontañas [pasamon'taɲas] *nm inv* balaclava helmet

pasaporte [pasa'porte] *nm* passport

pasar [pa'sar] *vt* to pass; (*tiempo*) to spend; (*desgracias*) to suffer, endure; (*noticia*) to give, pass on; (*río*) to cross; (*barrera*) to pass through; (*falta*) to overlook, tolerate; (*contrincante*) to surpass, do better than; (*coche*) to overtake; (*CINE*) to show; (*enfermedad*) to give, infect with ♦ *vi* (*gen*) to pass; (*terminarse*) to be over; (*ocurrir*) to happen; **pasarse** *vr* (*flores*) to fade; (*comida*) to go bad o off; (*fig*) to overdo it, go too far; **~ de** to go beyond, exceed; **~ por** (*LAm*) to fetch; **pasarlo bien/mal** to have a good/bad time; **¡pase!** come in!; **hacer ~** to show in; **lo que pasa es que ...** the thing is ...; **pasarse al enemigo** to go over to the enemy; **se me pasó** I forgot; **no se le pasa nada** he misses nothing; **pase lo que pase** come what may; **¿qué pasa?** what's going on?, what's up?; **¿qué te pasa?** what's wrong?

pasarela [pasa'rela] *nf* footbridge; (*en barco*) gangway

pasatiempo [pasa'tjempo] *nm* pastime, hobby

Pascua [pas'kwa] *nf* (*en Semana Santa*) Easter; **Pascuas** *nfpl* (*Navidad*) (time); **¡felices Pascuas!** Merry Christmas!

pase [pase] *nm* pass; (*CINE*) performance, showing

pasear [pase'ar] *vt* to take for a walk; (*exhibir*) to parade, show off ♦ *vi* to walk, go for a walk; **pasearse** *vr* to walk,

go for a walk; **~ en coche** to go for a drive □ **paseo** *nm* (*avenida*) avenue; (*distancia corta*) walk, stroll; **dar un** o **ir de paseo** to go for a walk ▶ **paseo marítimo** (*ESP*) promenade

pasillo [pa'siʎo] *nm* passage, corridor

pasión [pa'sjon] *nf* passion

pasivo, -a [pa'siβo, a] *adj* passive; (*inactivo*) inactive ♦ *nm* (*COM*) liabilities *pl*, debts *pl*

pasmoso, -a [pas'moso, a] *adj* amazing, astonishing

paso, -a ['paso, a] *adj* dried ♦ *nm* step; (*modo de andar*) walk; (*huella*) footprint; (*rapidez*) speed, pace, rate; (*camino accesible*) way through, passage; (*cruce*) crossing; (*pasaje*) passing, passage; (*GEO*) pass; (*estrecho*) strait; **a ese ~** (*fig*) at that rate; **salir al ~ de** o **a** to waylay; **estar de ~** to be passing through; **prohibido el ~** no entry; **ceda el ~** give way ▶ **paso a nivel** (*FERRO*) level-crossing ▶ **paso (de) cebra** (*ESP*) zebra crossing ▶ **paso de peatones** pedestrian crossing ▶ **paso elevado** flyover

pasota [pa'sota] (*ESP: fam*) *adj, nmf* **~** dropout; **ser un ~** to be a bit of a dropout; (*ser indiferente*) not to care about anything

pasta ['pasta] *nf* paste; (*CULIN: masa*) dough; (: *de bizcochos etc*) pastry; (*fam*) dough; **pastas** *nfpl* (*bizcochos*) pastries, small cakes; (*fideos, espaguetis etc*) pasta ▶ **pasta dentífrica** o **de dientes** toothpaste

pastar [pas'tar] *vt, vi* to graze

pastel [pas'tel] *nm* (*dulce*) cake; (*ARTE*) pastel ▶ **pastel de carne** meat pie □ **pastelería** *nf* cake shop

pastilla [pas'tiʎa] *nf* (*de jabón, chocolate*) bar; (*píldora*) tablet, pill

pasto ['pasto] *nm* (*hierba*) grass; (*lugar*) pasture, field □ **pastor, a** [pas'tor, a] *nm/f* shepherd/ess ♦ *nm* (*REL*) clergyman, pastor ▶ **pastor alemán** Alsatian

pata ['pata] nf (pierna) leg; (pie) foot; (de muebles) leg; **patas arriba** upside down; **metedura de ~** (fam) gaffe; **meter la ~** (fam) to put one's foot in it; **tener buena/mala ~** to be lucky/ unlucky ▶ **pata de cabra** (TEC) crowbar ❑ **patada** nf kick; (en el suelo) stamp

patata [pa'tata] nf (de tata) potato ▶ **patatas fritas** chips, French fries; (de bolsa) crisps

paté [pa'te] nm pâté

patente [pa'tente] adj obvious, evident; (COM) patent ♦ nf patent

paternal [pater'nal] adj fatherly, paternal ❑ **paterno, -a** adj paternal

patético, -a [pa'tetiko, a] adj pathetic, moving

patilla [pa'tiʎa] nf (de gafas) side(piece); **patillas** nfpl sideburns

patín [pa'tin] nm skate; (de trineo) runner ❑ **patinaje** nm skating ❑ **patinar** vi to skate; (resbalarse) to skid, slip; (fam) to slip up, blunder

patines de ruedas nmpl rollerskates

patineta nf (MÉX: patinete) scooter; (CS: monopatín) skateboard

patinete [pati'nete] nm scooter

patio ['patjo] nm (de casa) patio, courtyard ▶ **patio de recreo** playground

pato ['pato] nm duck; **pagar el ~** (fam) to take the blame, carry the can

patoso, -a [pa'toso, a] (fam) adj clumsy

patotero (CS) nm hooligan, lout

patraña [pa'traɲa] nf story, fib

patria ['patrja] nf native land, mother country

patrimonio [patri'monjo] nm inheritance; (fig) heritage

patriota [pa'trjota] nmf patriot

patrocinar [patroθi'nar] vt to sponsor

patrón, -ona [pa'tron, ona] nm/f (jefe) boss, chief, master(mistress); (propietario) landlord/lady; (REL) patron saint ♦ nm (TEC, COSTURA) pattern

patronato [patro'nato] nm sponsorship; (acto) patronage; (fundación benéfica) trust, foundation

patrulla [pa'truʎa] nf patrol

pausa ['pausa] nf pause, break

pauta ['pauta] nf line, guide line

pava (RPI) ['paβa] nf kettle

pavimento [paβi'mento] nm (de losa) pavement, paving

pavo ['paβo] nm turkey ▶ **pavo real** peacock

payaso, -a [pa'jaso, a] nm/f clown

payo, -a ['pajo, a] nm/f non-gipsy

paz [paθ] nf peace; (tranquilidad) peacefulness, tranquillity; **hacer las paces** to make peace; (fig) to make up; **¡déjame en ~!** leave me alone!

PC nm PC, personal computer

P.D. abr (= posdata) P.S., p.s.

peaje [pe'axe] nm toll

peatón [pea'ton] nm pedestrian

peatonal adj pedestrian

peca ['peka] nf freckle

pecado [pe'kaðo] nm sin ❑ **pecador, a** adj sinful ♦ nm/f sinner

pecaminoso, -a [pekami'noso, a] adj sinful

pecar [pe'kar] vi (REL) to sin; **peca de generoso** he is generous to a fault

pecera [pe'θera] nf fish tank; (redonda) goldfish bowl

pecho ['petʃo] nm (ANAT) chest; (de mujer) breast; **dar el ~ a** to breast-feed; **tomar algo a ~** to take sth to heart

pechuga [pe'tʃuʝa] nf breast

peculiar [peku'ljar] adj special, peculiar; (característico) typical, characteristic

pedal [pe'ðal] nm pedal ❑ **pedalear** vi to pedal

pedante [pe'ðante] adj pedantic ♦ nmf pedant

pedazo [pe'ðaθo] *nm* piece, bit; **hacerse pedazos** to smash, shatter

pediatra [pe'ðjatra] *nmf* paediatrician

pedido [pe'ðiðo] *nm* (COM) order; (*petición*) request

pedir [pe'ðir] *vt* to ask for, request; (*comida*, COM: *mandar*) to order; (*necesitar*) to need, demand, require ♦ *vi* to ask; **me pidió que cerrara la puerta** he asked me to shut the door; **¿cuánto piden por el coche?** how much are they asking for the car?

pedo ['peðo] (*fam!*) *nm* fart

pega ['peɣa] *nf* snag; **poner pegas (a)** to complain (about)

pegadizo, -a [peɣa'ðiθo, a] *adj* (MÚS) catchy

pegajoso, -a [peɣa'xoso, a] *adj* sticky, adhesive

pegamento [peɣa'mento] *nm* gum, glue

pegar [pe'ɣar] *vt* (*papel, sellos*) to stick (on); (*cartel*) to stick up; (*coser*) to sew (on); (*unir: partes*) to join, fix together; (COMPUT) to paste; (MED) to give, infect with; (*dar: golpe*) to give, deal ♦ *vi* (*adherirse*) to stick, adhere; (*ir juntos: colores*) to match, go together; (*golpear*) to hit; (*quemar: el sol*) to strike hot, burn; **pegarse** *vr* (*gen*) to stick; (*dos personas*) to hit each other, fight; (*fam*): **~ un grito** to let out a yell; **~ un salto** to jump (with fright); **~ en** to touch; **pegarse un tiro** to shoot o.s.

pegatina [peɣa'tina] *nf* sticker

pegote [pe'ɣote] (*fam*) *nm* eyesore, sight

peinado [pei'naðo] *nm* hairstyle

peinar [pei'nar] *vt* to comb; (*hacer estilo*) to style; **peinarse** *vr* to comb one's hair

peine ['peine] *nm* comb □ **peineta** *nf* ornamental comb

p.ej. *abr* (= *por ejemplo*) e.g.

Pekín [pe'kin] *n* Pekin(g)

pelado, -a [pe'laðo, a] *adj* (*fruta, patata etc*) peeled; (*cabeza*) shorn; (*campo, fig*) bare; (*fam: sin dinero*) broke

pelar [pe'lar] *vt* (*fruta, patatas etc*) to peel; (*cortar el pelo a*) to cut the hair of; (*quitar la piel: animal*) to skin; **pelarse** *vr* (*la piel*) to peel off; **voy a pelarme** I'm going to get my hair cut

peldaño [pel'daɲo] *nm* step

pelea [pe'lea] *nf* (*lucha*) fight; (*discusión*) quarrel, row □ **peleado, -a** [pele'aðo, a] *adj*: **estar peleado (con algn)** to have fallen out (with sb) □ **pelear** [pele'ar] *vi* to fight; **pelearse** *vr* to fight; (*reñirse*) to fall out, quarrel

pelela (CS) *nf* potty

peletería [pelete'ria] *nf* furrier's, fur shop

pelícano [pe'likano] *nm* pelican

película [pe'likula] *nf* film; (*cobertura ligera*) thin covering; (FOTO: *rollo*) roll o reel of film ▸ **película de dibujos (animados)/del oeste** cartoon/western

peligro [pe'liɣro] *nm* danger; (*riesgo*) risk; **correr ~ de** to run the risk of □ **peligroso, -a** *adj* dangerous; risky

pelirrojo, -a [peli'rroxo, a] *adj* red-haired, red-headed ♦ *nm/f* redhead

pellejo [pe'ʎexo] *nm* (*de animal*) skin, hide

pellizcar [peʎiθ'kar] *vt* to pinch, nip

pelma ['pelma] (ESP: *fam*) *nmf* pain (in the neck) □ **pelmazo** [pel'maθo] (*fam*) *nm* = **pelma**

pelo ['pelo] *nm* (*cabellos*) hair; (*de barba, bigote*) whisker; (*de animal: pellejo*) hair, fur, coat; **venir al ~** to be exactly what one needs; **un hombre de ~ en pecho** a brave man; **por los pelos** by the skin of one's teeth; **no tener pelos en la lengua** to be outspoken, not to mince one's words; **con pelos y señales** in minute detail; **tomar el ~ a algn** to pull sb's leg

pelota [pe'lota] nf ball; **en ~** stark naked; **hacer la ~ (a algn)** (ESP: fam) to creep (to sb) ▸ **pelota vasca** pelota

pelotón [pelo'ton] nm (MIL) squad, detachment

peluca [pe'luka] nf wig

peluche [pe'lutʃe] nm: **oso/muñeco de ~** teddy bear/soft toy

peludo, -a [pe'luðo, a] adj hairy, shaggy

peluquería [peluke'ria] nf hairdresser's ▸ **peluquero, -a** nm/f hairdresser

pelusa [pe'lusa] nf (BOT) down; (en tela) fluff

pena ['pena] nf (congoja) grief, sadness; (remordimiento) regret; (dificultad) trouble; (dolor) pain; (JUR) sentence; **merecer o valer la ~** to be worthwhile; **a duras penas** with great difficulty; **¡qué ~!** what a shame! ▸ **pena capital** capital punishment ▸ **pena de muerte** death penalty

penal [pe'nal] adj penal ◆ nm (cárcel) prison

penalidad [penali'ðað] nf (problema, dificultad) trouble, hardship; (JUR) penalty, punishment; **penalidades** nfpl trouble sg, hardship sg

penalti [pe'nalti] nm = **penalty**

penalty [pe'nalti] (pl **penaltys** o **penalties**) nm penalty (kick)

pendiente [pen'djente] adj pending, unsettled ◆ nm earring ◆ nf hill, slope

pene ['pene] nm penis

penetrante [pene'trante] adj (herida) deep; (persona, arma) sharp; (sonido) penetrating, piercing; (mirada) searching; (viento, ironía) biting

penetrar [pene'trar] vt to penetrate, pierce; (entender) to grasp ◆ vi to penetrate, go in; (entrar) to enter, go in; (líquido) to soak in; (fig) to pierce

penicilina [peniθi'lina] nf penicillin

península [pe'ninsula] nf peninsula ▸ **peninsular** adj peninsular

penique [pe'nike] nm penny

penitencia [peni'tenθja] nf penance

penoso, -a [pe'noso, a] adj (lamentable) distressing; (difícil) arduous, difficult

pensador, a [pensa'ðor, a] nm/f thinker

pensamiento [pensa'mjento] nm thought; (mente) mind; (idea) idea

pensar [pen'sar] vt to think; (considerar) to think over, think out; (proponerse) to intend, plan; (imaginarse) to think up, invent ◆ vi to think; **~ en** to aim at, aspire to ▸ **pensativo, -a** adj thoughtful, pensive

pensión [pen'sjon] nf (casa) boarding o guest house; (dinero) pension; (cama y comida) board and lodging; **media ~** half-board ▸ **pensión completa** full board ▸ **pensionista** nmf (jubilado) (old-age) pensioner; (huésped) lodger

penúltimo, -a [pe'nultimo, a] adj penultimate, last but one

penumbra [pe'numbra] nf half-light

peña ['pena] nf (roca) rock; (cuesta) cliff, crag; (grupo) group, circle; (LAm: club) folk club

peñasco [pe'nasko] nm large rock, boulder

peñón [pe'non] nm wall of rock; **el P~** the Rock of Gibraltar

peón [pe'on] nm labourer; (LAm AGR) farm labourer, farmhand; (AJEDREZ) pawn

peonza [pe'onθa] nf spinning top

peor [pe'or] adj (comparativo) worse; (superlativo) worst ◆ adv worse; worst; **de mal en ~** from bad to worse

pepinillo [pepi'niʎo] nm gherkin

pepino [pe'pino] nm cucumber; **(no) me importa un ~** I don't care one bit

pepita [pe'pita] nf (BOT) pip; (MINERÍA) nugget

pepito [pe'pito] (ESP) nm (tb: **~ de ternera**) steak sandwich

pequeño, -a [pe'keɲo, a] *adj* small, little

pera ['pera] *nf* pear ◆ **peral** *nm* pear tree

percance [per'kanθe] *nm* setback, misfortune

percatarse [perka'tarse] *vr*: ~ **de** to notice, take note of

percebe [per'θeβe] *nm* barnacle

percepción [perθep'θjon] *nf* (*vista*) perception; (*idea*) notion, idea

percha ['pertʃa] *nf* (*coat*)hanger; (*ganchos*) coat hooks *pl*; (*de ave*) perch

percibir [perθi'βir] *vt* to perceive, notice; (*COM*) to earn, get

percusión [perku'sjon] *nf* percussion

perdedor, -a [perde'ðor, a] *adj* losing ◆ *nm/f* loser

perder [per'ðer] *vt* to lose; (*tiempo, palabras*) to waste; (*oportunidad*) to lose, miss; (*tren*) to miss ◆ *vi* to lose; **perderse** *vr* (*extraviarse*) to get lost; (*desaparecer*) to disappear, be lost to view; (*arruinarse*) to be ruined; **echar a ~** (*comida*) to spoil, ruin; (*oportunidad*) to waste

pérdida ['perðiða] *nf* loss; (*de tiempo*) waste; **pérdidas** *nfpl* (*COM*) losses

perdido, -a [per'ðiðo, a] *adj* lost

perdiz [per'ðiθ] *nf* partridge

perdón [per'ðon] *nm* (*disculpa*) pardon, forgiveness; (*clemencia*) mercy; **¡~!** sorry!, I beg your pardon! ◆ **perdonar** *vt* to pardon, forgive; (*la vida*) to spare; (*excusar*) to exempt, excuse; **¡perdone (usted)!** sorry!, I beg your pardon!

perecedero, -a [pereθe'ðero, a] *adj* perishable

perecer [pere'θer] *vi* to perish, die

peregrinación [pereɣrina'θjon] *nf* (*REL*) pilgrimage

peregrino, -a [pere'ɣrino, a] *adj* (*idea*) strange, absurd ◆ *nm/f* pilgrim

perejil [pere'xil] *nm* parsley

perenne [pe'renne] *adj* everlasting, perennial

pereza [pe'reθa] *nf* laziness, idleness ◆ **perezoso, -a** *adj* lazy, idle

perfección [perfek'θjon] *nf* perfection ◆ **perfeccionar** *vt* to perfect; (*mejorar*) to improve; (*acabar*) to complete, finish

perfecto, -a [per'fekto, a] *adj* perfect; (*total*) complete

perfil [per'fil] *nm* profile; (*contorno*) silhouette, outline; (*ARQ*) (*cross*) section; **perfiles** *nmpl* features

perforación [perfora'θjon] *nf* perforation; (*con taladro*) drilling ◆ **perforadora** *nf* punch

perforar [perfo'rar] *vt* to perforate; (*agujero*) to drill, bore; (*papel*) to punch a hole in ◆ *vi* to drill, bore

perfume [per'fume] *nm* perfume, scent

periferia [peri'ferja] *nf* periphery; (*de ciudad*) outskirts *pl*

periférico [peri'feriko] (*LAm*) *nm* ring road (*BRIT*), beltway (*US*)

perilla [pe'riʎa] *nf* (*barba*) goatee; (*LAm: de puerta*) doorknob, door handle

perímetro [pe'rimetro] *nm* perimeter

periódico, -a [pe'rjoðiko, a] *adj* periodic(al) ◆ *nm* newspaper

periodismo [perjo'ðismo] *nm* journalism ◆ **periodista** *nmf* journalist

periodo [pe'rjoðo] *nm* period

período [pe'rioðo] *nm* = **periodo**

periquito [peri'kito] *nm* budgerigar, budgie

perito, -a [pe'rito, a] *adj* (*experto*) expert; (*diestro*) skilled, skilful ◆ *nm/f* expert; skilled worker; (*técnico*) technician

perjudicar [perxuði'kar] *vt* (*gen*) to damage, harm; ◆ **perjudicial** *adj* damaging, harmful; (*en detrimento*) detrimental ◆ **perjuicio** *nm* damage, harm

perjurar [perxu'rar] *vi* to commit perjury

perla ['perla] *nf* pearl; **me viene de perlas** it suits me fine

permanecer [permane'θer] *vi* (*quedarse*) to stay, remain; (*seguir*) to continue to be

permanente [perma'nente] *adj* permanent, constant ♦ *nf* perm

permiso [per'miso] *nm* permission; (*licencia*) permit, licence; **con ~** excuse me; **estar de ~** (*MIL*) to be on leave
▶ **permiso de conducir** driving licence (*BRIT*), driver's license (*US*)
▶ **permiso por enfermedad** (*LAm*) sick leave

permitir [permi'tir] *vt* to permit, allow

pernera [per'nera] *nf* trouser leg

pero ['pero] *conj* but; (*aún*) yet ♦ *nm* (*defecto*) flaw, defect; (*reparo*) objection

perpendicular [perpendiku'lar] *adj* perpendicular

perpetuo, -a [per'petwo, a] *adj* perpetual

perplejo, -a [per'plexo, a] *adj* perplexed, bewildered

perra ['perra] *nf* (*ZOOL*) bitch; **estar sin una ~** (*ESP: fam*) to be flat broke

perrera [pe'rrera] *nf* kennel

perrito [pe'rrito] *nm* (*tb:* **~ caliente**) hot dog

perro ['perro] *nm* dog

persa ['persa] *adj, nmf* Persian

persecución [perseku'θjon] *nf* pursuit, chase; (*REL, POL*) persecution

perseguir [perse'γir] *vt* to pursue, hunt; (*cortejar*) to chase after; (*molestar*) to pester, annoy; (*REL, POL*) to persecute

persiana [per'sjana] *nf* (Venetian) blind

persistente [persis'tente] *adj* persistent

persistir [persis'tir] *vi* to persist

persona [per'sona] *nf* person
▶ **persona mayor** elderly person

personaje [perso'naxe] *nm* important person, celebrity; (*TEATRO etc*) character

personal [perso'nal] *adj* (*particular*) personal; (*para una persona*) single, for one person ♦ *nm* personnel, staff
□ **personalidad** *nf* personality

personarse [perso'narse] *vr* to appear in person

personificar [personifi'kar] *vt* to personify

perspectiva [perspek'tiβa] *nf* perspective; (*vista, panorama*) view, panorama; (*posibilidad futura*) outlook, prospect

persuadir [perswa'ðir] *vt* (*gen*) to persuade; (*convencer*) to convince; **persuadirse** *vr* to become convinced
□ **persuasión** *nf* persuasion

pertenecer [pertene'θer] *vi* to belong; (*fig*) to concern □ **perteneciente** *adj:* **perteneciente a** belonging to
□ **pertenencia** *nf* ownership; **pertenencias** *nfpl* (*bienes*) possessions, property *sg*

pertenezca *etc* [perte'neθka] *vb ver* **pertenecer**

pértiga ['pertiγa] *nf:* **salto de ~** pole vault

pertinente [perti'nente] *adj* relevant, pertinent; (*apropiado*) appropriate; **~ a** concerning, relevant to

perturbación [perturβa'θjon] *nf* (*POL*) disturbance; (*MED*) upset, disturbance

Perú [pe'ru] *nm* Peru □ **peruano, -a** *adj, nm/f* Peruvian

perversión [perβer'sjon] *nf* perversion □ **perverso, -a** *adj* perverse; (*depravado*) depraved

pervertido, -a [perβer'tiðo, a] *adj* perverted ♦ *nm/f* pervert

pervertir [perβer'tir] *vt* to pervert, corrupt

pesa ['pesa] *nf* weight; (*DEPORTE*) shot

pesadez [pesa'ðeθ] nf (peso) heaviness; (lentitud) slowness; (aburrimiento) tediousness

pesadilla [pesa'ðiʎa] nf nightmare, bad dream

pesado, -a [pe'saðo, a] adj heavy; (lento) slow; (difícil, duro) tough, hard; (aburrido) boring, tedious; (tiempo) sultry

pésame ['pesame] nm expression of condolence, message of sympathy; **dar el ~** to express one's condolences

pesar [pe'sar] vt to weigh; (ser pesado) to weigh a lot, be heavy; (fig: opinión) to carry weight; **no pesa mucho** it's not very heavy ♦ nm (arrepentimiento) regret; (pena) grief, sorrow; **a ~ de** or **pese a (que)** in spite of, despite

pesca ['peska] nf (acto) fishing; (lo pescado) catch; **ir de ~** to go fishing

pescadería [peskaðe'ria] nf fish shop, fishmonger's (BRIT)

pescadilla [peska'ðiʎa] nf whiting

pescado [pes'kaðo] nm fish

pescador, a [peska'ðor, a] nm/f fisherman/woman

pescar [pes'kar] vt (tomar) to catch; (intentar tomar) to fish for; (conseguir: trabajo) to manage to get ♦ vi to fish, go fishing

pesebre [pe'seβre] nm manger

peseta [pe'seta] nf (HIST) peseta

pesimista [pesi'mista] adj pessimistic ♦ nmf pessimist

pésimo, -a ['pesimo, a] adj awful, dreadful

peso ['peso] nm weight; (balanza) scales pl; (moneda) peso; **vender al ~** to sell by weight ♦ **peso bruto/neto** gross/ net weight ♦ **peso pesado/pluma** heavyweight/featherweight

pesquero, -a [pes'kero, a] adj fishing cpd

pestaña [pes'taɲa] nf (ANAT) eyelash; (borde) rim

peste ['peste] nf plague; (mal olor) stink, stench

pesticida [pesti'θiða] nm pesticide

pestillo [pes'tiʎo] nm (cerrojo) bolt; (picaporte) door handle

petaca [pe'taka] nf (de cigarros) cigarette case; (de pipa) tobacco pouch; (MÉX: maleta) suitcase

pétalo ['petalo] nm petal

petardo [pe'tarðo] nm firework, firecracker

petición [peti'θjon] nf (pedido) request, plea; (memorial) petition; (JUR) plea

peto (ESP) ['peto] nm dungarees pl, overalls pl (US)

petróleo [pe'troleo] nm oil, petroleum ❐ **petrolero, -a** adj petroleum cpd ♦ nm (oil) tanker

peyorativo, -a [pejora'tiβo, a] adj pejorative

pez [peθ] nm fish ▶ **pez espada** swordfish

pezón [pe'θon] nm teat, nipple

pezuña [pe'θuɲa] nf hoof

pianista [pja'nista] nmf pianist

piano ['pjano] nm piano

piar [pjar] vi to cheep

pibe, -a ['piβe, a] (RPl) nm/f boy/girl

picadero [pika'ðero] nm riding school

picadillo [pika'ðiʎo] nm mince, minced meat

picado, -a [pi'kaðo, a] adj pricked, punctured; (CULIN) minced, chopped; (mar) choppy; (diente) bad; (tabaco) cut; (enfadado) cross

picador [pika'ðor] nm (TAUR) picador; (minero) faceworker

picadura [pika'ðura] nf (pinchazo) puncture; (de abeja) sting; (de mosquito) bite; (tabaco picado) cut tobacco

picante [pi'kante] adj hot; (comentario) racy, spicy

picaporte [pika'porte] nm (manija) doorhandle; (pestillo) latch

picar [pi'kar] vt (agujerear, perforar) to prick, puncture; (abeja) to sting; (mosquito, serpiente) to bite; (CULIN) to mince, chop; (incitar) to incite, goad; (dañar, irritar) to annoy, bother; (quemar: lengua) to burn, sting ♦ vi (pez) to bite, take the bait; (sol) to burn, scorch; (abeja, MED) to sting; (mosquito) to bite; **picarse** vr (agriarse) to turn sour, go off; (ofenderse) to take offence

picardía [pikar'ðia] nf villainy; (astucia) slyness, craftiness; (una picardía) dirty trick; (palabra) rude/bad word o expression

pícaro, -a ['pikaro, a] adj (malicioso) villainous; (travieso) mischievous ♦ nm (astuto) crafty sort; (sinvergüenza) rascal, scoundrel

pichi (ESP) nm pinafore dress (BRIT), jumper (US)

pichón [pi'tʃon] nm young pigeon

pico ['piko] nm (de ave) beak; (punta) sharp point; (TEC) pick, pickaxe; (GEO) peak, summit; **y ~** and a bit; **las seis y ~** six and a bit

picor [pi'kor] nm itch

picoso, -a (MÉX) [pi'koso, a] adj (comida) hot

picudo, -a [pi'kuðo, a] adj pointed, with a point

pidió etc vb ver **pedir**

pido etc vb ver **pedir**

pie [pje] (pl **pies**) nm foot; (fig: motivo) motive, basis; (: fundamento) foothold; **ir a ~** to go on foot, walk; **estar de ~** to be standing (up); **ponerse de ~** to stand up; **de pies a cabeza** from top to bottom; **al ~ de la letra** (citar) literally, verbatim; (copiar) exactly, word for word; **en ~ de guerra** on a war footing; **dar ~ a** to give cause for; **hacer ~** (en el agua) to touch (the) bottom

piedad [pje'ðað] nf (lástima) pity, compassion; (clemencia) mercy; (devoción) piety, devotion

piedra ['pjeðra] nf stone; (roca) rock; (de mechero) flint; (METEOROLOGÍA) hailstone ▶ **piedra preciosa** precious stone

piel [pjel] nf (ANAT) skin; (ZOOL) skin, hide, fur; (cuero) leather; (BOT) skin, peel

pienso etc [pi'penso] vb ver **pensar**

pierdo etc vb ver **perder**

pierna ['pjerna] nf leg

pieza ['pjeθa] nf piece; (habitación) room ▶ **pieza de recambio** o **repuesto** spare (part)

pigmeo, -a [piɣ'meo, a] adj, nm/f pigmy

pijama [pi'xama] nm pyjamas pl (BRIT), pajamas pl (US)

pila ['pila] nf (ELEC) battery; (montón) heap, pile; (lavabo) sink

píldora ['pildora] nf pill; **la ~ (anticonceptiva)** the (contraceptive) pill

pileta [pi'leta] (RPl) nf (fregadero) (kitchen) sink; (piscina) swimming pool

pillar [pi'ʎar] vt (saquear) to pillage, plunder; (fam: coger) to catch; (: agarrar) to grasp, seize; (: entender) to grasp, catch on to; **pillarse** vr: **pillarse un dedo con la puerta** to catch one's finger in the door

pillo, -a ['piʎo, a] adj villainous; (astuto) sly, crafty ♦ nm/f rascal, rogue, scoundrel

piloto [pi'loto] nm pilot; (de aparato) (pilot) light; (AUTO: luz) tail o rear light; (: conductor) driver ▶ **piloto automático** automatic pilot

pimentón [pimen'ton] nm paprika

pimienta [pi'mjenta] nf pepper

pimiento [pi'mjento] nm pepper, pimiento

pin [pin] (pl **pins**) nm badge

pinacoteca [pinako'teka] nf art gallery

pinar [pi'nar] nm pine forest (BRIT), pine grove (US)

pincel [pin'θel] nm paintbrush

pinchadiscos [pintʃa'ðiskos] (ESP) nmf inv disc-jockey, DJ

pinchar [pin'tʃar] vt (perforar) to prick, pierce; (neumático) to puncture; (fig) to prod; (INFORM) to click

pinchazo [pin'tʃaθo] nm (perforación) prick; (de neumático) puncture; (fig) prod

pincho ['pintʃo] nm savoury (snack) ▶ **pincho de tortilla** small slice of omelette ▶ **pincho moruno** shish kebab

ping-pong ['pin'pon] nm table tennis

pingüino [pin'gwino] nm penguin

pino ['pino] nm pine (tree)

pinta ['pinta] nf spot; (de líquidos) spot, drop; (aspecto) appearance, look(s) (pl) ❑ **pintado, -a** adj spotted; (de colores) colourful; **pintadas** nfpl graffiti sg

pintalabios (ESP) nm inv lipstick

pintar [pin'tar] vt to paint ♦ vi to paint; (fam) to count, be important; **pintarse** vr to put on make-up

pintor, a [pin'tor, a] nm/f painter

pintoresco, -a [pinto'resko, a] adj picturesque

pintura [pin'tura] nf painting ▶ **pintura al óleo** oil painting

pinza [pinθa] nf (ZOOL) claw; (para colgar ropa) clothes peg; (TEC) pincers pl; **pinzas** nfpl (para depilar etc) tweezers pl

piña ['pina] nf (de pino) pine cone; (fruta) pineapple; (fig) group

piñata nf container hung up at parties to be beaten with sticks until sweets or presents fall out

piñón [pi'non] nm (fruto) pine nut; (TEC) pinion

pío, -a ['pio, a] adj (devoto) pious, devout; (misericordioso) merciful

piojo ['pjoxo] nm louse

pipa ['pipa] nf pipe; **pipas** nfpl (BOT) (edible) sunflower seeds

pipí [pi'pi] (fam) nm: **hacer pipí** to have a wee(-wee) (BRIT), to go (wee-wee) (US)

pique ['pike] nm (resentimiento) pique, resentment; (rivalidad) rivalry, competition; **irse a ~** to sink; (esperanza, familia) to be ruined

piqueta [pi'keta] nf pick(axe)

piquete [pi'kete] nm (MIL) squad, party; (de obreros) picket; (MÉX: de insecto) bite ❑ **piquetear** (LAm) vt to picket

pirado, -a [pi'raðo, a] (fam) adj round the bend ♦ nm/f nutter

piragua [pi'raɣwa] nf canoe ❑ **piragüismo** nm canoeing

pirámide [pi'ramiðe] nf pyramid

pirata [pi'rata] adj, nmf pirate ▶ **pirata informático** hacker

Pirineo(s) [piri'neo(s)] nm(pl) Pyrenees pl

pirómano, -a [pi'romano, a] nm/f (MED, JUR) arsonist

piropo [pi'ropo] nm compliment, (piece of) flattery

pirueta [pi'rweta] nf pirouette

piruleta (*ESP*) *nf* lollipop

pis [pis] (*fam*) *nm* pee, piss; **hacer ~** to have a pee; (*para niños*) to wee-wee

pisada [pi'saða] *nf* (*paso*) footstep; (*huella*) footprint

pisar [pi'sar] *vt* (*caminar sobre*) to walk on, tread on; (*apretar con el pie*) to press; (*fig*) to trample on, walk all over ♦ *vi* to tread, step, walk

piscina [pis'θina] *nf* swimming pool

Piscis ['pisθis] *nm* Pisces

piso ['piso] *nm* (*suelo, planta*) floor; (*ESP: apartamento*) flat (*BRIT*), apartment; **primer ~** (*ESP*) first floor; (: *LAm: planta baja*) ground floor

pisotear [pisote'ar] *vt* to trample (on o underfoot)

pista ['pista] *nf* track, trail; (*indicio*) clue ▶ **pista de aterrizaje** runway ▶ **pista de baile** dance floor ▶ **pista de hielo** ice rink ▶ **pista de tenis** (*ESP*) tennis court

pistola [pis'tola] *nf* pistol; (*TEC*) spray-gun

pistón [pis'ton] *nm* (*TEC*) piston; (*MÚS*) key

pitar [pi'tar] *vt* (*silbato*) to blow; (*rechiflar*) to whistle at, boo ♦ *vi* to whistle; (*AUTO*) to sound o toot one's horn; (*LAm: fumar*) to smoke

pitillo [pi'tiʎo] *nm* cigarette

pito ['pito] *nm* whistle; (*de coche*) horn

pitón [pi'ton] *nm* (*ZOOL*) python

pitonisa [pito'nisa] *nf* fortune-teller

pitorreo [pito'rreo] *nm* joke; **estar de ~** to be joking

piyama (*LAm*) ['pi'jama] *nm* pyjamas *pl* (*BRIT*), pajamas (*US*)

pizarra [pi'θarra] *nf* (*piedra*) slate; (*ESP: encerado*) blackboard

pizarrón (*LAm*) *nm* blackboard

pizca ['piθka] *nf* pinch, spot; (*fig*) spot, speck; **ni ~** not a bit

placa ['plaka] *nf* plate; (*distintivo*) badge, insignia ▶ **placa de matrícula** (*LAm*) number plate

placard (*RPl*) [pla'kar] *nm* cupboard

placer [pla'θer] *nm* pleasure ♦ *vt* to please

plaga ['plaɣa] *nf* pest; (*MED*) plague; (*abundancia*) abundance

plagio ['plaxjo] *nm* plagiarism

plan [plan] *nm* (*esquema, proyecto*) plan; (*idea, intento*) idea, intention; **tener ~** (*fam*) to have a date; **tener un ~** (*fam*) to have an affair; **en ~ económico** (*fam*) on the cheap; **vamos en ~ de turismo** we're going as tourists; **si te pones en ese ~ ...** if that's your attitude ...

plana ['plana] *nf* sheet (of paper), page; (*TEC*) trowel; **en primera ~** on the front page

plancha ['plantʃa] *nf* (*para planchar*) iron; (*rótulo*) plate, sheet; (*NÁUT*) gangway; **a la ~** (*CULIN*) grilled ❑ **planchar** *vt* to iron ♦ *vi* to do the ironing

planear [plane'ar] *vt* to plan ♦ *vi* to glide

planeta [pla'neta] *nm* planet

plano, -a ['plano, a] *adj* flat, level, even ♦ *nm* (*MAT, TEC*) plane; (*FOTO*) shot; (*ARQ*) plan; (*GEO*) map; (*de ciudad*) map, street plan; **primer ~** close-up

planta ['planta] *nf* (*BOT, TEC*) plant; (*ANAT*) sole of the foot, bottom; (*piso*) floor; (*LAm: personal*) staff ▶ **planta baja** ground floor

plantar [plan'tar] *vt* (*BOT*) to plant; (*levantar*) to erect, set up; **plantarse** *vr* to stand firm; **~ a algn en la calle** to throw sb out; **dejar plantado a algn** (*fam*) to stand sb up

plantear [plante'ar] *vt* (*problema*) to pose; (*dificultad*) to raise

plantilla [plan'tiʎa] *nf* (*de zapato*) insole; (*ESP: personal*) personnel; **ser de ~** (*ESP*) to be on the staff

plantón [plan'ton] *nm* (*MIL*) guard, sentry; (*fam*) long wait; **dar (un) ~ a algn** to stand sb up

plasta ['plasta] (*ESP: fam*) *adj inv* boring
♦ *nmf* bore

plástico, -a ['plastiko, a] *adj* plastic
♦ *nm* plastic

Plastilina® [plasti'lina] *nf* Plasticine®

plata ['plata] *nf* (*metal*) silver; (*cosas hechas de plata*) silverware; (*CS: dinero*) cash, dough

plataforma [plata'forma] *nf* platform
▶ **plataforma de lanzamiento/ perforación** launch(ing) pad/drilling rig

plátano ['platano] *nm* (*fruta*) banana; (*árbol*) plane tree; banana tree

platea [pla'tea] *nf* (*TEATRO*) pit

plática ['platika] *nf* talk, chat
❏ **platicar** *vi* to talk, chat

platillo [pla'ti.ʎo] *nm* saucer; **platillos** *nmpl* (*MÚS*) cymbals ▶ **platillo volante** flying saucer

platino [pla'tino] *nm* platinum; **platinos** *nmpl* (*AUTO*) contact points

plato ['plato] *nm* plate, dish; (*parte de comida*) course; (*comida*) dish; **primer ~** first course ▶ **plato combinado** set main course (*served on one plate*)
▶ **plato fuerte** main course

playa ['plaja] *nf* beach; (*costa*) seaside ▶ **playa de estacionamiento** (*CS*) car park (*BRIT*), parking lot (*US*)

playera [pla'jera] *nf* (*MÉX: camiseta*) T-shirt; **playeras** *nfpl* (*zapatos*) canvas shoes

plaza ['plaθa] *nf* square; (*mercado*) market(place); (*sitio*) room, space; (*de vehículo*) seat, place; (*colocación*) job ▶ **plaza de toros** bullring

plazo ['plaθo] *nm* (*lapso de tiempo*) time, period; (*fecha de vencimiento*) expiry date; (*pago parcial*) instalment; **a corto/largo ~** short-/long-term; **comprar algo a plazos** to buy sth on hire purchase (*BRIT*) o on time (*US*)

plazoleta [plaθo'leta] *nf* small square

plebeyo, -a [ple'βejo, a] *adj* plebeian; (*pey*) coarse, common

plegable [ple'ɣaβle] *adj* collapsible; (*silla*) folding

pleito ['pleito] (*JUR*) *nm* lawsuit, case; (*fig*) dispute, feud

plenitud [pleni'tuð] *nf* plenitude, fullness; (*abundancia*) abundance

pleno, -a ['pleno, a] *adj* full; (*completo*) complete ♦ *nm* plenum; **en ~ día** in broad daylight; **en ~ verano** at the height of summer; **en plena cara** full in the face

pliego *etc* ['pljeɣo] *vb ver* **plegar** ♦ *nm* (*hoja*) sheet (of paper); (*carta*) sealed letter/document ▶ **pliego de condiciones** details *pl*, specifications *pl*

pliegue *etc* ['pljeɣe] *vb ver* **plegar** ♦ *nm* fold, crease; (*de vestido*) pleat

plomería (*LAm*) *nf* plumbing
❏ **plomero** [plo'mero] (*LAm*) *nm* plumber

plomo ['plomo] *nm* (*metal*) lead; (*ELEC*) fuse; **sin ~** unleaded

pluma ['pluma] *nf* feather; (*para escribir*): **~ (estilográfica)** jnk pen; **~ fuente** (*LAm*) fountain pen

plumero [plu'mero] *nm* (*para el polvo*) feather duster

plumón [plu'mon] *nm* (*de ave*) down

plural [plu'ral] *adj* plural

pluriempleo [pluriem'pleo] *nm* having more than one job

plus [plus] *nm* bonus

población [poβla'θjon] *nf* population; (*pueblo, ciudad*) town, city

poblado, -a [po'blaðo, a] *adj* inhabited ♦ *nm* (*aldea*) village; (*pueblo*) (small) town; **densamente ~** densely populated

poblador, a [poβla'ðor, a] *nm/f* settler, colonist

pobre ['poβre] *adj* poor ♦ *nmf* poor person ❏ **pobreza** *nf* poverty

pocilga [po'θilɣa] *nf* pigsty

poco, -a

PALABRA CLAVE

['poko, a] *adj*

1 (*sg*) little, not much; **poco tiempo** little o not much time; **de poco interés** of little interest, not very interesting; **poca cosa** not much

2 (*pl*) few, not many; **unos pocos** a few, some; **pocos niños comen lo que les conviene** few children eat what they should

♦ *adv*

1 little, not much; **cuesta poco** it doesn't cost much

2 (+ *adj: negativo, antónimo*): **poco amable/inteligente** not very nice/ intelligent

3 **por poco me caigo** I almost fell

4 **a poco: a poco de haberse casado** shortly after getting married

5 **poco a poco** little by little

♦ *nm* a little, a bit; **un poco triste/de dinero** a little sad/money

podar [po'ðar] *vt* to prune

poder

PALABRA CLAVE

[po'ðer] *vi*

1 (*tener capacidad*) can, be able to; **no puedo hacerlo** I can't do it, I'm unable to do it

2 (*tener permiso*) can, may, be allowed to; **¿se puede?** may I (o we)?; **puedes irte ahora** you may go now; **no se puede fumar en este hospital** smoking is not allowed in this hospital

3 (*tener posibilidad*) may, might, could; **puede llegar mañana** he may o might arrive tomorrow; **pudiste haberte hecho daño** you might o could have hurt yourself; **¡podías**

habérmelo dicho antes!** you might have told me before!

4: **puede ser: puede ser** perhaps; **puede ser que lo sepa Tomás** Tomás may o might know

5: **¡no puedo más!** I've had enough!; **es tonto a más no poder** he's as stupid as they come

6: **poder con: no puedo con este crío** this kid's too much for me

♦ *nm* power; **detentar** o **ocupar** o **estar en el poder** to be in power

▶ **poder adquisitivo/ejecutivo/ legislativo** purchasing/executive/ legislative power ▶ **poder judicial** judiciary

poderoso, -a [poðe'roso, a] *adj* (*político, país*) powerful

podio ['poðjo] *nm* (*DEPORTE*) podium

podium ['poðjum] = **podio**

podrido, -a [po'ðriðo, a] *adj* rotten, bad; (*fig*) rotten, corrupt

podrir [po'ðrir] = **pudrir**

poema [po'ema] *nm* poem

poesía [poe'sia] *nf* poetry

poeta [po'eta] *nmf* poet ❑ **poético, -a** *adj* poetic(al)

poetisa [poe'tisa] *nf* (woman) poet

póker ['poker] *nm* poker

polaco, -a [po'lako, a] *adj* Polish ♦ *nm/ f,* Pole

polar [po'lar] *adj* polar

polea [po'lea] *nf* pulley

polémica [po'lemika] *nf* polemics *sg*; (*una polémica*) controversy, polemic

polen ['polen] *nm* pollen

policía [poli'θia] *nmf* policeman/ woman ♦ *nf* police ❑ **policíaco, -a** *adj* police *cpd*; **novela policíaca** detective story ❑ **policial** *adj* police *cpd*

polideportivo [poliðepor'tiβo] *nm* sports centre o complex

polígono [po'liɣono] nm (MAT)
polygon ▶ **polígono industrial** (ESP)
industrial estate

polilla [po'liʎa] nf moth

polio ['poljo] nf polio

política [po'litika] nf politics sg;
(económica, agraria etc) policy; ver tb
político

político, -a [po'litiko, a] adj political;
(discreto) tactful; (de familia) -in-law
♦ nm/f politician; **padre ~** father-in-law

póliza [po'liθa] nf certificate, voucher;
(impuesto) tax stamp ▶ **póliza de
seguro(s)** insurance policy

polizón [poli'θon] nm stowaway

pollera [po'ʎera] nf (CS) nf skirt

pollo ['poʎo] nm chicken

polo ['polo] nm (GEO, ELEC) pole;
(helado) ice lolly (BRIT), Popsicle® (US);
(DEPORTE) polo; (suéter) polo-neck
▶ **polo Norte/Sur** North/South Pole

Polonia [po'lonja] nf Poland

poltrona [pol'trona] nf easy chair

polución [polu'θjon] nf pollution

polvera [pol'βera] nf powder compact

polvo [polβo] nm dust; (QUÍM, CULIN,
MED) powder; **polvos** nmpl (maquillaje)
powder sg; **en ~** powdered; **quitar el ~**
to dust; **estar hecho ~** (fam) to be worn
out o exhausted ▶ **polvos de talco**
talcum powder sg

pólvora [polβora] nf gunpowder

polvoriento, -a [polβo'rjento, a] adj
(superficie) dusty; (sustancia) powdery

pomada [po'maða] nf cream, ointment

pomelo [po'melo] nm grapefruit

pómez [pomeθ] nf: **piedra ~** pumice
stone

pomo ['pomo] nm doorknob

pompa [pompa] nf (burbuja) bubble;
(bomba) pump; (esplendor) pomp,
splendour

pómulo [pomulo] nm cheekbone

pon [pon] vb ver **poner**

ponchadura (MÉX) nf puncture (BRIT),
flat (US) ❏ **ponchar** (MÉX) vt (llanta) to
puncture

ponche ['pontʃe] nm punch

poncho ['pontʃo] nm poncho

pondré etc [pon'dre] vb ver **poner**

poner

PALABRA CLAVE

[po'ner] vt

1 (colocar) to put; (telegrama) to
send; (obra de teatro) to put on;
(película) to show; **ponlo más fuerte**
turn it up; **¿qué ponen en el
Excelsior?** what's on at the Excelsior?

2 (tienda) to open; (instalar: gas etc)
to put in; (radio, TV) to switch o turn
on

3 (suponer): **pongamos que ...** let's
suppose that ...

4 (contribuir): **el gobierno ha puesto
otro millón** the government has
contributed another million

5 (TEL): **póngame con el Sr. López**
can you put me through to Mr.
López?

6: **poner de: le han puesto de
director general** they've appointed
him general manager

7 (+ adj): to make; **me estás
poniendo nerviosa** you're making
me nervous

8 (dar nombre): **al hijo le pusieron
Diego** they called their son Diego
♦ vi (gallina) to lay

ponerse vr

1 (colocarse): **se puso a mi lado** he
came and stood beside me; **tú ponte
en esa silla** you go and sit on that
chair

2 (vestido, cosméticos) to put on; **¿por
qué no te pones el vestido nuevo?**
why don't you put on o wear your

new dress?

3 + adj, to turn; to get, become; **se puso muy serio** he got very serious; **después de lavarla la tela se puso azul** after washing it the material turned blue

4: **ponerse a**: **se puso a llorar** he started to cry; **tienes que ponerte a estudiar** you must get down to studying

pongo etc ['pongo] vb ver **poner**

poniente [po'njente] nm (occidente) west; (viento) west wind

pontífice [pon'tifiθe] nm pope, pontiff

popa ['popa] nf stern

popote (MÉX) nm straw

popular [popu'lar] adj popular; (cultura) of the people, folk cpd ▫ **popularidad** nf popularity

por

[por] prep

1 (objetivo) for; **luchar por la patria** to fight for one's country

2 (+ infin): **por no llegar tarde** so as not to arrive late; **por citar unos ejemplos** to give a few examples

3 (causa) out of, because of; **por escasez de fondos** through o for lack of funds

4 (tiempo): **por la mañana/noche** in the morning/at night; **se queda por una semana** she's staying (for) a week

5 (lugar): **pasar por Madrid** to pass through Madrid; **ir a Guayaquil por Quito** to go to Guayaquil via Quito; **caminar por la calle** to walk along the street; ver tb **todo**

6 (cambio, precio): **te doy uno nuevo por el que tienes** I'll give you a new one (in return) for the one you've got

7 (valor distributivo): **6 euros por hora/cabeza** 6 euros an o per hour/a o per head

8 (modo, medio) by; **por correo/ avión** by post/air; **entrar por la entrada principal** to go in through the main entrance

9: **10 por 10 son 100** 10 times 10 is 100

10 (en lugar de): **vino él por su jefe** he came instead of his boss

11: **por mí que revienten** as far as I'm concerned they can drop dead

12: **¿por qué?** why?; **¿por qué no?** why not?

porcelana [porθe'lana] nf porcelain; (china) china

porcentaje [porθen'taxe] nm percentage

porción [por'θjon] nf (parte) portion, share; (cantidad) quantity, amount

porfiar [por'fjar] vi to persist, insist; (disputar) to argue stubbornly

pormenor [porme'nor] nm detail, particular

pornografía [pornoɣra'fia] nf pornography

poro ['poro] nm pore

pororó (RPl) nm popcorn

poroso, -a [po'roso, a] adj porous

poroto (CS) [po'roto] nm bean

porque ['porke] conj (a causa de) because; (ya que) since; (con el fin de) so that, in order that

porqué [por'ke] nm reason, cause

porquería [porke'ria] nf (suciedad) filth, dirt; (acción) dirty trick; (objeto) small thing, trifle; (fig) rubbish

porra ['porra] (ESP) nf (arma) stick, club

porrazo [po'rraθo] nm blow, bump

porro ['porro] (fam) nm (droga) joint (fam)

porrón [po'rron] nm glass wine jar with a long spout

portaaviones [porta(a)βjones] nm inv aircraft carrier

portada [por'taða] nf (de revista) cover

portador, a [porta'ðor, a] nm/f carrier, bearer; (COM) bearer, payee

portaequipajes [portaeki'paxes] nm inv (AUTO: maletero) boot; (: baca) luggage rack

portafolio (LAm) [porta'foljo] nm briefcase

portal [por'tal] nm (entrada) vestibule, hall; (portada) porch, doorway; (puerta de entrada) main door; (INTERNET) portal; **portales** nmpl (LAm) arcade sg

portamaletas [portama'letas] nm inv (AUTO: maletero) boot; (: baca) roof rack

portarse [por'tarse] vr to behave, conduct o.s.

portátil [por'tatil] adj portable

portavoz [porta'βoθ] nmf spokesman/ woman

portazo [por'taθo] nm: **dar un ~** to slam the door

porte ['porte] nm (COM) transport; (precio) transport charges pl

portentoso, -a [porten'toso, a] adj marvellous, extraordinary

porteño, -a [por'teno, a] adj of o from Buenos Aires

portería [porte'ria] nf (oficina) porter's office; (DEPORTE) goal

portero, -a [por'tero, a] nm/f porter; (conserje) caretaker; (ujier) doorman; (DEPORTE) goalkeeper ▶ **portero automático** (ESP) entry phone

pórtico ['portiko] nm (patio) portico, porch; (fig) gateway; (arcada) arcade

portorriqueño, -a [portorri'keno, a] adj Puerto Rican

Portugal [portu'yal] nm Portugal
❏ **portugués, -esa** adj nm/f Portuguese ♦ nm (LING) Portuguese

porvenir [porβe'nir] nm future

pos [pos] prep: **en ~ de** after, in pursuit of

posaderas [posa'ðeras] nfpl backside sg, buttocks

posar [po'sar] vt (en el suelo) to lay down, put down; (la mano) to place, put gently ♦ vi (modelo) to sit, pose; **posarse** vr to settle; (pájaro) to perch; (avión) to land, come down

posavasos [posa'basos] nm inv coaster; (para cerveza) beermat

posdata [pos'ðata] nf postscript

pose ['pose] nf pose

poseedor, a [posee'ðor, a] nm/f owner, possessor; (de récord, puesto) holder

poseer [pose'er] vt to possess, own; (ventaja) to enjoy; (récord, puesto) to hold

posesivo, -a [pose'siβo, a] adj possessive

posibilidad [posiβili'ðað] nf possibility; (oportunidad) chance
❏ **posibilitar** vt to make possible; (hacer realizable) to make feasible

posible [po'siβle] adj possible; (realizable) feasible; **de ser ~** if possible; **en lo ~** as far as possible

posición [posi'θjon] nf position; (rango social) status

positivo, -a [posi'tiβo, a] adj positive

poso ['poso] nm sediment; (heces) dregs pl

posponer [pospo'ner] vt (relegar) to put behind/below; (aplazar) to postpone

posta ['posta] nf: **a ~** deliberately, on purpose

postal [pos'tal] adj postal ♦ nf postcard

poste ['poste] nm (de telégrafos etc) post, pole; (columna) pillar

póster ['poster] (pl **pósteres, pósters**) nm poster

posterior [poste'rjor] adj back, rear; (siguiente) following, subsequent; (más tarde) later

postgrado [post'graðo] nm = **posgrado**

postizo, -a [pos'tiθo, a] adj false, artificial ♦ nm hairpiece

postre ['postre] nm sweet, dessert

póstumo, -a ['postumo, a] adj posthumous

postura [pos'tura] nf (del cuerpo) posture, position; (fig) attitude, position

potable [po'taβle] adj drinkable; **agua ~** drinking water

potaje [po'taxe] nm thick vegetable soup

potencia [po'tenθja] nf power ❑ **potencial** [poten'θjal] adj, nm potential

potente [po'tente] adj powerful

potro, -a ['potro, a] nm/f (ZOOL) colt/ filly ♦ nm (de gimnasia) vaulting horse

pozo [po'θo] nm well; (de río) deep pool; (de mina) shaft

PP (ESP) nm abr = **Partido Popular**

práctica ['praktika] nf practice; (método) method; (arte, capacidad) skill; **en la ~** in practice

practicable [prakti'kaβle] adj practicable; (camino) passable

practicante [prakti'kante] nmf (MED: ayudante de doctor) medical assistant; (: enfermero) nurse; (quien practica algo) practitioner ♦ adj practising

practicar [prakti'kar] vt to practise; (DEPORTE) to play; (realizar) to carry out, perform

práctico, -a ['praktiko, a] adj practical; (instruido: persona) skilled, expert

practique etc [prak'tike] vb ver **practicar**

pradera [pra'ðera] nf meadow; (US etc) prairie

prado ['praðo] nm (campo) meadow, field; (pastizal) pasture

Praga ['praɣa] n Prague

pragmático, -a [praɣ'matiko, a] adj pragmatic

precario, -a [pre'karjo, a] adj precarious

precaución [prekau'θjon] nf (medida preventiva) preventive measure, precaution; (prudencia) caution, wariness

precedente [preθe'ðente] adj preceding; (anterior) former ♦ nm precedent

preceder [preθe'ðer] vt, vi to precede, go before, come before

precepto [pre'θepto] nm precept

precinto [pre'θinto] nm (tb: ~ **de garantía**) seal

precio [pre'θjo] nm price; (costo) cost; (valor) value, worth; (de viaje) fare
  ► **precio al contado/de coste/de oportunidad** cash/cost/bargain price
  ► **precio al por menor** retail price
  ► **precio de ocasión** bargain price
  ► **precio de venta al público** retail price ► **precio tope** top price

preciosidad [preθjosi'ðað] nf (valor) (high) value, (great) worth; (encanto) charm; (cosa bonita) beautiful thing; **es una ~** it's lovely, it's really beautiful

precioso, -a [pre'θjoso, a] adj precious; (de mucho valor) valuable; (fam) lovely, beautiful

precipicio [preθi'piθjo] nm cliff, precipice; (fig) abyss

precipitación [preθipita'θjon] nf haste; (lluvia) rainfall

precipitado, -a [preθipi'taðo, a] adj (conducta) hasty, rash; (salida) hasty, sudden

precipitar [preθipi'tar] vt (arrojar) to hurl down, throw; (apresurar) to hasten; (acelerar) to speed up, accelerate; **precipitarse** vr to throw o.s.; (apresurarse) to rush; (actuar sin pensar) to act rashly

precisamente [preθisa'mente] adv precisely; (exactamente) precisely, exactly

precisar [preθi'sar] vt (necesitar) to need, require; (fijar) to determine exactly, fix; (especificar) to specify

precisión [preθi'sjon] nf (exactitud) precision

preciso, -a [pre'θiso, a] adj (exacto) precise; (necesario) necessary, essential

preconcebido, -a [prekonθe'βiðo, a] adj preconceived

precoz [pre'koθ] adj (persona) precocious; (calvicie etc) premature

predecir [preðe'θir] vt to predict, forecast

predestinado, -a [preðesti'naðo, a] adj predestined

predicar [preði'kar] vt, vi to preach

predicción [preðik'θjon] nf prediction

predilecto, -a [preði'lekto, a] adj favourite

predisposición [preðisposi'θjon] nf inclination; prejudice, bias

predominar [preðomi'nar] vt to dominate ♦ vi to predominate; (prevalecer) to prevail ❑ **predominio** nm predominance; prevalence

preescolar [pre(e)sko'lar] adj preschool

prefabricado, -a [prefaβri'kaðo, a] adj prefabricated

prefacio [pre'faθjo] nm preface

preferencia [prefe'renθja] nf preference; **de ~** preferably, for preference

preferible [prefe'riβle] adj preferable

preferir [prefe'rir] vt to prefer

prefiero etc vb ver **preferir**

prefijo [pre'fixo] nm (TEL) (dialling) code

pregunta [pre'ɣunta] nf question; **hacer una ~** to ask a question ▶ **preguntas frecuentes** FAQs, frequently asked questions ❑ **preguntar** [preɣun'tar] vt to ask; (cuestionar) to question ♦ vi to ask; **preguntarse** vr to wonder; **preguntar**

por algn to ask for sb ❑ **preguntón, -ona** [preɣun'ton, ona] adj inquisitive

prehistórico, -a [preis'toriko, a] adj prehistoric

prejuicio [pre'xwiθjo] nm (acto) prejudgment; (idea preconcebida) preconception; (parcialidad) prejudice, bias

preludio [pre'luðjo] nm prelude

prematuro, -a [prema'turo, a] adj premature

premeditar [premeði'tar] vt to premeditate

premiar [pre'mjar] vt to reward; (en un concurso) to give a prize to

premio ['premjo] nm reward; prize; (COM) premium

prenatal [prena'tal] adj antenatal, prenatal

prenda ['prenda] nf (ropa) garment, article of clothing; (garantía) pledge; **prendas** nfpl (talentos) talents, gifts

prender [pren'der] vt (captar) to catch, capture; (detener) to arrest; (COSTURA) to pin, attach; (sujetar) to fasten ♦ vi to catch; (arraigar) to take root; **prenderse** vr (encenderse) to catch fire

prendido, -a [pren'diðo, a] (LAm) adj (luz etc) on

prensa ['prensa] nf press; **la ~** the press

preñado, -a [pre'ɲaðo, a] adj pregnant; **~ de** pregnant with, full of

preocupación [preokupa'θjon] nf worry, concern; (ansiedad) anxiety

preocupado, -a [preoku'paðo, a] adj worried, concerned; (ansioso) anxious

preocupar [preoku'par] vt to worry; **preocuparse** vr to worry; **preocuparse de algo** (hacerse cargo) to take care of sth

preparación [prepara'θjon] nf (acto) preparation; (estado) readiness; (entrenamiento) training

preparado, -a [prepa'raðo, a] adj (dispuesto) prepared; (CULIN) ready (to serve) ♦ nm preparation

preparar [prepa'rar] vt (disponer) to prepare, get ready; (TEC: tratar) to prepare, process; (entrenar) to teach, train; **prepararse** vr: **prepararse o para** to prepare to o for, get ready to o for □ **preparativo, -a** adj preparatory, preliminary □ **preparativos** nmpl preparations □ **preparatoria** (MÉX) nf sixth-form college (BRIT), senior high school (US)

presa ['presa] nf (cosa apresada) catch; (víctima) victim; (de animal) prey; (de agua) dam

presagiar [presa'xjar] vt to presage, forebode □ **presagio** nm omen

prescindir [presθin'dir] vi: ~ **de** (privarse de) to do o go without; (descartar) to dispense with

prescribir [preskri'βir] vt to prescribe

presencia [pre'senθja] nf presence □ **presenciar** vt to be present at; (asistir a) to attend; (ver) to see, witness

presentación [presenta'θjon] nf presentation; (introducción) introduction

presentador, a [presenta'ðor, a] nm/f presenter, compère

presentar [presen'tar] vt to present; (ofrecer) to offer; (mostrar) to show, display; (a una persona) to introduce; **presentarse** vr (llegar inesperadamente) to appear, turn up; (ofrecerse: como candidato) to run, stand; (aparecer) to show, appear; (solicitar empleo) to apply

presente [pre'sente] adj present ♦ nm present; **hacer** ~ to state, declare; **tener** ~ to remember, bear in mind

presentimiento [presenti'mjento] nm premonition, presentiment

presentir [presen'tir] vt to have a premonition of

preservación [preserβa'θjon] nf protection, preservation

preservar [preser'βar] vt to protect, preserve □ **preservativo** nm sheath, condom

presidencia [presi'ðenθja] nf presidency; (de comité) chairmanship

presidente [presi'ðente] nmf president; (de comité) chairman/ woman

presidir [presi'ðir] vt (dirigir) to preside at, preside over; (: comité) to take the chair at; (dominar) to dominate, rule ♦ vi to preside; to take the chair

presión [pre'sjon] nf pressure ▶ **presión atmosférica** atmospheric o air pressure □ **presionar** vt to press; (fig) to press, put pressure on ♦ vi: **presionar para** to press for

preso, -a ['preso, a] nm/f prisoner; **tomar** o **llevar** a **algn** to arrest sb, take sb prisoner

prestación [presta'θjon] nf service; (subsidio) benefit □ **prestaciones** nfpl (TEC, AUTO) performance features

prestado, -a [pres'taðo, a] adj on loan; **pedir** ~ to borrow

prestamista [presta'mista] nmf moneylender

préstamo ['prestamo] nm loan ▶ **préstamo hipotecario** mortgage

prestar [pres'tar] vt to lend, loan; (atención) to pay; (ayuda) to give

prestigio [pres'tixjo] nm prestige □ **prestigioso, -a** adj (honorable) prestigious; (famoso, renombrado) renowned, famous

presumido, -a [presu'miðo, a] adj (persona) vain

presumir [presu'mir] vt to presume ♦ vi (tener aires) to be conceited □ **presunto, -a** adj (supuesto) supposed, presumed; (así llamado) so-called □ **presuntuoso, -a** adj conceited, presumptuous

presupuesto [presu'pwesto] pp de **presuponer** ♦ nm (FINANZAS) budget; (estimación: de costo) estimate

pretencioso, -a [preten'θjoso, a] adj pretentious

pretender [preten'der] vt (intentar) to try to, seek to; (reivindicar) to claim; (buscar) to seek, try for; (cortejar) to woo, court; **~ que** to expect that □ **pretendiente** nmf (amante) suitor; (al trono) pretender □ **pretensión** nf (aspiración) aspiration; (reivindicación) claim; (orgullo) pretension

⚠ No confundir **pretender** con la palabra inglesa pretend.

pretexto [pre'teksto] nm pretext; (excusa) excuse

prevención [preßen'θjon] nf prevention; (precaución) precaution

prevenido, -a [preße'niðo, a] adj prepared, ready; (cauteloso) cautious

prevenir [preße'nir] vt (impedir) to prevent; (predisponer) to prejudice, bias; (avisar) to warn; (preparar) to prepare, get ready; **prevenirse** vr to get ready, prepare; **prevenirse contra** to take precautions against □ **preventivo, -a** adj preventive, precautionary

prever [pre'ßer] vt to foresee

previo, -a ['preßjo, a] adj (anterior) previous; (preliminar) preliminary
♦ prep: **~ acuerdo de los otros** subject to the agreement of the others

previsión [preßi'sjon] nf (perspicacia) foresight; (predicción) forecast □ **previsto, -a** adj anticipated, forecast

prima ['prima] nf (COM) bonus; (de seguro) premium; ver tb **primo**

primario, -a [pri'marjo, a] adj primary

primavera [prima'ßera] nf spring(-time)

primera [pri'mera] nf (AUTO) first gear; (FERRO: tb: ~ **clase**) first class; **de ~** (fam) first-class, first-rate

primero, -a [pri'mero, a] (delante de nmsg **primer**) adj first; (principal) prime

♦ adv first; (más bien) sooner, rather
▶ **primera plana** front page

primitivo, -a [primi'tißo, a] adj primitive; (original) original

primo, -a ['primo, a] adj prime ♦ nm/f cousin; (fam) fool, idiot; **materias primas** raw materials ▶ **primo hermano** first cousin

primogénito, -a [primo'xenito, a] adj first-born

primoroso, -a [primo'roso, a] adj exquisite, delicate

princesa [prin'θesa] nf princess

principal [prinθi'pal] adj principal, main ♦ nm (jefe) chief, principal

príncipe ['prinθipe] nm prince

principiante [prinθi'pjante] nmf beginner

principio [prin'θipjo] nm (comienzo) beginning, start; (origen) origin; (primera etapa) rudiment, basic idea; (moral) principle; **desde el ~** from the first; **en un ~** at first; **a principios de** at the beginning of

pringue ['pringe] nm (grasa) grease, fat, dripping

prioridad [priori'ðað] nf priority

prisa ['prisa] nf (apresuramiento) hurry, haste; (rapidez) speed; (urgencia) (sense of) urgency; **a o de ~** quickly; **correr ~** to be urgent; **darse ~** to hurry up; **tener ~** to be in a hurry

prisión [pri'sjon] nf (cárcel) prison; (período de cárcel) imprisonment □ **prisionero, -a** nm/f prisoner

prismáticos [pris'matikos] nmpl binoculars

privado, -a [pri'ßaðo, a] adj private

privar [pri'ßar] vt to deprive □ **privativo, -a** adj exclusive

privilegiar [prißile'xjar] vt to grant a privilege to; (favorecer) to favour

privilegio [prißi'lexjo] nm privilege; (concesión) concession

pro [pro] nm o f profit, advantage
♦ prep: **asociación ~ ciegos** association

for the blind ♦ *prefijo:* ~ **americano**
pro-American; **en ~ de** on behalf of,
for; **los pros y los contras** the pros and
cons

proa ['proa] *nf* bow, prow; **de ~** bow
cpd, fore

probabilidad [proβaβili'ðað] *nf*
probability, likelihood; (*oportunidad,
posibilidad*) chance, prospect
□ **probable** *adj* probable, likely

probador [proβa'ðor] *nm* (*en tienda*)
fitting room

probar [pro'βar] *vt* (*demostrar*) to
prove; (*someter a prueba*) to test, try
out; (*ropa*) to try on; (*comida*) to taste
♦ *vi* to try; **probarse un traje** to try on a
suit

probeta [pro'βeta] *nf* test tube

problema [pro'βlema] *nm* problem

procedente [proθe'ðente] *adj*
(*razonable*) reasonable; (*conforme a
derecho*) proper, fitting; ~ **de** coming
from, originating in

proceder [proθe'ðer] *vi* (*avanzar*) to
proceed; (*actuar*) to act; (*ser correcto*)
to be right (and proper), be fitting
♦ *nm* (*comportamiento*) behaviour,
conduct; ~ **de** to come from, originate
in □ **procedimiento** *nm* procedure;
(*proceso*) process; (*método*) means *pl*,
method

procesador [proθesa'ðor] *nm*
processor ▶ **procesador de textos**
word processor

procesar [proθe'sar] *vt* to try, put on
trial

procesión [proθe'sjon] *nf* procession

proceso [pro'θeso] *nm* process; (*JUR*)
trial

proclamar [prokla'mar] *vt* to proclaim

procrear [prokre'ar] *vt, vi* to procreate

procurador, a [prokura'ðor, a] *nm/f*
attorney

procurar [proku'rar] *vt* (*intentar*) to try,
endeavour; (*conseguir*) to get, obtain;

(*asegurar*) to secure; (*producir*) to
produce

prodigio [pro'ðixjo] *nm* prodigy;
(*milagro*) wonder, marvel
□ **prodigioso, -a** *adj* prodigious,
marvellous

pródigo, -a ['proðiɣo, a] *adj:* **hijo ~**
prodigal son

producción [proðuk'θjon] *nf* (*gen*)
production; (*producto*) output
▶ **producción en serie** mass
production

producir [proðu'θir] *vt* to produce;
(*causar*) to cause, bring about;
producirse *vr* (*cambio*) to come about;
(*accidente*) to take place; (*problema etc*)
to arise; (*hacerse*) to be produced, be
made; (*estallar*) to break out

productividad [proðuktiβi'ðað] *nf*
productivity □ **productivo, -a** *adj*
productive; (*provechoso*) profitable

producto [pro'ðukto] *nm* product

productor, a [proðuk'tor, a] *adj*
productive, producing ♦ *nm/f*
producer

proeza [pro'eθa] *nf* exploit, feat

profano, -a [pro'fano, a] *adj* profane
♦ *nm/f* layman/woman

profecía [profe'θia] *nf* prophecy

profesión [profe'sjon] *nf* profession;
(*en formulario*) occupation
□ **profesional** *adj* professional

profesor, a [profe'sor, a] *nm/f* teacher
□ **profesorado** *nm* teaching
profession

profeta [pro'feta] *nmf* prophet

prófugo, -a ['profuɣo, a] *nm/f* fugitive;
(*MIL: desertor*) deserter

profundidad [profundi'ðað] *nf* depth
□ **profundizar** *vi: profundizar en* to
go deeply into □ **profundo, -a** *adj*
deep; (*misterio, pensador*) profound

progenitor [proxeni'tor] *nm* ancestor;
progenitores *mpl* (*padres*) parents

programa [pro'ɣrama] *nm*
programme (*BRIT*), program (*US*)

▶ **programa de estudios**
curriculum, syllabus
❏ **programación** nf programming
❏ **programador, a** nm/f
programmer ❏ **programar** vt to
program

progresar [proɣre'sar] vi to progress,
make progress ❏ **progresista** adj,
nmf progressive ❏ **progresivo, -a** adj
progressive; (gradual) gradual;
(continuo) continuous ❏ **progreso**
nm progress

prohibición [proiβi'θjon] nf
prohibition, ban

prohibir [proi'βir] vt to prohibit, ban,
forbid; **prohibido o se prohibe fumar**
no smoking; **"prohibido el paso"** "no
entry"

prójimo, -a ['proximo, a] nm/f fellow
man; (vecino) neighbour

prólogo ['proloɣo] nm prologue

prolongar [prolon'ɣar] vt to extend;
(reunión etc) to prolong; (calle, tubo) to
extend

promedio [pro'meðjo] nm average;
(de distancia) middle, mid-point

promesa [pro'mesa] nf promise

prometer [prome'ter] vt to promise
♦ vi to show promise; **prometerse** vr
(novios) to get engaged
❏ **prometido, -a** adj promised;
engaged ♦ nm/f fiancé/fiancée

prominente [promi'nente] adj
prominent

promoción [promo'θjon] nf
promotion

promotor [promo'tor] nm promoter;
(instigador) instigator

promover [promo'βer] vt to promote;
(causar) to cause; (instigar) to instigate,
stir up

promulgar [promul'ɣar] vt to
promulgate; (anunciar) to proclaim

pronombre [pro'nombre] nm
pronoun

pronosticar [pronosti'kar] vt to
predict, foretell, forecast
❏ **pronóstico** nm prediction, forecast
▶ **pronóstico del tiempo** weather
forecast

pronto, -a ['pronto, a] adj (rápido)
prompt, quick; (preparado) ready ♦ adv
quickly, promptly; (en seguida) at once,
right away; (dentro de poco) soon;
(temprano) early ♦ nm: **tiene unos
prontos muy malos** he gets ratty all of
a sudden (inf); **de ~** suddenly; **por lo ~**
meanwhile, for the present

pronunciación [pronun'θjar] nf
pronunciation

pronunciar [pronun'θjar] vt to
pronounce; (discurso) to make, deliver;
pronunciarse vr to revolt, rebel;
(declararse) to declare o.s.

propagación [propaɣa'θjon] nf
propagation

propaganda [propa'ɣanda] nf (POL)
propaganda; (COM) advertising

propenso, -a [pro'penso, a] adj
inclined to; **ser ~ a** to be inclined to,
have a tendency to

propicio, -a [pro'piθjo, a] adj
favourable, propitious

propiedad [propje'ðað] nf property;
(posesión) possession, ownership
▶ **propiedad particular** private
property

propietario, -a [propje'tarjo, a] nm/f
owner, proprietor

propina [pro'pina] nf tip

propio, -a ['propjo, a] adj own, of one's
own; (característico) characteristic,
typical; (debido) proper; (mismo)
selfsame, very; **el ~ ministro** the
minister himself; **¿tienes casa propia?**
have you a house of your own?

proponer [propo'ner] vt to propose,
put forward; (problema) to pose;
proponerse vr to propose, intend

proporción [propor'θjon] nf
proportion; (MAT) ratio; **proporciones**

nfpl (dimensiones) dimensions; *(fig)* size
sg ❑ **proporcionado, -a** *adj*
proportionate; *(regular)* medium,
middling; *(justo)* just right
❑ **proporcionar** *vt (dar)* to give,
supply, provide

proposición [proposi'θjon] *nf*
proposition; *(propuesta)* proposal

propósito [pro'posito] *nm* purpose;
(intento) aim, intention ♦ *adv:* **a ~** by
the way, incidentally; *(a posta)* on
purpose, deliberately; **a ~ de** about,
with regard to

propuesta [pro'pwesta] *vb ver*
proponer ♦ *nf* proposal

propulsar [propul'sar] *vt* to drive,
propel; *(fig)* to promote, encourage
❑ **propulsión** *nf* propulsion
▶ **propulsión a chorro** *o* **por
reacción** jet propulsion

prórroga ['prorroɣa] *nf* extension; *(JUR)*
stay; *(COM)* deferment; *(DEPORTE)* extra
time ❑ **prorrogar** *vt (período)* to
extend; *(decisión)* to defer, postpone

prosa ['prosa] *nf* prose

proseguir [prose'ɣir] *vt* to continue,
carry on ♦ *vi* to continue, go on

prospecto [pros'pekto] *nm* prospectus

prosperar [prospe'rar] *vi* to prosper,
thrive, flourish ❑ **prosperidad** *nf*
prosperity; *(éxito)* success
❑ **próspero, -a** *adj* prosperous,
flourishing; *(que tiene éxito)* successful

prostíbulo [pros'tiβulo] *nm* brothel
(BRIT), house of prostitution *(US)*

prostitución [prostitu'θjon] *nf*
prostitution

prostituir [prosti'twir] *vt* to prostitute;
prostituirse *vr* to prostitute o.s.,
become a prostitute

prostituta [prosti'tuta] *nf* prostitute

protagonista [protaɣo'nista] *nmf*
protagonist

protección [protek'θjon] *nf* protection

protector, a [protek'tor, a] *adj*
protective, protecting ♦ *nm/f*
protector

proteger [prote'xer] *vt* to protect
❑ **protegido, -a** *nm/f* protégé/
protégée

proteína [prote'ina] *nf* protein

protesta [pro'testa] *nf* protest;
(declaración) protestation

protestante [protes'tante] *adj*
Protestant

protestar [protes'tar] *vt* to protest,
declare ♦ *vi* to protest

protocolo [proto'kolo] *nm* protocol

prototipo [proto'tipo] *nm* prototype

provecho [pro'βetʃo] *nm* advantage,
benefit; *(FINANZAS)* profit; **¡buen ~!** bon
appétit!; **en ~ de** to the benefit of;
sacar ~ de to benefit from, profit by

provenir [proβe'nir] *vi:* **~ de** to come *o*
stem from

proverbio [pro'βerβjo] *nm* proverb

providencia [proβi'ðenθja] *nf*
providence

provincia [pro'βinθja] *nf* province

provisión [proβi'sjon] *nf* provision;
(abastecimiento) provision, supply;
(medida) measure, step

provisional [proβisjo'nal] *adj*
provisional

provocar [proβo'kar] *vt* to provoke;
(alentar) to tempt, invite; *(causar)* to
bring about, lead to; *(promover)* to
promote; *(estimular)* to rouse,
stimulate; **¿te provoca un café?** *(CAm)*
would you like a coffee?
❑ **provocativo, -a** *adj* provocative

proxeneta [prokse'neta] *nm* pimp

próximamente [proksima'mente]
adv shortly, soon

proximidad [proksimi'ðað] *nf*
closeness, proximity ❑ **próximo, -a**
adj near, close; *(vecino)* neighbouring;
(siguiente) next

proyectar [projek'tar] vt (objeto) to hurl, throw; (luz) to cast, shed; (CINE) to screen, show; (planear) to plan

proyectil [projek'til] nm projectile, missile

proyecto [pro'jekto] nm plan; (estimación de costo) detailed estimate

proyector [projek'tor] nm (CINE) projector

prudencia [pru'ðenθja] nf (sabiduría) wisdom; (cuidado) care ▢ **prudente** adj sensible, wise; (conductor) careful

prueba etc ['prweβa] vb ver **probar ♦** nf proof; (ensayo) test, trial; (degustación) tasting, sampling; (de ropa) fitting; a ~ on trial; a ~ de proof against; a ~ de agua/fuego waterproof/fireproof; someter a ~ to put to the test

psico... [siko] prefijo psycho-
▢ **psicología** nf psychology
▢ **psicológico, -a** adj psychological
▢ **psicólogo, -a** nm/f psychologist
▢ **psicópata** nmf psychopath
▢ **psicosis** nf inv psychosis

psiquiatra [si'kjatra] nmf psychiatrist
▢ **psiquiátrico, -a** adj psychiatric

PSOE [pe'soe] (ESP) nm abr = **Partido Socialista Obrero Español**

púa ['pua] nf (BOT, ZOOL) prickle, spine; (para guitarra) plectrum (BRIT), pick (US); **alambre de ~** barbed wire

pubertad [puβer'tað] nf puberty

publicación [puβlika'θjon] nf publication

publicar [puβli'kar] vt (editar) to publish; (hacer público) to publicize; (divulgar) to make public, divulge

publicidad [puβliθi'ðað] nf publicity; (COM: propaganda) advertising ▢ **publicitario, -a** adj publicity cpd; advertising cpd

público, -a ['puβliko, a] adj public ♦ nm public; (TEATRO etc) audience

puchero [pu'tʃero] nm (CULIN: guiso) stew; (: olla) cooking pot; **hacer pucheros** to pout

pucho (CS: fam) ['putʃo] nm cigarette, fag (BRIT)

pude etc vb ver **poder**

pudiente [pu'ðjente] adj (rico) wealthy, well-to-do

pudiera etc vb ver **poder**

pudor [pu'ðor] nm modesty

pudrir [pu'ðrir] vt to rot; **pudrirse** vr to rot, decay

pueblo ['pweβlo] nm people; (nación) nation; (aldea) village

puedo etc vb ver **poder**

puente ['pwente] nm bridge; **hacer ~** (fam) to take extra days off work between two public holidays; to take a long weekend ▶ **puente aéreo** shuttle service ▶ **puente colgante** suspension bridge ▶ **puente levadizo** drawbridge

---

HACER PUENTE

When a public holiday in Spain falls on a Tuesday or Thursday it is common practice for employers to make the Monday or Friday a holiday as well and to give everyone a four-day weekend. This is known as **hacer puente**. When a named public holiday such as the **Día de la Constitución** falls on a Tuesday or Thursday, people refer to the whole holiday period as e.g. the **puente de la Constitución**.

---

puerco, -a ['pwerko, a] nm/f pig/sow ♦ adj (sucio) dirty, filthy; (obsceno) disgusting ▶ **puerco espín** porcupine

pueril [pwe'ril] adj childish

puerro ['pwerro] nm leek

puerta ['pwerta] nf door; (de jardín) gate; (portal) doorway; (fig) gateway; (portería) goal; **a la ~** at the door; **a ~ cerrada** behind closed doors ▶ **puerta giratoria** revolving door

puerto ['pwerto] nm port; (paso) pass; (fig) haven, refuge

Puerto Rico [pwerto'riko] *nm* Puerto Rico ❑ **puertorriqueño, -a** *adj, nm/f* Puerto Rican

pues [pwes] *adv* (*entonces*) then; (*bueno*) well, well then; (*así que*) so ♦ *conj* (*ya que*) since; **¡~ sí!** yes!, certainly!

puesta ['pwesta] *nf* (*apuesta*) bet, stake ▶ **puesta al día** updating ▶ **puesta a punto** fine tuning ▶ **puesta de sol** sunset ▶ **puesta en marcha** starting

puesto, -a ['pwesto, a] *pp de* **poner** ♦ *adj*: **tener algo ~** to have sth on, be wearing sth ♦ *nm* (*lugar, posición*) place; (*trabajo*) post, job; (*COM*) stall ♦ *conj*: **~ que** since, as

púgil [puxil] *nm* boxer

pulga ['pulγa] *nf* flea

pulgada [pul'γaða] *nf* inch

pulgar [pul'γar] *nm* thumb

pulir [pu'lir] *vt* to polish; (*alisar*) to smooth; (*fig*) to polish up, touch up

pulmón [pul'mon] *nm* lung ❑ **pulmonía** *nf* pneumonia

pulpa ['pulpa] *nf* pulp; (*de fruta*) flesh, soft part

pulpería [pulpe'ria] *nf* (*LAm*) (*tienda*) small grocery store

púlpito ['pulpito] *nm* pulpit

pulpo ['pulpo] *nm* octopus

pulque [pulke] *nm* pulque

PULQUE

Pulque is a thick, white, alcoholic drink which is very popular in Mexico. In ancient times it was considered sacred by the Aztecs. It is produced by fermenting the juice of the **maguey**, a Mexican cactus similar to the agave. It can be drunk by itself or mixed with fruit or vegetable juice.

---

pulsación [pulsa'θjon] *nf* beat; **pulsaciones** pulse rate

pulsar [pul'sar] *vt* (*tecla*) to touch, tap; (*MÚS*) to play; (*botón*) to press, push ♦ *vi* to pulsate; (*latir*) to beat, throb

pulsera [pul'sera] *nf* bracelet

pulso ['pulso] *nm* (*ANAT*) pulse; (*fuerza*) strength; (*firmeza*) steadiness, steady hand

pulverizador [pulβeriθa'ðor] *nm* spray, spray gun

pulverizar [pulβeri'θar] *vt* to pulverize; (*líquido*) to spray

puna ['puna] *nf* (*CAm*) mountain sickness

punta ['punta] *nf* point, tip; (*extremo*) end; (*fig*) touch, trace; **horas ~** peak o rush hours; **sacar ~ a** to sharpen

puntada [pun'taða] *nf* (*COSTURA*) stitch

puntal [pun'tal] *nm* prop, support

puntapié [punta'pje] *nm* kick

puntería [punte'ria] *nf* (*de arma*) aim, aiming; (*destreza*) marksmanship

puntero, -a [pun'tero, a] *adj* leading ♦ *nm* (*palo*) pointer

puntiagudo, -a [puntja'γuðo, a] *adj* sharp, pointed

puntilla [pun'tiλa] *nf* (*encaje*) lace edging o trim; (*andar*) **de puntillas** (to walk) on tiptoe

punto ['punto] *nm* (*gen*) point; (*señal diminuta*) spot, dot; (*COSTURA, MED*) stitch; (*lugar*) spot, place; (*momento*) point, moment; **a ~** ready; **estar a ~ de** to be on the point of o about to; **en ~** on the dot; **hasta cierto ~** to some extent; **hacer ~** (*ESP: tejer*) to knit; **dos puntos** (*LING*) colon ▶ **punto de interrogación** question mark ▶ **punto de vista** point of view, viewpoint ▶ **punto final** full stop (*BRIT*), period (*US*) ▶ **punto muerto** dead center; (*AUTO*) neutral (gear) ▶ **punto y aparte** (*en dictado*) full stop, new paragraph ▶ **punto y coma** semicolon

puntocom, punto.com *adj inv, nf inv* dotcom, dot.com

puntuación [puntwa'θjon] *nf* punctuation; (*puntos: en examen*) mark(s) (*pl*); (DEPORTE) score

puntual [pun'twal] *adj* (*a tiempo*) punctual; (*exacto*) exact, accurate ❏ **puntualidad** *nf* punctuality; exactness, accuracy

puntuar [pun'twar] *vi* (DEPORTE) to score, count

punzante [pun'θante] *adj* (*dolor*) shooting, sharp; (*herramienta*) sharp

puñado [pu'naðo] *nm* handful

puñal [pu'nal] *nm* dagger ❏ **puñalada** *nf* stab

puñetazo [pune'taθo] *nm* punch

puño ['puno] *nm* (ANAT) fist; (*cantidad*) fistful, handful; (COSTURA) cuff; (*de herramienta*) handle

pupila [pu'pila] *nf* pupil

pupitre [pu'pitre] *nm* desk

puré [pu're] *nm* purée; (*sopa*) (thick) soup ▶ **puré de papas** (LAm) mashed potatoes ▶ **puré de patatas** (ESP) mashed potatoes

purga ['purɣa] *nf* purge ❏ **purgante** *adj, nm* purgative

purgatorio [purɣa'torjo] *nm* purgatory

purificar [purifi'kar] *vt* to purify; (*refinar*) to refine

puritano, -a [puri'tano, a] *adj* (*actitud*) puritanical; (*iglesia, tradición*) puritan ♦ *nm/f* puritan

puro, -a ['puro, a] *adj* pure; (*verdad*) simple, plain ♦ *nm* cigar

púrpura ['purpura] *nf* purple

pus [pus] *nm* pus

puse *etc* ['puse] *vb ver* **poder**

pusiera *etc vb ver* **poder**

puta ['puta] (*fam!*) *nf* whore, prostitute

putrefacción [putrefak'θjon] *nf* rotting, putrefaction

PVP *nm abr* (= *precio de venta al público*) RRP

pyme, PYME ['pime] *nf abr* (= *Pequeña y Mediana Empresa*) SME

Q, q

que
PALABRA CLAVE

[ke] *conj*

1 (*con oración subordinada: muchas veces no se traduce*) that; **dijo que vendría** he said (that) he would come; **espero que lo encuentres** I hope (that) you find it; *ver tb* **el**

2 (*en oración independiente*): **¡que entre!** send him in; **¡Que aproveche!** enjoy your meal!; **¡que se mejore tu padre!** I hope your father gets better

3 (*enfático*): **¿me quieres? — ¡que sí!** do you love me? — of course!

4 (*consecutivo: muchas veces no se traduce*) that; **es tan grande que no lo puedo levantar** it's so big (that) I can't lift it

5 (*comparaciones*) than; **yo que tú/él** if I were you/him; *ver tb* **más**; **menos**; **mismo**

6 (*valor disyuntivo*): **que le guste o no** whether he likes it or not; **que venga o que no venga** whether he comes or not

7 (*porque*): **no puedo, que tengo que quedarme en casa** I can't, I've got to stay in

♦ *pron*

1 (*cosa*) that, which; (+ *prep*) which; **el sombrero que te compraste** the hat (that o which) you bought; **la cama en que dormí** the bed (that o which) I slept in

2 (*persona: suj*) that, who; (: *objeto*)

that, whom; **el amigo que me acompañó al museo** the friend that o who went to the museum with me; **la chica que invité** the girl (that o whom) I invited

qué [ke] *adj* what?, which? ♦ *pron* what?; **¡qué divertido!** how funny!; **¿qué edad tienes?** how old are you?; **¿de qué me hablas?** what are you saying to me?; **¿qué tal?** how are you?, how are things?; **¿qué hay (de nuevo)?** what's new?

quebrado, -a [ke'βraðo, a] *adj* (*roto*) broken ♦ *nm/f* bankrupt ♦ *nm* (*MAT*) fraction

quebrantar [keβran'tar] *vt* (*infringir*) to violate, transgress

quebrar [ke'βrar] *vt* to break, smash ♦ *vi* to go bankrupt

quedar [ke'ðar] *vi* to stay, remain; (*encontrarse: sitio*) to be; (*haber aún*) to remain, be left; **quedarse** *vr* to remain, stay (behind); **quedarse (con) algo** to keep sth; ~ **en** (*acordar*) to agree on/to; ~ **en nada** to come to nothing; ~ **por hacer** to be still to be done; ~ **ciego/mudo** to be left blind/dumb; **no te queda bien ese vestido** that dress doesn't suit you; **eso queda muy lejos** that's a long way (away); **quedamos a las seis** we agreed to meet at six

quedo, -a [ˈkeðo, a] *adj* still ♦ *adv* softly, gently

quehacer [kea'θer] *nm* task, job; **quehaceres (domésticos)** *nmpl* household chores

queja [ˈkexa] *nf* complaint ◻ **quejarse** *vr* (*enfermo*) to moan, groan; (*protestar*) to complain; **quejarse de que** to complain (about the fact) that ◻ **quejido** *nm* moan

quemado, -a [ke'maðo, a] *adj* burnt

quemadura [kema'ðura] *nf* burn, scald

quemar [ke'mar] *vt* to burn; (*fig: malgastar*) to burn up, squander ♦ *vi* to

be burning hot; **quemarse** *vr* (*consumirse*) to burn (up); (*del sol*) to get sunburnt

quemarropa [kema'rropa]: **a** ~ *adv* point-blank

quepo *etc* [ˈkepo] *vb ver* **caber**

querella [ke'reʎa] *nf* (*JUR*) charge; (*disputa*) dispute

querer [ke'rer] *vt*

1 (*desear*) to want; **quiero más dinero** I want more money; **quisiera** o **querría un té** I'd like a tea; **sin querer** unintentionally; **quiero ayudar/que vayas** I want to help/you to go

2 (*preguntas: para pedir algo*): **¿quiere abrir la ventana?** could you open the window?; **¿quieres echarme una mano?** can you give me a hand?

3 (*amar*) to love; (*tener cariño a*) to be fond of; **quiere mucho a sus hijos** he's very fond of his children

4: **le pedí que me dejara ir pero no quiso** I asked him to let me go but he refused

querido, -a [ke'riðo, a] *adj* dear ♦ *nm/f* darling; (*amante*) lover

queso [ˈkeso] *nm* cheese ▸ **queso crema** (*LAm*) cream cheese ▸ **queso de untar** (*ESP*) cream cheese ▸ **queso manchego** sheep's milk cheese made in La Mancha ▸ **queso rallado** grated cheese

quicio [ˈkiθjo] *nm* hinge; **sacar a algn de** ~ to get on sb's nerves

quiebra [ˈkjeβra] *nf* break, split; (*COM*) bankruptcy; (*ECON*) slump

quiebro [ˈkjeβro] *nm* (*del cuerpo*) swerve

quien [kjen] *pron* who; **hay ~ piensa que** there are those who think that; **no hay ~ lo haga** no-one will do it

quién [kjen] *pron* who, whom; **¿~ es?** who's there?

quienquiera [kjen'kjera] *(pl* **quienesquiera)** *pron* whoever

quiero *etc vb ver* **querer**

quieto, -a ['kjeto, a] *adj* still; *(carácter)* placid ❑ **quietud** *nf* stillness

⚠ No confundir **quieto** con la palabra inglesa *quiet.*

quilate [ki'late] *nm* carat

químico, -a ['kimiko, a] *adj* chemical ♦ *nm/f* chemist ♦ *nf* chemistry

quincalla [kin'kaʎa] *nf* hardware, ironmongery *(BRIT)*

quince [kin'θe] *num* fifteen; **~ días** a fortnight ❑ **quinceañero, -a** *nm/f* teenager ❑ **quincena** *nf* fortnight; *(pago)* fortnightly pay ❑ **quincenal** *adj* fortnightly

quiniela [ki'njela] *nf* football pools *pl*; **quinielas** *nfpl (impreso)* pools coupon *sg*

quinientos, -as [ki'njentos, as] *adj, num* five hundred

quinto, -a ['kinto, a] *adj* fifth ♦ *nf* country house; *(MIL)* call-up, draft

quiosco ['kjosko] *nm (de música)* bandstand; *(de periódicos)* news stand

quirófano [ki'rofano] *nm* operating theatre

quirúrgico, -a [ki'rurxiko, a] *adj* surgical

quise *etc* ['kise] *vb ver* **querer**

quisiera *etc vb ver* **querer**

quisquilloso, -a [kiski'ʎoso, a] *adj (susceptible)* touchy; *(meticuloso)* pernickety

quiste ['kiste] *nm* cyst

quitaesmalte [kitaes'malte] *nm* nail-polish remover

quitamanchas [kita'mantʃas] *nm inv* stain remover

quitanieves [kita'njeβes] *nm inv* snowplough *(BRIT)*, snowplow *(US)*

quitar [ki'tar] *vt* to remove, take away; *(ropa)* to take off; *(dolor)* to relieve; **¡quita de ahí!** get away!; **quitarse** *vr* to withdraw; *(ropa)* to take off; **se quitó el sombrero** he took off his hat

Quito ['kito] *n* Quito

quizá(s) [ki'θa(s)] *adv* perhaps, maybe

R, r

rábano ['raβano] *nm* radish; **me importa un ~** I don't give a damn

rabia ['raβja] *nf (MED)* rabies *sg*; *(ira)* fury, rage ❑ **rabiar** *vi* to have rabies; to rage, be furious; **rabiar por algo** to long for sth

rabieta [ra'βjeta] *nf* tantrum, fit of temper

rabino [ra'βino] *nm* rabbi

rabioso, -a [ra'βjoso, a] *adj* rabid; *(fig)* furious

rabo ['raβo] *nm* tail

racha ['ratʃa] *nf* gust of wind; **buena/ mala ~** spell of good/bad luck

racial [ra'θjal] *adj* racial, race *cpd*

racimo [ra'θimo] *nm* bunch

ración [ra'θjon] *nf* portion; **raciones** *nfpl* rations

racional [raθjo'nal] *adj (razonable)* reasonable; *(lógico)* rational

racionar [raθjo'nar] *vt* to ration (out)

racismo [ra'θismo] *nm* racism ❑ **racista** *adj, nm* racist

radar [ra'ðar] *nm* radar

radiador [raðja'ðor] *nm* radiator

radiante [ra'ðjante] *adj* radiant

radical [raði'kal] *adj, nmf* radical

radicar [raði'kar] *vi*: ~ **en** *(dificultad, problema)* to lie in; *(solución)* to consist in

radio ['raðjo] nf radio; (aparato) radio (set) ♦ nm (MAT) radius; (QUIM) radium
❏ **radioactividad** nf radioactivity
❏ **radioactivo, -a** adj radioactive
❏ **radiografía** nf X-ray
❏ **radioterapia** nf radiotherapy
❏ **radioyente** nmf listener

ráfaga ['rafaɣa] nf gust; (de luz) flash; (de tiros) burst

raíz [ra'iθ] nf root; **a ~ de** as a result of ► **raíz cuadrada** square root

raja ['raxa] nf (de melón etc) slice; (grieta) crack ❏ **rajar** vt to split; (fam) to slash; **rajarse** vr to split, crack; **rajarse de** to back out of

rajatabla [raxa'taβla]: **a ~** adv (estrictamente) strictly, to the letter

rallador [raʎa'ðor] nm grater

rallar [ra'ʎar] vt to grate

rama ['rama] nf branch ❏ **ramaje** nm branches pl, foliage ❏ **ramal** nm (de cuerda) strand; (FERRO) branch line (BRIT); (AUTO) branch (road) (BRIT)

rambla ['rambla] nf (avenida) avenue

ramo ['ramo] nm branch; (sección) department, section

rampa ['rampa] nf ramp ► **rampa de acceso** entrance ramp

rana ['rana] nf frog; **salto de ~** leapfrog

ranchero [ran'tʃero] (MÉX) nm (hacendado) rancher; smallholder

rancho ['rantʃo] nm (grande) ranch; (pequeño) small farm

rancio, -a ['ranθjo, a] adj (comestibles) rancid; (vino) aged, mellow; (fig) ancient

rango ['rango] nm rank, standing

ranura [ra'nura] nf groove; (de teléfono etc) slot

rapar [ra'par] vt to shave; (los cabellos) to crop

rapaz [ra'paθ] nf (▷ **rapaza**) nmf young boy/girl ♦ adj (ZOOL) predatory

rape ['rape] nm (pez) monkfish; **al ~** cropped

rapé [ra'pe] nm snuff

rapidez [rapi'ðeθ] nf speed, rapidity
❏ **rápido, -a** adj fast, quick ♦ adv quickly ♦ nm (FERRO) express
❏ **rápidos** nmpl rapids

rapiña [ra'piɲa] nm robbery; **ave de ~** bird of prey

raptar [rap'tar] vt to kidnap ❏ **rapto** nm kidnapping; (impulso) sudden impulse; (éxtasis) ecstasy, rapture

raqueta [ra'keta] nf racquet

raquítico, -a [ra'kitiko, a] adj stunted; (fig) poor, inadequate

rareza [ra'reθa] nf rarity; (fig) eccentricity

raro, -a ['raro, a] adj (poco común) rare; (extraño) odd, strange; (excepcional) remarkable

ras [ras] nm: **a ~** level with; **a ~ de tierra** at ground level

rasar [ra'sar] vt (igualar) to level

rascacielos [raska'θjelos] nm inv skyscraper

rascar [ras'kar] vt (con las uñas etc) to scratch; (raspar) to scrape; **rascarse** vr to scratch (o.s.)

rasgar [ras'ɣar] vt to tear, rip (up)

rasgo ['rasɣo] nm (con pluma) stroke; **rasgos** nmpl (facciones) features, characteristics; **a grandes rasgos** in outline, broadly

rasguño [ras'ɣuɲo] nm scratch

raso, -a ['raso, a] adj (liso) flat, level; (a baja altura) very low ♦ nm satin; **cielo ~** clear sky

raspadura [raspa'ðura] nf (acto) scrape, scraping; (marca) scratch; **raspaduras** nfpl (de papel etc) scrapings

raspar [ras'par] vt to scrape; (arañar) to scratch; (limar) to file

rastra ['rastra] nf (AGR) rake; **a rastras** by dragging; (fig) unwillingly

rastrear [rastre'ar] vt (seguir) to track

rastrero, -a [ras'trero, a] adj (BOT, ZOOL) creeping; (fig) despicable, mean

rastrillo [ras'triʎo] nm rake

rastro ['rastro] nm (AGR) rake; (pista) track, trail; (vestigio) trace; **el R~** (ESP) the Madrid fleamarket

rasurado (MÉX) nm shaving ❏ **rasuradora** [rasuraˈðora] (MÉX) nf electric shaver ❏ **rasurar** [rasuˈrar] (MÉX) vt to shave; **rasurarse** vr to shave

rata ['rata] nf rat

ratear [rateˈar] vt (robar) to steal

ratero, -a [raˈtero, a] adj light-fingered ♦ nm/f (carterista) pickpocket; (ladrón) petty thief

rato ['rato] nm while, short time; **a ratos** from time to time; **hay para ~** there's still a long way to go; **al poco ~** soon afterwards; **pasar el ~** to kill time; **pasar un buen/mal ~** to have a good/rough time; **en mis ratos libres** in my spare time

ratón [raˈton] nm mouse ❏ **ratonera** nf mousetrap

raudal [rauˈðal] nm torrent; **a raudales** in abundance

raya ['raja] nf line; (marca) scratch; (en tela) stripe; (de pelo) parting; (límite) boundary; (pez) ray; (puntuación) dash; **a rayas** striped; **pasarse de la ~** to go too far; **tener a ~** to keep in check ❏ **rayar** vt to line; to scratch; (subrayar) to underline ♦ vi: **rayar en o con** to border on

rayo ['rajo] nm (del sol) ray, beam; (de luz) shaft; (en una tormenta) (flash of) lightning ▸ **rayos X** X-rays

raza ['raθa] nf race ▸ **raza humana** human race

razón [raˈθon] nf reason; (justicia) right, justice; (razonamiento) reasoning; (motivo) reason, motive; (MAT) ratio; **a ~ de 10 cada día** at the rate of 10 a day; **en ~ de** with regard to; **dar ~ a algn** to agree that sb is right; **tener ~** to be right ▸ **razón de ser** raison d'être ▸ **razón directa/inversa** direct/inverse proportion ❏ **razonable** adj reasonable; (justo, moderado) fair ❏ **razonamiento** nm (juicio)

judg(e)ment; (argumento) reasoning ❏ **razonar** vt, vi to reason, argue

re nm (MÚS) D

reacción [reakˈθjon] nf reaction; **avión a ~** jet plane ▸ **reacción en cadena** chain reaction ❏ **reaccionar** vi to react

reacio, -a [reˈaθjo, a] adj stubborn

reactivar [reaktiˈβar] vt to revitalize

reactor [reakˈtor] nm reactor

real [reˈal] adj real; (del rey, fig) royal

realidad [realiˈðað] nf reality, fact; (verdad) truth

realista [reaˈlista] nmf realist

realización [realiθaˈθjon] nf fulfilment

realizador, a [realiθaˈðor, a] nm/f film-maker

realizar [realiˈθar] vt (objetivo) to achieve; (plan) to carry out; (viaje) to make, undertake; **realizarse** vr to come about, come true

realmente [realˈmente] adv really, actually

realzar [realˈθar] vt to enhance; (acentuar) to highlight

reanimar [reaniˈmar] vt to revive; (alentar) to encourage; **reanimarse** vr to revive

reanudar [reanuˈðar] vt (renovar) to renew; (historia, viaje) to resume

reaparición [reapariˈθjon] nf reappearance

rearme [reˈarme] nm rearmament

rebaja [reˈβaxa] nf (COM) reduction; (: descuento) discount; **rebajas** nfpl (COM) sale ❏ **rebajar** vt (bajar) to lower; (reducir) to reduce; (disminuir) to lessen; (humillar) to humble

rebanada [reβaˈnaða] nf slice

rebañar [reβaˈnar] vt (comida) to scrape up; (plato) to scrape clean

rebaño [reˈβano] nm herd; (de ovejas) flock

rebatir [reβaˈtir] vt to refute

rebeca [reˈβeka] nf cardigan

rebelarse [reβe'larse] *vr* to rebel, revolt

rebelde [re'βelde] *adj* rebellious; (*niño*) unruly ♦ *nmf* rebel ▫ **rebeldía** *nf* rebelliousness; (*desobediencia*) disobedience

rebelión [reβe'ljon] *nf* rebellion

reblandecer [reβlande'θer] *vt* to soften

rebobinar [reβoβi'nar] *vt* (*cinta, película de vídeo*) to rewind

rebosante [reβo'sante] *adj* overflowing

rebosar [reβo'sar] *vi* (*líquido, recipiente*) to overflow; (*abundar*) to abound, be plentiful

rebotar [reβo'tar] *vt* to bounce; (*rechazar*) to repel ♦ *vi* (*pelota*) to bounce; (*bala*) to ricochet ▫ **rebote** *nm* bounce; (*de bala*) rebound; **de rebote** on the rebound

rebozado, -a [reβo'θaðo, a] *adj* fried in batter *o* breadcrumbs

rebozar [reβo'θar] *vt* to wrap up; (*CULIN*) to fry in batter *o* breadcrumbs

rebuscado, -a [reβus'kaðo, a] *adj* (*amanerado*) affected; (*palabra*) recherché; (*idea*) far-fetched

rebuscar [reβus'kar] *vi*: ~ **(en/por)** to search carefully (in/for)

recado [re'kaðo] *nm* (*mensaje*) message; (*encargo*) errand; **tomar un** ~ (*TEL*) to take a message

recaer [reka'er] *vi* to relapse; ~ **en** to fall to *o* on; (*criminal etc*) to fall back into, relapse into ▫ **recaída** *nf* relapse

recalcar [rekal'kar] *vt* (*fig*) to stress, emphasize

recalentar [rekalen'tar] *vt* (*volver a calentar*) to reheat; (*calentar demasiado*) to overheat

recámara [re'kamara] (*MÉX*) *nf* bedroom

recambio [re'kambjo] *nm* spare; (*de pluma*) refill

recapacitar [rekapaθi'tar] *vi* to reflect

recargado, -a [rekar'γaðo, a] *adj* overloaded

recargar [rekar'γar] *vt* to overload; (*batería*) to recharge ▫ **recargo** *nm* surcharge; (*aumento*) increase

recatado, -a [reka'taðo, a] *adj* (*modesto*) modest, demure; (*prudente*) cautious

recaudación [rekauða'θjon] *nf* (*acción*) collection; (*cantidad*) takings *pl*; (*en deporte*) gate ▫ **recaudador, a** *nm/f* tax collector

recelar [reθe'lar] *vt*: ~ **que ...** (*sospechar*) to suspect that ...; (*temer*) to fear that ... ♦ *vi*: ~ **de** to distrust ▫ **recelo** *nm* distrust, suspicion

recepción [reθep'θjon] *nf* reception ▫ **recepcionista** *nmf* receptionist

receptor, a [reθep'tor, a] *nm/f* recipient ♦ *nm* (*TEL*) receiver

recesión [reθe'sjon] *nf* (*COM*) recession

receta [re'θeta] *nf* (*CULIN*) recipe; (*MED*) prescription

⚠ No confundir **receta** con la palabra inglesa *receipt*.

rechazar [retʃa'θar] *vt* to reject; (*oferta*) to turn down; (*ataque*) to repel

rechazo [re'tʃaθo] *nm* rejection

rechinar [retʃi'nar] *vi* to creak; (*dientes*) to grind

rechistar [retʃis'tar] *vi*: **sin** ~ without a murmur

rechoncho, -a [re'tʃontʃo, a] (*fam*) *adj* thickset (*BRIT*), heavy-set (*US*)

rechupete [retʃu'pete]: **de** ~ (*comida*) delicious, scrumptious

recibidor [reθiβi'ðor] *nm* entrance hall

recibimiento [reθiβi'mjento] *nm* reception, welcome

recibir [reθi'βir] *vt* to receive; (*dar la bienvenida*) to welcome ♦ *vi* to entertain ▫ **recibo** *nm* receipt

reciclable *adj* recyclable

reciclar [reθi'klar] *vt* to recycle

recién [re'θjen] *adv* recently, newly; **los ~ casados** the newly-weds; **el ~ llegado** the newcomer; **el ~ nacido** the newborn child

reciente [re'θjente] *adj* recent; (*fresco*) fresh

recinto [re'θinto] *nm* enclosure; (*área*) area, place

recio, -a ['reθjo, a] *adj* strong, tough; (*voz*) loud ♦ *adv* hard, loud(ly)

recipiente [reθi'pjente] *nm* receptacle

recíproco, -a [re'θiproko, a] *adj* reciprocal

recital [reθi'tal] *nm* (*MÚS*) recital; (*LITERATURA*) reading

recitar [reθi'tar] *vt* to recite

reclamación [reklama'θjon] *nf* claim, demand; (*queja*) complaint

reclamar [rekla'mar] *vt* to claim, demand ♦ *vi*: **~ contra** to complain about ❑ **reclamo** *nm* (*anuncio*) advertisement; (*tentación*) attraction

reclinar [rekli'nar] *vt* to recline, lean; **reclinarse** *vr* to lean back

reclusión [reklu'sjon] *nf* (*prisión*) prison; (*refugio*) seclusion

recluta [re'kluta] *nmf* recruit ♦ *nf* recruitment ❑ **reclutar** *vt* (*datos*) to collect; (*dinero*) to collect up ❑ **reclutamiento** *nm* recruitment

recobrar [reko'βrar] *vt* (*salud*) to recover; (*rescatar*) to get back; **recobrarse** *vr* to recover

recodo [re'koðo] *nm* (*de río, camino*) bend

recogedor [rekoxe'ðor] *nm* dustpan

recoger [reko'xer] *vt* to collect; (*AGR*) to harvest; (*levantar*) to pick up; (*juntar*) to gather; (*pasar a buscar*) to come for, get; (*dar asilo*) to give shelter to; (*faldas*) to gather up; (*pelo*) to put up; **recogerse** *vr* (*retirarse*) to retire ❑ **recogido, -a** *adj* (*lugar*) quiet, secluded; (*pequeño*) small ♦ *nf* (*CORREOS*) collection; (*AGR*) harvest

recolección [rekolek'θjon] *nf* (*AGR*) harvesting; (*colecta*) collection

recomendación [rekomenda'θjon] *nf* (*sugerencia*) suggestion, recommendation; (*referencia*) reference

recomendar [rekomen'dar] *vt* to suggest, recommend; (*confiar*) to entrust

recompensa [rekom'pensa] *nf* reward, recompense ❑ **recompensar** *vt* to reward, recompense

reconciliación [rekonθilja'θjon] *nf* reconciliation

reconciliar [rekonθi'ljar] *vt* to reconcile; **reconciliarse** *vr* to become reconciled

recóndito, -a [re'kondito, a] *adj* (*lugar*) hidden, secret

reconocer [rekono'θer] *vt* to recognize; (*registrar*) to search; (*MED*) to examine ❑ **reconocido, -a** *adj* recognized; (*agradecido*) grateful ❑ **reconocimiento** *nm* recognition; search; examination; gratitude; (*confesión*) admission

reconquista [rekon'kista] *nf* reconquest; **la R~** the Reconquest (of Spain)

reconstituyente [rekonstitu'jente] *nm* tonic

reconstruir [rekonstru'ir] *vt* to reconstruct

reconversión [rekonβer'sjon] *nf* (*reestructuración*) restructuring ▸ **reconversión industrial** industrial rationalization

recopilación [rekopila'θjon] *nf* (*resumen*) summary; (*compilación*) compilation ❑ **recopilar** *vt* to compile

récord ['rekorð] (*pl* **récords**) *adj inv, nm* record

recordar [rekor'ðar] vt (*acordarse de*) to remember; (*acordar a otro*) to remind ♦ vi to remember

⚠ No confundir **recordar** con la palabra inglesa *record*.

recorrer [reko'rrer] vt (*país*) to cross, travel through; (*distancia*) to cover; (*registrar*) to search; (*repasar*) to look over ❑ **recorrido** nm run, journey; **tren de largo recorrido** main-line train

recortar [rekor'tar] vt to cut out ❑ **recorte** nm (*acción, de prensa*) cutting; (*de telas, chapas*) trimming ► **recorte presupuestario** budget cut

recostar [rekos'tar] vt to lean; **recostarse** vr to lie down

recoveco [reko'βeko] nm (*de camino, río etc*) bend; (*en casa*) cubby hole

recreación [rekrea'θjon] nf recreation

recrear [rekre'ar] vt (*entretener*) to entertain; (*volver a crear*) to recreate ❑ **recreativo, -a** adj recreational ❑ **recreo** nm recreation; (*ESCOL*) break, playtime

recriminar [rekrimi'nar] vt to reproach ♦ vi to recriminate; **recriminarse** vr to reproach each other

recrudecer [rekruðe'θer] vt, vi to worsen; **recrudecerse** vr to worsen

recta ['rekta] nf straight line

rectángulo, -a [rek'tangulo, a] adj rectangular ♦ nm rectangle

rectificar [rektifi'kar] vt to rectify; (*volverse recto*) to straighten ♦ vi to correct o.s.

rectitud [rekti'tuð] nf straightness

recto, -a ['rekto, a] adj straight; (*persona*) honest, upright; **siga todo ~** go straight on ♦ nm rectum

rector, a [rek'tor, a] adj governing

recuadro [re'kwaðro] nm box; (*TIP*) inset

recubrir [reku'βrir] vt: **~ (con)** (*pintura, crema*) to cover (with)

recuento [re'kwento] nm inventory; **hacer el ~ de** to count o reckon up

recuerdo [re'kwerðo] nm souvenir; **recuerdos** nmpl (*memorias*) memories; **¡recuerdos a tu madre!** give my regards to your mother!

recular [reku'lar] vi to back down

recuperación [rekupera'θjon] nf recovery

recuperar [rekupe'rar] vt to recover; (*tiempo*) to make up; **recuperarse** vr to recuperate

recurrir [reku'rrir] vi (*JUR*) to appeal; **~ a** to resort to; (*persona*) to turn to ❑ **recurso** nm resort; (*medios*) means pl, resources pl; (*JUR*) appeal

red [reð] nf net, mesh; (*FERRO etc*) network; (*trampa*) trap; **la R~** (*Internet*) the Net

redacción [reðak'θjon] nf (*acción*) editing; (*personal*) editorial staff; (*ESCOL*) essay, composition

redactar [reðak'tar] vt to draw up, draft; (*periódico*) to edit

redactor, a [reðak'tor, a] nm/f editor

redada [re'ðaða] nf (*de policía*) raid, round-up

rededor [reðe'ðor] nm: **al o en ~** around, round about

redoblar [reðo'βlar] vt to redouble ♦ vi (*tambor*) to roll

redonda [re'ðonda] nf: **a la ~** around, round about

redondear [reðonde'ar] vt to round, round off

redondel [reðon'del] nm (*círculo*) circle; (*TAUR*) bullring, arena

redondo, -a [re'ðondo, a] adj (*circular*) round; (*completo*) complete

reducción [reðuk'θjon] nf reduction

reducido, -a [reðu'ðiðo, a] adj reduced; (*limitado*) limited; (*pequeño*) small

reducir [reðu'θir] vt to reduce; to limit; **reducirse** vr to diminish

redundancia [reðun'danθja] nf
redundancy

reembolsar [re(e)mbol'sar] vt
(persona) to reimburse; (dinero) to
repay, pay back; (depósito) to refund
❏ **reembolso** nm reimbursement;
refund

reemplazar [re(e)mpla'θar] vt to
replace ❏ **reemplazo** nm
replacement; **de reemplazo** (MIL)
reserve

reencuentro [re(e)n'kwentro] nm
reunion

refacción (MEX) [refak'θjon] nf spare
(part)

referencia [refe'renθja] nf reference;
con ~ a with reference to

referéndum [refe'rendum] (pl
referéndums) nm referendum

referente [refe'rente] adj: **~ a**
concerning, relating to

réferi (LAm) nmf referee

referir [refe'rir] vt (contar) to tell,
recount; (relacionar) to refer, relate;
referirse vr: **referirse a** to refer to

refilón [refi'lon]: **de ~** adv obliquely

refinado, -a [refi'naðo, a] adj refined

refinar [refi'nar] vt to refine
❏ **refinería** nf refinery

reflejar [refle'xar] vt to reflect
❏ **reflejo, -a** adj reflected;
(movimiento) reflex ♦ nm reflection;
(ANAT) reflex

reflexión [reflek'sjon] nf reflection
❏ **reflexionar** vt to reflect on ♦ vi to
reflect; (detenerse) to pause (to think)

reflexivo, -a [reflek'siβo, a] adj
thoughtful; (LING) reflexive

reforma [re'forma] nf reform; (ARQ etc)
repair ▶ **reforma agraria** agrarian
reform

reformar [refor'mar] vt to reform;
(modificar) to change, alter; (ARQ) to
repair; **reformarse** vr to mend one's
ways

reformatorio [reforma'torjo] nm
reformatory

reforzar [refor'θar] vt to strengthen;
(ARQ) to reinforce; (fig) to encourage

refractario, -a [refrak'tarjo, a] adj
(TEC) heat-resistant

refrán [re'fran] nm proverb, saying

refregar [refre'ɣar] vt to scrub

refrescante [refres'kante] adj
refreshing, cooling

refrescar [refres'kar] vt to refresh ♦ vi
to cool down; **refrescarse** vr to get
cooler; (tomar aire fresco) to go out for
a breath of fresh air; (beber) to have a
drink

refresco [re'fresko] nm soft drink, cool
drink; **"refrescos"** refreshments"

refriega [re'frjeɣa] nf scuffle, brawl

refrigeración [refrixera'θjon] nf
refrigeration; (de sala) air-conditioning

refrigerador [refrixera'ðor] nm
refrigerator (BRIT), icebox (US)

refrigerar [refrixe'rar] vt to refrigerate;
(sala) to air-condition

refuerzo [re'fwerθo] nm
reinforcement; (TEC) support

refugiado, -a [refu'xjaðo, a] nm/f
refugee

refugiarse [refu'xjarse] vr to take
refuge, shelter

refugio [re'fuxjo] nm refuge;
(protección) shelter

refunfuñar [refunfu'ɲar] vi to grunt,
growl; (quejarse) to grumble

regadera [reɣa'ðera] nf watering can

regadío [reɣa'ðio] nm irrigated land

regalado, -a [reɣa'laðo, a] adj
comfortable, luxurious; (gratis) free, for
nothing

regalar [reɣa'lar] vt (dar) to give (as a
present); (entregar) to give away;
(mimar) to pamper, make a fuss of

regaliz [reɣa'liθ] nm liquorice

regalo [re'ɣalo] nm (obsequio) gift,
present; (gusto) pleasure

regañadientes [reɣaɲa'ðjentes]: **a ~** adv reluctantly

regañar [reɣa'ɲar] vt to scold ♦ vi to grumble □ **regañón, -ona** adj nagging

regar [re'ɣar] vt to water, irrigate; (fig) to scatter, sprinkle

regatear [reɣate'ar] vt (COM) to bargain over; (escatimar) to be mean with ♦ vi to bargain, haggle; (DEPORTE) to dribble □ **regateo** nm bargaining; dribbling; (del cuerpo) swerve, dodge

regazo [re'ɣaθo] nm lap

regenerar [rexene'rar] vt to regenerate

régimen ['reximen] (pl **regímenes**) nm regime; (MED) diet

regimiento [rexi'mjento] nm regiment

regio, -a ['rexjo, a] adj royal, regal; (fig: suntuoso) splendid; (CS: fam) great, terrific

región [re'xjon] nf region

regir [re'xir] vt to govern, rule; (dirigir) to manage, run ♦ vi to apply, be in force

registrar [rexis'trar] vt (buscar) to search; (: en cajón) to look through; (inspeccionar) to inspect; (anotar) to register, record; (INFORM) to log; **registrarse** vr to register; (ocurrir) to happen

registro [re'xistro] nm (acto) registration; (MÚS, libro) register; (inspección) inspection, search ▶ **registro civil** registry office

regla ['reɣla] nf (ley) rule, regulation; (de medir) ruler, rule; (MED: periodo) period; **en ~** in order

reglamentación [reɣlamenta'θjon] nf (acto) regulation; (lista) rules pl

reglamentar [reɣlamen'tar] vt to regulate □ **reglamentario, -a** adj statutory □ **reglamento** nm rules pl, regulations pl

regocijarse [reɣoθi'xarse] vr (alegrarse) to rejoice □ **regocijo** nm joy, happiness

regresar [reɣre'sar] vi to come back, go back, return □ **regreso** nm return

reguero [re'ɣero] nm (de sangre etc) trickle; (de humo) trail

regulador [reɣula'ðor] nm regulator; (de radio etc) knob, control

regular [reɣu'lar] adj regular; (normal) normal, usual; (común) ordinary; (organizado) regular, orderly; (mediano) average; (fam) not bad, so-so ♦ adv so-so, alright ♦ vt (controlar) to control, regulate; (TEC) to adjust; **por lo ~** as a rule □ **regularidad** nf regularity □ **regularizar** vt to regularize

rehabilitación [reaβilita'θjon] nf rehabilitation; (ARQ) restoration

rehabilitar [reaβili'tar] vt to rehabilitate; (ARQ) to restore; (reintegrar) to reinstate

rehacer [rea'θer] vt (reparar) to mend, repair; (volver a hacer) to redo, repeat; **rehacerse** vr (MED) to recover

rehén [re'en] nm hostage

rehuir [reu'ir] vt to avoid, shun

rehusar [reu'sar] vt, vi to refuse

reina ['reina] nf queen □ **reinado** nm reign

reinar [rei'nar] vi to reign

reincidir [reinθi'ðir] vi to relapse

reincorporarse [reinkorpo'rarse] vr: **~ a** to rejoin

reino ['reino] nm kingdom ▶ **reino animal/vegetal** animal/plant kingdom ▶ **el Reino Unido** the United Kingdom

reintegrar [reinte'ɣrar] vt (reconstituir) to reconstruct; (persona) to reinstate; (dinero) to refund, pay back; **reintegrarse** vr: **reintegrarse a** to return to

reír [re'ir] vi to laugh; **reírse** vr to laugh; **reírse de** to laugh at

reiterar [reite'rar] vt to reiterate

reivindicación [reiβindika'θjon] nf (demanda) claim, demand; (justificación) vindication

reivindicar [reiβindi'kar] vt to claim

reja ['rexa] nf (de ventana) grille, bars pl; (en la calle) grating

rejilla [re'xiʎa] nf grating, grille; (muebles) wickerwork; (de ventilación) vent; (de coche etc) luggage rack

rejoneador [rexonea'ðor] nm mounted bullfighter

rejuvenecer [rexuβene'θer] vt, vi to rejuvenate

relación [rela'θjon] nf relation, relationship; (MAT) ratio; (narración) report; **con ~, en ~ con** in relation to ▶ **relaciones públicas** public relations ◻ **relacionar** vt to relate, connect; **relacionarse** vr to be connected, be linked

relajación [relaxa'θjon] nf relaxation

relajar [rela'xar] vt to relax; **relajarse** vr to relax

relamerse [rela'merse] vr to lick one's lips

relámpago [re'lampayo] nm flash of lightning; **visita ~** lightning visit

relatar [rela'tar] vt to tell, relate

relativo, -a [rela'tiβo, a] adj relative; **en lo ~ a** concerning

relato [re'lato] nm (narración) story, tale

relegar [rele'yar] vt to relegate

relevante [rele'βante] adj eminent, outstanding

relevar [rele'βar] vt (sustituir) to relieve; **relevarse** vr to relay; **~ a algn de un cargo** to relieve sb of his post

relevo [re'leβo] nm relief; **carrera de relevos** relay race

relieve [re'ljeβe] nm (ARTE, TEC) relief; (fig) prominence, importance; **bajo ~** bas-relief

religión [reli'xjon] nf religion ◻ **religioso, -a** adj religious ◆ nm/f monk/nun

relinchar [relin'tʃar] vi to neigh

reliquia [re'likja] nf relic ▶ **reliquia de familia** heirloom

rellano [re'ʎano] nm (ARQ) landing

rellenar [reʎe'nar] vt (llenar) to fill up; (CULIN) to stuff; (COSTURA) to fill ◻ **relleno, -a** adj full up; stuffed ◆ nm stuffing; (de tapicería) padding

reloj [re'lo(x)] nm clock; **poner el ~ (en hora)** to set one's watch (o the clock) ▶ **reloj (de pulsera)** wristwatch ▶ **reloj despertador** alarm (clock) ▶ **reloj digital** digital watch ◻ **relojero, -a** nm/f clockmaker; watchmaker

reluciente [relu'θjente] adj brilliant, shining

relucir [relu'θir] vi to shine; (fig) to excel

remachar [rema'tʃar] vt to rivet; (fig) to hammer home, drive home ◻ **remache** nm rivet

remangar [reman'gar] vt to roll up

remanso [re'manso] nm pool

remar [re'mar] vi to row

rematado, -a [rema'taðo, a] adj complete, utter

rematar [rema'tar] vt to finish off; (COM) to sell off cheap ◆ vi to end, finish off; (DEPORTE) to shoot

remate [re'mate] nm end, finish; (punta) tip; (DEPORTE) shot; (ARQ) top; **de o para ~** to crown it all (BRIT), to top it off

remedar [reme'ðar] vt to imitate

remediar [reme'ðjar] vt to remedy; (subsanar) to make good, repair; (evitar) to avoid

remedio [re'meðjo] nm remedy; (alivio) help, relief; (JUR) recourse, remedy; **poner ~ a** to correct, stop; **no tener más ~** to have no alternative;

¡qué ~! there's no choice!; **sin ~**
hopeless

remendar [remen'dar] vt to repair;
(con parche) to patch

remiendo [re'mjendo] nm mend; (con
parche) patch; (cosido) darn

remilgado, -a [remil'yaðo, a] adj prim;
(afectado) affected

remiso, -a [re'miso, a] adj slack, slow

remite [re'mite] nm (en sobre) name
and address of sender

remitente nmf sender

remitir [remi'tir] vt to remit, send ♦ vi
to slacken; (en carta): **remite: X** sender:
X ▷ **remitente** nmf sender

remo ['remo] nm (de barco) oar;
(DEPORTE) rowing

remojar [remo'xar] vt to steep, soak;
(galleta etc) to dip, dunk

remojo [re'moxo] nm: **dejar la ropa en
~** to leave clothes to soak

remolacha [remo'latʃa] nf beet,
beetroot

remolcador [remolka'ðor] nm (NÁUT)
tug; (AUTO) breakdown lorry

remolcar [remol'kar] vt to tow

remolino [remo'lino] nm eddy; (de
agua) whirlpool; (de viento) whirlwind;
(de gente) crowd

remolque [re'molke] nm tow, towing;
(cuerda) towrope; **llevar a ~** to tow

remontar [remon'tar] vt to mend;
remontarse vr to soar; **remontarse a**
(COM) to amount to; **~ el vuelo** to soar

remorder [remor'ðer] vt to distress,
disturb; **remorderle la conciencia a
algn** to have a guilty conscience
▷ **remordimiento** nm remorse

remoto, -a [re'moto, a] adj remote

remover [remo'ßer] vt to stir; (tierra) to
turn over; (objetos) to move round

remuneración [remunera'θjon] nf
remuneration

remunerar [remune'rar] vt to
remunerate; (premiar) to reward

renacer [rena'θer] vi to be reborn; (fig)
to revive ▷ **renacimiento** nm rebirth;
el Renacimiento the Renaissance

renacuajo [rena'kwaxo] nm (ZOOL)
tadpole

renal [re'nal] adj renal, kidney cpd

rencilla [ren'θiʎa] nf quarrel

rencor [ren'kor] nm rancour, bitterness
▷ **rencoroso, -a** adj spiteful

rendición [rendi'θjon] nf surrender

rendido, -a [ren'diðo, a] adj (sumiso)
submissive; (cansado) worn-out,
exhausted

rendija [ren'dixa] nf (hendedura) crack,
cleft

rendimiento [rendi'mjento] nm
(producción) output; (TEC, COM)
efficiency

rendir [ren'dir] vt (vencer) to defeat;
(producir) to produce; (dar beneficio) to
yield; (agotar) to exhaust ♦ vi to pay;
rendirse vr (someterse) to surrender;
(cansarse) to wear o.s. out; **~ homenaje
o culto a** to pay homage to

renegar [rene'yar] vi (renunciar) to
renounce; (blasfemar) to blaspheme;
(quejarse) to complain

RENFE ['renfe] nf abr = **Red Nacional
de los Ferrocarriles Españoles**

renglón [ren'glon] nm (línea) line;
(COM) item, article; **a ~ seguido**
immediately after

renombre [re'nombre] nm renown

renovación [renoβa'θjon] nf (de
contrato) renewal; (ARQ) renovation

renovar [reno'ßar] vt to renew; (ARQ) to
renovate

renta ['renta] nf (ingresos) income;
(beneficio) profit; (alquiler) rent
▸ **renta vitalicia** annuity
▷ **rentable** adj profitable

renuncia [re'nunθja] nf resignation

renunciar [renun'θjar] vt to
renounce; (tabaco, alcohol etc):
renunciar a to give up; (oferta,

oportunidad) to turn down; (*puesto*) to resign ♦ *vi* to resign

reñido, -a [re'niðo, a] *adj* (*batalla*) bitter, hard-fought; **estar ~ con algn** to be on bad terms with sb

reñir [re'nir] *vt* (*regañar*) to scold ♦ *vi* (*estar peleado*) to quarrel, fall out; (*combatir*) to fight

reo ['reo] *nmf* culprit, offender; (*acusado*) accused, defendant

reojo [re'oxo]: **de ~** *adv* out of the corner of one's eye

reparación [repara'θjon] *nf* (*acto*) mending, repairing; (*TEC*) repair; (*fig*) amends *pl*, reparation

reparar [repa'rar] *vt* to repair; (*fig*) to make amends for; (*observar*) to observe ♦ *vi*: **~ en** (*darse cuenta de*) to notice; (*prestar atención a*) to pay attention to

reparo [re'paro] *nm* (*advertencia*) observation; (*duda*) doubt; (*dificultad*) difficulty; **poner reparos (a)** to raise objections (to)

repartidor, a [reparti'ðor, a] *nm/f* distributor

repartir [repar'tir] *vt* to distribute, share out; (*CORREOS*) to deliver □ **reparto** *nm* distribution; delivery; (*TEATRO, CINE*) cast; (*CAm: urbanización*) housing estate (*BRIT*), real estate development (*US*)

repasar [repa'sar] *vt* (*ESCOL*) to revise; (*MECÁNICA*) to check, overhaul; (*COSTURA*) to mend □ **repaso** *nm* revision; overhaul, checkup; mending

repecho [re'petʃo] *nm* steep incline

repelente [repe'lente] *adj* repellent, repulsive

repeler [repe'ler] *vt* to repel

repente [re'pente] *nm*: **de ~** suddenly

repentino, -a [repen'tino, a] *adj* sudden

repercusión [reperku'sjon] *nf* repercussion

repercutir [reperku'tir] *vi* (*objeto*) to rebound; (*sonido*) to echo; **~ en** (*fig*) to have repercussions on

repertorio [reper'torjo] *nm* list; (*TEATRO*) repertoire

repetición [repeti'θjon] *nf* repetition

repetir [repe'tir] *vt* to repeat; (*plato*) to have a second helping of ♦ *vi* to repeat; (*sabor*) to come back; **repetirse** *vr* (*volver sobre un tema*) to repeat o.s.

repetitivo, a [repeti'tiβo, a] *adj* repetitive, repetitious

repique [re'pike] *nm* pealing, ringing □ **repiqueteo** *nm* pealing; (*de tambor*) drumming

repisa [re'pisa] *nf* ledge, shelf; (*de ventana*) windowsill; **la ~ de la chimenea** the mantelpiece

repito *etc vb ver* **repetir**

replantearse [replante'arse] *vr*: **~ un problema** to reconsider a problem

repleto, -a [re'pleto, a] *adj* replete, full up

réplica ['replika] *nf* answer; (*ARTE*) replica

replicar [repli'kar] *vi* to answer; (*objetar*) to argue, answer back

repliegue [re'pljeɣe] *nm* (*MIL*) withdrawal

repoblación [repoβla'θjon] *nf* repopulation; (*de río*) restocking ▶ **repoblación forestal** reafforestation

repoblar [repo'βlar] *vt* to repopulate; (*con árboles*) to reafforest

repollito (*CS*) *nm*: **repollitos de Bruselas** (Brussels) sprouts

repollo [re'poʎo] *nm* cabbage

reponer [repo'ner] *vt* to replace, put back; (*TEATRO*) to revive; **reponerse** *vr* to recover; **~ que ...** to reply that ...

reportaje [repor'taxe] *nm* report, article

reportero, -a [repor'tero, a] *nm/f* reporter

reposacabezas [reposaka'βeθas] *nm inv* headrest

reposar [repo'sar] *vi* to rest, repose

reposera (*RPl*) [repo'sera] *nf* deck chair

reposición [reposi'θjon] *nf* replacement; (*CINE*) remake

reposo [re'poso] *nm* rest

repostar [repos'tar] *vt* to replenish; (*AUTO*) to fill up (with petrol (*BRIT*) o gasoline (*US*))

repostería [reposte'ria] *nf* confectioner's (shop)

represa [re'presa] *nf* dam; (*lago artificial*) lake, pool

represalia [repre'salja] *nf* reprisal

representación [representa'θjon] *nf* representation; (*TEATRO*) performance □ **representante** *nmf* representative; performer

representar [represen'tar] *vt* to represent; (*TEATRO*) to perform; (*edad*) to look; **representarse** *vr* to imagine □ **representativo, -a** *adj* representative

represión [repre'sjon] *nf* repression

reprimenda [repri'menda] *nf* reprimand, rebuke

reprimir [repri'mir] *vt* to repress

reprobar [repro'βar] *vt* to censure, reprove

reprochar [repro'tʃar] *vt* to reproach □ **reproche** *nm* reproach

reproducción [reproðuk'θjon] *nf* reproduction

reproducir [reproðu'θir] *vt* to reproduce; **reproducirse** *vr* to breed; (*situación*) to recur

reproductor, a [reproðuk'tor, a] *adj* reproductive

reptil [rep'til] *nm* reptile

república [re'puβlika] *nf* republic
  ▶ **República Dominicana** Dominican Republic □ **republicano, -a** *adj, nm* republican

repudiar [repu'ðjar] *vt* to repudiate; (*fe*) to renounce

repuesto [re'pwesto] *nm* (*pieza de recambio*) spare (part); (*abastecimiento*) supply; **rueda de ~** spare wheel

repugnancia [repuɣ'nanθja] *nf* repugnance □ **repugnante** *adj* repugnant, repulsive

repugnar [repuɣ'nar] *vt* to disgust

repulsa [re'pulsa] *nf* rebuff

repulsión [repul'sjon] *nf* repulsion, aversion □ **repulsivo, -a** *adj* repulsive

reputación [reputa'θjon] *nf* reputation

requerir [reke'rir] *vt* (*pedir*) to ask, request; (*exigir*) to require; (*llamar*) to send for, summon

requesón [reke'son] *nm* cottage cheese

requete... [re'kete] *prefijo* extremely

réquiem ['rekjem] (*pl* **réquiems**) *nm* requiem

requisito [reki'sito] *nm* requirement, requisite

res [res] *nf* beast, animal

resaca [re'saka] *nf* (*de mar*) undertow, undercurrent; (*fam*) hangover

resaltar [resal'tar] *vi* to project, stick out; (*fig*) to stand out

resarcir [resar'θir] *vt* to compensate; **resarcirse** *vr* to make up for

resbaladero (*MÉX*) *nm* slide

resbaladizo, -a [resβala'ðiθo, a] *adj* slippery

resbalar [resβa'lar] *vi* to slip, slide; (*fig*) to slip (up); **resbalarse** *vr* to slip, slide; to slip (up) □ **resbalón** *nm* (*acción*) slip

rescatar [reska'tar] *vt* (*salvar*) to save, rescue; (*objeto*) to get back, recover; (*cautivos*) to ransom

rescate [res'kate] *nm* rescue; (*de objeto*) recovery; **pagar un ~** to pay a ransom

rescindir [resθin'dir] *vt* to rescind

rescisión [resθi'sjon] *nf* cancellation

resecar [rese'kar] vt to dry thoroughly; (MED) to cut out, remove; **resecarse** vr to dry up

reseco, -a [re'seko, a] adj very dry; (fig) skinny

resentido, -a [resen'tiðo, a] adj resentful

resentimiento [resenti'mjento] nm resentment, bitterness

resentirse [resen'tirse] vr (debilitarse: persona) to suffer; **~ de** (consecuencias) to feel the effects of; **~ de (o por) algo** to resent sth, be bitter about sth

reseña [re'seɲa] nf (cuenta) account; (informe) report; (LITERATURA) review □ **reseñar** [rese'ɲar] vt to describe; (LITERATURA) to review

reserva [re'serβa] nf reserve; (reservación) reservation

reservado, -a [reser'βaðo, a] adj reserved; (retraído) cold, distant ♦ nm private room

reservar [reser'βar] vt (guardar) to keep; (habitación, entrada) to reserve; **reservarse** vr to save o.s.; (callar) to keep to o.s.

resfriado [resfri'aðo] nm cold □ **resfriarse** vr to cool; (MED) to catch a cold

resguardar [reswar'ðar] vt to protect, shield; **resguardarse** vr: **resguardarse de** to guard against □ **resguardo** nm defence; (vale) voucher; (recibo) receipt, slip

residencia [resi'ðenθja] nf residence
▶ **residencia de ancianos** residential home, old people's home
▶ **residencia universitaria** hall of residence □ **residencial** nf (urbanización) housing estate

residente [resi'ðente] adj, nmf resident

residir [resi'ðir] vi to reside, live; **~ en** to reside in, lie in

residuo [re'siðwo] nm residue

resignación [resiɣna'θjon] nf resignation □ **resignarse** vr:

resignarse a o con to resign o.s. to, be resigned to

resina [re'sina] nf resin

resistencia [resis'tenθja] nf (dureza) endurance, strength; (oposición, ELEC) resistance □ **resistente** adj strong, hardy; resistant

resistir [resis'tir] vt (soportar) to bear; (oponerse a) to resist, oppose; (aguantar) to put up with ♦ vi to resist; (aguantar) to last, endure; **resistirse** vr: **resistirse a** to refuse to, resist

resoluto, -a [reso'luto, a] adj resolute

resolver [resol'βer] vt to resolve; (solucionar) to solve, resolve; (decidir) to decide, settle; **resolverse** vr to make up one's mind

resonar [reso'nar] vi to ring, echo

resoplar [reso'plar] vi to snort □ **resoplido** nm heavy breathing

resorte [re'sorte] nm spring; (fig) lever

resortera [resor'tera] nf (MÉX) catapult

respaldar [respal'dar] vt to back (up), support; **respaldarse** vr to lean back; **respaldarse con o en** (fig) to take one's stand on □ **respaldo** nm (de sillón) back; (fig) support, backing

respectivo, -a [respek'tiβo, a] adj respective; **en lo ~ a** with regard to

respecto [res'pekto] nm: **al ~** on this matter; **con ~ a, ~ de** with regard to, in relation to

respetable [respe'taβle] adj respectable

respetar [respe'tar] vt to respect □ **respeto** nm respect; (acatamiento) deference; **respetos** nmpl respects □ **respetuoso, -a** adj respectful

respingo [res'pingo] nm start, jump

respiración [respira'θjon] nf breathing; (MED) respiration; (ventilación) ventilation ▶ **respiración asistida** artificial respiration (by machine)

respirar [respi'rar] vi to breathe □ **respiratorio, -a** adj respiratory

❏ **respiro** nm breathing; (fig: descanso) respite

resplandecer [resplande'θer] vi to shine ❏ **resplandeciente** adj resplendent, shining ❏ **resplandor** nm brilliance, brightness; (de luz, fuego) blaze

responder [respon'der] vt to answer ♦ vi to answer; (fig) to respond; (pey) to answer back; **~ de** o **por** to answer for ❏ **respondón, -ona** adj cheeky

responsabilidad [responsaβili'ðað] nf responsibility

responsabilizarse [responsaβili'θarse] vr to make o.s. responsible, take charge

responsable [respon'saβle] adj responsible

respuesta [res'pwesta] nf answer, reply

resquebrajar [reskeβra'xar] vt to crack, split; **resquebrajarse** vr to crack, split

resquicio [res'kiθjo] nm chink; (hendedura) crack

resta ['resta] nf (MAT) remainder

restablecer [restaβle'θer] vt to re-establish, restore; **restablecerse** vr to recover

restante [res'tante] adj remaining; **lo ~** the remainder

restar [res'tar] vt (MAT) to subtract; (fig) to take away ♦ vi to remain, be left

restauración [restaura'θjon] nf restoration

restaurante [restau'rante] nm restaurant

restaurar [restau'rar] vt to restore

restituir [restitu'ir] vt (devolver) to return, give back; (rehabilitar) to restore

resto ['resto] nm (residuo) rest, remainder; (apuesta) stake; **restos** nmpl remains

restorán nm (LAm) restaurant

restregar [restre'ɣar] vt to scrub, rub

restricción [restrik'θjon] nf restriction

restringir [restrin'xir] vt to restrict, limit

resucitar [resuθi'tar] vt, vi to resuscitate, revive

resuelto, -a [re'swelto, a] pp de **resolver** ♦ adj resolute, determined

resultado [resul'taðo] nm result; (conclusión) outcome ❏ **resultante** adj resulting, resultant

resultar [resul'tar] vi (ser) to be; (llegar a ser) to turn out to be; (salir bien) to turn out well; (COM) to amount to; **~ de** to stem from; **me resulta difícil hacerlo** it's difficult for me to do it

resumen [re'sumen] (pl **resúmenes**) nm summary, résumé; **en ~** in short

resumir [resu'mir] vt to sum up; (cortar) to abridge, cut down; (condensar) to summarize

⚠ No confundir **resumir** con la palabra inglesa *resume*.

resurgir [resur'xir] vi (reaparecer) to reappear

resurrección [resurre(k)'θjon] nf resurrection

retablo [re'taβlo] nm altarpiece

retaguardia [reta'ɣwarðja] nf rearguard

retahíla [reta'ila] nf series, string

retal [re'tal] nm remnant

retar [re'tar] vt to challenge; (desafiar) to defy, dare

retazo [re'taθo] nm snippet (BRIT), fragment

retención [reten'θjon] nf (tráfico) hold-up ▸ **retención fiscal** deduction for tax purposes

retener [rete'ner] vt (intereses) to withhold

reticente [reti'θente] adj (tono) insinuating; (postura) reluctant; **ser ~ a hacer algo** to be reluctant o unwilling to do sth

retina [re'tina] nf retina

retintín [retin'tin] nm jangle, jingle

retirada [reti'raða] nf (MIL, refugio) retreat; (de dinero) withdrawal; (de embajador) recall ☐ **retirado, -a** adj (lugar) remote; (vida) quiet; (jubilado) retired

retirar [reti'rar] vt to withdraw; (quitar) to remove; (jubilar) to retire, pension off; **retirarse** vr to retreat, withdraw; to retire; (acostarse) to retire, go to bed ☐ **retiro** nm retreat; retirement; (pago) pension

reto ['reto] nm dare, challenge

retocar [reto'kar] vt (fotografía) to touch up, retouch

retoño [re'toɲo] nm sprout, shoot; (fig) offspring, child

retoque [re'toke] nm retouching

retorcer [retor'θer] vt to twist; (manos, lavado) to wring; **retorcerse** vr to become twisted; (mover el cuerpo) to writhe

retorcido, -a [retor'θiðo, a] adj (persona) devious

retorción (LAm) nm (tb: ~ de tripas) stomach cramp

retórica [re'torika] nf rhetoric; (pey) affectedness

retorno [re'torno] nm return

retortijón [retorti'xon] (ESP) nm (tb: ~ de tripas) stomach cramp

retozar [reto'θar] vi (juguetear) to frolic, romp; (saltar) to gambol

retracción [retrak'θjon] nf retraction

retraerse [retra'erse] vr to retreat, withdraw ☐ **retraído, -a** adj shy, retiring ☐ **retraimiento** nm retirement; (timidez) shyness

retransmisión [retransmi'sjon] nf repeat (broadcast)

retransmitir [retransmi'tir] vt (mensaje) to relay; (TV etc) to repeat, retransmit; (: en vivo) to broadcast live

retrasado, -a [retra'saðo, a] adj late; (MED) mentally retarded; (país etc) backward, underdeveloped

retrasar [retra'sar] vt (demorar) to postpone, put off; (retardar) to slow down ♦ vi (atrasarse) to be late; (reloj) to be slow; (producción) to fall (off); (quedarse atrás) to lag behind; **retrasarse** vr to be late; to be slow; to fall (off); to lag behind

retraso [re'traso] nm (demora) delay; (lentitud) slowness; (tardanza) lateness; (atraso) backwardness; **retrasos** nmpl (FINANZAS) arrears; **llegar con ~** to arrive late ▶ **retraso mental** mental deficiency

retratar [retra'tar] vt (ARTE) to paint the portrait of; (fotografiar) to photograph; (fig) to depict, describe ☐ **retrato** nm portrait; (fig) likeness ☐ **retrato-robot** (ESP) nm Identikit®

retrete [re'trete] nm toilet

retribuir [retri'βwir] vt (recompensar) to reward; (pagar) to pay

retro... ['retro] prefijo retro...

retroceder [retroθe'ðer] vi (echarse atrás) to move back(wards); (fig) to back down

retroceso [retro'θeso] nm backward movement; (MED) relapse; (fig) backing down

retrospectivo, -a [retrospek'tiβo, a] adj retrospective

retrovisor [retroβi'sor] nm (tb: **espejo ~**) rear-view mirror

retumbar [retum'bar] vi to echo, resound

reúma [re'uma], **reuma** ['reuma] nm rheumatism

reunión [reu'njon] nf (asamblea) meeting; (fiesta) party

reunir [reu'nir] vt (juntar) to reunite, join (together); (recoger) to gather (together); (personas) to get together; (cualidades) to combine; **reunirse** vr (personas: en asamblea) to meet, gather

revalidar [reβali'ðar] vt (ratificar) to confirm, ratify

revalorizar [reβaloriˈθar] vt to revalue, reassess

revancha [reˈβantʃa] nf revenge

revelación [reβelaˈθjon] nf revelation

revelado [reβeˈlaðo] nm developing

revelar [reβeˈlar] vt to reveal; (FOTO) to develop

reventa [reˈβenta] nf (de entradas: para concierto) touting

reventar [reβenˈtar] vt to burst, explode

reventón [reβenˈton] nm (AUTO) blowout (BRIT), flat (US)

reverencia [reβeˈrenθja] nf reverence ❑ **reverenciar** vt to revere

reverendo, -a [reβeˈrendo, a] adj reverend

reverente [reβeˈrente] adj reverent

reversa [MÉX, CAm] nf (reverse) gear

reversible [reβerˈsiβle] adj (prenda) reversible

reverso [reˈβerso] nm back, other side; (de moneda) reverse

revertir [reβerˈtir] vi to revert

revés [reˈβes] nm back, wrong side; (fig) reverse, setback; (DEPORTE) backhand; **al** ~ the wrong way round; (de arriba abajo) upside down; (ropa) inside out; **volver algo del** ~ to turn sth round; (ropa) to turn sth inside out

revisar [reβiˈsar] vt (examinar) to check; (texto etc) to revise ❑ **revisión** nf revision ▸ **revisión salarial** wage review

revisor, a [reβiˈsor, a] nm/f inspector; (FERRO) ticket collector

revista [reˈβista] nf magazine, review; (TEATRO) revue; (inspección) inspection; **pasar** ~ **a** to review, inspect ▸ **revista del corazón** magazine featuring celebrity gossip and real-life romance stories

revivir [reβiˈβir] vi to revive

revolcarse [reβolˈkarse] vr to roll about

revoltijo [reβolˈtixo] nm mess, jumble

revoltoso, -a [reβolˈtoso, a] adj (travieso) naughty, unruly

revolución [reβoluˈθjon] nf revolution ❑ **revolucionario, -a** adj, nm/f revolutionary

revolver [reβolˈβer] vt (desordenar) to disturb, mess up; (mover) to move about ♦ vi: **~ en** to go through, rummage (about) in; **revolverse** vr (volver contra) to turn on o against

revólver [reˈβolβer] nm revolver

revuelo [reˈβwelo] nm fluttering; (fig) commotion

revuelta [reˈβwelta] nf (motín) revolt; (agitación) commotion

revuelto, -a [reˈβwelto, a] pp de **revolver** ♦ adj (mezclado) mixed-up, in disorder

rey [rei] nm king; **Día de Reyes** Twelfth Night; **los Reyes Magos** the Three Wise Men, the Magi

---

REYES MAGOS

On the night before the 6th January (the Epiphany), children go to bed expecting **los Reyes Magos** (the Three Wise Men) to bring them presents. Twelfth Night processions, known as **cabalgatas**, take place that evening when 3 people dressed as **los Reyes Magos** arrive in the town by land or sea to the delight of the children.

---

reyerta [reˈjerta] nf quarrel, brawl

rezagado, -a [reθaˈɣaðo, a] nm/f straggler

rezar [reˈθar] vi to pray; **~ con** (fam) to concern, have to do with ❑ **rezo** nm prayer

rezumar [reθuˈmar] vt to ooze

ría [ˈria] nf estuary

riada [riˈaða] nf flood

ribera [riˈβera] nf (de río) bank; (: área) riverside

ribete [riˈβete] nm (de vestido) border; (fig) addition

ricino [ri'θino] *nm*: **aceite de ~** castor oil

rico, -a ['riko, a] *adj* rich; (*adinerado*) wealthy, rich; (*lujoso*) luxurious; (*comida*) delicious; (*niño*) lovely, cute ♦ *nm/f* rich person

ridiculez [riðiku'leθ] *nf* absurdity

ridiculizar [riðikuli'θar] *vt* to ridicule

ridículo, -a [ri'ðikulo, a] *adj* ridiculous; **hacer el ~** to make a fool of o.s.; **poner a algn en ~** to make a fool of sb

riego ['rjeɣo] *nm* (*aspersión*) watering; (*irrigación*) irrigation ▶ **riego sanguíneo** blood flow o circulation

riel [rjel] *nm* rail

rienda ['rjenda] *nf* rein; **dar ~ suelta a** to give free rein to

riesgo ['rjesɣo] *nm* risk; **correr el ~ de** to run the risk of

rifa ['rifa] *nf* (*lotería*) raffle ❑ **rifar** *vt* to raffle

rifle ['rifle] *nm* rifle

rigidez [rixi'ðeθ] *nf* rigidity, stiffness; (*fig*) strictness ❑ **rígido, -a** *adj* rigid, stiff; strict, inflexible

rigor [ri'ɣor] *nm* strictness, rigour; (*inclemencia*) harshness; **de ~** de rigueur, essential ❑ **riguroso, -a** *adj* rigorous; harsh; (*severo*) severe

rimar [ri'mar] *vi* to rhyme

rimbombante [rimbom'bante] *adj* pompous

rímel ['rimel] *nm* mascara

rimmel ['rimel] *nm* = **rímel**

rin (*MÉX*) *nm* (wheel) rim

rincón [rin'kon] *nm* corner (inside)

rinoceronte [rinoθe'ronte] *nm* rhinoceros

riña ['riɲa] *nf* (*disputa*) argument; (*pelea*) brawl

riñón [ri'ɲon] *nm* kidney

río *etc* ['rio] *vb ver* **reír** ♦ *nm* river; (*fig*) torrent, stream ▶ **río abajo/arriba** downstream/upstream ▶ **Río de la Plata** River Plate

rioja [ri'oxa] *nm* (*vino*) rioja (wine)

rioplatense [riopla'tense] *adj* of o from the River Plate region

riqueza [ri'keθa] *nf* wealth, riches *pl*; (*cualidad*) richness

risa ['risa] *nf* laughter; (*una risa*) laugh; **¡qué ~!** what a laugh!

risco ['risko] *nm* crag, cliff

ristra ['ristra] *nf* string

risueño, -a [ri'sweɲo, a] *adj* (*sonriente*) smiling; (*contento*) cheerful

ritmo ['ritmo] *nm* rhythm; **a ~ lento** slowly; **trabajar a ~ lento** to go slow ▶ **ritmo cardíaco** heart rate

rito ['rito] *nm* rite

ritual [ri'twal] *adj, nm* ritual

rival [ri'βal] *adj, nmf* rival ❑ **rivalidad** *nf* rivalry ❑ **rivalizar** *vi*: **rivalizar con** to rival, vie with

rizado, -a [ri'θaðo, a] *adj* curly ♦ *nm* curls *pl*

rizar [ri'θar] *vt* to curl; **rizarse** *vr* (*pelo*) to curl; (*agua*) to ripple ❑ **rizo** *nm* curl; ripple

RNE *nf abr* = **Radio Nacional de España**

robar [ro'βar] *vt* to rob; (*objeto*) to steal; (*casa etc*) to break into; (*NAIPES*) to draw

roble ['roβle] *nm* oak ❑ **robledal** *nm* oakwood

robo ['roβo] *nm* robbery, theft

robot [ro'βot] *nm* robot ▶ **robot (de cocina)** (*ESP*) food processor

robustecer [roβuste'θer] *vt* to strengthen

robusto, -a [ro'βusto, a] *adj* robust, strong

roca ['roka] *nf* rock

roce ['roθe] *nm* (*caricia*) brush; (*TEC*) friction; (*en la piel*) graze; **tener ~ con** to be in close contact with

rociar [ro'θjar] *vt* to spray

rocín [ro'θin] *nm* nag, hack

rocío [ro'θio] *nm* dew

rocola (*LAm*) *nf* jukebox

rocoso, -a [ro'koso, a] *adj* rocky

rodaballo [roða'βaʎo] *nm* turbot

rodaja [ro'ðaxa] *nf* slice

rodaje [ro'ðaxe] *nm* (*CINE*) shooting, filming; (*AUTO*): **en ~** running in

rodar [ro'ðar] *vt* (*vehículo*) to wheel (along); (*escalera*) to roll down; (*viajar por*) to travel (over) ♦ *vi* to roll; (*coche*) to go, run; (*CINE*) to shoot, film

rodear [roðe'ar] *vt* to surround ♦ *vi* to go round; **rodearse** *vr*: **rodearse de amigos** to surround o.s. with friends

rodeo [ro'ðeo] *nm* (*ruta indirecta*) detour; (*evasión*) evasion; (*DEPORTE*) rodeo; **hablar sin rodeos** to come to the point, speak plainly

rodilla [ro'ðiʎa] *nf* knee; **de rodillas** kneeling; **ponerse de rodillas** to kneel (down)

rodillo [ro'ðiʎo] *nm* roller; (*CULIN*) rolling-pin

roedor, a [roe'ðor, a] *adj* gnawing ♦ *nm* rodent

roer [ro'er] *vt* (*masticar*) to gnaw; (*corroer, fig*) to corrode

rogar [ro'ɣar] *vt, vi* (*pedir*) to ask for; (*suplicar*) to beg, plead; **se ruega no fumar** please do not smoke

rojizo, -a [ro'xiθo, a] *adj* reddish

rojo, -a ['roxo, a] *adj, nm* red; **al ~ vivo** red-hot

rol [rol] *nm* list, roll; (*papel*) role

rollito [ro'ʎito] *nm* (*tb*: **~ de primavera**) spring roll

rollizo, -a [ro'ʎiθo, a] *adj* (*objeto*) cylindrical; (*persona*) plump

rollo ['roʎo] *nm* roll; (*de cuerda*) coil; (*madera*) log; (*ESP: fam*) bore; **¡qué ~!** (*ESP: fam*) what a carry-on!

Roma ['roma] *nf* Rome

romance [ro'manθe] *nm* (*amoroso*) romance; (*LITERATURA*) ballad

romano, -a [ro'mano, a] *adj, nm/f* Roman; **a la romana** in batter

romanticismo [romanti'θismo] *nm* romanticism

romántico, -a [ro'mantiko, a] *adj* romantic

rombo ['rombo] *nm* (*GEOM*) rhombus

romería [rome'ria] *nf* (*REL*) pilgrimage; (*excursión*) trip, outing

---

ROMERÍA

Originally a pilgrimage to a shrine or church to express devotion to the Virgin Mary or a local Saint, the **romería** has also become a rural festival which accompanies the pilgrimage. People come from all over to attend, bringing their own food and drink, and spend the day in celebration.

---

romero, -a [ro'mero, a] *nm/f* pilgrim ♦ *nm* rosemary

romo, -a ['romo, a] *adj* blunt; (*fig*) dull

rompecabezas [rompeka'βeθas] *nm inv* riddle, puzzle; (*juego*) jigsaw (puzzle)

rompehuelgas (*LAm*) [rompe'welɣas] *nm inv* strikebreaker, scab

rompeolas [rompe'olas] *nm inv* breakwater

romper [rom'per] *vt* to break; (*hacer pedazos*) to smash; (*papel, tela etc*) to tear, rip ♦ *vi* (*olas*) to break; (*sol, diente*) to break through; **romperse** *vr* to break; **~ un contrato** to break a contract; **~ a** (*empezar a*) to start (suddenly) to; **~ a llorar** to burst into tears; **~ con algn** to fall out with sb

ron [ron] *nm* rum

roncar [ron'kar] *vi* to snore

ronco, -a ['ronko, a] *adj* (*afónico*) hoarse; (*áspero*) raucous

ronda ['ronda] *nf* (*gen*) round; (*patrulla*) patrol ☐ **rondar** *vt* to patrol ♦ *vi* to patrol; (*fig*) to prowl round

ronquido [ron'kiðo] *nm* snore, snoring

ronronear [ronrone'ar] *vi* to purr

roña ['roɲa] *nf* (*VETERINARIA*) mange; (*mugre*) dirt, grime; (*óxido*) rust

roñoso, -a [roˈɲoso, a] adj (mugriento) filthy; (tacaño) mean

ropa [ˈropa] nf clothes pl, clothing ▶ **ropa blanca** linen ▶ **ropa de cama** bed linen ▶ **ropa de color** coloureds pl ▶ **ropa interior** underwear ▶ **ropa sucia** dirty washing ❑ **ropaje** nm gown, robes pl

ropero [roˈpero] nm linen cupboard; (guardarropa) wardrobe

rosa [ˈrosa] adj pink ♦ nf rose

rosado, -a [roˈsaðo, a] adj pink ♦ nm rosé

rosal [roˈsal] nm rosebush

rosario [roˈsarjo] nm (REL) rosary; **rezar el ~** to say the rosary

rosca [ˈroska] nf (de tornillo) thread; (de humo) coil, spiral; (pan, postre) ring-shaped roll/pastry

rosetón [roseˈton] nm rosette; (ARQ) rose window

rosquilla [rosˈkiʎa] nf doughnut-shaped fritter

rostro [ˈrostro] nm (cara) face

rotativo, -a [rotaˈtiβo, a] adj rotary

roto, -a [ˈroto, a] pp de **romper** ♦ adj broken

rotonda [roˈtonda] nf roundabout

rótula [ˈrotula] nf kneecap; (TEC) ball-and-socket joint

rotulador [rotulaˈðor] nm felt-tip pen

rótulo [ˈrotulo] nm heading, title; label; (letrero) sign

rotundamente [rotundaˈmente] adv (negar) flatly; (responder, afirmar) emphatically ❑ **rotundo, -a** adj round; (enfático) emphatic

rotura [roˈtura] nf (acto) breaking; (MED) fracture

rozadura [roθaˈðura] nf abrasion, graze

rozar [roˈθar] vt (frotar) to rub; (arañar) to scratch; (tocar ligeramente) to shave, touch lightly; **rozarse** vr to rub (together); **rozarse con** (fam) to rub shoulders with

rte. abr (= remite, remitente) sender

RTVE nf abr = **Radiotelevisión Española**

rubí [ruˈβi] nm ruby; (de reloj) jewel

rubio, -a [ˈruβjo, a] adj fair-haired, blond(e) ♦ nm/f blond/blonde; **tabaco ~** Virginia tobacco

rubor [ruˈβor] nm (sonrojo) blush; (timidez) bashfulness ❑ **ruborizarse** vr to blush

rúbrica [ˈruβrika] nf (de la firma) flourish ❑ **rubricar** vt (firmar) to sign with a flourish; (concluir) to sign and seal

rudimentario, -a [ruðimenˈtarjo, a] adj rudimentary

rudo, -a [ˈruðo, a] adj (sin pulir) unpolished; (grosero) coarse; (violento) violent; (sencillo) simple

rueda [ˈrweða] nf wheel; (círculo) ring, circle; (rodaja) slice, round ▶ **rueda de auxilio** (RPl) spare tyre ▶ **rueda delantera/trasera/de repuesto** front/back/spare wheel ▶ **rueda de prensa** press conference ▶ **rueda gigante** (LAm) big (BRIT) o Ferris (US) wheel

ruedo [ˈrweðo] nm (círculo) circle; (TAUR) arena, bullring

ruego etc [ˈrweɣo] vb ver **rogar** ♦ nm request

rugby [ˈruɣβi] nm rugby

rugido [ruˈxiðo] nm roar

rugir [ruˈxir] vi to roar

rugoso, -a [ruˈɣoso, a] adj (arrugado) wrinkled; (áspero) rough; (desigual) ridged

ruido [ˈrwiðo] nm noise; (sonido) sound; (alboroto) racket, row; (escándalo) commotion, rumpus ❑ **ruidoso, -a** adj noisy, loud; (fig) sensational

ruin [rwin] adj contemptible, mean

ruina [ˈrwina] nf ruin; (colapso) collapse; (de persona) ruin, downfall

ruinoso, -a [rwi'noso, a] *adj* ruinous; *(destartalado)* dilapidated, tumbledown; *(COM)* disastrous

ruiseñor [rwise'ɲor] *nm* nightingale

rulero *(RPl)* *nm* roller

ruleta [ru'leta] *nf* roulette

rulo ['rulo] *nm (para el pelo)* curler

Rumanía [ruma'nia] *nf* Rumania

rumba ['rumba] *nf* rumba

rumbo ['rumbo] *nm (ruta)* route, direction; *(ángulo de dirección)* course, bearing; *(fig)* course of events; **ir con ~ a** to be heading for

rumiante [ru'mjante] *nm* ruminant

rumiar [ru'mjar] *vt* to chew; *(fig)* to chew over ♦ *vi* to chew the cud

rumor [ru'mor] *nm (ruido sordo)* low sound; *(murmuración)* murmur, buzz □ **rumorearse** *vr:* **se rumorea que ...** it is rumoured that ...

rupestre [ru'pestre] *adj* rock *cpd*

ruptura [rup'tura] *nf* rupture

rural [ru'ral] *adj* rural

Rusia ['rusja] *nf* Russia □ **ruso, -a** *adj, nm/f* Russian

rústico, -a ['rustiko, a] *adj* rustic; *(ordinario)* coarse, uncouth ♦ *nm/f* yokel

ruta ['ruta] *nf* route

rutina [ru'tina] *nf* routine

S, s

S *abr* (= **santo, a**) St; (= **sur**) S

s. *abr* (= **siglo**) C.; (= **siguiente**) foll

S.A. *abr* (= **Sociedad Anónima**) Ltd. *(BRIT)*, Inc. *(US)*

sábado ['saβaðo] *nm* Saturday

sábana ['saβana] *nf* sheet

sabañón [saβa'ɲon] *nm* chilblain

saber [sa'βer] *vt* to know; *(llegar a conocer)* to find out, learn; *(tener capacidad de)* to know how to ♦ *vi:* **~ a** to taste of, taste like ♦ *nm* knowledge, learning; **a ~** namely; **¿sabes conducir/ nadar?** can you drive/swim?; **¿sabes francés?** do you speak French?; **~ de memoria** to know by heart; **hacer ~ algo a algn** to inform sb of sth, let sb know sth

sabiduría [saβiðu'ria] *nf (conocimientos)* wisdom; *(instrucción)* learning

sabiendas [sa'βjendas]: **a ~** *adv* knowingly

sabio, -a ['saβjo,a] *adj (docto)* learned; *(prudente)* wise, sensible

sabor [sa'βor] *nm* taste, flavour □ **saborear** *vt* to taste, savour; *(fig)* to relish

sabotaje [saβo'taxe] *nm* sabotage

sabré *etc* [sa'βre] *vb ver* **saber**

sabroso, -a [sa'βroso, a] *adj* tasty; *(fig: fam)* racy, salty

sacacorchos [saka'kortʃos] *nm inv* corkscrew

sacapuntas [saka'puntas] *nm inv* pencil sharpener

sacar [sa'kar] *vt* to take out; *(fig: extraer)* to get (out); *(quitar)* to remove, get out; *(hacer salir)* to bring out; *(conclusión)* to draw; *(novela etc)* to publish, bring out; *(ropa)* to take off; *(obra)* to make; *(premio)* to receive; *(entradas)* to get; *(TENIS)* to serve; **~ adelante** *(niño)* to bring up; *(negocio)* to carry on, go on with; **~ a algn a bailar** to get sb up to dance; **~ una foto** to take a photo; **~ la lengua** to stick out one's tongue; **~ buenas/ malas notas** to get good/bad marks

sacarina [saka'rina] *nf* saccharin(e)

sacerdote [saθer'ðote] *nm* priest

saciar [sa'θjar] *vt (hambre, sed)* to satisfy; **saciarse** *vr (de comida)* to get full up

saco ['sako] *nm* bag; *(grande)* sack; *(su contenido)* bagful; *(LAm: chaqueta)* jacket ▶ **saco de dormir** sleeping bag

sacramento [sakra'mento] nm sacrament

sacrificar [sakrifi'kar] vt to sacrifice □ **sacrificio** nm sacrifice

sacristía [sakris'tia] nf sacristy

sacudida [saku'ðiða] nf (agitación) shake, shaking; (sacudimiento) jolt, bump ▶ **sacudida eléctrica** electric shock

sacudir [saku'ðir] vt to shake; (golpear) to hit

Sagitario [saxi'tarjo] nm Sagittarius

sagrado, -a [sa'ɣraðo, a] adj sacred, holy

Sáhara ['saara] nm: **el ~** the Sahara (desert)

sal [sal] vb ver **salir** ♦ nf salt ▶ **sales de baño** bath salts

sala ['sala] nf room; (tb: **~ de estar**) living room; (TEATRO) house, auditorium; (de hospital) ward ▶ **sala de espera** waiting room ▶ **sala de estar** living room ▶ **sala de fiestas** dance hall

salado, -a [sa'laðo, a] adj salty; (fig) witty, amusing; **agua salada** salt water

salar [sa'lar] vt to salt, add salt to

salario [sa'larjo] nm wage, pay

salchicha [sal'tʃitʃa] nf (pork) sausage □ **salchichón** nm (salami-type) sausage

saldo ['saldo] nm (pago) settlement; (de una cuenta) balance; (lo restante) remnant(s) (pl), remainder; (de móvil) credit; **saldos** nmpl (en tienda) sale

saldré etc [sal'dre] vb ver **salir**

salero [sa'lero] nm salt cellar

salgo etc vb ver **salir**

salida [sa'liða] nf (puerta etc) exit, way out; (acto) leaving, going out; (de tren, AVIAC) departure; (TEC) output, production; (fig) way out; (COM) opening; (GEO, ELEC) outlet; (de gas) leak; **calle sin ~** cul-de-sac ▶ **salida de baño** (RPI) bathrobe ▶ **salida de**

emergencia/incendios emergency exit/fire escape

salir [sa'lir] vi

1 (partir: tb: **salir de**) to leave; **Juan ha salido** Juan is out; **salió de la cocina** he came out of the kitchen

2 (aparecer) to appear; (disco, libro) to come out; **anoche salió en la tele** she appeared o was on TV last night; **salió en todos los periódicos** it was in all the papers

3 (resultar): **la muchacha nos salió muy trabajadora** the girl turned out to be a very hard worker; **la comida le ha salido exquisita** the food was delicious; **sale muy caro** it's very expensive

4: **salirle a uno algo: la entrevista que hice me salió bien/mal** the interview I did went o turned out well/badly

5: **salir adelante: no sé como haré para salir adelante** I don't know how I'll get by

♦ **salirse** vr (líquido) to spill; (animal) to escape

saliva [sa'liβa] nf saliva

salmo ['salmo] nm psalm

salmón [sal'mon] nm salmon

salmonete [salmo'nete] nm red mullet

salón [sa'lon] nm (de casa) living room, lounge; (muebles) lounge suite ▶ **salón de baile** dance hall ▶ **salón de belleza** beauty parlour

salpicadera (MÉX) [salpika'ðera] nf mudguard (BRIT), fender (US)

salpicadero [salpika'ðero] nm (AUTO) dashboard

salpicar [salpi'kar] vt (rociar) to sprinkle, spatter; (esparcir) to scatter

salpicón [salpi'kon] nm (tb: **~ de marisco**) seafood salad

salsa ['salsa] nf sauce; (con carne asada) gravy; (fig) spice

saltamontes [salta'montes] nm inv grasshopper

saltar [sal'tar] vt to jump (over), leap (over); (dejar de lado) to skip, miss out ♦ vi to jump, leap; (pelota) to bounce; (al aire) to fly up; (quebrarse) to break; (al agua) to dive; (fig) to explode, blow up

salto ['salto] nm jump, leap; (al agua) dive ▶ **salto de agua** waterfall ▶ **salto de altura/longitud** high/long jump

salud [sa'luð] nf health; **¡(a su) ~!** cheers!, good health! ❑ **saludable** adj (de buena salud) healthy; (provechoso) good, beneficial

saludar [salu'ðar] vt to greet; (MIL) to salute ❑ **saludo** nm greeting; **"saludos"** (en carta) "best wishes", "regards"

salvación [salβa'θjon] nf salvation; (rescate) rescue

salvado [sal'βaðo] nm bran

salvaje [sal'βaxe] adj wild; (tribu) savage

salvamanteles nm inv table mat

salvamento [salβa'mento] nm rescue

salvapantallas nm inv screen saver

salvar [sal'βar] vt (rescatar) to save, rescue; (resolver) to overcome, resolve; (cubrir distancias) to cover, travel; (hacer excepción) to except, exclude; (barco) to salvage

salvavidas [salβa'βiðas] adj inv: **bote/ chaleco ~** lifeboat/life jacket

salvo, -a ['salβo, a] adj safe ♦ adv except (for), save; **a ~** out of danger; **~ que** unless

san [san] adj saint; **S~ Juan** St John

sanar [sa'nar] vt (herida) to heal; (persona) to cure ♦ vi (persona) to get well, recover; (herida) to heal

sanatorio [sana'torjo] nm sanatorium

sanción [san'θjon] nf sanction

sancochado, -a (MÉX) adj (CULIN) underdone, rare

sandalia [san'dalja] nf sandal

sandía [san'dia] nf watermelon

sandwich ['sandwitʃ] (pl **sandwichs**, **sandwiches**) nm sandwich

sanfermines nmpl festivities in celebration of San Fermín (Pamplona)

sangrar [san'grar] vt, vi to bleed ❑ **sangre** nf blood

sangría [san'gria] nf sangria, sweetened drink of red wine with fruit

sangriento, -a [san'grjento, a] adj bloody

sanguíneo, -a [san'gineo, a] adj blood cpd

sanidad [sani'ðað] nf (tb: ~ **pública**) public health

San Isidro nm patron saint of Madrid

sanitario, -a [saniˈtarjo, a] adj health cpd ❑ **sanitarios** nmpl toilets (BRIT), washroom (US)

sano, -a [ˈsano, a] adj healthy; (sin daños) sound; (comida) wholesome; (entero) whole, intact; **~ y salvo** safe and sound

⚠ No confundir **sano** con la palabra inglesa **sane**.

Santiago [sanˈtjaɣo] nm: **~ (de Chile)** Santiago

santiamén [santjaˈmen] nm: **en un ~** in no time at all

santidad [santiˈðað] nf holiness, sanctity

santiguarse [santiˈɣwarse] vr to make the sign of the cross

santo, -a [ˈsanto, a] adj holy; (fig) wonderful, miraculous ♦ nm/f saint ♦ nm saint's day; (fig) **~ y seña** password

santuario [sanˈtwarjo] nm sanctuary, shrine

sapo [ˈsapo] nm toad

saque [ˈsake] nm (TENIS) service, serve; (FUTBOL) throw-in ▸ **saque de esquina** corner (kick)

saquear [sakeˈar] vt (MIL) to sack; (robar) to loot, plunder; (fig) to ransack

sarampión [saramˈpjon] nm measles sg

sarcástico, -a [sarˈkastiko, a] adj sarcastic

sardina [sarˈðina] nf sardine

sargento [sarˈxento] nm sergeant

sarmiento [sarˈmjento] nm (BOT) vine shoot

sarna [ˈsarna] nf itch; (MED) scabies

sarpullido [sarpuˈʎiðo] nm (MED) rash

sarro [ˈsarro] nm (en dientes) tartar, plaque

sartén [sarˈten] nf frying pan

sastre [ˈsastre] nm tailor ❑ **sastrería** nf (arte) tailoring; (tienda) tailor's (shop)

Satanás [sataˈnas] nm Satan

satélite [saˈtelite] nm satellite

sátira [ˈsatira] nf satire

satisfacción [satisfakˈθjon] nf satisfaction

satisfacer [satisfaˈθer] vt to satisfy; (gastos) to meet; (pérdida) to make good; **satisfacerse** vr to satisfy o.s., be satisfied; (vengarse) to take revenge ❑ **satisfecho, -a** adj satisfied; (contento) content(ed), happy; (tb: **satisfecho de sí mismo**) self-satisfied, smug

saturar [satuˈrar] vt to saturate; **saturarse** vr (mercado, aeropuerto) to reach saturation point

sauce [ˈsauθe] nm willow ▸ **sauce llorón** weeping willow

sauna [ˈsauna] nf sauna

savia [ˈsaβja] nf sap

saxofón [saksoˈfon] nm saxophone

sazonar [saθoˈnar] vt to ripen; (CULIN) to flavour, season

scooter (ESP) nf scooter

Scotch® (LAm) nm Sellotape® (BRIT), Scotch tape® (US)

SE abr (= sudeste) SE

---

se

PALABRA CLAVE

[se] pron

1 (reflexivo: sg: m) himself; (: f) herself; (: pl) themselves; (: cosa) itself; (: de Vd) yourself; (: pl de Vds) yourselves; **se está preparando** she's preparing herself

2 (con complemento indirecto) to him; to her; to them; to it; to you; **a usted se lo dije ayer** I told you yesterday; **se compró un sombrero** he bought himself a hat; **se rompió la pierna** he broke his leg

3 (uso recíproco) each other, one another; **se miraron (el uno al otro)** they looked at each other o one another

4 (en oraciones pasivas): **se han vendido muchos libros** a lot of books have been sold

B (*impers*): **se dice que ...** people say that ...; it is said that ...; **allí se come muy bien** the food there is very good, you can eat very well there

sé *etc* [se] *vb ver* **saber**; **ser**

sea *etc* ['sea] *vb ver* **ser**

sebo ['seβo] *nm* fat, grease

secador [seka'ðor] *nm*: ~ **de pelo** hair-dryer

secadora [seka'ðora] *nf* tumble dryer

secar [se'kar] *vt* to dry; **secarse** *vr* to dry (off); (*río, planta*) to dry up

sección [sek'θjon] *nf* section

seco, -a ['seko, a] *adj* dry; (*carácter*) cold; (*respuesta*) sharp, curt; **parar en ~** to stop dead; **decir algo a secas** to say sth curtly

secretaría [sekreta'ria] *nf* secretariat

secretario, -a [sekre'tarjo, a] *nm/f* secretary

secreto, -a [se'kreto, a] *adj* secret; (*persona*) secretive ♦ *nm* secret; (*calidad*) secrecy

secta ['sekta] *nf* sect

sector [sek'tor] *nm* sector

secuela [se'kwela] *nf* consequence

secuencia [se'kwenθja] *nf* sequence

secuestrar [sekwes'trar] *vt* to kidnap; (*bienes*) to seize, confiscate ❏ **secuestro** *nm* kidnapping; seizure, confiscation

secundario, -a [sekun'darjo, a] *adj* secondary

sed [seð] *nf* thirst; **tener ~** to be thirsty

seda ['seða] *nf* silk

sedal [se'ðal] *nm* fishing line

sedán (*LAm*) [se'ðan] *nm* saloon (*BRIT*), sedan (*US*)

sedante [se'ðante] *nm* sedative

sede ['seðe] *nf* (*de gobierno*) seat; (*de compañía*) headquarters *pl*; **Santa S~** Holy See

sedentario, -a [seðen'tarjo, a] *adj* sedentary

sediento, -a [se'ðjento, a] *adj* thirsty

sedimento [seði'mento] *nm* sediment

seducción [seðuk'θjon] *nf* seduction

seducir [seðu'θir] *vt* to seduce; (*cautivar*) to charm, fascinate; (*atraer*) to attract ❏ **seductor, a** *adj* seductive; charming, fascinating; attractive ♦ *nm/f* seducer

segar [se'ɣar] *vt* (*mies*) to reap, cut; (*hierba*) to mow, cut

seglar [se'ɣlar] *adj* secular, lay

seguida [se'ɣiða] *nf*: **en ~** at once, right away

seguido, -a [se'ɣiðo, a] *adj* (*continuo*) straight, unbroken; (*recto*) straight ♦ *adv* (*directo*) straight (on); (*después*) after; (*LAm: a menudo*) often; **seguidos** consecutive, successive; **5 días seguidos** 5 days running, 5 days in a row

seguir [se'ɣir] *vt* to follow; (*venir después*) to follow on, come after; (*proseguir*) to continue; (*perseguir*) to chase, pursue ♦ *vi* (*gen*) to follow; (*continuar*) to continue, carry o go on; **seguirse** *vr* to follow; **sigo sin comprender** I still don't understand; **sigue lloviendo** it's still raining

según [se'ɣun] *prep* according to ♦ *adv*: **¿irás? — ~** are you going? — it all depends ♦ *conj* as; **~ caminamos** while we walk

segundo, -a [se'ɣundo, a] *adj* second ♦ *nm* second ♦ *nf* second meaning; **de segunda mano** second-hand; **segunda (clase)** second class; **segunda (marcha)** (*AUTO*) second (gear)

seguramente [seɣura'mente] *adv* surely; (*con certeza*) for sure, with certainty

seguridad [seɣuri'ðað] *nf* safety; (*del estado, de casa etc*) security; (*certidumbre*) certainty; (*confianza*)

confidence; (*estabilidad*) stability
▶ **seguridad social** social security

seguro, -a [se'ɣuro, a] *adj* (*cierto*) sure, certain; (*fiel*) trustworthy; (*libre de peligro*) safe; (*bien defendido, firme*) secure ♦ *adv* for sure, certainly ♦ *nm* (COM) insurance ▶ **seguro contra terceros/a todo riesgo** third party/ comprehensive insurance ▶ **seguros sociales** social security *sg*

seis [seis] *num* six

seísmo [se'ismo] *nm* tremor, earthquake

selección [selek'θjon] *nf* selection ❏ **seleccionar** *vt* to pick, choose, select

selectividad [selektiβi'ðað] (*ESP*) *nf* university entrance examination

selecto, -a [se'lekto, a] *adj* select, choice; (*escogido*) selected

sellar [se'ʎar] *vt* (*documento oficial*) to seal; (*pasaporte, visado*) to stamp

sello ['seʎo] *nm* stamp; (*precinto*) seal

selva ['selβa] *nf* (*bosque*) forest, woods *pl*; (*jungla*) jungle

semáforo [se'maforo] *nm* (AUTO) traffic lights *pl*; (FERRO) signal

semana [se'mana] *nf* week; **entre ~** during the week ▶ **Semana Santa** Holy Week ❏ **semanal** *adj* weekly ❏ **semanario** *nm* weekly magazine

---

SEMANA SANTA

In Spain celebrations for **Semana Santa** (Holy Week) are often spectacular. "Viernes Santo", "Sábado Santo" and "Domingo de Resurrección" (Good Friday, Holy Saturday, Easter Sunday) are all national public holidays, with additional days being given as local holidays. There are fabulous **procesiones** all over the country, with members of "cofradías" (brotherhoods) dressing in hooded robes and parading their "pasos"

(religious floats and sculptures) through the streets. Seville has the most famous Holy Week processions.

sembrar [sem'brar] *vt* to sow; (*objetos*) to sprinkle, scatter about; (*noticias etc*) to spread

semejante [seme'xante] *adj* (*parecido*) similar ♦ *nm* fellow man, fellow creature; **semejantes** alike, similar; **nunca hizo cosa ~** he never did any such thing ❏ **semejanza** *nf* similarity, resemblance

semejar [seme'xar] *vi* to seem like, resemble; **semejarse** *vr* to look alike, be similar

semen ['semen] *nm* semen

semestral [semes'tral] *adj* half-yearly, bi-annual

semicírculo [semi'θirkulo] *nm* semicircle

semidesnatado, -a [semiðesna'taðo, a] *adj* semi-skimmed

semifinal [semifi'nal] *nf* semifinal

semilla [se'miʎa] *nf* seed

seminario [semi'narjo] *nm* (REL) seminary; (ESCOL) seminar

sémola ['semola] *nf* semolina

senado [se'naðo] *nm* senate ❏ **senador, a** *nm/f* senator

sencillez [senθi'ʎeθ] *nf* simplicity; (*de persona*) naturalness ❏ **sencillo, -a** *adj* simple; natural, unaffected

senda ['senda] *nf* path, track

senderismo [sende'rismo] *nm* hiking

sendero [sen'dero] *nm* path, track

sendos, -as ['sendos, as] *adj pl*: **les dio ~ golpes** he hit both of them

senil [se'nil] *adj* senile

seno ['seno] *nm* (ANAT) bosom, bust; (*fig*) bosom; **senos** breasts

sensación [sensa'θjon] *nf* sensation; (*sentido*) sense; (*sentimiento*) feeling ❏ **sensacional** *adj* sensational

sensato, -a [sen'sato, a] *adj* sensible

sensible [sen'sible] adj sensitive; (apreciable) perceptible, appreciable; (pérdida) considerable □ **sensiblero, -a** adj sentimental

⚠ No confundir **sensible** con la palabra inglesa *sensible*.

sensitivo, -a [sensi'tiβo, a] adj sense cpd

sensorial [senso'rjal] adj sensory

sensual [sen'swal] adj sensual

sentada [sen'taða] nf sitting; (protesta) sit-in

sentado, -a [sen'taðo, a] adj: **estar ~** to sit, be sitting (down); **dar por ~** to take for granted, assume

sentar [sen'tar] vt to sit, seat; (fig) to establish ♦ vi (vestido) to suit; (alimento): **~ bien/mal a** to agree/ disagree with; **sentarse** vr (persona) to sit, sit down; (los depósitos) to settle

sentencia [sen'tenθja] nf (máxima) maxim, saying; (JUR) sentence □ **sentenciar** vt to sentence

sentido, -a [sen'tiðo, a] adj (pérdida) regrettable; (carácter) sensitive ♦ nm sense; (sentimiento) feeling; (significado) sense, meaning; (dirección) direction; **mi más ~ pésame** my deepest sympathy; **tener ~** to make sense ▶ **sentido común** common sense ▶ **sentido del humor** sense of humour ▶ **sentido único** one-way (street)

sentimental [sentimen'tal] adj sentimental; **vida ~** love life

sentimiento [senti'mjento] nm feeling

sentir [sen'tir] vt to feel; (percibir) to perceive, sense; (lamentar) to regret, be sorry for ♦ vi (tener la sensación) to feel; (lamentarse) to feel sorry ♦ nm opinion, judgement; **sentirse bien/ mal** to feel well/ill; **lo siento** I'm sorry

seña ['sena] nf sign; (MIL) password; **señas** nfpl (dirección) address sg

▶ **señas personales** personal description sg

señal [se'nal] nf sign; (síntoma) symptom; (FERRO, TEL) signal; (marca) mark; (COM) deposit; **en ~ de** as a token o sign of □ **señalar** vt to mark; (indicar) to point out, indicate

señor [se'nor] nm (hombre) man; (caballero) gentleman; (dueño) owner, master; (trato: antes de nombre propio) Mr; (: hablando directamente) sir; **muy ~ mío** Dear Sir; **el ~ alcalde/presidente** the mayor/president

señora [se'nora] nf (dama) lady; (trato: antes de nombre propio) Mrs; (: hablando directamente) madam; (esposa) wife; **Nuestra S~** Our Lady

señorita [seno'rita] nf (con nombre y/o apellido) Miss; (mujer joven) young lady

señorito [seno'rito] nm young gentleman; (pey) rich kid

sepa etc ['sepa] vb ver **saber**

separación [separa'θjon] nf separation; (división) division; (hueco) gap

separar [sepa'rar] vt to separate; (dividir) to divide; **separarse** vr (parte) to come away; (partes) to come apart; (persona) to leave, go away; (matrimonio) to separate □ **separatismo** nm separatism

sepia ['sepja] nf cuttlefish

septentrional [septentrjo'nal] adj northern

septiembre [sep'tjembre] nm September

séptimo, -a ['septimo, a] adj, nm seventh

sepulcral [sepul'kral] adj (fig: silencio, atmósfera) deadly □ **sepulcro** nm tomb, grave

sepultar [sepul'tar] vt to bury □ **sepultura** nf (acto) burial; (tumba) grave, tomb

sequía [se'kia] nf drought

séquito ['sekito] nm (de rey etc) retinue; (seguidores) followers pl

ser

PALABRA CLAVE

[ser] vi

1 (descripción) to be; **es médica/muy alta** she's a doctor/very tall; **la familia es de Cuzco** his (o her etc) family is from Cuzco; **soy Ana** (TEL) Ana speaking o here

2 (propiedad): **es de Joaquín** it's Joaquín's, it belongs to Joaquín

3 (horas, fechas, números): **es la una** it's one o'clock; **son las seis y media** it's half-past six; **es el 1 de junio** it's the first of June; **somos/son seis** there are six of us/them

4 (en oraciones pasivas): **ha sido descubierto ya** it's already been discovered

5: **es de esperar que ...** it is to be hoped o I etc hope that ...

6 (locuciones con sub): **o sea** that is to say; **sea él sea su hermana** either him or his sister

7: **a no ser por él ...** but for him ...

8: **a no ser que: a no ser que tenga uno ya** unless he's got one already

♦ nm being ▶ **ser humano** human being

sereno, -a [se'reno, a] adj (persona) calm, unruffled; (el tiempo) fine, settled; (ambiente) calm, peaceful ♦ nm night watchman

serial [ser'jal] nm serial

serie ['serje] nf series; (cadena) sequence, succession; **fuera de ~** out of order; (fig) special, out of the ordinary; **fabricación en ~** mass production

seriedad [serje'ðað] nf seriousness; (formalidad) reliability □ **serio, -a** adj

serious; reliable, dependable; grave, serious; **en serio** adv seriously

serigrafía [seriɣra'fia] nf silk-screen printing

sermón [ser'mon] nm (REL) sermon

seropositivo, -a [seroposi'tiβo] adj HIV positive

serpentear [serpente'ar] vi to wriggle; (camino, río) to wind, snake

serpentina [serpen'tina] nf streamer

serpiente [ser'pjente] nf snake ▶ **serpiente de cascabel** rattlesnake

serranía [serra'nia] nf mountainous area

serrar [se'rrar] vt = **aserrar**

serrín [se'rrin] nm sawdust

serrucho [se'rrutʃo] nm saw

service (RPl) nm (AUTO) service

servicio [ser'βiθjo] nm service; (LAm AUTO) service; **servicios** nmpl (ESP) toilet(s) ▶ **servicio incluido** service charge included ▶ **servicio militar** military service

servidumbre [serβi'ðumbre] nf (sujeción) servitude; (criados) servants pl, staff

servil [ser'βil] adj servile

servilleta [serβi'ʎeta] nf serviette, napkin

servir [ser'βir] vt to serve ♦ vi to serve; (tener utilidad) to be of use, be useful; **servirse** vr to serve o help o.s.; **servirse de algo** to make use of sth, use sth; **sírvase pasar** please come in

sesenta [se'senta] num sixty

sesión [se'sjon] nf (POL) session, sitting; (CINE) showing

seso ['seso] nm brain □ **sesudo, -a** adj sensible, wise

seta ['seta] nf mushroom ▶ **seta venenosa** toadstool

setecientos, -as [sete'θjentos, as] adj, num seven hundred

setenta [se'tenta] num seventy

seto ['seto] nm hedge

severo, -a [se'βero, a] adj severe

Sevilla [se'βiʎa] n Seville ♦ **sevillano, -a** adj of o from Seville ♦ nm/f native o inhabitant of Seville

sexo ['sekso] nm sex

sexto, -a ['seksto, a] adj, nm sixth

sexual [sek'swal] adj sexual; **vida ~** sex life

si [si] conj if ♦ nm (MÚS) B; **me pregunto si ...** I wonder if o whether ...

sí [si] adv yes ♦ nm consent ♦ pron (uso impersonal) oneself; (sg: m) himself; (: f) herself; (: de cosa) itself; (de usted) yourself; (pl) themselves; (de ustedes) yourselves; (recíproco) each other; **él no quiere pero yo sí** he doesn't want to but I do; **ella sí vendrá** she will certainly come, she is sure to come; **claro que sí** of course; **creo que sí** I think so

siamés, -esa [sja'mes, esa] adj, nm/f Siamese

SIDA ['siða] nm abr (= Síndrome de Inmunodeficiencia Adquirida) AIDS

siderúrgico, -a [siðe'rurxico, a] adj iron and steel; **~** cpd

sidra ['siðra] nf cider

siembra ['sjembra] nf sowing

siempre ['sjempre] adv always; (todo el tiempo) all the time; **~ que** (cada vez) whenever; (dado que) provided that; **como ~** as usual; **para ~** for ever

sien [sjen] nf temple

siento etc ['sjento] vb ver **sentar**; **sentir**

sierra ['sjerra] nf (TEC) saw; (cadena de montañas) mountain range

siervo, -a ['sjerβo, a] nm/f slave

siesta ['sjesta] nf siesta, nap; **echar la ~** to have an afternoon nap o siesta

siete ['sjete] num seven

sifón [si'fon] nm syphon

sigla ['siɣla] nf abbreviation; acronym

siglo ['siɣlo] nm century; (fig) age

significado [siɣnifi'kaðo] nm (de palabra etc) meaning

significar [siɣnifi'kar] vt to mean, signify; (notificar) to make known, express

signo ['siɣno] nm sign ▶ **signo de admiración** o **exclamación** exclamation mark ▶ **signo de interrogación** question mark

sigo etc vb ver **seguir**

siguiente [si'ɣjente] adj next, following

siguió etc vb ver **seguir**

sílaba ['silaβa] nf syllable

silbar [sil'βar] vt, vi to whistle □ **silbato** nm whistle □ **silbido** nm whistle, whistling

silenciador [silenθja'ðor] nm silencer

silenciar [silen'θjar] vt (persona) to silence; (escándalo) to hush up □ **silencio** nm silence, quiet □ **silencioso, -a** adj silent, quiet

silla ['siʎa] nf (asiento) chair; (tb: **~ de montar**) saddle ▶ **silla de ruedas** wheelchair

sillón [si'ʎon] nm armchair, easy chair

silueta [si'lweta] nf silhouette; (de edificio) outline; (figura) figure

silvestre [sil'βestre] adj wild

simbólico, -a [sim'boliko, a] adj symbolic(al)

simbolizar [simboli'θar] vt to symbolize

símbolo ['simbolo] nm symbol

similar [simi'lar] adj similar

simio ['simjo] nm ape

simpatía [simpa'tia] nf liking; (afecto) affection; (amabilidad) kindness □ **simpático, -a** adj nice, pleasant; kind

⚠ No confundir **simpático** con la palabra inglesa sympathetic.

simpatizante [simpati'θante] nmf sympathizer

simpatizar [simpati'θar] vi: ~ **con** to get on well with

simple ['simple] adj simple; (elemental) simple, easy; (mero) mere; (puro) pure, sheer ♦ nmf simpletón ▪ **simpleza** nf simpleness; (necedad) silly thing ▪ **simplificar** vt to simplify

simposio [sim'posjo] nm symposium

simular [simu'lar] vt to simulate

simultáneo, -a [simul'taneo, a] adj simultaneous

sin [sin] prep without; **la ropa está ~ lavar** the clothes are unwashed; ~ **que** without; ~ **embargo** however, still

sinagoga [sina'ɣoɣa] nf synagogue

sinceridad [sinθeri'ðað] nf sincerity ▪ **sincero, -a** adj sincere

sincronizar [sinkroni'θar] vt to synchronize

sindical [sindi'kal] adj union cpd, trade-union cpd ▪ **sindicalista** adj, nmf trade unionist

sindicato [sindi'kato] nm (de trabajadores) trade(s) union; (de negociantes) syndicate

síndrome ['sindrome] nm (MED) syndrome ▪ **síndrome de abstinencia** (MED) withdrawal symptoms ▪ **síndrome de la clase turista** (MED) economy-class syndrome

sinfín [sin'fin] nm: **un ~ de** a great many, no end of

sinfonía [sinfo'nia] nf symphony

singular [singu'lar] adj singular; (fig) outstanding, exceptional; (raro) peculiar, odd

siniestro, -a [si'njestro, a] adj sinister ♦ nm (accidente) accident

sinnúmero [sin'numero] nm = **sinfín**

sino ['sino] nm fate, destiny ♦ conj (pero) but; (salvo) except, save

sinónimo, -a [si'nonimo, a] adj synonymous ♦ nm synonym

síntesis ['sintesis] nf synthesis ▪ **sintético, -a** adj synthetic

sintió vb ver **sentir**

síntoma ['sintoma] nm symptom

sintonía [sinto'nia] nf (RADIO, MÚS: de programa) tuning ▪ **sintonizar** vt (RADIO: emisora) to tune (in)

sinvergüenza [simber'ɣwenθa] nmf rogue, scoundrel; **¡es un ~!** he's got a nerve!

siquiera [si'kjera] conj even if, even though ♦ adv at least; **ni ~** not even

Siria ['sirja] nf Syria

sirviente, -a [sir'βjente, a] nm/f servant

sirvo etc vb ver **servir**

sistema [sis'tema] nm system; (método) method ▪ **sistema educativo** education system ▪ **sistemático, -a** adj systematic

---

SISTEMA EDUCATIVO

The reform of the Spanish **sistema educativo** (education system) begun in the early 90s has replaced the courses **EGB**, **BUP** and **COU** with the following: "Primaria" a compulsory 6 years; "Secundaria" a compulsory 4 years and "Bachillerato" an optional 2-year secondary school course, essential for those wishing to go on to higher education.

---

sitiar [si'tjar] vt to besiege, lay siege to

sitio ['sitjo] nm (lugar) place; (espacio) room, space; (MIL) siege ▪ **sitio de taxis** (MÉX: parada) taxi stand o rank (BRIT) ▪ **sitio Web** (INFORM) website

situación [sitwa'θjon] nf situation, position; (estatus) position, standing

situado, -a [si'twaðo] adj situated, placed

situar [si'twar] vt to place, put; (edificio) to locate, situate

slip [slip] nm pants pl, briefs pl

smoking ['smokɪŋ, es'mokɪn] (pl **smokings**) nm dinner jacket (BRIT), tuxedo (US)

⚠ No confundir **smoking** con la palabra inglesa *smoking*.

SMS nm (mensaje) text message, SMS message

snob [es'nob] = **esnob**

SO abr (= suroeste) SW

sobaco [so'βako] nm armpit

sobar [so'βar] vt (ropa) to rumple; (comida) to play around with

soberanía [soβera'nia] nf sovereignty ❑ **soberano, -a** adj sovereign; (fig) supreme ♦ nm/f sovereign

soberbia [so'βerβja] nf pride; haughtiness, arrogance; magnificence

soberbio, -a [so'βerβjo, a] adj (orgulloso) proud; (altivo) arrogant; (estupendo) magnificent, superb

sobornar [soβor'nar] vt to bribe ❑ **soborno** nm bribe

sobra ['soβra] nf excess, surplus; **sobras** nfpl left-overs, scraps; **de ~** surplus, extra; **tengo de ~** I've more than enough ❑ **sobrado, -a** adj (más que suficiente) more than enough; (superfluo) excessive ❑ **sobrante** adj remaining, extra ♦ nm surplus, remainder ❑ **sobrar** [so'βrar] vt to exceed, surpass ♦ vi (tener de más) to be more than enough; (quedar) to remain, be left (over)

sobrasada [soβra'saða] nf pork sausage spread

sobre ['soβre] prep (gen) on; (encima) on (top of); (por encima de, arriba de) over, above; (más que) more than; (además) in addition to, besides; (alrededor de) about ♦ nm envelope; **~ todo** above all

sobrecama [soβre'kama] nf bedspread

sobrecargar [soβrekar'yar] vt (camión) to overload; (COM) to overcharge

sobredosis [soβre'ðosis] nf inv overdose

sobreentender [soβre(e)nten'der] vt to deduce, infer; **sobreentenderse** vr: **se sobreentiende que ...** it is implied that ...

sobrehumano, -a [soβreu'mano, a] adj superhuman

sobrellevar [soβreʎe'βar] vt to bear, endure

sobremesa [soβre'mesa] nf: **durante la ~** after dinner

sobrenatural [soβrenatu'ral] adj supernatural

sobrenombre [soβre'nombre] nm nickname

sobrepasar [soβrepa'sar] vt to exceed, surpass

sobreponerse [soβrepo'nerse] vr: **~ a** to overcome

sobresaliente [soβresa'ljente] adj outstanding, excellent

sobresalir [soβresa'lir] vi to project, jut out; (fig) to stand out, excel

sobresaltar [soβresal'tar] vt (asustar) to scare, frighten; (sobrecoger) to startle ❑ **sobresalto** nm (movimiento) start; (susto) scare; (turbación) sudden shock

sobretodo [soβre'todo] nm overcoat

sobrevenir [soβreβe'nir] vi (ocurrir) to happen (unexpectedly); (resultar) to follow, ensue

sobrevivir [soβreβi'βir] vi to survive

sobrevolar [soβreβo'lar] vi to fly over

sobriedad [soβrje'ðað] nf sobriety, soberness; (moderación) moderation, restraint

sobrino, -a [so'βrino, a] nm/f nephew/niece

sobrio, -a ['soβrjo, a] adj sober; (moderado) moderate, restrained

socarrón, -ona [soka'rron, ona] adj (sarcástico) sarcastic, ironic(al)

socavón [soka'βon] nm (hoyo) hole

sociable [so'θjaβle] adj (persona) sociable, friendly; (animal) social

social [so'θjal] *adj* social; (COM) company cpd

socialdemócrata [soθjalde'mokrata] *nmf* social democrat

socialista [soθja'lista] *adj, nm* socialist

socializar [soθjali'θar] *vt* to socialize

sociedad [soθje'ðað] *nf* society; (COM) company ▶ **sociedad anónima** limited company ▶ **sociedad de consumo** consumer society

socio, -a ['soθjo, a] *nm/f* (miembro) member; (COM) partner

sociología [soθjolo'xia] *nf* sociology □ **sociólogo, -a** *nm/f* sociologist

socorrer [soko'rrer] *vt* to help □ **socorrista** *nmf* first aider; (en piscina, playa) lifeguard □ **socorro** *nm* (ayuda) help, aid; (MIL) relief; **¡socorro!** help!

soda ['soða] *nf* (sosa) soda; (bebida) soda (water)

sofá [so'fa] (pl **~s**) *nm* sofa, settee □ **sofá-cama** *nm* studio couch; sofa bed

sofocar [sofo'kar] *vt* to suffocate; (apagar) to smother, put out; **sofocarse** *vr* to suffocate; (fig) to blush, feel embarrassed □ **sofoco** *nm* suffocation; embarrassment

sofreír [sofre'ir] *vt* (CULIN) to fry lightly

soga ['soɣa] *nf* rope

sois etc [sois] *vb ver* **ser**

soja ['soxa] *nf* soya

sol [sol] *nm* sun; (luz) sunshine, sunlight; (MÚS) G; **hace ~** it's sunny

solamente [sola'mente] *adv* only, just

solapa [so'lapa] *nf* (de chaqueta) lapel; (de libro) jacket

solapado, -a [sola'paðo, a] *adj* (intenciónes) underhand; (gestos, movimiento) sly

solar [so'lar] *adj* solar, sun cpd ♦ *nm* (terreno) plot (of ground)

soldado [sol'daðo] *nm* soldier ▶ **soldado raso** private

soldador [solda'ðor] *nm* soldering iron; (persona) welder

soldar [sol'dar] *vt* to solder, weld

soleado, -a [sole'aðo, a] *adj* sunny

soledad [sole'ðað] *nf* solitude; (estado infeliz) loneliness

solemne [so'lemne] *adj* solemn

soler [so'ler] *vi* to be in the habit of, be accustomed to; **suele salir a las ocho** she usually goes out at eight o'clock

solfeo [sol'feo] *nm* solfa

solicitar [soliθi'tar] *vt* (permiso) to ask for, seek; (puesto) to apply for; (votos) to canvass for; (atención) to attract

solícito, -a [so'liθito, a] *adj* (diligente) diligent; (cuidadoso) careful □ **solicitud** *nf* (calidad) great care; (petición) request; (a un puesto) application

solidaridad [soliðari'ðað] *nf* solidarity □ **solidario, -a** *adj* (participación) joint, common; (compromiso) mutually binding

sólido, -a [so'liðo, a] *adj* solid

soliloquio [soli'lokjo] *nm* soliloquy

solista [so'lista] *nmf* soloist

solitario, -a [soli'tarjo, a] *adj* (persona) lonely, solitary; (lugar) lonely, desolate ♦ *nm/f* (recluso) recluse; (en la sociedad) loner ♦ *nm* solitaire

sollozar [soλo'θar] *vi* to sob □ **sollozo** *nm* sob

solo, -a ['solo, a] *adj* (único) single, sole; (sin compañía) alone; (solitario) lonely; **hay una sola dificultad** there is just one difficulty; **a solas** alone, by oneself

sólo ['solo] *adv* only, just

solomillo [solo'miλo] *nm* sirloin

soltar [sol'tar] *vt* (dejar ir) to let go of; (desprender) to unfasten, loosen; (librar) to release, set free; (risa etc) to let out

soltero, -a [sol'tero, a] *adj* single, unmarried ♦ *nm/f* bachelor/single woman □ **solterón, -ona** *nm/f* old bachelor/spinster

soltura [sol'tura] nf looseness, slackness; (de los miembros) agility, ease of movement; (en el hablar) fluency, ease

soluble [so'luβle] adj (QUÍM) soluble; (problema) solvable; ~ **en agua** soluble in water

solución [solu'θjon] nf solution □ **solucionar** vt (problema) to solve; (asunto) to settle, resolve

solventar [solβen'tar] vt (pagar) to settle, pay; (resolver) to resolve □ **solvente** adj (ECON: empresa, persona) solvent

sombra ['sombra] nf shadow; (como protección) shade; (oscuridad) darkness sg, shadows; **tener buena/mala ~** to be lucky/unlucky

sombrero [som'brero] nm hat

sombrilla [som'briʎa] nf parasol, sunshade

sombrío, -a [som'brio, a] adj (oscuro) dark; (triste) sombre, sad; (persona) gloomy

someter [some'ter] vt (país) to conquer; (persona) to subject to one's will; (informe) to present, submit; **someterse** vr to give in, yield, submit; ~ **a** to subject to

somier [so'mjer] (pl somiers) n spring mattress

somnífero [som'nifero] nm sleeping pill

somos ['somos] vb ver **ser**

son [son] vb ver **ser** ♦ nm sound

sonaja (MÉX) nf = **sonajero**

sonajero [sona'xero] nm (baby's) rattle

sonambulismo [sonambu'lismo] nm sleepwalking □ **sonámbulo, -a** nm/f sleepwalker

sonar [so'nar] vt to ring ♦ vi to make a noise; (hacer ruido) to make a noise; (pronunciarse) to be sounded, be pronounced; (ser conocido) to sound familiar; (campana) to ring; (reloj) to

strike, chime; **sonarse** vr: **sonarse (las narices)** to blow one's nose; **me suena ese nombre** that name rings a bell

sonda ['sonda] nf (NÁUT) sounding; (TEC) bore, drill; (MED) probe

sondear [sonde'ar] vt to sound; to bore (into), drill; to probe, sound out; (fig) to sound out □ **sondeo** nm sounding; boring, drilling; (fig) poll, enquiry

sonido [so'niðo] nm sound

sonoro, -a [so'noro, a] adj sonorous; (resonante) loud, resonant

sonreír [sonre'ir] vi to smile; **sonreírse** vr to smile □ **sonriente** adj smiling □ **sonrisa** nf smile

sonrojarse [sonro'xarse] vr to blush, go red □ **sonrojo** nm blush

soñador, a [soɲa'ðor, a] nm/f dreamer

soñar [so'ɲar] vt, vi to dream; ~ **con** to dream about o of

soñoliento, -a [soɲo'ljento, a] adj sleepy, drowsy

sopa ['sopa] nf soup

soplar [so'plar] vt (polvo) to blow away, blow off; (inflar) to blow up; (vela) to blow out ♦ vi to blow □ **soplo** nm blow, puff; (de viento) puff, gust

soplón, -ona [so'plon, ona] (fam) nm/f (niño) telltale; (de policía) grass (fam)

soporífero [sopo'rifero] nm sleeping pill

soportable [sopor'taβle] adj bearable

soportar [sopor'tar] vt to bear, carry; (fig) to bear, put up with □ **soporte** nm support; (fig) pillar, support

> ⚠ No confundir **soportar** con la palabra inglesa support.

soprano [so'prano] nf soprano

sorber [sor'βer] vt (chupar) to sip; (absorber) to soak up, absorb

sorbete [sor'βete] nm iced fruit drink

sorbo ['sorβo] nm (trago: grande) gulp, swallow; (: pequeño) sip

sordera [sor'ðera] nf deafness

sórdido, -a ['sorðiðo, a] *adj* dirty, squalid

sordo, -a ['sorðo, a] *adj* (*persona*) deaf ♦ *nm/f* deaf person ❑ **sordomudo, -a** *adj* deaf and dumb

sorna ['sorna] *nf* sarcastic tone

soroche [so'rotʃe] (*CAm*) *nm* mountain sickness

sorprendente [sorpren'dente] *adj* surprising

sorprender [sorpren'der] *vt* to surprise ❑ **sorpresa** *nf* surprise

sortear [sorte'ar] *vt* to draw lots for; (*rifar*) to raffle; (*dificultad*) to avoid ❑ **sorteo** *nm* (*en lotería*) draw; (*rifa*) raffle

sortija [sor'tixa] *nf* ring; (*rizo*) ringlet, curl

sosegado, -a [sose'ɣaðo, a] *adj* quiet, calm

sosiego [so'sjeɣo] *nm* quiet(ness), calm(ness)

soso, -a ['soso, a] *adj* (*CULIN*) tasteless; (*aburrido*) dull, uninteresting

sospecha [sos'petʃa] *nf* suspicion ❑ **sospechar** *vt* to suspect ❑ **sospechoso, -a** *adj* suspicious; (*testimonio, opinión*) suspect ♦ *nm/f* suspect

sostén [sos'ten] *nm* (*apoyo*) support; (*sujetador*) bra; (*alimentación*) sustenance, food

sostener [soste'ner] *vt* to support; (*mantener*) to keep up, maintain; (*alimentar*) to sustain, keep going; **sostenerse** *vr* to support o.s.; (*seguir*) to continue, remain ❑ **sostenido, -a** *adj* continuous, sustained; (*prolongado*) prolonged

sotana [so'tana] *nf* (*REL*) cassock

sótano ['sotano] *nm* basement

soy [soi] *vb ver* **ser**

soya (*LAm*) ['soja] *nf* soya (*BRIT*), soy (*US*)

Sr. *abr* (= *Señor*) Mr

Sra. *abr* (= *Señora*) Mrs

Sres. *abr* (= *Señores*) Messrs

Srta. *abr* (= *Señorita*) Miss

Sta. *abr* (= *Santa*) St

Sto. *abr* (= *Santo*) St

su [su] *pron* (*de él*) his; (*de ella*) her; (*de una cosa*) its; (*de ellos, ellas*) their; (*de usted, ustedes*) your

suave ['swaβe] *adj* gentle; (*superficie*) smooth; (*trabajo*) easy; (*música, voz*) soft, sweet ❑ **suavidad** *nf* gentleness; smoothness; softness; sweetness ❑ **suavizante** *nm* (*de ropa*) softener; (*del pelo*) conditioner ❑ **suavizar** *vt* to soften; (*quitar la aspereza*) to smooth (out)

subasta [su'βasta] *nf* auction ❑ **subastar** *vt* to auction (off)

subcampeón, -ona [suβkampe'on, ona] *nm/f* runner-up

subconsciente [suβkons'θjente] *adj, nm* subconscious

subdesarrollado, -a [suβðesarro'λaðo, a] *adj* underdeveloped

subdesarrollo [suβðesa'rroλo] *nm* underdevelopment

subdirector, -a [suβðirek'tor, a] *nm/f* assistant director

súbdito, -a ['suβðito, a] *nm/f* subject

subestimar [suβesti'mar] *vt* to underestimate, underrate

subida [su'βiða] *nf* (*de montaña etc*) ascent, climb; (*de precio*) rise, increase; (*pendiente*) slope, hill

subir [su'βir] *vt* (*objeto*) to raise, lift up; (*cuesta, calle*) to go up; (*colina, montaña*) to climb; (*precio*) to raise, put up ♦ *vi* to go up, come up; (*a un coche*) to get in; (*a un autobús, tren o avión*) to get on, board; (*precio*) to rise, go up; (*río, marea*) to rise; **subirse** *vr* to get up, climb

súbito, -a ['suβito, a] *adj* (*repentino*) sudden; (*imprevisto*) unexpected

subjetivo, -a [suβxe'tiβo, a] *adj* subjective

sublevar [suβle'βar] *vt* to rouse to revolt; **sublevarse** *vr* to revolt, rise

sublime [su'βlime] *adj* sublime

submarinismo [suβmari'nismo] *nm* scuba diving

submarino, -a [suβma'rino, a] *adj* underwater ♦ *nm* submarine

subnormal [suβnor'mal] *adj* subnormal ♦ *nmf* subnormal person

subordinado, -a [suβorði'naðo, a] *adj, nm/f* subordinate

subrayar [suβra'jar] *vt* to underline

subsanar [suβsa'nar] *vt* to rectify

subsidio [suβ'siðjo] *nm (ayuda)* aid, financial help; *(subvención)* subsidy, grant; *(de enfermedad, paro etc)* benefit, allowance

subsistencia [suβsis'tenθja] *nf* subsistence

subsistir [suβsis'tir] *vi* to subsist; *(sobrevivir)* to survive, endure

subte *(RPl)* [suβte] *nm* underground *(BRIT)*, subway *(US)*

subterráneo, -a [suβte'rraneo, a] *adj* underground, subterranean ♦ *nm* underpass, underground passage

subtítulo [suβ'titulo] *nm (CINE)* subtitle

suburbio [su'βurβjo] *nm (barrio)* slum quarter

subvención [suββen'θjon] *nf (ECON)* subsidy, grant ❑ **subvencionar** *vt* to subsidize

sucedáneo, -a [suθe'ðaneo, a] *adj* substitute ♦ *nm* substitute (food)

suceder [suθe'ðer] *vt, vi* to succeed, follow; *(seguir)* to succeed, follow; **lo que sucede es que ...** the fact is that ... ❑ **sucesión** *nf* succession; *(serie)* sequence, series

sucesivamente [suθesiβa'mente] *adv*: **y así ~** and so on

sucesivo, -a [suθe'siβo, a] *adj* successive, following; **en lo ~** in future, from now on

suceso [su'θeso] *nm (hecho)* event, happening; *(incidente)* incident

⚠ No confundir **suceso** con la palabra inglesa **success**.

suciedad [suθje'ðað] *nf (estado)* dirtiness; *(mugre)* dirt, filth

sucio, -a ['suθjo, a] *adj* dirty

suculento, -a [suku'lento, a] *adj* succulent

sucumbir [sukum'bir] *vi* to succumb

sucursal [sukur'sal] *nf* branch (office)

sudadera [suða'ðera] *nf* sweatshirt

Sudáfrica [suð'afrika] *nf* South Africa

Sudamérica [suða'merika] *nf* South America ❑ **sudamericano, -a** *adj, nm/f* South American

sudar [su'ðar] *vt, vi* to sweat

sudeste [su'ðeste] *nm* south-east

sudoeste [suðo'este] *nm* south-west

sudor [su'ðor] *nm* sweat ❑ **sudoroso, -a** *adj* sweaty, sweating

Suecia ['sweθja] *nf* Sweden ❑ **sueco, -a** *adj* Swedish ♦ *nm/f* Swede

suegro, -a ['sweɣro, a] *nm/f* father-/mother-in-law

suela ['swela] *nf* sole

sueldo ['sweldo] *nm* pay, wage(s) *(pl)*

suele *etc vb ver* **soler**

suelo ['swelo] *nm (tierra)* ground; *(de casa)* floor

suelto, -a ['swelto, a] *adj* loose; *(libre)* free; *(separado)* detached; *(ágil)* quick, agile ♦ *nm (loose)* change, small change

sueñito *(LAm)* *nm* nap

sueño *etc* ['sweɲo] *vb ver* **soñar** ♦ *nm* sleep; *(somnolencia)* sleepiness, drowsiness; *(lo soñado, fig)* dream; **tener ~** to be sleepy

suero ['swero] *nm (MED)* serum; *(de leche)* whey

suerte ['swerte] *nf (fortuna)* luck; *(azar)* chance; *(destino)* fate, destiny; *(especie)* sort, kind; **tener ~** to be lucky

suéter ['sweter] nm sweater

suficiente [sufi'θjente] adj enough, sufficient ♦ nm (ESCOL) pass

sufragio [su'fraxjo] nm (voto) vote; (derecho de voto) suffrage

sufrido, -a [su'friðo, a] adj (persona) tough; (paciente) long-suffering, patient

sufrimiento [sufri'mjento] nm (dolor) suffering

sufrir [su'frir] vt (padecer) to suffer; (soportar) to bear, put up with; (apoyar) to hold up, support ♦ vi to suffer

sugerencia [suxe'renθja] nf suggestion

sugerir [suxe'rir] vt to suggest; (sutilmente) to hint

sugestión [suxes'tjon] nf suggestion; (sutil) hint □ **sugestionar** vt to influence

sugestivo, -a [suxes'tiβo, a] adj stimulating; (fascinante) fascinating

suicida [sui'θiða] adj suicidal ♦ nmf suicidal person; (muerto) suicide, person who has committed suicide □ **suicidarse** vr to commit suicide, kill o.s. □ **suicidio** nm suicide

Suiza ['swiθa] nf Switzerland □ **suizo, -a** adj, nm/f Swiss

sujeción [suxe'θjon] nf subjection

sujetador [suxeta'ðor] nm (sostén) bra

sujetar [suxe'tar] vt (fijar) to fasten, (detener) to hold down; **sujetarse** vr to subject o.s. □ **sujeto, -a** adj fastened, secure ♦ nm subject; (individuo) individual; **sujeto a** subject to

suma ['suma] nf (cantidad) total, sum; (de dinero) sum; (acto) adding (up), addition; **en ~** in short

sumamente [suma'mente] adv extremely, exceedingly

sumar [su'mar] vt to add (up) ♦ vi to add up

sumergir [sumer'xir] vt to submerge; (hundir) to sink

suministrar [sumini'strar] vt to supply, provide □ **suministro** nm supply; (acto) supplying, providing

sumir [su'mir] vt to sink, submerge; (fig) to plunge

sumiso, -a [su'miso, a] adj submissive, docile

sumo, -a ['sumo, a] adj great, extreme; (autoridad) highest, supreme

suntuoso, -a [sun'twoso, a] adj sumptuous, magnificent

supe etc ['supe] vb ver **saber**

super... [super] prefijo super..., over...

superbueno [super'bweno] adj great, fantastic

súper ['super] nf (gasolina) four-star (petrol)

superar [supe'rar] vt (sobreponerse a) to overcome; (rebasar) to surpass, do better than; (pasar) to go beyond; **superarse** vr to excel o.s.

superficial [superfi'θjal] adj superficial; (medida) surface cpd, of the surface

superficie [super'fiθje] nf surface; (área) area

superfluo, -a [su'perflwo, a] adj superfluous

superior [supe'rjor] adj (piso, clase) upper; (temperatura, número, nivel) higher; (mejor: calidad, producto) superior, better ♦ nmf superior □ **superioridad** nf superiority

supermercado [supermer'kaðo] nm supermarket

superponer [superpo'ner] vt to superimpose

superstición [supersti'θjon] nf superstition □ **supersticioso, -a** adj superstitious

supervisar [superβi'sar] vt to supervise

supervivencia [superβi'βenθja] nf survival

superviviente [superβi'βjente] adj surviving

supiera etc vb ver **saber**

suplantar [suplan'tar] vt to supplant

suplemento [suple'mento] nm
supplement

suplente [su'plente] adj, nm substitute

supletorio, -a [suple'torjo, a] adj
supplementary ♦ nm supplement;
teléfono ~ extension

súplica ['suplika] nf request; (JUR)
petition

suplicar [supli'kar] vt (cosa) to request
(for), plead for; (persona) to beg, plead
with

suplicio [su'pliθjo] nm torture

suplir [su'plir] vt (compensar) to make
good, make up for; (reemplazar) to
replace, substitute ♦ vi: **~ a** to take the
place of, substitute for

supo etc ['supo] vb ver **saber**

suponer [supo'ner] vt to suppose
❑ **suposición** nf supposition

suprimir [supri'mir] vt to suppress;
(derecho, costumbre) to abolish;
(palabra etc) to delete; (restricción) to
cancel, lift

supuesto, -a [su'pwesto, a] pp de
suponer ♦ adj (hipotético) supposed
♦ nm assumption, hypothesis; **~ que**
since; **por ~** of course

sur [sur] nm south

surcar [sur'kar] vt to plough ❑ **surco**
nm (en metal, disco) groove; (AGR)
furrow

surgir [sur'xir] vi to arise, emerge; (
dificultad) to come up, crop up

suroeste [suro'este] nm south-west

surtido, -a [sur'tiðo, a] adj mixed,
assorted ♦ nm (selección) selection,
assortment; (abastecimiento) supply,
stock ❑ **surtidor** nm (tb: **surtidor de
gasolina**) petrol pump (BRIT), gas
pump (US)

surtir [sur'tir] vt to supply, provide ♦ vi
to spout, spurt

susceptible [susθep'tiβle] adj
susceptible; (sensible) sensitive; **~ de**
capable of

suscitar [susθi'tar] vt to cause,
provoke; (interés, sospechas) to arouse

suscribir [suskri'βir] vt (firmar) to sign;
(respaldar) to subscribe to, endorse;
suscribirse vr to subscribe
❑ **suscripción** nf subscription

susodicho, -a [suso'ðitʃo, a] adj
above-mentioned

suspender [suspen'der] vt (objeto) to
hang (up), suspend; (trabajo) to stop,
suspend; (ESCOL) to fail; (interrumpir) to
adjourn; (atrasar) to postpone

suspense (ESP) [sus'pense] nm
suspense; **película/novela de ~** thriller

suspensión [suspen'sjon] nf
suspension; (fig) stoppage, suspension

suspenso, -a [sus'penso, a] adj
hanging, suspended; (ESP ESCOL) failed
♦ nm (ESP ESCOL) fail; **película o novela
de ~** (LAm) thriller; **quedar o estar en ~**
to be pending

suspicaz [suspi'kaθ] adj suspicious,
distrustful

suspirar [suspi'rar] vi to sigh
❑ **suspiro** nm sigh

sustancia [sus'tanθja] nf substance

sustento [sus'tento] nm support;
(alimento) sustenance, food

sustituir [sustitu'ir] vt to substitute,
replace ❑ **sustituto, -a** nm/f
substitute, replacement

susto ['susto] nm fright, scare

sustraer [sustra'er] vt to remove, take
away; (MAT) to subtract

susurrar [susu'rrar] vi to whisper
❑ **susurro** nm whisper

sutil [su'til] adj (aroma, diferencia)
subtle; (tenue) thin; (inteligencia,
persona) sharp

suyo, -a ['sujo, a] (con articulo o después
del verbo ser) adj (de él) his; (de ella)
hers; (de ellos, ellas) theirs; (de Ud, Uds)
yours; **un amigo ~** a friend of his (o
hers o theirs o yours)

T, t

Tabacalera [taβakaˈlera] nf Spanish state tobacco monopoly

tabaco [taˈβako] nm tobacco; (ESP: fam) cigarettes pl

tabaquería (LAm) [tabakeˈria] nf tobacconist's (shop) (BRIT), smoke shop (US) ❏ **tabaquero, -a** (LAm) nm/f tobacconist

taberna [taˈβerna] nf bar, pub (BRIT)

tabique [taˈβike] nm partition (wall)

tabla [ˈtaβla] nf (de madera) plank; (estante) shelf; (de vestido) pleat; (ARTE) panel; **tablas** nfpl: **estar** o **quedar en tablas** to draw ❏ **tablado** nm (plataforma) platform; (TEATRO) stage

tablao [taˈβlao] nm (tb: **~ flamenco**) flamenco show

tablero [taˈβlero] nm (de madera) plank, board; (de ajedrez, damas) board ▶ **tablero de mandos** (LAm AUTO) dashboard

tableta [taˈβleta] nf (MED) tablet; (de chocolate) bar

tablón [taˈβlon] nm (de suelo) plank; (de techo) beam ▶ **tablón de anuncios** notice (BRIT) o bulletin (US) board

tabú [taˈβu] nm taboo

taburete [taβuˈrete] nm stool

tacaño, -a [taˈkaɲo, a] adj mean

tacha [ˈtatʃa] nf flaw; (TEC) stud ❏ **tachar** vt (borrar) to cross out; **tachar de** to accuse of

tacho (CS) [ˈtatʃo] nm (balde) bucket ▶ **tacho de la basura** rubbish bin (BRIT), trash can (US)

taco [ˈtako] nm (BILLAR) cue; (de billetes) book; (CS: de zapato) heel; (tarugo) peg; (palabrota) swear word

tacón [taˈkon] nm heel; **de ~ alto** high-heeled

táctica [ˈtaktika] nf tactics pl

táctico, -a [ˈtaktiko, a] adj tactical

tacto [ˈtakto] nm touch; (fig) tact

tajada [taˈxaða] nf slice

tajante [taˈxante] adj sharp

tajo [ˈtaxo] nm (corte) cut; (GEO) cleft

tal [tal] adj such ♦ pron such a one; (cosa) something, such a thing ♦ adv: **~ como** (igual) just as ♦ conj: **con ~ de que** provided that; **~ cual** (como es) just as it is; **~ vez** perhaps; **~ como** such as; **~ para cual** (dos iguales) two of a kind; **¿qué ~?** how are things?; **¿qué ~ te gusta?** how do you like it?

taladrar [talaˈðrar] vt to drill ❏ **taladro** nm drill

talante [taˈlante] nm (humor) mood; (voluntad) will, willingness

talar [taˈlar] vt to fell, cut down; (devastar) to devastate

talco [ˈtalko] nm (polvos) talcum powder

talento [taˈlento] nm talent; (capacidad) ability

TALGO [ˈtalɣo] (ESP) nm abr (= tren articulado ligero Goicoechea-Oriol) = HST (BRIT)

talismán [talisˈman] nm talisman

talla [ˈtaʎa] nf (estatura, fig, MED) height, stature; (palo) measuring rod; (ARTE) carving; (medida) size

tallar [taˈʎar] vt (madera) to carve; (metal etc) to engrave; (medir) to measure

tallarines [taʎaˈrines] nmpl noodles

talle [ˈtaʎe] nm (ANAT) waist; (fig) appearance

taller [taˈʎer] nm (TEC) workshop; (de artista) studio

tallo [ˈtaʎo] nm (de planta) stem; (de hierba) blade; (brote) shoot

talón [taˈlon] nm (ANAT) heel; (COM) counterfoil; (cheque) cheque (BRIT), check (US)

talonario [taloˈnarjo] nm (de cheques) chequebook (BRIT), checkbook (US); (de recibos) receipt book

tamaño, -a [ta'maɲo, a] *adj* (*tan grande*) such a big; (*tan pequeño*) such a small ♦ *nm* size; **de ~ natural** full-size

tamarindo [tama'rindo] *nm* tamarind

tambalearse [tambale'arse] *vr* (*persona*) to stagger; (*vehículo*) to sway

también [tam'bjen] *adv* (*igualmente*) also, too, as well; (*además*) besides

tambor [tam'bor] *nm* drum; (*ANAT*) eardrum ▶ **tambor del freno** brake drum

tamizar [tami'θar] *vt* to sieve

tampoco [tam'poko] *adv* nor, neither; **yo ~ lo compré** I didn't buy it either

tampón [tam'pon] *nm* tampon

tan [tan] *adv* so; **es así que ...** so much so that ...

tanda ['tanda] *nf* (*gen*) series; (*turno*) shift

tangente [tan'xente] *nf* tangent

tangerina (*LAm*) *nf* tangerine

tangible [tan'xiβle] *adj* tangible

tanque ['tanke] *nm* (*cisterna*, *MIL*) tank; (*AUTO*) tanker

tantear [tante'ar] *vt* (*calcular*) to reckon (up); (*medir*) to take the measure of; (*probar*) to test, try out; (*tomar la medida: persona*) to take the measurements of; (*situación*) to sound out ♦ *vi* (*DEPORTE*) to score □ **tanteo** *nm* (*cálculo*) (rough) calculation; (*prueba*) test, trial; (*DEPORTE*) scoring

tanto, -a ['tanto, a] *adj* (*cantidad*) so much, as much ♦ *adv* (*cantidad*) so much, as much; (*tiempo*) so long, as long ♦ *conj*: **en ~ que** while ♦ *nm* (*suma*) certain amount; (*proporción*) so much; (*punto*) point; (*gol*) goal; **un ~ perezoso** somewhat lazy ♦ *pron*: **cado uno paga** = each one pays so much; **tantos** so many, as many; **20 y tantos** 20-odd; **hasta ~ (que)** until such time as; **~ tú como yo** both you and I; **~ como eso** as much as that; **~ más ... cuanto que** all the more ... because; **~**

mejor/peor so much the better/the worse; **~ si viene como si va** whether he comes or he goes; **~ es así que** so much so that; **por (lo) ~** therefore; **entre ~** meanwhile; **estar al ~** to be up to date; **me he vuelto ronco de o con ~ hablar** I have become hoarse with so much talking; **a tantos de agosto** on such and such a day in August

tapa ['tapa] *nf* (*de caja*, *olla*) lid; (*de botella*) top; (*de libro*) cover; (*comida*) snack

tapadera [tapa'ðera] *nf* lid, cover

tapar [ta'par] *vt* (*cubrir*) to cover; (*envolver*) to wrap o cover up; (*la vista*) to obstruct; (*persona*, *falta*) to conceal; (*MÉX*, *CAm: diente*) to fill; **taparse** *vr* to wrap o.s. up

taparrabo [tapa'rraβo] *nm* loincloth

tapete [ta'pete] *nm* table cover

tapia ['tapja] *nf* (garden) wall

tapicería [tapiθe'ria] *nf* tapestry; (*para muebles*) upholstery; (*tienda*) upholsterer's (shop)

tapiz [ta'piθ] *nm* (*alfombra*) carpet; (*tela tejida*) tapestry □ **tapizar** *vt* (*muebles*) to upholster

tapón [ta'pon] *nm* (*de botella*) top; (*de lavabo*) plug ▶ **tapón de rosca** screw-top

taquigrafía [takiɣra'fia] *nf* shorthand □ **taquígrafo, -a** *nm/f* shorthand writer, stenographer

taquilla [ta'kiʎa] *nf* (*donde se compra*) booking office; (*suma recogida*) takings *pl*

tarántula [ta'rantula] *nf* tarantula

tararear [tarare'ar] *vi* to hum

tardar [tar'ðar] *vi* (*tomar tiempo*) to take a long time; (*llegar tarde*) to be late; (*demorar*) to delay; **¿tarda mucho el tren?** does the train take (very) long?; **a más ~** at the latest; **no tardes en venir** come soon

tarde ['tarðe] adv late ♦ nf (de día) afternoon; (al anochecer) evening; **de ~ en ~** from time to time; **¡buenas tardes!** good afternoon!; **a o por la ~** in the afternoon; in the evening

tardío, -a [tar'ðio, a] adj (retrasado) late; (lento) slow to arrive

tarea [ta'rea] nf task; (faena) chore; (ESCOL) homework

tarifa [ta'rifa] nf (lista de precios) price list; (precio) tariff

tarima [ta'rima] nf (plataforma) platform

tarjeta [tar'xeta] nf card ▶ **tarjeta de crédito/de Navidad/postal/ telefónica** credit card/Christmas card/postcard/phonecard ▶ **tarjeta de embarque** boarding pass

tarro ['tarro] nm jar, pot

tarta ['tarta] nf (pastel) cake; (de base dura) tart

tartamudear [tartamuðe'ar] vi to stammer ◻ **tartamudo, -a** adj stammering ♦ nm/f stammerer

tártaro, -a ['tartaro, a] adj: **salsa tártara** tartar(e) sauce

tasa ['tasa] nf (precio) (fixed) price, rate; (valoración) valuation; (medida, norma) measure, standard ▶ **tasa de cambio/interés** exchange/interest rate ▶ **tasas de aeropuerto** airport tax ▶ **tasas universitarias** university fees ◻ **tasar** [ta'sar] vt (arreglar el precio) to fix a price for; (valorar) to value, assess

tasca ['taska] (fam) nf pub

tatarabuelo, -a [tatara'βwelo, a] nm/f great-great-grandfather/mother

tatuaje [ta'twaxe] nm (dibujo) tattoo; (acto) tattooing

tatuar [ta'twar] vt to tattoo

taurino, -a [tau'rino, a] adj bullfighting cpd

Tauro ['tauro] nm Taurus

tauromaquia [tauro'makja] nf tauromachy, (art of) bullfighting

taxi ['taksi] nm taxi ◻ **taxista** [tak'sista] nmf taxi driver

taza [ta'θa] nf cup; (de retrete) bowl; ~ **para café** coffee cup ▶ **taza de café** cup of coffee ◻ **tazón** nm (taza grande) mug, large cup; (de fuente) basin

te [te] pron (complemento de objeto) you; (complemento indirecto) (to) you; (reflexivo) (to) yourself; **¿te duele mucho el brazo?** does your arm hurt a lot?; **te equivocas** you're wrong; **¡cálmate!** calm down!

té [te] nm tea

teatral [tea'tral] adj theatre cpd; (fig) theatrical

teatro [te'atro] nm theatre; (LITERATURA) plays pl, drama

tebeo [te'βeo] nm comic

techo [tetʃo] nm (externo) roof; (interno) ceiling ▶ **techo corredizo** sunroof

tecla ['tekla] nf key ◻ **teclado** nm keyboard ◻ **teclear** vi (MÚS) to strum; (con los dedos) to tap ♦ vt (INFORM) to key in

técnica [teknika] nf technique; (tecnología) technology; ver tb **técnico**

técnico, -a [tekniko, a] adj technical ♦ nm/f technician; (experto) expert

tecnología [teknolu'xia] nf technology ◻ **tecnológico, -a** adj technological

tecolote (MÉX) [teko'lote] nm owl

tedioso, -a [te'ðjoso, a] adj boring, tedious

teja ['texa] nf tile; (BOT) lime (tree) ◻ **tejado** nm (tiled) roof

tejemaneje [texema'nexe] nm (lío) fuss; (intriga) intrigue

tejer [te'xer] vt to weave; (hacer punto) to knit; (fig) to fabricate ◻ **tejido** nm (tela) material, fabric; (telaraña) web; (ANAT) tissue

tel [tel] abr (= teléfono) tel

tela ['tela] nf (tejido) material; (telaraña) web; (en líquido) skin ☐ **telar** nm (máquina) loom

telaraña [tela'raɲa] nf cobweb

tele ['tele] (fam) nf telly (BRIT), tube (US)

tele... ['tele] prefijo tele...
☐ **telecomunicación** nf telecommunication ☐ **telediario** nm television news ☐ **teledirigido, -a** adj remote-controlled

teleférico [tele'feriko] nm (de esquí) ski-lift

telefonear [telefone'ar] vi to telephone

telefónico, -a [tele'foniko, a] adj telephone cpd

telefonillo [telefo'niʎo] nm (de puerta) intercom

telefonista [telefo'nista] nmf telephonist

teléfono [te'lefono] nm (tele)phone; **estar hablando al ~** to be on the phone; **llamar a algn por ~** to ring sb (up) o phone sb (up) ► **teléfono celular** (LAm) mobile phone ► **teléfono inalámbrico** cordless phone ► **teléfono móvil** (ESP) mobile phone

telégrafo [te'leɣrafo] nm telegraph

telegrama [tele'ɣrama] nm telegram

tele: **telenovela** nf soap (opera) ☐ **teleobjetivo** nm telephoto lens ☐ **telepatía** nf telepathy ☐ **telepático, -a** adj telepathic ☐ **telescopio** nm telescope ☐ **telesilla** nm chairlift ☐ **telespectador, a** nm/f viewer ☐ **telesquí** nm ski-lift ☐ **teletarjeta** nf phonecard ☐ **teletipo** nm teletype ☐ **teletrabajador, a** nm/f teleworker ☐ **teletrabajo** nm teleworking ☐ **televentas** nfpl telesales

televidente [teleβi'ðente] nmf viewer

televisar [teleβi'sar] vt to televise

televisión [teleβi'sjon] nf television ► **televisión digital** digital television

televisor [teleβi'sor] nm television set

télex ['teleks] nm inv telex

telón [te'lon] nm curtain ► **telón de acero** (POL) iron curtain ► **telón de fondo** backcloth, background

tema ['tema] nm (asunto) subject, topic; (MÚS) theme ☐ **temático, -a** adj thematic

temblar [tem'blar] vi to shake, tremble; (por frío) to shiver ☐ **temblor** nm trembling; (de tierra) earthquake ☐ **tembloroso, -a** adj trembling

temer [te'mer] vt to fear ♦ vi to be afraid; **temo que llegue tarde** I am afraid he may be late

temible [te'miβle] adj fearsome

temor [te'mor] nm (miedo) fear; (duda) suspicion

témpano ['tempano] nm (tb: ~ **de hielo**) ice-floe

temperamento [tempera'mento] nm temperament

temperatura [tempera'tura] nf temperature

tempestad [tempes'taθ] nf storm

templado, -a [tem'plaðo, a] adj (moderado) moderate; (frugal) frugal; (agua) lukewarm; (clima) mild; (MÚS) well-tuned ☐ **templanza** nf moderation; mildness

templar [tem'plar] vt (moderar) to moderate; (furia) to restrain; (calor) to reduce; (afinar) to tune (up); (acero) to temper; (tuerca) to tighten up ☐ **temple** nm (ajuste) tempering; (afinación) tuning; (pintura) tempera

templo ['templo] nm (iglesia) church; (pagano etc) temple

temporada [tempo'raða] nf time, period; (estación) season

temporal [tempo'ral] adj (no permanente) temporary ♦ nm storm

temprano, -a [tem'prano, a] adj early; (demasiado pronto) too soon, too early

ten [ten] vb ver **tener**

tenaces [te'naθes] adj pl ver **tenaz**

tenaz [te'naθ] adj (material) tough; (persona) tenacious; (resistencia) stubborn

tenaza(s) [te'naθa(s)] nf(pl) (MED) forceps; (TEC) pliers; (ZOOL) pincers

tendedero [tende'ðero] nm (para ropa) drying place; (cuerda) clothes line

tendencia [ten'denθja] nf tendency; **tener ~ a** to tend to, have a tendency to

tender [ten'der] vt (extender) to spread out; (colgar) to hang out; (vía férrea, cable) to lay; (estirar) to stretch ♦ vi: **~ a** to tend to, have a tendency towards; **tenderse** vr to lie down; **~ la cama/mesa** (LAm) to make the bed/lay (BRIT) o set (US) the table

tenderete [tende'rete] nm (puesto) stall; (exposición) display of goods

tendero, -a [ten'dero, a] nm/f shopkeeper

tendón [ten'don] nm tendon

tendré etc [ten'dre] vb ver **tener**

tenebroso, -a [tene'βroso, a] adj (oscuro) dark; (fig) gloomy

tenedor [tene'ðor] nm (CULIN) fork

tenencia [te'nenθja] nf (de casa) tenancy; (de oficio) tenure; (de propiedad) possession

tener

PALABRA CLAVE

[te'ner] vt

1 (poseer, gen) to have; (en la mano) to hold; ¿**tienes un boli?** have you got a pen?; **va a tener un niño** she's going to have a baby; ¡**ten** (o **tenga**)!, ¡**aquí tienes** (o **tiene**)! here you are!

2 (edad, medidas) to be; **tiene 7 años** she's 7 (years old); **tiene 15 cm de largo** it's 15 cm long; ver **calor**; **hambre** etc

3 (considerar): **lo tengo por brillante** I consider him to be brilliant; **tener en mucho a algn** to think very highly of sb

4 (+ pp: = pretérito): **tengo terminada ya**

la mitad del trabajo I've done half the work already

5: **tener que hacer algo** to have to do sth; **tengo que acabar este trabajo hoy** I have to finish this job today

6: ¿**qué tienes, estás enfermo?** what's the matter with you, are you ill?

♦ **tenerse** vr

1: **tenerse en pie** to stand up

2: **tenerse por** to think o.s.

tengo etc vb ver **tener**

tenia ['tenja] nf tapeworm

teniente [te'njente] nm (rango) lieutenant; (ayudante) deputy

tenis ['tenis] nm tennis ▶ **tenis de mesa** table tennis ❑ **tenista** nmf tennis player

tenor [te'nor] nm (sentido) meaning; (MÚS) tenor; **a ~ de** on the lines of

tensar [ten'sar] vt to tighten; (arco) to draw

tensión [ten'sjon] nf tension; (TEC) stress; **tener la ~ alta** to have high blood pressure ▶ **tensión arterial** blood pressure

tenso, -a ['tenso, a] adj tense

tentación [tenta'θjon] nf temptation

tentáculo [ten'takulo] nm tentacle

tentador, a [tenta'ðor, a] adj tempting

tentar [ten'tar] vt (seducir) to tempt; (atraer) to attract

tentempié [tentem'pje] nm snack

tenue ['tenwe] adj (delgado) thin, slender; (neblina) light; (lazo, vínculo) slight

teñir [te'nir] vt to dye; (fig) to tinge; **teñirse** vr to dye; **teñirse el pelo** to dye one's hair

teología [teolo'xia] nf theology

teoría [teo'ria] nf theory; **en ~** in theory ❑ **teórico, -a** adj theoretic(al) ♦ nm/f theoretician, theorist ❑ **teorizar** vi to theorize

terapéutico, -a [tera'peutiko, a] *adj* therapeutic

terapia [te'rapja] *nf* therapy

tercer [ter'θer] *adj ver* **tercero**

tercermundista [terθermun'dista] *adj* Third World *cpd*

tercero, -a [ter'θero, a] *(delante de nmsg:* **tercer***) adj* third ♦ *nm (JUR)* third party

terceto [ter'θeto] *nm* trio

terciar [ter'θjar] *vi (participar)* to take part; *(hacer de árbitro)* to mediate
❑ **terciario, -a** *adj* tertiary

tercio ['terθjo] *nm* third

terciopelo [terθjo'pelo] *nm* velvet

terco, -a ['terko, a] *adj* obstinate

tergal® [ter'yal] *nm type of polyester*

tergiversar [terxiβer'sar] *vt* to distort

termal [ter'mal] *adj* thermal

termas ['termas] *nfpl* hot springs

térmico, -a ['termiko, a] *adj* thermal

terminal [termi'nal] *adj, nm, nf* terminal

terminante [termi'nante] *adj (final)* final, definitive; *(tajante)* categorical
❑ **terminantemente** *adv:* **terminantemente prohibido** strictly forbidden

terminar [termi'nar] *vt (completar)* to complete, finish; *(concluir)* to end ♦ *vi (llegar a su fin)* to end; *(parar)* to stop; *(acabar)* to finish; **terminarse** *vr* to come to an end; **por hacer algo** to end up (by) doing sth

término ['termino] *nm* end, conclusion; *(parada)* terminus; *(límite)* boundary; **en último ~** *(a fin de cuentas)* in the last analysis; *(como último recurso)* as a last resort ► **término medio** average; *(fig)* middle way

termómetro [ter'mometro] *nm* thermometer

termo(s)® ['termo(s)] *nm* Thermos®

termostato [termos'tato] *nm* thermostat

ternero, -a [ter'nero, a] *nm/f (animal)* calf ♦ *nf (carne)* veal

ternura [ter'nura] *nf (trato)* tenderness; *(palabra)* endearment; *(cariño)* fondness

terrado [te'rraðo] *nm* terrace

terraplén [terra'plen] *nm* embankment

terrateniente [terrate'njente] *nmf* landowner

terraza [te'rraθa] *nf (balcón)* balcony; *(tejado)* (flat) roof; *(AGR)* terrace

terremoto [terre'moto] *nm* earthquake

terrenal [terre'nal] *adj* earthly

terreno [te'rreno] *nm (tierra)* land; *(parcela)* plot; *(suelo)* soil; *(fig)* field; **un ~ a piece of land**

terrestre [te'rrestre] *adj* terrestrial; *(ruta)* land *cpd*

terrible [te'rriβle] *adj* terrible, awful

territorio [terri'torjo] *nm* territory

terrón [te'rron] *nm (de azúcar)* lump; *(de tierra)* clod, lump

terror [te'rror] *nm* terror
❑ **terrorífico, -a** *adj* terrifying
❑ **terrorista** *adj, nmf* terrorist

terso, -a ['terso, a] *adj (liso)* smooth; *(pulido)* polished

tertulia [ter'tulja] *nf (reunión informal)* social gathering; *(grupo)* group, circle

tesis ['tesis] *nf inv* thesis

tesón [te'son] *nm (firmeza)* firmness; *(tenacidad)* tenacity

tesorero, -a [teso'rero, a] *nm/f* treasurer

tesoro [te'soro] *nm* treasure; *(COM, POL)* treasury

testamento [testa'mento] *nm* will

testarudo, -a [testa'ruðo, a] *adj* stubborn

testículo [tes'tikulo] *nm* testicle

testificar [testifi'kar] *vt* to testify; *(fig)* to attest ♦ *vi* to give evidence

testigo [tes'tiɣo] *nmf* witness
▸ **testigo de cargo/descargo** witness for the prosecution/defence
▸ **testigo ocular** eye witness

testimonio [testi'monjo] *nm* testimony

teta ['teta] *nf* (de biberón) teat; (ANAT: fam) breast

tétanos ['tetanos] *nm* tetanus

tetera [te'tera] *nf* teapot

tétrico, -a ['tetriko, a] *adj* gloomy, dismal

textil [teks'til] *adj* textile

texto ['teksto] *nm* text □ **textual** *adj* textual

textura [teks'tura] *nf* (de tejido) texture

tez [teθ] *nf* (cutis) complexion

ti [ti] *pron* you; (reflexivo) yourself

tía ['tia] *nf* (pariente) aunt; (fam) chick, bird

tibio, -a ['tiβjo, a] *adj* lukewarm

tiburón [tiβu'ron] *nm* shark

tic [tik] *nm* (ruido) click; (de reloj) tick; (MED): **~ nervioso** nervous tic

tictac [tik'tak] *nm* (de reloj) tick tock

tiempo ['tjempo] *nm* time; (época, periodo) age, period; (METEOROLOGÍA) weather; (LING) tense; (DEPORTE) half; **a ~** in time; **a un al mismo ~** at the same time; **al poco ~** very soon (after); **se quedó poco ~** he didn't stay very long; **hace poco ~** not long ago; **mucho ~** a long time; **de ~ en ~** from time to time; **hace buen/mal ~** the/ weather is fine/bad; **estar a ~** to be in time; **hace ~** some time ago; **hacer ~** to while away the time; **motor de 2 tiempos** two-stroke engine; **primer ~** first half

tienda ['tjenda] *nf* shop, store ▸ **tienda de abarrotes** (MÉX, CAm) grocer's (BRIT), grocery store (US) ▸ **tienda de alimentación o comestibles** grocer's (BRIT), grocery store (US) ▸ **tienda de campaña** tent

tienes *etc vb ver* **tener**

tienta *etc* ['tjenta] *vb ver* **tentar** ♦ *nf*: **andar a tientas** to grope one's way along

tiento *etc* ['tjento] *vb ver* **tentar** ♦ *nm* (tacto) touch; (precaución) wariness

tierno, -a ['tjerno, a] *adj* (blando) tender; (fresco) fresh; (amable) sweet

tierra ['tjerra] *nf* earth; (suelo) soil; (mundo) earth, world; (país) country, land; **~ adentro** inland

tieso, -a ['tjeso, a] *adj* (rígido) rigid; (duro) stiff; (fam: orgulloso) conceited

tiesto ['tjesto] *nm* flowerpot

tifón [ti'fon] *nm* typhoon

tifus ['tifus] *nm* typhus

tigre ['tiɣre] *nm* tiger

tijera [ti'xera] *nf* scissors pl; (ZOOL) claw; **tijeras** *nfpl* scissors; (para plantas) shears

tila ['tila] *nf* lime blossom tea

tildar [til'dar] *vt*: **~ de** to brand as

tilde ['tilde] *nf* (TIP) tilde

tilín [ti'lin] *nm* tinkle

timar [ti'mar] *vt* (estafar) to swindle

timbal [tim'bal] *nm* small drum

timbre ['timbre] *nm* (sello) stamp; (campanilla) bell; (tono) timbre; (COM) stamp duty

timidez [timi'ðeθ] *nf* shyness □ **tímido, -a** *adj* shy

timo ['timo] *nm* swindle

timón [ti'mon] *nm* helm, rudder □ **timonel** *nm* helmsman

tímpano ['timpano] *nm* (ANAT) eardrum; (MÚS) small drum

tina ['tina] *nf* tub; (baño) bath(tub) □ **tinaja** *nf* large jar

tinieblas [ti'njeβlas] *nfpl* darkness sg; (sombras) shadows

tino ['tino] *nm* (habilidad) skill; (juicio) insight

tinta ['tinta] *nf* ink; (TEC) dye; (ARTE) colour

tinte ['tinte] *nm* dye

tintero [tin'tero] *nm* inkwell

tinto ['tinto] *nm* red wine

tintorería [tintore'ria] *nf* dry cleaner's

tío ['tio] *nm* (*pariente*) uncle; (*fam: individuo*) bloke (*BRIT*), guy

tiovivo [tio'βiβo] *nm* merry-go-round

típico, -a ['tipiko, a] *adj* typical

tipo ['tipo] *nm* (*clase*) type, kind; (*hombre*) fellow; (*ANAT: de hombre*) build; (: *de mujer*) figure; (*IMPRENTA*) type ▶ **tipo bancario/de descuento/ de interés/de cambio** bank/ discount/interest/exchange rate

tipografía [tipoɣra'fia] *nf* printing *cpd*

tíquet ['tiket] *nm* ticket; (*en tienda*) cash slip

tiquismiquis [tikis'mikis] *nm inv* fussy person ♦ *nmpl* (*querellas*) squabbling *sg*; (*escrúpulos*) silly scruples

tira ['tira] *nf* strip; (*fig*) abundance ▶ **tira y afloja** give and take

tirabuzón [tiraβu'θon] *nm* (*rizo*) curl

tirachinas [tira'tʃinas] *nm inv* catapult

tirada [ti'raða] *nf* (*acto*) cast, throw; (*serie*) series; (*TIP*) printing, edition; **de una** ~ at one go

tirado, -a [ti'raðo, a] *adj* (*barato*) dirt-cheap; (*fam: fácil*) very easy

tirador [tira'ðor] *nm* (*mango*) handle

tirano, -a [ti'rano, a] *adj* tyrannical ♦ *nm/f* tyrant

tirante [ti'rante] *adj* (*cuerda etc*) tight, taut; (*relaciónes*) strained ♦ *nm* (*ARQ*) brace; (*TEC*) stay; **tirantes** *nmpl* (*de pantalón*) braces (*BRIT*), suspenders (*US*) ❑ **tirantez** *nf* tightness; (*fig*) tension

tirar [ti'rar] *vt* to throw; (*dejar caer*) to drop; (*volcar*) to upset; (*derribar*) to knock down *o* over; (*desechar*) to throw out *o* away; (*dinero*) to squander; (*imprimir*) to print ♦ *vi* (*disparar*) to shoot; (*de la guerra etc*) to pull; (*fam: andar*) to go; (*tender a, buscar realizar*) to tend to; (*DEPORTE*) to shoot; **tirarse** *vr* to throw o.s.; ~ **abajo** to bring down, destroy; **tira más a su**

padre he takes more after his father; **ir tirando** to manage

tirita [ti'rita] *nf* (sticking) plaster (*BRIT*), Bandaid® (*US*)

tiritar [tiri'tar] *vi* to shiver

tiro ['tiro] *nm* (*lanzamiento*) throw; (*disparo*) shot; (*DEPORTE*) shot; (*GOLF, TENIS*) drive; (*alcance*) range; **caballo de** ~ cart-horse ▶ **tiro al blanco** target practice

tirón [ti'ron] *nm* (*sacudida*) pull, tug; **de un** ~ in one go, all at once

tiroteo [tiro'teo] *nm* exchange of shots, shooting

tisis ['tisis] *nf inv* consumption, tuberculosis

títere ['titere] *nm* puppet

titubear [tituβe'ar] *vi* to stagger; to stammer; (*fig*) to hesitate ❑ **titubeo** *nm* staggering; stammering; hesitation

titulado, -a [titu'laðo, a] *adj* (*libro*) entitled; (*persona*) titled

titular [titu'lar] *adj* titular ♦ *nmf* holder ♦ *nm* headline ♦ *vt* to title; **titularse** *vr* to be entitled ❑ **título** *nm* title; (*de diario*) headline; (*certificado*) professional qualification; (*universitario*) (university) degree; **a título de** in the capacity of

tiza ['tiθa] *nf* chalk

toalla [to'aʎa] *nf* towel

tobillo [to'βiʎo] *nm* ankle

tobogán [toβo'ɣan] *nm* (*montaña rusa*) roller-coaster; (*de niños*) chute, slide

tocadiscos [toka'ðiskos] *nm inv* record player

tocado, -a [to'kaðo, a] *adj* (*fam*) touched ♦ *nm* headdress

tocador [toka'ðor] *nm* (*mueble*) dressing table; (*cuarto*) boudoir; (*fam*) ladies' toilet (*BRIT*) *o* room (*US*)

tocar [to'kar] *vt* to touch; (*MÚS*) to play; (*referirse a*) to allude to; (*timbre*) to ring ♦ *vi* (*a la puerta*) to knock (on *o* at the door); (*ser de turno*) to fall to, be the turn off; (ser hora) to be due; **tocarse** vr (cubrirse la cabeza) to cover one's head; (tener contacto) to touch (each other); **por lo que a mí me toca** as far as I am concerned; **te toca a ti** it's your turn

tocayo, -a [to'kajo, a] nm/f namesake

tocino [to'θino] nm bacon

todavía [toða'βia] adv (aun) even; (aún) still, yet; **~ más** yet more; **~ no** not yet

todo, -a

PALABRA CLAVE

['toðo, a] adj

1 (con artículo sg) all; **toda la carne** all the meat; **toda la noche** all night, the whole night; **todo el libro** the whole book; **toda una botella** a whole bottle; **todo lo contrario** quite the opposite; **está toda sucia** she's all dirty; **por todo el país** throughout the whole country

2 (con artículo pl) all; every; **todos los libros** all the books; **todas las noches** every night; **todos los que quieran salir** all those who want to leave

♦ pron

1 everything, all; **todos** everyone, everybody; **lo sabemos todo** we know everything; **todos querían más tiempo** everybody o everyone wanted more time; **nos marchamos todos** all of us left

2: **con todo: con todo él me sigue gustando** even so I still like him

♦ adv all; **vaya todo seguido** keep straight on o ahead

♦ nm: **como un todo** as a whole; **del todo: no me agrada del todo** I don't entirely like it

todopoderoso, -a [toðopoðe'roso, a] adj all powerful; (REL) almighty

toga ['toɣa] nf toga; (ESCOL) gown

Tokio ['tokjo] n Tokyo

toldo ['toldo] nm (para el sol) sunshade (BRIT); parasol; (tienda) marquee

tolerancia [tole'ranθja] nf tolerance
❏ **tolerante** adj (sociedad) liberal; (persona) open-minded

tolerar [tole'rar] vt to tolerate; (resistir) to endure

toma ['toma] nf (acto) taking; (MED) dose ▶ **toma de corriente** socket ▶ **toma de tierra** earth (wire) ❏ **tomacorriente** (LAm) nm socket

tomar [to'mar] vt to take; (aspecto) to take on; (beber) to drink ♦ vi to take; (LAm: beber) to drink; **tomarse** vr to take; **tomarse por** to consider o.s. to be; **a bien/mal** to take well/badly; **~ en serio** to take seriously; **~ el pelo a algn** to pull sb's leg; **tomarla con algn** to pick a quarrel with sb; **¡tome!** here you are!; **~ el sol** to sunbathe

tomate [to'mate] nm tomato

tomillo [to'miʎo] nm thyme

tomo ['tomo] nm (libro) volume

ton [ton] abr = **tonelada** ♦ nm: **sin ~ ni son** without rhyme or reason

tonalidad [tonali'ðað] nf tone

tonel [to'nel] nm barrel

tonelada [tone'laða] nf ton ❏ **tonelaje** nm tonnage

tónica ['tonika] nf (MÚS) tonic; (fig) keynote

tónico, -a ['toniko, a] adj tonic ♦ nm (MED) tonic

tono ['tono] nm tone; **fuera de ~** inappropriate

tontería [tonte'ria] nf (estupidez) foolishness; (cosa) stupid thing; (acto) foolish act; **tonterías** nfpl (disparates) rubbish sg, nonsense sg

tonto, -a ['tonto, a] adj stupid, silly ♦ nm/f fool

topar [to'par] vi: **~ contra** o **en** to run into; **~ con** to run up against

tope ['tope] adj maximum ♦ nm (fin) end; (límite) limit; (FERRO) buffer; (AUTO) bumper; **al ~** end to end

tópico, -a ['topiko, a] *adj* topical ♦ *nm* platitude

topo ['topo] *nm* (ZOOL) mole; (*fig*) blunderer

toque *etc* ['toke] *vb ver* **tocar** ♦ *nm* touch; (MÚS) beat; (*de campana*) peal; **dar un ~ a** to warn ▶ **toque de queda** curfew

toqué *etc vb ver* **tocar**

toquetear [tokete'ar] *vt* to finger

toquilla [to'kiʎa] *nf* (*pañuelo*) headscarf; (*chal*) shawl

tórax ['toraks] *nm* thorax

torbellino [torbe'ʎino] *nm* whirlwind; (*fig*) whirl

torcedura [torθe'ðura] *nf* twist; (MED) sprain

torcer [tor'θer] *vt* to twist; (*la esquina*) to turn; (MED) to sprain ♦ *vi* (*desviar*) to turn off; **torcerse** *vr* (*ladearse*) to bend; (*desviarse*) to go astray; (*fracasar*) to go wrong ▢ **torcido, -a** *adj* twisted; (*fig*) crooked ♦ *nm* curl

tordo, -a ['torðo, a] *adj* dappled ♦ *nm* thrush

torear [tore'ar] *vt* (*fig*: *evadir*) to avoid; (*jugar con*) to tease ♦ *vi* to fight bulls ▢ **toreo** *nm* bullfighting ▢ **torero, -a** *nm/f* bullfighter

tormenta [tor'menta] *nf* storm; (*fig*: *confusión*) turmoil

tormento [tor'mento] *nm* torture; (*fig*) anguish

tornar [tor'nar] *vt* (*devolver*) to return, give back; (*transformar*) to transform ♦ *vi* to go back

tornasolado, -a [tornaso'laðo, a] *adj* (*brillante*) iridescent; (*reluciente*) shimmering

torneo [tor'neo] *nm* tournament

tornillo [tor'niʎo] *nm* screw

torniquete [torni'kete] *nm* (MED) tourniquet

torno ['torno] *nm* (TEC) winch; (*tambor*) drum; **en ~ (a)** round, about

toro ['toro] *nm* bull; (*fam*) he-man; **los toros** bullfighting

toronja [to'ronxa] *nf* grapefruit

torpe ['torpe] *adj* (*poco hábil*) clumsy, awkward; (*necio*) dim; (*lento*) slow

torpedo [tor'peðo] *nm* torpedo

torpeza [tor'peθa] *nf* (*falta de agilidad*) clumsiness; (*lentitud*) slowness; (*error*) mistake

torre ['torre] *nf* tower; (*de petróleo*) derrick

torrefacto, -a [torre'fakto, a] *adj* roasted

torrente [to'rrente] *nm* torrent

torrija [to'rrixa] *nf* French toast

torsión [tor'sjon] *nf* twisting

torso ['torso] *nm* torso

torta ['torta] *nf* cake; (*fam*) slap

tortícolis [tor'tikolis] *nm inv* stiff neck

tortilla [tor'tiʎa] *nf* omelette; (LAm: *de maíz*) maize pancake ▶ **tortilla de papas** (LAm) potato omelette ▶ **tortilla de patatas** (ESP) potato omelette ▶ **tortilla francesa** (ESP) plain omelette

tórtola ['tortola] *nf* turtledove

tortuga [tor'tuɣa] *nf* tortoise

tortuoso, -a [tor'twoso, a] *adj* winding

tortura [tor'tura] *nf* torture ▢ **torturar** *vt* to torture

tos [tos] *nf* cough ▶ **tos ferina** whooping cough

toser [to'ser] *vi* to cough

tostada [tos'taða] *nf* piece of toast ▢ **tostado, -a** *adj* toasted; (*por el sol*) dark brown; (*piel*) tanned

tostador [tosta'ðor] (ESP) *nm* toaster ▢ **tostadora** (LAm) *nf* = **tostador**

tostar [tos'tar] *vt* to toast; (*café*) to roast; (*persona*) to tan; **tostarse** *vr* to get brown

total [to'tal] *adj* total ♦ *adv* in short; (*al fin y al cabo*) when all is said and done ♦ *nm* total; **en ~** in all; **~ que ...** to cut (BRIT) o make (US) a long story short ...

totalidad [totali'ðað] nf whole

totalitario, -a [totali'tarjo, a] adj totalitarian

tóxico, -a ['toksiko, a] adj toxic ♦ nm poison ☐ **toxicómano, -a** nm/f drug addict

toxina [to'ksina] nf toxin

tozudo, -a [to'θuðo, a] adj obstinate

trabajador, a [traβaxa'ðor, a] adj hard-working ♦ nm/f worker ▶ **trabajador autónomo** o **por cuenta propia** self-employed person

trabajar [traβa'xar] vt to work; (AGR) to till; (empeñarse en) to work at; (convencer) to persuade ♦ vi to work; (esforzarse) to strive ☐ **trabajo** nm work; (tarea) task; (POL) labour; (fig) effort; **tomarse el trabajo de** to take the trouble to ▶ **trabajo a destajo** piecework ▶ **trabajo en equipo** teamwork ▶ **trabajo por turnos** shift work ▶ **trabajos forzados** hard labour sg

trabalenguas [traβa'lengwas] nm inv tongue twister

tracción [trak'θjon] nf traction ▶ **tracción delantera/trasera** front-wheel/rear-wheel drive

tractor [trak'tor] nm tractor

tradición [traði'θjon] nf tradition ☐ **tradicional** adj traditional

traducción [traðuk'θjon] nf translation

traducir [traðu'θir] vt to translate ☐ **traductor, a** nm/f translator

traer [tra'er] vt to bring; (llevar) to carry; (llevar puesto) to wear; (incluir) to carry; (causar) to cause; **traerse** vr: **traerse algo** to be up to sth

traficar [trafi'kar] vi to trade

tráfico ['trafiko] nm (COM) trade; (AUTO) traffic

tragaluz [traɣa'luθ] nm skylight

tragamonedas (LAm) [traɣamo'neðas] nf inv slot machine

tragaperras [traɣa'perras] (ESP) nf inv slot machine

tragar [tra'ɣar] vt to swallow; (devorar) to devour, bolt down; **tragarse** vr to swallow

tragedia [tra'xeðja] nf tragedy ☐ **trágico, -a** adj tragic

trago ['traɣo] nm (líquido) drink; (bocado) gulp; (fam: de bebida) swig; (desgracia) blow; **echar un ~** to have a drink

traición [trai'θjon] nf treachery; (JUR) treason; (una traición) act of treachery ☐ **traicionar** vt to betray

traidor, a [trai'ðor, a] adj treacherous ♦ nm/f traitor

traigo etc vb ver **traer**

traje ['traxe] vb ver **traer** ♦ nm (de hombre) suit; (de mujer) dress; (vestido típico) costume ▶ **traje de baño/chaqueta** swimsuit/suit ▶ **traje de etiqueta** dress suit ▶ **traje de luces** bullfighter's costume

trajera etc [tra'xera] vb ver **traer**

trajín [tra'xin] nm (fam: movimiento) bustle ☐ **trajinar** vi (moverse) to bustle about

trama ['trama] nf (intriga) plot; (de tejido) weft (BRIT), woof (US) ☐ **tramar** vt to plot; (TEC) to weave

tramitar [trami'tar] vt (asunto) to transact; (negociar) to negotiate

trámite ['tramite] nm (paso) step; (JUR) transaction; **trámites** nmpl (burocracia) procedure sg; (JUR) proceedings

tramo ['tramo] nm (de tierra) plot; (de escalera) flight; (de vía) section

trampa ['trampa] nf trap; (en el suelo) trapdoor; (truco) trick; (engaño) fiddle ☐ **trampear** vt, vi to cheat

trampolín [trampo'lin] nm (de piscina etc) diving board

tramposo, -a [tram'poso, a] adj crooked, cheating ♦ nm/f crook, cheat

tranca ['traŋka] nf (palo) stick; (de puerta, ventana) bar ♦ **trancar** vt to bar

trance ['tranθe] nm (momento difícil) difficult moment o juncture; (estado hipnotizado) trance

tranquilidad [traŋkili'ðað] nf (calma) calmness, stillness; (paz) peacefulness

tranquilizar [traŋkili'θar] vt (calmar) to calm (down); (asegurar) to reassure; **tranquilizarse** vr to calm down □ **tranquilo, -a** adj (calmado) calm; (apacible) peaceful; (mar) calm; (mente) untroubled

transacción [transak'θjon] nf transaction

transbordador [transβorða'ðor] nm ferry

transbordo [trans'βorðo] nm transfer; **hacer ~** to change (trains etc)

transcurrir [transku'rrir] vi (tiempo) to pass; (hecho) to take place

transcurso [trans'kurso] nm: **~ del tiempo** lapse (of time)

transeúnte [transe'unte] nmf passer-by

transferencia [transfe'renθja] nf transference; (COM) transfer

transferir [transfe'rir] vt to transfer

transformador [transforma'ðor] nm (ELEC) transformer

transformar [transfor'mar] vt to transform; (convertir) to convert

transfusión [transfu'sjon] nf transfusion

transgénico, -a [trans'xeniko, a] adj genetically modified, GM

transición [transi'θjon] nf transition

transigir [transi'xir] vi to compromise, make concessions

transitar [transi'tar] vi to go (from place to place) □ **tránsito** nm transit; (AUTO) traffic □ **transitorio, -a** adj transitory

transmisión [transmi'sjon] nf (TEC) transmission; (transferencia) transfer

▸ **transmisión exterior/en directo** outside/live broadcast

transmitir [transmi'tir] vt to transmit; (RADIO, TV) to broadcast

transparencia [transpa'renθja] nf transparency; (claridad) clearness, clarity; (foto) slide

transparentar [transparen'tar] vt to reveal ♦ vi to be transparent □ **transparente** adj transparent; (claro) clear

transpirar [transpi'rar] vi to perspire

transportar [transpor'tar] vt to transport; (llevar) to carry □ **transporte** nm transport; (COM) haulage

transversal [transβer'sal] adj transverse, cross

tranvía [tram'bia] nm tram

trapeador (LAm) nm mop □ **trapear** (LAm) vt to mop

trapecio [tra'peθjo] nm trapeze □ **trapecista** nmf trapeze artist

trapero, -a [tra'pero, a] nm/f ragman

trapicheo [trapi'tʃeo] (fam) nm scheme, fiddle

trapo ['trapo] nm (tela) rag; (de cocina) cloth

tráquea ['trakea] nf windpipe

traqueteo [trake'teo] nm rattling

tras [tras] prep (detrás) behind; (después) after

trasatlántico [trasat'lantiko] nm (barco) (cabin) cruiser

trascendencia [trasθen'denθja] nf (importancia) importance; (FILOSOFÍA) transcendence

trascendental [trasθenden'tal] adj important; (FILOSOFÍA) transcendental

trasero, -a [tra'sero, a] adj back, rear ♦ nm (ANAT) bottom

trasfondo [tras'fondo] nm background

trasgredir [trasγre'ðir] vt to contravene

trashumante [trasu'mante] *adj* (*animales*) migrating

trasladar [trasla'ðar] *vt* to move; (*persona*) to transfer; (*postergar*) to postpone; (*copiar*) to copy; **trasladarse** *vr* (*mudarse*) to move ▷ **traslado** *nm* move; (*mudanza*) move, removal

traslucir [traslu'θir] *vt* to show

trasluz [tras'luθ] *nm* reflected light; **al ~** against o up to the light

trasnochador, a [trasnotʃa'ðor, a] *nm/f* night owl

trasnochar [trasno'tʃar] *vi* (*acostarse tarde*) to stay up late

traspapelar [traspape'lar] *vt* (*documento, carta*) to mislay, misplace

traspasar [traspa'sar] *vt* (*suj: bala etc*) to pierce, go through; (*propiedad*) to sell, transfer; (*calle*) to cross over; (*límites*) to go beyond; (*ley*) to break ▷ **traspaso** *nm* (*venta*) transfer, sale

traspatio [LAm] *nm* backyard

traspié [tras'pje] *nm* (*tropezón*) trip; (*error*) blunder

trasplantar [trasplan'tar] *vt* to transplant

traste ['traste] *nm* (*MÚS*) fret; **dar al ~ con algo** to ruin sth

trastero [tras'tero] *nm* storage room

trastienda [tras'tjenda] *nf* back of shop

trasto ['trasto] (*pey*) *nm* (*cosa*) piece of junk; (*persona*) dead loss

trastornado, -a [trastor'naðo, a] *adj* (*loco*) mad, crazy

trastornar [trastor'nar] *vt* (*fig: planes*) to disrupt; (*: nervios*) to shatter; (*: persona*) to drive crazy; **trastornarse** *vr* (*volverse loco*) to go mad o crazy ▷ **trastorno** *nm* (*acto*) overturning; (*confusión*) confusion

tratable [tra'taβle] *adj* friendly

tratado [tra'taðo] *nm* (*POL*) treaty; (*COM*) agreement

tratamiento [trata'mjento] *nm* treatment ▷ **tratamiento de textos** (*INFORM*) word processing *cpd*

tratar [tra'tar] *vt* (*ocuparse de*) to treat; (*manejar, TEC*) to handle; (*MED*) to treat; (*dirigirse a: persona*) to address ▷ *vi*: **~ de** (*hablar sobre*) to deal with, be about; (*intentar*) to try; **tratarse de**: **~ con** (*COM*) to trade in; (*negociar*) to negotiate with; (*tener contactos*) to have dealings with; **¿de qué se trata?** what's it about? ▷ **trato** *nm* dealings *pl*; (*relaciones*) relationship; (*comportamiento*) manner; (*COM*) agreement

trauma ['trauma] *nm* trauma

través [tra'βes] *nm* (*fig*) reverse; **al ~** across, crossways; **a ~ de** across; (*sobre*) over; (*por*) through

travesaño [traβe'saɲo] *nm* (*ARQ*) crossbeam; (*DEPORTE*) crossbar

travesía [traβe'sia] *nf* (*calle*) cross-street; (*NÁUT*) crossing

travesura [traβe'sura] *nf* (*broma*) prank; (*ingenio*) wit

travieso, -a [tra'βjeso, a] *adj* (*niño*) naughty

trayecto [tra'jekto] *nm* (*ruta*) road, way; (*viaje*) journey; (*tramo*) stretch ▷ **trayectoria** *nf* trajectory; (*fig*) path

traza ['traθa] *nf* (*aspecto*) looks *pl*; (*señal*) sign ▷ **trazado, -a** *adj*: **bien trazado** shapely, well-formed ♦ *nm* (*ARQ*) plan, design; (*fig*) outline

trazar [tra'θar] *vt* (*ARQ*) to plan; (*ARTE*) to sketch; (*fig*) to trace; (*plan*) to draw up ▷ **trazo** *nm* (*línea*) line; (*bosquejo*) sketch

trébol [tre'βol] *nm* (*BOT*) clover

trece ['treθe] *num* thirteen

trecho ['tretʃo] *nm* (*distancia*) distance; (*tiempo*) while

tregua ['treɣwa] *nf* (*MIL*) truce; (*fig*) respite

treinta ['treinta] *num* thirty

tremendo, -a [tre'mendo, a] *adj* (*terrible*) terrible; (*imponente: cosa*) imposing; (*fam: fabuloso*) tremendous

tren [tren] *nm* train ► **tren de aterrizaje** undercarriage ► **tren de cercanías** suburban train

trenca ['trenka] *nf* duffel coat

trenza ['trenθa] *nf* (*de pelo*) plait (BRIT), braid (US)

trepadora [trepa'ðora] *nf* (BOT) climber

trepar [tre'par] *vt, vi* to climb

tres [tres] *num* three

tresillo [tre'siʎo] *nm* three-piece suite; (MÚS) triplet

treta ['treta] *nf* trick

triángulo ['trjanɣulo] *nm* triangle

tribu ['triβu] *nf* tribe

tribuna [tri'βuna] *nf* (*plataforma*) platform; (DEPORTE) (grand)stand

tribunal [triβu'nal] *nm* (JUR) court; (*comisión, fig*) tribunal; **~ popular** jury

tributo [tri'βuto] *nm* (COM) tax

trigal [tri'ɣal] *nm* wheat field

trigo ['triɣo] *nm* wheat

trigueño, -a [tri'ɣeɲo, a] *adj* (*pelo*) corn-coloured

trillar [tri'ʎar] *vt* (AGR) to thresh

trimestral [trimes'tral] *adj* quarterly; (ESCOL) termly

trimestre [tri'mestre] *nm* (ESCOL) term

trinar [tri'nar] *vi* (*pájaros*) to sing; (*rabiar*) to fume, be angry

trinchar [trin'tʃar] *vt* to carve

trinchera [trin'tʃera] *nf* (*fosa*) trench

trineo [tri'neo] *nm* sledge

trinidad [trini'ðað] *nf* trio; (REL): **la T~** the Trinity

tripa ['tripa] *nf* (ANAT) intestine; (*fam: tb:* **tripas**) insides *pl*

triple ['triple] *adj* triple

triplicado, -a [tripli'kaðo, a] *adj:* **por ~** in triplicate

triplicación [triplika'θjon] *nf* crew

tripulante [tripu'lante] *nmf* crewman/woman

tripular [tripu'lar] *vt* (*barco*) to man; (AUTO) to drive

triquiñuela [triki'ɲwela] *nf* trick

tris [tris] *nm inv* crack

triste ['triste] *adj* sad; (*lamentable*) sorry, miserable □ **tristeza** *nf* (*aflicción*) sadness; (*melancolía*) melancholy

triturar [tritu'rar] *vt* (*moler*) to grind; (*mascar*) to chew

triunfar [trjun'far] *vi* (*tener éxito*) to triumph; (*ganar*) to win □ **triunfo** *nm* triumph

trivial [tri'βjal] *adj* trivial

triza ['triθa] *nf:* **hacer trizas** to smash to bits; (*papel*) to tear to shreds

trocear [troθe'ar] *vt* (*carne, manzana*) to cut up, cut into pieces

trocha ['trotʃa] *nf* short cut

trofeo [tro'feo] *nm* (*premio*) trophy; (*éxito*) success

tromba ['tromba] *nf* downpour

trombón [trom'bon] *nm* trombone

trombosis [trom'bosis] *nf inv* thrombosis

tromba ['trompa] *nf* horn; (*trompo*) humming top; (*hocico*) snout; (*fam:*) **cogerse una** ~ to get tight

trompazo [trom'paθo] *nm* bump, bang

trompeta [trom'peta] *nf* trumpet; (*clarín*) bugle

trompicón [trompi'kon]: **a trompicones** *adv* in fits and starts

trompo ['trompo] *nm* spinning top

trompón [trom'pon] *nm* bump

tronar [tro'nar] *vt* (MÉX, CAm: *fusilar*) to shoot; (MÉX: *examen*) to flunk ♦ *vi* to thunder; (*fig*) to rage

tronchar [tron'tʃar] *vt* (*árbol*) to chop down; (*fig: vida*) to cut short; (*: esperanza*) to shatter; (*persona*) to tire out; **troncharse** *vr* to fall down

tronco ['tronko] *nm* (*de árbol, ANAT*) trunk

trono ['trono] nm throne

tropa ['tropa] nf (MIL) troop; (soldados) soldiers pl

tropezar [trope'θar] vi to trip, stumble; (error) to slip up; ~ **con** to run into; (topar con) to bump into □ **tropezón** nm trip; (fig) blunder

tropical [tropi'kal] adj tropical

trópico ['tropiko] nm tropic

tropiezo [tro'pjeθo] vb ver **tropezar**
♦ nm (error) slip, blunder; (desgracia) misfortune; (obstáculo) snag

trotamundos [trota'mundos] nm inv globetrotter

trotar [tro'tar] vi to trot □ **trote** nm trot; (fam) travelling; **de mucho trote** hard-wearing

trozar (LAm) vt to cut up, cut into pieces

trozo ['troθo] nm bit, piece

trucha ['trutʃa] nf trout

truco ['truko] nm (habilidad) knack; (engaño) trick

trueno ['trweno] nm thunder; (estampido) bang

trueque etc ['trweke] vb ver **trocar**
♦ nm exchange; (COM) barter

trufa ['trufa] nf (BOT) truffle

truhán, -ana [tru'an, ana] nm/f rogue

truncar [trun'kar] vt (cortar) to truncate; (fig: la vida etc) to cut short; (: el desarrollo) to stunt

tu [tu] adj your

tú [tu] pron you

tubérculo [tu'βerkulo] nm (BOT) tuber

tuberculosis [tuβerku'losis] nf inv tuberculosis

tubería [tuβe'ria] nf pipes pl; (conducto) pipeline

tubo ['tuβo] nm tube, pipe ▶ **tubo de ensayo** test tube ▶ **tubo de escape** exhaust (pipe)

tuerca ['twerka] nf nut

tuerto, -a ['twerto, a] adj blind in one eye ♦ nm/f one-eyed person

tuerza etc ['twerθa] vb ver **torcer**

tuétano ['twetano] nm marrow; (BOT) pith

tufo ['tufo] nm (hedor) stench

tul [tul] nm tulle

tulipán [tuli'pan] nm tulip

tullido, -a [tu'ʎiðo, a] adj crippled

tumba ['tumba] nf (sepultura) tomb

tumbar [tum'bar] vt to knock down; **tumbarse** vr (echarse) to lie down; (extenderse) to stretch out

tumbo ['tumbo] nm: **dar tumbos** to stagger

tumbona [tum'bona] nf (butaca) easy chair; (de playa) deckchair (BRIT), beach chair (US)

tumor [tu'mor] nm tumour

tumulto [tu'multo] nm turmoil

tuna ['tuna] nf (MÚS) student music group; ver tb **tuno**

tunante [tu'nante] nmf rascal

túnel ['tunel] nm tunnel

Túnez ['tuneθ] nm Tunisia; (ciudad) Tunis

tuno, -a ['tuno, a] nm/f (fam) rogue
♦ nm member of student music group

tupido, -a [tu'piðo, a] adj (denso) dense; (tela) close-woven

turbante [tur'βante] nm turban

turbar [tur'βar] vt (molestar) to disturb; (incomodar) to upset

turbina [tur'βina] nf turbine

turbio, -a ['turβjo, a] adj cloudy; (tema etc) confused

turbulencia [turβu'lenθja] nf turbulence; (fig) restlessness ❑ **turbulento, -a** adj turbulent; (fig: intranquilo) restless; (: ruidoso) noisy

turco, -a ['turko, a] adj Turkish ♦ nm/f Turk

turismo [tu'rismo] nm tourism; (coche) car ❑ **turista** nmf tourist ❑ **turístico, -a** adj tourist cpd

turnar [tur'nar] vi to take (it in) turns; **turnarse** vr to take (it in) turns ❑ **turno** nm (de trabajo) shift; (en juegos etc) turn

turquesa [tur'kesa] nf turquoise

Turquía [tur'kia] nf Turkey

turrón [tu'rron] nm (dulce) nougat

tutear [tute'ar] vt to address as familiar "tú"; **tutearse** vr to be on familiar terms

tutela [tu'tela] nf (legal) guardianship ❑ **tutelar** adj tutelary ♦ vt to protect

tutor, -a [tu'tor, a] nm/f (legal) guardian; (ESCOL) tutor

tuve etc ['tuβe] vb ver **tener**

tuviera etc vb ver **tener**

tuyo, -a ['tujo, a] adj yours, of yours ♦ pron yours; **un amigo ~** a friend of yours; **los tuyos** (fam) your relations o family

TV nf abr (= televisión) TV

TVE nf abr = **Televisión Española**

U, u

u [u] conj or

ubicar [uβi'kar] vt to place, situate; (LAm: encontrar) to find; **ubicarse** vr (LAm: encontrarse) to lie, be located

ubre ['uβre] nf udder

UCI nf abr (= Unidad de Cuidados Intensivos) ICU

Ud(s) abr = **usted(es)**

UE nf abr (= Unión Europea) EU

ufanarse [ufa'narse] vr to boast ❑ **ufano, -a** adj (arrogante) arrogant; (presumido) conceited

UGT (ESP) nf abr = **Unión General de Trabajadores**

úlcera ['ulθera] nf ulcer

ulterior [ulte'rjor] adj (más allá) farther, further; (subsecuente, siguiente) subsequent

últimamente ['ultimamente] adv (recientemente) lately, recently

ultimar [ulti'mar] vt to finish; (finalizar) to finalize; (LAm: matar) to kill

ultimátum [ulti'matum] (pl ultimátums) nm ultimatum

último, -a ['ultimo, a] adj last; (más reciente) latest, most recent; (más bajo) bottom; (más alto) top; **en las últimas** on one's last legs; **por último** finally

ultra ['ultra] adj ultra ♦ nmf extreme right-winger

ultraje [ul'traxe] nm outrage; insult

ultramar [ultra'mar] nm: **de o en ~** abroad, overseas

ultramarinos [ultrama'rinos] nmpl groceries; **tienda de ~** grocer's (shop)

ultranza [ul'tranθa]: **a ~** adv (a todo trance) at all costs; (completo) outright

umbral [um'bral] nm (gen) threshold

un, una

[un, 'una] art indef a; (antes de vocal) an; **una mujer/naranja** a woman/an orange ♦ adj: **unos** (o **unas**), **hay unos regalos para ti** there are some presents for you; **hay unas cervezas en la nevera** there are some beers in the fridge

unánime [u'nanime] adj unanimous ❑ **unanimidad** nf unanimity

undécimo, -a [un'deθimo, a] adj eleventh

ungir [un'xir] vt to anoint

ungüento [un'gwento] nm ointment

único, -a ['uniko, a] adj only, sole; (sin par) unique

unidad [uni'ðað] nf unity; (COM, TEC etc) unit

unido, -a [u'niðo, a] adj joined, linked; (fig) united

unificar [unifi'kar] vt to unite, unify

uniformar [unifor'mar] vt to make uniform, level up; (persona) to put into uniform

uniforme [uni'forme] adj uniform, equal; (superficie) even ♦ nm uniform

unilateral [unilate'ral] adj unilateral

unión [u'njon] nf union; (acto) uniting, joining; (unidad) unity; (TEC) joint
▶ **Unión Europea** European Union

unir [u'nir] vt (juntar) to join, unite; (atar) to tie, fasten; (combinar) to combine; **unirse** vr to join together, unite; (empresas) to merge

unísono [u'nisono] nm: **al ~** in unison

universal [uniβer'sal] adj universal; (mundial) world cpd

universidad [uniβersi'ðað] nf university

universitario, -a [uniβersi'tarjo, a] adj university cpd ♦ nm/f (profesor) lecturer; (estudiante) (university) student; (graduado) graduate

universo [uni'βerso] nm universe

uno, -a

['uno, a] adj one; **unos pocos** a few; **unos cien** about a hundred

♦ pron

1 one; **quiero sólo uno** I only want one; **uno de ellos** one of them

2 (alguien) somebody, someone; **conozco a uno que se te parece** I know somebody o someone who looks like you; **uno mismo** oneself; **unos querían quedarse** some (people) wanted to stay

3: **(los) unos ... (los) otros ...** some ... others

♦ nf one; **es la una** it's one o'clock

♦ nm (number) one

untar [un'tar] vt (mantequilla) to spread; (engrasar) to grease, oil

uña ['uɲa] nf (ANAT) nail; (garra) claw; (casco) hoof; (arrancaclavos) claw

uranio [u'ranjo] nm uranium

urbanización [urβaniθa'θjon] nf (barrio, colonia) housing estate

urbanizar [urβani'θar] vt (zona) to develop, urbanize

urbano, -a [ur'βano, a] adj (de ciudad) urban; (cortés) courteous, polite

urbe ['urβe] nf large city

urdir [ur'ðir] vt to warp; (complot) to plot, contrive

urgencia [ur'xenθja] nf urgency; (prisa) haste, rush; (emergencia) emergency; **servicios de ~** emergency services; **"Urgencias"** "Casualty" ❑ **urgente** adj urgent

urgir [ur'xir] vi to be urgent; **me urge** I'm in a hurry for it

urinario, -a [uri'narjo, a] adj urinary ♦ nm urinal

urna ['urna] nf urn; (POL) ballot box

urraca [u'rraka] nf magpie

URSS [urs] nf (HIST): **la ~** the USSR

Uruguay [uru'ɣwai] nm (tb: **el ~**) Uruguay ❑ **uruguayo, -a** adj, nm/f Uruguayan

usado, -a [u'saðo, a] adj used; (de segunda mano) secondhand

usar [u'sar] vt to use; (ropa) to wear; (tener costumbre) to be in the habit of; **usarse** vr to be used ❑ **uso** nm use; wear; (costumbre) usage, custom; (moda) fashion; **al uso** in keeping with custom; **al uso de** in the style of; **de uso externo** (MED) for external use

usted [us'teð] pron (sg) you sg; (pl): **ustedes** you pl

usual [u'swal] adj usual

usuario, -a [usu'arjo, a] nm/f user

usura [u'sura] nf usury □ **usurero, -a** nm/f usurer

usurpar [usur'par] vt to usurp

utensilio [uten'siljo] nm tool; (CULIN) utensil

útero ['utero] nm uterus, womb

útil ['util] adj useful ♦ nm tool □ **utilidad** nf usefulness; (COM) profit □ **utilizar** vt to use, utilize

utopía [uto'pia] nf Utopia □ **utópico, -a** adj Utopian

uva ['uβa] nf grape

V, v

v abr (= voltio) v

va [ba] vb ver **ir**

vaca ['baka] nf (animal) cow; **carne de ~** beef

vacaciones [baka'θjones] nfpl holidays

vacante [ba'kante] adj vacant, empty ♦ nf vacancy

vaciar [ba'θjar] vt to empty out; (ahuecar) to hollow out; (moldear) to cast; **vaciarse** vr to empty

vacilar [baθi'lar] vi to be unsteady; (al hablar) to falter; (dudar) to hesitate, waver; (memoria) to fail

vacío, -a [ba'θio, a] adj empty; (puesto) vacant; (desocupado) idle; (vano) vain ♦ nm emptiness; (FÍSICA) vacuum; (un vacío) (empty) space

vacuna [ba'kuna] nf vaccine □ **vacunar** vt to vaccinate

vacuno, -a [ba'kuno, a] adj cow cpd; **ganado ~** cattle

vadear [baðe'ar] vt (río) to ford □ **vado** nm ford

vagabundo, -a [baɣa'βundo, a] adj wandering ♦ nm tramp

vagancia [ba'ɣanθja] nf (pereza) idleness, laziness

vagar [ba'ɣar] vi to wander; (no hacer nada) to idle

vagina [ba'xina] nf vagina

vago, -a ['baɣo, a] adj vague; (perezoso) lazy ♦ nm/f (vagabundo) tramp; (flojo) lazybones sg, idler

vagón [ba'ɣon] nm (FERRO: de pasajeros) carriage; (: de mercancías) wagon

vaho ['bao] nm (vapor) vapour, steam; (respiración) breath

vaina ['baina] nf sheath

vainilla [bai'niʎa] nf vanilla

vais [bais] vb ver **ir**

vaivén [bai'βen] nm to-and-fro movement; (de tránsito) coming and going; **vaivenes** nmpl (fig) ups and downs

vajilla [ba'xiʎa] nf crockery, dishes pl; (juego) service, set

valdré etc vb ver **valer**

vale ['bale] nm voucher; (recibo) receipt; (pagaré) IOU

valedero, -a [bale'ðero, a] adj valid

valenciano, -a [balen'θjano, a] adj Valencian

valentía [balen'tia] nf courage, bravery

valer [ba'ler] vt to be worth; (MAT) to equal; (costar) to cost ♦ vi (ser útil) to be useful; (ser válido) to be valid; **valerse** vr to take care of oneself; **valerse de** to make use of, take advantage of; **~ la pena** to be worthwhile; **¿vale?** (ESP) OK?; **más vale que nos vayamos** we'd better go; **¡eso a mí no me vale!** (MÉX: fam: no importar) I couldn't care less about that

valeroso, -a [bale'roso, a] adj brave, valiant

valgo etc vb ver **valer**

valía [ba'lia] nf worth, value

validar [bali'ðar] vt to validate □ **validez** nf validity □ **válido, -a** adj valid

valiente [ba'ljente] adj brave, valiant ♦ nm hero

valija [ba'lixa] nf (CS) (suit)case

valioso, -a [ba'ljoso, a] adj valuable

valla ['baʎa] nf fence; (DEPORTE) hurdle
  ▶ **valla publicitaria** hoarding
  ❏ **vallar** vt to fence in

valle ['baʎe] nm valley

valor [ba'lor] nm value, worth; (precio) price; (valentía) valour, courage; (importancia) importance; **valores** nmpl (COM) securities ❏ **valorar** vt to value

vals [bals] nm inv waltz

válvula ['balβula] nf valve

vamos ['bamos] vb ver **ir**

vampiro, -resa [bam'piro, 'resa] nm/f vampire

van [ban] vb ver **ir**

vanguardia [ban'gwardja] nf vanguard; (ARTE etc) avant-garde

vanidad [bani'ðað] nf vanity
  ❏ **vanidoso, -a** adj vain, conceited

vano, -a ['bano, a] adj vain

vapor [ba'por] nm vapour; (vaho) steam; **al ~** (CULIN) steamed ▶ **vapor de agua** water vapour
  ❏ **vaporizador** nm atomizer
  ❏ **vaporizar** vt to vaporize
  ❏ **vaporoso, -a** adj vaporous

vaquero, -a [ba'kero, a] adj cattle cpd ♦ nm cowboy; **vaqueros** nmpl (pantalones) jeans

vaquilla [ba'kiʎa] nf (ZOOL) heifer

vara ['bara] nf stick; (TEC) rod

variable [ba'rjaβle] adj, nf variable

variación [barja'θjon] nf variation

variar [bar'jar] vt to vary; (modificar) to modify; (cambiar de posición) to switch around ♦ vi to vary

varicela [bari'θela] nf chickenpox

varices [ba'riθes] nfpl varicose veins

variedad [barje'ðað] nf variety

varilla [ba'riʎa] nf stick; (BOT) twig; (TEC) rod; (de rueda) spoke

vario, -a ['barjo, a] adj varied; **varios** various, several

varita [ba'rita] nf (tb: ~ mágica) magic wand

varón [ba'ron] nm male, man
  ❏ **varonil** adj manly, virile

Varsovia [bar'soβja] n Warsaw

vas [bas] vb ver **ir**

vasco, -a ['basko, a] adj, nm/f Basque
  ❏ **vascongado, -a** [baskon'gaðo, a] adj Basque; **las Vascongadas** the Basque Country

vaselina [base'lina] nf Vaseline®

vasija [ba'sixa] nf container, vessel

vaso ['baso] nm glass, tumbler; (ANAT) vessel

⚠ No confundir **vaso** con la palabra inglesa *vase*.

vástago ['bastaɣo] nm (BOT) shoot; (TEC) rod; (fig) offspring

vasto, -a ['basto, a] adj vast, huge

Vaticano [bati'kano] nm: **el ~** the Vatican

vatio ['batjo] nm (ELEC) watt

vaya etc ['baja] vb ver **ir**

Vd(s) abr = **usted(es)**

ve [be] vb ver **ir; ver**

vecindad [beθin'dað] nf neighbourhood; (habitantes) residents pl

vecindario [beθin'darjo] nm neighbourhood; residents pl

vecino, -a [be'θino, a] adj neighbouring ♦ nm/f neighbour; (residente) resident

veda ['beða] nf prohibition ❏ **vedar** [be'ðar] vt (prohibir) to ban, prohibit; (impedir) to stop, prevent

vegetación [bexeta'θjon] nf vegetation

vegetal [bexe'tal] adj, nm vegetable

vegetariano, -a [bexeta'rjano, a] adj, nm/f vegetarian

vehículo [be'ikulo] nm vehicle; (MED) carrier

veía etc vb ver **ver**

veinte ['beinte] num twenty

vejar [be'xar] vt (irritar) to annoy, vex; (humillar) to humiliate

vejez [be'xeθ] nf old age

vejiga [be'xiɣa] nf (ANAT) bladder

vela ['bela] nf (de cera) candle; (NÁUT) sail; (insomnio) sleeplessness; (vigilia) vigil; (MIL) sentry duty; **estar a dos velas** (fam: sin dinero) to be skint

velado, -a [be'laðo, a] adj veiled; (sonido) muffled; (FOTO) blurred ♦ nf soirée

velar [be'lar] vt (vigilar) to keep watch over ♦ vi to stay awake; **~ por** to watch over, look after

velatorio [bela'torjo] nm (funeral) wake

velero [be'lero] nm (NÁUT) sailing ship; (AVIAC) glider

veleta [be'leta] nf weather vane

veliz [be'lis] (MÉX) nm (suit)case

vello ['beʎo] nm down, fuzz

velo ['belo] nm veil

velocidad [beloθi'ðað] nf speed; (TEC, AUTO) gear

velocímetro [belo'θimetro] nm speedometer

velorio (LAm) nm (funeral) wake

veloz [be'loθ] adj fast

ven [ben] vb ver **venir**

vena ['bena] nf vein

venado [be'naðo] nm deer

vencedor, a [benθe'ðor, a] adj victorious ♦ nm/f victor, winner

vencer [ben'θer] vt (dominar) to defeat, beat; (derrotar) to vanquish; (superar, controlar) to overcome, master ♦ vi (triunfar) to win (through), triumph; (plazo) to expire ■ **vencido, -a** adj (derrotado) defeated, beaten; (COM) due ♦ adv: **pagar vencido** to pay in arrears

venda ['benda] nf bandage ■ **vendaje** nm bandage, dressing ■ **vendar** vt to bandage; **vendar los ojos** to blindfold

vendaval [benda'βal] nm (viento) gale

vendedor, a [bende'ðor, a] nm/f seller

vender [ben'der] vt to sell; **venderse** vr (estar a la venta) to be on sale; **~ al contado/al por mayor/al por menor** to sell for cash/wholesale/retail; **"se vende"** "for sale"

vendimia [ben'dimja] nf grape harvest

vendré etc [ben'dre] vb ver **venir**

veneno [be'neno] nm poison; (de serpiente) venom ■ **venenoso, -a** adj poisonous; venomous

venerable [bene'raβle] adj venerable ■ **venerar** vt (respetar) to revere; (adorar) to worship

venéreo, -a [be'nereo, a] adj: **enfermedad venérea** venereal disease

venezolano, -a [beneθo'lano, a] adj Venezuelan

Venezuela [bene'θwela] nf Venezuela

venganza [ben'ganθa] nf vengeance, revenge ■ **vengar** vt to avenge; **vengarse** vr to take revenge ■ **vengativo, -a** adj (persona) vindictive

vengo etc vb ver **venir**

venia ['benja] nf (perdón) pardon; (permiso) consent

venial [be'njal] adj venial

venida [be'niða] nf (llegada) arrival; (regreso) return

venidero, -a [beni'ðero, a] adj coming, future

venir [be'nir] vi to come; (llegar) to arrive; (ocurrir) to happen; (fig): **~ de** to stem from; **~ bien/mal** to be suitable/unsuitable; **el año que viene** next year; **venirse abajo** to collapse

venta ['benta] nf (COM) sale; **"en ~"** "for sale"; **estar a la o en ~** to be (up) for sale o on the market ▸ **venta a domicilio** door-to-door selling ▸ **venta a plazos** hire purchase ▸ **venta al contado/al por mayor/al por menor** cash sale/wholesale/retail

ventaja [ben'taxa] nf advantage
 ❏ **ventajoso, -a** adj advantageous

ventana [ben'tana] nf window
 ❏ **ventanilla** nf (de taquilla) window
 (of booking office etc)

ventilación [bentila'θjon] nf
 ventilation; (corriente) draught

ventilador [bentila'ðor] nm fan

ventilar [benti'lar] vt to ventilate; (para
 secar) to put out to dry; (asunto) to air,
 discuss

ventisca [ben'tiska] nf blizzard

ventrílocuo, -a [ben'trilokwo, a] nm/f
 ventriloquist

ventura [ben'tura] nf (felicidad)
 happiness; (buena suerte) luck;
 (destino) fortune; **a la (buena) ~** at
 random; (afortunado) lucky, fortunate

veo etc vb ver **ver**

ver [ber] vt to see; (mirar) to look at,
 watch; (entender) to understand;
 (investigar) to look into ♦ vi to see; to
 understand; **verse** vr (encontrarse) to
 meet; (dejarse ver) to be seen; (hallarse:
 en un apuro) to find o.s., be; **(vamos) a
 ~** let's see; **no tener nada que ~** con to
 have nothing to do with; **a mi modo de
 ~** as I see it; **ya veremos** we'll see

vera ['bera] nf edge, verge; (de río) bank

veranear [berane'ar] vi to spend the
 summer ❏ **veraneo** nm summer
 holiday ❏ **veraniego, -a** adj summer
 cpd

verano [be'rano] nm summer

veras ['beras] nfpl truth sg; **de ~** really,
 truly

verbal [ber'βal] adj verbal

verbena [ber'βena] nf (baile) open-air
 dance

verbo ['berβo] nm verb

verdad [ber'ðað] nf truth; (fiabilidad)
 reliability; **de ~** real, proper; **a decir ~**
 to tell the truth ❏ **verdadero, -a** adj
 (veraz) true, truthful; (fiable) reliable;
 (fig) real

verde ['berðe] adj green; (chiste) blue,
 dirty ♦ nm green; **viejo ~** dirty old man
 ❏ **verdear** vi to turn green ❏ **verdor**
 nm greenness

verdugo [ber'ðuɣo] nm executioner

verdulero, -a [berðu'lero, a] nm/f
 greengrocer

verduras [ber'ðuras] nfpl (CULIN)
 greens

vereda [be'reða] nf path; (CS: acera)
 pavement (BRIT), sidewalk (US)

veredicto [bere'ðikto] nm verdict

vergonzoso, -a [berɣon'θoso, a] adj
 shameful; (timido) timid, bashful

vergüenza [ber'ɣwenθa] nf shame,
 sense of shame; (timidez) bashfulness;
 (pudor) modesty; **me da ~** I'm ashamed

verídico, -a [be'riðiko, a] adj true,
 truthful

verificar [berifi'kar] vt to check;
 (corroborar) to verify; (llevar a cabo) to
 carry out; **verificarse** vr (predicción) to
 prove to be true

verja ['berxa] nf (cancela) iron gate;
 (valla) iron railings pl; (de ventana)
 grille

vermut [ber'mut] (pl **vermuts**) nm
 vermouth

verosímil [bero'simil] adj likely,
 probable; (relato) credible

verruga [be'rruɣa] nf wart

versátil [ber'satil] adj versatile

versión [ber'sjon] nf version

verso ['berso] nm verse; **un ~** a line of
 poetry

vértebra ['berteβra] nf vertebra

verter [ber'ter] vt (líquido: adrede) to
 empty, pour (out); (: sin querer) to spill;
 (basura) to dump ♦ vi to flow

vertical [berti'kal] adj vertical

vértice ['bertiθe] nm vertex, apex

vertidos [ber'tiðos] nmpl waste sg

vertiente [ber'tjente] nf slope; (fig)
 aspect

vértigo [ˈbertiɣo] nm vertigo; (mareo) dizziness

vesícula [beˈsikula] nf blister

vespino® [besˈpino] nm o nf moped

vestíbulo [besˈtiβulo] nm hall; (de teatro) foyer

vestido [besˈtiðo] nm (ropa) clothes pl, clothing; (de mujer) dress, frock ♦ pp de **vestir**; **~ de azul/marinero** dressed in blue/as a sailor

vestidor (MÉX) nm (DEPORTE) changing (BRIT) o locker (US) room

vestimenta [bestiˈmenta] nf clothing

vestir [besˈtir] vt (poner: ropa) to put on; (llevar: ropa) to wear; (proveer de ropa a) to clothe; (sastre) to make clothes for ♦ vi to dress; (verse bien) to look good; **vestirse** vr to get dressed, dress o.s.

vestuario [besˈtwarjo] nm clothes pl, wardrobe; (TEATRO: cuarto) dressing room; (DEPORTE) changing (BRIT) o locker (US) room

vetar [beˈtar] vt to veto

veterano, -a [beteˈrano, a] adj, nm veteran

veterinaria [beteriˈnarja] nf veterinary science; ver tb **veterinario**

veterinario, -a [beteriˈnarjo, a] nm/f vet(erinary surgeon)

veto [ˈbeto] nm veto

vez [beθ] nf time; (turno) turn; **a la ~ que** at the same time as; **a su ~** in its turn; **otra ~** again; **una ~** once; **de una ~** in one go; **de una ~ para siempre** once and for all; **en ~ de** instead of; **a o algunas veces** sometimes; **una y otra ~** repeatedly; **de ~ en cuando** from time to time; **7 veces 9** 7 times 9; **hacer las veces de** to stand in for; **tal ~** perhaps

vía [ˈbia] nf track, route; (FERRO) line; (fig) way; (ANAT) passage, tube ♦ prep via, by way of; **por ~ judicial** by legal means; **en vías de** in the process of ► **vía aérea** airway ► **Vía Láctea**

Milky Way ► **vía pública** public road o thoroughfare

viable [ˈbjaβle] adj (solución, plan, alternativa) feasible

viaducto [bjaˈðukto] nm viaduct

viajante [bjaˈxante] nm commercial traveller

viajar [bjaˈxar] vi to travel □ **viaje** nm journey; (gira) tour; (NÁUT) voyage; **estar de viaje** to be on a trip ► **viaje de ida y vuelta** round trip ► **viaje de novios** honeymoon □ **viajero, -a** adj travelling; (ZOOL) migratory ♦ nm/f (quien viaja) traveller; (pasajero) passenger

víbora [ˈbiβora] nf (ZOOL) viper; (: MÉX: venenoso) poisonous snake

vibración [biβraˈθjon] nf vibration

vibrar [biˈβrar] vt, vi to vibrate

vicepresidente [biθepresiˈðente] nmf vice-president

viceversa [biθeˈβersa] adv vice versa

vicio [ˈbiθjo] nm vice; (mala costumbre) bad habit □ **vicioso, -a** adj (muy malo) vicious; (corrompido) depraved ♦ nm/f depraved person

víctima [ˈbiktima] nf victim

victoria [bikˈtorja] nf victory □ **victorioso, -a** adj victorious

vid [bið] nf vine

vida [ˈbiða] nf (gen) life; (duración) lifetime; **de por ~** for life; **en la o mi ~** never; **estar con ~** to be still alive; **ganarse la ~** to earn one's living

vídeo [ˈbiðeo] nm video ♦ adj inv: **película de ~** video film □ **videocámara** nf camcorder □ **videocasete** nm video cassette, videotape □ **videoclub** nm video club □ **videojuego** nm video game

vidrio [ˈbiðrjo] nm glass

vieira [ˈbjeira] nf scallop

viejo, -a [ˈbjexo, a] adj old ♦ nm/f old man/woman; **hacerse ~** to get old

Viena [ˈbjena] n Vienna

vienes etc vb ver **venir**

vienés, -esa [bje'nes, esa] *adj* Viennese

viento ['bjento] *nm* wind; **hacer ~** to be windy

vientre ['bjentre] *nm* belly; (*matriz*) womb

viernes ['bjernes] *nm inv* Friday
▶ **Viernes Santo** Good Friday

Vietnam [bjet'nam] *nm* Vietnam
☐ **vietnamita** *adj* Vietnamese

viga ['biɣa] *nf* beam, rafter; (*de metal*) girder

vigencia [bi'xenθja] *nf* validity; **estar en ~** to be in force ☐ **vigente** *adj* valid, in force; (*imperante*) prevailing

vigésimo, -a [bi'xesimo, a] *adj* twentieth

vigía [bi'xia] *nm* look-out

vigilancia [bixi'lanθja] *nf*: **tener a algn bajo ~** to keep watch on sb

vigilar [bixi'lar] *vt* to watch over ♦ *vi* (*gen*) to be vigilant; (*hacer guardia*) to keep watch; **~ por** to take care of

vigilia [vi'xilja] *nf* wakefulness, being awake; (*REL*) fast

vigor [bi'ɣor] *nm* vigour, vitality; **en ~** in force; **entrar/poner en ~** to come/put into effect ☐ **vigoroso, -a** *adj* vigorous

VIH *nm abr* (= *virus de la inmunodeficiencia humana*) HIV ▶ **VIH negativo/positivo** HIV-negative/-positive

vil [bil] *adj* vile, low

villa ['biʎa] *nf* (*casa*) villa; (*pueblo*) small town; (*municipalidad*) municipality

villancico [biʎan'θiko] *nm* (Christmas) carol

vilo ['bilo]: **en ~** *adv* in the air, suspended; (*fig*) on tenterhooks, in suspense

vinagre [bi'nayre] *nm* vinegar

vinagreta [bina'ɣreta] *nf* vinaigrette, French dressing

vinculación [binkula'θjon] *nf* (*lazo*) link, bond; (*acción*) linking

vincular [binku'lar] *vt* to link, bind
☐ **vínculo** *nm* link, bond

vine *etc vb ver* **venir**

vinicultura [binikul'tura] *nf* wine growing

viniera *etc vb ver* **venir**

vino ['bino] *vb ver* **venir** ♦ *nm* wine
▶ **vino blanco/tinto** white/red wine

viña ['biɲa] *nf* vineyard ☐ **viñedo** *nm* vineyard

viola ['bjola] *nf* viola

violación [bjola'θjon] *nf* violation; (*sexual*) rape

violar [bjo'lar] *vt* to violate; (*sexualmente*) to rape

violencia [bjo'lenθja] *nf* violence, force; (*incomodidad*) embarrassment; (*acto injusto*) unjust act ☐ **violentar** *vt* to force; (*casa*) to break into; (*agredir*) to assault; (*violar*) to violate ☐ **violento, -a** *adj* violent; (*furioso*) furious; (*situación*) embarrassing; (*acto*) forced, unnatural

violeta [bjo'leta] *nf* violet

violín [bjo'lin] *nm* violin

violón [bjo'lon] *nm* double bass

virar [bi'rar] *vt* to change direction

virgen ['birxen] *adj, nf* virgin

Virgo ['birɣo] *nm* Virgo

viril [bi'ril] *adj* virile ☐ **virilidad** *nf* virility

virtud [bir'tuð] *nf* virtue; **en ~ de** by virtue of ☐ **virtuoso, -a** *adj* virtuous ♦ *nm/f* virtuoso

viruela [bi'rwela] *nf* smallpox

virulento, -a [biru'lento, a] *adj* virulent

virus ['birus] *nm inv* virus

visa ['bisa] (*LAm*) *nf* = **visado**

visado [bi'saðo] (*ESP*) *nm* visa

víscera ['bisθera] *nf* (*ANAT, ZOOL*) gut, bowel; **vísceras** *nfpl* entrails

visceral [bisθe'ral] *adj* (*odio*) intense; **reacción ~** gut reaction

visera [bi'sera] *nf* visor

visibilidad [bisiβili'ðað] nf visibility
❏ **visible** adj visible; (fig) obvious

visillos [bi'siʎos] nmpl lace curtains

visión [bi'sjon] nf (ANAT) vision,
(eye)sight; (fantasía) vision, fantasy

visita [bi'sita] nf call, visit; (persona)
visitor; **hacer una ~** to pay a visit
❏ **visitar** [bisi'tar] vt to visit, call on

visón [bi'son] nm mink

visor [bi'sor] nm (FOTO) viewfinder

víspera [bispera] nf: **la ~ de ...** the day
before ...

vista [bista] nf sight, vision; (capacidad
de ver) (eye)sight; (mirada) look(s) (pl);
a primera ~ at first glance; **hacer la ~
gorda** to turn a blind eye; **volver la ~**
to look back; **está a la ~ que** it's
obvious that; **en ~ de** in view of; **~
de que** in view of the fact that; **¡hasta
la ~!** so long!, see you!; **con vistas a**
with a view to ❏ **vistazo** nm glance;
dar o echar un vistazo a to glance at

visto, -a [bisto, a] pp de **ver** ♦ vb ver tb
vestir ♦ adj seen; (considerado)
considered ♦ nm: **~ bueno** approval;
por lo ~ apparently; **está ~ que** it's
clear that; **está bien/mal ~** it's
acceptable/unacceptable; **~ que** since,
considering that

vistoso, -a [bis'toso, a] adj colourful

visual [bi'swal] adj visual

vital [bi'tal] adj life cpd, living cpd; (fig)
vital; (persona) lively, vivacious
❏ **vitalicio, -a** adj for life ❏ **vitalidad**
nf (de persona, negocio) energy; (de
ciudad) liveliness

vitamina [bita'mina] nf vitamin

vitorear [bitore'ar] vt to cheer, acclaim

vitrina [bi'trina] nf show case; (LAm:
escaparate) shop window

viudo, -a [bjuðo, a] nm/f widower/
widow

viva [biβa] excl hurrah!; **¡~ el rey!** long
live the king!

vivaracho, -a [biβa'ratʃo, a] adj jaunty,
lively; (ojos) bright, twinkling

vivaz [bi'βaθ] adj lively

víveres [biβeres] nmpl provisions

vivero [bi'βero] nm (para plantas)
nursery; (para peces) fish farm; (fig)
hotbed

viveza [bi'βeθa] nf liveliness; (agudeza:
mental) sharpness

vivienda [bi'βjenda] nf housing; (una
vivienda) house; (piso) flat (BRIT),
apartment (US)

viviente [bi'βjente] adj living

vivir [bi'βir] vt, vi to live ♦ nm life, living

vivo, -a [biβo, a] adj living, alive; (fig:
descripción) vivid; (persona: astuto)
smart, clever; **en ~** (transmisión etc) live

vocablo [bo'kaβlo] nm (palabra) word;
(término) term

vocabulario [bokaβu'larjo] nm
vocabulary

vocación [boka'θjon] nf vocation
❏ **vocacional** (LAm) nf ~ technical
college

vocal [bo'kal] adj vocal ♦ nf vowel
❏ **vocalizar** vt to vocalize

vocero [bo'θero] (LAm) nmf
spokesman/woman

voces [boθes] pl de **voz**

vodka ['boðka] nm o f vodka

vol abr = **volumen**

volado (MÉX) [bo'laðo] adv in a rush,
hastily

volador, a [bola'ðor, a] adj flying

volandas [bo'landas]: **en ~** adv in the
air

volante [bo'lante] adj flying ♦ nm (de
coche) steering wheel; (de reloj)
balance

volar [bo'lar] vt (edificio) to blow up ♦ vi
to fly

volátil [bo'latil] adj volatile

volcán [bol'kan] nm volcano
❏ **volcánico, -a** adj volcanic

volcar [bol'kar] vt to upset, overturn;
(tumbar, derribar) to knock over;

(*vaciar*) to empty out ♦ *vi* to overturn;
volcarse *vr* to tip over

voleibol [bolei'βol] *nm* volleyball

volqué *etc* [bol'ke] *vb ver* **volcar**

voltaje [bol'taxe] *nm* voltage

voltear [bolte'ar] *vt* to turn over;
(*volcar*) to turn upside down

voltereta [bolte'reta] *nf* somersault

voltio ['boltjo] *nm* volt

voluble [bo'luβle] *adj* fickle

volumen [bo'lumen] (*pl* **volúmenes**)
nm volume; (*de libro*) volume

voluminoso, -a [bolumi'noso, a] *adj*
voluminous; (*enorme*) massive

voluntad [bolun'tað] *nf* will;
(*resolución*) willpower; (*deseo*) desire,
wish

voluntario, -a [bolun'tarjo, a] *adj*
voluntary ♦ *nm/f* volunteer

volver [bol'βer] *vt* (*gen*) to turn; (*dar
vuelta a*) to turn (over); (*voltear*) to
turn round, turn upside down; (*poner al
revés*) to turn inside out; (*devolver*) to
return ♦ *vi* to return, go back, come
back; **volverse** *vr* to turn round; **~ la
espalda** to turn one's back; **~ triste** *etc*
a algn to make so sad *etc*; **~ a hacer**
to do again; **~ en sí** to come to;
volverse insoportable/muy caro to get o
become unbearable/very expensive;
volverse loco to go mad

vomitar [bomi'tar] *vt*, *vi* to vomit
❏ **vómito** *nm* vomiting

voraz [bo'raθ] *adj* voracious

vos [bos] (*LAm*) *pron* you

vosotros, -as [bo'sotros, as] (*ESP*) *pron*
you; (*reflexivo*): **entre/para ~** among/
for yourselves

votación [bota'θjon] *nf* (*acto*) voting;
(*voto*) vote

votar [bo'tar] *vi* to vote ❏ **voto** *nm*
vote; (*promesa*) vow; **votos** *nmpl*
(*good*) wishes

voy [boi] *vb ver* **ir**

voz [boθ] *nf* voice; (*grito*) shout; (*rumor*)
rumour; (*LING*) word; **dar voces** to
shout, yell; **de viva ~** verbally; **en ~ alta**

aloud; **en ~ baja** in a low voice, in a
whisper ▶ **voz de mando** command

vuelco ['bwelko] *vb ver* **volcar** ♦ *nm*
spill, overturning

vuelo ['bwelo] *vb ver* **volar** ♦ *nm* flight;
(*encaje*) lace, frill; **coger al ~** to catch in
flight ▶ **vuelo chárter/regular**
charter/scheduled flight ▶ **vuelo
libre** (*DEPORTE*) hang-gliding

vuelque *etc* ['bwelke] *vb ver* **volcar**

vuelta ['bwelta] *nf* (*gen*) turn; (*curva*)
bend, curve; (*regreso*) return; (*curva*)
(*revolución*) revolution; (*de circuito*) lap;
(*de papel, tela*) reverse; (*cambio*)
change; **a la ~** on one's return; **a la ~
(de la esquina)** round the corner; **a ~
de correo** by return of post; **dar
vueltas** (*cabeza*) to spin; (*volverse*) to turn round; **dar vueltas a
una idea** to turn over an idea (in one's
head); **estar de ~** to be back; **dar una ~**
to go for a walk; (*en coche*) to go for a
drive ▶ **vuelta ciclista** (*DEPORTE*)
(cycle) tour

vuelto ['bwelto] *pp de* **volver**

vuelvo *etc vb ver* **volver**

vuestro, -a ['bwestro, a] *adj pos* your;
un amigo ~ a friend of yours ♦ *pron*: **el
~/la vuestra, los vuestros/las vuestras**
yours

vulgar [bul'ɣar] *adj* (*ordinario*) vulgar;
(*común*) common ▶ **vulgaridad** *nf*
commonness; (*acto*) vulgarity;
(*expresión*) coarse expression

vulnerable [bulne'raβle] *adj*
vulnerable

vulnerar [bulne'rar] *vt* (*ley, acuerdo*) to
violate, breach; (*derechos, intimidad*) to
violate; (*reputación*) to damage

W, w

walkie-talkie [walki–'talki] (*pl*
walkie-talkies) *nm* walkie-talkie

Walkman® ['walkman] *nm* Walkman®

wáter ['bater] *nm* (*taza*) toilet; (*LAm: lugar*) toilet (BRIT), rest room (US)

web [web] *nm o f* (*página*) website; (*red*) (World Wide) Web ◆ **webcam** *nf* webcam ◆ **webmaster** *nmf* webmaster ◆ **website** *nm* website

western (*pl* **westerns**) *nm* western

whisky ['wiski] *nm* whisky, whiskey

windsurf ['winsurf] *nm* windsurfing; **hacer ~** to go windsurfing

X, x

xenofobia [kseno'foβja] *nf* xenophobia

xilófono [ksi'lofono] *nm* xylophone

xocoyote, -a (*MÉX*) *nm/f* baby of the family, youngest child

Y, y

y [i] *conj* and

ya [ja] *adv* (*gen*) already; (*ahora*) now; (*en seguida*) at once; (*pronto*) soon ◆ *excl* all right! ◆ *conj* (*ahora que*) now that; **ya lo sé** I know; **ya que ...** since; **¡ya está bien!** that's (quite) enough!; **¡ya voy!** coming!

yacaré (*CS*) [jaka're] *nm* cayman

yacer [ja'θer] *vi* to lie

yacimiento [jaθi'mjento] *nm* (*de mineral*) deposit; (*arqueológico*) site

yanqui [janki] *adj, nmf* Yankee

yate [jate] *nm* yacht

yazco etc *vb ver* **yacer**

yedra ['jeðra] *nf* ivy

yegua ['jeɣwa] *nf* mare

yema ['jema] *nf* (*del huevo*) yolk; (*BOT*) leaf bud; (*fig*) best part ▸ **yema del dedo** fingertip

yerno ['jerno] *nm* son-in-law

yeso ['jeso] *nm* plaster

yo [jo] *pron* I; **soy yo** it's me

yodo ['joðo] *nm* iodine

yoga ['joɣa] *nm* yoga

yogur(t) [jo'ɣur(t)] *nm* yoghurt

yuca ['juka] *nf* (*alimento*) cassava, manioc root

Yugoslavia [juɣos'laβja] *nf* (HIST) Yugoslavia

yugular [juɣu'lar] *adj* jugular

yunque ['junke] *nm* anvil

yuyo (*RPl*) ['jujo] *nm* (*mala hierba*) weed

Z, z

zafar [θa'far] *vt* (*soltar*) to untie; (*superficie*) to clear; **zafarse** *vr* (*escaparse*) to escape; (*TEC*) to slip off

zafiro [θa'firo] *nm* sapphire

zaga ['θaɣa] *nf*: **a la ~** behind, in the rear

zaguán [θa'ɣwan] *nm* hallway

zalamero, -a [θala'mero, a] *adj* flattering; (*cobista*) suave

zamarra [θa'marra] *nf* (*chaqueta*) sheepskin jacket

zambullirse [θambu'ʎirse] *vr* to dive

zampar [θam'par] *vt* to gobble down

zanahoria [θana'orja] *nf* carrot

zancadilla [θanka'ðiʎa] *nf* trip

zanco ['θanko] *nm* stilt

zángano ['θanɣano] *nm* drone

zanja ['θanxa] *nf* ditch ▢ **zanjar** *vt* (*resolver*) to resolve

zapata [θa'pata] *nf* (MECÁNICA) shoe

zapatería [θapate'ria] *nf* (*oficio*) shoemaking; (*tienda*) shoe shop; (*fábrica*) shoe factory ▢ **zapatero, -a** *nm/f* shoemaker

zapatilla [θapa'tiʎa] *nf* slipper ▸ **zapatilla de deporte** training shoe

zapato [θa'pato] *nm* shoe

zapping ['θapin] nm channel-hopping; **hacer ~** to flick through the channels

zar [θar] nm tsar, czar

zarandear [θarande'ar] (fam) vt to shake vigorously

zarpa ['θarpa] nf (garra) claw

zarpar [θar'par] vi to weigh anchor

zarza ['θarθa] nf (BOT) bramble

zarzamora [θarθa'mora] nf blackberry

zarzuela [θar'θwela] nf Spanish light opera

zigzag [θiɣ'θaɣ] nm zigzag

zinc [θink] nm zinc

zíper (MÉX, CAm) ['θiper] zip (fastener) (BRIT), zipper (US)

zócalo ['θokalo] nm (ARQ) plinth; base; (de pared) skirting board (BRIT), baseboard (US); (MÉX: plaza) main o public square

zoclo (MÉX) ['θoklo] nm skirting board (BRIT), baseboard (US)

zodíaco [θo'ðiako] nm (ASTROLOGÍA) zodiac

zona ['θona] nf zone ▶ **zona fronteriza** border area ▶ **zona roja** (LAm) red-light district

zonzo, -a (LAm: fam) ['θonθo, a] adj silly ♦ nm/f fool

zoo ['θoo] nm zoo

zoología [θoolo'xia] nf zoology ❑ **zoológico, -a** adj zoological ♦ nm (tb: **parque zoológico**) zoo ❑ **zoólogo, -a** nm/f zoologist

zoom [θum] nm zoom lens

zopilote [θopi'lote] (MÉX, CAm) nm buzzard

zoquete [θo'kete] nm (fam) blockhead

zorro, -a ['θorro, a] adj crafty ♦ nm/f fox/vixen

zozobrar [θoθo'βrar] vi (hundirse) to capsize; (fig) to fail

zueco ['θweko] nm clog

zumbar [θum'bar] vt (golpear) to hit ♦ vi to buzz ❑ **zumbido** nm buzzing

zumo ['θumo] nm juice

zurcir [θur'θir] vt (coser) to darn

zurdo, -a ['θurðo, a] adj (persona) left-handed

zurrar [θu'rrar] (fam) vt to wallop

ENGLISH - SPANISH
ESPAÑOL - INGLÉS

Aa

A [eɪ] n (MUS) la m

a

KEYWORD

[ə] (before vowel or silent h: an) indef art

1 un(a); **a book** un libro; **an apple** una manzana; **she's a doctor** (ella) es médica

2 (instead of the number "one") un(a); **a year ago** hace un año; **a hundred/thousand etc pounds** cien/mil etc libras

3 (in expressing ratios, prices etc): **3 a day/week** 3 al día/a la semana; **10 km an hour** 10 km por hora; **£5 a person** £5 por persona; **30p a kilo** 30p el kilo

A.A. n abbr = **Automobile Association**; (BRIT) = RACE m (SP); (= Alcoholics Anonymous) Alcohólicos Anónimos

A.A.A. (US) n abbr (= American Automobile Association) = RACE m (SP)

aback [əˈbæk] adv: **to be taken ~** quedar desconcertado

abandon [əˈbændən] vt abandonar; (give up) renunciar a

abattoir [ˈæbətwɑː] (BRIT) n matadero

abbey [ˈæbɪ] n abadía

abbreviation [əˌbriːvɪˈeɪʃən] n (short form) abreviatura

abdomen [ˈæbdəmən] n abdomen m

abduct [æbˈdʌkt] vt raptar, secuestrar

abide [əˈbaɪd] vt: **I can't ~ it/him** no lo/le puedo ver ▶ **abide by** vt fus atenerse a

ability [əˈbɪlɪtɪ] n habilidad f, capacidad f; (talent) talento

able [ˈeɪbl] adj capaz; (skilled) hábil; **to be ~ to do sth** poder hacer algo

abnormal [æbˈnɔːməl] adj anormal

aboard [əˈbɔːd] adv a bordo ♦ prep a bordo de

abolish [əˈbɒlɪʃ] vt suprimir, abolir

abolition [æbəˈlɪʃən] n supresión f, abolición f

abort [əˈbɔːt] vt, vi abortar ❑ **abortion** [əˈbɔːʃən] n aborto; **to have an abortion** abortar, hacerse abortar

about

KEYWORD

[əˈbaut] adv

1 (approximately) más o menos, aproximadamente; **about a hundred/thousand etc** unos(unas) cien/mil etc; **it takes about 10 hours** se tarda unas or más o menos 10 horas; **at about 2 o'clock** sobre las dos; **I've just about finished** casi he terminado

2 (referring to place) por todas partes; **to leave things lying about** dejar las cosas (tiradas) por ahí; **to run about** correr por todas partes; **to walk about** pasearse, ir y venir

3: **to be about to do sth** estar a punto de hacer algo

♦ prep

1 (relating to) de, sobre, acerca de; **a book about London** un libro sobre or acerca de Londres; **what is it about?** ¿de qué se trata?; **we talked about it** hablamos de eso or ello; **what or how about doing this?** ¿qué tal si hacemos esto?

2 (referring to place) por; **to walk about the town** caminar por la ciudad

above [əˈbʌv] adv encima, por encima, arriba ♦ prep encima de; (greater than: in number) más de; (: in rank) superior a; **mentioned ~** susodicho; **~ all** sobre todo

abroad [əˈbrɔːd] adv (to be) en el extranjero; (to go) al extranjero

abrupt [əˈbrʌpt] adj (sudden) brusco; (curt) áspero

abscess [ˈæbsɪs] n absceso

absence [ˈæbsəns] n ausencia

absent [ˈæbsənt] adj ausente ❏ **absent-minded** adj distraído

absolute [ˈæbsəluːt] adj absoluto ❏ **absolutely** [-ˈluːtlɪ] adv (totally) totalmente; (certainly!) ¡por supuesto (que sí)!

absorb [əbˈzɔːb] vt absorber; **to be absorbed in a book** estar absorto en un libro ❏ **absorbent cotton** (US) n algodón m hidrófilo ❏ **absorbing** adj absorbente

abstain [əbˈsteɪn] vi: **to ~ (from)** abstenerse (de)

abstract [ˈæbstrækt] adj abstracto

absurd [əbˈsəːd] adj absurdo

abundance [əˈbʌndəns] n abundancia

abundant [əˈbʌndənt] adj abundante

abuse [n əˈbjuːs, vb əˈbjuːz] n (insults) insultos mpl, injurias fpl; (ill-treatment) malos tratos mpl; (misuse) abuso ♦ vt insultar; maltratar; abusar de ❏ **abusive** adj ofensivo

abysmal [əˈbɪzməl] adj pésimo; (failure) garrafal; (ignorance) supino

academic [ækəˈdemɪk] adj académico, universitario; (pej: issue) puramente teórico ♦ n estudioso(-a), profesor(a) m/f universitario(-a) ❏ **academic year** n (UNIV) año m académico; (SCOL) año m escolar

academy [əˈkædəmɪ] n (learned body) academia; (school) instituto, colegio; **~ of music** conservatorio

accelerate [ækˈseləreɪt] vt, vi acelerar ❏ **acceleration** [ækseləˈreɪʃən] n aceleración f ❏ **accelerator** (BRIT) n acelerador m

accent [ˈæksənt] n acento; (fig) énfasis m

accept [əkˈsept] vt aceptar; (responsibility, blame) admitir ❏ **acceptable** adj aceptable ❏ **acceptance** n aceptación f

access [ˈækses] n acceso; **to have ~ to** tener libre acceso a ❏ **accessible** [-ˈsesəbl] adj (place, person) accesible; (knowledge etc) asequible

accessory [ækˈsesərɪ] n accesorio; (LAW): **~ to** cómplice de

accident [ˈæksɪdənt] n accidente m; (chance event) casualidad f; **by ~** (unintentionally) sin querer; (by chance) por casualidad ❏ **accidental** [-ˈdentl] adj accidental, fortuito ❏ **accidentally** [-ˈdentlɪ] adv sin querer; por casualidad ❏ **Accident and Emergency Department** n (BRIT) Urgencias fpl ❏ **accident insurance** n seguro contra accidentes

acclaim [əˈkleɪm] vt aclamar, aplaudir ♦ n aclamación f, aplausos mpl

accommodate [əˈkɔmədeɪt] vt (person) alojar, hospedar; (: car, hotel etc) tener cabida para; (oblige, help) complacer

accommodation [əkɔməˈdeɪʃən] (US **accommodations**) n alojamiento

accompaniment [əˈkʌmpənɪmənt] n acompañamiento

accompany [əˈkʌmpənɪ] vt acompañar

accomplice [əˈkʌmplɪs] n cómplice mf

accomplish [əˈkʌmplɪʃ] vt (finish) concluir; (achieve) lograr ❏ **accomplishment** n (skill: gen pl) talento; (completion) realización f

accord [ə'kɔːd] n acuerdo ♦ vt conceder; **of his own ~** espontáneamente ♦ **accordance** n: **in accordance with** de acuerdo con □ **according: according to** prep según; (in accordance with) conforme a □ **accordingly** adv (appropriately) de acuerdo con esto; (as a result) en consecuencia

account [ə'kaunt] n (COMM) cuenta; (report) informe m; **accounts** npl (COMM) cuentas fpl; **of no ~** de ninguna importancia; **on ~** a cuenta; **on no ~** bajo ningún concepto; **on ~ of** a causa de, por motivo de; **to take into ~, to take ~ of** tener en cuenta ▶ **account for** vt fus (explain) explicar; (represent) representar □ **accountable** adj: **accountable (to)** responsable (ante) □ **accountant** n contable mf, contador(a) m/f □ **account number** n (at bank etc) número de cuenta

accumulate [ə'kjuːmjuleɪt] vt acumular ♦ vi acumularse

accuracy ['ækjurəsɪ] n (of total) exactitud f; (of description etc) precisión f

accurate ['ækjurɪt] adj (total) exacto; (description) preciso; (device) de precisión □ **accurately** adv con precisión

accusation [ækju'zeɪʃən] n acusación f

accuse [ə'kjuːz] vt: **to ~ sb (of sth)** acusar a algn (de algo) □ **accused** n (LAW) acusado(-a)

accustomed [ə'kʌstəmd] adj: **~ to** acostumbrado a

ace [eɪs] n as m

ache [eɪk] n dolor m ♦ vi doler; **my head aches** me duele la cabeza

achieve [ə'tʃiːv] vt (aim, result) alcanzar; (success) lograr, conseguir □ **achievement** n (completion) realización f; (success) éxito

acid ['æsɪd] adj ácido; (taste) agrio ♦ n (CHEM, inf: LSD) ácido

acknowledge [ək'nɔlɪdʒ] vt (letter: also: ~ **receipt of**) acusar recibo de; (fact, situation, person) reconocer □ **acknowledgement** n acuse m de recibo

acne ['æknɪ] n acné m

acorn ['eɪkɔːn] n bellota

acoustic [ə'kuːstɪk] adj acústico

acquaintance [ə'kweɪntəns] n (person) conocido(-a); (with person, subject) conocimiento

acquire [ə'kwaɪə*] vt adquirir □ **acquisition** [ækwɪ'zɪʃən] n adquisición f

acquit [ə'kwɪt] vt absolver, exculpar; **to ~ o.s. well** salir con éxito

acre ['eɪkə*] n acre m

acronym ['ækrənɪm] n siglas fpl

across [ə'krɔs] prep (on the other side) al otro lado de, del otro lado de; (crosswise) a través de ♦ adv de un lado a otro, de una parte a otra; a través, al través; (measurement): **the road is 10m ~** la carretera tiene 10m de ancho; **to run/swim ~** atravesar corriendo/ nadando; **~ from** enfrente de

acrylic [ə'krɪlɪk] adj acrílico ♦ n acrílica

act [ækt] n acto, acción f; (of play) acto; (in music hall etc) número; (LAW) decreto, ley f ♦ vi (behave) comportarse; (have effect: drug, chemical) hacer efecto; (THEATRE) actuar; (pretend) fingir; (take action) obrar ♦ vt (part) hacer el papel de; **in the ~ of**, **to catch sb in the ~ of ...** pillar a algn en el momento en que ...; **to ~ as** actuar or hacer de ▶ **act up** (inf) vi (person) portarse mal □ **acting** adj suplente ♦ n (activity) actuación f; (profession) profesión f de actor

action ['ækʃən] n acción f, acto; (MIL) acción f, batalla; (LAW) proceso, demanda; **out of ~** (person) fuera de combate; (thing) estropeado; **to take ~** tomar medidas □ **action replay** n (TV) repetición f

activate ['æktɪveɪt] *vt* activar

active ['æktɪv] *adj* activo, enérgico; *(volcano)* en actividad ♦ **actively** *adv* *(participate)* activamente; *(discourage, dislike)* enérgicamente

activist ['æktɪvɪst] *n* activista *m/f*

activity [-'tɪvɪtɪ] *n* actividad *f*
□ **activity holiday** *n* vacaciones con actividades organizadas

actor ['æktə] *n* actor *m*

actress ['æktrɪs] *n* actriz *f*

actual ['æktjʊəl] *adj* verdadero, real; *(emphatic term)* propiamente dicho

⚠ Be careful not to translate **actual** by the Spanish word *actual*.

actually ['æktjʊəlɪ] *adv* realmente, en realidad; *(even)* incluso

⚠ Be careful not to translate **actually** by the Spanish word *actualmente*.

acupuncture ['ækjʊpʌŋktʃə'] *n* acupuntura

acute [ə'kju:t] *adj* agudo

ad [æd] *n abbr* = **advertisement**

A.D. *adv abbr* (= *anno Domini*) DC

adamant ['ædəmənt] *adj* firme, inflexible

adapt [ə'dæpt] *vt* adaptar ♦ *vi*: **to ~ (to)** adaptarse (a), ajustarse (a) □ **adapter, adaptor** *n* (ELEC) adaptador *m*; *(for several plugs)* ladrón

add [æd] *vt* añadir, agregar ▶ **add up** *vt* *(figures)* sumar ♦ *vi* *(fig)*: **it doesn't add up** no tiene sentido ▶ **add up to** *vt fus* (MATH) sumar, ascender a; *(fig: mean)* querer decir, venir a ser

addict ['ædɪkt] *n* adicto(-a); *(enthusiast)* entusiasta *mf* □ **addicted** [ə'dɪktɪd] *adj*: **to be addicted to** ser adicto a, ser fanático de □ **addiction** [ə'dɪkʃən] *n* *(to drugs etc)* adicción *f* □ **addictive** [ə'dɪktɪv] *adj* que causa adicción

addition [ə'dɪʃən] *n (adding up)* adición *f*; *(thing added)* añadidura, añadido; **in ~** además, por añadidura; **in ~ to**

además de □ **additional** *adj* adicional

additive ['ædɪtɪv] *n* aditivo

address [ə'drɛs] *n* dirección *f*, señas *fpl*; *(speech)* discurso ♦ *vt (letter)* dirigir; *(speak to)* dirigirse a, dirigir la palabra a; *(problem)* tratar □ **address book** *n* agenda (de direcciones)

adequate ['ædɪkwɪt] *adj (satisfactory)* adecuado; *(enough)* suficiente

adhere [əd'hɪə'] *vi*: **to ~ to** *(stick to)* pegarse a; *(fig: abide by)* observar; *(: belief etc)* ser partidario de

adhesive [əd'hi:zɪv] *n* adhesivo □ **adhesive tape** *n* (BRIT) cinta adhesiva; *(US MED)* esparadrapo

adjacent [ə'dʒeɪsənt] *adj*: **~ to** contiguo a, inmediato a

adjective ['ædʒɛktɪv] *n* adjetivo

adjoining [ə'dʒɔɪnɪŋ] *adj* contiguo, vecino

adjourn [ə'dʒə:n] *vt* aplazar ♦ *vi* suspenderse

adjust [ə'dʒʌst] *vt (change)* modificar; *(clothing)* arreglar; *(machine)* ajustar ♦ *vi*: **to ~ (to)** adaptarse (a) □ **adjustable** *adj* ajustable □ **adjustment** *n* adaptación *f*; *(to machine, prices)* ajuste *m*

administer [əd'mɪnɪstə'] *vt* administrar □ **administration** [-'treɪʃən] *n (management)* administración *f*; *(government)* gobierno □ **administrative** [-trətɪv] *adj* administrativo

administrator [əd'mɪnɪstreɪtə'] *n* administrador(a) *m/f*

admiral ['ædmərəl] *n* almirante *m*

admiration [ædmə'reɪʃən] *n* admiración *f*

admire [əd'maɪə'] *vt* admirar □ **admirer** *n (fan)* admirador(a) *m/f*

admission [əd'mɪʃən] *n (to university, club)* ingreso; *(entry fee)* entrada; *(confession)* confesión *f*

admit [əd'mɪt] vt (confess) confesar; (permit to enter) dejar entrar, dar entrada a; (to club, organization) admitir; (accept: defeat) reconocer; **to be admitted to hospital** ingresar en el hospital ▸ **admit to** vt fus confesarse culpable de □ **admittance** n entrada □ **admittedly** adv es cierto or verdad que

adolescent [ædəu'lɛsnt] adj, n adolescente mf

adopt [ə'dɒpt] vt adoptar □ **adopted** adj adoptivo □ **adoption** [ə'dɒpʃən] n adopción f

adore [ə'dɔ:r] vt adorar

adorn [ə'dɔ:n] vt adornar

Adriatic [eɪdrɪ'ætɪk] n: **the ~ (Sea)** el (Mar) Adriático

adrift [ə'drɪft] adv a la deriva

adult ['ædʌlt] n adulto(-a) ♦ adj (grown-up) adulto; (for adults) para adultos □ **adult education** n educación f para adultos

adultery [ə'dʌltərɪ] n adulterio

advance [əd'vɑ:ns] n (progress) adelanto, progreso; (money) anticipo, préstamo; (MIL) avance m ♦ adj: ~ **booking** venta anticipada; ~ **notice, ~ warning** previo aviso ♦ vt (money) anticipar; (theory, idea) proponer (para la discusión) ♦ vi avanzar, adelantarse; **to make advances (to sb)** hacer proposiciones (a algn); **in ~** por adelantado □ **advanced** adj avanzado; (SCOL: studies) adelantado

advantage [əd'vɑ:ntɪdʒ] n (also TENNIS) ventaja; **to take ~ of** (person) aprovecharse de; (opportunity) aprovechar

advent ['ædvənt] n advenimiento; **A~** Adviento

adventure [əd'vɛntʃər] n aventura □ **adventurous** [-tʃərəs] adj atrevido; aventurero

adverb ['ædvə:b] n adverbio

adversary ['ædvəsərɪ] n adversario, contrario

adverse ['ædvə:s] adj adverso, contrario

advert ['ædvə:t] (BRIT) n abbr = **advertisement**

advertise ['ædvətaɪz] vi (in newspaper etc) anunciar, hacer publicidad; **to ~ for** (staff, accommodation etc) buscar por medio de anuncios ♦ vt anunciar □ **advertisement** [əd'və:tɪsmənt] n (COMM) anuncio □ **advertiser** n anunciante mf □ **advertising** n publicidad f, anuncios mpl; (industry) industria publicitaria

advice [əd'vaɪs] n consejo, consejos mpl; (notification) aviso; **a piece of ~** un consejo; **to take legal ~** consultar con un abogado

advisable [əd'vaɪzəbl] adj aconsejable, conveniente

advise [əd'vaɪz] vt aconsejar; (inform): **to ~ sb of sth** informar a algn de algo; **to ~ sb against sth/doing sth** desaconsejar algo a algn/aconsejar a algn que no haga algo □ **adviser**, **advisor** n consejero(-a); (consultant) asesor(a) m/f □ **advisory** adj consultivo

advocate [vb 'ædvəkeɪt, -kɪt] vt abogar por ♦ n (lawyer) abogado(-a); (supporter): ~ **of** defensor(a) m/f de

Aegean [i:'dʒi:ən] n: **the ~ (Sea)** el (Mar) Egeo

aerial ['ɛərɪəl] n antena ♦ adj aéreo

aerobics [ɛə'rəubɪks] n aerobic m

aeroplane ['ɛərəpleɪn] (BRIT) n avión m

aerosol ['ɛərəsɔl] n aerosol m

affair [ə'fɛər] n asunto; (also: **love ~**) aventura (amorosa)

affect [ə'fɛkt] vt (influence) afectar, influir en; (afflict, concern) afectar; (move) conmover □ **affected** adj afectado □ **affection** n afecto, cariño □ **affectionate** adj afectuoso, cariñoso

afflict [ə'flɪkt] vt afligir

affluent ['æfluənt] adj (wealthy) acomodado; **the ~ society** la sociedad opulenta

afford [ə'fɔːd] vt (provide) proporcionar; **can we ~ (to buy) it?** ¿tenemos bastante dinero para comprarlo? ❑ **affordable** adj asequible

Afghanistan [æf'gænɪstæn] n Afganistán m

afraid [ə'freɪd] adj: **to be ~ of** (person) tener miedo a; (thing) tener miedo de; **to be ~ to** tener miedo de, temer; **I am ~ that** me temo que; **I am ~ not/so** lo siento, pero no/es así

Africa ['æfrɪkə] n África ❑ **African** adj, n africano(-a) m/f ❑ **African-American** adj, n afroamericano(-a)

after ['ɑːftə'] prep (time) después de; (place, order) detrás de, tras ♦ adv después ♦ conj después (de) que; **what/who are you ~?** ¿qué/a quién busca usted?; **~ having done/he left** después de haber hecho/después de que se marchó; **to name sb ~ sb** llamar a algn después por algn; **it's twenty ~ eight** (US) son las ocho y veinte; **to ask ~ sb** preguntar por algn; **~ all** después de todo, al fin y al cabo; **~ you!** ¡pase usted! ❑ **after-effects** fpl consecuencias fpl, efectos mpl ❑ **aftermath** n consecuencias fpl, resultados mpl ❑ **afternoon** n tarde f ❑ **after-shave (lotion)** n aftershave m ❑ **aftersun (lotion/cream)** n loción f/crema para después del sol, aftersun m ❑ **afterwards** (US **afterward**) adv después, más tarde

again [ə'gen] adv otra vez, de nuevo; **to do sth ~** volver a hacer algo; **~ and ~** una y otra vez

against [ə'genst] prep (in opposition to) en contra de; (leaning on, touching) contra, junto a

age [eɪdʒ] n edad f; (period) época ♦ vi envejecer(se) ♦ vt envejecer; **she is 20**

years of ~ tiene 20 años; **to come of ~** llegar a la mayoría de edad; **it's been ages since I saw you** hace siglos que no te veo; **aged 10** de 10 años de edad ❑ **age group** n: **to be in the same age group** tener la misma edad ❑ **age limit** n edad f mínima (or máxima)

agency ['eɪdʒənsɪ] n agencia

agenda [ə'dʒendə] n orden m del día

⚠ Be careful not to translate **agenda** by the Spanish word agenda.

agent ['eɪdʒənt] n agente mf; (COMM: holding concession) representante mf, delegado(-a); (CHEM, fig) agente m

aggravate ['ægrəveɪt] vt (situation) agravar; (person) irritar

aggression [ə'greʃən] n agresión f

aggressive [ə'gresɪv] adj (belligerent) agresivo; (assertive) enérgico

agile ['ædʒaɪl] adj ágil

agitated ['ædʒɪteɪtɪd] adj agitado

AGM n abbr (= annual general meeting) asamblea anual

ago [ə'gəu] adv: **2 days ~** hace 2 días; **not long ~** hace poco; **how long ~?** ¿hace cuánto tiempo?

agony ['ægənɪ] n (pain) dolor m agudo; (distress) angustia; **to be in ~** retorcerse de dolor

agree [ə'griː] vt (price, date) acordar, quedar en ♦ vi (have same opinion): **to ~ (with/that)** estar de acuerdo (con/que); (correspond) coincidir, concordar; (consent) acceder; **to ~ with** (person) estar de acuerdo con, ponerse de acuerdo con; (: food) sentar bien a; (LING) concordar con; **to ~ to sth/to do sth** consentir en algo/aceptar hacer algo; **to ~ that** (admit) estar de acuerdo en que ❑ **agreeable** adj (sensation) agradable; (person) simpático; (willing) de acuerdo, conforme ❑ **agreed** adj (time, place) convenido ❑ **agreement** n acuerdo; (contract) contrato; **in agreement** de acuerdo, conforme

agricultural [ægrɪˈkʌltʃərəl] *adj*
agrícola

agriculture [ˈægrɪkʌltʃə] *n* agricultura

ahead [əˈhed] *adv* (*in front*) delante;
(*into the future*): **she had no time to
think ~** no tenía tiempo de hacer
planes para el futuro; **~ of** delante de;
(*in advance of*) antes de; **~ of time**
antes de la hora; **go right** *or* **straight ~**
(*direction*) siga adelante; (*permission*)
hazlo (*or* hágalo)

aid [eɪd] *n* ayuda, auxilio; (*device*)
aparato ♦ *vt* ayudar, auxiliar; **in ~ of** a
beneficio de

aide [eɪd] *n* (*person, also MIL*) ayudante
mf

AIDS [eɪdz] *n abbr* (= *acquired immune
deficiency syndrome*) SIDA *m*

ailing [ˈeɪlɪŋ] *adj* (*person, economy*)
enfermizo

ailment [ˈeɪlmənt] *n* enfermedad *f*,
achaque *m*

aim [eɪm] *vt* (*gun, camera*) apuntar;
(*missile, remark*) dirigir; (*blow*) asestar
♦ *vi* (*also*: **take ~**) apuntar ♦ *n* (*in
shooting*: *skill*) puntería; (*objective*)
propósito, meta; **to ~ at** (*with weapon*)
apuntar a; (*objective*) aspirar a,
pretender; **to ~ to do** tener la
intención de hacer

ain't [eɪnt] (*inf*) = **am not; aren't; isn't**

air [ɛə] *n* aire *m*; (*appearance*) aspecto
♦ *vt* (*room*) ventilar; (*clothes, ideas*)
airear ♦ *cpd* aéreo; **to throw sth into
the ~** (*ball etc*) lanzar algo al aire; **by ~**
(*travel*) en avión; **to be on the ~** (*RADIO,
TV*) estar en antena □ **airbag** *n* airbag
m inv □ **airbed** (*BRIT*) *n* colchón *m*
neumático □ **airborne** *adj* (*in the air*)
en el aire; **as soon as the plane was
airborne** tan pronto como el avión
estuvo en el aire □ **air-conditioned**
adj climatizado □ **air conditioning** *n*
aire acondicionado □ **aircraft** *n inv*
avión *m* □ **airfield** *n* campo de
aviación □ **Air Force** *n* fuerzas *fpl*
aéreas, aviación *f* □ **air hostess** (*BRIT*)

n azafata □ **airing cupboard** *n* (*BRIT*)
armario *m* para oreo □ **airlift** *n*
puente *m* aéreo □ **airline** *n* línea
aérea □ **airliner** *n* avión *m* de
pasajeros □ **airmail** *n*: **by airmail** por
avión □ **airplane** (*US*) *n* avión *m*
□ **airport** *n* aeropuerto □ **air raid** *n*
ataque *m* aéreo □ **airsick** *adj*: **to be
airsick** marearse (en avión)
□ **airspace** *n* espacio aéreo
□ **airstrip** *n* pista de aterrizaje □ **air
terminal** *n* terminal *f* □ **airtight** *adj*
hermético □ **air-traffic controller** *n*
controlador(a) *m/f*aéreo(-a) □ **airy** *adj*
(*room*) bien ventilado; (*fig: manner*)
desenfadado

aisle [aɪl] *n* (*of church*) nave *f*; (*of theatre,
supermarket*) pasillo □ **aisle seat** *n*
(*on plane*) asiento de pasillo

ajar [əˈdʒɑː] *adj* entreabierto

à la carte [æləˈkɑːt] *adv* a la carta

alarm [əˈlɑːm] *n* (*in shop, bank*) alarma;
(*anxiety*) inquietud *f* ♦ *vt* asustar,
inquietar □ **alarm call** *n* (*in hotel etc*)
alarma □ **alarm clock** *n* despertador
m □ **alarmed** *adj* (*person*) alarmado,
asustado; (*house, car etc*) con alarma
□ **alarming** *adj* alarmante

Albania [ælˈbeɪnɪə] *n* Albania

albeit [ɔːlˈbiːɪt] *conj* aunque

album [ˈælbəm] *n* álbum *m*; (*L.P.*) elepé
m

alcohol [ˈælkəhɒl] *n* alcohol *m*
□ **alcohol-free** *adj* sin alcohol
□ **alcoholic** [-ˈhɒlɪk] *adj, n*
alcohólico(-a) *m/f*

alcove [ˈælkəʊv] *n* nicho, hueco

ale [eɪl] *n* cerveza

alert [əˈlɜːt] *adj* (*attentive*) atento; (*to
danger, opportunity*) alerta ♦ *n* alerta *m*,
alarma ♦ *vt* poner sobre aviso; **to be on
the ~** (*also MIL*) estar alerta o sobre
aviso

algebra [ˈældʒɪbrə] *n* álgebra

Algeria [ælˈdʒɪərɪə] *n* Argelia

alias ['eılıəs] adv alias, conocido por ♦ n (of criminal) apodo; (of writer) seudónimo

alibi ['ælıbaı] n coartada

alien ['eılıən] n (foreigner) extranjero(-a); (extraterrestrial) extraterrestre mf ♦ adj: ~ **to** ajeno a ❑ **alienate** vt enajenar, alejar

alight [ə'laıt] adj ardiendo; (eyes) brillante ♦ vi (person) apearse, bajar; (bird) posarse

align [ə'laın] vt alinear

alike [ə'laık] adj semejantes, iguales ♦ adv igualmente, del mismo modo; **to look ~** parecerse

alive [ə'laıv] adj vivo; (lively) alegre

all

KEYWORD

[ɔːl] adj (sg) todo(-a); (pl) todos(-as); **all day** todo el día; **all night** toda la noche; **all men** todos los hombres; **all five came** vinieron los cinco; **all the books** todos los libros; **all his life** toda su vida

♦ pron

1 todo; **I ate it all, I ate all of it** me lo comí todo; **all of us went** fuimos todos; **all the boys went** fueron todos los chicos; **is that all?** ¿eso es todo?, ¿algo más?; (in shop) ¿algo más?, ¿alguna cosa más?

2 (in phrases): **above all** sobre todo; por encima de todo; **after all** después de todo; **at all: not at all** (in answer to question) en absoluto; (in answer to thanks) ¡de nada!, ¡no hay de qué!; **I'm not at all tired** no estoy nada cansado(-a); **anything at all will do** cualquier cosa viene bien; **all in all** a fin de cuentas

♦ adv: **all alone** completamente solo(-a); **it's not as hard as all that** no es tan difícil como lo pintas; **the**

more/the better tanto más/mejor; **all but** casi; **the score is 2 all** están empatados a 2

Allah ['ælə] n Alá m

allegation [ælı'ɡeıʃən] n alegato

alleged [ə'ledʒd] adj supuesto, presunto ❑ **allegedly** adv supuestamente, según se afirma

allegiance [ə'liːdʒəns] n lealtad f

allergic [ə'lɜːdʒık] adj: ~ **to** alérgico a

allergy ['ælədʒı] n alergia

alleviate [ə'liːvıeıt] vt aliviar

alley ['ælı] n callejuela

alliance [ə'laıəns] n alianza

allied ['ælaıd] adj aliado

alligator ['ælıɡeıtə^r] n (ZOOL) caimán m

all-in (BRIT) ['ɔːlın] adj, adv (charge) todo incluido

allocate ['æləkeıt] vt (money etc) asignar

allot [ə'lɒt] vt asignar

all-out ['ɔːlaut] adj (effort etc) supremo

allow [ə'lau] vt permitir, dejar; (a claim) admitir; (sum, time etc) dar, conceder; (concede): **to ~ that** reconocer que; **to ~ sb to do** permitir a algn hacer; **he is allowed to ...** se le permite ... ► **allow for** vt fus tener en cuenta ❑ **allowance** n subvención f; (welfare payment) subsidio, pensión f; (pocket money) dinero de bolsillo; (tax allowance) desgravación f; **to make allowances for** (person) disculpar a; (thing) tener en cuenta ❑ **all right** adv bien; (as answer) ¡conforme!, ¡está bien!

ally ['ælaı] n aliado(-a ♦ vt: **to ~ o.s. with** aliarse con

almighty [ɔːl'maıtı] adj todopoderoso; (row etc) imponente

almond ['ɑːmənd] n almendra

almost ['ɔːlməust] adv casi

alone [ə'ləun] adj, adv solo; **to leave sb ~** dejar a algn en paz; **to leave sth ~** no

tocar algo, dejar algo sin tocar; **let ~ ...** y mucho menos ...

along [ə'lɒŋ] *prep* a lo largo de, por ♦ *adv*: **is he coming ~ with us?** ¿viene con nosotros?; **he was limping ~** iba cojeando; **~ with** junto con; **all ~** *(all the time)* desde el principio ❑ **alongside** *prep* al lado de ♦ *adv* al lado

aloof [ə'luːf] *adj* reservado ♦ *adv*: **to stand ~** mantenerse apartado

aloud [ə'laʊd] *adv* en voz alta

alphabet ['ælfəbet] *n* alfabeto

Alps [ælps] *npl*: **the ~** los Alpes

already [ɔːl'redɪ] *adv* ya

alright [ɔːl'raɪt] *(BRIT) adv* = **all right**

also ['ɔːlsəu] *adv* también, además

altar ['ɒltə'] *n* altar *m*

alter ['ɒltə'] *vt* cambiar, modificar ♦ *vi* cambiar ❑ **alteration** [ɒltə'reɪʃən] *n* cambio; *(to clothes)* arreglo; *(to building)* arreglos *mpl*

alternate [adj al'tə:nɪt, vb 'ɒltə:neɪt] *adj (actions etc)* alternativo; *(events)* alterno; *(US)* = **alternative** ♦ *vi*: **to ~ (with)** alternar (con); **on ~ days** un día sí y otro no ...

alternative [ɒl'tə:nətɪv] *adj* alternativo ♦ *n* alternativa; **~ medicine** medicina alternativa ❑ **alternatively** *adv*: **alternatively one could ...** por otra parte se podría ...

although [ɔːl'ðəu] *conj* aunque

altitude ['æltɪtjuːd] *n* altura

altogether [ɔːltə'geðə'] *adv* completamente, del todo; *(on the whole)* en total, en conjunto

aluminium ['æljʊ'mɪnɪəm] *(BRIT)*, **aluminum** [ə'luːmɪnəm] *(US) n* aluminio

always ['ɔːlweɪz] *adv* siempre

Alzheimer's (disease) ['æltshaɪməz-] *n* enfermedad *f* de Alzheimer

am [æm] *vb see* **be**

amalgamate [ə'mælgəmeɪt] *vi* amalgamarse ♦ *vt* amalgamar, unir

amass [ə'mæs] *vt* amontonar, acumular

amateur ['æmətə'] *n* aficionado(-a), amateur *mf*

amaze [ə'meɪz] *vt* asombrar, pasmar; **to be amazed (at)** quedar pasmado (de) ❑ **amazed** *adj* asombrado ❑ **amazement** *n* asombro, sorpresa ❑ **amazing** *adj* extraordinario, *(fantastic)* increíble

Amazon [æməzən] *n (GEO)* Amazonas *m*

ambassador [æm'bæsədə'] *n* embajador(a) *m/f*

amber ['æmbə'] *n* ámbar *m*; **at ~** *(BRIT AUT)* en el amarillo

ambiguous [æm'bɪgjuəs] *adj* ambiguo

ambition [æm'bɪʃən] *n* ambición *f* ❑ **ambitious** [-ʃəs] *adj* ambicioso

ambulance ['æmbjʊləns] *n* ambulancia

ambush ['æmbʊʃ] *n* emboscada ♦ *vt* tender una emboscada a

amen [ɑ:'mɛn] *excl* amén

amend [ə'mɛnd] *vt* enmendar; **to make amends** dar cumplida satisfacción ❑ **amendment** *n* enmienda

amenities [ə'mi:nɪtɪz] *npl* comodidades *fpl*

America [ə'mɛrɪkə] *n (USA)* Estados *mpl* Unidos ❑ **American** *adj*, *n* norteamericano(-a); estadounidense *mf* ❑ **American football** *n (BRIT)* fútbol *m* americano

amicable ['æmɪkəbl] *adj* amistoso, amigable

amid(st) [ə'mɪd(st)] *prep* entre, en medio de

ammunition [æmju'nɪʃən] *n* municiones *fpl*

amnesty [æmnɪstɪ] *n* amnistía

among(st) [ə'mʌŋ(st)] *prep* entre, en medio de

amount [ə'maunt] *n (gen)* cantidad *f*; *(of bill etc)* suma, importe *m* ♦ *vi*: **to ~ to**

sumar; (be same as) equivaler a, significar

amp(ère) ['æmp(eə')] n amperio

ample ['æmpl] adj (large) grande; (abundant) abundante; (enough) bastante, suficiente

amplifier ['æmplıfaıə'] n amplificador m

amputate ['æmpjuteıt] vt amputar

Amtrak ['æmtræk] (US) n empresa nacional de ferrocarriles de los EEUU

amuse [ə'mju:z] vt divertir; (distract) distraer, entretener □ **amusement** n diversión f; (pastime) pasatiempo; (laughter) risa □ **amusement arcade** n salón m de juegos □ **amusement park** n parque m de atracciones

amusing [ə'mju:zıŋ] adj divertido

an [æn] indef art see **a**

anaemia [ə'ni:mıə] (US anemia) n anemia

anaemic [ə'ni:mık] (US anemic) adj anémico; (fig) soso, insípido

anaesthetic [ænıs'θetık] (US anesthetic) n anestesia

analog(ue) ['ænaləg] adj (computer, watch) analógico

analogy [ə'nælədʒı] n analogía

analyse ['ænəlaız] (US analyze) vt analizar □ **analysis** [ə'nælısıs] (pl analyses) n análisis m inv □ **analyst** [-lıst] n (political analyst, psychoanalyst) analista mf

analyze ['ænəlaız] (US) vt = **analyse**

anarchy ['ænəkı] n anarquía, desorden m

anatomy [ə'nætəmı] n anatomía

ancestor ['ænsıstə'] n antepasado

anchor ['æŋkə'] n ancla, áncora ♦ vi (also: **to drop** ~) anclar ♦ vt anclar; **to weigh** ~ levar anclas

anchovy ['æntʃəvı] n anchoa

ancient ['eınʃənt] adj antiguo

and [ænd] conj y; (before i-, hi- + consonant) e; **men** ~ **women** hombres

y mujeres; **father** ~ **son** padre e hijo; **trees** ~ **grass** árboles y hierba; ~ **so on** etcétera, y así sucesivamente; **try** ~ **come** procura venir; **he talked** ~ **talked** habló sin parar; **better** ~ **better** cada vez mejor

Andes ['ændi:z] npl: **the** ~ los Andes

Andorra [æn'dɔ:rə] n Andorra

anemia etc [ə'ni:mıə] (US) = **anaemia** etc

anesthetic [ænıs'θetık] (US) = **anaesthetic**

angel ['eındʒəl] n ángel m

anger ['æŋgə'] n cólera

angina [æn'dʒaınə] n angina (del pecho)

angle ['æŋgl] n ángulo; **from their** ~ desde su punto de vista

angler ['æŋglə'] n pescador(a) m/f (de caña)

Anglican ['æŋglıkən] adj, n anglicano(-a) m/f

angling ['æŋglıŋ] n pesca con caña

angrily ['æŋgrılı] adv coléricamente, airadamente

angry ['æŋgrı] adj enfadado, airado; (wound) inflamado; **to be** ~ **with sb/at sth** estar enfadado con algn/por algo; **to get** ~ enfadarse, enojarse

anguish ['æŋgwıʃ] n (physical) tormentos mpl; (mental) angustia

animal ['ænıməl] n animal m; (pej: person) bestia ♦ adj animal

animated [-meıtıd] adj animado

animation [ænı'meıʃən] n animación f

aniseed ['ænısi:d] n anís m

ankle ['æŋkl] n tobillo

annex [n 'æneks, vb æ'neks] n (BRIT: also: annexe: building) edificio anexo ♦ vt (territory) anexionar

anniversary [ænı'və:sərı] n aniversario

announce [ə'nauns] vt anunciar □ **announcement** n anuncio; (official) declaración f □ **announcer** n (RADIO) locutor(a) m/f; (TV) presentador(a)

annoy [əˈnɔɪ] vt molestar, fastidiar; **don't get annoyed!** ¡no se enfade! ❑ **annoying** adj molesto, fastidioso; (person) pesado

annual [ˈænjuəl] adj anual ♦ n (BOT) anual m; (book) anuario ❑ **annually** adv anualmente, cada año

annum [ˈænəm] n see **per**

anonymous [əˈnɒnɪməs] adj anónimo

anorak [ˈænəræk] n anorak m

anorexia [ænəˈreksɪə] n (MED: also: **~ nervosa**) anorexia

anorexic [ænəˈreksɪk] adj, n anoréxico(-a) m/f

another [əˈnʌðə*] adj (one more, a different one) otro ♦ pron otro; see **one**

answer [ˈɑːnsə*] n contestación f, respuesta; (to problem) solución f ♦ vi contestar, responder ♦ vt (reply to) contestar a, responder a; (problem) resolver; (prayer) escuchar; **in ~ to your letter** contestando or en contestación a su carta; **to ~ the phone** contestar or coger el teléfono; **to ~ the bell** or **the door** acudir a la puerta ▶ **answer back** vi replicar, ser respondón(-ona) ❑ **answerphone** n (esp BRIT) contestador m (automático)

ant [ænt] n hormiga

Antarctic [æntˈɑːktɪk] n: **the ~** el Antártico

antelope [ˈæntɪləʊp] n antílope m

antenatal [ˈæntɪˈneɪtl] adj antenatal, prenatal

antenna [ænˈtɛnə, pl -niː] (pl **antennae**) n antena

anthem [ˈænθəm] n: **national ~** himno nacional

anthology [ænˈθɒlədʒɪ] n antología

anthrax [ˈænθræks] n ántrax m

anthropology [ænθrəˈpɒlədʒɪ] n antropología

anti [ˈæntɪ] prefix anti ❑ **antibiotic** [-baɪˈɒtɪk] n antibiótico ❑ **antibody** [ˈæntɪbɒdɪ] n anticuerpo

anticipate [ænˈtɪsɪpeɪt] vt prever; (expect) esperar, contar con; (look forward to) esperar con ilusión; (do first) anticiparse a, adelantarse a ❑ **anticipation** [-ˈpeɪʃən] n (expectation) previsión f; (eagerness) ilusión f, expectativa f

anticlimax [æntɪˈklaɪmæks] n decepción f

anticlockwise [æntɪˈklɒkwaɪz] (BRIT) adv en dirección contraria a la de las agujas del reloj

antics [ˈæntɪks] npl gracias fpl

anti: antidote [ˈæntɪdəʊt] n antídoto ❑ **antifreeze** [ˈæntɪfriːz] n anticongelante m ❑ **antihistamine** [-ˈhɪstəmiːn] n antihistamínico ❑ **antiperspirant** [ˈæntɪpəːspɪrənt] n antitranspirante m

antique [ænˈtiːk] n antigüedad f ♦ adj antiguo ❑ **antique shop** n tienda de antigüedades

antiseptic [æntɪˈseptɪk] adj, n antiséptico

antisocial [æntɪˈsəʊʃəl] adj antisocial

antlers [ˈæntləz] npl cuernas fpl, cornamenta sg

anxiety [æŋˈzaɪətɪ] n inquietud f; (MED) ansiedad f; **~ to do** deseo de hacer

anxious [ˈæŋkʃəs] adj inquieto, preocupado; (worrying) preocupante; (keen): **to be ~ to do** tener muchas ganas de hacer

any
KEYWORD
[ˈenɪ] adj

1 (in questions etc) algún/alguna; **have you any butter/children?** ¿tienes mantequilla/hijos?; **if there are any tickets left** si quedan billetes, si queda algún billete

2 (with negative): **I haven't any money/books** no tengo dinero/libros

3 (no matter which) cualquier; **any**

excuse will do valdrá or servirá cualquier excusa; **choose any book you like** escoge el libro que quieras; **any teacher you ask will tell you** cualquier profesor al que preguntes te lo dirá

4 (in phrases): **in any case** de todas formas, en cualquier caso; **any day now** cualquier día (de estos); **at any moment** en cualquier momento, de un momento a otro; **at any rate** en todo caso; **any time, come (at) any time** ven cuando quieras; **he might come (at) any time** podría llegar de un momento a otro

♦ pron

1 (in questions etc): **have you got any?** ¿tienes alguno(s)/a(s)?; **can any of you sing?** ¿sabe cantar alguno de vosotros/ustedes?

2 (with negative): **I haven't any (of them)** no tengo ninguno

3 (no matter which one(s)): **take any of those books (you like)** toma el libro que quieras de ésos

♦ adv

1 (in questions etc): **do you want any more soup/sandwiches?** ¿quieres más sopa/bocadillos?; **are you feeling any better?** ¿te sientes algo mejor?

2 (with negative): **I can't hear him any more** ya no le oigo; **don't wait any longer** no esperes más

any: **anybody** pron cualquiera; (in interrogative sentences) alguien; (in negative sentences): **I don't see anybody** no veo a nadie; **if anybody should phone ...** si llama alguien ... ❑ **anyhow** adv (at any rate) de todos modos, de todas formas; (haphazard): **do it anyhow you like** hazlo como

quieras; **she leaves things just anyhow** deja las cosas como quiera or de cualquier modo; **I shall go anyhow** de todos modos iré ❑ **anyone** pron = **anybody** ❑ **anything** pron (in questions etc) algo, alguna cosa; (with negative) nada; **can you see anything?** ¿ves algo?; **if anything happens to me ...** si algo me ocurre ...; (no matter what): **you can say anything you like** puedes decir lo que quieras; **anything will do** vale todo or cualquier cosa; **he'll eat anything** come de todo or lo que sea ❑ **anytime** adv (at any moment) en cualquier momento, de un momento a otro; (whenever) no importa cuándo, cuando quiera ❑ **anyway** adv (at any rate) de todos modos, de todas formas; **I shall go anyway** iré de todos modos; (besides): **anyway, I couldn't come even if I wanted to** además, no podría venir aunque quisiera; **why are you phoning anyway?** ¿entonces, por qué llamas?, ¿por qué llamas, pues? ❑ **anywhere** adv (in questions etc): **can you see him anywhere?** ¿le ves por algún lado?; **are you going anywhere?** ¿vas a algún sitio?; (with negative): **I can't see him anywhere** no le veo por ninguna parte; **anywhere in the world** (no matter where) en cualquier parte (del mundo); **put the books down anywhere** deja los libros donde quieras

apart [əˈpɑːt] adv (aside) aparte; (situation): **~ (from)** separado (de); (movement): **to pull ~** separar; **10 miles ~** separados por 10 millas; **to take ~** desmontar; ♦ prep aparte de

apartment [əˈpɑːtmənt] n (US) piso (SP), departamento (LAm), apartamento; (room) cuarto ❑ **apartment building** (US) n edificio de apartamentos

apathy [ˈæpəθɪ] n apatía, indiferencia

ape [eɪp] n mono ♦ vt imitar, remedar

aperitif [əˈperɪtɪf] n aperitivo

aperture

aperture [ˈæpətʃjuə⁺] n rendija, resquicio; (PHOT) abertura

APEX [ˈeɪpeks] n abbr (= Advanced Purchase Excursion Fare) tarifa f APEX

apologize [əˈpɒlədʒaɪz] vi: **to ~ (for sth to sb)** disculparse (con algn de algo)

apology [əˈpɒlədʒɪ] n disculpa, excusa

⚠ Be careful not to translate **apology** by the Spanish word *apología*.

apostrophe [əˈpɒstrəfɪ] n apóstrofo

appal [əˈpɔːl] (US **appall**) vt horrorizar, espantar ❑ **appalling** adj espantoso; (awful) pésimo

apparatus [æpəˈreɪtəs] n (equipment) equipo; (organization) aparato; (in gymnasium) aparatos mpl

apparent [əˈpærənt] adj aparente; (obvious) evidente ❑ **apparently** adv por lo visto, al parecer

appeal [əˈpiːl] vi (LAW) apelar ♦ n (LAW) apelación f; (request) llamamiento; (plea) petición f; (charm) atractivo; **to ~ for** reclamar; **to ~ to** (be attractive to) atraer; **it doesn't ~ to me** no me atrae, no me llama la atención ❑ **appealing** adj (attractive) atractivo

appear [əˈpɪə⁺] vi aparecer, presentarse; (LAW) comparecer; (publication) salir (a luz), publicarse; (seem) parecer; **to ~ on TV/in "Hamlet"** salir por la tele/hacer un papel en "Hamlet"; **it would ~ that** parecería que ❑ **appearance** n aparición f; (look) apariencia, aspecto

appendices [əˈpendɪsiːz] npl of **appendix**

appendicitis [əpendɪˈsaɪtɪs] n apendicitis f

appendix [əˈpendɪks] (pl **appendices**) n apéndice m

appetite [ˈæpɪtaɪt] n apetito; (fig) deseo, anhelo

appetizer [ˈæpɪtaɪzə⁺] n (drink) aperitivo; (food) tapas fpl (SP)

applaud [əˈplɔːd] vt, vi aplaudir

approach

applause [əˈplɔːz] n aplausos mpl

apple [ˈæpl] n manzana ❑ **apple pie** n pastel m de manzana, pay m de manzana (LAm)

appliance [əˈplaɪəns] n aparato

applicable [əˈplɪkəbl] adj (relevant): **to be ~ (to)** referirse (a)

applicant [ˈæplɪkənt] n candidato(-a); solicitante mf

application [æplɪˈkeɪʃən] n aplicación f; (for a job etc) solicitud f, petición f ❑ **application form** n solicitud f

apply [əˈplaɪ] vt (paint etc) poner; (law etc: put into practice) poner en vigor ♦ vi: **to ~ to** (ask) dirigirse a; (be applicable) ser aplicable a; **to ~ for** (permit, grant, job) solicitar; **to ~ o.s. to** aplicarse a, dedicarse a

appoint [əˈpɔɪnt] vt (to post) nombrar ❑ **appointment** n (with client) cita; (act) nombramiento; (post) puesto; (at hairdresser etc): **to have an appointment** tener hora; **to make an appointment (with sb)** citarse (con algn)

⚠ Be careful not to translate **appoint** by the Spanish word *apuntar*.

appraisal [əˈpreɪzl] n valoración f

appreciate [əˈpriːʃɪeɪt] vt apreciar, tener en mucho; (be grateful for) agradecer; (be aware) comprender ♦ vi (COMM) aumentar(se) en valor ❑ **appreciation** [-ˈeɪʃən] n apreciación f; (gratitude) reconocimiento, agradecimiento; (COMM) aumento en valor

apprehension [æprɪˈhenʃən] n (fear) aprensión f

apprehensive [æprɪˈhensɪv] adj aprensivo

apprentice [əˈprentɪs] n aprendiz(a) m/f

approach [əˈprəʊtʃ] vi acercarse ♦ vt acercarse a; (ask, apply to) dirigirse a; (situation, problem) abordar ♦ n acercamiento; (access) acceso; (to *problem, situation*: ~ **(to)** actitud f (ante)

appropriate [*adj* ə'prəuprɪɪt, *vb* ə'prəuprɪeɪt] *adj* apropiado, conveniente ♦ *vt (take)* apropiarse de

approval [ə'pruːvəl] *n* aprobación f, visto bueno; *(permission)* consentimiento; **on** ~ *(COMM)* a prueba

approve [ə'pruːv] *vt* aprobar
  ► **approve of** *vt fus (thing)* aprobar; *(person)*: **they don't approve of her** (ella) no les parece bien

approximate [ə'prɒksɪmɪt] *adj* aproximado ♦ **approximately** *adv* aproximadamente, más o menos

Apr. *abbr* (= *April*) abr

apricot ['eɪprɪkɒt] *n* albaricoque m, chabacano *(MEX)*, damasco *(RPI)*

April ['eɪprɪl] *n* abril m ♦ **April Fools' Day** *n* el primero de abril, ≈ día m de los Inocentes *(28 December)*

apron ['eɪprən] *n* delantal m

apt [æpt] *adj* acertado, apropiado; *(likely)*: ~ **to do** propenso a hacer

aquarium [ə'kwɛərɪəm] *n* acuario

Aquarius [ə'kwɛərɪəs] *n* Acuario

Arab ['ærəb] *adj, n* árabe mf

Arabia [ə'reɪbɪə] *n* Arabia ♦ **Arabian** *adj* árabe ♦ **Arabic** ['ærəbɪk] *adj* árabe; *(numerals)* arábigo ♦ *n* árabe m

arbitrary ['ɑːbɪtrərɪ] *adj* arbitrario

arbitration [ɑːbɪ'treɪʃən] *n* arbitraje m

arc [ɑːk] *n* arco

arcade [ɑː'keɪd] *n (round a square)* soportales mpl; *(shopping mall)* galería comercial

arch [ɑːtʃ] *n* arco; *(of foot)* arco del pie ♦ *vt* arquear

archaeology [ɑːkɪ'ɒlədʒɪ] *(US* **archeology**) *n* arqueología

archbishop [ɑːtʃ'bɪʃəp] *n* arzobispo

archeology [ɑːkɪ'ɒlədʒɪ] *(US)* = **archaeology**

architect ['ɑːkɪtekt] *n* arquitecto(-a) ♦ **architectural** [ɑːkɪ'tektʃərəl]

arquitectónico ♦ **architecture** *n* arquitectura

archive ['ɑːkaɪv] *n (often pl: also COMPUT)* archivo

Arctic ['ɑːktɪk] *adj* ártico ♦ *n*: **the** ~ el Ártico

are [ɑː*] *vb see* **be**

area ['ɛərɪə] *n* área, región f; *(part of place)* zona; *(MATH etc)* área, superficie f; *(in room: e.g. dining area)* parte f; *(of knowledge, experience)* campo ♦ **area code** *n (TEL)* prefijo

arena [ə'riːnə] *n* estadio; *(of circus)* pista

aren't [ɑːnt] = **are not**

Argentina [ɑːdʒən'tiːnə] *n* Argentina ♦ **Argentinian** ['tɪnɪən] *adj, n* argentino(-a) m/f

arguably ['ɑːgjuəblɪ] *adv* posiblemente

argue [ɑː'gjuː] *vi (quarrel)* discutir, pelearse; *(reason)* razonar, argumentar; to ~ **that** sostener que

argument ['ɑːgjumənt] *n* discusión f, pelea; *(reasons)* argumento

Aries ['ɛərɪz] *n* Aries m

arise [ə'raɪz] *(pt* arose, *pp* arisen) *vi* surgir, presentarse

arithmetic [ə'rɪθmətɪk] *n* aritmética

arm [ɑːm] *n* brazo ♦ *vt* armar; **arms** *npl* armas fpl; ~ **in** ~ cogidos del brazo ♦ **armchair** ['ɑːmtʃɛə*] *n* sillón m, butaca

armed [ɑːmd] *adj* armado ♦ **armed robbery** *n* robo a mano armada

armour ['ɑːmə*] *(US* **armor**) *n* armadura; *(MIL: tanks)* blindaje m ♦ **armpit** ['ɑːmpɪt] *n* sobaco, axila ♦ **armrest** ['ɑːmrest] *n* apoyabrazos *m inv*

army ['ɑːmɪ] *n* ejército; *(fig)* multitud f

A road *n (BRIT)* ≈ carretera f nacional

aroma [ə'rəumə] *n* aroma m, fragancia ♦ **aromatherapy** *n* aromaterapia

arose [ə'rəuz] *pt of* **arise**

around [ə'raund] *adv* alrededor; *(in the area)*: **there is no one else** ~ no hay nadie más por aquí ♦ *prep* alrededor de

arouse [əˈrauz] *vt* despertar; *(anger)* provocar

arrange [əˈreɪndʒ] *vt* arreglar, ordenar; *(organize)* organizar; **to ~ to do sth** quedar en hacer algo ❑ **arrangement** *n* arreglo; *(agreement)* acuerdo; **arrangements** *npl (preparations)* preparativos *mpl*

array [əˈreɪ] *n*: **~ of** *(things)* serie *f* de; *(people)* conjunto de

arrears [əˈrɪəz] *npl* atrasos *mpl*; **to be in ~ with one's rent** estar retrasado en el pago del alquiler

arrest [əˈrɛst] *vt* detener; *(sb's attention)* llamar ♦ *n* detención *f*; **under ~** detenido

arrival [əˈraɪvl] *n* llegada; **new ~** recién llegado(-a); *(baby)* recién nacido

arrive [əˈraɪv] *vi* llegar; *(baby)* nacer ► **arrive at** *vt fus (decision, solution)* llegar a

arrogance [ˈærəɡəns] *n* arrogancia, prepotencia *(LAm)*

arrogant [ˈærəɡənt] *adj* arrogante

arrow [ˈærəʊ] *n* flecha

arse [ɑːs] *(BRIT: inf!)* *n* culo, trasero

arson [ˈɑːsn] *n* incendio premeditado

art [ɑːt] *n* arte *m*; *(skill)* destreza ❑ **art college** *n* escuela *f* de Bellas Artes

artery [ˈɑːtərɪ] *n* arteria

art gallery *n* pinacoteca; *(saleroom)* galería de arte

arthritis [ɑːˈθraɪtɪs] *n* artritis *f*

artichoke [ˈɑːtɪtʃəʊk] *n* alcachofa; **Jerusalem ~** aguaturma

article [ˈɑːtɪkl] *n* artículo

articulate [*adj* ɑːˈtɪkjʊlɪt, *vb* ɑːˈtɪkjʊleɪt] *adj* claro, bien expresado ♦ *vt* expresar

artificial [ɑːtɪˈfɪʃl] *adj* artificial; *(affected)* afectado

artist [ˈɑːtɪst] *n* artista *mf*; *(MUS)* intérprete *mf* ❑ **artistic** [ɑːˈtɪstɪk] *adj* artístico

art school *n* escuela de bellas artes

as

[æz] *conj*

1 *(referring to time)* cuando, mientras; a medida que; **as the years went by** con el paso de los años; **he came in as I was leaving** entró cuando me marchaba; **as from tomorrow** desde *or* a partir de mañana

2 *(in comparisons)*: **as big as** tan grande como; **twice as big as** el doble de grande que; **as much money/many books as** tanto dinero/tantos libros como; **as soon as** en cuanto

3 *(since, because)* como, ya que; **he left early as he had to be home by 10** se fue temprano ya que tenía que estar en casa a las 10

4 *(referring to manner, way)*: **do as you wish** haz lo que quieras; **as she said** como dijo; **he gave it to me as a present** me lo dio de regalo

5 *(in the capacity of)*: **he works as a barman** trabaja de barman; **as chairman of the company, he ...** como presidente de la compañía ...

6 *(concerning)*: **as for** *or* **to that** por *or* en lo que respecta a eso

7: **as if** *or* **though** como si; **he looked as if he was ill** parecía como si estuviera enfermo, tenía aspecto de enfermo; *see also* **long**; **such**; **well**

a.s.a.p. *abbr* (= *as soon as possible*) cuanto antes

asbestos [æzˈbɛstəs] *n* asbesto, amianto

ascent [əˈsɛnt] *n* subida; *(slope)* cuesta, pendiente *f*

ash [æʃ] *n* ceniza; *(tree)* fresno

ashamed [ə'ʃeɪmd] adj avergonzado, apenado (LAm); **to be ~ of** avergonzarse de

ashore [ə'ʃɔː'] adv en tierra; (swim etc) a tierra

ashtray ['æʃtreɪ] n cenicero

Ash Wednesday n miércoles m de Ceniza

Asia ['eɪʃə] n Asia ❏ **Asian** adj, n asiático(-a) m/f

aside [ə'saɪd] adv a un lado ♦ n aparte m

ask [ɑːsk] vt (question) preguntar; (invite) invitar; **to ~ sb sth/to do sth** preguntar algo a algn/pedir a algn que haga algo; **to ~ sb about sth** preguntar algo a algn; **to ~ (sb) a question** hacer una pregunta (a algn); **to ~ sb out to dinner** invitar a cenar a algn ► **ask for** vt fus pedir; (trouble) buscar

asleep [ə'sliːp] adj dormido; **to fall ~** dormirse, quedarse dormido

asparagus [əs'pærəgəs] n (plant) espárrago; (food) espárragos mpl

aspect ['æspekt] n aspecto, apariencia; (direction in which a building etc faces) orientación f

aspirations [æspə'reɪʃənz] npl aspiraciones fpl; (ambition) ambición f

aspire [əs'paɪə'] vi: **to ~ to** aspirar a, ambicionar

aspirin ['æsprɪn] n aspirina

ass [æs] n asno, burro; (inf: idiot) imbécil mf; (US: inf!) culo, trasero

assassin [ə'sæsɪn] n asesino(-a) ❏ **assassinate** vt asesinar

assault [ə'sɔːlt] n asalto; (LAW) agresión f ♦ vt asaltar, atacar; (sexually) violar

assemble [ə'sembl] vt reunir, juntar; (TECH) montar ♦ vi reunirse, juntarse

assembly [ə'semblɪ] n reunión f, asamblea; (parliament) parlamento; (construction) montaje m

assert [ə'sɜːt] vt afirmar; (authority) hacer valer ❏ **assertion** [-ʃən] n afirmación f

assess [ə'ses] vt valorar, calcular; (tax, damages) fijar; (for tax) gravar ❏ **assessment** n valoración f; (for tax) gravamen m

asset ['æset] n ventaja; **assets** npl (COMM) activo; (property, funds) fondos mpl

assign [ə'saɪn] vt: **to ~ (to)** (date) fijar (para); (task) asignar (a); (resources) destinar (a) ❏ **assignment** n tarea

assist [ə'sɪst] vt ayudar ❏ **assistance** n ayuda, auxilio ❏ **assistant** n ayudante mf; (BRIT: also: **shop assistant**) dependiente(-a) m/f

associate [adj, n ə'səuʃɪt, vb ə'səuʃɪeɪt] adj asociado ♦ n (at work) colega mf ♦ vt asociar; (ideas) relacionar ♦ vi: **to ~ with sb** tratar con algn

association [əsəusɪ'eɪʃən] n asociación f

assorted [ə'sɔːtɪd] adj surtido, variado

assortment [ə'sɔːtmənt] n (of shapes, colours) surtido; (of books) colección f; (of people) mezcla

assume [ə'sjuːm] vt suponer; (responsibilities) asumir; (attitude) adoptar, tomar

assumption [ə'sʌmpʃən] n suposición f, presunción f; (of power etc) toma

assurance [ə'ʃuərəns] n garantía, promesa; (confidence) confianza, aplomo; (insurance) seguro

assure [ə'ʃuə'] vt asegurar

asterisk ['æstərɪsk] n asterisco

asthma ['æsmə] n asma

astonish [ə'stɒnɪʃ] vt asombrar, pasmar ❏ **astonished** adj estupefacto, pasmado; **to be astonished (at)** asombrarse (de) ❏ **astonishing** adj asombroso, pasmoso; **I find it astonishing that ...** me asombra or pasma que ... ❏ **astonishment** n asombro, sorpresa

astound [ə'staund] vt asombrar, pasmar

astray [ə'streɪ] adv: **to go ~** extraviarse; **to lead ~** (morally) llevar por mal camino

astrology [æs'trɒlədʒɪ] n astrología

astronaut [æstrənɔ:t] n astronauta mf

astronomer [əs'trɒnəmə'] n astrónomo(-a)

astronomical [æstrə'nɒmɪkəl] adj astronómico

astronomy [əs'trɒnəmɪ] n astronomía

astute [əs'tju:t] adj astuto

asylum [ə'saɪləm] n (refuge) asilo; (mental hospital) manicomio

at

KEYWORD

[æt] prep

1 (referring to position) en; (direction) a; **at the top** en lo alto; **at home/ school** en casa/la escuela; **to look at sth/sb** mirar algo/a algn

2 (referring to time): **at 4 o'clock** a las 4; **at night** por la noche; **at Christmas** en Navidad; **at times** a veces

3 (referring to rates, speed etc): **at £1 a kilo** a una libra el kilo; **two at a time** de dos en dos; **at 50 km/h** a 50 km/h

4 (referring to manner): **at a stroke** de un golpe; **at peace** en paz

5 (referring to activity): **to be at work** estar trabajando; (in the office etc) estar en el trabajo; **to play at cowboys** jugar a los vaqueros; **to be good at sth** ser bueno en algo

6 (referring to cause): **shocked/ surprised/annoyed at sth** asombrado/sorprendido/fastidiado por algo; **I went at his suggestion** fui a instancias suyas

ate [eɪt] pt of **eat**

atheist ['eɪθɪɪst] n ateo(-a)

Athens ['æθɪnz] n Atenas

athlete ['æθli:t] n atleta mf

athletic [æθ'letɪk] adj atlético ❏ **athletics** n atletismo

Atlantic [ət'læntɪk] adj atlántico ♦ n: **the ~ (Ocean)** el (Océano) Atlántico

atlas ['ætləs] n atlas m

A.T.M. n abbr (= automated telling machine) cajero automático

atmosphere ['ætməsfɪə'] n atmósfera; (of place) ambiente m

atom ['ætəm] n átomo ❏ **atomic** [ə'tɒmɪk] adj atómico ❏ **atom(ic) bomb** n bomba atómica

A to Z® n (map) callejero

atrocity [ə'trɒsɪtɪ] n atrocidad f

attach [ə'tætʃ] vt (fasten) atar; (join) unir, sujetar; (document, letter) adjuntar; (importance etc) dar, conceder; **to be attached to sb/sth** (to like) tener cariño a algn/algo ❏ **attachment** n (tool) accesorio; (COMPUT) archivo, documento adjunto; (love): **attachment (to)** apego (a)

attack [ə'tæk] vt (MIL) atacar; (criminal) agredir, asaltar; (criticize) criticar; (task) emprender ♦ n ataque m, asalto; (on sb's life) atentado; (fig: criticism) crítica; (of illness) ataque m; **heart ~** infarto (de miocardio) ❏ **attacker** n agresor(a) m/f, asaltante mf

attain [ə'teɪn] vt (also: **~ to**) alcanzar; (achieve) lograr, conseguir

attempt [ə'tɛmpt] n tentativa, intento; (attack) atentado ♦ vt intentar

attend [ə'tend] vt asistir a; (patient) atender ▶ **attend to** vt fus ocuparse de; (customer, patient) atender a ❏ **attendance** n asistencia, presencia; (people present) concurrencia ❏ **attendant** n ayudante mf; (in garage etc) encargado(-a) ♦ adj (dangers) concomitante

attention [ə'tenʃən] n atención f; (care) atenciones fpl ♦ excl (MIL) ¡firme(s)!; **for the ~ of ...** (ADMIN) atención ...

attic ['ætɪk] n desván m

attitude [ˈætɪtjuːd] n actitud f; (disposition) disposición f

attorney [əˈtɜːnɪ] n (lawyer) abogado(-a) □ **Attorney General** n (BRIT) ≈ Presidente m del Consejo del Poder Judicial (SP); (US) ≈ ministro de Justicia

attract [əˈtrækt] vt atraer; (sb's attention) llamar □ **attraction** [əˈtrækʃən] n encanto; (gen pl: amusements) diversiones fpl; (PHYSICS) atracción f □ **attractive** adj atractivo; (interesting) atrayente

attribute [n ˈætrɪbjuːt, vb əˈtrɪbjuːt] n atributo ♦ vt: **to ~ sth to** atribuir algo a

aubergine [ˈəʊbəʒiːn] (BRIT) n berenjena; (colour) morado

auburn [ˈɔːbən] adj color castaño rojizo

auction [ˈɔːkʃən] n (also: **sale by ~**) subasta ♦ vt subastar

audible [ˈɔːdɪbl] adj audible, que se puede oír

audience [ˈɔːdɪəns] n público; (RADIO) radioescuchas mpl; (TV) telespectadores mpl; (interview) audiencia

audit [ˈɔːdɪt] vt revisar, intervenir

audition [ɔːˈdɪʃən] n audición f

auditor [ˈɔːdɪtə*] n interventor(a) m/f, censor(a) m/f de cuentas

auditorium [ɔːdɪˈtɔːrɪəm] n auditorio

Aug. abbr (= August) ag

August [ˈɔːgəst] n agosto

aunt [ɑːnt] n tía □ **auntie** n diminutive of **aunt** □ **aunty** n diminutive of **aunt**

au pair [ˈəʊˈpɛə*] n (also: **~ girl**) (chica) au pair f

aura [ˈɔːrə] n aura; (atmosphere) ambiente m

austerity [ɔˈstɛrɪtɪ] n austeridad f

Australia [ɔsˈtreɪlɪə] n Australia □ **Australian** adj, n australiano(-a) m/f

Austria [ˈɔstrɪə] n Austria □ **Austrian** adj, n austríaco(-a) m/f

authentic [ɔːˈθentɪk] adj auténtico

author [ˈɔːθə*] n autor(a) m/f

authority [ɔːˈθɒrɪtɪ] n autoridad f; (official permission) autorización f; **the authorities** npl las autoridades

authorize [ˈɔːθəraɪz] vt autorizar

auto [ˈɔːtəʊ] (US) n coche m (SP), carro (LAm), automóvil m

auto-: autobiography [ɔːtəbaɪˈɒɡrəfɪ] n autobiografía □ **autograph** [ˈɔːtəgrɑːf] n autógrafo ♦ vt (photo etc) dedicar; (programme) firmar □ **automatic** [ɔːtəˈmætɪk] adj automático ♦ n (gun) pistola automática; (car) coche m automático □ **automatically** adv automáticamente □ **automobile** [ˈɔːtəməbiːl] (US) n coche m (SP), carro (LAm), automóvil m □ **autonomous** [ɔːˈtɒnəməs] adj autónomo □ **autonomy** [ɔːˈtɒnəmɪ] n autonomía

autumn [ˈɔːtəm] n otoño

auxiliary [ɔːgˈzɪlɪərɪ] adj, n auxiliar mf

avail [əˈveɪl] vt: **to ~ o.s. of** aprovechar(se) de ♦ n: **to no ~** en vano, sin resultado

availability [əveɪləˈbɪlɪtɪ] n disponibilidad f

available [əˈveɪləbl] adj disponible; (unoccupied) libre; (person: unattached) soltero y sin compromiso

avalanche [ˈævəlɑːnʃ] n alud m, avalancha

Ave. abbr = **avenue**

avenue [ˈævənjuː] n avenida; (fig) camino

average [ˈævərɪdʒ] n promedio, término medio ♦ adj medio, de término medio; (ordinary) regular, corriente ♦ vt sacar un promedio de; **on ~** por regla general

avert [əˈvɜːt] vt prevenir; (blow) desviar; (one's eyes) apartar

avid [ˈævɪd] adj ávido

avocado [ævəˈkɑːdəʊ] n (also: BRIT: also: **~ pear**) aguacate m, palta (SC)

avoid [əˈvɔɪd] vt evitar, eludir

await [əˈweɪt] *vt* esperar, aguardar

awake [əˈweɪk] (*pt* awoke, *pp* awoken or awaked) *adj* despierto ♦ *vt* despertar ♦ *vi* despertarse; **to be ~** estar despierto

award [əˈwɔːd] *n* premio; (*LAW*: *damages*) indemnización *f* ♦ *vt* otorgar, conceder; (*LAW*: *damages*) adjudicar

aware [əˈwɛə] *adj*: **~ (of)** consciente (de); **to become ~ of/that** (*realize*) darse cuenta de/de que; (*learn*) enterarse de/de que ❑ **awareness** *n* conciencia; (*knowledge*) conocimiento

away [əˈweɪ] *adv* fuera; (*movement*): **she went ~** se marchó; **far ~** lejos; **two kilometres ~** a dos kilómetros de distancia; **two hours ~ by car** a dos horas en coche; **the holiday was two weeks ~** faltaban dos semanas para las vacaciones; **he's ~ for a week** estará ausente una semana; **to take ~ (from)** quitar (a); (*subtract*) substraer (de); **to work/pedal ~** seguir trabajando/ pedaleando; **to fade ~** (*colour*) desvanecerse; (*sound*) apagarse

awe [ɔː] *n* admiración *f* respetuosa ❑ **awesome** [ˈɔːsəm] (*US*) *adj* (*excellent*) formidable

awful [ˈɔːfəl] *adj* horroroso; (*quantity*): **an ~ lot of** cantidad (de) ❑ **awfully** *adv* (*very*) terriblemente

awkward [ˈɔːkwəd] *adj* desmañado, torpe; (*shape*) incómodo; (*embarrassing*) delicado, difícil

awoke [əˈwəuk] *pt of* **awake**

awoken [əˈwəukən] *pp of* **awake**

axe [æks] (*US* **ax**) *n* hacha ♦ *vt* (*project*) cortar; (*jobs*) reducir

axle [ˈæksl] *n* eje *m*, árbol *m*

ay(e) [aɪ] *excl* sí

azalea [əˈzeɪlɪə] *n* azalea

B, b

B [biː] *n* (*MUS*) si *m*

B.A. *abbr* = **Bachelor of Arts**

baby [ˈbeɪbɪ] *n* bebé *mf*; (*US*: inf: *darling*) mi amor ❑ **baby carriage** (*US*) *n* cochecito ❑ **baby-sit** *vi* hacer de canguro ❑ **baby-sitter** *n* canguro(-a) ❑ **baby wipe** *n* toallita húmeda (*para bebés*)

bachelor [ˈbætʃələ] *n* soltero; **B~ of Arts/Science** licenciado(-a) en Filosofía y Letras/Ciencias

back [bæk] *n* (*of person*) espalda; (*of animal*) lomo; (*of hand*) dorso; (*as opposed to front*) parte *f* de atrás; (*of chair*) respaldo; (*of page*) reverso; (*of book*) final *m*; (*FOOTBALL*) defensa *m*; (*of crowd*): **the ones at the ~** los del fondo ♦ *vt* (*candidate: also:* **~ up**) respaldar, apoyar; (*horse: at races*) apostar a; (*car*) dar marcha atrás a *or* con ♦ *vi* (*car etc*) ir (*or* salir *or* entrar) marcha atrás ♦ *adj* (*payment, rent*) atrasado; (*seats, wheels*) de atrás ♦ *adv* (*not forward*) (hacia) atrás; (*returned*): **he's ~** está de vuelta, ha vuelto; **he ran ~** volvió corriendo; (*restitution*): **throw the ball ~** devuelve la pelota; **can I have it ~?** ¿me lo devuelve?; (*again*): **he called ~** llamó de nuevo ► **back down** *vi* echarse atrás ► **back out** *vi* (*of promise*) volverse atrás ► **back up** *vt* (*person*) apoyar, respaldar; (*theory*) defender; (*COMPUT*) hacer una copia preventiva *or* de reserva ❑ **backache** *n* dolor *m* de espalda ❑ **backbencher** (*BRIT*) *n* miembro del parlamento sin cargo relevante ❑ **backbone** *n* columna vertebral ❑ **back door** *n* puerta *f* trasera ❑ **backfire** *vi* (*AUT*) petardear; (*plans*) fallar, salir mal ❑ **backgammon** *n* backgammon *m* ❑ **background** *n* fondo; (*of events*) antecedentes *mpl*; (*basic knowledge*) bases *fpl*; (*experience*) conocimientos *mpl*, educación *f*; **family background** origen *m*, antecedentes *mpl* ❑ **backing** *n* (*fig*) apoyo, respaldo ❑ **backlog** *n*: **backlog of work** trabajo atrasado ❑ **backpack** *n* mochila ❑ **backpacker** *n* mochilero(-a) ❑ **backslash** *n* pleca, barra inversa ❑ **backstage** *adv* entre bastidores ❑ **backstroke** *n* espalda ❑ **backup** *adj* suplementario *o* (*COMPUT*: *support*) apoyo *o* (*also*: **backup file**) copia preventiva *or* de reserva ❑ **backward** *adj* (*person, country*) atrasado ❑ **backwards** *adv* hacia atrás; (*read a list*) al revés; (*fall*) de espaldas ❑ **backyard** *n* traspatio

bacon ['beikən] *n* tocino, beicon *m*

bacteria [bæk'tɪərɪə] *npl* bacterias *fpl*

bad [bæd] *adj* malo; (*mistake, accident*) grave; (*food*) podrido, pasado; **his ~ leg** su pierna lisiada; **to go ~** pasarse

badge [bædʒ] *n* insignia; (*policeman's*) chapa, placa

badger ['bædʒə*r*] *n* tejón *m*

badly ['bædlɪ] *adv* mal; **to reflect ~ on sb** influir negativamente en la reputación de algn; **~ wounded** gravemente herido; **he needs it ~** le hace gran falta; **to be ~ off (for money)** andar mal de dinero

bad-mannered ['bæd'mænəd] *adj* mal educado

badminton ['bædmɪntən] *n* bádminton *m*

bad-tempered ['bæd'tempəd] *adj* de mal genio *or* carácter; (*temporarily*) de mal humor

bag [bæg] *n* bolsa; (*handbag*) bolso; (*satchel*) mochila; (*case*) maleta; **bags of** (*inf*) un montón de ❑ **baggage** *n* equipaje *m* ❑ **baggage allowance** *n* límite *m* de equipaje ❑ **baggage reclaim** *n* recogida de equipajes ❑ **baggy** *adj* amplio ❑ **bagpipes** *npl* gaita

bail [beil] *n* fianza ♦ *vt* (*prisoner: gen: grant bail to*) poner en libertad bajo

fianza; (*boat: also:* **~ out**) achicar; **on ~** (*prisoner*) bajo fianza; **to ~ sb out** obtener la libertad de algn bajo fianza

bait [beit] *n* cebo ♦ *vt* poner cebo en; (*tease*) tomar el pelo a

bake [beik] *vt* cocer (al horno) ♦ *vi* cocerse ❑ **baked beans** *npl* judías *fpl* en salsa de tomate ❑ **baked potato** *n* patata al horno ❑ **baker** *n* panadero ❑ **bakery** *n* panadería; (*for cakes*) pastelería ❑ **baking** *n* (*act*) amasar *m*; (*batch*) hornada ❑ **baking powder** *n* levadura (en polvo)

balance ['bæləns] *n* equilibrio; (*COMM: sum*) balance *m*; (*remainder*) resto; (*scales*) balanza ♦ *vt* equilibrar; (*budget*) nivelar; (*account*) saldar; (*make equal*) equilibrar; **~ of trade/ payments** balanza de comercio/ pagos ❑ **balanced** *adj* (*personality, diet*) equilibrado; (*report*) objetivo ❑ **balance sheet** *n* balance *m*

balcony ['bælkənɪ] *n* (*open*) balcón *m*; (*closed*) galería; (*in theatre*) anfiteatro

bald [bɔːld] *adj* calvo; (*tyre*) liso

Balearics [bælɪ'ærɪks] *npl*: **the ~ las** Baleares

ball [bɔːl] *n* pelota; (*football*) balón *m*; (*of wool, string*) ovillo; (*dance*) baile *m*; **to play ~** (*fig*) cooperar

ballerina [bælə'riːnə] *n* bailarina

ballet ['bæleɪ] *n* ballet *m* ❑ **ballet dancer** *n* bailarín(-ina) *m/f*

balloon [bə'luːn] *n* globo

ballot ['bælət] *n* votación *f*

ballpoint (pen) ['bɔːlpɔɪnt-] *n* bolígrafo

ballroom ['bɔːlrum] *n* salón *m* de baile

Baltic ['bɔːltɪk] *n*: **the ~ (Sea)** el (Mar) Báltico

bamboo [bæm'buː] *n* bambú *m*

ban [bæn] *n* prohibición *f*, proscripción *f* ♦ *vt* prohibir, proscribir

banana [bə'nɑːnə] *n* plátano, banana (*LAm*), banano (*CAm*)

band [bænd] n grupo; (strip) faja, tira; (stripe) lista; (MUS: jazz) orquesta; (: rock) grupo; (MIL) banda

bandage ['bændɪdʒ] n venda, vendaje m ♦ vt vendar

Band-Aid® ['bændeɪd] (US) n tirita

bandit ['bændɪt] n bandido

bang [bæŋ] n (of gun, exhaust) estallido, detonación f; (of door) portazo; (blow) golpe m ♦ vt (door) cerrar de golpe; (one's head) golpear ♦ vi estallar; (door) cerrar de golpe

Bangladesh [bɑːŋglə'deʃ] n Bangladesh m

bangle ['bæŋgl] n brazalete m, ajorca

bangs [bæŋz] (US) npl flequillo

banish ['bænɪʃ] vt desterrar

banister(s) ['bænɪstə(z)] n(pl) barandilla, pasamanos m inv

banjo ['bændʒəʊ] (pl **banjoes** or **banjos**) n banjo

bank [bæŋk] n (COMM) banco; (of river, lake) ribera, orilla; (of earth) terraplén m ♦ vi (AVIAT) ladearse ▸ **bank on** vt fus contar con ☐ **bank account** n cuenta de banco ☐ **bank balance** n saldo ☐ **bank card** n tarjeta bancaria ☐ **bank charges** npl comisión fsg ☐ **banker** n banquero ☐ **bank holiday** n (BRIT) día m festivo or de fiesta ☐ **banking** n banca ☐ **bank manager** n director(a) m/f (de sucursal) de banco ☐ **banknote** n billete m de banco

bankrupt ['bæŋkrʌpt] adj quebrado, insolvente; **to go ~** hacer bancarrota; **to be ~** estar en quiebra ☐ **bankruptcy** n quiebra

bank statement n balance m or detalle m de cuenta

banner ['bænə'] n pancarta

bannister(s) ['bænɪstə(z)] n(pl) = **banister(s)**

banquet ['bæŋkwɪt] n banquete m

baptism ['bæptɪzəm] n bautismo; (act) bautizo

baptize [bæp'taɪz] vt bautizar

bar [bɑː'] n (pub) bar m; (counter) mostrador m; (rod) barra; (of window, cage) reja; (of soap) pastilla; (of chocolate) tableta; (fig: hindrance) obstáculo; (prohibition) proscripción f; (MUS) barra ♦ vt (road) obstruir; (person) excluir; (activity) prohibir; **the B~** (LAW) la abogacía; **behind bars** entre rejas; **~ none** sin excepción

barbaric [bɑː'bærɪk] adj bárbaro

barbecue ['bɑːbɪkjuː] n barbacoa

barbed wire ['bɑːbd-] n alambre m de púas

barber ['bɑːbə'] n peluquero, barbero ☐ **barber's (shop)** (US **barber (shop)**) n peluquería

bar code n código de barras

bare [bɛə'] adj desnudo; (trees) sin hojas; (necessities etc) básico ♦ vt desnudar; (teeth) enseñar ☐ **barefoot** adj, adv descalzo ☐ **barely** adv apenas

bargain ['bɑːgɪn] n pacto, negocio; (good buy) ganga ♦ vi negociar; (haggle) regatear; **into the ~** además, por añadidura ▸ **bargain for** vt fus: **he got more than he bargained for** le resultó peor de lo que esperaba

barge [bɑːdʒ] n barcaza ▸ **barge in** vi irrumpir; (interrupt: conversation) interrumpir

bark [bɑːk] n (of tree) corteza; (of dog) ladrido ♦ vi ladrar

barley ['bɑːlɪ] n cebada

barmaid ['bɑːmeɪd] *n* camarera

barman ['bɑːmən] (*irreg*) *n* camarero, barman *m*

barn [bɑːn] *n* granero

barometer [bə'rɒmɪtə'] *n* barómetro

baron ['bærən] *n* barón *m*; (*press baron etc*) magnate *m* ❑ **baroness** *n* baronesa

barracks ['bærəks] *npl* cuartel *m*

barrage ['bærɑːʒ] *n* (*in MIL*) descarga, bombardeo; (*dam*) presa; (*of criticism*) lluvia, aluvión *m*

barrel ['bærəl] *n* barril *m*; (*of gun*) cañón *m*

barren ['bærən] *adj* estéril

barrette [bə'ret] (*US*) *n* pasador *m* (*LAm, SP*), broche *m* (*MEX*)

barricade [bærɪ'keɪd] *n* barricada

barrier ['bærɪə'] *n* barrera

barring ['bɑːrɪŋ] *prep* excepto, salvo

barrister ['bærɪstə'] (*BRIT*) *n* abogado(-a)

barrow ['bærəʊ] *n* (*cart*) carretilla (de mano)

bartender ['bɑːtendə'] (*US*) *n* camarero, barman *m*

base [beɪs] *n* base *f* ♦ *vt*: **to ~ sth on** basar *or* fundar algo en ♦ *adj* bajo, infame

baseball ['beɪsbɔːl] *n* béisbol *m* ❑ **baseball cap** *n* gorra *f* de béisbol

basement ['beɪsmənt] *n* sótano

bases¹ ['beɪsiːz] *npl of* **basis**

bases² ['beɪsɪz] *npl of* **base**

bash [bæʃ] (*inf*) *vt* golpear

basic ['beɪsɪk] *adj* básico ❑ **basically** *adv* fundamentalmente, en el fondo; (*simply*) sencillamente ❑ **basics** *npl*: **the basics** los fundamentos

basil ['bæzl] *n* albahaca

basin ['beɪsn] *n* cuenco, tazón *m*; (*GEO*) cuenca; (*also:* **washbasin**) lavabo

basis ['beɪsɪs] (*pl* **bases**) *n* base *f*; **on a part-time/trial ~** a tiempo parcial/a prueba

basket ['bɑːskɪt] *n* cesta, cesto; canasta ❑ **basketball** *n* baloncesto

bass [beɪs] *n* (*MUS: instrument*) bajo; (*double bass*) contrabajo; (*singer*) bajo

bastard ['bɑːstəd] *n* bastardo; (*inf!*) hijo de puta (*!*)

bat [bæt] *n* (*ZOOL*) murciélago; (*for ball games*) pala; (*BRIT: for table tennis*) pala ♦ *vt*: **he didn't ~ an eyelid** ni pestañeó

batch [bætʃ] *n* (*of bread*) hornada; (*of letters etc*) lote *m*

bath [bɑːθ, *pl* bɑːðz] *n* (*action*) baño; (*bathtub*) bañera (*SP*), tina (*LAm*), bañadera (*RPl*) ♦ *vt* bañar; **to have a ~** bañarse, tomar un baño; *see also* **baths**

bathe [beɪð] *vi* bañarse ♦ *vt* (*wound*) lavar

bathing ['beɪðɪŋ] *n* el bañarse ❑ **bathing costume** (*US* **bathing suit**) *n* traje *m* de baño

bath: bathrobe (*man's*) batín *m*; (*woman's*) bata ❑ **bathroom** *n* (cuarto de) baño ❑ **baths** [bɑːðz] *npl* (*also:* **swimming baths**) piscina ❑ **bath towel** *n* toalla de baño ❑ **bathtub** *n* bañera

baton ['bætən] *n* (*MUS*) batuta; (*ATHLETICS*) testigo; (*weapon*) porra

batter ['bætə'] *vt* maltratar; (*rain etc*) azotar ♦ *n* masa (para rebozar) ❑ **battered** *adj* (*hat, pan*) estropeado

battery ['bætərɪ] *n* (*AUT*) batería; (*of torch*) pila ❑ **battery farming** *n* cría intensiva

battle ['bætl] *n* batalla; (*fig*) lucha ♦ *vi* luchar ❑ **battlefield** *n* campo *m* de batalla

bay [beɪ] *n* (*GEO*) bahía; **B~ of Biscay** ≈ mar Cantábrico; **to hold sb at ~** mantener a algn a raya

bazaar [bə'zɑː'] *n* bazar *m*; (*fete*) venta con fines benéficos

B. & B. *n abbr* = **bed and breakfast**; (*place*) pensión *f*; (*terms*) cama y desayuno

BBC n abbr (= British Broadcasting Corporation) cadena de radio y televisión estatal británica

B.C. adv abbr (= before Christ) a. de C.

be

KEYWORD

[biː] (pt **was, were,** pp **been**) aux vb

1 (with present participle: forming continuous tenses): **what are you doing?** ¿qué estás haciendo?, ¿qué haces?; **they're coming tomorrow** vienen mañana; **I've been waiting for you for hours** llevo horas esperándote

2 (with pp: forming passives) ser (but often replaced by active or reflexive constructions); **to be murdered** ser asesinado; **the box had been opened** habían abierto la caja; **the thief was nowhere to be seen** no se veía al ladrón por ninguna parte

3 (in tag questions): **it was fun, wasn't it?** fue divertido, ¿no? or ¿verdad?; **he's good-looking, isn't he?** es guapo, ¿no te parece?; **she's back again, is she?** entonces, ¿ha vuelto?

4 (+to +infin): **the house is to be sold** (necessity) hay que vender la casa; (future) van a vender la casa; **he's not to open it** no tiene que abrirlo

♦ vb +complement

1 (with n or num complement, but see also **3, 4, 5** and impers vb below: ser); **he's a doctor** es médico; **2 and 2 are 4** 2 y 2 son 4

2 (with adj complement: expressing permanent or inherent quality) ser; (: expressing state seen as temporary or reversible) estar; **I'm English** soy inglés(-esa); **she's tall/pretty** es alta/bonita; **he's young** es joven; **be careful/good/quiet** ten cuidado/

pórtate bien/cállate; **I'm tired** estoy cansado(-a); **it's dirty** está sucio(-a)

3 (of health) estar; **how are you?** ¿cómo estás?; **he's very ill** está muy enfermo; **I'm better now** ya estoy mejor

4 (of age) tener; **how old are you?** ¿cuántos años tienes?; **I'm sixteen (years old)** tengo dieciséis años

5 (cost) costar; ser; **how much was the meal?** ¿cuánto fue or costó la comida?; **that'll be £5.75, please** son £5.75, por favor; **this shirt is £17** esta camisa cuesta £17

♦ vi

1 (exist, occur etc) existir, haber; **the best singer that ever was** el mejor cantante que existió jamás; **is there a God?** ¿hay un Dios?, ¿existe Dios?; **be that as it may** sea como sea; **so be it** así sea

2 (referring to place) estar; **I won't be here tomorrow** no estaré aquí mañana

3 (referring to movement): **where have you been?** ¿dónde has estado?

♦ impers vb

1 (referring to time): **it's 5 o'clock** son las 5; **it's the 28th of April** estamos a 28 de abril

2 (referring to distance): **it's 10 km to the village** el pueblo está a 10 km

3 (referring to the weather): **it's too hot/cold** hace demasiado calor/frío; **it's windy today** hace viento hoy

4 (emphatic): **it's me** soy yo; **it was Maria who paid the bill** fue María la que pagó la cuenta

beach [biːtʃ] n playa ♦ vt varar

beacon [ˈbiːkən] n (lighthouse) faro; (marker) guía

bead [biːd] n cuenta; (of sweat etc) gota; **beads** npl (necklace) collar m

beak [biːk] n pico

beam [biːm] n (ARCH) viga, travesaño; (of light) rayo, haz m de luz ♦ vi brillar; (smile) sonreír

bean [biːn] n judía; **runner/broad ~** habichuela/haba; **coffee ~** grano de café □ **beansprouts** npl brotes mpl de soja

bear [beəʳ] (pt bore, pp borne) n oso ♦ vt (weight etc) llevar; (cost) pagar; (responsibility) tener; (endure) soportar, aguantar; (children) parir, tener; (fruit) dar ♦ vi: to ~ right/left torcer a la derecha/izquierda

beard [bɪəd] n barba

bearer ['bɛərəʳ] n portador(a) m/f

bearing ['bɛərɪŋ] n porte m, comportamiento; (connection) relación f

beast [biːst] n bestia; (inf) bruto, salvaje m

beat [biːt] (pt ~, pp beaten) n (of heart) latido; (MUS) ritmo, compás m; (of policeman) ronda ♦ vt pegar, golpear; (eggs) batir; (defeat: opponent) vencer, derrotar; (: record) sobrepasar ♦ vi (heart) latir; (drum) redoblar; (rain, wind) azotar; **off the beaten track** aislado; **to ~ it** (inf) largarse ▶ **beat up** vt (attack) dar una paliza a □ **beating** n paliza

beautiful ['bjuːtɪful] adj precioso, hermoso, bello □ **beautifully** adv maravillosamente

beauty ['bjuːtɪ] n belleza □ **beauty parlour** (US beauty parlor) n salón m there too de belleza □ **beauty salon** n salón m de belleza □ **beauty spot** n (TOURISM) lugar m pintoresco

beaver ['biːvəʳ] n castor m

became [bɪ'keɪm] pt of become

because [bɪ'kɒz] conj porque; ~ **of** debido a, a causa de

beckon ['bɛkən] vt (also: ~ to) llamar con señas

become [bɪ'kʌm] (pt became, pp ~) vt (suit) favorecer, sentar bien a ♦ vi (+ n) hacerse, llegar a ser; (+ adj) ponerse, volverse; **to ~ fat** engordar

bed [bɛd] n cama; (of flowers) macizo; (of coal, clay) capa; (of river) lecho; (of sea) fondo; **to go to ~** acostarse □ **bed and breakfast** n (place) pensión f; (terms) cama y desayuno □ **bedclothes** npl ropa de cama □ **bedding** n ropa de cama □ **bed linen** n (BRIT) ropa f de cama

BED AND BREAKFAST

Se llama **bed and breakfast** a una forma de alojamiento, en el campo o la ciudad, que ofrece cama y desayuno a precios inferiores a los de un hotel. El servicio se suele anunciar con carteles en los que a menudo se usa únicamente la abreviatura **B. & B.**

bed: bedroom n dormitorio □ **bedside** n: **at the bedside of** a la cabecera de □ **bedside lamp** n lámpara de noche □ **bedside table** n mesilla de noche □ **bedsit(ter)** (BRIT) n cuarto de alquiler □ **bedspread** n cubrecama m, colcha □ **bedtime** n hora de acostarse

bee [biː] n abeja

beech [biːtʃ] n haya

beef [biːf] n carne f de vaca; **roast ~** rosbif m □ **beefburger** n hamburguesa □ **Beefeater** n alabardero de la Torre de Londres

been [biːn] pp of be

beer [bɪəʳ] n cerveza □ **beer garden** n (BRIT) terraza f de verano, jardín m (de un bar)

beet [biːt] n (US) (also: **red ~**) remolacha

beetle ['biːtl] n escarabajo

beetroot ['biːtruːt] n (BRIT) remolacha

before [bɪ'fɔːʳ] prep (of time) antes de; (of space) delante de ♦ conj antes (de) que ♦ *adv* antes, anteriormente; delante, adelante; **~ going** antes de marcharse; **~ she goes** antes de que se vaya; **the week ~** la semana anterior; **I've never seen it ~** no lo he visto nunca ▫ **beforehand** *adv* de antemano, con anticipación

beg [beg] *vi* pedir limosna ♦ *vt* pedir, rogar; (*entreat*) suplicar; **to ~ sb to do sth** rogar a algn que haga algo; *see also* **pardon**

began [bɪˈgæn] *pt of* **begin**

beggar [ˈbegəˈ] *n* mendigo(-a)

begin [bɪˈgɪn] (*pt* **began**, *pp* **begun**) *vt, vi* empezar, comenzar; **to ~ doing** *or* **to do sth** empezar a hacer algo ▫ **beginner** *n* principiante *mf* ▫ **beginning** *n* principio, comienzo

begun [bɪˈgʌn] *pp of* **begin**

behalf [bɪˈhɑːf] *n*: **on ~ of** en nombre de, por; (*for benefit of*) en beneficio de; **on my/his ~** por mí/él

behave [bɪˈheɪv] *vi* (*person*) portarse, comportarse; (*well: also*: **~ o.s.**) portarse bien ▫ **behaviour** (*US* **behavior**) *n* comportamiento, conducta

behind [bɪˈhaɪnd] *prep* detrás de; (*supporting*): **to be ~ sb** apoyar a algn ♦ *adv* detrás, por detrás, atrás ♦ *n* trasero *m*; **to be ~ (schedule)** ir retrasado; **~ the scenes** (*fig*) entre bastidores

beige [beɪʒ] *adj* color beige

Beijing [ˈbeɪˈdʒɪŋ] *n* Pekín *m*

being [ˈbiːɪŋ] *n* ser *m*; (*existence*): **in ~** existente; **to come into ~** aparecer

belated [bɪˈleɪtɪd] *adj* atrasado, tardío

belch [beltʃ] *vi* eructar ♦ *vt* (*gen*: belch out: smoke etc) arrojar

Belgian [ˈbeldʒən] *adj, n* belga *mf*

Belgium [ˈbeldʒəm] *n* Bélgica

belief [bɪˈliːf] *n* opinión f; (*faith*) fe f

believe [bɪˈliːv] *vt, vi* creer; **to ~ in** creer en ▫ **believer** *n* partidario(-a); (*REL*) creyente *mf*, fiel *mf*

bell [bel] *n* campana; (*small*) campanilla; (*on door*) timbre *m*

bellboy [ˈbelbɔɪ] (*BRIT*) *n* botones *m inv*

bellhop [ˈbelhɔp] (*US*) *n* = **bellboy**

bellow [ˈbeləʊ] *vi* bramar; (*person*) rugir

bell pepper *n* (*esp US*) pimiento, pimentón *m* (*LAm*)

belly [ˈbelɪ] *n* barriga, panza ▫ **belly button** (*inf*) *n* ombligo

belong [bɪˈlɔŋ] *vi*: **to ~ to** pertenecer a; (*club etc*) ser socio de; **this book belongs here** este libro va aquí ▫ **belongings** *npl* pertenencias *fpl*

beloved [bɪˈlʌvɪd] *adj* querido(-a)

below [bɪˈləʊ] *prep* bajo, debajo de; (*less than*) inferior a ♦ *adv* abajo, (por) debajo; **see ~** véase más abajo

belt [belt] *n* cinturón *m*; (*TECH*) correa, cinta ♦ *vt* (*thrash*) pegar con correa ▫ **beltway** (*US*) *n* (*AUT*) carretera de circunvalación

bemused [bɪˈmjuːzd] *adj* perplejo

bench [bentʃ] *n* banco; (*BRIT POL*): **the Government/Opposition benches** (los asientos *m* de) los miembros del Gobierno/de la Oposición; **the B~** (*LAW: judges*) magistratura

bend [bend] (*pt, pp* **bent**) *vt* doblar ♦ *vi* inclinarse ♦ *n* (*BRIT: in road, river*) curva; (*in pipe*) codo ▶ **bend down** *vi* inclinarse, doblarse ▶ **bend over** *vi* inclinarse

beneath [bɪˈniːθ] *prep* bajo, debajo de; (*unworthy*) indigno de ♦ *adv* abajo, (por) debajo

beneficial [benɪˈfɪʃəl] *adj* beneficioso

benefit [ˈbenɪfɪt] *n* beneficio; (*allowance of money*) subsidio ♦ *vt* beneficiar ♦ *vi*: **he'll ~ from it** le sacará provecho

benign [bɪˈnaɪn] *adj* benigno; (*smile*) afable

bent [bent] *pt, pp of* **bend** ♦ *n* inclinación f ♦ *adj*: **to be ~ on** estar empeñado en

bereaved [bɪˈriːvd] *npl*: **the ~** los íntimos de una persona afligidos por su muerte

beret [ˈbereɪ] *n* boina

Berlin [bəːˈlɪn] *n* Berlín

Bermuda [bəːˈmjuːdə] *n* las Bermudas

berry [ˈberɪ] *n* baya

berth [bəːθ] *n* (*bed*) litera; (*cabin*) camarote *m*; (*for ship*) amarradero ♦ *vi* atracar, amarrar

beside [bɪˈsaɪd] *prep* junto a, al lado de; **to be ~ o.s. with anger** estar fuera de sí; **that's ~ the point** eso no tiene nada que ver ❑ **besides** *adv* además ♦ *prep* además de

best [best] *adj* (el/la) mejor ♦ *adv* (lo) mejor; **the ~ part of** (*quantity*) la mayor parte de; **at ~** en el mejor de los casos; **to make the ~ of sth** sacar el mejor partido de algo; **to do one's ~** hacer todo lo posible; **to the ~ of my knowledge** que yo sepa; **to the ~ of my ability** como mejor puedo ❑ **best-before date** *n* fecha de consumo preferente ❑ **best man** (*irreg*) *n* padrino de boda ❑ **bestseller** *n* éxito de librería, bestseller *m*

bet [bet] (*pt, pp* **~** *or* **betted**) *n* apuesta ♦ *vt*: **~ money on** apostar dinero en ♦ *vi* apostar; **to ~ sb sth** apostar algo a algn

betray [bɪˈtreɪ] *vt* traicionar; (*trust*) faltar a

better [ˈbetə] *adj, adv* mejor ♦ *vt* superar ♦ *n*: **to get the ~ of sb** quedar por encima de algn; **you had ~ do it** más vale que lo hagas; **he thought ~ of it** cambió de parecer; **to get ~** (*MED*) mejorar(se)

betting [ˈbetɪŋ] *n* juego, el apostar ❑ **betting shop** (*BRIT*) *n* agencia de apuestas

between [bɪˈtwiːn] *prep* entre ♦ *adv* (*time*) mientras tanto; (*place*) en medio

beverage [ˈbevərɪdʒ] *n* bebida

beware [bɪˈweə] *vi*: **to ~ (of)** tener cuidado (con); **"~ of the dog"** "perro peligroso"

bewildered [bɪˈwɪldəd] *adj* aturdido, perplejo

beyond [bɪˈjɔnd] *prep* más allá de; (*past: understanding*) fuera de; (*after: date*) después de, más allá de; (*above*) superior a ♦ *adv* (*in space*) más allá; (*in time*) posteriormente; **~ doubt** fuera de toda duda; **~ repair** irreparable

bias [ˈbaɪəs] *n* (*prejudice*) prejuicio, pasión *f*; (*preference*) predisposición *f* ❑ **bias(s)ed** *adj* parcial

bib [bɪb] *n* babero

Bible [ˈbaɪbl] *n* Biblia

bicarbonate of soda [baɪˈkɑːbənɪt-] *n* bicarbonato sódico

biceps [ˈbaɪseps] *n* bíceps *m*

bicycle [ˈbaɪsɪkl] *n* bicicleta ❑ **bicycle pump** *n* bomba de bicicleta

bid [bɪd] (*pt* **bade** *or* **~**, *pp* **bidden** *or* **~**) *n* oferta, postura; (*in tender*) licitación *f*; (*attempt*) tentativa, conato ♦ *vi* hacer una oferta ♦ *vt* (*offer*) ofrecer; **to ~ sb good day** dar a algn los buenos días ❑ **bidder** *n*: **the highest bidder** el mejor postor

bidet [ˈbiːdeɪ] *n* bidet *m*

big [bɪg] *adj* grande; (*brother, sister*) mayor ❑ **bigheaded** *adj* engreído ❑ **big toe** *n* dedo gordo (del pie)

bike [baɪk] *n* bici *f* ❑ **bike lane** *n* carril-bici *m*

bikini [bɪˈkiːnɪ] *n* bikini *m*

bilateral [baɪˈlætərl] *adj* (*agreement*) bilateral

bilingual [baɪˈlɪŋgwəl] *adj* bilingüe

bill [bɪl] *n* cuenta; (*invoice*) factura; (*POL*) proyecto de ley; (*US: banknote*) billete *m*; (*of bird*) pico; (*of show*) programa *m*; **"post no bills"** "prohibido fijar carteles"; **to fit** *or* **fill the ~** (*fig*) cumplir con los requisitos ❑ **billboard** (*US*) *n* cartelera ❑ **billfold** [ˈbɪlfəuld] (*US*) *n* cartera

billiards ['biljədz] n billar m

billion ['biljən] n (BRIT) billón m (millón de millones); (US) mil millones mpl

bin [bin] n (for rubbish) cubo o bote m (MEX) or tacho (SC) de la basura; (container) recipiente m

bind [baind] (pt, pp **bound**) vt atar; (book) encuadernar; (oblige) obligar ♦ n (inf: nuisance) lata

binge [bindʒ] (inf) n: **to go on a ~** ir de juerga

bingo ['bingəu] n bingo m

binoculars [bi'nɔkjuləz] npl prismáticos mpl

bio... [baiə] prefix: **biochemistry** n bioquímica ❏ **biodegradable** [baiəudi'greidəbl] adj biodegradable ❏ **biography** [bai'ɔgrəfi] n biografía ❏ **biological** adj biológico ❏ **biology** [bai'ɔlədʒi] n biología

birch [bə:tʃ] n (tree) abedul m

bird [bə:d] n ave f, pájaro; (BRIT: inf: girl) chica ❏ **bird of prey** n ave f de presa ❏ **birdwatching** n: **he likes to go birdwatching on Sundays** los domingos le gusta ir a ver pájaros

Biro® ['baiərəu] n boli

birth [bə:θ] n nacimiento; **to give ~ to** parir, dar a luz ❏ **birth certificate** n partida de nacimiento ❏ **birth control** n (policy) control m de natalidad; (methods) métodos mpl anticonceptivos ❏ **birthday** n cumpleaños m inv ♦ cpd (cake, card etc) de cumpleaños ❏ **birthmark** n antojo, marca de nacimiento ❏ **birthplace** n lugar m de nacimiento

biscuit ['biskit] (BRIT) n galleta

bishop ['biʃəp] n obispo; (CHESS) alfil m

bistro ['bi:strəu] n café-bar m

bit [bit] pt of **bite** ♦ n trozo, pedazo, pedacito; (COMPUT) bit m, bitio (for horse) freno, bocado; **a ~** of un poco de; **a ~ mad** un poco loco; **~ by ~** poco a poco

bitch [bitʃ] n perra; (inf: woman) zorra (!)

bite [bait] (pt **bit**, pp **bitten**) vt, vi morder; (insect etc) picar ♦ n (insect bite) picadura; (mouthful) bocado; **to ~ one's nails** comerse las uñas; **let's have a ~ (to eat)** (inf) vamos a comer algo

bitten ['bitn] pp of **bite**

bitter ['bitə'] adj amargo; (wind) cortante, penetrante; (battle) encarnizado ♦ n (BRIT: beer) cerveza típica británica a base de lúpulos

bizarre [bi'za:'] adj raro, extraño

black [blæk] adj negro; (tea, coffee) solo ♦ n color m negro; (person): **B~negro(-a)** ♦ vt (BRIT INDUSTRY) boicotear; **to give sb a ~ eye** ponerle a algn el ojo morado; **~ and blue** (bruised) amoratado; **to be in the ~** (bank account) estar en números negros ▶ **black out** vi (faint) desmayarse ❏ **blackberry** n zarzamora ❏ **blackbird** n mirlo ❏ **blackboard** n pizarra ❏ **black coffee** n café m solo ❏ **blackcurrant** n grosella negra ❏ **black ice** n hielo invisible en la carretera ❏ **blackmail** n chantaje m ♦ vt chantajear ❏ **black market** n mercado negro ❏ **blackout** n (MIL) oscurecimiento; (power cut) apagón m; (TV, RADIO) interrupción f de programas; (fainting) desvanecimiento ❏ **black pepper** n pimienta f negra ❏ **black pudding** n morcilla ❏ **Black Sea** n: **the Black Sea** el Mar Negro

bladder ['blædə'] n vejiga

blade [bleid] n hoja; (of propeller) paleta; **a ~ of grass** una brizna de hierba

blame [bleim] n culpa ♦ vt: **to ~ sb for sth** echar a algn la culpa de algo; **to be to ~ (for)** tener la culpa de

bland [blænd] adj (music, taste) soso

blank [blæŋk] adj en blanco; (look) sin expresión ♦ n **my mind is**

a ~ no puedo recordar nada; (on form) blanco, espacio en blanco; (cartridge) cartucho sin bala or de fogueo

blanket ['blæŋkɪt] n manta (SP), cobija (LAm); (of snow) capa; (of fog) manto

blast [blɑːst] n (of wind) ráfaga, soplo; (of explosive) explosión f ♦ vt (blow up) volar

blatant ['bleɪtənt] adj descarado

blaze [bleɪz] n (fire) fuego; (fig: of colour) despliegue m; (: of glory) esplendor m ♦ vi arder en llamas; (fig) brillar ♦ vt: to **~ a trail** (fig) abrir (un) camino; **in a ~ of publicity** con gran publicidad

blazer ['bleɪzə*] n chaqueta de uniforme de colegial o de socio de club

bleach [bliːtʃ] n (also: **household ~**) lejía ♦ vt blanquear ♦ **bleachers** (US) npl (SPORT) gradas fpl al sol

bleak [bliːk] adj (countryside) desierto; (prospect) poco prometedor(a); (weather) crudo; (smile) triste

bled [bled] pt, pp of **bleed**

bleed [bliːd] (pt, pp bled) vt, vi sangrar; **my nose is bleeding** me está sangrando la nariz

blemish ['blemɪʃ] n marca, mancha; (on reputation) tacha

blend [blend] n mezcla ♦ vt mezclar; (colours etc) combinar, mezclar ♦ vi (colours etc: also: **~ in**) combinarse, mezclarse ♦ **blender** n (CULIN) batidora

bless [bles] (pt, pp blessed or blest) vt bendecir; **~ you!** (after sneeze) ¡Jesús! ♦ **blessing** n (approval) aprobación f; (godsend) don m del cielo, bendición f; (advantage) beneficio, ventaja

blew [bluː] pt of **blow**

blight [blaɪt] vt (hopes etc) frustrar, arruinar

blind [blaɪnd] adj ciego; (fig): **~ (to)** ciego (a) ♦ n (for window) persiana ♦ vt cegar; (dazzle) deslumbrar; (deceive): **to ~ sb to ...** cegar a algn a ...; **the ~** npl los ciegos ♦ **blind alley** n callejón m

sin salida ♦ **blindfold** n venda ♦ adv con los ojos vendados ♦ vt vendar los ojos a

blink [blɪŋk] vi parpadear, pestañear; (light) oscilar

bliss [blɪs] n felicidad f

blister ['blɪstə*] n ampolla ♦ vi (paint) ampollarse

blizzard ['blɪzəd] n ventisca

bloated ['bləʊtɪd] adj hinchado; (person: full) ahíto

blob [blɒb] n (drop) gota; (indistinct object) bulto

block [blɒk] n bloque m; (in pipes) obstáculo; (of buildings) manzana (SP), cuadra (LAm) ♦ vt obstruir, cerrar; (progress) estorbar; **~ of flats** (BRIT) bloque m de pisos; **mental ~** bloqueo mental ▶ **block up** vt tapar, obstruir; (pipe) atascar ♦ **blockade** [-'keɪd] n bloqueo ♦ vt bloquear ♦ **blockage** n estorbo, obstrucción f ♦ **blockbuster** n (book) bestseller m; (film) éxito de público ♦ **block capitals** npl mayúsculas fpl ♦ **block letters** npl mayúsculas fpl

bloke [bləʊk] (BRIT: inf) n tipo, tío

blond(e) [blɒnd] adj, n rubio(-a) m/f

blood [blʌd] n sangre f ♦ **blood donor** n donante m/f de sangre ♦ **blood group** n grupo sanguíneo ♦ **blood poisoning** n envenenamiento de la sangre ♦ **blood pressure** n presión f sanguínea ♦ **bloodshed** n derramamiento de sangre ♦ **bloodshot** adj inyectado en sangre ♦ **bloodstream** n corriente f sanguínea ♦ **blood test** n análisis m inv de sangre ♦ **blood transfusion** n transfusión f de sangre ♦ **blood type** n grupo sanguíneo ♦ **blood vessel** n vaso sanguíneo ♦ **bloody** adj sangriento; (nose etc) lleno de sangre; (BRIT: inf!): **this bloody ...** es condenado o puñetero ... (!) ♦ adv:

bloody strong/good (BRIT: infl) terriblemente fuerte/bueno

bloom [bluːm] n flor f ♦ vi florecer

blossom ['blɒsəm] n flor f ♦ vi florecer

blot [blɒt] n borrón m; (fig) mancha ♦ vt (stain) manchar

blouse [blauz] n blusa

blow [bləu] (pt **blew**, pp **blown**) n golpe m; (with sword) espadazo ♦ vi soplar; (dust, sand etc) volar; (fuse) fundirse ♦ vt (wind) llevarse; (fuse) quemar; (instrument) tocar; to ~ **one's nose** sonarse ► **blow away** vt llevarse, arrancar ► **blow out** vi apagarse ► **blow up** vi estallar ♦ vt volar; (tyre) inflar; (PHOT) ampliar ❑ **blow-dry** n moldeado (con secador)

blown [bləun] pp of **blow**

blue [bluː] adj azul; (depressed) deprimido; ~ **film/joke** película/chiste m verde; **out of the** ~ (fig) de repente ❑ **bluebell** n campanilla, campánula azul ❑ **blueberry** n arándano ❑ **blue cheese** n queso azul ❑ **blues** npl: **the blues** (MUS) el blues; **to have the blues** estar triste ❑ **bluetit** n herrerillo m (común)

bluff [blʌf] vi tirarse un farol, farolear ♦ n farol m; **to call sb's** ~ coger a algn la palabra

blunder ['blʌndə'] n patinazo, metedura de pata ♦ vi cometer un error, meter la pata

blunt [blʌnt] adj (pencil) despuntado, (knife) desafilado, romo; (person) franco, directo

blur [bləː'] n (shape): **to become a** ~ hacerse borroso ♦ vt (vision) enturbiar; (distinction) borrar ❑ **blurred** adj borroso

blush [blʌʃ] vi ruborizarse, ponerse colorado ♦ n rubor m ❑ **blusher** n colorete m

board [bɔːd] n (cardboard) cartón m; (wooden) tabla, tablero; (on wall) tablón m; (for chess etc) tablero;

(committee) junta, consejo; (in firm) mesa or junta directiva; (NAUT, AVIAT): **on** ~ a bordo ♦ vt (ship) embarcarse en; (train) subir a; **full** ~ (BRIT) pensión completa; **half** ~ (BRIT) media pensión; **to go by the** ~ (fig) ser abandonado or olvidado ❑ **board game** n juego de tablero ❑ **boarding card** (BRIT) n tarjeta de embarque ❑ **boarding pass** (US) n = **boarding card** ❑ **boarding school** n internado ❑ **board room** n sala de juntas

boast [bəust] vi: **to** ~ (**about** or **of**) alardear (de)

boat [bəut] n barco, buque m; (small) barca, bote m

bob [bɒb] vi (also: ~ **up and down**) menearse, balancearse

bobby pin (US) n horquilla

body ['bɒdi] n cuerpo; (corpse) cadáver m; (of car) caja, carrocería; (fig: group) grupo; (: organization) organismo ❑ **body-building** n culturismo ❑ **bodyguard** n guardaespaldas m inv ❑ **bodywork** n carrocería

bog [bɒg] n pantano, ciénaga ♦ vt: **to get bogged down** (fig) empantanarse, atascarse

bogus ['bəugəs] adj falso, fraudulento

boil [bɔil] vt (water) hervir; (eggs) pasar por agua, cocer ♦ vi hervir; (fig: with anger) estar furioso; (: with heat) asfixiarse ♦ n (MED) furúnculo, divieso; **to come to the** ~, **to come to a** ~ (US) comenzar a hervir; **to** ~ **down to** (fig) reducirse a ❑ **boil over** vi salirse, rebosar; (anger etc) llegar al colmo ❑ **boiled egg** n (soft) huevo tibio (MEX) or pasado por agua or a la copa (SC); (hard) huevo duro ❑ **boiled potatoes** npl patatas fpl (SP) or papas fpl (LAm) cocidas ❑ **boiler** n caldera ❑ **boiling** ['bɔiliŋ] adj: **I'm boiling (hot)** (inf) estoy asado ❑ **boiling point** n punto de ebullición

bold [bəuld] adj valiente, audaz; (pej) descarado; (colour) llamativo

Bolivia [bə'lɪvɪə] n Bolivia ❑ **Bolivian** adj, n boliviano(-a) m/f

bollard ['bɔləd] (BRIT) n (AUT) poste m

bolt [bəʊlt] n (lock) cerrojo; (with nut) perno, tornillo ♦ adv: ~ **upright** rígido, erguido ♦ vt (door) echar el cerrojo a; (also: ~ **together**) sujetar con tornillos; (food) engullir ♦ vi fugarse; (horse) desbocarse

bomb [bɔm] n bomba ♦ vt bombardear ❑ **bombard** [bɔm'bɑːd] vt bombardear; (fig) asediar ❑ **bomber** n (AVIAT) bombardero ❑ **bomb scare** n amenaza de bomba

bond [bɔnd] n (promise) fianza; (FINANCE) bono; (link) vínculo, lazo; (COMM): **in ~** en depósito bajo fianza; **bonds** (chains) cadenas fpl

bone [bəʊn] n hueso; (of fish) espina ♦ vt deshuesar; quitar las espinas a

bonfire ['bɔnfaɪə'] n hoguera, fogata

bonnet ['bɔnɪt] n gorra; (BRIT: of car) capó m

bonus ['bəʊnəs] n (payment) paga extraordinaria, plus m; (fig) bendición f

boo [buː] excl ¡uh! ♦ vt abuchear, rechiflar

book [buk] n libro; (of tickets) taco; (of stamps etc) librito ♦ vt (ticket) sacar; (seat, room) reservar; **books** npl (COMM) cuentas fpl, contabilidad f ▶ **book in** vi (at hotel) registrarse ▶ **book up** vt: **to be booked up** (hotel) estar completo ❑ **bookcase** n librería, estante m para libros ❑ **booking** n reserva ❑ **booking office** n (BRIT: RAIL) despacho de billetes (SP) or boletos (LAm); (THEATRE) taquilla (SP), boletería (LAm) ❑ **book-keeping** n contabilidad f ❑ **booklet** n folleto ❑ **bookmaker** n corredor m de apuestas ❑ **bookmark** n (also: COMPUT) marcador m ❑ **bookseller** n librero ❑ **bookshelf** n estante m (para libros) ❑ **bookshop**, **book store** n librería

boom [buːm] n (noise) trueno, estampido; (in prices etc) alza rápida; (ECON, in population) boom m ♦ vi (cannon) hacer gran estruendo, retumbar; (ECON) estar en alza

boost [buːst] n estímulo, empuje m ♦ vt estimular, empujar

boot [buːt] n bota; (BRIT: of car) maleta, maletero ♦ vt (COMPUT) arrancar; **to ~** (in addition) además, por añadidura

booth [buːð] n (telephone booth, voting booth) cabina

booze [buːz] (inf) n bebida

border ['bɔːdə'] n borde m, margen m; (of a country) frontera; (for flowers) arriate m ♦ vt (road) bordear; (another country: also: ~ **on**) lindar con ❑ **borderline** n: **on the borderline** en el límite

bore [bɔː'] pt of **bear** ♦ vt (hole) hacer un agujero en; (well) perforar; (person) aburrir ♦ n (person) pelmazo, pesado; (of gun) calibre m ❑ **bored** adj aburrido; **he's bored to tears** or **to death** or **stiff** está aburrido como una ostra, está muerto de aburrimiento ❑ **boredom** n aburrimiento

boring ['bɔːrɪŋ] adj aburrido

born [bɔːn] adj: **to be ~** nacer; **I was ~ in 1960** nací en 1960

borne [bɔːn] pp of **bear**

borough ['bʌrə] n municipio

borrow ['bɔrəʊ] vt: **to ~ sth (from sb)** tomar algo prestado (a algn)

Bosnia(-Herzegovina) ['bɔznɪə(herzə'gəʊvɪːnə)] n Bosnia(-Herzegovina) ❑ **Bosnian** ['bɔznɪən] adj, n bosnio(-a)

bosom ['buzəm] n pecho

boss [bɔs] n jefe m ♦ vt (also: ~ **about** or **around**) mangonear ❑ **bossy** adj mandón(-ona)

both [bəʊθ] adj, pron ambos(-as), los dos; ~ **of us went**, **we** ~ **went** fuimos los dos, ambos fuimos ♦ adv: **A and B** tanto A como B

bother ['bɒðə'] vt (worry) preocupar; (disturb) molestar, fastidiar ♦ vi (also: ~ o.s.) molestarse ♦ n (trouble) dificultad f; (nuisance) molestia, lata; **to ~ doing** tomarse la molestia de hacer

bottle ['bɒtl] n botella; (small) frasco; (baby's) biberón m ♦ vt embotellar □ **bottle bank** n contenedor m de vidrio □ **bottle-opener** n abrebotellas m inv

bottom ['bɒtəm] n (of box, sea) fondo; (buttocks) trasero, culo; (of page) pie m; (of list) final m; (of class) último(-a) ♦ adj (lowest) más bajo; (last) último

bought [bɔːt] pt, pp of **buy**

boulder ['bəuldə'] n canto rodado

bounce [bauns] vi (ball) (re)botar; (cheque) ser rechazado ♦ vt hacer (re)botar ♦ n (rebound) (re)bote m □ **bouncer** (inf) n gorila m (que echa a los alborotadores de un bar, club etc)

bound [baund] pt, pp of **bind** ♦ n (leap) salto; (gen pl: limit) límite m ♦ vi (leap) saltar ♦ vt (border) rodear ♦ adj: ~ **by** rodeado de; **to be ~ to do sth** (obliged) tener el deber de hacer algo; **he's ~ to come** es seguro que vendrá; **out of bounds** prohibido el paso; ~ **for** con destino a

boundary ['baundrɪ] n límite m

bouquet ['bukeɪ] n (of flowers) ramo

bourbon ['buəbən] (US) n (also: ~ whiskey) whisky m americano, bourbon m

bout [baut] n (of malaria etc) ataque m; (of activity) período; (BOXING etc) combate m, encuentro

boutique [buː'tiːk] n boutique f, tienda de ropa

bow¹ [bəu] n (knot) lazo; (weapon, MUS) arco

bow² [bau] n (of the head) reverencia; (NAUT: also: **bows**) proa ♦ vi inclinarse, hacer una reverencia

bowels [bauəlz] npl intestinos mpl, vientre m; (fig) entrañas fpl

bowl [bəul] n tazón m, cuenco; (ball) bola ♦ vi (CRICKET) arrojar la pelota; see also **bowls** □ **bowler** n (CRICKET) lanzador m (de la pelota); (BRIT: also: **bowler hat**) hongo, bombín m □ **bowling** n (game) bochas fpl, bolos mpl □ **bowling alley** n bolera □ **bowling green** n pista para bochas □ **bowls** n juego de las bochas, bolos mpl

bow tie ['bəu-] n corbata de lazo, pajarita

box [bɒks] n (also: **cardboard ~**) caja, cajón m; (THEATRE) palco ♦ vt encajonar ♦ vi (SPORT) boxear □ **boxer** n (person) boxeador m □ **boxer shorts** ['bɒksəʃɔːts] pl n bóxers; **a pair of boxer shorts** unos bóxers □ **boxing** ['bɒksɪŋ] n (SPORT) boxeo □ **Boxing Day** (BRIT) n día en que se dan los aguinaldos, 26 de diciembre □ **boxing gloves** npl guantes mpl de boxeo □ **boxing ring** n ring m, cuadrilátero □ **box office** n taquilla (SP), boletería (LAm)

boy [bɔɪ] n (young) niño; (older) muchacho, chico; (son) hijo

boycott ['bɔɪkɒt] n boicot m ♦ vt boicotear

boyfriend ['bɔɪfrɛnd] n novio

bra [brɑː] n sostén m, sujetador m

brace [breɪs] n (BRIT: also: **braces**: on teeth) corrector m, aparato; (tool) berbiquí m ♦ vt (knees, shoulders) tensionar; **braces** npl (BRIT) tirantes mpl; **to ~ o.s.** (fig) prepararse

bracelet ['breɪslɪt] n pulsera, brazalete m

bracket ['brækɪt] n (TECH) soporte m, puntal m; (group) clase f, categoría; (also: **brace ~**) soporte m, abrazadera; (also: **round ~**) paréntesis m inv; (also: **square ~**) corchete m ♦ vt (word etc) poner entre paréntesis

brag [bræg] vi jactarse

braid [breɪd] n (trimming) galón m; (of hair) trenza

brain [breɪn] n cerebro; **brains** npl sesos mpl; **she's got brains** es muy lista

braise [breɪz] vt cocer a fuego lento

brake [breɪk] n (on vehicle) freno ♦ vi frenar ❑ **brake light** n luz f de frenado

bran [bræn] n salvado

branch [brɑːntʃ] n rama; (COMM) sucursal f ▸ **branch off** vi: **a small road branches off to the right** hay una carretera pequeña que sale hacia la derecha ▸ **branch out** vi (fig) extenderse

brand [brænd] n marca; (fig: type) tipo ♦ vt (cattle) marcar con hierro candente ❑ **brand name** n marca ❑ **brand-new** adj flamante, completamente nuevo

brandy [brændɪ] n coñac m

brash [bræʃ] adj (forward) descarado

brass [brɑːs] n latón m; **the ~** (MUS) los cobres ❑ **brass band** n banda de metal

brat [bræt] (pej) n mocoso(-a)

brave [breɪv] adj valiente, valeroso ♦ vt (face up to) desafiar ❑ **bravery** n valor m, valentía

brawl [brɔːl] n pelea, reyerta

Brazil [brəˈzɪl] n (el) Brasil ❑ **Brazilian** adj, n brasileño(-a) m/f

breach [briːtʃ] vt abrir brecha en ♦ n (gap) brecha; (breaking): **~ of contract** infracción f de contrato; **~ of the peace** perturbación f del orden público

bread [bred] n pan m ❑ **breadbin** n panera ❑ **breadbox** (US) n panera ❑ **breadcrumbs** npl migajas fpl; (CULIN) pan rallado

breadth [bretθ] n anchura; (fig) amplitud f

break [breɪk] (pt **broke**, pp **broken**) vt romper; (promise) faltar a; (law) infringir; (record) batir ♦ vi romperse, quebrarse; (storm) estallar; (weather) cambiar; (dawn) despuntar; (news etc) darse a conocer ♦ n (gap) abertura;

(fracture) fractura; (time) intervalo; (: at school) (período de) recreo; (chance) oportunidad f; **to ~ the news to sb** comunicar la noticia a algn ▸ **break down** vt (figures, data) analizar, descomponer ♦ vi (machine) estropearse; (AUT) averiarse; (person) romper a llorar; (talks) fracasar ▸ **break in** vt (horse etc) domar ♦ vi (burglar) forzar una entrada; (interrupt) interrumpir ▸ **break into** vt fus (house) forzar ▸ **break off** vi (speaker) pararse, detenerse; (branch) partir ▸ **break out** vi estallar; (prisoner) escaparse; **to break out in spots** salirle a algn granos ▸ **break up** vi (ship) hacerse pedazos; (crowd, meeting) disolverse; (marriage) deshacerse; (SCOL) terminar (el curso) ♦ vt (rocks etc) partir; (journey) partir; (fight etc) acabar con ❑ **breakdown** n (AUT) avería; (in communications) interrupción f; (MED: also: **nervous breakdown**) colapso, crisis f nerviosa; (of marriage, talks) fracaso; (of statistics) análisis m inv ❑ **breakdown truck, breakdown van** n (camión m) grúa

breakfast [brekfəst] n desayuno

break: break-in n robo con allanamiento de morada ❑ **breakthrough** n (also fig) avance m

breast [brest] n (of woman) pecho, seno; (chest) pecho; (of bird) pechuga ❑ **breast-feed** (pt, pp **breast-fed**) vt, vi amamantar, criar a los pechos ❑ **breast-stroke** n braza (de pecho)

breath [breθ] n aliento, respiración f; **to take a deep ~** respirar hondo; **out of ~** sin aliento, sofocado

Breathalyser® [breθəlaɪzə] (BRIT) n alcoholímetro

breathe [briːð] vt, vi respirar ▸ **breathe in** vt, vi aspirar ▸ **breathe out** vt, vi espirar ❑ **breathing** n respiración f

breath: breathless adj sin aliento, jadeante ❑ **breathtaking** adj

imponente, pasmoso ❏ **breath test**
n prueba de la alcoholemia

bred [bred] pt, pp of **breed**

breed [bri:d] (pt, pp **bred**) vt criar ♦ vi
reproducirse, procrear ♦ n (ZOOL) raza,
casta; (type) tipo

breeze [bri:z] n brisa

breezy ['bri:zi] adj de mucho viento,
ventoso; (person) despreocupado

brew [bru:] vt (tea) hacer; (beer)
elaborar ♦ vi (fig: trouble) prepararse;
(storm) amenazar ❏ **brewery** n
fábrica de cerveza, cervecería

bribe [braib] n soborno ♦ vt sobornar,
cohechar ❏ **bribery** n soborno,
cohecho

bric-a-brac ['brɪkəbræk] n inv baratijas
fpl

brick [brik] n ladrillo ❏ **bricklayer** n
albañil m

bride [braid] n novia ❏ **bridegroom** n
novio ❏ **bridesmaid** n dama de
honor

bridge [brɪdʒ] n puente m; (NAUT)
puente m de mando; (of nose)
caballete m; (CARDS) bridge m ♦ vt (fig):
to ~ a gap llenar un vacío

bridle ['braidl] n brida, freno

brief [bri:f] adj breve, corto ♦ n (LAW)
escrito; (task) cometido, encargo ♦ vt
informar; **briefs** npl (for men)
calzoncillos mpl; (for women) bragas
fpl ❏ **briefcase** n cartera (SP),
portafolio (LAm) ❏ **briefing** n (PRESS)
informe m ❏ **briefly** adv (glance)
fugazmente; (say) en pocas palabras

brigadier [brɪgə'dɪəʳ] n general m de
brigada

bright [brait] adj brillante; (room)
luminoso; (day) de sol; (person: clever)
listo, inteligente; (: lively) alegre;
(colour) vivo; (future) prometedor(a)

brilliant ['brɪljənt] adj brillante; (inf)
fenomenal

brim [brim] n borde m; (of hat) ala

brine [brain] n (CULIN) salmuera

bring [brɪŋ] (pt, pp **brought**) vt (thing,
person: with you) traer; (: to sb) llevar,
conducir; (trouble, satisfaction) causar
▶ **bring about** vt ocasionar, producir
▶ **bring back** vt volver a traer; (return)
devolver ▶ **bring down** vt
(government, plane) derribar; (price)
rebajar ▶ **bring in** vt (harvest) recoger;
(person) hacer entrar o pasar; (object)
traer; (POL: bill, law) presentar;
(produce: income) producir, rendir
▶ **bring on** vt (illness, attack) producir,
causar; (player, substitute) sacar (de la
reserva), hacer salir ▶ **bring out** vt
sacar; (book etc) publicar; (meaning)
subrayar ▶ **bring up** vt subir; (person)
educar, criar; (question) sacar a
colación; (food: vomit) devolver,
vomitar

brink [brɪŋk] n borde m

brisk [brisk] adj (abrupt: tone) brusco;
(person) enérgico, vigoroso; (pace)
rápido; (trade) activo

bristle ['brisl] n cerda ♦ vi: **to ~ in anger**
temblar de rabia

Brit [brit] n abbr (inf: = British person)
británico(-a)

Britain ['britən] n (also: **Great ~**) Gran
Bretaña

British ['britiʃ] adj británico ♦ npl: **the ~**
los británicos ❏ **British Isles** npl: **the
British Isles** las Islas Británicas

Briton ['britən] n británico(-a)

brittle ['britl] adj quebradizo, frágil

broad [brɔ:d] adj ancho; (range)
amplio; (smile) abierto; (general:
outlines etc) general; (accent) cerrado;
in ~ daylight en pleno día
❏ **broadband** n banda ancha
❏ **broad bean** n haba ❏ **broadcast**
(pt, pp ~) n emisión f ♦ vt (RADIO) emitir;
(TV) transmitir ♦ vi emitir; transmitir
❏ **broaden** vt ampliar ♦ vi
ensancharse; **to broaden one's mind**
hacer más tolerante a algn ❏ **broadly**
adv en general ❏ **broad-minded** adj
tolerante, liberal

broccoli ['brɒkəlɪ] n brécol m

brochure ['brəʊʃjʊə'] n folleto

broil [brɔɪl] vt (CULIN) asar a la parrilla

broiler ['brɔɪlə'] n (grill) parrilla

broke [brəʊk] pt of **break** ◆ adj (inf)
pelado, sin blanca

broken ['brəʊkən] pp of **break** ◆ adj
roto; (machine: also: ~ **down**) averiado;
~ leg pierna rota; **in ~ English** en un
inglés imperfecto

broker ['brəʊkə'] n agente mf, bolsista
mf; (insurance broker) agente de
seguros

bronchitis [brɒŋ'kaɪtɪs] n bronquitis f

bronze [brɒnz] n bronce m

brooch [brəʊtʃ] n prendedor m, broche
m

brood [bruːd] n camada, cría ◆ vi
(person) dejarse obsesionar

broom [brum] n escoba; (BOT) retama

Bros. abbr (= Brothers) Hnos

broth [brɒθ] n caldo

brothel ['brɒθl] n burdel m

brother ['brʌðə'] n hermano
❑ **brother-in-law** n cuñado

brought [brɔːt] pt, pp of **bring**

brow [braʊ] n (forehead) frente m;
(eyebrow) ceja; (of hill) cumbre f

brown [braʊn] adj (colour) marrón m;
(hair) castaño; (tanned) bronceado,
moreno ◆ n (colour) color m marrón or
pardo ◆ vt (CULIN) dorar ❑ **brown
bread** n pan integral

Brownie ['braʊnɪ] n niña exploradora

brown rice n arroz m integral

brown sugar n azúcar m terciado

browse [braʊz] vi (through book)
hojear; (in shop) mirar ❑ **browser** n
(COMPUT) navegador m

bruise [bruːz] n cardenal m (SP),
moretón m ◆ vt magullar

brunette [bruː'net] n morena

brush [brʌʃ] n cepillo; (for painting,
shaving etc) brocha; (artist's) pincel m;
(with police etc) roce m ◆ vt (sweep)

barrer; (groom) cepillar; (also: ~
against) rozar al pasar

Brussels ['brʌslz] n Bruselas

Brussels sprout n col f de Bruselas

brutal ['bruːtl] adj brutal

B.Sc. abbr (= Bachelor of Science)
licenciado en Ciencias

BSE n abbr (= bovine spongiform
encephalopathy) encefalopatía
espongiforme bovina

bubble ['bʌbl] n burbuja ◆ vi
burbujear, borbotar ❑ **bubble bath** n
espuma para el baño ❑ **bubble gum**
n chicle m de globo ❑ **bubblejet
printer** ['bʌbldʒet-] n impresora de
inyección por burbujas

buck [bʌk] n (rabbit) conejo macho;
(deer) gamo; (US: inf) dólar m ◆ vi
corcovear; **to pass the ~ (to sb)** echar
(a algn) el muerto

bucket ['bʌkɪt] n cubo, balde m

buckle ['bʌkl] n hebilla ◆ vt abrochar
con hebilla ◆ vi combarse

bud [bʌd] n (of plant) brote m, yema; (of
flower) capullo ◆ vi brotar, echar brotes

Buddhism ['bʊdɪzm] n Budismo

Buddhist ['bʊdɪst] adj, n budista m/f

buddy ['bʌdɪ] (US) n compañero,
compinche m

budge [bʌdʒ] vt mover; (fig) hacer
ceder ◆ vi moverse, ceder

budgerigar ['bʌdʒərɪɡɑː'] n periquito

budget ['bʌdʒɪt] n presupuesto ◆ vi: **to
~ for sth** presupuestar algo

budgie ['bʌdʒɪ] n = **budgerigar**

buff [bʌf] adj (colour) color de ante ◆ n
(inf: enthusiast) entusiasta mf

buffalo ['bʌfələʊ] (pl ~ or **buffaloes**)
(BRIT) búfalo; (US: bison) bisonte m

buffer ['bʌfə'] n (COMPUT) memoria
intermedia; (RAIL) tope m

buffet[1] ['bʌfɪt] vt golpear

buffet[2] ['bʊfeɪ] n (BRIT: in station) bar m,
cafetería; (food) buffet m ❑ **buffet car**
(BRIT) n coche-comedor m

bug [bʌg] n (esp US: insect) bicho, sabandija; (COMPUT) error m; (germ) microbio, bacilo; (spy device) micrófono oculto ♦ vt (inf: annoy) fastidiar; (room) poner micrófono oculto en

buggy ['bʌgɪ] n cochecito de niño

build [bɪld] (pt, pp **built**) n (of person) tipo ♦ vt construir, edificar ▶ **build up** vt (morale, forces, production) acrecentar; (stocks) acumular ❑ **builder** n (contractor) contratista mf ❑ **building** n construcción f; (structure) edificio ❑ **building site** n obra ❑ **building society** n (BRIT) sociedad f inmobiliaria

built [bɪlt] pt, pp of **build** ❑ **built-in** adj (cupboard) empotrado; (device) interior, incorporado ❑ **built-up** adj (area) urbanizado

bulb [bʌlb] n (BOT) bulbo; (ELEC) bombilla, foco (MEX), bujía (CAm), bombita (RPl)

Bulgaria [bʌlˈgɛərɪə] n Bulgaria ❑ **Bulgarian** adj, n búlgaro(-a) m/f

bulge [bʌldʒ] n bulto, protuberancia ♦ vi bombearse, pandearse; (pocket etc): **to ~ (with)** rebosar (de)

bulimia [bəˈlɪmɪə] n bulimia

bulimic [bjuːˈlɪmɪk] adj, n bulímico(-a) m/f

bulk [bʌlk] n masa, mole f; **in ~** (COMM) a granel; **the ~ of** la mayor parte de ❑ **bulky** adj voluminoso, abultado

bull [bʊl] n toro; (male elephant, whale) macho

bulldozer [ˈbʊldəʊzəʳ] n bulldozer m

bullet [ˈbʊlɪt] n bala

bulletin [ˈbʊlɪtɪn] n anuncio, parte m; (journal) boletín m ❑ **bulletin board** n (US) tablón m de anuncios; (COMPUT) tablero de noticias

bullfight [ˈbʊlfaɪt] n corrida de toros ❑ **bullfighter** n torero ❑ **bullfighting** n los toros, el toreo

bully [ˈbʊlɪ] n valentón m, matón m ♦ vt intimidar, tiranizar

bum [bʌm] n (inf: backside) culo; (esp US: tramp) vagabundo

bumblebee [ˈbʌmblbiː] n abejorro

bump [bʌmp] n (blow) tope m, choque m; (jolt) sacudida; (on road etc) bache m; (on head etc) chichón m ♦ vt (strike) chocar contra ▶ **bump into** vt fus chocar contra, tropezar con; (person) topar con ❑ **bumper** n (AUT) parachoques m inv ♦ adj: **bumper crop** or **harvest** cosecha abundante ❑ **bumpy** adj (road) lleno de baches

bun [bʌn] n (BRIT: cake) pastel m; (US: bread) bollo; (of hair) moño

bunch [bʌntʃ] n (of flowers) ramo; (of keys) manojo; (of bananas) piña; (of people) grupo; (pej) pandilla; **bunches** npl (in hair) coletas fpl

bundle [ˈbʌndl] n bulto, fardo; (of sticks) haz m; (of papers) legajo ♦ vt (also: ~ up) atar, envolver; **to ~ sth/sb into** meter algo/a algn precipitadamente en

bungalow [ˈbʌŋgələʊ] n bungalow m, chalé m

bungee jumping [ˈbʌndʒiːˈdʒʌmpɪŋ] n puenting m, banyi m

bunion [ˈbʌnjən] n juanete m

bunk [bʌŋk] n litera ❑ **bunk beds** npl literas fpl

bunker [ˈbʌŋkəʳ] n (coal store) carbonera; (MIL) refugio; (GOLF) bunker m

bunny [ˈbʌnɪ] n (inf: also: ~ **rabbit**) conejito

buoy [bɔɪ] n boya ❑ **buoyant** adj (ship) capaz de flotar; (economy) boyante; (person) optimista

burden [ˈbɜːdn] n carga ♦ vt cargar

bureau [bjʊəˈrəʊ] n (pl **bureaux**) n (BRIT: writing desk) escritorio, buró m; (US: chest of drawers) cómoda; (office) oficina, agencia

bureaucracy [bjuə'rɔkrəsɪ] n burocracia

bureaucrat ['bjuərəkræt] n burócrata m/f

bureau de change [-də'ʃɔʒ] (pl **bureaux de change**) n caja f de cambio

bureaux ['bjuərəuz] npl of **bureau**

burger ['bɜːgə] n hamburguesa

burglar ['bɜːglə] n ladrón(-ona) m/f ❑ **burglar alarm** n alarma f antirrobo ❑ **burglary** n robo con allanamiento, robo de una casa

burial ['bɛrɪəl] n entierro

burn [bɜːn] (pt, pp **burned** or **burnt**) vt quemar; (house) incendiar ♦ vi quemarse, arder; incendiarse; (sting) escocer ♦ n quemadura ▸ **burn down** vt incendiar ▸ **burn out** vt (writer etc): **to burn o.s. out** agotarse ❑ **burning** adj (building etc) en llamas; (hot: sand etc) abrasador(a); (ambition) ardiente

Burns' Night [bɜːnz-] n see **recuadro**

BURNS' NIGHT

Cada veinticinco de enero los escoceses celebran la llamada **Burns' Night** (noche de Burns), en honor al poeta escocés Robert Burns (1759-1796). Es tradición hacer una cena en la que, al son de la música de la gaita escocesa, se sirve "haggis", plato tradicional de asadura de cordero cocida en el estómago del animal, acompañado de nabos y puré de patatas. Durante la misma se recitan poemas del autor y varios discursos conmemorativos de carácter festivo.

---

burnt [bɜːnt] pt, pp of **burn**

burp [bɜːp] (inf) n eructo ♦ vi eructar

burrow ['bʌrəu] n madriguera ♦ vi hacer una madriguera; (rummage) hurgar

burst [bɜːst] (pt, pp ~) vt reventar; (river: banks etc) romper ♦ vi reventarse; (tyre) pincharse ♦ n (of gunfire) ráfaga; (also: ~ **pipe**) reventón m ▸ **a ~ of energy/**

speed/enthusiasm una explosión de energía/un ímpetu de velocidad/un arranque de entusiasmo; **to ~ into flames** estallar en llamas; **to ~ out laughing** soltar la carcajada; **to ~ out crying** deshacerse en lágrimas; **to ~ open** abrirse de golpe; **to be bursting with** (container) estar lleno a rebosar de; (: person) reventar por o de ❑ **burst into** vt fus (room etc) irrumpir en

bury ['bɛrɪ] vt enterrar; (body) enterrar, sepultar

bus [bʌs] (pl **buses**) n autobús m ❑ **bus conductor** n cobrador(a) m/f

bush [buʃ] n arbusto; (scrub land) monte m; **to beat about the ~** andar(se) con rodeos

business ['bɪznɪs] n (matter) asunto; (trading) comercio, negocios mpl; (firm) empresa, casa; (occupation) oficio; **to be away on ~** estar en viaje de negocios; **it's my ~ to ...** me toca o corresponde ...; **it's none of my ~** yo no tengo nada que ver; **he means ~** habla en serio ❑ **business class** n (Aer) clase f preferente ❑ **businesslike** adj eficiente ❑ **businessman** (irreg) n hombre m de negocios ❑ **business trip** n viaje m de negocios ❑ **businesswoman** (irreg) n mujer f de negocios

busker ['bʌskə] n (BRIT) músico(-a) ambulante

bus: **bus pass** n bonobús m ❑ **bus shelter** n parada cubierta ❑ **bus station** n estación f de autobuses ❑ **bus-stop** n parada de autobús

bust [bʌst] n (ANAT) pecho; (sculpture) busto ♦ adj (inf: broken) roto, estropeado; **to go ~** quebrar

bustling ['bʌslɪŋ] adj (town) animado, bullicioso

busy ['bɪzɪ] adj ocupado, atareado; (shop, street) concurrido, animado; (TEL: line) comunicando ♦ vt: **to ~ o.s. with** ocuparse en ❑ **busy signal** (US) n (TEL) señal f de comunicado

but

KEYWORD

[bʌt] *conj*

1 pero; **he's not very bright, but he's hard-working** no es muy inteligente, pero es trabajador

2 (*in direct contradiction*) sino; **he's not English but French** no es inglés sino francés; **he didn't sing but he shouted** no cantó sino que gritó

3 (*showing disagreement, surprise etc*): **but that's far too expensive!** ¡pero eso es carísimo!; **but it does work!** ¡(pero) sí que funciona!

♦ *prep* (*apart from, except*) menos, salvo; **we've had nothing but trouble** no hemos tenido más que problemas; **no-one but him can do it** nadie más que él puede hacerlo; **who but a lunatic would do such a thing?** ¡sólo un loco haría una cosa así!; **but for you/your help** si no fuera por ti/tu ayuda; **anything but that** cualquier cosa menos eso

♦ *adv* (*just, only*): **she's but a child** no es más que una niña; **had I but known** si lo hubiera sabido; **I can but try** al menos lo puedo intentar; **it's all but finished** está casi acabado

butcher ['bʊtʃə'] *n* carnicero ♦ *vt* hacer una carnicería con; (*cattle etc*) matar ❑ **butcher's (shop)** *n* carnicería

butler ['bʌtlə'] *n* mayordomo

butt [bʌt] *n* (*barrel*) tonel *m*; (*of gun*) culata; (*of cigarette*) colilla; (*BRIT: fig: target*) blanco ♦ *vt* dar cabezadas contra, top(et)ar

butter ['bʌtə'] *n* mantequilla ♦ *vt* untar con mantequilla ❑ **buttercup** *n* botón *m* de oro

butterfly ['bʌtəflaɪ] *n* mariposa; (*SWIMMING: also:* ~ **stroke**) braza de mariposa

buttocks ['bʌtəks] *npl* nalgas *fpl*

button ['bʌtn] *n* botón *m*; (*US*) placa, chapa ♦ *vt* (*also:* ~ **up**) abotonar, abrochar ♦ *vi* abrocharse

buy [baɪ] (*pt, pp* **bought**) *vt* comprar ♦ *n* compra; **to ~ sb sth/sth from sb** comprarle algo a algn; **to ~ sb a drink** invitar a algn a tomar algo ► **buy out** *vt* (*partner*) comprar la parte de ► **buy up** *vt* (*property*) acaparar; (*stock*) comprar todas las existencias de ❑ **buyer** *n* comprador(a) *m/f*

buzz [bʌz] *n* zumbido; (*inf: phone call*) llamada (por teléfono) ♦ *vi* zumbar ❑ **buzzer** *n* timbre *m*

by

KEYWORD

[baɪ] *prep*

1 (*referring to cause, agent*) por; de; **killed by lightning** muerto por un relámpago; **a painting by Picasso** un cuadro de Picasso

2 (*referring to method, manner, means*): **by bus/car/train** en autobús/coche/tren; **to pay by cheque** pagar con un cheque; **by moonlight/candlelight** a la luz de la luna/una vela; **by saving hard he ...** ahorrando ...

3 (*via, through*) por; **we came by Dover** vinimos por Dover

4 (*close to, past*): **the house by the river** la casa junto al río; **she rushed by me** pasó a mi lado como una exhalación; **I go by the post office every day** paso por delante de Correos todos los días

5 (*time: not later than*) para; (: *during*): **by daylight** de día; **by 4 o'clock** para las cuatro; **by this time tomorrow** mañana a estas horas; **by the time I**

got here it was too late cuando llegué ya era demasiado tarde
6 (*amount*): **by the metre/kilo** por metro/kilo; **paid by the hour** pagado por hora
7 (*MATH, measure*): **to divide/multiply by 3** dividir/multiplicar por 3; **a room 3 metres by 4** una habitación de 3 metros por 4; **it's broader by a metre** es un metro más ancho
8 (*according to*) según, de acuerdo con; **it's three by my watch** según mi reloj, son las tres; **it's all right by me** por mí, está bien
9: (**all**) **by oneself** *etc* todo solo; **he did it (all) by himself** lo hizo él solo; **he was standing by himself in a corner** estaba de pie solo en un rincón
10: **by the way** a propósito, por cierto; **this wasn't my idea, by the way** pues, no fue idea mía
♦ *adv*
11 *see* **go, pass** *etc*
12: **by and** finalmente; **they'll come back by and by** acabarán volviendo; **by and large** en líneas generales, en general

bye(-bye) ['baɪ('baɪ)] *excl* adiós, hasta luego ◻ **by-election** (*BRIT*) *n* elección *f* parcial
bypass ['baɪpɑːs] *n* carretera de circunvalación; (*MED*) operación *f* de by-pass *m* ♦ *vt* evitar
byte [baɪt] *n* (*COMPUT*) byte *m*, octeto

C, c

C [siː] *n* (*MUS*) do *m*
cab [kæb] *n* taxi *m*; (*of truck*) cabina

cabaret ['kæbəreɪ] *n* cabaret *m*
cabbage ['kæbɪdʒ] *n* col *f*, berza
cabin ['kæbɪn] *n* cabaña; (*on ship*) camarote *m*; (*on plane*) cabina ◻ **cabin crew** *n* tripulación *f* de cabina
cabinet ['kæbɪnɪt] *n* (*POL*) consejo de ministros; (*furniture*) armario; (*also:* **display ~**) vitrina ◻ **cabinet minister** *n* ministro(-a) (del gabinete)
cable ['keɪbl] *n* cable *m* ♦ *vt* cablegrafiar ◻ **cable car** *n* teleférico ◻ **cable television** *n* televisión *f* por cable
cactus ['kæktəs] *n* (*pl* **cacti**) *n* cacto
café ['kæfeɪ] *n* café *m*
cafeteria [kæfɪ'tɪərɪə] *n* cafetería
caffein(e) ['kæfiːn] *n* cafeína
cage [keɪdʒ] *n* jaula
cagoule [kə'guːl] *n* chubasquero
cake [keɪk] *n* (*CULIN: large*) tarta; (*: small*) pastel *m*; (*of soap*) pastilla
calcium ['kælsɪəm] *n* calcio
calculate ['kælkjuleɪt] *vt* calcular ◻ **calculation** [-'leɪʃən] *n* cálculo, cómputo ◻ **calculator** *n* calculadora
calendar ['kæləndə*] *n* calendario
calf [kɑːf] *n* (*pl* **calves**) *n* (*of cow*) ternero, becerro; (*of other animals*) cría; (*also:* **calfskin**) piel *f* de becerro; (*ANAT*) pantorrilla
calibre ['kælɪbə*] (*US* **caliber**) *n* calibre *m*
call [kɔːl] *vt* llamar; (*meeting*) convocar ♦ *vi* (*shout*) llamar; (*TEL*) llamar (por teléfono); (*visit: also:* **~ in**, **~ round**) hacer una visita ♦ *n* llamada; (*of bird*) canto; **to be called** llamarse; **on ~** (*on duty*) de guardia ◻ **call back** *vi* (*return*) volver; (*TEL*) volver a llamar ▶ **call for** *vt fus* (*demand*) pedir, exigir; (*fetch*) pasar a recoger ▶ **call in** *vt* (*doctor, expert, police*) llamar ▶ **call off** *vt* (*cancel: meeting, race*) cancelar; (*: deal*) anular; (*: strike*) desconvocar ▶ **call on** *vt fus* (*visit*) visitar; (*turn to*) acudir a

▶ **call out** *vi* gritar ▶ **call up** *vt* (MIL) llamar al servicio militar; (TEL) llamar
❏ **callbox** (BRIT) *n* cabina telefónica
❏ **call centre** (US **call center**) *n* centro de atención al cliente ▶ **caller** *n* visita; (TEL) usuario(-a)

callous ['kæləs] *adj* insensible, cruel

calm [kɑːm] *adj* tranquilo; (sea) liso, en calma ♦ *n* calma, tranquilidad *f* ♦ *vt* calmar, tranquilizar ▶ **calm down** *vi* calmarse, tranquilizarse ♦ *vt* calmar, tranquilizar ❏ **calmly** ['kɑːmlɪ] *adv* tranquilamente, con calma

Calor gas® ['kælə'-] *n* butano

calorie ['kælərɪ] *n* caloría

calves [kɑːvz] *npl of* **calf**

camcorder ['kæmkɔːdə'] *n* videocámara

came [keɪm] *pt of* **come**

camel ['kæməl] *n* camello

camera ['kæmərə] *n* máquina fotográfica; (CINEMA, TV) cámara; **in ~** (LAW) a puerta cerrada ❏ **cameraman** (irreg) *n* cámara *m*

camouflage ['kæməflɑːʒ] *n* camuflaje *m* ♦ *vt* camuflar

camp [kæmp] *n* campamento, camping *m*; (MIL) campamento; (for prisoners) campo; (fig: faction) bando ♦ *vi* acampar ♦ *adj* afectado, afeminado

campaign [kæm'peɪn] *n* (MIL, POL etc) campaña ♦ *vi* hacer campaña
❏ **campaigner** *n*: **campaigner for** defensor(a) *m/f* de

camp: campbed (BRIT) *n* cama de campaña ❏ **camper** *n* campista *mf*; (vehicle) caravana ❏ **campground** (US) *n* camping *m*, campamento
❏ **camping** *n* camping *m*; **to go camping** hacer camping ❏ **campsite** *n* camping *m*

campus ['kæmpəs] *n* ciudad *f* universitaria

can¹ [kæn] *n* (of oil, water) bidón *m*; (tin) lata, bote *m* ♦ *vt* enlatar

can²

KEYWORD

[kæn] (negative **cannot**, **can't**, conditional and pt **could**) aux vb

1 (be able to) poder; **you can do it if you try** puedes hacerlo si lo intentas; **I can't see you** no te veo

2 (know how to) saber; **I can swim/ play tennis/drive** sé nadar/jugar al tenis/conducir; **can you speak French?** ¿hablas or sabes hablar francés?

3 (may) poder; **can I use your phone?** ¿me dejas or puedo usar tu teléfono?

4 (expressing disbelief, puzzlement etc): **it can't be true!** ¡no puede ser (verdad)!; **what CAN he want?** ¿qué querrá?

5 (expressing possibility, suggestion etc): **he could be in the library** podría estar en la biblioteca; **she could have been delayed** pudo haberse retrasado

Canada ['kænədə] *n* (el) Canadá
❏ **Canadian** [kə'neɪdɪən] *adj*, *n* canadiense *mf*

canal [kə'næl] *n* canal *m*

canary [kə'nɛərɪ] *n* canario

Canary Islands [kə'nɛərɪ'aɪləndz] *npl*: **the ~** (las Islas) Canarias

cancel ['kænsəl] *vt* cancelar; (train) suprimir; (cross out) tachar, borrar
❏ **cancellation** [-'leɪʃən] *n* cancelación *f*; supresión *f*

Cancer ['kænsə'] *n* (ASTROLOGY) Cáncer *m*

cancer ['kænsə'] *n* cáncer *m*

candidate ['kændɪdeɪt] *n* candidato(-a)

candle ['kændl] *n* vela; (in church) cirio
❏ **candlestick** *n* (single) candelero; (low) palmatoria; (bigger, ornate) candelabro

candy ['kændɪ] n azúcar m cande; (US) caramelo ❏ **candy bar** (US) n barrita (dulce) ❏ **candyfloss** (BRIT) n algodón m (azucarado)

cane [keɪn] n (BOT) caña; (stick) vara, palmeta; (for furniture) mimbre f ♦ vt (BRIT: SCOL) castigar (con vara)

canister ['kænɪstə*] n bote m, lata; (of gas) bombona

cannabis ['kænəbɪs] n marijuana

canned [kænd] adj en lata, de lata

cannon ['kænən] (pl ~ or **cannons**) n cañón m

cannot ['kænɔt] = **can not**

canoe [kə'nuː] n canoa; (SPORT) piragua ❏ **canoeing** n piragüismo

canon ['kænən] n (clergyman) canónigo; (standard) canon m

can-opener ['kænəʊpnə*] n abrelatas m inv

can't [kɑːnt] = **can not**

canteen [kæn'tiːn] n (eating place) cantina; (BRIT: of cutlery) juego

canter ['kæntə*] vi ir a medio galope

canvas ['kænvəs] n (material) lona; (painting) lienzo; (NAUT) velas fpl

canvass ['kænvəs] vt (POL): **to ~ for** solicitar votos por ♦ vt (COMM) sondear

canyon ['kænjən] n cañón m

cap [kæp] n (hat) gorra; (of pen) capuchón m; (of bottle) tapa, tapón m; (contraceptive) diafragma m; (for toy gun) cápsula ♦ vt (outdo) superar; (limit) recortar

capability [keɪpə'bɪlɪtɪ] n capacidad f

capable ['keɪpəbl] adj capaz

capacity [kə'pæsɪtɪ] n capacidad f; (position) calidad f

cape [keɪp] n capa; (GEO) cabo

caper ['keɪpə*] n (CULIN: gen pl) alcaparra; (prank) broma

capital ['kæpɪtl] n (also: ~ **city**) capital f; (money) capital m; (also: ~ **letter**) mayúscula ❏ **capitalism** n capitalismo ❏ **capitalist** adj, n

capitalista mf ❏ **capital punishment** n pena de muerte

Capitol ['kæpɪtl] n see **recuadro**

CAPITOL

El Capitolio (**Capitol**) es el edificio del Congreso (**Congress**) de los Estados Unidos, situado en la ciudad de Washington. Por extensión, también se suele llamar así al edificio en el que tienen lugar las sesiones parlamentarias de la cámara de representantes de muchos de los estados.

Capricorn ['kæprɪkɔːn] n Capricornio

capsize [kæp'saɪz] vt volcar, hacer zozobrar ♦ vi volcarse, zozobrar

capsule ['kæpsjuːl] n cápsula

captain ['kæptɪn] n capitán m

caption ['kæpʃən] n (heading) título; (to picture) leyenda

captivity [kæp'tɪvɪtɪ] n cautiverio

capture ['kæptʃə*] vt prender, apresar; (animal, COMPUT) capturar; (place) tomar; (attention) captar, llamar ♦ n apresamiento; captura; toma; (data capture) formulación f de datos

car [kɑː*] n coche m, carro (LAm), automóvil m; (US RAIL) vagón m

carafe [kə'ræf] n jarra

caramel ['kærəməl] n caramelo

carat ['kærət] n quilate m

caravan ['kærəvæn] n (BRIT) caravana, ruló f; (in desert) caravana ❏ **caravan site** (BRIT) n camping m para caravanas

carbohydrate [kɑːbəʊ'haɪdreɪt] n hidrato de carbono; (food) fécula

carbon ['kɑːbən] n carbono ❏ **carbon dioxide** n dióxido de carbono, anhídrido carbónico ❏ **carbon monoxide** n monóxido de carbono

car boot sale n mercadillo organizado en un aparcamiento, en el que se exponen las mercancías en el maletero del coche

carburettor [ka:bjuˈrɛtə] (*US* **carburetor**) *n* carburador *m*

card [ka:d] *n* (*material*) cartulina; (*index card etc*) ficha; (*playing card*) carta, naipe *m*; (*visiting card, greetings card etc*) tarjeta ◆ **cardboard** *n* cartón *m* ❏ **card game** *n* juego de naipes or cartas

cardigan [ˈka:dɪgən] *n* rebeca

cardinal [ˈka:dɪnl] *adj* (*importance, principal*) esencial ◆ *n* cardenal *m*

cardphone [ˈka:dfəun] *n* cabina que funciona con tarjetas telefónicas

care [kɛə] *n* cuidado; (*worry*) inquietud *f*; (*charge*) custodia ◆ *vi*: **to ~ about** (*person, animal*) tener cariño a; (*thing, idea*) preocuparse por; **~ of** en casa de, al cuidado de; **in sb's ~** a cargo de algn; **to take ~** to cuidarse de, tener cuidado de; **to take ~ of** cuidar; (*problem etc*) ocuparse de; **I don't ~** no me importa; **I couldn't ~ less** eso me trae sin cuidado ▶ **care for** *vt fus* cuidar a; (*like*) querer

career [kəˈrɪə] *n* profesión *f*; (*in work, school*) carrera ◆ *vi* (*also*: **~ along**) correr a toda velocidad

care: **carefree** *adj* despreocupado ❏ **careful** *adj* cuidadoso; (*cautious*) cauteloso; **(be) careful!** ¡ten cuidado! ❏ **carefully** *adv* con cuidado, cuidadosamente; con cautela ❏ **caregiver** (*US*) *n* (*professional*) enfermero(-a) *m/f*; (*unpaid*) persona que cuida a un pariente o vecino ❏ **careless** *adj* descuidado; (*heedless*) poco atento ❏ **carelessness** *n* descuido, falta de atención ❏ **carer** [ˈkɛərə] *n* (*professional*) enfermero(-a) *m/f*; (*unpaid*) persona que cuida a un pariente o vecino ❏ **caretaker** *n* portero(-a), conserje *mf*

car-ferry [ˈka:fɛrɪ] *n* transbordador *m* para coches

cargo [ˈka:gəu] (*pl* **cargoes**) *n* cargamento, carga

car hire *n* alquiler *m* de automóviles

Caribbean [kærɪˈbi:ən] *n*: **the ~ (Sea)** el (Mar) Caribe

caring [ˈkɛərɪŋ] *adj* humanitario; (*behaviour*) afectuoso

carnation [ka:ˈneɪʃən] *n* clavel *m*

carnival [ˈka:nɪvəl] *n* carnaval *m*; (*US: funfair*) parque *m* de atracciones

carol [ˈkærəl] *n*: **(Christmas) ~** villancico

carousel [kærəˈsɛl] (*US*) *n* tiovivo, caballitos *mpl*

carpenter [ˈka:pɪntə] *n* carpintero(-a)

carpet [ˈka:pɪt] *n* alfombra; (*fitted*) moqueta ◆ *vt* alfombrar

car rental (*US*) *n* alquiler *m* de coches

carriage [ˈkærɪdʒ] *n* (*BRIT RAIL*) vagón *m*; (*horse-drawn*) coche *m*; (*of goods*) transporte *m*; (*: cost*) porte *m*, flete *m* ❏ **carriageway** (*BRIT*) *n* (*part of road*) calzada

carrier [ˈkærɪə] *n* (*transport company*) transportista, empresa de transportes; (*MED*) portador *m* ❏ **carrier bag** (*BRIT*) *n* bolsa de papel or plástico

carrot [ˈkærət] *n* zanahoria

carry [ˈkærɪ] *vt* (*person*) llevar; (*transport*) transportar; (*involve: responsibilities etc*) entrañar, implicar; (*MED*) ser portador de ◆ *vi* (*sound*) oírse; **to get carried away** (*fig*) entusiasmarse ▶ **carry on** *vi* (*continue*) seguir (adelante), continuar ◆ *vt* proseguir, continuar ▶ **carry out** *vt* (*orders*) cumplir; (*investigation*) llevar a cabo, realizar

cart [ka:t] *n* carro, carreta ◆ *vt* (*inf: transport*) acarrear

carton [ˈka:tən] *n* (*box*) caja (de cartón); (*of milk etc*) bote *m* or tarro; (*of yogurt*) tarrina

cartoon [ka:ˈtu:n] *n* (*PRESS*) caricatura; (*comic strip*) tira cómica; (*film*) dibujos *mpl* animados

cartridge [ˈkɑːtrɪdʒ] n cartucho; (of pen) recambio

carve [kɑːv] vt (meat) trinchar; (wood, stone) cincelar, esculpir; (initials etc) grabar ❑ **carving** n (object) escultura; (design) talla; (art) tallado

car wash n lavado de coches

case [keɪs] n (container) caja; (MED) caso; (for jewels etc) estuche m; (LAW) causa, proceso; (BRIT: also: **suitcase**) maleta; **in ~ of** en caso de; **in any ~** en todo caso; **just in ~** por si acaso

cash [kæʃ] n dinero en efectivo, dinero contante ♦ vt cobrar, hacer efectivo; **to pay (in) ~** pagar al contado; **~ on delivery** cóbrese al entregar ❑ **cashback** n (discount) devolución f; (at supermarket etc) retirada de dinero en efectivo de un establecimiento donde se ha pagado con tarjeta; también dinero retirado ❑ **cash card** n tarjeta f dinero ❑ **cash desk** (BRIT) n caja ❑ **cash dispenser** n cajero automático

cashew [kæˈʃuː] n (also: **~ nut**) anacardo

cashier [kæˈʃɪə] n cajero(-a)

cashmere [ˈkæʃmɪə] n cachemira

cash point n cajero automático

cash register n caja

casino [kəˈsiːnəu] n casino

casket [ˈkɑːskɪt] n cofre m, estuche m; (US: coffin) ataúd m

casserole [ˈkæsərəul] n (food, pot) cazuela

cassette [kæˈset] n casete f ❑ **cassette player**, **cassette recorder** n casete m

cast [kɑːst] n (pt, pp ~) vt (throw) echar, arrojar, lanzar; (glance, eyes) dirigir; (THEATRE): **to ~ sb as Othello** dar a algn el papel de Otelo ♦ vi (FISHING) lanzar ♦ n (THEATRE) reparto; (also: **plaster ~**) vaciado; **to ~ one's vote** votar; **to ~ doubt on** suscitar dudas acerca de ► **cast off** vi (NAUT) desamarrar; (KNITTING) cerrar (los puntos)

castanets [kæstəˈnets] npl castañuelas fpl

caster sugar [ˈkɑːstə-] (BRIT) n azúcar m extrafino

Castile [kæsˈtiːl] n Castilla ❑ **Castilian** adj, n castellano(-a) m/f

cast-iron [ˈkɑːstaɪən] adj (lit) (hecho) de hierro fundido; (fig: case) irrebatible

castle [ˈkɑːsl] n castillo; (CHESS) torre f

casual [ˈkæʒjul] adj fortuito; (irregular: work etc) eventual, temporero; (unconcerned) despreocupado; (clothes) informal

⚠ Be careful not to translate **casual** by the Spanish word casual.

casualty [ˈkæʒjultɪ] n víctima, herido; (dead) muerto; (MED: department) urgencias fpl

cat [kæt] n gato; (big cat) felino

Catalan [ˈkætəlæn] adj, n catalán(-ana) m/f

catalogue [ˈkætəlɔg] (US **catalog**) n catálogo ♦ vt catalogar

Catalonia [kætəˈləunɪə] n Cataluña

catalytic converter [kætəˈlɪtɪkənˈvɜːtə] n catalizador m

cataract [ˈkætərækt] n (MED) cataratas fpl

catarrh [kəˈtɑː] n catarro

catastrophe [kəˈtæstrəfi] n catástrofe f

catch [kætʃ] (pt, pp **caught**) vt coger (SP), agarrar (LAm); (arrest) detener; (grasp) asir; (breath) contener; (surprise: person) sorprender; (attract: attention) captar; (hear) oír; (MED) contagiarse de, coger; (also: **~ up**) alcanzar ♦ vi (fire) encenderse; (in brambles etc) enredarse ♦ n (fish etc) pesca; (act of catching) cogida; (hidden problem) dificultad f; (game) pilla-pilla; (of lock) pestillo, cerradura; **to ~ fire** encenderse; **to ~ sight of** divisar ► **catch up** vi (fig) ponerse al día ❑ **catching** [ˈkætʃɪŋ] adj (MED) contagioso

category ['kætɪgərɪ] n categoría, clase f

cater ['keɪtə] vi: to ~ **for** (BRIT) abastecer a; (needs) atender a; (COMM: parties etc) proveer comida a

caterpillar ['kætəpɪlə] n oruga, gusano

cathedral [kə'θiːdrəl] n catedral f

Catholic ['kæθəlɪk] adj, n (REL) católico(-a) m/f

Catseye® ['kæts'aɪ] (BRIT) n (AUT) catafoto

cattle ['kætl] npl ganado

catwalk ['kætwɔːk] n pasarela

caught [kɔːt] pt, pp of **catch**

cauliflower ['kɒlɪflaʊə] n coliflor f

cause [kɔːz] n causa, motivo, razón f; (principle: also POL) causa ♦ vt causar

caution ['kɔːʃən] n cautela, prudencia; (warning) advertencia, amonestación f ♦ vt amonestar □ **cautious** adj cauteloso, prudente, precavido

cave [keɪv] n cueva, caverna ▶ **cave in** vi (roof etc) derrumbarse, hundirse

caviar(e) ['kævɪɑː] n caviar m

cavity ['kævɪtɪ] n hueco, cavidad f

cc abbr (= cubic centimetres) c.c.; (= carbon copy) copia hecha con papel del carbón

CCTV n abbr (= closed-circuit television) circuito cerrado de televisión

CD n abbr (= compact disc) DC m; (player) (reproductor m de) disco compacto □ **CD player** n reproductor m de discos compactos □ **CD-ROM** [siːdiː'rɒm] n abbr CD-ROM m

cease [siːs] vt, vi cesar □ **ceasefire** n alto m el fuego

cedar ['siːdə] n cedro

ceilidh ['keɪlɪ] n baile con música y danzas tradicionales escocesas o irlandesas

ceiling ['siːlɪŋ] n techo; (fig) límite m

celebrate ['selɪbreɪt] vt celebrar ♦ vi divertirse □ **celebration** [-'breɪʃən] n fiesta, celebración f

celebrity [sɪ'lebrɪtɪ] n celebridad f

celery ['selərɪ] n apio

cell [sel] n celda; (BIOL) célula; (ELEC) elemento

cellar ['selə] n sótano; (for wine) bodega

cello ['tʃeləʊ] n violoncelo

Cellophane® ['seləfeɪn] n celofán m

cellphone ['selfəʊn] n teléfono celular

Celsius ['selsɪəs] adj centígrado

Celtic ['keltɪk] adj celta

cement [sə'ment] n cemento

cemetery ['semɪtrɪ] n cementerio

censor ['sensə] n censor m ♦ vt (cut) censurar □ **censorship** n censura

census ['sensəs] n censo

cent [sent] n (unit of dollar) centavo, céntimo; (unit of euro) céntimo; see also **per**

centenary [sen'tiːnərɪ] n centenario

centennial [sen'tenɪəl] (US) n centenario

center ['sentə] (US) = **centre**

centi... [sentɪ] prefix: **centigrade** adj centígrado □ **centimetre** (US **centimeter**) n centímetro □ **centipede** ['sentɪpiːd] n ciempiés m inv

central ['sentrəl] adj central; (of house etc) céntrico □ **Central America** n Centroamérica □ **central heating** n calefacción f central □ **central reservation** n (BRIT AUT) mediana

centre ['sentə] (US **center**) n centro; (fig) núcleo ♦ vt centrar □ **centre-forward** n (SPORT) delantero centro □ **centre-half** n (SPORT) medio centro

century ['sentʃʊrɪ] n siglo; **20th ~** siglo veinte

CEO n abbr = **chief executive officer**

ceramic [sɪ'ræmɪk] adj cerámico

cereal ['sɪərɪəl] n cereal m

ceremony ['serɪmənɪ] n ceremonia; **to stand on ~** hacer ceremonias, estar de cumplido

certain [ˈsɜːtən] *adj* seguro; (*person*): **a ~ Mr Smith** un tal Sr Smith; (*particular, some*) cierto; **for ~** a ciencia cierta ❑ **certainly** *adv* (*undoubtedly*) ciertamente; (*of course*) desde luego, por supuesto ❑ **certainty** *n* certeza, certidumbre *f*, seguridad *f*; (*inevitability*) certeza

certificate [səˈtɪfɪkɪt] *n* certificado

certify [ˈsɜːtɪfaɪ] *vt* certificar; (*award diploma to*) conceder un diploma a; (*declare insane*) declarar loco

cf. *abbr* (= *compare*) cfr

CFC *n abbr* (= *chlorofluorocarbon*) CFC *m*

chain [tʃeɪn] *n* cadena; (*of mountains*) cordillera; (*of events*) sucesión *f* ♦ *vt* (*also:* **~ up**) encadenar ❑ **chain-smoke** *vi* fumar un cigarrillo tras otro

chair [tʃeəʳ] *n* silla; (*armchair*) sillón *m*, butaca; (*of university*) cátedra; (*of meeting etc*) presidencia ♦ *vt* (*meeting*) presidir ❑ **chairlift** *n* telesilla ❑ **chairman** (*irreg*) *n* presidente *m* ❑ **chairperson** *n* presidente(-a) *m/f* ❑ **chairwoman** (*irreg*) *n* presidenta

chalet [ˈʃæleɪ] *n* chalet *m* (de madera)

chalk [tʃɔːk] *n* (GEO) creta; (*for writing*) tiza, gis *m* (MEX) ❑ **chalkboard** (US) *n* pizarrón (LAm), pizarra (SP)

challenge [ˈtʃælɪndʒ] *n* desafío, reto ♦ *vt* desafiar, retar; (*statement, right*) poner en duda; **to ~ sb to do sth** retar a algn a que haga algo ❑ **challenging** *adj* exigente; (*tone*) de desafío

chamber [ˈtʃeɪmbəʳ] *n* cámara, sala; (POL) cámara; (BRIT LAW: *gen pl*) despacho; **~ of commerce** cámara de comercio ❑ **chambermaid** *n* camarera

champagne [ʃæmˈpeɪn] *n* champaña *m*, champán *m*

champion [ˈtʃæmpɪən] *n* campeón(-ona) *m/f*; (*of cause*) defensor(a) *m/f* ❑ **championship** *n* campeonato

chance [tʃɑːns] *n* (*opportunity*) ocasión *f*, oportunidad *f*; (*likelihood*) posibilidad *f*; (*risk*) riesgo ♦ *vt* arriesgar, probar ♦ *adj* fortuito, casual; **to ~ it** arriesgarse, intentarlo; **to take a ~** arriesgarse; **by ~** por casualidad

chancellor [ˈtʃɑːnsələʳ] *n* canciller *m* ❑ **Chancellor of the Exchequer** (BRIT) *n* Ministro de Hacienda

chandelier [ʃændəˈlɪəʳ] *n* araña (de luces)

change [tʃeɪndʒ] *vt* cambiar; (*replace*) cambiar, reemplazar; (*gear, clothes, job*) cambiar de; (*transform*) transformar ♦ *vi* cambiar(se); (*change trains*) hacer transbordo; (*traffic lights*) cambiar de color; (*be transformed*): **to ~ into** transformarse en ♦ *n* cambio; (*alteration*) modificación *f*; (*transformation*) transformación *f*; (*of clothes*) muda; (*coins*) suelto, sencillo; (*money returned*) vuelta; **to ~ gear** (AUT) cambiar de marcha; **to ~ one's mind** cambiar de opinión o idea; **for a ~** para variar ♦ **change over** *vi* (*from sth to sth*) cambiar; (*players etc*) cambiar(se) ♦ *vt* cambiar ❑ **changeable** *adj* (*weather*) cambiable ❑ **change machine** *n* máquina de cambio ❑ **changing room** (BRIT) *n* vestuario

channel [ˈtʃænl] *n* (TV) canal *m*; (*of river*) cauce *m*; (*groove*) conducto; (*fig: medium*) medio ♦ *vt* (*river etc*) encauzar; **the (English) C~** el Canal (de la Mancha); **the C~ Islands** las Islas Normandas ❑ **Channel Tunnel** *n*: **the Channel Tunnel** el túnel del Canal de la Mancha, el Eurotúnel

chant [tʃɑːnt] *n* (*of crowd*) gritos *mpl*; (REL) canto ♦ *vt* (*slogan, word*) repetir a gritos

chaos [ˈkeɪɒs] *n* caos *m*

chaotic [keɪˈɒtɪk] *adj* caótico

chap [tʃæp] (BRIT: *inf*) *n* (*man*) tío, tipo

chapel [ˈtʃæpəl] *n* capilla

chapped [tʃæpt] *adj* agrietado

chapter ['tʃæptə] n capítulo

character ['kærɪktə] n carácter m, naturaleza, índole f; (moral strength, personality) carácter m; (in novel, film) personaje m ❏ **characteristic** [-'rɪstɪk] adj característico ♦ n característica ❏ **characterize** ['kærɪktəraɪz] vt caracterizar

charcoal ['tʃɑːkəʊl] n carbón m vegetal; (ART) carboncillo

charge [tʃɑːdʒ] n (LAW) cargo, acusación f; (cost) precio, coste m; (responsibility) cargo ♦ vt (LAW): **to ~ (with)** acusar (de); (battery) cargar; (price) pedir; (customer) cobrar ♦ vi precipitarse; (MIL) cargar, atacar ❏ **charge card** n tarjeta de cuenta ❏ **charger** n (also: **battery charger**) cargador m (de baterías)

charismatic [kærɪz'mætɪk] adj carismático

charity ['tʃærɪtɪ] n caridad f; (organization) sociedad f benéfica; (money, gifts) limosnas fpl ❏ **charity shop** n (BRIT) tienda de artículos de segunda mano que dedica su recaudación a causas benéficas

charm [tʃɑːm] n encanto, atractivo; (talisman) hechizo; (on bracelet) dije m ♦ vt encantar ❏ **charming** adj encantador(a)

chart [tʃɑːt] n (diagram) cuadro; (graph) gráfica; (map) carta de navegación ♦ vt (course) trazar; (progress) seguir; **charts** npl (Top 40): **the charts** = los 40 principales (SP)

charter ['tʃɑːtə] vt (plane) alquilar; (ship) fletar ♦ n (document) carta; (of university, company) estatutos mpl ❏ **chartered accountant** (BRIT) n contable m/f diplomado(-a) ❏ **charter flight** n vuelo chárter

chase [tʃeɪs] vt (pursue) perseguir; (also: **~ away**) ahuyentar ♦ n persecución f

chat [tʃæt] vi (also: **have a ~**) charlar ♦ n charla ▶ **chat up** vt (inf: girl) ligar con, enrollarse con ❏ **chat room** n

(INTERNET) chat m, canal m de charla ❏ **chat show** n (BRIT) n programa m de entrevistas

chatter ['tʃætə] vi (person) charlar; (teeth) castañetear ♦ n (of birds) parloteo; (of people) charla, cháchara

chauffeur ['ʃəʊfə] n chófer m

chauvinist ['ʃəʊvɪnɪst] n (male chauvinist) machista m; (nationalist) chovinista mf

cheap [tʃiːp] adj barato; (joke) de mal gusto; (poor quality) de mala calidad ♦ adv barato ❏ **cheap day return** n billete de ida y vuelta el mismo día ❏ **cheaply** adv barato, a bajo precio

cheat [tʃiːt] vi hacer trampa ♦ vt: **to ~ sb (out of sth)** estafar (algo) a algn ♦ n (person) tramposo(-a) ♦ **cheat on** vt fus engañar

Chechnya [tʃɪtʃ'njɑː] n Chechenia

check [tʃek] vt (examine) controlar; (facts) comprobar; (halt) parar, detener; (restrain) refrenar, restringir ♦ n (inspection) control m, inspección f; (curb) freno; (US: bill) nota, cuenta; (US) = **cheque**; (pattern: gen pl) cuadro ▶ **check in** vi (at hotel) firmar el registro; (at airport) facturar el equipaje ♦ vt (luggage) facturar ▶ **check off** vt (esp US: check) comprobar; (cross off) tachar ▶ **check out** vi (of hotel) marcharse ▶ **check up** vi: **to check up on sth** comprobar algo; **to check up on sb** investigar a algn ❏ **checkbook** (US) = **chequebook** ❏ **checked** adj a cuadros ❏ **checkers** (US) n juego de damas ❏ **check-in** n (also: **check-in desk**: at airport) mostrador m de facturación ❏ **checking account** (US) n cuenta corriente ❏ **checklist** n lista (de control) ❏ **checkmate** n jaque m mate ❏ **checkout** n caja ❏ **checkpoint** n (punto de) control m ❏ **checkroom** (US) n consigna ❏ **checkup** n (MED) reconocimiento general

cheddar [ˈtʃedə] n (also: ~ cheese) queso m cheddar

cheek [tʃiːk] n mejilla; (impudence) descaro; **what a ~!** ¡qué cara! □ **cheekbone** n pómulo □ **cheeky** adj fresco, descarado

cheer [tʃɪə] vt vitorear, aplaudir; (gladden) alegrar, animar ♦ vi dar vivas ♦ n viva m ► **cheer up** vi animarse ♦ vt alegrar, animar □ **cheerful** adj alegre

cheerio [tʃɪərɪˈəu] (BRIT) excl ¡hasta luego!

cheerleader [ˈtʃɪəliːdə] n animador(a) m/f

cheese [tʃiːz] n queso □ **cheeseburger** n hamburguesa con queso □ **cheesecake** n pastel m de queso

chef [ʃef] n jefe(-a) m/f de cocina

chemical [ˈkemɪkəl] adj químico ♦ n producto químico

chemist [ˈkemɪst] n (BRIT: pharmacist) farmacéutico(-a); (scientist) químico(-a) □ **chemistry** n química □ **chemist's (shop)** (BRIT) n farmacia

cheque [tʃek] (US check) n cheque m □ **chequebook** n talonario de cheques (SP), chequera (LAm) □ **cheque card** n tarjeta de cheque

cherry [ˈtʃerɪ] n cereza; (also: ~ tree) cerezo

chess [tʃes] n ajedrez m

chest [tʃest] n (ANAT) pecho; (box) cofre m, cajón m

chestnut [ˈtʃesnʌt] n castaña; (also: ~ tree) castaño

chest of drawers n cómoda

chew [tʃuː] vt mascar, masticar □ **chewing gum** n chicle m

chic [ʃiːk] adj elegante

chick [tʃɪk] n pollito, polluelo; (inf: girl) chica

chicken [ˈtʃɪkɪn] n gallina, pollo; (food) pollo; (inf: coward) gallina mf ► **chicken out** (inf) vi rajarse □ **chickenpox** n varicela

chickpea [ˈtʃɪkpiː] n garbanzo

chief [tʃiːf] n jefe(-a) m/f ♦ adj principal □ **chief executive (officer)** n director(a) m/f general □ **chiefly** adv principalmente

child [tʃaɪld] (pl **children**) n niño(-a); (offspring) hijo(-a) □ **child abuse** n (with violence) malos tratos mpl a niños; (sexual) abuso m sexual de niños □ **child benefit** n (BRIT) subsidio por cada hijo pequeño □ **childbirth** n parto □ **child-care** n cuidado de los niños □ **childhood** n niñez f, infancia □ **childish** adj pueril, aniñado □ **child minder** (BRIT) n madre f de día □ **children** [ˈtʃɪldrən] npl of **child**

Chile [ˈtʃɪlɪ] n Chile m □ **Chilean** adj, n chileno(-a) m/f

chill [tʃɪl] n frío; (MED) resfriado ♦ vt enfriar; (CULIN) congelar ► **chill out** vi (esp US: inf) tranquilizarse

chil(l)i [ˈtʃɪlɪ] (BRIT) n chile m, ají m (SC)

chilly [ˈtʃɪlɪ] adj frío

chimney [ˈtʃɪmnɪ] n chimenea

chimpanzee [tʃɪmpænˈziː] n chimpancé m

chin [tʃɪn] n mentón m, barbilla

China [ˈtʃaɪnə] n China

china [ˈtʃaɪnə] n porcelana; (crockery) loza

Chinese [tʃaɪˈniːz] adj chino ♦ n inv chino(-a) m/f; (LING) chino

chip [tʃɪp] n (gen pl: CULIN: BRIT) patata (SP) o papa (LAm) frita; (: US: also: **potato** ~) patata o papa frita; (of wood) astilla; (of glass, stone) lasca; (at poker) ficha; (COMPUT) chip m ♦ vt (cup, plate) desconchar □ **chip shop** n pescadería (donde se vende principalmente pescado rebozado y patatas fritas)

chiropodist [kɪˈrɔpədɪst] n (BRIT) pedicuro(-a), callista m/f

chisel [ˈtʃɪzl] n (for wood) escoplo; (for stone) cincel m

chives [tʃaɪvz] npl cebollinos mpl

chlorine ['klɔ:ri:n] n cloro

choc-ice ['tʃɒkaɪs] n (BRIT) helado m cubierto de chocolate

chocolate ['tʃɒklɪt] n chocolate m; (sweet) bombón m

choice [tʃɔɪs] n elección f, selección f; (option) opción f; (preference) preferencia ♦ adj escogido

choir ['kwaɪə'] n coro

choke [tʃəʊk] vi ahogarse; (on food) atragantarse ♦ vt estrangular, ahogar; (block): **to be choked with** estar atascado de ♦ n (AUT) estárter m

cholesterol [kə'lestərɒl] n colesterol m

choose [tʃu:z] (pt **chose**, pp **chosen**) vt escoger, elegir; (team) seleccionar; **to ~ to do sth** optar por hacer algo

chop [tʃɒp] vt (wood) cortar, tajar; (CULIN: also: ~ **up**) picar ♦ n (CULIN) chuleta ▶ **chop down** vt (tree) talar ▶ **chop off** vt cortar (de un tajo) ❏ **chopsticks** ['tʃɒpstɪks] npl palillos mpl

chord [kɔ:d] n (MUS) acorde m

chore [tʃɔ:'] n faena, tarea; (routine task) trabajo rutinario

chorus ['kɔ:rəs] n coro; (repeated part of song) estribillo

chose [tʃəʊz] pt of **choose**

chosen ['tʃəʊzn] pp of **choose**

Christ [kraɪst] n Cristo

christen ['krɪsn] vt bautizar ❏ **christening** n bautizo

Christian ['krɪstɪən] adj, n cristiano(-a) m/f ❏ **Christianity** [-ʃɪ'ænɪtɪ] n cristianismo ❏ **Christian name** n nombre m de pila

Christmas ['krɪsməs] n Navidad f; **Merry ~!** ¡Felices Pascuas! ❏ **Christmas card** n crismas m inv, tarjeta de Navidad ❏ **Christmas carol** n villancico m ❏ **Christmas Day** n día m de Navidad ❏ **Christmas Eve** n Nochebuena ❏ **Christmas pudding** n (esp BRIT) pudin m de

Navidad ❏ **Christmas tree** n árbol m de Navidad

chrome [krəʊm] n cromo

chronic ['krɒnɪk] adj crónico

chrysanthemum [krɪ'sænθəməm] n crisantemo

chubby ['tʃʌbɪ] adj regordete

chuck [tʃʌk] (inf) vt lanzar, arrojar; (BRIT: also: ~ **up**) abandonar ▶ **chuck out** vt (person) echar (fuera); (rubbish etc) tirar

chuckle ['tʃʌkl] vi reírse entre dientes

chum [tʃʌm] n compañero(-a)

chunk [tʃʌŋk] n pedazo, trozo

church [tʃə:tʃ] n iglesia ❏ **churchyard** n cementerio

churn [tʃə:n] n (for butter) mantequera; (for milk) lechera

chute [ʃu:t] n (also: **rubbish ~**) vertedero; (for coal etc) rampa de caída

chutney ['tʃʌtnɪ] n condimento a base de frutas de la India

CIA (US) n abbr (= Central Intelligence Agency) CIA f

CID (BRIT) n abbr (= Criminal Investigation Department) = B.I.C. f (SP)

cider ['saɪdə'] n sidra

cigar [sɪ'gɑ:'] n puro

cigarette [sɪgə'ret] n cigarrillo ❏ **cigarette lighter** n mechero

cinema ['sɪnəmə] n cine m

cinnamon ['sɪnəmən] n canela

circle ['sə:kl] n círculo; (in theatre) anfiteatro ♦ vi dar vueltas ♦ vt (surround) rodear, cercar; (move round) dar la vuelta a

circuit ['sə:kɪt] n circuito; (tour) gira; (track) pista; (lap) vuelta

circular ['sə:kjulə'] adj circular ♦ n circular f

circulate ['sə:kjuleɪt] vi circular; (person: at party etc) hablar con los invitados ♦ vt poner en circulación ❏ **circulation** [-'leɪʃən] n circulación f; (of newspaper) tirada

circumstances ['sɜ:kəmstənsɪz] npl circunstancias fpl; (financial condition) situación f económica

circus ['sɜ:kəs] n circo m

cite [saɪt] vt citar

citizen ['sɪtɪzn] n (POL) ciudadano(-a); (of city) vecino(-a), habitante mf ❑ **citizenship** n ciudadanía

citrus fruits ['sɪtrəs] npl agrios mpl

city ['sɪtɪ] n ciudad f; **the C~** centro financiero de Londres ❑ **city centre** (BRIT) n centro de la ciudad ❑ **city technology college** n centro de formación profesional (centro de enseñanza secundaria que da especial importancia a la ciencia y tecnología.)

civic ['sɪvɪk] adj cívico; (authorities) municipal

civil ['sɪvɪl] adj civil; (polite) atento, cortés ❑ **civilian** [sɪ'vɪlɪən] adj civil (no militar) ♦ n civil mf, paisano(-a)

civilization [sɪvɪlaɪ'zeɪʃən] n civilización f

civilized ['sɪvɪlaɪzd] adj civilizado

civil: civil law n derecho civil ❑ **civil rights** npl derechos mpl civiles ❑ **civil servant** n funcionario(-a) del Estado ❑ **Civil Service** n administración f pública ❑ **civil war** n guerra civil

CJD n abbr (= Creutzfeldt-Jakob disease) enfermedad f de Creutzfeldt-Jakob

claim [kleɪm] vt exigir, reclamar; (rights etc) reivindicar; (assert) pretender ♦ vi (for insurance) reclamar ♦ n reclamación f; pretensión f ❑ **claim form** n solicitud f

clam [klæm] n almeja

clamp [klæmp] n abrazadera, grapa ♦ vt (two things together) cerrar fuertemente; (one thing on another) afianzar (con abrazadera); (AUT: wheel) poner el cepo a

clan [klæn] n clan m

clap [klæp] vi aplaudir

claret ['klærət] n burdeos m inv

clarify ['klærɪfaɪ] vt aclarar

clarinet [klærɪ'net] n clarinete m

clarity ['klærɪtɪ] n claridad f

clash [klæʃ] n enfrentamiento; choque m; desacuerdo; estruendo ♦ vi (fight) enfrentarse; (beliefs) chocar; (disagree) estar en desacuerdo; (colours) desentonar; (two events) coincidir

clasp [klɑ:sp] n (hold) apretón m; (of necklace, bag) cierre m ♦ vt apretar; abrazar

class [klɑ:s] n clase f ♦ vt clasificar

classic ['klæsɪk] adj, n clásico ❑ **classical** adj clásico

classification [klæsɪfɪ'keɪʃən] n clasificación f

classify ['klæsɪfaɪ] vt clasificar

classmate ['klɑ:smeɪt] n compañero(-a) de clase

classroom ['klɑ:srʊm] n aula

classy ['klɑ:sɪ] adj (inf) elegante, con estilo

clatter ['klætə] n estrépito ♦ vi hacer ruido or estrépito

clause [klɔ:z] n cláusula; (LING) oración f

claustrophobic [klɔ:strə'fəʊbɪk] adj claustrofóbico; **I feel ~** me entra claustrofobia

claw [klɔ:] n (of cat) uña; (of bird of prey) garra; (of lobster) pinza

clay [kleɪ] n arcilla

clean [kli:n] adj limpio; (record, reputation) bueno, intachable; (joke) decente ♦ vt limpiar; (hands etc) lavar ▶ **clean up** vt limpiar, asear ❑ **cleaner** n (person) asistenta; (substance) producto para la limpieza ❑ **cleaner's** n tintorería ❑ **cleaning** n limpieza

cleanser ['klenzə] n (for face) crema limpiadora

clear [klɪə] adj claro; (road, way) libre; (conscience) limpio, tranquilo; (skin) terso; (sky) despejado ♦ vt (space) despejar, limpiar; (LAW: suspect) absolver; (obstacle) salvar, saltar por encima de; (cheque) aceptar ♦ vi (fog *etc*) despejarse ♦ *adv*: ~ **of** a distancia de; **to ~ the table** recoger *or* levantar la mesa ► **clear away** *vt* (*things, clothes etc*) quitar (de en medio); (*dishes*) retirar ► **clear up** *vt* limpiar; (*mystery*) aclarar, resolver ❑ **clearance** *n* (*removal*) despeje *m*; (*permission*) acreditación *f* ❑ **clear-cut** *adj* bien definido, nítido ❑ **clearing** *n* (*in wood*) claro ❑ **clearly** *adv* claramente; (*evidently*) sin duda ❑ **clearway** (BRIT) *n* carretera donde no se puede parar

clench [klentʃ] *vt* apretar, cerrar

clergy ['klɜːdʒɪ] *n* clero

clerk [klɑːk, (US) klɜːrk] *n* (BRIT) oficinista *mf*; (US) dependiente(-a) *m/f*

clever ['klevər] *adj* (*intelligent*) inteligente, listo; (*skilful*) hábil; (*device, arrangement*) ingenioso

cliché ['kliːʃeɪ] *n* cliché *m*, frase *f* hecha

click [klɪk] *vt* (*tongue*) chasquear; (*heels*) taconear ♦ *vi* (COMPUT) hacer clic; **to ~ on an icon** hacer clic en un icono

client ['klaɪənt] *n* cliente *m/f*

cliff [klɪf] *n* acantilado

climate ['klaɪmɪt] *n* clima *m*

climax ['klaɪmæks] *n* (*of battle, career*) apogeo; (*of film, book*) punto culminante; (*sexual*) orgasmo

climb [klaɪm] *vi* subir; (*plant*) trepar; (*move with effort*): **to ~ over a wall/into a car** trepar a una tapia/subir a un coche ♦ *vt* (*stairs*) subir; (*tree*) trepar a; (*mountain*) escalar ♦ *n* subida ► **climb down** *vi* (*fig*) volverse atrás ❑ **climber** *n* alpinista *mf* (SP, MEX), andinista *mf* (LAm) ❑ **climbing** *n* alpinismo (SP, MEX), andinismo (LAm)

clinch [klɪntʃ] *vt* (*deal*) cerrar; (*argument*) remachar

cling [klɪŋ] (*pt, pp* **clung**) *vi*: **to ~ to** agarrarse a; (*clothes*) pegarse a

Clingfilm® ['klɪŋfɪlm] *n* plástico adherente

clinic ['klɪnɪk] *n* clínica

clip [klɪp] *n* (*for hair*) horquilla; (*also*: **paper ~**) sujetapapeles *m inv*, clip *m*; (TV, CINEMA) fragmento ♦ *vt* (*cut*) cortar; (*also*: ~ **together**) unir ❑ **clipping** *n* (*newspaper*) recorte *m*

cloak [kləʊk] *n* capa, manto ♦ *vt* (*fig*) encubrir, disimular ❑ **cloakroom** *n* guardarropa; (BRIT: WC) lavabo (SP), aseos *mpl* (SP), baño (LAm)

clock [klɒk] *n* reloj *m* ► **clock in** *or* **on** *vi* (*with manual*) fichar, picar; (*start work*) entrar a trabajar ► **clock off** *or* **out** *vi* (*with manual*) fichar *or* picar la salida; (*leave work*) salir del trabajar ❑ **clockwise** *adv* en el sentido de las agujas del reloj ❑ **clockwork** *n* aparato de relojería ♦ *adj* (*toy*) de cuerda

clog [klɒg] *n* zueco, chanclo ♦ *vt* atascar ♦ *vi* (*also*: ~ **up**) atascarse

clone [kləʊn] *n* clon *m* ♦ *vt* clonar

close¹ [kləʊs] *adj* (*near*): ~ **(to)** cerca (de); (*friend*) íntimo; (*connection*) estrecho; (*examination*) detallado, minucioso; (*weather*) bochornoso ♦ *adv* cerca; **~ by, ~ at hand** muy cerca; **to have a ~ shave** (*fig*) escaparse por un pelo

close² [kləʊz] *vt* (*shut*) cerrar; (*end*) concluir, terminar ♦ *vi* (*shop etc*) cerrarse; (*end*) concluirse, terminarse ♦ *n* (*end*) fin *m*, final *m*, conclusión *f* ► **close down** *vi* cerrarse definitivamente ❑ **closed** *adj* (*shop etc*) cerrado

closely ['kləʊslɪ] *adv* (*study*) con detalle; (*watch*) de cerca; (*resemble*) estrechamente

closet ['klɒzɪt] *n* armario

close-up ['kləʊsʌp] *n* primer plano

closing time *n* hora de cierre

closure ['kləʊʒər] *n* cierre *m*

clot [klɒt] *n* (*gen*) coágulo; (*inf: idiot*) imbécil *m/f* ♦ *vi* (*blood*) coagularse

cloth [klɒθ] *n* (*material*) tela, paño; (*rag*) trapo

clothes [kləʊðz] *npl* ropa ◻ **clothes line** *n* cuerda (para tender la ropa) ◻ **clothes peg** (*US* **clothes pin**) *n* pinza

clothing [kləʊðɪŋ] *n* = **clothes**

cloud [klaʊd] *n* nube *f* ► **cloud over** *vi* (*also fig*) nublarse ◻ **cloudy** *adj* nublado, nuboso; (*liquid*) turbio

clove [kləʊv] *n* clavo; ~ **of garlic** diente *m* de ajo

clown [klaʊn] *n* payaso ♦ *vi* (*also*: ~ **about**, ~ **around**) hacer el payaso

club [klʌb] *n* (*society*) club *m*; (*weapon*) porra, cachiporra; (*also*: **golf** ~) palo ♦ *vt* aporrear ♦ *vi*: **to** ~ **together** (*for gift*) comprar entre todos; **clubs** *npl* (*CARDS*) tréboles *mpl* ◻ **club class** *n* (*AVIAT*) clase *f* preferente

clue [kluː] *n* pista; (*in crosswords*) indicación *f*; **I haven't a** ~ no tengo ni idea

clump [klʌmp] *n* (*of trees*) grupo

clumsy [klʌmzɪ] *adj* (*person*) torpe, desmañado; (*tool*) difícil de manejar; (*movement*) desgarbado

clung [klʌŋ] *pt, pp of* **cling**

cluster [klʌstə] *n* grupo ♦ *vi* agruparse, apiñarse

clutch [klʌtʃ] *n* (*AUT*) embrague *m*; (*grasp*): **clutches** garras *fpl* ♦ *vt* asir, agarrar

cm *abbr* (= *centimetre*) cm

Co. *abbr* = **county**, = **company**

c/o *abbr* (= *care of*) c/a, a/c

coach [kəʊtʃ] *n* autocar *m* (*SP*), coche *m* de línea; (*horse-drawn*) coche *m*; (*of train*) vagón *m*, coche *m*; (*SPORT*) entrenador(a) *m/f*, instructor(a) *m/f*; (*tutor*) profesor(a) *m/f* particular ♦ *vt* (*SPORT*) entrenar; (*student*) preparar, enseñar ◻ **coach station** *n* (*BRIT*) estación *f* de autobuses *etc* ◻ **coach trip** *n* excursión *f* en autocar

coal [kəʊl] *n* carbón *m*

coalition [kəʊəˈlɪʃən] *n* coalición *f*

coarse [kɔːs] *adj* basto, burdo; (*vulgar*) grosero, ordinario

coast [kəʊst] *n* costa, litoral *m* ♦ *vi* (*AUT*) ir en punto muerto ◻ **coastal** *adj* costero, costanero ◻ **coastguard** *n* guardacostas *m inv* ◻ **coastline** *n* litoral *m*

coat [kəʊt] *n* abrigo; (*of animal*) pelaje *m*, lana; (*of paint*) mano *f*, capa ♦ *vt* cubrir, revestir ◻ **coat hanger** *n* percha (*SP*), gancho (*LAm*) ◻ **coating** *n* capa, baño

coax [kəʊks] *vt* engatusar

cob [kɔb] *n see* **corn**

cobbled [kɔbld] *adj*: ~ **street** calle *f* empedrada, calle *f* adoquinada

cobweb [kɔbweb] *n* telaraña

cocaine [kəˈkeɪn] *n* cocaína

cock [kɔk] *n* (*rooster*) gallo; (*male bird*) macho *m* ♦ *vt* (*gun*) amartillar ◻ **cockerel** *n* gallito

cockney [kɔknɪ] *n* habitante *m* de ciertos barrios de Londres

cockpit [kɔkpɪt] *n* cabina

cockroach [kɔkrəʊtʃ] *n* cucaracha

cocktail [kɔkteɪl] *n* coctel *m*, cóctel *m*

cocoa [kəʊkəʊ] *n* cacao; (*drink*) chocolate *m*

coconut [kəʊkənʌt] *n* coco

cod [kɔd] *n* bacalao

C.O.D. *abbr* (= *cash on delivery*) C.A.E.

code [kəʊd] *n* código; (*cipher*) clave *f*; (*dialling code*) prefijo; (*post code*) código postal

coeducational [kəʊedjuˈkeɪʃənl] *adj* mixto

coffee [kɔfɪ] *n* café *m* ◻ **coffee bar** *n* (*BRIT*) cafetería ◻ **coffee bean** *n* grano de café ◻ **coffee break** *n* descanso (para tomar café) ◻ **coffee maker** *n* máquina de hacer café, cafetera ◻ **coffeepot** *n* cafetera ◻ **coffee shop** *n* café *m* ◻ **coffee table** *n* mesita (para servir el café)

coffin [kɔfɪn] *n* ataúd *m*

cog [kɔg] n (wheel) rueda dentada; (tooth) diente m

cognac [ˈkɔnjæk] n coñac m

coherent [kəuˈhɪərənt] adj coherente

coil [kɔɪl] n rollo; (ELEC) bobina, carrete m; (contraceptive) espiral f ♦ vt enrollar

coin [kɔɪn] n moneda ♦ vt (word) inventar, idear

coincide [kəuɪnˈsaɪd] vi coincidir; (agree) estar de acuerdo ❑ **coincidence** [kəuˈɪnsɪdəns] n casualidad f

Coke® [kəuk] n Coca-Cola®

coke [kəuk] n (coal) coque m

colander [ˈkɔləndə] n colador m, escurridor m

cold [kəuld] adj frío ♦ n frío; (MED) resfriado; **it's ~** hace frío; **to be ~** (person) tener frío; **to catch (a) ~** resfriarse; **in ~ blood** a sangre fría ❑ **cold sore** n herpes mpl or fpl

coleslaw [ˈkəulslɔ:] n especie de ensalada de col

colic [ˈkɔlɪk] n cólico

collaborate [kəˈlæbəreɪt] vi colaborar

collapse [kəˈlæps] vi hundirse, derrumbarse; (MED) sufrir un colapso ♦ n hundimiento, derrumbamiento; (MED) colapso

collar [ˈkɔlə] n (of coat, shirt) cuello; (for dog etc) collar ❑ **collarbone** n clavícula

colleague [ˈkɔli:g] n colega mf; (at work) compañero(-a)

collect [kəˈlekt] vt (litter, mail etc) recoger; (as a hobby) coleccionar; (BRIT: call and pick up) recoger; (debts, subscriptions etc) recaudar ♦ vi reunirse; (dust) acumularse; **to call ~** (US TEL) llamar a cobro revertido ❑ **collection** [kəˈlekʃən] n colección f; (of mail, for charity) recogida ❑ **collective** [kəˈlektɪv] adj colectivo ❑ **collector** [kəˈlektə] n coleccionista mf

college [ˈkɔlɪdʒ] n colegio mayor; (of agriculture, technology) escuela universitaria

collide [kəˈlaɪd] vi chocar

collision [kəˈlɪʒən] n choque m

cologne [kəˈləun] n (also: **eau de ~**) (agua de) colonia

Colombia [kəˈlɔmbɪə] n Colombia ❑ **Colombian** adj, n colombiano(-a)

colon [ˈkəulən] n (sign) dos puntos; (MED) colon m

colonel [ˈkə:nl] n coronel m

colonial [kəˈləunɪəl] adj colonial

colony [ˈkɔlənɪ] n colonia

colour etc [ˈkʌlə] (US **color** etc) n color m ♦ vt color(e)ar; (dye) teñir; (fig: account) adornar; (: judgement) distorsionar ♦ vi (blush) sonrojarse ▸ **colour in** vt colorear ❑ **colour-blind** adj daltónico ❑ **coloured** adj de color; (photo) en color ❑ **colour film** n película en color ❑ **colourful** adj lleno de color; (story) fantástico; (person) excéntrico ❑ **colouring** n (complexion) tez f; (in food) colorante m ❑ **colour television** n televisión f en color

column [ˈkɔləm] n columna

coma [ˈkəumə] n coma m

comb [kəum] n peine m; (ornamental) peineta f ♦ vt (hair) peinar; (area) registrar a fondo

combat [ˈkɔmbæt] n combate m ♦ vt combatir

combination [kɔmbɪˈneɪʃən] n combinación f

combine [vb kəmˈbaɪn, n ˈkɔmbaɪn] vt combinar; (qualities) reunir ♦ vi combinarse ♦ n (ECON) cartel m

---

come

KEYWORD

[kʌm] (pt **came**, pp **come**) vi

1 (movement towards) venir; **to come running** venir corriendo

2 (arrive) llegar; **he's come here to**

work ha venido aquí para trabajar; **to come home** volver a casa

3 (reach): **to come to** llegar a; **the bill came to £40** la cuenta ascendía a cuarenta libras

4 (occur): **an idea came to me** se me ocurrió una idea

5 (be, become): **to come loose/ undone** etc aflojarse/desabrocharse/ desatarse etc; **I've come to like him** por fin ha llegado a gustarme

▶ **come across** vt fus (person) topar con; (thing) dar con

▶ **come along** vi (BRIT: progress) ir

▶ **come back** vi (return) volver

▶ **come down** vi (price) bajar; (tree, building) ser derribado

▶ **come from** vt fus (place, source) ser de

▶ **come in** vi (visitor) entrar; (train, report) llegar; (fashion) ponerse de moda; (on deal etc) entrar

▶ **come off** vi (button) soltarse, desprenderse; (attempt) salir bien

▶ **come on** vi (pupil) progresar; (work, project) desarrollarse; (lights) encenderse; (electricity) volver; **come on!** ¡vamos!

▶ **come out** vi (fact) salir a la luz; (book, sun) salir; (stain) quitarse

▶ **come round** vi (after faint, operation) volver en sí

▶ **come to** vi (wake) volver en sí

▶ **come up** vi (sun) salir; (problem) surgir; (event) aproximarse; (in conversation) mencionarse

▶ **come up with** vt fus (idea) sugerir; (money) conseguir

comeback ['kʌmbæk] n: **to make a ~** (THEATRE) volver a las tablas

comedian [kə'miːdɪən] n humorista mf

comedy ['kɒmɪdɪ] n comedia f; (humour) comicidad f

comet ['kɒmɪt] n cometa m

comfort ['kʌmfət] n bienestar m; (relief) alivio ♦ vt consolar ❑ **comfortable** adj cómodo; (financially) acomodado; (easy) fácil ♦ **comfort station** (US) n servicios mpl

comic ['kɒmɪk] adj (also: **comical**) cómico ♦ n (comedian) cómico; (BRIT: for children) tebeo; (BRIT: for adults) comic m ❑ **comic book** (US) n libro de cómics ❑ **comic strip** n tira cómica

comma ['kɒmə] n coma

command [kə'mɑːnd] n orden f, mandato; (MIL: authority) mando; (mastery) dominio ♦ vt (troops) mandar; (give orders to): **to ~ sb to do** mandar or ordenar a algn hacer ❑ **commander** n (MIL) comandante mf, jefe(-a) m/f

commemorate [kə'meməreɪt] vt conmemorar

commence [kə'mens] vt, vi comenzar, empezar ❑ **commencement** (US) n (UNIV) (ceremonia de) graduación f

commend [kə'mend] vt elogiar, alabar; (recommend) recomendar

comment ['kɒment] n comentario ♦ vi: **to ~ on** hacer comentarios sobre; **"no ~"** (written) "sin comentarios"; (spoken) "no tengo nada que decir" ❑ **commentary** ['kɒməntəri] n comentario ❑ **commentator** ['kɒmənteɪtə'] n comentarista mf

commerce ['kɒmɜːs] n comercio

commercial [kə'mɜːʃəl] adj comercial ♦ n (TV, RADIO) anuncio ♦ **commercial break** n intermedio para publicidad

commission [kə'mɪʃən] n (committee, fee) comisión f ♦ vt (work of art) encargar; **out of ~** fuera de servicio ❑ **commissioner** n (POLICE) comisario de policía

commit [kə'mɪt] vt (act) cometer; (resources) dedicar; (to sb's care) entregar; **to ~ o.s. (to do)** comprometerse (a hacer); **to ~ suicide** suicidarse ❑ **commitment** n compromiso; (to ideology etc) entrega

committee [kə'mɪtɪ] n comité m

commodity [kə'mɒdɪtɪ] n mercancía

common ['kɒmən] adj común; (pej) ordinario ♦ n campo común ❑ **commonly** adv comúnmente ❑ **commonplace** adj de lo más común ❑ **Commons** (BRIT) npl (POL): **the Commons** (la Cámara de) los Comunes ❑ **common sense** n sentido común ❑ **Commonwealth** n: **the Commonwealth** la Commonwealth

communal ['kɒmjuːnl] adj (property) comunal; (kitchen) común

commune [n 'kɒmjuːn, vb kə'mjuːn] n (group) comuna ♦ vi: **to ~ with** comulgar or conversar con

communicate [kə'mjuːnɪkeɪt] vt comunicar ♦ vi: **to ~ (with)** comunicarse (con); (in writing) estar en contacto (con)

communication [kəmjuːnɪ'keɪʃən] n comunicación f

communion [kə'mjuːnɪən] n (also: **Holy C~**) comunión f

communism ['kɒmjuːnɪzəm] n comunismo ❑ **communist** adj, n comunista mf

community [kə'mjuːnɪtɪ] n comunidad f; (large group) colectividad f ❑ **community centre** (US **community center**) n centro social ❑ **community service** n trabajo m comunitario (prestado en lugar de cumplir una pena de prisión)

commute [kə'mjuːt] vi viajar a diario de la casa al trabajo ♦ vt conmutar ❑ **commuter** n persona que viaja a diario de la casa al trabajo

compact [adj kəm'pækt, n 'kɒmpækt] adj compacto ♦ n (also: **powder ~**)

polvera ❑ **compact disc** n compact disc m ❑ **compact disc player** n reproductor m de disco compacto, compact disc m

companion [kəm'pænɪən] n compañero(-a)

company ['kʌmpənɪ] n compañía; (COMM) sociedad f, compañía; **to keep sb ~** acompañar a algn ❑ **company car** n coche m de la empresa ❑ **company director** n director(a) m/f de empresa

comparable ['kɒmpərəbl] adj comparable

comparative [kəm'pærətɪv] adj relativo; (study) comparativo ❑ **comparatively** adv (relatively) relativamente

compare [kəm'pɛə'] vt: **to ~ sth/sb with** or **to** comparar algo/a algn con ♦ vi: **to ~ (with)** compararse (con) ❑ **comparison** [-'pærɪsn] n comparación f

compartment [kəm'pɑːtmənt] n (also: RAIL) compartim(i)ento

compass ['kʌmpəs] n brújula; **compasses** npl (MATH) compás m

compassion [kəm'pæʃən] n compasión f

compatible [kəm'pætɪbl] adj compatible

compel [kəm'pɛl] vt obligar ❑ **compelling** adj (fig: argument) convincente

compensate ['kɒmpənseɪt] vt compensar ♦ vi: **to ~ for** compensar ❑ **compensation** [-'seɪʃən] n (for loss) indemnización f

compete [kəm'piːt] vi (take part) tomar parte, concurrir; (vie with): **to ~ with** competir con, hacer competencia a

competent ['kɒmpɪtənt] adj competente, capaz

competition [kɒmpɪ'tɪʃən] n (contest) concurso; (rivalry) competencia

competitive [kəm'petɪtɪv] adj (ECON, SPORT) competitivo

competitor [kəm'petɪtə'] n (rival) competidor(a) m/f; (participant) concursante mf

complacent [kəm'pleɪsənt] adj autocomplaciente

complain [kəm'pleɪn] vi quejarse; (COMM) reclamar ❑ **complaint** n queja; reclamación f; (MED) enfermedad f

complement [n 'kɒmplɪmənt, vb 'kɒmplɪmɛnt] n complemento; (esp of ship's crew) dotación f ♦ vt (enhance) complementar ❑ **complementary** [kɒmplɪ'mɛntərɪ] adj complementario

complete [kəm'pli:t] adj (full) completo; (finished) acabado ♦ vt (fulfil) completar; (finish) acabar; (a form) llenar ❑ **completely** adv completamente ❑ **completion** [-'pli:ʃən] n terminación f; (of contract) realización f

complex ['kɒmplɛks] adj, n complejo

complexion [kəm'plɛkʃən] n (of face) tez f, cutis m

compliance [kəm'plaɪəns] n (submission) sumisión f; (agreement) conformidad f; **in ~ with** de acuerdo con

complicate ['kɒmplɪkeɪt] vt complicar ❑ **complicated** adj complicado ❑ **complication** [-'keɪʃən] n complicación f

compliment [n 'kɒmplɪmənt] n (formal) cumplido ♦ vt felicitar ❑ **complimentary** [-'mɛntərɪ] adj lisonjero; (free) de favor

comply [kəm'plaɪ] vi: **to ~ with** cumplir con

component [kəm'pəʊnənt] adj componente ♦ n (TECH) pieza

compose [kəm'pəʊz] vt: **to be composed of** componerse de; (music etc) componer; **to ~ o.s.** tranquilizarse ❑ **composer** n (MUS) compositor(a) m/

f ❑ **composition** [kɒmpə'zɪʃən] n composición f

composure [kəm'pəʊʒə'] n serenidad f, calma

compound ['kɒmpaʊnd] n (CHEM) compuesto; (LING) palabra compuesta; (enclosure) recinto ♦ adj compuesto; (fracture) complicado

comprehension [-'hɛnʃən] n comprensión f

comprehensive [kɒmprɪ'hɛnsɪv] adj exhaustivo; (INSURANCE) contra todo riesgo ❑ **comprehensive (school)** n centro estatal de enseñanza secundaria, ≈ Instituto Nacional de Bachillerato (SP)

compress [vb kəm'prɛs, n 'kɒmprɛs] vt comprimir; (information) condensar ♦ n (MED) compresa

comprise [kəm'praɪz] vt (also: **be comprised of**) comprender, constar de; (constitute) constituir

compromise ['kɒmprəmaɪz] n (agreement) arreglo ♦ vt comprometer ♦ vi transigir

compulsive [kəm'pʌlsɪv] adj compulsivo; (viewing, reading) obligado

compulsory [kəm'pʌlsərɪ] adj obligatorio

computer [kəm'pju:tə'] n ordenador m, computador m, computadora f ❑ **computer game** n juego para ordenador ❑ **computer-generated** adj realizado por ordenador, creado por ordenador ❑ **computerize** vt (data) computerizar; (system) informatizar; **we're computerized now** ya nos hemos informatizado ❑ **computer programmer** n programador(a) m/f ❑ **computer programming** n programación f ❑ **computer science** n informática ❑ **computer studies** npl informática fsg, computación fsg (LAm) ❑ **computing** [kəm'pju:tɪŋ] n (activity, science) informática

con [kɒn] vt (deceive) engañar; (cheat) estafar ♦ n estafa

conceal [kən'siːl] vt ocultar

concede [kən'siːd] vt (point, argument) reconocer; (territory) ceder; to ~ (defeat) darse por vencido; to ~ that admitir que

conceited [kən'siːtid] adj presumido

conceive [kən'siːv] vt, vi concebir

concentrate ['kɒnsəntreit] vi concentrarse ♦ vt concentrar

concentration [kɒnsən'treiʃən] n concentración f

concept ['kɒnsept] n concepto

concern [kən'sɜːn] n (matter) asunto; (COMM) empresa; (anxiety) preocupación f ♦ vt (worry) preocupar; (involve) afectar; (relate to) tener que ver con; to be concerned (about) interesarse (por), preocuparse (por)
□ **concerning** prep sobre, acerca de

concert ['kɒnsət] n concierto
□ **concert hall** n sala de conciertos

concerto [kən'tʃɜːtəu] n concierto

concession [kən'seʃən] n concesión f; tax ~ privilegio fiscal

concise [kən'sais] adj conciso

conclude [kən'kluːd] vt concluir; (treaty etc) firmar; (agreement) llegar a; (decide) llegar a la conclusión de
□ **conclusion** [-'kluːʒən] n conclusión f; firma

concrete ['kɒnkriːt] n hormigón m ♦ adj de hormigón; (fig) concreto

concussion [kən'kʌʃən] n conmoción f cerebral

condemn [kən'dem] vt condenar; (building) declarar en ruina

condensation [kɒnden'seiʃən] n condensación f

condense [kən'dens] vi condensarse ♦ vt condensar, abreviar

condition [kən'diʃən] n condición f, estado; (requirement) condición f ♦ vt condicionar; on ~ that a condición (de) que □ **conditional** [kən'diʃənl] adj

conditional □ **conditioner** n suavizante

condo ['kɒndəu] (US) n (inf) = **condominium**

condom ['kɒndəm] n condón m

condominium [kɒndə'miniəm] (US) n (building) bloque m de pisos o apartamentos (propiedad de quienes lo habitan), condominio (LAm); (apartment) piso or apartamento (en propiedad), condominio (LAm)

condone [kən'dəun] vt condonar

conduct [n 'kɒndʌkt, vb kən'dʌkt] n conducta, comportamiento ♦ vt (lead) conducir; (manage) llevar a cabo, dirigir; (MUS) dirigir; to ~ o.s. comportarse □ **conducted tour** (BRIT) n visita acompañada
□ **conductor** n (of orchestra) director m; (US: on train) revisor/a m/f; (on bus) cobrador m; (ELEC) conductor m

cone [kəun] n cono; (pine cone) piña; (on road) pivote m; (for ice-cream) cucurucho

confectionery [kən'fekʃənri] n dulces mpl

confer [kən'fɜː] vt: to ~ sth on otorgar algo a ♦ vi conferenciar

conference ['kɒnfərns] n (meeting) reunión f; (convention) congreso

confess [kən'fes] vt confesar ♦ vi admitir □ **confession** [-'feʃən] n confesión f

confide [kən'faid] vi: to ~ in confiar en

confidence ['kɒnfidns] n (secret) confianza; (also: **self-~**) confianza f; **in ~** (speak, write) en confianza
□ **confident** adj seguro de sí mismo; (certain) seguro □ **confidential** [kɒnfi'denʃəl] adj confidencial

confine [kən'fain] vt (limit) limitar; (shut up) encerrar □ **confined** adj (space) reducido

confirm [kən'fɜːm] vt confirmar
□ **confirmation** [kɒnfə'meiʃən] n confirmación f

confiscate ['kɒnfɪskeɪt] vt confiscar

conflict [n 'kɒnflɪkt, vb kən'flɪkt] n conflicto ♦ vi (opinions) chocar

conform [kən'fɔːm] vi conformarse; **to ~ to** ajustarse a

confront [kən'frʌnt] vt (problems) hacer frente a; (enemy, danger) enfrentarse con ❏ **confrontation** [kɒnfrən'teɪʃən] n enfrentamiento

confuse [kən'fjuːz] vt (perplex) aturdir, desconcertar; (mix up) confundir; (complicate) complicar ❏ **confused** adj confuso; (person) perplejo ❏ **confusing** adj confuso ❏ **confusion** [-'fjuːʒən] n confusión f

congestion [kən'dʒestʃən] n congestión f

congratulate [kən'grætjuleɪt] vt: **to ~ sb (on)** felicitar a algn (por) ❏ **congratulations** [-'leɪʃənz] npl felicitaciones fpl; **congratulations!** ¡enhorabuena!

congregation [-'geɪʃən] n (of a church) feligreses mpl

congress ['kɒngres] n congreso; (US): **C~** Congreso ❏ **congressman** (irreg: US) n miembro del Congreso ❏ **congresswoman** (irreg: US) n diputada, miembro del Congreso

conifer ['kɒnɪfə'] n conífera

conjugate ['kɒndʒugeɪt] vt conjugar

conjugation [kɒndʒə'geɪʃən] n conjugación f

conjunction [kən'dʒʌŋkʃən] n conjunción f; **in ~ with** junto con

conjure ['kʌndʒə'] vi hacer juegos de manos

connect [kə'nekt] vt juntar, unir; (ELEC) conectar; (TEL: subscriber) poner; (: caller) poner al habla; (fig) relacionar, asociar ♦ vi: **to ~ with** (train) enlazar con; **to be connected with** (associated) estar relacionado con ❏ **connecting flight** n vuelo m de enlace ❏ **connection** [-ʃən] n juntura, unión f;

(ELEC) conexión f; (RAIL) enlace m; (TEL) comunicación f; (fig) relación f

conquer ['kɒŋkə'] vt (territory) conquistar; (enemy, feelings) vencer **conquest** ['kɒŋkwest] n conquista

cons [kɒnz] npl see **convenience**; **pro**

conscience ['kɒnʃəns] n conciencia

conscientious [kɒnʃɪ'enʃəs] adj concienzudo; (objection) de conciencia

conscious ['kɒnʃəs] adj (deliberate) deliberado; (awake, aware) consciente ❏ **consciousness** n conciencia; (MED) conocimiento

consecutive [kən'sekjutɪv] adj consecutivo; **on 3 ~ occasions** en 3 ocasiones consecutivas

consensus [kən'sensəs] n consenso

consent [kən'sent] n consentimiento ♦ vi: **to ~ (to)** consentir (en)

consequence ['kɒnsɪkwəns] n consecuencia; (significance) importancia

consequently ['kɒnsɪkwəntlɪ] adv por consiguiente

conservation [kɒnsə'veɪʃən] n conservación f

conservative [kən'sɜːvətɪv] adj conservador(a); (estimate etc) cauteloso ❏ **Conservative** (BRIT) adj, n (POL) conservador(a) m/f

conservatory [kən'sɜːvətrɪ] n invernadero; (MUS) conservatorio

consider [kən'sɪdə'] vt considerar; (take into account) tener en cuenta; (study) estudiar, examinar; **to ~ doing sth** pensar en (la posibilidad de) hacer algo ❏ **considerable** adj considerable ❏ **considerably** adv notablemente ❏ **considerate** adj considerado ❏ **consideration** [-'reɪʃən] n consideración f; (factor) factor m; **to give sth further consideration** estudiar algo más a fondo ❏ **considering** prep teniendo en cuenta

consignment [kən'saɪnmənt] n envío

consist [kən'sɪst] vi: **to ~ of** consistir en
consistency [kən'sɪstənsɪ] n (of argument etc) coherencia; consecuencia; (thickness) consistencia
consistent [kən'sɪstənt] adj (person) consecuente; (argument etc) coherente
consolation [kɒnsə'leɪʃən] n consuelo
console[1] [kən'səul] vt consolar
console[2] ['kɒnsəul] n consola
consonant ['kɒnsənənt] n consonante f
conspicuous [kən'spɪkjuəs] adj (visible) visible
conspiracy [kən'spɪrəsɪ] n conjura, complot m
constable ['kʌnstəbl] (BRIT) n policía mf; **chief ~** = jefe m de policía
constant ['kɒnstənt] adj constante ❑ **constantly** adv constantemente
constipated ['kɒnstɪpeɪtəd] adj estreñido ❑ **constipation** [kɒnstɪ'peɪʃən] n estreñimiento

⚠ Be careful not to translate **constipated** by the Spanish word constipado.

constituency [kən'stɪtjuənsɪ] n (POL: area) distrito electoral; (: electors) electorado
constitute ['kɒnstɪtjuːt] vt constituir
constitution [kɒnstɪ'tjuːʃən] n constitución f
constraint [kən'streɪnt] n obligación f; (limit) restricción f
construct [kən'strʌkt] vt construir ❑ **construction** [-ʃən] n construcción f ❑ **constructive** adj constructivo
consul ['kɒnsl] n cónsul mf ❑ **consulate** ['kɒnsjulɪt] n consulado
consult [kən'sʌlt] vt consultar ❑ **consultant** n (BRIT MED) especialista mf; (other specialist) asesor(a) m/f ❑ **consultation** [kɒnsəl'teɪʃən] n consulta ❑ **consulting room** (BRIT) n consultorio

consume [kən'sjuːm] vt (eat) comerse; (drink) beberse; (fire etc, COMM) consumir ❑ **consumer** n consumidor(a) m/f
consumption [kən'sʌmpʃən] n consumo
cont. abbr (= continued) sigue
contact ['kɒntækt] n contacto; (person) contacto; (: pej) enchufe m ♦ vt ponerse en contacto con ❑ **contact lenses** npl lentes fpl de contacto
contagious [kən'teɪdʒəs] adj contagioso
contain [kən'teɪn] vt contener; **to ~ o.s.** contenerse ❑ **container** n recipiente m; (for shipping etc) contenedor m
contaminate [kən'tæmɪneɪt] vt contaminar
cont'd abbr (= continued) sigue
contemplate ['kɒntəmpleɪt] vt contemplar; (reflect upon) considerar
contemporary [kən'tempərərɪ] adj, n contemporáneo(-a) m/f
contempt [kən'tempt] n desprecio; **~ of court** (LAW) desacato (a los tribunales)
contend [kən'tend] vt (argue) afirmar ♦ vi: **to ~ with/for** luchar contra/por
content [adj, vb kən'tent, n 'kɒntent] adj (happy) contento; (satisfied) satisfecho ♦ vt contentar; satisfacer ♦ n contenido; **contents** npl contenido; **(table of) contents** índice m de materias ❑ **contented** adj contento; satisfecho
contest [n 'kɒntest, vb kən'test] n lucha; (competition) concurso ♦ vt (dispute) impugnar; (POL) presentarse como candidato(-a) en ❑ **contestant** [kən'testənt] n concursante mf; (in fight) contendiente mf

⚠ Be careful not to translate **con** by the Spanish word contest

context ['kɒntekst] n contexto

continent ['kɔntɪnənt] n continente m; **the C~** (BRIT) el continente europeo ☐ **continental** [-'nentl] adj continental ☐ **continental breakfast** n desayuno estilo europeo ☐ **continental quilt** (BRIT) n edredón m

continual [kən'tɪnjuəl] adj continuo ☐ **continually** adv constantemente

continue [kən'tɪnju:] vi, vt seguir, continuar

continuity [kɔntɪ'nju:ɪtɪ] n (also CINE) continuidad f

continuous [kən'tɪnjuəs] adj continuo ☐ **continuous assessment** n (BRIT) evaluación f continua ☐ **continuously** adv continuamente

contour ['kɔntuə] n contorno; (also: ~ **line**) curva de nivel

contraception [kɔntrə'sepʃən] n contracepción f

contraceptive [kɔntrə'septɪv] adj, n anticonceptivo

contract [n 'kɔntrækt, vb kən'trækt] n contrato ♦ vi (COMM): **to ~ to do sth** comprometerse por contrato a hacer algo; (become smaller) contraerse, encogerse ♦ vt contraer ☐ **contractor** n contratista mf

contradict [kɔntrə'dɪkt] vt contradecir ☐ **contradiction** [-ʃən] n contradicción f

contrary[1] ['kɔntrərɪ] adj contrario ♦ n lo contrario; **on the ~** al contrario; **unless you hear to the ~** a no ser que le digan lo contrario

contrary[2] [kən'treərɪ] adj (perverse) terco

ontrast [n 'kɔntrɑːst, vt kən'trɑːst] n ntraste m ♦ vt comparar; **in ~ to** en ntraste con

tribute [kən'trɪbjuːt] vi contribuir : **to ~ £10/an article to** contribuir 10 libras/un artículo a; **to ~ to** rity) donar a; (newspaper) escribir a; (discussion) intervenir en

☐ **contribution** [kɔntrɪ'bjuːʃən] n (donation) donativo; (BRIT: for social security) cotización f; (to debate) intervención f; (to journal) colaboración f ☐ **contributor** n (to newspaper) colaborador(a) m/f

control [kən'trəul] vt controlar; (process etc) dirigir; (machinery) manejar; (temper) dominar; (disease) contener ♦ n control m; **controls** npl (of vehicle) instrumentos mpl de mando; (of radio) controles mpl; (governmental) medidas fpl de control; **under ~** bajo control; **to be in ~ of** tener el mando de; **the car went out of ~** se perdió el control del coche ☐ **control tower** n (AVIAT) torre f de control

controversial [kɔntrə'vəːʃl] adj polémico

controversy ['kɔntrəvəːsɪ] n polémica

convenience [kən'viːnɪəns] n (easiness) comodidad f; (suitability) idoneidad f; (advantage) ventaja; **at your ~** cuando le sea conveniente; **all modern conveniences, all mod cons** (BRIT) todo confort

convenient [kən'viːnɪənt] adj (useful) útil; (place, time) conveniente

convent ['kɔnvənt] n convento

convention [kən'venʃən] n convención f; (meeting) asamblea; (agreement) convenio ☐ **conventional** adj convencional

conversation [kɔnvə'seɪʃən] n conversación f

conversely [-'vəːslɪ] adv a la inversa

conversion [kən'vəːʃən] n conversión f

convert [vb kən'vəːt, n 'kɔnvəːt] vt (REL, COMM) convertir; (alter): **to ~ sth into/ to** transformar algo en/convertir algo a ♦ n converso(-a) ☐ **convertible** adj convertible ♦ n descapotable m

convey [kən'veɪ] vt llevar; (thanks) comunicar; (idea) expresar ☐ **conveyor belt** n cinta transportadora

convict [vb kən'vɪkt, n 'kɒnvɪkt] vt (find guilty) declarar culpable a ♦ n presidiario(-a) □ **conviction** [-ʃən] n condena; (belief, certainty) convicción f

convince [kən'vɪns] vt convencer □ **convinced** adj: **convinced of/that** convencido de/de que □ **convincing** adj convincente

convoy ['kɒnvɔɪ] n convoy m

cook [kuk] vt (stew etc) guisar; (meal) preparar ♦ vi cocer; (person) cocinar ♦ n cocinero(-a) □ **cook book** n libro de cocina □ **cooker** n cocina □ **cookery** n cocina □ **cookery book** (BRIT) n = **cook book** □ **cookie** (US) n galleta □ **cooking** n cocina

cool [kuːl] adj fresco; (not afraid) tranquilo; (unfriendly) frío ♦ vt enfriar ♦ vi enfriarse ► **cool down** vi enfriarse; (fig: person, situation) calmarse ► **cool off** vi (become calmer) calmarse, apaciguarse; (lose enthusiasm) perder (el) interés, enfriarse

cop [kɒp] (inf) n poli mf (SP), tira mf (MEX)

cope [kəup] vi: **to ~ with** (problem) hacer frente a

copper ['kɒpə*] n (metal) cobre m; (BRIT: inf) poli mf, tira mf (MEX)

copy ['kɒpɪ] n copia; (of book etc) ejemplar m ♦ vt copiar □ **copyright** n derechos mpl de autor

coral ['kɒrəl] n coral m

cord [kɔːd] n cuerda; (ELEC) cable m; (fabric) pana; **cords** npl (trousers) pantalones mpl de pana □ **cordless** adj sin hilos

corduroy ['kɔːdərɔɪ] n pana

core [kɔː*] n centro, núcleo; (of fruit) corazón m; (of problem) meollo ♦ vt quitar el corazón de

coriander [kɒrɪ'ændə*] n culantro

cork [kɔːk] n corcho; (tree) alcornoque m □ **corkscrew** n sacacorchos m inv

corn [kɔːn] n (BRIT: cereal crop) trigo; (US: maize) maíz m; (on foot) callo; **~ on the**

cob (CULIN) mazorca, elote m (MEX), choclo (SC)

corned beef ['kɔːnd-] n carne f acecinada (en lata)

corner ['kɔːnə*] n (outside) esquina; (inside) rincón m; (in road) curva; (FOOTBALL) córner m; (BOXING) esquina ♦ vt (trap) arrinconar; (COMM) acaparar ♦ vi (in car) tomar las curvas □ **corner shop** (BRIT) tienda de la esquina

cornflakes ['kɔːnfleɪks] npl copos mpl de maíz, cornflakes mpl

cornflour ['kɔːnflauə*] (BRIT) n harina de maíz

cornstarch ['kɔːnstɑːtʃ] (US) n = **cornflour**

Cornwall ['kɔːnwəl] n Cornualles m

coronary ['kɒrənərɪ] n (also: ~ **thrombosis**) infarto

coronation [kɒrə'neɪʃən] n coronación f

coroner ['kɒrənə*] n juez mf de instrucción

corporal ['kɔːpərl] n cabo ♦ adj: **~ punishment** castigo corporal

corporate ['kɔːpərɪt] adj (action, ownership) colectivo; (finance, image) corporativo

corporation [kɔːpə'reɪʃən] n (of town) ayuntamiento; (COMM) corporación f

corps [kɔː, pl kɔːz] n inv cuerpo; **diplomatic ~** cuerpo diplomático; **press ~** gabinete m de prensa

corpse [kɔːps] n cadáver m

correct [kə'rekt] adj justo, exacto; (proper) correcto ♦ vt corregir; (exam) corregir, calificar □ **correction** [-ʃən] n (act) corrección f; (instance) rectificación f

correspond [kɒrɪs'pɒnd] vi (write): **to ~ (with)** escribirse (con); (be equivalent to): **to ~ (to)** corresponder (a); (be in accordance): **to ~ (with)** corresponder (con) □ **correspondence** n correspondencia □ **correspondent** n corresponsal mf ❑ **corresponding** adj correspondiente

corridor ['kɒrɪdɔ:ʳ] n pasillo

corrode [kə'rəud] vt corroer ♦ vi corroerse

corrupt [kə'rʌpt] adj (person) corrupto; (COMPUT) corrompido ♦ vt corromper; (COMPUT) degradar ❑ **corruption** n corrupción f; (of data) alteración f

Corsica ['kɔ:sɪkə] n Córcega

cosmetic [kɒz'metɪk] adj, n cosmético ❑ **cosmetic surgery** n cirugía f estética

cosmopolitan [kɒzmə'pɒlɪtn] adj cosmopolita

cost [kɒst] (pt, pp ~) n (price) precio ♦ vi costar, valer ♦ vt preparar el presupuesto de; **how much does it ~?** ¿cuánto cuesta?; **to ~ sb time/effort** costarle a algn tiempo/esfuerzo; **it ~ him his life** le costó la vida; **at all costs** cueste lo que cueste; **costs** npl (COMM) costes mpl, (LAW) costas fpl

co-star ['kəustɑ:ʳ] n coprotagonista mf

Costa Rica ['kɒstə'ri:kə] n Costa Rica ❑ **Costa Rican** adj, n costarriqueño(-a)

costly ['kɒstlɪ] adj costoso

cost of living ['kɒstjɔv'lɪvɪŋ] n costo o coste m (Sp) de la vida

costume ['kɒstju:m] n traje m; (BRIT: also: **swimming ~**) traje de baño

cosy ['kəuzɪ] (US **cozy**) adj (person) cómodo; (room) acogedor(a)

cot [kɒt] n (BRIT: child's) cuna; (US: campbed) cama de campaña

cottage ['kɒtɪdʒ] n casita de campo; (rustic) barraca ❑ **cottage cheese** n requesón m

cotton ['kɒtn] n algodón m; (thread) hilo ▸ **cotton on** vi (inf): **to cotton on (to sth)** caer en la cuenta (de algo) ❑ **cotton bud** (BRIT) n bastoncillo m de algodón ❑ **cotton candy** (US) n algodón m (azucarado) ❑ **cotton wool** (BRIT) n algodón m (hidrófilo)

couch [kautʃ] n sofá m; (doctor's etc) diván m

cough [kɒf] vi toser ♦ n tos f ❑ **cough mixture** n jarabe m para la tos

could [kud] pt of **can²** ❑ **couldn't** = **could not**

council ['kaunsl] n consejo; **city** or **town ~** consejo municipal ❑ **council estate** (BRIT) n urbanización de viviendas municipales de alquiler ❑ **council house** (BRIT) n vivienda municipal de alquiler ❑ **councillor** (US **councilor**) n concejal(a) m/f ❑ **council tax** (BRIT) n contribución f municipal (dependiente del valor de la vivienda)

counsel ['kaunsl] n (advice) consejo; (lawyer) abogado(-a) ♦ vt aconsejar ❑ **counselling** (US **counseling**) n (PSYCH) asistencia f psicológica ❑ **counsellor** (US **counselor**) n consejero(-a), abogado(-a)

count [kaunt] vt contar; (include) incluir ♦ vi contar ♦ n cuenta; (of votes) escrutinio; (level) nivel m; (nobleman) conde m ▸ **count in** (inf) vt: **to count sb in on sth** contar con algn para algo ▸ **count on** vt fus contar con ❑ **countdown** n cuenta atrás

counter ['kauntəʳ] n (in shop) mostrador m; (in games) ficha ♦ vt contrarrestar ♦ adv: **to run ~ to** contrario a, ir en contra de ❑ **counter clockwise** (US) adv en sentido contrario al de las agujas del reloj

counterfeit ['kauntəfɪt] n falsificación f, simulación f ♦ vt falsificar ♦ adj falso, falsificado

counterpart ['kauntəpɑ:t] n homólogo(-a)

countess ['kauntɪs] n condesa

countless ['kauntlɪs] adj innumerable

country ['kʌntrɪ] n país m; (native land) patria; (as opposed to town) campo; (region) región f, tierra ❑ **country and western (music)** n música country ❑ **country house** n casa de campo ❑ **countryside** n campo

county ['kaʊntɪ] n condado

coup [kuː] (pl **coups**) n (also: ~ **d'état**) golpe m (de estado); (achievement) éxito

couple ['kʌpl] n (of things) par m; (of people) pareja; (married couple) matrimonio; **a ~ of** un par de

coupon ['kuːpɔn] n cupón m; (voucher) valé m

courage ['kʌrɪdʒ] n valor m, valentía
❑ **courageous** [kə'reɪdʒəs] adj valiente

courgette [kʊə'ʒet] (BRIT) n calabacín m, calabacita (MEX)

courier ['kʊrɪə] n mensajero(-a); (for tourists) guía mf (de turismo)

course [kɔːs] n (direction) dirección f; (of river, SCOL) curso; (process) transcurso; (MED): ~ **of treatment** tratamiento m; (of ship) rumbo; (part of meal) plato; (GOLF) campo; **of ~** desde luego, naturalmente; **of ~!** ¡claro!

court [kɔːt] n (royal) corte f; (LAW) tribunal m, juzgado; (TENNIS etc) pista, cancha ♦ vt (woman) cortejar; **to take to ~** demandar

courtesy ['kəːtəsɪ] n cortesía; (by) **of** por cortesía de ❑ **courtesy bus**, **courtesy coach** n autobús m gratuito

court: **court-house** ['kɔːthaus] (US) n palacio de justicia ❑ **courtroom** ['kɔːtrum] n sala de justicia ❑ **courtyard** ['kɔːtjɑːd] n patio

cousin ['kʌzn] n primo(-a); **first ~** primo(-a) carnal, primo(-a) hermano(-a)

cover ['kʌvə] vt cubrir; (feelings, mistake) ocultar; (with lid) tapar; (book etc) forrar; (distance) recorrer; (include) abarcar; (protect: also: INSURANCE) cubrir; (PRESS) investigar; (discuss) tratar ♦ n cubierta; (lid) tapa; (for chair etc) funda; (envelope) sobre m; (for book) forro; (of magazine) portada; (shelter) abrigo; (INSURANCE) cobertura; (of spy) cobertura; **covers** npl (on bed) sábanas; mantas; **to take ~** (shelter)

protegerse, resguardarse; **under ~** (indoors) bajo techo; **under ~ of darkness** al amparo de la oscuridad; **under separate ~** (COMM) por separado ▸ **cover up** vi: **to cover up for sb** encubrir a algn ❑ **coverage** n (TV, PRESS) cobertura ❑ **cover charge** n precio del cubierto ❑ **cover-up** n encubrimiento

cow [kaʊ] n vaca; (inf!: woman) bruja ♦ vt intimidar

coward ['kaʊəd] n cobarde mf
❑ **cowardly** adj cobarde

cowboy ['kaʊbɔɪ] n vaquero

cozy ['kəʊzɪ] (US) adj = **cosy**

crab [kræb] n cangrejo

crack [kræk] n grieta; (noise) crujido; (drug) crack m ♦ vt agrietar, romper; (nut) cascar; (solve: problem) resolver; (: code) descifrar; (whip etc) chasquear; (knuckles) crujir; (joke) contar ♦ adj (expert) de primera ▸ **crack down on** vt fus adoptar fuertes medidas contra ❑ **cracked** adj (cup, window) rajado; (wall) resquebrajado ❑ **cracker** n (biscuit) cráquer m; (Christmas cracker) petardo sorpresa

crackle ['krækl] vi crepitar

cradle ['kreɪdl] n cuna

craft [krɑːft] n (skill) arte m; (trade) oficio; (cunning) astucia; (boat: pl inv) barco; (plane: pl inv) avión m
❑ **craftsman** (irreg) n artesano
❑ **craftsmanship** n (quality) destreza

cram [kræm] vt (fill): **to ~ sth with** llenar algo (a reventar) de; (put): **to ~ sth into** meter algo a la fuerza en ♦ vi (for exams) empollar

cramp [kræmp] n (MED) calambre m
❑ **cramped** adj apretado, estrecho

cranberry ['krænbərɪ] n arándano agrio

crane [kreɪn] n (TECH) grúa; (bird) grulla

crap [kræp] n (inf!) mierda (!)

crash [kræʃ] n (noise) estrépito; (of car etc) choque m; (of plane) accidente de aviación; (COMM) quiebra ♦ vt (car, plane) estrellar ♦ vi (car, plane) estrellarse; (two cars) chocar; (COMM) quebrar ❏ **crash course** n curso acelerado ❏ **crash helmet** n casco (protector)

crate [kreɪt] n cajón m de embalaje; (for bottles) caja

crave [kreɪv] vt, vi: **to ~ (for)** ansiar, anhelar

crawl [krɔ:l] vi (drag o.s.) arrastrarse; (child) andar a gatas, gatear; (vehicle) avanzar (lentamente) ♦ n (SWIMMING) crol m

crayfish ['kreɪfɪʃ] n inv (freshwater) cangrejo de río; (saltwater) cigala

crayon ['kreɪən] n lápiz m de color

craze [kreɪz] n (fashion) moda

crazy ['kreɪzɪ] adj (person) loco; (idea) disparatado; (inf: keen): **~ about sb/sth** loco por algn/algo

creak [kri:k] vi (floorboard) crujir; (hinge etc) chirriar, rechinar

cream [kri:m] n (of milk) nata, crema; (lotion) crema; (fig) flor f y nata ♦ adj (colour) color crema ❏ **cream cheese** n queso blanco ❏ **creamy** adj cremoso; (colour) color crema

crease [kri:s] n (fold) pliegue m; (in trousers) raya; (wrinkle) arruga ♦ vt (wrinkle) arrugar ♦ vi (wrinkle up) arrugarse

create [kri:'eɪt] vt crear ❏ **creation** [-ʃən] n creación f ❏ **creative** adj creativo ❏ **creator** n creador(a) m/f

creature ['kri:tʃə'] n (animal) animal m, bicho; (person) criatura

crèche [kreʃ] n guardería (infantil)

credentials [krɪ'denʃlz] npl (references) referencias fpl; (identity papers) documentos mpl de identidad

credibility [kredɪ'bɪlɪtɪ] n credibilidad f

credible ['kredɪbl] adj creíble; (trustworthy) digno de confianza

credit ['kredɪt] n crédito; (merit) honor m, mérito ♦ vt (COMM) abonar; (believe: also: **give ~ to**) creer, prestar fe a ♦ adj crediticio; **credits** npl (CINEMA) fichas fpl técnicas; (to sb) (person) tener saldo a favor; **to ~ sb with** (fig) reconocer a algn el mérito de ❏ **credit card** n tarjeta de crédito

creek [kri:k] n cala, ensenada; (US) riachuelo

creep [kri:p] (pt, pp **crept**) vi arrastrarse

cremate [krɪ'meɪt] vt incinerar

crematorium [kremə'tɔ:rɪəm] (pl **crematoria**) n crematorio

crept [krept] pt, pp of **creep**

crescent ['kresnt] n media luna; (street) calle f (en forma de semicírculo)

cress [kres] n berro

crest [krest] n (of bird) cresta; (of hill) cima, cumbre f; (of coat of arms) blasón m

crew [kru:] n (of ship etc) tripulación f; (TV, CINEMA) equipo ❏ **crew-neck** n cuello a la caja

crib [krɪb] n cuna ♦ vt (inf) plagiar

cricket ['krɪkɪt] n (insect) grillo; (game) críquet m ❏ **cricketer** n jugador(a) m/f de críquet

crime [kraɪm] n (no pl: illegal activities) crimen m; (illegal action) delito ❏ **criminal** ['krɪmɪnl] n criminal mf, delincuente mf ♦ adj criminal; (illegal) delictivo; (law) penal

crimson ['krɪmzn] adj carmesí

cringe [krɪndʒ] vi agacharse, encogerse

cripple ['krɪpl] n lisiado(-a), cojo(-a) ♦ vt lisiar, mutilar

crisis ['kraɪsɪs] (pl **crises**) n crisis f inv

crisp [krɪsp] adj fresco; (vegetables etc) crujiente; (manner) seco ❏ **crispy** adj crujiente

criterion [kraɪ'tɪərɪən] (pl **criteria**) n criterio

critic ['krɪtɪk] n crítico(-a) ❏ **critical** adj crítico; (illness) grave ❏ **criticism** ['krɪtɪsɪzm] n crítica ❏ **criticize** ['krɪtɪsaɪz] vt criticar

Croat [ˈkrəʊæt] adj, n = **Croatian**

Croatia [krəʊˈeɪʃə] n Croacia
  ❑ **Croatian** adj, n croata m/f ♦ n (LING) croata m

crockery [ˈkrɔkərɪ] n loza, vajilla

crocodile [ˈkrɔkədaɪl] n cocodrilo

crocus [ˈkrəʊkəs] n croco, crocus m

croissant [ˈkrwæs] n croissant m, medialuna (esp LAm)

crook [krʊk] n ladrón(-ona) m/f; (of shepherd) cayado ♦ **crooked** [ˈkrʊkɪd] adj torcido; (dishonest) nada honrado

crop [krɔp] n (produce) cultivo; (amount produced) cosecha; (riding crop) látigo de montar ♦ vt cortar, recortar ▶ **crop up** vi surgir, presentarse

cross [krɔs] n cruz f; (hybrid) cruce m ♦ vt (street etc) cruzar, atravesar ♦ adj de mal humor, enojado ▶ **cross off** vt tachar ▶ **cross out** vt tachar ▶ **cross over** vi cruzar ❑ **cross-Channel ferry** [ˈkrɔsˈtʃænl-] n transbordador m que cruza el Canal de la Mancha ❑ **crosscountry** (race) n carrera a campo traviesa, cross m ❑ **crossing** n (sea passage) travesía f; (also: **pedestrian crossing**) paso para peatones ❑ **crossing guard** (US) n persona encargada de ayudar a los niños a cruzar la calle ❑ **crossroads** n cruce m, encrucijada f ❑ **crosswalk** (US) n paso de peatones ❑ **crossword** n crucigrama m

crotch [krɔtʃ] n (ANAT, of garment) entrepierna

crouch [kraʊtʃ] vi agacharse, acurrucarse

crouton [ˈkruːtɒn] n cubito de pan frito

crow [krəʊ] n (bird) cuervo; (of cock) canto, cacareo ♦ vi (cock) cantar

crowd [kraʊd] n muchedumbre f, multitud f ♦ vt (fill) llenar ♦ vi (gather): **to ~ round** reunirse en torno a; (cram): **to ~ in** entrar en tropel ❑ **crowded** adj (full) atestado; (densely populated) superpoblado

crown [kraʊn] n corona; (of head) coronilla; (for tooth) funda; (of hill) cumbre f ♦ vt coronar; (fig) completar, rematar ❑ **crown jewels** npl joyas fpl reales

crucial [ˈkruːʃl] adj decisivo

crucifix [ˈkruːsɪfɪks] n crucifijo

crude [kruːd] adj (materials) bruto; (fig: basic) tosco; (: vulgar) ordinario ❑ **crude (oil)** n (petróleo) crudo

cruel [krʊəl] adj cruel ❑ **cruelty** n crueldad f

cruise [kruːz] n crucero ♦ vi (ship) hacer un crucero; (car) ir a velocidad de crucero

crumb [krʌm] n miga, migaja

crumble [ˈkrʌmbl] vt desmenuzar ♦ vi (building, also fig) desmoronarse

crumpet [ˈkrʌmpɪt] n ≈ bollo para tostar

crumple [ˈkrʌmpl] vt (paper) estrujar; (material) arrugar

crunch [krʌntʃ] vt (with teeth) mascar; (underfoot) hacer crujir ♦ n (fig) hora o momento de la verdad ❑ **crunchy** adj crujiente

crush [krʌʃ] n (crowd) aglomeración f; (infatuation): **to have a ~ on sb** estar loco por algn; (drink): **lemon ~** limonada ♦ vt (squeeze) estrujar; (paper) estrujar; (cloth) arrugar; (fruit) exprimir; (opposition) aplastar; (hopes) destruir

crust [krʌst] n corteza; (of snow, ice) costra ❑ **crusty** adj (bread) crujiente; (person) de mal carácter

crutch [krʌtʃ] n muleta

cry [kraɪ] vi llorar ♦ n (shriek) chillido; (shout) grito ▶ **cry out** vi (call out, shout) lanzar un grito, echar un grito ♦ vt gritar

crystal [ˈkrɪstl] n cristal m

cub [kʌb] n cachorro; (also: ~ **scout**) niño explorador

Cuba [ˈkjuːbə] n Cuba ❑ **Cuban** adj, n cubano(-a) m/f

cube [kjuːb] n cubo ♦ vt (MATH) cubicar

cubicle ['kju:bɪkl] n (at pool) caseta; (for bed) cubículo

cuckoo ['kuku:] n cuco

cucumber ['kju:kʌmbə'] n pepino

cuddle ['kʌdl] vt abrazar ♦ vi abrazarse

cue [kju:] n (snooker cue) taco; (THEATRE etc) señal f

cuff [kʌf] n (of sleeve) puño; (US: of trousers) vuelta; (blow) bofetada; **off the ~** adv de improviso □ **cufflinks** npl gemelos mpl

cuisine [kwɪ'zi:n] n cocina

cul-de-sac ['kʌldəsæk] n callejón m sin salida

cull [kʌl] vt (idea) sacar ♦ n (of animals) matanza selectiva

culminate ['kʌlmɪneɪt] vi: **to ~ in** terminar en

culprit ['kʌlprɪt] n culpable mf

cult [kʌlt] n culto

cultivate ['kʌltɪveɪt] vt cultivar

cultural ['kʌltʃərəl] adj cultural

culture ['kʌltʃə'] n (also fig) cultura; (BIOL) cultivo

cumin ['kʌmɪn] n (spice) comino

cunning ['kʌnɪŋ] n astucia ♦ adj astuto

cup [kʌp] n taza; (as prize) copa

cupboard ['kʌbəd] n armario; (in kitchen) alacena

cup final n (FOOTBALL) final f de copa

curator [kjuə'reɪtə'] n director(a) m/f

curb [kə:b] vt refrenar; (person) reprimir ♦ n freno; (US) bordillo

curdle ['kə:dl] vi cuajarse

cure [kjuə'] vt curar ♦ n cura, curación f; (fig: solution) remedio

curfew ['kə:fju:] n toque m de queda

curiosity [kjuərɪ'ɒsɪtɪ] n curiosidad f

curious ['kjuərɪəs] adj curioso; (person: interested): **to be ~** sentir curiosidad

curl [kə:l] n rizo ♦ vt (hair) rizar ♦ vi rizarse ► **curl up** vi (person) hacerse un ovillo □ **curler** n rulo □ **curly** adj rizado

currant ['kʌrnt] n pasa (de Corinto); (blackcurrant, redcurrant) grosella

currency ['kʌrnsɪ] n moneda; **to gain ~** (fig) difundirse

current ['kʌrnt] n corriente f ♦ adj (accepted) corriente; (present) actual □ **current account** (BRIT) n cuenta corriente □ **current affairs** npl noticias fpl de actualidad □ **currently** adv actualmente

curriculum [kə'rɪkjuləm] n (pl **curriculums** or **curricula**) n plan m de estudios □ **curriculum vitae** n currículum m

curry ['kʌrɪ] n curry m ♦ vt: **to ~ favour with** buscar favores con □ **curry powder** n curry m en polvo

curse [kə:s] vi soltar tacos ♦ vt maldecir ♦ n maldición f; (swearword) palabrota, taco

cursor ['kə:sə'] n (COMPUT) cursor m

curt [kə:t] adj corto, seco

curtain ['kə:tn] n cortina; (THEATRE) telón m

curve [kə:v] n curva ♦ vi (road) hacer una curva; (line etc) curvarse □ **curved** adj curvo

cushion ['kuʃən] n cojín m; (of air) colchón m ♦ vt (shock) amortiguar

custard ['kʌstəd] n natillas fpl

custody ['kʌstədɪ] n custodia; **to take into ~** detener

custom ['kʌstəm] n costumbre f; (COMM) clientela

customer ['kʌstəmə'] n cliente m/f

customized ['kʌstəmaɪzd] adj (car etc) hecho a encargo

customs ['kʌstəmz] npl aduana □ **customs officer** n aduanero(-a)

cut [kʌt] (pt, pp **~**) vt cortar; (price) rebajar; (text, programme) acortar; (reduce) reducir ♦ vi cortar ♦ n (of garment) corte m; (in skin) cortadura; (in salary etc) rebaja; (in spending) reducción f, recorte m; (slice of meat) tajada; **to ~ a tooth** echar un diente; **to**

~ **and paste** (COMPUT) cortar y pegar ▶ **cut back** vt (plants) podar; (production, expenditure) reducir ▶ **cut down** vt (tree) derribar; (reduce) reducir ▶ **cut off** vt cortar; (person, place) aislar; (TEL) desconectar ▶ **cut out** vt (shape) recortar; (stop: activity etc) dejar; (remove) quitar ▶ **cut up** vt cortar (en pedazos) ❑ **cutback** n reducción f

cute [kjuːt] adj mono

cutlery ['kʌtlərɪ] n cubiertos mpl

cutlet ['kʌtlɪt] n chuleta; (nut etc cutlet) plato vegetariano hecho con nueces y verdura en forma de chuleta

cut: cut-price (BRIT) ['kʌt'praɪs] adj a precio reducido

cut-rate (US) ['kʌt'reɪt] adj = **cut-rate**

cutting ['kʌtɪŋ] adj (remark) mordaz ♦ n (BRIT: from newspaper) recorte m; (from plant) esqueje m

CV n abbr = **curriculum vitae**

cwt abbr = **hundredweight(s)**

cybercafé ['saɪbəkæfeɪ] n cibercafé m

cyberspace ['saɪbəspeɪs] n ciberespacio m

cycle ['saɪkl] n ciclo m; (bicycle) bicicleta ♦ vi ir en bicicleta ❑ **cycle hire** n alquiler m de bicicletas ❑ **cycle lane** n carril-bici m ❑ **cycle path** n carril-bici m ❑ **cycling** n ciclismo ❑ **cyclist** n ciclista m/f

cyclone ['saɪkləʊn] n ciclón m

cylinder ['sɪlɪndə*] n cilindro; (of gas) bombona

cymbal ['sɪmbl] n címbalo, platillo

cynical ['sɪnɪkl] adj cínico

Cypriot ['sɪprɪət] adj, n chipriota m/f

Cyprus ['saɪprəs] n Chipre f

cyst [sɪst] n quiste m ❑ **cystitis** [-'taɪtɪs] n cistitis f

czar [zɑː*] n zar m

Czech [tʃek] adj, n checo(-a) m/f ❑ **Czech Republic** n: **the Czech Republic** la República Checa

D, d

D [diː] n (MUS) re m

dab [dæb] vt (eyes, wound) tocar (ligeramente); (paint, cream) poner un poco de

dad [dæd] n = **daddy**

daddy ['dædɪ] n papá m

daffodil ['dæfədɪl] n narciso

daft [dɑːft] adj tonto

dagger ['dægə*] n puñal m, daga

daily ['deɪlɪ] adj diario, cotidiano ♦ adv todos los días, cada día

dairy ['dɛərɪ] n (shop) lechería; (on farm) vaquería ❑ **dairy produce** n productos mpl lácteos

daisy ['deɪzɪ] n margarita

dam [dæm] n presa ♦ vt construir una presa sobre, represar

damage ['dæmɪdʒ] n lesión f; daño; (dents etc) desperfectos mpl; (fig) perjuicio ♦ vt dañar, perjudicar; (spoil, break) estropear; **damages** npl (LAW) daños mpl y perjuicios

damn [dæm] vt condenar; (curse) maldecir ♦ n (inf): **I don't give a ~** me importa un pito ♦ adj (inf: also: **damned**) maldito; **~ (it)!** ¡maldito sea!

damp [dæmp] adj húmedo, mojado ♦ n humedad f ♦ vt (also: **dampen**: cloth, rag) mojar; (: enthusiasm) enfriar

dance [dɑːns] n baile m ♦ vi bailar ❑ **dance floor** n pista f de baile ❑ **dancer** n bailador(a) m/f; (professional) bailarín(-ina) m/f ❑ **dancing** n baile m

dandelion ['dændɪlaɪən] n diente m de león

dandruff ['dændrəf] n caspa

Dane [deɪn] n danés(-esa) m/f

danger ['deɪndʒə*] n peligro; (risk) riesgo; **~!** (on sign) ¡peligro de muerte!; **to be in ~ of** correr riesgo de ❑ **dangerous** adj peligroso

dangle ['dæŋgl] vt colgar ♦ vi pender, colgar

Danish ['deɪnɪʃ] adj danés(-esa) ♦ n (LING) danés m

dare [dɛə'] vt: to ~ sb to do desafiar a algn a hacer ♦ vi: to ~ (to) do sth atreverse a hacer algo; I ~ say (I suppose) puede ser (que) □ **daring** adj atrevido, osado ♦ n atrevimiento, osadía

dark [dɑ:k] adj oscuro; (hair, complexion) moreno ♦ n: in the ~ in the dark; to be in the ~ about (fig) no saber nada de; after ~ después del anochecer □ **darken** vt (colour) hacer más oscuro ♦ vi oscurecerse □ **darkness** n oscuridad f □ **darkroom** n cuarto oscuro

darling ['dɑ:lɪŋ] adj, n querido(-a) m/f

dart [dɑ:t] n dardo; (in sewing) sisa ♦ vi precipitarse □ **dartboard** n diana □ **darts** n (game) dardos mpl

dash [dæʃ] n (small quantity: of liquid) gota, chorrito; (sign) raya ♦ vt (throw) tirar; (hopes) defraudar ♦ vi precipitarse, ir de prisa

dashboard ['dæʃbɔːd] n (AUT) salpicadero

data ['deɪtə] npl datos mpl □ **database** n base f de datos □ **data processing** n proceso de datos

date [deɪt] n (day) fecha; (with friend) cita; (fruit) dátil m ♦ vt fechar; (person) salir con; ~ of birth fecha de nacimiento; to ~ adv hasta la fecha □ **dated** adj anticuado

daughter ['dɔːtə'] n hija □ **daughter-in-law** n nuera, hija política

daunting ['dɔːntɪŋ] adj desalentador(a)

dawn [dɔːn] n alba, amanecer m; (fig) nacimiento ♦ vi (day) amanecer; (fig): it dawned on him that ... cayó en la cuenta de que ...

day [deɪ] n día m; (working day) jornada; (heyday) tiempos mpl, días mpl; the ~

before/after el día anterior/siguiente; the ~ after tomorrow pasado mañana; the ~ before yesterday anteayer; the following ~ el día siguiente; by ~ de día □ **day-care centre** ['deɪkeə-] n centro de día; (for children) guardería infantil □ **daydream** vi soñar despierto □ **daylight** n luz f (del día) □ **day return** (BRIT) n billete m de ida y vuelta (en un día) □ **daytime** n día m □ **day-to-day** adj cotidiano □ **day trip** n excursión f (de un día)

dazed [deɪzd] adj aturdido

dazzle ['dæzl] vt deslumbrar □ **dazzling** adj (light, smile) deslumbrante; (colour) fuerte

DC abbr (= direct current) corriente f continua

dead [ded] adj muerto; (limb) dormido; (telephone) cortado; (battery) agotado ♦ adv (completely) totalmente; (exactly) exactamente; to shoot sb ~ matar a algn a tiros; ~ tired muerto (de cansancio); to stop ~ parar en seco □ **dead end** n callejón m sin salida □ **deadline** n fecha (or hora) tope □ **deadly** adj mortal, fatal □ **Dead Sea** n: the Dead Sea el Mar Muerto

deaf [def] adj sordo □ **deafen** vt ensordecer □ **deafening** adj ensordecedor(a)

deal [diːl] (pt, pp dealt) n (agreement) pacto, convenio; (business deal) trato ♦ vt dar; (card) repartir; a great ~ (of) bastante, mucho ► **deal with** vt fus (people) tratar con; (problem) ocuparse de; (subject) tratar de □ **dealer** n comerciante m/f; (CARDS) mano f □ **dealings** npl (COMM) transacciones fpl; (relations) relaciones fpl

dealt [delt] pt, pp of deal

dean [diːn] n (REL) deán m; (SCOL: BRIT) decano; (: US) decano; rector m

dear [dɪə'] adj querido; (expensive) caro ♦ n: my ~ mi querido(-a) ♦ excl: ~ me! ¡Dios mío!; D~ Sir/Madam (in letter) Muy Señor Mío, Estimado Señor/

Estimada Señora; D~ Mr/Mrs X Estimado(-a) Señor(a) X ❑ **dearly** adv (love) mucho; (pay) caro

death [deθ] n muerte f ❑ **death penalty** n pena de muerte ❑ **death sentence** n condena a muerte

debate [dɪˈbeɪt] n debate m ♦ vt discutir

debit [ˈdebɪt] n debe m ♦ vt: **to ~ a sum to sb** or **to sb's account** cargar una suma en cuenta a algn ❑ **debit card** n tarjeta de débito

debris [ˈdebriː] n escombros mpl

debt [det] n deuda; **to be in ~** tener deudas

debut [ˈdeɪbjuː] n presentación f

Dec. abbr (= December) dic

decade [ˈdekeɪd] n decenio, década

decaffeinated [dɪˈkæfɪneɪtɪd] adj descafeinado

decay [dɪˈkeɪ] n (of building) desmoronamiento f; (of tooth) caries f inv ♦ vi (rot) pudrirse

deceased [dɪˈsiːst] n: **the ~** el (la) difunto(-a)

deceit [dɪˈsiːt] n engaño ❑ **deceive** [dɪˈsiːv] vt engañar

December [dɪˈsembə⁰] n diciembre m

decency [ˈdiːsənsɪ] n decencia

decent [ˈdiːsənt] adj (proper) decente; (person: kind) amable, bueno

deception [dɪˈsepʃən] n engaño

deceptive [dɪˈseptɪv] adj engañoso

⚠️ Be careful not to translate **deception** by the Spanish word *decepción*.

decide [dɪˈsaɪd] vt (person) decidir; (question, argument) resolver ♦ vi decidir; **to ~ to do/that** decidir hacer/que; **to ~ on sth** decidirse por algo

decimal [ˈdesɪməl] adj decimal ♦ n decimal m

decision [dɪˈsɪʒən] n decisión f

decisive [dɪˈsaɪsɪv] adj decisivo; (person) decidido

deck [dek] n (NAUT) cubierta; (of bus) piso; (record deck) platina; (of cards) baraja ❑ **deckchair** n tumbona

declaration [deklaˈreɪʃən] n declaración f

declare [dɪˈkleə⁰] vt declarar

decline [dɪˈklaɪn] n disminución f, descenso ♦ vt rehusar ♦ vi (person, business) decaer; (strength) disminuir

decorate [ˈdekəreɪt] vt (adorn): **to ~ (with)** adornar (de), decorar (de); (paint) pintar; (paper) empapelar ❑ **decoration** [-ˈreɪʃən] n adorno; (act) decoración f; (medal) condecoración f ❑ **decorator** n (workman) pintor m (decorador)

decrease [n ˈdiːkriːs, vb dɪˈkriːs] n: **~ (in)** disminución f (de) ♦ vt disminuir, reducir ♦ vi reducirse

decree [dɪˈkriː] n decreto

dedicate [ˈdedɪkeɪt] vt dedicar ❑ **dedicated** adj dedicado; (COMPUT) especializado; **dedicated word processor** procesador m de textos especializado or dedicado ❑ **dedication** [-ˈkeɪʃən] n (devotion) dedicación f; (in book) dedicatoria

deduce [dɪˈdjuːs] vt deducir

deduct [dɪˈdʌkt] vt restar, descontar ❑ **deduction** [dɪˈdʌkʃən] n (amount deducted) descuento; (conclusion) deducción f, conclusión f

deed [diːd] n hecho, acto; (feat) hazaña; (LAW) escritura

deem [diːm] vt (formal) juzgar, considerar

deep [diːp] adj profundo; (expressing measurements) de profundidad; (voice) bajo; (breath) profundo; (colour) intenso ♦ adv: **the spectators stood 20 ~** los espectadores se formaron de 20 en fondo; **to be 4 metres ~** tener 4 metros de profundidad ❑ **deep-fry** vt freír en aceite abundante ❑ **deeply** adv (breathe) a pleno pulmón; (interested, moved, grateful) profundamente, hondamente

deer [dɪə'] *n inv* ciervo

default [dɪ'fɔːlt] *n*: **by ~** (win) por incomparecencia ♦ *adj* (COMPUT) por defecto

defeat [dɪ'fiːt] *n* derrota ♦ *vt* derrotar, vencer

defect [*n* 'diːfekt, *vb* dɪ'fekt] *n* defecto ♦ *vi*: **to ~ to the enemy** pasarse al enemigo ☐ **defective** [dɪ'fektɪv] *adj* defectuoso

defence [dɪ'fens] (*US* **defense**) *n* defensa

defend [dɪ'fend] *vt* defender ☐ **defendant** *n* acusado(-a); (*in civil case*) demandado(-a) ☐ **defender** *n* defensor(a) *m/f*; (SPORT) defensa *mf*

defense [dɪ'fens] (*US*) = **defence**

defensive [dɪ'fensɪv] *adj* defensivo ♦ *n*: **on the ~** a la defensiva

defer [dɪ'fəː'] *vt* aplazar

defiance [dɪ'faɪəns] *n* desafío; **in ~ of** en contra de ☐ **defiant** [dɪ'faɪənt] *adj* (*challenging*) desafiante, retador(a)

deficiency [dɪ'fɪʃənsɪ] *n* (*lack*) falta; (*defect*) defecto ☐ **deficient** [dɪ'fɪʃənt] *adj* deficiente

deficit ['defɪsɪt] *n* déficit *m*

define [dɪ'faɪn] *vt* (*word etc*) definir; (*limits etc*) determinar

definite ['defɪnɪt] *adj* (*fixed*) determinado, (*obvious*) claro; (*certain*) indudable; **he was ~ about it** no dejó lugar a dudas (sobre ello) ☐ **definitely** *adv* desde luego, por supuesto

definition [defɪ'nɪʃən] *n* definición *f*; (*clearness*) nitidez *f*

deflate [diː'fleɪt] *vt* desinflar

deflect [dɪ'flekt] *vt* desviar

defraud [dɪ'frɔːd] *vt*: **to ~ sb of sth** estafar algo a algn

defrost [diː'frɒst] *vt* descongelar

defuse [diː'fjuːz] *vt* desactivar; (*situation*) calmar

defy [dɪ'faɪ] *vt* (*resist*) oponerse a; (*challenge*) desafiar; (*fig*): **it defies description** resulta imposible describirlo

degree [dɪ'griː] *n* grado; (SCOL) título; **to have a ~ in maths** tener una licenciatura en matemáticas; **by degrees** (*gradually*) poco a poco, por etapas; **to some ~** hasta cierto punto

dehydrated [diːhaɪ'dreɪtɪd] *adj* deshidratado; (*milk*) en polvo

de-icer [diː'aɪsə'] *n* descongelador *m*

delay [dɪ'leɪ] *vt* demorar, aplazar; (*person*) entretener; (*train*) retrasar ♦ *vi* tardar ♦ *n* demora, retraso; **to be delayed** retrasarse; **without ~** en seguida, sin tardar

delegate [*n* 'delɪgɪt, *vb* 'delɪgeɪt] *n* delegado(-a) ♦ *vt* (*person*) delegar en; (*task*) delegar

delete [dɪ'liːt] *vt* suprimir, tachar

deli ['delɪ] *n* = **delicatessen**

deliberate [*adj* dɪ'lɪbərɪt, *vb* dɪ'lɪbəreɪt] *adj* (*intentional*) intencionado; (*slow*) pausado, lento ♦ *vi* deliberar ☐ **deliberately** *adv* (*on purpose*) a propósito

delicacy ['delɪkəsɪ] *n* delicadeza; (*choice food*) manjar *m*

delicate ['delɪkɪt] *adj* delicado; (*fragile*) frágil

delicatessen [delɪkə'tesn] *n* ultramarinos *mpl* finos

delicious [dɪ'lɪʃəs] *adj* delicioso

delight [dɪ'laɪt] *n* (*feeling*) placer *m*, deleite *m*; (*person, experience etc*) encanto, delicia ♦ *vt* encantar, deleitar; **to take ~ in** deleitarse en ☐ **delighted** *adj*: **delighted (at or with/to do)** encantado (con/de hacer) ☐ **delightful** *adj* encantador(a), delicioso

delinquent [dɪ'lɪŋkwənt] *adj, n* delincuente *mf*

deliver [dɪ'lɪvə'] *vt* (*distribute*) repartir; (*hand over*) entregar; (*message*) comunicar; (*speech*) pronunciar; (MED) asistir al parto de ☐ **delivery** *n* reparto; entrega; (of speaker) modo de expresarse; (MED) parto, alumbramiento; **to take delivery of** recibir

delusion [dɪ'lu:ʒən] n ilusión f, engaño

de luxe [də'lʌks] adj de lujo

delve [dɛlv] vi: **to ~ into** hurgar en

demand [dɪ'mɑ:nd] vt (gen) exigir; (rights) reclamar ♦ n exigencia; (claim) reclamación f; (ECON) demanda; **to be in** = ser muy solicitado; **on ~** a solicitud ◻ **demanding** adj (boss) exigente; (work) absorbente

demise [dɪ'maɪz] n (death) fallecimiento

demo ['dɛməʊ] (inf) n abbr (= demonstration) manifestación f

democracy [dɪ'mɔkrəsɪ] n democracia ◻ **democrat** ['dɛməkræt] n demócrata mf ◻ **democratic** [dɛmə'krætɪk] adj democrático; (US) demócrata

demolish [dɪ'mɔlɪʃ] vt derribar, demoler; (fig: argument) destruir ◻ **demolition** [dɛmə'lɪʃən] n derribo, demolición f

demon ['di:mən] n (evil spirit) demonio

demonstrate ['dɛmənstreɪt] vt demostrar; (skill, appliance) mostrar ♦ vi manifestarse ◻ **demonstration** [-'streɪʃən] n (POL) manifestación f; (proof, exhibition) demostración f ◻ **demonstrator** n (POL) manifestante mf; (COMM) demostrador(a) m/f; vendedor(a) m/f

demote [dɪ'məʊt] vt degradar

den [dɛn] n (of animal) guarida; (room) habitación f

denial [dɪ'naɪəl] n (refusal) negativa; (of report etc) negación f

denim ['dɛnɪm] n tela vaquera; **denims** npl vaqueros mpl

Denmark ['dɛnmɑ:k] n Dinamarca

denomination [dɪnɔmɪ'neɪʃən] n valor m; (REL) confesión f

denounce [dɪ'naʊns] vt denunciar

dense [dɛns] adj (crowd) denso; (thick) espeso; (: foliage etc) tupido; (inf: stupid) torpe

density ['dɛnsɪtɪ] n densidad f; **single/ double-~ disk** n (COMPUT) disco de densidad sencilla/de doble densidad

dent [dɛnt] n abolladura ♦ vt (also: **make a ~ in**) abollar

dental ['dɛntl] adj dental ◻ **dental floss** [-flɔs] n seda dental ◻ **dental surgery** n clínica f dental, consultorio m dental

dentist ['dɛntɪst] n dentista mf

dentures ['dɛntʃəz] npl dentadura (postiza)

deny [dɪ'naɪ] vt negar; (charge) rechazar

deodorant [di:'əʊdərənt] n desodorante m

depart [dɪ'pɑ:t] vi irse, marcharse; (train) salir; **to ~ from** (fig: differ from) apartarse de

department [dɪ'pɑ:tmənt] n (COMM) sección f; (SCOL) departamento; (POL) ministerio ◻ **department store** n gran almacén m

departure [dɪ'pɑ:tʃə'] n partida, ida; (of train) salida; (of employee) marcha; **a new ~** un nuevo rumbo ◻ **departure lounge** n (at airport) sala de embarque

depend [dɪ'pɛnd] vi: **to ~ on** depender de; (rely on) contar con; **it depends** depende, según; **depending on the result** según el resultado ◻ **dependant** n dependiente mf ◻ **dependent** adj: **to be dependent on** depender de ♦ n = **dependant**

depict [dɪ'pɪkt] vt (in picture) pintar; (describe) representar

deport [dɪ'pɔ:t] vt deportar

deposit [dɪ'pɔzɪt] n depósito; (CHEM) sedimento; (of ore, oil) yacimiento ♦ vt (gen) depositar ◻ **deposit account** (BRIT) n cuenta de ahorros

depot ['dɛpəʊ] n (storehouse) depósito; (for vehicles) parque m; (US) estación f

depreciate [dɪ'pri:ʃɪeɪt] vi depreciarse, perder valor

depress [dɪ'pres] vt deprimir; (wages etc) hacer bajar; (press down) apretar
❏ **depressed** adj deprimido
❏ **depressing** adj deprimente
❏ **depression** [-ʃən] n depresión f

deprive [dɪ'praɪv] vt: **to ~ sb of** privar a algn de ❏ **deprived** adj necesitado

dept. abbr (= department) dto

depth [depθ] n profundidad f; (of cupboard) fondo; **to be in the depths of despair** sentir la mayor desesperación; **to be out of one's ~** (in water) no hacer pie; (fig) sentirse totalmente perdido

deputy ['depjutɪ] adj: **~ head** subdirector(a) m/f ♦ n sustituto(-a), suplente mf; (US POL) diputado(-a), (US: also: **~ sheriff**) agente m del sheriff

derail [dɪ'reɪl] vt: **to be derailed** descarrilarse

derelict ['derɪlɪkt] adj abandonado

derive [dɪ'raɪv] vt (benefit etc) obtener ♦ vi: **to ~ from** derivarse de

descend [dɪ'send] vt, vi descender, bajar; **to ~ from** descender de; **to ~ to** rebajarse a ❏ **descendant** n descendiente mf

descent [dɪ'sent] n descenso; (origin) descendencia

describe [dɪs'kraɪb] vt describir
❏ **description** [-'krɪpʃən] n descripción f; (sort) clase f, género

desert [n 'dezət, vb dɪ'zə:t] n desierto ♦ vt abandonar ♦ vi (MIL) desertar
❏ **deserted** [dɪ'zə:tɪd] adj desierto

deserve [dɪ'zə:v] vt merecer, ser digno de

design [dɪ'zaɪn] n (sketch) bosquejo; (layout, shape) diseño; (pattern) dibujo; (intention) intención f ♦ vt diseñar

designate [vb 'dezɪgneɪt, adj 'dezɪgnɪt] vt (appoint) nombrar; (destine) designar ♦ adj designado

designer [dɪ'zaɪnə] n diseñador(a) m/f; (fashion designer) modisto(-a), diseñador(a) m/f de moda

desirable [dɪ'zaɪərəbl] adj (proper) deseable; (attractive) atractivo

desire [dɪ'zaɪə] n deseo ♦ vt desear

desk [desk] n (in office) escritorio; (for pupil) pupitre m; (in hotel, at airport) recepción f; (BRIT: in shop, restaurant) caja ❏ **desk-top publishing** ['desktɒp-] n autoedición f

despair [dɪs'pεə] n desesperación f ♦ vi: **to ~ of** perder la esperanza de

dispatch [dɪs'pætʃ] n, vt = **dispatch**

desperate ['despərɪt] adj desesperado; (fugitive) peligroso; **to be ~ for sth/to do** necesitar urgentemente algo/ hacer ❏ **desperately** adv desesperadamente; (very) terriblemente, gravemente

desperation [despə'reɪʃən] n desesperación f; **in (sheer) ~** (absolutamente) desesperado

despise [dɪs'paɪz] vt despreciar

despite [dɪs'paɪt] prep a pesar de, pese a

dessert [dɪ'zə:t] n postre m
❏ **dessertspoon** n cuchara (de postre)

destination [destɪ'neɪʃən] n destino

destined ['destɪnd] adj: **~ for London** con destino a Londres

destiny ['destɪnɪ] n destino

destroy [dɪs'trɔɪ] vt destruir; (animal) sacrificar

destruction [dɪs'trʌkʃən] n destrucción f

destructive [dɪs'trʌktɪv] adj destructivo, destructor(a)

detach [dɪ'tætʃ] vt separar; (unstick) despegar ❏ **detached** adj (attitude) objetivo, imparcial ❏ **detached house** n = chalé m, ≈ chalet m

detail ['di:teɪl] n detalle m; (no pl: in picture etc) detalles mpl; (trifle) pequeñez f ♦ vt detallar; (MIL) destacar;

in ~ detalladamente ❏ **detailed** adj detallado

detain [dɪ'teɪn] vt retener; (in captivity) detener

detect [dɪ'tɛkt] vt descubrir; (MED, POLICE) identificar; (MIL, RADAR, TECH) detectar ❏ **detection** [dɪ'tɛkʃən] n descubrimiento; identificación f ❏ **detective** n detective mf ❏ **detective story** n novela policíaca

detention [dɪ'tɛnʃən] n detención f, arresto; (SCOL) castigo

deter [dɪ'tə:'] vt (dissuade) disuadir

detergent [dɪ'tə:dʒənt] n detergente m

deteriorate [dɪ'tɪərɪəreɪt] vi deteriorarse

determination [dɪtə:mɪ'neɪʃən] n resolución f

determine [dɪ'tə:mɪn] vt determinar ❏ **determined** adj (person) resuelto, decidido; **determined to do** resuelto a hacer

deterrent [dɪ'tɛrənt] n (MIL) fuerza de disuasión

detest [dɪ'tɛst] vt aborrecer

detour ['di:tuə'] n (gen, US AUT) desviación f

detract [dɪ'trækt] vt: **to ~ from** quitar mérito a, desvirtuar

detrimental [dɛtrɪ'mɛntl] adj: **~ (to)** perjudicial (a)

devastating [dɛvəsteɪtɪŋ] adj devastador(a); (fig) arrollador(a)

develop [dɪ'vɛləp] vt desarrollar; (PHOT) revelar; (disease) coger; (habit) adquirir; (fault) empezar a tener ♦ vi desarrollarse; (advance) progresar; (facts, symptoms) aparecer ❏ **developing country** n país m en (vías de) desarrollo ❏ **development** n desarrollo; (advance) progreso; (of affair, case) desenvolvimiento; (of land) urbanización f

device [dɪ'vaɪs] n (apparatus) aparato, mecanismo

devil ['dɛvl] n diablo, demonio

devious ['di:vɪəs] adj taimado

devise [dɪ'vaɪz] vt idear, inventar

devote [dɪ'vəut] vt: **to ~ sth** to dedicar algo a ❏ **devoted** adj (loyal) leal, fiel; **to be devoted to sb** querer con devoción a algn; **the book is devoted to politics** el libro trata de la política ❏ **devotion** n dedicación f; (REL) devoción f

devour [dɪ'vauə'] vt devorar

devout [dɪ'vaut] adj devoto

dew [dju:] n rocío

diabetes [daɪə'bi:ti:z] n diabetes f

diabetic [daɪə'bɛtɪk] adj, n diabético(-a) m/f

diagnose ['daɪəgnəuz] vt diagnosticar

diagnosis [daɪəg'nəusɪs] (pl **-ses**) n diagnóstico

diagonal [daɪ'ægənl] adj, n diagonal f

diagram ['daɪəgræm] n diagrama m, esquema m

dial ['daɪəl] n esfera (SP), cara (LAm); (on radio etc) dial m; (of phone) disco ♦ vt (number) marcar

dialect ['daɪəlɛkt] n dialecto

dialling code ['daɪəlɪŋ-] n prefijo

dialling tone (US **dial tone**) n (BRIT) señal f or tono de marcar

dialogue ['daɪəlɔg] (US **dialog**) n diálogo

diameter [daɪ'æmɪtə'] n diámetro

diamond ['daɪəmənd] n diamante m; (shape) rombo; **diamonds** npl (CARDS) diamantes mpl

diaper ['daɪəpə'] (US) n pañal m

diarrhoea [daɪə'ri:ə] (US **diarrhea**) n diarrea

diary ['daɪərɪ] n (daily account) diario; (book) agenda

dice [daɪs] n inv dados mpl ♦ vt (CULIN) cortar en cuadritos

dictate [dɪk'teɪt] vt dictar; (conditions) imponer ❑ **dictation** [-'teɪʃən] n dictado; (giving of orders) órdenes fpl

dictator [dɪk'teɪtə'] n dictador m

dictionary ['dɪkʃənrɪ] n diccionario

did [dɪd] pt of **do**

didn't ['dɪdənt] = **did not**

die [daɪ] vi morir; (fig: fade) desvanecerse, desaparecer; **to be dying for sth/to do sth** morirse por algo/de ganas de hacer algo ▸ **die down** vi apagarse; (wind) amainar ▸ **die out** vi desaparecer

diesel ['di:zəl] n vehículo con motor Diesel

diet ['daɪət] n dieta; (restricted food) régimen m ♦ vi (also: **be on a ~**) estar a dieta, hacer régimen

differ ['dɪfə'] vi: **to ~ (from)** (be different) ser distinto a, diferenciarse (de); (disagree) discrepar (de) ❑ **difference** n diferencia; (disagreement) desacuerdo ❑ **different** adj diferente, distinto ❑ **differentiate** [-'renʃɪeɪt] vi: **to differentiate (between)** distinguir (entre) ❑ **differently** adv de otro modo, en forma distinta

difficult ['dɪfɪkəlt] adj difícil ❑ **difficulty** n dificultad f

dig [dɪg] (pt, pp **dug**) vt (hole, ground) cavar ♦ n (prod) empujón m; (archaeological) excavación f; (remark) indirecta; **to ~ one's nails into** clavar las uñas en ▸ **dig up** vt (information) desenterrar; (plant) desarraigar

digest [vb daɪ'dʒest, n'daɪdʒest] vt (food) digerir; (facts) asimilar ♦ n resumen m ❑ **digestion** [dɪ'dʒestʃən] n digestión f

digit ['dɪdʒɪt] n (number) dígito; (finger) dedo ❑ **digital** adj digital ❑ **digital camera** n cámara digital ❑ **digital TV** n televisión f digital

dignified ['dɪgnɪfaɪd] adj grave, solemne

dignity ['dɪgnɪtɪ] n dignidad f

digs [dɪgz] (BRIT: inf) npl pensión f, alojamiento

dilemma [daɪ'lemə] n dilema m

dill [dɪl] n eneldo

dilute [daɪ'luːt] vt diluir

dim [dɪm] adj (light) débil; (outline) indistinto; (room) oscuro; (inf: stupid) lerdo ♦ vt (light) bajar

dime [daɪm] n (US) moneda de diez centavos

dimension [dɪ'menʃən] n dimensión f

diminish [dɪ'mɪnɪʃ] vt, vi disminuir

din [dɪn] n estruendo, estrépito

dine [daɪn] vi cenar ❑ **diner** n (person) comensal mf

dinghy ['dɪŋgɪ] n bote m; (also: **rubber ~**) lancha (neumática)

dingy ['dɪndʒɪ] adj (room) sombrío; (colour) sucio

dining car ['daɪnɪŋ-] (BRIT) n (RAIL) coche-comedor m

dining room ['daɪnɪŋ-] n comedor m

dining table n mesa f de comedor

dinner ['dɪnə'] n (evening meal) cena; (lunch) comida; (public) cena, banquete m ❑ **dinner jacket** n smoking m ❑ **dinner party** n cena ❑ **dinner time** n (evening) hora de cenar; (midday) hora de comer

dinosaur ['daɪnəsɔː'] n dinosaurio

dip [dɪp] n (slope) pendiente m; (in sea) baño; (CULIN) salsa ♦ vt (in water) mojar; (ladle etc) meter; (BRIT AUT): **to ~ one's lights** poner luces de cruce ♦ vi (road etc) descender, bajar

diploma [dɪ'pləumə] n diploma m

diplomacy [dɪ'pləuməsɪ] n diplomacia

diplomat ['dɪpləmæt] n diplomático(-a) ❑ **diplomatic** [dɪplə'mætɪk] adj diplomático

dipstick ['dɪpstɪk] (BRIT) n (AUT) varilla de nivel (del aceite)

dire [daɪə'] adj calamitoso

direct [daɪ'rekt] adj directo; (person) franco ♦ vt dirigir;

(*order*): **to ~ sb to do sth** mandar a algn hacer algo ♦ *adv* derecho; **can you ~ me to ...?** ¿puede indicarme dónde está ...? ❏ **direct debit** (*BRIT*) *n* domiciliación *f* bancaria de recibos

direction [dɪˈrɛkʃən] *n* dirección *f*; **sense of ~** sentido de la dirección; **directions** *npl* (*instructions*) instrucciones *fpl*; **directions for use** modo de empleo

directly [dɪˈrɛktlɪ] *adv* (*in straight line*) directamente; (*at once*) en seguida

director [dɪˈrɛktə*] *n* director(a) *m/f*

directory [dɪˈrɛktərɪ] *n* (*TEL*) guía (telefónica); (*COMPUT*) directorio ❏ **directory enquiries** (*US* **directory assistance**) *n* (servicio de) información *f*

dirt [dɜːt] *n* suciedad *f*; (*earth*) tierra ❏ **dirty** *adj* sucio; (*joke*) verde, colorado (*MEX*) ♦ *vt* ensuciar; (*stain*) manchar

disability [dɪsəˈbɪlɪtɪ] *n* incapacidad *f*

disabled [dɪsˈeɪbld] *adj*: **to be physically ~** ser minusválido(-a); **to be mentally ~** ser deficiente mental

disadvantage [dɪsədˈvɑːntɪdʒ] *n* desventaja, inconveniente *m*

disagree [dɪsəˈɡriː] *vi* (*differ*) discrepar; **to ~ (with)** no estar de acuerdo (con) ❏ **disagreeable** *adj* desagradable; (*person*) antipático ❏ **disagreement** *n* desacuerdo

disappear [dɪsəˈpɪə*] *vi* desaparecer ❏ **disappearance** *n* desaparición *f*

disappoint [dɪsəˈpɔɪnt] *vt* decepcionar, defraudar ❏ **disappointed** *adj* decepcionado ❏ **disappointing** *adj* decepcionante ❏ **disappointment** *n* decepción *f*

disapproval [dɪsəˈpruːvəl] *n* desaprobación *f*

disapprove [dɪsəˈpruːv] *vi*: **to ~ of** ver mal

disarm [dɪsˈɑːm] *vt* desarmar ❏ **disarmament** [dɪsˈɑːməmənt] *n* desarme *m*

disaster [dɪˈzɑːstə*] *n* desastre *m*

disastrous [dɪˈzɑːstrəs] *adj* desastroso

disbelief [dɪsbəˈliːf] *n* incredulidad *f*

disc [dɪsk] *n* disco; (*COMPUT*) = **disk**

discard [dɪsˈkɑːd] *vt* (*old things*) tirar; (*fig*) descartar

discharge [*vb* dɪsˈtʃɑːdʒ, *n* ˈdɪstʃɑːdʒ] *vt* (*task, debt*) cumplir; (*waste*) verter; (*patient*) dar de alta; (*employee*) despedir; (*soldier*) licenciar; (*defendant*) poner en libertad ♦ *n* (*ELEC*) descarga; (*MED*) supuración *f*; (*dismissal*) despedida; (*of duty*) desempeño; (*of debt*) pago, descargo

discipline [ˈdɪsɪplɪn] *n* disciplina ♦ *vt* disciplinar; (*punish*) castigar

disc jockey *n* pinchadiscos *mf inv*

disclose [dɪsˈkləʊz] *vt* revelar

disco [ˈdɪskəʊ] *n abbr* discoteca

discoloured [dɪsˈkʌləd] (*US* **discolored**) *adj* descolorido

discomfort [dɪsˈkʌmfət] *n* incomodidad *f*; (*unease*) inquietud *f*; (*physical*) malestar *m*

disconnect [dɪskəˈnɛkt] *vt* separar; (*ELEC etc*) desconectar

discontent [dɪskənˈtɛnt] *n* descontento

discontinue [dɪskənˈtɪnjuː] *vt* interrumpir; (*payments*) suspender; **"discontinued"** (*COMM*) "ya no se fabrica"

discount [*n* ˈdɪskaʊnt, *vb* dɪsˈkaʊnt] *n* descuento ♦ *vt* descontar

discourage [dɪsˈkʌrɪdʒ] *vt* desalentar; (*advise against*): **to ~ sb from doing** disuadir a algn de hacer

discover [dɪsˈkʌvə*] *vt* descubrir; (*error*) darse cuenta de ❏ **discovery** *n* descubrimiento

discredit [dɪsˈkrɛdɪt] *vt* desacreditar

discreet [dɪsˈkriːt] *adj* (*tactful*) discreto; (*careful*) circunspecto, prudente

discrepancy [dɪsˈkrɛpənsɪ] *n* diferencia

discretion [dɪ'skreʃən] n (tact) discreción f; **at the ~ of** a criterio de

discriminate [dɪ'skrɪmɪneɪt] vi: **to ~ between** distinguir entre; **to ~ against** discriminar contra ❏ **discrimination** [-'neɪʃən] n (discernment) perspicacia; (bias) discriminación f

discuss [dɪ'skʌs] vt discutir; (a theme) tratar ❏ **discussion** [dɪ'skʌʃən] n discusión f

disease [dɪ'ziːz] n enfermedad f

disembark [dɪsɪm'bɑːk] vt, vi desembarcar

disgrace [dɪs'greɪs] n ignominia; (shame) vergüenza, escándalo ♦ vt deshonrar ❏ **disgraceful** adj vergonzoso

disgruntled [dɪs'grʌntld] adj disgustado, descontento

disguise [dɪs'gaɪz] n disfraz m ♦ vt disfrazar; **in ~** disfrazado

disgust [dɪs'gʌst] n repugnancia ♦ vt repugnar, dar asco a

⚠ Be careful not to translate *disgust* by the Spanish word *disgustar*.

disgusted [dɪs'gʌstɪd] adj indignado

⚠ Be careful not to translate *disgusted* by *disgustado*.

disgusting [dɪs'gʌstɪŋ] adj repugnante, asqueroso; (behaviour etc) vergonzoso

dish [dɪʃ] n (gen) plato; **to do** or **wash the dishes** fregar los platos ❏ **dishcloth** n estropajo

dishonest [dɪs'ɒnɪst] adj (person) poco honrado, tramposo; (means) fraudulento

dishtowel ['dɪʃtaʊəl] (US) n estropajo

dishwasher ['dɪʃwɒʃə*] n lavaplatos m inv

disillusion [dɪsɪ'luːʒən] vt desilusionar

disinfectant [dɪsɪn'fektənt] n desinfectante m

disintegrate [dɪs'ɪntɪgreɪt] vi disgregarse, desintegrarse

disk [dɪsk] n (esp US) = **disc**; (COMPUT) disco, disquete m; **single-/double-sided ~** disco de una cara/dos caras ❏ **disk drive** n disc drive m ❏ **diskette** n = **disk**

dislike [dɪs'laɪk] n antipatía, aversión f ♦ vt tener antipatía a

dislocate ['dɪsləkeɪt] vt dislocar

disloyal [dɪs'lɔɪəl] adj desleal

dismal ['dɪzml] adj (gloomy) deprimente, triste; (very bad) malísimo, fatal

dismantle [dɪs'mæntl] vt desmontar, desarmar

dismay [dɪs'meɪ] n consternación f ♦ vt consternar

dismiss [dɪs'mɪs] vt (worker) despedir; (pupils) dejar marchar; (soldiers) dar permiso para irse; (idea, LAW) rechazar; (possibility) descartar ❏ **dismissal** n despido

disobedient [dɪsə'biːdɪənt] adj desobediente

disobey [dɪsə'beɪ] vt desobedecer

disorder [dɪs'ɔːdə*] n desorden m; (rioting) disturbios mpl; (MED) trastorno

disorganized [dɪs'ɔːgənaɪzd] adj desorganizado

disown [dɪs'əʊn] vt (action) renegar de; (person) negar cualquier tipo de relación con

dispatch [dɪs'pætʃ] vt enviar ♦ n (sending) envío; (PRESS) informe m; (MIL) parte m

dispel [dɪs'pel] vt disipar

dispense [dɪs'pens] vt (medicines) preparar ▸ **dispense with** vt fus prescindir de ❏ **dispenser** n (container) distribuidor m automático

disperse [dɪs'pɜːs] vt dispersar ♦ vi dispersarse

display [dɪs'pleɪ] n (in shop window) escaparate m; (exhibition) exposición f; (COMPUT) visualización f; (of feeling) manifestación f ♦ vt exponer; manifestar; (*ostentatiously*) lucir

displease [dɪsˈpliːz] vt (*offend*) ofender; (*annoy*) fastidiar

disposable [dɪsˈpəʊzəbl] adj desechable; (*income*) disponible

disposal [dɪsˈpəʊzl] n (*of rubbish*) destrucción f; **at one's ~** a su disposición

dispose [dɪsˈpəʊz] vi: **to ~ of** (*unwanted goods*) deshacerse de; (*problem etc*) resolver ☐ **disposition** [dɪspəˈzɪʃən] n (*nature*) temperamento f; (*inclination*) propensión f

disproportionate [dɪsprəˈpɔːʃənət] adj desproporcionado

dispute [dɪsˈpjuːt] n disputa; (*also:* **industrial ~**) conflicto (laboral) ♦ vt (*argue*) disputar, discutir; (*question*) cuestionar

disqualify [dɪsˈkwɒlɪfaɪ] vt (SPORT) desclasificar; **to ~ sb for sth/from doing sth** incapacitar a algn para algo/ hacer algo

disregard [dɪsrɪˈgɑːd] vt (*ignore*) no hacer caso de

disrupt [dɪsˈrʌpt] vt (*plans*) desbaratar, trastornar; (*conversation*) interrumpir ☐ **disruption** [dɪsˈrʌpʃən] n desbaratamiento; interrupción f

dissatisfaction [dɪssætɪsˈfækʃən] n disgusto, descontento

dissatisfied [dɪsˈsætɪsfaɪd] adj insatisfecho

dissect [dɪˈsekt] vt disecar

dissent [dɪˈsent] n disensión f

dissertation [dɪsəˈteɪʃən] n tesina

dissolve [dɪˈzɒlv] vt disolver ♦ vi disolverse; **to ~ in(to) tears** deshacerse en lágrimas

distance [ˈdɪstəns] n distancia; **in the ~** a lo lejos

distant [ˈdɪstənt] adj lejano; (*manner*) reservado, frío

distil [dɪsˈtɪl] (US **distill**) vt destilar ☐ **distillery** n destilería

distinct [dɪsˈtɪŋkt] adj (*different*) distinto; (*clear*) claro; (*unmistakeable*) inequívoco; **as ~ from** a diferencia de ☐ **distinction** [dɪsˈtɪŋkʃən] n distinción f; (*honour*) honor m; (*in exam*) sobresaliente m ☐ **distinctive** adj distintivo

distinguish [dɪsˈtɪŋgwɪʃ] vt distinguir; **to ~ o.s.** destacarse ☐ **distinguished** adj (*eminent*) distinguido

distort [dɪsˈtɔːt] vt distorsionar; (*shape, image*) deformar

distract [dɪsˈtrækt] vt distraer ☐ **distracted** adj distraído ☐ **distraction** [dɪsˈtrækʃən] n distracción f; (*confusion*) aturdimiento

distraught [dɪsˈtrɔːt] adj loco de inquietud

distress [dɪsˈtres] n (*anguish*) angustia, aflicción f ♦ vt afligir ☐ **distressing** adj angustioso; doloroso

distribute [dɪsˈtrɪbjuːt] vt distribuir; (*share out*) repartir ☐ **distribution** [-ˈbjuːʃən] n distribución f, reparto ☐ **distributor** n (AUT) distribuidor m; (COMM) distribuidora

district [ˈdɪstrɪkt] n (*of country*) zona, región f; (*of town*) barrio; (ADMIN) distrito ☐ **district attorney** (US) n fiscal mf

distrust [dɪsˈtrʌst] n desconfianza ♦ vt desconfiar de

disturb [dɪsˈtɜːb] vt (*person: bother, interrupt*) molestar; (: *upset*) perturbar, inquietar; (*disorganize*) alterar ☐ **disturbance** n (*upheaval*) perturbación f; (*political etc: gen pl*) disturbio; (*of mind*) trastorno ☐ **disturbed** adj (*worried, upset*) preocupado, angustiado; **emotionally disturbed** trastornado; (*childhood*) inseguro ☐ **disturbing** adj inquietante, perturbador(a)

ditch [dɪtʃ] n zanja; (*irrigation ditch*) acequia ♦ vt (inf: *partner*) deshacerse de; (: *plan, car etc*) abandonar

ditto [ˈdɪtəʊ] adv ídem, lo mismo

dive [daɪv] n (from board) salto; (underwater) buceo; (of submarine) sumersión f ♦ vi (swimmer: into water) saltar; (: under water) zambullirse, bucear; (fish, submarine) sumergirse; (bird) lanzarse en picado; **to ~ into** (bag etc) meter la mano en; (place) meterse de prisa en ☐ **diver** n (underwater) buzo

diverse [daɪˈvɜːs] adj diversos(-as), varios(-as)

diversion [daɪˈvɜːʃən] n (BRIT AUT) desviación f; (distraction, MIL) diversión f; (of funds) distracción f

diversity [daɪˈvɜːsɪtɪ] n diversidad f

divert [daɪˈvɜːt] vt (turn aside) desviar

divide [dɪˈvaɪd] vt dividir; (separate) separar ♦ vi dividirse; (road) bifurcarse ☐ **divided highway** (US) n carretera de doble calzada

divine [dɪˈvaɪn] adj (also fig) divino

diving [ˈdaɪvɪŋ] n (SPORT) salto; (underwater) buceo ☐ **diving board** n trampolín m

division [dɪˈvɪʒən] n división f; (sharing out) reparto; (disagreement) diferencias fpl; (COMM) sección f

divorce [dɪˈvɔːs] n divorcio ♦ vt divorciarse de ☐ **divorced** adj divorciado ☐ **divorcee** [-ˈsiː] n divorciado(-a)

D.I.Y. (BRIT) adj, n abbr = **do-it-yourself**

dizzy [ˈdɪzɪ] adj (spell) de mareo; **to feel ~** marearse

DJ n abbr = **disc jockey**

DNA n abbr (= deoxyribonucleic acid) ADN m

do

KEYWORD

[duː] (pt **did**, pp **done**) n (inf: party etc): **we're having a little do on Saturday** damos una fiestecita el sábado; **it was rather a grand do** fue un acontecimiento a lo grande
♦ aux vb

1 (in negative constructions: not translated): **I don't understand** no entiendo

2 (to form questions: not translated): **didn't you know?** ¿no lo sabías?; **what do you think?** ¿qué opinas?

3 (for emphasis, in polite expressions): **people do make mistakes sometimes** sí que se cometen errores a veces; **she does seem rather late** a mí también me parece que se ha retrasado; **do sit down/help yourself** siéntate/sírvete por favor; **do take care!** ¡ten cuidado(, te pido)!

4 (used to avoid repeating vb): **she sings better than I do** canta mejor que yo; **do you agree? — yes, I do/ no, I don't** ¿estás de acuerdo? — sí (lo estoy)/no (lo estoy); **she lives in Glasgow — so do I** vive en Glasgow — yo también; **he didn't like it and neither did we** no le gustó y a nosotros tampoco; **who made this mess? — I did** ¿quién hizo esta chapuza? — yo; **he asked me to help him and I did** me pidió que le ayudara y lo hice

5 (in question tags): **you like him, don't you?** te gusta, ¿verdad? or ¿no?; **I don't know him, do I?** creo que no le conozco
♦ vt

1 (gen, carry out, perform etc): **what are you doing tonight?** ¿qué haces esta noche?; **what can I do for you?** ¿en qué puedo servirle?; **to do the washing-up/cooking** fregar los platos/cocinar; **to do one's teeth/ hair/nails** lavarse los dientes/ arreglarse el pelo/arreglarse las uñas

2 (AUT etc): **the car was doing 100** el coche iba a 100; **we've done 200 km**

already ya hemos hecho 200 km; **he can do 100 in that car** puede ir a 100 en ese coche
♦ vi
1 (act, behave) hacer; **do as I do** haz como yo
2 (get on, fare): **he's doing well/badly at school** va bien/mal en la escuela; **the firm is doing well** la empresa anda or va bien; **how do you do?** mucho gusto; (less formal) ¿qué tal?
3 (suit): **will it do?** ¿sirve?, ¿está or va bien?
4 (be sufficient) bastar; **will £10 do?** ¿será bastante con £10?; **that'll do** así está bien; **that'll do!** (in annoyance) ¡ya está bien!, ¡basta ya!; **to make do (with)** arreglárselas (con)
► **do up** vt (laces) atar; (zip, dress, shirt) abrochar; (renovate: room, house) renovar
► **do with** vt fus (need): **I could do with a drink/some help** no me vendría mal un trago/un poco de ayuda; (be connected) tener que ver con; **what has it got to do with you?** ¿qué tiene que ver contigo?
► **do without** vi pasar sin; **if you're late for tea then you'll do without** si llegas tarde tendrás que quedarte sin cenar ♦ vt fus pasar sin; **I can do without a car** puedo pasar sin coche

dock [dɔk] n (NAUT) muelle m; (LAW) banquillo m (de los acusados) ♦ vi (enter dock) atracar (la) muelle; (SPACE) acoplarse ► **docks** npl (NAUT) muelles mpl, puerto sg

doctor ['dɔktə'] n médico(-a); (Ph.D. etc) doctor(a) m/f ♦ vt (drink etc) adulterar ► **Doctor of Philosophy** n Doctor en Filosofía y Letras

document ['dɔkjumənt] n documento ► **documentary** [-'mentəri] adj

documental ♦ n documental m
► **documentation** [-men'teɪʃən] n documentación f

dodge [dɔdʒ] n (fig) truco ♦ vt evadir; (blow) esquivar

dodgy ['dɔdʒɪ] adj (inf: uncertain) dudoso; (suspicious) sospechoso; (risky) arriesgado

does [dʌz] vb see **do**

doesn't ['dʌznt] = **does not**

dog [dɔg] n perro ♦ vt seguir los pasos de; (bad luck) perseguir ► **doggy bag** ['dɔgɪ-] n bolsa para llevarse las sobras de la comida

do-it-yourself ['du:ɪtjɔ:'self] n bricolaje m

dole [dəul] (BRIT) n (payment) subsidio de paro; **on the ~** parado

doll [dɔl] n muñeca; (US: inf: woman) muñeca, gachí f

dollar ['dɔlə'] n dólar m

dolphin ['dɔlfɪn] n delfín m

dome [dəum] n (ARCH) cúpula

domestic [də'mestɪk] adj (animal, duty) doméstico; (flight, policy) nacional ► **domestic appliance** n aparato doméstico, aparato m de uso doméstico

dominant ['dɔmɪnənt] adj dominante

dominate ['dɔmɪneɪt] vt dominar

domino ['dɔmɪnəu] (pl dominoes) n ficha de dominó ► **dominoes** n (game) dominó

donate [də'neɪt] vt donar ► **donation** [də'neɪʃən] n donativo

done [dʌn] pp of **do**

donkey ['dɔŋkɪ] n burro

donor ['dəunə'] n donante m/f ► **donor card** n carnet m de donante

don't [dəunt] = **do not**

donut ['dəunʌt] (US) n = **doughnut**

doodle ['du:dl] vi hacer dibujitos or garabatos

doom [du:m] n (fate) suerte f ♦ vt: **to be doomed to failure** estar condenado al fracaso

door [dɔ:ʳ] n puerta ❑ **doorbell** n timbre m ❑ **door handle** n tirador m; (of car) manija ❑ **doorknob** n pomo m de la puerta, manilla f (LAm) ❑ **doorstep** n peldaño ❑ **doorway** n entrada, puerta

dope [dəup] n (inf: illegal drug) droga; (: person) imbécil mf ♦ vt (horse etc) drogar

dormitory [ˈdɔːmɪtrɪ] n (BRIT) dormitorio; (US) colegio mayor

DOS n abbr (= disk operating system) DOS m

dosage [ˈdəusɪdʒ] n dosis f inv

dose [dəus] n dosis f inv

dot [dɔt] n punto ♦ vi: **dotted with** salpicado de; **on the ~** en punto ❑ **dotted line** [ˈdɔtɪd-] n: **to sign on the dotted line** firmar

double [ˈdʌbl] adj doble ♦ adv (twice): **to cost ~** costar el doble ♦ n doble m ♦ vt doblar ♦ vi doblarse; **on the ~, at the ~** (BRIT) corriendo ▶ **double back** vi (person) volver sobre sus pasos ❑ **double bass** n contrabajo ❑ **double bed** n cama de matrimonio ❑ **double-check** vt volver a revisar ♦ vi: **I'll double-check** voy a revisarlo otra vez ❑ **double-click** vi (COMPUT) hacer doble clic ❑ **double-cross** vt (trick) engañar; (betray) traicionar ❑ **doubledecker** n autobús m de dos pisos ❑ **double glazing** (BRIT) n doble acristalamiento ❑ **double room** n habitación f doble ❑ **doubles** n (TENNIS) juego de dobles ❑ **double yellow lines** npl (BRIT: AUT) línea doble amarilla de prohibido aparcar; = línea fsg amarilla continua

doubt [daut] n duda ♦ vt dudar; (suspect) dudar de; **to ~ that** dudar que ❑ **doubtful** adj dudoso; (person): **to be doubtful about sth** tener dudas sobre algo ❑ **doubtless** adv sin duda

dough [dəu] n masa, pasta ❑ **doughnut** (US **donut**) n = rosquilla

dove [dʌv] n paloma

down [daun] n (feathers) plumón m, flojel m ♦ adv (downwards) abajo, hacia abajo; (on the ground) por el suelo, en tierra ♦ prep abajo ♦ vt (inf: drink) beberse; **~ with X!** ¡abajo X! ❑ **down-and-out** n vagabundo(-a) ❑ **downfall** n caída, ruina ❑ **downhill** adv: **to go downhill** (also fig) ir cuesta abajo

Downing Street [ˈdaunɪŋ-] n (BRIT) Downing Street f

down: download vt (COMPUT) bajar ❑ **downright** adj (nonsense, lie) manifiesto; (refusal) terminante

Down's syndrome [ˈdaunz-] n síndrome m de Down

down: downstairs adv (below) (en la piso de) abajo; (downwards) escaleras abajo ❑ **down-to-earth** adj práctico ❑ **downtown** adv en el centro de la ciudad ❑ **down under** adv en Australia (or Nueva Zelanda) ❑ **downward** [-wəd] adj, adv hacia abajo ❑ **downwards** [-wədz] adv hacia abajo

doz. abbr = **dozen**

doze [dəuz] vi dormitar

dozen [ˈdʌzn] n docena; **a ~ books** una docena de libros; **dozens of** cantidad de

Dr. abbr = **doctor; drive**

drab [dræb] adj gris, monótono

draft [drɑ:ft] n (first copy) borrador m; (POL: of bill) anteproyecto; (US: call-up) quinta ♦ vt (plan) esbozar; (write roughly) hacer un borrador de; see also **draught**

drag [dræg] vt arrastrar; (river) dragar, rastrear ♦ vi (time) pasar despacio; (play, film etc) hacerse pesado ♦ n (inf) lata; (women's clothing): **in ~** vestido de travesti; **to ~ and drop** (COMPUT) arrastrar y soltar

dragon [ˈdrægən] n dragón m

dragonfly ['drægənflaɪ] n libélula

drain [dreɪn] n desaguadero; (in street) sumidero; (source of loss): **to be a ~ on** consumir, agotar ♦ vt (land, marshes) desaguar; (reservoir) desecar; (vegetables) escurrir ♦ vi escurrirse □ **drainage** n (act) desagüe m; (MED, AGR) drenaje m; (sewage) alcantarillado □ **drainpipe** n tubo de desagüe

drama ['drɑːmə] n (art) teatro; (play) drama m; (excitement) emoción f □ **dramatic** [drə'mætɪk] adj dramático; (sudden, marked) espectacular

drank [dræŋk] pt of **drink**

drape [dreɪp] vt (cloth) colocar; (flag) colgar; **drapes** npl (US) cortinas fpl

drastic ['dræstɪk] adj (measure) severo; (change) radical, drástico

draught [drɑːft] (US **draft**) n (of air) corriente f de aire; (NAUT) calado; **on ~** (beer) de barril □ **draught beer** n cerveza de barril □ **draughts** (BRIT) n (game) juego de damas

draw [drɔː] (pt **drew**, pp **drawn**) vt (picture) dibujar; (cart) tirar de; (curtain) correr; (take out) sacar; (attract) atraer; (money) retirar; (wages) cobrar ♦ vi (SPORT) empatar ♦ n (SPORT) empate m; (lottery) sorteo ▸ **draw out** vi (lengthen) alargarse ♦ vt sacar ▸ **draw up** vi (stop) pararse ♦ vt (chair) acercar; (document) redactar □ **drawback** n inconveniente m, desventaja

drawer [drɔː[r]] n cajón m

drawing ['drɔːɪŋ] n dibujo □ **drawing pin** (BRIT) n chincheta □ **drawing room** n salón m

drawn [drɔːn] pp of **draw**

dread [drɛd] n pavor m, terror m ♦ vt temer, tener miedo or pavor a □ **dreadful** adj horroroso

dream [driːm] (pt, pp **dreamed** or **dreamt**) n sueño ♦ vt, vi soñar □ **dreamer** n soñador(a) m/f

dreamt [drɛmt] pt, pp of **dream**

dreary ['drɪərɪ] adj monótono

drench [drɛntʃ] vt empapar

dress [drɛs] n vestido; (clothing) ropa ♦ vt vestir; (wound) vendar ♦ vi vestirse; **to get dressed** vestirse ▸ **dress up** vi vestirse de etiqueta; (in fancy dress) disfrazarse □ **dress circle** (BRIT) n principal m □ **dresser** n (furniture) aparador m; (: US) cómoda (con espejo) □ **dressing** n (MED) vendaje m; (CULIN) aliño □ **dressing gown** (BRIT) n bata □ **dressing room** n (THEATRE) camarín m; (SPORT) vestuario □ **dressing table** n tocador m □ **dressmaker** n modista, costurera

drew [druː] pt of **draw**

dribble ['drɪbl] vi (baby) babear ♦ vt (ball) regatear

dried [draɪd] adj (fruit) seco; (milk) en polvo

drier ['draɪə[r]] n = **dryer**

drift [drɪft] n (of current etc) flujo; (of snow) ventisquero; (meaning) significado ♦ vi (boat) ir a la deriva; (sand, snow) amontonarse

drill [drɪl] n (drill bit) broca; (tool for DIY etc) taladro; (of dentist) fresa; (for mining etc) perforadora, barrena, (MIL) instrucción f ♦ vt perforar, taladrar; (troops) enseñar la instrucción a ♦ vi (for oil) perforar

drink [drɪŋk] (pt **drank**, pp **drunk**) n bebida; (sip) trago ♦ vt, vi beber; **to have a ~** tomar algo; tomar una copa or un trago; **a ~ of water** un trago de agua □ **drink-driving: to be charged with drink-driving** ser acusado de conducir borracho or en estado de embriaguez □ **drinker** n bebedor(a) m/f □ **drinking water** n agua potable

drip [drɪp] n (act) goteo; (one drip) gota; (MED) gota a gota m ♦ vi gotear

drive [draɪv] (pt **drove**, pp **driven**) n (journey) viaje m (en coche); (also:

driveway) entrada; (*energy*) energía, vigor m; (COMPUT: also: **disk ~**) drive m ♦ vt (*car*) conducir (SP), manejar (LAm); (*nail*) clavar; (*push*) empujar; (TECH: *motor*) impulsar ♦ vi (AUT: *at controls*) conducir; (: *travel*) pasearse en coche; **left-/right-hand ~** conducción f a la izquierda/derecha; **to ~ sb mad** volverle loco a algn ► **drive out** vt (*force out*) expulsar, echar □ **drive-in** adj (esp US): **drive-in cinema** autocine m

driven ['drɪvn] pp of **drive**

driver ['draɪvəʳ] n conductor(a) m/f (SP), chofer mf (LAm); (of taxi, bus) chófer mf (SP), chofer mf (LAm); **driver's license** (US) n carnet m de conducir

driveway ['draɪvweɪ] n entrada

driving ['draɪvɪŋ] n conducir (SP), el manejar (LAm) □ **driving instructor** n profesor(a) m/f de autoescuela (SP), instructor(a) m/f de manejo (LAm) □ **driving lesson** n clase f de conducir (SP) or manejar (LAm) □ **driving licence** (BRIT) n licencia de manejo (LAm), carnet m de conducir (SP) □ **driving test** n examen m de conducir (SP) or manejar (LAm)

drizzle ['drɪzl] n llovizna

droop [druːp] vi (*flower*) marchitarse; (*shoulders*) encorvarse; (*head*) inclinarse

drop [drɔp] n (of water) gota; (*lessening*) baja; (*fall*) caída ♦ vt dejar caer; (*voice, eyes, price*) bajar; (*passenger*) dejar; (*omit*) omitir ♦ vi (*object*) caer; (*wind*) amainar ► **drop in** vi (inf: *visit*): **to drop in (on)** pasar por casa (de) ► **drop off** vi (*sleep*) dormirse ♦ vt (*passenger*) dejar ► **drop out** vi (*withdraw*) retirarse

drought [draut] n sequía

drove [drəuv] pt of **drive**

drown [draun] vt ahogar ♦ vi ahogarse

drowsy ['drauzɪ] adj soñoliento; **to be ~** tener sueño

drug [drʌg] n medicamento; (*narcotic*) droga ♦ vt drogar; **to be on drugs** drogarse □ **drug addict** n drogadicto(-a) □ **drug dealer** n traficante mf de drogas □ **druggist** (US) n farmacéutico □ **drugstore** (US) n farmacia

drum [drʌm] n tambor m; (for oil, petrol) bidón m; **drums** npl batería □ **drummer** n tambor m

drunk [drʌŋk] pp of **drink** ♦ adj borracho ♦ n (also: **drunkard**) borracho(-a) □ **drunken** adj borracho; (*laughter, party*) de borrachos

dry [draɪ] adj seco; (*day*) batería sin lluvia; (*climate*) árido, seco ♦ vt secar; (*tears*) enjugarse ♦ vi secarse □ **dry off** vi secarse ♦ vt secar ► **dry up** vi (*river*) secarse □ **dry-cleaner's** n tintorería □ **dry-cleaning** n lavado en seco □ **dryer** n (for hair) secador m; (US: for clothes) secadora

DSS n abbr = **Department of Social Security**

DTP n abbr (= desk-top publishing) autoedición f

dual ['djuəl] adj doble □ **dual carriageway** (BRIT) n carretera de doble calzada

dubious ['djuːbɪəs] adj indeciso; (*reputation, company*) sospechoso

duck [dʌk] n pato ♦ vi agacharse

due [djuː] adj (owed): **he is ~ £10** se le deben 10 libras; (expected: *event*): **the meeting is ~ on Wednesday** la reunión tendrá lugar el miércoles; (: *arrival*): **the train is ~ at 8am** el tren tiene su llegada para las 8; (*proper*) debido ♦ n: **to give sb his (or her) ~** ser justo con algn ♦ adv: **~ north** derecho al norte

duel ['djuəl] n duelo

duet [djuːˈɛt] n dúo

dug [dʌg] pt, pp of **dig**

duke [djuːk] n duque m

dull [dʌl] adj (light) débil; (stupid) torpe; (boring) pesado; (sound, pain) sordo; (weather, day) gris ♦ vt (pain, grief) aliviar; (mind, senses) entorpecer

dumb [dʌm] adj mudo; (pej: stupid) estúpido

dummy ['dʌmɪ] n (tailor's dummy) maniquí m; (mock-up) maqueta; (BRIT: for baby) chupete m ♦ adj falso, postizo

dump [dʌmp] n (also: **rubbish ~**) basurero, vertedero; (inf: place) cuchitril m ♦ vt (put down) dejar; (get rid of) deshacerse de; (COMPUT: data) transferir

dumpling ['dʌmplɪŋ] n bola de masa hervida

dune [djuːn] n duna

dungarees [dʌŋgə'riːz] npl mono

dungeon ['dʌndʒən] n calabozo

duplex ['djuːpleks] n dúplex m

duplicate [n 'djuːplɪkət, vb 'djuːplɪkeɪt] n duplicado ♦ vt duplicar; (photocopy) fotocopiar; (repeat) repetir; **in ~** por duplicado

durable ['djuərəbl] adj duradero

duration [djuə'reɪʃən] n duración f

during ['djuərɪŋ] prep durante

dusk [dʌsk] n crepúsculo, anochecer m

dust [dʌst] n polvo ♦ vt quitar el polvo a, desempolvar; (cake etc): to ~ **with** espolvorear de □ **dustbin** (BRIT) n cubo or bote m (MEX) or tacho (SC) de la basura □ **duster** n paño, trapo □ **dustman** (BRIT: irreg) n basurero □ **dustpan** n cogedor m □ **dusty** adj polvoriento

Dutch [dʌtʃ] adj holandés(-esa) ♦ n (LING) holandés m; **the ~** npl los holandeses; **to go ~** (inf) pagar cada uno lo suyo □ **Dutchman** (irreg) n holandés m □ **Dutchwoman** (irreg) n holandésa

duty ['djuːtɪ] n deber m; (tax) derechos mpl de aduana; **on ~** de servicio; (at night etc) de guardia; **off ~** libre de

servicio) □ **duty-free** adj libre de impuestos

duvet ['duːveɪ] (BRIT) n edredón m

DVD n abbr (= digital versatile or video disc) DVD m □ **DVD player** n lector m (de) DVD

dwarf [dwɔːf] (pl **dwarves**) n enano(-a) ♦ vt empequeñecer

dwell [dwel] (pt, pp **dwelt**) vi morar ▸ **dwell on** vt fus explayarse en

dwelt [dwelt] pt, pp of **dwell**

dwindle ['dwɪndl] vi disminuir

dye [daɪ] n tinte m ♦ vt teñir

dying ['daɪɪŋ] adj moribundo

dynamic [daɪ'næmɪk] adj dinámico

dynamite ['daɪnəmaɪt] n dinamita

dyslexia [dɪs'leksɪə] n dislexia

dyslexic [dɪs'leksɪk] adj, n disléxico(-a) m/f

E, e

E [iː] n (MUS) mi m

E111 n abbr (= form E111) impreso E111

each [iːtʃ] adj cada inv ♦ pron cada uno; **~ other** el uno al otro; **they hate ~ other** se odian (entre ellos or mutuamente); **they have 2 books ~** tienen 2 libros por persona

eager ['iːgə'] adj (keen) entusiasmado; **to be ~ to do sth** tener muchas ganas de hacer algo, impacientarse por hacer algo; **to be ~ for** tener muchas ganas de

eagle ['iːgl] n águila

ear [ɪə'] n oreja; oído; (of corn) espiga □ **earache** n dolor m de oídos □ **eardrum** n tímpano

earl [əːl] n conde m

earlier ['əːlɪə'] adj anterior ♦ adv antes

early ['əːlɪ] adv temprano; (before time) con antelación, con anticipación ♦ adj temprano; (settlers etc) primitivo;

(*death, departure*) prematuro; (*reply*) pronto; **to have an ~ night** acostarse temprano; **in the ~ or ~ in the spring/19th century** a principios de primavera/del siglo diecinueve ❏ **early retirement** *n* jubilación *f* anticipada

earmark ['ɪɑːmɑːk] *vt*: **to ~ (for)** reservar (para), destinar (a)

earn [ɜːn] *vt* (*salary*) percibir; (*interest*) devengar; (*praise*) merecerse

earnest ['ɜːnɪst] *adj* (*wish*) fervoroso; (*person*) serio, formal; **in ~** en serio

earnings ['ɜːnɪŋz] *npl* (*personal*) sueldo, ingresos *mpl*; (*company*) ganancias *fpl*

ear: earphones *npl* auriculares *mpl* ❏ **earplugs** *npl* tapones *mpl* para los oídos ❏ **earring** *n* pendiente *m*, arete *m*

earth [ɜːθ] *n* tierra; (*BRIT ELEC*) cable *m* de toma de tierra ♦ *vt* (*BRIT ELEC*) conectar a tierra ❏ **earthquake** *n* terremoto

ease [iːz] *n* facilidad *f*; (*comfort*) comodidad *f* ♦ *vt* (*lessen: problem*) mitigar; (*: pain*) aliviar; (*: tension*) reducir; **to ~ sth in/out** meter/sacar algo con cuidado; **at ~!** (*MIL*) ¡descansen!

easily ['iːzɪlɪ] *adv* fácilmente

east [iːst] *n* este *m* ♦ *adj* del este, oriental; (*wind*) este ♦ *adv* al este, hacia el este; **the E~** el Oriente; (*POL*) los países del Este ❏ **eastbound** *adj* en dirección este

Easter ['iːstə'] *n* Pascua (de Resurrección) ❏ **Easter egg** *n* huevo de Pascua

eastern ['iːstən] *adj* del este, oriental; (*oriental*) oriental

Easter Sunday *n* Domingo de Resurrección

easy ['iːzɪ] *adj* fácil; (*simple*) sencillo; (*comfortable*) holgado, cómodo; (*relaxed*) tranquilo ♦ *adv*: **to take it** or

things ~ (*not worry*) tomarlo con calma; (*rest*) descansar ❏ **easy-going** *adj* acomodadizo

eat [iːt] (*pt* **ate**, *pp* **eaten**) *vt* comer ► **eat out** *vi* comer fuera

eavesdrop ['iːvzdrɒp] *vi*: **to ~ (on)** escuchar a escondidas

e-book ['iːbuk] *n* libro electrónico

e-business ['iːbɪznɪs] *n* (*company*) negocio electrónico; (*commerce*) comercio electrónico

EC *n abbr* (= *European Community*) CE *f*

eccentric [ɪk'sentrɪk] *adj*, *n* excéntrico(-a) *m/f*

echo ['ekəu] (*pl* **echoes**) *n* eco ♦ *vt* (*sound*) repetir ♦ *vi* resonar, hacer eco

eclipse [ɪ'klɪps] *n* eclipse *m*

eco-friendly ['iːkəufrendlɪ] *adj* ecológico

ecological [iːkə'lɒdʒɪkl] *adj* ecológico

ecology [ɪ'kɒlədʒɪ] *n* ecología

e-commerce *n abbr* comercio electrónico

economic [iːkə'nɒmɪk] *adj* económico; (*business etc*) rentable ❏ **economical** *adj* económico ❏ **economics** *n* (*SCOL*) economía ♦ *npl* (*of project etc*) rentabilidad *f*

economist [ɪ'kɒnəmɪst] *n* economista *m/f*

economize [ɪ'kɒnəmaɪz] *vi* economizar, ahorrar

economy [ɪ'kɒnəmɪ] *n* economía ❏ **economy class** *n* (*AVIAT*) clase *f* económica ❏ **economy class syndrome** *n* síndrome *m* de la clase turista

ecstasy ['ekstəsɪ] *n* éxtasis *m inv*; (*drug*) éxtasis *m inv* ❏ **ecstatic** [eks'tætɪk] *adj* extático

eczema ['eksɪmə] *n* eczema *m*

edge [edʒ] *n* (*of knife*) filo; (*of object*) borde *m*; (*of lake*) orilla ♦ *vt* (*SEWING*) ribetear; *vi* ~ (*fig*) = edge; **to ~ away from** alejarse poco a poco de

edgy ['edʒɪ] *adj* nervioso, inquieto

edible ['edɪbl] adj comestible

Edinburgh ['edɪnbərə] n Edimburgo

edit ['edɪt] vt (be editor of) dirigir; (text, report) corregir, preparar ❑ **edition** [ɪ'dɪʃən] n edición f ❑ **editor** n (of newspaper) director(a) m/f; (of column): **foreign/political editor** encargado de la sección de extranjero/política; (of book) redactor(a) m/f ❑ **editorial** [-'tɔːrɪəl] adj editorial ♦ n editorial m

educate ['edjʊkeɪt] vt (gen) educar; (instruct) instruir ❑ **educated** ['edjʊkeɪtɪd] adj culto

education [edjʊ'keɪʃən] n educación f; (schooling) enseñanza; (SCOL) pedagogía ❑ **educational** adj (policy etc) educacional; (experience) docente; (toy) educativo

eel [iːl] n anguila

eerie ['ɪərɪ] adj misterioso

effect [ɪ'fekt] n efecto ❑ **effortless** vt efectuar, llevar a cabo; **to take ~** (law) entrar en vigor o vigencia; (drug) surtir efecto; **in ~** en realidad; **effects** npl (property) efectos mpl ❑ **effective** adj eficaz; (actual) verdadero ❑ **effectively** adv eficazmente; (in reality) efectivamente

efficiency [ɪ'fɪʃənsɪ] n eficiencia; rendimiento

efficient [ɪ'fɪʃənt] adj eficiente; (machine) de buen rendimiento ❑ **efficiently** adv eficientemente, de manera eficiente

effort ['efət] n esfuerzo ❑ **effortless** adj sin ningún esfuerzo; (style) natural

e.g. adv abbr (= exempli gratia) p. ej.

egg [eg] n huevo; **hard-boiled/soft-boiled ~** huevo duro/pasado por agua ❑ **eggcup** n huevera ❑ **egg plant** n (esp US) n berenjena ❑ **eggshell** n cáscara de huevo ❑ **egg white** n clara de huevo ❑ **egg yolk** n yema de huevo

ego ['iːgəʊ] n ego

Egypt ['iːdʒɪpt] n Egipto ❑ **Egyptian** [ɪ'dʒɪpʃən] adj, n egipcio(-a) m/f

eight [eɪt] num ocho ❑ **eighteen** num diez y ocho, dieciocho ❑ **eighteenth** adj decimoctavo; **the eighteenth floor** la planta dieciocho; **the eighteenth of August** el dieciocho de agosto ❑ **eighth** num octavo ❑ **eightieth** ['eɪtɪɪθ] adj octogésimo

eighty ['eɪtɪ] num ochenta

Eire ['eərə] n Eire m

either ['aɪðə] adj cualquiera de los dos; (both, each) cada ♦ pron: **~ (of them)** cualquiera (de los dos) ♦ adv tampoco ♦ conj: **~ yes or no** o sí o no; **on ~ side** en ambos lados; **I don't like ~** no me gusta ninguno/-a de los (las) dos; **no, I don't ~** no, yo tampoco

eject [ɪ'dʒekt] vt echar, expulsar; (tenant) desahuciar

elaborate [adj ɪ'læbərɪt, vb ɪ'læbəreɪt] adj (complex) complejo ♦ vt (expand) ampliar; (refine) refinar ♦ vi explicar con más detalles

elastic [ɪ'læstɪk] n elástico ♦ adj elástico; (fig) flexible ❑ **elastic band** (BRIT) n gomita

elbow ['elbəʊ] n codo

elder ['eldə] adj mayor ♦ n (tree) saúco; (person) mayor ❑ **elderly** adj de edad, mayor ♦ npl: **the elderly** los mayores

eldest ['eldɪst] adj, n el (la) mayor

elect [ɪ'lekt] vt elegir ♦ adj: **the president ~** el presidente electo; **to ~ to do** optar por hacer ❑ **election** n elección f ❑ **electoral** adj electoral ❑ **electorate** n electorado

electric [ɪ'lektrɪk] adj eléctrico ❑ **electrical** adj eléctrico ❑ **electric blanket** n manta eléctrica ❑ **electric fire** n estufa eléctrica ❑ **electrician** [ɪlek'trɪʃən] n electricista mf ❑ **electricity** [ɪlek'trɪsɪtɪ] n electricidad f ❑ **electric shock** n electrochoque m ❑ **electrify** [ɪ'lektrɪfaɪ] vt (RAIL) electrificar; (fig: audience) electrizar

electronic [ɪlek'trɒnɪk] adj electrónico ❑ **electronic mail** n correo electrónico ❑ **electronics** n electrónica

elegance ['elɪgəns] n elegancia

elegant ['elɪgənt] adj elegante

element ['elɪmənt] n elemento; (of kettle etc) resistencia

elementary [elɪ'mentərɪ] adj elemental; (primitive) rudimentario ❑ **elementary school** (US) n escuela de enseñanza primaria

elephant ['elɪfənt] n elefante m

elevate ['elɪveɪt] vt (gen) elevar; (in rank) ascender

elevator ['elɪveɪtə°] (US) n ascensor m; (in warehouse etc) montacargas m inv

eleven [ɪ'levn] num once ❑ **eleventh** num undécimo

eligible ['elɪdʒəbl] adj: **an ~ young man/woman** un buen partido; **to be ~ for sth** llenar los requisitos para algo

eliminate [ɪ'lɪmɪneɪt] vt (suspect, possibility) descartar

elm [elm] n olmo

eloquent ['eləkwənt] adj elocuente

else [els] adv: **something ~** otra cosa; **somewhere ~** en otra parte; **everywhere ~** en todas partes menos aquí; **where ~?** ¿dónde más?, ¿en qué otra parte?; **there was little ~ to do** apenas quedaba otra cosa que hacer; **nobody ~ spoke** no habló nadie más ❑ **elsewhere** adv (be) en otra parte; (go) a otra parte

elusive [ɪ'luːsɪv] adj esquivo; (quality) difícil de encontrar

e-mail [iːmeɪl] n abbr (= electronic mail) correo electrónico, e-mail m ❑ **e-mail address** n dirección f electrónica, email m

embankment [ɪm'bæŋkmənt] n terraplén m

embargo [ɪm'bɑːgəʊ] (pl embargoes) n (COMM, NAUT) embargo; (prohibition) prohibición f; **to put an ~ on sth** poner un embargo en algo

embark [ɪm'bɑːk] vi embarcarse ♦ vt embarcar; **to ~ on** (journey) emprender; (course of action) lanzarse a

embarrass [ɪm'bærəs] vt avergonzar; (government etc) dejar en mal lugar ❑ **embarrassed** (laugh, silence) embarazoso ❑ **embarrassing** adj (situation) violento; (question) embarazoso ❑ **embarrassment** n (shame) vergüenza; (problem): **to be an embarrassment for sb** poner en un aprieto a algn

⚠ Be careful not to translate **embarrassed** by the Spanish word **embarazada**.

embassy ['embəsɪ] n embajada

embrace [ɪm'breɪs] vt abrazar, dar un abrazo a; (include) abarcar ♦ vi abrazarse ♦ n abrazo

embroider [ɪm'brɔɪdə°] vt bordar ❑ **embroidery** n bordado

embryo ['embrɪəʊ] n embrión m

emerald ['emərəld] n esmeralda

emerge [ɪ'mɜːdʒ] vi salir; (arise) surgir

emergency [ɪ'mɜːdʒənsɪ] n crisis f inv; **in an ~** en caso de urgencia; **state of ~** estado de emergencia ❑ **emergency brake** (US) n freno de mano ❑ **emergency exit** n salida de emergencia ❑ **emergency landing** n aterrizaje m forzoso ❑ **emergency room** (US: MED) n sala f de urgencias ❑ **emergency services** npl (fire, police, ambulance) servicios mpl de urgencia or emergencia

emigrate ['emɪgreɪt] vi emigrar ❑ **emigration** [emɪ'greɪʃən] n emigración f

eminent ['emɪnənt] adj eminente

emissions [ɪ'mɪʃənz] npl emisión f

emit [ɪ'mɪt] vt emitir; (smoke) arrojar; (smell) despedir; (sound) producir

emotion [ɪ'məʊʃən] n emoción f ❑ **emotional** adj (needs) emocional;

(*person*) sentimental; (*scene*) conmovedor(a), emocionante; (*speech*) emocionado

emperor ['empərə'] *n* emperador *m*

emphasis ['emfəsis] (*pl* -ses) *n* énfasis *m inv*

emphasize ['emfəsaɪz] *vt* (*word, point*) subrayar, recalcar; (*feature*) hacer resaltar

empire ['empaɪə'] *n* imperio

employ [ɪm'plɔɪ] *vt* emplear ❏ **employee** [-'iː] *n* empleado(-a) ❏ **employer** *n* patrón(-ona) *m/f*; empresario ❏ **employment** *n* (*work*) trabajo ❏ **employment agency** *n* agencia de colocaciones

empower [ɪm'pauə'] *vt*: to ~ sb to do sth autorizar a algn para hacer algo

empress ['emprɪs] *n* emperatriz *f*

emptiness ['emptɪnɪs] *n* vacío; (*of life etc*) vaciedad *f*

empty ['empti] *adj* vacío; (*place*) desierto; (*house*) desocupado; (*threat*) vano ♦ *vt* vaciar; (*place*) dejar vacío ♦ *vi* vaciarse; (*house etc*) quedar desocupado ❏ **empty-handed** *adj* con las manos vacías

EMU *n abbr* (= *European Monetary Union*) UME *f*

emulsion [ɪ'mʌlʃən] *n* emulsión *f*; (*also*: ~ **paint**) pintura emulsión

enable [ɪ'neɪbl] *vt*: to ~ sb to do sth permitir a algn hacer algo

enamel [ɪ'næməl] *n* esmalte *m*; (*also*: ~ **paint**) pintura esmaltada

enchanting [ɪn'tʃɑːntɪŋ] *adj* encantador(a)

encl. *abbr* (= *enclosed*) adj

enclose [ɪn'kləuz] *vt* (*land*) cercar; (*letter etc*) adjuntar; **please find enclosed** le mandamos adjunto

enclosure [ɪn'kləuʒə'] *n* cercado, recinto

encore [ɔŋ'kɔː'] *excl* ¡otra!, ¡bis! ♦ *n* bis *m*

encounter [ɪn'kauntə'] *n* encuentro ♦ *vt* encontrar, encontrarse con; (*difficulty*) tropezar con

encourage [ɪn'kʌrɪdʒ] *vt* alentar, animar; (*activity*) fomentar; (*growth*) estimular ❏ **encouragement** *n* estímulo; (*of industry*) fomento

encouraging [ɪn'kʌrɪdʒɪŋ] *adj* alentador(a)

encyclop(a)edia [ɛnsaɪkləu'piːdɪə] *n* enciclopedia

end [end] *n* fin *m*; (*of table*) extremo; (*of street*) final *m*; (*SPORT*) lado ♦ *vt* terminar, acabar; (*also*: **bring to an ~, put an ~ to**) acabar con ♦ *vi* terminar, acabar; **in the ~** al fin; **on ~** (*object*) de punta, de cabeza; **to stand on ~** (*hair*) erizarse; **for hours on ~** hora tras hora ▸ **end up** *vi*: **to end up in** terminar en; (*place*) ir a parar en

endanger [ɪn'deɪndʒə'] *vt* poner en peligro; **an endangered species** una especie en peligro de extinción

endearing [ɪn'dɪərɪŋ] *adj* simpático, atractivo

endeavour [ɪn'devə'] (*US* **endeavor**) *n* esfuerzo; (*attempt*) tentativa ♦ *vt*: **to ~ to do** esforzarse por hacer; (*try*) procurar hacer

ending ['endɪŋ] *n* (*of book*) desenlace *m*; (*LING*) terminación *f*

endless ['endlɪs] *adj* interminable, inacabable

endorse [ɪn'dɔːs] *vt* (*cheque*) endosar; (*approve*) aprobar ❏ **endorsement** *n* (*on driving licence*) nota de inhabilitación

endurance [ɪn'djuərəns] *n* resistencia

endure [ɪn'djuə'] *vt* (*bear*) aguantar, soportar ♦ *vi* (*last*) durar

enemy ['enəmɪ] *adj, n* enemigo(-a) *m/f*

energetic [enə'dʒetɪk] *adj* enérgico

energy ['enədʒɪ] *n* energía

enforce [ɪn'fɔːs] *vt* (*LAW*) hacer cumplir

engaged [ɪn'geɪdʒd] *adj* (*BRIT*: busy, in use*) ocupado; (*betrothed*) prometido;

to get ~ prometerse ❑ **engaged tone** (BRIT) n (TEL) señal f de comunicando

engagement [ɪnˈgeɪdʒmənt] n (appointment) compromiso, cita; (booking) contratación f; (to marry) compromiso; (period) noviazgo ❑ **engagement ring** n anillo de prometida

engaging [ɪnˈgeɪdʒɪŋ] adj atractivo

engine [ˈendʒɪn] n (AUT) motor m; (RAIL) locomotora

engineer [endʒɪˈnɪə*] n ingeniero; (BRIT: for repairs) mecánico; (on ship, US RAIL) maquinista m ❑ **engineering** n ingeniería

England [ˈɪŋglənd] n Inglaterra

English [ˈɪŋglɪʃ] adj inglés(-esa) ♦ n (LING) inglés m; **the** ~ npl los ingleses mpl ❑ **English Channel** n: **the English Channel** (el Canal de) la Mancha ❑ **Englishman** (irreg) n inglés m ❑ **Englishwoman** (irreg) n inglésa

engrave [ɪnˈgreɪv] vt grabar

engraving [ɪnˈgreɪvɪŋ] n grabado

enhance [ɪnˈhɑːns] vt (gen) aumentar; (beauty) realzar

enjoy [ɪnˈdʒɔɪ] vt (health, fortune) disfrutar de, gozar de; (like) gustarle a algn; **to** ~ **o.s.** divertirse ❑ **enjoyable** adj agradable; (amusing) divertido ❑ **enjoyment** n (joy) placer m; (activity) diversión f

enlarge [ɪnˈlɑːdʒ] vt aumentar; (broaden) extender; (PHOT) ampliar ♦ vi: **to** ~ **on** (subject) tratar con más detalles ❑ **enlargement** n (PHOT) ampliación f

enlist [ɪnˈlɪst] vt alistar; (support) conseguir ♦ vi alistarse

enormous [ɪˈnɔːməs] adj enorme

enough [ɪˈnʌf] adj: ~ **time/books** bastante tiempo/bastantes libros ♦ pron bastante(s) ♦ adv: **big** ~ bastante grande; **he has not worked** ~

no ha trabajado bastante; **have you got** ~? ¿tiene usted bastante(s)?; ~ **to eat** (lo) suficiente o (lo) bastante para comer; ~! ¡basta ya!; **that's** ~, **thanks** con eso basta, gracias; **I've had** ~ **of him** estoy harto de él; ~, **which, funnily** or **oddly** ~ ... ... lo que, por extraño que parezca ...

enquire [ɪnˈkwaɪə*] vt, vi = **inquire**

enquiry [ɪnˈkwaɪərɪ] n (official investigation) investigación

enrage [ɪnˈreɪdʒ] vt enfurecer

enrich [ɪnˈrɪtʃ] vt enriquecer

enrol [ɪnˈrəʊl] (US **enroll**) vt (members) inscribir; (SCOL) matricular ♦ vi inscribirse; matricularse ❑ **enrolment** (US **enrollment**) n inscripción f; matriculación f

en route [ɔnˈruːt] adv durante el viaje

en suite [ɔnˈswiːt] adj: **with** ~ **bathroom** con baño

ensure [ɪnˈʃʊə*] vt asegurar

entail [ɪnˈteɪl] vt suponer

enter [ˈentə*] vt (room) entrar en; (club) hacerse socio de; (army) alistarse en; (sb for a competition) inscribir; (write down) anotar, apuntar; (COMPUT) meter ♦ vi entrar

enterprise [ˈentəpraɪz] n empresa; (spirit) iniciativa; **free** ~ la libre empresa; **private** ~ la iniciativa privada ❑ **enterprising** adj emprendedor(a)

entertain [entəˈteɪn] vt (amuse) divertir; (invite: guest) invitar (a casa); (idea) abrigar ❑ **entertainer** n artista mf ❑ **entertaining** adj divertido, entretenido ❑ **entertainment** n (amusement) diversión f; (show) espectáculo

enthusiasm [ɪnˈθuːzɪæzəm] n entusiasmo

enthusiast [ɪnˈθuːzɪæst] n entusiasta mf ❑ **enthusiastic** [-ˈæstɪk] adj entusiasta; **to be enthusiastic about** entusiasmarse por

entire [ɪn'taɪə] *adj* entero ❏ **entirely** *adv* totalmente

entitle [ɪn'taɪtl] *vt*: **to ~ sb to sth** dar a algn derecho a algo ❏ **entitled** *adj* (*book*) titulado; **to be entitled to do** tener derecho a hacer

entrance [*n* 'entrəns, *vb* ɪn'trɑːns] *n* entrada ♦ *vt* encantar, hechizar; **to gain ~ to** (*university etc*) ingresar en ❏ **entrance examination** *n* examen *m* de ingreso ❏ **entrance fee** *n* cuota ❏ **entrance ramp** (*US*) *n* (*AUT*) rampa de acceso

entrant ['entrənt] *n* (*in race, competition*) participante *mf*; (*in examination*) candidato(-a)

entrepreneur [ɔntrəprə'nɜː] *n* empresario

entrust [ɪn'trʌst] *vt*: **to ~ sth to sb** confiar algo a algn

entry ['entrɪ] *n* entrada; (*in competition*) participación *f*; (*in register*) apunte *m*; (*in account*) partida; (*in reference book*) artículo; **"no ~"** "prohibido el paso"; (*AUT*) "dirección prohibida" ❏ **entry phone** *n* portero automático

envelope ['envələup] *n* sobre *m*

envious ['envɪəs] *adj* envidioso; (*look*) de envidia

environment [ɪn'vaɪərnmənt] *n* (*surroundings*) entorno; (*natural world*): **the ~** el medio ambiente ❏ **environmental** [-'mentl] *adj* ambiental; medioambiental ❏ **environmentally** [-'mentlɪ] *adv*: **environmentally sound/friendly** ecológico

envisage [ɪn'vɪzɪdʒ] *vt* prever

envoy ['envɔɪ] *n* enviado

envy ['envɪ] *n* envidia ♦ *vt* tener envidia a; **to ~ sb sth** envidiar algo a algn

epic ['epɪk] *n* épica ♦ *adj* épico

epidemic [epɪ'demɪk] *n* epidemia

epilepsy ['epɪlepsɪ] *n* epilepsia

epileptic [epɪ'leptɪk] *adj*, *n* epiléptico(-a) *m/f* ❏ **epileptic fit**

[epɪ'leptɪk-] *n* ataque *m* de epilepsia, acceso *m* epiléptico

episode ['epɪsəud] *n* episodio

equal ['iːkwl] *adj* igual; (*treatment*) equitativo ♦ *n* igual *mf* ♦ *vt* ser igual a; (*fig*) igualar; **to be ~ to** (*task*) estar a la altura de ❏ **equality** [iː'kwɔlɪtɪ] *n* igualdad *f* ❏ **equalize** *vi* (*SPORT*) empatar ❏ **equally** *adv* igualmente; (*share etc*) a partes iguales

equation [ɪ'kweɪʒən] *n* (*MATH*) ecuación *f*

equator [ɪ'kweɪtə'] *n* ecuador *m*

equip [ɪ'kwɪp] *vt* equipar; (*person*) proveer; **to be well equipped** estar bien equipado ❏ **equipment** *n* equipo; (*tools*) avíos *mpl*

equivalent [ɪ'kwɪvələnt] *adj*: **~ (to)** equivalente (a) ♦ *n* equivalente *m*

ER *abbr* (*BRIT*: = *Elizabeth Regina*) la reina Isabel; (*US*: *Med*) = **emergency room**

era ['ɪərə] *n* era, época

erase [ɪ'reɪz] *vt* borrar ❏ **eraser** *n* goma de borrar

erect [ɪ'rekt] *adj* erguido ♦ *vt* erigir, levantar; (*assemble*) montar ❏ **erection** [-ʃən] *n* construcción *f*; (*assembly*) montaje *m*; (*PHYSIOL*) erección *f*

ERM *n* abbr (= *Exchange Rate Mechanism*) tipo de cambio europeo

erode [ɪ'rəud] *vt* (*GEO*) erosionar; (*metal*) corroer, desgastar; (*fig*) desgastar

erosion [ɪ'rəuʒən] *n* erosión *f*; desgaste *m*

erotic [ɪ'rɔtɪk] *adj* erótico

errand ['ernd] *n* recado (*SP*), mandado (*LAm*)

erratic [ɪ'rætɪk] *adj* desigual, poco uniforme

error ['erə'] *n* error *m*, equivocación *f*

erupt [ɪ'rʌpt] *vi* entrar en erupción; (*fig*) estallar ❏ **eruption** [ɪ'rʌpʃən] *n* erupción *f*; (*of war*) estallido

escalate ['eskəleɪt] *vi* extenderse, intensificarse

escalator [ˈeskəleɪtə] n escalera móvil

escape [ɪˈskeɪp] n fuga ♦ vi escaparse; (flee) huir, evadirse; (leak) fugarse ♦ vt (responsibility etc) evitar, eludir; (consequences) escapar a; (elude): **his name escapes me** no me sale su nombre; **to ~ from** (place) escaparse de; (person) escaparse a

escort [n ˈeskɔːt, vb ɪˈskɔːt] n acompañante mf; (MIL) escolta mf ♦ vt acompañar

especially [ɪˈspeʃlɪ] adv (above all) sobre todo; (particularly) en particular, especialmente

espionage [ˈespɪənɑːʒ] n espionaje m

essay [ˈeseɪ] n (LITERATURE) ensayo; (SCOL: short) redacción f; (: long) trabajo

essence [ˈesns] n esencia

essential [ɪˈsenʃl] adj (necessary) imprescindible; (basic) esencial
❏ **essentially** adv esencialmente
❏ **essentials** npl lo imprescindible, lo esencial

establish [ɪˈstæblɪʃ] vt establecer; (prove) demostrar; (relations) entablar; (reputation) ganarse
❏ **establishment** n establecimiento; **the Establishment** la clase dirigente

estate [ɪˈsteɪt] n (land) finca, hacienda; (inheritance) herencia; (BRIT: also: **housing ~**) urbanización f ❏ **estate agent** (BRIT) n agente mf inmobiliario(-a) ❏ **estate car** (BRIT) n furgoneta

estimate [n ˈestɪmət, vb ˈestɪmeɪt] n estimación f, apreciación f; (assessment) tasa, cálculo; (COMM) presupuesto ♦ vt estimar, tasar; calcular

etc abbr (= et cetera) etc

eternal [ɪˈtɜːnl] adj eterno

eternity [ɪˈtɜːnɪtɪ] n eternidad f

ethical [ˈeθɪkl] adj ético ❏ **ethics** [ˈeθɪks] n ética ♦ npl moralidad f

Ethiopia [iːθɪˈəʊpɪə] n Etiopía

ethnic [ˈeθnɪk] adj étnico ❏ **ethnic minority** n minoría étnica

etiquette [ˈetɪket] n etiqueta

EU n abbr (= European Union) UE f

euro n euro

Europe [ˈjuərəp] n Europa
❏ **European** [-ˈpiːən] adj, n europeo(-a) m/f ❏ **European Community** n Comunidad f Europea ❏ **European Union** n Unión f Europea

Eurostar® [ˈjuərəʊstɑːʳ] n Eurostar® m

evacuate [ɪˈvækjueɪt] vt (people) evacuar; (place) desocupar

evade [ɪˈveɪd] vt evadir, eludir

evaluate [ɪˈvæljueɪt] vt evaluar; (value) tasar; (evidence) interpretar

evaporate [ɪˈvæpəreɪt] vi evaporarse; (fig) desvanecerse

eve [iːv] n: **on the ~ of** en vísperas de

even [ˈiːvn] adj (level) llano; (smooth) liso; (speed, temperature) uniforme; (number) par ♦ adv hasta, incluso; (introducing a comparison) aún, todavía; **~ if, ~ though** aunque +subjun; **~ more** aún más; **~ so** aun así; **not ~** ni siquiera; **~ he was there** hasta él estuvo allí; **~ on Sundays** incluso los domingos; **to get ~ with sb** ajustar cuentas con algn

evening [ˈiːvnɪŋ] n tarde f; (late) noche f; **in the ~** por la tarde ❏ **evening class** n clase f nocturna ❏ **evening dress** n (no pl: formal clothes) traje m de etiqueta; (woman's) traje m de noche

event [ɪˈvent] n suceso, acontecimiento; (SPORT) prueba; **in the ~ of** en caso de ❏ **eventful** adj (life) activo; (day) ajetreado

eventual [ɪˈventʃuəl] adj final ❏ **eventually** adv (finally) finalmente; (in time) con el tiempo

⚠️ Be careful not to translate **eventual** by the Spanish word *eventual*.

ever ['ɛvəʳ] *adv* (*at any time*) nunca, jamás; (*at all times*) siempre; (*in question*): **why ~ not?** ¿y por qué no?; **the best ~** lo nunca visto; **have you ~ seen it?** ¿lo ha visto usted alguna vez?; **better than ~** mejor que nunca; **~ since** *adv* desde entonces ♦ *conj* después de que ♦ **evergreen** *n* árbol *m* de hoja perenne

every
KEYWORD
['ɛvrɪ] *adj*
1 (*each*) cada; **every one of them** (*persons*) todos ellos(-as); (*objects*) cada uno de ellos(-as); **every shop in the town was closed** todas las tiendas de la ciudad estaban cerradas
2 (*all possible*) todo(-a); **I gave you every assistance** te di toda la ayuda posible; **I have every confidence in him** tiene en mí toda mi confianza; **we wish you every success** te deseamos toda suerte de éxitos
3 (*showing recurrence*) todo(-a); **every day/week** todos los días/todas las semanas; **every other car had been broken into** habían forzado uno de cada dos coches; **she visits me every other/third day** me visita cada dos/tres días; **every now and then** de vez en cuando

every: everybody *pron* = **everyone** ♦ **everyday** *adj* (*daily*) cotidiano, de todos los días; (*usual*) acostumbrado ♦ **everyone** *pron* todos(-as), todo el mundo ♦ **everything** *pron* todo; **this shop sells everything** esta tienda vende de todo ♦ **everywhere** *adv*: **I've been looking for you everywhere** te he estado buscando por todas partes; **everywhere you go you meet ...** en todas partes encuentras ...

evict [ɪ'vɪkt] *vt* desahuciar

evidence ['ɛvɪdəns] *n* (*proof*) prueba; (*of witness*) testimonio; (*sign*) indicios *mpl*; **to give ~** prestar declaración, dar testimonio

evident ['ɛvɪdənt] *adj* evidente, manifiesto ❑ **evidently** *adv* por lo visto

evil ['iːvl] *adj* malo; (*influence*) funesto ♦ *n* mal *m*

evoke [ɪ'vəuk] *vt* evocar

evolution [iːvə'luːʃən] *n* evolución *f*

evolve [ɪ'vɔlv] *vt* desarrollar ♦ *vi* evolucionar, desarrollarse

ewe [juː] *n* oveja

ex (*inf*) [ɛks] *n*: **my ex** mi ex

ex- [ɛks] *prefix* ex

exact [ɪg'zækt] *adj* exacto; (*person*) meticuloso ♦ *vt*: **to ~ sth (from)** exigir algo (de) ❑ **exactly** *adv* exactamente; (*indicating agreement*) exacto

exaggerate [ɪg'zædʒəreɪt] *vt, vi* exagerar ❑ **exaggeration** [-'reɪʃən] *n* exageración *f*

exam [ɪg'zæm] *n abbr* (SCOL) = **examination**

examination [ɪgzæmɪ'neɪʃən] *n* examen *m*; (MED) reconocimiento

examine [ɪg'zæmɪn] *vt* examinar; (*inspect*) inspeccionar, escudriñar; (MED) reconocer ❑ **examiner** *n* examinador(a) *m/f*

example [ɪg'zɑːmpl] *n* ejemplo; **for ~** por ejemplo

exasperated [ɪg'zɑːspəreɪtɪd] *adj* exasperado

excavate ['ɛkskəveɪt] *vt* excavar

exceed [ɪk'siːd] *vt* (*amount*) exceder; (*number*) pasar de; (*speed limit*) sobrepasar; (*powers*) excederse en; (*hopes*) superar ❑ **exceedingly** *adv* sumamente, sobremanera

excel [ɪk'sɛl] *vi* sobresalir; **to ~ o.s** lucirse

excellence ['ɛksələns] *n* excelencia

excellent ['ɛksələnt] *adj* excelente

except [ɪkˈsɛpt] prep (also: ~ **for,**
excepting) excepto, salvo ♦ vt
exceptuar, excluir; ~ **if/when** excepto
si/cuando; ~ **that** salvo que
❏ **exception** [ɪkˈsɛpʃən] n excepción f;
to take exception to ofenderse por
❏ **exceptional** [ɪkˈsɛpʃənl] adj
excepcional ❏ **exceptionally**
[ɪkˈsɛpʃənəlɪ] adv excepcionalmente,
extraordinariamente

excerpt [ˈɛksɜːpt] n extracto

excess [ɪkˈsɛs] n exceso ❏ **excess
baggage** n exceso de equipaje
❏ **excessive** adj excesivo

exchange [ɪksˈtʃeɪndʒ] n intercambio;
(conversation) diálogo; (also:
telephone ~) central f (telefónica) ♦ vt:
to ~ (for) cambiar (por) ❏ **exchange
rate** n tipo de cambio

excite [ɪkˈsaɪt] vt (stimulate) estimular;
(arouse) excitar ❏ **excited** adj: **to get
excited** emocionarse ❏ **excitement**
n (agitation) excitación f; (exhilaration)
emoción f ❏ **exciting** adj
emocionante

exclaim [ɪkˈskleɪm] vi exclamar
❏ **exclamation** [ɛkskləˈmeɪʃən] n
exclamación f ❏ **exclamation mark**
n punto de admiración
❏ **exclamation point** (US) =
exclamation mark

exclude [ɪkˈskluːd] vt excluir; exceptuar

excluding [ɪksˈkluːdɪŋ] prep: ~ **VAT** IVA
no incluido

exclusion [ɪkˈskluːʒən] n exclusión f; **to
the ~ of** con exclusión de

exclusive [ɪkˈskluːsɪv] adj exclusivo;
(club, district) selecto; ~ **of tax**
excluyendo impuestos ❏ **exclusively**
adv únicamente

excruciating [ɪkˈskruːʃieɪtɪŋ] adj (pain)
agudísimo, atroz; (noise,
embarrassment) horrible

excursion [ɪkˈskɜːʃən] n (tourist
excursion) excursión f

excuse [n ɪkˈskjuːs, vb ɪkˈskjuːz] n
disculpa, excusa; (pretext) pretexto ♦ vt

(justify) justificar; (forgive) disculpar,
perdonar; **to ~ sb from doing sth**
dispensar a algn de hacer algo; ~ **me!**
(attracting attention) ¡por favor!;
(apologizing) ¡perdón!; **if you will ~ me**
con su permiso

ex-directory [ˈɛksdɪˈrɛktərɪ] (BRIT) adj
que no consta en la guía

execute [ˈɛksɪkjuːt] vt (plan) realizar;
(order) cumplir; (person) ajusticiar,
ejecutar ❏ **execution** [-ˈkjuːʃən] n
realización f; cumplimiento; ejecución
f

executive [ɪɡˈzɛkjʊtɪv] n (person,
committee) ejecutivo; (POL: committee)
poder m ejecutivo ♦ adj ejecutivo

exempt [ɪɡˈzɛmpt] adj: ~ **from** exento
de ♦ vt: **to ~ sb from** eximir a algn de

exercise [ˈɛksəsaɪz] n ejercicio ♦ vt
(patience) usar de; (right) valerse de;
(dog) llevar de paseo; (mind)
preocupar ♦ vi (also: **to take ~**) hacer
ejercicio(s) ❏ **exercise book** n
cuaderno

exert [ɪɡˈzɜːt] vt ejercer; **to ~ o.s.**
esforzarse ❏ **exertion** [-ʃən] n
esfuerzo

exhale [ɛksˈheɪl] vt despedir ♦ vi
exhalar

exhaust [ɪɡˈzɔːst] n (AUT: also: ~ **pipe**)
escape m; (: fumes) gases mpl de
escape ♦ vt agotar ❏ **exhausted** adj
agotado ❏ **exhaustion** [ɪɡˈzɔːstʃən] n
agotamiento; **nervous exhaustion**
postración f nerviosa

exhibit [ɪɡˈzɪbɪt] n (ART) obra expuesta;
(LAW) objeto expuesto ♦ vt (show:
emotions) manifestar; (: courage, skill)
demostrar; (paintings) exponer
❏ **exhibition** [ɛksɪˈbɪʃən] n exposición
f; (of talent etc) demostración f

exhilarating [ɪɡˈzɪləreɪtɪŋ] adj
estimulante, tónico

exile [ˈɛksaɪl] n exilio; (person)
exiliado(-a) ♦ vt desterrar, exiliar

exist [ɪg'zɪst] vi existir; (live) vivir
❑ **existence** n existencia ❑ **existing**
adj existente, actual

exit ['eksɪt] n salida ♦ vi (THEATRE) hacer
mutis; (COMPUT) salir (del sistema)
❑ **exit ramp** (US) n (AUT) vía de acceso

⚠ Be careful not to translate **exit** by
the Spanish word *éxito*.

exotic [ɪg'zɔtɪk] adj exótico

expand [ɪk'spænd] vt ampliar; (number)
aumentar ♦ vi (population) aumentar;
(trade etc) expandirse; (gas, metal)
dilatarse

expansion [ɪk'spænʃən] n (of
population) aumento; (of trade)
expansión f

expect [ɪk'spekt] vt esperar; (require)
contar con; (suppose) suponer ♦ vi: **to
be expecting** (pregnant woman) estar
embarazada ❑ **expectation**
[ekspek'teɪʃən] n (hope) esperanza;
(belief) expectativa

expedition [ekspə'dɪʃən] n expedición
f

expel [ɪk'spel] vt arrojar; (from place)
expulsar

expenditure [ɪk'spendɪtʃə*] n gastos
mpl, desembolso; consumo

expense [ɪk'spens] n gasto, gastos mpl;
(high cost) costa; **expenses** npl (COMM)
gastos mpl; **at the ~ of** a costa de
❑ **expense account** n cuenta de
gastos

expensive [ɪk'spensɪv] adj caro,
costoso

experience [ɪk'spɪərɪəns] n
experiencia ♦ vt experimentar; (suffer)
sufrir ❑ **experienced** adj
experimentado

experiment [ɪk'sperɪmənt] n
experimento ♦ vi hacer experimentos
❑ **experimental** [-'mentl] adj
experimental; **the process is still at
the experimental stage** el proceso
está todavía en prueba

expert ['ekspə:t] adj experto, perito ♦ n
experto(-a), perito(-a); (specialist)
especialista mf ❑ **expertise** [-'ti:z] n
pericia

expire [ɪk'spaɪə*] vi caducar, vencer
❑ **expiry** n vencimiento ❑ **expiry
date** n (of medicine, food item) fecha de
caducidad

explain [ɪk'spleɪn] vt explicar
❑ **explanation** [eksplə'neɪʃən] n
explicación f

explicit [ɪk'splɪsɪt] adj explícito

explode [ɪk'spləud] vi estallar,
explotar; (population) crecer
rápidamente; (with anger) reventar

exploit [n 'eksplɔɪt, vb ɪk'splɔɪt] n
hazaña ♦ vt explotar ❑ **exploitation**
[-'teɪʃən] n explotación f

explore [ɪk'splɔ:*] vt explorar; (fig)
examinar; investigar ❑ **explorer** n
explorador(a) m/f

explosion [ɪk'spləuʒən] n explosión f
❑ **explosive** [ɪks'pləusɪv] adj, n
explosivo

export [vb ek'spɔ:t, n, cpd 'ekspɔ:t] vt
exportar ♦ n (process) exportación f;
(product) producto de exportación
♦ cpd de exportación ❑ **exporter** n
exportador m

expose [ɪk'spəuz] vt exponer; (unmask)
desenmascarar ❑ **exposed** adj
expuesto

exposure [ɪk'spəuʒə*] n exposición f,
(publicity) publicidad f; (PHOT: speed)
velocidad f de obturación; (: shot)
fotografía; **to die from ~** (MED) morir de
frío

express [ɪk'spres] adj (definite) expreso,
explícito; (BRIT: letter etc) urgente ♦ n
(train) rápido ♦ vt expresar
❑ **expression** [ɪk'spreʃən] n expresión
f; (of actor etc) sentimiento
❑ **expressway** (US) n (urban
motorway) autopista

exquisite [ek'skwɪzɪt] adj exquisito

extend [ɪk'stɛnd] vt (visit, street)
prolongar; (building) ampliar;
(invitation) ofrecer ♦ vi (land)
extenderse; (period of time)
prolongarse

extension [ɪk'stɛnʃən] n extensión f;
(building) ampliación f; (of time)
prolongación f; (TEL: in private house)
línea derivada; (: in office) extensión f
❏ **extension lead** n alargador m,
alargadera

extensive [ɪk'stɛnsɪv] adj extenso;
(damage) importante; (knowledge)
amplio

extent [ɪk'stɛnt] n (breadth) extensión f;
(scope) alcance m; **to some ~** hasta
cierto punto; **to the ~ of ...** hasta el
punto de ...; **to such an ~ that ...** hasta
tal punto que ...; **to what ~?** ¿hasta qué
punto?

exterior [ɛk'stɪərɪəʳ] adj exterior,
externo ♦ n exterior m

external [ɛk'stə:nl] adj externo

extinct [ɪk'stɪŋkt] adj (volcano)
extinguido; (race) extinto
❏ **extinction** n extinción f

extinguish [ɪk'stɪŋgwɪʃ] vt extinguir,
apagar

extra ['ɛkstrə] adj adicional ♦ adv (in
addition) de más ♦ n (luxury, addition)
extra m; (CINEMA, THEATRE) extra mf,
comparsa mf

extract [vb ɪk'strækt, n 'ɛkstrækt] vt
sacar; (tooth) extraer; (money, promise)
obtener ♦ n extracto m

extradite ['ɛkstrədaɪt] vt extraditar
❏ **extraordinary** [ɪk'strɔ:dnrɪ] adj
extraordinario; (odd) raro

extravagance [ɪk'strævəgəns] n
derroche m, despilfarro; (thing bought)
extravagancia

extravagant [ɪk'strævəgənt] adj
(lavish: person) pródigo; (: gift)
(demasiado) caro; (wasteful)
despilfarrador(a)

extreme [ɪk'stri:m] adj extremo,
extremado ♦ n extremo ❏ **extremely**
adv sumamente, extremadamente

extremist [ɪk'stri:mɪst] adj, n
extremista m/f

extrovert ['ɛkstrəvə:t] n
extrovertido(-a)

eye [aɪ] n ojo ♦ vt mirar de soslayo,
ojear; **to keep an ~ on** vigilar
❏ **eyeball** n globo ocular ❏ **eyebrow**
n ceja ❏ **eyedrops** npl gotas fpl para
los ojos, colino ❏ **eyelash** n pestaña
❏ **eyelid** n párpado ❏ **eyeliner** n
delineador m de ojos ❏ **eyeshadow**
n sombreador m de ojos ❏ **eyesight** n
vista ❏ **eye witness** n testigo mf
presencial

F, f

F [ɛf] n (MUS) fa m

fabric ['fæbrɪk] n tejido, tela

⚠ Be careful not to translate **fabric**
by the Spanish word *fábrica*.

fabulous ['fæbjuləs] adj fabuloso

face [feɪs] n (ANAT) cara, rostro; (of clock)
esfera (SP), cara (LAm); (of mountain)
cara, ladera; (of building) fachada ♦ vt
(direction) estar de cara a; (situation)
hacer frente a; (facts) aceptar; **~ down**
(person, card) boca abajo; **to lose ~**
desprestigiarse; **to make** or **pull a ~**
hacer muecas; **in the ~ of** (difficulties
etc) ante; **on the ~ of it** a primera vista;
~ to ~ cara a cara ▶ **face up to** vt fus
hacer frente a, arrostrar ❏ **face cloth**
(BRIT) n manopla ❏ **face pack** n (BRIT)
mascarilla

facial ['feɪʃəl] adj de la cara ♦ n (also:
beauty ~) tratamiento facial, limpieza

facilitate [fə'sɪlɪteɪt] vt facilitar

facilities [fə'sɪlɪtɪz] npl (buildings)
instalaciones fpl; (equipment) servicios
mpl; **credit ~** facilidades fpl de crédito

fact [fækt] n hecho; **in ~** en realidad

faction ['fækʃən] n facción f

factor ['fæktə'] n factor m

factory ['fæktəri] n fábrica

factual ['fæktjuəl] adj basado en los hechos

faculty ['fækəlti] n facultad f; (US: teaching staff) personal m docente

fad [fæd] n novedad f, moda

fade [feɪd] vi (colour) destenirse; (sound, smile) desvanecerse; (light) apagarse; (flower) marchitarse; (hope, memory) perderse
  ▶ **fade away** vi (sound) apagarse

fag [fæg] (BRIT: inf) n (cigarette) pitillo (SP), cigarro

Fahrenheit ['fɑːrənhaɪt] n Fahrenheit m

fail [feɪl] vt (candidate, test) suspender (SP), reprobar (LAm); (memory etc) fallar a ♦ vi suspender (SP), reprobar (LAm); (be unsuccessful) fracasar; (strength, brakes) fallar; (light) acabarse; **to ~ to do sth** (neglect) dejar de hacer algo; (be unable) no poder hacer algo; **without ~** sin falta □ **failing** n falta, defecto ♦ prep a falta de □ **failure** ['feɪljə'] n fracaso; (person) fracasado(-a); (mechanical etc) fallo

faint [feɪnt] adj (recollection) vago; (mark) apenas visible ♦ n desmayo ♦ vi desmayarse; **to feel ~** estar mareado, marearse □ **faintest** adj: **I haven't the faintest idea** no tengo la más remota idea □ **faintly** adv débilmente; (vaguely) vagamente

fair [feə'] adj (just) justo; (hair, person) rubio; (weather) bueno; (good enough) regular; (considerable) considerable ♦ adv (play) limpio ♦ n feria; (BRIT: funfair) parque m de atracciones □ **fairground** n recinto ferial □ **fair-haired** adj (person) rubio □ **fairly** adv (justly) con justicia; (quite) bastante □ **fairway** n (GOLF) calle f

fairy ['feəri] n hada □ **fairy tale** n cuento de hadas

faith [feɪθ] n fe f; (trust) confianza; (sect) religión f □ **faithful** adj (loyal: troops etc) leal; (spouse) fiel; (account) exacto □ **faithfully** adv fielmente; **yours faithfully** (BRIT: in letters) le saluda atentamente

fake [feɪk] n (painting etc) falsificación f; (person) impostor(a) m/f ♦ adj falso ♦ vt fingir; (painting etc) falsificar

falcon ['fɔːlkən] n halcón m

fall [fɔːl] (pt fell, pp fallen) n caída; (in price etc) descenso; (US) otoño ♦ vi caer(se); (price) bajar, descender; **falls** npl (waterfall) cascada, salto de agua; **to ~ flat** (on one's face) caerse (boca abajo); (plan) fracasar; (joke, story) no hacer gracia ▶ **fall apart** vi deshacerse ▶ **fall down** vi (person) caerse; (building, hopes) derrumbarse ▶ **fall for** vt fus (trick) dejarse engañar por; (person) enamorarse de ▶ **fall off** vi caerse; (diminish) disminuir ▶ **fall out** vi (friends etc) renir; (hair, teeth) caerse ▶ **fall over** vi caer(se) ▶ **fall through** vi (plan, project) fracasar

fallen ['fɔːlən] pp of **fall**

fallout ['fɔːlaʊt] n lluvia radioactiva

false [fɔːls] adj falso; **under ~ pretences** con engaños □ **false alarm** n falsa alarma □ **false teeth** (BRIT) npl dentadura postiza

fame [feɪm] n fama

familiar [fə'mɪlɪə'] adj conocido, familiar; (tone) de confianza; **to be ~ with** (subject) conocer (bien) □ **familiarize** [fə'mɪlɪəraɪz] vt: **to familiarize o.s.** with familiarizarse con

family ['fæmɪlɪ] n familia □ **family doctor** n médico(-a) de cabecera □ **family planning** n planificación f familiar

famine ['fæmɪn] n hambre f, hambruna

famous ['feɪməs] adj famoso, célebre

fan [fæn] n abanico; (ELEC) ventilador m; (of pop star) fan m/f; (SPORT) hincha m/f ♦ vt abanicar; (fire, quarrel) atizar

fanatic [fəˈnætɪk] n fanático(-a)

fan belt n correa del ventilador

fan club n club m de fans

fancy [ˈfænsɪ] n (whim) capricho, antojo; (imagination) imaginación f ♦ adj (luxury) lujoso, de lujo ♦ vt (feel like, want) tener ganas de; (imagine) imaginarse; (think) creer; **to take a ~ to sb** tomar cariño a algn; **he fancies her** (inf) le gusta (ella) mucho ♦ **fancy dress** n disfraz m

fan heater n calefactor m de aire

fantasize [ˈfæntəsaɪz] vi fantasear, hacerse ilusiones

fantastic [fænˈtæstɪk] adj (enormous) enorme; (strange, wonderful) fantástico

fantasy [ˈfæntəsɪ] n (dream) sueño; (unreality) fantasía

fanzine [ˈfænziːn] n fanzine m

FAQs abbr (= frequently asked questions) preguntas frecuentes

far [fɑːʳ] adj (distant) lejano ♦ adv lejos; (much, greatly) mucho; **~ away, ~ off** (a lo) lejos; **~ better** mucho mejor; **~ from** lejos de; **by ~** con mucho; **go as ~ as the farm** vaya hasta la granja; **as ~ as I know** que yo sepa; **how ~?** ¿hasta dónde?; (fig) ¿hasta qué punto?

farce [fɑːs] n farsa

fare [fɛəʳ] n (on trains, buses) precio (del billete); (in taxi: cost) tarifa; (food) comida; **half ~** medio pasaje m; **full ~** pasaje completo

Far East n: **the ~** el Extremo Oriente

farewell [fɛəˈwɛl] excl, n adiós m

farm [fɑːm] n cortijo (SP), hacienda (LAm), rancho (MEX), estancia (RPl) ♦ vt cultivar ❑ **farmer** n granjero, hacendado (LAm), ranchero (MEX), estanciero (RPl) ❑ **farmhouse** n granja, casa del hacendado (LAm), rancho (MEX), casco de la estancia (RPl) ❑ **farming** n agricultura; (of crops) cultivo; (of animals) cría ❑ **farmyard** n corral m

far-reaching [fɑːˈriːtʃɪŋ] adj (reform, effect) de gran alcance

fart [fɑːt] (inf!) vi tirarse un pedo (!)

farther [ˈfɑːðəʳ] adv más lejos, más allá ♦ adj más lejano

farthest [ˈfɑːðɪst] superlative of **far**

fascinate [ˈfæsɪneɪt] vt fascinar ❑ **fascinated** adj fascinado

fascinating [ˈfæsɪneɪtɪŋ] adj fascinante

fascination [-ˈneɪʃən] n fascinación f

fascist [ˈfæʃɪst] adj, n fascista m/f

fashion [ˈfæʃən] n moda; (fashion industry) industria de la moda; (manner) manera ♦ vt formar; **in ~** a la moda; **out of ~** pasado de moda ❑ **fashionable** adj de moda ❑ **fashion show** n desfile m de modelos

fast [fɑːst] adj rápido; (dye, colour) resistente; (clock): **to be ~** estar adelantado ♦ adv rápidamente, de prisa; (stuck, held) firmemente ♦ n ayuno ♦ vi ayunar; **~ asleep** profundamente dormido

fasten [ˈfɑːsn] vt atar, sujetar; (coat, belt) abrochar ♦ vi atarse; abrocharse

fast food n comida rápida, platos mpl preparados

fat [fæt] adj gordo; (book) grueso; (profit) grande, pingüe ♦ n grasa; (on person) carnes fpl; (lard) manteca

fatal [ˈfeɪtl] adj (mistake) fatal; (injury) mortal ❑ **fatality** [fəˈtælɪtɪ] n (road death etc) víctima ❑ **fatally** adv fatalmente; mortalmente

fate [feɪt] n destino; (of person) suerte f

father [ˈfɑːðəʳ] n padre m ❑ **Father Christmas** n Papá m Noel ❑ **father-in-law** n suegro

fatigue [fəˈtiːg] n fatiga, cansancio

fattening [ˈfætnɪŋ] adj (food) que hace engordar

fatty [ˈfætɪ] adj (food) graso ♦ n (inf) gordito(-a), gordinflón(-ona) (inf)

faucet ['fɔːsɪt] (US) n grifo (SP), llave f, canilla (RPl)

fault [fɔːlt] n (blame) culpa f; (defect: in person, machine) defecto; (GEO) falla ♦ vt criticar; **it's my ~** es culpa mía; **to find ~ with** criticar, poner peros a; **at ~** culpable ❑ **faulty** adj defectuoso

fauna ['fɔːnə] n fauna

favour etc ['feɪvəʳ] (US **favor** etc) n favor m; (approval) aprobación f ♦ vt (proposition) estar a favor de, aprobar; (assist) ser propicio a; **to do sb a ~** hacer un favor a algn; **to find ~ with sb** caer en gracia a algn; **in ~ of** a favor de ❑ **favourable** adj favorable ❑ **favourite** ['feɪvrɪt] adj, n favorito, preferido

fawn [fɔːn] n cervato ♦ adj (also: **~-coloured**) color de cervato, leonado ♦ vi: **to ~ (up)on** adular

fax [fæks] n (document) fax m; (machine) telefax m ♦ vt mandar por telefax

FBI (US) n abbr (= Federal Bureau of Investigation) = BIC f (SP)

fear [fɪəʳ] n miedo, temor m ♦ vt tener miedo a, temer; **for ~ of** por si ❑ **fearful** adj temeroso, miedoso; (awful) terrible ❑ **fearless** adj audaz

feasible ['fiːzəbl] adj factible

feast [fiːst] n banquete m; (REL: also: **~ day**) fiesta ♦ vi festejar

feat [fiːt] n hazaña

feather ['feðəʳ] n pluma

feature ['fiːtʃəʳ] n característica; (article) artículo de fondo ♦ vt (film) presentar ♦ vi: **to ~ in** tener un papel destacado en; **features** npl (of face) facciones fpl ❑ **feature film** n largometraje m

Feb. abbr (= February) feb

February ['fɛbruəri] n febrero

fed [fed] pt, pp of **feed**

federal ['fedərəl] adj federal

federation [fedə'reɪʃən] n federación f

fed up [fed'ʌp] adj: **to be ~ (with)** estar harto (de)

fee [fiː] n pago; (professional) derechos mpl, honorarios mpl; (of club) cuota; **school fees** matrícula

feeble ['fiːbl] adj débil; (joke) flojo

feed [fiːd] (pt, pp **fed**) n comida; (of animal) pienso; (on printer) dispositivo de alimentación f ♦ vt alimentar; (BRIT: baby: breastfeed) dar el pecho a; (animal) dar de comer a; (data, information): **to ~ into** meter en ❑ **feedback** n reacción f, feedback m

feel [fiːl] (pt, pp **felt**) n (sensation) sensación f; (sense of touch) tacto; (impression): **to have the ~ of** parecerse a ♦ vt tocar; (pain etc) sentir; (think, believe) creer; **to ~ hungry/cold** tener hambre/frío; **to ~ lonely/better** sentirse solo/mejor; **I don't ~ well** no me siento bien; **it feels soft** es suave al tacto; **to ~ like** (want) tener ganas de ❑ **feeling** n (physical) sensación f; (foreboding) presentimiento; (emotion) sentimiento

feet [fiːt] npl of **foot**

fell [fel] pt of **fall** ♦ vt (tree) talar

fellow ['feləu] n tipo, tío (SP); (comrade) compañero; (of learned society) socio(-a) ❑ **fellow citizen** n conciudadano(-a) ❑ **fellow countryman** (irreg) n compatriota m ❑ **fellow men** npl semejantes mpl ❑ **fellowship** n compañerismo; (grant) beca

felony ['feləni] n crimen m

felt [felt] pt, pp of **feel** ♦ n fieltro ❑ **felt-tip** n (also: **felt-tip pen**) rotulador m

female ['fiːmeɪl] n (pej: woman) mujer f, tía; (ZOOL) hembra ♦ adj femenino; hembra

feminine ['feminɪn] adj femenino

feminist ['feminɪst] n feminista

fence [fens] n valla, cerca ♦ vt (also: **~ in**) cercar ♦ vi (SPORT) hacer esgrima ❑ **fencing** n esgrima

fend [fɛnd] vi: to ~ **for o.s.** valerse por sí mismo ▶ **fend off** vt (attack) rechazar; (questions) evadir

fender ['fɛndər] (US) n guardafuego; (AUT) parachoques m inv

fennel ['fɛnl] n hinojo

ferment [vb fə'mɛnt, n 'fə:mɛnt] vi fermentar ♦ n (fig) agitación f

fern [fə:n] n helecho

ferocious [fə'rəuʃəs] adj feroz

ferret ['fɛrɪt] n hurón m

ferry ['fɛrɪ] n (small) barca (de pasaje), balsa; (large: also: **ferryboat**) transbordador m, ferry m ♦ vt transportar

fertile ['fə:taɪl] adj fértil; (BIOL) fecundo □ **fertilize** ['fə:tɪlaɪz] vt (BIOL) fecundar; (AGR) abonar □ **fertilizer** n abono

festival ['fɛstɪvəl] n (REL) fiesta; (ART, MUS) festival m

festive ['fɛstɪv] adj festivo; **the ~ season** (BRIT: Christmas) las Navidades

fetch [fɛtʃ] vt ir a buscar; (sell for) venderse por

fête [feɪt] n fiesta

fetus ['fi:təs] (US) n = **foetus**

feud [fju:d] n (hostility) enemistad f; (quarrel) disputa

fever ['fi:vər] n fiebre f □ **feverish** adj febril

few [fju:] adj (not many) pocos ♦ pron pocos; algunos; **a ~** adj unos pocos, algunos □ **fewer** adj menos □ **fewest** adj los (las) menos

fiancé [fɪ'ɑ̃ːnseɪ] n novio, prometido □ **fiancée** n novia, prometida

fiasco [fɪ'æskəu] n fiasco

fib [fɪb] n mentirilla

fibre ['faɪbər] (US **fiber**) n fibra □ **fibreglass** (US **Fiberglass®**) n fibra de vidrio

fickle ['fɪkl] adj inconstante

fiction ['fɪkʃən] n ficción f □ **fictional** adj novelesco

fiddle ['fɪdl] n (MUS) violín m; (cheating) trampa ♦ vt (BRIT: accounts) falsificar ▶ **fiddle with** vt fus juguetear con

fidelity [fɪ'dɛlɪtɪ] n fidelidad f

field [fi:ld] n campo; (fig) campo, esfera; (SPORT) campo (SP), cancha (LAm) □ **field marshal** n mariscal m

fierce [fɪəs] adj feroz; (wind, heat) fuerte; (fighting, enemy) encarnizado

fifteen [fɪf'ti:n] num quince □ **fifteenth** adj decimoquinto; **the fifteenth floor** la planta quince; **the fifteenth of August** el quince de agosto

fifth [fɪfθ] num quinto

fiftieth ['fɪftɪɪθ] adj quincuagésimo

fifty ['fɪftɪ] num cincuenta □ **fifty-fifty** (deal, split) a medias ♦ adv a medias, mitad por mitad

fig [fɪg] n higo

fight [faɪt] (pt, pp **fought**) n (gen) pelea; (MIL) combate m; (struggle) lucha ♦ vt luchar contra; (cancer, alcoholism) combatir; (election) intentar ganar; (emotion) resistir ♦ vi pelear, luchar ▶ **fight back** vi defenderse; (after illness) recuperarse ♦ vt (tears) contener ▶ **fight off** vt (attack, attacker) rechazar; (disease, sleep, urge) luchar contra □ **fighting** n combate m, pelea

figure ['fɪgər] n (DRAWING, GEOM) figura, dibujo; (number, cipher) cifra; (body, outline) tipo; (personality) figura ♦ vt (esp US) imaginar ♦ vi (appear) figurar ▶ **figure out** vt (work out) resolver

file [faɪl] n (tool) lima; (dossier) expediente m; (folder) carpeta; (COMPUT) fichero; (row) fila ♦ vt limar; (LAW: claim) presentar; (store) archivar □ **filing cabinet** n fichero, archivador m

Filipino [fɪlɪ'pi:nəu] adj filipino ♦ n (person) filipino(-a); m/f; (LING) tagalo

fill [fɪl] vt (space): **to ~ (with)** llenar (de); (vacancy, need) cubrir ♦ n: **to eat one's**

~ llenarse ▶ **fill in** vt rellenar ♦ **fill out** vt (form, receipt) rellenar ♦ **fill up** vt llenar (hasta el borde) ♦ vi (AUT) poner gasolina

fillet ['fılıt] n filete m ❑ **fillet steak** n filete m de ternera

filling ['fılıŋ] n (CULIN) relleno; (for tooth) empaste m ❑ **filling station** n estación f de servicio

film [fılm] n (gen) película ♦ vt (scene) filmar ♦ vi rodar (una película) ❑ **film star** n astro, estrella de cine

filter ['fıltə^r] n filtro ♦ vt filtrar ❑ **filter lane** (BRIT) n carril m de selección

filth [fılθ] n suciedad f ❑ **filthy** adj sucio; (language) obsceno

fin [fın] n (gen) aleta

final ['faınl] adj (last) final, último; (definitive) definitivo, terminante ♦ n (BRIT SPORT) final f; **finals** npl (SCOL) examen m final; (US SPORT) final f

finale [fı'nɑːlɪ] n final m

final: **finalist** n (SPORT) finalista mf ❑ **finalize** vt concluir, completar ❑ **finally** adv (lastly) por último, finalmente; (eventually) por fin

finance [faı'næns] n (money) fondos mpl ♦ vt financiar; **finances** npl finanzas fpl; (personal finances) situación f económica ❑ **financial** [-'nænʃəl] adj financiero ❑ **financial year** n ejercicio (financiero)

find [faınd] (pt, pp found) vt encontrar, hallar; (come upon) descubrir ♦ n hallazgo; descubrimiento; **to ~ sb guilty** (LAW) declarar culpable a algn ▶ **find out** vt averiguar; (truth, secret) descubrir; **to find out about** (subject) informarse sobre; (by chance) enterarse de ❑ **findings** npl (LAW) veredicto, fallo; (of report) recomendaciones fpl

fine [faın] adj excelente; (thin) fino ♦ adv (well) bien ♦ n (LAW) multa ♦ vt (LAW) multar; **to be ~** (person) estar bien; (weather) hacer buen tiempo ❑ **fine arts** npl bellas artes fpl

~ **llenarse** ▶ **finger** ['fıŋgə^r] n dedo ♦ vt (touch) manosear; **little/index ~** (dedo) meñique m/índice m ❑ **fingernail** n uña ❑ **fingerprint** n huella dactilar ❑ **fingertip** n yema del dedo

finish ['fınıʃ] n (end) fin m; (SPORT) meta; (polish etc) acabado ♦ vt, vi terminar; **to ~ doing sth** acabar de hacer algo; **to ~ third** llegar el tercero ▶ **finish off** vt acabar, terminar; (kill) acabar con ▶ **finish up** vt acabar, terminar ♦ vi ir a parar, terminar

Finland ['fınlənd] n Finlandia

Finn [fın] n finlandés(-esa) m/f ❑ **Finnish** adj finlandés(-esa) ♦ n (LING) finlandés m

fir [fə:^r] n abeto

fire ['faıə^r] n fuego; (in hearth) lumbre f; (accidental) incendio; (heater) estufa ♦ vt (gun) disparar; (interest) despertar; (inf: dismiss) despedir ♦ vi (shoot) disparar; **on ~** ardiendo, en llamas ❑ **fire alarm** n alarma de incendios ❑ **firearm** n arma de fuego ❑ **fire brigade** (US **fire department**) n (cuerpo de) bomberos mpl ❑ **fire engine** (BRIT) n coche m de bomberos ❑ **fire escape** n escalera de incendios ❑ **fire exit** n salida de incendios ❑ **fire extinguisher** n extintor m (de incendios) ❑ **fireman** (irreg) n bombero ❑ **fireplace** n chimenea ❑ **fire station** n parque m de bomberos ❑ **firetruck** (US) n = **fire engine** ❑ **firewall** n (INTERNET) firewall m ❑ **firewood** n leña ❑ **fireworks** npl fuegos mpl artificiales

firm [fə:m] adj firme; (look, voice) resuelto ♦ n firma, empresa ❑ **firmly** adv firmemente; resueltamente

first [fə:st] adj primero ♦ adv (before others) primero; (when listing reasons etc) en primer lugar, primeramente ♦ n (person: in race) primero(-a); (AUT) primera; (BRIT SCOL) título de licenciado con calificación de sobresaliente; **at ~** al principio; **~ of all** ante todo ❏ **first aid** n primera ayuda, primeros auxilios mpl ❏ **first-aid kit** n botiquín m ❏ **first-class** adj (excellent) de primera (categoría); (ticket etc) de primera clase ❏ **first-hand** adj de primera mano ❏ **first lady** n (esp US) primera dama ❏ **firstly** adv en primer lugar ❏ **first name** n nombre m (de pila) ❏ **first-rate** adj estupendo

fiscal ['fɪskəl] adj fiscal ❏ **fiscal year** n año fiscal, ejercicio

fish [fɪʃ] n inv pez m; (food) pescado ♦ vt, vi pescar; **to go fishing** ir de pesca; **~ and chips** pescado frito con patatas fritas ❏ **fisherman** (irreg) n pescador m ❏ **fish fingers** (BRIT) npl croquetas fpl de pescado ❏ **fishing** n pesca ❏ **fishing boat** n barca de pesca ❏ **fishing line** n sedal m ❏ **fishmonger** (BRIT) n pescadero(-a) ❏ **fishmonger's (shop)** (BRIT) n pescadería ❏ **fish sticks** (US) npl = **fish fingers** ❏ **fishy** (inf) adj sospechoso

fist [fɪst] n puño

fit [fɪt] adj (healthy) en (buena) forma; (proper) adecuado, apropiado ♦ vt (clothes) estar or sentar bien a; (install) poner; (equip) proveer, dotar; (facts) cuadrar or corresponder con ♦ vi (clothes) sentar bien; (in space, gap) caber; (facts) coincidir ♦ n (MED) ataque m; **~ to** (ready) a punto de; **~ for** apropiado para; **a ~ of anger/pride** un arranque de cólera/orgullo; **this dress is a good ~** este vestido me sienta bien; **by fits and starts** a rachas ► **fit in** vi (fig: person) llevarse bien (con todos) ❏ **fitness** n (MED) salud f ❏ **fitted** adj (jacket, shirt) entallado; (sheet) de cuatro picos ❏ **fitted carpet** n moqueta ❏ **fitted kitchen** n cocina amueblada ❏ **fitting** adj apropiado ♦ n (of dress) prueba; (of piece of equipment) instalación f

❏ **fitting room** n probador m ❏ **fittings** npl instalaciones fpl

five [faɪv] num cinco ❏ **fiver** (inf) n (BRIT) billete m de cinco libras; (US) billete m de cinco dólares

fix [fɪks] vt (secure) fijar, asegurar; (mend) arreglar; (prepare) preparar ♦ n: **to be in a ~** estar en un aprieto ► **fix up** vt (meeting) arreglar; **to fix sb up with sth** proveer a algn de algo ❏ **fixed** adj (prices etc) fijo ❏ **fixture** n (SPORT) encuentro

fizzy ['fɪzɪ] adj (drink) gaseoso

flag [flæg] n bandera; (stone) losa ♦ vi decaer ♦ vt: **to ~ sb down** hacer señas a algn para que se pare ❏ **flagpole** n asta de bandera

flair [fleə'] n aptitud f especial

flak [flæk] n (MIL) fuego antiaéreo; (inf: criticism) lluvia de críticas

flake [fleɪk] n (of rust, paint) escama; (of snow, soap powder) copo ♦ vi (also: ~ off) descamarse

flamboyant [flæm'bɔɪənt] adj (dress) vistoso; (person) extravagante

flame [fleɪm] n llama

flamingo [flə'mɪŋgəu] n flamenco

flammable ['flæməbl] adj inflamable

flan [flæn] (BRIT) n tarta

⚠ Be careful not to translate **flan** by the Spanish word flan.

flank [flæŋk] n (of animal) ijar m; (of army) flanco ♦ vt flanquear

flannel ['flænl] n (BRIT: also: **face ~**) manopla; (fabric) franela

flap [flæp] n (of pocket, envelope) solapa ♦ vt (wings, arms) agitar ♦ vi (sail, flag) ondear

flare [fleə'] n llamarada; (MIL) bengala; (in skirt etc) vuelo; **flares** (trousers) pantalones mpl de campana ► **flare up** vi encenderse; (fig: person) encolerizarse; (: revolt) estallar

flash [flæʃ] n relámpago; (also: **news ~**) noticias fpl de última hora; (PHOT) flash m ♦ vt (light, headlights) lanzar un destello con; (news, message) transmitir; (smile) lanzar ♦ vi brillar; (hazard light etc) lanzar destellos; **in a ~** en un instante; **he flashed by** o **past** pasó como un rayo ❏ **flashback** n (CINEMA) flashback m ❏ **flashbulb** n bombilla fusible ❏ **flashlight** n linterna

flask [flɑːsk] n frasco; (also: **vacuum ~**) termo

flat [flæt] adj llano; (smooth) liso; (tyre) desinflado; (battery) descargado; (beer) muerto; (refusal etc) rotundo; (MUS) desafinado; (rate) fijo ♦ n (BRIT: apartment) piso (SP), departamento (LAm), apartamento; (AUT) pinchazo; (MUS) bemol m; **to work ~ out** trabajar a toda mecha ❏ **flatten** vt (also: **flatten out**) allanar; (smooth out) alisar; (building, plants) arrasar

flatter [ˈflætə*] vt adular, halagar ❏ **flattering** adj halagüeño; (dress) que favorece

flaunt [flɔːnt] vt ostentar, lucir

flavour etc [ˈfleɪvə*] (US **flavor** etc) n sabor m, gusto ♦ vt sazonar, condimentar; **strawberry-flavoured** con sabor a fresa ❏ **flavouring** n (in product) aromatizante m

flaw [flɔː] n defecto ❏ **flawless** adj impecable

flea [fliː] n pulga ❏ **flea market** n rastro, mercadillo

flee [fliː] (pt, pp **fled**) vt huir de ♦ vi huir, fugarse

fleece [fliːs] n vellón m; (wool) lana; (top) forro polar ♦ vt (inf) desplumar

fleet [fliːt] n flota; (of lorries etc) escuadra

fleeting [ˈfliːtɪŋ] adj fugaz

Flemish [ˈflemɪʃ] adj flamenco

flesh [fleʃ] n carne f; (skin) piel f; (of fruit) pulpa

flew [fluː] pt of **fly**

flex [fleks] n cordón m ♦ vt (muscles) tensar ❏ **flexibility** n flexibilidad f ❏ **flexible** adj flexible ❏ **flexitime** (US **flextime**) n horario flexible

flick [flɪk] n capirotazo; chasquido ♦ vt (with hand) dar un capirotazo a; (whip etc) chasquear; (switch) accionar
▶ **flick through** vt fus hojear

flicker [ˈflɪkə*] vi (light) parpadear; (flame) vacilar

flies [flaɪz] npl of **fly**

flight [flaɪt] n vuelo; (escape) huida, fuga; (also: **~ of steps**) tramo (de escaleras) ❏ **flight attendant** n auxiliar mf de vuelo

flimsy [ˈflɪmzɪ] adj (thin) muy ligero; (building) endeble; (excuse) flojo

flinch [flɪntʃ] vi encogerse; **to ~ from** retroceder ante

fling [flɪŋ] (pt, pp **flung**) vt arrojar

flint [flɪnt] n pedernal m; (in lighter) piedra

flip [flɪp] vt dar la vuelta a; (switch: turn on) encender; (turn) apagar; (coin) echar a cara o cruz

flip-flops [ˈflɪpflɒps] npl (esp BRIT) chancletas fpl

flipper [ˈflɪpə*] n aleta

flirt [flɜːt] vi coquetear, flirtear ♦ n coqueta

float [fləʊt] n flotador m; (in procession) carroza; (money) reserva ♦ vi flotar; (swimmer) hacer la plancha

flock [flɒk] n (of sheep) rebaño; (of birds) bandada ♦ vi: **to ~ to** acudir en tropel a

flood [flʌd] n inundación f; (of letters, imports etc) avalancha ♦ vt inundar ♦ vi (place) inundarse; (people): **to ~ into** inundar ❏ **flooding** n inundaciones fpl ❏ **floodlight** n foco

floor [flɔː*] n suelo; (storey) piso; (of sea) fondo ♦ vt (question) dejar sin respuesta; (: blow) derribar; **ground ~, first ~** (US) planta baja; **first ~, second ~** (US) primer piso ❏ **floorboard** n tabla □ **flooring** n suelo; (material) solería □ **floor show** n cabaret m

flop [flɒp] n fracaso ♦ vi (fail) fracasar; (fall) derrumbarse □ **floppy** adj flojo ♦ n (COMPUT: also: **floppy disk**) floppy m

flora ['flɔːrə] n flora

floral ['flɔːrl] adj (pattern) floreado

florist ['flɒrɪst] n florista mf □ **florist's (shop)** n floristería

flotation [fləu'teɪʃən] n (of shares) emisión f; (of company) lanzamiento

flour ['flauə] n harina

flourish ['flʌrɪʃ] vi florecer ♦ n ademán m, movimiento (ostentoso)

flow [fləu] n (movement) flujo; (of traffic) circulación f; (tide) corriente f ♦ vi (river, blood) fluir; (traffic) circular

flower ['flauə] n flor f ♦ vi florecer □ **flower bed** n macizo □ **flowerpot** n tiesto

flown [fləun] pp of **fly**

fl. oz. abbr = **fluid ounce**

flu [fluː] n: **to have ~** tener la gripe

fluctuate ['flʌktjueɪt] vi fluctuar

fluent ['fluːənt] adj (linguist) que habla perfectamente; (speech) elocuente; **he speaks ~ French, he's ~ in French** domina el francés

fluff [flʌf] n pelusa □ **fluffy** adj de pelo suave

fluid ['fluːɪd] adj (movement) fluido, líquido; (situation) inestable ♦ n fluido, líquido □ **fluid ounce** n onza f líquida

fluke [fluːk] (inf) n chiripa

flung [flʌŋ] pt, pp of **fling**

fluorescent [fluə'resnt] adj fluorescente

fluoride ['fluəraɪd] n fluoruro

flurry ['flʌrɪ] n (of snow) temporal m; **~ of activity** frenesí m de actividad

flush [flʌʃ] n rubor m; (fig: of youth etc) resplandor m ♦ vt limpiar con agua ♦ vi ruborizarse ♦ adj: **~ with** a ras de; **to ~ the toilet** hacer funcionar la cisterna

flute [fluːt] n flauta

flutter ['flʌtə*] n (of wings) revoloteo, aleteo; (fig): **a ~ of panic/excitement** una oleada de pánico/excitación ♦ vi revolotear

fly [flaɪ] (pt **flew**, pp **flown**) n mosca; (on trousers: also: **flies**) bragueta f ♦ vt (plane) pilot(e)ar; (cargo) transportar (en avión); (distances) recorrer (en avión) ♦ vi volar; (passengers) ir en avión; (escape) evadirse; (flag) ondear ▶ **fly away**, **fly off** vi emprender el vuelo □ **fly-drive** n: **fly-drive holiday** vacaciones que incluyen vuelo y alquiler de coche □ **flying** n (activity) (el) volar; (action) vuelo ♦ adj: **flying visit** visita relámpago; **with flying colours** con lucimiento □ **flying saucer** n platillo volante □ **flyover** (BRIT) n paso a desnivel or superior

FM abbr (RADIO: = frequency modulation) FM

foal [fəul] n potro

foam [fəum] n espuma ♦ vi hacer espuma

focus ['fəukəs] (pl **focuses**) n foco; (centre) centro ♦ vt (field glasses etc) enfocar ♦ vi: **to ~ (on)** enfocar a; (issue etc) centrarse en; **in/out of ~** enfocado/desenfocado

foetus ['fiːtəs] (US **fetus**) n feto

fog [fɒg] n niebla □ **foggy** adj: **it's foggy** hay niebla, está brumoso □ **fog lamp** (US **fog light**) n (AUT) faro de niebla

foil [fɔɪl] n vt frustrar ♦ n hoja; (kitchen foil) papel m (de) aluminio; (complement) complemento; (FENCING) florete m

fold [fəuld] n (bend, crease) pliegue m; (AGR) redil m ♦ vt doblar; (arms) cruzar ▶ **fold up** vi plegarse, doblarse; (business) quebrar ♦ vt (map etc) plegar □ **folder** n (for papers) carpeta; (COMPUT) directorio □ **folding** adj (chair, bed) plegable

foliage ['fəulɪdʒ] n follaje m

folk [fəʊk] *npl* gente f ♦ *adj* popular, folklórico; **folks** *npl* (*family*) familia *sg*, parientes *mpl* ❏ **folklore** ['fəʊklɔː*] *n* folklore *m* ❏ **folk music** *n* música folk ❏ **folk song** *n* canción f popular

follow ['fɒləʊ] *vt* seguir ♦ *vi* seguir; (*result*) resultar; **to ~ suit** hacer lo mismo ► **follow up** *vt* (*letter, offer*) responder a; (*case*) investigar ❏ **follower** *n* (*of person, belief*) partidario(-a) ❏ **following** *adj* siguiente ♦ *n* afición f, partidarios *mpl* ❏ **follow-up** *n* continuación f

fond [fɒnd] *adj* (*memory, smile etc*) cariñoso; (*hopes*) ilusorio; **to be ~ of** tener cariño a; (*pastime, food*) ser aficionado a

food [fuːd] *n* comida ❏ **food mixer** *n* batidora ❏ **food poisoning** *n* intoxicación f alimenticia ❏ **food processor** *n* robot *m* de cocina ❏ **food stamp** (*US*) *n* vale *m* para comida

fool [fuːl] *n* tonto(-a); (*CULIN*) puré *m* de frutas con nata ♦ *vt* engañar ♦ *vi* (*gen*) bromear ► **fool about, fool around** *vi* hacer el tonto ❏ **foolish** *adj* tonto; (*careless*) imprudente ❏ **foolproof** *adj* (*plan etc*) infalible

foot [fʊt] (*pl* **feet**) *n* pie *m*; (*measure*) pie *m* (= 304 mm); (*of animal*) pata ♦ *vt* (*bill*) pagar; **on ~** a pie ❏ **footage** *n* (*CINEMA*) imágenes *fpl* ❏ **foot-and-mouth (disease)** [fʊtænd'maʊθ-] *n* fiebre f aftosa ❏ **football** *n* balón *m*; (*game: BRIT*) fútbol *m*; (*US*) fútbol *m* americano ❏ **footballer** (*BRIT*) = **football player** ❏ **football match** *n* partido de fútbol ❏ **football player** *n* (*BRIT*) futbolista *mf*; (*US*) jugador *m* de fútbol americano ❏ **footbridge** *n* puente *m* para peatones ❏ **foothills** *npl* estribaciones *fpl* ❏ **foothold** *n* pie *m* firme ❏ **footing** *n* (*fig*) posición f; **to lose one's footing** perder el pie ❏ **footnote** *n* nota (al pie de la página) ❏ **footpath** *n* sendero

❏ **footprint** *n* huella, pisada ❏ **footstep** *n* paso ❏ **footwear** *n* calzado

forbid [fə'bɪd] (*pt* **forbad(e)**, *pp* **forbidden**) *vt* prohibir; **to ~ sb to do sth** prohibir a algn hacer algo ❏ **forbidden** *pt of* **forbid** ♦ *adj* (*food, area*) prohibido; (*word, subject*) tabú

force [fɔːs] *n* fuerza ♦ *vt* forzar; (*push*) meter a la fuerza; **to ~ o.s. to do** hacer un esfuerzo por hacer ❏ **forced** *adj* forzado ❏ **forceful** *adj* enérgico

ford [fɔːd] *n* vado

fore [fɔː*] *n*: **to come to the ~** empezar a destacar ❏ **forearm** *n* antebrazo ❏ **forecast** (*pt, pp* **forecast**) *n* pronóstico ♦ *vt* pronosticar ❏ **forecourt** *n* patio ❏ **forefinger** *n* (dedo) índice *m* ❏ **forefront** *n*: **in the forefront of** en la vanguardia de ❏ **foreground** *n* primer plano ❏ **forehead** ['fɒrɪd] *n* frente f

foreign ['fɒrɪn] *adj* extranjero; (*trade*) exterior; (*object*) extraño ❏ **foreign currency** *n* divisas *fpl* ❏ **foreigner** *n* extranjero(-a) ❏ **foreign exchange** *n* divisas *fpl* ❏ **Foreign Office** (*BRIT*) *n* Ministerio de Asuntos Exteriores ❏ **Foreign Secretary** (*BRIT*) *n* Ministro de Asuntos Exteriores

fore: **foreman** (*irreg*) *n* capataz *m*; (*in construction*) maestro de obras ❏ **foremost** *adj* principal ♦ *adv*: **first and foremost** ante todo ❏ **forename** *n* nombre *m* (de pila)

forensic [fə'rensɪk] *adj* forense

foresee [fɔː'siː] (*pt* **foresaw**, *pp* **foreseen**) *vt* prever ❏ **foreseeable** *adj* previsible

forest ['fɒrɪst] *n* bosque *m* ❏ **forestry** *n* silvicultura

forever [fə'revə*] *adv* para siempre; (*endlessly*) constantemente

foreword ['fɔːwəːd] *n* prefacio

forfeit ['fɔːfɪt] *vt* perder

forgave [fə'geɪv] *pt of* **forgive**

forge [fɔːdʒ] n herrería ♦ vt (*signature, money*) falsificar; (*metal*) forjar
❑ **forger** n falsificador(a) m/f
❑ **forgery** n falsificación f

forget [fəˈgɛt] (*pt* forgot, *pp* forgotten) vt olvidar ♦ vi olvidarse ❑ **forgetful** adj despistado

forgive [fəˈgɪv] (*pt* forgave, *pp* forgiven) vt perdonar; **to ~ sb for sth** perdonar algo a algn

forgot [fəˈgɒt] pt of **forget**

forgotten [fəˈgɒtn] pp of **forget**

fork [fɔːk] n (*for eating*) tenedor m; (*for gardening*) horca; (*of roads*) bifurcación f ♦ vi (*road*) bifurcarse

forlorn [fəˈlɔːn] adj (*person*) triste, melancólico; (*place*) abandonado; (*attempt, hope*) desesperado

form [fɔːm] n forma; (*BRIT SCOL*) clase f; (*document*) formulario ♦ vt formar; (*idea*) concebir; (*habit*) adquirir; **in top ~** en plena forma; **to ~ a queue** hacer cola

formal [ˈfɔːməl] adj (*offer, receipt*) por escrito; (*person etc*) correcto; (*occasion, dinner*) de etiqueta; (*dress*) correcto; (*garden*) de estilo clásico
❑ **formality** [-ˈmælɪtɪ] n (*procedure*) trámite m; corrección f; etiqueta

format [ˈfɔːmæt] n formato ♦ vt (*COMPUT*) formatear

formation [fɔːˈmeɪʃən] n formación f

former [ˈfɔːmə'] adj anterior; (*earlier*) antiguo; (*ex*) ex; **the ~ ... the latter ...** aquél ... éste ... ❑ **formerly** adv antes

formidable [ˈfɔːmɪdəbl] adj formidable

formula [ˈfɔːmjulə] n fórmula

fort [fɔːt] n fuerte m

forthcoming [fɔːˈθkʌmɪŋ] adj próximo, venidero; (*help, information*) disponible; (*character*) comunicativo

fortieth [ˈfɔːtɪɪθ] adj cuadragésimo

fortify [ˈfɔːtɪfaɪ] vt (*city*) fortificar; (*person*) fortalecer

fortnight [ˈfɔːtnaɪt] (*BRIT*) n quince días mpl; quincena ❑ **fortnightly** adj de cada quince días, quincenal ♦ adv cada quince días, quincenalmente

fortress [ˈfɔːtrɪs] n fortaleza

fortunate [ˈfɔːtʃənɪt] adj afortunado; **it is ~ that ...** (es una) suerte que ...
❑ **fortunately** adv afortunadamente

fortune [ˈfɔːtʃən] n suerte f; (*wealth*) fortuna ❑ **fortune-teller** n adivino(-a)

forty [ˈfɔːtɪ] num cuarenta

forum [ˈfɔːrəm] n foro

forward [ˈfɔːwəd] adj (*movement, position*) avanzado; (*front*) delantero; (*in time*) adelantado; (*not shy*) atrevido ♦ n (*SPORT*) delantero ♦ vt (*letter*) remitir; (*career*) promocionar; **to move ~** avanzar ❑ **forwarding address** n destinatario ❑ **forward(s)** adv (hacia) adelante

forward slash n barra diagonal

fossil [ˈfɒsl] n fósil m

foster [ˈfɒstə'] vt (*child*) acoger en una familia; fomentar ❑ **foster child** n hijo(-a) adoptivo(-a) ❑ **foster mother** n madre f adoptiva

fought [fɔːt] pt, pp of **fight**

foul [faul] adj sucio, puerco; (*weather, smell etc*) asqueroso; (*language*) grosero; (*temper*) malísimo ♦ n (*SPORT*) falta ♦ vt (*dirty*) ensuciar ❑ **foul play** n (*LAW*) muerte f violenta

found [faund] pt, pp of **find** ♦ vt fundar ❑ **foundation** [-ˈdeɪʃən] n (*act*) fundación f; (*basis*) base f; (*also:* **foundation cream**; crema base; **foundations** npl (*of building*) cimientos mpl

founder [ˈfaundə'] n fundador(a) m/f ♦ vi hundirse

fountain [ˈfauntɪn] n fuente f ❑ **fountain pen** n (*pluma*) estilográfica (*SP*), pluma-fuente f (*LAm*)

four [fɔː'] num cuatro; **on all fours** a gatas ❑ **four-letter word** n taco

❏ **four-poster** n (also: **four-poster bed**) cama de columnas ❏ **fourteen** num catorce ❏ **fourteenth** adj decimocuarto ❏ **fourth** num cuarto ❏ **four-wheel drive** n tracción f a las cuatro ruedas

fowl [faul] n ave f (de corral)

fox [fɔks] n zorro ♦ vt confundir

foyer ['fɔɪeɪ] n vestíbulo

fraction ['frækʃən] n fracción f

fracture ['fræktʃə'] n fractura

fragile ['frædʒaɪl] adj frágil

fragment ['frægmənt] n fragmento

fragrance ['freɪgrəns] n fragancia

frail [freɪl] adj frágil; (person) débil

frame [freɪm] n (TECH) armazón m; (of person) cuerpo; (of picture, door etc) marco; (of spectacles: also: **frames**) montura ♦ vt enmarcar ❏ **framework** n marco

France [frɑːns] n Francia

franchise ['fræntʃaɪz] n (POL) derecho de votar, sufragio; (COMM) licencia, concesión f

frank [fræŋk] adj franco ♦ vt (letter) franquear ❏ **frankly** adv francamente

frantic ['fræntɪk] adj (distraught) desesperado; (hectic) frenético

fraud [frɔːd] n fraude m; (person) impostor(a) m/f

fraught [frɔːt] adj: ~ **with** lleno de

fray [freɪ] vi deshilacharse

freak [friːk] n (person) fenómeno; (event) suceso anormal

freckle ['frekl] n peca

free [friː] adj libre; (gratis) gratuito ♦ vt (prisoner etc) poner en libertad; (jammed object) soltar; ~ **(of charge)**, **for** ~ gratis ❏ **freedom** n libertad f ❏ **Freefone®** n número gratuito ❏ **free gift** n prima ❏ **free kick** n tiro libre ❏ **freelance** adj independiente ♦ adv por cuenta propia ❏ **freely** adv libremente; (liberally) generosamente ❏ **Freepost®** n porte m pagado ❏ **free-range** adj (hen, eggs) de granja

❏ **freeway** (US) n autopista ❏ **free will** n libre albedrío; **of one's own free will** por su propia voluntad

freeze [friːz] (pt **froze**, pp **frozen**) vi (weather) helar; (liquid, pipe, person) helarse, congelarse ♦ vt helar; (food, prices, salaries) congelar ♦ n helada; (on arms, wages) congelación f ❏ **freezer** n congelador m, freezer m (SC)

freezing ['friːzɪŋ] adj helado; **three degrees below** ~ tres grados bajo cero ❏ **freezing point** n punto de congelación

freight [freɪt] n (goods) carga; (money charged) flete m ❏ **freight train** (US) n tren m de mercancías

French [frentʃ] adj francés(-esa) ♦ n (LING) francés m; **the** ~ npl los franceses ❏ **French bean** n judía verde ❏ **French bread** n pan m francés ❏ **French dressing** n (CULIN) vinagreta ❏ **French fried potatoes**, **French fries** (US) npl patatas fpl (SP) or papas fpl (LAm) fritas ❏ **Frenchman** (irreg) n francés m ❏ **Frenchwoman** (irreg) n francesa ❏ **French stick** n barra de pan ❏ **French window** n puerta de cristal

frenzy ['frenzɪ] n frenesí m

frequency ['friːkwənsɪ] n frecuencia

frequent [adj 'friːkwənt, vb frɪ'kwent] adj frecuente ♦ vt frecuentar ❏ **frequently** [-əntlɪ] adv frecuentemente, a menudo

fresh [freʃ] adj fresco; (bread) tierno; (new) nuevo ❏ **freshen** vi (wind, air) soplar más recio ▶ **freshen up** vi (person) arreglarse, lavarse ❏ **fresher** (BRIT: inf) n (UNIV) estudiante mf de primer año ❏ **freshly** adv (made, painted etc) recién ❏ **freshman** (US: irreg) n = **fresher** ❏ **freshwater** (fish) de agua dulce

fret [fret] vi inquietarse

Fri abbr (= Friday) vier

friction ['frɪkʃən] n fricción f

Friday ['fraɪdɪ] n viernes m inv

fridge [frɪdʒ] (BRIT) n frigorífico (SP), nevera (SP), refrigerador m (LAm), heladera (RPl)

fried [fraɪd] adj frito

friend [frɛnd] n amigo(-a) ❑ **friendly** adj simpático; (government) amigo; (place) acogedor(a); (match) amistoso ❑ **friendship** n amistad f

fries [fraɪz] (esp US) npl = **French fried potatoes**

frigate [ˈfrɪɡɪt] n fragata f

fright [fraɪt] n (terror) terror m; (scare) susto; **to take ~** asustarse ❑ **frighten** vt asustar ❑ **frightened** adj asustado ❑ **frightening** adj espantoso ❑ **frightful** adj espantoso, horrible

frill [frɪl] n volante m

fringe [frɪndʒ] n (BRIT: of hair) flequillo; (on lampshade etc) flecos mpl; (of forest etc) borde m, margen m

Frisbee® [ˈfrɪzbɪ] n frisbee® m

fritter [ˈfrɪtə*] n buñuelo

frivolous [ˈfrɪvələs] adj frívolo

fro [frəʊ] see **to**

frock [frɒk] n vestido

frog [frɒɡ] n rana ❑ **frogman** (irreg) n hombre-rana m

from

KEYWORD

[frɒm] prep

1 (indicating starting place) de, desde; **where do you come from?** ¿de dónde eres?; **from London to Glasgow** de Londres a Glasgow; **to escape from sth/sb** escaparse de algo/algn

2 (indicating origin etc): **a letter/ telephone call from my sister** una carta/llamada de mi hermana; **tell him from me that ...** dígale de mi parte que ...

3 (indicating time): **from one o'clock to** or **until** or **till two** de(sde) la una a or hasta las dos; **from January (on)** a partir de enero

4 (indicating distance) de; **the hotel is 1 km from the beach** el hotel está a 1 km de la playa

5 (indicating price, number etc) de; **prices range from £10 to £50** los precios van desde £10 a or hasta £50; **the interest rate was increased from 9% to 10%** el tipo de interés fue incrementado un 9% a un 10%

6 (indicating difference) de; **he can't tell red from green** no sabe distinguir el rojo del verde; **to be different from sb/sth** ser diferente a algn/algo

7 (because of, on the basis of): **from what he says** por lo que dice; **weak from hunger** debilitado por el hambre

front [frʌnt] n (foremost part) parte f delantera; (of house) fachada; (of dress) delantero; (promenade: also: **sea ~**) paseo marítimo; (MIL, POL, METEOROLOGY) frente m; (fig: appearances) apariencias fpl ♦ adj (wheel, leg) delantero; (row, line) primero; **in ~ (of)** delante (de) ❑ **front door** n puerta principal ❑ **frontier** [ˈfrʌntɪə*] n frontera ❑ **front page** n primera plana ❑ **front-wheel drive** n tracción f delantera

frost [frɒst] n helada; (also: **hoarfrost**) escarcha ❑ **frostbite** n congelación f ❑ **frosting** n (esp US: icing) glaseado ❑ **frosty** adj (weather) de helada; (welcome etc) glacial

froth [frɒθ] n espuma

frown [fraʊn] vi fruncir el ceño

froze [frəʊz] pt of **freeze**

frozen [ˈfrəʊzn] pp of **freeze**

fruit [fruːt] n inv fruta; fruto; (fig) fruto; resultados mpl ❑ **fruit juice** n zumo (SP) or jugo (LAm) de fruta ❑ **fruit machine** (BRIT) n máquina f

tragaperras ❑ **fruit salad** n
macedonia (SP) or ensalada (LAm) de
frutas

frustrate [frʌs'treɪt] vt frustrar
❑ **frustrated** adj frustrado

fry [fraɪ] (pt, pp **fried**) vt freír; **small ~**
gente f menuda ❑ **frying pan** n
sartén f

ft. abbr = **foot; feet**

fudge [fʌdʒ] n (CULIN) caramelo blando

fuel [fjʊəl] n (for heating) combustible
m; (coal) carbón m; (wood) leña; (for
engine) carburante m ❑ **fuel tank** n
depósito (de combustible)

fulfil [fʊl'fɪl] vt (function) cumplir con;
(condition) satisfacer; (wish, desire)
realizar

full [fʊl] adj lleno; (fig) pleno; (complete)
completo; (maximum) máximo;
(information) detallado; (price) íntegro;
(skirt) amplio ♦ adv: **to know ~ well
that** saber perfectamente que; **I'm ~
(up)** no puedo más; **~ employment**
pleno empleo; **a ~ two hours** dos
horas completas; **at ~ speed** a máxima
velocidad, **in ~** (reproduce, quote)
íntegramente ❑ **full-length** adj
(novel etc) entero; (coat) largo;
(portrait) de cuerpo entero ❑ **full
moon** n luna llena ❑ **full-scale** adj
(attack, war) en gran escala; (model) de
tamaño natural ❑ **full stop** n punto
❑ **full-time** adj (work) de tiempo
completo ♦ adv: **to work full-time**
trabajar a tiempo completo ❑ **fully**
adv completamente; (at least) por lo
menos

fumble ['fʌmbl] vi: **to ~ with** manejar
torpemente

fume [fjuːm] vi (rage) estar furioso
❑ **fumes** npl humo, gases mpl

fun [fʌn] n (amusement) diversión f; **to
have ~** divertirse; **for ~** en broma; **to
make ~ of** burlarse de

function ['fʌŋkʃən] n función f ♦ vi
funcionar

fund [fʌnd] n fondo n; (reserve) reserva;
funds npl (money) fondos mpl

fundamental [fʌndə'mentl] adj
fundamental

funeral ['fjuːnərəl] n (burial) entierro;
(ceremony) funerales mpl ❑ **funeral
director** n director(a) m/f de pompas
fúnebres ❑ **funeral parlour** (BRIT) n
funeraria

funfair ['fʌnfeəʳ] (BRIT) n parque m de
atracciones

fungus ['fʌŋgəs] (pl **fungi**) n hongo;
(mould) moho

funnel ['fʌnl] n embudo; (of ship)
chimenea

funny ['fʌnɪ] adj gracioso, divertido;
(strange) curioso, raro

fur [fəːʳ] n piel f; (BRIT: in kettle etc) sarro
❑ **fur coat** n abrigo de pieles

furious ['fjʊərɪəs] adj furioso; (effort)
violento

furnish ['fəːnɪʃ] vt amueblar; (supply)
suministrar; (information) facilitar
❑ **furnishings** npl muebles mpl

furniture ['fəːnɪtʃəʳ] n muebles mpl;
piece of ~ mueble m

furry ['fəːrɪ] adj peludo

further ['fəːðəʳ] adj (new) nuevo,
adicional ♦ adv más lejos; (more) más;
(moreover) además ♦ vt promover,
adelantar ❑ **further education** n
educación f superior ❑ **furthermore**
adv además

furthest ['fəːðɪst] superlative of **far**

fury ['fjʊərɪ] n furia

fuse [fjuːz] (US **fuze**) n fusible m; (for
bomb etc) mecha ♦ vt (metal) fundir;
(fig) fusionar ♦ vi fundirse; fusionarse;
(BRIT ELEC): **to ~ the lights** fundir los
plomos ❑ **fuse box** n caja de fusibles

fusion ['fjuːʒən] n fusión f

fuss [fʌs] n (excitement) conmoción f;
(trouble) alboroto; **to make a ~** armar
un lío or jaleo; **to make a ~ of sb** mimar
a algn ❑ **fussy** adj (person) exigente;
(too ornate) recargado

future ['fju:tʃə] adj futuro; (coming) venidero ♦ n futuro; (prospects) porvenir m; **in ~** de ahora en adelante; **futures** npl (COMM) operaciones fpl a término, futuros mpl

fuze [fju:z] US = **fuse**

fuzzy ['fʌzɪ] adj (PHOT) borroso; (hair) muy rizado

G, g

G [dʒi:] n (MUS) sol m

g. abbr (= gram(s)) gr.

gadget ['gædʒɪt] n aparato

Gaelic ['geɪlɪk] adj, n (LING) gaélico

gag [gæg] n (on mouth) mordaza; (joke) chiste m ♦ vt amordazar

gain [geɪn] n: **~ (in)** aumento (de); (profit) ganancia ♦ vt ganar ♦ vi (watch) adelantarse; **to ~ from/by sth** sacar provecho de algo; **to ~ on sb** ganar terreno a algn; **to ~ 3 lbs (in weight)** engordar 3 libras

gal. abbr = **gallon**

gala ['gɑ:lə] n fiesta

galaxy ['gæləksɪ] n galaxia

gale [geɪl] n (wind) vendaval m

gall bladder ['gɔ:l-] n vesícula biliar

gallery ['gælərɪ] n (also: **art ~**: public) pinacoteca; (: private) galería de arte; (for spectators) tribuna

gallon ['gælən] n galón m (BRIT = 4,546 litros, US = 3,785 litros)

gallop ['gæləp] n galope m ♦ vi galopar

gallstone ['gɔ:lstəun] n cálculo biliar

gamble ['gæmbl] n (risk) riesgo ♦ vt jugar, apostar ♦ vi (take a risk) jugárselas; (bet) apostar; **to ~ on** apostar a; (success etc) contar con □ **gambler** n jugador(a) m/f □ **gambling** n juego

game [geɪm] n juego; (match) partido; (of cards) partida; (HUNTING) caza ♦ adj (willing): **to be ~ for anything**

atreverse a todo; **big ~** caza mayor; **games** (contest) juegos; (BRIT: SCOL) deportes mpl □ **games console** [geɪmz-] n consola de juegos □ **game show** n programa m concurso inv, concurso

gammon ['gæmən] n (bacon) tocino ahumado; (ham) jamón m ahumado

gang [gæŋ] n (of criminals) pandilla; (of friends etc) grupo; (of workmen) brigada

gangster ['gæŋstə] n gángster m

gap [gæp] n vacío (SP), hueco (LAm); (in trees, traffic) claro; (in time) intervalo; (difference): **~ (between)** diferencia (entre)

gape [geɪp] vi mirar boquiabierto; (shirt etc) abrirse (completamente)

gap year n año sabático (antes de empezar a estudiar en la universidad)

garage ['gærɑ:ʒ] n garaje m; (for repairs) taller m □ **garage sale** n venta de objetos usados (en el jardín de una casa particular)

garbage ['gɑ:bɪdʒ] n (US) basura; (inf: nonsense) tonterías fpl □ **garbage can** n cubo or bote m (MEX) or tacho (SC) de la basura □ **garbage collector** (US) n basurero(-a)

garden ['gɑ:dn] n jardín m; **gardens** npl (park) parque m □ **garden centre** (BRIT) n centro de jardinería □ **gardener** n jardinero(-a) □ **gardening** n jardinería

garlic ['gɑ:lɪk] n ajo

garment ['gɑ:mənt] n prenda (de vestir)

garnish ['gɑ:nɪʃ] vt (CULIN) aderezar

garrison ['gærɪsn] n guarnición f

gas [gæs] n gas m; (fuel) combustible m; (US: gasoline) gasolina ♦ vt asfixiar con gas □ **gas cooker** (BRIT) n cocina de gas □ **gas cylinder** n bombona de gas □ **gas fire** n estufa de gas

gasket ['gæskɪt] n (AUT) junta de culata

gasoline ['gæsəli:n] (US) n gasolina

gasp [gɑːsp] n boqueada; (of shock etc) grito sofocado ♦ vi (pant) jadear

gas: **gas pedal** n (esp US) acelerador m □ **gas station** (US) n gasolinera □ **gas tank** (US) n (AUT) depósito m (de gasolina)

gate [geɪt] n puerta; (iron gate) verja

gateau ['gætəʊ] (pl **gateaux**) n tarta

gatecrash ['geɪtkræʃ] (BRIT) vt colarse en

gateway ['geɪtweɪ] n puerta

gather ['gæðə'] vt (flowers, fruit) coger (SP), recoger; (assemble) reunir; (pick up) recoger; (SEWING) fruncir; (understand) entender ♦ vi (assemble) reunirse; **to ~ speed** ganar velocidad □ **gathering** n reunión f, asamblea

gauge [geɪdʒ] n (instrument) indicador m ♦ vt medir; (fig) juzgar

gave [geɪv] pt of **give**

gay [geɪ] adj (homosexual) gay; (joyful) alegre; (colour) vivo

gaze [geɪz] n mirada fija ♦ vi: **to ~ at sth** mirar algo fijamente

GB abbr = **Great Britain**

GCSE (BRIT) n abbr (= General Certificate of Secondary Education) examen de reválida que se hace a los 16 años

gear [gɪə'] n equipo, herramientas fpl; (TECH) engranaje m; (AUT) velocidad f, marcha ♦ vt (fig: adapt): **to ~ sth to** adaptar o ajustar algo a; **top** or **high** (US)/**low** ~ cuarta/primera velocidad; **in** ~ en marcha ► **gear up** vi prepararse □ **gear box** n caja de cambios □ **gear lever** n palanca de cambio □ **gear shift** (US) n = **gear lever** □ **gear stick** (US) n palanca de cambios

geese [giːs] npl of **goose**

gel [dʒel] n gel m

gem [dʒem] n piedra preciosa

Gemini ['dʒemɪnaɪ] n Géminis m, Gemelos mpl

gender ['dʒendə'] n género

gene [dʒiːn] n gen(e) m

general ['dʒenərl] n general m ♦ adj general; **in ~** en general □ **general anaesthetic** (US **general anesthetic**) n anestesia general □ **general election** n elecciones fpl generales □ **generalize** vi generalizar □ **generally** adv generalmente, en general □ **general practitioner** n médico general □ **general store** n tienda (que vende de todo), almacén m (SC, SP)

generate ['dʒenəreɪt] vt (ELEC) generar; (jobs, profits) producir

generation [dʒenə'reɪʃən] n generación f

generator ['dʒenəreɪtə'] n generador m

generosity [dʒenə'rɔsɪtɪ] n generosidad f

generous ['dʒenərəs] adj generoso

genetic [dʒɪ'netɪk] adj: **~ engineering** ingeniería genética; **~ fingerprinting** identificación f genética □ **genetically modified** adj transgénico □ **genetics** n genética

genitals ['dʒenɪtlz] npl (órganos mpl) genitales mpl

genius ['dʒiːnɪəs] n genio

gent [dʒent] n abbr (BRIT inf) = **gentleman**

gentle ['dʒentl] adj apacible, dulce; (animal) manso; (breeze, curve etc) suave

> ⚠ Be careful not to translate **gentle** by the Spanish word **gentil**.

gentleman ['dʒentlmən] (irreg) n señor m; (well-bred man) caballero

gently ['dʒentlɪ] adv dulcemente; suavemente

gents [dʒents] n aseos mpl (de caballeros)

genuine ['dʒenjuɪn] adj auténtico; (person) sincero □ **genuinely** adv sinceramente

geographic(al) [dʒɪə'græfɪk(l)] adj geográfico

geography [dʒɪˈɒɡrəfɪ] n geografía
geology [dʒɪˈɒlədʒɪ] n geología
geometry [dʒɪˈɒmɪtrɪ] n geometría
geranium [dʒɪˈreɪnjəm] n geranio
geriatric [dʒerɪˈætrɪk] adj, n
geriátrico(-a) m/f
germ [dʒɜːm] n (microbe) microbio,
bacteria; (seed, fig) germen m
German [ˈdʒɜːmən] adj alemán(-ana)
♦ n alemán(-ana) m/f; (LING) alemán m
❑ **German measles** n rubéola
Germany [ˈdʒɜːmənɪ] n Alemania
gesture [ˈdʒestjəʳ] n gesto; (symbol)
muestra

get

KEYWORD

[get] (pt, pp **got**, pp **gotten** (US)) vi
1 (become, be) ponerse, volverse; **to
get old/tired** envejecer/cansarse; **to
get drunk** emborracharse; **to get
dirty** ensuciarse; **to get married**
casarse; **when do I get paid?** ¿cuándo
me pagan or se me paga?; **it's getting
late** se está haciendo tarde
2 (go): **to get to/from** llegar a/de; **to
get home** llegar a casa
3 (begin) empezar a; **to get to know
sb** (llegar a) conocer a algn; **I'm
getting to like him** me está
empezando a gustar; **let's get going
or started** ¡vamos (a empezar)!
4 (modal aux vb): **you've got to do it**
tienes que hacerlo
♦ vt
1: **to get sth done** (finish) terminar
algo; (have done) mandar hacer algo;
to get one's hair cut cortarse el pelo;
to get the car going or to go arrancar
el coche; **to get sb to do sth**
conseguir or hacer que algn haga
algo; **to get sth/sb ready** preparar
algo/a algn
2 (obtain: money, permission, results)

conseguir; (find: job, flat) encontrar;
(fetch: person, doctor) buscar; (object)
ir a buscar, traer; **to get sth for sb**
conseguir algo para algn; **get me Mr
Jones, please** (TEL) póngame (SP) or
comuníqueme (LAm) con el Sr. Jones,
por favor; **can I get you a drink?**
¿quieres algo de beber?
3 (receive: present, letter) recibir;
(acquire: reputation) alcanzar; (: prize)
ganar; **what did you get for your
birthday?** ¿qué te regalaron por tu
cumpleaños?; **how much did you get
for the painting?** ¿cuánto sacaste
por el cuadro?
4 (catch) coger (SP), agarrar (LAm);
(hit: target etc) dar en; **to get sb by the
arm/throat** coger or agarrar a algn
por el brazo/cuello; **get him!** ¡cógelo!
(SP), ¡atrápalo! (LAm); **the bullet got
him in the leg** la bala le dio en la
pierna
5 (take, move) llevar; **to get sth to sb**
hacer llegar algo a algn; **do you think
we'll get it through the door?** ¿crees
que lo podremos meter por la
puerta?
6 (catch, take: plane, bus etc) coger
(SP), tomar (LAm); **where do I get the
train for Birmingham?** ¿dónde se
coge or se toma el tren para
Birmingham?
7 (understand) entender; (hear) oír;
I've got it! ¡ya lo tengo!, ¡eureka!; **I
don't get your meaning** no te
entiendo; **I'm sorry, I didn't get your
name** lo siento, no cogí tu nombre
8 (have, possess): **to have got** tener
▶ **get away** vi marcharse; (escape)
escaparse
▶ **get away with** vt fus hacer
impunemente

▶ **get back** vi (return) volver ♦ vt recobrar

▶ **get in** vi entrar; (train) llegar; (arrive home) volver a casa, regresar

▶ **get into** vt fus entrar en; (vehicle) subir a; **to get into a rage** enfadarse

▶ **get off** vi (from train etc) bajar; (depart: person, car) marcharse ♦ vt (remove) quitar ♦ vt fus (train, bus) bajar de

▶ **get on** vi (at exam etc): **how are you getting on?** ¿cómo te va?; (agree): **to get on (with)** llevarse bien (con) ♦ vt fus subir a

▶ **get out** vi salir; (of vehicle) bajar ♦ vt sacar

▶ **get out of** vt fus salir de; (duty etc) escaparse de

▶ **get over** vt fus (illness) recobrarse de

▶ **get through** vi (TEL) (lograr) comunicarse

▶ **get up** vi (rise) levantarse ♦ vt fus subir

getaway ['gɛtəweɪ] n fuga

Ghana ['gɑːnə] n Ghana

ghastly ['gɑːstlɪ] adj horrible

ghetto ['gɛtəu] n gueto

ghost [gəust] n fantasma m

giant ['dʒaɪənt] n gigante mf ♦ adj gigantesco, gigante

gift [gɪft] n regalo; (ability) talento □ **gifted** adj dotado □ **gift shop** (US **gift store**) n tienda de regalos □ **gift token**, **gift voucher** n vale m canjeable por un regalo

gig [gɪg] n (inf: concert) actuación f

gigabyte ['dʒɪgəbaɪt] n gigabyte m

gigantic [dʒaɪ'gæntɪk] adj gigantesco

giggle ['gɪgl] vi reírse tontamente

gills [gɪlz] npl (of fish) branquias fpl, agallas fpl

gilt [gɪlt] adj, n dorado

gimmick ['gɪmɪk] n truco

gin [dʒɪn] n ginebra

ginger ['dʒɪndʒə'] n jengibre m

gipsy ['dʒɪpsɪ] n = **gypsy**

giraffe [dʒɪ'rɑːf] n jirafa

girl [gɜːl] n (small) niña; (young woman) chica, joven f, muchacha; (daughter) hija; **an English ~** una (chica) inglesa □ **girlfriend** n (of girl) amiga; (of boy) novia □ **Girl Scout** (US) n = **Girl Guide**

gist [dʒɪst] n lo esencial

give [gɪv] (pt **gave**, pp **given**) vt dar; (deliver) entregar; (as gift) regalar ♦ vi (break) romperse; (stretch: fabric) dar de sí; **to ~ sb sth**, **~ sth to sb** dar algo a algn ▶ **give away** vt (give free) regalar; (betray) traicionar; (disclose) revelar

▶ **give back** vt devolver ▶ **give in** vi ceder ♦ vt entregar ▶ **give out** vt distribuir ▶ **give up** vi rendirse, darse por vencido ♦ vt renunciar a; **to give up smoking** dejar de fumar; **to give o.s. up** entregarse

given ['gɪvn] pp of **give** ♦ adj (fixed: time, amount) determinado ♦ conj: ~ **(that) ...** dado (que ...); ~ **the circumstances ...** dadas las circunstancias ...

glacier ['glæsɪə'] n glaciar m

glad [glæd] adj contento □ **gladly** ['-lɪ] adv con mucho gusto

glamour ['glæmə'] (US **glamor**) n encanto, atractivo □ **glamorous** adj encantador(a), atractivo

glance [glɑːns] n ojeada, mirada ♦ vi: **to ~ at** echar una ojeada a

gland [glænd] n glándula

glare [glɛə'] n (of anger) mirada feroz; (of light) deslumbramiento, brillo; **to be in the ~ of publicity** ser el foco de la atención pública ♦ vi deslumbrar; **to ~ at** mirar con odio a □ **glaring** adj (mistake) manifiesto

glass [glɑ:s] n vidrio, cristal m; (for drinking) vaso; (+ stem) copa; **glasses** npl (spectacles) gafas fpl

glaze [gleɪz] vt (window) poner cristales a; (pottery) vidriar ♦ n vidriado

gleam [gli:m] vi brillar

glen [glen] n cañada

glide [glaɪd] vi deslizarse; (AVIAT, birds) planear ◻ **glider** n (AVIAT) planeador m

glimmer ['glɪmə*] n luz f tenue; (of interest) muestra; (of hope) rayo

glimpse [glɪmps] n vislumbre m ♦ vt vislumbrar, entrever

glint [glɪnt] vi centellear

glisten ['glɪsn] vi relucir, brillar

glitter ['glɪtə*] vi relucir, brillar

global ['glaʊbl] adj mundial ◻ **global warming** n (re)calentamiento global or de la tierra

globe [glaʊb] n globo; (model) globo terráqueo

gloom [glu:m] n oscuridad f; (sadness) tristeza ◻ **gloomy** adj (dark) oscuro; (sad) triste; (pessimistic) pesimista

glorious ['glɔ:rɪəs] adj glorioso; (weather etc) magnífico

glory ['glɔ:rɪ] n gloria

gloss [glɒs] n (shine) brillo; (paint) pintura de aceite

glossary ['glɒsərɪ] n glosario

glossy ['glɒsɪ] adj lustroso; (magazine) de lujo

glove [glʌv] n guante m ◻ **glove compartment** n (AUT) guantera

glow [glaʊ] vi brillar

glucose ['glu:kəʊs] n glucosa

glue [glu:] n goma (de pegar), cemento ♦ vt pegar

GM adj abbr (= genetically modified) transgénico

gm abbr (= gram) g

GMO n abbr (= genetically modified organism) organismo transgénico

GMT abbr (= Greenwich Mean Time) GMT

gnaw [nɔ:] vt roer

go [gəʊ] (pt went, pp gone, pl goes) vi ir; (travel) viajar; (depart) irse, marcharse; (work) funcionar, marchar; (be sold) venderse; (time) pasar; (fit, suit): **to go with** hacer juego con; (become) ponerse; (break etc) estropearse, romperse ♦ n: **to have a go (at)** probar suerte (con); **to be on the go** no parar; **whose go is it?** ¿a quién le toca?; **he's going to do it** va a hacerlo; **to go for a walk** ir de paseo; **to go dancing** ir a bailar; **how did it go?** ¿qué tal salió or resultó?, ¿cómo ha ido?; **to go round the back** pasar por detrás ► **go ahead** vi seguir adelante ► **go away** vi irse, marcharse ► **go back** vi volver ► **go by** vi (time) pasar ♦ vt fus guiarse por ► **go down** vi bajar; (ship) hundirse; (sun) ponerse ♦ vt fus bajar ► **go for** vt fus (fetch) ir por; (like) gustar; (attack) atacar ► **go in** vi entrar ► **go into** vt fus entrar en; (investigate) investigar; (embark on) dedicarse a ► **go off** vi irse, marcharse; (food) pasarse; (explode) estallar; (event) realizarse ♦ vt fus dejar de gustar; **I'm going off him/ the idea** ya no me gusta tanto él/la idea ► **go on** vi (continue) seguir, continuar; (happen) pasar, ocurrir; **to go on doing sth** seguir haciendo algo ► **go out** vi salir; (fire, light) apagarse ► **go over** vi (ship) zozobrar ♦ vt fus (check) revisar ► **go past** vi, vt fus pasar ► **go round** vi (circulate: news, rumour) correr; (suffice) alcanzar, bastar; (revolve) girar, dar vueltas; (visit): **to go round (to sb's)** pasar a ver (a algn); **to go round (by)** (make a detour) dar la vuelta (por) ► **go through** vt fus (town etc) atravesar ► **go up** vi, vt fus subir ► **go with** vt fus (accompany) ir con, acompañar a ► **go without** vt fus pasarse sin

go-ahead ['gəʊəhɛd] adj (person) dinámico; (firm) innovador(a) ♦ n luz f verde

goal [gəʊl] n meta; (score) gol m □ **goalkeeper** n portero □ **goalpost** n poste m (de la portería)

goat [gəʊt] n cabra

gobble ['gɒbl] vt (also: ~ **down**, ~ **up**) tragarse, engullir

God [gɒd] n Dios m □ **godchild** n ahijado(-a) □ **goddaughter** n ahijada □ **goddess** n diosa □ **godfather** n padrino □ **godmother** n madrina □ **godson** n ahijado

goggles ['gɒglz] npl gafas fpl

going ['gəʊɪŋ] n (conditions) estado del terreno ♦ adj: **the ~ rate** la tarifa corriente o en vigor

gold [gəʊld] n oro ♦ adj de oro □ **golden** adj (made of gold) de oro; (gold in colour) dorado □ **goldfish** n pez m de colores □ **goldmine** n (also fig) mina de oro □ **gold-plated** adj chapado en oro

golf [gɒlf] n golf m □ **golf ball** n (for game) pelota de golf; (on typewriter) esfera □ **golf club** n club m de golf; (stick) palo de golf □ **golf course** n campo de golf □ **golfer** n golfista mf

gone [gɒn] pp of **go**

gong [gɒŋ] n gong m

good [gʊd] adj bueno; (pleasant) agradable; (kind) bueno, amable; (well-behaved) educado ♦ n bien m, provecho; **goods** npl (COMM) mercancías fpl; **~!** ¡qué bien!; **to be ~ at** tener aptitud para; **to be ~ for** servir para; **it's ~ for you** te hace bien; **would you be ~ enough to ...?** ¿podría hacerme el favor de ...?; ¿sería tan amable de ...?; **a ~ deal (of)** mucho; **a ~ many** muchos; **to make ~** reparar; **it's no ~ complaining** no vale la pena (de) quejarse; **for ~** para siempre, definitivamente; **~ morning/afternoon!** ¡buenos días/buenas

tardes!; **~ evening!** ¡buenas noches!; **~ night!** ¡buenas noches!

goodbye [gʊd'baɪ] excl ¡adiós!; **to say ~ (to)** (person) despedirse (de)

good: **Good Friday** n Viernes m Santo □ **good-looking** adj guapo □ **good-natured** adj amable, simpático □ **goodness** n (of person) bondad f; **for goodness sake!** ¡por Dios!; **goodness gracious!** ¡Dios mío! □ **goods train** n (BRIT) n tren m de mercancías □ **goodwill** n buena voluntad f

goose [guːs] (pl **geese**) n ganso, oca

gooseberry ['guzbərɪ] n grosella espinosa; **to play ~** hacer de carabina

goose bumps, **goose pimples** npl carne f de gallina

gorge [gɔːdʒ] n barranco ♦ vr: **to ~ o.s. (on)** atracarse (de)

gorgeous ['gɔːdʒəs] adj (thing) precioso; (weather) espléndido; (person) guapísimo

gorilla [gə'rɪlə] n gorila m

gosh [gɒʃ] (inf) [gɒʃ] excl ¡cielos!

gospel ['gɒspl] n evangelio

gossip ['gɒsɪp] n (scandal) cotilleo, chismes mpl; (chat) charla; (scandalmonger) cotilla m/f, chismoso(-a) ♦ vi cotillear □ **gossip column** n ecos mpl de sociedad

got [gɒt] pt, pp of **get**

gotten (US) ['gɒtn] pp of **get**

gourmet ['guəmeɪ] n gastrónomo(-a) m/f

govern ['gʌvən] vt gobernar; (influence) dominar □ **government** n gobierno □ **governor** n gobernador(a) m/f; (of school etc) miembro del consejo; (of jail) director(a) m/f

gown [gaʊn] n traje m; (of teacher, BRIT: of judge) toga

G.P. n abbr = **general practitioner**

grab [græb] vt coger (SP), agarrar (LAm), arrebatar ♦ vi: **to ~ at** intentar agarrar

grace [greɪs] n gracia ♦ vt honrar; (adorn) adornar; **5 days' ~** un plazo de 5 días ❏ **graceful** adj grácil, ágil; (style, shape) elegante, gracioso ❏ **gracious** ['greɪʃəs] adj amable

grade [greɪd] n (quality) clase f, calidad f; (in hierarchy) grado; (SCOL: mark) nota; (US: school class) curso ♦ vt clasificar ❏ **grade crossing** (US) n paso a nivel ❏ **grade school** (US) n escuela primaria

gradient ['greɪdɪənt] n pendiente f

gradual ['grædjuəl] adj paulatino ❏ **gradually** adv paulatinamente

graduate [n 'grædjuɪt, vb 'grædjueɪt] n (US: of high school) graduado(-a); (of university) licenciado(-a) ♦ vi graduarse; licenciarse ❏ **graduation** [-'eɪʃən] n (ceremony) entrega del título

graffiti [grə'fiːtiː] n pintadas fpl

graft [grɑːft] n (AGR, MED) injerto; (BRIT: inf) trabajo duro; (bribery) corrupción f ♦ vt injertar

grain [greɪn] n (single particle) grano; (corn) granos mpl, cereales mpl; (of wood) fibra

gram [græm] n gramo

grammar ['græmə'] n gramática ❏ **grammar school** (BRIT) n ≈ instituto de segunda enseñanza, liceo (SP)

gramme [græm] n = **gram**

gran (inf) [græn] n (BRIT) abuelita

grand [grænd] adj magnífico, imponente; (wonderful) estupendo, (gesture etc) grandioso ❏ **grandad** (inf) n = **granddad** ❏ **grandchild** (pl **grandchildren**) n nieto(-a) m/f ❏ **granddad** (inf) n yayo, abuelito ❏ **granddaughter** n nieta ❏ **grandfather** n abuelo ❏ **grandma** (inf) n yaya, abuelita ❏ **grandmother** n abuela ❏ **grandpa** (inf) n = **granddad** ❏ **grandparents** npl abuelos mpl ❏ **grand piano** n piano de cola ❏ **Grand Prix** ['grɑ̃:'priː] n

(AUT) gran premio, Grand Prix m ❏ **grandson** n nieto

granite ['grænɪt] n granito

granny ['grænɪ] (inf) n abuelita, yaya

grant [grɑːnt] vt (concede) conceder; (admit) reconocer ♦ n (SCOL) beca; (ADMIN) subvención f; **to take sth/sb for granted** dar algo por sentado/no hacer ningún caso a algn

grape [greɪp] n uva

grapefruit ['greɪpfruːt] n pomelo (SP, SC), toronja (LAm)

graph [grɑːf] n gráfica ❏ **graphic** ['græfɪk] adj gráfico ❏ **graphics** n artes fpl gráficas ♦ npl (drawings) dibujos mpl

grasp [grɑːsp] vt agarrar, asir; (understand) comprender ♦ n (grip) asimiento; (understanding) comprensión f

grass [grɑːs] n hierba; (lawn) césped m ❏ **grasshopper** n saltamontes m inv

grate [greɪt] n parrilla de chimenea ♦ vi: **to ~ (on)** chirriar (sobre) ♦ vt (CULIN) rallar

grateful ['greɪtful] adj agradecido

grater ['greɪtə'] n rallador m

gratitude ['grætɪtjuːd] n agradecimiento

grave [greɪv] n tumba ♦ adj serio, grave

gravel ['grævl] n grava

gravestone ['greɪvstəun] n lápida

graveyard ['greɪvjɑːd] n cementerio

gravity ['grævɪtɪ] n gravedad f

gravy ['greɪvɪ] n salsa de carne

gray [greɪ] adj (US) = **grey**

graze [greɪz] vi pacer ♦ vt (touch lightly) rozar; (scrape) raspar ♦ n (MED) abrasión f

grease [griːs] n (fat) grasa; (lubricant) lubricante m ♦ vt engrasar; lubrificar ❏ **greasy** adj grasiento

great [greɪt] adj grande; (inf) magnífico, estupendo ❏ **Great Britain** n Gran Bretaña ❏ **great-grandfather** n bisabuelo ❑ **great-grandmother** n

bisabuela ❑ **greatly** adv muy; (with verb) mucho

Greece [griːs] n Grecia

greed [griːd] n (also: **greediness**) codicia, avaricia; (for food) gula; (for power etc) avidez f ❑ **greedy** adj avaro; (for food) glotón(-ona)

Greek [griːk] adj griego ♦ n griego(-a); (LING) griego

green [griːn] adj (also POL) verde; (inexperienced) novato ♦ n verde m; (stretch of grass) césped m; (GOLF) green m; **greens** npl (vegetables) verduras fpl ❑ **green card** n (AUT) carta verde; (US: work permit) permiso de trabajo para los extranjeros en EE. UU. ❑ **greengage** n (ciruela) claudia ❑ **greengrocer** (BRIT) n verdulero(-a) ❑ **greenhouse** n invernadero ❑ **greenhouse effect** n efecto invernadero

Greenland ['griːnlənd] n Groenlandia

green salad n ensalada f (de lechuga, pepino, pimiento verde, etc)

greet [griːt] vt (welcome) dar la bienvenida a; (receive: news) recibir ❑ **greeting** n (welcome) bienvenida ❑ **greeting(s) card** n tarjeta de felicitación

grew [gruː] pt of **grow**

grey [greɪ] (US **gray**) adj gris; (weather) sombrío ❑ **grey-haired** adj canoso ❑ **greyhound** n galgo

grid [grɪd] n reja; (ELEC) red f ❑ **gridlock** n (traffic jam) retención f

grief [griːf] n dolor m, pena

grievance ['griːvəns] n motivo de queja, agravio

grieve [griːv] vi afligirse, acongojarse ♦ vt dar pena a; **to ~ for** (BRIT) llorar la muerte de

grill [grɪl] n (on cooker) parrilla; (also: **mixed ~**) parrillada ♦ vt (BRIT) asar a la parrilla; (inf: question) interrogar

grille [grɪl] n reja; (AUT) rejilla

grim [grɪm] adj (place) sombrío; (situation) triste; (person) ceñudo

grime [graɪm] n mugre f, suciedad f

grin [grɪn] n sonrisa abierta ♦ vi sonreír abiertamente

grind [graɪnd] (pt, pp **ground**) vt (coffee, pepper etc) moler; (US: meat) picar; (make sharp) afilar ♦ n (work) rutina

grip [grɪp] n (hold) asimiento; (control) control m, dominio; (of tyre etc): **to have a good/bad ~** agarrarse bien/mal; (handle) asidero; (holdall) maletín m ♦ vt agarrar; (viewer, reader) fascinar; **to get to grips with** enfrentarse con ❑ **gripping** adj absorbente

grit [grɪt] n gravilla; (courage) valor m ♦ vt (road) poner gravilla en; **to ~ one's teeth** apretar los dientes

grits [grɪts] (US) npl maíz msg a medio moler

groan [grəʊn] n gemido; quejido ♦ vi gemir; quejarse

grocer ['grəʊsə'] n tendero de ultramarinos (SP)) ❑ **groceries** npl comestibles mpl ❑ **grocer's (shop)** n tienda de comestibles or (MEX, CAM) abarrotes, almacén (SC) ❑ **grocery** n (shop) tienda de ultramarinos

groin [grɔɪn] n ingle f

groom [gruːm] n mozo(-a) de cuadra; (also: **bridegroom**) novio ♦ vt (horse) almohazar; (fig): **to ~ sb for** preparar a algn para; **well-groomed** de buena presencia

groove [gruːv] n ranura, surco

grope [grəʊp] vi: **to ~ for** buscar a tientas

gross [grəʊs] adj (neglect, injustice) grave; (vulgar: behaviour) grosero; (: appearance) de mal gusto; (COMM) bruto ❑ **grossly** adv (greatly) enormemente

grotesque [grə'tɛsk] adj grotesco

ground [graʊnd] pt, pp of **grind** ♦ n suelo, tierra; (SPORT) campo, terreno; (reason: gen pl) causa, razón f; (US: also:

~ wire) tierra ♦ vt (plane) mantener en tierra; (US ELEC) conectar con tierra; **grounds** npl (of coffee etc) poso; (gardens etc) jardines mpl, parque m; **on the ~** en el suelo; **to the ~** al suelo; **to gain/lose ~** ganar/perder terreno □ **ground floor** (BRIT) planta baja □ **groundsheet** (BRIT) n tela impermeable; suelo □ **groundwork** n preparación f

group [gruːp] n grupo; (musical) conjunto ♦ vt (also: ~ **together**) agrupar ♦ vi (also: ~ **together**) agruparse

grouse [graus] n inv (bird) urogallo ♦ vi (complain) quejarse

grovel ['grɒvl] vi (fig): **to ~ before** humillarse ante

grow [grəu] (pt **grew**, pp **grown**) vi crecer; (increase) aumentar; (expand) desarrollarse; (become) volverse; **to ~ rich/weak** enriquecerse/debilitarse ♦ vt cultivar; (hair, beard) dejar crecer
▶ **grow on** vt fus: **that painting is growing on me** ese cuadro me gusta cada vez más ▶ **grow up** vi crecer, hacerse hombre/mujer

growl [graul] vi gruñir

grown [grəun] pp of **grow** □ **grown-up** n adulto(-a), mayor m/f

growth [grəuθ] n crecimiento, desarrollo; (what has grown) brote m; (MED) tumor m

grub [grʌb] n larva, gusano; (inf: food) comida

grubby ['grʌbɪ] adj sucio, mugriento

grudge [grʌdʒ] n (motivo de) rencor m ♦ vt: **to ~ sb sth** dar algo a algn de mala gana; **to bear sb a ~** guardar rencor a algn

gruelling ['gruəlɪŋ] (US **grueling**) adj penoso, duro

gruesome ['gruːsəm] adj horrible

grumble ['grʌmbl] vi refunfuñar, quejarse

grumpy ['grʌmpɪ] adj gruñón(-ona)

grunt [grʌnt] vi gruñir

guarantee [gærən'tiː] n garantía ♦ vt garantizar

guard [gɑːd] n (squad) guardia; (one man) guardia m/f; (BRIT RAIL) jefe m de tren; (on machine) dispositivo de seguridad; (also: **fireguard**) rejilla de protección ♦ vt guardar; (prisoner) vigilar; **to be on one's ~** estar alerta □ **guardian** n guardián(-ana) m/f; (of minor) tutor(a) m/f

guerrilla [gə'rɪlə] n guerrillero(-a)

guess [ges] vt adivinar; (US) suponer ♦ vt adivinar; suponer ♦ n suposición f, conjetura; **to take** or **have a ~** tratar de adivinar

guest [gest] n invitado(-a); (in hotel) huésped m/f □ **guest house** n casa de huéspedes, pensión f □ **guest room** n cuarto de huéspedes

guidance ['gaɪdəns] n (advice) consejos mpl

guide [gaɪd] n (person) guía m/f; (book, fig) guía; (also: **Girl G~**) guía f ♦ vt (round museum etc) guiar; (lead) conducir; (direct) orientar □ **guidebook** n guía □ **guide dog** n perro m guía □ **guided tour** n visita f con guía □ **guidelines** npl (advice) directrices fpl

guild [gɪld] n gremio

guilt [gɪlt] n culpabilidad f □ **guilty** adj culpable

guinea pig ['gɪnɪ-] n cobaya; (fig) conejillo de Indias

guitar [gɪ'tɑː] n guitarra □ **guitarist** n guitarrista m/f

gulf [gʌlf] n golfo; (abyss) abismo

gull [gʌl] n gaviota

gulp [gʌlp] vi tragar saliva ♦ vt (also: ~ **down**) tragarse

gum [gʌm] n (ANAT) encía; (glue) goma, cemento; (sweet) caramelo de goma; (also: **chewing-~**) chicle m ♦ vt pegar con goma

gun

gun [gʌn] n (*small*) pistola, revólver m; (*shotgun*) escopeta; (*rifle*) fusil m; (*cannon*) cañón m ❏ **gunfire** n disparos mpl ❏ **gunman** (irreg) n pistolero ❏ **gunpoint** n: **at gunpoint** a mano armada ❏ **gunpowder** n pólvora ❏ **gunshot** n escopetazo

gush [gʌʃ] vi salir a raudales; (*person*) deshacerse en efusiones

gust [gʌst] n (*of wind*) ráfaga

gut [gʌt] n intestino; **guts** npl (ANAT) tripas fpl; (*courage*) valor m

gutter [ˈgʌtə] n (*of roof*) canalón m; (*in street*) cuneta

guy [gai] n (*also*: **guyrope**) cuerda; (*inf*: *man*) tío (SP), tipo; (*figure*) monigote m

Guy Fawkes' Night [gaiˈfɔːks-] n ver recuadro

GUY FAWKES' NIGHT

La noche del cinco de noviembre, **Guy Fawkes' Night**, se celebra en el Reino Unido el fracaso de la conspiración de la pólvora ("Gunpowder Plot"), un intento fallido de volar el parlamento de Jaime I en 1605. Esa noche se lanzan fuegos artificiales y se hacen hogueras en las que se queman unos muñecos de trapo que representan a **Guy Fawkes**, uno de los cabecillas de la revuelta. Días antes, los niños tienen por costumbre pedir a los transeúntes **a penny for the guy**, dinero que emplean en comprar cohetes y petardos.

gym [dʒim] n gimnasio ❏ **gymnasium** n gimnasio mf ❏ **gymnast** n gimnasta mf ❏ **gymnastics** n gimnasia ❏ **gym shoes** npl zapatillas fpl (de deporte)

gynaecologist [gainiˈkɔlədʒist] (US **gynecologist**) n ginecólogo(-a)

gypsy [ˈdʒipsi] n gitano(-a)

H, h

haberdashery [hæbəˈdæʃəri] (BRIT) n mercería

habit [ˈhæbit] n hábito, costumbre f; (*drug habit*) adicción f; (*costume*) hábito

habitat [ˈhæbitæt] n hábitat m

hack [hæk] vt (*cut*) cortar; (*slice*) tajar ♦ n (*pej*: *writer*) escritor(a) m/f a sueldo ❏ **hacker** n (COMPUT) pirata mf informático(-a)

had [hæd] pt, pp of **have**

haddock [ˈhædək] n (pl ~ or **haddocks**) n especie de merluza

hadn't [ˈhædnt] = **had not**

haemorrhage [ˈhemərɪdʒ] (US **hemorrhage**) n hemorragia

haemorrhoids [ˈheməˌrɔidz] (US **hemorrhoids**) npl hemorroides fpl

haggle [ˈhægl] vi regatear

Hague [heig] n: **The ~** La Haya

hail [heil] n granizo; (*fig*) lluvia ♦ vt saludar; (*taxi*) llamar a; (*acclaim*) aclamar ♦ vi granizar ❏ **hailstone** n (piedra) de granizo

hair [heə] n pelo, cabellos mpl; (*one hair*) pelo, cabello; (*on legs etc*) vello; **to do one's ~** arreglarse el pelo; **to have grey ~** tener canas fpl ❏ **hairband** n cinta ❏ **hairbrush** n cepillo (para el pelo) ❏ **haircut** n corte m (de pelo) ❏ **hairdo** n peinado ❏ **hairdresser** n peluquero(-a) ❏ **hairdresser's** n peluquería ❏ **hair dryer** n secador m de pelo ❏ **hair gel** n fijador ❏ **hair spray** n laca ❏ **hairstyle** n peinado ❏ **hairy** adj peludo; velludo; (*inf*: *frightening*) espeluznante

hake [heik] n (pl ~ or **hakes**) n merluza

half [hɑːf] n (pl **halves**) n mitad f; (*of beer*) ≈ caña (SP), media pinta; (RAIL, BUS) billete m de niño ♦ adj medio ♦ adv medio, a medias; **two and a ~** dos y media; **~ a dozen** media docena; **~ a**

pound media libra; **to cut sth in ~** cortar algo por la mitad ◻ **half board** n (BRIT: in hotel) media pensión ◻ **half-brother** n hermanastro ◻ **half day** n medio día m, media jornada ◻ **half fare** n medio pasaje m ◻ **half-hearted** adj indiferente, poco entusiasta ◻ **half-hour** n media hora ◻ **half-price** adj, adv a mitad de precio ◻ **half term** (BRIT) n (SCOL) vacaciones de mediados del trimestre ◻ **half-time** n descanso ◻ **halfway** adv a medio camino; (halfway through) a mitad de

hall [hɔːl] n (for concerts) sala; (entrance way) hall m; vestíbulo

hallmark [ˈhɔːlmɑːk] n sello

hallo [həˈləʊ] excl = **hello**

hall of residence (BRIT) n residencia

Hallowe'en [hæləʊˈiːn] n víspera de Todos los Santos

hallucination [həluːsɪˈneɪʃən] n alucinación f

hallway [ˈhɔːlweɪ] n vestíbulo

halo [ˈheɪləʊ] n (of saint) halo, aureola

halt [hɔːlt] n (stop) alto, parada ◆ vt parar; interrumpir ◆ vi pararse

halve [hɑːv] vt partir por la mitad

halves [hɑːvz] npl of **half**

ham [hæm] n jamón m (cocido)

hamburger [ˈhæmbɜːgəʳ] n hamburguesa

hamlet [ˈhæmlɪt] n aldea

hammer [ˈhæməʳ] n martillo ◆ vt (nail) clavar; (force): **to ~ an idea into sb/a message home** meter una idea en la cabeza a algn/machacar una idea ◆ vi dar golpes

hammock [ˈhæmək] n hamaca

hamper [ˈhæmpəʳ] vt estorbar ◆ n cesto

hamster [ˈhæmstəʳ] n hámster m

hamstring [ˈhæmstrɪŋ] n (ANAT) tendón m de la corva

hand [hænd] n mano f; (of clock) aguja; (writing) letra; (worker) obrero ◆ vt dar, pasar; **to give** o **lend sb a ~** echar una mano a algn, ayudar a algn; **at ~** in a mano; in ~ (time) libre; (job etc) entre manos; **on ~** (person, services) a mano, al alcance; **to ~** (information etc) a mano; **on the one ~ ..., on the other ~** ... por una parte ... por otra (parte) ...
▶ **hand down** vt pasar, bajar; (tradition) transmitir; (heirloom) dejar en herencia; (US: sentence, verdict) imponer ▶ **hand in** vt entregar ▶ **hand out** vt distribuir ▶ **hand over** vt (deliver) entregar ◻ **handbag** n bolso (SP), cartera (LAm), bolsa (MEX) ◻ **hand baggage** n = **hand luggage** ◻ **handbook** n manual m ◻ **handbrake** n freno de mano ◻ **handcuffs** npl esposas fpl ◻ **handful** n puñado

handicap [ˈhændɪkæp] n minusvalía; (disadvantage) desventaja; (SPORT) handicap m ◆ vt estorbar; **to be mentally handicapped** ser mentalmente m/f discapacitado; **to be physically handicapped** ser minusválido(-a)

handkerchief [ˈhæŋkətʃɪf] n pañuelo

handle [ˈhændl] n (of door etc) tirador m; (of cup etc) asa; (of knife etc) mango; (for winding) manivela ◆ vt (touch) tocar; (deal with) encargarse de; (treat:

people) manejar; **"~ with care"** "(manéjese) con cuidado"; **to fly off the ~** perder los estribos ❏ **handlebar(s)** n(pl) manillar m

hand: hand luggage n equipaje m de mano ❏ **handmade** adj hecho a mano ❏ **handout** n *(money etc)* limosna; *(leaflet)* folleto

handsome [ˈhænsəm] adj guapo; *(building)* bello; *(fig: profit)* considerable

handwriting [ˈhændraɪtɪŋ] n letra

handy [ˈhændɪ] adj *(close at hand)* a la mano; *(tool etc)* práctico; *(skilful)* hábil, diestro

hang [hæŋ] *(pt, pp hung)* vt colgar; *(criminal: pt, pp hanged)* ahorcar ♦ vi *(painting, coat etc)* colgar; *(hair, drapery)* caer; **to get the ~ of sth** *(inf)* lograr dominar algo ► **hang about** *or* **around** vi haraganear ► **hang down** vi colgar, pender ► **hang on** vi *(wait)* esperar ► **hang out** vt *(washing)* tender, colgar ♦ vi *(inf: live)* vivir; *(spend time)* pasar el rato; **to hang out of sth** colgar fuera de algo ► **hang round** vi = **hang around** ► **hang up** vi *(TEL)* colgar ♦ vt colgar

hanger [ˈhæŋəʳ] n percha

hang-gliding [ˈ–glaɪdɪŋ] n vuelo libre

hangover [ˈhæŋəʊvəʳ] n *(after drinking)* resaca

hankie [ˈhæŋkɪ], **hanky** [ˈhæŋkɪ] n abbr = **handkerchief**

happen [ˈhæpən] vi suceder, ocurrir; *(chance)*: **he happened to hear/see** dió la casualidad de que oyó/vió; **as it happens** da la casualidad de que

happily [ˈhæpɪlɪ] adv *(luckily)* afortunadamente; *(cheerfully)* alegremente

happiness [ˈhæpɪnɪs] n felicidad f; *(cheerfulness)* alegría

happy [ˈhæpɪ] adj feliz; *(cheerful)* alegre; **to be ~ (with)** estar contento (con); **to**

be ~ **to do** estar encantado de hacer; ~ **birthday!** ¡feliz cumpleaños!

harass [ˈhærəs] vt acosar, hostigar ❏ **harassment** n persecución f

harbour *(US* **harbor)** [ˈhɑːbəʳ] n puerto ♦ vt *(fugitive)* dar abrigo a; *(hope etc)* abrigar

hard [hɑːd] adj duro; *(difficult)* difícil; *(work)* arduo; *(person)* severo; *(fact)* innegable ♦ adv *(think)* mucho, duro; *(think)* profundamente; **to look** ~ **at** clavar los ojos en; **to try** ~ esforzarse; **no ~ feelings!** ¡sin rencor(es)!; **to be** ~ **of hearing** ser duro de oído; **to be** ~ **done by** ser tratado injustamente ❏ **hardback** n libro en cartoné ❏ **hardboard** n aglomerado m *(de madera)* ❏ **hard disk** n *(COMPUT)* disco duro o rígido ❏ **harden** vt endurecer; *(fig)* curtir ♦ vi endurecerse; curtirse

hardly [ˈhɑːdlɪ] adv apenas; ~ **ever** casi nunca

hard: hardship n privación f ❏ **hard shoulder** *(BRIT)* n *(AUT)* arcén m ❏ **hard-up** *(inf)* adj sin un duro *(SP)*, pelado, sin un centavo *(MEX)*, pato *(SC)* ❏ **hardware** n ferretería; *(COMPUT)* hardware m; *(MIL)* armamento ❏ **hardware shop** *(US* **hardware store)** ferretería ❏ **hard-working** adj trabajador(a)

hardy [ˈhɑːdɪ] adj fuerte; *(plant)* resistente

hare [hɛəʳ] n liebre f

harm [hɑːm] n daño, mal m ♦ vt *(person)* hacer daño a; *(health, interests)* perjudicar; *(thing)* dañar; **out of ~'s way** a salvo ❏ **harmful** adj dañino ❏ **harmless** adj *(person)* inofensivo; *(joke etc)* inocente

harmony [ˈhɑːmənɪ] n armonía

harness [ˈhɑːnɪs] n arreos mpl; *(for child)* arnés m; *(safety harness)* arneses mpl ♦ vt *(horse)* enjaezar; *(resources)* aprovechar

harp [hɑːp] n arpa ♦ vi: **to ~ on (about)** machacar con

harsh [hɑːʃ] *adj* (*cruel*) duro, cruel; (*severe*) severo; (*sound*) áspero; (*light*) deslumbrador(a)

harvest [ˈhɑːvɪst] *n* (*harvest time*) siega; (*of cereals etc*) cosecha; (*of grapes*) vendimia ♦ *vt* cosechar

has [hæz] *vb see* **have**

hasn't [ˈhæznt] = **has not**

hassle [ˈhæsl] (*inf*) *n* lata

haste [heɪst] *n* prisa ❑ **hasten** [ˈheɪsn] *vt* acelerar ♦ *vi* darse prisa ❑ **hastily** *adv* de prisa; precipitadamente ❑ **hasty** *adj* apresurado; (*rash*) precipitado

hat [hæt] *n* sombrero

hatch [hætʃ] *n* (*NAUT: also*: **hatchway**) escotilla; (*also*: **service ~**) ventanilla ♦ *vi* (*bird*) salir del cascarón ♦ *vt* incubar; (*plot*) tramar; **5 eggs have hatched** han salido 5 pollos

hatchback [ˈhætʃbæk] *n* (*AUT*) tres *or* cinco puertas *m*

hate [heɪt] *vt* odiar, aborrecer ♦ *n* odio ❑ **hatred** [ˈheɪtrɪd] *n* odio

haul [hɔːl] *vt* tirar ♦ *n* (*of fish*) redada; (*of stolen goods etc*) botín *m*

haunt [hɔːnt] *vt* (*ghost*) aparecerse en; (*obsess*) obsesionar ♦ *n* guarida ❑ **haunted** *adj* (*castle etc*) embrujado; (*look*) de angustia

have

KEYWORD

[hæv] (*pt, pp* **had**) *aux vb*

1 (*gen*) haber; **to have arrived/eaten** haber llegado/comido; **having finished** *or* **when he had finished, he left** cuando hubo acabado, se fue

2 (*in tag questions*): **you've done it, haven't you?** lo has hecho, ¿verdad? or ¿no?

3 (*in short answers and questions*): **I haven't** no; **yes we have!** sí, es verdad; **we haven't paid — yes we have!** no hemos pagado — ¡sí que hemos

pagado!; **I've been there before, have you?** he estado allí antes, ¿y tú?

♦ *modal aux vb* (*be obliged*): **to have (got) to do sth** tener que hacer algo; **you haven't to tell her** no hay que *or* no debes decírselo

♦ *vt*

1 (*possess*): **he has (got) blue eyes/dark hair** tiene los ojos azules/el pelo negro

2 (*referring to meals etc*): **to have breakfast/lunch/dinner** desayunar/comer/cenar; **to have a drink/a cigarette** tomar algo/fumar un cigarrillo

3 (*receive*) recibir; (*obtain*) obtener; **may I have your address?** ¿puedes darme tu dirección?; **you can have it for £5** te lo puedes quedar por £5; **I must have it by tomorrow** lo necesito para mañana; **to have a baby** tener un niño *or* bebé

4 (*maintain, allow*): **I won't have it/this nonsense!** ¡no lo permitiré!/¡no permitiré estas tonterías!; **we can't have that** no podemos permitir eso

5: **to have sth done** hacer *or* mandar hacer algo; **to have one's hair cut** cortarse el pelo; **to have sb do sth** hacer que algn haga algo

6 (*experience, suffer*): **to have a cold/flu** tener un resfriado/la gripe; **she had her bag stolen/her arm broken** le robaron el bolso/se rompió un brazo; **to have an operation** operarse

7 (+ *noun*): **to have a swim/walk/bath/rest** nadar/dar un paseo/darse un baño/descansar; **let's have a look** vamos a ver; **to have a meeting/party** celebrar una reunión/una fiesta; **let me have a try** déjame intentarlo

haven ['heɪvn] n puerto; (fig) refugio

haven't ['hævnt] = **have not**

havoc ['hævək] n estragos mpl

Hawaii [hə'waɪiː] n (Islas fpl) Hawai m

hawk [hɔːk] n halcón m

hawthorn ['hɔːθɔːn] n espino

hay [heɪ] n heno ☐ **hay fever** n fiebre f
del heno ☐ **haystack** n almiar m

hazard ['hæzəd] n peligro ♦ vt
aventurar ☐ **hazardous** adj peligroso
☐ **hazard warning lights** npl (AUT)
señales fpl de emergencia

haze [heɪz] n neblina

hazel ['heɪzl] n (tree) avellano ♦ adj
(eyes) color m de avellano ☐ **hazelnut**
n avellana

hazy ['heɪzɪ] adj brumoso, (idea) vago

he [hiː] pron él; **he who ...** él que ...,
quien ...

head [hed] n cabeza; (leader) jefe(-a) m/
f; (of school) director(a) m/f ♦ vt (list)
encabezar; (group) capitanear;
(company) dirigir; **heads (or tails)** cara
(o cruz); ~ **first** de cabeza; ~ **over
heels** (in love) perdidamente; **to ~ the
ball** cabecear (la pelota) ♦ **head for** vt fus
dirigirse a; (disaster) ir camino de
▶ **head off** vt (threat, danger) evitar
☐ **headache** n dolor m de cabeza
☐ **heading** n título ☐ **headlamp**
(BRIT) n = **headlight** ☐ **headlight** n
faro ☐ **headline** n titular m ☐ **head
office** n oficina central, central f
☐ **headphones** npl auriculares mpl
☐ **headquarters** npl sede f central;
(MIL) cuartel m general ☐ **headroom**
n (in car) altura interior; (under bridge)
(límite m de) altura ☐ **headscarf** n
pañuelo ☐ **headset** n cascos mpl
☐ **headteacher** n director ☐ **head
waiter** n maître m

heal [hiːl] vt curar ♦ vi cicatrizarse

health [helθ] n salud f ☐ **health care** n
asistencia sanitaria ☐ **health centre**
(BRIT) n ambulatorio, centro médico
☐ **health food** n alimentos mpl

orgánicos ☐ **Health Service** (BRIT) n el
servicio de salud pública, ≈ el Insalud
(SP) ☐ **healthy** adj sano, saludable

heap [hiːp] n montón m ♦ vt: **to ~ (up)**
amontonar; **to ~ sth with** llenar algo
hasta arriba de; **heaps of** un montón de
de

hear [hɪə*] (pt, pp **heard**) vt (also LAW)
oír; (news) saber ♦ vi oír; **to ~ about** oír
hablar de; **to ~ from sb** tener noticias
de algn

heard [hɜːd] pt, pp of **hear**

hearing ['hɪərɪŋ] n (sense) oído; (LAW)
vista ☐ **hearing aid** n audífono

hearse [hɜːs] n coche m fúnebre

heart [hɑːt] n corazón m; (fig) valor m;
(of lettuce) cogollo; **hearts** npl (CARDS)
corazones mpl; **to lose/take ~**
descorazonarse/cobrar ánimo; **at ~** en
el fondo; **by ~** (learn, know) de
memoria ☐ **heart attack** n infarto (de
miocardio) ☐ **heartbeat** n latido (del
corazón) ☐ **heartbroken** adj: **she was
heartbroken about it** esto le partió el
corazón ☐ **heartburn** n acedía
☐ **heart disease** n enfermedad f
cardíaca

hearth [hɑːθ] n (fireplace) chimenea

heartless ['hɑːtlɪs] adj despiadado

hearty ['hɑːtɪ] adj (person)
campechano; (laugh) sano; (dislike,
support) absoluto

heat [hiːt] n calor m; (SPORT: also:
qualifying ~) prueba eliminatoria ♦ vt
calentar ▶ **heat up** vi calentarse ♦ vt
calentar ☐ **heated** adj caliente; (fig)
acalorado ☐ **heater** n estufa; (in car)
calefacción f

heather ['heðə*] n brezo

heating ['hiːtɪŋ] n calefacción f

heatwave ['hiːtweɪv] n ola de calor

heaven ['hevn] n cielo; (fig) una
maravilla ☐ **heavenly** adj celestial;
(fig) maravilloso

heavily ['hevɪlɪ] adv pesadamente; (drink, smoke) con exceso; (sleep, sigh) profundamente; (depend) mucho

heavy ['hevɪ] adj pesado; (work, blow) duro; (sea, rain, meal) fuerte; (drinker, smoker) grande; (responsibility) grave; (schedule) ocupado; (weather) bochornoso

Hebrew ['hi:bru:] adj, n (LING) hebreo

hectare ['hektɑː'] n (BRIT) hectárea

hectic ['hektɪk] adj agitado

he'd [hi:d] = **he would**; **he had**

hedge [hedʒ] n seto ♦ vi contestar con evasivas; **to ~ one's bets** (fig) cubrirse

hedgehog ['hedʒhɒg] n erizo

heed [hi:d] vt también: **take ~**: **pay attention to**) hacer caso de

heel [hi:l] n talón m; (of shoe) tacón m ♦ vt (shoe) poner tacón a

hefty ['heftɪ] adj (person) fornido; (parcel, profit) gordo

height [haɪt] n (of person) estatura; (of building) altura; (high ground) cerro; (altitude) altitud f; (fig: of season): **at the ~ of summer** en los días más calurosos del verano; (: of power etc) cúspide f; (: of stupidity etc) colmo □ **heighten** vt elevar; (fig) aumentar

heir [εə'] n heredero □ **heiress** n heredera

held [held] pt, pp of **hold**

helicopter ['helɪkɒptə'] n helicóptero

hell [hel] n infierno; **~!** (inf) ¡demonios!

he'll [hi:l] = **he will**; **he shall**

hello [hə'ləu] excl ¡hola!; (to attract attention) ¡oiga!; (surprise) ¡caramba!

helmet ['helmɪt] n casco

help [help] n ayuda; (cleaner etc) criada, asistenta ♦ vt ayudar; **~!** ¡socorro!; **~ yourself** sírvete; **he can't ~ it** no es culpa suya ▶ **help out** vi ayudar, echar una mano ♦ vt: **to ~ sb out** ayudar a algn, echar una mano a algn □ **helper** n ayudante mf □ **helpful** adj útil; (person) servicial; (advice) útil □ **helping** n ración f □ **helpless** adj

(incapable) incapaz; (defenceless) indefenso □ **helpline** n teléfono de asistencia al público

hem [hem] n dobladillo ♦ vt poner or coser el dobladillo de

hemisphere ['hemɪsfɪə'] n hemisferio

hemorrhage ['hemərɪdʒ] (US) n = **haemorrhage**

hemorrhoids ['hemərɔɪdz] (US) npl = **haemorrhoids**

hen [hen] n gallina; (female bird) hembra

hence [hens] adv (therefore) por lo tanto; **2 years ~** de aquí a 2 años

hen night, **hen party** n (inf) despedida de soltera

hepatitis [hepə'taɪtɪs] n hepatitis f

her [hə:'] pron (direct) la; (indirect) le; (stressed, after prep) ella ♦ adj su; see also **me**; **my**

herb [hə:b] n hierba □ **herbal** adj de hierbas □ **herbal tea** n infusión f de hierbas

herd [hə:d] n rebaño

here [hɪə'] adv aquí; (at this point) en este punto; **~!** (present) ¡presente!; **~ is/~ are** aquí está/están; **~ she is** aquí está

hereditary [hɪ'redɪtrɪ] adj hereditario

heritage ['herɪtɪdʒ] n patrimonio

hernia ['hə:nɪə] n hernia

hero ['hɪərəu] (pl **heroes**) n héroe m; (in book, film) protagonista m □ **heroic** [hɪ'rəuɪk] adj heroico

heroin ['herəuɪn] n heroína

heroine ['herəuɪn] n heroína; (in book, film) protagonista

heron ['herən] n garza

herring ['herɪŋ] n arenque m

hers[1] [hə:z] pron (el) suyo ((la) suya) etc; see also **mine**

herself [hə:'self] pron (reflexive) se; (emphatic) ella misma; (after prep) sí (misma); see also **oneself**

he's [hi:z] = **he is**; **he has**

hesitant ['hezɪtənt] adj vacilante

hesitate ['hezɪteɪt] vi vacilar; (in speech) titubear; (be unwilling) resistirse a ❑ **hesitation** ['-teɪʃən] n indecisión f; titubeo; dudas fpl

heterosexual [hetərəu'seksjuəl] adj heterosexual

hexagon ['heksəgən] n hexágono

hey [heɪ] excl ¡oye!, ¡oiga!

heyday ['heɪdeɪ] n: **the ~ of** el apogeo de

HGV n abbr (= heavy goods vehicle) vehículo pesado

hi [haɪ] excl ¡hola!; (to attract attention) ¡oiga!

hibernate ['haɪbəneɪt] vi invernar

hiccough ['hɪkʌp] = **hiccup**

hiccup ['hɪkʌp] n hipar

hid [hɪd] pt of **hide**

hidden ['hɪdn] pp of **hide** ♦ adj: ~ **agenda** plan m encubierto

hide [haɪd] (pt **hid**, pp **hidden**) n (skin) piel f ♦ vt esconder, ocultar ♦ vi: **to ~ (from sb)** esconderse or ocultarse (de algn)

hideous ['hɪdɪəs] adj horrible

hiding ['haɪdɪŋ] n (beating) paliza; **to be in ~** (concealed) estar escondido

hi-fi ['haɪfaɪ] n estéreo, hifi m ♦ adj de alta fidelidad

high [haɪ] adj alto; (speed, number) grande; (price) elevado; (wind) fuerte; (voice) agudo ♦ adv alto, a gran altura; **it is 20 m ~** tiene 20 m de altura; **~ in the air** en las alturas ❑ **highchair** n silla alta ❑ **high-class** adj (hotel) de lujo; (person) distinguido, de categoría; (food) de alta categoría; ❑ **higher education** n educación f or enseñanza superior ❑ **high heels** npl (heels) tacones mpl altos; (shoes) zapatos mpl de tacón ❑ **high jump** n (SPORT) salto de altura ❑ **highlands** ['haɪləndz] npl tierras fpl altas; **the Highlands** (in Scotland) las Tierras Altas de Escocia ❑ **highlight** n (fig: of event) punto culminante ♦ vt subrayar;

highlights npl (in hair) reflejos mpl ❑ **highlighter** n rotulador ❑ **highly** adv (paid) muy bien; (critical, confidential) sumamente; (a lot): **to speak/think highly of** hablar muy bien de/tener en mucho a ❑ **highness** n altura; **Her/His Highness** Su Alteza ❑ **high-rise** n (also: **high-rise block, high-rise building**) torre f de pisos ❑ **high school** n ≈ Instituto Nacional de Bachillerato (SP) ❑ **high season** (BRIT) n temporada alta ❑ **high street** (BRIT) n calle f mayor ❑ **high-tech** (inf) adj altec (inf), de alta tecnología

highway n carretera; (US) carretera nacional; autopista ❑ **Highway Code** (BRIT) n código de la circulación

hijack ['haɪdʒæk] vt secuestrar ❑ **hijacker** n secuestrador(a) m/f

hike [haɪk] vi (go walking) ir de excursión (a pie) ♦ n caminata ❑ **hiker** n excursionista mf ❑ **hiking** n senderismo

hilarious [hɪ'leərɪəs] adj divertidísimo

hill [hɪl] n colina; (high) montaña; (slope) cuesta ❑ **hillside** n ladera ❑ **hill walking** n senderismo de montaña ❑ **hilly** adj montañoso

him [hɪm] pron (direct) le, lo; (indirect) le; (stressed, after prep) él; see also **me** ❑ **himself** pron (reflexive) se; (emphatic) él mismo; (after prep) sí (mismo); see also **oneself**

hind [haɪnd] adj posterior

hinder ['hɪndə'] vt estorbar, impedir

hindsight ['haɪndsaɪt] n: **with ~** en retrospectiva

Hindu ['hɪnduː] n hindú mf ❑ **Hinduism** n (REL) hinduismo

hinge [hɪndʒ] n bisagra, gozne m ♦ vi (fig): **to ~ on** depender de

hint [hɪnt] n indirecta; (advice) consejo; (sign) dejo ♦ vt: **to ~ that** insinuar que ♦ vi: **to ~ at** hacer alusión a

hip [hɪp] n cadera

hippie ['hɪpɪ] n hippie m/f, jipi m/f

hippo ['hɪpəʊ] (PL **hippos**) n
hipopótamo

hippopotamus [hɪpə'pɒtəməs] (pl
hippopotamuses or **hippopotami**) n
hipopótamo

hippy ['hɪpɪ] n = **hippie**

hire ['haɪə] vt (BRIT: car, equipment)
alquilar; (worker) contratar ♦ n alquiler
m; **for** ~ se alquila; (taxi) libre
❑ **hire(d) car** (BRIT) n coche m de
alquiler ❑ **hire purchase** (BRIT) n
compra a plazos

his [hɪz] pron (el) suyo ((la) suya) etc
♦ adj su; see also **mine¹**; **my**

Hispanic [hɪs'pænɪk] adj hispánico

hiss [hɪs] vi silbar

historian [hɪ'stɔːrɪən] n historiador(a)
m/f

historic(al) [hɪ'stɔrɪk(l)] adj histórico

history ['hɪstərɪ] n historia

hit [hɪt] (pt, pp ~) vt (strike) golpear,
pegar; (reach: target) alcanzar; (collide
with: car) chocar contra; (fig: affect)
afectar ♦ n golpe m; (success) éxito; **to**
~ **it off with sb** llevarse bien con algn
▶ **hit back** vi defenderse; (fig)
devolver golpe por golpe

hitch [hɪtʃ] vt (fasten) atar, amarrar;
(also: ~ **up**) remangar ♦ n (difficulty)
dificultad f; **to ~ a lift** hacer autostop

hitch-hike [hɪtʃhaɪk] vi hacer
autostop ❑ **hitch-hiker** n
autostopista m/f ❑ **hitch-hiking** n
autostop m

hi-tech [haɪ'tek] adj de alta tecnología

hitman ['hɪtmæn] (irreg) n asesino a
sueldo

HIV n abbr (= human immunodeficiency
virus) VIH m; **~-negative/positive** VIH
negativo/positivo

hive [haɪv] n colmena

hoard [hɔːd] n (treasure) tesoro,
(stockpile) provisión f ♦ vt acumular;
(goods in short supply) acaparar

hoarse [hɔːs] adj ronco

hoax [həʊks] n trampa

hob [hɒb] n quemador m

hobble ['hɒbl] vi cojear

hobby ['hɒbɪ] n pasatiempo, afición f

hobo ['həʊbəʊ] (US) n vagabundo

hockey ['hɒkɪ] n hockey m ❑ **hockey
stick** n palo m de hockey

hog [hɒg] n cerdo, puerco ♦ vt (fig)
acaparar; **to go the whole** ~ poner
toda la carne en el asador

Hogmanay [hɒgmə'neɪ] n see
recuadro

hoist [hɔɪst] n (crane) grúa ♦ vt levantar,
alzar; (flag, sail) izar

hold [həʊld] (pt, pp **held**) vt sostener;
(contain) contener; (have: power,
qualification) tener; (keep back)
retener; (believe) sostener; (consider)
considerar; (keep in position): **to** ~ **one's
head up** mantener la cabeza alta;
(meeting) celebrar ♦ vi (withstand
pressure) resistir; (be valid) valer ♦ n
(grasp) asimiento; (fig) dominio; ~ **the
line!** (TEL) ¡no cuelgue!; **to** ~ **one's own**
(fig) defenderse; **to catch** or **get (a)** ~ **of**
agarrarse o asirse de ▶ **hold back** vt
retener; (secret) ocultar ▶ **hold on** vi
agarrarse bien; (wait) esperar; **hold on!**
(TEL) ¡(espere) un momento! ▶ **hold
out** vt ofrecer ♦ vi (resist) resistir
▶ **hold up** vt (raise) levantar; (support)
apoyar; (delay) retrasar; (rob) asaltar

holdall (BRIT) n bolsa ❏ **holder** n (container) receptáculo; (of ticket, record) poseedor(a) m/f; (of office, title etc) titular mf

hole [həul] n agujero

holiday ['hɔlɪdɪ] n vacaciones fpl; (public holiday) (día m de) fiesta, día m feriado; **on** ~ de vacaciones ❏ **holiday camp** n (BRIT: also: **holiday centre**) centro de vacaciones ❏ **holiday job** n (BRIT) trabajillo extra para las vacaciones ❏ **holiday-maker** n (BRIT) turista mf ❏ **holiday resort** n centro turístico

Holland ['hɔlənd] n Holanda

hollow ['hɔləu] adj hueco; (claim) vacío; (eyes) hundido; (sound) sordo ♦ n hueco; (in ground) hoyo ♦ vt: **to** ~ **out** excavar

holly ['hɔlɪ] n acebo

Hollywood ['hɔlɪwud] n Hollywood m

holocaust ['hɔləkɔːst] n holocausto

holy ['həulɪ] adj santo, sagrado; (water) bendito

home [həum] n (gen) casa; (country) patria; (institution) asilo ♦ cpd (domestic) casero, de casa; (ECON, POL) nacional ♦ adv (direction) a casa; (right in: nail etc) a fondo; **at** ~ en casa; (in country) en el país; (fig) como pez en el agua; **to go/come** ~ ir/volver a casa; **make yourself at** ~ ¡estás en tu casa! ❏ **home address** n domicilio ❏ **homeland** n tierra natal ❏ **homeless** adj sin hogar, sin casa ❏ **homely** adj (simple) sencillo ❏ **home-made** adj casero ❏ **home match** n partido en casa ❏ **Home Office** (BRIT) n Ministerio del Interior ❏ **home owner** n propietario-a m/f de una casa ❏ **home page** n página de inicio ❏ **Home Secretary** (BRIT) n Ministro del Interior ❏ **homesick** adj: **to be homesick** tener morriña, sentir nostalgia ❏ **home town** n ciudad f natal ❏ **homework** n deberes mpl

homicide ['hɔmɪsaɪd] (US) n homicidio

homoeopathic [həumɪɔ'pæθɪk] (US **homeopathic**) adj homeopático

homoeopathy [həumɪ'ɔpəθɪ] (US **homeopathy**) n homeopatía

homosexual [hɔməu'seksjuəl] adj, n homosexual mf

honest ['ɔnɪst] adj honrado; (sincere) franco, sincero ❏ **honestly** adv honradamente; francamente ❏ **honesty** n honradez f

honey ['hʌnɪ] n miel f ❏ **honeymoon** n luna de miel ❏ **honeysuckle** n madreselva

Hong Kong ['hɔŋ'kɔŋ] n Hong-Kong m

honorary ['ɔnərərɪ] adj (member, president) de honor; (title) honorífico; ~ **degree** doctorado honoris causa

honour ['ɔnə] (US **honor**) vt (commitment, promise) cumplir con ♦ n honor m, honra; **to graduate with honours** = licenciarse con matrícula (de honor) ❏ **honourable** (US **honor**) adj honorable ❏ **honours degree** n (SCOL) título de licenciado con calificación alta

hood [hud] n capucha; (BRIT AUT) capota; (US AUT) capó m; (of cooker) campana de humos

hoof [huːf] (pl **hooves**) n pezuña

hook [huk] n gancho; (on dress) corchete m, broche m; (for fishing) anzuelo ♦ vt enganchar; (fish) pescar

hooligan ['huːlɪgən] n gamberro

hoop [huːp] n aro

hooray [hu'reɪ] excl = **hurray**

hoot [huːt] (BRIT) vi (AUT) tocar el pito, pitar; (siren) sonar; (owl) ulular

Hoover® ['huːvə] (BRIT) n aspiradora ♦ vt: **to hoover** pasar la aspiradora por

hooves [huːvz] npl of **hoof**

hop [hɔp] vi saltar, brincar; (on one foot) saltar con un pie

hope [həup] vt, vi esperar ♦ n esperanza; **I** ~ **so/not** espero que sí/no ❏ **hopeful** adj (person) optimista; (situation) prometedor(a)

□ **hopefully** adv con esperanza; (one hopes): **hopefully he will recover** esperamos que se recupere
□ **hopeless** adj desesperado; (person): **to be hopeless** ser un desastre

hops [hɒps] npl lúpulo

horizon [həˈraɪzn] n horizonte m
□ **horizontal** [hɔrɪˈzɒntl] adj horizontal

hormone [ˈhɔːməʊn] n hormona

horn [hɔːn] n cuerno; (MUS: also: **French ~**) trompa; (AUT) pito, claxon m

horoscope [ˈhɒrəskəʊp] n horóscopo

horrendous [həˈrɛndəs] adj horrendo

horrible [ˈhɒrɪbl] adj horrible

horrid [ˈhɒrɪd] adj horrible, horroroso

horrific [hɒˈrɪfɪk] adj (accident) horroroso; (film) horripilante

horrifying [ˈhɒrɪfaɪɪŋ] adj horroroso

horror [ˈhɒrə*] n horror m □ **horror film** n película de horror

hors d'oeuvre [ɔːˈdəːvrə] n entremeses mpl

horse [hɔːs] n caballo □ **horseback**: **on horseback** a caballo □ **horse chestnut** n (tree) castaño de Indias; (nut) castaña de Indias
□ **horsepower** n caballo (de fuerza)
□ **horse-racing** n carreras fpl de caballos □ **horseradish** n rábano picante □ **horse riding** n (BRIT) equitación f

hose [həʊz] n manguera □ **hosepipe** n manguera

hospital [ˈhɒspɪtl] n hospital m

hospitality [hɒspɪˈtælɪtɪ] n hospitalidad f

host [həʊst] n anfitrión m; (TV, RADIO) presentador m; (REL) hostia; (large number): **a ~ of** multitud de

hostage [ˈhɒstɪdʒ] n rehén m

hostel [ˈhɒstl] n hostal m; (youth) **~** albergue m juvenil

hostess [ˈhəʊstɪs] n anfitriona; (BRIT: air hostess) azafata; (TV, RADIO) presentadora

hostile [ˈhɒstaɪl] adj hostil

hostility [hɒˈstɪlɪtɪ] n hostilidad f

hot [hɒt] adj caliente; (weather) caluroso, de calor; (as opposed to warm) muy caliente; (spicy) picante; **to be ~** (person) tener calor; (object) estar caliente; (weather) hacer calor □ **hot dog** n perro caliente

hotel [həʊˈtel] n hotel m

hot-water bottle [hɒtˈwɔːtə*-] n bolsa de agua caliente

hound [haʊnd] vt acosar ♦ n perro de caza)

hour [ˈaʊə*] n hora □ **hourly** adj (de) cada hora

house [n haʊs, pl ˈhaʊzɪz, vb haʊz] n (gen, firm) casa; (POL) cámara; (THEATRE) sala ♦ vt (person) alojar; (collection) albergar; **on the ~** (fig) la casa invita □ **household** n familia; (home) casa □ **householder** n propietario(-a); (head of house) cabeza de familia □ **housekeeper** n ama de llaves □ **housekeeping** n (work) trabajos mpl domésticos □ **housewife** (irreg) n ama de casa □ **house wine** n vino m de la casa □ **housework** n faenas fpl (de la casa)

housing [ˈhaʊzɪŋ] n (act) alojamiento; (houses) viviendas fpl □ **housing development, housing estate** (BRIT) n urbanización f

hover [ˈhɒvə*] vi flotar (en el aire) □ **hovercraft** n aerodeslizador m

how [haʊ] adv (in what way) cómo; **~ are you?** ¿cómo estás?; **~ much milk/many people?** ¿cuánta leche/gente?; **~ much does it cost?** ¿cuánto cuesta?; **~ long have you been here?** ¿cuánto hace que estás aquí?; **~ old are you?** ¿cuántos años tienes?; **~ tall is he?** ¿cómo es de alto?; **~ is school?** ¿cómo (te) va (en) la escuela?; **~ was the film?** ¿qué tal la película?; **~ lovely/awful!** ¡qué bonito/horror!

however [haʊˈɛvə*] adv: **~ I do it** lo haga como lo haga; **~ cold it is** por mucho frío que haga; **~ fast he runs** por muy rápido que corra; **~ did you do it?** ¿cómo lo hiciste? ♦ *conj* sin embargo, no obstante

howl [haul] *n* aullido ♦ *vi* aullar; (*person*) dar alaridos; (*wind*) ulular

H.P. *n, abbr* = **hire purchase**

h.p. *abbr* = **horsepower**

HQ *n, abbr* = **headquarters**

hr(s) *abbr* (= *hour(s)*) h

HTML *n abbr* (= *hypertext markup language*) lenguaje *m* de hipertexto

hubcap ['hʌbkæp] *n* tapacubos *m inv*

huddle ['hʌdl] *vi:* **to ~ together** acurrucarse

huff [hʌf] *n:* **in a ~** enojado

hug [hʌɡ] *vt* abrazar; (*thing*) apretar con los brazos

huge [hju:dʒ] *adj* enorme

hull [hʌl] *n* (*of ship*) casco

hum [hʌm] *vt* tararear, canturrear ♦ *vi* tararear, canturrear; (*insect*) zumbar

human ['hju:mən] *adj, n* humano

humane [hju:'meɪn] *adj* humano, humanitario

humanitarian [hju:mænɪ'tɛərɪən] *adj* humanitario

humanity [hju:'mænɪtɪ] *n* humanidad *f* □ **human rights** *npl* derechos *mpl* humanos

humble ['hʌmbl] *adj* humilde

humid ['hju:mɪd] *adj* húmedo □ **humidity** ['-mɪdɪtɪ] *n* humedad *f*

humiliate [hju:'mɪlɪeɪt] *vt* humillar

humiliating [hju:'mɪlɪeɪtɪŋ] *adj* humillante, vergonzoso

humiliation [hju:mɪlɪ'eɪʃən] *n* humillación *f*

hummus ['huməs] *n* paté de garbanzos

humorous ['hju:mərəs] *adj* gracioso, divertido

humour [hju:'mə'] (*US* **humor**) *n* humorismo, sentido del humor; (*mood*) humor *m* ♦ *vt* (*person*) complacer

hump [hʌmp] *n* (*in ground*) montículo; (*camel's*) giba

hunch [hʌntʃ] *n* (*premonition*) presentimiento

hundred ['hʌndrəd] *num* ciento; (*before a*) cien; **hundreds of** centenares de □ **hundredth** [-ɪdθ] *adj* centésimo

hung [hʌŋ] *pt, pp of* **hang**

Hungarian [hʌŋ'gɛərɪən] *adj, n* húngaro(-a) *m/f*

Hungary ['hʌŋgərɪ] *n* Hungría

hunger ['hʌŋgə'] *n* hambre *f* ♦ *vi:* **to ~ for** (*fig*) tener hambre de, anhelar

hungry ['hʌŋgrɪ] *adj:* **~ (for)** hambriento (de); **to be ~** tener hambre

hunt [hʌnt] *vt* (*seek*) buscar; (*SPORT*) cazar ♦ *vi* (*search*): **to ~ (for)** buscar; (*SPORT*) cazar ♦ *n* búsqueda; caza, cacería □ **hunter** *n* cazador(a) *m/f* □ **hunting** *n* caza

hurdle ['hə:dl] *n* (*SPORT*) valla; (*fig*) obstáculo

hurl [hə:l] *vt* lanzar, arrojar

hurrah [hu:'rɑ:] *excl* = **hurray**

hurray [hu'reɪ] *excl* ¡viva!

hurricane ['hʌrɪkən] *n* huracán *m*

hurry ['hʌrɪ] *n* prisa ♦ *vt* (*also:* **~ up:** *person*) dar prisa a; (: *work*) apresurar, hacer de prisa; **to be in a ~** tener prisa ▶ **hurry up** *vi* darse prisa, apurarse (*LAm*)

hurt [hə:t] (*pt, pp* **~**) *vt* hacer daño a ♦ *vi* doler ♦ *adj* lastimado

husband ['hʌzbənd] *n* marido

hush [hʌʃ] *n* silencio ♦ *vt* hacer callar; **~!** ¡chitón!, ¡cállate!

husky ['hʌskɪ] *adj* ronco ♦ *n* perro esquimal

hut [hʌt] *n* cabaña; (*shed*) cobertizo

hyacinth ['haɪəsɪnθ] *n* jacinto

hydrangea [haɪ'dreɪndʒə] *n* hortensia

hydrofoil ['haɪdrəfɔɪl] *n* aerodeslizador *m*

hydrogen ['haɪdrədʒən] *n* hidrógeno

hygiene ['haɪdʒi:n] n higiene f
❏ **hygienic** [-'dʒi:nɪk] adj higiénico

hymn [hɪm] n himno

hype [haɪp] (inf) n bombardeo publicitario

hyphen ['haɪfn] n guión m

hypnotize ['hɪpnətaɪz] vt hipnotizar

hypocrite ['hɪpəkrɪt] n hipócrita mf

hypocritical [hɪpə'krɪtɪkl] adj hipócrita

hypothesis [haɪ'pɒθɪsɪs] (pl **hypotheses** [-si:z]) n hipótesis f inv

hysterical [hɪ'sterɪkl] adj histérico; (funny) para morirse de risa

hysterics [hɪ'sterɪks] npl histeria f; **to be in ~** (fig) morirse de risa

I, i

I [aɪ] pron yo

ice [aɪs] n hielo; (ice cream) helado ♦ vt (cake) alcorzar ♦ vi (also: **~ over, ~ up**) helarse ❏ **iceberg** n iceberg m ❏ **ice cream** n helado ❏ **ice cube** n cubito de hielo ❏ **ice hockey** n hockey m sobre hielo

Iceland ['aɪslənd] n Islandia
❏ **Icelander** n islandés(-esa) m/f
❏ **Icelandic** [aɪs'lændɪk] adj islandés(-esa) ♦ n (LING) islandés m

ice: ice lolly (BRIT) n polo ❏ **ice rink** n pista de hielo ❏ **ice skating** n patinaje m sobre hielo

icing ['aɪsɪŋ] n (CULIN) alcorza ❏ **icing sugar** (BRIT) n azúcar m glas(eado)

icon ['aɪkɒn] n icono

icy ['aɪsɪ] adj helado

I'd [aɪd] = I would; I had

ID card n (identity card) DNI m

idea [aɪ'dɪə] n idea

ideal [aɪ'dɪəl] n ideal m ♦ adj ideal
❏ **ideally** [-dɪəlɪ] adv idealmente; **they're ideally suited** hacen una pareja ideal

identical [aɪ'dentɪkl] adj idéntico

identification [aɪdentɪfɪ'keɪʃən] n identificación f; **(means of) ~** documentos mpl personales

identify [aɪ'dentɪfaɪ] vt identificar

identity [aɪ'dentɪtɪ] n identidad f
❏ **identity card** n carnet m de identidad

ideology [aɪdɪ'ɒlədʒɪ] n ideología

idiom ['ɪdɪəm] n modismo; (style of speaking) lenguaje m

⚠ Be careful not to translate **idiom** by the Spanish word **idioma**.

idiot ['ɪdɪət] n idiota mf

idle ['aɪdl] adj (inactive) ocioso; (lazy) holgazán(-ana); (unemployed) parado, desocupado; (machinery etc) parado; (talk etc) frívolo ♦ vi (machine) marchar en vacío

idol ['aɪdl] n ídolo

idyllic [ɪ'dɪlɪk] adj idílico

i.e. abbr (= that is) esto es

if [ɪf] conj si; **if necessary** si fuera necesario, si hiciese falta; **if I were you** yo en tu lugar; **if so** not de ser así/si no; **if only I could!** ¡ojalá pudiera!; see also **as**; **even**

ignite [ɪg'naɪt] vt (set fire to) encender ♦ vi encenderse

ignition [ɪg'nɪʃən] n (AUT: process) ignición f; (: mechanism) encendido; **to switch on/off the ~** arrancar/apagar el motor

ignorance ['ɪgnərəns] n ignorancia

ignorant ['ɪgnərənt] adj ignorante; **to be ~ of** ignorar

ignore [ɪg'nɔ:'] vt (person, advice) no hacer caso de; (fact) pasar por alto

I'll [aɪl] = I will; I shall

ill [ɪl] adj enfermo, malo ♦ n mal m ♦ adv mal; **to be taken ~** ponerse enfermo

illegal [ɪ'li:gl] adj ilegal

illegible [ɪ'ledʒɪbl] adj ilegible

illegitimate [ɪlɪ'dʒɪtɪmət] adj ilegítimo

ill health n mala salud f; **to be in ~** estar mal de salud

illiterate [ɪ'lɪtərət] adj analfabeto

illness ['ɪlnɪs] n enfermedad f

illuminate [ɪ'lu:mɪneɪt] vt (room, street) iluminar, alumbrar

illusion [ɪ'lu:ʒən] n ilusión f; (trick) truco

illustrate ['ɪləstreɪt] vt ilustrar

illustration [ɪlə'streɪʃən] n (act of illustrating) ilustración f; (example) ejemplo, ilustración f; (in book) lámina

I'm [aɪm] = **I am**

image ['ɪmɪdʒ] n imagen f

imaginary [ɪ'mædʒɪnərɪ] adj imaginario

imagination [ɪmædʒɪ'neɪʃən] n imaginación f; (inventiveness) inventiva

imaginative [ɪ'mædʒɪnətɪv] adj imaginativo

imagine [ɪ'mædʒɪn] vt imaginarse

imbalance [ɪm'bæləns] n desequilibrio

imitate ['ɪmɪteɪt] vt imitar
□ **imitation** [ɪmɪ'teɪʃən] n imitación f; (copy) copia

immaculate [ɪ'mækjulət] adj inmaculado

immature [ɪmə'tjuə'] adj (person) inmaduro

immediate [ɪ'mi:dɪət] adj inmediato; (pressing) urgente, apremiante; (nearest: family) próximo; (: neighbourhood) inmediato
□ **immediately** adv (at once) en seguida; (directly) inmediatamente; **immediately next to** muy junto a

immense [ɪ'mens] adj inmenso, enorme; (importance) enorme
□ **immensely** adv enormemente

immerse [ɪ'mɜ:s] vt (submerge) sumergir; **to be immersed in** (fig) estar absorto en

immigrant ['ɪmɪɡrənt] n inmigrante mf □ **immigration** [ɪmɪ'ɡreɪʃən] n inmigración f

imminent ['ɪmɪnənt] adj inminente

immoral [ɪ'mɒrəl] adj inmoral

immortal [ɪ'mɔ:tl] adj inmortal

immune [ɪ'mju:n] adj: **~ (to)** inmune (a) □ **immune system** n sistema m inmunitario

immunize ['ɪmjunaɪz] vt inmunizar

impact ['ɪmpækt] n impacto

impair [ɪm'pɛə'] vt perjudicar

impartial [ɪm'pɑ:ʃl] adj imparcial

impatience [ɪm'peɪʃəns] n impaciencia

impatient [ɪm'peɪʃənt] adj impaciente; **to get** or **grow ~** impacientarse

impeccable [ɪm'pekəbl] adj impecable

impending [ɪm'pendɪŋ] adj inminente

imperative [ɪm'perətɪv] adj (tone) imperioso; (need) imprescindible ♦ n (LING: also: **~ tense**) imperativo

imperfect [ɪm'pɜ:fɪkt] adj (goods etc) defectuoso ♦ n (LING: also: **~ tense**) imperfecto

imperial [ɪm'pɪərɪəl] adj imperial

impersonal [ɪm'pɜ:sənl] adj impersonal

impersonate [ɪm'pɜ:səneɪt] vt hacerse pasar por; (THEATRE) imitar

impetus ['ɪmpɪtəs] n ímpetu m; (fig) impulso

implant [ɪm'plɑ:nt] vt (MED) injertar, implantar; (fig: idea, principle) inculcar

implement [n 'ɪmplɪmənt, vb 'ɪmplɪment] n herramienta f; (for cooking) utensilio ♦ vt (regulation) hacer efectivo; (plan) realizar

implicate ['ɪmplɪkeɪt] vt (compromise) comprometer; **to ~ sb in sth** comprometer a algn en algo

implication [ɪmplɪ'keɪʃən] n consecuencia f; **by ~** indirectamente

implicit [ɪm'plɪsɪt] adj implícito; (belief, trust) absoluto

imply [ɪm'plaɪ] vt (involve) suponer; (hint) dar a entender que

impolite [ɪmpə'laɪt] adj mal educado

import [vb ɪm'pɔ:t, n 'ɪmpɔ:t] vt importar ♦ n (COMM) importación f;

(: *article*) producto importado; (*meaning*) significado, sentido

importance [ɪmˈpɔːtəns] *n* importancia

important [ɪmˈpɔːtənt] *adj* importante; **it's not** ~ no importa, no tiene importancia

importer [ɪmˈpɔːtəʳ] *n* importador(a) *m/f*

impose [ɪmˈpəuz] *vt* imponer ♦ *vi*: **to ~ on sb** abusar de algn ❑ **imposing** *adj* imponente, impresionante

impossible [ɪmˈpɒsɪbl] *adj* imposible; (*person*) insoportable

impotent [ˈɪmpətənt] *adj* impotente

impoverished [ɪmˈpɒvərɪʃt] *adj* necesitado

impractical [ɪmˈpræktɪkl] *adj* (*person*, *plan*) poco práctico

impress [ɪmˈpres] *vt* impresionar; (*mark*) estampar; **to ~ sth on sb** hacer entender algo a algn

impression [ɪmˈpreʃən] *n* impresión *f*; (*imitation*) imitación *f*; **to be under the ~ that** tener la impresión de que

impressive [ɪmˈpresɪv] *adj* impresionante

imprison [ɪmˈprɪzn] *vt* encarcelar ❑ **imprisonment** *n* encarcelamiento; (*term of imprisonment*) cárcel *f*

improbable [ɪmˈprɒbəbl] *adj* improbable, inverosímil

improper [ɪmˈprɒpəʳ] *adj* (*unsuitable*: *conduct etc*) incorrecto; (: *activities*) deshonesto

improve [ɪmˈpruːv] *vt* mejorar; (*foreign language*) perfeccionar ♦ *vi* mejorarse ❑ **improvement** *n* mejoramiento; perfección *f*; progreso

improvise [ˈɪmprəvaɪz] *vt, vi* improvisar

impulse [ˈɪmpʌls] *n* impulso; **to act on ~** obrar sin reflexión ❑ **impulsive** [ɪmˈpʌlsɪv] *adj* irreflexivo

in

[ɪn] *prep*

1 (*indicating place, position, with place names*) en; **in the house/garden** en (la) casa/el jardín; **in here/there** aquí/allí or allá dentro; **in London/ England** en Londres/Inglaterra

2 (*indicating time*) en; **in spring** en (la) primavera; **in the afternoon** por la tarde; **at 4 o'clock in the afternoon** a las 4 de la tarde; **I did it in 3 hours/ days** lo hice en 3 horas/días; **I'll see you in 2 weeks** or **in 2 weeks' time** te veré dentro de 2 semanas

3 (*indicating manner etc*) en; **in a loud/soft voice** en voz alta/baja; **in pencil/ink** a lápiz/bolígrafo; **the boy in the blue shirt** el chico de la camisa azul

4 (*indicating circumstances*): **in the sun/shade/rain** al sol/a la sombra/ bajo la lluvia; **a change in policy** un cambio de política

5 (*indicating mood, state*): **in tears** en lágrimas, llorando; **in anger/despair** enfadado/desesperado; **to live in luxury** vivir lujosamente

6 (*with ratios, numbers*): **1 in 10 households, 1 household in 10** una de cada 10 familias; **20 pence in the pound** 20 peniques por libra; **they lined up in twos** se alinearon de dos en dos

7 (*referring to people, works*) en; entre; **the disease is common in children** la enfermedad es común entre los niños; **in (the works of) Dickens** en (las obras de) Dickens

8 (*indicating profession etc*): **to be in teaching** estar en la enseñanza

9 (*after superlative*) de; **the best pupil**

in the class el (la) mejor alumno(-a) de la clase
16 (with present participle): **in saying this** al decir esto
♦ adv: **to be in** (person: at home) estar en casa; (at work) estar; (train, ship, plane) haber llegado; (in fashion) estar de moda; **she'll be in later today** llegará más tarde hoy; **to ask sb in** hacer pasar a algn; **to run/limp** etc **in** entrar corriendo/cojeando etc
♦ n: **the ins and outs** (of proposal, situation etc) los detalles

inability [ɪnəˈbɪlɪtɪ] n: ~ **(to do)** incapacidad f (de hacer)

inaccurate [ɪnˈækjʊrət] adj inexacto, incorrecto

inadequate [ɪnˈædɪkwət] adj (income, reply etc) insuficiente; (person) incapaz

inadvertently [ɪnədˈvɜːtntlɪ] adv por descuido

inappropriate [ɪnəˈprəʊprɪət] adj inadecuado; (improper) poco oportuno

inaugurate [ɪˈnɔːgjʊreɪt] vt inaugurar; (president, official) investir

Inc. (US) abbr (= incorporated) S.A.

incapable [ɪnˈkeɪpəbl] adj incapaz

incense [n ˈɪnsens, vb ɪnˈsens] n incienso ♦ vt (anger) indignar, encolerizar

incentive [ɪnˈsentɪv] n incentivo, estímulo

inch [ɪntʃ] n pulgada; **to be within an ~ of** estar a dos dedos de; **he didn't give an ~** no dio concesión alguna

incidence [ˈɪnsɪdns] n (of crime, disease) incidencia

incident [ˈɪnsɪdnt] n incidente m

incidentally [ɪnsɪˈdentəlɪ] adv (by the way) a propósito

inclination [ɪnklɪˈneɪʃən] n (tendency) tendencia, inclinación f; (desire) deseo; (disposition) propensión f

incline [n ˈɪnklaɪn, vb ɪnˈklaɪn] n pendiente m, cuesta ♦ vt (head) poner de lado ♦ vi inclinarse; **to be inclined to** (tend) tener tendencia a hacer algo

include [ɪnˈkluːd] vt (incorporate) incluir; (in letter) adjuntar □ **including** prep incluso, inclusive

inclusion [ɪnˈkluːʒən] n inclusión f

inclusive [ɪnˈkluːsɪv] adj inclusivo; **~ of tax** incluidos los impuestos

income [ˈɪnkʌm] n (earned) ingresos mpl; (from property etc) renta; (from investment etc) rédito □ **income support** n (BRIT) ≈ ayuda familiar □ **income tax** n impuesto sobre la renta

incoming [ˈɪnkʌmɪŋ] adj (flight, government etc) entrante

incompatible [ɪnkəmˈpætɪbl] adj incompatible

incompetence [ɪnˈkɒmpɪtəns] n incompetencia

incompetent [ɪnˈkɒmpɪtənt] adj incompetente

incomplete [ɪnkəmˈpliːt] adj (partial: achievement etc) incompleto; (unfinished: painting etc) inacabado

inconsistent [ɪnkənˈsɪstənt] adj inconsecuente; (contradictory) incongruente; **~ with** (que) no concuerda con

inconvenience [ɪnkənˈviːnjəns] n inconveniencias mpl, (trouble) molestia, incomodidad f ♦ vt incomodar

inconvenient [ɪnkənˈviːnjənt] adj incómodo, poco práctico; (time, place, visitor) inoportuno

incorporate [ɪnˈkɔːpəreɪt] vt incorporar; (contain) comprender; (add) agregar

incorrect [ɪnkəˈrekt] adj incorrecto

increase [n ˈɪnkriːs, vb ɪnˈkriːs] n aumento ♦ vi aumentar; (grow) crecer; (price) subir ♦ vt aumentar; (price) subir □ **increasingly** adv cada vez más, más y más

incredible [ɪnˈkrɛdɪbl] adj increíble □ **incredibly** adv increíblemente

incur [ɪnˈkəː] vt (expenditure) incurrir; (loss) sufrir; (anger, disapproval) provocar

indecent [ɪnˈdiːsnt] adj indecente

indeed [ɪnˈdiːd] adv efectivamente, en realidad; (in fact) en efecto; (furthermore) es más; **yes ~!** ¡claro que sí!

indefinitely [ɪnˈdɛfɪnɪtlɪ] adv (wait) indefinidamente

independence [ɪndɪˈpɛndns] n independencia □ **Independence Day** (US) n Día m de la Independencia

INDEPENDENCE DAY

El cuatro de julio es **Independence Day**, la fiesta nacional de Estados Unidos, que se celebra en conmemoración de la Declaración de Independencia, escrita por Thomas Jefferson y aprobada en 1776. En ella se proclamaba la independencia total de Gran Bretaña de las trece colonias americanas que serían el origen de los Estados Unidos de América.

independent [ɪndɪˈpɛndnt] adj independiente □ **independent school** n (BRIT) escuela f privada, colegio m privado

index [ˈɪndɛks] (pl **indexes**) n (in book) índice m; (: in library etc) catálogo; (pl **indices**: ratio, sign) exponente m

India [ˈɪndɪə] n la India □ **Indian** adj, n indio(-a); **Red Indian** piel roja mf

indicate [ˈɪndɪkeɪt] vt indicar □ **indication** [-ˈkeɪʃən] n indicio, señal f □ **indicative** [ɪnˈdɪkətɪv] adj; **to be indicative of** indicar □ **indicator** n indicador m; (AUT) intermitente m

indices [ˈɪndɪsiːz] npl of **index**

indict [ɪnˈdaɪt] vt acusar □ **indictment** n acusación f

indifference [ɪnˈdɪfrəns] n indiferencia

indifferent [ɪnˈdɪfrənt] adj indiferente; (mediocre) regular

indigenous [ɪnˈdɪdʒɪnəs] adj indígena

indigestion [ɪndɪˈdʒɛstʃən] n indigestión f

indignant [ɪnˈdɪgnənt] adj: **to be ~ at sth/with sb** indignarse por algo/con algn

indirect [ɪndɪˈrɛkt] adj indirecto

indispensable [ɪndɪsˈpɛnsəbl] adj indispensable, imprescindible

individual [ɪndɪˈvɪdjuəl] n individuo ♦ adj individual; (personal) personal; (particular) particular □ **individually** adv (singly) individualmente

Indonesia [ɪndəˈniːzɪə] n Indonesia

indoor [ˈɪndɔː] adj (swimming pool) cubierto; (plant) de interior; (sport) bajo cubierta □ **indoors** [ɪnˈdɔːz] adv dentro

induce [ɪnˈdjuːs] vt inducir, persuadir; (bring about) producir; (labour) provocar

indulge [ɪnˈdʌldʒ] vt (whim) satisfacer; (person) complacer; (child) mimar ♦ vi: **to ~ in** darse el gusto de □ **indulgent** adj indulgente

industrial [ɪnˈdʌstrɪəl] adj industrial □ **industrial estate** (BRIT) n polígono (SP) or zona (LAm) industrial □ **industrialist** n industrial mf □ **industrial park** (US) n = **industrial estate**

industry [ˈɪndəstrɪ] n industria; (diligence) aplicación f

inefficient [ɪnɪˈfɪʃnt] adj ineficaz, ineficiente

inequality [ɪnɪˈkwɔlɪtɪ] n desigualdad f

inevitable [ɪnˈɛvɪtəbl] adj inevitable □ **inevitably** adv inevitablemente

inexpensive [ɪnɪkˈspɛnsɪv] adj económico

inexperienced [ɪnɪkˈspɪərɪənst] adj inexperto

inexplicable [ɪnɪkˈsplɪkəbl] adj inexplicable

infamous ['ɪnfəməs] *adj* infame

infant ['ɪnfənt] *n* niño(-a); *(baby)* niño(-a) pequeño(-a), bebé *mf*; *(pej)* aniñado

infantry ['ɪnfəntrɪ] *n* infantería

infant school *(BRIT) n* parvulario

infect [ɪn'fɛkt] *vt (wound)* infectar; *(food)* contaminar; *(person, animal)* contagiar ❑ **infection** [ɪn'fɛkʃən] *n* infección *f*; *(fig)* contagio ❑ **infectious** [ɪn'fɛkʃəs] *adj (also fig)* contagioso

infer [ɪn'fə:] *vt* deducir, inferir

inferior [ɪn'fɪərɪə] *adj, n* inferior *mf*

infertile [ɪn'fə:taɪl] *adj* estéril; *(person)* infecundo ❑ **infertility** [ɪnfə:'tɪlɪtɪ] *n* esterilidad *f*; infecundidad *f*

infested [ɪn'fɛstɪd] *adj:* ~ **with** plagado de

infinite ['ɪnfɪnɪt] *adj* infinito ❑ **infinitely** *adv* infinitamente

infirmary [ɪn'fə:mərɪ] *n* hospital *m*

inflamed [ɪn'fleɪmd] *adj:* **to become** ~ inflamarse

inflammation [ɪnflə'meɪʃən] *n* inflamación *f*

inflatable [ɪn'fleɪtəbl] *adj (ball, boat)* inflable

inflate [ɪn'fleɪt] *vt (tyre, price etc)* inflar; *(fig)* hinchar ❑ **inflation** [ɪn'fleɪʃən] *n (ECON)* inflación *f*

inflexible [ɪn'flɛksəbl] *adj (rule)* rígido; *(person)* inflexible

inflict [ɪn'flɪkt] *vt:* **to ~ sth on sb** infligir algo en algn

influence ['ɪnfluəns] *n* influencia ♦ *vt* influir en, influenciar; **under the ~ of alcohol** en estado de embriaguez ❑ **influential** [-'ɛnʃl] *adj* influyente

influx ['ɪnflʌks] *n* afluencia

info *(inf)* ['ɪnfəu] *n* = **information**

inform [ɪn'fɔ:m] *vt:* **to ~ sb of sth** informar a algn sobre *or* de algo ♦ *vi:* **to ~ on sb** delatar a algn

informal [ɪn'fɔ:məl] *adj (manner, tone)* familiar; *(dress, interview, occasion)* informal; *(visit, meeting)* extraoficial

information [ɪnfə'meɪʃən] *n* información *f*; *(knowledge)* conocimientos *mpl*; **a piece of** ~ un dato ❑ **information office** *n* información *f* ❑ **information technology** *n* informática

informative [ɪn'fɔ:mətɪv] *adj* informativo

infra-red [ɪnfrə'rɛd] *adj* infrarrojo

infrastructure ['ɪnfrəstrʌktʃə'] *n (of system etc)* infraestructura

infrequent [ɪn'fri:kwənt] *adj* infrecuente

infuriate [ɪn'fjuərɪeɪt] *vt:* **to become infuriated** ponerse furioso

infuriating [ɪn'fjuərɪeɪtɪŋ] *adj (habit, noise)* enloquecedor(a)

ingenious [ɪn'dʒi:njəs] *adj* ingenioso

ingredient [ɪn'gri:dɪənt] *n* ingrediente *m*

inhabit [ɪn'hæbɪt] *vt* vivir en ❑ **inhabitant** *n* habitante *mf*

inhale [ɪn'heɪl] *vt* inhalar ♦ *vi (breathe in)* aspirar; *(in smoking)* tragar ❑ **inhaler** *n* inhalador *m*

inherent [ɪn'hɪərənt] *adj:* ~ **in** *or* **to** inherente a

inherit [ɪn'hɛrɪt] *vt* heredar ❑ **inheritance** *n* herencia *f*; *(fig)* patrimonio

inhibit [ɪn'hɪbɪt] *vt* inhibir, impedir ❑ **inhibition** [-'bɪʃən] *n* cohibición *f*

initial [ɪ'nɪʃl] *adj* primero ♦ *n* inicial *f* ♦ *vt* firmar con las iniciales; **initials** *npl (as signature)* iniciales *fpl*; *(abbreviation)* siglas *fpl* ❑ **initially** *adv* al principio

initiate [ɪ'nɪʃɪeɪt] *vt* iniciar; **to ~ proceedings against sb** *(LAW)* entablar proceso contra algn

initiative [ɪ'nɪʃətɪv] *n* iniciativa

inject [ɪn'dʒɛkt] vt inyectar; **to ~ sb with sth** inyectar algo a algn □ **injection** [ɪn'dʒɛkʃən] n inyección f

injure ['ɪndʒə*] vt (hurt) herir, lastimar; (fig: reputation etc) perjudicar □ **injured** adj (person, arm) herido, lastimado □ **injury** n herida, lesión f; (wrong) perjuicio, daño

⚠ Be careful not to translate **injury** by the Spanish word **injuria**.

injustice [ɪn'dʒʌstɪs] n injusticia

ink [ɪŋk] n tinta □ **ink-jet printer** ['ɪŋkdʒɛt-] n impresora f de chorro de tinta

inland [adj 'ɪnlənd, adv ɪn'lænd] adj (waterway, port etc) interior ♦ adv tierra adentro □ **Inland Revenue** (BRIT) n departamento de impuestos, ≈ Hacienda (SP)

in-laws ['ɪnlɔ:z] npl suegros mpl

inmate ['ɪnmeɪt] n (in prison) preso(-a), presidiario(-a); (in asylum) internado(-a)

inn [ɪn] n posada, mesón m

inner ['ɪnə*] adj (courtyard, calm) interior; (feelings) íntimo □ **inner-city** adj (schools, problems) de las zonas céntricas pobres, de los barrios céntricos pobres

inning ['ɪnɪŋ] n (US: BASEBALL) inning m, entrada; **innings** (CRICKET) entrada, turno

innocence ['ɪnəsns] n inocencia

innocent ['ɪnəsnt] adj inocente

innovation [ɪnəʊ'veɪʃən] n novedad f

innovative ['ɪnəʊ'veɪtɪv] adj innovador

in-patient ['ɪnpeɪʃənt] n paciente m/f interno(-a)

input ['ɪnpʊt] n entrada; (of resources) inversión f; (COMPUT) entrada de datos

inquest ['ɪnkwɛst] n (coroner's) encuesta judicial

inquire [ɪn'kwaɪə*] vi preguntar ♦ vt: **to ~ whether** preguntar si; **to ~ about** (person) preguntar por; (fact) informarse de □ **inquiry** n pregunta; (investigation) investigación f, pesquisa; **"Inquiries"** "Información"

ins. abbr = **inches**

insane [ɪn'seɪn] adj loco; (MED) demente

insanity [ɪn'sænɪtɪ] n demencia, locura

insect ['ɪnsɛkt] n insecto □ **insect repellent** n loción f contra insectos

insecure [ɪnsɪ'kjʊə*] adj inseguro

insecurity [ɪnsɪ'kjʊərɪtɪ] n inseguridad f

insensitive [ɪn'sɛnsɪtɪv] adj insensible

insert [vb ɪn'sɜːt, n 'ɪnsɜːt] vt (into sth) introducir ♦ n encarte m

inside ['ɪn'saɪd] n interior m ♦ adj interior, interno ♦ adv (be) (por) dentro; (go) hacia dentro ♦ prep dentro de; (of time): **~ 10 minutes** en menos de 10 minutos □ **inside lane** n (AUT: in Britain) carril m izquierdo; (: in US, Europe etc) carril m derecho □ **inside out** adv (turn) al revés; (know) a fondo

insight ['ɪnsaɪt] n perspicacia

insignificant [ɪnsɪg'nɪfɪkənt] adj insignificante

insincere [ɪnsɪn'sɪə*] adj poco sincero

insist [ɪn'sɪst] vi insistir; **to ~ on** insistir en; **to ~ that** insistir en que; (claim) exigir que □ **insistent** adj insistente; (noise, action) persistente

insomnia [ɪn'sɒmnɪə] n insomnio

inspect [ɪn'spɛkt] vt inspeccionar, examinar; (troops) pasar revista a □ **inspection** [ɪn'spɛkʃən] n inspección f, examen m; (of troops) revista □ **inspector** n inspector(a) m/f; (BRIT: on buses, trains) revisor(a) m/f

inspiration [ɪnspə'reɪʃən] n inspiración f □ **inspire** [ɪn'spaɪə*] vt □ **inspiring** adj inspirador(a)

instability [ɪnstə'bɪlɪtɪ] n inestabilidad f

install [ɪnˈstɔːl] (*US* **instal**) *vt* instalar; (*official*) nombrar □ **installation** [ɪnstəˈleɪʃən] *n* instalación *f*

instalment [ɪnˈstɔːlmənt] (*US* **installment**) *n* plazo; (*of story*) entrega; (*of TV serial etc*) capítulo; **in instalments** (*pay, receive*) a plazos

instance [ˈɪnstəns] *n* ejemplo, caso; **for ~** por ejemplo; **in the first ~** en primer lugar

instant [ˈɪnstənt] *n* instante *m*, momento ♦ *adj* inmediato; (*coffee etc*) instantáneo □ **instantly** *adv* en seguida

instead [ɪnˈsted] *adv* en cambio; **~ of** en lugar de, en vez de

instinct [ˈɪnstɪŋkt] *n* instinto □ **instinctive** *adj* instintivo

institute [ˈɪnstɪtjuːt] *n* instituto; (*professional body*) colegio ♦ *vt* (*begin*) iniciar, empezar; (*proceedings*) entablar; (*system, rule*) establecer

institution [ɪnstɪˈtjuːʃən] *n* institución *f*; (*MED: home*) asilo; (: *asylum*) manicomio; (*of system etc*) establecimiento; (*of custom*) iniciación *f*

instruct [ɪnˈstrʌkt] *vt*: **to ~ sb in sth** instruir a algn en *o* sobre algo; **to ~ sb to do sth** dar instrucciones a algn de hacer algo □ **instruction** [ɪnˈstrʌkʃən] *n* (*teaching*) instrucción *f*; **instructions** *npl* (*orders*) órdenes *fpl*; **instructions (for use)** modo de empleo □ **instructor** *n* instructor(a) *m/f*

instrument [ˈɪnstrəmənt] *n* instrumento □ **instrumental** [-ˈmentl] *adj* (*MUS*) instrumental; **to be instrumental in** ser (el) artífice de

insufficient [ɪnsəˈfɪʃənt] *adj* insuficiente

insulate [ˈɪnsjuleɪt] *vt* aislar □ **insulation** [-ˈleɪʃən] *n* aislamiento *m*

insulin [ˈɪnsjulɪn] *n* insulina

insult [*n* ˈɪnsʌlt, *vb* ɪnˈsʌlt] *n* insulto ♦ *vt* insultar □ **insulting** *adj* insultante

insurance [ɪnˈʃuərəns] *n* seguro; **fire/ life ~** seguro contra incendios/sobre la vida □ **insurance company** *n* compañía *f* de seguros □ **insurance policy** *n* póliza (de seguros)

insure [ɪnˈʃuə] *vt* asegurar

intact [ɪnˈtækt] *adj* íntegro; (*unharmed*) intacto

intake [ˈɪnteɪk] *n* (*of food*) ingestión *f*; (*of air*) consumo; (*BRIT SCOL*): **an ~ of 200 a year** 200 matriculados al año

integral [ˈɪntɪɡrəl] *adj* (*whole*) íntegro; (*part*) integrante

integrate [ˈɪntɪɡreɪt] *vt* integrar ♦ *vi* integrarse

integrity [ɪnˈteɡrɪtɪ] *n* honradez *f*, rectitud *f*

intellect [ˈɪntəlekt] *n* intelecto □ **intellectual** [-ˈlektjuəl] *adj, n* intelectual *mf*

intelligence [ɪnˈtelɪdʒəns] *n* inteligencia

intelligent [ɪnˈtelɪdʒənt] *adj* inteligente

intend [ɪnˈtend] *vt* (*gift etc*): **to ~ sth for** destinar algo a; **to ~ to do sth** tener intención de *or* pensar hacer algo

intense [ɪnˈtens] *adj* intenso

intensify [ɪnˈtensɪfaɪ] *vt* intensificar; (*increase*) aumentar

intensity [ɪnˈtensɪtɪ] *n* (*gen*) intensidad *f*

intensive [ɪnˈtensɪv] *adj* intensivo □ **intensive care** *n*: **to be in intensive care** estar bajo cuidados intensivos □ **intensive care unit** *n* unidad *f* de vigilancia intensiva

intent [ɪnˈtent] *n* propósito; (*LAW*) premeditación *f* ♦ *adj* (*absorbed*) absorto; (*attentive*) atento; **to all intents and purposes** prácticamente; **to be ~ on doing sth** estar resuelto a hacer algo

intention [ɪnˈtenʃən] *n* intención *f*, propósito □ **intentional** *adj* deliberado

interact [ɪntər'ækt] *vi* influirse mutuamente □ **interaction** [ɪntər'ækʃən] *n* interacción *f*, acción *f* recíproca □ **interactive** *adj* (COMPUT) interactivo

intercept [ɪntə'sept] *vt* interceptar; (*stop*) detener

interchange ['ɪntətʃeɪndʒ] *n* intercambio; (*on motorway*) intersección *f*

intercourse ['ɪntəkɔːs] *n* (*sexual*) relaciones *fpl* sexuales

interest ['ɪntrɪst] *n* (*also COMM*) interés *m* ♦ *vt* interesar □ **interested** *adj* interesado; **to be interested in** interesarse por □ **interesting** *adj* interesante □ **interest rate** *n* tipo or tasa de interés

interface ['ɪntəfeɪs] *n* (COMPUT) junción *f*

interfere [ɪntə'fɪə] *vi*: **to ~ in** entrometerse en; **to ~ with** (*hinder*) estorbar; (*damage*) estropear

interference [ɪntə'fɪərəns] *n* intromisión *f*; (RADIO, TV) interferencia *f*

interim ['ɪntərɪm] *n*: **in the ~** en el interín ♦ *adj* provisional

interior [ɪn'tɪərɪə] *n* interior *m* ♦ *adj* interior □ **interior design** *n* interiorismo, decoración *f* de interiores

intermediate [ɪntə'miːdɪət] *adj* intermedio

intermission [ɪntə'mɪʃən] *n* intermisión *f*; (THEATRE) descanso

intern [*vb* ɪn'tɜːn, *n* 'ɪntɜːn] (US) *vt* internar ♦ *n* interno(-a)

internal [ɪn'tɜːnl] *adj* (*layout, pipes, security*) interior; (*injury, structure, memo*) internal □ **Internal Revenue Service** (US) *n* departamento de impuestos, ≈ Hacienda (SP)

international [ɪntə'næʃənl] *adj* internacional ♦ *n* (BRIT: *match*) partido internacional

Internet ['ɪntənet] *n*: **the ~ Internet** *m* or *f* □ **Internet café** *n* cibercafé *m* □ **Internet Service Provider** *n* proveedor *m* de (acceso a) Internet □ **Internet user** *n* internauta *mf*

interpret [ɪn'tɜːprɪt] *vt* interpretar; (*translate*) traducir; (*understand*) entender ♦ *vi* hacer de intérprete □ **interpretation** [ɪntəːprɪ'teɪʃən] *n* interpretación *f*; traducción *f* □ **interpreter** *n* intérprete *mf*

interrogate [ɪn'terəʊgeɪt] *vt* interrogar □ **interrogation** [-'geɪʃən] *n* interrogatorio □ **interrogative** [ɪntə'rɒgətɪv] *adj* interrogativo

interrupt [ɪntə'rʌpt] *vt, vi* interrumpir □ **interruption** [-'rʌpʃən] *n* interrupción *f*

intersection [ɪntə'sekʃən] *n* (*of roads*) cruce *m*

interstate ['ɪntəsteɪt] (US) *n* carretera interestatal

interval ['ɪntəvl] *n* intervalo; (BRIT THEATRE, SPORT) descanso; (SCOL) recreo; **at intervals** a ratos, de vez en cuando

intervene [ɪntə'viːn] *vi* intervenir; (*event*) interponerse; (*time*) transcurrir

interview ['ɪntəvjuː] *n* entrevista ♦ *vt* entrevistarse con □ **interviewer** *n* entrevistador(a) *m/f*

intimate [*adj* 'ɪntɪmət, *vb* 'ɪntɪmeɪt] *adj* íntimo; (*friendship*) estrecho; (*knowledge*) profundo ♦ *vt* dar a entender

intimidate [ɪn'tɪmɪdeɪt] *vt* intimidar, amedrentar

intimidating [ɪn'tɪmɪdeɪtɪŋ] *adj* amedrentador, intimidante

into ['ɪntuː] *prep* en; (*towards*) a; (*inside*) hacia el interior de; **~ 3 pieces/French** en 3 pedazos/al francés

intolerant [ɪn'tɒlərnt] *adj*: **~ (of)** intolerante (con o para)

intranet ['ɪntrənet] *n* intranet *f*

intransitive [ɪnˈtrænsɪtɪv] *adj*
intransitivo

intricate [ˈɪntrɪkət] *adj (design, pattern)*
intrincado

intrigue [ɪnˈtriːg] *n* intriga ♦ *vt* fascinar
❏ **intriguing** *adj* fascinante

introduce [ɪntrəˈdjuːs] *vt* introducir,
meter; *(speaker, TV show etc)* presentar;
to ~ sb (to sb) presentar a algn (a algn);
to ~ sb to *(pastime, technique)*
introducir a algn a ❏ **introduction**
[-ˈdʌkʃən] *n* introducción f; *(of person)*
presentación f ❏ **introductory**
[-ˈdʌktərɪ] *adj* introductorio; *(lesson,
offer)* de introducción

intrude [ɪnˈtruːd] *vi (person)*
entrometerse; **to ~ on** estorbar
❏ **intruder** *n* intruso(-a)

intuition [ɪntjuːˈɪʃən] *n* intuición f

inundate [ˈɪnʌndeɪt] *vt:* **to ~ with**
inundar de

invade [ɪnˈveɪd] *vt* invadir

invalid [*n* ˈɪnvəlɪd, *adj* ɪnˈvælɪd] *n (MED)*
minusválido(-a) ♦ *adj (not valid)*
inválido, nulo

invaluable [ɪnˈvæljuəbl] *adj*
inestimable

invariably [ɪnˈvɛərɪəblɪ] *adv* sin
excepción, siempre; **she is ~ late**
siempre llega tarde

invasion [ɪnˈveɪʒən] *n* invasión f

invent [ɪnˈvent] *vt* inventar
❏ **invention** [ɪnˈvenʃən] *n* invento;
(lie) ficción f, mentira ❏ **inventor** *n*
inventor(a) *m/f*

inventory [ˈɪnvəntrɪ] *n* inventario

inverted commas [ɪnˈvɜːtɪd-] *(BRIT)*
npl comillas *fpl*

invest [ɪnˈvest] *vt* invertir ♦ *vi:* **to ~ in**
(company etc) invertir dinero en; *(fig:*
sth useful) comprar

investigate [ɪnˈvestɪgeɪt] *vt* investigar
❏ **investigation** [-ˈgeɪʃən] *n*
investigación f, pesquisa

investigator [ɪnˈvestɪgeɪtə'] *n*
investigador(a) *m/f;* **private ~**
investigador(a) *m/f* privado(-a)

investment [ɪnˈvestmənt] *n* inversión
f

investor [ɪnˈvestə'] *n* inversionista *mf*

invisible [ɪnˈvɪzɪbl] *adj* invisible

invitation [ɪnvɪˈteɪʃən] *n* invitación f

invite [ɪnˈvaɪt] *vt* invitar; *(opinions etc)*
solicitar, pedir ❏ **inviting** *adj*
atractivo; *(food)* apetitoso

invoice [ˈɪnvɔɪs] *n* factura ♦ *vt* facturar

involve [ɪnˈvɒlv] *vt* suponer, implicar;
tener que ver con; *(concern, affect)*
corresponder; **to ~ sb (in sth)**
comprometer a algn (con algo)
❏ **involved** *adj* complicado; **to be
involved in** *(take part)* tomar parte en;
(be engrossed) estar muy metido en
❏ **involvement** *n* participación f;
dedicación f

inward [ˈɪnwəd] *adj (movement)*
interior, interno; *(thought, feeling)*
íntimo ❏ **inward(s)** *adv* hacia dentro

IQ *n abbr (= intelligence quotient)*
cociente *m* intelectual

IRA *n abbr (= Irish Republican Army)* IRA
m

Iran [ɪˈrɑːn] *n* Irán *m* ❏ **Iranian**
[ɪˈreɪnɪən] *adj, n* iraní *mf*

Iraq [ɪˈrɑːk] *n* Iraq ❏ **Iraqi** *adj,* iraquí
mf

Ireland [ˈaɪələnd] *n* Irlanda

iris [ˈaɪrɪs] *(pl* **irises)** *n (ANAT)* iris *m;* *(BOT)*
lirio

Irish [ˈaɪrɪʃ] *adj* irlandés(-esa) ♦ *npl:* **the
~ los irlandeses** ❏ **Irishman** *(irreg)* *n*
irlandés *m* ❏ **Irishwoman** *(irreg)* *n*
irlandésa

iron [ˈaɪən] *n* hierro; *(for clothes)*
plancha ♦ *cpd* de hierro ♦ *vt (clothes)*
planchar

ironic(al) [aɪˈrɒnɪk(l)] *adj* irónico
❏ **ironically** *adv* irónicamente

ironing [ˈaɪənɪŋ] *n (activity)* planchado;
(clothes: ironed) ropa planchada; *(: to be*

ironed) ropa por planchar ❑ **ironing board** *n* tabla de planchar

irony ['aɪrənɪ] *n* ironía

irrational [ɪ'ræʃənl] *adj* irracional

irregular [ɪ'regjulə*] *adj* irregular; (*surface*) desigual; (*action, event*) anómalo; (*behaviour*) poco ortodoxo

irrelevant [ɪ'reləvənt] *adj* fuera de lugar, inoportuno

irresistible [ɪrɪ'zɪstɪbl] *adj* irresistible

irresponsible [ɪrɪ'spɒnsɪbl] *adj* (*act*) irresponsable; (*person*) poco serio

irrigation [ɪrɪ'geɪʃən] *n* riego

irritable ['ɪrɪtəbl] *adj* (*person*) de mal humor

irritate ['ɪrɪteɪt] *vt* fastidiar; (*MED*) picar ❑ **irritating** *adj* fastidioso ❑ **irritation** [-'teɪʃən] *n* fastidio; enfado; picazón *f*

IRS (*US*) *n abbr* = **Internal Revenue Service**

is [ɪz] *vb see* **be**

ISDN *n abbr* (= *Integrated Services Digital Network*) RDSI *f*

Islam ['ɪzlɑːm] *n* Islam *m* ❑ **Islamic** [ɪz'læmɪk] *adj* islámico

island ['aɪlənd] *n* isla ❑ **islander** *n* isleño/a-*)

isle [aɪl] *n* isla

isn't ['ɪznt] = **is not**

isolated ['aɪsəleɪtɪd] *adj* aislado

isolation [aɪsə'leɪʃən] *n* aislamiento

ISP *n abbr* = **Internet Service Provider**

Israel ['ɪzreɪl] *n* Israel *m* ❑ **Israeli** [ɪz'reɪlɪ] *adj, n* israelí *mf*

issue ['ɪʃjuː] *n* (*problem, subject*) cuestión *f*; (*outcome*) resultado; (*of banknotes etc*) emisión *f*; (*of newspaper etc*) edición *f* ♦ *vt* (*rations, equipment*) distribuir, repartir; (*orders*) dar; (*certificate, passport*) expedir; (*decree*) promulgar; (*magazine*) publicar; (*cheques*) extender; (*banknotes, stamps*) emitir; **at** ~ en cuestión; **to take** ~ **with sb** (*over*) estar en

desacuerdo con algn (sobre); **to make an** ~ **of sth** hacer una cuestión de algo

IT *n abbr* = **information technology**

---

it

[ɪt] *pron*

1 (*specific subject: not generally translated*) él (ella); (: *direct object*) lo, la; (: *indirect object*) le; (*after prep*) él (ella); (*abstract concept*) ello; **it's on the table** está en la mesa; **I can't find it** no lo (*or* la) encuentro; **give it to me** dámelo (*or* dámela); **I spoke to him about it** le hablé del asunto; **what did you learn from it?** ¿qué aprendiste de él (*or* ella)?; **did you go to it?** (*party, concert etc*) ¿fuiste?

2 (*impersonal*) **it's raining** llueve, está lloviendo; **it's 6 o'clock/the 10th of August** son las 6/es el 10 de agosto; **how far is it?** — **it's 10 miles/2 hours on the train** ¿a qué distancia está? — a 10 millas/2 horas en tren; **who is it?** — **it's me** ¿quién es? — soy yo

---

Italian [ɪ'tæljən] *adj* italiano ♦ *n* italiano/a-); (*LING*) italiano

italics [ɪ'tælɪks] *npl* cursiva

Italy ['ɪtəlɪ] *n* Italia

itch [ɪtʃ] *n* picazón *f* ♦ *vi* (*part of body*) picar; **to** ~ **to do sth** rabiar por hacer algo ❑ **itching** *adj*: **my hand is itchy** me pica la mano

it'd ['ɪtd] = **it would; it had**

item ['aɪtəm] *n* artículo; (*on agenda*) asunto (*a tratar*); (*also:* **news** ~) noticia

itinerary [aɪ'tɪnərərɪ] *n* itinerario

it'll ['ɪtl] = **it will; it shall**

its [ɪts] *adj* su; sus *pl*

it's [ɪts] = **it is; it has**

itself [ɪt'self] *pron* (*reflexive*) sí mismo(-a); (*emphatic*) él mismo (ella misma)

ITV n abbr (BRIT: = Independent Television) cadena de televisión comercial independiente del Estado

I've [aɪv] = **I have**

ivory ['aɪvərɪ] n marfil m

ivy ['aɪvɪ] n (BOT) hiedra

J, j

jab [dʒæb] vt: **to ~ sth into sth** clavar algo en algo ♦ n (inf: MED) pinchazo

jack [dʒæk] n (AUT) gato; (CARDS) sota

jacket ['dʒækɪt] n chaqueta, americana (SP), saco (LAm); (of book) sobrecubierta ❑ **jacket potato** n patata asada (con piel)

jackpot ['dʒækpɔt] n premio gordo

Jacuzzi® [dʒə'ku:zɪ] n jacuzzi® m

jagged ['dʒægɪd] adj dentado

jail [dʒeɪl] n cárcel f ♦ vt encarcelar ❑ **jail sentence** n pena f de cárcel

jam [dʒæm] n mermelada; (also: **traffic ~**) embotellamiento; (inf: difficulty) apuro ♦ vt (passage etc) obstruir; (mechanism, drawer etc) atascar; (RADIO) interferir ♦ vi atascarse, trabarse; **to ~ sth into sth** meter algo a la fuerza en algo

Jamaica [dʒə'meɪkə] n Jamaica

jammed [dʒæmd] adj atascado

Jan abbr (= January) ene

janitor ['dʒænɪtə*] n (caretaker) portero, conserje m

January ['dʒænjuərɪ] n enero

Japan [dʒə'pæn] n (el) Japón ❑ **Japanese** [dʒæpə'ni:z] adj japonés(-esa) ♦ n inv japonés(-esa) m/f; (LING) japonés m

jar [dʒa:*] n tarro, bote m ♦ vi (sound) chirriar; (colours) desentonar

jargon ['dʒa:gən] n jerga

javelin ['dʒævlɪn] n jabalina

jaw [dʒɔ:] n mandíbula

jazz [dʒæz] n jazz m

jealous ['dʒeləs] adj celoso; (envious) envidioso ❑ **jealousy** n celos mpl; envidia

jeans [dʒi:nz] npl vaqueros mpl, tejanos mpl

Jello® ['dʒeləu] (US) n gelatina

jelly ['dʒelɪ] n (jam) jalea; (dessert etc) gelatina ❑ **jellyfish** n inv medusa, aguaviva (RPl)

jeopardize ['dʒepədaɪz] vt arriesgar, poner en peligro

jerk [dʒə:k] n (jolt) sacudida; (wrench) tirón m; (inf) imbécil m/f ♦ vt tirar bruscamente de ♦ vi (vehicle) traquetear

Jersey ['dʒə:zɪ] n Jersey m

jersey ['dʒə:zɪ] n jersey m; (fabric) (tejido de) punto

Jesus ['dʒi:zəs] n Jesús m

jet [dʒet] n (of gas, liquid) chorro; (AVIAT) avión m a reacción ❑ **jet lag** n desorientación f después de un largo vuelo ❑ **jet-ski** vi practicar el motociclismo acuático

jetty ['dʒetɪ] n muelle m, embarcadero

Jew [dʒu:] n judío(-a)

jewel ['dʒu:əl] n joya; (in watch) rubí m ❑ **jeweller** (US **jeweler**) n joyero(-a) ❑ **jeweller's (shop)** (US **jewelry store**) n joyería ❑ **jewellery** (US **jewelry**) n joyas fpl, alhajas fpl

Jewish ['dʒu:ɪʃ] adj judío

jigsaw ['dʒigsɔ:] n (also: **~ puzzle**) rompecabezas m inv, puzle m

job [dʒɔb] n (task) tarea; (post) empleo; **it's not my ~** no me incumbe a mí; **it's a good ~ that ...** menos mal que ...; **just the ~!** ¡estupendo! ❑ **job centre** (BRIT) n oficina estatal de colocaciones ❑ **jobless** adj sin trabajo

jockey ['dʒɔkɪ] n jockey m/f ♦ vi: **to ~ for position** maniobrar para conseguir una posición

jog [dʒɔg] vt empujar (ligeramente) ♦ vi (run) hacer footing; **to ~ sb's memory**

refrescar la memoria a algn ❑ **jogging** n *footing m*

join [dʒɔɪn] vt *(things)* juntar, unir; *(club)* hacerse socio de; *(POL: party)* afiliarse a; *(queue)* ponerse en; *(meet: people)* reunirse con ♦ vi *(roads)* juntarse; *(rivers)* confluir ♦ n juntura ▸ **join in** vi tomar parte, participar ♦ vt fus tomar parte o participar en ▸ **join up** vi reunirse; *(MIL)* alistarse

joiner [ˈdʒɔɪnə³] *(BRIT)* n carpintero(-a)

joint [dʒɔɪnt] n *(TECH)* junta, unión f; *(ANAT)* articulación f; *(BRIT CULIN)* pieza de carne (para asar); *(inf: place)* tugurio; *(: of cannabis)* porro ♦ adj *(common)* común; *(combined)* combinado ❑ **joint account** n *(with bank etc)* cuenta común ❑ **jointly** adv *(gen)* en común; *(together)* conjuntamente

joke [dʒəuk] n chiste m; *(also: practical ~)* broma ♦ vi bromear; **to play a ~ on** gastar una broma a ❑ **joker** n *(CARDS)* comodín m

jolly [ˈdʒɔlɪ] adj *(merry)* alegre; *(enjoyable)* divertido ♦ adv *(BRIT: inf)* muy, terriblemente

jolt [dʒəult] n *(jerk)* sacudida; *(shock)* susto ♦ vt *(physically)* sacudir; *(emotionally)* asustar

Jordan [ˈdʒɔːdən] n *(country)* Jordania; *(river)* Jordán m

journal [ˈdʒɜːnl] n *(magazine)* revista; *(diary)* periódico, diario ❑ **journalism** n periodismo ❑ **journalist** n periodista mf, reportero(-a)

journey [ˈdʒɜːnɪ] n viaje m; *(distance covered)* trayecto

joy [dʒɔɪ] n alegría ❑ **joyrider** n gamberro que roba un coche para dar una vuelta y luego abandonarlo ❑ **joy stick** n *(AVIAT)* palanca de mando; *(COMPUT)* palanca de control

Jr abbr = **junior**

judge [dʒʌdʒ] n juez mf; *(fig: expert)* perito ♦ vt juzgar; *(consider)* considerar

judo [ˈdʒuːdəu] n judo

jug [dʒʌɡ] n jarra

juggle [ˈdʒʌɡl] vi hacer juegos malabares ❑ **juggler** n malabarista mf

juice [dʒuːs] n zumo (SP), jugo (LAm) ❑ **juicy** adj jugoso

Jul abbr (= July) jul

July [dʒuːˈlaɪ] n julio

jumble [ˈdʒʌmbl] n revoltijo ♦ vt *(also: ~ up)* revolver ❑ **jumble sale** n *(BRIT)* venta de objetos usados con fines benéficos

JUMBLE SALE

Los **jumble sales** son unos mercadillos que se organizan con fines benéficos en los locales de un colegio, iglesia u otro centro público. En ellos puede comprarse todo tipo de artículos baratos de segunda mano, sobre todo ropa, juguetes, libros, vajillas o muebles.

jumbo [ˈdʒʌmbəu] n *(also: ~ jet)* jumbo

jump [dʒʌmp] vi saltar, dar saltos; *(with fear etc)* pegar un bote; *(increase)* aumentar ♦ vt saltar ♦ n salto; aumento; **to ~ the queue** *(BRIT)* colarse

jumper [ˈdʒʌmpə³] n *(BRIT: pullover)* suéter m, jersey m; *(US: dress)* mandil m

jumper cables (US) npl = **jump leads**

jump leads *(BRIT)* npl cables mpl puente de batería

Jun. abbr = **junior**

junction [ˈdʒʌŋkʃən] n *(BRIT: of roads)* cruce m; *(RAIL)* empalme m

June [dʒuːn] n junio

jungle [ˈdʒʌŋɡl] n selva, jungla

junior [ˈdʒuːnɪə³] adj *(in age)* menor, más joven; *(position)* subalterno ♦ n menor mf, joven mf ❑ **junior high school** (US) n centro de educación secundaria; see also **high school** ❑ **junior school** *(BRIT)* n escuela primaria

junk [dʒʌŋk] n (cheap goods) baratijas fpl; (rubbish) basura ◻ **junk food** n alimentos preparados y envasados de escaso valor nutritivo

junkie ['dʒʌŋki] (inf) n drogadicto(-a), yonqui mf

junk mail n propaganda de buzón

Jupiter ['dʒuːpɪtə'] n (MYTHOLOGY, ASTROLOGY) Júpiter m

jurisdiction [dʒuərɪs'dɪkʃən] n jurisdicción f; **it falls or comes within/ outside our ~** es/no es de nuestra competencia

jury ['dʒuərɪ] n jurado

just [dʒʌst] adj justo ♦ adv (exactly) exactamente; (only) sólo, solamente; **he's ~ done it/left** acaba de hacerlo/irse; **~ right** perfecto; **~ two o'clock** las dos en punto; **she's ~ as clever as you** (ella) es tan lista como tú; **~ as well that ...** menos mal que ...; **~ as he was leaving** en el momento en que se marchaba; **~ before/enough** justo antes/lo suficiente; **~ here** aquí mismo; **he ~ missed** ha fallado por poco; **~ listen to this** escucha esto un momento

justice ['dʒʌstɪs] n justicia; (US: judge) juez mf; **to do ~ to** (fig) hacer justicia a

justification [dʒʌstɪfɪ'keɪʃən] n justificación f

justify ['dʒʌstɪfaɪ] vt justificar; (text) alinear

jut [dʒʌt] vi (also: ~ **out**) sobresalir

juvenile ['dʒuːvənaɪl] adj (court) de menores; (humour, mentality) infantil ♦ n menor m de edad

K, k

K abbr (= one thousand) mil; (= kilobyte) kilobyte m, kilocoteto

kangaroo [kæŋgə'ruː] n canguro

karaoke [kɑːrə'əukɪ] n karaoke m

karate [kə'rɑːtɪ] n karate m

kebab [kə'bæb] n pincho moruno

keel [kiːl] n quilla; **on an even ~** (fig) en equilibrio

keen [kiːn] adj (interest, desire) grande, vivo; (eye, intelligence) agudo; (competition) reñido; (edge) afilado; (eager) entusiasta; **to be ~ to do or doing sth** tener muchas ganas de hacer algo; **to be ~ on sth/sb** interesarse por algo/algn

keep [kiːp] (pt, pp kept) vt (preserve, store) guardar; (hold back) quedarse con; (maintain) mantener; (detain) detener; (shop) ser propietario de; (feed: family etc) mantener; (promise) cumplir; (chickens, bees etc) criar; (accounts) llevar; (diary) escribir; (prevent): **to ~ sb from doing sth** impedir a algn hacer algo ♦ vi (food) conservarse; (remain) seguir, continuar ♦ n (of castle) torreón m; (food etc) comida, subsistencia; (inf): **for keeps** para siempre; **to ~ doing sth** seguir haciendo algo; **to ~ sb happy** tener a algn contento; **to ~ a place tidy** mantener un lugar limpio; **to ~ sth to o.s.** guardar algo para sí mismo; **to ~ sth (back) from sb** ocultar algo a algn; **to ~ time** (clock) mantener la hora exacta ▸ **keep away** vt: **to keep sth/ sb away from sb** mantener algo/a algn apartado de algn ♦ vi: **to keep away (from)** mantenerse apartado (de) ▸ **keep back** vt (crowd, tears) contener; (money) quedarse con; (conceal: information): **to keep sth back from sb** ocultar algo a algn ♦ vi hacerse a un lado ▸ **keep off** vt (dog, person) mantener a distancia ♦ vi: **if the rain keeps off** si no llueve; **keep your hands off!** ¡no toques!; "**keep off the grass**" "prohibido pisar el césped" ▸ **keep on** vi: **to keep on doing** seguir or continuar haciendo; **to keep on (about sth)** no parar de hablar (de algo) ▸ **keep out** vi (stay out) permanecer fuera; **"keep out"** "prohibida la entrada" ▶ **keep up** vt mantener, conservar ♦ vi no retrasarse; **to keep up with** (pace) ir al paso de; (level) mantenerse a la altura de ❏ **keeper** n guardián(-ana) m/f ❏ **keeping** n (care) cuidado; **in keeping with** de acuerdo con

kennel ['kenl] n perrera; **kennels** npl residencia canina

Kenya ['kenjə] n Kenia

kept [kept] pt, pp of **keep**

kerb [kə:b] n (BRIT) bordillo

kerosene ['kerəsi:n] n keroseno

ketchup ['ketʃəp] n salsa de tomate, catsup m

kettle ['ketl] n hervidor m de agua

key [ki:] n llave f; (MUS) tono; (of piano, typewriter) tecla ♦ adj (issue etc) clave inv ♦ vt (also: ~ **in**) teclear ❏ **keyboard** n teclado ❏ **keyhole** n ojo (de la cerradura) ❏ **keyring** n llavero

kg abbr (= kilogram) kg

khaki ['kɑ:kɪ] n caqui

kick [kɪk] vt dar una patada or un puntapié a; (inf: habit) quitarse de ♦ vi (horse) dar coces ♦ n patada; puntapié m; (of animal) coz f; (thrill; inf): **he does it for kicks** lo hace por pura diversión ▶ **kick off** vi (SPORT) hacer el saque inicial ❏ **kick-off** n saque inicial; **the kick-off is at 10 o'clock** el partido empieza a las diez

kid [kɪd] n (inf: child) chiquillo(-a); (animal) cabrito; (leather) cabritilla ♦ vi (inf) bromear

kidnap ['kɪdnæp] vt secuestrar ❏ **kidnapping** n secuestro

kidney ['kɪdnɪ] n riñón m ❏ **kidney bean** n judía, alubia

kill [kɪl] vt matar; (murder) asesinar ♦ n matanza; **to ~ time** matar el tiempo ❏ **killer** n asesino(-a) ❏ **killing** n (one) asesinato; (several) matanza; **to make a killing** (fig) hacer su agosto

kiln [kɪln] n horno

kilo ['ki:ləu] n kilo ❏ **kilobyte** n (COMPUT) kilobyte m, kilococteto ❏ **kilogram(me)** n kilo, kilogramo ❏ **kilometre** ['kɪləmi:tə] (US **kilometer**) n kilómetro ❏ **kilowatt** n kilovatio

kilt [kɪlt] n falda escocesa

kin [kɪn] n see **next-of-kin**

kind [kaɪnd] adj amable, atento ♦ n clase f, especie f; (species) género; **in ~** (COMM) en especie; **a ~ of** una especie de; **to be two of a ~** ser tal para cual

kindergarten ['kɪndəgɑ:tn] n jardín m de la infancia

kindly ['kaɪndlɪ] adj bondadoso; cariñoso ♦ adv bondadosamente, amablemente; **will you ~ ...** sea usted tan amable de ...

kindness ['kaɪndnɪs] n (quality) bondad f, amabilidad f; (act) favor m

king [kɪŋ] n rey m ❏ **kingdom** n reino ❏ **kingfisher** n martín m pescador ❏ **king-size(d) bed** n cama de matrimonio extragrande

kiosk ['ki:ɔsk] n quiosco; (BRIT TEL) cabina

kipper ['kɪpə'] n arenque m ahumado

kiss [kɪs] n beso ♦ vt besar; **to ~ (each other)** besarse ❏ **kiss of life** n respiración f boca a boca

kit [kɪt] n (equipment) equipo; (tools etc) (caja de herramientas fpl; (assembly kit) juego de armar

kitchen ['kɪtʃɪn] n cocina

kite [kaɪt] n (toy) cometa

kitten ['kɪtn] n gatito(-a)

kiwi ['ki:wi:-] n (also: ~ **fruit**) kiwi m

km abbr (= kilometre) km

km/h abbr (= kilometres per hour) km/h

knack [næk] n: **to have the ~ of doing sth** tener el don de hacer algo

knee [ni:] n rodilla ❏ **kneecap** n rótula

kneel [ni:l] (pt, pp knelt) vi (also: ~ **down**) arrodillarse

knelt [nelt] pt, pp of **kneel**

knew [njuː] *pt of* **know**

knickers ['nɪkəz] (*BRIT*) *npl* bragas *fpl*

knife [naɪf] (*pl* **knives**) *n* cuchillo ♦ *vt* acuchillar

knight [naɪt] *n* caballero; (*CHESS*) caballo

knit [nɪt] *vt* tejer, tricotar ♦ *vi* hacer punto, tricotar; (*bones*) soldarse; **to ~ one's brows** fruncir el ceño
❏ **knitting** *n* labor *f* de punto
❏ **knitting needle** *n* aguja de hacer punto ❏ **knitwear** *n* prendas *fpl* de punto

knives [naɪvz] *npl of* **knife**

knob [nɔb] *n* (*of door*) tirador *m*; (*of stick*) puño; (*on radio, TV*) botón *m*

knock [nɔk] *vt* (*strike*) golpear; (*bump into*) chocar contra; (*inf*) criticar ♦ *vi* (*at door etc*): **to ~ at/on** llamar a ♦ *n* golpe *m*; (*on door*) llamada ► **knock down** *vt* atropellar ► **knock off** (*inf*) *vi* (*finish*) salir del trabajo ♦ *vt* (*from price*) descontar; (*inf: steal*) birlar ► **knock out** *vt* dejar sin sentido; (*BOXING*) poner fuera de combate, dejar K.O.; (*in competition*) eliminar ► **knock over** *vt* (*object*) tirar; (*person*) atropellar
❏ **knockout** *n* (*BOXING*) K.O. *m*, knockout *m* ♦ *cpd* (*competition etc*) eliminatorio

knot [nɔt] *n* nudo ♦ *vt* anudar

know [nəu] (*pt* **knew**, *pp* **known**) *vt* (*facts*) saber; (*be acquainted with*) conocer; (*recognize*) reconocer, conocer; **to ~ how to swim** saber nadar; **to ~ about** or **of sb/sth** saber de algn/algo ❏ **know-all** *n* sabelotodo *mf* ❏ **know-how** *n* conocimientos *mpl* ❏ **knowing** *adj* (*look*) de complicidad ❏ **knowingly** *adv* (*purposely*) adrede; (*smile, look*) con complicidad ❏ **know-it-all** (*US*) *n* = **know-all**

knowledge ['nɔlɪdʒ] *n* conocimiento; (*learning*) saber *m*, conocimientos *mpl*
❏ **knowledgeable** *adj* entendido

known [nəun] *pp of* **know** ♦ *adj* (*thief, facts*) conocido; (*expert*) reconocido

knuckle ['nʌkl] *n* nudillo

koala [kəu'ɑːlə] *n* (*also*: **~ bear**) koala *m*

Koran [kɔ'rɑːn] *n* Corán *m*

Korea [kə'rɪə] *n* Corea ❏ **Korean** *adj*, *n* coreano(-a) *m/f*

kosher ['kəuʃə] *adj* autorizado por la ley judía

Kosovar, Kosovan *adj* kosovar

Kosovo ['kusəvəu] *n* Kosovo

Kremlin ['kremlɪn] *n*: **the ~** el Kremlin

Kuwait [ku'weɪt] *n* Kuwait *m*

L, l

L (*BRIT*) *abbr* = **learner driver**

l. *abbr* (= *litre*) l

lab [læb] *n abbr* = **laboratory**

label ['leɪbl] *n* etiqueta ♦ *vt* poner etiqueta a

labor *etc* ['leɪbə] (*US*) = **labour** *etc*

laboratory [lə'bɔrətərɪ] *n* laboratorio

Labor Day (*US*) *n* día *m* de los trabajadores (*primer lunes de septiembre*)

labor union (*US*) *n* sindicato

labour ['leɪbə] (*US* **labor**) *n* (*hard work*) trabajo; (*labour force*) mano *f* de obra; (*MED*): **to be in ~** estar de parto ♦ *vi*: **to ~ (at sth)** trabajar (en algo) ♦ *vt*: **to ~ a point** insistir en un punto; **L~, the L~ party** (*BRIT*) el partido laborista, los laboristas *mpl* ❏ **labourer** *n* peón *m*; **farm labourer** peón *m* de campo; (*day labourer*) jornalero

lace [leɪs] *n* encaje *m*; (*of shoe etc*) cordón *m* ♦ *vt* (*shoes: also*: **~ up**) atarse (los zapatos)

lack [læk] *n* (*absence*) falta ♦ *vt* faltarle a algn, carecer de; **through** or **for ~ of** por falta de; **to be lacking** faltar, no haber; **to be lacking in sth** faltarle a algn algo

lacquer ['lækəʳ] n laca

lacy ['leɪsɪ] adj (of lace) de encaje; (like lace) como de encaje

lad [læd] n muchacho, chico

ladder ['lædəʳ] n escalera (de mano); (BRIT: in tights) carrera

ladle ['leɪdl] n cucharón m

lady ['leɪdɪ] n señora; (dignified, graceful) dama; "**ladies and gentlemen ...**" "señoras y caballeros ..."; **young ~** señorita; **the ladies' (room)** los servicios de señoras □ **ladybird** (US **ladybug**) n mariquita

lag [læg] n retraso ♦ vi (also: ~ **behind**) retrasarse, quedarse atrás ♦ vt (pipes) revestir

lager ['lɑːɡəʳ] n cerveza (rubia)

lagoon [lə'ɡuːn] n laguna

laid [leɪd] pt, pp of **lay** □ **laid back** (inf) adj relajado

lain [leɪn] pp of **lie**

lake [leɪk] n lago

lamb [læm] n cordero; (meat) (carne f de) cordero

lame [leɪm] adj cojo; (excuse) poco convincente

lament [lə'mɛnt] n quejo ♦ vt lamentarse de

lamp [læmp] n lámpara □ **lamppost** (BRIT) n (poste m de) farol m □ **lampshade** n pantalla

land [lænd] n tierra; (country) país m; (piece of land) terreno; (estate) tierras fpl, finca f ♦ vi (from ship) desembarcar; (AVIAT) aterrizar; (fig: fall) caer, terminar ♦ vt (passengers, goods) desembarcar; **to ~ sb with sth** (inf) hacer cargar a algn con algo □ **landing** n aterrizaje m; (of staircase) rellano □ **landing card** n tarjeta de desembarque □ **landlady** n (of rented house, pub etc) dueña □ **landlord** n propietario; (of pub etc) patrón m □ **landmark** n lugar m conocido; **to be a landmark** (fig) marcar un hito histórico □ **landowner** n terrateniente mf

□ **landscape** n paisaje m □ **landslide** n (GEO) corrimiento de tierras; (fig: POL) victoria arrolladora

lane [leɪn] n (in country) camino; (AUT) carril m; (in race) calle f

language ['læŋɡwɪdʒ] n lenguaje m; (national tongue) idioma m, lengua; **bad ~** palabrotas fpl □ **language laboratory** n laboratorio de idiomas

lantern ['læntn] n linterna, farol m

lap [læp] n (of track) vuelta; (of body) regazo ♦ vt (also: ~ **up**) beber a lengüetadas ♦ vi (waves) chapotear; **to sit on sb's ~** sentarse en las rodillas de algn

lapel [lə'pɛl] n solapa

lapse [læps] n fallo; (moral) desliz m; (of time) intervalo ♦ vi (expire) caducar; (time) pasar, transcurrir; **to ~ into bad habits** caer en malos hábitos

laptop (computer) ['læptɔp-] n (ordenador m) portátil m

lard [lɑːd] n manteca (de cerdo)

larder ['lɑːdəʳ] n despensa

large [lɑːdʒ] adj grande; **at ~** (free) en libertad; (generally) en general □ **largely** adv (mostly) en su mayor parte; (introducing reason) en gran parte □ **large-scale** adj (map) en gran escala; (fig) importante

⚠ Be careful not to translate **large** by the Spanish word largo.

lark [lɑːk] n (bird) alondra; (joke) broma

laryngitis [lærɪn'dʒaɪtɪs] n laringitis f

lasagne [lə'zænjə] n lasaña

laser ['leɪzəʳ] n láser m □ **laser printer** n impresora (por) láser

lash [læʃ] n latigazo; (also: **eyelash**) pestaña ♦ vt azotar; (tie: **to ~ to/together** atar a/atar ► **lash out** vi: **to lash out (at sb)** (hit) arremeter (contra algn); **to lash out against sb** lanzar invectivas contra algn

lass [læs] (BRIT) n chica

last [lɑːst] *adj* último; (*end: of series etc*) final ♦ *adv* (*most recently*) la última vez; (*finally*) por último ♦ *vi* durar; (*continue*) continuar, seguir; **~ night** anoche; **~ week** la semana pasada; **at ~** por fin; **~ but one** penúltimo □ **lastly** *adv* por último, finalmente □ **last-minute** *adj* de última hora

latch [lætʃ] *n* pestillo ▶ **latch onto** *vt fus* (*person, group*) pegarse a; (*idea*) agarrarse a

late [leɪt] *adj* (*far on: in time, process etc*) al final de; (*not on time*) tarde, atrasado; (*dead*) fallecido ♦ *adv* tarde; (*behind time, schedule*) con retraso; **of ~** últimamente; **~ at night** a última hora de la noche; **in ~ May** hacia fines de mayo; **the ~ Mr X** el difunto Sr X □ **latecomer** *n* recién llegado(-a) □ **lately** *adv* últimamente □ **later** *adj* (*date etc*) posterior; (*version etc*) más reciente ♦ *adv* más tarde, después □ **latest** [ˈleɪtɪst] *adj* último; **at the latest** a más tardar

lather [ˈlɑːðəʳ] *n* espuma (de jabón) ♦ *vt* enjabonar

Latin [ˈlætɪn] *n* latín *m* ♦ *adj* latino □ **Latin America** *n* América latina □ **Latin American** *adj, n* latinoamericano(-a) *m/f*

latitude [ˈlætɪtjuːd] *n* latitud *f*; (*fig*) libertad *f*

latter [ˈlætəʳ] *adj* último; (*of two*) segundo ♦ *n*: **the ~** éste, éste

laugh [lɑːf] *n* risa ♦ *vi* reír(se); (**to do sth**) **for a ~** (*hacer algo*) en broma ▶ **laugh at** *vt fus* reírse de □ **laughter** *n* risa

launch [lɔːntʃ] *n* lanzamiento; (*boat*) lancha ♦ *vt* (*ship*) botar; (*rocket etc*) lanzar; (*fig*) comenzar ▶ **launch into** *vt fus* lanzarse a

launder [ˈlɔːndəʳ] *vt* lavar

Launderette® [lɔːnˈdret] (*BRIT*) *n* lavandería (automática)

Laundromat® [ˈlɔːndrəmæt] (*US*) *n* = **Launderette**

laundry [ˈlɔːndrɪ] *n* (*dirty*) ropa sucia; (*clean*) colada; (*room*) lavadero

lava [ˈlɑːvə] *n* lava

lavatory [ˈlævətərɪ] *n* wáter *m*

lavender [ˈlævəndəʳ] *n* lavanda

lavish [ˈlævɪʃ] *adj* (*amount*) abundante; (*person*): **~ with** pródigo en ♦ *vt*: **to ~ sth on sb** colmar a algn de algo

law [lɔː] *n* ley *f*; (*SCOL*) derecho; (*a rule*) regla; (*professions connected with law*) jurisprudencia □ **lawful** *adj* legítimo, lícito □ **lawless** *adj* (*action*) criminal

lawn [lɔːn] *n* césped *m* □ **lawnmower** *n* cortacésped *m*

lawsuit [ˈlɔːsuːt] *n* pleito

lawyer [ˈlɔːjəʳ] *n* abogado(-a); (*for sales, wills etc*) notario(-a)

lax [læks] *adj* laxo

laxative [ˈlæksətɪv] *n* laxante *m*

lay [leɪ] (*pt, pp* **laid**) *pp of* **lie** ♦ *adj* laico; (*not expert*) lego ♦ *vt* (*place*) colocar; (*eggs, table*) poner; (*cable*) tender; (*carpet*) extender ▶ **lay down** *vt* (*pen etc*) dejar; (*rules etc*) establecer; **to lay down the law** (*pej*) imponer las normas ▶ **lay off** *vt* (*workers*) despedir ▶ **lay on** *vt* (*meal, facilities*) proveer ▶ **lay out** *vt* (*spread out*) disponer, exponer □ **lay-by** (*BRIT AUT*) *n* área de aparcamiento

layer [ˈleɪəʳ] *n* capa

layman [ˈleɪmən] (*irreg*) *n* lego

layout [ˈleɪaut] *n* (*design*) plan *m*, trazado; (*PRESS*) composición *f*

lazy [ˈleɪzɪ] *adj* perezoso, vago; (*movement*) lento

lb. *abbr* = **pound** (*weight*)

lead¹ [liːd] (*pt, pp* **led**) *n* (*front position*) delantera; (*clue*) pista; (*ELEC*) cable *m*; (*for dog*) correa; (*THEATRE*) papel principal ♦ *vt* (*walk etc in front*) ir a la cabeza de; (*guide*): **to ~ sb somewhere** conducir a algn a algún sitio; (*be leader*) dirigir; (*start, guide: activity*) protagonizar ♦ *vi* (*road, pipe etc*) conducir y, primero; (*SPORT*) llevar la delantera; **to be in**

the ~ (SPORT) llevar la delantera; (fig) ir a la cabeza; **to ~ the way** llevar la delantera ▶ **lead up to** vt fus (events) conducir a; (in conversation) preparar el terreno para

lead² [lɛd] n (metal) plomo; (in pencil) mina

leader ['li:dəʳ] n jefe(-a) m/f, líder mf; (SPORT) líder mf □ **leadership** n dirección f; (position) mando; (quality) iniciativa

lead-free ['lɛdfri:] adj sin plomo

leading ['li:dɪŋ] adj (main) principal; (first) primero; (front) delantero

lead singer [li:d-] n cantante mf

leaf [li:f] (pl **leaves**) n hoja ♦ vi: **to ~ through** hojear; **to turn over a new ~** reformarse

leaflet ['li:flɪt] n folleto

league [li:g] n sociedad f; (FOOTBALL) liga; **to be in ~ with** haberse confabulado con

leak [li:k] n (of liquid, gas) escape m, fuga; (in pipe) agujero; (in roof) gotera; (in security) filtración f ♦ vi (shoes, ship) hacer agua; (pipe) tener (un) escape; (roof) gotear; (liquid, gas) escaparse, fugarse; (fig) divulgarse ♦ vt (fig) filtrar

lean [li:n] (pt, pp **leaned** or **leant**) adj (thin) flaco; (meat) magro ♦ vt: **to ~ sth on sth** apoyar algo en algo ♦ vi (slope) inclinarse; **to ~ against** apoyarse contra; **to ~ on** apoyarse en ▶ **lean forward** vi inclinarse hacia adelante ▶ **lean over** vi inclinarse □ **leaning** n: **leaning (towards)** inclinación f (hacia)

leant [lɛnt] pt, pp of **lean**

leap [li:p] (pt, pp **leaped** or **leapt**) n salto ♦ vi saltar

leapt [lɛpt] pt, pp of **leap**

leap year n año bisiesto

learn [lə:n] (pt, pp **learned** or **learnt**) vt aprender ♦ vi aprender; **to ~ about sth** enterarse de algo; **to ~ to do sth** aprender a hacer algo □ **learner** n (BRIT: also: **learner driver**) principiante

mf □ **learning** n el saber m, conocimientos mpl

learnt [lə:nt] pp of **learn**

lease [li:s] n arriendo ♦ vt arrendar

leash [li:ʃ] n correa

least [li:st] adj: **the ~** (slightest) el menor, el más pequeño; (smallest amount of) mínimo ♦ adv (+ vb) menos; (+ adj): **the ~ expensive** el (la) menos costoso(-a); **the ~ possible effort** el menor esfuerzo posible; **at ~** por lo menos, al menos; **you could at ~ have written** por lo menos podías haber escrito; **not in the ~** en absoluto

leather ['lɛðəʳ] n cuero

leave [li:v] (pt, pp **left**) vt dejar; (go away from) abandonar; (place etc: permanently) salir de ♦ vi irse; (train etc) salir ♦ n permiso; **to ~ sth to sb** (money etc) legar algo a algn; (responsibility etc) encargar a algn de algo; **to be left** quedar, sobrar; **there's some milk left over** sobra or queda algo de leche; **on ~** de permiso ▶ **leave behind** vt (on purpose) dejar; (accidentally) dejarse ▶ **leave out** vt omitir

leaves [li:vz] npl of **leaf**

Lebanon ['lɛbənən] n: **the ~** el Líbano

lecture ['lɛktʃəʳ] n conferencia; (SCOL) clase f ♦ vi dar una clase ♦ vt (scold): **to ~ sb on** or **about sth** echar una reprimenda a algn por algo; **to give a ~ on** dar una conferencia sobre □ **lecture hall** n sala de conferencias; (UNIV) aula □ **lecturer** n conferenciante mf; (BRIT: at university) profesor(a) m/f □ **lecture theatre** n = **lecture hall**

led [lɛd] pt, pp of **lead¹**

ledge [lɛdʒ] n repisa; (of window) alféizar m; (of mountain) saliente m

leek [li:k] n puerro

left [lɛft] pt, pp of **leave** ♦ adj izquierdo; (remaining): **there are two ~** quedan dos ♦ n izquierda ♦ adv a la izquierda; **on** or **to the ~** a la izquierda; **the L~**

(POL) la izquierda ❑ **left-hand** adj: **the left-hand side** la izquierda ❑ **left-hand drive** adj: **a left-hand drive car** un coche con el volante a la izquierda ❑ **left-handed** adj zurdo ❑ **left-luggage locker** n (BRIT) consigna f automática ❑ **left-luggage (office)** (BRIT) n consigna ❑ **left-overs** npl sobras fpl ❑ **left-wing** adj (POL) de izquierdas, izquierdista

leg [lɛg] n (person; of animal, chair) pata; (trouser leg) pernera; (CULIN: of lamb) pierna; (: of chicken) pata; (of journey) etapa

legacy ['lɛgəsɪ] n herencia

legal ['liːgl] adj (permitted by law) lícito; (of law) legal ❑ **legal holiday** (US) n fiesta oficial ❑ **legalize** vt legalizar ❑ **legally** adv legalmente

legend ['lɛdʒənd] n (also fig: person) leyenda ❑ **legendary** [-ərɪ] adj legendario

leggings ['lɛgɪŋz] npl mallas fpl, leggins mpl

legible ['lɛdʒəbl] adj legible

legislation [lɛdʒɪs'leɪʃən] n legislación f

legislative ['lɛdʒɪslətɪv] adj legislativo

legitimate [lɪ'dʒɪtɪmət] adj legítimo

leisure ['lɛʒə*] n ocio, tiempo libre; **at ~** con tranquilidad ❑ **leisure centre** (BRIT) n centro de recreo ❑ **leisurely** adj sin prisa; lento

lemon ['lɛmən] n limón m ❑ **lemonade** (fizzy) gaseosa ❑ **lemon tea** n té m con limón

lend [lɛnd] (pt, pp lent) vt: **to ~ sth to sb** prestar algo a algn

length [lɛŋθ] n (size) largo, longitud f; (distance): **the ~ of** todo lo largo de; (of swimming pool, cloth) largo; (of wood, string) trozo; (amount of time) duración f; **at ~** (at last) por fin, finalmente; (lengthily) largamente ❑ **lengthen** vt alargar ♦ vi alargarse ❑ **lengthways**

adv a lo largo ❑ **lengthy** adj largo, extenso

lens [lɛnz] n (of spectacles) lente f; (of camera) objetivo

Lent [lɛnt] n Cuaresma

lent [lɛnt] pt, pp of **lend**

lentil ['lɛntl] n lenteja

Leo ['liːəu] n Leo

leopard ['lɛpəd] n leopardo

leotard ['liːəutɑːd] n mallas fpl

leprosy ['lɛprəsɪ] n lepra

lesbian ['lɛzbɪən] n lesbiana

less [lɛs] adj (in size, degree etc) menor; (in quality) menos ♦ pron, adv menos ♦ prep: **~ tax/10% discount** menos impuestos/el 10 por ciento de descuento; **~ than half** menos de la mitad; **~ than ever** menos que nunca; **~ and ~** cada vez menos; **the ~ he works …** cuanto menos trabaja … ❑ **lessen** vi disminuir, reducirse ♦ vt disminuir, reducir ❑ **lesser** ['lɛsə*] adj menor; **to a lesser extent** en menor grado

lesson ['lɛsn] n clase f; (warning) lección f

let [lɛt] (pt, pp ~) vt (allow) dejar, permitir; (BRIT: lease) alquilar; **to ~ sb do sth** dejar que algn haga algo; **to ~ sb know sth** comunicar algo a algn; **~'s go** ¡vamos!; **~ him** come que venga; **"to ~"** "se alquila" ▶ **let down** vt (tyre) desinflar; (person) defraudar ▶ **let in** vt dejar entrar; (visitor etc) hacer pasar ▶ **let off** vt (culprit) dejar escapar; (gun) disparar; (bomb) accionar; (firework) hacer estallar ▶ **let out** vt dejar salir; (sound) soltar

lethal ['liːθl] adj (weapon) mortífero; (poison, wound) mortal

letter ['lɛtə*] n (of alphabet) letra; (correspondence) carta ❑ **letterbox** (BRIT) n buzón m

lettuce ['lɛtɪs] n lechuga

leukaemia [luː'kiːmɪə] (US **leukemia**) n leucemia

level ['lɛvl] adj (flat) llano ♦ adv: **to draw ~** with llegar a la altura de ♦ n nivel m; (height) altura ♦ vt nivelar; allanar; (destroy: building) derribar; (: forest) arrasar; **to be ~ with** estar a nivel de; **"A" levels** (BRIT) = exámenes mpl de bachillerato superior, B.U.P.; **on the ~** (fig: honest) serio ❑ **level crossing** (BRIT) n paso a nivel

lever ['liːvəʳ] n (also fig) palanca ♦ vt: **to ~ up** levantar con palanca ❑ **leverage** n (using bar etc) apalancamiento; (fig: influence) influencia

levy ['lɛvɪ] n impuesto ♦ vt exigir, recaudar

liability [laɪə'bɪlɪtɪ] n (pej: person, thing) estorbo, lastre m; (JUR: responsibility) responsabilidad f

liable ['laɪəbl] adj (subject): **~ for** sujeto a; (responsible): **~ for** responsable de; (likely): **~ to do** propenso a hacer

liaise [lɪ'eɪz] vt: **to ~ with** enlazar con

liar ['laɪəʳ] n mentiroso(-a)

liberal ['lɪbərəl] adj liberal; (offer, amount etc) generoso ❑ **Liberal Democrat** n (BRIT) demócrata m/f liberal

liberate ['lɪbəreɪt] vt (people: from poverty etc) librar; (prisoner) libertar; (country) liberar ❑ **liberation** [lɪbə'reɪʃən] n liberación f

liberty ['lɪbətɪ] n libertad f; **to be at ~** (criminal) estar en libertad; **to be at ~ to do** estar libre para hacer; **to take the ~ of doing sth** tomarse la libertad de hacer algo

Libra ['liːbrə] n Libra

librarian [laɪ'breərɪən] n bibliotecario(-a)

library ['laɪbrərɪ] n biblioteca

⚠ Be careful not to translate **library** by the Spanish word *librería*.

Libya ['lɪbɪə] n Libia

lice [laɪs] npl of **louse**

licence ['laɪsəns] (US **license**) n licencia; (permit) permiso; (also: **driving ~**) carnet m de conducir (SP), licencia de manejo (LAm)

license ['laɪsəns] n (US) = **licence** ♦ vt autorizar, dar permiso a ❑ **licensed** adj (for alcohol) autorizado para vender bebidas alcohólicas; (car) matriculado ❑ **license plate** (US) n placa (de matrícula) ❑ **licensing hours** (BRIT) npl horas durante las cuales se permite la venta y consumo de alcohol (en un bar etc)

lick [lɪk] vt lamer; (inf: defeat) dar una paliza a; **to ~ one's lips** relamerse

lid [lɪd] n (of box, case) tapa; (of pan) tapadera

lie [laɪ] (pt **lay**, pp **lain**) vi (rest) estar echado, estar acostado; (of object: be situated) estar, encontrarse; (tell lies: pt, pp **lied**) mentir ♦ n mentira; **to ~ low** (fig) mantenerse a escondidas ▶ **lie about** or **around** vi (things) estar tirado; (BRIT: people) estar tumbado ▶ **lie down** vi echarse, tumbarse

Liechtenstein ['lɪktənstaɪn] n Liechtenstein m

lie-in ['laɪɪn] (BRIT) n: **to have a ~** quedarse en la cama

lieutenant [lɛf'tɛnənt, US luː'tɛnənt] n (MIL) teniente mf

life [laɪf] (pl **lives**) n vida; **to come to ~** animarse ❑ **life assurance** (BRIT) n seguro de vida ❑ **lifeboat** n lancha de socorro ❑ **lifeguard** n vigilante mf, socorrista mf ❑ **life insurance** n = **life assurance** ❑ **life jacket** n chaleco salvavidas ❑ **lifelike** adj (model etc) que parece vivo; (realistic) realista ❑ **life preserver** (US) n cinturón m/chaleco salvavidas ❑ **life sentence** n cadena perpetua ❑ **lifestyle** n estilo de vida ❑ **lifetime** n (of person) vida; (of thing) período de vida

lift [lɪft] vt levantar; (end: ban, rule) levantar, suprimir ♦ vi (fog) disiparse

♦ *n* (BRIT: *machine*) ascensor *m*; **to give sb a ~** (BRIT) llevar a algn en el coche ▶ **lift up** *vt* levantar ☐ **lift-off** *n* despegue *m*

light [laɪt] (*pt, pp* **lighted** *or* **lit**) *n* luz *f*; (*lamp*) luz *f*, lámpara; (AUT) faro; (*for cigarette etc*): **have you got a ~?** ¿tienes fuego? ♦ *vt* (*candle, cigarette, fire*) encender (SP), prender (LAm); (*room*) alumbrar ♦ *adj* (*colour*) claro; (*not heavy, also fig*) ligero; (*room*) con mucha luz; (*gentle, graceful*) ágil; **lights** *npl* (*traffic lights*) semáforos *mpl*; **to come to ~** salir a luz; **in the ~ of** (*new evidence etc*) a la luz de ▶ **light up** *vi* (*smoke*) encender un cigarrillo; (*face*) iluminarse ♦ *vt* (*illuminate*) iluminar, alumbrar; (*set fire to*) encender ☐ **light bulb** *n* bombilla (SP), foco (MEX), bujía (CAm), bombita (RPl) ☐ **lighten** *vt* (*make less heavy*) aligerar ☐ **lighter** *n* (*also*: **cigarette lighter**) encendedor *m*, mechero ☐ **light-hearted** *adj* (*person*) alegre; (*remark etc*) divertido ☐ **lighthouse** *n* faro ☐ **lighting** *n* (*system*) alumbrado ☐ **lightly** *adv* ligeramente; (*not seriously*) con poca seriedad; **to get off lightly** ser castigado con poca severidad

lightning [ˈlaɪtnɪŋ] *n* relámpago, rayo ☐ **lightweight** *adj* (*suit*) ligero ♦ *n* (BOXING) peso ligero

like [laɪk] *vt* gustarle a algn ♦ *prep* como ♦ *adj* parecido, semejante ♦ *n*: **and the ~** y otros por el estilo; **his likes and dislikes** sus gustos y aversiones; **I would ~, I'd ~** me gustaría; (*for purchase*) quisiera; **would you ~ a coffee?** ¿te apetece un café?; **I ~ swimming** me gusta nadar; **she likes apples** le gustan las manzanas; **to be or look ~ sb/sth** parecerse a algn/algo; **what does it look/taste/sound ~?** ¿cómo es/a qué sabe/cómo suena ~? ; **that's just ~ him** es muy de él, es característico de él; **do it ~ this** hazlo así; **it is nothing ~ ...** no tiene parecido

alguno con ... ☐ **likeable** *adj* simpático, agradable

likelihood [ˈlaɪklɪhʊd] *n* probabilidad *f*

likely [ˈlaɪklɪ] *adj* probable; **he's ~ to leave** es probable que se vaya; **not ~!** ¡ni hablar!

likewise [ˈlaɪkwaɪz] *adv* igualmente; **to do ~** hacer lo mismo

liking [ˈlaɪkɪŋ] *n*: **~ (for)** (*person*) cariño (a); (*thing*) afición (a); **to be to sb's ~** ser del gusto de algn

lilac [ˈlaɪlək] *n* (*tree*) lilo; (*flower*) lila

Lilo® [ˈlaɪləʊ] *n* colchoneta inflable

lily [ˈlɪlɪ] *n* lirio, azucena; **~ of the valley** *n* lirio de los valles

limb [lɪm] *n* miembro

limbo [ˈlɪmbəʊ] *n*: **to be in ~** (*fig*) quedar a la expectativa

lime [laɪm] *n* (*tree*) limero; (*fruit*) lima; (GEO) cal *f*

limelight [ˈlaɪmlaɪt] *n*: **to be in the ~** (*fig*) ser el centro de atención

limestone [ˈlaɪmstəʊn] *n* piedra caliza

limit [ˈlɪmɪt] *n* límite *m* ♦ *vt* limitar ☐ **limited** *adj* limitado; **to be limited to** limitarse a

limousine [ˈlɪməziːn] *n* limusina

limp [lɪmp] *n*: **to have a ~** tener cojera ♦ *vi* cojear ♦ *adj* flojo; (*material*) fláccido

line [laɪn] *n* línea; (*rope*) cuerda; (*for fishing*) sedal *m*; (*wire*) hilo; (*row, series*) fila, hilera; (*of writing*) renglón *m*, línea; (*of song*) verso; (*on face*) arruga; (RAIL) vía ♦ *vt* (*road etc*) llenar; (SEWING) forrar; **to ~ the streets** llenar las aceras; **in ~ with** alineado con; (*according to*) de acuerdo con ▶ **line up** *vi* hacer cola ♦ *vt* alinear; (*prepare*) preparar; organizar

linear [ˈlɪnɪər] *adj* lineal

linen [ˈlɪnɪn] *n* ropa blanca; (*cloth*) lino

liner [ˈlaɪnər] *n* vapor *m* de línea, transatlántico; (*for bin*) bolsa (de basura)

line-up ['laɪnʌp] *n* (*US: queue*) cola; (*SPORT*) alineación *f*

linger ['lɪŋgə] *vi* retrasarse, tardar en marcharse; (*smell, tradition*) persistir

lingerie ['lænʒəri:] *n* lencería

linguist ['lɪŋgwɪst] *n* lingüista *mf* ❑ **linguistic** *adj* lingüístico

lining ['laɪnɪŋ] *n* forro; (*ANAT*) (membrana) mucosa

link [lɪŋk] *n* (*of a chain*) eslabón *m*; (*relationship*) relación *f*, vínculo; (*INTERNET*) link *m*, enlace *m* ♦ *vt* vincular, unir; (*associate*): **to ~ with** *or* **to** relacionar con; **links** *npl* (*GOLF*) campo de golf ► **link up** *vt* acoplar ♦ *vi* unirse

lion ['laɪən] *n* león *m* ❑ **lioness** *n* leona

lip [lɪp] *n* labio ❑ **lipread** *vi* leer los labios ❑ **lip salve** *n* crema protectora para labios ❑ **lipstick** *n* lápiz *m* de labios, carmín *m*

liqueur [lɪ'kjuə] *n* licor *m*

liquid ['lɪkwɪd] *adj, n* líquido ❑ **liquidizer** [-aɪzə] *n* licuadora

liquor ['lɪkə] *n* licor *m*, bebidas *fpl* alcohólicas ❑ **liquor store** (*US*) *n* bodega, *tienda de vinos y bebidas alcohólicas*

Lisbon ['lɪzbən] *n* Lisboa

lisp [lɪsp] *n* ceceo ♦ *vi* cecear

list [lɪst] *n* lista ♦ *vt* (*mention*) enumerar; (*put on a list*) poner en una lista

listen ['lɪsn] *vi* escuchar, oír; **to ~ to sb/ sth** escuchar a algn/algo ❑ **listener** *n* oyente *mf*; (*RADIO*) radioyente *mf*

lit [lɪt] *pt, pp of* **light**

liter ['li:tə] (*US*) *n* = **litre**

literacy ['lɪtərəsɪ] *n* capacidad *f* de leer y escribir

literal ['lɪtərl] *adj* literal ❑ **literally** *adv* literalmente

literary ['lɪtərərɪ] *adj* literario

literate ['lɪtərət] *adj* que sabe leer y escribir; (*educated*) culto

literature ['lɪtərɪtʃə] *n* literatura *f*; (*brochures etc*) folletos *mpl*

litre ['li:tə] (*US* **liter**) *n* litro

litter ['lɪtə] *n* (*rubbish*) basura; (*young animals*) camada, cría ❑ **litter bin** (*BRIT*) *n* papelera ❑ **littered** *adj*: **littered with** (*scattered*) lleno de

little ['lɪtl] *adj* (*small*) pequeño; (*not much*) poco ♦ *adv* poco; **a ~** un poco (de); **~ house/bird** casita/pajarito; **a ~ bit** un poquito; **~ by ~** poco a poco ❑ **little finger** *n* dedo meñique

live[1] [laɪv] *adj* (*animal*) vivo; (*wire*) conectado; (*broadcast*) en directo; (*shell*) cargado

live[2] [lɪv] *vi* vivir ► **live together** *vi* vivir juntos ► **live up to** *vt fus* (*fulfil*) cumplir con

livelihood ['laɪvlɪhud] *n* sustento

lively ['laɪvlɪ] *adj* vivo; (*interesting: place, book etc*) animado

liven up ['laɪvn-] *vt* animar ♦ *vi* animarse

liver ['lɪvə] *n* hígado

lives ['laɪvz] *npl of* **life**

livestock ['laɪvstɔk] *n* ganado

living ['lɪvɪŋ] *adj* (*alive*) vivo ♦ *n*: **to earn** *or* **make a ~** ganarse la vida ❑ **living room** *n* sala (de estar)

lizard ['lɪzəd] *n* lagarto; (*small*) lagartija

load [ləud] *n* carga; (*weight*) peso ♦ *vt* (*COMPUT*) cargar; (*also*: **~ up**): **to ~ (with)** cargar (con or de); **a ~ of** *or* **~s of** (*inf*) tonterías *fpl*; **a ~ of rubbish** (*inf*) tonterías *fpl*; **a ~ of, loads of** (*fig*) (gran) cantidad de, montones de ❑ **loaded** *adj* (*vehicle*): **to be loaded with** estar cargado de

loaf [ləuf] (*pl* **loaves**) *n* (barra de) pan *m*

loan [ləun] *n* préstamo ♦ *vt* prestar; **on ~** prestado

loathe [ləuð] *vt* aborrecer; (*person*) odiar

loaves [ləuvz] *npl of* **loaf**

lobby ['lɔbɪ] *n* vestíbulo, sala de espera; (*POL: pressure group*) grupo de presión ♦ *vt* presionar

lobster ['lɔbstə] *n* langosta

local ['ləukl] *adj* local ♦ *n* (*pub*) bar *m*; **the locals** *npl* los vecinos, los del lugar ❑ **local anaesthetic** *n* (*MED*) anestesia local ❑ **local authority** *n* municipio, ayuntamiento (*SP*) ❑ **local government** *n* gobierno municipal ❑ **locally** [-kəlɪ] *adv* en la vecindad; por aquí

locate [ləu'keɪt] *vt* (*find*) localizar; (*situate*): **to be located in** estar situado en

location [ləu'keɪʃən] *n* situación *f*; **on ~** (*CINEMA*) en exteriores

loch [lɔx] *n* lago

lock [lɔk] *n* (*of door, box*) cerradura; (*of canal*) esclusa; (*of hair*) mechón *m* ♦ *vt* (*with key*) cerrar (con llave) ♦ *vi* (*door etc*) cerrarse (con llave), (*wheels*) trabarse ► **lock in** *vt* encerrar ► **lock out** *vt* (*person*) cerrar la puerta a ► **lock up** *vt* (*criminal*) meter en la cárcel; (*mental patient*) encerrar; (*house*) cerrar (con llave) ♦ *vi* echar la llave

locker ['lɔkə] *n* casillero ❑ **locker-room** (*US*) *n* (*SPORT*) vestuario

locksmith ['lɔksmɪθ] *n* cerrajero(-a)

locomotive [ləukə'məutɪv] *n* locomotora

lodge [lɔdʒ] *n* casita (del guarda) ♦ *vi* (*person*): **to ~ (with)** alojarse (en casa de); (*bullet, bone*) incrustarse ♦ *vt* presentar ❑ **lodger** *n* huésped *mf*

lodging ['lɔdʒɪŋ] *n* alojamiento, hospedaje *m*

loft [lɔft] *n* desván *m*

log [lɔg] *n* (*of wood*) leño, tronco; (*written account*) diario ♦ *vt* anotar ► **log in, log on** *vi* (*COMPUT*) entrar en el sistema ► **log off, log out** *vi* (*COMPUT*) salir del sistema

logic ['lɔdʒɪk] *n* lógica ❑ **logical** *adj* lógico

logo ['ləugəu] *n* logotipo

lollipop ['lɔlɪpɔp] *n* piruli *m* ❑ **lollipop man/lady** (*BRIT: irreg*) *n* persona

encargada de ayudar a los niños a cruzar la calle

lolly ['lɔlɪ] *n* (*inf: ice cream*) polo; (*: lollipop*) piruleta; (*: money*) guita

London ['lʌndən] *n* Londres ❑ **Londoner** *n* londinense *mf*

lone [ləun] *adj* solitario

loneliness ['ləunlɪnɪs] *n* soledad *f*; aislamiento

lonely ['ləunlɪ] *adj* (*situation*) solitario; (*person*) solo; (*place*) aislado

long [lɔŋ] *adj* largo ♦ *adv* mucho tiempo, largamente ♦ *vi*: **to ~ for sth** anhelar algo; **so** *or* **as ~ as** mientras, con tal que; **don't be ~!** ¡no tardes!, ¡vuelve pronto!; **how ~ is the street?** ¿cuánto tiene la calle de largo?; **how ~ is the lesson?** ¿cuánto dura la clase?; **6 metres ~** que mide 6 metros, de 6 metros de largo; **6 months ~** que dura 6 meses, de 6 meses de duración; **all night ~** toda la noche; **he no longer comes** ya no viene; **I can't stand it any longer** ya no lo aguanto más; **~ before** mucho antes; **before ~** (+ *future*) dentro de poco; (+ *past*) poco tiempo después; **at ~ last** al fin, por fin ❑ **long-distance** *adj* (*race*) de larga distancia; (*call*) interurbano ❑ **long-haul** *adj* (*flight*) de larga distancia ❑ **longing** *n* anhelo, ansia; (*nostalgia*) nostalgia ♦ *adj* anhelante

longitude ['lɔŋgɪtju:d] *n* longitud *f*

long: long jump *n* salto de longitud ❑ **long-life** *adj* (*batteries*) de larga duración; (*milk*) uperizado ❑ **long-sighted** (*BRIT*) *adj* présbita ❑ **long-standing** *adj* de mucho tiempo ❑ **long-term** *adj* a largo plazo

loo [lu:] (*BRIT: inf*) *n* wáter *m*

look [luk] *vi* mirar; (*seem*) parecer; (*building etc*): **to ~ south/on to the sea** dar al sur/al mar ♦ *n* (*gen*): **to have a ~** mirar; (*glance*) mirada; (*appearance*) aire *m*, aspecto; **looks** *npl* (*good looks*) belleza; **~ (here)!** (*expressing annoyance etc*) ¡oye!; **~!** (*expressing* surprise) ¡mira! ► **look after** vt fus (care for) cuidar a; (deal with) encargarse de ► **look around** vi echar una mirada alrededor ► **look at** vt fus mirar; (read quickly) echar un vistazo a ► **look back** vi mirar hacia atrás ► **look down on** vt fus (fig) despreciar, mirar con desprecio ► **look for** vt fus buscar ► **look forward to** vt fus esperar con ilusión; (in letters): **we look forward to hearing from you** quedamos a la espera de sus gratas noticias ► **look into** vt investigar ► **look out** vi (beware): **to look out (for)** tener cuidado (de) ► **look out for** vt fus (seek) buscar; (await) esperar ► **look round** vi volver la cabeza ► **look through** vt fus (examine) examinar ► **look up** vi mirar hacia arriba; (improve) mejorar ♦ vt (word) buscar ► **look up to** vt fus admirar ❑ **lookout** n (tower etc) puesto de observación; (person) vigía mf; **to be on the lookout for sth** estar al acecho de algo

loom [luːm] vi: ~ **(up)** (threaten) surgir, amenazar; (event: approach) aproximarse

loony ['luːnɪ] (inf) n, adj loco(-a) m/f

loop [luːp] n lazo ♦ vt: **to ~ sth round sth** pasar algo alrededor de algo ❑ **loophole** n escapatoria

loose [luːs] adj suelto; (clothes) ancho; (morals, discipline) relajado; **to be on the ~** estar en libertad; **to be at a ~ end** or **at ~ ends** (US) no saber qué hacer ❑ **loosely** adv libremente, aproximadamente ❑ **loosen** vt aflojar

loot [luːt] n botín m ♦ vt saquear

lop-sided ['lɔp'saɪdɪd] adj torcido

lord [lɔːd] n señor m; **L~ Smith** Lord Smith; **the L~** el Señor; **my ~** (to bishop) Ilustrísima; (to noble etc) Señor; **good L~!** ¡Dios mío! ❑ **Lords** npl (BRIT: POL): **the (House of) Lords** la Cámara de los Lores

lorry ['lɔrɪ] (BRIT) n camión m ❑ **lorry driver** (BRIT) n camionero(-a)

lose [luːz] (pt, pp **lost**) vt perder ♦ vi perder, ser vencido; **to ~ (time)** (clock) atrasarse ► **lose out** vi salir perdiendo ❑ **loser** n perdedor(a) m/f

loss [lɔs] n pérdida; **heavy losses** (MIL) grandes pérdidas; **to be at a ~** no saber qué hacer; **to make a ~** sufrir pérdidas

lost [lɔst] pt, pp of **lose** ♦ adj perdido ❑ **lost property** (US **lost and found**) n objetos mpl perdidos

lot [lɔt] n (group: of things) grupo; (at auctions) lote m; **the ~** el todo, todos; **a ~ (large number: of books etc)** muchos; (a great deal) mucho, bastante; **a ~ of**, **lots of** mucho(s) (pl); **I read a ~** leo bastante; **to draw lots (for sth)** echar suertes (para decidir algo)

lotion ['ləʊʃən] n loción f

lottery ['lɔtərɪ] n lotería

loud [laʊd] adj (voice, sound) fuerte; (laugh, shout) estrepitoso; (condemnation etc) enérgico; (gaudy) chillón(-ona) ♦ adv (speak etc) fuerte; **out~** en voz alta ❑ **loudly** adv (noisily) fuerte; (aloud) en voz alta ❑ **loudspeaker** n altavoz m

lounge [laʊndʒ] n salón m, sala (de estar); (at airport etc) sala; (BRIT: also: ~ **bar**) salón-bar m ♦ vi (also: ~ **about** or **around**) reposar, holgazanear

louse [laʊs] (pl **lice**) n piojo

lousy ['laʊzɪ] (inf) adj (bad quality) malísimo, asqueroso; (ill) fatal

love [lʌv] n (romantic, sexual) amor m; (kind, caring) cariño ♦ vt amar, querer; (thing, activity) encantarle a algn; **"~ from Anne"** (on letter) "un abrazo (de) Anne"; **to ~ to do** encantarle a algn hacer; **to be/fall in ~ with** estar enamorado/enamorarse de algn; **to make ~ to** hacer el amor; **for the ~ of** por amor de; **"15 ~"** (TENNIS) "15 a cero"; **I ~ paella** me encanta la paella ❑ **love affair** n aventura sentimental ❑ **love life** n vida sentimental

lovely ['lʌvlɪ] adj (delightful) encantador(a); (beautiful) precioso

lover ['lʌvə'] n amante mf; (person in love) enamorado; (amateur): **a ~ of** un(a) aficionado(-a) o un(a) amante de

loving ['lʌvɪŋ] adj amoroso, cariñoso; (action) tierno

low [ləʊ] adj, adv bajo ♦ n (METEOROLOGY) área de baja presión; **to be ~ on** (supplies etc) andar mal de; **to feel ~** sentirse deprimido; **to turn (down)** → bajar □ **low-alcohol** adj de bajo contenido en alcohol □ **low-calorie** adj bajo en calorías

lower ['ləʊə'] adj más bajo; (less important) menos importante ♦ vt bajar; (reduce) reducir ♦ vr: **to ~ o.s. to** (fig) rebajarse a

low-fat adj (milk, yoghurt) desnatado; (diet) bajo en calorías

loyal ['lɔɪəl] adj leal □ **loyalty** n lealtad f □ **loyalty card** n tarjeta cliente

L.P. n abbr (= long-playing record) elepé m

L-plates ['el-] (BRIT) npl placas fpl de aprendiz de conductor

L-PLATES

En el Reino Unido las personas que están aprendiendo a conducir deben llevar en la parte delantera y trasera de su vehículo unas placas blancas con una L en rojo conocidas como **L-Plates** (de learner). No es necesario que asistan a clases teóricas sino que, desde el principio, se les entrega un carnet de conducir provisional ("provisional driving licence") para que realicen sus prácticas, aunque no pueden circular por las autopistas y deben ir siempre acompañadas por un conductor con carnet definitivo ("full driving licence").

Lt abbr (= lieutenant) Tte.

Ltd abbr (= limited company) S.A.

luck [lʌk] n suerte f; **bad ~** mala suerte; **good ~!** ¡que tengas suerte!, ¡suerte!; **bad** or **hard** or **tough ~!** ¡qué pena! □ **luckily** adv afortunadamente □ **lucky** adj afortunado; (at cards etc) con suerte; (object) que trae suerte

lucrative ['luːkrətɪv] adj lucrativo

ludicrous ['luːdɪkrəs] adj absurdo

luggage ['lʌgɪdʒ] n equipaje m □ **luggage rack** n (on car) baca, portaequipajes m inv

lukewarm ['luːkwɔːm] adj tibio

lull [lʌl] n tregua ♦ vt: **to ~ sb to sleep** arrullar a algn; **to ~ sb into a false sense of security** dar a algn una falsa sensación de seguridad

lullaby ['lʌləbaɪ] n nana

lumber ['lʌmbə'] n (junk) trastos mpl viejos; (wood) maderos mpl

luminous ['luːmɪnəs] adj luminoso

lump [lʌmp] n terrón m; (fragment) trozo; (swelling) bulto ♦ vt (also: **~ together**) juntar □ **lump sum** n suma global □ **lumpy** adj (sauce) lleno de grumos; (mattress) lleno de bultos

lunatic ['luːnətɪk] adj loco

lunch [lʌntʃ] n almuerzo, comida ♦ vi almorzar □ **lunch break**, **lunch hour** n hora del almuerzo □ **lunch time** n hora de comer

lung [lʌŋ] n pulmón m

lure [luə'] n (attraction) atracción f ♦ vt tentar

lurk [lɜːk] vi (person, animal) estar al acecho; (fig) acechar

lush [lʌʃ] adj exuberante

lust [lʌst] n lujuria; (greed) codicia

Luxembourg ['lʌksəmbəːg] n Luxemburgo

luxurious [lʌg'zjʊərɪəs] adj lujoso

luxury ['lʌkʃərɪ] n lujo ♦ cpd de lujo

Lycra® ['laɪkrə] n licra®

lying ['laɪŋ] n mentiras fpl ♦ adj mentiroso

lyrics ['lɪrɪks] npl (of song) letra

M, m

m. *abbr* = **metre**; **mile**; **million**

M.A. *abbr* = **Master of Arts**

ma (*inf*) [maː] *n* mamá

mac [mæk] (*BRIT*) *n* impermeable *m*

macaroni [mækəˈrəuni] *n* macarrones *mpl*

Macedonia [mæsiˈdəuniə] *n* Macedonia □ **Macedonian** [-ˈdəuniən] *adj* macedonio *n* macedonio(-a); (*LING*) macedonio

machine [məˈʃiːn] *n* máquina ♦ *vt* (*dress etc*) coser a máquina; (*TECH*) hacer a máquina □ **machine gun** *n* ametralladora □ **machinery** *n* maquinaria; (*fig*) mecanismo □ **machine washable** *adj* lavable a máquina

macho [ˈmætʃəu] *adj* machista

mackerel [ˈmækrl] *n inv* caballa

mackintosh [ˈmækintɔʃ] (*BRIT*) *n* impermeable *m*

mad [mæd] *adj* loco; (*idea*) disparatado; (*angry*) furioso; (*keen*): **to be ~ about sth** volverse loco a algn algo

Madagascar [mædəˈgæskəʳ] *n* Madagascar *m*

madam [ˈmædəm] *n* señora

mad cow disease *n* encefalopatía espongiforme bovina

made [meɪd] *pt, pp of* **make** □ **made-to-measure** (*BRIT*) *adj* hecho a la medida □ **made-up** [ˈmeɪdʌp] *adj* (*story*) ficticio

madly [ˈmædlɪ] *adv* locamente

madman [ˈmædmən] (*irreg*) *n* loco

madness [ˈmædnɪs] *n* locura

Madrid [məˈdrɪd] *n* Madrid *m*

Mafia [ˈmæfiə] *n* Mafia

mag [mæg] *n abbr* (*BRIT inf*) = **magazine**

magazine [mægəˈziːn] *n* revista; (*RADIO, TV*) programa *m* magazina

maggot [ˈmægət] *n* gusano

magic [ˈmædʒɪk] *n* magia ♦ *adj* mágico □ **magical** *adj* mágico □ **magician** [məˈdʒɪʃən] *n* mago(-a); (*conjurer*) prestidigitador(a) *m/f*

magistrate [ˈmædʒistreit] *n* juez *mf* (municipal)

magnet [ˈmægnit] *n* imán *m* □ **magnetic** [-ˈnetik] *adj* magnético; (*personality*) atrayente

magnificent [mægˈnifisant] *adj* magnífico

magnify [ˈmægnifai] *vt* (*object*) ampliar; (*sound*) aumentar □ **magnifying glass** *n* lupa

magpie [ˈmægpai] *n* urraca

mahogany [məˈhɔgəni] *n* caoba

maid [meid] *n* criada; **old ~** (*pej*) solterona

maiden name *n* nombre *m* de soltera

mail [meil] *n* correo; (*letters*) cartas *fpl* ♦ *vt* echar al correo □ **mailbox** (*US*) *n* buzón *m* □ **mailing list** *n* lista de direcciones □ **mailman** (*US: irreg*) *n* cartero □ **mail-order** *n* pedido postal

main [mein] *adj* principal, mayor ♦ *n* (*pipe*) cañería maestra; (*US*) red *f* eléctrica; **the mains** *npl* (*BRIT ELEC*) la red eléctrica; **in the ~** en general □ **main course** (*CULIN*) plato principal □ **mainland** *n* tierra firme □ **mainly** *adv* principalmente □ **main road** *n* carretera □ **mainstream** *n* corriente *f* principal □ **main street** *n* calle *f* mayor

maintain [mein'tein] *vt* mantener □ **maintenance** [ˈmeintənəns] *n* mantenimiento; (*LAW*) manutención *f*

maisonette [meizəˈnet] *n* dúplex *m*

maize [meiz] (*BRIT*) *n* maíz *m*, choclo (*SC*)

majesty [ˈmædʒisti] *n* majestad *f*; (*title*): **Your M~** Su Majestad

major [ˈmeidʒəʳ] *n* (*MIL*) comandante *mf* ♦ *adj* principal; (*MUS*) mayor

Majorca [məˈjɔːkə] *n* Mallorca

majority [məˈdʒɔriti] *n* mayoría

make [meɪk] (*pt, pp* **made**) *vt* hacer; (*manufacture*) fabricar; (*mistake*) cometer; (*speech*) pronunciar; (*cause to be*): **to ~ sb sad** poner triste a algn; (*force*): **to ~ sb do sth** obligar a algn a hacer algo; (*earn*) ganar; (*equal*): **2 and 2 ~ 4** 2 y 2 son 4 ♦ *n* marca; **to ~ the bed** hacer la cama; **to ~ a fool of sb** poner a algn en ridículo; **to ~ a profit/loss** obtener ganancias/sufrir pérdidas; **to ~ it** (*arrive*) llegar; (*achieve sth*) tener éxito; **what time do you ~ it?** ¿qué hora tienes?; **to ~ do with** contentarse con ▶ **make off** *vi* largarse ▶ **make out** *vt* (*decipher*) descifrar; (*understand*) entender; (*see*) distinguir; (*cheque*) extender ▶ **make up** *vt* (*invent*) inventar; (*prepare*) hacer; (*constitute*) constituir ♦ *vi* reconciliarse; (*with cosmetics*) maquillarse ▶ **make up for** *vt fus* compensar ▶ **makeover** ['meɪkəʊvə*r*] *n* (*by beautician*) sesión *f* de maquillaje y peluquería; (*change of image*) lavado de cara □ **maker** *n* fabricante *mf*; (*of film, programme*) autor(a) *m/f* □ **makeshift** *adj* improvisado □ **make-up** *n* maquillaje *m*

making ['meɪkɪŋ] *n* (*fig*): **in the ~** en vías de formación; **to have the makings of** (*person*) tener madera de

malaria [mə'lɛərɪə] *n* malaria

Malaysia [mə'leɪzɪə] *n* Malasia, Malaysia

male [meɪl] *n* (BIOL) macho ♦ *adj* (*sex, attitude*) masculino; (*child etc*) varón

malicious [mə'lɪʃəs] *adj* malicioso; rencoroso

malignant [mə'lɪgnənt] *adj* (MED) maligno

mall [mɔːl] (US) *n* (*also*: **shopping ~**) centro comercial

mallet ['mælɪt] *n* mazo

malnutrition [mælnjuː'trɪʃən] *n* desnutrición *f*

malpractice [mæl'præktɪs] *n* negligencia profesional

malt [mɔːlt] *n* malta; (*whisky*) whisky *m* de malta

Malta ['mɔːltə] *n* Malta □ **Maltese** [-'tiːz] *adj, n inv* maltés(-esa) *m/f*

mammal ['mæml] *n* mamífero

mammoth ['mæməθ] *n* mamut *m* ♦ *adj* gigantesco

man [mæn] (*pl* **men**) *n* hombre *m*; (*mankind*) el hombre ♦ *vt* (NAUT) tripular; (MIL) guarnecer; (*operate: machine*) manejar; **an old ~** un viejo; **~ and wife** marido y mujer

manage ['mænɪdʒ] *vi* arreglárselas, ir tirando ♦ *vt* (*be in charge of*) dirigir; (*control: person*) manejar; (*: ship*) gobernar □ **manageable** *adj* manejable □ **management** *n* dirección *f* □ **manager** *n* director(a) *m/f*; (*of pop star*) mánager *mf*; (SPORT) entrenador(a) *m* □ **manageress** *n* directora; entrenadora □ **managerial** [-'dʒɪərɪəl] *adj* directivo □ **managing director** *n* director *m/f* general

mandarin ['mændərɪn] *n* (*also*: **~ orange**) mandarina; (*person*) mandarín *m*

mandate ['mændeɪt] *n* mandato

mandatory ['mændətərɪ] *adj* obligatorio

mane [meɪn] *n* (*of horse*) crin *f*; (*of lion*) melena

maneuver [mə'nuːvə*r*] (US) = **manoeuvre**

mangetout [mɔnʒ'tuː] *n* tirabeque *m*

mango ['mæŋgəʊ] (*pl* **mangoes**) *n* mango

man: **manhole** *n* agujero de acceso □ **manhood** *n* edad *f* viril; (*state*) virilidad *f*

mania ['meɪnɪə] *n* manía □ **maniac** ['meɪnɪæk] *n* maníaco(-a); (*fig*) maniático

manic ['mænɪk] *adj* frenético

manicure ['mænɪkjʊə*r*] *n* manicura

manifest ['mænɪfest] vt manifestar, mostrar ♦ adj manifiesto

manifesto [mænɪ'festəu] n manifiesto

manipulate [mə'nɪpjuleɪt] vt manipular

man: mankind [mæn'kaɪnd] n humanidad f, género humano ❑ **manly** adj varonil ❑ **man-made** adj artificial

manner ['mænə'] n manera, modo; (behaviour) conducta, manera de ser; (type): **all ~ of things** toda clase de cosas; **manners** npl (behaviour) modales mpl; **bad manners** mala educación

manoeuvre [mə'nuːvə'] (US **maneuver**) vt, vi maniobrar ♦ n maniobra

manpower ['mænpauə'] n mano f de obra

mansion ['mænʃən] n palacio, casa grande

manslaughter ['mænslɔːtə'] n homicidio no premeditado

mantelpiece ['mæntlpiːs] n repisa, chimenea

manual ['mænjuəl] adj manual ♦ n manual m

manufacture [mænju'fæktʃə'] vt fabricar ♦ n fabricación f ❑ **manufacturer** n fabricante mf

manure [mə'njuə'] n estiércol m

manuscript ['mænjuskrɪpt] n manuscrito

many ['menɪ] adj, pron muchos(-as); **a great ~** muchísimos, un buen número de; **~ a time** muchas veces

map [mæp] n mapa m; **to ~ out** vt proyectar

maple ['meɪpl] n arce m, maple m (LAm)

Mar abbr (= **March**) mar

mar [mɑː'] vt estropear

marathon ['mærəθən] n maratón m

marble ['mɑːbl] n mármol m; (toy) canica

March [mɑːtʃ] n marzo

march [mɑːtʃ] vi (MIL) marchar; (demonstrators) manifestarse ♦ n marcha; (demonstration) manifestación f

mare [meə'] n yegua

margarine [mɑːdʒə'riːn] n margarina

margin ['mɑːdʒɪn] n margen m; (COMM: profit margin) margen m de beneficios ❑ **marginal** adj marginal ❑ **marginally** adv ligeramente

marigold ['mærɪgəuld] n caléndula

marijuana [mærɪ'wɑːnə] n marijuana

marina [mə'riːnə] n puerto deportivo

marinade [mærɪ'neɪd] n adobo

marinate ['mærɪneɪt] vt marinar

marine [mə'riːn] adj marino ♦ n soldado de marina

marital ['mærɪtl] adj matrimonial ❑ **marital status** n estado m civil

maritime ['mærɪtaɪm] adj marítimo

marjoram ['mɑːdʒərəm] n mejorana

mark [mɑːk] n marca, señal f; (in snow, mud etc) huella; (stain) mancha; (BRIT SCOL) nota ♦ vt marcar; manchar; (damage: furniture) rayar; (indicate: place etc) señalar; (BRIT SCOL) calificar, corregir; **to ~ time** marcar el paso; (fig) marcar(se) un ritmo ❑ **marked** adj (obvious) marcado, acusado ❑ **marker** n (sign) marcador m; (bookmark) señal f (de libro)

market ['mɑːkɪt] n mercado ♦ vt (COMM) comercializar ❑ **marketing** n márketing m ❑ **marketplace** n mercado ❑ **market research** n análisis m inv de mercados

marmalade ['mɑːməleɪd] n mermelada de naranja

maroon [mə'ruːn] vt: **to be marooned** quedar aislado; (fig) quedar abandonado ♦ n (colour) granate m

marquee [mɑː'kiː] n entoldado

marriage ['mærɪdʒ] n (relationship, institution) matrimonio; (wedding) boda; (act) casamiento ❑ **marriage certificate** n partida de casamiento

married ['mærɪd] adj casado; (life, love) conyugal

marrow ['mærəʊ] n médula; (vegetable) calabacín m

marry ['mærɪ] vt casarse con; (father, priest etc) casar ♦ vi (also: **get married**) casarse

Mars [mɑːz] n Marte m

marsh [mɑːʃ] n pantano; (salt marsh) marisma

marshal ['mɑːʃl] n (MIL) mariscal m; (at sports meeting etc) oficial m; (US: of police, fire department) jefe(-a) m/f ♦ vt (thoughts etc) ordenar; (soldiers) formar

martyr ['mɑːtə'] n mártir mf

marvel ['mɑːvl] n maravilla, prodigio ♦ vi: **to ~ (at)** maravillarse (de) ❏ **marvellous** (US **marvelous**) adj maravilloso

Marxism ['mɑːksɪzm] n marxismo

Marxist ['mɑːksɪst] adj, n marxista mf

marzipan ['mɑːzɪpæn] n mazapán m

mascara [mæs'kɑːrə] n rímel m

mascot ['mæskət] n mascota

masculine ['mæskjulɪn] adj masculino

mash [mæʃ] vt machacar ❏ **mashed potato(es)** n(pl) puré m de patatas (SP) or papas (LAm)

mask [mɑːsk] n máscara ♦ vt (cover): **to ~ one's face** ocultarse la cara; (hide: feelings) esconder

mason ['meɪsn] n (also: **stonemason**) albañil m; (also: **freemason**) masón m ❏ **masonry** n (in building) mampostería

mass [mæs] n (people) muchedumbre f; (of air, liquid etc) masa; (of detail, hair etc) gran cantidad f; (REL) misa ♦ cpd masivo ♦ vi reunirse; concentrarse; **the masses** npl las masas; **masses of** (inf) montones de

massacre ['mæsəkə'] n masacre f

massage ['mæsɑːʒ] n masaje m ♦ vt dar masaje en

massive ['mæsɪv] adj enorme; (support, changes) masivo

mass media npl medios mpl de comunicación

mass-produce ['mæsprə'djuːs] vt fabricar en serie

mast [mɑːst] n (NAUT) mástil m; (RADIO etc) torre f

master ['mɑːstə'] n (of servant) amo; (of situation) dueño, maestro; (in primary school) maestro; (in secondary school) profesor m; (title for boys): **M~ X** Señorito X ♦ vt dominar ❏ **mastermind** n inteligencia superior ♦ vt dirigir, planear ❏ **Master of Arts/Science** n licenciatura superior en Letras/Ciencias ❏ **masterpiece** n obra maestra

masturbate ['mæstəbeɪt] vi masturbarse

mat [mæt] n estera; (also: **doormat**) felpudo; (also: **table ~**) salvamanteles m inv, posavasos m inv ♦ adj = **matt**

match [mætʃ] n cerilla, fósforo; (game) partido; (equal) igual m/f ♦ vt (go well with) hacer juego con; (equal) igualar; (correspond to) corresponderse con; (pair: also: **~ up**) casar con ♦ vi hacer juego; **to be a good ~** hacer juego ❏ **matchbox** n caja de cerillas ❏ **matching** adj que hace juego

mate [meɪt] n (workmate) colega mf; (inf: friend) amigo(-a); (animal) macho/ hembra; (in merchant navy) segundo de a bordo ♦ vi acoplarse, aparearse ♦ vt aparear

material [mə'tɪərɪəl] n (substance) materia; (information) material m; (cloth) tela, tejido ♦ adj material; (important) esencial; **materials** npl materiales mpl

materialize [mə'tɪərɪəlaɪz] vi materializarse

maternal [mə'təːnl] adj maternal

maternity [mə'təːnɪtɪ] n maternidad f ❏ **maternity hospital** n hospital m de maternidad ❏ **maternity leave** n baja por maternidad

math [mæθ] (US) n = **mathematics**

mathematical [mæθə'mætɪkl] adj matemático

mathematician [mæθəmə'tɪʃən] n matemático(-a)

mathematics [mæθə'mætɪks] n matemáticas fpl

maths [mæθs] (BRIT) n = **mathematics**

matinée ['mætɪneɪ] n sesión f de tarde

matron ['meɪtrən] n enfermera f jefe; (in school) ama de llaves

matt [mæt] adj mate

matter ['mætə*] n cuestión f, asunto; (PHYSICS) sustancia, materia; (reading matter) material m; (MED: pus) pus m ♦ vi importar; **matters** npl (affairs) asuntos mpl, temas mpl; **it doesn't** ~ no importa; **what's the** ~? ¿qué pasa?; **no** ~ **what** pase lo que pase; **as a** ~ **of course** por rutina; **as a** ~ **of fact** de hecho

mattress ['mætrɪs] n colchón m

mature [mə'tjuə*] adj maduro ♦ vi madurar ❑ **mature student** n estudiante de más de 21 años ❑ **maturity** n madurez f

maul [mɔːl] vt magullar

mauve [məuv] adj de color malva (SP) or guinda (LAm)

max abbr = **maximum**

maximize ['mæksɪmaɪz] vt (profits etc) llevar al máximo; (chances) maximizar

maximum ['mæksɪməm] (pl **maxima**) adj máximo ♦ n máximo

May [meɪ] n mayo

may [meɪ] (conditional **might**) vi (indicating possibility): **he** ~ **come** puede que venga; (be allowed to): ~ **I smoke?** ¿puedo fumar?; (wishes): ~ **God bless you!** ¡que Dios le bendiga!; **you** ~ **as well go** bien puedes irte

maybe ['meɪbiː] adv quizá(s)

May Day n el primero de Mayo

mayhem ['meɪhem] n caos m total

mayonnaise [meɪə'neɪz] n mayonesa

mayor [mɛə*] n alcalde m ❑ **mayoress** n alcaldesa

maze [meɪz] n laberinto

MD n abbr = **managing director**

me [miː] pron (direct) me; (stressed, after pron) mí; **can you hear me?** ¿me oyes?; **he heard me** ¡me oyó a mí!; **it's me** soy yo; **give them to me** dámelos/las; **with/without me** conmigo/sin mí

meadow ['mɛdəu] n prado, pradera

meagre ['miːgə*] (US **meager**) adj escaso, pobre

meal [miːl] n comida; (flour) harina ❑ **mealtime** n hora de comer

mean [miːn] (pt, pp **meant**) adj (with money) tacaño; (unkind) mezquino, malo; (shabby) humilde; (average) medio ♦ vt (signify) querer decir, significar; (refer to) referirse a; (intend): **to** ~ **to do sth** pensar o pretender hacer algo ♦ n medio, término medio; **means** npl (way) medio, manera; (money) recursos mpl, medios mpl; **by means of** mediante, por medio de; **by all means!** ¡naturalmente!, ¡claro que sí!; **do you** ~ **it?** ¿lo dices en serio?; **what do you** ~? ¿qué quiere decir?; **to be meant for sb/sth** ser para algn/algo

meaning ['miːnɪŋ] n significado, sentido; (purpose) sentido, propósito ❑ **meaningful** adj significativo ❑ **meaningless** adj sin sentido

meant [mɛnt] pt, pp of **mean**

meantime ['miːntaɪm] adv (also: **in the** ~) mientras tanto

meanwhile ['miːnwaɪl] adv = **meantime**

measles ['miːzlz] n sarampión m

measure ['mɛʒə*] vt, vi medir ♦ n medida; (ruler) regla ❑ **measurement** ['mɛʒəmənt] n (measure) medida; (act) medición f; **to take sb's measurements** tomar las medidas a algn

meat [miːt] n carne f; **cold** ~ fiambre m ❑ **meatball** n albóndiga

Mecca ['mɛkə] n La Meca

mechanic [mɪˈkænɪk] n mecánico(-a)
❏ **mechanical** adj mecánico

mechanism [ˈmɛkənɪzəm] n
mecanismo

medal [ˈmɛdl] n medalla ❏ **medallist**
(US **medalist**) n (SPORT) medallista mf

meddle [ˈmɛdl] vi: to ~ in entrometerse
en; to ~ with sth manosear algo

media [ˈmiːdɪə] npl medios mpl de
comunicación ♦ npl of **medium**

mediaeval [mɛdɪˈiːvl] adj = **medieval**

mediate [ˈmiːdɪeɪt] vi mediar

medical [ˈmɛdɪkl] adj médico ♦ n
reconocimiento médico ❏ **medical
certificate** n certificado m médico

medicated [ˈmɛdɪkeɪtɪd] adj medicinal

medication [mɛdɪˈkeɪʃən] n
medicación f

medicine [ˈmɛdsɪn] n medicina; (drug)
medicamento

medieval [mɛdɪˈiːvl] adj medieval

mediocre [miːdɪˈəʊkəʳ] adj mediocre

meditate [ˈmɛdɪteɪt] vi meditar

meditation [mɛdɪˈteɪʃən] n
meditación f

Mediterranean [mɛdɪtəˈreɪnɪən] adj
mediterráneo; **the ~ (Sea)** el (Mar)
Mediterráneo

medium [ˈmiːdɪəm] (pl **media**) adj
mediano, regular ♦ n (means) medio;
(pl **mediums**: person) médium mf
❏ **medium-sized** adj de tamaño
mediano; (clothes) de (la) talla
mediana ❏ **medium wave** n onda
media

meek [miːk] adj manso, sumiso

meet [miːt] (pt, pp **met**) vt encontrar;
(accidentally) encontrarse con,
tropezar con; (by arrangement)
reunirse con; (for the first time) conocer;
(go and fetch) ir a buscar; (opponent)
enfrentarse con; (obligations) cumplir;
(encounter: problem) hacer frente a;
(need) satisfacer ♦ vi encontrarse; (in
session) reunirse; (join: objects) unirse;
(for the first time) conocerse ▶ **meet**

up vi: **to meet up with sb** reunirse con
algn ▶ **meet with** vt fus (difficulty)
tropezar con; **to meet with success**
tener éxito ❏ **meeting** n encuentro;
(arranged) cita, compromiso; (business
meeting) reunión f; (POL) mitin m
❏ **meeting place** n lugar m de
reunión o encuentro

megabyte [ˈmɛgəbaɪt] n (COMPUT)
megabyte m, megaocteto

megaphone [ˈmɛgəfəʊn] n megáfono

melancholy [ˈmɛlənkəlɪ] n melancolía
♦ adj melancólico

melody [ˈmɛlədɪ] n melodía

melon [ˈmɛlən] n melón m

melt [mɛlt] vi (metal) fundirse; (snow)
derretirse ♦ vt fundir

member [ˈmɛmbəʳ] n (gen, ANAT)
miembro; (of club) socio(-a)
❏ **Member of Congress** (US) n
miembro mf del Congreso
❏ **Member of Parliament** (BRIT)
diputado(-a) m/f, parlamentario(-a) m/
f ❏ **Member of the European
Parliament** n diputado(-a) m/f del
Parlamento Europeo,
eurodiputado(-a) m/f ❏ **Member of
the Scottish Parliament** (BRIT)
diputado(-a) del Parlamento escocés
❏ **membership** n (members) número
de miembros; (state) filiación f
❏ **membership card** n carnet m de
socio

memento [məˈmɛntəʊ] n recuerdo

memo [ˈmɛməʊ] n apunte m, nota

memorable [ˈmɛmərəbl] adj
memorable

memorandum [mɛməˈrændəm] (pl
memoranda) n apunte m, nota;
(official note) acta

memorial [mɪˈmɔːrɪəl] n monumento
conmemorativo ♦ adj conmemorativo

memorize [ˈmɛməraɪz] vt aprender de
memoria

memory ['mɛmərɪ] n (also: COMPUT) memoria; (instance) recuerdo; (of dead person): **in ~ of** a la memoria de

men [mɛn] npl of **man**

menace ['mɛnəs] n amenaza ♦ vt amenazar

mend [mɛnd] vt reparar, arreglar; (darn) zurcir ♦ vi reponerse ♦ n arreglo, reparación f zurcido ♦ n: **to be on the ~** ir mejorando; **to ~ one's ways** enmendarse

meningitis [mɛnɪn'dʒaɪtɪs] n meningitis f

menopause ['mɛnəupɔːz] n menopausia

men's room (US) n: **the ~** el servicio de caballeros

menstruation [mɛnstru'eɪʃən] n menstruación f

menswear ['mɛnzwɛə'] n confección f de caballero

mental ['mɛntl] adj mental ❑ **mental hospital** n (hospital m) psiquiátrico ❑ **mentality** [mɛn'tælɪtɪ] n mentalidad f ❑ **mentally** adv: **to be mentally ill** tener una enfermedad mental

menthol ['mɛnθɒl] n mentol m

mention ['mɛnʃən] n mención f ♦ vt mencionar; (speak) hablar de; **don't ~ it!** ¡de nada!

menu ['mɛnjuː] n (set menu) menú m; (printed) carta; (COMPUT) menú m

MEP n abbr = **Member of the European Parliament**

mercenary ['mɜːsɪnərɪ] adj, n mercenario(-a)

merchandise ['mɜːtʃəndaɪz] n mercancías fpl

merchant ['mɜːtʃənt] n comerciante mf ❑ **merchant navy** (US **merchant marine**) n marina mercante

merciless ['mɜːsɪlɪs] adj despiadado

mercury ['mɜːkjʊrɪ] n mercurio

mercy ['mɜːsɪ] n compasión f; (REL) misericordia; **at the ~ of** a la merced de

mere [mɪə'] adj simple, mero ❑ **merely** adv simplemente, sólo

merge [mɜːdʒ] vt (join) unir ♦ vi unirse; (COMM) fusionarse; (colours etc) fundirse ❑ **merger** n (COMM) fusión f

meringue [mə'ræŋ] n merengue m

merit ['mɛrɪt] n mérito ♦ vt merecer

mermaid ['mɜːmeɪd] n sirena

merry ['mɛrɪ] adj alegre; **M~ Christmas!** ¡Felices Pascuas! ❑ **merry-go-round** n tiovivo

mesh [mɛʃ] n malla

mess [mɛs] n (muddle: of situation) confusión f; (: of room) revoltijo; (dirt) porquería; (MIL) comedor m ▸ **mess about** or **around** (inf) vi perder el tiempo; (pass the time) entretenerse ▸ **mess up** vt (spoil) estropear; (dirty) ensuciar ▸ **mess with** (inf) vt fus (challenge, confront) meterse con (inf); (interfere with) interferir con

message ['mɛsɪdʒ] n recado, mensaje m

messenger ['mɛsɪndʒə'] n mensajero(-a)

Messrs abbr (on letters: = Messieurs) Sres

messy ['mɛsɪ] adj (dirty) sucio; (untidy) desordenado

met [mɛt] pt, pp of **meet**

metabolism [mɛ'tæbəlɪzəm] n metabolismo

metal ['mɛtl] n metal m ❑ **metallic** [-'tælɪk] adj metálico

metaphor ['mɛtəfə'] n metáfora

meteor ['miːtɪə'] n meteoro ❑ **meteorite** [-aɪt] n meteorito

meteorology [miːtɪə'rɒlədʒɪ] n meteorología

meter ['miːtə'] n (instrument) contador m; (US: unit) = **metre** ♦ vt (US POST) franquear

method ['mɛθəd] n método ❑ **methodical** [mɪ'θɒdɪkl] adj metódico

meths [meθs] n (BRIT) alcohol m metilado or desnaturalizado

meticulous [me'tɪkjʊləs] adj meticuloso

metre ['miːtə'] (US **meter**) n metro

metric ['metrɪk] adj métrico

metro ['metrəʊ] n metro

metropolitan [metrə'pɒlɪtən] adj metropolitano; **the M~ Police** (BRIT) la policía londinense

Mexican ['meksɪkən] adj, n mejicano(-a), mexicano(-a)

Mexico ['meksɪkəʊ] n Méjico (SP), México (LAm)

mg abbr (= milligram) mg

mice [maɪs] npl of **mouse**

micro... [maɪkrəʊ] prefix micro...
❏ **microchip** n microplaqueta
❏ **microphone** n micrófono
❏ **microscope** n microscopio
❏ **microwave** n (also: **microwave oven**) horno microondas

mid [mɪd] adj: **in ~ May** a mediados de mayo; **in ~ afternoon** a media tarde; **in ~ air** en el aire ❏ **midday** n mediodía m

middle ['mɪdl] n centro; (half-way point) medio; (waist) cintura ♦ adj de en medio; (course, way) intermedio; **in the ~ of the night** en plena noche ❏ **middle-aged** adj de mediana edad ❏ **Middle Ages** npl: **the Middle Ages** la Edad Media ❏ **middle-class** adj de clase media; **the middle class(es)** la clase media ❏ **Middle East** n Oriente m Medio ❏ **middle name** n segundo nombre ❏ **middle school** n (US) colegio para niños de doce a catorce años; (BRIT) colegio para niños de ocho o nueve a doce o trece años

midge [mɪdʒ] n mosquito

midget ['mɪdʒɪt] n enano(-a)

midnight ['mɪdnaɪt] n medianoche f

midst [mɪdst] n: **in the ~ of** (crowd) en medio de; (situation, action) en mitad de

midsummer [mɪd'sʌmə'] n: **in ~** en pleno verano

midway [mɪd'weɪ] adj, adv: **~ (between)** a medio camino (entre); **~ through** a la mitad (de)

midweek [mɪd'wiːk] adv entre semana

midwife ['mɪdwaɪf] (irreg) n comadrona, partera

midwinter [mɪd'wɪntə'] n: **in ~** en pleno invierno

might [maɪt] vb see **may** ♦ n fuerza, poder m ❏ **mighty** adj fuerte, poderoso

migraine [ˈmiːgreɪn] n jaqueca

migrant ['maɪgrənt] n, adj (bird) migratorio; (worker) emigrante

migrate [maɪ'greɪt] vi emigrar

migration [maɪ'greɪʃən] n emigración f

mike [maɪk] n abbr (= microphone) micro

mild [maɪld] adj (person) apacible; (climate) templado; (slight) ligero; (taste) suave; (illness) leve ❏ **mildly** ['-lɪ] adv ligeramente; suavemente; **to put it mildly** para no decir más

mile [maɪl] n milla ❏ **mileage** n número de millas, ≈ kilometraje m ❏ **mileometer** [maɪ'lɒmɪtə'] n ≈ cuentakilómetros m inv ❏ **milestone** n mojón m

military ['mɪlɪtərɪ] adj militar

militia [mɪ'lɪʃə] n milicia

milk [mɪlk] n leche f ♦ vt (cow) ordeñar; (fig) chupar ❏ **milk chocolate** n chocolate m con leche ❏ **milkman** (irreg) n lechero ❏ **milky** adj lechoso

mill [mɪl] n (windmill etc) molino; (coffee mill) molinillo; (factory) fábrica ♦ vt moler ♦ vi (also: **~ about**) arremolinarse

millennium [mɪ'lenɪəm] (pl **millenniums** or **millennia**) n milenio, milenario

milli... ['mɪlɪ] prefix: **milligram(me)** n miligramo ❏ **millilitre** ['mɪlɪliːtə'] (US

millilete) n mililitro ❑ **millimetre** (US **millimeter**) n milímetro

million ['mɪljən] n millón m; **a ~ times** un millón de veces ❑ **millionaire** [-jə'neə*] n millonario(-a) ❑ **millionth** [-θ] adj millonésimo

milometer [maɪ'lɒmɪtə*] (BRIT) n = **mileometer**

mime [maɪm] n mímica; (actor) mimo(-a) ♦ vt remedar ♦ vi actuar de mimo

mimic ['mɪmɪk] n imitador(a) m/f ♦ adj mímico ♦ vt remedar, imitar

min. abbr = **minimum**; **minute(s)**

mince [mɪns] vt picar ♦ n (BRIT CULIN) carne f picada ❑ **mincemeat** n conserva de fruta picada; (US: meat) carne f picada ❑ **mince pie** n empanadilla rellena de fruta picada

mind [maɪnd] n mente f; (intellect) intelecto; (contrasted with matter) espíritu m ♦ vt (attend to, look after) ocuparse de, cuidar; (be careful) tener cuidado con; (object to): **I don't ~ the noise** no me molesta el ruido; **it is on my ~** me preocupa; **to bear sth in ~** tomar or tener algo en cuenta; **to make up one's ~** decidirse; **I don't ~** me es igual; **~ you ...** te advierto que ...; **never ~!** ¡es igual!, ¡no importa!; (don't worry) ¡no te preocupes!; **"~ the step"** "cuidado con el escalón" ❑ **mindless** adj (crime) sin motivo; (work) de autómata

mine¹ [maɪn] pron el mío/la mía etc; **a friend of ~** un(a) amigo(-a) mío/mía ♦ adj: **this book is ~** = este libro es mío

mine² [maɪn] n mina ♦ vt (coal) extraer; (bomb: beach etc) minar ❑ **minefield** n campo de minas ❑ **miner** n minero(-a)

mineral ['mɪnərəl] adj mineral ♦ n mineral m ❑ **mineral water** n agua mineral

mingle ['mɪŋgl] vi: **to ~ with** mezclarse con

miniature ['mɪnətʃə*] adj (en) miniatura ♦ n miniatura

minibar ['mɪnibɑ:*] n minibar m

minibus ['mɪnibʌs] n microbús m

minicab ['mɪnikæb] n taxi m (que sólo puede pedirse por teléfono)

minimal ['mɪnɪml] adj mínimo

minimize ['mɪnɪmaɪz] vt minimizar; (play down) empequeñecer

minimum ['mɪnɪməm] (pl **minima**) n, adj mínimo

mining ['maɪnɪŋ] n explotación f minera

miniskirt ['mɪniskɜ:t] n minifalda

minister ['mɪnɪstə*] n (BRIT POL) ministro(-a) (SP), secretario(-a) (LAm); (REL) pastor m ♦ vi: **to ~ to** atender a

ministry ['mɪnɪstri] n (BRIT POL) ministerio, secretaría (MEX); (REL) sacerdocio

minor ['maɪnə*] adj (repairs, injuries) leve; (poet, planet) menor; (MUS) menor ♦ n (LAW) menor m de edad

Minorca [mɪ'nɔ:kə] n Menorca

minority [maɪ'nɒrɪti] n minoría

mint [mɪnt] n (plant) menta, hierbabuena; (sweet) caramelo de menta ♦ vt (coins) acuñar; **the (Royal) M~, the (US) M~** la Casa de la Moneda; **in ~ condition** en perfecto estado

minus ['maɪnəs] n (also: **~ sign**) signo de menos ♦ prep menos; **12 ~ 6 equals 6** 12 menos 6 son 6; **~ 24°C** menos 24 grados

minute¹ ['mɪnɪt] n minuto; (fig) momento; **minutes** npl (of meeting) actas fpl; **at the last ~** a última hora

minute² [maɪ'nju:t] adj diminuto; (search) minucioso

miracle ['mɪrəkl] n milagro

miraculous [mɪ'rækjuləs] adj milagroso

mirage ['mɪrɑ:ʒ] n espejismo

mirror ['mɪrə*] n espejo; (in car) retrovisor m

misbehave
455
misuse

misbehave [mɪsbɪ'heɪv] vi portarse mal

misc. abbr = **miscellaneous**

miscarriage ['mɪskærɪdʒ] n (MED) aborto; ~ **of justice** error m judicial

miscellaneous [mɪsɪ'leɪnɪəs] adj varios(-as), diversos(-as)

mischief ['mɪstʃɪf] n travesuras fpl, diabluras fpl; (maliciousness) malicia ❏ **mischievous** [-fɪvəs] adj travieso

misconception [mɪskən'sepʃən] n idea equivocada; equivocación f

misconduct [mɪs'kɒndʌkt] n mala conducta; **professional ~** falta profesional

miser ['maɪzə*] n avaro(-a)

miserable ['mɪzərəbl] adj (unhappy) triste, desgraciado; (unpleasant, contemptible) miserable

misery ['mɪzərɪ] n tristeza, (wretchedness) miseria, desdicha

misfortune [mɪs'fɔːtʃən] n desgracia

misgiving [mɪs'gɪvɪŋ] n (apprehension) presentimiento; **to have misgivings about sth** tener dudas acerca de algo

misguided [mɪs'gaɪdɪd] adj equivocado

mishap ['mɪshæp] n desgracia, contratiempo

misinterpret [mɪsɪn'tɜːprɪt] vt interpretar mal

misjudge [mɪs'dʒʌdʒ] vt juzgar mal

mislay [mɪs'leɪ] vt extraviar, perder

mislead [mɪs'liːd] vt llevar a conclusiones erróneas ❏ **misleading** adj engañoso

misplace [mɪs'pleɪs] vt extraviar

misprint ['mɪsprɪnt] n errata, error m de imprenta

misrepresent [mɪsreprɪ'zent] vt falsificar

Miss [mɪs] n Señorita

miss [mɪs] vt (train etc) perder; (fail to hit: target) errar; (regret the absence of): **I ~ him** (yo) le echo de menos or a

faltar; (fail to see): **you can't ~ it** no tiene pérdida ♦ vi fallar ♦ n (shot) tiro fallido or perdido ▶ **miss out** (BRIT) vt omitir ▶ **miss out on** vt fus (fun, party, opportunity) perderse

missile ['mɪsaɪl] n (AVIAT) mísil m; (object thrown) proyectil m

missing ['mɪsɪŋ] adj (pupil) ausente; (thing) perdido (MIL): **~ in action** desaparecido en combate

mission ['mɪʃən] n misión f; (official representation) delegación f ❏ **missionary** n misionero(-a)

misspell [mɪs'spel] (pt, pp **misspelt** (Brit) or **misspelled**) vt escribir mal

mist [mɪst] n (light) neblina; (heavy) niebla; (at sea) bruma ♦ vi (eyes: also: ~ **over**, ~ **up**) llenarse de lágrimas; (BRIT: windows: also: ~ **over**, ~ **up**) empañarse

mistake [mɪs'teɪk] (vt: irreg) n error m ♦ vt entender mal; **by ~** por equivocación; **to make a ~** equivocarse; **to ~ A for B** confundir A con B ❏ **mistaken** pp of **mistake** ♦ adj equivocado; **to be mistaken** equivocarse, engañarse

mister ['mɪstə*] (inf) n señor m; see **Mr**

mistletoe ['mɪsltəʊ] n muérdago

mistook [mɪs'tʊk] pt of **mistake**

mistress ['mɪstrɪs] n (lover) amante f; (of house) señora (de la casa); (BRIT: in primary school) maestra; (in secondary school) profesora; (of situation) dueña

mistrust [mɪs'trʌst] vt desconfiar de

misty ['mɪstɪ] adj (day) de niebla; (glasses etc) empañado

misunderstand [mɪsʌndə'stænd] (irreg) vt, vi entender mal ❏ **misunderstanding** n malentendido

misunderstood [mɪsʌndə'stʊd] pt, pp of **misunderstand** ♦ adj (person) incomprendido

misuse [n mɪs'juːs, vb mɪs'juːz] n mal uso; (of power) abuso; (of funds) malversación f ♦ vt abusar de; malversar

mitt(en) ['mɪt(n)] n manopla

mix [mɪks] vt mezclar; (combine) unir ♦ vi mezclarse; (people) llevarse bien ♦ n mezcla ▶ **mix up** vt mezclar; (confuse) confundir ❑ **mixed** adj mixto; (feelings etc) encontrado ❑ **mixed grill** n (BRIT) parrillada mixta ❑ **mixed salad** n ensalada mixta ❑ **mixed-up** adj (confused) confuso, revuelto ❑ **mixer** n (for food) licuadora; (for drinks) coctelera; (person): **he's a good mixer** tiene don de gentes ❑ **mixture** n mezcla; (also: **cough mixture**) jarabe m ❑ **mix-up** n confusión f

ml abbr (= millilitre(s)) ml

mm abbr (= millimetre) mm

moan [məʊn] n gemido ♦ vi gemir; (inf: complain): **to ~ (about)** quejarse (de)

moat [məʊt] n foso

mob [mɔb] n multitud f ♦ vt acosar

mobile ['məʊbaɪl] adj móvil ♦ n móvil m ❑ **mobile home** n caravana ❑ **mobile phone** n teléfono móvil

mobility [məʊ'bɪlɪtɪ] n movilidad f

mobilize ['məʊbɪlaɪz] vt movilizar

mock [mɔk] vt (ridicule) ridiculizar; (laugh at) burlarse de ♦ adj fingido; **~ exam** examen preparatorio antes de los exámenes oficiales; **mocks** (BRIT: SCOL: inf) exámenes mpl de prueba ❑ **mockery** n burla

mod cons ['mɔd'kɒnz] npl abbr = **modern conveniences**; see **convenience**

mode [məʊd] n modo

model ['mɔdl] n modelo; (fashion model, artist's model) modelo mf ♦ adj modelo ♦ vt (with clay etc) modelar; (copy): **to ~ o.s. on** tomar como modelo a ♦ vi ser modelo; **to ~ clothes** pasar modelos, ser modelo

modem ['məʊdəm] n modem m

moderate [adj 'mɔdərət, vb 'mɔdəreɪt] adj moderado(-a) ♦ vi moderarse, calmarse ♦ vt moderar

moderation [mɔdə'reɪʃən] n moderación f; **in ~** con moderación

modern ['mɔdən] adj moderno ❑ **modernize** vt modernizar ❑ **modern languages** npl lenguas fpl modernas

modest ['mɔdɪst] adj modesto; (small) módico ❑ **modesty** n modestia

modification [mɔdɪfɪ'keɪʃən] n modificación f

modify ['mɔdɪfaɪ] vt modificar

module ['mɔdjuːl] n (unit, component, SPACE) módulo

mohair ['məʊheə'] n mohair m

Mohammed [mə'hæmed] n Mahoma m

moist [mɔɪst] adj húmedo ❑ **moisture** ['mɔɪstʃə'] n humedad f ❑ **moisturizer** ['mɔɪstʃəraɪzə'] n crema hidratante

mold etc [məʊld] (US) = **mould** etc

mole [məʊl] n (animal, spy) topo; (spot) lunar m

molecule ['mɔlɪkjuːl] n molécula

molest [mə'lest] vt importunar; (assault sexually) abusar sexualmente de

> ⚠ Be careful not to translate **molest** by the Spanish word *molestar*.

molten ['məʊltən] adj fundido; (lava) líquido

mom [mɔm] (US) n = **mum**

moment ['məʊmənt] n momento; **at the ~** de momento, por ahora ❑ **momentarily** ['məʊməntrɪlɪ] adv momentáneamente; (US: very soon) de un momento a otro ❑ **momentary** adj momentáneo ❑ **momentous** [-'mentəs] adj trascendental, importante

momentum [mə'mentəm] n momento; (fig) ímpetu m; **to gather ~** cobrar velocidad; (fig) ganar fuerza

mommy ['mɔmɪ] (US) n = **mummy**

Mon abbr (= Monday) lun

Monaco ['mɔnəkəu] n Mónaco

monarch ['mɔnək] n monarca mf
❏ **monarchy** n monarquía

monastery ['mɔnəstərɪ] n monasterio

Monday ['mʌndɪ] n lunes m inv

monetary ['mʌnɪtərɪ] adj monetario

money ['mʌnɪ] n dinero m; (currency) moneda; **to make ~** ganar dinero
❏ **money belt** n riñonera ❏ **money order** n giro

mongrel ['mʌŋɡrəl] n (dog) perro mestizo

monitor ['mɔnɪtə*] n (SCOL) monitor m; (also: **television ~**) receptor m de control; (of computer) monitor m ◆ vt controlar

monk [mʌŋk] n monje m

monkey ['mʌŋkɪ] n mono m

monologue ['mɔnəlɔɡ] n monólogo

monopoly [mə'nɔpəlɪ] n monopolio

monosodium glutamate
[mɔnə'səudɪəm'ɡluːtəmeɪt] n glutamato monosódico

monotonous [mə'nɔtənəs] adj monótono

monsoon [mɔn'suːn] n monzón m

monster ['mɔnstə*] n monstruo m

month [mʌnθ] n mes m ❏ **monthly** adj mensual ◆ adv mensualmente

monument ['mɔnjumənt] n monumento

mood [muːd] n humor m; (of crowd, group) clima m; **to be in a good/bad ~** estar de buen/mal humor ❏ **moody** adj (changeable) de humor variable; (sullen) malhumorado

moon [muːn] n luna ❏ **moonlight** n luz f de la luna

moor [muə*] n páramo ◆ vt (ship) amarrar ◆ vi echar las amarras

moose [muːs] n inv alce m

mop [mɔp] n fregona; (of hair) greña, melena ◆ vt fregar ▶ **mop up** vt limpiar

mope [məup] vi estar or andar deprimido

moped ['məuped] n ciclomotor m

moral ['mɔrl] adj moral ◆ n moraleja; **morals** npl moralidad f, moral f

morale [mɔ'rɑːl] n moral f

morality [mə'rælɪtɪ] n moralidad f

morbid ['mɔːbɪd] adj (interest) morboso; (MED) mórbido

more

KEYWORD

[mɔː*] adj

1 (greater in number etc) más; **more people/work than before** más gente/trabajo que antes

2 (additional) más; **do you want (some) more tea?** ¿quieres más té?; **is there any more wine?** ¿queda vino?; **it'll take a few more weeks** tardará unas semanas más; **it's 2 kms more to the house** faltan 2 kms para la casa; **more time/letters than we expected** más tiempo del que/más cartas de las que esperábamos

◆ pron (greater amount, additional amount) más; **more than 10** más de 10; **it cost more than the other one/than we expected** costó más que el otro/más de lo que esperábamos; **is there any more?** ¿hay más?; **many/much more** muchos(as)/mucho(a) más

◆ adv más; **more dangerous/easily (than)** más peligroso/fácilmente (que); **more and more expensive** cada vez más caro; **more or less** más o menos; **more than ever** más que nunca

moreover [mɔː'rəʊvə'] adv además, por otra parte

morgue [mɔːɡ] n depósito de cadáveres

morning [ˈmɔːnɪŋ] n mañana; (early morning) madrugada ♦ cpd matutino, de la mañana; in the ~ por la mañana; **7 o'clock in the ~** las 7 de la mañana ❏ **morning sickness** n náuseas fpl matutinas

Moroccan [məˈrɒkən] adj, n marroquí m/f

Morocco [məˈrɒkəʊ] n Marruecos m

moron [ˈmɔːrɒn] (inf) n imbécil m/f

morphine [ˈmɔːfiːn] n morfina

Morse [mɔːs] n (also: ~ code) (código) Morse

mortal [ˈmɔːtl] adj, n mortal m

mortar [ˈmɔːtə'] n argamasa

mortgage [ˈmɔːɡɪdʒ] n hipoteca ♦ vt hipotecar

mortician [mɔːˈtɪʃən] (US) n director(-a) m/f de pompas fúnebres

mortified [ˈmɔːtɪfaɪd] adj: **I was ~** me dio muchísima vergüenza

mortuary [ˈmɔːtjʊərɪ] n depósito de cadáveres

mosaic [məʊˈzeɪɪk] n mosaico

Moslem [ˈmɒzləm] adj, n = **Muslim**

mosque [mɒsk] n mezquita

mosquito [mɒsˈkiːtəʊ] (pl **mosquitoes**) n mosquito (SP), zancudo (LAm)

moss [mɒs] n musgo

most [məʊst] adj la mayor parte de, la mayoría de ♦ pron la mayor parte, la mayoría de ♦ adv el más; (very) muy; the ~ (also: + adj) el más; **~ of them** la mayor parte de ellos; **I saw the ~** yo vi el que más; **at the (very) ~** a lo sumo, todo lo más; **to make the ~ of** aprovechar (al máximo); **a ~ interesting book** un libro interesantísimo ❏ **mostly** adv en su mayor parte, principalmente

MOT (BRIT) n abbr = **Ministry of Transport; the ~ (test)** inspección (anual) obligatoria de coches y camiones

motel [məʊˈtel] n motel m

moth [mɒθ] n mariposa nocturna; (clothes moth) polilla

mother [ˈmʌðə'] n madre f ♦ adj materno ♦ vt (care for) cuidar (como una madre) ❏ **motherhood** n maternidad f ❏ **mother-in-law** n suegra ❏ **mother-of-pearl** n nácar m ❏ **Mother's Day** n Día m de la Madre ❏ **mother-to-be** n futura madre f ❏ **mother tongue** n lengua materna

motif [məʊˈtiːf] n motivo

motion [ˈməʊʃən] n movimiento; (gesture) ademán m, señal f; (at meeting) moción f ♦ vt, vi: **to ~ (to) sb to do sth** hacer señas a algn para que haga algo ❏ **motionless** adj inmóvil ❏ **motion picture** n película

motivate [ˈməʊtɪveɪt] vt motivar

motivation [məʊtɪˈveɪʃən] n motivación f

motive [ˈməʊtɪv] n motivo

motor [ˈməʊtə'] n motor m; (BRIT: inf: vehicle) coche m (SP), carro (LAm), automóvil m ♦ adj motor (f: motora or motriz) ❏ **motorbike** n moto f ❏ **motorboat** n lancha motora ❏ **motorcar** (BRIT) n coche m, carro, automóvil m ❏ **motorcycle** n motocicleta ❏ **motorcyclist** n motociclista m/f ❏ **motoring** (BRIT) n automovilismo ❏ **motorist** n conductor(a) m/f, automovilista mf ❏ **motor racing** (BRIT) n carreras fpl de coches, automovilismo ❏ **motorway** (BRIT) n autopista

motto [ˈmɒtəʊ] (pl **mottoes**) n lema m; (watchword) consigna

mould [məʊld] (US **mold**) n molde m; (mildew) moho ♦ vt moldear; (fig) formar ❏ **mouldy** adj enmohecido

mound [maʊnd] n montón m, montículo

mount [maʊnt] n monte m ♦ vt montar, subir a; (jewel) engarzar; (picture) enmarcar; (exhibition etc)

organizar ♦ vi (increase) aumentar
▶ **mount up** vi aumentar

mountain ['mauntin] n montaña
♦ cpd de montaña ❏ **mountain bike** n bicicleta de montaña
❏ **mountaineer** n alpinista mf (SP, MEX), andinista mf (LAm)
❏ **mountaineering** n alpinismo (SP, MEX), andinismo (LAm)
❏ **mountainous** adj montañoso
❏ **mountain range** n sierra

mourn [mɔ:n] vt llorar, lamentar ♦ vi: **to ~ for** llorar la muerte de
❏ **mourner** n doliente mf; dolorido(-a) ❏ **mourning** n luto; **in mourning** de luto

mouse [maus] (pl mice) n (ZOOL, COMPUT) ratón m ❏ **mouse mat** n (COMPUT) alfombrilla

moussaka [mu'sɑːkə] n musaca

mousse [mu:s] n (CULIN) crema batida; (for hair) espuma (moldeadora)

moustache [məs'tɑːʃ] (US **mustache**) n bigote m

mouth [mauθ, pl mauðz] n boca; (of river) desembocadura ❏ **mouthful** n bocado ❏ **mouth organ** n armónica ❏ **mouthpiece** n (of musical instrument) boquilla; (spokesman) portavoz mf ❏ **mouthwash** n enjuague m

move [mu:v] n (movement) movimiento; (in game) jugada; (: turn to play) turno; (change: of house) mudanza; (: of job) cambio de trabajo ♦ vt mover; (emotionally) conmover; (POL: resolution etc) proponer ♦ vi moverse; (traffic) circular; (also: ~ house) trasladarse, mudarse; **to ~ sb to do sth** mover a algn a hacer algo; **to get a ~ on** darse prisa ▶ **move back** vi retroceder ▶ **move in** vi (to a house) instalarse ▶ **move off** vi ponerse en camino ▶ **move on** vi ponerse en camino ▶ **move out** vi (of house) mudarse ▶ **move over** vi apartarse, hacer sitio

▶ **move up** vi (employee) ser ascendido ❏ **movement** n movimiento

movie ['mu:vɪ] n película; **to go to the movies** ir al cine ❏ **movie theater** (US) n cine m

moving ['mu:vɪŋ] adj (emotional) conmovedor(a); (that moves) móvil

mow [məu] (pt **mowed**, pp **mowed** or **mown**) vt (grass, corn) cortar, segar ❏ **mower** n (also: **lawnmower**) cortacéspedes m inv

Mozambique [məuzæm'biːk] n Mozambique m

MP n abbr = **Member of Parliament**

MP3 n MP3 ❏ **MP3 player** n reproductor m (de) MP3

mpg n abbr = **miles per gallon**

m.p.h. abbr = **miles per hour** (60 m.p.h. = 96 k.p.h.)

Mr ['mɪstə'] (US **Mr.**) n: **Mr Smith** (el) Sr. Smith

Mrs ['mɪsɪz] (US **Mrs.**) n: ~ **Smith** (la) Sra. Smith

Ms [mɪz] (US **Ms.**) n = **Miss** or **Mrs**; **Ms Smith** (la) Sr(t)a. Smith

MSP n abbr = **Member of the Scottish Parliament**

Mt abbr (GEO: = **mount**) m

much [mʌtʃ] adj mucho ♦ adv mucho; (before pp) muy ♦ n or pron mucho; **how ~ is it?** ¿cuánto es?, ¿cuánto cuesta?; **too ~** demasiado; **it's not ~** no es mucho; **as ~ as** tanto como; **however ~ he tries** por mucho que se esfuerce

muck [mʌk] n suciedad f ▶ **muck up** (inf) vt arruinar, estropear ❏ **mucky** adj (dirty) sucio

mucus ['mju:kəs] n mucosidad f, moco

mud [mʌd] n barro, lodo

muddle ['mʌdl] n desorden m, confusión f; (mix-up) embrollo, lío ♦ vt (also: ~ up) embrollar, confundir

muddy ['mʌdɪ] adj fangoso, cubierto de lodo

mudguard ['mʌdgɑːd] n guardabarros m inv

muesli ['mjuːzlɪ] n muesli m

muffin ['mʌfɪn] n panecillo dulce

muffled ['mʌfld] adj (noise etc) amortiguado, apagado

muffler (US) ['mʌflə'] n (AUT) silenciador m

mug [mʌg] n taza grande (sin platillo); (for beer) jarra; (inf: face) jeta ♦ vt (assault) asaltar ❑ **mugger** ['mʌgə'] n atracador(a) m/f ❑ **mugging** n asalto

muggy ['mʌgɪ] adj bochornoso

mule [mjuːl] n mula

multicoloured ['mʌltɪkʌləd] (US **multicolored**) adj multicolor

multimedia [mʌltɪ'miːdɪə] adj multimedia

multinational [mʌltɪ'næʃənl] n multinacional f ♦ adj multinacional

multiple ['mʌltɪpl] adj múltiple ♦ n múltiplo ❑ **multiple choice (test)** n examen m de tipo test ❑ **multiple sclerosis** n esclerosis f múltiple

multiplex cinema ['mʌltɪpleks-] n multicines mpl

multiplication [mʌltɪplɪ'keɪʃən] n multiplicación f

multiply ['mʌltɪplaɪ] vt multiplicar ♦ vi multiplicarse

multistorey [mʌltɪ'stɔːrɪ] (BRIT) adj de muchos pisos

mum [mʌm] (BRIT: inf) n mamá ♦ adj: **to keep ~** mantener la boca cerrada

mumble ['mʌmbl] vt, vi hablar entre dientes, refunfuñar

mummy ['mʌmɪ] n (BRIT: mother) mamá; (embalmed) momia

mumps [mʌmps] n paperas fpl

munch [mʌntʃ] vt, vi mascar

municipal [mjuː'nɪsɪpl] adj municipal

mural ['mjuərl] n (pintura) mural m

murder ['mɜːdə'] n asesinato; (in law) homicidio ♦ vt asesinar, matar ❑ **murderer** n asesino

murky ['mɜːkɪ] adj (water) turbio; (street, night) lóbrego

murmur ['mɜːmə'] n murmullo ♦ vt, vi murmurar

muscle ['mʌsl] n músculo; (fig: strength) garra, fuerza ❑ **muscular** ['mʌskjulə'] adj muscular; (person) musculoso

museum [mjuː'zɪəm] n museo

mushroom ['mʌʃrum] n seta, hongo; (CULIN) champiñón m ♦ vi crecer de la noche a la mañana

music ['mjuːzɪk] n música ❑ **musical** adj musical; (sound) melodioso; (person) con talento musical ♦ n (show) comedia musical ❑ **musical instrument** n instrumento musical ❑ **musician** [-'zɪʃən] n músico(-a)

Muslim ['mʌzlɪm] adj, n musulmán(-ana) m/f

muslin ['mʌzlɪn] n muselina

mussel ['mʌsl] n mejillón m

must [mʌst] aux vb (obligation): **I ~ do it** debo hacerlo, tengo que hacerlo; (probability): **he ~ be there by now** ya debe (de) estar allí ♦ n: **it's a ~** es imprescindible

mustache ['mʌstæʃ] (US) n = **moustache**

mustard ['mʌstəd] n mostaza

mustn't ['mʌsnt] = **must not**

mute [mjuːt] adj, n mudo(-a) m/f

mutilate ['mjuːtɪleɪt] vt mutilar

mutiny ['mjuːtɪnɪ] n motín m ♦ vi amotinarse

mutter ['mʌtə'] vt, vi murmurar

mutton ['mʌtn] n carne f de cordero

mutual ['mjuːtʃuəl] adj mutuo; (interest) común

muzzle ['mʌzl] n hocico; (for dog) bozal m; (of gun) boca ♦ vt (dog) poner un bozal a

my [maɪ] adj mi(s); **my house/brother/ sisters** mi casa/mi hermano/mis hermanas; **I've washed my hair/cut my finger** me he lavado el pelo/

cortado un dedo; **is this my pen or yours?** ¿es este bolígrafo mío o tuyo?

myself [maɪˈsɛlf] *pron (reflexive)* me; *(emphatic)* yo mismo; *(after prep)* mí (mismo); *see also* **oneself**

mysterious [mɪsˈtɪərɪəs] *adj* misterioso

mystery [ˈmɪstərɪ] *n* misterio

mystical [ˈmɪstɪkl] *adj* místico

mystify [ˈmɪstɪfaɪ] *vt (perplex)* dejar perplejo

myth [mɪθ] *n* mito ◻ **mythology** [mɪˈθɒlədʒɪ] *n* mitología

N, n

n/a *abbr* (= *not applicable*) no interesa

nag [næɡ] *vt (scold)* regañar

nail [neɪl] *n (human)* uña; *(metal)* clavo ◆ *vt* clavar; **to ~ sth to sth** clavar algo en algo; **to ~ sb down to doing sth** comprometer a algn a que haga algo ◻ **nailbrush** *n* cepillo para las uñas ◻ **nailfile** *n* lima para las uñas ◻ **nail polish** *n* esmalte *m* or laca para las uñas ◻ **nail polish remover** *n* quitaesmalte *m* ◻ **nail scissors** *npl* tijeras *fpl* para las uñas ◻ **nail varnish** *(BRIT) n* = **nail polish**

naïve [naɪˈiːv] *adj* ingenuo

naked [ˈneɪkɪd] *adj (nude)* desnudo; *(flame)* expuesto al aire

name [neɪm] *n* nombre *m*; *(surname)* apellido; *(reputation)* fama, renombre *m* ◆ *vt (child)* poner nombre a; *(criminal)* identificar; *(price, date etc)* fijar; **what's your ~?** ¿cómo se llama?; **by ~** de nombre; **in the ~ of** en nombre de; **to give one's ~ and address** dar sus señas ◻ **namely** *adv* a saber

nanny [ˈnænɪ] *n* niñera

nap [næp] *n (sleep)* sueñecito, siesta

napkin [ˈnæpkɪn] *n (also:* **table ~)** servilleta

nappy [ˈnæpɪ] *(BRIT) n* pañal *m*

narcotics *npl (illegal drugs)* estupefacientes *mpl*, narcóticos *mpl*

narrative [ˈnærətɪv] *n* narrativa ◆ *adj* narrativo

narrator [nəˈreɪtə] *n* narrador(a) *m/f*

narrow [ˈnærəʊ] *adj* estrecho, angosto; *(fig: majority etc)* corto; (: *ideas etc)* estrecho ◆ *vi (road)* estrecharse; *(diminish)* reducirse; **to have a ~ escape** escaparse por los pelos ▶ **narrow down** *vt (search, investigation, possibilities)* restringir, limitar; *(list)* reducir ◻ **narrowly** *adv (miss)* por poco ◻ **narrow-minded** *adj* de miras estrechas

nasal [ˈneɪzl] *adj* nasal

nasty [ˈnɑːstɪ] *adj (remark)* feo; *(person)* antipático; *(revolting: taste, smell)* asqueroso; *(wound, disease etc)* peligroso, grave

nation [ˈneɪʃən] *n* nación *f*

national [ˈnæʃənl] *adj, n* nacional *m/f* ◻ **national anthem** *n* himno nacional ◻ **national dress** *n* vestido nacional ◻ **National Health Service** *(BRIT) n* servicio nacional de salud pública, = Insalud *m (SP)* ◻ **National Insurance** *(BRIT) n* seguro social nacional ◻ **nationalist** *adj, n* nacionalista *m/f* ◻ **nationality** [-ˈnælɪtɪ] *n* nacionalidad *f* ◻ **nationalize** *vt* nacionalizar ◻ **national park** *(BRIT) n* parque *m* nacional ◻ **National Trust** *n (BRIT)* organización encargada de preservar el patrimonio histórico británico

nationwide [ˈneɪʃənwaɪd] *adj* en escala or a nivel nacional

native [ˈneɪtɪv] *n (local inhabitant)* natural *mf*, nacional *mf* ◆ *adj (indigenous)* indígena; *(country)* natal; *(innate)* natural, innato; **a ~ of Russia** un(a) natural de Rusia ◻ **Native American** *n* americano(-a) indígena, amerindio(-a) ◻ **native speaker** *n* hablante *mf* nativo(-a)

NATO ['neɪtəu] n abbr (= North Atlantic Treaty Organization) OTAN f

natural ['nætʃrəl] adj natural ❑ **natural gas** n gas m natural ❑ **natural history** n historia natural ❑ **naturally** adv (speak etc) naturalmente; (of course) desde luego, por supuesto ❑ **natural resources** npl recursos mpl naturales

nature ['neɪtʃə'] n (also: **N~**) naturaleza; (group, sort) género, clase; (character) carácter m, genio; **by ~** por or de naturaleza ❑ **nature reserve** n reserva natural

naughty ['nɔːtɪ] adj (child) travieso

nausea ['nɔːsɪə] n náuseas fpl

naval ['neɪvl] adj naval, de marina

navel ['neɪvl] n ombligo

navigate ['nævɪɡeɪt] vt gobernar ♦ vi navegar; (AUT) ir de copiloto ❑ **navigation** [-'ɡeɪʃən] n (action) navegación f; (science) náutica

navy ['neɪvɪ] n marina de guerra; (ships) armada, flota

Nazi ['nɑːtsɪ] n nazi mf

NB abbr (= nota bene) nótese

near [nɪə'] adj (place, relation) cercano; (time) próximo ♦ adv cerca ♦ prep (also: **~ to**: space) cerca de, junto a; (: time) cerca de ♦ vt acercarse a, aproximarse a ❑ **nearby** [nɪə'baɪ] adj cercano, próximo ♦ adv cerca ❑ **nearly** adv casi, por poco; **I nearly fell** por poco me caigo ❑ **near-sighted** adj miope, corto de vista

neat [niːt] adj (place) ordenado, bien cuidado; (person) pulcro; (plan) ingenioso; (spirits) solo ❑ **neatly** adv (tidily) con esmero; (skilfully) ingeniosamente

necessarily ['nesɪsrɪlɪ] adv necesariamente

necessary ['nesɪsrɪ] adj necesario, preciso

necessity [nɪ'sesɪtɪ] n necesidad f

neck [nek] n (of person, garment, bottle) cuello; (of animal) pescuezo ♦ vi (inf) besuquearse; **~ and ~** parejos ❑ **necklace** ['neklɪs] n collar m ❑ **necktie** ['nektaɪ] n corbata

nectarine ['nektərɪn] n nectarina

need [niːd] n (lack) escasez f, falta; (necessity) necesidad f ♦ vt (require) necesitar; **I ~ to do it** tengo que or debo hacerlo; **you don't ~ to go** no hace falta que (te) vayas

needle ['niːdl] n aguja ♦ vt (fig: inf) picar, fastidiar

needless ['niːdlɪs] adj innecesario; **~ to say** huelga decir que

needlework ['niːdlwɜːk] n (activity) costura, labor f de aguja

needn't ['niːdnt] = **need not**

needy ['niːdɪ] adj necesitado

negative ['neɡətɪv] n (PHOT) negativo; (LING) negación f ♦ adj negativo

neglect [nɪ'ɡlekt] vt (one's duty) faltar a, no cumplir con; (child) descuidar, desatender ♦ n (of house, garden etc) abandono; (of child) desatención f; (of duty) incumplimiento

negotiate [nɪ'ɡəʊʃɪeɪt] vt (treaty, loan) negociar; (obstacle) franquear; (bend in road) tomar ♦ vi: **to ~ (with)** negociar (con)

negotiations [nɪɡəʊʃɪ'eɪʃənz] pl n negociaciones

negotiator [nɪ'ɡəʊʃɪeɪtə'] n negociador(a) m/f

neighbour ['neɪbə'] (US **neighbor** etc) n vecino(-a) ❑ **neighbourhood** n (place) vecindad f, barrio; (people) vecindario ❑ **neighbouring** adj vecino

neither ['naɪðə'] adj ni ♦ conj: **I didn't move and ~ did John** no me he movido, ni Juan tampoco ♦ pron ninguno ♦ adv: **~ good nor bad** ni bueno ni malo; **~ is true** ninguno(-a) de los (las) dos es cierto(-a)

neon ['niːɔn] n neón m

Nepal [nɪˈpɔːl] n Nepal m

nephew [ˈnɛvjuː] n sobrino

nerve [nɜːv] n (ANAT) nervio; (courage) valor m; (impudence) descaro, frescura; **nerves** (nervousness) nerviosismo msg, nervios mpl; **a fit of nerves** un ataque de nervios

nervous [ˈnɜːvəs] adj (anxious, ANAT) nervioso; (timid) miedoso ❑ **nervous breakdown** n crisis f nerviosa

nest [nɛst] n (of bird) nido; (wasps' nest) avispero ♦ vi anidar

net [nɛt] n (gen) red f; (fabric) tul m ♦ adj (COMM) neto, líquido ♦ vt coger (SP) or agarrar (LAm) con red; (SPORT) marcar ❑ **netball** n básquet m

Netherlands [ˈnɛðələndz] npl: **the ~** los Países Bajos

nett [nɛt] adj = **net**

nettle [ˈnɛtl] n ortiga

network [ˈnɛtwɜːk] n red f

neurotic [njuəˈrɔtɪk] adj neurótico(-a)

neuter [ˈnjuːtəʳ] adj (LING) neutro ♦ vt castrar, capar

neutral [ˈnjuːtrəl] adj (person) neutral; (colour etc, ELEC) neutro ♦ n (AUT) punto muerto

never [ˈnɛvəʳ] adv nunca, jamás; **I ~ went** no fui nunca; **~ in my life** jamás en la vida; see also **mind** ❑ **never-ending** adj interminable, sin fin ❑ **nevertheless** [nɛvəðəˈlɛs] adv sin embargo, no obstante

new [njuː] adj nuevo; (brand new) a estrenar; (recent) reciente ❑ **New Age** n Nueva Era ❑ **newborn** adj recién nacido ❑ **newcomer** [ˈnjuːkʌməʳ] n recién venido(-a) or llegado(-a) ❑ **newly** adv nuevamente, recién

news [njuːz] n noticias fpl; **a piece of ~** una noticia; **the ~** (RADIO, TV) las noticias fpl ❑ **news agency** n agencia de noticias ❑ **newsagent** (BRIT) n vendedor(a) m/f de periódicos ❑ **newscaster** n presentador(a) m/f,

locutor(a) m/f ❑ **news dealer** (US) n = **newsagent** ❑ **newsletter** n hoja informativa, boletín m ❑ **newspaper** n periódico, diario ❑ **newsreader** n = **newscaster**

newt [njuːt] n tritón m

New Year n Año Nuevo ❑ **New Year's Day** n Día m de Año Nuevo ❑ **New Year's Eve** n Nochevieja

New Zealand [njuːˈziːlənd] n Nueva Zelanda ❑ **New Zealander** n neozelandés(-esa) m/f

next [nɛkst] adj (house, room) vecino; (bus stop, meeting) próximo; (following: page etc) siguiente ♦ adv después; **the ~ day** el día siguiente; **~ time** la próxima vez; **~ year** el año próximo or que viene; **~ to** junto a, al lado de; **~ to nothing** casi nada; **~ please!** ¡el siguiente! ❑ **next door** adv en la casa de al lado ♦ adj vecino, de al lado ❑ **next-of-kin** n pariente m más cercano

NHS n abbr = **National Health Service**

nibble [ˈnɪbl] vt mordisquear, mordiscar

nice [naɪs] adj (likeable) simpático; (kind) amable; (pleasant) agradable; (attractive) bonito, lindo (LAm) ❑ **nicely** adv amablemente; bien

niche [niːʃ] n (ARCH) nicho, hornacina

nick [nɪk] n (wound) rasguño; (cut, indentation) mella, muesca ♦ vt (inf) birlar, robar; **in the ~ of time** justo a tiempo

nickel [ˈnɪkl] n níquel m; (US) moneda de 5 centavos

nickname [ˈnɪkneɪm] n apodo, mote m ♦ vt apodar

nicotine [ˈnɪkətiːn] n nicotina

niece [niːs] n sobrina

Nigeria [naɪˈdʒɪərɪə] n Nigeria

night [naɪt] n noche f; (evening) tarde f; **the ~ before last** anteanoche; **at ~, by ~** de noche, por la noche ❑ **night**

club n cabaret m ❑ **nightdress** (BRIT) n camisón m ❑ **nightie** ['naɪtɪ] n =
nightdress ❑ **nightlife** n vida nocturna ♦ adj de todas las noches ❑ **nightly** adj de todas las noches ❑ **nightmare** n pesadilla ❑ **night school** n clase(s) f(pl) nocturna(s) ❑ **night shift** n turno nocturno or de noche ❑ **night-time** n noche f

nil [nɪl] (BRIT) (SPORT) n cero, nada

nine [naɪn] num nueve ❑ **nineteen** num diecinueve, diez y nueve ❑ **nineteenth** [naɪn'tiːnθ] adj decimonoveno, decimonono ❑ **ninetieth** ['naɪntɪɪθ] adj nonagésimo ❑ **ninety** num noventa

ninth [naɪnθ] adj noveno

nip [nɪp] vt (pinch) pellizcar; (bite) morder

nipple ['nɪpl] n (ANAT) pezón m

nitrogen ['naɪtrədʒən] n nitrógeno

no

KEYWORD

[nəʊ] (pl noes) adv (opposite of "yes")
no; **are you coming? — no (I'm not)**
¿vienes? — no; **would you like some**
more? — no thank you ¿quieres
más? — no gracias

♦ adj (not any): **I have no money/**
time/books no tengo dinero/
tiempo/libros; **no other man would**
have done it ningún otro lo hubiera
hecho; **"no entry"** "prohibido el
paso"; **"no smoking"** "prohibido
fumar"

♦ n no m

nobility [nəʊ'bɪlɪtɪ] n nobleza
noble ['nəʊbl] adj noble
nobody ['nəʊbədɪ] pron nadie
nod [nɒd] vi saludar con la cabeza; (in agreement) decir que sí con la cabeza; (doze) dar cabezadas ♦ vt: **to ~ one's head** inclinar la cabeza ♦ n inclinación

f de cabeza ▶ **nod off** vi dar cabezadas

noise [nɔɪz] n ruido; (din) escándalo, estrépito ❑ **noisy** adj ruidoso; (child) escandaloso

nominal ['nɒmɪnl] adj nominal

nominate ['nɒmɪneɪt] vt (propose) proponer; (appoint) nombrar ❑ **nomination** [nɒmɪ'neɪʃən] n propuesta; nombramiento ❑ **nominee** [-'niː] n candidato(-a)

none [nʌn] pron ninguno(-a) ♦ adv de ninguna manera; **~ of you** ninguno de vosotros; **I've ~ left** no me queda ninguno(-a); **he's ~ the worse for it** no le ha hecho ningún mal

nonetheless [nʌnðə'les] adv sin embargo, no obstante

non-fiction [nɒn'fɪkʃən] n literatura no novelesca

nonsense ['nɒnsəns] n tonterías fpl, disparates mpl; **~!** ¡qué tonterías!

non: **non-smoker** n no fumador(a) m/f ❑ **non-smoking** adj (de) no fumador ❑ **non-stick** adj (pan, surface) antiadherente

noodles ['nuːdlz] npl tallarines mpl

noon [nuːn] n mediodía m

no-one ['nəʊwʌn] pron = **nobody**

nor [nɔːʳ] conj = **neither** ♦ adv see **neither**

norm [nɔːm] n norma

normal ['nɔːml] adj normal ❑ **normally** adv normalmente

north [nɔːθ] n norte m ♦ adj del norte, norteño ♦ adv al or hacia el norte ❑ **North America** n América del Norte ❑ **North American** adj, n norteamericano(-a) m/f ❑ **northbound** ['nɔːθbaʊnd] adj (traffic) que se dirige al norte; (carriageway) de dirección norte ❑ **north-east** n nor(d)este m ❑ **northeastern** adj nor(d)este, del nor(d)este ❑ **northern** ['nɔːðən] adj del norte ❑ **Northern**

Ireland n Irlanda del Norte ❑ **North Korea** n Corea del Norte ❑ **North Pole** n Polo Norte ❑ **North Sea** n Mar m del Norte ❑ **north-west** n nor(d)oeste m ❑ **northwestern** ['nɔːθ'westən] adj noroeste, del noroeste

Norway ['nɔːweɪ] n Noruega ❑ **Norwegian** [-'wiːdʒən] adj noruego(-a) ♦ n noruego(-a); (LING) noruego

nose [nəʊz] n (ANAT) nariz f; (ZOOL) hocico; (sense of smell) olfato ♦ vi: to ~ **about** curiosear ❑ **nosebleed** n hemorragia nasal ❑ **nosey** (inf) adj curioso, fisgón(-ona)

nostalgia [nɔs'tældʒɪə] n nostalgia

nostalgic [nɔs'tældʒɪk] adj nostálgico

nostril ['nɔstrɪl] n ventana de la nariz

nosy ['nəʊzɪ] (inf) adj = **nosey**

not [nɔt] adv no; ~ **that** ... no es que ...; **it's too late, isn't it?** es demasiado tarde, ¿verdad or no?; ~ **yet/now** todavía/ahora no; **why** ~? ¿por qué no?; see also **all**; **only**

notable ['nəʊtəbl] adj notable ❑ **notably** adv especialmente

notch [nɔtʃ] n muesca, corte m

note [nəʊt] n (MUS, record, letter) nota; (banknote) billete m; (tone) tono ♦ vt (observe) notar, observar; (write down) apuntar, anotar ❑ **notebook** n libreta, cuaderno ❑ **noted** ['nəʊtɪd] adj célebre, conocido ❑ **notepad** n bloc m ❑ **notepaper** n papel m para cartas

nothing ['nʌθɪŋ] n nada; (zero) cero; **he does** ~ no hace nada; ~ **new** nada nuevo; ~ **much** no mucho; **for** ~ (free) gratis, sin pago; (in vain) en balde

notice ['nəʊtɪs] n (announcement) anuncio; (warning) aviso; (dismissal) despido; (resignation) dimisión f; (period of time) plazo ♦ vt (observe) notar, observar; **to bring sth to sb's** ~ (attention) llamar la atención de algn sobre algo; **to take** ~ **of** tomar nota de,

prestar atención a; **at short** ~ con poca anticipación; **until further** ~ hasta nuevo aviso; **to hand in one's** ~ dimitir ❑ **noticeable** adj evidente, obvio

⚠ Be careful not to translate **notice** by the Spanish word **noticia**.

notify ['nəʊtɪfaɪ] vt: **to** ~ **sb (of sth)** comunicar (algo) a algn

notion ['nəʊʃən] n idea; (opinion) opinión f; **notions** npl (US) mercería

notorious [nəʊ'tɔːrɪəs] adj notorio

notwithstanding [nɔtwɪθ'stændɪŋ] adv no obstante, sin embargo; ~ **this** a pesar de esto

nought [nɔːt] n cero

noun [naʊn] n nombre m, sustantivo

nourish ['nʌrɪʃ] vt nutrir; (fig) alimentar ❑ **nourishment** n alimento, sustento

Nov. abbr (= November) nov

novel ['nɔvl] n novela ♦ adj (new) nuevo, original; (unexpected) insólito ❑ **novelist** n novelista mf ❑ **novelty** n novedad f

November [nəʊ'vembə°] n noviembre m

novice ['nɔvɪs] n (REL) novicio(-a)

now [naʊ] adv (at the present time) ahora; (these days) actualmente, hoy día ♦ conj: ~ **(that)** ya que, ahora que; **right** ~ ahora mismo; **by** ~ ya; **just** ~ ahora mismo; ~ **and then**, ~ **and again** de vez en cuando; **from** ~ **on** de ahora en adelante ❑ **nowadays** ['naʊədeɪz] adv hoy (en) día, actualmente

nowhere ['nəʊweə°] adv (direction) a ninguna parte; (location) en ninguna parte

nozzle ['nɔzl] n boquilla

nr abbr (BRIT) = **near**

nuclear ['njuːklɪə°] adj nuclear

nucleus ['njuːklɪəs] (pl **nuclei**) n núcleo

nude [njuːd] adj, n desnudo(-a) m/f; **in the** ~ desnudo

nudge [nʌdʒ] vt dar un codazo a

nudist ['njuːdɪst] n nudista mf

nudity ['nju:dɪtɪ] n desnudez f

nuisance ['nju:sns] n molestia, fastidio; (person) pesado, latoso; **what a ~!** ¡qué lata!

numb [nʌm] adj: ~ **with cold/fear** entumecido por el frío/paralizado de miedo

number ['nʌmbə'] n número; (quantity) cantidad f ♦ vt (pages etc) numerar, poner número a; (amount to) sumar, ascender a; **to be numbered among** figurar entre; **a ~ of** varios, algunos; **they were ten in ~** eran diez ☐ **number plate** (BRIT) n matrícula, placa ☐ **Number Ten** n (BRIT: 10 Downing Street) residencia del primer ministro

numerical [nju:'merɪkl] adj numérico

numerous ['nju:mərəs] adj numeroso

nun [nʌn] n monja, religiosa

nurse [nə:s] n enfermero(-a); (also: **nursemaid**) niñera ♦ vt (patient) cuidar, atender

nursery ['nə:sərɪ] n (institution) guardería infantil; (room) cuarto de los niños; (for plants) criadero, semillero ☐ **nursery rhyme** n canción f infantil ☐ **nursery school** n parvulario, escuela de párvulos ☐ **nursery slope** (BRIT) n (SKI) cuesta para principiantes

nursing ['nə:sɪŋ] n (profession) profesión f de enfermera; (care) asistencia, cuidado ☐ **nursing home** n clínica de reposo

nurture ['nə:tʃə'] vt (child, plant) alimentar, nutrir

nut [nʌt] n (TECH) tuerca; (BOT) nuez f

nutmeg ['nʌtmeg] n nuez f moscada

nutrient ['nju:trɪənt] adj nutritivo ♦ n elemento nutritivo

nutrition [nju:'trɪʃən] n nutrición f, alimentación f

nutritious [nju:'trɪʃəs] adj nutritivo, alimenticio

nuts [nʌts] (inf) adj loco

NVQ n abbr (BRIT) = **National Vocational Qualification**

nylon ['naɪlɔn] n nilón m ♦ adj de nilón

O, o

oak [əuk] n roble m ♦ adj de roble

O.A.P. (BRIT) n, abbr = **old-age pensioner**

oar [ɔ:'] n remo

oasis [əu'eɪsɪs] (pl **oases**) n oasis m inv

oath [əuθ] n juramento; (swear word) palabrota; **on** (BRIT) **or under ~** bajo juramento

oatmeal ['əutmi:l] n harina de avena

oats [əuts] npl avena

obedience [ə'bi:dɪəns] n obediencia

obedient [ə'bi:dɪənt] adj obediente

obese [əu'bi:s] adj obeso

obesity [əu'bi:sɪtɪ] n obesidad f

obey [ə'beɪ] vt obedecer; (instructions, regulations) cumplir

obituary [ə'bɪtjuərɪ] n necrología

object [n 'ɔbdʒɪkt, vb əb'dʒɛkt] n objeto; (purpose) objeto, propósito; (LING) complemento ♦ vi: **to ~ to** estar en contra de; (proposal) oponerse a; **to ~ that** objetar que; **expense is no ~** no importa cuánto cuesta; **I ~!** ¡yo protesto! ☐ **objection** [əb'dʒɛkʃən] n protesta; **I have no objection to ...** no tengo inconveniente en que ... ☐ **objective** adj, n objetivo

obligation [ɔblɪ'geɪʃən] n obligación f; (debt) deber m; **without ~** sin compromiso

obligatory [ə'blɪɡətərɪ] adj obligatorio

oblige [ə'blaɪdʒ] vt (do a favour for) complacer, hacer un favor a; **to ~ sb to do sth** forzar or obligar a algn a hacer algo; **to be obliged to sb for sth** estarle agradecido a algn por algo

oblique [ə'bli:k] adj oblicuo; (allusion) indirecto

obliterate 467 **of**

obliterate [əˈblɪtəreɪt] vt borrar

oblivious [əˈblɪvɪəs] adj: ~ of inconsciente de

oblong [ˈɒblɒŋ] adj rectangular ♦ n rectángulo

obnoxious [əbˈnɒkʃəs] adj odioso, detestable; (smell) nauseabundo

oboe [ˈəubəu] n oboe m

obscene [əbˈsiːn] adj obsceno

obscure [əbˈskjuə] adj oscuro ♦ vt oscurecer; (hide: sun) esconder

observant [əbˈzəːvnt] adj observador(a)

observation [ɒbzəˈveɪʃən] n observación f; (MED) examen m

observatory [əbˈzəːvətrɪ] n observatorio

observe [əbˈzəːv] vt observar; (rule) cumplir □ **observer** n observador(a) m/f

obsess [əbˈses] vt obsesionar □ **obsession** [əbˈseʃən] n obsesión f □ **obsessive** adj obsesivo, obsesionante

obsolete [ˈɒbsəliːt] adj: to be ~ estar en desuso

obstacle [ˈɒbstəkl] n obstáculo; (nuisance) estorbo

obstinate [ˈɒbstɪnɪt] adj terco, porfiado; (determined) empecinado

obstruct [əbˈstrʌkt] vt obstruir; (hinder) estorbar, obstaculizar □ **obstruction** [əbˈstrʌkʃən] n (action) obstrucción f; (object) estorbo

obtain [əbˈteɪn] vt obtener; (achieve) conseguir

obvious [ˈɒbvɪəs] adj obvio, evidente □ **obviously** adv evidentemente, naturalmente; **obviously not** por supuesto que no

occasion [əˈkeɪʒən] n oportunidad f, ocasión f; (event) acontecimiento □ **occasional** adj poco frecuente, ocasional □ **occasionally** adv de vez en cuando

occult [ɔˈkʌlt] adj (gen) oculto

occupant [ˈɒkjupənt] n (of house) inquilino(-a); (of car) ocupante mf

occupation [ɒkjuˈpeɪʃən] n ocupación f; (job) trabajo; (pastime) ocupaciones fpl

occupy [ˈɒkjupaɪ] vt (seat, post, time) ocupar; (house) habitar; **to ~ o.s. in doing** pasar el tiempo haciendo

occur [əˈkəː] vi pasar, suceder; **to ~ to sb** ocurrírsele a algn □ **occurrence** [əˈkʌrəns] n acontecimiento; (existence) existencia

ocean [ˈəuʃən] n océano

o'clock [əˈklɒk] adv: **it is 5 ~** son las 5

Oct. abbr (= October) oct

October [ɔkˈtəubə] n octubre m

octopus [ˈɒktəpəs] n pulpo

odd [ɒd] adj extraño, raro; (number) impar; (sock, shoe etc) suelto; **60—60** y pico; **at ~ times** de vez en cuando; **to be the ~ one out** estar de más □ **oddly** adv curiosamente, extrañamente; see also **enough** □ **odds** npl (in betting) puntos mpl de ventaja; **it makes no odds** da lo mismo; **at odds** reñidos(-as); **odds and ends** minucias fpl

odometer [ɔˈdɒmɪtə] (US) n cuentakilómetros m inv

odour [ˈəudə] (US **odor**) n olor m; (unpleasant) hedor m

of

KEYWORD

[ɒv, əv] prep

1 (gen) de; **a friend of ours** un amigo nuestro; **a boy of 10** un chico de 10 años; **that was kind of you** eso fue muy amable por o de tu parte

2 (expressing quantity, amount, dates etc) de; **a kilo of flour** un kilo de harina; **there were three of them** había tres; **three of us went** tres de nosotros fuimos; **the 5th of July** el 5 de julio

3 (*from, out of*) de; **made of wood** (hecho) de madera

off [ɔf] *adj, adv* (*engine*) desconectado; (*light*) apagado; (*tap*) cerrado; (BRIT: *food: bad*) pasado, malo; (: *milk*) cortado; (*cancelled*) cancelado ♦ *prep* de; **to be ~** (*to leave*) irse, marcharse; **to be ~ sick** estar enfermo or de baja; **a day ~** un día libre *or* sin trabajar; **to have an ~ day** tener un día malo; **he had his coat ~** se había quitado el abrigo; **10% ~** (COMM) con el 10% de descuento; **5 km ~ (the road)** a 5 km (de la carretera); **~ the coast** frente a la costa; **I'm ~ meat** (*no longer eat/like it*) paso de la carne; **on the ~ chance** por si acaso; **~ and on** de vez en cuando

offence [əˈfɛns] (US **offense**) *n* (*crime*) delito; **to take ~ at** ofenderse por

offend [əˈfɛnd] *vt* (*person*) ofender
❑ **offender** *n* delincuente *mf*

offense [əˈfɛns] (US) *n* = **offence**

offensive [əˈfɛnsɪv] *adj* ofensivo; (*smell etc*) repugnante ♦ *n* (MIL) ofensiva

offer [ˈɔfə*] *n* oferta, ofrecimiento; (*proposal*) propuesta ♦ *vt* ofrecer; (*opportunity*) facilitar; **"on ~"** (COMM) "en oferta"

offhand [ɔfˈhænd] *adj* informal ♦ *adv* de improviso

office [ˈɔfɪs] *n* (*place*) oficina; (*room*) despacho; (*position*) carga, oficio; **doctor's ~** (US) consultorio; **to take ~** entrar en funciones ❑ **office block** (US **office building**) *n* bloque *m* de oficinas ❑ **office hours** *npl* horas *fpl* de oficina; (US MED) horas *fpl* de consulta

officer [ˈɔfɪsə*] *n* (MIL etc) oficial *mf*; (*also*: **police ~**) agente *mf* de policía; (*of organization*) director(a) *m/f*

office worker *n* oficinista *mf*

official [əˈfɪʃl] *adj* oficial, autorizado ♦ *n* funcionario(-a), oficial
❑ **officer** *n* delincuente *mf*

off: **off-licence** (BRIT) *n* (*shop*) bodega, tienda de vinos y bebidas alcohólicas

❑ **off-line** *adj, adv* (COMPUT) fuera de línea ❑ **off-peak** *adj* (*electricity*) de banda económica; (*ticket*) billete *m* de precio reducido *por viajar fuera de las horas punta* ❑ **off-putting** (BRIT) *adj* (*person*) asqueroso; (*remark*) desalentador(a) ❑ **off-season** *adj, adv* fuera de temporada

offset [ˈɔfsɛt] *vt* contrarrestar, compensar

offshore [ɔfˈʃɔː*] *adj* (*breeze, island*) costera; (*fishing*) de bajura

offside [ˈɔfsaɪd] *adj* (SPORT) fuera de juego; (AUT: *in UK*) del lado derecho; (: *in US, Europe etc*) del lado izquierdo

offspring [ˈɔfsprɪŋ] *n inv* descendencia

often [ˈɔfn] *adv* a menudo, con frecuencia; **how ~ do you go?** ¿cada cuánto vas?

oh [əu] *excl* ¡ah!

oil [ɔɪl] *n* aceite *m*; (*petroleum*) petróleo; (*for heating*) aceite *m* combustible ♦ *vt* engrasar ❑ **oil filter** *n* (AUT) filtro de aceite ❑ **oil painting** *n* pintura al óleo ❑ **oil refinery** *n* refinería de petróleo ❑ **oil rig** *n* torre *f* de perforación ❑ **oil slick** *n* marea negra ❑ **oil tanker** *n* petrolero; (*truck*) camión *m* cisterna ❑ **oil well** *n* pozo (de petróleo) ❑ **oily** *adj* aceitoso; (*food*) grasiento

ointment ['ɔɪntmənt] n ungüento

O.K., okay ['əʊ'keɪ] excl O.K., ¡está bien!, ¡vale! (SP) ♦ adj bien ♦ vt dar el visto bueno a

old [əʊld] adj viejo; (former) antiguo; **how ~ are you?** ¿cuántos años tienes?, ¿qué edad tienes?; **he's 10 years ~** tiene 10 años; **older brother** hermano mayor ❏ **old age** n vejez f ❏ **old-age pension** n (BRIT) jubilación f, pensión f ❏ **old-age pensioner** (BRIT) n jubilado(-a) ❏ **old-fashioned** adj anticuado, pasado de moda ❏ **old people's home** n (esp BRIT) residencia f de ancianos

olive ['ɔlɪv] n (fruit) aceituna; (tree) olivo ♦ adj (also: **~-green**) verde oliva ❏ **olive oil** n aceite m de oliva

Olympic [əʊ'lɪmpɪk] adj olímpico; **the ~ Games, the Olympics** las Olimpiadas

omelet(te) ['ɔmlɪt] n tortilla francesa (SP), omelette f (LAm)

omen ['əʊmən] n presagio

ominous ['ɔmɪnəs] adj de mal agüero, amenazador(a)

omit [əʊ'mɪt] vt omitir

on

[ɔn] prep
1 (indicating position) en; sobre; **on the wall** en la pared; **it's on the table** está sobre or en la mesa; **on the left** a la izquierda

2 (indicating means, method, condition etc): **on foot** a pie; **on the train/plane** (go) en tren/avión; (be) en el tren/el avión; **on the radio/ television/telephone** por or en la radio/televisión/al teléfono; **to be on drugs** drogarse; (MED) estar a tratamiento; **to be on holiday/ business** estar de vacaciones/en viaje de negocios

3 (referring to time): **on Friday** el

viernes; **on Fridays** los viernes; **on June 20th** el 20 de junio; **a week on Friday** del viernes en una semana; **on arrival** al llegar; **on seeing this** al ver esto

4 (about, concerning) sobre, acerca de; **a book on physics** un libro de or sobre física
♦ adv

1 (referring to dress): **to have one's coat on** tener or llevar el abrigo puesto; **she put her gloves on** se puso los guantes

2 (referring to covering): **"screw the lid on tightly"** "cerrar bien la tapa"

3 (further, continuously): **to walk** etc **on** seguir caminando etc
♦ adj

1 (functioning, in operation: machine, radio, TV, light) encendido(-a) (SP), prendido(-a) (LAm); (: tap) abierto(-a); (: brakes) echado(-a), puesto(-a); **is the meeting still on?** (in progress) ¿todavía continúa la reunión?; (not cancelled) ¿va a haber reunión al fin?; **there's a good film on at the cinema** ponen una buena película en el cine

2: **that's not on!** (inf: not possible) ¡eso ni hablar!; (: not acceptable) ¡eso no se hace!

once [wʌns] adv una vez; (formerly) antiguamente ♦ conj una vez que; **~ he had left/it was done** una vez que se había marchado/se hizo; **at ~** en seguida, inmediatamente; (simultaneously) a la vez; **~ a week** una vez por semana; **~ more** otra vez; **~ and for all** de una vez por todas; **~ upon a time** érase una vez

oncoming ['ɔnkʌmɪŋ] adj (traffic) que viene de frente

one

KEYWORD

[wʌn] num un(o)/una; **one hundred and fifty** ciento cincuenta; **one by one** uno a uno

♦ adj

1 (*sole*) único; **the one book which** el único libro que; **the one man who** el único que

2 (*same*) mismo(-a); **they came in the one car** vinieron en un solo coche

♦ pron

1: **this one** éste (ésta); **that one** ése (ésa); (*more remote*) aquél (aquella); **I've already got (a red) one** ya tengo uno(-a) rojo(-a); **one by one** uno(-a) por uno(-a)

2: **one another** os (*SP*), se (+ *el uno al otro, unos a otros etc*); **do you two ever see one another?** ¿vosotros dos os veis alguna vez? (*SP*), ¿se ven ustedes dos alguna vez?; **the boys didn't dare look at one another** los chicos no se atrevieron a mirarse (el uno al otro); **they all kissed one another** se besaron unos a otros

3 (*impers*): **one never knows** nunca se sabe; **to cut one's finger** cortarse el dedo; **one needs to eat** hay que comer ◻ **one-off** (*BRIT: inf*) n (*event*) acontecimiento único

oneself [wʌn'sɛlf] pron (*reflexive*) se; (*after prep*) sí; (*emphatic*) uno(-a) mismo(-a); **to hurt** ~ hacerse daño; **to keep sth for** ~ guardarse algo; **to talk to** ~ hablar solo

one: **one-shot** [wʌn'ʃɔt] (*US*) n = **one-off** ◻ **one-sided** adj (*argument*) parcial ◻ **one-to-one** adj (*relationship*) de dos ◻ **one-way** adj (*street*) de sentido único

ongoing ['ɔngəʊɪŋ] adj continuo

onion ['ʌnjən] n cebolla

on-line ['ɔnlaɪn] adj, adv (*COMPUT*) en línea

onlooker ['ɔnlukə^r] n espectador(a) m/f

only ['əʊnlɪ] adv solamente, sólo ♦ adj único, solo ♦ conj solamente que, pero; **an ~ child** un hijo único; **not ~ ... but also ...** no sólo ... sino también ...

on-screen [ɔn'skri:n] adj (*COMPUT etc*) en pantalla; (*romance, kiss*) cinematográfico

onset ['ɔnsɛt] n comienzo

onto ['ɔntu] prep = **on to**

onward(s) ['ɔnwəd(z)] adv (*move*) (hacia) adelante; **from that time onward(s)** desde entonces en adelante

oops [ups] excl (*also: ~-a-daisy!*) ¡huy!

ooze [u:z] vi rezumar

opaque [əʊ'peɪk] adj opaco

open ['əʊpn] adj abierto; (*car*) descubierto; (*road, view*) despejado; (*meeting*) público; (*admiration*) manifiesto ♦ vt abrir ♦ vi abrirse; (*book etc: commence*) comenzar; **in the ~ (air)** al aire libre ► **open up** vt abrir; (*blocked road*) despejar ♦ vi abrirse, empezar ◻ **open-air** adj al aire libre ◻ **opening** n abertura; (*start*) comienzo; (*opportunity*) oportunidad f ◻ **opening hours** npl horario de apertura ◻ **open learning** n enseñanza flexible a tiempo parcial ◻ **openly** adv abiertamente ◻ **open-minded** adj imparcial ◻ **open-necked** adj (*shirt*) desabrochado; sin corbata ◻ **open-plan** adj: **open-plan office** gran oficina sin particiones ◻ **Open University** n (*BRIT*) ≈ Universidad f Nacional de Enseñanza a Distancia, UNED f

OPEN UNIVERSITY

La **Open University**, fundada en 1969, está especializada en impartir cursos a distancia que no exigen una dedicación exclusiva. Cuenta con sus propios materiales de apoyo, entre ellos programas de radio y televisión emitidos por la **BBC** y para conseguir los créditos de la licenciatura es necesaria la presentación de unos trabajos y la asistencia a los cursos de verano.

opera ['ɔpərə] n ópera ❑ **opera house** n teatro de la ópera ❑ **opera singer** n cantante m/f de ópera

operate ['ɔpəreɪt] vt (machine) hacer funcionar; (company) dirigir ♦ vi funcionar; **to ~ on sb** (MED) operar a algn

operating room ['ɔpəreɪtɪŋ-] (US) n quirófano, sala de operaciones

operating theatre (BRIT) n sala de operaciones

operation [ɔpə'reɪʃən] n operación f; (of machine) funcionamiento; **to be in ~** estar funcionando or en funcionamiento; **to have an ~** (MED) ser operado ❑ **operational** adj operacional, en buen estado

operative ['ɔpərətɪv] adj en vigor

operator ['ɔpəreɪtə*] n (of machine) maquinista m/f, operario(-a); (TEL) operador(a) m/f, telefonista m/f

opinion [ə'pɪnɪən] n opinión f; **in my ~** en mi opinión, a mi juicio ❑ **opinion poll** n encuesta, sondeo

opponent [ə'pəunənt] n adversario(-a), contrincante m/f

opportunity [ɔpə'tju:nɪtɪ] n oportunidad f; **to take the ~ of doing** aprovechar la ocasión para hacer

oppose [ə'pəuz] vt oponerse a; **to be opposed to sth** oponerse a algo; **as opposed to** a diferencia de

opposite ['ɔpəzɪt] adj opuesto, contrario a; (house etc) de enfrente ♦ adv en frente ♦ prep en frente de, frente a ♦ n lo contrario

opposition [ɔpə'zɪʃən] n oposición f

oppress [ə'pres] vt oprimir

opt [ɔpt] vi: **to ~ to** or **for** optar por; **to ~ to do** optar por hacer ▶ **opt out** vi: **to opt out of** optar por no hacer

optician [ɔp'tɪʃən] n óptico m/f

optimism ['ɔptɪmɪzəm] n optimismo

optimist ['ɔptɪmɪst] n optimista m/f ❑ **optimistic** [-'mɪstɪk] adj optimista

optimum ['ɔptɪməm] adj óptimo

option ['ɔpʃən] n opción f ❑ **optional** adj facultativo, discrecional

or [ɔː*] conj o; (before o, ho) u; (with negative): **he hasn't seen or heard anything** no ha visto ni oído nada; **or else** ni no

oral ['ɔːrəl] adj oral ♦ n examen m oral

orange ['ɔrɪndʒ] n (fruit) naranja ♦ adj color naranja ❑ **orange juice** n jugo m de naranja, zumo m de naranja (SP) ❑ **orange squash** n naranjada

orbit ['ɔːbɪt] n órbita ♦ vt, vi orbitar

orchard ['ɔːtʃəd] n huerto

orchestra ['ɔːkɪstrə] n orquesta; (US: seating) platea

orchid ['ɔːkɪd] n orquídea

ordeal [ɔː'diːl] n experiencia horrorosa

order ['ɔːdə*] n orden m; (command) orden f; (good order) buen estado; (COMM) pedido ♦ vt (also: **put in ~**) arreglar, poner en orden; (COMM) pedir; (command) mandar, ordenar; **in ~** en orden; (of document) en regla; **in (working) ~** en funcionamiento; **in ~ to do/that** para hacer/que; **on ~** (COMM) pedido; **to be out of ~** estar desordenado; (not working) no funcionar; **to ~ sb to do** sth mandar a algn hacer algo ❑ **order form** n hoja de pedido ❑ **orderly** n (MIL) ordenanza m; (MED) enfermero(-a) (auxiliar) ♦ adj ordenado

ordinary ['ɔːdnrɪ] adj corriente, normal; (pej) común y corriente; **out of the** ~ fuera de lo común

ore [ɔː'] n mineral m

oregano [ɒrɪ'gɑːnəʊ] n orégano

organ ['ɔːgən] n órgano ❑ **organic** [ɔː'gænɪk] adj orgánico ❑ **organism** n organismo

organization [ˌɔːgənaɪ'zeɪʃən] n organización f

organize ['ɔːgənaɪz] vt organizar ❑ **organized** ['ɔːgənaɪzd] adj organizado ❑ **organizer** n organizador(a) m/f

orgasm ['ɔːgæzəm] n orgasmo

orgy ['ɔːdʒɪ] n orgía

oriental [ɔːrɪ'entl] adj oriental

orientation [ˌɔːrɪen'teɪʃən] n orientación f

origin ['ɒrɪdʒɪn] n origen m

original [ə'rɪdʒɪnl] adj original; (first) primero; (earlier) primitivo ♦ n original m ❑ **originally** adv al principio

originate [ə'rɪdʒɪneɪt] vi: **to** ~ **from, to** ~ **in** surgir de, tener su origen en

Orkneys ['ɔːknɪz] npl: **the** ~ (also: **the Orkney Islands**) las Orcadas

ornament ['ɔːnəmənt] n adorno; (trinket) chuchería ❑ **ornamental** [-'mentl] adj decorativo, de adorno

ornate [ɔː'neɪt] adj muy ornado, vistoso

orphan ['ɔːfn] n huérfano(-a)

orthodox ['ɔːθədɒks] adj ortodoxo

orthopaedic [ɔːθə'piːdɪk] (US **orthopedic**) adj ortopédico

osteopath ['ɒstɪəpæθ] n osteópata mf

ostrich ['ɒstrɪtʃ] n avestruz m

other ['ʌðə'] adj otro ♦ pron: **the** ~ **(one)** el (la) otro(-a) ♦ adv: ~ **than** aparte de ❑ **otherwise** adv de otra manera ♦ conj (if not) si no

otter ['ɒtə'] n nutria

ouch [aʊtʃ] excl ¡ay!

ought [ɔːt] (pt ~) aux vb: **I** ~ **to do it** debería hacerlo; **this** ~ **to have been corrected** esto debiera haberse corregido; **he** ~ **to win** (probability) debe o debiera ganar

ounce [aʊns] n onza (28.35g)

our [aʊə'] adj nuestro; see also **my** ❑ **ours** pron (el) nuestro/(la) nuestra etc; see also **mine**[1] ❑ **ourselves** pron pl (reflexive, after prep) nosotros; (emphatic) nosotros mismos; see also **oneself**

oust [aʊst] vt desalojar

out [aʊt] adv fuera, afuera; (not at home) fuera (de casa); (light, fire) apagado; ~ **there** allí (fuera); **he's** ~ (absent) no está, ha salido; **to be** ~ **in one's calculations** equivocarse en sus cálculos; **to run** ~ salir corriendo; ~ **loud** en alta voz; ~ **of** (outside) fuera de; (because of: anger etc) por; ~ **of petrol** sin gasolina; "~ **of order**" "no funciona" ❑ **outback** n interior m ❑ **outbound** adj (flight) de salida; (flight: not return) de ida ❑ **outbreak** n (of war) comienzo; (of disease) epidemia; (of violence etc) ola ❑ **outburst** n explosión f, arranque m ❑ **outcast** n paria mf ❑ **outcome** n resultado ❑ **outcry** n protestas fpl ❑ **outdated** adj anticuado, fuera de moda ❑ **outdoor** adj exterior, de aire libre; (clothes) de calle ❑ **outdoors** adv al aire libre

outer ['aʊtə'] adj exterior, externo ❑ **outer space** n espacio exterior

outfit ['aʊtfɪt] n (clothes) conjunto

out: outgoing adj (character) extrovertido; (retiring: president etc) saliente ❑ **outgoings** (BRIT) npl gastos mpl ❑ **outhouse** n dependencia

outing ['aʊtɪŋ] n excursión f, paseo

out: outlaw n proscrito ♦ vt proscribir ❑ **outlay** n inversión f ❑ **outlet** n salida; (of pipe) desagüe m; (US ELEC) toma de corriente; (also: **retail outlet**) punto de venta ❑ **outline** n (shape) contorno, perfil m; (sketch, plan) esbozo ♦ vt (plan etc) esbozar; **in outline** (fig) a grandes rasgos ❑ **outlook** n (fig: prospects) perspectivas fpl; (: for weather) pronóstico ♦ **outnumber** vt superar en número ❑ **out-of-date** adj (passport) caducado; (clothes) pasado de moda ❑ **out-of-doors** adv al aire libre ❑ **out-of-the-way** adj apartado ❑ **out-of-town** adj (shopping centre etc) en las afueras ❑ **outpatient** n paciente mf externo(-a) ❑ **outpost** n puesto avanzado ❑ **output** n (volumen m de) producción f, rendimiento; (COMPUT) salida

outrage ['autreɪdʒ] n escándalo; (atrocity) atrocidad f ♦ vt ultrajar ❑ **outrageous** [-'reɪdʒəs] adj monstruoso

outright [adv aut'raɪt, adj 'autraɪt] adv (ask, deny) francamente; (refuse) rotundamente; (win) de manera absoluta; (be killed) en el acto ♦ adj franco; rotundo

outset ['autset] n principio

outside [aut'saɪd] n exterior m ♦ adj exterior, externo ♦ adv fuera ♦ prep fuera de; (beyond) más allá de; **at the ~** (fig) a lo sumo ❑ **outside lane** n (AUT: in Britain) carril m de la derecha; (: in US, Europe etc) carril m de la izquierda ❑ **outside line** n (TEL) línea (exterior) ❑ **outsider** n (stranger) extraño, forastero

out: outsize adj (clothes) de talla grande ❑ **outskirts** npl alrededores mpl, afueras fpl ❑ **outspoken** adj muy franco ❑ **outstanding** adj excepcional, destacado; (remaining) pendiente

outward ['autwəd] adj externo; (journey) de ida ❑ **outwards** adv (esp BRIT) = **outward**

outweigh [aut'weɪ] vt pesar más que

oval ['əuvl] adj ovalado ♦ n óvalo

ovary ['əuvərɪ] n ovario

oven ['ʌvn] n horno ❑ **oven glove** n guante m para el horno, manopla para el horno ❑ **ovenproof** adj resistente al horno ❑ **oven-ready** adj listo para el horno

over ['əuvə*] adv encima, por encima ♦ adj or adv (finished) terminado; (surplus) de sobra ♦ prep (por) encima de; (above) sobre; (on the other side of) al otro lado de; (more than) más de; (during) durante; **~ here** (por) aquí; **~ there** (por) allí o allá; **all ~** (everywhere) por todas partes; **~ and ~ (again)** una y otra vez; **~ and above** además de; **to ask sb ~** invitar a algn a casa; **to bend ~** inclinarse

overall [adj, n 'əuvərɔ:l, adv əuvər'ɔ:l] adj (length etc) total; (study) de conjunto ♦ adv en conjunto ♦ n (BRIT) guardapolvo; **overalls** npl (boiler suit) mono (SP) or overol m (LAm) (de trabajo)

overboard adv (NAUT) por la borda

overcame [əuvə'keɪm] pt of **overcome**

overcast [əuvə'ka:st] adj encapotado

overcharge [əuvə'tʃɑ:dʒ] vt: **to ~ sb** cobrar un precio excesivo a algn

overcoat ['əuvəkəut] n abrigo, sobretodo

overcome [əuvə'kʌm] vt vencer; (difficulty) superar

over: overcrowded adj atestado de gente; (city, country) superpoblado ❑ **overdo** (irreg) vt exagerar; (overcook) cocer demasiado; **to overdo it** (work etc) pasarse ❑ **overdone** [əuvə'dʌn] adj (vegetables) recocido; (steak) demasiado hecho ❑ **overdose** n sobredosis f inv ❑ **overdraft** n saldo deudor ❑ **overdrawn** adj (account) en descubierto ❑ **overdue** adj retrasado ❑ **overestimate** vt sobreestimar

overflow [vb əuvəˈfləu, n ˈəuvəfləu] vi desbordarse ♦ n (also: ~ **pipe**) (cañería de) desagüe m

overgrown [əuvəˈɡrəun] adj (garden) invadido por la vegetación

overhaul [vb əuvəˈhɔːl, n ˈəuvəhɔːl] vt revisar, repasar ♦ n revisión f

overhead [adv əuvəˈhed, adj, n ˈəuvəhed] adv por arriba or encima ♦ adj (cable) aéreo ♦ n (US) = **overheads** ❑ **overhead projector** n retroproyector ❑ **overheads** npl (expenses) gastos mpl generales

over: overhear (irreg) vt oír por casualidad ❑ **overheat** vi (engine) recalentarse ❑ **overland** adj, adv por tierra ❑ **overlap** [əuvəˈlæp] vi traslaparse ❑ **overleaf** adv al dorso ❑ **overload** vt sobrecargar ❑ **overlook** vt (have view of) dar a, tener vistas a; (miss: by mistake) pasar por alto; (excuse) perdonar

overnight [əuvəˈnaɪt] adv durante la noche; (fig) de la noche a la mañana ♦ adj de noche; **to stay ~** pasar la noche ❑ **overnight bag** n film de semana, neceser m de viaje

overpass (US) [ˈəuvəpɑːs] n paso superior

overpower [əuvəˈpauə] vt dominar; (fig) embargar ❑ **overpowering** adj (heat) agobiante; (smell) penetrante

over: overreact [əuvəriˈækt] vi reaccionar de manera exagerada ❑ **overrule** vt (decision) anular; (claim) denegar ❑ **overrun** (irreg) vt (country) invadir; (time limit) rebasar, exceder

overseas [əuvəˈsiːz] adv (abroad: live) en el extranjero; (travel) al extranjero ♦ adj (trade) exterior; (visitor) extranjero

oversee [əuvəˈsiː] (irreg) vt supervisar

overshadow [əuvəˈʃædəu] vt: **to be overshadowed by** estar a la sombra de

oversight [ˈəuvəsaɪt] n descuido

oversleep [əuvəˈsliːp] (irreg) vi quedarse dormido

overspend [əuvəˈspend] (irreg) vi gastar más de la cuenta; **we have overspent by 5 pounds** hemos excedido el presupuesto en 5 libras

overt [əuˈvɜːt] adj abierto

overtake [əuvəˈteɪk] (irreg) vt sobrepasar; (BRIT AUT) adelantar

over: overthrow (irreg) vt (government) derrocar ❑ **overtime** n horas fpl extraordinarias

overtook [əuvəˈtuk] pt of **overtake**

over: overturn vt volcar; (fig: plan) desbaratar; (: government) derrocar ♦ vi volcar ❑ **overweight** adj demasiado gordo or pesado ❑ **overwhelm** vt aplastar; (emotion) sobrecoger ❑ **overwhelming** adj (victory, defeat) arrollador(a); (feeling) irresistible

ow [au] excl ¡ay!

owe [əu] vt: **to ~ sb sth, to ~ sth to sb** deber algo a algn ❑ **owing to** prep debido a, por causa de

owl [aul] n búho, lechuza

own [əun] vt tener, poseer ♦ adj propio; **a room of my ~** una habitación propia; **to get one's ~ back** tomar revancha; **on one's ~** solo, a solas ► **own up** vi confesar ❑ **owner** n dueño(-a) ❑ **ownership** n posesión f

ox [ɒks] (pl **oxen**) n buey m

Oxbridge [ˈɒksbrɪdʒ] n universidades de Oxford y Cambridge

oxen [ˈɒksən] npl of **ox**

oxygen [ˈɒksɪdʒən] n oxígeno

oyster [ˈɔɪstə] n ostra

oz. abbr = **ounce(s)**

ozone [ˈəuzəun] n ozono ❑ **ozone friendly** adj que no daña la capa de ozono ❑ **ozone layer** n capa f de ozono

P, p

p [pi:] *abbr* = **penny**; **pence**

P.A. *n abbr* = **personal assistant**; **public address system**

p.a. *abbr* = **per annum**

pace [peɪs] *n* paso ♦ *vi*: to ~ **up and down** pasearse de un lado a otro; **to keep ~ with** llevar el mismo paso que
❑ **pacemaker** *n* (MED) regulador *m* cardíaco, marcapasos *m inv*; (SPORT: *also*: **pacesetter**) liebre *f*

Pacific [pə'sɪfɪk] *n*: **the ~ (Ocean)** el (Océano) Pacífico

pacifier ['pæsɪfaɪə'] (US) *n* (dummy) chupete *m*

pack [pæk] *n* (packet) paquete *m*; (of hounds) jauría; (of people) manada, bando; (of cards) baraja; (bundle) fardo; (US: of cigarettes) paquete *m*; (back pack) mochila ♦ *vt* (fill) llenar; (in suitcase etc) meter, poner; (cram) llenar, atestar; **to ~ (one's bags)** hacerse la maleta; **to ~ sb off** despachar a algn ♦ *n pack in vi* (watch, car) estropearse ♦ *vt* (inf) dejar; **pack it in!** ¡para!, ¡basta ya! ♦ *pack up vi* (inf: machine) estropearse; (person) irse ♦ *vt* (belongings, clothes) recoger; (goods, presents) empaquetar, envolver

package ['pækɪdʒ] *n* paquete *m*; (bulky) bulto; (also: ~ **deal**) acuerdo global
❑ **package holiday** *n* vacaciones *fpl* organizadas ❑ **package tour** *n* viaje *m* organizado

packaging ['pækɪdʒɪŋ] *n* envase *m*

packed [pækt] *adj* abarrotado
❑ **packed lunch** *n* almuerzo frío

packet ['pækɪt] *n* paquete *m*

packing ['pækɪŋ] *n* embalaje *m*

pact [pækt] *n* pacto

pad [pæd] *n* (of paper) bloc *m*; (cushion) cojinete *m*; (inf: home) casa ♦ *vt* rellenar ❑ **padded** *adj* (jacket) acolchado; (bra) reforzado

paddle ['pædl] *n* (oar) canalete *m*; (US: for table tennis) paleta ♦ *vt* impulsar con canalete ♦ *vi* (with feet) chapotear
❑ **paddling pool** (BRIT) *n* estanque *m* de juegos

paddock ['pædək] *n* corral *m*

padlock ['pædlɒk] *n* candado

paedophile ['pi:dəufaɪl] (US **pedophile**) *adj* de pedófilos ♦ *n* pedófilo(-a)

page [peɪdʒ] *n* (of book) página; (of newspaper) plana; (also: ~ **boy**) paje *m* ♦ *vt* (in hotel etc) llamar por altavoz a

pager ['peɪdʒə'] *n* (TEL) busca *m*

paid [peɪd] *pt, pp of* **pay** ♦ *adj* (work) remunerado; (holiday) pagado; (official etc) a sueldo; **to put ~ to** (BRIT) acabar con

pain [peɪn] *n* dolor *m*; **to be in ~** sufrir; **to take pains to do sth** tomarse grandes molestias en hacer algo
❑ **painful** *adj* doloroso; (difficult) penoso; (disagreeable) desagradable
❑ **painkiller** *n* analgésico
❑ **painstaking** ['peɪnzteɪkɪŋ] *adj* (person) concienzudo, esmerado

paint [peɪnt] *n* pintura ♦ *vt* pintar; **to ~ the door blue** pintar la puerta de azul
❑ **paintbrush** *n* (of artist) pincel *m*; (of decorator) brocha ❑ **painter** *n* pintor(a) *m/f* ❑ **painting** *n* pintura

pair [peə'] *n* (of shoes, gloves etc) par *m*; (of people) pareja; **a ~ of scissors** unas tijeras; **a ~ of trousers** unos pantalones, un pantalón

pajamas [pə'dʒɑ:məz] (US) *npl* pijama *m*

Pakistan [pɑ:kɪ'stɑ:n] *n* Paquistán *m*
❑ **Pakistani** *adj, n* paquistaní *mf*

pal [pæl] (inf) *n* compinche *mf*, compañero(-a)

palace ['pæləs] *n* palacio

pale [peɪl] *adj* (gen) pálido; (colour) claro ♦ *n*: **to be beyond the ~** pasarse de la raya

Palestine ['pælɪstaɪn] n Palestina
 ❑ **Palestinian** [-'tɪnɪən] adj, n
palestino(-a) m/f

palm [pɑːm] n (ANAT) palma; (also: ~
tree) palmera, palma ♦ vt: **to ~ sth off
on sb** (inf) encajar algo a algn

pamper ['pæmpə⁹] vt mimar

pamphlet ['pæmflət] n folleto

pan [pæn] n (also: **saucepan**) cacerola,
cazuela, olla; (also: **frying ~**) sartén f

pancake ['pænkeɪk] n crepe f

panda ['pændə] n panda m

pane [peɪn] n cristal m

panel ['pænl] n (of wood etc) panel m;
(RADIO, TV) panel m de invitados

panhandler ['pænhændlə⁹] (US) n (inf)
mendigo(-a)

panic ['pænɪk] n terror m pánico ♦ vi
dejarse llevar por el pánico

panorama [pænə'rɑːmə] n panorama m

pansy ['pænzɪ] n (BOT) pensamiento;
(inf, pej) maricón m

pant [pænt] vi jadear

panther ['pænθə⁹] n pantera

panties ['pæntɪz] npl bragas fpl, pantis
mpl

pantomime ['pæntəmaɪm] (BRIT) n
revista musical representada en Navidad,
basada en cuentos de hadas

PANTOMIME

En época navideña se ponen en escena
en los teatros británicos las llamadas
pantomimes, que son versiones libres
de cuentos tradicionales como Aladino
o El gato con botas. En ella nunca faltan
personajes como la dama ("dame"),
papel que siempre interpreta un actor,
el protagonista joven ("principal boy"),
normalmente interpretado por una
actriz, y el malvado ("villain"). Es un
espectáculo familiar en el que se anima
al público a participar y aunque va
dirigido principalmente a los niños,
cuenta con grandes dosis de humor
para adultos

---

pants [pænts] n (BRIT: underwear:
woman's) bragas fpl; (: man's)
calzoncillos mpl; (US: trousers)
pantalones mpl

paper ['peɪpə⁹] n papel m; (also:
newspaper) periódico, diario;
(academic essay) ensayo; (exam)
examen m ♦ adj de papel ♦ vt
empapelar, tapizar (MEX); **papers** npl
(also: **identity papers**) papeles mpl,
documentos mpl ❑ **paperback** n libro
en rústica ❑ **paper bag** n bolsa de
papel ❑ **paper clip** n clip m ❑ **paper
shop** (BRIT) n tienda de periódicos
❑ **paperwork** n trabajo
administrativo

paprika ['pæprɪkə] n pimentón m

par [pɑː⁹] n par f; (GOLF) par m; **to be on
a ~ with** estar a la par con

paracetamol [pærə'siːtəmɒl] (BRIT) n
paracetamol m

parachute ['pærəʃuːt] n paracaídas m
inv

parade [pə'reɪd] n desfile m ♦ vt (show)
hacer alarde de ♦ vi desfilar; (MIL) pasar
revista

paradise ['pærədaɪs] n paraíso

paradox ['pærədɒks] n paradoja

paraffin ['pærəfɪn] (BRIT) n (also: ~ **oil**)
parafina

paragraph ['pærəgrɑːf] n párrafo

parallel ['pærəlɛl] adj en paralelo; (fig)
semejante ♦ n (line) paralela; (fig, GEO)
paralelo

paralysed ['pærəlaɪzd] adj paralizado

paralysis [pə'rælɪsɪs] n parálisis f inv

paramedic [pærə'mɛdɪk] n auxiliar m/f
sanitario(-a)

paranoid ['pærənɔɪd] adj (person,
feeling) paranoico

parasite ['pærəsaɪt] n parásito(-a)

parcel ['pɑːsl] n paquete m ♦ vt (also: ~
up) empaquetar, embalar

pardon ['pɑːdn] n (LAW) indulto ♦ vt
perdonar; **~ me!, I beg your ~!** (I'm

sorry!) ¡perdone usted!; **(I beg your) ~?, ~ me?** (US: what did you say?) ¿cómo?

parent ['pɛərənt] n (mother) madre f; (father) padre m; **parents** npl padres mpl ❑ **parental** [pə'rɛntl] adj paternal/maternal

⚠ Be careful not to translate **parent** by the Spanish word *pariente*.

Paris ['pærɪs] n París

parish ['pærɪʃ] n parroquia

Parisian [pə'rɪzən] adj, n parisiense mf

park [pɑːk] n parque m ♦ vt aparcar, estacionar ♦ vi aparcar, estacionarse

parking ['pɑːkɪŋ] n aparcamiento, estacionamiento; **"no ~"** "prohibido estacionarse" ❑ **parking lot** (US) n parking m ❑ **parking meter** n parquímetro ❑ **parking ticket** n multa de aparcamiento

parkway ['pɑːkweɪ] (US) n alameda

parliament ['pɑːləmənt] n parlamento; (Spanish) Cortes fpl ❑ **parliamentary** [-'mɛntərɪ] adj parlamentario

PARLIAMENT

El Parlamento británico (**Parliament**) tiene como sede el palacio de Westminster, también llamado "Houses of Parliament" y consta de dos cámaras. La Cámara de los Comunes ("House of Commons"), compuesta por 650 diputados (**Members of Parliament**) elegidos por sufragio universal en su respectiva circunscripción electoral (**constituency**), se reúne 175 días al año y sus sesiones son moderadas por el Presidente de la Cámara (**Speaker**). La cámara alta es la Cámara de los Lores ("House of Lords") y está formada por miembros que han sido nombrados por el monarca o que han heredado su escaño. Su poder es limitado, aunque actúa como tribunal supremo de apelación, excepto en Escocia.

Parmesan [pɑːmɪ'zæn] n (also: ~ cheese) queso parmesano

parole [pə'rəul] n: **on ~** libre bajo palabra

parrot ['pærət] n loro, papagayo

parsley ['pɑːslɪ] n perejil m

parsnip ['pɑːsnɪp] n chirivía

parson ['pɑːsn] n cura m

part [pɑːt] n (gen, MUS) parte f; (bit) trozo; (of machine) pieza; (THEATRE etc) papel m; (of serial) entrega; (US: in hair) raya ♦ adv = **partly** ♦ vt separar ♦ vi (people) separarse; (crowd) apartarse; **to take ~** in tomar parte o participar en; **to take sth in good** ~ tomar algo en buena parte; **to take sb's** ~ defender a algn; **for my** ~ por mi parte; **for the most** ~ en su mayor parte; **to ~ one's hair** hacerse la raya ► **part with** vt fus ceder, entregar; (money) pagar ❑ **part of speech** n parte f de la oración, categoría f gramatical

partial ['pɑːʃl] adj parcial; **to be ~ to** ser aficionado a

participant [pɑː'tɪsɪpənt] n (in competition) concursante mf; (in campaign etc) participante mf

participate [pɑː'tɪsɪpeɪt] vi: **to ~ in** participar en

particle ['pɑːtɪkl] n partícula; (of dust) grano

particular [pə'tɪkjulə°] adj (special) particular; (concrete) concreto; (given) determinado; (fussy) quisquilloso; (demanding) exigente; **in ~** en particular ❑ **particularly** adv (in particular) sobre todo; (especially, good etc) especialmente ❑ **particulars** npl (information) datos mpl; (details) pormenores mpl

parting ['pɑːtɪŋ] n (act) separación f; (farewell) despedida; (BRIT: in hair) raya ♦ adj de despedida

partition [pɑː'tɪʃən] n (POL) división f; (wall) tabique m

partly ['pɑːtlɪ] adv en parte

partner ['pɑːtnəʳ] n (COMM) socio(-a); (SPORT, at dance) pareja; (spouse) cónyuge mf; (lover) compañero(-a) ❏ **partnership** n asociación f; (COMM) sociedad f

partridge ['pɑːtrɪdʒ] n perdiz f

part-time ['pɑːt'taɪm] adj, adv a tiempo parcial

party ['pɑːtɪ] n (POL) partido; (celebration) fiesta; (group) grupo; (LAW) parte f interesada ♦ cpd (POL) de partido

pass [pɑːs] vt (time, object) pasar; (place) pasar por; (overtake) rebasar; (exam) aprobar; (approve) aprobar ♦ vi pasar; (SCOL) aprobar, ser aprobado ♦ n (permit) permiso; (membership card) carnet m; (in mountains) puerto, desfiladero; (SPORT) pase m; (SCOL: also: ~ mark): **to get a ~ in** aprobar en; **to ~ sth through sth** pasar algo por algo; **to make a ~ at sb** (inf) hacer proposiciones a algn ► **pass away** vi fallecer ► **pass by** vi pasar ♦ vt (ignore) pasar por alto ► **pass on** vt transmitir ► **pass out** vi desmayarse ► **pass over** vi, vt omitir, pasar por alto ► **pass up** vt (opportunity) renunciar a ❏ **passable** adj (road) transitable; (tolerable) pasable

passage ['pæsɪdʒ] n (also: **passageway**) pasillo; (act of passing) tránsito; (fare, in book) pasaje m; (by boat) travesía; (ANAT) tubo

passenger ['pæsɪndʒəʳ] n pasajero(-a), viajero(-a)

passer-by [pɑːsə'baɪ] n transeúnte mf

passing place n (AUT) apartadero

passion ['pæʃən] n pasión f ❏ **passionate** adj apasionado ❏ **passion fruit** n fruta de la pasión, granadilla

passive ['pæsɪv] adj (gen, also LING) pasivo

passport ['pɑːspɔːt] n pasaporte m ❏ **passport control** n control m de pasaporte ❏ **passport office** n oficina de pasaportes

password ['pɑːswɜːd] n contraseña

past [pɑːst] prep (in front of) por delante de; (further than) más allá de; (later than) después de ♦ adj pasado; (president etc) antiguo ♦ n (time) pasado; (of person) antecedentes mpl; **he's ~ forty** tiene más de cuarenta años; **ten/quarter ~ eight** las ocho y diez/cuarto; **for the ~ few/days** durante los últimos días/últimos 3 días; **to run ~ sb** pasar a algn corriendo

pasta ['pæstə] n pasta

paste [peɪst] n pasta; (glue) engrudo ♦ vt pegar

pastel ['pæstl] adj pastel; (painting) al pastel

pasteurized ['pæstəraɪzd] adj pasteurizado

pastime ['pɑːstaɪm] n pasatiempo

pastor ['pɑːstəʳ] n pastor m

past participle [-'pɑːtɪsɪpl] n (LING) participio m (de) pasado or (de) pretérito or pasivo

pastry ['peɪstrɪ] n (dough) pasta; (cake) pastel m

pasture ['pɑːstʃəʳ] n pasto

pasty¹ ['pæstɪ] n empanada

pasty² ['peɪstɪ] adj (complexion) pálido

pat [pæt] vt dar una palmadita a; (dog etc) acariciar

patch [pætʃ] n (of material, eye patch) parche n; (mended part) remiendo; (of land) terreno ♦ vt remendar; **(to go through) a bad ~** (pasar por) una mala racha ❏ **patchy** adj desigual

pâté ['pæteɪ] n paté m

patent ['peɪtnt] n patente f ♦ vt patentar ♦ adj patente, evidente

paternal [pə'tɜːnl] adj paternal; (relation) paterno

paternity leave [pə'tɜːnɪtɪ-] n permiso m por paternidad, licencia por paternidad

path [pɑːθ] n camino, sendero; (trail, track) pista; (of missile) trayectoria

pathetic [pə'θetɪk] adj patético, lastimoso; (very bad) malísimo

pathway ['pɑːθweɪ] n sendero, vereda

patience ['peɪʃns] n paciencia; (BRIT CARDS) solitario

patient ['peɪʃnt] n paciente mf ♦ adj paciente, sufrido

patio ['pætɪəu] n patio

patriotic [pætrɪ'ɔtɪk] adj patriótico

patrol [pə'trəul] n patrulla ♦ vt patrullar por **□ patrol car** n coche m patrulla

patron ['peɪtrən] n (in shop) cliente m/f; (of charity) patrocinador(a) m/f; **~ of the arts** mecenas m

patronizing ['pætrənaɪzɪŋ] adj condescendiente

pattern ['pætən] n (SEWING) patrón m; (design) dibujo **□ patterned** adj (material) estampado

pause [pɔːz] n pausa ♦ vi hacer una pausa

pave [peɪv] vt pavimentar; **to ~ the way for** preparar el terreno para

pavement ['peɪvmənt] (BRIT) n acera, banqueta (MEX), andén m (CAm), vereda (SC)

pavilion [pə'vɪlɪən] n (SPORT) caseta

paving ['peɪvɪŋ] n pavimento, enlosado

paw [pɔː] n pata

pawn [pɔːn] n (CHESS) peón m; (fig) instrumento ♦ vt empeñar **□ pawn broker** n prestamista mf

pay [peɪ] (pt, pp **paid**) n (wage etc) sueldo, salario ♦ vt pagar ♦ vi (be profitable) rendir; **to ~ attention (to)** prestar atención (a); **to ~ sb a visit** hacer una visita a algn; **to ~ one's respects to sb** presentar sus respetos a algn ► **pay back** vt (money) reembolsar; (person) pagar ► **pay for** vt fus pagar ► **pay in** vt ingresar ► **pay off** vt saldar ♦ vi (scheme, decision) dar resultado ► **pay out** vt (money) gastar,

desembolsar ► **pay up** vt pagar (de mala gana) **□ payable** adj: **payable to** pagadero a **□ pay day** n día m de paga **□ pay envelope** (US) n = **pay packet □ payment** n pago; **monthly payment** mensualidad f **□ payout** n pago; (in competition) premio en metálico **□ pay packet** (BRIT) n sobre m (de paga) **□ pay phone** n teléfono público **□ payroll** n nómina **□ pay slip** n recibo de sueldo **□ pay television** n televisión f de pago

PC n abbr = **personal computer**; (BRIT: = police constable) policía mf ♦ adv abbr = **politically correct**

p.c. abbr = **per cent**

PDA n abbr (= personal digital assistant) agenda electrónica

PE n abbr (= physical education) ed. física

pea [piː] n guisante m (SP), arveja (LAm), chícharo (MEX, CAm)

peace [piːs] n paz f; (calm) paz f, tranquilidad f **□ peaceful** adj (gentle) pacífico; (calm) tranquilo, sosegado

peach [piːtʃ] n melocotón m (SP), durazno (LAm)

peacock ['piːkɔk] n pavo real

peak [piːk] n (of mountain) cumbre f, cima; (of cap) visera; (fig) cumbre f **□ peak hours** npl horas fpl punta

peanut ['piːnʌt] n cacahuete m (SP), maní m (LAm), cacahuate m (MEX) **□ peanut butter** n manteca de cacahuete or maní

pear [peər] n pera

pearl [pɜːl] n perla

peasant ['peznt] n campesino(-a)

peat [piːt] n turba

pebble ['pebl] n guijarro

peck [pek] vt (also: **~ at**) picotear ♦ n picotazo; (kiss) besito **□ peckish** (BRIT: inf) adj: **I feel peckish** tengo ganas de picar algo

peculiar [pɪ'kjuːlɪər] adj (odd) extraño, raro; (typical) propio, característico; **~ to** propio de

pedal ['pɛdl] n pedal m ♦ vi pedalear

pedalo ['pedaləu] n patín m a pedal

pedestal ['pedəstl] n pedestal m

pedestrian [pɪ'destrɪən] n
peatón(-ona) m/f ♦ adj pedestre
❏ **pedestrian crossing** (BRIT) n paso
de peatones ❏ **pedestrianized** adj: **a
pedestrianized street** una calle
peatonal ❏ **pedestrian precinct** (US
pedestrian zone) n zona peatonal

pedigree ['pedɪgriː] n genealogía; (of
animal) raza, pedigrí m ♦ cpd (animal)
de raza, de casta

pedophile ['piːdəʊfaɪl] (US) n =
paedophile

pee [piː] (inf) vi mear

peek [piːk] vi mirar a hurtadillas

peel [piːl] n piel f; (of orange, lemon)
cáscara; (: removed) peladuras fpl ♦ vt
pelar ♦ vi (paint etc) desconchar;
(wallpaper) despegarse, desprenderse;
(skin) pelar

peep [piːp] n (BRIT: look) mirada furtiva;
(sound) pío ♦ vi (BRIT: look) mirar
furtivamente

peer [pɪə'] vi: **to ~ at** esudriñar ♦ n
(noble) par m; (equal) igual m;
(contemporary) contemporáneo(-a)

peg [peg] n (for coat etc) gancho,
colgador; (BRIT: also: **clothes ~**) pinza

pelican ['pelɪkən] n pelícano
❏ **pelican crossing** (BRIT) n (AUT) paso
de peatones señalizado

pelt [pelt] vt: **to ~ sb with sth** arrojarle
algo a algn ♦ vi (rain) llover a cántaros;
(inf: run) correr ♦ n pellejo

pelvis ['pelvɪs] n pelvis f

pen [pen] n (fountain pen) pluma;
(ballpoint pen) bolígrafo; (for sheep)
redil m

penalty ['penltɪ] n (gen) pena; (fine)
multa

pence [pens] npl of **penny**

pencil ['pensl] n lápiz m ♦ **pencil in** vt
(appointment) apuntar con carácter
provisional ❏ **pencil case** n estuche

m ❏ **pencil sharpener** n sacapuntas
m inv

pendant ['pendnt] n pendiente m

pending ['pendɪŋ] prep antes de ♦ adj
pendiente

penetrate ['penɪtreɪt] vt penetrar

penfriend ['penfrend] (BRIT) n
amigo(-a) por carta

penguin ['peŋgwɪn] n pingüino

penicillin [penɪ'sɪlɪn] n penicilina

peninsula [pə'nɪnsjulə] n península

penis ['piːnɪs] n pene m

penitentiary [penɪ'tenʃərɪ] (US) n
cárcel f, presidio

penknife ['pennaɪf] n navaja

penniless ['penɪlɪs] adj sin dinero

penny ['penɪ] (pl **pennies** or **pence**
(BRIT)) n penique m; (US) centavo

penpal ['penpæl] n amigo(-a) por carta

pension ['penʃən] n (state benefit)
jubilación f ❏ **pensioner** (BRIT) n
jubilado(-a)

pentagon ['pentəgən] (US) n: **the P~**
(POL) el Pentágono

PENTAGON

Se conoce como **Pentagon** al edificio
de planta pentagonal que acoge las
dependencias del Ministerio de
Defensa estadounidense
("Department of Defense") en
Arlington, Virginia. En lenguaje
periodístico se aplica también a la
dirección militar del país.

---

penthouse ['penthaus] n ático de lujo

penultimate [pe'nʌltɪmət] adj
penúltimo

people ['piːpl] npl gente f; (citizens)
pueblo, ciudadanos mpl; (POL): **the ~** el
pueblo ♦ n (nation, race) pueblo,
nación f; **several ~ came** vinieron
varias personas; **~ say that ...** dice la
gente que ...

pepper ['pepə'] n (spice) pimienta;
(vegetable) pimiento ♦ vt: **to ~ with**

(fig) salpicar de ❑ **peppermint** *n*
(sweet) pastilla de menta

per [pɜːʳ] *prep* por; **~ day/person** por
día/persona; **~ annum** al año

perceive [pəˈsiːv] *vt* percibir; *(realize)*
darse cuenta de

per cent *n* por ciento

percentage [pəˈsentɪdʒ] *n* porcentaje
m

perception [pəˈsepʃən] *n* percepción *f*;
(insight) perspicacia; *(opinion etc)*
opinión *f*

perch [pɜːtʃ] *n (fish)* perca; *(for bird)*
percha ♦ *vi*: **to ~ (on)** *(bird)* posarse
(en); *(person)* encaramarse (en)

percussion [pəˈkʌʃən] *n* percusión *f*

perfect [*adj, n* ˈpɜːfɪkt, *vb* pəˈfekt] *adj*
perfecto ♦ *n (also: ~ tense)* perfecto
♦ *vt* perfeccionar ❑ **perfection**
[pəˈfekʃən] *n* perfección *f* ❑ **perfectly**
[ˈpɜːfɪktlɪ] *adv* perfectamente

perform [pəˈfɔːm] *vt (carry out)* realizar,
llevar a cabo; *(THEATRE)* representar;
(piece of music) interpretar ♦ *vi (well,
badly)* funcionar ❑ **performance** *n*
(of a play) representación *f*; *(of actor,
athlete etc)* actuación *f*; *(of car, engine,
company)* rendimiento; *(of economy)*
resultados *mpl* ❑ **performer** *n (actor)*
actor *m*, actriz *f*

perfume [ˈpɜːfjuːm] *n* perfume *m*

perhaps [pəˈhæps] *adv* quizá(s), tal vez

perimeter [pəˈrɪmɪtəʳ] *n* perímetro

period [ˈpɪərɪəd] *n* período; *(SCOL)* clase
f; *(full stop)* punto; *(MED)* regla ♦ *adj*
(costume, furniture) de época
❑ **periodical** [pɪərɪˈɒdɪkl] *n* periódico
❑ **periodically** *adv* de vez en cuando,
cada cierto tiempo

perish [ˈperɪʃ] *vi* perecer; *(decay)*
echarse a perder

perjury [ˈpɜːdʒərɪ] *n (LAW)* perjurio

perk [pɜːk] *n* extra *m*

perm [pɜːm] *n* permanente *f*

permanent [ˈpɜːmənənt] *adj*
permanente ❑ **permanently** *adv*

(lastingly) para siempre, de modo
definitivo; *(all the time)*
permanentemente

permission [pəˈmɪʃən] *n* permiso

permit [*n* ˈpɜːmɪt, *vt* pəˈmɪt] *n* permiso,
licencia ♦ *vt* permitir

perplex [pəˈpleks] *vt* dejar perplejo

persecute [ˈpɜːsɪkjuːt] *vt* perseguir
persecution [pɜːsɪˈkjuːʃən] *n*
persecución *f*

persevere [pɜːsɪˈvɪəʳ] *vi* persistir

Persian [ˈpɜːʃən] *adj, n* persa *mf*; **the ~
Gulf** el Golfo Pérsico

persist [pəˈsɪst] *vi*: **to ~ (in doing sth)**
persistir (en hacer algo) ❑ **persistent**
adj persistente; *(determined)* porfiado

person [ˈpɜːsn] *n* persona; **in ~** en
persona ❑ **personal** *adj* personal;
individual; *(visit)* en persona
❑ **personal assistant** *n* ayudante *mf*
personal ❑ **personal computer** *n*
ordenador *m* personal ❑ **personality**
[ˈnælɪtɪ] *n* personalidad *f*
❑ **personally** *adv* personalmente; *(in
person)* en persona; **to take sth
personally** tomarse algo a mal
❑ **personal organizer** *n* agenda
❑ **personal stereo** *n* Walkman® *m*

personnel [pɜːsəˈnel] *n* personal *m*

perspective [pəˈspektɪv] *n* perspectiva

perspiration [pɜːspɪˈreɪʃən] *n*
transpiración *f*

persuade [pəˈsweɪd] *vt*: **to ~ sb to do
sth** persuadir a algn para que haga
algo

persuasion [pəˈsweɪʒən] *n* persuasión
f; *(persuasiveness)* persuasiva

persuasive [pəˈsweɪsɪv] *adj* persuasivo

perverse [pəˈvɜːs] *adj* perverso;
(wayward) travieso

pervert [*n* ˈpɜːvɜːt, *vb* pəˈvɜːt] *n*
pervertido(-a) ♦ *vt* pervertir; *(truth, sb's
words)* tergiversar

pessimism [ˈpesɪmɪzəm] *n* pesimismo

pessimist [ˈpesɪmɪst] *n* pesimista *mf*
❑ **pessimistic** [ˈmɪstɪk] *adj* pesimista

pest [pest] n (insect) insecto nocivo; (fig) lata, molestia

pester ['pestə'] vt molestar, acosar

pesticide ['pestisaid] n pesticida m

pet [pet] n animal m doméstico ♦ cpd favorito ♦ vt acariciar; **teacher's ~** favorito(-a) (del profesor); **~ hate** manía

petal ['petl] n pétalo

petite [pə'ti:t] adj chiquita

petition [pə'tɪʃən] n petición f

petrified ['petrifaɪd] adj horrorizado

petrol ['petrəl] (BRIT) n gasolina

petroleum [pə'trəuliəm] n petróleo

petrol: petrol pump (BRIT) n (in garage) surtidor m de gasolina □ **petrol station** (BRIT) n gasolinera □ **petrol tank** (BRIT) n depósito (de gasolina)

petticoat ['petikəut] n enaguas fpl

petty ['peti] adj (mean) mezquino; (unimportant) insignificante

pew [pju:] n banco

pewter ['pju:tə'] n peltre m

phantom ['fæntəm] n fantasma m

pharmacist ['fɑ:məsist] n farmacéutico(-a)

pharmacy ['fɑ:məsi] n farmacia

phase [feiz] n fase f ▶ **phase in** vt introducir progresivamente ▶ **phase out** vt (machinery, product) retirar progresivamente; (job, subsidy) eliminar por etapas

Ph.D. abbr = **Doctor of Philosophy**

pheasant ['feznt] n faisán m

phenomena [fə'nɔmɪnə] npl of **phenomenon**

phenomenal [fɪ'nɔmɪnl] adj fenomenal, extraordinario

phenomenon [fə'nɔmɪnən] (pl **phenomena**) n fenómeno

Philippines ['filipi:nz] npl: **the ~** las Filipinas

philosopher [fɪ'lɔsəfə'] n filósofo(-a)

philosophical [filə'sɔfɪkl] adj filosófico

philosophy [fɪ'lɔsəfi] n filosofía

phlegm [flem] n flema

phobia ['fəubjə] n fobia

phone [fəun] n teléfono ♦ vt telefonear, llamar por teléfono; **to be on the ~** tener teléfono; (be calling) estar hablando por teléfono ▶ **phone back** vt, vi volver a llamar ▶ **phone up** vt, vi llamar por teléfono □ **phone book** n guía telefónica □ **phone booth** n cabina telefónica □ **phone box** (BRIT) n = **phone booth** □ **phone call** n llamada (telefónica) □ **phonecard** n teletarjeta □ **phone number** n número de teléfono

phonetics [fə'netɪks] n fonética

phoney ['fəuni] adj falso

photo ['fəutəu] n foto f □ **photo album** n álbum m de fotos □ **photocopier** n fotocopiadora □ **photocopy** n fotocopia ♦ vt fotocopiar

photograph ['fəutəgrɑ:f] n fotografía ♦ vt fotografiar □ **photographer** [fə'tɔgrəfə'] n fotógrafo □ **photography** [fə'tɔgrəfi] n fotografía

phrase [freɪz] n frase f ♦ vt expresar □ **phrase book** n libro de frases

physical ['fɪzɪkl] adj físico □ **physical education** n educación f física □ **physically** adv físicamente

physician [fɪ'zɪʃən] n médico(-a)

physicist ['fɪzɪsɪst] n físico(-a)

physics ['fɪzɪks] n física

physiotherapist [fɪzɪəu'θerəpɪst] n fisioterapeuta

physiotherapy [fɪzɪəu'θerəpɪ] n fisioterapia

physique [fɪ'zi:k] n físico

pianist ['pɪənɪst] n pianista mf

piano [pɪ'ænəu] n piano

pick [pɪk] n (tool: also: **~axe**) pico, piqueta ♦ vt (select) elegir, escoger;

(gather) coger (SP), recoger; (remove, take out) sacar, quitar; (lock) abrir con ganzúa; **take your ~** escoja lo que quiera; **the ~ of** lo mejor de; **to ~ one's nose/teeth** hurgarse las narices/limpiarse los dientes; **to ~ a quarrel with sb** meterse con algn ▶ **pick on vt fus** (person) meterse con ▶ **pick out vt** escoger; (distinguish) identificar ▶ **pick up vi** (improve: sales) ir mejor; (: patient) reponerse; (FINANCE) recobrarse ♦ vt recoger; (learn) aprender; (POLICE: arrest) detener; (person: for sex) ligar; (RADIO) captar; **to pick up speed** acelerarse; **to pick o.s. up** levantarse

pickle ['pɪkl] n (also: **pickles**: as condiment) escabeche m; (fig: mess) apuro ♦ vt encurtir

pickpocket ['pɪkpɔkɪt] n carterista mf

pick-up ['pɪkʌp] n (also: **~ truck**) furgoneta, camioneta

picnic ['pɪknɪk] n merienda ♦ vi ir de merienda ❑ **picnic area** n zona de picnic; (AUT) área de descanso

picture ['pɪktʃə'] n cuadro; (painting) pintura; (photograph) fotografía; (TV) imagen f; (film) película; (fig: description) descripción f; (: situation) situación f ♦ vt (imagine) imaginar; **pictures** npl: **the pictures** (BRIT) el cine ❑ **picture frame** n marco ❑ **picture messaging** n (envío de) mensajes con imágenes

picturesque [pɪktʃə'resk] adj pintoresco

pie [paɪ] n pastel m; (open) tarta; (small: of meat) empanada

piece [piːs] n pedazo, trozo; (of cake) trozo; (item): **a ~ of clothing/furniture/advice** una prenda (de vestir)/un mueble/un consejo ♦ vt: **to ~ together** juntar; (TECH) armar; **to take to pieces** desmontar

pie chart n gráfico de sectores or tarta

pier [pɪə'] n muelle m, embarcadero

pierce [pɪəs] vt perforar ❑ **pierced** adj: **I've got pierced ears** tengo los agujeros hechos en las orejas

pig [pɪg] n cerdo, chancho (LAm); (pej: unkind person) asqueroso; (: greedy person) glotón(-ona) m/f

pigeon ['pɪdʒən] n paloma; (as food) pichón m

piggy bank ['pɪgɪ-] n hucha (en forma de cerdito) ❑ **pigsty** ['pɪgstaɪ] n pocilga ❑ **pigtail** n (girl's) trenza

pike [paɪk] n (fish) lucio

pilchard ['pɪltʃəd] n sardina

pile [paɪl] n montón m; (of carpet, cloth) pelo ▶ **pile up** vi +adv (accumulate: work) amontonarse, acumularse ♦ vt +adv (put in a heap: books, clothes) apilar, amontonar; (accumulate) acumular ❑ **piles** npl (MED) almorranas fpl, hemorroides mpl ❑ **pile-up** n (AUT) accidente m múltiple

pilgrimage ['pɪlgrɪmɪdʒ] n peregrinación f, romería

pill [pɪl] n píldora; **the ~** la píldora

pillar ['pɪlə'] n pilar m

pillow ['pɪləu] n almohada ❑ **pillowcase** n funda

pilot ['paɪlət] n piloto ♦ cpd (scheme etc) piloto ♦ vt pilotar ❑ **pilot light** n piloto

pimple ['pɪmpl] n grano

PIN n abbr (= personal identification number) número personal

pin [pɪn] n alfiler m ♦ vt prender (con alfiler); **pins and needles** hormigueo; **to ~ sb down** (fig) hacer que algn concrete; **to ~ sth on sb** (fig) colgarle a algn el sambenito de algo

pinafore ['pɪnəfɔː'] n delantal m

pinch [pɪntʃ] n (of salt etc) pizca ♦ vt pellizcar; (inf: steal) birlar; **at a ~** en caso de apuro

pine [paɪn] n (also: **~ tree**) pino ♦ vi: **to ~ for** suspirar por

pineapple ['paɪnæpl] n piña, ananás m

ping [pɪŋ] n (noise) sonido agudo
❑ **ping-pong®** m

pink [pɪŋk] adj rosado, (color de) rosa
♦ n (colour) rosa; (BOT) clavel m,
clavellina

pinpoint ['pɪnpɔɪnt] vt precisar

pint [paɪnt] n pinta (BRIT = 568cc, US =
473cc); (BRIT: inf: of beer) pinta de
cerveza, = jarra (SP)

pioneer [paɪə'nɪə²] n pionero(-a)

pious ['paɪəs] adj piadoso, devoto

pip [pɪp] n (seed) pepita; **the pips** (BRIT)
la señal

pipe [paɪp] n tubo, caño; (for smoking)
pipa ♦ vt conducir en cañerías
❑ **pipeline** n (for oil) oleoducto; (for
gas) gasoducto ❑ **piper** n gaitero(-a)

pirate ['paɪərət] n pirata mf ♦ vt
(cassette, book) piratear

Pisces ['paɪsi:z] n Piscis m

piss [pɪs] (inf!) vi mear ❑ **pissed** (inf!)
adj (drunk) borracho

pistol ['pɪstl] n pistola

piston ['pɪstən] n pistón m, émbolo

pit [pɪt] n hoyo; (also: **coal ~**) mina; (in
garage) foso de inspección; (also:
orchestra ~) platea ♦ vt: **to ~ one's
wits against sb** medir fuerzas con algn

pitch [pɪtʃ] n (MUS) tono; (BRIT SPORT)
campo, terreno; (fig) punto; (tar) brea
♦ vt (throw) arrojar, lanzar ♦ vi (fall)
caer(se); **to ~ a tent** montar una tienda
(de campaña) ❑ **pitch-black** adj
negro como boca de lobo

pitfall ['pɪtfɔːl] n riesgo

pith [pɪθ] n (of orange) médula

pitiful ['pɪtɪful] adj (touching)
lastimoso, conmovedor(a)

pity ['pɪtɪ] n compasión f, piedad f ♦ vt
compadecer(se de); **what a ~!** ¡qué
pena!

pizza ['piːtsə] n pizza

placard ['plækɑːd] n letrero; (in march
etc) pancarta

place [pleɪs] n lugar m, sitio; (seat)
plaza, asiento; (post) puesto; (home):

at/to his ~ en/a su casa; (role: in society
etc) papel m ♦ vt (object) poner,
colocar; (identify) reconocer; **to take ~**
tener lugar; **to be placed** (in race,
exam) colocarse; **out of ~** (not suitable)
fuera de lugar; **in the first ~** en primer
lugar; **to change places with sb**
cambiarse de sitio con algn; **~ of birth**
lugar m de nacimiento ❑ **place mat** n
(wooden etc) salvamanteles m inv;
(linen etc) mantel m individual
❑ **placement** n (positioning)
colocación f; (at work) emplazamiento

placid ['plæsɪd] adj apacible

plague [pleɪg] n plaga; (MED) peste f
♦ vt (fig) acosar, atormentar

plaice [pleɪs] n inv platija

plain [pleɪn] adj (unpatterned) liso;
(clear) claro, evidente; (simple) sencillo;
(not handsome) poco atractivo ♦ adv
claramente ♦ n llano, llanura ❑ **plain
chocolate** n chocolate m amargo
❑ **plainly** adv claramente

plaintiff ['pleɪntɪf] n demandante mf

plait [plæt] n trenza

plan [plæn] n (drawing) plano; (scheme)
plan m, proyecto ♦ vt proyectar,
planificar ♦ vi hacer proyectos; **to ~ to
do** pensar hacer

plane [pleɪn] n (AVIAT) avión m; (MATH,
fig) plano; (also: **~ tree**) plátano; (tool)
cepillo

planet ['plænɪt] n planeta m

plank [plæŋk] n tabla

planning ['plænɪŋ] n planificación f;
family ~ planificación familiar

plant [plɑːnt] n planta; (machinery)
maquinaria; (factory) fábrica ♦ vt
plantar; (field) sembrar; (bomb) colocar

plantation [plæn'teɪʃən] n plantación
f; (estate) hacienda

plaque [plæk] n placa

plaster ['plɑːstə²] n (for walls) yeso;
(also: **~ of Paris**) yeso mate, escayola
(SP); (BRIT: also: **sticking ~**) tirita (SP),
curita (LAm) ♦ vt enyesar; (cover): **to ~**

with llenar or cubrir □ **plaster cast** n (MED) escayola; (model, statue) vaciado de yeso

plastic ['plæstɪk] n plástico ♦ adj de plástico □ **plastic bag** n bolsa de plástico □ **plastic surgery** n cirugía plástica

plate [pleɪt] n (dish) plato; (metal, in book) lámina; (dental plate) placa de dentadura postiza

plateau ['plætəʊ] n (pl plateaus or plateaux) n meseta, altiplanicie f

platform ['plætfɔːm] n (RAIL) andén m; (stage, BRIT: on bus) plataforma; (at meeting) tribuna; (POL) programa m (electoral)

platinum ['plætɪnəm] adj, n platino

platoon [plə'tuːn] n pelotón m

platter ['plætə*] n fuente f

plausible ['plɔːzɪbl] adj verosímil; (person) convincente

play [pleɪ] n (THEATRE) obra, comedia ♦ vt (game) jugar; (compete against) jugar contra; (instrument) tocar; (part: in play etc) hacer el papel de; (tape, record) poner ♦ vi jugar; (band) tocar; (tape, record) sonar; **to ~ safe** n ir a lo seguro ► **play back** vt (tape) poner ► **play up** vi (cause trouble to) dar guerra □ **player** n jugador(a) m/f; (THEATRE) actor (actriz) m/f; (MUS) músico(-a) □ **playful** adj juguetón(-ona) □ **playground** n (in school) patio de recreo; (in park) parque m infantil □ **playgroup** n jardín m de niños □ **playing card** n naipe m, carta □ **playing field** n campo de deportes □ **playschool** n = playgroup □ **playtime** n (SCOL) recreo □ **playwright** n dramaturgo(-a)

plc abbr (= public limited company) = S.A.

plea [pliː] n súplica, petición f; (LAW) alegato, defensa

plead [pliːd] vt (LAW): **to ~ sb's case** defender a algn; (give as excuse) poner

como pretexto ♦ vi (LAW) declararse; (beg): **to ~ with sb** suplicar or rogar a algn

pleasant ['plɛznt] adj agradable

please [pliːz] excl ¡por favor! ♦ vt (give pleasure to) dar gusto a, agradar ♦ vi (think fit): **do as you ~** haz lo que quieras; **~ yourself!** (inf) ¡haz lo que quieras!; ¡como quieras! □ **pleased** adj (happy) alegre, contento; **pleased (with)** satisfecho (de); **pleased to meet you** ¡encantado!, ¡tanto gusto!

pleasure ['plɛʒə*] n placer m, gusto; **"it's a ~"** "el gusto es mío"

pleat [pliːt] n pliegue m

pledge [plɛdʒ] n (promise) promesa, voto ♦ vt prometer

plentiful ['plɛntɪful] adj copioso, abundante

plenty ['plɛntɪ] n: **~ of** mucho(s)/a(s)

pliers ['plaɪəz] npl alicates mpl, tenazas fpl

plight [plaɪt] n situación f difícil

plod [plɔd] vi caminar con paso pesado; (fig) trabajar laboriosamente

plonk [plɔŋk] (inf) n (BRIT: wine) vino peleón ♦ vt: **to ~ sth down** dejar caer algo

plot [plɔt] n (scheme) complot m, conjura; (of story, play) argumento; (of land) terreno ♦ vt (mark out) trazar; (conspire) tramar, urdir ♦ vi conspirar

plough [plaʊ] (US **plow**) n arado ♦ vt (earth) arar; **to ~ money into** invertir dinero en □ **ploughman's lunch** (BRIT) n almuerzo de pub a base de pan, queso y encurtidos

plow [plaʊ] (US) = **plough**

ploy [plɔɪ] n truco, estratagema

pluck [plʌk] vt (fruit) coger (SP), recoger (LAm); (musical instrument) puntear; (bird) desplumar; (eyebrows) depilar; **to ~ up courage** hacer de tripas corazón

plug [plʌg] n tapón m; (ELEC) enchufe m, clavija; (AUT: also: **spark(ing)** n) bujía ♦ vt (hole) tapar; (inf: advertise) dar publicidad a ▸ **plug in** vt (ELEC) enchufar ❑ **plughole** n desagüe m

plum [plʌm] n (fruit) ciruela

plumber ['plʌmə'] n fontanero(-a) (SP, CAm), plomero(-a) (LAm)

plumbing ['plʌmɪŋ] n (trade) fontanería, plomería; (piping) cañería

plummet ['plʌmɪt] vi: **to ~ (down)** caer a plomo

plump [plʌmp] adj rechoncho, rollizo ◆ vt señalar; (gun etc): **to ~ sth at sb** apuntar algo a algn ◆ vi: **to ~ for** (inf: choose) optar por

plunge [plʌndʒ] n zambullida ◆ vt sumergir, hundir ◆ vi (fall) caer; (dive) saltar; (person) arrojarse; **to take the ~** lanzarse

plural ['pluərl] adj plural ◆ n plural m

plus [plʌs] n (also: **~ sign**) signo más ◆ prep más, y, además de; **ten/twenty ~** más de diez/veinte

ply [plaɪ] vt (a trade) ejercer ◆ vi (ship) ir y venir ◆ n (of wool, rope) cabo; **to ~ sb with drink** insistir en ofrecer a algn muchas copas ❑ **plywood** n madera contrachapada

P.M. n abbr = **Prime Minister**

p.m. adv abbr (= post meridiem) de la tarde or noche

PMS n abbr (= premenstrual syndrome) SPM m

PMT n abbr (= premenstrual tension) SPM m

pneumatic drill [njuː'mætɪk-] n martillo neumático

pneumonia [njuː'məʊnɪə] n pulmonía

poach [pəʊtʃ] vt (cook) escalfar; (steal) cazar (or pescar) en vedado ◆ vi cazar (or pescar) en vedado ❑ **poached** adj escalfado

P.O. Box n abbr (= Post Office Box) apdo., aptdo.

pocket ['pɒkɪt] n bolsillo; (fig: small area) bolsa ◆ vt meter en el bolsillo; (steal) embolsar; **to be out of ~** (BRIT) salir perdiendo ❑ **pocketbook** (US) n cartera ❑ **pocket money** n asignación f

pod [pɒd] n vaina

podiatrist [pɒ'diːətrɪst] (US) n pedicuro(-a)

podium ['pəʊdɪəm] n podio

poem ['pəʊɪm] n poema m

poet ['pəʊɪt] n poeta m/f ❑ **poetic** [-'etɪk] adj poético ❑ **poetry** n poesía

poignant ['pɔɪnjənt] adj conmovedor(a)

point [pɔɪnt] n punto; (tip) punta; (purpose) fin m, propósito; (use) utilidad f; (significant part) lo significativo; (moment) momento; (ELEC) toma de corriente; (also: **decimal ~**): **2 ~ 3 (2.3)** dos coma tres (2,3) ◆ vt señalar; (gun etc): **to ~ sth at sb** apuntar algo a algn ◆ vi: **to ~ at** señalar; **points** npl (AUT) contactos mpl; (RAIL) agujas fpl; **to be on the ~ of doing sth** estar a punto de hacer algo; **to make a ~ of** poner empeño en; **to get/miss the ~** comprender/no comprender; **to come to the ~** ir al meollo; **there's no ~ (in doing)** no tiene sentido (hacer) ▸ **point out** vt señalar ❑ **point-blank** adv (say, refuse) sin más hablar; (also: **at point-blank range**) a quemarropa ❑ **pointed** adj (shape) puntiagudo, afilado; (remark) intencionado ❑ **pointer** n (needle) aguja, indicador m ❑ **pointless** adj sin sentido ❑ **point of view** n punto de vista

poison ['pɔɪzn] n veneno ◆ vt envenenar ❑ **poisonous** adj venenoso; (fumes etc) tóxico

poke [pəʊk] vt (jab with finger, stick etc) empujar; (put): **to ~ sth in(to)** introducir algo en ▸ **poke about** or **around** vi fisgonear ▸ **poke out** vi (stick out) salir

poker ['pəʊkə'] n atizador m; (CARDS) póker m

Poland ['pəʊlənd] n Polonia

polar ['pəʊlə'] adj polar ❑ **polar bear** n oso polar

Pole [pəʊl] n polaco(-a)

pole [pəul] n palo; (*fixed*) poste m; (GEO) polo ❑ **pole bean** (US) n ≈ judía verde ❑ **pole vault** n salto con pértiga

police [pə'liːs] n policía ◆ vt vigilar ❑ **police car** n coche-patrulla m ❑ **police constable** (BRIT) n guardia m, policía m ❑ **police force** n cuerpo de policía ❑ **policeman** (*irreg*) n policía m, guardia m ❑ **police officer** n guardia m, policía m ❑ **police station** n comisaría ❑ **policewoman** (*irreg*) n mujer f policía

policy ['pɒlɪsɪ] n política f; (*also*: **insurance ~**) póliza

polio ['pəulɪəu] n polio f

Polish ['pəulɪʃ] adj polaco ◆ n (LING) polaco

polish ['pɒlɪʃ] n (for shoes) betún m; (for floor) cera (de lustrar); (shine) brillo, lustre m; (fig: refinement) educación f ◆ vt (shoes) limpiar; (make shiny) pulir, sacar brillo a ▶ **polish off** vt (food) despachar ❑ **polished** adj (fig: person) elegante

polite [pə'laɪt] adj cortés, atento ❑ **politeness** n cortesía

political [pə'lɪtɪkl] adj político ❑ **politically** adv políticamente; **politically correct** políticamente correcto

politician [pɒlɪ'tɪʃən] n político(-a)

politics ['pɒlɪtɪks] n política

poll [pəul] n (election) votación f; (*also*: **opinion ~**) sondeo, encuesta ◆ vt encuestar; (votes) obtener

pollen ['pɒlən] n polen m

polling station ['pəulɪŋ-] n centro electoral

pollute [pə'luːt] vt contaminar

pollution [pə'luːʃən] n polución f, contaminación f del medio ambiente

polo ['pəuləu] n (sport) polo ❑ **polo-neck** adj de cuello vuelto ◆ n (sweater) suéter m de cuello vuelto ❑ **polo shirt** n polo, niqui m

polyester [pɒlɪ'estə'] n poliéster m

polystyrene [pɒlɪ'staɪriːn] n poliestireno

polythene ['pɒlɪθiːn] (BRIT) n politeno ❑ **polythene bag** n bolsa de plástico

pomegranate ['pɒmɪgrænɪt] n granada

pompous ['pɒmpəs] adj pomposo

pond [pɒnd] n (natural) charca; (artificial) estanque m

ponder ['pɒndə'] vt meditar

pony ['pəunɪ] n poni m ❑ **ponytail** n coleta ❑ **pony trekking** (BRIT) n excursión f a caballo

poodle ['puːdl] n caniche m

pool [puːl] n (natural) charca; (*also*: **swimming ~**) piscina, alberca (MEX), pileta (RPl); (fig: of light etc) charco; (SPORT) chapolín m ◆ vt juntar; **pools** npl quinielas fpl

poor [puə'] adj pobre; (bad) de mala calidad ◆ npl: **the ~** los pobres ❑ **poorly** adj mal, enfermo ◆ adv mal

pop [pɒp] n (sound) ruido seco; (MUS) (música) pop m; (inf: father) papá m; (drink) gaseosa ◆ vt (put quickly) meter (de prisa) ◆ vi reventar; (cork) saltar ▶ **pop in** vi entrar un momento ▶ **pop out** vi salir un momento ❑ **popcorn** n palomitas fpl

poplar ['pɒplə'] n álamo

popper ['pɒpə'] (BRIT) n automático

poppy ['pɒpɪ] n amapola

Popsicle® ['pɒpsɪkl] (US) n polo

pop star n estrella del pop

popular ['pɒpjulə'] adj popular ❑ **popularity** [pɒpju'lærɪtɪ] n popularidad f

population [pɒpju'leɪʃən] n población f

porcelain ['pɔːslɪn] n porcelana

porch [pɔːtʃ] n pórtico, entrada; (US) veranda

pore [pɔː'] n poro ◆ vi: **to ~ over** engolfarse en

pork [pɔːk] n carne f de cerdo or (LAm) chancho □ **pork chop** n chuleta de cerdo □ **pork pie** n (BRIT: CULIN) empanada de carne de cerdo

porn [pɔːn] adj (inf) porno inv ♦ n porno □ **pornographic** [pɔːnəˈgræfɪk] adj pornográfico □ **pornography** [pɔːˈnɔgrəfɪ] n pornografía

porridge [ˈpɔrɪdʒ] n gachas fpl de avena

port [pɔːt] n puerto; (NAUT: left side) babor m; (wine) vino de Oporto; ~ **of call** puerto de escala

portable [ˈpɔːtəbl] adj portátil

porter [ˈpɔːtə'] n (for luggage) maletero; (doorkeeper) portero(-a), conserje m/f

portfolio [pɔːtˈfəʊlɪəʊ] n cartera

portion [ˈpɔːʃən] n porción f; (of food) ración f

portrait [ˈpɔːtreɪt] n retrato

portray [pɔːˈtreɪ] vt retratar; (actor) representar

Portugal [ˈpɔːtjʊgl] n Portugal m

Portuguese [pɔːtjuˈgiːz] adj portugués(-esa) ♦ n inv portugués(-esa) m/f; (LING) portugués m

pose [pəʊz] n postura, actitud f ♦ vi (pretend): **to** ~ **as** hacerse pasar por ♦ vt (question) plantear; **to** ~ **for** posar para

posh [pɔʃ] (inf) adj elegante, de lujo

position [pəˈzɪʃən] n posición f; (job) puesto; (situation) situación f ♦ vt colocar

positive [ˈpɔzɪtɪv] adj positivo; (certain) seguro; (definite) definitivo □ **positively** adv (affirmatively, enthusiastically) de forma positiva; (inf: really) absolutamente

possess [pəˈzes] vt poseer □ **possession** [pəˈzeʃən] n posesión f; **possessions** npl (belongings) pertenencias fpl □ **possessive** adj posesivo

possibility [pɔsɪˈbɪlɪtɪ] n posibilidad f

possible [ˈpɔsɪbl] adj posible; **as big as** ~ lo más grande posible □ **possibly** adv posiblemente; **I cannot possibly come** me es imposible venir

post [pəʊst] n (BRIT: system) correos mpl; (BRIT: letters, delivery) correo; (job, situation) puesto; (pole) poste m ♦ vt (BRIT: send by post) echar al correo; (BRIT: appoint): **to** ~ **to** enviar a □ **postage** n porte m, franqueo □ **postal** adj postal, de correos □ **postal order** n giro postal □ **postbox** (BRIT) n buzón m □ **postcard** n tarjeta postal □ **postcode** (BRIT) n código postal

poster [ˈpəʊstə'] n cartel m

postgraduate [pəʊstˈgrædjuət] n posgraduado(-a)

postman [ˈpəʊstmən] (BRIT: irreg) n cartero

postmark [ˈpəʊstmɑːk] n matasellos m inv

post-mortem [-ˈmɔːtəm] n autopsia

post office n (building) (oficina de) correos m; (organization): **the Post Office** Correos m inv (SP), Dirección f General de Correos (LAm)

postpone [pəsˈpəʊn] vt aplazar

posture [ˈpɔstʃə'] n postura, actitud f

postwoman [ˈpəʊstwʊmən] (BRIT: irreg) n cartera

pot [pɔt] n (for cooking) olla; (teapot) tetera; (coffeepot) cafetera; (for flowers) maceta; (for jam) tarro, pote m; (inf: marijuana) chocolate m ♦ vt (plant) poner en tiesto; **to go to** ~ (inf) irse al traste

potato [pəˈteɪtəʊ] (pl **potatoes**) n patata (SP), papa (LAm) □ **potato peeler** n pelapatatas m inv

potent [ˈpəʊtnt] adj potente, poderoso; (drink) fuerte

potential [pəˈtenʃl] adj potencial, posible ♦ n potencial m

pothole [ˈpɔthəʊl] n (in road) bache m; (BRIT: underground) gruta

pot plant ['pɔtplɑːnt] n planta de interior

potter ['pɔtə'] n alfarero(-a) ♦ vi: **to ~ around** or **about** (BRIT) hacer trabajitos ❑ **pottery** n cerámica; (factory) alfarería

potty ['pɔti] n orinal m de niño

pouch [pautʃ] n (ZOOL) bolsa; (for tobacco) petaca

poultry ['pəultri] n aves fpl de corral; (meat) pollo

pounce [pauns] vi: **to ~ on** precipitarse sobre

pound [paund] n libra (weight = 453g or 16oz; money = 100 pence) ♦ vt (beat) golpear; (crush) machacar ♦ vi (heart) latir ❑ **pound sterling** n libra esterlina

pour [pɔː'] vt echar; (tea etc) servir ♦ vi correr, fluir; **to ~ sb a drink** servirle a algn una copa ▶ **pour in** vi (people) entrar en tropel ▶ **pour out** vi salir en tropel ♦ vt (drink) echar, servir; (fig): **to pour out one's feelings** desahogarse ❑ **pouring** adj: **pouring rain** lluvia torrencial

pout [paut] vi hacer pucheros

poverty ['pɔvəti] n pobreza, miseria

powder ['paudə'] n polvo; (also: **face~**) polvos mpl ♦ vt polvorear; **to ~ one's face** empolvarse la cara ❑ **powdered milk** n leche f en polvo

power ['pauə'] n poder m; (strength) fuerza; (nation, TECH) potencia; (drive) empuje m; (ELEC) fuerza, energía ♦ vt impulsar; **to be in ~** (POL) estar en el poder ❑ **power cut** n apagón m ❑ **power failure** n = **power cut** ❑ **powerful** adj poderoso; (engine) potente; (speech etc) convincente ❑ **powerless** adj: **powerless (to do)** incapaz (de hacer) ❑ **power point** (BRIT) n enchufe m ❑ **power station** n central f eléctrica

p.p. abbr = **per procurationem**; **p.p. J. Smith** p.p. (por poder de) J. Smith; (= pages) págs

PR n abbr = **public relations**

practical ['præktɪkl] adj práctico ❑ **practical joke** n broma pesada ❑ **practically** adv (almost) casi

practice ['præktɪs] n (habit) costumbre f; (exercise) práctica, ejercicio; (training) adiestramiento; (MED: of profession) práctica, ejercicio; (MED, LAW: business) consulta ♦ vt, vi (US) = **practise**; **in ~** (in reality) en la práctica; **out of ~** desentrenado

practise ['præktɪs] (US **practice**) vt (carry out) practicar; (profession) ejercer; (train at) practicar ♦ vi ejercer; (train) practicar ❑ **practising** adj (Christian etc) practicante; (lawyer) en ejercicio

practitioner [præk'tɪʃənə'] n (MED) médico(-a)

pragmatic [præg'mætɪk] adj pragmático

prairie ['preəri] n pampa

praise [preiz] n alabanza(s) f(pl), elogio(s) m(pl) ♦ vt alabar, elogiar

pram [præm] (BRIT) n cochecito de niño

prank [præŋk] n travesura

prawn [prɔːn] n gamba ❑ **prawn cocktail** n cóctel m de gambas

pray [prei] vi rezar ❑ **prayer** [preə'] n oración f, rezo; (entreaty) ruego, súplica

preach [priːtʃ] vi predicar ❑ **preacher** n predicador(a) m/f

precarious [prɪ'keəriəs] adj precario

precaution [prɪ'kɔːʃən] n precaución f

precede [prɪ'siːd] vt, vi preceder ❑ **precedent** ['presɪdənt] n precedente m ❑ **preceding** [prɪ'siːdɪŋ] adj anterior

precinct ['priːsɪŋkt] n recinto

precious ['preʃəs] adj precioso

precise [prɪ'saɪs] adj preciso, exacto ❑ **precisely** adv precisamente, exactamente

precision [prɪ'sɪʒən] n precisión f

predator ['predətə'] n depredador m

predecessor [ˈpriːdɪsesəʳ] n antecesor(a) m/f

predicament [prɪˈdɪkəmənt] n apuro

predict [prɪˈdɪkt] vt pronosticar ❑ **predictable** adj previsible ❑ **prediction** [-ˈdɪkʃən] n predicción f

predominantly [prɪˈdɒmɪnəntlɪ] adv en su mayoría

preface [ˈprefəs] n prefacio

prefect [ˈpriːfekt] (BRIT) n (in school) monitor(a) m/f

prefer [prɪˈfəːʳ] vt preferir; **to ~ doing** or **to do** preferir hacer ❑ **preferable** [ˈprefrəbl] adj preferible ❑ **preferably** [ˈprefrəblɪ] adv de preferencia ❑ **preference** [ˈprefrəns] n preferencia; (priority) prioridad f

prefix [ˈpriːfɪks] n prefijo

pregnancy [ˈpregnənsɪ] n (of woman) embarazo; (of animal) preñez f

pregnant [ˈpregnənt] adj (woman) embarazada; (animal) preñada

prehistoric [ˈpriːhɪsˈtɒrɪk] adj prehistórico

prejudice [ˈpredʒʊdɪs] n prejuicio ❑ **prejudiced** adj (person) predispuesto

preliminary [prɪˈlɪmɪnərɪ] adj preliminar

prelude [ˈpreljuːd] n preludio

premature [ˈprematjʊəʳ] adj prematuro

premier [ˈpremɪəʳ] adj primero, principal ♦ n (POL) primer(a) ministro(-a)

première [ˈpremɪəʳ] n estreno

Premier League [premɪəˈliːg] n primera división

premises [ˈpremɪsɪz] npl (of business etc) local m; **on the ~** en el lugar mismo

premium [ˈpriːmɪəm] n premio; (insurance) prima; **to be at a ~** ser muy solicitado

premonition [preməˈnɪʃən] n resentimiento

preoccupied [prɪˈɒkjʊpaɪd] adj ensimismado

prepaid [priːˈpeɪd] adj porte pagado

preparation [prepəˈreɪʃən] n preparación f; **preparations** npl preparativos mpl

preparatory school [prɪˈpærətərɪ-] n escuela preparatoria

prepare [prɪˈpeəʳ] vt preparar, disponer; (CULIN) preparar ♦ vi: **to ~ for** (action) prepararse or disponerse para; (event) hacer preparativos para; **prepared to** dispuesto a; **prepared for** listo para

preposition [prepəˈzɪʃən] n preposición f

prep school [prep-] n = **preparatory school**

prerequisite [priːˈrekwɪzɪt] n requisito

preschool [ˈpriːskuːl] adj preescolar

prescribe [prɪˈskraɪb] vt (MED) recetar

prescription [prɪˈskrɪpʃən] n (MED) receta

presence [ˈprezns] n presencia; **in sb's ~** en presencia de algn; **~ of mind** aplomo

present [adj, n ˈpreznt, vb prɪˈzent] adj (in attendance) presente; (current) actual ♦ n (gift) regalo; (actuality): **the ~** la actualidad, el presente ♦ vt (introduce, describe) presentar; (expound) exponer; (give) presentar, dar, ofrecer; (THEATRE) representar; **to give sb a ~** regalar algo a algn; **at ~** actualmente ❑ **presentable** [prɪˈzentəbl] adj: **to make o.s. presentable** arreglarse ❑ **presentation** [-ˈteɪʃən] n presentación f; (of report etc) exposición f; (formal ceremony) entrega de un regalo ❑ **present-day** adj actual ❑ **presenter** (RADIO, TV) locutor(a) m/f ❑ **presently** adv (soon) dentro de poco; (now) ahora ❑ **present participle** n participio (de) presente

preservation [prezə'veɪʃən] n
conservación f

preservative [prɪ'zɜːvətɪv] n
conservante m

preserve [prɪ'zɜːv] vt (keep safe)
preservar, proteger; (maintain)
mantener; (food) conservar ♦ n (for
game) coto, vedado; (often pl: jam)
conserva, confitura

preside [prɪ'zaɪd] vi presidir

president ['prezɪdənt] n presidente m/
f □ **presidential** [-'denʃl] adj
presidencial

press [pres] n (newspapers): **the P~** la
prensa; (printer's) imprenta; (of button)
pulsación f ♦ vt empujar; (button etc)
apretar; (clothes: iron) planchar; (put
pressure on: person) presionar; (insist):
to ~ sth on sb insistir en que algn
acepte algo ♦ vi (squeeze) apretar;
(pressurize): **to ~** for presionar por; **we
are pressed for time/money** estamos
apurados de tiempo/dinero □ **press
conference** n rueda de prensa
□ **pressing** adj apremiante □ **press
stud** (BRIT) n botón m de presión
□ **press-up** (BRIT) n plancha

pressure ['preʃə*] n presión f; **to put ~
on sb** presionar a algn □ **pressure
cooker** n olla a presión □ **pressure
group** n grupo de presión

prestige [pres'tiːʒ] n prestigio

prestigious [pres'tɪdʒəs] adj
prestigioso

presumably [prɪ'zjuːməblɪ] adv es de
suponer que, cabe presumir que

presume [prɪ'zjuːm] vt: **to ~ (that)**
presumir (que), suponer (que)

pretence [prɪ'tens] (US **pretense**) n
fingimiento; **under false pretences**
con engaños

pretend [prɪ'tend] vt, vi (feign) fingir

⚠ Be careful not to translate **pretend**
by the Spanish word *pretender*.

pretense [prɪ'tens] (US) n = **pretence**

pretentious [prɪ'tenʃəs] adj
presumido; (ostentatious) ostentoso,
aparatoso

pretext ['priːtekst] n pretexto

pretty ['prɪtɪ] adj bonito, lindo (LAm)
♦ adv bastante

prevail [prɪ'veɪl] vi (gain mastery)
prevalecer; (be current) predominar
□ **prevailing** adj (dominant)
predominante

prevalent ['prevələnt] adj (widespread)
extendido

prevent [prɪ'vent] vt: **to ~ sb from
doing sth** impedir a algn hacer algo; **to
~ sth from happening** evitar que
ocurra algo □ **prevention**
[prɪ'venʃən] n prevención f
□ **preventive** adj preventivo

preview ['priːvjuː] n (of film)
preestreno

previous ['priːvɪəs] adj previo, anterior
□ **previously** adv antes

prey [preɪ] n presa ♦ vi: **to ~ on** (feed on)
alimentarse de; **it was preying on his
mind** le preocupaba, le obsesionaba

price [praɪs] n precio ♦ vt (goods) fijar el
precio de □ **priceless** adj que no
tiene precio □ **price list** n tarifa

prick [prɪk] n (sting) picadura ♦ vt
pinchar; (hurt) picar; **to ~ up one's ears**
aguzar el oído

prickly ['prɪklɪ] adj espinoso; (fig:
person) enojadizo

pride [praɪd] n orgullo; (pej) soberbia
♦ vt: **to ~ o.s. on** enorgullecerse de

priest [priːst] n sacerdote m

primarily ['praɪmərɪlɪ] adv ante todo

primary ['praɪmərɪ] adj (first in
importance) principal ♦ n (US POL)
elección f primaria □ **primary school**
(BRIT) n escuela primaria

prime [praɪm] adj primero, principal;
(excellent) selecto, de primera clase
♦ n: **in the ~ of life** en la flor de la vida
♦ vt (wood: fig) preparar; **~ example**

ejemplo típico ❏ **Prime Minister** n primer(a) ministro(-a)

primitive ['prɪmɪtɪv] adj primitivo; (crude) rudimentario

primrose ['prɪmrəuz] n primavera, prímula

prince [prɪns] n príncipe m

princess [prɪn'ses] n princesa

principal ['prɪnsɪpl] adj principal, mayor ♦ n director(a) m/f ❏ **principally** adv principalmente

principle ['prɪnsɪpl] n principio; **in ~** en principio; **on ~** por principio

print [prɪnt] n (footprint) huella; (fingerprint) huella dactilar; (letters) letra de molde; (fabric) estampado; (ART) grabado; (PHOT) impresión f ♦ vt imprimir; (cloth) estampar; (write in capitals) escribir en letras de molde; **out of ~** agotado ▶ **print out** vt (COMPUT) imprimir ❏ **printer** n (person) impresor(a) m/f; (machine) impresora ❏ **printout** n (COMPUT) impresión f

prior ['praɪə*] adj anterior, previo; (more important) más importante; **~ to** antes de

priority [praɪ'ɔrɪtɪ] n prioridad f; **to have ~ (over)** tener prioridad (sobre)

prison ['prɪzn] n cárcel f, prisión f ♦ cpd carcelario ❏ **prisoner** n (in prison) preso(-a); (captured person) prisionero ❏ **prisoner-of-war** n prisionero de guerra

pristine ['prɪstiːn] adj prístino

privacy ['prɪvəsɪ] n intimidad f

private ['praɪvɪt] adj (personal) particular; (property, industry, discussion etc) privado; (place) reservado; (place) tranquilo ♦ n soldado raso; **"~"** (on envelope) "confidencial"; (on door) "prohibido el [paso]"; **in ~** en privado ❏ **privately** adv en privado; (in o.s.) en secreto ❏ **private property** n propiedad f

privada ❏ **private school** n colegio particular

privatize ['praɪvɪtaɪz] vt privatizar

privilege ['prɪvɪlɪdʒ] n privilegio; (prerogative) prerrogativa

prize [praɪz] n premio ♦ adj de primera clase ♦ vt apreciar, estimar ❏ **prize-giving** n distribución f de premios ❏ **prizewinner** n premiado(-a)

pro [prəu] n (SPORT) profesional mf ♦ prep a favor de; **the pros and cons** los pros y los contras

probability [prɔbə'bɪlɪtɪ] n probabilidad f; **in all ~** con toda probabilidad

probable ['prɔbəbl] adj probable

probably ['prɔbəblɪ] adv probablemente

probation [prə'beɪʃən] n: **on ~** (employee) a prueba; (LAW) en libertad condicional

probe [prəub] n (MED, SPACE) sonda; (enquiry) encuesta, investigación f ♦ vt sondar; (investigate) investigar

problem ['prɔbləm] n problema m

procedure [prə'siːdʒə*] n procedimiento; (bureaucratic) trámites mpl

proceed [prə'siːd] vi (do afterwards): **to ~ to do sth** proceder a hacer algo; (continue): **to ~ (with)** continuar or seguir (con) ❏ **proceedings** npl acto(s) (pl); (LAW) proceso ❏ **proceeds** ['prəusiːdz] npl (money) ganancias fpl, ingresos mpl

process ['prəuses] n proceso ♦ vt tratar, elaborar

procession [prə'seʃən] n desfile m; **funeral ~** cortejo fúnebre

proclaim [prə'kleɪm] vt (announce) anunciar

prod [prɔd] vt empujar ♦ n empujón m

produce [n 'prɔdjuːs, vt prə'djuːs] n (AGR) productos mpl agrícolas ♦ vt producir; (play, film, programme) presentar ❏ **producer** n productor(a) m/f; (of film, programme) director(a) m/f; (of record) productor(a) m/f

product ['prɒdʌkt] n producto ❑ **production** [prə'dʌkʃən] n producción f; (THEATRE) presentación f ❑ **productive** [prə'dʌktɪv] adj productivo ❑ **productivity** [prɒdʌk'tɪvɪtɪ] n productividad f

Prof. [prɒf] abbr (= professor) Prof

profession [prə'feʃən] n profesión f ❑ **professional** adj profesional ♦ n profesional mf; (skilled person) perito

professor [prə'fesə'] n (BRIT) catedrático(-a); (US, Canada) profesor(a) m/f

profile ['prəʊfaɪl] n perfil m

profit ['prɒfɪt] n (COMM) ganancia f ♦ vi: **to ~ by** or **from** aprovechar or sacar provecho de ❑ **profitable** [ECON] rentable

profound [prə'faʊnd] adj profundo

programme ['prəʊgræm] (US **program**) n programa m ♦ vt programar ❑ **programmer** (US **programer**) n programador(a) m/f ❑ **programming** (US **programing**) n programación f

progress [n 'prəʊgres, vi prə'gres] n progreso; (development) desarrollo ♦ vi progresar, avanzar; **in ~** en curso ❑ **progressive** [-'gresɪv] adj progresivo; (person) progresista

prohibit [prə'hɪbɪt] vt prohibir; **to ~ sb from doing sth** prohibir a algn hacer algo

project [n 'prɒdʒekt, vb prə'dʒekt] n proyecto ♦ vt proyectar ♦ vi (stick out) salir, sobresalir ❑ **projection** [prə'dʒekʃən] n proyección f; (overhang) saliente m ❑ **projector** [prə'dʒektə'] n proyector m

prolific [prə'lɪfɪk] adj prolífico

prolong [prə'lɒŋ] vt prolongar, extender

prom [prɒm] n abbr = **promenade**; (US: ball) baile m de gala; **the Proms** ver recuadro

PROM

El ciclo de conciertos de música clásica más conocido de Londres es el llamado **the Proms** (promenade concerts), que se celebra anualmente en el Royal Albert Hall. Su nombre se debe a que originalmente el público paseaba durante las actuaciones, costumbre que en la actualidad se mantiene de forma simbólica, permitiendo que parte de los asistentes permanezcan de pie. En Estados Unidos se llama **prom** a un baile de gala en un centro de educación secundaria o universitaria.

promenade [prɒmə'nɑːd] n (by sea) paseo marítimo

prominent ['prɒmɪnənt] adj (standing out) saliente; (important) eminente, importante

promiscuous [prə'mɪskjʊəs] adj (sexually) promiscuo

promise ['prɒmɪs] n promesa ♦ vt, vi prometer ❑ **promising** adj prometedor(a)

promote [prə'məʊt] vt (employee) ascender; (product, pop star) hacer propaganda por; (ideas) fomentar ❑ **promotion** [-'məʊʃən] n (advertising campaign) campaña f de promoción; (in rank) ascenso

prompt [prɒmpt] adj rápido ♦ adv: **at 6 o'clock** a las seis en punto ♦ n (COMPUT) aviso ♦ vt (urge) mover, incitar; (when talking) instar; (THEATRE) apuntar; **to ~ sb to do sth** instar a algn a hacer algo ❑ **promptly** adv rápidamente; (exactly) puntualmente

prone [prəʊn] adj (lying) postrado; **~ to** propenso a

prong [prɒŋ] n diente m, punta

pronoun ['prəʊnaʊn] n pronombre m

pronounce [prə'nauns] vt pronunciar

pronunciation [prənʌnsɪ'eɪʃən] n pronunciación f

proof [pruːf] n prueba ♦ adj: **~ against** a prueba de

prop [prɒp] n apoyo; (fig) sostén m; **props** accesorios mpl, at(t)rezzo msg ▶ **prop up** vt (roof, structure) apuntalar; (economy) respaldar

propaganda [prɒpə'gændə] n propaganda

propeller [prə'pelə'] n hélice f

proper ['prɒpə'] adj (suited, right) propio; (exact) justo; (seemly) correcto, decente; (authentic) verdadero; (referring to place): **the village ~** el pueblo mismo ❑ **properly** adv (adequately) correctamente; (decently) decentemente ❑ **proper noun** n nombre m propio

property ['prɒpətɪ] n propiedad f; (personal) bienes mpl muebles

prophecy ['prɒfɪsɪ] n profecía

prophet ['prɒfɪt] n profeta m

proportion [prə'pɔːʃən] n proporción f; (share) parte f; **proportions** npl (size) dimensiones fpl ❑ **proportional** adj: **proportional (to)** en proporción (con)

proposal [prə'pəuzl] n (offer of marriage) oferta de matrimonio; (plan) proyecto

propose [prə'pəuz] vt proponer ♦ vi declararse; **to ~ to do** tener intención de hacer

proposition [prɒpə'zɪʃən] n propuesta

proprietor [prə'praɪətə'] n propietario(-a), dueño(-a)

prose [prəuz] n prosa

prosecute ['prɒsɪkjuːt] vt (LAW) procesar ❑ **prosecution** [-'kjuːʃən] n proceso, causa; (accusing side) acusación f ❑ **prosecutor** n acusador(a) m/f; (also: **public prosecutor**) fiscal mf

prospect [n 'prɒspekt, vb prə'spekt] n (possibility) posibilidad f; (outlook)

perspectiva ♦ vi: **to ~ for** buscar; **prospects** npl (for work etc) perspectivas fpl ❑ **prospective** [prə'spektɪv] adj futuro

prospectus [prə'spektəs] n prospecto

prosper ['prɒspə'] vi prosperar ❑ **prosperity** [-'sperɪtɪ] n prosperidad f ❑ **prosperous** adj próspero

prostitute ['prɒstɪtjuːt] n prostituta; (male) hombre que se dedica a la prostitución

protect [prə'tekt] vt proteger ❑ **protection** [-'tekʃən] n protección f ❑ **protective** adj protector(a)

protein ['prəutiːn] n proteína

protest [n 'prəutest, vb prə'test] n protesta ♦ vi: **to ~ about** or **at/against** protestar de/contra ♦ vt (insist): **to ~ (that)** insistir en (que)

Protestant ['prɒtɪstənt] adj, n protestante mf

protester [prə'testə'] n manifestante mf

protractor [prə'træktə'] n (GEOM) transportador m

proud [praud] adj orgulloso; (pej) soberbio, altanero

prove [pruːv] vt probar; (show) demostrar ♦ vi: **to ~ (to be) correct** resultar correcto; **to ~ o.s.** probar su valía

proverb ['prɒvɜːb] n refrán m

provide [prə'vaɪd] vt proporcionar, dar; **to ~ sb with sth** proveer a algn de algo ▶ **provide for** vt fus (person) mantener a; (problem etc) tener en cuenta ❑ **provided** conj: **provided (that)** con tal de que, a condición de que ❑ **providing** [prə'vaɪdɪŋ] conj: **providing (that)** a condición de que, con tal de que

province ['prɒvɪns] n provincia; (fig) esfera ❑ **provincial** [prə'vɪnʃəl] adj provincial; (pej) provinciano

provision [prə'vɪʒən] n (supplying) suministro, abastecimiento; (of

contract etc) disposición *f*; **provisions** *npl* (*food*) comestibles *mpl*
❏ **provisional** *adj* provisional

provocative [prə'vɒkətɪv] *adj* provocativo

provoke [prə'vəʊk] *vt* (*cause*) provocar, incitar; (*anger*) enojar

prowl [praʊl] *vi* (*also*: ~ **about**, ~ **around**) merodear ♦ *n*: **on the** ~ de merodeo

proximity [prɒk'sɪmɪtɪ] *n* proximidad *f*

proxy ['prɒksɪ] *n*: **by** ~ por poderes

prudent ['pru:dənt] *adj* prudente

prune [pru:n] *n* ciruela pasa ♦ *vt* podar

pry [praɪ] *vi*: **to** ~ (**into**) entrometerse (en)

PS *n abbr* (= *postscript*) P.D.

pseudonym ['sju:dənɪm] *n* seudónimo

psychiatric [saɪkɪ'ætrɪk] *adj* psiquiátrico

psychiatrist [saɪ'kaɪətrɪst] *n* psiquiatra *mf*

psychic ['saɪkɪk] *adj* (*also*: **psychical**) psíquico

psychoanalysis [saɪkəʊə'nælɪsɪs] *n* psicoanálisis *m inv*

psychological [saɪkə'lɒdʒɪkl] *adj* psicológico

psychologist [saɪ'kɒlədʒɪst] *n* psicólogo(-a)

psychology [saɪ'kɒlədʒɪ] *n* psicología *f*

psychotherapy [saɪkəʊ'θerəpɪ] *n* psicoterapia

pt *abbr* = **pint(s)**; **point(s)**

PTO *abbr* (= *please turn over*) sigue

pub [pʌb] *n abbr* (= *public house*) pub *m*, bar *m*

puberty ['pju:bətɪ] *n* pubertad *f*

public ['pʌblɪk] *adj* público ♦ *n*: **the** ~ el público; **in** ~ en público; **to make** ~ hacer público

publication [pʌblɪ'keɪʃən] *n* publicación *f*

public: **public company** *n* sociedad *f* anónima ❏ **public convenience** (*BRIT*) *n* aseos *mpl* públicos (*SP*), sanitarios *mpl* (*LAm*) ❏ **public holiday** *n* (día *m* de) fiesta (*SP*), (día *m*) feriado (*LAm*) ❏ **public house** (*BRIT*) *n* bar *m*, pub *m*

publicity [pʌb'lɪsɪtɪ] *n* publicidad *f*

publicize ['pʌblɪsaɪz] *vt* publicitar

public: **public limited company** *n* sociedad *f* anónima (S.A.) ❏ **publicly** *adv* públicamente, en público ❏ **public opinion** *n* opinión *f* pública ❏ **public relations** *n* relaciones *fpl* públicas ❏ **public school** *n* (*BRIT*) escuela privada; (*US*) instituto ❏ **public transport** *n* transporte *m* público

publish ['pʌblɪʃ] *vt* publicar
❏ **publisher** *n* (*person*) editor(a) *m/f*; (*firm*) editorial *f* ❏ **publishing** *n* (*industry*) industria del libro

pub lunch *n* almuerzo *que se sirve en un pub*; **to go for a** ~ almorzar o comer en un pub

pudding ['pʊdɪŋ] *n* pudín *m*; (*BRIT*: *dessert*) postre *m*; **black** ~ morcilla

puddle ['pʌdl] *n* charco

Puerto Rico [pweː'tɔʊ'riːkəʊ] *n* Puerto Rico

puff [pʌf] *n* soplo; (*of smoke, air*) bocanada; (*of breathing*) resoplido ♦ *vt*: **to** ~ **one's pipe** chupar la pipa ♦ *vi* (*pant*) jadear ❏ **puff pastry** *n* hojaldre *m*

pull [pʊl] *n* (*tug*): **to give sth a** ~ dar un tirón a algo ♦ *vt* tirar de; (*press: trigger*) apretar; (*haul*) tirar, arrastrar; (*close: curtain*) echar ♦ *vi* tirar; **to** ~ **to pieces** hacer pedazos; **not to** ~ **one's punches** no andarse con bromas; **to** ~ **one's weight** hacer su parte; **to** ~ **o.s. together** sobreponerse; **to** ~ **sb's leg** tomar el pelo a algn ▶ **pull apart** *vt* (*break*) romper ▶ **pull away** *vi* (*vehicle: move off*) salir, arrancar; (*draw back*) apartarse bruscamente ▶ **pull**

back vt (lever etc) tirar hacia sí; (curtains) descorrer ♦ vi (refrain) contenerse; (MIL: withdraw) retirarse ▸ **pull down** vt (building) derribar ▸ **pull in** vi (car etc) parar (junto a la acera); (train) llegar a la estación ▸ **pull off** vt (deal etc) cerrar ▸ **pull out** vi (car, train etc) salir ♦ vt sacar, arrancar ▸ **pull over** vi (AUT) hacerse a un lado ▸ **pull up** vi (stop) parar ♦ vt (raise) levantar; (uproot) arrancar, desarraigar

pulley ['puli] n polea

pullover ['puləuvə'] n jersey m, suéter m

pulp [pʌlp] n (of fruit) pulpa

pulpit ['pulpit] n púlpito

pulse [pʌls] n (ANAT) pulso; (rhythm) pulsación f; (BOT) legumbre f; **pulses** pl n legumbres

puma ['pju:mə] n puma m

pump [pʌmp] n bomba; (shoe) zapatilla ♦ vt sacar con una bomba ▸ **pump up** vt inflar

pumpkin ['pʌmpkin] n calabaza

pun [pʌn] n juego de palabras

punch [pʌntʃ] n (blow) golpe m, puñetazo; (tool) punzón m; (drink) ponche m ♦ vt (hit): **to ~ sb/sth** dar un puñetazo or golpear a algn/algo ▢ **punch-up** (BRIT: inf) n riña

punctual ['pʌŋktjuəl] adj puntual

punctuation [pʌŋktju'eiʃən] n puntuación f

puncture ['pʌŋktʃə'] (BRIT) n pinchazo ♦ vt pinchar

punish ['pʌniʃ] vt castigar ▢ **punishment** n castigo

punk [pʌŋk] n (also: **~ rocker**) punki mf; (also: **~ rock**) música punk; (US: inf: hoodlum) rufián m

pup [pʌp] n cachorro

pupil ['pju:pl] n alumno(-a); (of eye) pupila

puppet ['pʌpit] n títere m

puppy ['pʌpi] n cachorro, perrito

purchase ['pə:tʃis] n compra ♦ vt comprar

pure [pjuə'] adj puro ▢ **purely** adv puramente

purify ['pjuərifai] vt purificar, depurar

purity ['pjuəriti] n pureza

purple ['pə:pl] adj purpúreo; morado

purpose ['pə:pəs] n propósito; **on ~** a propósito, adrede

purr [pə:'] vi ronronear

purse [pə:s] n monedero; (US: handbag) bolso (SP), cartera (LAm), bolsa (MEX) ♦ vt fruncir

pursue [pə'sju:] vt seguir

pursuit [pə'sju:t] n (chase) caza; (occupation) actividad f

pus [pʌs] n pus m

push [puʃ] n empuje m, empujón m; (of button) presión f; (drive) empuje m ♦ vt empujar; (button) apretar; (promote) promover ♦ vi empujar; (demand): **to ~ for** luchar por ▸ **push in** vi colarse ▸ **push off** (inf) vi largarse ▸ **push on** vi seguir adelante ▸ **push over** vt (cause to fall) hacer caer, derribar; (knock over) volcar ▸ **push through** vt (crowd) abrirse paso a empujones ♦ vt (measure) despachar ▢ **pushchair** (BRIT) n sillita de ruedas ▢ **pusher** n (drug pusher) traficante mf de drogas ▢ **push-up** (US) n plancha

pussy(-cat) ['pusi-] (inf) n minino (inf)

put [put] (pt, pp ~) vt (place) poner, colocar; (put into) meter; (say) expresar; (a question) hacer; (estimate) estimar ▸ **put aside** vt (lay down: book etc) dejar or poner a un lado; (save) ahorrar; (in shop) guardar ▸ **put away** vt (store) guardar ▸ **put back** vt (replace) devolver a su lugar; (postpone) aplazar ▸ **put by** vt (money) guardar ▸ **put down** vt (on ground) poner en el suelo; (animal) sacrificar; (in writing) apuntar; (revolt etc) sofocar; (attribute): **to ~ sth down to** atribuir algo a ▸ **put forward** vt (ideas) presentar, proponer ▸ **put in** vt (complaint) presentar; (time) dedicar ▸ **put off** vt (postpone) aplazar; (discourage) desanimar ▸ **put on** vt ponerse; (light etc) encender; (play etc) presentar; (gain): **to put on weight** engordar; (brake) echar; (record, kettle etc) poner; (assume) adoptar ▸ **put out** vt (fire, light) apagar; (rubbish etc) sacar; (cat etc) echar; (one's hand) alargar; (inf: person): **to be put out** alterarse ▸ **put through** vt (TEL) poner; (plan etc) hacer aprobar ▸ **put together** vt unir, reunir; (assemble: furniture) armar, montar; (meal) preparar ▸ **put up** vt (raise) levantar, alzar; (hang) colgar; (build) construir; (increase) aumentar; (accommodate) alojar ▸ **put up with** vt fus aguantar

putt [pʌt] n putt m, golpe m corto ▫ **putting green** n green m; minigolf m

puzzle ['pʌzl] n rompecabezas m inv; (also: **crossword ~**) crucigrama m; (mystery) misterio ♦ vt dejar perplejo, confundir ♦ vi: **to ~ over sth** devanarse los sesos con algo ▫ **puzzled** adj perplejo ▫ **puzzling** adj misterioso, extraño

pyjamas [pɪ'dʒɑːməz] (BRIT) npl pijama m

pylon ['paɪlən] n torre f de conducción eléctrica

pyramid ['pɪrəmɪd] n pirámide f

Q, q

quack [kwæk] n graznido; (pej: doctor) curandero(-a)

quadruple [kwɒ'druːpl] vt, vi cuadruplicar

quail [kweɪl] n codorniz f ♦ vi: **to ~ at** o **before** amedrentarse ante

quaint [kweɪnt] adj extraño; (picturesque) pintoresco

quake [kweɪk] vi temblar ♦ n abbr = **earthquake**

qualification [kwɒlɪfɪ'keɪʃən] n (ability) capacidad f; (often pl: diploma etc) título; (reservation) salvedad f

qualified ['kwɒlɪfaɪd] adj capacitado; (professionally) titulado; (limited) limitado ·

qualify ['kwɒlɪfaɪ] vt (make competent) capacitar; (modify) modificar ♦ vi (in competition): **to ~ (for)** calificarse (para); (pass examination(s)): **to ~ (as)** calificarse de, graduarse (en); (be eligible): **to ~ (for)** reunir los requisitos (para)

quality ['kwɒlɪtɪ] n calidad f; (of person) cualidad f

qualm [kwɑːm] n escrúpulo

quantify ['kwɒntɪfaɪ] vt cuantificar

quantity ['kwɒntɪtɪ] n cantidad f; **in ~** en grandes cantidades

quarantine ['kwɒrntiːn] n cuarentena f

quarrel ['kwɒrl] n riña, pelea ♦ vi reñir, pelearse

quarry ['kwɒrɪ] n cantera f

quart [kwɔːt] n ≈ litro

quarter ['kwɔːtə*] n cuarto, cuarta parte f; (US: coin) moneda de 25 centavos; (of year) trimestre m; (district) barrio ♦ vt dividir en cuartos; (MIL: lodge) alojar; **quarters** npl (barracks) cuartel m; (living quarters) alojamiento; **a ~ of an hour** un cuarto de hora ▫ **quarter final** n cuarto de final ▫ **quarterly** adj trimestral ♦ adv cada 3 meses, trimestralmente

quartet(te) [kwɔː'tet] n cuarteto

quartz [kwɔːts] n cuarzo

quay [kiː] n (also: **quayside**) muelle m

queasy ['kwiːzɪ] adj: **to feel ~** tener náuseas

queen [kwiːn] n reina; (CARDS etc) dama

queer [kwɪə*] adj raro, extraño ♦ n (inf: highly offensive) maricón m

quench [kwentʃ] vt: **to ~ one's thirst** apagar la sed

query ['kwɪərɪ] n (question) pregunta
♦ vt dudar de

quest [kwɛst] n busca, búsqueda

question ['kwɛstʃən] n pregunta;
(doubt) duda; (matter) asunto, cuestión
f ♦ vt (doubt) dudar de; (interrogate)
interrogar, hacer preguntas a; **beyond
~** fuera de toda duda; **out of the ~**
imposible; ni hablar ❏ **questionable**
adj dudoso ❏ **question mark** n
punto de interrogación
❏ **questionnaire** [-'nɛəʳ] n
cuestionario

queue [kju:] (BRIT) n cola ♦ vi (also: ~
up) hacer cola

quiche [ki:ʃ] n quiche m

quick [kwɪk] adj rápido; (agile) ágil;
(mind) listo ♦ n: **cut it to the ~** (fig) herido
en lo vivo; **be ~!** ¡date prisa! ❏ **quickly**
adv rápidamente, de prisa

quid [kwɪd] (BRIT: inf) n inv libra

quiet ['kwaɪət] adj (voice, music etc)
bajo; (person, place) tranquilo;
(ceremony) íntimo ♦ n silencio;
(calm) tranquilidad f ♦ vt, vi (US) = **quieten**
❏ **quietly** adv tranquilamente;
(silently) silenciosamente

⚠ Be careful not to translate **quiet** by
the Spanish word *quieto*.

quilt [kwɪlt] n edredón m

quirky ['kwɜ:kɪ] adj raro, estrafalario

quit [kwɪt] (pt, pp or **quitted**) vt dejar,
abandonar ♦ vt (premises) desocupar ♦ vi
(give up) renunciar; (resign) dimitir

quite [kwaɪt] adv (rather) bastante;
(entirely) completamente; **that's not ~
big enough** no acaba de ser lo
bastante grande; **~ a few of them** un
buen número de ellos; **~ (so)!** ¡así es!,
¡exactamente!

quits [kwɪts] adj: **~ (with)** en paz (con);
let's call it ~ dejémoslo en tablas

quiver ['kwɪvəʳ] vi estremecerse

quiz [kwɪz] n concurso ♦ vt interrogar

quota ['kwəʊtə] n cuota

quotation [kwəʊ'teɪʃən] n cita;
(estimate) presupuesto ❏ **quotation
marks** npl comillas fpl

quote [kwəʊt] n cita; (estimate)
presupuesto ♦ vt citar; (price) cotizar
♦ vi: **to ~ from** citar de; **quotes** npl
(inverted commas) comillas fpl

R, r

rabbi ['ræbaɪ] n rabino

rabbit ['ræbɪt] n conejo

rabies ['reɪbi:z] n rabia

RAC (BRIT) n abbr (= Royal Automobile
Club) ≈ RACE m

rac(c)oon [rə'ku:n] n mapache m

race [reɪs] n carrera; (species) raza ♦ vt
(horse) hacer correr; (engine) acelerar
♦ vi (compete) competir; (run) correr;
(pulse) latir a ritmo acelerado ❏ **race
car** (US) n = **racing car** ❏ **racecourse**
n hipódromo ❏ **racehorse** n caballo
de carreras ❏ **racetrack** n pista; (for
cars) autódromo

racial ['reɪʃl] adj racial

racing ['reɪsɪŋ] n carreras fpl ❏ **racing
car** (BRIT) n coche m de carreras
❏ **racing driver** (BRIT) n piloto mf de
carreras

racism ['reɪsɪzəm] n racismo ❏ **racist**
[-sɪst] adj, n racista mf

rack [ræk] n (also: **luggage ~**) rejilla;
(shelf) estante m; (also: **roof ~**) baca,
portaequipajes m inv; (dish rack)
escurreplatos m inv; (clothes rack)
percha ♦ vt atormentar; **to ~ one's
brains** devanarse los sesos

racket ['rækɪt] n (for tennis) raqueta;
(noise) ruido, estrépito; (swindle)
estafa, timo

racquet ['rækɪt] n raqueta

radar ['reɪdɑ:ʳ] n radar m

radiation [reɪdɪ'eɪʃən] n radiación f

radiator ['reɪdɪeɪtəʳ] n radiador m

radical ['rædɪkl] *adj* radical

radio ['reɪdɪəʊ] *n* radio f; **on the ~** por radio ❏ **radioactive** *adj* radioactivo ❏ **radio station** *n* emisora

radish ['rædɪʃ] *n* rábano

RAF *n abbr* (= *Royal Air Force*) las Fuerzas Aéreas Británicas

raffle ['ræfl] *n* rifa, sorteo

raft [rɑːft] *n* balsa; (*also:* **life ~**) balsa salvavidas

rag [ræg] *n* (*piece of cloth*) trapo; (*torn cloth*) harapo; (*pej: newspaper*) periodicucho; (*for charity*) actividades estudiantiles benéficas; **rags** *npl* (*torn clothes*) harapos *mpl*

rage [reɪdʒ] *n* rabia, furor *m* ♦ *vi* (*person*) rabiar, estar furioso; (*storm*) bramar; **it's all the ~** (*very fashionable*) está muy de moda

ragged ['rægɪd] *adj* (*edge*) desigual, mellado; (*appearance*) andrajoso, harapiento

raid [reɪd] *n* (MIL) incursión f; (*criminal*) asalto; (*by police*) redada ♦ *vt* invadir, atacar; asaltar

rail [reɪl] *n* (*on stair*) barandilla, pasamanos *m inv*; (*on bridge, balcony*) pretil *m*; (*of ship*) barandilla; (*also:* **towel ~**) toallero ❏ **railcard** *n* (BRIT) tarjeta para obtener descuentos en el tren ❏ **railing(s)** *n(pl)* vallado ❏ **railroad** (US) *n* = **railway** ❏ **railway** (BRIT) *n* ferrocarril *m*, vía férrea ❏ **railway line** (BRIT) *n* línea (de ferrocarril) ❏ **railway station** (BRIT) *n* estación f de ferrocarril

rain [reɪn] *n* lluvia ♦ *vi* llover; **in the ~** bajo la lluvia; **it's raining** llueve, está lloviendo ❏ **rainbow** *n* arco iris ❏ **raincoat** *n* impermeable *m* ❏ **raindrop** *n* gota de lluvia ❏ **rainfall** *n* lluvia ❏ **rainforest** *n* selvas *fpl* tropicales ❏ **rainy** *adj* lluvioso

raise [reɪz] *n* aumento ♦ *vt* levantar; (*increase*) aumentar; (*improve: morale*) subir; (*: standards*) mejorar; (*doubts*)

suscitar; (*a question*) plantear; (*cattle, family*) criar; (*crop*) cultivar; (*army*) reclutar; (*loan*) obtener; **to ~ one's voice** alzar la voz

raisin ['reɪzn] *n* pasa de Corinto

rake [reɪk] *n* (*tool*) rastrillo; (*person*) libertino ♦ *vt* (*garden*) rastrillar

rally ['rælɪ] *n* (POL etc) reunión f, mitin *m*; (AUT) rallye *m*; (TENNIS) peloteo ♦ *vt* reunir ♦ *vi* recuperarse

RAM [ræm] *n abbr* (= *random access memory*) RAM f

ram [ræm] *n* carnero; (*also:* **battering ~**) ariete *m* ♦ *vt* (*crash into*) dar contra, chocar con; (*push: fist etc*) empujar con fuerza

Ramadan [ræmə'dæn] *n* ramadán *m*

ramble ['ræmbl] *n* caminata, excursión f en el campo ♦ *vi* (*pej: also:* **~ on**) divagar ❏ **rambler** *n* excursionista *mf*; (BOT) trepadora ❏ **rambling** *adj* (*speech*) inconexo; (*house*) laberíntico; (BOT) trepador(a)

ramp [ræmp] *n* rampa; **on/off ~** (US AUT) vía de acceso/salida

rampage [ræm'peɪdʒ] *n*: **to be on the ~** desmandarse ♦ *vi*: **they went rampaging through the town** recorrieron la ciudad armando alboroto

ran [ræn] *pt of* **run**

ranch [rɑːntʃ] *n* hacienda, estancia

random ['rændəm] *adj* fortuito, sin orden; (COMPUT, MATH) aleatorio ♦ *n*: **at ~** al azar

rang [ræŋ] *pt of* **ring**

range [reɪndʒ] *n* (*of mountains*) cadena de montañas, cordillera; (*of missile*) alcance *m*; (*of voice*) registro; (*series*) serie f; (*of products*) surtido; (MIL: *also:* **shooting ~**) campo de tiro; (*also:* **kitchen ~**) fogón *m* ♦ *vt* (*place*) colocar; (*arrange*) arreglar ♦ *vi*: **to ~ over** (*extend*) extenderse por; **to ~ from ... to ...** oscilar entre ... y ...

ranger ['reɪndʒəʳ] n guardabosques mf inv

rank [ræŋk] n (row) fila; (MIL) rango; (status) categoría; (BRIT: also: **taxi ~**) parada de taxis ♦ vi: **to ~ among** figurar entre ♦ adj fétido, rancio; **the ~ and file** (fig) la base

ransom ['rænsəm] n rescate m; **to hold to ~** (fig) hacer chantaje a

rant [rænt] vi divagar, desvariar

rap [ræp] vt golpear, dar un golpecito ♦ n (music) rap m

rape [reɪp] n violación f; (BOT) colza ♦ vt violar

rapid ['ræpɪd] adj rápido ❏ **rapidly** adv rápidamente ❏ **rapids** npl (GEO) rápidos mpl

rapist ['reɪpɪst] n violador m

rapport [ræ'pɔː] n simpatía

rare [rɛəʳ] adj raro, poco común; (CULIN: steak) poco hecho ❏ **rarely** adv pocas veces

rash [ræʃ] adj imprudente, precipitado ♦ n (MED) sarpullido, erupción f (cutánea); (of events) serie f

rasher ['ræʃəʳ] n lonja

raspberry ['rɑːzbərɪ] n frambuesa

rat [ræt] n rata

rate [reɪt] n (ratio) razón f; (price) precio; (: of hotel etc) tarifa; (of interest) tipo; (speed) velocidad f ♦ vt (value) tasar; (estimate) estimar; **rates** npl (BRIT: property tax) impuesto municipal; (fees) tarifa; **to ~ sth/sb as** considerar algo/a algn como

rather ['rɑːðəʳ] adv: **it's ~ expensive** es algo caro; (too much) es demasiado caro; (to some extent) más bien; **there's ~ a lot** hay bastante; **I would ~ or I'd ~ go** preferiría ir; **or ~** mejor dicho

rating ['reɪtɪŋ] n tasación f; (score) índice m; (of ship) clase f; **ratings** npl (RADIO, TV) niveles mpl de audiencia

ratio ['reɪʃɪəu] n razón f; **in the ~ of 100 to 1** a razón de 100 a 1

ration ['ræʃən] n ración f ♦ vt racionar; **rations** npl víveres mpl

rational ['ræʃənl] adj (solution, reasoning) lógico, razonable; (person) cuerdo, sensato

rattle ['rætl] n golpeteo; (of train etc) traqueteo; (for baby) sonaja, sonajero ♦ vi castañetear; (car, bus): **to ~ along** traquetear ♦ vt hacer sonar agitando

rave [reɪv] vi (in anger) encolerizarse; (with enthusiasm) entusiasmarse; (MED) delirar, desvariar ♦ n (inf: party) rave m

raven ['reɪvn] n cuervo

ravine [rə'viːn] n barranco

raw [rɔː] adj crudo; (not processed) bruto; (sore) vivo; (inexperienced) novato, inexperto; **~ materials** materias primas

ray [reɪ] n rayo; **~ of hope** (rayo de) esperanza

razor ['reɪzəʳ] n (open) navaja; (safety razor) máquina de afeitar; (electric razor) máquina (eléctrica) de afeitar ❏ **razor blade** n hoja de afeitar

Rd abbr = **road**

RE n abbr (BRIT) = **religious education**

re [riː] prep con referencia a

reach [riːtʃ] n alcance m; (of river etc) extensión f entre dos recodos ♦ vt alcanzar, llegar a; (achieve) lograr ♦ vi extenderse; **within ~** al alcance (de la mano); **out of ~** fuera del alcance ▶ **reach out** vt (hand) tender ♦ vi: **to reach out for sth** alargar o tender la mano para tomar algo

react [riː'ækt] vi reaccionar ❏ **reaction** [-'ækʃən] n reacción f ❏ **reactor** [riː'æktəʳ] n (also: **nuclear reactor**) reactor m (nuclear)

read [riːd, pt, pp red] (pt, pp ~) vi leer ♦ vt (understand) entender; (study) estudiar ▶ **read out** vt leer en alta voz ❏ **reader** n lector(a) m/f; (BRIT: at university) profesor(a) m/f adjunto(-a)

readily ['rɛdɪlɪ] adv (willingly) de buena gana; (easily) fácilmente; (quickly) en seguida

reading ['riːdɪŋ] n lectura; (on instrument) indicación f

ready ['rɛdɪ] adj listo, preparado; (willing) dispuesto; (available) disponible ♦ adv: **~-cooked** listo para comer ♦ n: **at the ~** (MIL) listo para tirar; **to get ~** vi prepararse ♦ vt preparar ❏ **ready-made** adj confeccionado

real [rɪəl] adj verdadero, auténtico; **in ~ terms** en términos reales ❏ **real ale** n cerveza elaborada tradicionalmente ❏ **real estate** n bienes mpl raíces ❏ **realistic** [-'lɪstɪk] adj realista ❏ **reality** [riː'ælɪtɪ] n realidad f

realization [rɪəlaɪ'zeɪʃən] n comprensión f; (fulfilment, COMM) realización f

realize [rɪəlaɪz] vt (understand) darse cuenta de

really ['rɪəlɪ] adv realmente; (for emphasis) verdaderamente; (actually): **what ~ happened** lo que pasó en realidad; **~?** ¿de veras?; **~!** (annoyance) ¡vamos!, ¡por favor!

realm [rɛlm] n reino; (fig) esfera

realtor ['rɪəltɔː'] (US) n agente mf inmobiliario/-a

reappear [riːə'pɪə'] vi reaparecer

rear [rɪə'] adj trasero ♦ n parte f trasera ♦ vt (cattle, family) criar ♦ vi (also: **~ up**: animal) encabritarse

rearrange [riːə'reɪndʒ] vt ordenar or arreglar de nuevo

rear: **rear-view mirror** n (AUT) (espejo) retrovisor m ❏ **rear-wheel drive** n tracción f trasera

reason ['riːzn] n razón f ♦ vi: **to ~ with sb** tratar de que algn entre en razón; **it stands to ~ that ...** es lógico que ... ❏ **reasonable** adj razonable; (sensible) sensato ❏ **reasonably** adv razonablemente; (sensible) ❏ **reasoning** n razonamiento, argumentos mpl

reassurance [riːə'ʃʊərəns] n consuelo

reassure [riːə'ʃʊə'] vt tranquilizar, alentar; **to ~ sb that ...** tranquilizar a algn asegurando que ...

rebate ['riːbeɪt] n (on tax etc) desgravación f

rebel [n 'rɛbl, vi rɪ'bɛl] n rebelde mf ♦ vi rebelarse, sublevarse ❏ **rebellion** [rɪ'bɛljən] n rebelión f, sublevación f ❏ **rebellious** [rɪ'bɛljəs] adj rebelde; (child) revoltoso

rebuild [riː'bɪld] vt reconstruir

recall [vb rɪ'kɔːl, n 'riːkɔːl] vt (remember) recordar; (ambassador etc) retirar ♦ n recuerdo; retirada

rec'd abbr (= received) rbdo

receipt [rɪ'siːt] n (document) recibo; (for parcel etc) acuse m de recibo; (act of receiving) recepción f; **receipts** npl (COMM) ingresos mpl

⚠ Be careful not to translate **receipt** by the Spanish word **receta**.

receive [rɪ'siːv] vt recibir; (guest) acoger; (wound) sufrir ❏ **receiver** n (TEL) auricular m; (RADIO) receptor m; (of stolen goods) perista mf; (COMM) administrador m y jurídico

recent ['riːsnt] adj reciente ❏ **recently** adv recientemente; **recently arrived** recién llegado

reception [rɪ'sɛpʃən] n recepción f; (welcome) acogida ❏ **reception desk** n recepción f ❏ **receptionist** n recepcionista m

recession [rɪ'sɛʃən] n recesión f

recharge [riː'tʃɑːdʒ] vt (battery) recargar

recipe ['rɛsɪpɪ] n receta; (for disaster, success) fórmula

recipient [rɪ'sɪpɪənt] n recibidor(a) m/f; (of letter) destinatario/-a

recital [rɪ'saɪtl] n recital m

recite [rɪ'saɪt] vt (poem) recitar

reckless ['rɛkləs] adj temerario, imprudente; (driving, driver) peligroso

reckon ['rɛkən] vt calcular; (consider) considerar; (think): **I ~ that ...** me parece que ...

reclaim [rɪ'kleɪm] vt (land, waste) recuperar; (from sea) rescatar; (demand back) reclamar

recline [rɪ'klaɪn] vi reclinarse

recognition [rɛkəg'nɪʃən] n reconocimiento; **transformed beyond ~** irreconocible

recognize ['rɛkəgnaɪz] vt: **to ~ (by/as)** reconocer (por/como)

recollection [rɛkə'lɛkʃən] n recuerdo

recommend [rɛkə'mɛnd] vt recomendar ❑ **recommendation** [rɛkəmən'deɪʃən] n recomendación f

reconcile ['rɛkənsaɪl] vt (two people) reconciliar; (two facts) compaginar; **to ~ o.s. to sth** conformarse a algo

reconsider [ri:kən'sɪdə'] vt repensar

reconstruct [ri:kən'strʌkt] vt reconstruir

record [n, adj 'rɛkɔːd, vt rɪ'kɔːd] n (MUS) disco; (of meeting etc) acta; (register) registro, partida; (file) archivo; (also: **criminal ~**) antecedentes mpl; (written) expediente m; (SPORT, COMPUT) récord m ◆ adj récord, sin precedentes ◆ vt registrar; (MUS: song etc) grabar; **in ~ time** en un tiempo récord; **off the ~** adj no oficial ◆ adv confidencialmente ❑ **recorded delivery** (BRIT) n (POST) entrega con acuse de recibo ❑ **recorder** n (MUS) flauta de pico ❑ **recording** n (MUS) grabación f ❑ **record player** n tocadiscos m inv

recount [rɪ'kaunt] vt contar

recover [rɪ'kʌvə'] vt recuperar ◆ vi (from illness, shock) recuperarse ❑ **recovery** n recuperación f

recreate [ri:krɪ'eɪt] vt recrear

recreation [rɛkrɪ'eɪʃən] n recreo ❑ **recreational vehicle** (US) n caravan or rulota pequeña; **recreational drug** droga recreativa

recruit [rɪ'kruːt] n recluta mf ◆ vt reclutar; (staff) contratar ❑ **recruitment** n reclutamiento

rectangle ['rɛktæŋgl] n rectángulo ❑ **rectangular** [-'tæŋgjulə'] adj rectangular

rectify ['rɛktɪfaɪ] vt rectificar

rector ['rɛktə'] n (REL) párroco

recur [rɪ'kə:'] vi repetirse; (pain, illness) producirse de nuevo ❑ **recurring** adj (problem) repetido, constante

recyclable [ri:'saɪklæbl] adj reciclable

recycle [ri:'saɪkl] vt reciclar

recycling [ri:'saɪklɪŋ] n reciclaje

red [red] n rojo ◆ adj rojo; (hair) pelirrojo; (wine) tinto; **to be in the ~** (account) estar en números rojos; (business) tener un saldo negativo; **to give sb the ~ carpet treatment** recibir a algn con todos los honores ❑ **Red Cross** n Cruz f Roja ❑ **redcurrant** n grosella roja

redeem [rɪ'di:m] vt redimir; (promises) cumplir; (sth in pawn) desempeñar; (fig, also REL) rescatar

red: red-haired adj pelirrojo ❑ **redhead** n pelirrojo(-a) ❑ **red-hot** adj candente ❑ **red light** n: **to go through a red light** (AUT) pasar la luz roja ❑ **red-light district** n barrio chino

red meat n carne f roja

reduce [rɪ'dju:s] vt reducir; **to ~ sb to tears** hacer llorar a algn; **"~ speed now"** (AUT) "reduzca la velocidad" ❑ **reduced** adj (decreased) reducido, rebajado; **at a reduced price** con rebaja or descuento; **"greatly reduced prices"** "grandes rebajas" ❑ **reduction** [rɪ'dʌkʃən] n reducción f; (of price) rebaja; (discount) descuento; (smaller-scale copy) copia reducida

redundancy [rɪ'dʌndənsɪ] n (dismissal) despido; (unemployment) desempleo

redundant [rɪ'dʌndnt] adj (BRIT: worker) parado, sin trabajo; (detail, object) superfluo; **to be made ~** quedar(se) sin trabajo

reed [riːd] n (BOT) junco, caña; (MUS) lengüeta

reef [riːf] n (at sea) arrecife m

reek [riːk] n carrete m, bobina; (of film) rollo; (dance) baile escocés ♦ vt (also: **~ up**) devanar; (also: **~ in**) sacar ♦ vi (sway) tambalear(se)

ref [ref] (inf) n abbr = **referee**

refectory [rɪˈfɛktərɪ] n comedor m

refer [rɪˈfɜː] vt (send: patient) referir; (: matter) remitir ♦ vi: **to ~ to** (allude to) referirse a, aludir a; (apply to) relacionarse con; (consult) consultar

referee [refəˈriː] n árbitro; (BRIT: for job application): **to be a ~ for sb** proporcionar referencias a algn ♦ vt (match) arbitrar

reference [ˈrefrəns] n referencia; (for job application: letter) carta de recomendación; **with ~ to** (COMM: in letter) me remito a ❏ **reference number** n número de referencia

refill [vt riːˈfɪl, n ˈriːfɪl] vt rellenar ♦ n repuesto, recambio

refine [rɪˈfaɪn] vt refinar ❏ **refined** adj (person) fino ❏ **refinery** n refinería

reflect [rɪˈflɛkt] vt reflejar ♦ vi (think) reflexionar, pensar; **it reflects badly/well on him** le perjudica/le hace honor ❏ **reflection** [-ˈflɛkʃən] n (act) reflexión f; (image) reflejo; (criticism) crítica; **on reflection** pensándolo bien

reflex [ˈriːflɛks] adj, n reflejo

reform [rɪˈfɔːm] n reforma ♦ vt reformar

refrain [rɪˈfreɪn] vi: **to ~ from doing** abstenerse de hacer ♦ n estribillo

refresh [rɪˈfreʃ] vt refrescar ❏ **refreshing** adj refrescante ❏ **refreshments** npl refrescos mpl

refrigerator [rɪˈfrɪdʒəreɪtə] n frigorífico (SP), nevera (SP), refrigerador m (LAm), heladera (RPl)

refuel [riːˈfjuəl] vi repostar (combustible)

refuge [ˈrefjuːdʒ] n refugio, asilo; **to take ~ in** refugiarse en ❏ **refugee** [refjʊˈdʒiː] n refugiado(-a)

refund [n ˈriːfʌnd, vb rɪˈfʌnd] n reembolso ♦ vt devolver, reembolsar

refurbish [riːˈfɜːbɪʃ] vt restaurar, renovar

refusal [rɪˈfjuːzəl] n negativa; **to have first ~ on** tener la primera opción a

refuse[1] [ˈrefjuːs] n basura

refuse[2] [rɪˈfjuːz] vt rechazar; (invitation) declinar; (permission) denegar ♦ vi: **to do sth** negarse a hacer algo; (horse) rehusar

regain [rɪˈgeɪn] vt recobrar, recuperar

regard [rɪˈgɑːd] n mirada; (esteem) respeto; (attention) consideración f ♦ vt (consider) considerar; **to give one's regards to** saludar de su parte a; **"with kindest regards"** "con muchos recuerdos"; **as regards, with ~ to** con respecto a, en cuanto a ❏ **regarding** prep con respecto a, en cuanto a ❏ **regardless** adv a pesar de todo; **regardless of** sin reparar en

regenerate [rɪˈdʒenəreɪt] vt regenerar

reggae [ˈregeɪ] n reggae m

regiment [ˈredʒɪmənt] n regimiento

region [ˈriːdʒən] n región f; **in the ~ of** (fig) alrededor de ❏ **regional** adj regional

register [ˈredʒɪstə] n registro ♦ vt registrar; (birth) declarar; (car) matricular; (letter) certificar; (instrument) marcar, indicar ♦ vi (at hotel) registrarse; (as student) matricularse; (make impression) producir impresión ❏ **registered** adj (letter, parcel) certificado

registrar [ˈredʒɪstrɑː] n secretario(-a) (del registro civil)

registration [redʒɪsˈtreɪʃən] n (act) declaración f; (AUT: also: **~ number**) matrícula

registry office ['redʒɪstrɪ-] (BRIT) n registro civil; **to get married in a ~** casarse por lo civil

regret [rɪ'gret] n sentimiento, pesar m ♦ vt sentir, lamentar □ **regrettable** adj lamentable

regular ['regjulə'] adj regular; (soldier) profesional; (usual) habitual; (: doctor) de cabecera ♦ n (client etc) cliente(-a) m/f habitual □ **regularly** adv con regularidad; (often) repetidas veces

regulate ['regjuleɪt] vt controlar □ **regulation** [-'leɪʃən] n (rule) regla, reglamento

rehabilitation ['ri:əbɪlɪ'teɪʃən] n rehabilitación f

rehearsal [rɪ'hə:səl] n ensayo

rehearse [rɪ'hə:s] vt ensayar

reign [reɪn] n reinado; (fig) predominio ♦ vi reinar; (fig) imperar

reimburse [ri:ɪm'bə:s] vt reembolsar

rein [reɪn] n (for horse) rienda

reincarnation [ri:ɪnkɑ:'neɪʃən] n reencarnación f

reindeer ['reɪndɪə'] n inv reno

reinforce [ri:ɪn'fɔ:s] vt reforzar □ **reinforcements** npl (MIL) refuerzos mpl

reinstate [ri:ɪn'steɪt] vt reintegrar; (tax, law) reinstaurar

reject [n 'ri:dʒekt, vb rɪ'dʒekt] n (thing) desecho ♦ vt rechazar; (suggestion) descartar; (coin) expulsar □ **rejection** [rɪ'dʒekʃən] n rechazo

rejoice [rɪ'dʒɔɪs] vi: **to ~ at** or **over** regocijarse o alegrarse de

relate [rɪ'leɪt] vt (tell) contar, relatar; (connect) relacionar ♦ vi relacionarse □ **related** adj afín; (person) emparentado; **related to** (subject) relacionado con □ **relating to** prep referente a

relation [rɪ'leɪʃən] n (person) familiar mf, pariente mf; (link) relación f; **relations** npl (relatives) familiares mpl □ **relationship** n relación f; (personal)

relaciones fpl; (also: **family relationship**) parentesco

relative ['relətɪv] n pariente mf, familiar mf ♦ adj relativo □ **relatively** adv (comparatively) relativamente

relax [rɪ'læks] vi descansar; (unwind) relajarse ♦ vt (one's grip) soltar, aflojar; (control) relajar; (mind, person) descansar □ **relaxation** [ri:læk'seɪʃən] n descanso; (of rule, control) relajamiento; (entertainment) diversión f □ **relaxed** adj relajado; (tranquil) tranquilo □ **relaxing** adj relajante

relay ['ri:leɪ] n (race) carrera de relevos ♦ vt (RADIO, TV) retransmitir

release [rɪ'li:s] n (liberation) liberación f; (from prison) puesta en libertad; (of gas etc) escape m; (of film etc) estreno; (of record) lanzamiento ♦ vt (prisoner) poner en libertad; (gas) despedir, arrojar; (from wreckage) soltar; (catch, spring etc) desenganchar; (film) estrenar; (book) publicar; (news) difundir

relegate ['reləgeɪt] vt relegar; (BRIT SPORT): **to be relegated** to bajar a

relent [rɪ'lent] vi ablandarse □ **relentless** adj implacable

relevant ['reləvənt] adj (fact) pertinente; **~ to** relacionado con

reliable [rɪ'laɪəbl] adj (person, firm) de confianza, de fiar; (method, machine) seguro; (source) fidedigno

relic ['relɪk] n (REL) reliquia; (of the past) vestigio

relief [rɪ'li:f] n (from pain, anxiety) alivio; (help, supplies) socorro, ayuda; (ART, GEO) relieve m

relieve [rɪ'li:v] vt (pain) aliviar; (bring help to) ayudar, socorrer; (take over from) sustituir; (: guard) relevar; **to ~ sb of sth** quitar algo a algn; **to ~ o.s.** hacer sus necesidades □ **relieved** adj: **to be relieved** sentir un gran alivio

religion [rɪ'lɪdʒən] n religión f

religious [rɪˈlɪdʒəs] adj religioso
❏ **religious education** n educación f religiosa

relish [ˈrelɪʃ] n (CULIN) salsa; (enjoyment) entusiasmo ♦ vt (food etc) saborear; (enjoy): **to ~ sth** hacerle mucha ilusión a algn algo

relocate [riːləʊˈkeɪt] vt cambiar de lugar, mudar ♦ vi mudarse

reluctance [rɪˈlʌktəns] n renuencia.

reluctant [rɪˈlʌktənt] adj renuente
❏ **reluctantly** adv de mala gana

rely on [rɪˈlaɪ-] vt fus depender de; (trust) contar con

remain [rɪˈmeɪn] vi (survive) quedar; (be left) sobrar; (continue) quedar(se), permanecer ❏ **remainder** n resto
❏ **remaining** adj que queda(n); (surviving) restante(s) ❏ **remains** npl restos mpl

remand [rɪˈmɑːnd] n: **on ~** detenido (bajo custodia) ♦ vt: **to be remanded in custody** quedar detenido bajo custodia

remark [rɪˈmɑːk] n comentario ♦ vt comentar ❏ **remarkable** adj (outstanding) extraordinario

remarry [riːˈmærɪ] vi volver a casarse

remedy [ˈremədɪ] n remedio ♦ vt remediar, curar

remember [rɪˈmembə*] vt recordar, acordarse de; (bear in mind) tener presente; (send greetings to): **~ me to him** dale recuerdos de mi parte
❏ **Remembrance Day** n día en el que se recuerda a los caídos en las dos guerras mundiales

REMEMBRANCE DAY

En el Reino Unido el domingo más próximo al 11 de noviembre se conoce como **Remembrance Sunday** o **Remembrance Day**, aniversario de la firma del armisticio de 1918 que puso fin a la Primera Guerra Mundial. Ese día, a las once de la mañana (hora

en que se firmó el armisticio), se recuerda a los que murieron en las dos guerras mundiales con dos minutos de silencio ante los monumentos a los caídos. Allí se colocan coronas de amapolas, flor que también se suele llevar prendida en el pecho tras pagar un donativo destinado a los inválidos de guerra.

remind [rɪˈmaɪnd] vt: **to ~ sb to do sth** recordar a algn que haga algo; **to ~ sb of sth** (of fact) recordar algo a algn; **she reminds me of her mother** me recuerda a su madre ❏ **reminder** n notificación f; (memento) recuerdo

reminiscent [remɪˈnɪsnt] adj: **to be ~ of sth** recordar algo

remnant [ˈremnənt] n resto; (of cloth) retal m

remorse [rɪˈmɔːs] n remordimiento mpl

remote [rɪˈməʊt] adj (distant) lejano; (person) distante ❏ **remote control** n telecontrol m ❏ **remotely** adv remotamente; (slightly) levemente

removal [rɪˈmuːvəl] n (taking away) el quitar; (BRIT: from house) mudanza; (from office: dismissal) despido f; (MED) extirpación f ❏ **removal man** (irreg) n (BRIT) mozo de mudanzas
❏ **removal van** (BRIT) n camión m de mudanzas

remove [rɪˈmuːv] vt quitar; (employee) destituir; (name: from list) tachar, borrar; (doubt) disipar; (abuse) suprimir, acabar con; (MED) extirpar

Renaissance [rɪˈneɪsɑ̃s] n: **the ~** el Renacimiento

rename [riːˈneɪm] vt poner nuevo nombre a

render [ˈrendə*] vt (thanks) dar; (aid) proporcionar, prestar; (make): **to ~ sth useless** hacer algo inútil

rendezvous [ˈrɒndɪvuː] n cita

renew [rɪˈnjuː] vt renovar; (resume) reanudar; (loan etc) prorrogar

renovate ['renəveɪt] vt renovar

renowned [rɪ'naund] adj renombrado

rent [rent] n (for house) arriendo, renta
♦ vt alquilar □ **rental** n (for television, car) alquiler m

reorganize [riː'ɔːgənaɪz] vt reorganizar

rep [rep] n abbr = **representative**

repair [rɪ'peə] n reparación f, compostura f ♦ vt reparar, componer; (shoes) remendar; **in good/bad** ~ en buen/mal estado □ **repair kit** n caja de herramientas

repay [riː'peɪ] vt (money) devolver, reembolsar; (person) pagar; (debt) liquidar; (sb's efforts) devolver, corresponder a □ **repayment** n reembolso, devolución f; (sum of money) recompensa

repeat [rɪ'piːt] n (RADIO, TV) reposición f ♦ vt repetir ♦ vi repetirse
□ **repeatedly** adv repetidas veces
□ **repeat prescription** n (BRIT) receta renovada

repellent [rɪ'pelənt] adj repugnante
♦ n: **insect** ~ crema or loción f anti-insectos

repercussions [riːpə'kʌʃənz] npl consecuencias fpl

repetition [repɪ'tɪʃən] n repetición f

repetitive [rɪ'petɪtɪv] adj repetitivo

replace [rɪ'pleɪs] vt (put back) devolver a su sitio; (take the place) reemplazar, sustituir □ **replacement** n (act) reposición f; (thing) recambio; (person) suplente m/f

replay ['riːpleɪ] n (SPORT) desempate m; (of tape, film) repetición f

replica ['replɪkə] n copia, reproducción f (exacta)

reply [rɪ'plaɪ] n respuesta, contestación f ♦ vi contestar, responder

report [rɪ'pɔːt] n informe m; (PRESS etc) reportaje m; (BRIT: also: **school** ~) boletín m escolar; (of gun) estallido ♦ vt informar de; (PRESS etc) hacer un

reportaje sobre; (notify: accident, culprit) denunciar ♦ vi (make a report) presentar un informe; (present o.s.): **to ~ (to sb)** presentarse (ante algn)
□ **report card** n (US, Scottish) cartilla escolar □ **reportedly** adv según se dice □ **reporter** n periodista m/f

represent [reprɪ'zent] vt representar; (COMM) ser agente de; (describe): **to ~ sth as** describir algo como
□ **representation** [-'teɪʃən] n representación f □ **representative** n representante m/f; (US POL) diputado(-a) m/f ♦ adj representativo

repress [rɪ'pres] vt reprimir
□ **repression** [-'preʃən] n represión f

reprimand ['reprɪmɑːnd] n reprimenda ♦ vt reprender

reproduce [riːprə'djuːs] vt reproducir
♦ vi reproducirse □ **reproduction** [-'dʌkʃən] n reproducción f

reptile ['reptaɪl] n reptil m

republic [rɪ'pʌblɪk] n república
□ **republican** adj, n republicano(-a) m/f

reputable ['repjutəbl] adj (make etc) de renombre

reputation [repju'teɪʃən] n reputación f

request [rɪ'kwest] n petición f; (formal) solicitud f ♦ vt: **to ~ sth of or from sb** solicitar algo a algn □ **request stop** n (BRIT) parada discrecional

require [rɪ'kwaɪə] vt (need: person) necesitar, tener necesidad de; (: thing, situation) exigir; (want) pedir; **to ~ sb to do sth** pedir a algn que haga algo
□ **requirement** n requisito; (need) necesidad f

resat [riː'sæt] pt, pp of **resit**

rescue ['reskjuː] n rescate m ♦ vt rescatar

research [rɪ'sɜːtʃ] n investigaciones fpl
♦ vt investigar

resemblance [rɪ'zembləns] n parecido

resemble [rɪ'zembl] vt parecerse a

resent [rɪˈzɛnt] vt tomar a mal □ **resentful** adj resentido □ **resentment** n resentimiento

reservation [rɛzəˈveɪʃən] n reserva □ **reservation desk** (US) n (in hotel) recepción f

reserve [rɪˈzɜːv] n reserva; (SPORT) suplente mf ♦ vt (seats etc) reservar □ **reserved** adj reservado

reservoir [ˈrɛzəvwɑː] n (artificial lake) embalse m, tank; (small) depósito

residence [ˈrɛzɪdəns] n (formal: home) domicilio; (length of stay) permanencia □ **residence permit** (BRIT) n permiso de permanencia

resident [ˈrɛzɪdənt] n (of area) vecino(-a); (in hotel) huésped mf ♦ adj (population) permanente; (doctor) residente □ **residential** [-ˈdɛnʃəl] adj residencial

residue [ˈrɛzɪdjuː] n resto

resign [rɪˈzaɪn] vt renunciar a ♦ vi dimitir; **to ~ o.s. to** (situation) resignarse a □ **resignation** [rɛzɪɡˈneɪʃən] n dimisión f; (state of mind) resignación f

resin [ˈrɛzɪn] n resina

resist [rɪˈzɪst] vt resistir, oponerse a □ **resistance** n resistencia

resit [ˈriːsɪt] (BRIT) (pt, pp **resat**) vt (exam) volver a presentarse a; (subject) recuperar, volver a examinarse de (SP)

resolution [rɛzəˈluːʃən] n resolución f

resolve [rɪˈzɒlv] n resolución f ♦ vt resolver ♦ vi: **to ~ to do** resolver hacer

resort [rɪˈzɔːt] n (town) centro turístico; (recourse) recurso ♦ vi: **to ~ to** recurrir a; **in the last ~** como último recurso

resource [rɪˈsɔːs] n recurso □ **resourceful** adj despabilado, ingenioso

respect [rɪsˈpɛkt] n respeto ♦ vt respetar □ **respectable** adj respetable; (large: amount) apreciable; (passable) tolerable □ **respectful** adj respetuoso □ **respective** adj

respectivo □ **respectively** adv respectivamente

respite [ˈrɛspaɪt] n respiro

respond [rɪsˈpɒnd] vi responder; (react) reaccionar □ **response** [-ˈpɒns] n respuesta; reacción f

responsibility [rɪspɒnsɪˈbɪlɪtɪ] n responsabilidad f

responsible [rɪsˈpɒnsɪbl] adj (character) serio, formal; (job) de confianza; (liable): **~ (for)** responsable (de) □ **responsibly** adv con seriedad

responsive [rɪsˈpɒnsɪv] adj sensible

rest [rɛst] n descanso, reposo; (MUS, pause) pausa, silencio; (support) apoyo; (remainder) resto ♦ vi descansar; (be supported): **to ~ on** descansar sobre ♦ vt: **to ~ sth on/against** apoyar algo en or sobre/contra; **the ~ of them** (people, objects) los demás; **it rests with him to ...** depende de él el que ...

restaurant [ˈrɛstərɒŋ] n restaurante m □ **restaurant car** (BRIT) n (RAIL) coche-comedor m

restless [ˈrɛstlɪs] adj inquieto

restoration [rɛstəˈreɪʃən] n restauración f; devolución f

restore [rɪˈstɔː] vt (building) restaurar; (sth stolen) devolver; (health) restablecer; (to power) volver a poner a

restrain [rɪsˈtreɪn] vt (feeling) contener, refrenar; (person): **to ~ (from doing)** disuadir (de hacer) □ **restraint** n (restriction) restricción f; (moderation) moderación f; (of manner) reserva

restrict [rɪsˈtrɪkt] vt restringir, limitar □ **restriction** [-kʃən] n restricción f, limitación f

rest room (US) n aseos mpl

restructure [riːˈstrʌktʃə] vt reestructurar

result [rɪˈzʌlt] n resultado ♦ vi: **to ~ in** terminar en, tener por resultado; **as ~ of** a consecuencia de

resume [rɪ'zjuːm] vt reanudar ♦ vi comenzar de nuevo

⚠ Be careful not to translate **resume** by the Spanish word **resumir**.

résumé ['reɪzjuːmeɪ] n resumen m; (US) currículum m

resuscitate [rɪ'sʌsɪteɪt] vt (MED) resucitar

retail ['riːteɪl] adj, adv al por menor ❑ **retailer** n detallista mf

retain [rɪ'teɪn] vt (keep) retener, conservar

retaliation [rɪtælɪ'eɪʃən] n represalias fpl

retarded [rɪ'tɑːdɪd] adj retrasado

retire [rɪ'taɪə] vi (give up work) jubilarse; (withdraw) retirarse; (go to bed) acostarse ❑ **retired** adj (person) jubilado ❑ **retirement** n (giving up work: state) retiro; (: act) jubilación f

retort [rɪ'tɔːt] vi contestar

retreat [rɪ'triːt] n (place) retiro; (MIL) retirada ♦ vi retirarse

retrieve [rɪ'triːv] vt recobrar; (situation, honour) salvar; (COMPUT) recuperar; (error) reparar

retrospect ['retrəspekt] n: in ~ retrospectivamente ❑ **retrospective** [-'spektɪv] adj retrospectivo; (law) retroactivo

return [rɪ'tɜːn] n (going or coming back) vuelta, regreso; (of sth stolen etc) devolución f; (FINANCE: from land, shares) ganancia, ingresos mpl ♦ cpd (journey) de regreso; (BRIT: ticket) de ida y vuelta; (match) de vuelta ♦ vi (person etc: come or go back) volver, regresar; (symptoms etc) reaparecer; (regain): to ~ to recuperar ♦ vt devolver; (favour, love etc) corresponder a; (verdict) pronunciar; (POL: candidate) elegir; **returns** npl (COMM) ingresos mpl; in ~ (for) a cambio (de); by ~ of post a vuelta de correo; **many happy returns (of the day)!** ¡feliz cumpleaños! ❑ **return ticket** n (esp BRIT) billete m

(SP) or boleto m (LAm) de ida y vuelta, billete m redondo (MEX)

reunion [riː'juːnɪən] n (of family) reunión f; (of two people, school) reencuentro

reunite [riːjuː'naɪt] vt reunir; (reconcile) reconciliar

revamp [riː'væmp] vt renovar

reveal [rɪ'viːl] vt revelar ❑ **revealing** adj revelador(a)

revel ['revl] vi: to ~ in sth/in doing sth gozar de algo/con hacer algo

revelation [revə'leɪʃən] n revelación f

revenge [rɪ'vendʒ] n venganza; **to take ~ on** vengarse de

revenue ['revənjuː] n ingresos mpl, rentas fpl

Reverend ['revərənd] adj (in titles): **the ~ John Smith** (Anglican) el Reverendo John Smith; (Catholic) el Padre John Smith; (Protestant) el Pastor John Smith

reversal [rɪ'vɜːsl] n (of order) inversión f; (of direction, policy) cambio; (of decision) revocación f

reverse [rɪ'vɜːs] n (opposite) contrario; (back: of cloth) revés m; (: of coin) reverso; (: of paper) dorso; (AUT: also: ~ **gear**) marcha atrás, revés m ♦ adj (order) inverso; (direction) contrario; (process) opuesto ♦ vt (decision, AUT) dar marcha atrás a; (position, function) invertir ♦ vi (BRIT AUT) dar marcha atrás ❑ **reverse-charge call** (BRIT) n llamada a cobro revertido ❑ **reversing lights** (BRIT) npl (AUT) luces fpl de retroceso

revert [rɪ'vɜːt] vi: to ~ to volver a

review [rɪ'vjuː] n (magazine, MIL) revista; (of book, film) reseña; (US: examination) repaso, examen m ♦ vt repasar, examinar; (MIL) pasar revista a; (book, film) reseñar

revise [rɪ'vaɪz] vt (manuscript) corregir; (opinion) modificar; (price, procedure) revisar ♦ vi (study) repasar ❑ **revision**

[rɪ'vɪʒən] n corrección f; modificación f; (for exam) repaso

revival [rɪ'vaɪvəl] n (recovery) reanimación f; (of interest) renacimiento m; (THEATRE) reestreno m; (of faith) despertar m

revive [rɪ'vaɪv] vt resucitar; (custom) restablecer; (hope) despertar; (play) reestrenar ♦ vi (person) volver en sí; (business) reactivarse

revolt [rɪ'vəult] n rebelión f ♦ vi rebelarse, sublevarse ♦ vt dar asco a, repugnar ❏ **revolting** adj asqueroso, repugnante

revolution [rɛvə'luːʃən] n revolución f ❏ **revolutionary** adj, n revolucionario(-a) m/f

revolve [rɪ'vɒlv] vi dar vueltas, girar; (life, discussion): **to ~ (a)round** girar en torno a

revolver [rɪ'vɒlvə*] n revólver m

reward [rɪ'wɔːd] n premio, recompensa ♦ vt: **to ~ (for)** recompensar o premiar (por) ❏ **rewarding** adj (fig) valioso

rewind [riː'waɪnd] vt rebobinar

rewrite [riː'raɪt] (pt **rewrote**, pp **rewritten**) vt reescribir

rheumatism [ˈruːmətɪzəm] n reumatismo, reúma m

rhinoceros [raɪ'nɒsərəs] n rinoceronte m

rhubarb [ˈruːbɑːb] n ruibarbo

rhyme [raɪm] n rima; (verse) poesía

rhythm [ˈrɪðm] n ritmo

rib [rɪb] n (ANAT) costilla ♦ vt (mock) tomar el pelo a

ribbon [ˈrɪbən] n cinta; **in ribbons** (torn) hecho trizas

rice [raɪs] n arroz m ❏ **rice pudding** n arroz m con leche

rich [rɪtʃ] adj rico; (soil) fértil; (food) pesado; (: sweet) empalagoso; (abundant): **~ in** (minerals etc) rico en

rid [rɪd] (pt, pp ~) vt: **to ~ sb of sth** librar a algn de algo; **to get ~ of** deshacerse or desembarazarse de

riddle [ˈrɪdl] n (puzzle) acertijo; (mystery) enigma m, misterio ♦ vt: **to be riddled with** ser lleno or plagado de

ride [raɪd] (pt **rode**, pp **ridden**) n paseo; (distance covered) viaje m, recorrido ♦ vi (as sport) montar; (go somewhere: on horse, bicycle) dar un paseo, pasearse; (travel: on bicycle, motorcycle, bus) viajar ♦ vt (a horse) montar a; (a bicycle, motorcycle) andar en; (distance) recorrer; **to take sb for a ~** (fig) engañar a algn ❏ **rider** n (on horse) jinete mf; (on bicycle) ciclista mf; (on motorcycle) motociclista mf

ridge [rɪdʒ] n (of hill) cresta; (of roof) caballete m; (wrinkle) arruga

ridicule [ˈrɪdɪkjuːl] n irrisión f, burla f ♦ vt poner en ridículo, burlarse de ❏ **ridiculous** [-ˈdɪkjuləs] adj ridículo

riding [ˈraɪdɪŋ] n equitación f; **I like ~** me gusta montar a caballo ❏ **riding school** n escuela de equitación

rife [raɪf] adj: **to be ~** ser muy común; **to be ~ with** abundar en

rifle [ˈraɪfl] n rifle m, fusil m ♦ vt saquear

rift [rɪft] n (in clouds) claro; (fig: disagreement) desavenencia

rig [rɪg] n (also: **oil ~**: at sea) plataforma petrolera ♦ vt (election etc) amañar

right [raɪt] adj (correct) correcto, exacto; (suitable) indicado, debido; (proper) apropiado; (just) justo; (morally good) bueno; (not left) derecho ♦ n bueno; (title, claim) derecho; (not left) derecha ♦ adv bien, correctamente; (not left) a la derecha; (exactly): **~ now** ahora mismo ♦ vt enderezar; (correct) corregir ♦ excl ¡bueno!, ¡está bien! **to be ~** (person) tener razón; (answer) ser correcto; **is that the ~ time?** (of clock) ¿es esa la hora buena?; **by rights** en justicia; **on the ~** a la derecha; **to be in the ~** tener razón; **~ away** en seguida; **~ in the middle** exactamente en el

centro □ **right angle** *n* ángulo recto
□ **rightful** *adj* legítimo □ **right-hand**
adj: **right-hand drive** conducción *f* por
la derecha; **the right-hand side**
derecha □ **rightly** *adv* correctamente,
debidamente; (*with reason*) con razón
□ **right of way** *n* (*on path etc*)
derecho de paso; (*AUT*) prioridad *f*
□ **right-wing** *adj* (*POL*) derechista

rigid ['rɪdʒɪd] *adj* rígido; (*person, ideas*)
inflexible

rigorous ['rɪgərəs] *adj* riguroso

rim [rɪm] *n* borde *m*; (*of spectacles*) aro;
(*of wheel*) llanta

rind [raɪnd] *n* (*of bacon*) cáscara *f*; (*of
lemon etc*) cáscara; (*of cheese*) costra

ring [rɪŋ] (*pt* **rang**, *pp* **rung**) *n* (*of metal*)
aro; (*on finger*) anillo; (*of people*) corro;
(*of objects*) círculo; (*gang*) banda; (*for
boxing*) cuadrilátero; (*of circus*) pista;
(*bull ring*) ruedo, plaza; (*sound of bell*)
toque *m* ♦ *vi* (*on telephone*) llamar por
teléfono; (*bell*) repicar; (*doorbell,
phone*) sonar; (*also: ~ out*) sonar; (*ears*)
zumbar ♦ *vt* (*BRIT TEL*) llamar,
telefonear; (*bell etc*) hacer sonar;
(*doorbell*) tocar; **to give sb a ~** (*BRIT TEL*)
llamar o telefonear a algn ▶ **ring
back** (*BRIT*) *vt, vi* (*TEL*) devolver la
llamada ▶ **ring off** (*BRIT*) *vi* (*TEL*)
colgar, cortar la comunicación ▶ **ring
up** (*BRIT*) *vt* (*TEL*) llamar, telefonear
□ **ringing tone** *n* (*TEL*) tono de
llamada □ **ringleader** *n* (*of gang*)
cabecilla *m* □ **ring road** (*BRIT*) *n*
carretera periférica o de
circunvalación

rink [rɪŋk] *n* (*also*: **ice ~**) pista de hielo

rinse [rɪns] *n* aclarado; (*dye*) tinte *m* ♦ *vt*
aclarar; (*mouth*) enjuagar

riot ['raɪət] *n* motín *m*, disturbio ♦ *vi*
amotinarse; **to run ~** desmandarse

rip [rɪp] *n* rasgón *m*, rasgadura ♦ *vt*
rasgar, desgarrar ♦ *vi* rasgarse,
desgarrarse ▶ **rip off** *vt* (*inf: cheat*)
estafar ▶ **rip up** *vt* hacer pedazos

ripe [raɪp] *adj* maduro

rip-off ['rɪpɔf] *n* (*inf*): **it's a ~!** ¡es una
estafa!, ¡es un timo!

ripple ['rɪpl] *n* onda, rizo; (*sound*)
murmullo ♦ *vi* rizarse

rise [raɪz] (*pt* **rose**, *pp* **risen**) *n* (*slope*)
cuesta, pendiente *f*; (*hill*) altura; (*BRIT: in
wages*) aumento; (*in prices,
temperature*) subida; (*fig: to power etc*)
ascenso ♦ *vi* subir; (*waters*) crecer; (*sun,
moon*) salir; (*person: from bed etc*)
levantarse; (*also: ~ up: rebel*)
sublevarse; (*in rank*) ascender; **to give
~ to** dar lugar o origen a; **to ~ to the
occasion** ponerse a la altura de las
circunstancias □ **risen** ['rɪzn] *pp of*
rise □ **rising** *adj* (*increasing: number*)
creciente; (*: prices*) en aumento o alza;
(*tide*) creciente; (*sun, moon*) naciente

risk [rɪsk] *n* riesgo, peligro ♦ *vt*
arriesgar; (*run the risk of*) exponerse a;
to take o **run the ~ of doing** correr el
riesgo de hacer; **at ~** en peligro; **at
one's own ~** bajo su propia
responsabilidad □ **risky** *adj*
arriesgado, peligroso

rite [raɪt] *n* rito; **last rites** exequias *fpl*

ritual ['rɪtjuəl] *adj* ritual ♦ *n* ritual *m*, rito

rival ['raɪvl] *n* rival *mf*; (*in business*)
competidor(a) *m/f* ♦ *adj* rival, opuesto
♦ *vt* competir con □ **rivalry** *n*
competencia

river ['rɪvə'] *n* río ♦ *cpd* (*port*) de río;
(*traffic*) fluvial; **up/down ~** río arriba/
abajo □ **riverbank** *n* orilla (del río)

rivet ['rɪvɪt] *n* roblón *m*, remache *m* ♦ *vt*
(*fig*) captar

road [rəʊd] *n* camino; (*motorway etc*)
carretera; (*in town*) calle *f* ♦ *cpd*
(*accident*) de tráfico; **major/minor ~**
carretera principal/secundaria
□ **roadblock** *n* barricada □ **road
map** *n* mapa *m* de carreteras □ **road
rage** *n* agresividad *f* en la carretera
□ **road safety** *n* seguridad *f* vial
□ **roadside** *n* borde *m* (del camino)
□ **roadsign** *n* señal *f* de tráfico

❏ **road tax** n (BRIT) impuesto de rodaje ❏ **roadworks** npl obras fpl

roam [rəʊm] vi vagar

roar [rɔːʳ] n rugido; (of vehicle, storm) estruendo; (of laughter) carcajada ♦ vi rugir; hacer estruendo; **to ~ with laughter** reírse a carcajadas; **to do a roaring trade** hacer buen negocio

roast [rəʊst] n carne f asada, asado ♦ vt asar; (coffee) tostar ❏ **roast beef** n rosbif m

rob [rɒb] vt robar; **to ~ sb of sth** robar algo a algn; (fig: deprive) quitar algo a algn ❏ **robber** n ladrón(-ona) m/f ❏ **robbery** n robo

robe [rəʊb] n (for ceremony etc) toga; (also: **bathrobe**) albornoz m

robin ['rɒbɪn] n petirrojo

robot ['rəʊbɒt] n robot m

robust [rəʊˈbʌst] adj robusto, fuerte

rock [rɒk] n roca; (boulder) peña, peñasco; (US: small stone) piedrecita; (BRIT: sweet) = piruli ♦ vt (swing gently: cradle) balancear, mecer; (: child) arrullar; (shake) sacudir ♦ vi mecerse, balancearse; sacudirse; **on the rocks** (drink) con hielo; (marriage etc) en ruinas ❏ **rock and roll** n rocanrol m ❏ **rock climbing** n (SPORT) escalada

rocket ['rɒkɪt] n cohete m

rocking chair ['rɒkɪŋ-] n mecedora

rocky ['rɒkɪ] adj rocoso

rod [rɒd] n vara, varilla; (also: **fishing ~**) caña

rode [rəʊd] pt of **ride**

rodent ['rəʊdnt] n roedor m

rogue [rəʊg] n pícaro, pillo

role [rəʊl] n papel m ❏ **role-model** n modelo a imitar

roll [rəʊl] n rollo; (of bank notes) fajo; (also: **bread**) panecillo; (register, list) lista, nómina; (sound of drums etc) redoble m ♦ vt hacer rodar; (also: ~ **up**: string) enrollar; (cigarette) liar; (also: ~ **out**: pastry) aplanar; (flatten: road, lawn) apisonar ♦ vi rodar; (drum)

redoblar; (ship) balancearse ▸ **roll over** vi dar una vuelta ▸ **roll up** vi (inf: arrive) aparecer ♦ vt (carpet) arrollar; (: sleeves) arremangar ❏ **roller** n rodillo; (wheel) rueda; (for road) apisonadora; (for hair) rulo ❏ **Rollerblades®** npl patines mpl en línea ❏ **roller coaster** n montaña rusa ❏ **roller skates** npl patines mpl de rueda ❏ **roller-skating** n patinaje sobre ruedas; **to go roller-skating** (sobre ruedas) ir a patinar ❏ **rolling pin** n rodillo (de cocina)

ROM [rɒm] n abbr (COMPUT: = read only memory) ROM f

Roman ['rəʊmən] (irreg) adj romano(-a) ❏ **Roman Catholic** (irreg) adj, n católico(-a) m/f (romano(-a))

romance [rəˈmæns] n (love affair) amor m; (charm) lo romántico; (novel) novela de amor

Romania etc [ruːˈmeɪnɪə] n = **Rumania** etc

Roman numeral n número romano

romantic [rəˈmæntɪk] adj romántico

Rome [rəʊm] n Roma

roof [ruːf] (pl **roofs**) n techo; (of house) techo, tejado ♦ vt techar, poner techo a; **the ~ of the mouth** el paladar ❏ **roof rack** n (AUT) baca, portaequipajes m inv

rook [rʊk] n (bird) graja; (CHESS) torre f

room [ruːm] n cuarto, habitación f; (also: **bedroom**) dormitorio, recámara (MEX), pieza (SC); (in school etc) sala; (space, scope) sitio, cabida ❏ **roommate** n compañero(-a) de cuarto ❏ **room service** n servicio de habitaciones ❏ **roomy** adj espacioso; (garment) amplio

rooster ['ruːstəʳ] n gallo

root [ruːt] n raíz f ❏ vi arraigarse

rope [rəʊp] n cuerda; (NAUT) cable m ♦ vt (tie) atar o amarrar con (una) cuerda; (climbers: also: ~ **together**) encordarse; (an area: also: ~ **off**)

acordonar; **to know the ropes** (fig)
conocer los trucos (del oficio)

rose [rəʊz] pt of **rise** ♦ n rosa; (shrub)
rosal m; (on watering can) roseta

rosé ['rəʊzeɪ] n vino rosado

rosemary ['rəʊzmərɪ] n romero

rosy [rəʊzɪ] adj rosado, sonrosado; **a ~
future** un futuro prometedor

rot [rɒt] n podredumbre f; (fig: pej)
tonterías fpl ♦ vt pudrir ♦ vi pudrirse

rota ['rəʊtə] n (sistema m de) turnos mpl

rotate [rəʊ'teɪt] vt (revolve) hacer girar,
dar vueltas a; (jobs) alternar ♦ vi girar,
dar vueltas

rotten ['rɒtn] adj podrido; (dishonest)
corrompido; (inf: bad) pocho; **to feel ~**
(ill) sentirse fatal

rough [rʌf] adj (skin, surface) áspero;
(terrain) quebrado; (road) desigual;
(voice) bronco; (person, manner) tosco,
grosero; (weather) borrascoso;
(treatment) brutal; (sea) picado; (town,
area) peligroso; (cloth) basto; (plan)
preliminar; (guess) aproximado ♦ n
(GOLF): **in the ~** en las hierbas altas; **to ~
it** vivir sin comodidades; **to sleep ~**
(BRIT) pasar la noche al raso
❑ **roughly** adv (handle) torpemente;
(make) toscamente; (speak)
groseramente; (approximately)
aproximadamente

roulette [ruːˈlɛt] n ruleta

round [raʊnd] adj redondo ♦ n círculo;
(BRIT: of toast) rebanada f; (of policeman)
ronda; (of milkman) recorrido; (of
doctor) visitas fpl; (game: of cards, in
competition) partida; (of ammunition)
cartucho; (BOXING) asalto; (of talks)
ronda f ♦ vt (corner) doblar ♦ prep
alrededor de; (surrounding): **~ his
neck/the table** en su cuello/alrededor
de la mesa; (in a circular movement): **to
move ~ the room/sail ~ the world** dar
una vuelta a la habitación/
circunnavigar el mundo; (in various
directions): **to move ~ a room/house**
moverse por toda la habitación/casa;

(approximately) alrededor de ♦ adv: **all
~** por todos lados; **the long way ~** por
el camino menos directo; **all (the) year
~** durante todo el año; **it's just ~ the
corner** (fig) está a la vuelta de la
esquina; **~ the clock** adv las 24 horas;
to go ~ to sb's (house) ir a casa de algn;
to go ~ the back pasar por atrás;
enough to go ~ bastante (para todos);
a ~ of applause una salva de aplausos;
a ~ of drinks/sandwiches una ronda
de bebidas/bocadillos ▸ **round off** vt
(speech etc) acabar, poner término a
▸ **round up** vt (cattle) acorralar;
(people) reunir; (price) redondear
❑ **roundabout** (BRIT) n (AUT) isleta; (at
fair) tiovivo ♦ adj (route, means)
indirecto ❑ **round trip** n viaje m de
ida y vuelta ❑ **roundup** n rodeo; (of
criminals) redada; (of news) resumen m

rouse [raʊz] vt (wake up) despertar; (stir
up) suscitar

route [ruːt] n ruta, camino; (of bus)
recorrido; (of shipping) derrota

routine [ruːˈtiːn] adj rutinario ♦ n
rutina; (THEATRE) número

row¹ [rəʊ] n (line) fila, hilera; (KNITTING)
pasada ♦ vi (in boat) remar ♦ vt
conducir remando; **4 days in a ~** 4 días
seguidos

row² [raʊ] n (racket) escándalo;
(dispute) bronca, pelea; (scolding)
regaño ♦ vi pelear(se)

rowboat ['rəʊbəʊt] (US) = **rowing
boat**

rowing ['rəʊɪŋ] n remo ❑ **rowing
boat** (BRIT) n bote m de remos

royal ['rɔɪəl] adj real ❑ **royalty** n (royal
persons) familia real; (payment to
author) derechos mpl de autor

rpm abbr (= revs per minute) r.p.m.

R.S.V.P. abbr (= répondez s'il vous plaît)
SRC

Rt. Hon. abbr (BRIT: = Right Honourable)
título honorífico de diputado

rub [rʌb] vt frotar; (scrub) restregar ♦ n:
to give sth a ~ frotar algo; **to ~ sb up** or

~ sb (*US*) **the wrong way** entrarle algn por mal ojo ▶ **rub in** vt (*ointment*) aplicar frotando ▶ **rub off** vi borrarse ▶ **rub out** vt borrar

rubber ['rʌbə*] n caucho, goma; (*BRIT: eraser*) goma de borrar ❏ **rubber band** n goma, gomita ❏ **rubber gloves** npl guantes mpl de goma

rubbish ['rʌbɪʃ] n (*waste*) basura; (*fig: pej*) tonterías fpl; (*junk*) pacotilla ❏ **rubbish bin** (*BRIT*) n cubo o bote m (*MEX*) o tacho (*SC*) de la basura ❏ **rubbish dump** n vertedero, basurero

rubble ['rʌbl] n escombros mpl

ruby ['ruːbɪ] n rubí m

rucksack ['rʌksæk] n mochila

rudder ['rʌdə*] n timón m

rude [ruːd] adj (*impolite: person*) mal educado; (: *word, manners*) grosero; (*crude*) crudo; (*indecent*) indecente

ruffle ['rʌfl] vt (*hair*) despeinar; (*clothes*) arrugar; **to get ruffled** (*fig: person*) alterarse

rug [rʌg] n alfombra; (*BRIT: blanket*) manta

rugby ['rʌgbɪ] n rugby m

rugged ['rʌgɪd] adj (*landscape*) accidentado; (*features*) robusto

ruin ['ruːɪn] n ruina ♦ vt arruinar; (*spoil*) estropear; **ruins** npl ruinas fpl, restos mpl

rule [ruːl] n (*norm*) norma, costumbre f; (*regulation, ruler*) regla; (*government*) dominio ♦ vt (*country, person*) gobernar ♦ vi gobernar; (*law*) fallar; **as a ~** por regla general ▶ **rule out** vt excluir ❏ **ruler** n (*sovereign*) soberano; (*for measuring*) regla ❏ **ruling** adj (*party*) gobernante; (*class*) dirigente ♦ n (*LAW*) fallo m, decisión f

rum [rʌm] n ron m

Rumania [ruːˈmeɪnɪə] n Rumanía ❏ **Rumanian** adj rumano(-a) ♦ n rumano(-a) m/f; (*LING*) rumano

rumble ['rʌmbl] n (*noise*) ruido sordo ♦ vi retumbar, hacer un ruido sordo; (*stomach, pipe*) sonar

rumour ['ruːmə*] (*US* **rumor**) n rumor m ♦ vt: **it is rumoured that ...** se rumorea que ...

rump steak n filete m de lomo

run [rʌn] (pt **ran**, pp **~**) n (*fast pace*): **at a ~** corriendo; (*SPORT, in tights*) carrera; (*outing*) paseo, excursión f; (*distance travelled*) trayecto; (*series*) serie f; (*THEATRE*) temporada; (*SKI*) pista ♦ vt correr; (*operate: business*) dirigir; (: *competition, course*) organizar; (: *hotel, house*) administrar, llevar; (*COMPUT*) ejecutar; (*pass: hand*) pasar; (*PRESS: feature*) publicar ♦ vi correr; (*work: machine*) funcionar, marchar; (*bus, train*: *operate*) circular, ir; (: *travel*) ir; (*continue: play*) seguir; (*contract*) ser válido; (*flow: river*) fluir; (*colours, washing*) desteñirse; (*in election*) ser candidato; **there was a ~ on** (*meat, tickets*) hubo mucha demanda de; **in the long ~** a la larga; **on the ~** en fuga; **I'll ~ you to the station** te llevaré a la estación (en coche); **to ~ a risk** correr un riesgo; **to ~ a bath** llenar la bañera ▶ **run after** vt fus (*to catch up*) correr tras; (*chase*) perseguir ▶ **run away** vi huir ▶ **run down** vt (*production*) ir reduciendo; (*factory*) ir restringiendo la producción en; (*car*) atropellar; (*criticize*) criticar; **to be run down** (*person: tired*) estar debilitado ▶ **run into** vt fus (*meet: person, trouble*) tropezar con; (*collide with*) chocar con ▶ **run off** vt (*water*) dejar correr; (*copies*) sacar ♦ vi huir corriendo ▶ **run out** vi (*person*) salir corriendo; (*liquid*) irse; (*lease*) caducar, vencer; (*money etc*) acabarse ▶ **run out of** vt fus quedar sin ▶ **run over** vt (*AUT*) atropellar ♦ vt fus (*revise*) repasar ▶ **run through** vt fus (*instructions*) repasar ▶ **run up** vt (*debt*) contraer; **to run up against** (*difficulties*) tropezar con ❏ **runaway** *adj* (*horse*) desbocado; (*truck*) sin frenos; (*child*) escapado de casa

rung [rʌŋ] *pp of* **ring** ♦ *n* (*of ladder*) escalón *m*, peldaño

runner [rʌnəʳ] *n* (*in race: person*) corredor(a) *m/f*; (*: horse*) caballo; (*on sledge*) patín *m* ❏ **runner bean** (BRIT) *n* = judía verde ❏ **runner-up** *n* subcampeón(-ona) *m/f*

running [rʌnɪŋ] *n* (*sport*) atletismo; (*of business*) administración *f* ♦ *adj* (*water, costs*) corriente; (*commentary*) continuo; **to be in/out of the ~ for sth** tener/no tener posibilidades de ganar algo; **6 days ~** 6 días seguidos

runny [rʌnɪ] *adj* fluido; (*nose, eyes*) gastante

run-up [rʌnʌp] *n*: **~ to** (*election etc*) período previo a

runway [rʌnweɪ] *n* (AVIAT) pista de aterrizaje

rupture [rʌptʃəʳ] *n* (MED) hernia ♦ *vt*: **to ~ o.s** causarse una hernia

rural [rʊərl] *adj* rural

rush [rʌʃ] *n* ímpetu *m*; (*hurry*) prisa; (COMM) demanda repentina; (*current*) corriente *f* fuerte; (*of feeling*) torrente *m*; (BOT) junco ♦ *vt* apresurar; (*work*) hacer de prisa ♦ *vi* correr, precipitarse ❏ **rush hour** *n* horas *fpl* punta

Russia [rʌʃə] *n* Rusia ❏ **Russian** *adj* ruso(-a) ♦ *n* ruso(-a) *m/f*; (LING) ruso

rust [rʌst] *n* herrumbre *f*, moho ♦ *vi* oxidarse

rusty [rʌstɪ] *adj* oxidado

ruthless [ru:θlɪs] *adj* despiadado

RV (US) *n abbr* = **recreational vehicle**

rye [raɪ] *n* centeno

S, s

Sabbath [sæbəθ] *n* domingo; (*Jewish*) sábado

sabotage [sæbətɑːʒ] *n* sabotaje *m* ♦ *vt* sabotear

saccharin(e) [sækərɪn] *n* sacarina

sachet [sæʃeɪ] *n* sobrecito

sack [sæk] *n* (*bag*) saco, costal *m* ♦ *vt* (*dismiss*) despedir; (*plunder*) saquear; **to get the ~** ser despedido

sacred [seɪkrɪd] *adj* sagrado, santo

sacrifice [sækrɪfaɪs] *n* sacrificio ♦ *vt* sacrificar

sad [sæd] *adj* (*unhappy*) triste; (*deplorable*) lamentable

saddle [sædl] *n* silla (de montar); (*of cycle*) sillín *m* ♦ *vt* (*horse*) ensillar; **to be saddled with** (*inf*) quedar cargado con algo

sadistic [sədɪstɪk] *adj* sádico

sadly [sædlɪ] *adv* lamentablemente; **to be ~ lacking in** estar por desgracia carente de

sadness [sædnɪs] *n* tristeza

s.a.e. *abbr* = **stamped addressed envelope**) *sobre con las propias señas de uno y con sello*

safari [səfɑːrɪ] *n* safari *m*

safe [seɪf] *adj* (*out of danger*) fuera de peligro; (*not dangerous, sure*) seguro; (*unharmed*) ileso ♦ *n* caja de caudales, caja fuerte; **~ and sound** sano y salvo; **(just) to be on the ~ side** para mayor seguridad ❏ **safely** *adv* seguramente, con seguridad; **to arrive safely** llegar bien ❏ **safe sex** *n* sexo seguro *or* sin riesgo

safety [seɪftɪ] *n* seguridad *f* ❏ **safety belt** *n* cinturón *m* (de seguridad) ❏ **safety pin** *n* imperdible *m*, seguro (MEX), alfiler *m* de gancho (SC)

saffron [sæfrən] *n* azafrán *m*

sag [sæg] *vi* aflojarse

sage [seɪdʒ] *n* (*herb*) salvia; (*man*) sabio

Sagittarius [sædʒɪtɛərɪəs] *n* Sagitario

Sahara [səhɑːrə] *n*: **the ~** (*Desert*) el (desierto del) Sáhara

said [sɛd] *pt, pp of* **say**

sail [seɪl] n (on boat) vela; (trip): **to go for a ~** dar un paseo en barco ♦ vt (boat) gobernar ♦ vi (travel: ship) navegar; (SPORT) practicar la vela; (begin voyage) salir; **they sailed into Copenhagen** arribaron a Copenhague ❏ **sailboat** (US) n = **sailing boat** ❏ **sailing** n (SPORT) vela; **to go sailing** hacer vela ❏ **sailing boat** n barco de vela ❏ **sailor** n marinero, marino

saint [seɪnt] n santo

sake [seɪk] n: **for the ~ of** por

salad ['sæləd] n ensalada ❏ **salad cream** (BRIT) n (especie f de) mayonesa ❏ **salad dressing** n aliño

salami [sə'lɑːmɪ] n salami m, salchichón m

salary ['sælərɪ] n sueldo

sale [seɪl] n venta; (at reduced prices) liquidación f, saldo; (auction) subasta; **sales** npl (total amount sold) ventas fpl, facturación f; **"for ~"** "se vende"; **on ~** en venta; **on ~ or return** (goods) venta por reposición ❏ **sales assistant** (US **sales clerk**) n dependiente(-a) m/f ❏ **salesman/woman** (irreg) n (in shop) dependiente(-a) m/f ❏ **salesperson** (irreg) n vendedor(a) m/f, dependiente(-a) m/f ❏ **sales rep** n representante mf, agente mf comercial

saline ['seɪlaɪn] adj salino

saliva [sə'laɪvə] n saliva

salmon ['sæmən] n inv salmón m

salon ['sælɒn] n (hairdressing salon) peluquería; (beauty salon) salón m de belleza

saloon [sə'luːn] n (US) bar m, taberna; (BRIT AUT) coche m (de) turismo; (ship's lounge) cámara, salón m

salt [sɔːlt] n sal f ♦ vt salar; (put salt on) poner sal en ❏ **saltwater** adj de agua salada ❏ **salty** adj salado

salute [sə'luːt] n (MIL) saludo; (of guns) salva ♦ vt saludar

salvage ['sælvɪdʒ] n (saving) salvamento, recuperación f; (things saved) objetos mpl salvados ♦ vt salvar

Salvation Army [sæl'veɪʃən-] n Ejército de Salvación

same [seɪm] adj mismo ♦ pron: **the ~** el (la) mismo(-a), los (las) mismos(-as); **the ~ book** al mismo libro que; **at the ~ time** (at the same moment) al mismo tiempo; (yet) sin embargo; **all or just the ~** sin embargo, aun así; **to do the ~** (as sb) hacer lo mismo (que algn); **the ~ to you!** ¡igualmente!

sample ['sɑːmpl] n muestra ♦ vt (food) probar; (wine) catar

sanction ['sæŋkʃən] n aprobación f ♦ vt sancionar; aprobar; **sanctions** npl (POL) sanciones fpl

sanctuary ['sæŋktjuərɪ] n santuario; (refuge) asilo, refugio; (for wildlife) reserva

sand [sænd] n arena; (beach) playa ♦ vt (also: ~ down) lijar

sandal ['sændl] n sandalia

sand: sandbox (US) n = **sandpit** ❏ **sandcastle** n castillo de arena ❏ **sand dune** n duna ❏ **sandpaper** n papel m de lija ❏ **sandpit** n (for children) cajón m de arena ❏ **sands** npl playa sg de arena ❏ **sandstone** ['sændstəʊn] n piedra arenisca

sandwich ['sændwɪtʃ] n sandwich m ♦ vt intercalar; **sandwiched between** apretujado entre; **cheese/ham ~** sandwich de queso/jamón

sandy ['sændɪ] adj arenoso; (colour) rojizo

sane [seɪn] adj cuerdo; (sensible) sensato

⚠ Be careful not to translate **sane** by the Spanish word sano.

sang [sæŋ] pt of **sing**

sanitary towel (US **sanitary napkin**) n paño higiénico, compresa

sanity ['sænɪtɪ] n cordura; (of judgment) sensatez f

sank [sæŋk] pt of **sink**

Santa Claus ['sæntə'klɔːz] n San Nicolás, Papá Noel

sap [sæp] n (of plants) savia ♦ vt (strength) minar, agotar

sapphire ['sæfaɪə'] n zafiro

sarcasm ['sɑːkæzm] n sarcasmo

sarcastic [sɑː'kæstɪk] adj sarcástico

sardine [sɑː'diːn] n sardina

SASE (US) n abbr (= self-addressed stamped envelope) sobre con las propias señas de uno y con sello

Sat. abbr (= Saturday) sáb

sat [sæt] pt, pp of **sit**

satchel ['sætʃl] n (child's) mochila, cartera (SP)

satellite ['sætəlaɪt] n satélite m
☐ **satellite dish** n antena de televisión por satélite ☐ **satellite television** n televisión f vía satélite

satin ['sætɪn] n raso ♦ adj de raso

satire ['sætaɪə'] n sátira

satisfaction [sætɪs'fækʃən] n satisfacción f

satisfactory [sætɪs'fæktərɪ] adj satisfactorio

satisfied [ʹsætɪsfaɪd] adj satisfecho; **to be ~ (with sth)** estar satisfecho (de algo)

satisfy ['sætɪsfaɪ] vt satisfacer; (convince) convencer

Saturday ['sætədɪ] n sábado

sauce [sɔːs] n salsa; (sweet) crema; jarabe m ☐ **saucepan** n cacerola, olla

saucer ['sɔːsə'] n platillo

Saudi Arabia n Arabia Saudí or Saudita

sauna ['sɔːnə] n sauna

sausage ['sɒsɪdʒ] n salchicha
☐ **sausage roll** n empanadita de salchicha

sautéed ['səuteɪd] adj salteado

savage ['sævɪdʒ] adj (cruel, fierce) feroz, furioso; (primitive) salvaje ♦ n salvaje mf ♦ vt (attack) embestir

save [seɪv] vt (rescue) salvar, rescatar; (money, time) ahorrar; (put by, keep: seat) guardar; (COMPUT) salvar (y guardar); (avoid: trouble) evitar; (SPORT) parar ♦ vi (also: ~ up) ahorrar ♦ n (SPORT) parada ♦ prep salvo, excepto

savings ['seɪvɪŋz] npl ahorros mpl
☐ **savings account** n cuenta de ahorros ☐ **savings and loan association** (US) n sociedad f de ahorro y préstamo

savoury ['seɪvərɪ] (US **savory**) adj sabroso; (dish: not sweet) salado

saw [sɔː] (pt sawed, pp sawed or sawn) pt of **see** ♦ n (tool) sierra ♦ vt serrar ☐ **sawdust** n (a)serrín m

sawn [sɔːn] pp of **saw**

saxophone ['sæksəfəun] n saxófono

say [seɪ] (pt, pp said) n: **to have one's ~** expresar su opinión ♦ vt decir; **to have a** or **some ~ in sth** tener voz or tener que ver en algo; **to ~ yes/no** decir que sí/no; **could you ~ that again?** ¿podría repetir eso?; **that is to ~** es decir; **that goes without saying** ni que decir tiene ☐ **saying** n dicho, refrán m

scab [skæb] n costra; (pej) esquirol m

scaffolding ['skæfəldɪŋ] n andamio, andamiaje m

scald [skɔːld] n escaldadura ♦ vt escaldar

scale [skeɪl] n (gen, MUS) escala; (of fish) escama; (of salaries, fees etc) escalafón m ♦ vt (mountain) escalar; (tree) trepar ☐ **scales** npl (for weighing: small) balanza; (: large) báscula; **on a large ~** en gran escala; **~ of charges** tarifa, lista de precios

scallion ['skælɪən] (US) n cebolleta

scallop ['skɒləp] n (ZOOL) venera; (SEWING) festón m

scalp [skælp] n cabellera ♦ vt escalpar

scalpel ['skælpl] n bisturí m

scam [skæm] n (inf) estafa, timo

scampi ['skæmpɪ] npl gambas fpl

scan [skæn] vt (examine) escudriñar; (glance at quickly) dar un vistazo a; (TV, RADAR) explorar, registrar ♦ n (MED): **to have a ~** pasar por el escáner

scandal ['skændl] n escándalo; (gossip) chismes mpl

Scandinavia [skændɪ'neɪvɪə] n Escandinavia ❑ **Scandinavian** adj, n escandinavo(-a) m/f

scanner ['skænə'] n (RADAR, MED) escáner m

scapegoat ['skeɪpgəut] n cabeza de turco, chivo expiatorio

scar [skɑː'] n cicatriz f; (fig) señal f ♦ vt dejar señales en

scarce [skɛəs] adj escaso; **to make o.s. ~** (inf) esfumarse ❑ **scarcely** adv apenas

scare [skɛə'] n susto, sobresalto; (panic) pánico ♦ vt asustar, espantar; **to ~ sb stiff** dar a algn un susto de muerte; **bomb ~** amenaza de bomba ❑ **scarecrow** n espantapájaros m inv ❑ **scared** adj: **to be scared** estar asustado

scarf [skɑːf] (pl **scarfs** or **scarves**) n (long) bufanda; (square) pañuelo

scarlet ['skɑːlɪt] adj escarlata

scarves [skɑːvz] npl of **scarf**

scary ['skɛərɪ] (inf) adj espeluznante

scatter ['skætə'] vt (spread) esparcir, desparramar; (put to flight) dispersar ♦ vi desparramarse; dispersarse

scenario [sɪ'nɑːrɪəu] n (THEATRE) argumento; (CINEMA) guión m; (fig) escenario

scene [siːn] n (THEATRE, fig etc) escena; (of crime etc) escenario; (view) panorama m; (fuss) escándalo ❑ **scenery** (THEATRE) decorado; (landscape) paisaje m ❑ **scenic** adj pintoresco

⚠ Be careful not to translate **scenery** by the Spanish word **escenario**.

scent [sɛnt] n perfume m, olor m; (fig: track) rastro, pista

sceptical ['skɛptɪkl] adj escéptico

schedule ['ʃɛdjuːl, (US) 'skɛdjuːl] n (timetable) horario; (of events) programa m; (list) lista ♦ vt (visit) fijar la hora de; **to arrive on ~** llegar a la hora debida; **to be ahead of/behind ~** estar adelantado/en retraso ❑ **scheduled flight** n vuelo regular

scheme [skiːm] n (plan) plan m, proyecto; (plot) intriga; (arrangement) disposición f; (pension scheme etc) sistema m ♦ vi (intrigue) intrigar

schizophrenic [skɪtsə'frɛnɪk] adj esquizofrénico

scholar ['skɒlə'] n (pupil) alumno(-a); (learned person) sabio(-a), erudito(-a) ❑ **scholarship** n erudición f; (grant) beca

school [skuːl] n escuela, colegio; (in university) facultad f ♦ cpd escolar ❑ **schoolbook** n libro de texto ❑ **schoolboy** n alumno ❑ **school children** npl alumnos mpl ❑ **schoolgirl** n alumna ❑ **schooling** n enseñanza ❑ **schoolteacher** n (primary) maestro(-a); (secondary) profesor(-a) m/f

science ['saɪəns] n ciencia ❑ **science fiction** n ciencia-ficción f ❑ **scientific** ['tɪfɪk] adj científico(-a) ❑ **scientist** n científico(-a)

sci-fi ['saɪfaɪ] n abbr (inf) = **science fiction**

scissors ['sɪzəz] npl tijeras fpl; **a pair of ~** unas tijeras

scold [skəuld] vt regañar

scone [skɒn] n pastel de pan

scoop [skuːp] n (for flour etc) pala; (PRESS) exclusiva

scooter ['skuːtə'] n moto f; (toy) patinete m

scope [skəup] n (of plan) ámbito; (of person) competencia; (opportunity) libertad f (de acción)

scorching ['skɔːtʃɪŋ] *adj* (heat, sun) abrasador(a)

score [skɔːʳ] *n* (points etc) puntuación *f*; (MUS) partitura; (twenty) veintena ♦ *vt* (goal, point) ganar; (mark) rayar; (achieve: success) conseguir ♦ *vi* marcar un tanto; (FOOTBALL) marcar (un) gol; (keep score) llevar el tanteo; **scores of** (lots of) decenas de; **on that** ~ en lo que se refiere a eso; **to ~ 6 out of 10** obtener una puntuación de 6 sobre 10 ▶ **score out** *vt* tachar □ **scoreboard** *n* marcador *m* □ **scorer** *n* marcador *m*; (keeping score) encargado(-a) del marcador

scorn [skɔːn] *n* desprecio

Scorpio ['skɔːpɪəu] *n* Escorpión *m*

scorpion ['skɔːpɪən] *n* alacrán *m*

Scot [skɔt] *n* escocés(-esa) *m/f*

Scotch tape® (US) *n* cinta adhesiva, celo, scotch® *m*

Scotland ['skɔtlənd] *n* Escocia

Scots [skɔts] *adj* escocés(-esa) □ **Scotsman** (irreg) *n* escocés □ **Scotswoman** (irreg) *n* escocésa □ **Scottish** ['skɔtɪʃ] *adj* escocés(-esa) □ **Scottish Parliament** *n* Parlamento escocés

scout [skaut] *n* (MIL: also: **boy** ~) explorador *m*; **girl** ~ (US) niña exploradora

scowl [skaul] *vi* fruncir el ceño; **to** ~ **at sb** mirar con ceño a algn

scramble ['skræmbl] *n* (climb) subida (difícil); (struggle) pelea ♦ *vi*: **to** ~ **through/out** abrirse paso/salir de dificultad; **to** ~ **for** pelear por □ **scrambled eggs** *npl* huevos *mpl* revueltos

scrap [skræp] *n* (bit) pedacito; (fig) pizca; (fight) riña, bronca; (also: ~ **iron**) chatarra, hierro viejo ♦ *vt* desechar, descartar ♦ *vi* reñir, armar una bronca; **scraps** *npl* (waste) sobras *fpl*, desperdicios *mpl* □ **scrapbook** *n* álbum *m* de recortes

scrape [skreip] *n*: **to get into a** ~ meterse en un lío ♦ *vt* (skin etc) rasguñar; (scrape against) rozar ♦ *vi*: **to** ~ **through** (exam) aprobar por los pelos

scrap paper *n* pedazos *mpl* de papel

scratch [skrætʃ] *n* rasguño; (from claw) arañazo ♦ *vt* (paint, car) rayar; (with claw, nail) rascar, arañar; (rub: nose etc) rascarse ♦ *vi* rascarse; **to start from** ~ partir de cero; **to be up to** ~ cumplir con los requisitos □ **scratch card** *n* (BRIT) tarjeta *f* de "rasque y gane"

scream [skriːm] *n* chillido ♦ *vi* chillar

screen [skriːn] *n* (CINEMA, TV) pantalla; (movable barrier) biombo ♦ *vt* (conceal) tapar; (from the wind etc) proteger; (film) proyectar; (candidates etc) investigar □ **screening** *n* (MED) investigación *f* médica □ **screenplay** *n* guión *m* □ **screen saver** *n* (COMPUT) protector *m* de pantalla

screw [skruː] *n* tornillo ♦ *vt* (also: ~ **in**) atornillar ▶ **screw up** *vt* (paper etc) arrugar; **to screw up one's eyes** arrugar el entrecejo □ **screwdriver** *n* destornillador *m*

scribble ['skribl] *n* garabatos *mpl* ♦ *vt*, *vi* garabatear

script [skript] *n* (CINEMA etc) guión *m*; (writing) escritura, letra

scroll [skrəul] *n* rollo

scrub [skrʌb] *n* (land) maleza ♦ *vt* fregar, restregar; (inf: reject) cancelar, anular

scruffy ['skrʌfɪ] *adj* desaliñado, piojoso

scrum(mage) ['skrʌm(mɪdʒ)] *n* (RUGBY) melée *f*

scrutiny ['skruːtɪnɪ] *n* escrutinio, examen *m*

scuba diving ['skuːbə'daɪvɪŋ] *n* submarinismo

sculptor ['skʌlptəʳ] *n* escultor(a) *m/f*

sculpture ['skʌlptʃəʳ] *n* escultura

scum [skʌm] *n* (on liquid) espuma; (pej: people) escoria

scurry ['skʌrɪ] vi correr; **to ~ off** escabullirse

sea [si:] n mar m ♦ cpd de mar, marítimo; **by ~** (travel) en barco; **on the ~** (boat) en el mar; (town) junto al mar; **to be all at ~** (fig) estar despistado; **out to ~, at ~** en alta mar ❏ **seafood** n mariscos mpl ❏ **sea front** n paseo marítimo ❏ **seagull** n gaviota

seal [si:l] n (animal) foca; (stamp) sello ♦ vt (close) cerrar ▶ **seal off** vt (area) acordonar

sea level n nivel m del mar

seam [si:m] n costura; (of metal) juntura; (of coal) veta, filón m

search [sə:tʃ] n (for person, thing) busca, búsqueda; (COMPUT) búsqueda; (inspection: of sb's home) registro ♦ vt (look in) buscar en; (examine) examinar; (person, place) registrar ♦ vi: **to ~ for** buscar; **in ~ of** en busca de ❏ **search engine** n (COMPUT) buscador m ❏ **search party** n pelotón m de salvamento

sea: seashore n playa, orilla del mar ❏ **seasick** adj mareado ❏ **seaside** n playa, orilla del mar ❏ **seaside resort** n centro turístico costero

season ['si:zn] n (of year) estación f; (sporting etc) temporada; (of films etc) ciclo ♦ vt (food) sazonar; **in/out of ~** en sazón/fuera de temporada ❏ **seasonal** adj estacional ❏ **seasoning** n condimento, aderezo ❏ **season ticket** n abono

seat [si:t] n (in bus, train) asiento; (chair) silla; (PARLIAMENT) escaño; (buttocks) culo, trasero; (of trousers) culera ♦ vt sentar; (have room for) tener cabida para; **to be seated** sentarse ❏ **seat belt** n cinturón m de seguridad ❏ **seating** n asientos mpl

sea: sea water n agua del mar ❏ **seaweed** n alga marina

sec. abbr = **second(s)**

secluded [sɪ'klu:dɪd] adj retirado

second ['sɛkənd] adj segundo ♦ adv en segundo lugar ♦ n segundo; (AUT: also: ~ **gear**) segunda; (COMM) artículo con algún desperfecto; (BRIT SCOL: degree) título de licenciado con calificación de notable ♦ vt (motion) apoyar ❏ **secondary** adj secundario ❏ **secondary school** n escuela secundaria ❏ **second-class** adj de segunda clase ♦ adv (RAIL) en segunda ❏ **secondhand** adj de segunda mano, usado ❏ **secondly** adv en segundo lugar ❏ **second-rate** adj de segunda categoría ❏ **second thoughts: to have second thoughts** cambiar de opinión; **on second thoughts** or **thought** (US) pensándolo bien

secrecy ['si:krəsɪ] n secreto

secret ['si:krɪt] adj, n secreto; **in ~** en secreto

secretary ['sɛkrətərɪ] n secretario(-a); **S~ of State (for)** (BRIT POL) Ministro (de)

secretive ['si:krətɪv] adj reservado, sigiloso

secret service n servicio secreto

sect [sɛkt] n secta

section ['sɛkʃən] n sección f; (part) parte f; (of document) artículo; (of opinion) sector m; (cross-section) corte m transversal

sector ['sɛktə'] n sector m

secular ['sɛkjʊlə'] adj secular, seglar

secure [sɪ'kjʊə'] adj seguro; (firmly fixed) firme, fijo ♦ vt (fix) asegurar, afianzar; (get) conseguir

security [sɪ'kjʊərɪtɪ] n seguridad f; (for loan) fianza; (: object) prenda; **securities** npl (COMM) valores mpl, títulos mpl ❏ **security guard** n guardia m/f de seguridad

sedan [sɪ'dæn] (US) n (AUT) sedán m

sedate [sɪ'deɪt] adj tranquilo ♦ vt tratar con sedantes

sedative ['sɛdɪtɪv] n sedante m, sedativo

seduce [sɪ'dju:s] vt seducir ▫ **seductive** [-'dʌktɪv] adj seductor(a)

see [si:] (pt saw, pp seen) vt ver; (accompany): **to ~ sb to the door** acompañar a algn a la puerta; (understand) ver, comprender ♦ vi ver ♦ vt (arz)obispado: **to ~ that** (ensure) asegurar que; **~ you soon!** ¡hasta pronto! ► **see off** vt despedir ► **see out** vt (take to the door) acompañar hasta la puerta ► **see through** vt fus (fig) calar ♦ vt (plan) llevar a cabo ► **see to** vt fus atender a, encargarse de

seed [si:d] n semilla; (in fruit) pepita; (fig: gen pl) germen m; (TENNIS etc) preseleccionado(-a); **to go to ~** (plant) granar; (fig) descuidarse

seeing [si:ɪŋ] conj: **~ (that)** visto que, en vista de que

seek [si:k] (pt, pp sought) vt buscar; (post) solicitar

seem [si:m] vi parecer; **there seems to be ...** parece que hay ... ▫ **seemingly** adv aparentemente, según parece

seen [si:n] pp of **see**

seesaw [si:sɔ:] n subibaja

segment ['sɛgmənt] n (part) sección f; (of orange) gajo

segregate ['sɛgrɪgeɪt] vt segregar

seize [si:z] vt (grasp) agarrar, asir; (take possession of) secuestrar; (: territory) apoderarse de; (opportunity) aprovecharse de

seizure ['si:ʒər] n (MED) ataque m; (LAW, of power) incautación f

seldom ['sɛldəm] adv rara vez

select [sɪ'lɛkt] adj selecto, escogido ♦ vt escoger, elegir; (SPORT) seleccionar ▫ **selection** n selección f, elección f; (COMM) surtido ▫ **selective** adj selectivo

self [sɛlf] (pl **selves**) n uno mismo; **the ~** el yo ♦ prefix auto... ▫ **self-assured** adj seguro de sí mismo ▫ **self-catering** (BRIT) adj (flat etc) con cocina ▫ **self-centred** (US **self-centered**) adj

egocéntrico ▫ **self-confidence** n confianza en sí mismo ▫ **self-confident** adj seguro de sí (mismo), lleno de confianza en sí mismo ▫ **self-conscious** adj cohibido ▫ **self-contained** (BRIT) adj (flat) con entrada particular ▫ **self-control** n autodominio ▫ **self-defence** (US **self-defense**) n defensa propia ▫ **self-drive** adj (BRIT) sin chofer or (SP) chófer ▫ **self-employed** adj que trabaja por cuenta propia ▫ **self-esteem** n amor m propio ▫ **self-indulgent** adj autocomplaciente ▫ **self-interest** n egoísmo ▫ **self-ish** adj egoísta ▫ **self-pity** n lástima de sí mismo ▫ **self-raising** [self'reɪzɪŋ] (US **self-rising**) adj: **self-raising flour** harina con levadura ▫ **self-respect** n amor m propio ▫ **self-service** adj de autoservicio

sell [sɛl] (pt, pp sold) vt vender ♦ vi venderse; **to ~ at or for £10** venderse a 10 libras ► **sell off** vt liquidar ► **sell out** vi: **to sell out of tickets/milk** vender todas las entradas/toda la leche ▫ **sell-by date** n fecha de caducidad ▫ **seller** n vendedor(a) m/f

selves [sɛlvz] npl of **self**

semester [sɪ'mɛstər] n (US) semestre m

semi... [sɛmɪ] prefix semi..., medio... ▫ **semicircle** n semicírculo ▫ **semidetached (house)** n (casa) semiseparada ▫ **semi-final** n semifinal m

seminar ['sɛmɪnɑː'] n seminario

semi-skimmed [sɛmɪ'skɪmd] adj semidesnatado ▫ **semi-skimmed (milk)** n leche semidesnatada

senate ['sɛnɪt] n senado; **the S~** (US) el Senado ▫ **senator** n senador(a) m/f

send [sɛnd] (pt, pp sent) vt mandar, enviar; (signal) transmitir ► **send back** vt devolver ► **send for** vt fus mandar traer ▶ **send in** vt (report, application, resignation) mandar ▶ **send off** vt (goods) despachar; (BRIT SPORT: player) expulsar ▶ **send on** vt (letter, luggage) remitir; (person) mandar ▶ **send out** vt (invitation) mandar; (signal) emitir ▶ **send up** vt (person, price) hacer subir; (BRIT: parody) parodiar ☐ **sender** n remitente mf ☐ **send-off** n: **a good send-off** una buena despedida

senile ['siːnaɪl] adj senil

senior ['siːnɪə*] adj (older) mayor, más viejo; (: on staff) de más antigüedad; (of higher rank) superior ◆ **senior citizen** n persona de la tercera edad ☐ **senior high school** (US) n = instituto de enseñanza media; see also **high school**

sensation [sen'seɪʃən] n sensación f ☐ **sensational** adj sensacional

sense [sens] n (faculty, meaning) sentido; (feeling) sensación f; (good sense) sentido común, juicio ◆ vt sentir, percibir; **it makes ~** tiene sentido ☐ **senseless** adj estúpido, insensato; (unconscious) sin conocimiento ◆ **sense of humour** (BRIT) n sentido del humor

sensible ['sensɪbl] adj sensato; (reasonable) razonable, lógico

⚠ Be careful not to translate **sensible** by the Spanish word *sensible*.

sensitive ['sensɪtɪv] adj sensible; (touchy) susceptible

sensual ['sensjʊəl] adj sensual

sensuous ['sensjʊəs] adj sensual

sent [sent] pt, pp of **send**

sentence ['sentəns] n (LING) oración f; (LAW) sentencia, fallo ◆ vt: **to ~ sb to death/to 5 years (in prison)** condenar a algn a muerte/a 5 años de cárcel

sentiment ['sentɪmənt] n sentimiento; (opinion) opinión f ☐ **sentimental** [-'mentl] adj sentimental

Sep. abbr (= September) sep., set.

separate [adj 'seprɪt, vb 'sepəreɪt] adj separado; (distinct) distinto ◆ vt separar; (part) dividir ◆ vi separarse ☐ **separately** adv por separado ☐ **separates** npl (clothes) coordinados mpl ☐ **separation** [-'reɪʃən] n separación f

September [sep'tembə*] n se(p)tiembre m

septic ['septɪk] adj séptico ☐ **septic tank** n fosa séptica

sequel ['siːkwl] n consecuencia, resultado; (of story) continuación f

sequence ['siːkwəns] n sucesión f, serie f; (CINEMA) secuencia

sequin ['siːkwɪn] n lentejuela

Serb [səːb] adj, n = **Serbian**

Serbian ['səːbɪən] adj serbio ◆ n serbio(-a); (LING) serbio

sergeant ['sɑːdʒənt] n sargento

serial ['sɪərɪəl] n (TV) telenovela, serie f televisiva; (BOOK) serie f ☐ **serial killer** n asesino(-a) múltiple ☐ **serial number** n número de serie

series ['sɪəriːz] n inv serie f

serious ['sɪərɪəs] adj serio; (grave) grave ☐ **seriously** adv en serio; (ill, wounded etc) gravemente

sermon ['səːmən] n sermón m

servant ['səːvənt] n servidor(a) m/f; (house servant) criado(-a)

serve [səːv] vt servir; (customer) atender; (train) pasar por; (apprenticeship) hacer; (prison term) cumplir ◆ vi (at table) servir; (TENNIS) sacar; **to ~ as/for/to do** servir de/para/para hacer ◆ n (TENNIS) saque m; **it serves him right** se lo tiene merecido ☐ **server** n (COMPUT) servidor m

service ['səːvɪs] n servicio; (REL) misa; (AUT) mantenimiento; (dishes etc) juego ◆ vt (car etc) revisar; (: repair) reparar; **to be of ~ to sb** ser útil a algn; **~ included/not included** servicio incluido/no incluido; **services** (ECON: tertiary sector) sector m terciario o (de) servicios; (BRIT: on motorway) área de servicio; (MIL): **the Services** las fuerzas armadas ❑ **service area** n (on motorway) área de servicio ❑ **service charge** (BRIT) n servicio ❑ **serviceman** (irreg) n militar m ❑ **service station** n estación f de servicio

serviette [sɑːvɪˈet] (BRIT) n servilleta

session [ˈseʃən] n sesión f; **to be in ~** estar en sesión

set [set] (pt, pp ~) n juego; (RADIO) aparato; (TV) televisor m; (of utensils) batería; (of cutlery) cubierto; (of books) colección f; (TENNIS) set m; (group of people) grupo; (CINEMA) plató m; (THEATRE) decorado; (HAIRDRESSING) marcado ♦ adj (fixed) fijo; (ready) listo ♦ vt (place) poner, colocar; (fix) fijar; (adjust) ajustar, arreglar; (decide: rules etc) establecer, decidir ♦ vi (sun) ponerse; (jam, jelly) cuajarse; (concrete) fraguar; (bone) componerse; **to be ~ on doing sth** estar empeñado en hacer algo; **to ~ to music** poner música a; **to ~ on fire** incendiar, poner fuego a; **to ~ free** poner en libertad; **to ~ sth going** poner algo en marcha; **to ~ sail** zarpar, hacerse a la vela ► **set aside** vt poner aparte, dejar de lado; (money, time) reservar ► **set down** vt (bus, train) dejar ► **set in** vi (infection) declararse; (complications) comenzar; **the rain has set in for the day** parece que va a llover todo el día ► **set off** vi partir ♦ vt (bomb) hacer estallar; (events) poner en marcha; (show up well) hacer resaltar ► **set out** vi partir ♦ vt (arrange) disponer; (state) exponer; **set out to do sth** proponerse hacer algo ► **set up** vt establecer ❑ **setback** n revés m, contratiempo ❑ **set menu** n menú m

settee [seˈtiː] n sofá m

setting [ˈsetɪŋ] n (scenery) marco; (position) disposición f; (of sun) puesta; (of jewel) engaste m, montadura

settle [ˈsetl] vt (argument) resolver; (accounts) ajustar, liquidar; (MED: calm) calmar, sosegar ♦ vi (dust etc) depositarse; (weather) serenarse; **to ~ for sth** convenir en aceptar algo; **to ~ on sth** decidirse por algo ► **settle down** vi (get comfortable) ponerse cómodo, acomodarse; (calm down) calmarse, tranquilizarse; (live quietly) echar raíces ► **settle in** vi instalarse ► **settle up** vi: **to settle up with sb** ajustar cuentas con algn ❑ **settlement** n (payment) liquidación f; (agreement) acuerdo, convenio; (village etc) pueblo

setup [ˈsetʌp] n sistema m; (situation) situación f

seven [ˈsevn] num siete ❑ **seventeen** num diez y siete, diecisiete ❑ **seventeenth** [sevnˈtiːnθ] adj decimoséptimo ❑ **seventh** num séptimo ❑ **seventieth** [ˈsevntɪθ] adj septuagésimo ❑ **seventy** num setenta

sever [ˈsevə] vt cortar; (relations) romper

several [ˈsevərl] adj, pron varios(-as) m/fpl, algunos(-as) m/fpl; **~ of us** varios de nosotros

severe [sɪˈvɪə] adj (serious) severo; grave; (hard) duro; (pain) intenso

sew [səu] (pt sewed, pp sewn) vt, vi coser

sewage [ˈsuːɪdʒ] n aguas fpl residuales

sewer [ˈsuːə] n alcantarilla, cloaca

sewing [ˈsəuɪŋ] n costura ❑ **sewing machine** n máquina de coser

sewn [səun] pp of **sew**

sex [seks] n sexo; (lovemaking): **to have ~** hacer el amor ❑ **sexism** [ˈseksɪzəm] n sexismo ❑ **sexist** adj, n sexista mf ❑ **sexual** [ˈseksjuəl] adj sexual ❑ **sexual intercourse** n relaciones fpl sexuales ❑ **sexuality** [seksjuˈælɪtɪ] n sexualidad f ♦ **sexy** adj sexy

shabby [ˈʃæbɪ] adj (person) desharrapado; (clothes) raído, gastado; (behaviour) ruin sin/

shack [ʃæk] n choza, chabola

shade [ʃeɪd] n sombra; (for lamp) pantalla; (for eyes) visera; (of colour) matiz m, tonalidad f; (small quantity): **a ~ (too big/more)** un poquitín (grande/más) ♦ vt dar sombra a; (eyes) proteger del sol; **in the ~** en la sombra; **shades** npl (sunglasses) gafas fpl de sol

shadow [ʃædəu] n sombra ♦ vt (follow) seguir y vigilar ☐ **shadow cabinet** (BRIT) n (POL) gabinete paralelo formado por el partido de oposición

shady [ʃeɪdɪ] adj sombreado; (fig: dishonest) sospechoso; (: deal) turbio

shaft [ʃɑːft] n (of arrow, spear) astil m; (AUT, TECH) eje m, árbol m; (of mine) pozo; (of lift) hueco, caja; (of light) rayo

shake [ʃeɪk] (pt **shook**, pp **shaken**) vt sacudir; (building) hacer temblar; (bottle, cocktail) agitar ♦ vi (tremble) temblar; **to ~ one's head** (in refusal) negar con la cabeza; (in dismay) mover or menear la cabeza, incrédulo; **to ~ hands with sb** estrechar la mano a algn ▶ **shake off** vt sacudirse; (fig) deshacerse de ▶ **shake up** vt agitar, (fig) reorganizar ☐ **shaky** adj (hand, voice) trémulo; (building) inestable

shall [ʃæl] aux vb: **~ I help you?** ¿quieres que te ayude?; **I'll buy three, ~ I?** compro tres, ¿no te parece?

shallow [ʃæləu] adj poco profundo; (fig) superficial

sham [ʃæm] n fraude m, engaño

shambles [ʃæmblz] n confusión f

shame [ʃeɪm] n vergüenza ♦ vt avergonzar; **it is a ~ that/to do** es una lástima que/hacer; **what a ~!** ¡qué lástima! ☐ **shameful** adj vergonzoso ☐ **shameless** adj desvergonzado

shampoo [ʃæmˈpuː] n champú m ♦ vt lavar con champú

shandy [ʃændɪ] n mezcla de cerveza con gaseosa

shan't [ʃɑːnt] = **shall not**

shape [ʃeɪp] n forma ♦ vt formar, dar forma a; (sb's ideas) formar; (sb's life) determinar; **to take ~** tomar forma

share [ʃɛəʳ] n (part) parte f, porción f; (contribution) cuota; (COMM) acción f ♦ vt dividir; (have in common) compartir; **to ~ out** (among or between) repartir (entre) ☐ **shareholder** (BRIT) n accionista mf

shark [ʃɑːk] n tiburón m

sharp [ʃɑːp] adj (blade, nose) afilado; (point) puntiagudo; (outline) definido; (pain) intenso; (MUS) desafinado; (contrast) marcado; (voice) agudo; (person: quick-witted) astuto; (: dishonest) poco escrupuloso ♦ n (MUS) sostenido ♦ adv: **at 2 o'clock ~** a las 2 en punto ▶ **sharpen** vt afilar; (pencil) sacar punta a; (fig) agudizar ☐ **sharpener** n (also: **pencil sharpener**) sacapuntas m inv ☐ **sharply** adv (turn, stop) bruscamente; (stand out, contrast) claramente; (criticize, retort) severamente

shatter [ʃætəʳ] vt hacer añicos or pedazos; (fig: ruin) destruir, acabar con ♦ vi hacerse añicos ☐ **shattered** adj (grief-stricken) destrozado, deshecho; (exhausted) agotado, hecho polvo

shave [ʃeɪv] vt afeitar, rasurar ♦ vi afeitarse, rasurarse ♦ n: **to have a ~** afeitarse ☐ **shaver** n (also: **electric shaver**) máquina de afeitar (eléctrica)

shavings [ʃeɪvɪŋz] npl (of wood etc) virutas fpl

shaving cream [ʃeɪvɪŋ-] n crema de afeitar

shaving foam n espuma de afeitar

shawl [ʃɔːl] n chal m

she [ʃiː] pron ella

sheath [ʃiːθ] n vaina; (contraceptive) preservativo

shed [ʃed] (pt, pp ~) n cobertizo ♦ vt (skin) mudar; (tears, blood) derramar; (load) derramar; (workers) despedir

she'd [ʃi:d] = **she had; she would**

sheep [ʃi:p] n inv oveja □ **sheepdog** n perro pastor □ **sheepskin** n piel f de carnero

sheer [ʃɪəˠ] adj (utter) puro, completo; (steep) escarpado; (material) diáfano ♦ adv verticalmente

sheet [ʃi:t] n (on bed) sábana; (of paper) hoja; (of glass, metal) lámina; (of ice) capa

sheik(h) [ʃeɪk] n jeque m

shelf [ʃelf] (pl **shelves**) n estante m

shell [ʃel] n (on beach) concha; (of egg, nut etc) cáscara; (explosive) proyectil m, obús m; (of building) armazón f ♦ vt (peas) desenvainar; (MIL) bombardear

she'll [ʃi:l] = **she will; she shall**

shellfish [ʃelfɪʃ] n inv crustáceo m; (as food) mariscos mpl

shelter [ʃeltəˠ] n abrigo, refugio ♦ vt (aid) amparar, proteger; (give lodging to) abrigar ♦ vi abrigarse, refugiarse □ **sheltered** adj (life) protegido; (spot) abrigado

shelves [ʃelvz] npl of **shelf**

shelving [ʃelvɪŋ] n estantería

shepherd [ʃepəd] n pastor m ♦ vt (guide) guiar, conducir □ **shepherd's pie** (BRIT) n pastel de carne y patatas

sheriff [ʃerɪf] (US) n sheriff m

sherry [ʃerɪ] n jerez m

she's [ʃi:z] = **she is; she has**

Shetland [ʃetlənd] n (also: the **Shetlands, the ~ Isles**) las Islas de Zetlandia

shield [ʃi:ld] n escudo; (protection) blindaje m ♦ vt: to ~ (**from**) proteger (de)

shift [ʃɪft] n (change) cambio; (at work) turno ♦ vt trasladar; (remove) quitar ♦ vi moverse

shin [ʃɪn] n espinilla

shine [ʃaɪn] (pt, pp **shone**) n brillo, lustre m ♦ vi brillar, relucir ♦ vt (shoes) lustrar, sacar brillo a; to ~ **a torch on sth** dirigir una linterna hacia algo

shingles [ʃɪŋɡlz] n (MED) herpes mpl or fpl

shiny [ʃaɪnɪ] adj brillante, lustroso

ship [ʃɪp] n buque m, barco ♦ vt (goods) embarcar; (send) transportar or enviar por vía marítima □ **shipment** n (goods) envío □ **shipping** n (act) embarque m; (traffic) buques mpl □ **shipwreck** n naufragio ♦ vt: to be **shipwrecked** naufragar □ **shipyard** n astillero

shirt [ʃɔ:t] n camisa; **in (one's) ~ sleeves** en mangas de camisa

shit [ʃɪt] (inf!) excl ¡mierda! (!)

shiver [ʃɪvəˠ] n escalofrío ♦ vi temblar, estremecerse; (with cold) tiritar

shock [ʃɔk] n (impact) choque m; (ELEC) descarga (eléctrica); (emotional) conmoción f; (start) sobresalto, susto; (MED) postración f nerviosa ♦ vt dar un susto a; (offend) escandalizar □ **shocking** adj (awful) espantoso; (outrageous) escandaloso

shoe [ʃu:] (pt, pp **shod**) n zapato; (for horse) herradura ♦ vt (horse) herrar □ **shoelace** n cordón m □ **shoe polish** n betún m □ **shoeshop** n zapatería

shone [ʃɔn] pt, pp of **shine**

shook [ʃʊk] pt of **shake**

shoot [ʃu:t] (pt, pp **shot**) n (on branch, seedling) retoño, vástago ♦ vt disparar; (kill) matar a tiros; (wound) pegar un tiro; (execute) fusilar; (film) rodar, filmar ♦ vi (FOOTBALL) chutar ▸ **shoot down** vt (plane) derribar ▸ **shoot up** vi (prices) dispararse □ **shooting** n (shots) tiros mpl; (HUNTING) caza con escopeta

shop [ʃɔp] n tienda; (workshop) taller m ♦ vi (also: **go shopping**) ir de compras □ **shop assistant** (BRIT) n dependiente(-a) m/f □ **shopkeeper** n tendero(-a) □ **shoplifting** n mechería □ **shopping** n (goods) compras fpl □ **shopping bag** n bolsa (de compras) □ **shopping centre** (US

shopping center) n centro comercial
❑ **shopping mall** n centro comercial
❑ **shopping trolley** n (BRIT) carrito de
la compra ❑ **shop window** n
escaparate m (SP), vidriera (LAm)

shore [ʃɔːˀ] n orilla ♦ vt: **to ~ (up)**
reforzar; **on ~** en tierra

short [ʃɔːt] adj corto; (in time) breve, de
corta duración; (person) bajo; (curt)
brusco, seco; (insufficient) insuficiente;
(a pair of) shorts (unos) pantalones
mpl cortos; **to be ~ of sth** estar falto de
algo; **in ~** en pocas palabras; **~ of
doing ...** fuera de hacer ...; **it is ~ for** es
la forma abreviada de; **to cut ~** (speech,
visit) interrumpir, terminar
inesperadamente; **everything ~ of ...**
todo menos ...; **to fall ~ of** no alcanzar;
to run ~ of quedarle a algn poco; **to
stop ~** parar en seco; **to stop ~ of**
detenerse antes de ❑ **shortage** n: a
shortage of una falta de
❑ **shortbread** n especie de mantecada
❑ **shortcoming** n defecto,
deficiencia ❑ **short(crust) pastry**
(BRIT) n pasta quebradiza ❑ **shortcut**
n atajo ❑ **shorten** vt acortar; (visit)
interrumpir ❑ **shortfall** n déficit m
❑ **shorthand** (BRIT) n taquigrafía
❑ **short-lived** adj efímero ❑ **shortly**
adv en breve, dentro de poco ❑ **shorts**
npl pantalones mpl cortos;
(US) calzoncillos mpl ❑ **short-sighted**
(BRIT) adj miope; (fig) imprudente
❑ **short-sleeved** adj de manga corta
❑ **short story** n cuento ❑ **short-
tempered** adj enojadizo ❑ **short-
term** adj (effect) a corto plazo

shot [ʃɒt] pt, pp of **shoot** ♦ n (sound)
tiro, disparo; (try) tentativa; (injection)
inyección f; (PHOT) toma, fotografía; **to
be a good/poor ~** (person) tener
buena/mala puntería; **like a ~** (without
any delay) como un rayo ❑ **shotgun** n
escopeta

should [ʃʊd] aux vb: **I ~ go now** debo
irme ahora; **he ~ be there now** debe de

haber llegado (ya); **I ~ go if I were you**
yo en tu lugar me iría; **I ~ like to** me
gustaría

shoulder [ˈʃəʊldəˀ] n hombro ♦ vt (fig)
cargar con ❑ **shoulder blade** n
omóplato

shouldn't [ˈʃʊdnt] = **should not**

shout [ʃaʊt] n grito ♦ vt gritar ♦ vi gritar,
dar voces

shove [ʃʌv] n empujón m ♦ vt empujar;
(inf: put): **to ~ sth in** meter algo a
empellones

shovel [ˈʃʌvl] n pala; (mechanical)
excavadora ♦ vt mover con pala

show [ʃəʊ] (pt **showed**, pp **shown**) n (of
emotion) demostración f; (semblance)
apariencia; (exhibition) exposición f;
(THEATRE) función f, espectáculo; (TV)
show m ♦ vt mostrar, enseñar; (courage
etc) mostrar, manifestar; (exhibit)
exponer; (film) proyectar ♦ vi
mostrarse; (appear) aparecer; **for ~**
para impresionar; **on ~** (exhibits etc)
expuesto ▶ **show in** vt (person) hacer
pasar ▶ **show off** (pej) vi presumir ♦ vt
(display) lucir ▶ **show out** vt: **to show
sb out** acompañar a algn a la puerta
▶ **show up** vi (stand out) destacar; (inf:
turn up) aparecer ♦ vt (unmask)
desenmascarar ❑ **show business** n
mundo del espectáculo

shower [ˈʃaʊəˀ] n (rain) chaparrón m,
chubasco; (of stones etc) lluvia; (for
bathing) ducha, regadera (MEX) ♦ vi
llover ♦ vt (fig): **to ~ sb with sth** colmar
a algn de algo; **to have a ~** ducharse
❑ **shower cap** n gorro de baño
❑ **shower gel** n gcl m de ducha

showing [ˈʃəʊɪŋ] n (of film) proyección f

show jumping n hípica

shown [ʃəʊn] pp of **show**

show: **show-off** (inf) n (person)
presumido(-a) ❑ **showroom** n sala de
muestras

shrank [ʃræŋk] pt of **shrink**

shred [ʃred] n (gen pl) triza, jirón m ♦ vt hacer trizas; (CULIN) desmenuzar

shrewd [ʃruːd] adj astuto

shriek [ʃriːk] n chillido ♦ vi chillar

shrimp [ʃrɪmp] n camarón m

shrine [ʃraɪn] n santuario, sepulcro

shrink [ʃrɪŋk] (pt shrank, pp shrunk) vi encogerse; (be reduced) reducirse; (also: ~ away) retroceder ♦ vt encoger ♦ n (inf, pej) loquero(-a); to ~ from (doing) sth no atreverse a hacer algo

shrivel [ʃrɪvl] (also: ~ up) vt (dry) secar ♦ vi secarse

shroud [ʃraud] n sudario ♦ vt: **shrouded in mystery** envuelto en el misterio

Shrove Tuesday [ʃrəuv-] n martes m de carnaval

shrub [ʃrʌb] n arbusto

shrug [ʃrʌg] n encogimiento de hombros ♦ vt, vi: to ~ (one's shoulders) encogerse de hombros ► shrug off vt negar importancia a

shrunk [ʃrʌŋk] pp of shrink

shudder [ʃʌdə*] n estremecimiento, escalofrío ♦ vi estremecerse

shuffle [ʃʌfl] vt (cards) barajar ♦ vi: to ~ (one's feet) arrastrar los pies

shun [ʃʌn] vt rehuir, esquivar

shut [ʃʌt] (pt, pp ~) vt cerrar ♦ vi cerrarse ► shut down vt, vi cerrar ► shut up vi (inf: keep quiet) callarse ♦ vt (close) cerrar; (silence) hacer callar □ **shutter** n contraventana; (PHOT) obturador m

shuttle [ʃʌtl] n lanzadera; (also: ~ service) servicio rápido y continuo entre dos puntos; (AVIAT) puente m aéreo □ **shuttlecock** n volante m

shy [ʃaɪ] adj tímido

sibling [sɪblɪŋ] n (formal) hermano(-a)

Sicily [sɪsɪlɪ] n Sicilia

sick [sɪk] adj (ill) enfermo; (nauseated) mareado; (humour) negro; (vomiting): **to be ~** (BRIT) vomitar; **to feel ~** tener náuseas; **to be ~ of** (fig) estar harto de □ **sickening** adj (fig) asqueroso

□ **sick leave** n baja por enfermedad

□ **sickly** adj enfermizo; (smell) nauseabundo □ **sickness** n enfermedad f, mal m; (vomiting) náuseas fpl

side [saɪd] n (gen) lado; (of body) costado; (of lake) orilla; (of hill) ladera; (team) equipo ♦ adj (door, entrance) lateral ♦ vi: **to ~ with sb** tomar el partido de algn; **by the ~ of** al lado de; **~ by ~** juntos(-as); **from ~ to ~** de un lado para otro; **from all sides** de todos lados; **to take sides (with)** tomar partido (con) □ **sideboard** n aparador m □ **sideboards** (BRIT) npl = **sideburns** □ **sideburns** npl patillas fpl □ **sidelight** n (AUT) luz f lateral □ **sideline** n (SPORT) línea de banda; (fig) empleo suplementario □ **side order** n plato de acompañamiento □ **side road** n (BRIT) calle f lateral □ **side street** n calle f lateral □ **sidetrack** vt (fig) desviar (de su propósito) □ **sidewalk** (US) n acera □ **sideways** adv de lado

siege [siːdʒ] n cerco, sitio

sieve [sɪv] n colador m ♦ vt cribar

sift [sɪft] vt cribar; (fig: information) escudriñar

sigh [saɪ] n suspiro ♦ vi suspirar

sight [saɪt] n (faculty) vista; (spectacle) espectáculo; (on gun) mira, alza ♦ vt divisar; **in ~** a la vista; **out of ~** fuera de (la) vista; **on ~** (shoot) sin previo aviso □ **sightseeing** n excursionismo, turismo; **to go sightseeing** hacer turismo

sign [saɪn] n (with hand) señal f, seña; (trace) huella, rastro; (notice) letrero; (written) signo ♦ vt firmar; (SPORT) fichar; **to ~ sth over to sb** firmar el traspaso de algo a algn ► sign for vt fus (item) firmar el recibo de ► sign in vi firmar el registro (al entrar) ► sign on vi (BRIT: as unemployed) registrarse como desempleado; (for course) inscribirse ♦ vt (MIL) alistar; (employee) contratar ▶ **sign up** vi (MIL) alistarse; (for course) inscribirse ♦ vt (player) fichar

signal ['sɪɡnl] n señal f ♦ vi señalizar ♦ vt (person) hacer señas a; (message) comunicar por señales

signature ['sɪɡnətʃə'] n firma

significance [sɪɡ'nɪfɪkəns] n (importance) trascendencia

significant [sɪɡ'nɪfɪkənt] adj significativo; (important) trascendente

signify ['sɪɡnɪfaɪ] vt significar

sign language n lenguaje m para sordomudos

signpost ['saɪnpəust] n indicador m

Sikh [siːk] adj, n sij mf

silence ['saɪləns] n silencio ♦ vt acallar; (guns) reducir al silencio

silent ['saɪlənt] adj silencioso; (not speaking) callado; (film) mudo; **to remain ~** guardar silencio

silhouette [sɪluː'et] n silueta

silicon chip ['sɪlɪkən-] n plaqueta de silicio

silk [sɪlk] n seda ♦ adj de seda

silly ['sɪlɪ] adj (person) tonto; (idea) absurdo

silver ['sɪlvə'] n plata f; (money) moneda suelta ♦ adj de plata; (colour) plateado □ **silver-plated** adj plateado

similar ['sɪmɪlə'] adj: **~ (to)** parecido or semejante (a) □ **similarity** [-'lærɪtɪ] n semejanza □ **similarly** adv del mismo modo

simmer ['sɪmə'] vi hervir a fuego lento

simple ['sɪmpl] adj (easy) sencillo; (foolish, COMM: interest) simple □ **simplicity** [-'plɪsɪtɪ] n sencillez f □ **simplify** ['sɪmplɪfaɪ] vt simplificar □ **simply** adv (live, talk) sencillamente; (just, merely) sólo

simulate ['sɪmjuːleɪt] vt fingir, simular

simultaneous [sɪml'teɪnɪəs] adj simultáneo □ **simultaneously** adv simultáneamente

sin [sɪn] n pecado ♦ vi pecar

since [sɪns] adv desde entonces, después ♦ prep desde ♦ conj (time) desde que; (because) ya que, puesto que; **~ then, ever ~** desde entonces

sincere [sɪn'sɪə'] adj sincero □ **sincerely** adv: **yours sincerely** (in letters) le saluda atentamente

sing [sɪŋ] (pt **sang**, pp **sung**) vt, vi cantar

Singapore [sɪŋə'pɔː'] n Singapur m

singer ['sɪŋə'] n cantante mf

singing ['sɪŋɪŋ] n canto

single ['sɪŋɡl] adj único, solo; (unmarried) soltero; (not double) simple, sencillo ♦ n (BRIT: also: **~ ticket**) billete m sencillo; (record) sencillo, single m; **singles** npl (TENNIS) individual m ▶ **single out** vt (choose) escoger □ **single bed** n cama individual □ **single file** n: **in single file** en fila de uno □ **single-handed** adv sin ayuda □ **single-minded** adj resuelto, firme □ **single parent** n padre or soltero, madre f soltera (o divorciado etc); **single parent family** familia monoparental □ **single room** n cuarto individual

singular ['sɪŋɡjulə'] adj (odd) raro, extraño; (outstanding) excepcional ♦ n (LING) singular m

sinister ['sɪnɪstə'] adj siniestro

sink [sɪŋk] (pt **sank**, pp **sunk**) n fregadero ♦ vt (ship) hundir, echar a pique; (foundations) excavar ♦ vi hundirse; **to ~ sth into** hundir algo en ▶ **sink in** vi (fig) penetrar, calar

sinus ['saɪnəs] n (ANAT) seno

sip [sɪp] n sorbo ♦ vt sorber, beber a sorbitos

sir [sɜː'] n señor m; **S~ John Smith** Sir John Smith; **yes ~** sí, señor

siren ['saɪərn] n sirena

sirloin ['sɜːlɔɪn] n (also: **~ steak**) solomillo

sister ['sɪstə'] n hermana; (BRIT: nurse) enfermera jefe □ **sister-in-law** n cuñada

sit [sɪt] (pt, pp **sat**) vi sentarse; (be sitting) estar sentado; (assembly) reunirse; (for painter) posar ♦ vt (exam) presentarse a ▶ **sit back** vi (in seat) recostarse ▶ **sit down** vi sentarse ▶ **sit on** vt fus (jury, committee) ser miembro de, formar parte de ▶ **sit up** vi incorporarse; (not go to bed) velar

sitcom ['sɪtkɔm] n abbr (= situation comedy) comedia de situación

site [saɪt] n sitio m; (also: **building ~**) solar m ♦ vt situar

sitting ['sɪtɪŋ] n (of assembly etc) sesión f; (in canteen) turno ❑ **sitting room** n sala de estar

situated ['sɪtjueɪtɪd] adj situado

situation [sɪtjʊ'eɪʃən] n situación f; **"situations vacant"** (BRIT) "ofrecen trabajo"

six [sɪks] num seis ❑ **sixteen** num diez y seis, dieciséis ❑ **sixteenth** [sɪks'tiːnθ] adj decimosexto ❑ **sixth** [sɪksθ] num sexto ❑ **sixth form** n (BRIT) clase f de alumnos del sexto año (de 16 a 18 años de edad) ❑ **sixth-form college** n instituto m para alumnos de 16 a 18 años ❑ **sixtieth** ['sɪkstɪɪθ] adj sexagésimo ❑ **sixty** num sesenta

size [saɪz] n tamaño m; (extent) extensión f; (of clothing) talla; (of shoes) número ❑ **sizeable** adj importante, considerable

sizzle ['sɪzl] vi crepitar

skate [skeɪt] n patín m; (fish: pl inv) raya ♦ vi patinar ❑ **skateboard** n monopatín m ❑ **skateboarding** n monopatín m ❑ **skater** n patinador(a) m/f ❑ **skating** n patinaje m ❑ **skating rink** n pista de patinaje

skeleton ['skelɪtn] n esqueleto m; (TECH) armazón f; (outline) esquema m

skeptical ['skeptɪkl] (US) = **sceptical**

sketch [sketʃ] n (drawing) dibujo; (outline) esbozo, bosquejo; (THEATRE) sketch m ♦ vt dibujar; (plan etc: also: ~ **out**) esbozar

skewer ['skjuːə'] n broqueta

ski [skiː] n esquí m ♦ vi esquiar ❑ **ski boot** n bota de esquí

skid [skɪd] n patinazo m ♦ vi patinar

ski: skier n esquiador(a) m/f ❑ **skiing** n esquí m

ski lift n telesilla m, telesquí m

skilful ['skɪlful] (US **skillfull**) adj diestro, experto

ski pole n bastón m de esquiar

skill [skɪl] n destreza, pericia; técnica ❑ **skilled** adj hábil, diestro; (worker) cualificado

skim [skɪm] vt (milk) desnatar; (glide over) rozar, rasar ♦ vi: **to ~ through** (book) hojear ❑ **skimmed milk** (US **skim milk**) n leche f desnatada

skin [skɪn] n piel f; (complexion) cutis m ♦ vt (fruit etc) pelar; (animal) despellejar ❑ **skinhead** n cabeza m/f rapada, skin(head) m/f ❑ **skinny** adj flaco

skip [skɪp] n brinco, salto; (BRIT: container) contenedor m ♦ vi brincar; (with rope) saltar a la comba ♦ vt saltarse

ski: ski pass n forfait m (de esquí) ❑ **ski pole** n bastón m de esquiar

skipper ['skɪpə'] n (NAUT, SPORT) capitán m

skipping rope ['skɪpɪŋ-] (US **skip rope**) n comba

skirt [skəːt] n falda, pollera (SC) ♦ vt (go round) ladear

skirting board ['skəːtɪŋ-] (BRIT) n rodapié m

ski slope n pista de esquí

ski suit n traje m de esquiar

skull [skʌl] n calavera; (ANAT) cráneo

skunk [skʌŋk] n mofeta

sky [skaɪ] n cielo ❑ **skyscraper** n rascacielos m inv

slab [slæb] n (stone) bloque m; (flat) losa; (of cake) trozo

slack [slæk] adj (loose) flojo; (slow) de poca actividad; (careless) descuidado ❑ **slacks** npl pantalones mpl

slain [sleɪn] *pp of* **slay**

slam [slæm] *vt (throw)* arrojar (violentamente); *(criticize)* criticar duramente ♦ *vi (door)* cerrarse de golpe; **to ~ the door** dar un portazo

slander ['slɑːndə] *n* calumnia, difamación f

slang [slæŋ] *n* argot m; *(jargon)* jerga f

slant [slɑːnt] *n* sesgo, inclinación f; *(fig)* interpretación f

slap [slæp] *n* palmada; *(in face)* bofetada ♦ *vt* dar una palmada *or* bofetada a; *(paint etc)*: **to ~ sth on sth** embadurnar algo con algo ♦ *adv (directly)* exactamente, directamente

slash [slæʃ] *vt* acuchillar; *(fig: prices)* fulminar

slate [sleɪt] *n* pizarra ♦ *vt (fig: criticize)* criticar duramente

slaughter ['slɔːtə] *n (of animals)* matanza; *(of people)* carnicería ♦ *vt* matar □ **slaughterhouse** *n* matadero

Slav [slɑːv] *adj* eslavo

slave [sleɪv] *n* esclavo(-a) ♦ *vi (also: ~ away)* sudar tinta □ **slavery** *n* esclavitud f

slay [sleɪ] *(pt* **slew**, *pp* **slain**) *vt* matar

sleazy ['sliːzɪ] *adj* de mala fama

sled [sled] *(US)* = **sledge**

sledge [sledʒ] *n* trineo

sleek [sliːk] *adj (shiny)* lustroso; *(car etc)* elegante

sleep [sliːp] *(pt, pp* **slept**) *n* sueño ♦ *vi* dormir; **to go to ~** quedarse dormido ▶ **sleep in** *vi (oversleep)* quedarse dormido ▶ **sleep together** *vi (have sex)* acostarse juntos □ **sleeper** *n (person)* durmiente mf; *(BRIT RAIL: on track)* traviesa; *(: train)* coche-cama m □ **sleeping bag** *n* saco de dormir □ **sleeping car** *n* coche-cama m □ **sleeping pill** *n* somnífero □ **sleepover** *n*: **we're having a sleepover at Jo's** nos vamos a quedar a dormir en casa de Jo □ **sleepwalk** *vi*

caminar dormido; *(habitually)* ser sonámbulo □ **sleepy** *adj* soñoliento; *(place)* soporífero

sleet [sliːt] *n* aguanieve f

sleeve [sliːv] *n* manga; *(TECH)* manguito; *(of record)* portada □ **sleeveless** *adj* sin mangas

sleigh [sleɪ] *n* trineo

slender ['slendə] *adj* delgado; *(means)* escaso

slept [slept] *pt, pp of* **sleep**

slew [sluː] *pt of* **slay** ♦ *vi (BRIT: veer)* torcerse

slice [slaɪs] *n (of meat)* tajada; *(of bread)* rebanada; *(of lemon)* rodaja; *(utensil)* pala ♦ *vt* cortar (en tajos), rebanar

slick [slɪk] *adj (skilful)* hábil, diestro; *(clever)* astuto ♦ *n (also:* **oil ~**) marea negra

slide [slaɪd] *(pt, pp* **slid**) *n (movement)* descenso, desprendimiento; *(in playground)* tobogán m; *(PHOT)* diapositiva; *(BRIT: also:* **hair ~**) pasador m ♦ *vt* correr, deslizar ♦ *vi (slip)* resbalarse; *(glide)* deslizarse □ **sliding** *adj (door)* corredizo

slight [slaɪt] *adj (slim)* delgado; *(frail)* delicado; *(pain etc)* leve; *(trivial)* insignificante; *(small)* pequeño ♦ *n (insult)* desaire m ♦ *vt (insult)* ofender, desairar; **not in the slightest** en absoluto □ **slightly** *adv* ligeramente, un poco

slim [slɪm] *adj* delgado, esbelto; *(fig: chance)* remoto ♦ *vi* adelgazar □ **slimming** *n* adelgazamiento

slimy ['slaɪmɪ] *adj* cenagoso

sling [slɪŋ] *(pt, pp* **slung**) *n (MED)* cabestrillo; *(weapon)* honda ♦ *vt* tirar, arrojar

slip [slɪp] *n (slide)* resbalón m; *(mistake)* descuido; *(underskirt)* combinación f; *(of paper)* papelito ♦ *vt (slide)* deslizar ♦ *vi* deslizarse; *(stumble)* resbalar(se); *(decline)* decaer; *(move smoothly)*: **to ~ into/out of** *(room etc)* introducirse en/

salirse de; **to give sb the ~** eludir a algn; **a ~ of the tongue** un lapsus; **to ~ sth on/off** ponerse/quitarse algo
  ▶ **slip up** vi (make mistake) equivocarse; meter la pata

slipper ['slɪpə'] n zapatilla, pantufla

slippery ['slɪpəri] adj resbaladizo

slip road (BRIT) n carretera de acceso

slit [slɪt] (pt, pp ~) n raja; (cut) corte m ♦ vt rajar; cortar

slog [slɔg] (BRIT) vi sudar tinta; **it was a ~** costó trabajo (hacerlo)

slogan ['sləʊgən] n eslogan m, lema m

slope [sləʊp] n (up) cuesta, pendiente f; (down) declive m; (side of mountain) falda, vertiente m ♦ vi: **to ~ down** estar en declive; **to ~ up** inclinarse
  □ **sloping** adj en pendiente; en declive; (writing) inclinado

sloppy ['slɔpi] adj (work) descuidado; (appearance) desaliñado

slot [slɔt] n ranura ♦ vt: **to ~ into** encajar en □ **slot machine** n (BRIT: vending machine) distribuidor m automático; (for gambling) tragaperras m inv

Slovakia [sləʊ'vækɪə] n Eslovaquia

Slovene [sləʊ'viːn] adj esloveno ♦ n esloveno(-a); (LING) esloveno

Slovenia [sləʊ'viːnɪə] n Eslovenia
  □ **Slovenian** adj, n = **Slovene**

slow [sləʊ] adj lento; (not clever) lerdo; (watch): **to be ~** atrasar ♦ adv lentamente, despacio ♦ vt, vi retardar; **"~" (road sign)** "disminuir velocidad"
  ▶ **slow down** vi reducir la marcha
  □ **slowly** adv lentamente, despacio
  □ **slow motion** n: **in slow motion** a cámara lenta

slug [slʌg] n babosa; (bullet) posta □ **sluggish** adj lento; (person) perezoso

slum [slʌm] n casucha

slump [slʌmp] n (economic) depresión f ♦ vi hundirse; (prices) caer en picado

slung [slʌŋ] pt, pp of **sling**

slur [slɜː'] n: **to cast a ~ on** insultar ♦ vt (speech) pronunciar mal

sly [slaɪ] adj astuto; (smile) taimado

smack [smæk] n bofetada ♦ vt dar con la mano a; (child, on face) abofetear ♦ vi: **to ~ of** saber a, oler a

small [smɔːl] adj pequeño □ **small ads** (BRIT) npl anuncios mpl por palabras □ **small change** n suelto, cambio

smart [smɑːt] adj elegante; (clever) listo, inteligente; (quick) rápido, vivo ♦ vi escocer, picar □ **smartcard** n tarjeta inteligente

smash [smæʃ] n (also: ~-up) choque m; (MUS) exitazo ♦ vt (break) hacer pedazos; (car etc) estrellar; (SPORT: record) batir ♦ vi hacerse pedazos; (against wall etc) estrellarse □ **smashing** (inf) adj estupendo

smear [smɪə'] n mancha; (MED) frotis m inv ♦ vt untar □ **smear test** n (MED) citología, frotis m inv (cervical)

smell [smɛl] (pt, pp smelt or smelled) n olor m; (sense) olfato ♦ vt, vi oler □ **smelly** adj maloliente

smelt [smɛlt] pt, pp of **smell**

smile [smaɪl] n sonrisa ♦ vi sonreír

smirk [smɜːk] n sonrisa falsa or afectada

smog [smɔg] n esmog m

smoke [sməʊk] n humo ♦ vi fumar; (chimney) echar humo ♦ vt (cigarettes) fumar □ **smoke alarm** n detector m de humo, alarma contra incendios □ **smoked** adj (bacon, glass) ahumado □ **smoker** n fumador(a) m/f; (RAIL) coche m fumador □ **smoking** n: **"no smoking"** "prohibido fumar" □ **smoky** adj (room) lleno de humo; (taste) ahumado

⚠ Be careful not to translate **smoking** by the Spanish word smoking.

smooth [smuːð] adj liso; (sea) tranquilo; (flavour, movement) suave;

(*sauce*) fino; (*person: pej*) meloso ♦ *vt* (*also*: **~ out**) alisar; (*creases, difficulties*) allanar

smother ['smʌðə'] *vt* sofocar; (*repress*) contener

SMS *n abbr* (= *short message service*) (servicio) SMS ❑ **SMS message** *n* (mensaje *m*) SMS

smudge [smʌdʒ] *n* mancha ♦ *vt* manchar

smug [smʌg] *adj* presumido; orondo

smuggle ['smʌgl] *vt* pasar de contrabando ❑ **smuggling** *n* contrabando

snack [snæk] *n* bocado ❑ **snack bar** *n* cafetería

snag [snæg] *n* problema *m*

snail [sneɪl] *n* caracol *m*

snake [sneɪk] *n* serpiente *f*

snap [snæp] *n* (*sound*) chasquido; (*photograph*) foto *f* ♦ *adj* (*decision*) instantáneo ♦ *vt* (*break*) quebrar; (*fingers*) castañetear ♦ *vi* quebrarse; (*fig: speak sharply*) contestar bruscamente; **to ~ shut** cerrarse de golpe ► **snap at** *vt fus* (*dog*) intentar morder ► **snap up** *vt* agarrar ❑ **snapshot** *n* foto *f* (instantánea)

snarl [snɑːl] *vi* gruñir

snatch [snætʃ] *n* (*small piece*) fragmento ♦ *vt* (*snatch away*) arrebatar; (*fig*) agarrar; **to ~ some sleep** encontrar tiempo para dormir

sneak [sniːk] (*US: pt* **snuck**) *vi*: **to ~ in/ out** entrar/salir a hurtadillas ♦ *n* (*inf*) soplón(-ona) *m/f*; **to ~ up on sb** aparecérsele de improviso a algn ❑ **sneakers** *npl* zapatos *mpl* de lona

sneer [snɪə'] *vi* reír con sarcasmo; (*mock*): **to ~ at** burlarse de

sneeze [sniːz] *vi* estornudar

sniff [snɪf] *vi* sollozar ♦ *vt* husmear, oler; (*drugs*) esnifar

snigger ['snɪgə'] *vi* reírse con disimulo

snip [snɪp] *n* tijeretazo; (*BRIT: inf: bargain*) ganga ♦ *vt* tijeretear

sniper ['snaɪpə'] *n* francotirador(a) *m/f*

snob [snɔb] *n* (e)snob *mf*

snooker ['snuːkə'] *n* especie de billar

snoop [snuːp] *vi*: **to ~ about** fisgonear

snooze [snuːz] *n* siesta ♦ *vi* echar una siesta

snore [snɔː'] *n* ronquido ♦ *vi* roncar

snorkel ['snɔːkl] *n* (tubo) respirador *m*

snort [snɔːt] *n* bufido ♦ *vi* bufar

snow [snəʊ] *n* nieve *f* ♦ *vi* nevar ❑ **snowball** *n* bola de nieve ♦ *vi* (*fig*) agrandirse, ampliare ❑ **snowstorm** *n* nevada, nevasca

snub [snʌb] *vt* (*person*) desairar ♦ *n* desaire *m*, repulsa

snug [snʌg] *adj* (*cosy*) cómodo; (*fitted*) ajustado

KEYWORD

[səʊ] *adv*

1 (*thus, likewise*) así, de este modo; **if so** de ser así; **I like swimming — so do I** a mí me gusta nadar — a mí también; **I've got work to do — so has Paul** tengo trabajo que hacer — Paul también; **it's 5 o'clock — so it is!** son las cinco — ¡pues es verdad!; **I hope/think so** espero/creo que sí; **so far** hasta ahora; (*in past*) hasta este momento

2 (*in comparisons etc: to such a degree*) tan; **so quickly (that)** tan rápido (que); **so big (that)** tan grande (que); **she's not so clever as her brother** no es tan lista como su hermano; **we were so worried** estábamos preocupadísimos

3: **so much** *adj, adv* tanto; **so many** tantos(-as)

4 (*phrases*): **10 or so** unos 10, 10 o así; **so long!** (*inf: goodbye*) ¡hasta luego! ♦ *conj*

1 (*expressing purpose*): **so as to do**

para hacer; **so (that)** para que +*subjun*

2 (*expressing result*) así que; **so you see, I could have gone** así que ya ves, (yo) podría haber ido

soak [səuk] *vt* (*drench*) empapar; (*steep in water*) remojar ♦ *vi* remojarse, estar a remojo ▶ **soak up** *vt* absorber ❑ **soaking** *adj* (*also:* **soaking wet**) calado *or* empapado (hasta los huesos *or* el tuétano)

so-and-so [ˈsəuənsəu] *n* (*somebody*) fulano(-a) de tal

soap [səup] *n* jabón *m* ❑ **soap opera** *n* telenovela ❑ **soap powder** *n* jabón *m* en polvo

soar [sɔːʳ] *vi* (*on wings*) remontarse; (*rocket: prices*) dispararse; (*building etc*) elevarse

sob [sɒb] *n* sollozo ♦ *vi* sollozar

sober [ˈsəubəʳ] *adj* (*serious*) serio; (*not drunk*) sobrio; (*colour, style*) discreto ▶ **sober up** *vt* quitar la borrachera

so-called [ˈsəuˈkɔːld] *adj* así llamado

soccer [ˈsɒkəʳ] *n* fútbol *m*

sociable [ˈsəuʃəbl] *adj* sociable

social [ˈsəuʃl] *adj* social ♦ *n* velada, fiesta ❑ **socialism** *n* socialismo ❑ **socialist** *adj, n* socialista *mf* ❑ **to socialize** *vi*: **to socialize (with)** alternar (con) ❑ **social life** *n* vida social ❑ **socially** *adv* socialmente ❑ **social security** *n* seguridad *f* social ❑ **social services** *npl* servicios *mpl* sociales ❑ **social work** *n* asistencia social ❑ **social worker** *n* asistente(-a) *m/f* social

society [səˈsaɪətɪ] *n* sociedad *f*; (*club*) asociación *f*; (*also:* **high ~**) alta sociedad

sociology [səusɪˈɒlədʒɪ] *n* sociología

sock [sɒk] *n* calcetín *m*

socket [ˈsɒkɪt] *n* cavidad *f*; (*BRIT ELEC*) enchufe *m*

soda [ˈsəudə] *n* (*CHEM*) sosa; (*also: ~ water*) soda; (*US: also: ~ pop*) gaseosa

sodium [ˈsəudɪəm] *n* sodio

sofa [ˈsəufə] *n* sofá *m* ❑ **sofa bed** *n* sofá-cama *m*

soft [sɒft] *adj* (*lenient, not hard*) blando; (*gentle, not bright*) suave ❑ **soft drink** *n* bebida no alcohólica ❑ **soft drugs** *npl* drogas *fpl* blandas ❑ **soften** [ˈsɔfn] *vt* ablandar; suavizar; (*effect*) amortiguar ♦ *vi* ablandarse; suavizarse ❑ **softly** *adv* suavemente; (*gently*) delicadamente, con delicadeza ❑ **software** *n* (*COMPUT*) software *m*

soggy [ˈsɒgɪ] *adj* empapado

soil [sɔɪl] *n* (*earth*) tierra, suelo ♦ *vt* ensuciar

solar [ˈsəuləʳ] *adj* solar ❑ **solar power** *n* energía solar ❑ **solar system** *n* sistema *m* solar

sold [səuld] *pt, pp* of **sell**

soldier [ˈsəuldʒəʳ] *n* soldado; (*army man*) militar *m*

sold out *adj* (*COMM*) agotado

sole [səul] *n* (*of foot*) planta; (*of shoe*) suela; (*fish: pl inv*) lenguado ♦ *adj* único ❑ **solely** *adv* únicamente, sólo, solamente; **I will hold you solely responsible** le consideraré el único responsable

solemn [ˈsɒləm] *adj* solemne

solicitor [səˈlɪsɪtəʳ] (*BRIT*) *n* (*for wills etc*) ≈ notario(-a); (*in court*) ≈ abogado(-a)

solid [ˈsɒlɪd] *adj* sólido; (*gold etc*) macizo ♦ *n* sólido

solitary [ˈsɒlɪtərɪ] *adj* solitario, solo

solitude [ˈsɒlɪtjuːd] *n* soledad *f*

solo [ˈsəuləu] *n* solo ♦ *adv* (*fly*) en solitario ❑ **soloist** *n* solista *m/f*

soluble [ˈsɒljubl] *adj* soluble

solution [səˈluːʃən] *n* solución *f*

solve [sɒlv] *vt* resolver, solucionar

solvent [ˈsɒlvənt] *adj* (*COMM*) solvente ♦ *n* (*CHEM*) solvente *m*

sombre [ˈsɒmbəʳ] (*US* **somber**) *adj* sombrío

some

KEYWORD

[sʌm] adj

1 (a certain amount or number): **some tea/water/biscuits** té/agua/(unas) galletas; **there's some milk in the fridge** hay leche en el frigo; **there were some people outside** había algunas personas fuera; **I've got some money, but not much** tengo algo de dinero, pero no mucho

2 (certain: in contrasts) algunos(-as); **some people say that ...** hay quien dice que ...; **some films were excellent, but most were mediocre** hubo películas excelentes, pero la mayoría fueron mediocres

3 (unspecified): **some woman was asking for you** una mujer estuvo preguntando por ti; **he was asking for some book (or other)** pedía un libro; **some day** algún día; **some day next week** un día de la semana que viene

♦ pron

1 (a certain number): **I've got some** (books etc) tengo algunos(-as)

2 (a certain amount): **I've got some** (money, milk) tengo algo; **could I have some of that cheese?** ¿me puede dar un poco de ese queso?; **I've read some of the book** he leído parte del libro

♦ adv: **some 10 people** unas 10 personas, una decena de personas

some: **somebody** ['sʌmbədɪ] pron = **someone** ❑ **somehow** adv de alguna manera; (for some reason) por una u otra razón ❑ **someone** pron alguien ❑ **someplace** (US) adv = **somewhere** ❑ **something** pron algo; **would you like something to eat/drink?** ¿te gustaría cenar/tomar algo? ❑ **sometime** adv (in future) algún día, en algún momento; (in past): **sometime last month** durante el mes pasado ❑ **sometimes** adv a veces ❑ **somewhat** adv algo ❑ **somewhere** adv (be) en alguna parte; (go) a alguna parte; **somewhere else** (be) en otra parte; (go) a otra parte

son [sʌn] n hijo

song [sɒŋ] n canción f

son-in-law ['sʌnɪnlɔ:] n yerno

soon [su:n] adv pronto, dentro de poco; ~ **afterwards** poco después; see also **as** ❑ **sooner** adv (time) antes, más temprano; (preference: rather): **I would sooner do that** preferiría hacer eso; **sooner or later** tarde o temprano

soothe [su:ð] vt tranquilizar; (pain) aliviar

sophisticated [sə'fɪstɪkeɪtɪd] adj sofisticado

sophomore ['sɒfəmɔ:'] (US) n estudiante mf de segundo año

soprano [sə'prɑ:nəu] n soprano f

sorbet ['sɔ:beɪ] n sorbete m

sordid ['sɔ:dɪd] adj (place etc) sórdido; (motive etc) mezquino

sore [sɔ:'] adj (painful) doloroso, que duele ♦ n llaga

sorrow ['sɒrəu] n pena, dolor m

sorry ['sɒrɪ] adj (regretful) arrepentido; (condition, excuse) lastimoso; ~! ¡perdón!, ¡perdone!; ~? ¿cómo?; **to feel ~ for sb** tener lástima a algn; **I feel ~ for him** me da lástima

sort [sɔ:t] n clase f, género, tipo ► **sort out** vt +adv (papers) clasificar; (organize) ordenar, organizar; (resolve: problem, situation etc) arreglar, solucionar

SOS n SOS m

so-so ['səusəu] adv regular, así así

sought [sɔ:t] pt, pp of **seek**

soul [səul] n alma

sound [saund] n (noise) sonido, ruido; (volume: on TV etc) volumen m; (GEO) estrecho ♦ adj (healthy) sano; (safe, not damaged) en buen estado; (reliable: person) digno de confianza; (sensible) sensato, razonable ♦ adv: ~ asleep profundamente dormido ♦ vt (alarm) sonar ♦ vi sonar, resonar; (fig: seem) parecer; to ~ like sonar a □ **soundtrack** n (of film) banda sonora

soup [su:p] n (thick) sopa; (thin) caldo

sour ['sauə] adj agrio; (milk) cortado; it's ~ grapes es envidia

source [sɔ:s] n fuente f

south [sauθ] n sur m ♦ adj del sur, sureño ♦ adv al sur, hacia el sur □ **South Africa** n África del Sur □ **South African** adj, n sudafricano(-a) m/f □ **South America** n América del Sur, Sudamérica □ **South American** adj, n sudamericano(-a) m/f □ **southbound** adj (con) rumbo al sur □ **southeastern** [sauθ'i:stən] adj sureste, del sureste □ **southern** ['sʌðən] adj del sur, meridional □ **South Korea** n Corea del Sur □ **South Pole** n Polo Sur □ **southward(s)** adv hacia el sur □ **south-west** n suroeste □ **southwestern** [sauθ'westən] adj suroeste

souvenir [su:və'nɪə] n recuerdo

sovereign ['sɔvrɪn] adj, n soberano(-a) m/f

sow¹ [sau] (pt sowed, pp sown) vt sembrar

sow² [sau] n cerda, puerca

soya ['sɔɪə] (BRIT) n soja

spa [spa:] n balneario

space [speɪs] n espacio; (room) sitio ♦ cpd espacial ♦ vt (also: ~ out) espaciar □ **spacecraft** n nave f espacial □ **spaceship** n = spacecraft

spacious ['speɪʃəs] adj amplio

spade [speɪd] n (tool) pala, laya; **spades** npl (CARDS: British) picas fpl; (: Spanish) espadas fpl

spaghetti [spə'gɛti] n espaguetis mpl, fideos mpl

Spain [speɪn] n España

spam [spæm] n (junk e-mail) spam m

span [spæn] n (of bird, plane) envergadura; (of arch) luz f; (in time) lapso ♦ vt extenderse sobre, cruzar; (fig) abarcar

Spaniard ['spænjəd] n español(a) m/f

Spanish ['spænɪʃ] adj español(a) ♦ n (LING) español m, castellano; **the ~** npl los españoles

spank [spæŋk] vt zurrar

spanner ['spænə] (BRIT) n llave f (inglesa)

spare [speə] adj de reserva; (surplus) sobrante, de más ♦ n = spare part ♦ vt (do without) pasarse sin; (refrain from hurting) perdonar; **to ~** (surplus) sobrante, de sobra □ **spare part** n pieza de repuesto □ **spare room** n cuarto de los invitados □ **spare time** n tiempo libre □ **spare tyre** (US **spare tire**) n (AUT) neumático or llanta (LAm) de recambio □ **spare wheel** n (AUT) rueda de recambio

spark [spa:k] n chispa; (fig) chispazo □ **spark(ing) plug** n bujía

sparkle ['spa:kl] n centelleo, destello ♦ vi (shine) relucir, brillar

sparrow ['spærəu] n gorrión m

sparse [spa:s] adj esparcido, escaso

spasm ['spæzəm] n (MED) espasmo

spat [spæt] pt, pp of spit

spate [speɪt] n (fig): **a ~ of** un torrente de

spatula ['spætjulə] n espátula

speak [spi:k] (pt spoke, pp spoken) vt (language) hablar; (truth) decir ♦ vi hablar; (make a speech) intervenir; **to ~ to sb/of or about sth** hablar con algn/de or sobre algo; **~ up!** ¡habla fuerte! □ **speaker** n (in public) orador(a) m/f;

(also: **loudspeaker***)* altavoz *m*; *(for stereo etc)* bafle *m*; *(POL:)* **the Speaker** *(BRIT)* el Presidente de la Cámara de los Comunes; *(US)* el Presidente del Congreso

spear [spɪə^r] *n* lanza ♦ *vt* alancear

special ['spɛʃl] *adj* especial; *(edition etc)* extraordinario; *(delivery)* urgente ❑ **special delivery** *(POST):* **by special delivery** por entrega urgente ❑ **special effects** *npl (CINE)* efectos *mpl* especiales ❑ **specialist** *n* especialista *mf* ❑ **speciality** [speʃɪˈælɪtɪ] *(BRIT)* n especialidad *f* ❑ **to specialize (in)** especializarse (en) ❑ **specially** *adv* sobre todo, en particular ❑ **special needs** *npl (BRIT):* **children with special needs** niños que requieren una atención diferenciada ❑ **special offer** *n (COMM)* oferta especial ❑ **special school** *n (BRIT)* colegio *m* de educación especial ❑ **specialty** *(US)* n = **speciality**

species ['spiːʃiːz] *n inv* especie *f*

specific [spəˈsɪfɪk] *adj* específico ❑ **specifically** *adv* específicamente

specify ['spesɪfaɪ] *vt, vi* especificar, precisar

specimen ['spesɪmən] *n* ejemplar *m*; *(MED: of urine)* espécimen *m*; *(: of blood)* muestra

speck [spek] *n* grano, mota

spectacle ['spektəkl] *n* espectáculo; **spectacles** *npl (BRIT: glasses)* gafas *fpl* (SP), anteojos *mpl* ❑ **spectacular** [-'tækjulə^r] *adj* espectacular; *(success)* impresionante

spectator [spek'teɪtə^r] *n* espectador(a) *m/f*

spectrum ['spektrəm] *(pl* **spectra***) n* espectro

speculate ['spekjuleɪt] *vi:* **to ~ (on)** especular (en)

sped [sped] *pt, pp* of **speed**

speech [spiːtʃ] *n (faculty)* habla; *(formal talk)* discurso; *(spoken language)*

lenguaje *m* ❑ **speechless** *adj* mudo, estupefacto

speed [spiːd] *n* velocidad *f*; *(haste)* prisa; *(promptness)* rapidez *f*; **at full** or **top ~** a máxima velocidad ▶ **speed up** *vi* acelerarse ♦ *vt* acelerar ❑ **speedboat** *n* lancha motora ❑ **speeding** *n (AUT)* exceso de velocidad ❑ **speed limit** *n* límite *m* de velocidad, velocidad *f* máxima ❑ **speedometer** [spɪ'dɒmɪtə^r] *n* velocímetro ❑ **speedy** *adj (fast)* veloz, rápido; *(prompt)* pronto

spell [spel] *(pt, pp* **spelt** *(Brit)* or **spelled***) n (also:* **magic ~***)* encanto, hechizo; *(period of time)* rato, período ♦ *vt* deletrear; *(fig)* anunciar, presagiar; **to cast a ~ on sb** hechizar a algn; **he can't ~** pone faltas de ortografía ▶ **spell out** *vt (explain):* **to spell sth out for sb** explicar algo a algn en detalle ❑ **spellchecker** ['speltʃekə^r] *n* corrector *m* ortográfico ❑ **spelling** *n* ortografía

spelt [spelt] *pt, pp* of **spell**

spend [spend] *(pt, pp* **spent***) vt (money)* gastar; *(time)* pasar; *(life)* dedicar ❑ **spending** *n:* **government spending** gastos *mpl* del gobierno

spent [spent] *pt, pp* of **spend** ♦ *adj (cartridge, bullets, match)* usado

sperm [spɜːm] *n* esperma

sphere [sfɪə^r] *n* esfera

spice [spaɪs] *n* especia ♦ *vt* condimentar

spicy ['spaɪsɪ] *adj* picante

spider ['spaɪdə^r] *n* araña

spike [spaɪk] *n (point)* punta; *(BOT)* espiga

spill [spɪl] *(pt, pp* **spilt** *or* **spilled***) vt* derramar, verter ♦ *vi* derramarse; **to ~ over** desbordarse

spin [spɪn] *(pt, pp* **spun***) n (AVIAT)* barrena; *(trip in car)* paseo *(en coche)*; *(on ball)* efecto ♦ *vt (wool etc)* hilar; *(ball etc)* hacer girar ♦ *vi* girar, dar vueltas

spinach ['spɪnɪtʃ] n espinaca; (as food) espinacas fpl

spinal ['spaɪnl] adj espinal

spin doctor n informador(a) parcial al servicio de un partido político etc

spin-dryer (BRIT) n secador m centrifugo

spine [spaɪn] n espinazo, columna vertebral; (thorn) espina

spiral ['spaɪərl] n espiral f ♦ vi (fig: prices) subir desorbitadamente

spire ['spaɪə'] n aguja, chapitel m

♦ **spirit** ['spɪrɪt] n (soul) alma; (ghost) fantasma m; (attitude, sense) espíritu m; (courage) valor m, ánimo; **spirits** npl (drink) licor(es) m(pl); **in good spirits** alegre, de buen ánimo

spiritual ['spɪrɪtjuəl] adj espiritual ♦ n espiritual m

spit [spɪt] (pt, pp spat) n (for roasting) asador m, espetón m; (saliva) saliva ♦ vi escupir; (sound) chisporrotear; (rain) lloviznar

spite [spaɪt] n rencor m, ojeriza ♦ vt causar pena a, mortificar; **in ~ of** a pesar de, pese a □ **spiteful** adj rencoroso, malévolo

splash [splæʃ] n (sound) chapoteo; (of colour) mancha ♦ vt salpicar ♦ vi (also: ~ about) chapotear ▶ **splash out** (inf) vi (BRIT) derrochar dinero

splendid ['splendɪd] adj espléndido

splinter ['splɪntə'] n (of wood etc) astilla; (in finger) espigón m ♦ vi astillarse, hacer astillas

split [splɪt] (pt, pp ~~) n hendedura, raja; (fig) división f; (POL) escisión f ♦ vt partir, rajar; (party) dividir; (share) repartir ♦ vi dividirse, escindirse ▶ **split up** vi (couple) separarse; (meeting) acabarse

spoil [spɔɪl] (pt, pp spoilt or spoiled) vt (damage) dañar; (mar) estropear; (child) mimar, consentir

spoilt [spɔɪlt] pt, pp of **spoil** ♦ adj (child) mimado, consentido; (ballot paper) invalidado

spoke [spəʊk] pt of **speak** ♦ n rayo, radio

spoken ['spəʊkn] pp of **speak**

spokesman ['spəʊksmən] (irreg) n portavoz m

spokesperson ['spəʊkspɜːsn] (irreg) n portavoz m/f, vocero(-a) (LAm)

spokeswoman ['spəʊkswʊmən] (irreg) n portavoz f

sponge [spʌndʒ] n esponja; (also: ~ cake) bizcocho ♦ vt (wash) lavar con esponja ♦ vi: **to ~ off** or **on sb** vivir a costa de algn □ **sponge bag** (BRIT) n esponjera

sponsor ['spɒnsə'] n patrocinador(a) m/f ♦ vt (applicant, proposal etc) proponer □ **sponsorship** n patrocinio

spontaneous [spɒn'teɪnɪəs] adj espontáneo

spooky ['spuːkɪ] (inf) adj espeluznante, horripilante

spoon [spuːn] n cuchara □ **spoonful** n cucharada

sport [spɔːt] n deporte m; (person): **to be a good ~** ser muy majo ♦ vt (wear) lucir, ostentar □ **sport jacket** (US) n = **sports jacket** □ **sports car** n coche m deportivo □ **sports centre** (BRIT) n polideportivo □ **sports jacket** (BRIT) n chaqueta deportiva □ **sportsman** (irreg) n deportista m □ **sportswear** n trajes mpl de deporte or sport □ **sportswoman** (irreg) n deportista f □ **sporty** adj deportista

spot [spɒt] n sitio, lugar m; (dot: on pattern) punto, mancha; (pimple) grano; (RADIO) cuña publicitaria; (TV) espacio publicitario; (small amount): **a ~ of** un poquito de ♦ vt (notice) notar, observar; **on the ~** allí mismo □ **spotless** adj perfectamente limpio □ **spotlight** n foco, reflector m; (AUT) faro auxiliar

spouse [spauz] n cónyuge mf

sprain [spreɪn] n torcedura ♦ vt: **to ~ one's ankle/wrist** torcerse el tobillo/la muñeca

sprang [spræŋ] pt of **spring**

sprawl [sprɔːl] vi tumbarse

spray [spreɪ] n rociada; (of sea) espuma; (container) atomizador m; (for paint etc) pistola rociadora; (of flowers) ramita ♦ vt rociar; (crops) regar

spread [spred] (pt, pp ~) n extensión f; (for bread etc) pasta para untar; (inf: food) comilona ♦ vt extender; (butter) untar; (wings, sails) desplegar; (work, wealth) repartir; (scatter) esparcir ♦ vi (also: ~ **out**: stain) extenderse; (news) diseminarse ▶ **spread out** vi (move apart) separarse ❑ **spreadsheet** n hoja electrónica or de cálculo

spree [spriː] n: **to go on a ~** ir de juerga

spring [sprɪŋ] (pt **sprang**, pp **sprung**) n (season) primavera; (leap) salto, brinco; (coiled metal) resorte m; (of water) fuente f, manantial m ♦ vi saltar, brincar ▶ **spring up** vi (thing: appear) aparecer; (problem) surgir ❑ **spring onion** n cebolleta

sprinkle [sprɪŋkl] vt (pour: liquid) rociar; (: salt, sugar) espolvorear; **to ~ water etc on, ~ with water** etc rociar or salpicar de agua etc

sprint [sprɪnt] n esprint m ♦ vi esprintar

sprung [sprʌŋ] pp of **spring**

spun [spʌn] pt, pp of **spin**

spur [spəːʳ] n espuela; (fig) estímulo, aguijón m ♦ vt (also: ~ **on**) estimular, incitar; **on the ~ of the moment** de improviso

spurt [spəːt] n chorro; (of energy) arrebato ♦ vi chorrear

spy [spaɪ] n espía mf ♦ vi: **to ~ on** espiar a ♦ vt (see) divisar, lograr ver

sq. abbr = **square**

squabble [skwɔbl] vi reñir, pelear

squad [skwɔd] n (MIL) pelotón m; (POLICE) brigada; (SPORT) equipo

squadron [skwɔdrn] n (MIL) escuadrón m; (AVIAT, NAUT) escuadra

squander [skwɔndəʳ] vt (money) derrochar, despilfarrar; (chances) desperdiciar

square [skweəʳ] n cuadro; (in town) plaza; (inf: person) carca m/f ♦ adj cuadrado; (inf: ideas, tastes) trasnochado ♦ vt (arrange) arreglar; (MATH) cuadrar; (reconcile) compaginar; **all ~** igual(es); **to have a ~ meal** comer caliente; **2 metres ~** 2 metros en cuadro; **2 ~ metres** 2 metros cuadrados ❑ **square root** n raíz f cuadrada

squash [skwɔʃ] n (BRIT: drink): **lemon/orange ~** zumo (SP) or jugo (LAm) de limón/naranja; (US BOT: vegetable) calabacín m; (SPORT) squash m ♦ vt aplastar

squat [skwɔt] adj achaparrado ♦ vi (also: ~ **down**) agacharse, sentarse en cuclillas ❑ **squatter** n okupa mf (SP)

squeak [skwiːk] vi (hinge) chirriar, rechinar; (mouse) chillar

squeal [skwiːl] vi chillar, dar gritos agudos

squeeze [skwiːz] n presión f; (of hand) apretón m; (COMM) restricción f ♦ vt (hand, arm) apretar

squid [skwɪd] n inv calamar m; (CULIN) calamares mpl

squint [skwɪnt] vi bizquear, ser bizco ♦ n (MED) estrabismo

squirm [skwəːm] vi retorcerse, revolverse

squirrel [skwɪrəl] n ardilla

squirt [skwəːt] vi salir a chorros ♦ vt chiscar

Sr abbr = **senior**

Sri Lanka [srɪˈlæŋkə] n Sri Lanka m

St abbr = **saint**; **street**

stab [stæb] n (with knife) puñalada; (of pain) pinchazo; (inf: try): **to have a ~ at (doing) sth** intentar (hacer) algo ♦ vt apuñalar

stability [stəˈbɪlɪtɪ] n estabilidad f

stable ['steɪbl] adj estable ♦ n cuadra, caballeriza

stack [stæk] n montón m, pila ♦ vt amontonar, apilar

stadium ['steɪdɪəm] n estadio

staff [stɑːf] n (work force) personal m, plantilla; (BRIT SCOL) cuerpo docente ♦ vt proveer de personal

stag [stæg] n ciervo, venado

stage [steɪdʒ] n (in theatre) escena; (point) etapa; (platform) plataforma; (profession): **the ~** el teatro ♦ vt (play) poner en escena, representar; (organize) montar, organizar; **in stages** por etapas

stagger ['stægə'] vi tambalearse ♦ vt (amaze) asombrar; (hours, holidays) escalonar ❑ **staggering** adj asombroso

stagnant ['stægnənt] adj estancado

stag night, stag party n despedida de soltero

stain [steɪn] n mancha; (colouring) tintura ♦ vt manchar; (wood) teñir ❑ **stained glass** n vidrio m de color ❑ **stainless steel** n acero inoxidable

staircase ['steəkeɪs] n = **stairway**

stairs [steəz] npl escaleras fpl

stairway ['steəweɪ] n escalera

stake [steɪk] n estaca, poste m; (COMM) interés m; (BETTING) apuesta ♦ vt (money) apostar; (life) arriesgar; (reputation) poner en juego; (claim) presentar una reclamación; **to be at ~** estar en juego

stale [steɪl] adj (bread) duro; (food) pasado; (smell) rancio; (beer) agrio

stalk [stɔːk] n tallo, caña ♦ vt acechar, cazar al acecho

stall [stɔːl] n (in market) puesto; (in stable) casilla (de establo) ♦ vt (AUT) calar; (fig) dar largas a ♦ vi (AUT) calarse; (fig) andarse con rodeos

stamina ['stæmɪnə] n resistencia

stammer ['stæmə'] n tartamudeo ♦ vi tartamudear

stamp [stæmp] n sello (SP); estampilla (LAm); timbre m (MEX); (on document) timbre m ♦ vi (also: **~ one's foot**) patear ♦ vt (mark) marcar; (letter) franquear; (with rubber stamp) sellar ► **stamp out** vt (fire) apagar con el pie; (crime, opposition) acabar con ❑ **stamped addressed envelope** n (BRIT) sobre m sellado con las señas propias

stampede [stæm'piːd] n estampida

stance [stæns] n postura

stand [stænd] (pt, pp stood) n (position) posición f, postura; (for taxis) parada; (hall stand) perchero; (music stand) atril m; (SPORT) tribuna; (at exhibition) stand m ♦ vi (be) estar, encontrarse; (be on foot) estar de pie; (rise) levantarse; (remain) quedar en pie; (in election) presentar candidatura ♦ vt (place) poner, colocar; (withstand) aguantar, soportar; (invite to) invitar; **to take a ~** (fig) mantener una postura firme; **to ~ for parliament** (BRIT) presentarse (como candidato) a las elecciones ► **stand back** vi retirarse ► **stand by** vi (be ready) estar listo ♦ vt fus (opinion) aferrarse a; (person) apoyar ► **stand down** vi (withdraw) ceder el puesto ► **stand for** vt fus (signify) significar; (tolerate) aguantar, permitir ► **stand in for** vt fus suplir a ► **stand out** vi destacarse ► **stand up** vi levantarse, ponerse de pie ► **stand up for** vt fus defender ► **stand up to** vt fus hacer frente a

standard ['stændəd] n patrón m, norma; (level) nivel m; (flag) estandarte m ♦ adj (size etc) normal, corriente; (text) básico; **standards** npl (morals) valores mpl morales ❑ **standard of living** n nivel m de vida

standing ['stændɪŋ] adj (on foot) de pie, en pie; (permanent) permanente ♦ n reputación f; **of many years' ~** que lleva muchos años ❑ **standing order**

(BRIT) n (at bank) orden f de pago permanente

stand: standpoint n punto de vista ❏ **standstill** n: **at a standstill** (industry, traffic) paralizado; (car) parado; **to come to a standstill** quedar paralizado; pararse

stank [stæŋk] pt of **stink**

staple ['steɪpl] n (for papers) grapa ♦ adj (food etc) básico ♦ vt grapar

star [staː^r] n estrella; (celebrity) estrella, astro ♦ vt (THEATRE, CINEMA) ser el/la protagonista de; **the stars** npl (ASTROLOGY) el horóscopo

starboard ['staːbəd] n estribor m

starch [staːtʃ] n almidón m

stardom ['staːdəm] n estrellato

stare [steə^r] n mirada fija ♦ vi: **to ~ at** mirar fijo

stark [staːk] adj (bleak) severo, escueto ♦ adv: **~ naked** en cueros

start [staːt] n principio, comienzo; (departure) salida; (sudden movement) salto, sobresalto; (advantage) ventaja ♦ vt empezar, comenzar; (cause) causar; (found) fundar; (engine) poner en marcha ♦ vi comenzar, empezar; (with fright) asustarse, sobresaltarse; (train etc) salir; **to ~ doing** or **to do sth** empezar a hacer algo ► **start off** vi empezar, comenzar; (leave) salir, ponerse en camino ► **start out** vi (begin) empezar; (set out) partir, salir ► **start up** vi comenzar; (car) ponerse en marcha ♦ vt comenzar; poner en marcha ❏ **starter** n (AUT) botón m de arranque; (SPORT: official) juez mf de salida; (BRIT CULIN) entrante m ❏ **starting point** n punto de partida

startle ['staːtl] vt asustar, sobrecoger ❏ **startling** adj alarmante

starvation [staː'veɪʃən] n hambre f

starve [staːv] vi tener mucha hambre; (to death) morir de hambre ♦ vt hacer pasar hambre

state [steɪt] n estado ♦ vt (say, declare) afirmar; **the States** los Estados Unidos; **to be in a ~** estar agitado ❏ **statement** n afirmación f ❏ **state school** n escuela or colegio estatal ❏ **statesman** (irreg) n estadista m

static ['stætɪk] n (RADIO) parásitos mpl ♦ adj estático

station ['steɪʃən] n estación f (RADIO) emisora; (rank) posición f social ♦ vt colocar, situar; (MIL) apostar

stationary ['steɪʃnəri] adj estacionario, fijo

stationer's (shop) [BRIT] n papelería

stationery [-nəri] n papel m de escribir, artículos mpl de escritorio

station wagon (US) n ranchera

statistic [stə'tɪstɪk] n estadística ❏ **statistics** n (science) estadística

statue ['stætjuː] n estatua

stature ['stætʃə^r] n estatura; (fig) talla

status ['steɪtəs] n estado; (reputation) estatus m ❏ **status quo** n (e)statu quo m

statutory ['stætjutri] adj estatutario

staunch [stɔːntʃ] adj leal, incondicional

stay [steɪ] n estancia ♦ vi quedar(se), (us guest) hospedarse; **to ~ put** seguir en el mismo sitio; **to ~ the night/5 days** pasar la noche/estar 5 días ► **stay away** vi (from person, building) no acercarse; (from event) no acudir ► **stay behind** vi quedar atrás ► **stay in** vi quedarse en casa ► **stay on** vi quedarse ► **stay out** vi (of house) no volver a casa; (on strike) permanecer en huelga ► **stay up** vi (at night) velar, no acostarse

steadily ['stedɪlɪ] adv constantemente; (firmly) firmemente; (work, walk) sin parar; (gaze) fijamente

steady ['stedɪ] adj (firm) firme; (regular) regular; (person, character) sensato, juicioso; (boyfriend) formal; (look, voice) tranquilo ♦ vt (stabilize) estabilizar; (nerves) calmar

steak [steɪk] n filete m; (beef) bistec m

steal [stiːl] (pt **stole**, pp **stolen**) vt robar ♦ vi robar; (move secretly) andar a hurtadillas

steam [stiːm] n vapor m; (mist) vaho, humo ♦ vt (CULIN) cocer al vapor ♦ vi echar vapor ► **steam up** vi (window) empañarse; **to get steamed up about sth** (fig) ponerse negro por algo ❑ **steamy** adj (room) lleno de vapor; (window) empañado; (heat, atmosphere) bochornoso

steel [stiːl] n acero ♦ adj de acero

steep [stiːp] adj escarpado, abrupto; (stair) empinado; (price) exorbitante, excesivo ♦ vt empapar, remojar

steeple [stiːpl] n aguja

steer [stɪə*] vt (car) conducir (SP), manejar (LAm); (person) dirigir ♦ vi conducir, manejar ❑ **steering** n (AUT) dirección f ❑ **steering wheel** n volante m

stem [stem] n (of plant) tallo; (of glass) pie m ♦ vt detener; (blood) restañar ► **stem from** vt fus provenir or derivarse de

stench [stentʃ] n hedor m

stencil [stensl] n (typed) cliché m de mimeógrafo; (lettering) plantilla ♦ vt estarcir

step [stɛp] n paso; (on stair) peldaño, escalón m ♦ vi: **to ~ forward/back** dar un paso adelante/hacia atrás; **steps** npl (BRIT) = **stepladder**; **in/out of ~ (with)** acorde/en disonancia (con) ► **step down** vi (fig) retirarse ► **step in** vi entrar; (fig) intervenir ► **step up** vt (increase) aumentar ❑ **stepbrother** n hermanastro ❑ **stepchild** (pl **stepchildren**) n hijastro(-a) m/f ❑ **stepdaughter** n hijastra ❑ **stepfather** n padrastro ❑ **stepladder** n escalera doble or de tijera ❑ **stepmother** n madrastra ❑ **stepsister** n hermanastra ❑ **stepson** n hijastro

stereo [stɛrɪəu] n estéreo ♦ adj (also: **stereophonic**) estéreo, estereofónico

stereotype [stɛrɪətaɪp] n estereotipo ♦ vt estereotipar

sterile [stɛraɪl] adj estéril ❑ **sterilize** [stɛrɪlaɪz] vt esterilizar

sterling [stɜːlɪŋ] adj (silver) de ley ♦ n (ECON) libras fpl esterlinas fpl; **one pound ~** una libra esterlina

stern [stɜːn] adj severo, austero ♦ n (NAUT) popa

steroid [stɪərɔɪd] n esteroide m

stew [stjuː] n estofado, guiso ♦ vt estofar, guisar; (fruit) cocer

steward [stjuːəd] n camarero ❑ **stewardess** n (esp on plane) azafata

stick [stɪk] (pt, pp **stuck**) n palo; (of dynamite) barreno; (as weapon) porra; (also: **walking** ~) bastón m ♦ vt (glue) pegar; (inf: put) meter; (: tolerate) aguantar, soportar; (thrust): **to ~ sth into** clavar or hincar algo en ♦ vi pegarse; (be unmoveable) quedarse parado; (in mind) quedarse grabado ► **stick out** vi sobresalir ► **stick up** vi sobresalir ► **stick up for** vt fus defender ❑ **sticker** n (label) etiqueta engomada; (with slogan) pegatina ❑ **sticking plaster** n esparadrapo ❑ **stick shift** (US) n (AUT) palanca de cambios

sticky [stɪkɪ] adj pegajoso; (label) engomado; (fig) difícil

stiff [stɪf] adj rígido, tieso; (hard) duro; (manner) estirado; (difficult) difícil; (person) inflexible; (price) exorbitante ♦ adv: **scared/bored** ~ muerto de miedo/aburrimiento

stifling [staɪflɪŋ] adj (heat) sofocante, bochornoso

stigma [stɪgmə] n (fig) estigma m

stiletto [stɪlɛtəu] (BRIT) n (also: ~ **heel**) tacón m de aguja

still [stɪl] adj inmóvil, quieto ♦ adv todavía; (even so) aun así; (nonetheless) sin embargo, aun así

stimulate [stɪmjuleɪt] vt estimular

stimulus [stɪmjuləs] (pl **stimuli**) n estímulo, incentivo

sting [stɪŋ] (pt, pp **stung**) n picadura; (pain) escozor m, picazón f; (organ) aguijón m ♦ vt, vi picar

stink [stɪŋk] (pt **stank**, pp **stunk**) n hedor m, tufo ♦ vi heder, apestar

stir [stəːʳ] n (fig: agitation) conmoción f ♦ vt (tea etc) remover; (fig: emotions) provocar ♦ vi moverse ► **stir up** vt (trouble) fomentar □ **stir-fry** vt sofreír removiendo ♦ n plato preparado sofriendo y removiendo los ingredientes

stitch [stɪtʃ] n (SEWING) puntada; (KNITTING) punto; (MED) punto (de sutura); (pain) punzada ♦ vt coser; (MED) suturar

stock [stɔk] n (COMM: store) existencias fpl, stock m; (: selection) surtido; (AGR) ganado, ganadería; (CULIN) caldo; (descent) raza, estirpe f; (FINANCE) capital m ♦ adj (fig: reply etc) clásico ♦ vt (have in stock) tener existencias de; **stocks and shares** acciones y valores; **in** ~ en existencia or almacén; **out of** ~ agotado; **to take** ~ **of** (fig) asesorar, examinar □ **stockbroker** ['stɔkbrəukəʳ] n agente mf or corredor(a) m/f de bolsa □ **stock cube** (BRIT) n pastilla de caldo □ **stock exchange** n bolsa □ **stockholder** ['stɔkhəuldəʳ] (US) n accionista m/f

stocking ['stɔkɪŋ] n media

stock market n bolsa (de valores)

stole [stəul] pt of **steal** ♦ n estola

stolen ['stəuln] pp of **steal**

stomach ['stʌmək] n (ANAT) estómago; (belly) vientre m ♦ vt tragar, aguantar □ **stomachache** n dolor m de estómago

stone [stəun] n piedra; (in fruit) hueso (= 6.348 kg; 14 libras) ♦ adj de piedra ♦ vt apedrear; (fruit) deshuesar

stood [stud] pt, pp of **stand**

stool [stuːl] n taburete m

stoop [stuːp] vi (also: ~ **down**) doblarse, agacharse; (also: **have a** ~) ser cargado de espaldas

stop [stɔp] n parada; (in punctuation) punto ♦ vt parar, detener; (break) suspender; (block: pay) suspender; (:

cheque) invalidar; (also: **put a** ~ **to**) poner término a ♦ vi pararse, detenerse; (end) acabarse; **to** ~ **doing sth** dejar de hacer algo ► **stop by** vi pasar por ► **stop off** vi interrumpir el viaje □ **stopover** n parada; (AVIAT) escala □ **stoppage** n (strike) paro; (blockage) obstrucción f

storage ['stɔːrɪdʒ] n almacenaje m

store [stɔːʳ] n (stock) provisión f; (depot: BRIT: large shop) almacén m; (US) tienda; (reserve) reserva, repuesto ♦ vt almacenar; **stores** npl víveres mpl; **to be in** ~ **for sb** esperarle a algn □ **storekeeper** (US) n tendero(-a)

storey ['stɔːri] (US **story**) n piso

storm [stɔːm] n tormenta; (fig: of applause) salva; (: of criticism) nube f ♦ vi (fig) rabiar ♦ vt tomar por asalto □ **stormy** adj tempestuoso

story ['stɔːri] n historia; (lie) mentira; (US) = **storey**

stout [staut] adj (strong) sólido; (fat) gordo, corpulento; (resolute) resuelto ♦ n cerveza negra

stove [stəuv] n (for cooking) cocina; (for heating) estufa

straight [streɪt] adj recto, derecho; (frank) franco, directo; (simple) sencillo ♦ adv derecho, directamente; (drink) sin mezcla; **to put** or **get sth** ~ dejar algo en claro; ~ **away**, ~ **off** en seguida □ **straighten** vt (also: **straighten out**) enderezar, poner derecho ♦ vi (also: **straighten up**) enderezarse, ponerse derecho □ **straightforward** adj (simple) sencillo; (honest) honrado, franco

strain [streɪn] n tensión f; (TECH) presión f; (MED) torcedura; (breed) tipo, variedad f ♦ vt (back etc) torcerse; (resources) agotar; (food, tea) colar □ **strained** adj (muscle) torcido; (laugh) forzado; (relations) tenso □ **strainer** n colador m

strait [streɪt] n (GEO) estrecho; **straits** (fig): **to be in dire straits** estar en un gran apuro

strand [strænd] n (of thread) hebra; (of hair) trenza; (of rope) ramal m ❑ **stranded** adj (person: without money) desamparado, -a; (: without transport) colgado

strange [streɪndʒ] adj (not known) desconocido; (odd) extraño, raro ❑ **strangely** adv de un modo raro; see also **enough** ❑ **stranger** n desconocido(-a); (from another area) forastero(-a)

⚠ Be careful not to translate **stranger** by the Spanish word extranjero.

strangle ['stræŋgl] vt estrangular

strap [stræp] n correa; (of slip, dress) tirante m

strategic [strə'tiːdʒɪk] adj estratégico

strategy ['strætɪdʒɪ] n estrategia

straw [strɔː] n paja; (drinking straw) caña, pajita; **that's the last ~!** ¡eso es el colmo!

strawberry ['strɔːbərɪ] n fresa, frutilla (SC)

stray [streɪ] adj (animal) extraviado; (bullet) perdido; (scattered) disperso ♦ vi extraviarse, perderse

streak [striːk] n raya; (in hair) raya ♦ vt rayar ♦ vi: **to ~ past** pasar como un rayo

stream [striːm] n riachuelo, arroyo; (of people, vehicles) riada, caravana; (of smoke, insults etc) chorro ♦ vt (SCOL) dividir en grupos por habilidad ♦ vi correr, fluir; **to ~ in/out** (people) entrar/ salir en tropel

street [striːt] n calle f ❑ **streetcar** (US) n tranvía m ❑ **street light** n farol m (LAm), farola (SP) ❑ **street map** n plano (de la ciudad) ❑ **street plan** n plano

strength [streŋθ] n fuerza; (of girder, knot etc) resistencia; (fig: power) poder

m ❑ **strengthen** vt fortalecer, reforzar

strenuous ['strenjuəs] adj (energetic, determined) enérgico

stress [stres] n presión f; (mental strain) estrés m; (accent) acento ♦ vt subrayar, recalcar; (syllable) acentuar ❑ **stressed** adj (tense) estresado, agobiado; (syllable) acentuado ❑ **stressful** adj (job) estresante

stretch [stretʃ] n (of sand etc) trecho ♦ vi estirarse; (extend): **to ~ to or as far as** extenderse hasta ♦ vt extender, estirar; (make demands) exigir el máximo esfuerzo a ▶ **stretch out** vi tenderse ♦ vt (arm etc) extender; (spread) extender

stretcher ['stretʃəʳ] n camilla

strict [strɪkt] adj severo; (exact) estricto ❑ **strictly** adv severamente; estrictamente

stride [straɪd] (pt **strode**, pp **stridden**) n zancada, tranco ♦ vi dar zancadas, andar a trancos

strike [straɪk] (pt, pp **struck**) n huelga; (of oil etc) descubrimiento; (attack) ataque m ♦ vt golpear, pegar; (oil etc) descubrir; (bargain, deal) cerrar ♦ vi declarar la huelga; (attack) atacar; (clock) dar la hora; on ~ (workers) en huelga; **to ~ a match** encender un fósforo ❑ **striker** n huelguista mf; (SPORT) delantero ❑ **striking** adj llamativo

string [strɪŋ] (pt, pp **strung**) n cuerda; (row) hilera ♦ vt: **to ~ together** ensartar; **to ~ out** extender; **the strings** npl (MUS) los instrumentos de cuerda; **to pull strings** (fig) mover palancas

strip [strɪp] n tira; (of land) franja; (of metal) cinta, lámina ♦ vt desnudar; (paint) quitar; (also: ~ **down**: machine) desmontar ♦ vi desnudarse ▶ **strip off** vt (paint etc) quitar ♦ vi (person) desnudarse

stripe [straɪp] n raya; (MIL) galón m ❑ **striped** adj a rayas, rayado

stripper ['strɪpə'] n artista mf de striptease

strip-search ['strɪpsə:tʃ] vt: **to ~ sb** desnudar y registrar a algn

strive [straɪv] (pt **strove**, pp **striven**) vi: **to ~ for sth/to do sth** luchar por conseguir/hacer algo

strode [strəud] pt of **stride**

stroke [strəuk] n (blow) golpe m; (SWIMMING) brazada; (MED) apoplejía; (of paintbrush) toque m ♦ vt acariciar; **at a ~** de un solo golpe

stroll [strəul] n paseo, vuelta ♦ vi dar un paseo o una vuelta ❑ **stroller** (US) n (for child) sillita de ruedas

strong [strɔŋ] adj fuerte; **they are 50 ~** son 50 ❑ **stronghold** n fortaleza; (fig) baluarte m ❑ **strongly** adv fuertemente, con fuerza; (believe) firmemente

strove [strəuv] pt of **strive**

struck [strʌk] pt, pp of **strike**

structure ['strʌktʃə'] n estructura; (building) construcción f

struggle ['strʌgl] n lucha ♦ vi luchar

strung [strʌŋ] pt, pp of **string**

stub [stʌb] n (of ticket etc) talón m; (of cigarette) colilla; **to ~ one's toe** on dar con el dedo (del pie) contra algo ► **stub out** vt apagar

stubble ['stʌbl] n rastrojo; (on chin) barba (incipiente)

stubborn ['stʌbən] adj terco, testarudo

stuck [stʌk] pt, pp of **stick** ♦ adj (jammed) atascado

stud [stʌd] n (shirt stud) corchete m; (of boot) taco; (earring) pendiente m (de bolita); (also: ~ **farm**) caballeriza; (also: ~ **horse**) caballo semental ♦ vt (fig): **studded with** salpicado de

student ['stju:dənt] n estudiante mf ♦ adj estudiantil ❑ **student driver** (US) n conductor(a) mf en prácticas ❑ **students' union** n (building) centro de estudiantes; (BRIT: association) federación f de estudiantes

studio ['stju:dɪəu] n estudio; (artist's) taller m ❑ **studio flat** n estudio

study ['stʌdɪ] n estudio ♦ vt estudiar; (examine) examinar, investigar ♦ vi estudiar

stuff [stʌf] n materia; (substance) material m, sustancia; (things) cosas fpl ♦ vt llenar; (CULIN) rellenar; (animals) disecar; (inf: push) meter ❑ **stuffing** n relleno ❑ **stuffy** adj (room) mal ventilado; (person) de miras estrechas

stumble ['stʌmbl] vi tropezar, dar un traspié; **to ~ across, ~ on** (fig) tropezar con

stump [stʌmp] n (of tree) tocón m; (of limb) muñón m ♦ vt: **to be stumped for an answer** no saber qué contestar

stun [stʌn] vt dejar sin sentido

stung [stʌŋ] pt, pp of **sting**

stunk [stʌŋk] pp of **stink**

stunned [stʌnd] adj (dazed) aturdido, atontado; (amazed) asombrado; (shocked) anonadado

stunning ['stʌnɪŋ] adj (fig: news) pasmoso; (: outfit etc) sensacional

stunt [stʌnt] n (in film) escena peligrosa; (publicity stunt) truco publicitario

stupid ['stju:pɪd] adj estúpido, tonto ❑ **stupidity** [-'pɪdɪtɪ] n estupidez f

sturdy ['stə:dɪ] adj robusto, fuerte

stutter ['stʌtə'] n tartamudeo ♦ vi tartamudear

style [staɪl] n estilo ❑ **stylish** adj elegante, a la moda ❑ **stylist** n (hair stylist) peluquero(-a)

sub... [sʌb] prefix sub... ❑ **subconscious** adj subconsciente

subdued [səb'dju:d] adj (light) tenue; (person) sumiso, manso

subject [n 'sʌbdʒɪkt, vb səb'dʒɛkt] n súbdito; (SCOL) asignatura; (matter) tema m; (GRAMMAR) sujeto ♦ vt: **to ~ sb to sth** someter a algn a algo; **to be ~ to** (law) estar sujeto a; (person) ser propenso a ❑ **subjective** [-'dʒɛktɪv] *adj* subjetivo ❑ **subject matter** *n* (content) contenido

subjunctive [səbˈdʒʌŋktɪv] *adj, n* subjuntivo

submarine [ˌsʌbməˈriːn] *n* submarino

submission [səbˈmɪʃən] *n* sumisión *f*

submit [səbˈmɪt] *vt* someter ♦ *vi*: **to ~ to sth** someterse a algo

subordinate [səˈbɔːdɪnət] *adj, n* subordinado(-a) *m/f*

subscribe [səbˈskraɪb] *vi* suscribir; **to ~ to** (opinion, fund) suscribir, aprobar; (newspaper) suscribirse a

subscription [səbˈskrɪpʃən] *n* abono; (to magazine) suscripción *f*

subsequent [ˈsʌbsɪkwənt] *adj* subsiguiente, posterior ❑ **subsequently** *adv* posteriormente, más tarde

subside [səbˈsaɪd] *vi* hundirse; (flood) bajar; (wind) amainar

subsidiary [səbˈsɪdɪərɪ] *adj* secundario ♦ *n* sucursal *f*, filial *f*

subsidize [ˈsʌbsɪdaɪz] *vt* subvencionar

subsidy [ˈsʌbsɪdɪ] *n* subvención *f*

substance [ˈsʌbstəns] *n* sustancia

substantial [səbˈstænʃl] *adj* sustancial, sustancioso; (fig) importante

substitute [ˈsʌbstɪtjuːt] *n* (person) suplente *mf*; (thing) sustituto ♦ *vt*: **to ~ A for B** sustituir A por B, reemplazar B por A ❑ **substitution** *n* sustitución *f*

subtle [ˈsʌtl] *adj* sutil

subtract [səbˈtrækt] *vt* restar, sustraer

suburb [ˈsʌbəːb] *n* barrio residencial; **the suburbs** las afueras de (la ciudad) ❑ **suburban** [səˈbəːbən] *adj* suburbano; (train etc) de cercanías

subway [ˈsʌbweɪ] *n* (BRIT) paso subterráneo or inferior; (US) metro

succeed [səkˈsiːd] *vi* (person) tener éxito; (plan) salir bien ♦ *vt* suceder a; **to ~ in doing** lograr hacer

success [səkˈses] *n* éxito ❑ **successful** *adj* exitoso; (business) próspero; **to be**

successful (in doing) lograr (hacer) ❑ **successfully** *adv* con éxito

⚠ Be careful not to translate **success** by the Spanish word **suceso**.

succession [səkˈseʃən] *n* sucesión *f*, serie *f*

successive [səkˈsesɪv] *adj* sucesivo, consecutivo

successor [səkˈsesə?] *n* sucesor(a) *m/f*

succumb [səˈkʌm] *vi* sucumbir

such [sʌtʃ] *adj* tal, semejante; (of that kind): **~ a book** tal libro; (so much): **~ courage** tanto valor ♦ *adv* tan; **~ a long trip** un viaje tan largo; **~ a lot of** tanto(s)/a(s); **~ as** (like) tal como; **as ~** como tal ❑ **such-and-such** *adj* tal o cual

suck [sʌk] *vt* chupar; (bottle) sorber; (breast) mamar

Sudan [suˈdæn] *n* Sudán *m*

sudden [ˈsʌdn] *adj* (rapid) repentino, súbito; (unexpected) imprevisto; **all of a ~** de repente ❑ **suddenly** *adv* de repente

sue [suː] *vt* demandar

suede [sweɪd] *n* ante *m*, gamuza

suffer [ˈsʌfə?] *vt* sufrir, padecer; (tolerate) aguantar, soportar ♦ *vi* sufrir; **to ~ from** (illness etc) padecer ❑ **suffering** *n* sufrimiento

suffice [səˈfaɪs] *vi* bastar, ser suficiente

sufficient [səˈfɪʃənt] *adj* suficiente, bastante

suffocate [ˈsʌfəkeɪt] *vi* ahogarse, asfixiarse

sugar [ˈʃʊgə?] *n* azúcar *m* ♦ *vt* echar azúcar a, azucarar

suggest [səˈdʒest] *vt* sugerir ❑ **suggestion** [-ˈdʒestʃən] *n* sugerencia

suicide [ˈsuɪsaɪd] *n* suicidio; (person) suicida *mf*; see also **commit**; **~ bombing** atentado suicida

suit [suːt] *n* (man's) traje *m*; (woman's) conjunto; (LAW) pleito; (CARDS) palo

◆ vt convenir; (clothes) sentar a, ir bien a; (adapt): **to ~ sth to** adaptar or ajustar algo a; **well suited** (well matched: couple) hecho el uno para el otro ❏ **suitable** adj conveniente; (apt) indicado ❏ **suitcase** n maleta, valija (RPl)

suite [swiːt] n (of rooms, MUS) suite f; (furniture): **bedroom/dining room ~** (juego de) dormitorio/comedor; see also **three-piece suite**

sulfur ['sʌlfə] (US) n = **sulphur**

sulk [sʌlk] vi estar de mal humor

sulphur ['sʌlfə] (US **sulfur**) n azufre m

sultana [sʌl'tɑːnə] n (fruit) pasa de Esmirna

sum [sʌm] n suma; (total) total m
▶ **sum up** vt resumir ◆ vi hacer un resumen

summarize ['sʌməraɪz] vt resumir

summary ['sʌmərɪ] n resumen m ◆ adj (justice) sumario

summer ['sʌmə] n verano ◆ cpd de verano; **in ~** en verano ❏ **summer holidays** npl vacaciones fpl de verano ❏ **summertime** n (season) verano

summit ['sʌmɪt] n cima, cumbre f; (also: **~ conference, ~ meeting**) (conferencia) cumbre f

summon ['sʌmən] vt (person) llamar; (meeting) convocar; (LAW) citar

Sun. abbr (= Sunday) dom

sun [sʌn] n sol m ❏ **sunbathe** vi tomar el sol ❏ **sunbed** n cama solar ❏ **sunblock** n filtro solar ❏ **sunburn** n (painful) quemadura; (tan) bronceado ❏ **sunburned, sunburnt** adj (painfully) quemado por el sol; (tanned) bronceado

Sunday ['sʌndɪ] n domingo

sunflower ['sʌnflaʊə] n girasol m

sung [sʌŋ] pp of **sing**

sunglasses ['sʌnglɑːsɪz] npl gafas fpl (SP) or anteojos mpl (LAm) de sol

sunk [sʌŋk] pp of **sink**

sun: sunlight n luz f del sol ❏ **sun lounger** n tumbona, perezosa (LAm) ❏ **sunny** adj soleado; (day) de sol; (fig) alegre ❏ **sunrise** n salida del sol ❏ **sun roof** n (AUT) techo corredizo ❏ **sunscreen** n protector m solar ❏ **sunset** n puesta del sol ❏ **sunshade** n (over table) sombrilla ❏ **sunshine** n sol m ❏ **sunstroke** n insolación f ❏ **suntan** n bronceado ❏ **suntan lotion** n bronceador m ❏ **suntan oil** n aceite m bronceador

super ['suːpə] (inf) adj genial

superb [suː'pɜːb] adj magnífico, espléndido

superficial [suːpə'fɪʃəl] adj superficial

superintendent [suːpərɪn'tendənt] n director(a) m/f; (POLICE) subjefe(-a) m/f

superior [su'pɪərɪə] adj superior; (smug) desdeñoso ◆ n superior m

superlative [suː'pɜːlətɪv] n superlativo

supermarket ['suːpəmɑːkɪt] n supermercado

supernatural [suːpə'nætʃərəl] adj sobrenatural ◆ n: **the ~** lo sobrenatural

superpower ['suːpəpaʊə] n (POL) superpotencia

superstition [suːpə'stɪʃən] n superstición f

superstitious [suːpə'stɪʃəs] adj supersticioso

superstore ['suːpəstɔː] n (BRIT) hipermercado

supervise ['suːpəvaɪz] vt supervisar ❏ **supervision** [-'vɪʒən] n supervisión f ❏ **supervisor** n supervisor(a) m/f

supper ['sʌpə] n cena

supple ['sʌpl] adj flexible

supplement [n 'sʌplɪmənt, vb sʌplɪ'mənt] n suplemento ◆ vt suplir

supplier [sə'plaɪə] n (COMM) distribuidor m/f

supply [sə'plaɪ] vt (provide) suministrar; (equip): **to ~ (with)** proveer (de) ◆ n provisión f; (of gas, water etc) suministro; **supplies** npl (food) víveres mpl; (MIL) pertrechos mpl

support [sə'pɔːt] n apoyo; (TECH) soporte m ♦ vt apoyar; (financially) mantener; (uphold, TECH) sostener ❑ **supporter** n (POL etc) partidario(-a); (SPORT) aficionado(-a)

⚠ Be careful not to translate **support** by the Spanish word *soportar*.

suppose [sə'pəuz] vt suponer; (imagine) imaginarse; (duty): **to be supposed to do sth** deber hacer algo ❑ **supposedly** [sə'pəuzɪdlɪ] adv según cabe suponer ❑ **supposing** conj en caso de que

suppress [sə'prɛs] vt suprimir; (yawn) ahogar

supreme [su'priːm] adj supremo

surcharge [ˈsɜːtʃɑːdʒ] n sobretasa, recargo

sure [ʃuəˈ] adj seguro; (definite, convinced) cierto; **to make ~ of sth/ that** asegurarse de algo/asegurar que; **~!** (of course) ¡claro!; ¡por supuesto!; **~ enough** efectivamente ❑ **surely** adv (certainly) seguramente

surf [sɜːf] n olas fpl ♦ vt: **to ~ the Net** navegar por Internet

surface [ˈsɜːfɪs] n superficie f ♦ vt (road) revestir ♦ vi salir a la superficie; **by ~ mail** por vía terrestre

surfboard [ˈsɜːfbɔːd] n tabla (de surf)

surfing [ˈsɜːfɪŋ] n surf m

surge [sɜːdʒ] n oleada, oleaje m ♦ vi (wave) romper; (people) avanzar en tropel

surgeon [ˈsɜːdʒən] n cirujano(-a)

surgery [ˈsɜːdʒərɪ] n cirugía; (BRIT: room) consultorio m

surname [ˈsɜːneɪm] n apellido

surpass [sɜːˈpɑːs] vt superar, exceder

surplus [ˈsɜːpləs] n excedente m; (COMM) superávit m ♦ adj excedente, sobrante

surprise [sə'praɪz] n sorpresa ♦ vt sorprender ❑ **surprised** adj (look, smile) de sorpresa; **to be surprised** sorprenderse ❑ **surprising** adj sorprendente ❑ **surprisingly** adv: **it was surprisingly easy** me etc sorprendió lo fácil que fue

surrender [sə'rɛndəˈ] n rendición f, entrega ♦ vi rendirse, entregarse

surround [sə'raund] vt rodear, circundar; (MIL etc) cercar ❑ **surrounding** adj circundante ❑ **surroundings** npl alrededores mpl, cercanías fpl

surveillance [sɜːˈveɪləns] n vigilancia

survey [n sə:veɪ, vb sə:ˈveɪ] n inspección f, reconocimiento m; (inquiry) encuesta ♦ vt examinar, inspeccionar; (look at) mirar, contemplar ❑ **surveyor** n agrimensor(a) m/f

survival [sə'vaɪvl] n supervivencia

survive [sə'vaɪv] vi sobrevivir; (custom etc) perdurar ♦ vt sobrevivir a ❑ **survivor** n superviviente mf

suspect [adj, n 'sʌspɛkt, vb sə'spɛkt] adj, n sospechoso(-a) m/f ♦ vt (person) sospechar de; (think) sospechar

suspend [sə'spɛnd] vt suspender ❑ **suspended sentence** n (LAW) libertad f condicional ❑ **suspenders** npl (BRIT) ligas fpl; (US) tirantes mpl

suspense [sə'spɛns] n incertidumbre f, duda; (in film etc) suspense m; **to keep sb in ~** mantener a algn en suspense

suspension [sə'spɛnʃən] n (gen, AUT) suspensión f; (of driving licence) privación f ❑ **suspension bridge** n puente m colgante

suspicion [sə'spɪʃən] n sospecha; (distrust) recelo ❑ **suspicious** adj receloso; (causing suspicion) sospechoso

sustain [sə'steɪn] vt sostener, apoyar; (suffer) sufrir, padecer

swallow [ˈswɔləu] n (bird) golondrina ♦ vt tragar; (fig, pride) tragarse

swam [swæm] pt of **swim**

swamp [swɔmp] n pantano, ciénaga
♦ vt (with water etc) inundar; (fig)
abrumar, agobiar

swan [swɔn] n cisne m

swap [swɔp] n canje m, intercambio
♦ vt: **to ~** (**for**) cambiar (por)

swarm [swɔːm] n (of bees) enjambre m;
(fig) multitud f ♦ vi (bees) formar un
enjambre; (people) pulular; **to be
swarming with** ser un hervidero de

sway [sweɪ] vi mecerse, balancearse
♦ vt (influence) mover, influir en

swear [sweə] (pt **swore**, pp **sworn**) vi
(curse) maldecir; (promise) jurar ♦ vt
jurar ► **swear in** vt: **to be sworn in**
prestar juramento □ **swearword** n
taco, palabrota

sweat [swet] n sudor m ♦ vi sudar

sweater ['swetə] n suéter m

sweatshirt ['swetʃɜːt] n suéter m

sweaty ['swetɪ] adj sudoroso

Swede [swiːd] n sueco(-a)

swede [swiːd] (BRIT) n nabo

Sweden ['swiːdn] n Suecia □ **Swedish**
['swiːdɪʃ] adj sueco ♦ n (LING) sueco

sweep [swiːp] (pt, pp **swept**) n (act)
barrido; (also: **chimney ~**)
deshollinador(a) m/f ♦ vt barrer; (with
arm) empujar; (current) arrastrar ♦ vi
barrer; (arm etc) moverse
rápidamente; (wind) soplar con
violencia

sweet [swiːt] n (candy) dulce m,
caramelo; (BRIT: pudding) postre m
♦ adj dulce; (fig: kind) dulce, amable;
(: attractive) mono □ **sweetcorn** n
maíz m □ **sweetener** ['swiːtnə'] n
(CULIN) edulcorante m □ **sweetheart**
n novio(-a) □ **sweetshop** n (BRIT)
confitería, bombonería

swell [swel] (pt **swelled**, pp **swollen** or
swelled) n (of sea) marejada, oleaje m
♦ adj (US: inf: excellent) estupendo,
fenomenal ♦ vt hinchar, inflar ♦ vi (also:
~ up) hincharse; (numbers) aumentar;

(sound, feeling) ir aumentando
□ **swelling** n (MED) hinchazón f

swept [swept] pt, pp of **sweep**

swerve [swɜːv] vi desviarse
bruscamente

swift [swɪft] n (bird) vencejo ♦ adj
rápido, veloz

swim [swɪm] (pt **swam**, pp **swum**) n: **to
go for a ~** ir a nadar or a bañarse ♦ vi
nadar; (head, room) dar vueltas ♦ vt
nadar; (the Channel etc) cruzar a nado
□ **swimmer** n nadador(a) m/f
□ **swimming** n natación f
□ **swimming costume** (BRIT) n
bañador m, traje m de baño
□ **swimming pool** n piscina, alberca
(MEX), pileta (RPl) □ **swimming
trunks** npl bañador m (de hombre)
□ **swimsuit** n = **swimming
costume**

swing [swɪŋ] (pt, pp **swung**) n (in
playground) columpio; (movement)
balanceo, vaivén m; (change of
direction) viraje m; (rhythm) ritmo ♦ vt
balancear; (also: **~ round**) voltear, girar
♦ vi balancearse, columpiarse; (also: **~
round**) dar media vuelta; **to be in full ~**
estar en plena marcha

swipe card [swaɪp-] n tarjeta
magnética deslizante, tarjeta swipe

swirl [swɜːl] vi arremolinarse

Swiss [swɪs] adj, n inv suizo(-a) m/f

switch [swɪtʃ] n (for light etc)
interruptor m; (change) cambio ♦ vt
(change) cambiar de ► **switch off** vt
apagar; (engine) parar ► **switch on** vt
encender (SP), prender (LAm); (engine,
machine) arrancar □ **switchboard** n
(TEL) centralita (SP), conmutador m
(LAm)

Switzerland ['swɪtsələnd] n Suiza

swivel ['swɪvl] vi (also: **~ round**) girar

swollen ['swəʊlən] pp of **swell**

swoop [swuːp] n (by police etc) redada
♦ vi (also: **~ down**) calarse

swop [swɔp] = **swap**

sword [sɔːd] n espada ◻ **swordfish** n pez m espada

swore [swɔːʳ] pt of **swear**

sworn [swɔːn] pp of **swear** ♦ adj (statement) bajo juramento; (enemy) implacable

swum [swʌm] pp of **swim**

swung [swʌŋ] pt, pp of **swing**

syllable ['sɪləbl] n sílaba

syllabus ['sɪləbəs] n programa m de estudios

symbol ['sɪmbl] n símbolo ◻ **symbolic(al)** [sɪm'bɒlɪk(l)] adj simbólico; **to be symbolic(al) of sth** simbolizar algo

symmetrical [sɪ'metrɪkl] adj simétrico

symmetry ['sɪmɪtrɪ] n simetría

sympathetic [sɪmpə'θetɪk] adj (understanding) comprensivo; (showing support): **~ to(wards)** bien dispuesto hacia

⚠ Be careful not to translate **sympathetic** by the Spanish word simpático.

sympathize ['sɪmpəθaɪz] vi: **to ~ with** (person) compadecerse de; (feelings) comprender; (cause) apoyar

sympathy ['sɪmpəθɪ] n (pity) compasión f

symphony ['sɪmfənɪ] n sinfonía

symptom ['sɪmptəm] n síntoma m, indicio

synagogue ['sɪnəgɒg] n sinagoga

syndicate ['sɪndɪkɪt] n sindicato; (of newspapers) agencia (de noticias)

syndrome ['sɪndrəum] n síndrome m

synonym ['sɪnənɪm] n sinónimo

synthetic [sɪn'θetɪk] adj sintético

Syria ['sɪrɪə] n Siria

syringe [sɪ'rɪndʒ] n jeringa

syrup ['sɪrəp] n jarabe m; (also: **golden ~**) almíbar m

system ['sɪstəm] n sistema m; (ANAT) organismo ◻ **systematic** [-'mætɪk]

adj sistemático, metódico ◻ **systems analyst** n analista mf de sistemas

T, t

ta [tɑː] (BRIT: inf) excl ¡gracias!

tab [tæb] n lengüeta; (label) etiqueta; **to keep tabs on** (fig) vigilar

table ['teɪbl] n mesa; (of statistics etc) cuadro, tabla ♦ vt (BRIT: motion etc) presentar; **to lay** or **set the ~** poner la mesa ◻ **tablecloth** n mantel m ◻ **table d'hôte** [tɑːbl'dəut] adj del menú ◻ **table lamp** n lámpara de mesa ◻ **tablemat** n (for plate) posaplatos m inv; (for hot dish) salvamantel m ◻ **tablespoon** n cuchara de servir; (also: **tablespoonful**: as measurement) cucharada

tablet ['tæblɪt] n (MED) pastilla, comprimido; (of stone) lápida

table tennis n ping-pong m, tenis m de mesa

tabloid ['tæblɔɪd] n periódico popular sensacionalista

TABLOID PRESS

El término **tabloid press** o **tabloids** se usa para referirse a la prensa popular británica, por el tamaño más pequeño de los periódicos. A diferencia de los de la llamada **quality press**, estas publicaciones se caracterizan por un lenguaje sencillo, una presentación llamativa y un contenido sensacionalista, centrado a veces en los escándalos financieros y sexuales de los famosos, por lo que también reciben el nombre peyorativo de "gutter press".

taboo [tə'buː] adj, n tabú m

tack [tæk] n (nail) tachuela; (fig) rumbo
♦ vt (nail) clavar con tachuelas; (stitch)
hilvanar ♦ vi virar

tackle [tækl] n (fishing tackle) aparejo
(de pescar); (for lifting) aparejo ♦ vt
(difficulty) enfrentarse con; (challenge:
person) hacer frente a; (grapple with)
agarrar; (FOOTBALL) cargar; (RUGBY)
placar

tacky [tæki] adj pegajoso; (pej) cutre

tact [tækt] n tacto, discreción f
❏ **tactful** adj discreto, diplomático

tactics [tæktɪks] npl táctica

tactless [tæktlɪs] adj indiscreto

tadpole [tædpəul] n renacuajo

taffy [tæfɪ] (US) n melcocha

tag [tæg] n (label) etiqueta

tail [teɪl] n cola; (of shirt, coat) faldón m
♦ vt (follow) vigilar a; **tails** npl (formal
suit) levita

tailor [teɪlə] n sastre m

Taiwan [taɪwɑːn] n Taiwán m
❏ **Taiwanese** [taɪwɑːniːz] adj, n
taiwanés(-esa) m/f

take [teɪk] (pt **took**, pp **taken**) vt tomar;
(grab) coger (SP), agarrar (LAm); (gain:
prize) ganar; (require: effort, courage)
exigir; (tolerate: pain etc) aguantar;
(hold: passengers etc) tener cabida
para; (accompany, bring, carry) llevar;
(exam) presentarse a; **to ~ sth from**
(drawer etc) sacar algo de; (person)
quitar algo a; **I ~ it that ...** supongo que
... ▸ **take after** vt fus parecerse a
▸ **take apart** vt desmontar ▸ **take
away** vt (remove) llevar; (carry) llevar;
(MATH) restar ▸ **take back** vt (return)
devolver; (one's words) retractarse de
▸ **take down** vt (building) derribar;
(letter etc) apuntar ▸ **take in** vt
(deceive) engañar; (understand)
entender; (include) abarcar; (lodger)
acoger, recibir ▸ **take off** vi (AVIAT)
despegar ♦ vt (remove) quitar ▸ **take
on** vt (work) aceptar; (employee)
contratar; (opponent) desafiar ▸ **take
out** vt sacar ▸ **take over** vt (business)

tomar posesión de; (country) tomar el
poder ♦ vi: **to ~ over from sb**
reemplazar a algn ▸ **take up** vt (a
dress) acortar; (occupy: time, space)
ocupar; (engage in: hobby etc)
dedicarse a; (accept): **to take sb up on**
aceptar algo de algn ▸ **takeaway**
(BRIT) (US) (food) para llevar ♦ n tienda or
restaurante m de comida para llevar
❏ **taken** pp of **take** ❏ **takeoff** n
(AVIAT) despegue m ❏ **takeout** (US) n
= **takeaway** ❏ **takeover** n (COMM)
absorción f ❏ **takings** npl (COMM)
ingresos mpl

talc [tælk] n (also: **talcum powder**)
(polvos de) talco

tale [teɪl] n (story) cuento; (account)
relación f; **to tell tales** (fig) chivarse

talent [tælnt] n talento ❏ **talented**
adj de talento

talk [tɔːk] n charla; (conversation)
conversación f; (gossip) habladurías fpl,
chismes mpl ♦ vi hablar; **talks** npl (POL
etc) conversaciones fpl; **to ~ about**
hablar de; **to ~ sb into doing sth**
convencer a algn para que haga algo;
to ~ sb out of doing sth disuadir a algn
de que haga algo; **to ~ shop** hablar del
trabajo ▸ **talk over** vt discutir ❏ **talk
show** n programa m de entrevistas

tall [tɔːl] adj alto; (object) grande; **to be
6 feet ~** (person) ≈ medir 1 metro 80

tambourine [tæmbəriːn] n pandereta

tame [teɪm] adj domesticado; (fig)
mediocre

tamper [tæmpə] vi: **to ~ with** tocar,
andar con

tampon [tæmpən] n tampón m

tan [tæn] n (also: **suntan**) bronceado
♦ vi ponerse moreno ♦ adj (colour)
marrón

tandem [tændəm] n tándem m

tangerine [tændʒəriːn] n mandarina

tangle [tæŋgl] n enredo; **to get in(to) a
~** enredarse

tank [tæŋk] n (water tank) depósito, tanque m; (for fish) acuario; (MIL) tanque m

tanker ['tæŋkə] n (in ship) buque m; (truck) camión m cisterna

tanned [tænd] adj (skin) moreno

tantrum ['tæntrəm] n rabieta

Tanzania [tænzə'nɪə] n Tanzania

tap [tæp] n (BRIT: on sink etc) grifo (SP), llave f, canilla (RPl); (gas tap) llave f; (gentle blow) golpecito ♦ vt (hit gently) dar golpecitos en; (resources) utilizar, explotar; (telephone) intervenir; **on ~** (fig: resources) a mano ☐ **tap dancing** n claqué n

tape [teɪp] n (also: magnetic ~) cinta magnética; (cassette) cassette f, cinta; (sticky tape) cinta adhesiva; (for tying) cinta ♦ vt (record) grabar (en cinta); (stick with tape) pegar con cinta adhesiva ☐ **tape measure** n cinta métrica, metro ☐ **tape recorder** n grabadora

tapestry ['tæpɪstrɪ] n (object) tapiz m; (art) tapicería

tar [tɑː] n alquitrán m, brea

target ['tɑːgɪt] n blanco

tariff ['tærɪf] n (on goods) arancel m; (BRIT: in hotels etc) tarifa

tarmac ['tɑːmæk] n (BRIT: on road) asfaltado; (AVIAT) pista de aterrizaje

tarpaulin [tɑː'pɔːlɪn] n lona impermeabilizada

tarragon ['tærəgən] n estragón m

tart [tɑːt] n (CULIN) tarta; (BRIT: inf: prostitute) puta ♦ adj agrio, ácido

tartan ['tɑːtn] n tejido escocés m

tartar(e) sauce ['tɑːtə-] n salsa tártara

task [tɑːsk] n tarea; **to take to ~** reprender

taste [teɪst] n (sense) gusto; (flavour) sabor m; (sample): **have a ~!** ¡prueba un poquito!; (fig) muestra, idea ♦ vt probar ♦ vi: **to ~ of** or **like** (fish, garlic etc) saber a; **you can ~ the garlic (in it)** se nota el sabor a ajo; **in good/bad ~**

de buen/mal gusto ☐ **tasteful** adj de buen gusto ☐ **tasteless** adj (food) soso; (remark etc) de mal gusto ☐ **tasty** adj sabroso, rico

tatters ['tætəz] npl: **in ~** hecho jirones

tattoo [tə'tuː] n tatuaje m; (spectacle) espectáculo militar ♦ vt tatuar

taught [tɔːt] pt, pp of **teach**

taunt [tɔːnt] n burla ♦ vt burlarse de

Taurus ['tɔːrəs] n Tauro

taut [tɔːt] adj tirante, tenso

tax [tæks] n impuesto ♦ vt gravar (con un impuesto); (fig: memory) poner a prueba; (: patience) agotar ☐ **tax-free** adj libre de impuestos

taxi ['tæksɪ] n taxi m ♦ vi (AVIAT) rodar por la pista ☐ **taxi driver** n taxista mf ☐ **taxi rank** (BRIT) n = **taxi stand** ☐ **taxi stand** n parada de taxis

tax payer n contribuyente mf

TB n abbr = **tuberculosis**

tea [tiː] n té m; (BRIT: meal) = merienda (SP); cena; **high ~** (BRIT) merienda-cena (SP) ☐ **tea bag** n bolsita de té ☐ **tea break** (BRIT) n descanso para el té

teach [tiːtʃ] (pt, pp taught) vt: **to ~ sb sth, ~ sth to sb** enseñar algo a algn ♦ vi (be a teacher) ser profesor(a), enseñar ☐ **teacher** n (in secondary school) profesor(a) m/f; (in primary school) maestro(-a), profesor(a) de EGB ☐ **teaching** n enseñanza

tea: tea cloth n paño de cocina, trapo de cocina (LAm) ☐ **teacup** n taza para el té

tea leaves npl hojas de té

team [tiːm] n equipo; (of horses) tiro ▶ **team up** vi asociarse

teapot ['tiːpɒt] n tetera

tear¹ [tɪə] n lágrima; **in tears** llorando

tear² [tɛə] (pt **tore**, pp **torn**) n rasgón m, desgarrón m ♦ vt romper, rasgar ♦ vi rasgarse ▶ **tear apart** vt (also fig) hacer pedazos ▶ **tear down** vt +adv (building, statue) derribar; (poster, flag) arrancar ▶ **tear off** vt (sheet of paper *etc*) arrancar; (*one's clothes*) quitarse a tirones ▶ **tear up** *vt* (*sheet of paper etc*) romper

tearful ['tɪəfəl] *adj* lloroso

tear gas ['tɪə-] *n* gas *m* lacrimógeno

tearoom ['tiːruːm] *n* salón *m* de té

tease [tiːz] *vt* tomar el pelo a

tea: **teaspoon** *n* cucharita; (*also*: **teaspoonful**: *as measurement*) cucharada ❑ **teatime** *n* hora del té ❑ **tea towel** (BRIT) *n* paño de cocina

technical ['tɛknɪkl] *adj* técnico

technician [tɛk'nɪʃn] *n* técnico(-a)

technique [tɛk'niːk] *n* técnica

technology [tɛk'nɔlədʒɪ] *n* tecnología

teddy (bear) ['tɛdɪ-] *n* osito de felpa

tedious ['tiːdɪəs] *adj* pesado, aburrido

tee [tiː] *n* (GOLF) tee *m*

teen [tiːn] *adj* = **teenage** ♦ *n* (US) = **teenager**

teenage ['tiːneɪdʒ] *adj* (*fashions etc*) juvenil; (*children*) quinceañero ❑ **teenager** *n* adolescente *mf*

teens [tiːnz] *npl*: **to be in one's ~** ser adolescente

teeth [tiːθ] *npl of* **tooth**

teetotal ['tiːˈtəutl] *adj* abstemio

telecommunications [tɛlɪkəmjuːnɪ'keɪʃənz] *fpl* telecomunicaciones *fpl*

telegram ['tɛlɪɡræm] *n* telegrama *m*

telegraph pole ['tɛlɪɡrɑːf-] *n* poste *m* telegráfico

telephone ['tɛlɪfəun] *n* teléfono ♦ *vt* llamar por teléfono, telefonear; (*message*) dar por teléfono; **to be on the ~** (*talking*) hablar por teléfono; (*possessing telephone*) tener teléfono ❑ **telephone book** *n* guía *f* telefónica ❑ **telephone booth**, **telephone box** (BRIT) *n* cabina telefónica ❑ **telephone call** *n* llamada (telefónica) ❑ **telephone directory** *n* guía (telefónica) ❑ **telephone number** *n* número de teléfono

telesales ['tɛliːseɪlz] *npl* televenta(s) (*f(pl)*)

telescope ['tɛlɪskəup] *n* telescopio

televise ['tɛlɪvaɪz] *vt* televisar

television ['tɛlɪvɪʒən] *n* televisión *f*; **on ~** en la televisión ❑ **television programme** *n* programa *m* de televisión

tell [tɛl] (*pt, pp* **told**) *vt* decir; (*relate: story*) contar; (*distinguish*): **to ~ sth from** distinguir algo de ♦ *vi* (*talk*): **to ~ (of)** contar; (*have effect*) tener efecto; **to ~ sb to do sth** mandar a algn hacer algo ▶ **tell off** *vt*: **to tell sb off** regañar a algn ❑ **teller** *n* (*in bank*) cajero(-a)

telly ['tɛlɪ] (BRIT: *inf*) *n abbr* (= *television*) tele *f*

temp [tɛmp] *n abbr* (BRIT: = *temporary*) temporero(-a)

temper ['tɛmpə'] *n* (*nature*) carácter *m*; (*mood*) humor *m*; (*bad temper*) (mal) genio; (*fit of anger*) acceso de ira ♦ *vt* (*moderate*) moderar; **to be in a ~** estar furioso; **to lose one's ~** enfadarse, enojarse

temperament ['tɛmprəmənt] *n* (*nature*) temperamento ❑ **temperamental** [tɛmprə'mɛntl] *adj* temperamental

temperature ['tɛmprətʃə'] *n* temperatura; **to have** *o* **run a ~** tener fiebre

temple ['tɛmpl] *n* (*building*) templo; (ANAT) sien *f*

temporary ['tɛmpərərɪ] *adj* provisional; (*passing*) transitorio; (*worker*) temporero; (*job*) temporal

tempt [tɛmpt] *vt* tentar; **to ~ sb into doing sth** tentar *o* inducir a algn a hacer algo ❑ **temptation** *n* tentación *f* ❑ **tempting** *adj* tentador(a); (*food*) apetitoso(-a)

ten [tɛn] *num* diez

tenant ['tɛnənt] *n* inquilino(-a)

tend [tɛnd] vt cuidar ♦ vi: **to ~ to do sth** tener tendencia a hacer algo ❑ **tendency** ['tɛndənsɪ] n tendencia

tender ['tɛndə'] adj (person, care) tierno, cariñoso; (meat) tierno; (sore) sensible ♦ n (COMM: offer) oferta; (money): **legal ~** moneda de curso legal ♦ vt ofrecer

tendon ['tɛndən] n tendón m

tenner ['tɛnə'] n (inf) (billete m de) diez libras fpl

tennis ['tɛnɪs] n tenis m ❑ **tennis ball** n pelota de tenis ❑ **tennis court** n cancha de tenis ❑ **tennis match** n partido de tenis ❑ **tennis player** n tenista mf ❑ **tennis racket** n raqueta de tenis

tenor ['tɛnə'] n (MUS) tenor m

tenpin bowling ['tɛnpɪn-] n (juego de los) bolos

tense [tɛns] adj (person) nervioso; (moment, atmosphere) tenso; (muscle) tenso, en tensión ♦ n (LING) tiempo

tension ['tɛnʃən] n tensión f

tent [tɛnt] n tienda (de campaña) (SP), carpa (LAm)

tentative ['tɛntətɪv] adj (person, smile) indeciso; (conclusion, plans) provisional

tenth [tɛnθ] num décimo

tent: tent peg n clavija, estaca ❑ **tent pole** n mástil m

tepid ['tɛpɪd] adj tibio

term [tə:m] n (word) término; (period) periodo; (SCOL) trimestre ♦ vt llamar; **terms** npl (conditions, COMM) condiciones fpl; **in the short/long ~** a corto/largo plazo; **to be on good terms with sb** llevarse bien con algn; **to come to terms with** (problem) aceptar

terminal ['tə:mɪnl] adj (disease) mortal; (patient) terminal ♦ n (ELEC) borne m; (COMPUT) terminal m; (also: **air ~**) terminal f; (BRIT: also: **coach ~**) estación f terminal f

terminate ['tə:mɪneɪt] vt terminar

termini ['tə:mɪnaɪ] npl of **terminus**

terminology [tə:mɪ'nɔlədʒɪ] n terminología

terminus ['tə:mɪnəs] (pl **termini**) n término, (estación f) terminal f

terrace ['tɛrəs] n terraza; (BRIT: row of houses) hilera de casas adosadas; **the terraces** (BRIT SPORT) las gradas fpl ❑ **terraced** adj (garden) en terrazas; (house) adosado

terrain [tɛ'reɪn] n terreno

terrestrial [tɪ'rɛstrɪəl] adj (life) terrestre; (BRIT: channel) de transmisión (por) vía terrestre

terrible ['tɛrɪbl] adj terrible, horrible; (inf) atroz ❑ **terribly** adv terriblemente; (very badly) malísimamente

terrier ['tɛrɪə'] n terrier m

terrific [tə'rɪfɪk] adj (very great) tremendo; (wonderful) fantástico, fenomenal

terrified ['tɛrɪfaɪd] adj aterrorizado

terrify ['tɛrɪfaɪ] vt aterrorizar ❑ **terrifying** adj aterrador(a)

territorial [tɛrɪ'tɔ:rɪəl] adj territorial

territory ['tɛrɪtərɪ] n territorio

terror ['tɛrə'] n terror m ❑ **terrorism** n terrorismo ❑ **terrorist** n terrorista mf

test [tɛst] n (gen, CHEM) prueba; (MED) examen m; (SCOL) examen m, test m; (also: **driving ~**) examen m de conducir ♦ vt probar, poner a prueba; (MED, SCOL) examinar

testicle ['tɛstɪkl] n testículo

testify ['tɛstɪfaɪ] vi (LAW) prestar declaración; **to ~ to sth** atestiguar algo

testimony ['tɛstɪmənɪ] n (LAW) testimonio

test: test match n (CRICKET, RUGBY) partido internacional ❑ **test tube** n probeta

tetanus ['tɛtənəs] n tétano

text [tɛkst] n texto; (on mobile phone) mensaje m de texto ♦ vt: **to ~ sb** (inf) enviar un mensaje (de texto) *or* un SMS a algn □ **textbook** *n* libro de texto

textile ['tekstaɪl] *n* textil *m*, tejido

text message *n* mensaje *m* de texto

text messaging [-'mesɪdʒɪŋ] *n* (envío de) mensajes *mpl* de texto

texture ['tekstʃə'] *n* textura

Thai [taɪ] *adj, n* tailandés(-esa) *m/f*

Thailand ['taɪlænd] *n* Tailandia

than [ðæn] *conj* (*in comparisons*): **more ~ 10/once** más de 10/una vez; **I have more/less ~ you/Paul** tengo más/menos que tú/Paul; **she is older ~ you think** es mayor de lo que piensas

thank [θæŋk] *vt* dar las gracias a, agradecer; **~ you (very much)** muchas gracias; **~ God!** ¡gracias a Dios! ♦ *excl* (*also*: **many thanks, thanks a lot**) ¡gracias!; **thanks to** *prep* gracias a; **thanks** *npl* gracias *fpl* ♦ **thankfully** *adv* (*fortunately*) afortunadamente □ **Thanksgiving (Day)** *n* día *m* de Acción de Gracias

THANKSGIVING (DAY)

En Estados Unidos el cuarto jueves de noviembre es **Thanksgiving Day**, fiesta oficial en la que se recuerda la celebración que hicieron los primeros colonos norteamericanos ("Pilgrims" o "Pilgrim Fathers") tras la estupenda cosecha de 1621, por la que se dan gracias a Dios. En Canadá se celebra una fiesta semejante el segundo lunes de octubre, aunque no está relacionada con dicha fecha histórica.

that

KEYWORD

[ðæt] (*pl* **those**) *adj* (*demonstrative*) ese(-a); (*pl*) esos(-as); (*more remote*) aquel (aquella); (*pl*) aquellos(-as); **leave those books on the table** deja esos libros sobre la mesa; **that one** ése (ésa); (*more remote*) aquél

(aquélla); **that one over there** ése (ésa) de ahí; aquél (aquélla) de allí ♦ *pron*

1 (*demonstrative*) ése(-a); (*pl*) ésos(-as); (*neuter*) eso; (*more remote*) aquél (aquélla); (*pl*) aquéllos(-as); (*neuter*) aquello; **what's that?** ¿qué es eso (or aquello)?; **who's that?** ¿quién es ése(-a) (*or* aquél (aquélla))?; **is that you?** ¿eres tú?; **will you eat all that?** ¿vas a comer todo eso?; **that's my house** ésa es mi casa; **that's what he said** eso es lo que dijo; **that is (to say)** es decir

2 (*relative: subject, object*) que; (*with preposition*) (el ((la))) que *etc*, el (la) cual *etc*; **the book (that) I read** el libro que leí; **the books that are in the library** los libros que están en la biblioteca; **all (that) I have** todo lo que tengo; **the box (that) I put it in** la caja en la que *or* donde lo puse; **the people (that) I spoke to** la gente con la que hablé

3 (*relative: of time*) que; **the day (that) he came** el día (en) que vino ♦ *conj* que; **he thought that I was ill** creyó que yo estaba enfermo ♦ *adv* (*demonstrative*): **I can't work that much** no puedo trabajar tanto; **I didn't realise it was that bad** no creí que fuera tan malo; **that high** así de alto

thatched [θætʃt] *adj* (*roof*) de paja; (*cottage*) con tejado de paja

thaw [θɔː] *n* deshielo ♦ *vi* (*ice*) derretirse; (*food*) descongelarse ♦ *vt* (*food*) descongelar

the

KEYWORD

[ðiː, ðə] *def art*

1 (*gen*) el *f*, la *pl*, los *fpl*, las (*NB* 'el'

immediately before f n beginning with stressed (h)a; a + el = al; de + el = del); **the boy/girl** el chico/la chica; **the books/flowers** los libros/las flores; **to the postman/from the drawer** al cartero/del cajón; **I haven't the time/money** no tengo tiempo/dinero

2 (+*adj to form n*) los; lo; **the rich and the poor** los ricos y los pobres; **to attempt the impossible** intentar lo imposible

3 (*in titles*): **Elizabeth the First** Isabel primera; **Peter the Great** Pedro el Grande

4 (*in comparisons*): **the more he works the more he earns** cuanto más trabaja más gana

theatre ['θɪətə*] (*US* **theater**) *n* teatro; (*also:* **lecture ~**) *n* aula; (*MED: also:* **operating ~**) quirófano

theft [θeft] *n* robo

their [ðeə*] *adj* su □ **theirs** *pron* (el) suyo ((la) suya *etc*); *see also* **my**; **mine¹**

them [ðem, ðəm] *pron* (*direct*) los/las; (*indirect*) les; (*stressed, after prep*) ellos (ellas); *see also* **me**

theme [θiːm] *n* tema *m* □ **theme park** *n* parque de atracciones (*en torno a un tema central*)

themselves [ðəm'selvz] *pl pron* (*subject*) ellos mismos (ellas mismas); (*complement*) se; (*after prep*) sí (mismos (as)); *see also* **oneself**

then [ðen] *adv* (*at that time*) entonces; (*next*) después; (*later*) luego, después; (*and also*) además ♦ *conj* (*therefore*) en ese caso, entonces ♦ *adj*: **the ~ president** el entonces presidente; **by ~** para entonces; **from ~ on** desde entonces

theology [θɪ'ɒlədʒɪ] *n* teología

theory ['θɪərɪ] *n* teoría

therapist ['θerəpɪst] *n* terapeuta *mf*

therapy ['θerəpɪ] *n* terapia

KEYWORD

['ðeə*] *adv*

1: **there is, there are** hay; **there is no-one here/no bread left** no hay nadie aquí/no queda pan; **there has been an accident** ha habido un accidente

2 (*referring to place*) ahí; (*distant*) allí; **it's there** está ahí; **put it in/on/up/down there** ponlo ahí dentro/encima/arriba/abajo; **I want that book there** quiero ese libro de ahí; **there he is!** ¡ahí está!

3: **there, there** (*esp to child*) ea, ea

there: **thereabouts** *adv* por ahí
□ **thereafter** *adv* después
□ **thereby** *adv* así, de ese modo
□ **therefore** *adv* por lo tanto
□ **there's** = **there is**; **there has**

thermal ['θəːml] *adj* termal; (*paper*) térmico

thermometer [θə'mɒmɪtə*] *n* termómetro

thermostat ['θəːməʊstæt] *n* termostato

these [ðiːz] *pl adj* estos(-as) ♦ *pl pron* éstos(-as)

thesis ['θiːsɪs] (*pl* **theses**) *n* tesis *f inv*

they [ðeɪ] *pl pron* ellos (ellas); (*stressed*) ellos (mismos) (ellas (mismas)); **~ say that ...** (*it is said that*) se dice que ...
□ **they'd** = **they had**; **they would**
□ **they'll** = **they shall**; **they will**
□ **they're** = **they are** □ **they've** = **they have**

thick [θɪk] *adj* (*in consistency*) espeso; (*in size*) grueso; (*stupid*) torpe ♦ *n*: **in the ~ of the battle** en lo más reñido de la batalla; **it's 20 cm ~** tiene 20 cm de espesor □ **thicken** *vi* espesarse ♦ *vt* (*sauce etc*) espesar □ **thickness** *n* espesor *m*; grueso

thief [θi:f] (pl **thieves**) n ladrón(-ona) m/f

thigh [θaɪ] n muslo

thin [θɪn] adj (person, animal) flaco; (in size) delgado; (in consistency) poco espeso; (hair, crowd) escaso ♦ vt: **to ~ (down)** diluir

thing [θɪŋ] n cosa; (object) objeto, artículo; (matter) asunto; (mania): **to have a ~ about sb/sth** estar obsesionado con algn/algo; **things** npl (belongings) efectos mpl (personales); **the best ~ would be to ...** lo mejor sería ...; **how are things?** ¿qué tal?

think [θɪŋk] (pt, pp **thought**) vi pensar ♦ vt pensar, creer; **what did you ~ of them?** ¿qué te parecieron?; **to ~ about sth/sb** pensar en algo/algn; **I'll ~ about it** lo pensaré; **to ~ of doing sth** pensar en hacer algo; **I ~ so/not** creo que sí/no; **to ~ well of sb** tener buen concepto de algn ▶ **think over** vt reflexionar sobre, meditar ▶ **think up** vt (plan etc) idear

third [θɜ:d] adj (before n) tercer(a); (following n) tercero(-a) ♦ n tercero(-a); (fraction) tercio; (BRIT SCOL: degree) título de licenciado con calificación de aprobado ❑ **thirdly** adv en tercer lugar ❑ **third party insurance** (BRIT) n seguro contra terceros ❑ **Third World** n Tercer Mundo

thirst [θɜ:st] n sed f ❑ **thirsty** adj (person, animal) sediento; (work) que da sed; **to be thirsty** tener sed

thirteen ['θɜ:'ti:n] num trece ❑ **thirteenth** [-'ti:nθ] adj decimotercero

thirtieth ['θɜ:tɪəθ] adj trigésimo

thirty ['θɜ:tɪ] num treinta

this

KEYWORD

[ðɪs] (pl **these**) adj (demonstrative) este(-a) pl; estos(-as); (neuter) esto; **this man/woman** este hombre (esta mujer); **these children/flowers** estos

chicos/estas flores; **this one (here)** éste(-a), esto (de aquí)
♦ pron (demonstrative) éste(-a) pl, éstos(-as); (neuter) esto; **who is this?** ¿quién es éste/ésta?; **what is this?** ¿qué es esto?; **this is where I live** aquí vivo; **this is what he said** esto es lo que dijo; **this is Mr Brown** (in introductions) le presento al Sr. Brown; (photo) éste es el Sr. Brown; (on telephone) habla el Sr. Brown
♦ adv (demonstrative): **this high/long** etc así de alto/largo etc; **this far** hasta aquí

thistle ['θɪsl] n cardo

thorn [θɔ:n] n espina

thorough ['θʌrə] adj (search) minucioso; (wash) a fondo; (knowledge, research) profundo; (person) meticuloso ❑ **thoroughly** adv (search) minuciosamente; (study) profundamente; (wash) a fondo; (utterly: bad, wet etc) completamente, totalmente

those [ðəuz] pl adj esos (esas); (more remote) aquellos(-as)

though [ðəu] conj aunque ♦ adv sin embargo

thought [θɔ:t] pt, pp of **think** ♦ n pensamiento; (opinion) opinión f ❑ **thoughtful** adj pensativo; (serious) serio; (considerate) atento ❑ **thoughtless** adj desconsiderado

thousand ['θauzənd] num mil; **two ~** dos mil; **thousands of** miles de ❑ **thousandth** num milésimo

thrash [θræʃ] vt azotar; (defeat) derrotar

thread [θred] n hilo; (of screw) rosca ♦ vt (needle) enhebrar

threat [θret] n amenaza ❑ **threaten** vi amenazar ♦ vt: **to threaten sb with/to do** amenazar a algn con/con hacer

❏ **threatening** adj amenazador(a), amenazante

three [θriː] num tres ❏ **three-dimensional** adj tridimensional ❏ **three-piece suite** n tresillo ❏ **three-quarters** npl tres cuartas partes; **three-quarters full** tres cuartas partes lleno

threshold [ˈθrɛʃhəʊld] n umbral m

threw [θruː] pt of **throw**

thrill [θrɪl] n (excitement) emoción f; (shudder) estremecimiento ♦ vt emocionar; **to be thrilled** (with gift etc) estar encantado ❏ **thrilled** adj: **I was thrilled** estaba emocionada ❏ **thriller** n novela (or obra or película) de suspense ❏ **thrilling** adj emocionante

thriving [ˈθraɪvɪŋ] adj próspero

throat [θrəʊt] n garganta; **to have a sore ~** tener dolor de garganta

throb [θrɔb] vi latir; dar puntadas; vibrar

throne [θrəʊn] n trono

through [θruː] prep por, a través de; (time) durante; (by means of) por medio de, mediante; (owing to) gracias a ♦ adj (ticket, train) directo ♦ adv completamente, de parte a parte; de principio a fin; **to put sb ~ to sb** (TEL) poner a algn con algn; **to be ~** (TEL) tener comunicación; (have finished) haber terminado; **"no ~ road"** (BRIT) "calle sin salida" ❏ **throughout** prep (place) por todas partes de, por todo; (time) durante todo ♦ adv por or en todas partes

throw [θrəʊ] (pt **threw**, pp **thrown**) n tiro; (SPORT) lanzamiento ♦ vt tirar, echar; (SPORT) lanzar; (rider) derribar; (fig) desconcertar; **to ~ a party** dar una fiesta ► **throw away** vt tirar; (money) derrochar ► **throw in** vt (SPORT: ball) sacar; (include) incluir ► **throw off** vt deshacerse de ► **throw out** vt tirar; (person) echar; expulsar ► **throw up** vi vomitar

thru [θruː] (US) = **through**

thrush [θrʌʃ] n zorzal m, tordo

thrust [θrʌst] (pt, pp ~) vt empujar con fuerza

thud [θʌd] n golpe m sordo

thug [θʌɡ] n gamberro(-a)

thumb [θʌm] n (ANAT) pulgar m; **to ~ a lift** hacer autostop ❏ **thumbtack** (US) n chincheta (SP)

thump [θʌmp] n golpe m; (sound) ruido seco or sordo ♦ vt golpear ♦ vi (heart etc) palpitar

thunder [ˈθʌndəʳ] n trueno ♦ vi tronar; (train also): **to ~ past** pasar como un trueno ❏ **thunderstorm** n tormenta

Thur(s). abbr (= Thursday) juev

Thursday [ˈθɜːzdɪ] n jueves m inv

thus [ðʌs] adv así, de este modo

thwart [θwɔːt] vt frustrar

thyme [taɪm] n tomillo

Tibet [tɪˈbɛt] n el Tibet

tick [tɪk] n (sound: of clock) tictac m; (mark) palomita; (ZOOL) garrapata; (BRIT: inf): **in a ~** en un instante ♦ vi hacer tictac ♦ vt marcar ► **tick off** vt marcar; (person) reñir

ticket [ˈtɪkɪt] n billete m (SP), boleto (LAm); (for cinema etc) entrada; (in shop: on goods) etiqueta; (for raffle) papeleta; (for library) tarjeta; (parking ticket) multa de aparcamiento (SP) or por estacionamiento (indebido) (LAm) ❏ **ticket barrier** n (BRIT: RAIL) barrera más allá de la cual se necesita billete/boleto ❏ **ticket collector** n revisor(a) m/f ❏ **ticket inspector** n revisor(a) m/f, inspector(a) m/f de boletos (LAm) ❏ **ticket machine** n máquina de billetes (SP) or boletos (LAm) ❏ **ticket office** n (THEATRE) taquilla (SP), boletería (LAm); (RAIL) mostrador m de billetes (SP) or boletos (LAm)

tickle [ˈtɪkl] vt hacer cosquillas a ♦ vi hacer cosquillas ❏ **ticklish** adj (person) cosquilloso; (problem) delicado

tide [taɪd] n marea; (fig: of events etc) curso, marcha

tidy ['taɪdɪ] adj (room etc) ordenado; (dress, work) limpio; (person) (bien) arreglado ♦ vt (also: ~ **up**) poner en orden

tie [taɪ] n (string etc) atadura; (BRIT: also: **necktie**) corbata; (fig: link) vínculo, lazo; (SPORT etc: draw) empate m ♦ vt atar ♦ vi (SPORT etc) empatar; **to ~ in a bow** atar con un lazo; **to ~ a knot in sth** hacer un nudo en algo ▶ **tie down** vt (fig: person: restrict) atar; (: to price, date etc) obligar a ▶ **tie up** vt (dog, person) atar; (arrangements) concluir; **to be tied up** (busy) estar ocupado

tier [tɪə'] n grada; (of cake) piso

tiger ['taɪgə'] n tigre m

tight [taɪt] adj (rope) tirante; (money) escaso; (clothes) ajustado; (bend) cerrado; (shoes, schedule) apretado; (budget) ajustado; (security) estricto; (inf: drunk) borracho ♦ adv (squeeze) muy fuerte; (shut) bien ▶ **tighten** vt (rope) estirar; (screw, grip) apretar; (security) reforzar ♦ vi estirarse; apretarse ▶ **tightly** adv (grasp) muy fuerte ▶ **tights** (BRIT) npl panti mpl

tile [taɪl] n (on roof) teja; (on floor) baldosa; (on wall) azulejo

till [tɪl] n caja (registradora) ♦ vt (land) cultivar ♦ prep, conj = **until**

tilt [tɪlt] vt inclinar ♦ vi inclinarse

timber ['tɪmbə'] n (material) madera

time [taɪm] n tiempo; (epoch: often pl) época; (by clock) hora; (moment) momento; (occasion) vez f; (MUS) compás m ♦ vt calcular o medir el tiempo de; (race) cronometrar; (remark, visit etc) elegir el momento para; **a long ~** mucho tiempo; **4 at a ~** de 4 en 4; **4 a la vez**; **for the ~ being** de momento, por ahora; **from ~ to ~** de vez en cuando; **at times** a veces; **in ~** (soon enough) a tiempo; (after some time) con el tiempo; (MUS) al compás; **in a week's ~** dentro de una semana; **in**

no ~ en un abrir y cerrar de ojos; **any ~** cuando sea; **on ~** a la hora; **5 times 5** 5 por 5; **what ~ is it?** ¿qué hora es? **to have a good ~** pasarlo bien, divertirse ▶ **time limit** n plazo ▶ **timely** adj oportuno ▶ **timer** n (in kitchen etc) programador m horario ▶ **time-share** n apartamento (or casa) a tiempo compartido ▶ **timetable** n horario ▶ **time zone** n huso horario

timid ['tɪmɪd] adj tímido

timing ['taɪmɪŋ] n (SPORT) cronometraje m; **the ~ of his resignation** el momento que eligió para dimitir

tin [tɪn] n estaño; (also: ~ **plate**) hojalata; (BRIT: can) lata ▶ **tinfoil** n papel m de estaño

tingle ['tɪŋgl] vi (person): **to ~ (with)** estremecerse (de); (hands etc) hormiguear

tinker ['tɪŋkə']: **~ with** vt fus jugar con, tocar

tinned [tɪnd] (BRIT) adj (food) en lata, en conserva

tin opener [-'əupnə'] (BRIT) n abrelatas m inv

tint [tɪnt] n matiz m; (for hair) tinte m ▶ **tinted** adj (hair) teñido; (glass, spectacles) ahumado

tiny ['taɪnɪ] adj minúsculo, pequeñito

tip [tɪp] n (end) punta; (gratuity) propina; (BRIT: for rubbish) vertedero; (advice) consejo ♦ vt (waiter) dar una propina a; (tilt) inclinar; (empty: also: ~ **out**) vaciar, echar; (overturn: also: ~ **over**) volcar ▶ **tip off** vt avisar, poner sobreaviso a

tiptoe ['tɪptəu]: **on ~** de puntillas

tire ['taɪə'] n (US) = **tyre** ♦ vt cansar ♦ vi cansarse; (become bored) aburrirse ▶ **tired** adj cansado; **to be tired of sth** estar harto de algo ▶ **tire pressure** (US) = **tyre pressure** ▶ **tiring** adj cansado

tissue ['tɪʃuː] n tejido; (paper handkerchief) pañuelo de papel, kleenex® m ◻ **tissue paper** n papel m de seda

tit [tɪt] n (bird) herrerillo común; **to give ~ for tat** dar ojo por ojo

title ['taɪtl] n título

T-junction ['tiːdʒʌŋkʃən] n cruce m en T

TM abbr = **trademark**

to
KEYWORD
[tuː, tə] prep

1 (direction) a; **to go to France/ London/school/the station** ir a Francia/Londres/al colegio/a la estación; **to go to Claude's/the doctor's** ir a casa de Claude/al médico; **the road to Edinburgh** la carretera de Edimburgo

2 (as far as) hasta, a; **from here to London** de aquí a or hasta Londres; **to count to 10** contar hasta 10; **from 40 to 50 people** entre 40 y 50 personas

3 (with expressions of time): **a quarter/twenty to 5** las 5 menos cuarto/veinte

4 (for, of): **the key to the front door** la llave de la puerta principal; **she is secretary to the director** es la secretaria del director; **a letter to his wife** una carta a or para su mujer

5 (expressing indirect object): **to give sth to sb** darle algo a algn; **to talk to sb** hablar con algn; **to be a danger to sb** ser un peligro para algn; **to carry out repairs to sth** hacer reparaciones en algo

6 (in relation to): **3 goals to 2** 3 goles a 2; **30 miles to the gallon** ≈ 94 litros a los cien (kms)

7 (purpose, result): **to come to sb's aid** venir en auxilio or ayuda de algn; **to sentence sb to death** condenar a algn a muerte; **to my great surprise** con gran sorpresa mía

♦ **with vb**

1 (simple infin): **to go/eat** ir/comer

2 (following another vb): **to want/try/ start to do** querer/intentar/empezar a hacer

3 (with vb omitted): **I don't want to** no quiero

4 (purpose, result) para; **I did it to help you** lo hice para ayudarte; **he came to see you** vino a verte

5 (equivalent to relative clause): **I have things to do** tengo cosas que hacer; **the main thing is to try** lo principal es intentarlo

6 (after adj etc): **ready to go** listo para irse; **too old to ...** demasiado viejo (como) para ...

♦ **adv**: **pull/push the door to** tirar de/ empujar la puerta

toad [təud] n sapo ◻ **toadstool** n hongo venenoso

toast [təust] n (CULIN) tostada; (drink, speech) brindis m ♦ vt (CULIN) tostar; (drink) to sb brindar por ◻ **toaster** n tostador m

tobacco [tə'bækəu] n tabaco

toboggan [tə'bɔgən] n tobogán m

today [tə'deɪ] adv, n (also fig) hoy m

toddler ['tɔdlə²] n niño(-a) (que empieza a andar)

toe [təu] n dedo (del pie); (of shoe) punta; **to ~ the line** (fig) conformarse ◻ **toenail** n uña del pie

toffee ['tɔfɪ] n toffee m

together [tə'geðə²] adv juntos; (at same time) al mismo tiempo, a la vez; **~ with** junto con

toilet ['tɔɪlət] n inodoro; (BRIT: room) (cuarto de) baño, servicio ♦ cpd (soap etc) de aseo □ **toilet bag** n neceser m, bolsa de aseo □ **toilet paper** n papel m higiénico □ **toiletries** npl artículos mpl de tocador □ **toilet roll** n rollo de papel higiénico

token ['təukən] n (sign) señal f, muestra; (souvenir) recuerdo; (disc) ficha ♦ adj (strike, payment etc) simbólico; **book/record~** (BRIT) vale m para comprar libros/discos; **gift ~** (BRIT) vale-regalo

Tokyo ['təukjəu] n Tokio, Tokío

told [təuld] pt, pp of **tell**

tolerant ['tɔlərnt] adj: **~ of** tolerante con

tolerate ['tɔləreɪt] vt tolerar

toll [təul] n (of casualties) número de víctimas; (tax, charge) peaje m ♦ vi (bell) doblar □ **toll call** n (US TEL) conferencia, llamada interurbana □ **toll-free** (US) adj, adv gratis

tomato [tə'mɑːtəu] (pl tomatoes) n tomate m □ **tomato sauce** n salsa de tomate

tomb [tuːm] n tumba □ **tombstone** n lápida

tomorrow [tə'mɔrəu] adv, n (also: big) mañana; **the day after ~** pasado mañana; **~ morning** mañana por la mañana

ton [tʌn] n tonelada (BRIT = 1016 kg; US = 907 kg); (metric ton) tonelada métrica; **tons of** (inf) montones de

tone [təun] n tono ♦ vi (also: **~ in**) armonizar ▶ **tone down** vt (criticism) suavizar; (colour) atenuar

tongs [tɔŋz] npl (for coal) tenazas fpl; (curling tongs) tenacillas fpl

tongue [tʌŋ] n lengua; **~ in cheek** irónicamente

tonic ['tɔnɪk] n (MED) tónico; (also: **~ water**) (agua) tónica

tonight [tə'naɪt] adv, n esta noche; esta tarde

tonne [tʌn] n tonelada (métrica) (1.000kg)

tonsil ['tɔnsl] n amígdala □ **tonsillitis** [-'laɪtɪs] n amigdalitis f

too [tuː] adv (excessively) demasiado; (also) también; **~ much** demasiado; **~ many** demasiados(-as)

took [tuk] pt of **take**

tool [tuːl] n herramienta □ **tool box** n caja de herramientas □ **tool kit** n juego de herramientas

tooth [tuːθ] (pl teeth) n (ANAT, TECH) diente m; (molar) muela □ **toothache** n dolor m de muelas □ **toothbrush** n cepillo de dientes □ **toothpaste** n pasta de dientes □ **toothpick** n palillo

top [tɔp] n (of mountain) cumbre f, cima; (of tree) copa; (of head) coronilla; (of ladder, page) lo alto; (of table) superficie f; (of cupboard) parte f de arriba; (lid: of box) tapa; (: of bottle, jar) tapón m; (of list etc) cabeza; (toy) peonza; (garment) blusa; camiseta ♦ adj de arriba; (in rank) principal, primero; (best) mejor ♦ vt (exceed) exceder; (be first in) encabezar; **on ~ of** (above) sobre, encima de; (in addition to) además de; **from ~ to bottom** de pies a cabeza ▶ **top up** vt llenar □ **top floor** n último piso □ **top hat** n sombrero de copa

topic ['tɔpɪk] n tema m □ **topical** adj actual

topless ['tɔplɪs] adj (bather, bikini) topless inv

topping ['tɔpɪŋ] n (CULIN): **with a ~ of cream** con nata por encima

topple ['tɔpl] vt derribar ♦ vi caerse

torch [tɔːtʃ] n antorcha; (BRIT: electric) linterna

tore [tɔːʳ] pt of **tear²**

torment [n 'tɔːment, vt tɔː'ment] n tormento ♦ vt atormentar; (fig: annoy) fastidiar

torn [tɔːn] pp of **tear²**

tornado [tɔː'neɪdəʊ] (pl **tornadoes**) n tornado

torpedo [tɔː'piːdəʊ] (pl **torpedoes**) n torpedo

torrent ['tɒrnt] n torrente m
□ **torrential** [tɒ'renʃl] adj torrencial

tortoise ['tɔːtəs] n tortuga f

torture ['tɔːtʃə] n tortura ♦ vt torturar; (fig) atormentar

Tory ['tɔːrɪ] (BRIT) adj, n (POL) conservador(a) m/f

toss [tɒs] vt tirar, echar; (one's head) sacudir; **to ~ a coin** echar a cara o cruz; **to ~ up for sth** jugar a cara o cruz algo; **to ~ and turn** (in bed) dar vueltas

total ['təʊtl] adj total, entero; (emphatic: failure etc) completo, total ♦ n total m, suma ♦ vt (add up) sumar; (amount to) ascender a

totalitarian [təʊtælɪ'tɛərɪən] adj totalitario

totally ['təʊtəlɪ] adv totalmente

touch [tʌtʃ] n tacto; (contact) contacto ♦ vt tocar; (emotionally) conmover; **a ~** of (fig) un poquito de; **to get in ~ with sb** ponerse en contacto con algn; **to lose ~** (friends) perder contacto ▶ **touch down** vi (on land) aterrizar □ **touchdown** n aterrizaje m; (on sea) amerizaje m; (US FOOTBALL) ensayo □ **touched** adj (moved) conmovido □ **touching** adj (moving) conmovedor(a) □ **touchline** n (SPORT) línea de banda □ **touch-sensitive** adj sensible al tacto

tough [tʌf] adj (material) resistente; (meat) duro; (problem etc) difícil; (policy, stance) inflexible; (person) fuerte

tour [tʊə] n viaje m, vuelta; (also: **package ~**) viaje m todo comprendido; (of town, museum) visita; (by band etc) gira ♦ vt recorrer, visitar □ **tour guide** n guía mf turístico(-a)

tourism ['tʊərɪzm] n turismo

tourist ['tʊərɪst] n turista mf ♦ cpd turístico □ **tourist office** n oficina de turismo

tournament ['tʊənəmənt] n torneo

tour operator n touroperador(a) m/f, operador(a) m/f turístico(-a)

tow [təʊ] vt remolcar; **"on** or **in** (US) **~"** (AUT) "a remolque" ▶ **tow away** vt llevarse a remolque

toward(s) [tə'wɔːd(z)] prep hacia; (attitude) respecto a, con; (purpose) para

towel ['taʊəl] n toalla □ **towelling** n (fabric) felpa

tower ['taʊə] n torre f □ **tower block** (BRIT) n torre f (de pisos)

town [taʊn] n ciudad f; **to go to ~** ir a la ciudad; (fig) echar la casa por la ventana □ **town centre** (BRIT) n centro de la ciudad □ **town hall** n ayuntamiento

tow truck (US) n camión m grúa

toxic ['tɒksɪk] adj tóxico

toy [tɔɪ] n juguete m ▶ **toy with** vt fus jugar con; (idea) acariciar □ **toyshop** n juguetería

trace [treɪs] n rastro ♦ vt (draw) trazar, delinear; (locate) encontrar; (follow) seguir la pista de

track [træk] n (mark) huella, pista; (path: gen) camino, senda; (: of bullet etc) trayectoria; (: of suspect, animal) pista, rastro; (RAIL) vía; (SPORT) pista; (on tape, record) canción f ♦ vt seguir la pista de; **to keep ~** of mantenerse al tanto de, seguir ▶ **track down** vt (prey) seguir el rastro de; (sth lost) encontrar □ **tracksuit** n chandal m

tractor ['træktə] n tractor m

trade [treɪd] n comercio; (skill, job) oficio ♦ vi negociar, comerciar ♦ vt (exchange): **to ~ sth (for sth)** cambiar algo (por algo) ▶ **trade in** vt (old car etc) ofrecer como parte del pago □ **trademark** n marca de fábrica □ **trader** n comerciante m

❏ **tradesman** (*irreg*) *n* (*shopkeeper*) tendero ❏ **trade union** *n* sindicato *m*

trading ['treɪdɪŋ] *n* comercio

tradition [trə'dɪʃən] *n* tradición *f*
❏ **traditional** *adj* tradicional

traffic ['træfɪk] *n* (*gen*, *AUT*) tráfico, circulación *f* ♦ *vi*: **to ~ in** (*pej*: *liquor*, *drugs*) traficar en ❏ **traffic circle** (*US*) *n* isleta ❏ **traffic island** *n* refugio, isleta ❏ **traffic jam** *n* embotellamiento ❏ **traffic lights** *npl* semáforo ❏ **traffic warden** *n* guardia *mf* de tráfico

tragedy ['trædʒədɪ] *n* tragedia

tragic ['trædʒɪk] *adj* trágico

trail [treɪl] *n* (*tracks*) rastro, pista; (*path*) camino, sendero; (*dust*, *smoke*) estela ♦ *vt* (*drag*) arrastrar; (*follow*) seguir la pista de ♦ *vi* arrastrar; (*in contest etc*) ir perdiendo ❏ **trailer** *n* (*AUT*) remolque *m*; (*caravan*) caravana; (*CINEMA*) trailer *m*, avance *m*

train [treɪn] *n* tren *m*; (*of dress*) cola; (*series*) serie *f* ♦ *vt* (*educate*, *teach skills to*) formar; (*sportsman*) entrenar; (*dog*) adiestrar; (*point*: *gun etc*): **to ~ on** apuntar a ♦ *vi* (*SPORT*) entrenarse; (*learn a skill*): **to ~ as a teacher** *etc* estudiar para profesor *etc*; **one's ~ of thought** el razonamiento de algn ❏ **trainee** [treɪ'niː] *n* aprendiz(a) *m/f* ❏ **trainer** *n* (*SPORT*: *coach*) entrenador(a) *m/f*; (*of animals*) domador(a) *m/f*; **trainers** *npl* (*shoes*) zapatillas *fpl* (de deporte) ❏ **training** *n* formación *f*; entrenamiento; **to be in training** (*SPORT*) estar entrenando ❏ **training course** *n* curso de formación ❏ **training shoes** *npl* zapatillas *fpl* de deporte

trait [treɪt] *n* rasgo

traitor ['treɪtə] *n* traidor(a) *m/f*

tram [træm] (*BRIT*) *n* (*also*: **tramcar**) tranvía *m*

tramp [træmp] *n* (*person*) vagabundo(-a); (*inf*. *pej*: *woman*) puta

trample ['træmpl] *vt*: **to ~ (underfoot)** pisotear

trampoline ['træmpəliːn] *n* trampolín *m*

tranquil ['træŋkwɪl] *adj* tranquilo ❏ **tranquillizer** (*US* **tranquilizer**) *n* (*MED*) tranquilizante *m*

transaction [træn'zækʃən] *n* transacción *f*, operación *f*

transatlantic [trænzət'læntɪk] *adj* transatlántico

transcript ['trænskrɪpt] *n* copia

transfer [*n* 'trænsfə:, *vb* træns'fə:] *n* (*of employees*) traslado; (*of money*, *power*) transferencia; (*SPORT*) traspaso; (*picture*, *design*) calcomanía ♦ *vt* trasladar; transferir; **to ~ the charges** (*BRIT TEL*) llamar a cobro revertido

transform [træns'fɔ:m] *vt* transformar ❏ **transformation** *n* transformación *f*

transfusion [træns'fjuːʒən] *n* transfusión *f*

transit ['trænzɪt] *n*: **in ~** en tránsito

transition [træn'zɪʃən] *n* transición *f*

transitive ['trænzɪtɪv] *adj* (*LING*) transitivo

translate [trænz'leɪt] *vt* traducir ❏ **translation** [-'leɪʃən] *n* traducción *f* ❏ **translator** *n* traductor(a) *m/f*

transmission [trænz'mɪʃən] *n* transmisión *f*

transmit [trænz'mɪt] *vt* transmitir ❏ **transmitter** *n* transmisor *m*

transparent [træns'pærnt] *adj* transparente

transplant ['trænspla:nt] *n* (*MED*) transplante *m*

transport [*n* 'trænspɔ:t, *vt* træns'pɔ:t] *n* transporte *m*; (*car*) coche *m* (*SP*), carro (*LAm*), automóvil *m* ♦ *vt* transportar ❏ **transportation** [-'teɪʃən] *n* transporte *m*

transvestite [trænz'vestaɪt] *n* travestí *mf*

trap [træp] *n* (*snare*, *trick*) trampa; (*carriage*) cabriolé *m* ♦ *vt* coger (*SP*) or agarrar (*LAm*) (en una trampa); (*trick*) engañar; (*confine*) atrapar

trash [træʃ] *n* (*rubbish*) basura; (*nonsense*) tonterías *fpl*; (*pej*): **the book/film is ~** el libro/la película no vale nada ❏ **trash can** (*US*) *n* cubo o bote *m* (*MEX*) or tacho (*SC*) de la basura

trauma ['trɔːmə] *n* trauma *m* ❏ **traumatic** [trɔː'mætɪk] *adj* traumático

travel ['trævl] *n* el viajar ♦ *vi* viajar ♦ *vt* (*distance*) recorrer ❏ **travel agency** *n* agencia de viajes ❏ **travel agent** *n* agente *mf* de viajes ❏ **travel insurance** *n* seguro de viaje ❏ **traveller** (*US* **traveler**) *n* viajero(-a) ❏ **traveller's cheque** (*US* **traveler's check**) *n* cheque *m* de viajero ❏ **travelling** (*US* **traveling**) *n* los viajes, el viajar ❏ **travel-sick** *adj*: **to get travel-sick** marearse al viajar ❏ **travel sickness** *n* mareo

tray [treɪ] *n* bandeja; (*on desk*) cajón *m*

treacherous ['tretʃərəs] *adj* traidor, traicionero; (*dangerous*) peligroso

treacle ['triːkl] *n* (*BRIT*) melaza

tread [tred] (*pt* **trod**, *pp* **trodden**) *n* (*step*) paso, pisada; (*sound*) ruido de pasos; (*of stair*) escalón *m*; (*of tyre*) banda de rodadura ♦ *vi* pisar ▸ **tread on** *vt fus* pisar

treason ['triːzn] *n* traición *f*

treasure ['treʒə] *n* tesoro ♦ *vt* (*value*: *object, friendship*) apreciar; (: *memory*) guardar ❏ **treasurer** *n* tesorero(-a)

treasury ['treʒərɪ] *n*: **the T~** el Ministerio de Hacienda

treat [triːt] *n* (*present*) regalo ♦ *vt* tratar; **to ~ sb to sth** invitar a algn a algo ❏ **treatment** *n* tratamiento

treaty ['triːtɪ] *n* tratado

treble ['trebl] *adj* triple ♦ *vt* triplicar ♦ *vi* triplicarse

tree [triː] *n* árbol *m*; **~ trunk** tronco (de árbol)

trek [trek] *n* (*long journey*) viaje *m* largo y difícil; (*tiring walk*) caminata

tremble ['trembl] *vi* temblar

tremendous [trɪ'mendəs] *adj* tremendo, enorme; (*excellent*) estupendo

trench [trentʃ] *n* zanja

trend [trend] *n* (*tendency*) tendencia; (*of events*) curso; (*fashion*) moda ❏ **trendy** *adj* de moda

trespass ['trespəs] *vi*: **to ~ on** entrar sin permiso en; **"no trespassing"** "prohibido el paso"

trial ['traɪəl] *n* (*LAW*) juicio, proceso; (*test*: *of machine etc*) prueba ❏ **trial period** *n* periodo de prueba

triangle ['traɪæŋgl] *n* (*MATH, MUS*) triángulo

triangular [traɪ'æŋgjulə] *adj* triangular

tribe [traɪb] *n* tribu *f*

tribunal [traɪ'bjuːnl] *n* tribunal *m*

tribute ['trɪbjuːt] *n* homenaje *m*, tributo; **to pay ~ to** rendir homenaje a

trick [trɪk] *n* (*skill, knack*) tino, truco; (*conjuring trick*) truco; (*joke*) broma; (*CARDS*) baza ♦ *vt* engañar; **to play a ~ on sb** gastar una broma a algn; **that should do the ~** a ver si funciona así

trickle ['trɪkl] *n* (*of water etc*) goteo ♦ *vi* gotear

tricky ['trɪkɪ] *adj* difícil; delicado

tricycle ['traɪsɪkl] *n* triciclo

trifle ['traɪfl] *n* bagatela; (*CULIN*) dulce de bizcocho borracho, gelatina, fruta y natillas ♦ *adv*: **a ~ long** un poquito largo

trigger ['trɪgə] *n* (*of gun*) gatillo

trim [trɪm] *adj* (*house, garden*) en buen estado; (*person, figure*) esbelto ♦ *n* (*haircut etc*) recorte *m*; (*on car*) guarnición *f* ♦ *vt* (*neaten*) arreglar; (*cut*) recortar; (*decorate*) adornar; (*NAUT*: *sail*) orientar

trio ['triːəu] *n* trío

trip [trɪp] *n* viaje *m*; (*excursion*) excursión *f*; (*stumble*) traspié *m* ♦ *vi* (*stumble*) tropezar; (*go lightly*) andar a paso ligero; **on a ~** de viaje ▸ **trip up** *vi* tropezar, caerse ♦ vt hacer tropezar or caer

triple ['trɪpl] adj triple

triplets ['trɪplɪts] npl trillizos(-as) mpl/fpl

tripod ['traɪpɒd] n trípode m

triumph ['traɪʌmf] n triunfo ♦ vi: **to ~ (over)** vencer □ **triumphant** [traɪˈʌmfənt] adj (team etc) vencedor(a); (wave, return) triunfal

trivial ['trɪvɪəl] adj insignificante; (commonplace) banal

trod [trɒd] pt of **tread**

trodden ['trɒdn] pp of **tread**

trolley ['trɒlɪ] n carrito; (also: **~ bus**) trolebús m

trombone [trɒmˈbəʊn] n trombón m

troop [truːp] n grupo, banda; **troops** npl (MIL) tropas fpl

trophy ['trəʊfɪ] n trofeo m

tropical ['trɒpɪkl] adj tropical

trot [trɒt] n trote m ♦ vi trotar; **on the ~** (BRIT: fig) seguidos(-as)

trouble ['trʌbl] n problema m, dificultad f; (worry) preocupación f; (bother, effort) molestia, esfuerzo; (unrest) inquietud f; (MED): **stomach etc ~** mpl gástricos etc ♦ vt (disturb) molestar; (worry) preocupar, inquietar ♦ vi: **to ~ to do sth** molestarse en hacer algo; **troubles** npl (POL etc) conflictos mpl; (personal) problemas mpl; **to be in ~** estar en un apuro; **it's no ~!** ¡no es molestia (ninguna)!; **what's the ~?** (with broken TV etc) ¿cuál es el problema?; (doctor to patient) ¿qué pasa? □ **troubled** adj (person) preocupado; (country, epoch, life) agitado □ **troublemaker** n agitador(a) m/f; (child) alborotador m □ **troublesome** adj molesto

trough [trɒf] n (also: **drinking ~**) abrevadero; (also: **feeding ~**) comedero; (depression) depresión f

trousers ['traʊzəz] npl pantalones mpl; **short ~** pantalones mpl cortos

trout [traʊt] n inv trucha

trowel ['traʊəl] n (of gardener) palita; (of builder) paleta

truant ['truːənt] n: **to play ~** (BRIT) hacer novillos

truce [truːs] n tregua

truck [trʌk] n (lorry) camión m; (RAIL) vagón m □ **truck driver** n camionero

true [truː] adj verdadero; (accurate) exacto; (genuine) auténtico; (faithful) fiel; **to come ~** realizarse

truly ['truːlɪ] adv (really) realmente; (truthfully) verdaderamente; (faithfully): **yours ~** (in letter) le saluda atentamente

trumpet ['trʌmpɪt] n trompeta

trunk [trʌŋk] n (of tree, person) tronco; (of elephant) trompa; (case) baúl m; (US AUT) maletero; **trunks** npl (also: **swimming trunks**) bañador m (de hombre)

trust [trʌst] n confianza; (responsibility) responsabilidad f; (LAW) fideicomiso ♦ vt (rely on) tener confianza en; (hope) esperar; (entrust): **to ~ sth to sb** confiar algo a algn; **to take sth on ~** fiarse de algo □ **trusted** adj de confianza □ **trustworthy** adj digno de confianza

truth [truːθ, pl truːðz] n verdad f □ **truthful** adj veraz

try [traɪ] n tentativa, intento; (RUGBY) ensayo ♦ vt (attempt) intentar; (test: also: **~ out**) probar, someter a prueba; (LAW) juzgar, procesar; (strain: patience) hacer perder ♦ vi probar; **to have a ~** probar suerte; **to ~ to do sth** intentar hacer algo; **~ again!** ¡vuelve a probar!; **~ harder!** ¡esfuérzate más!; **well, I tried** al menos lo intenté ► **try on** vt (clothes) probarse □ **trying** adj (experience) cansado; (person) pesado

T-shirt ['tiːʃəːt] n camiseta

tub [tʌb] n cubo (SP), cubeta (SP, MEX), balde m (LAm); (bath) bañera (SP), tina (LAm), bañadera (RPl)

tube [tju:b] n tubo; (BRIT: underground) metro; (for tyre) cámara de aire

tuberculosis [tjubə:kju'ləusıs] n tuberculosis f inv

tube station (BRIT) n estación f de metro

tuck [tʌk] vt (put) poner ▶ **tuck away** vt (money) guardar; (building): **to be tucked away** esconderse, ocultarse ▶ **tuck in** vt meter dentro; (child) arropar ♦ vi (eat) comer con apetito ❏ **tuck shop** n (SCOL) tienda, ≈ bar m (del colegio) (SP)

Tue(s). abbr (= Tuesday) mart

Tuesday ['tju:zdı] n martes m inv

tug [tʌg] n (ship) remolcador m ♦ vt tirar de

tuition [tju:'ıʃən] n (BRIT) enseñanza; (: private tuition) clases fpl particulares; (US: school fees) matrícula

tulip ['tju:lıp] n tulipán m

tumble ['tʌmbl] n (fall) caída ♦ vi caer; **to ~ to sth** (inf) caer en la cuenta de algo ❏ **tumble dryer** (BRIT) n secadora

tumbler ['tʌmblə*] n (glass) vaso

tummy ['tʌmı] n (inf) barriga, tripa

tumour ['tju:mə*] (US **tumor**) n tumor m

tuna ['tju:nə] n inv (also: ~ **fish**) atún m

tune [tju:n] n melodía ♦ vt (MUS) afinar; (RADIO, TV, AUT) sintonizar; **to be in/out of** ~ (instrument) estar afinado/desafinado; (singer) cantar afinadamente/desafinar; **to be in/out of** ~ **with** (fig) estar de acuerdo/en desacuerdo con ▶ **tune in** vi: **to tune in (to)** (RADIO, TV) sintonizar (con) ❏ **tune up** vi (musician) afinar (su instrumento)

tunic ['tju:nık] n túnica

Tunisia [tju:'nızıə] n Túnez m

tunnel ['tʌnl] n túnel m; (in mine) galería ♦ vi construir un túnel/una galería

turbulence ['tə:bjuləns] n (AVIAT) turbulencia

turf [tə:f] n césped m; (clod) tepe m ♦ vt cubrir con césped

Turk [tə:k] n turco(-a)

Turkey ['tə:kı] n Turquía

turkey ['tə:kı] n pavo

Turkish ['tə:kıʃ] adj, n turco; (LING) turco

turmoil ['tə:mɔıl] n: **in ~** revuelto

turn [tə:n] n turno; (in road) curva; (of mind, events) rumbo; (THEATRE) número; (MED) ataque m ♦ vt girar, volver; (collar, steak) dar la vuelta a; (page) pasar; (change): **to ~** sth **into** convertir algo en ♦ vi volver; (person: look back) volverse; (reverse direction) dar la vuelta; (milk) cortarse; (become): **to ~ nasty/forty** ponerse feo/cumplir los cuarenta; **a good ~** un favor; **it gave me quite a ~** me dio un susto; **"no left ~"** (AUT) "prohibido girar a la izquierda"; **it's your ~** te toca a ti; **in ~** por turnos; **to take turns (at)** turnarse (en) ▶ **turn around** vi (person) volverse, darse la vuelta ♦ vt (object) dar la vuelta a, voltear (LAM) ▶ **turn away** vi apartar la vista ♦ vt rechazar ▶ **turn back** vi volverse atrás ♦ vt hacer retroceder; (clock) retrasar ▶ **turn down** vt (refuse) rechazar; (reduce) bajar; (fold) doblar ▶ **turn in** vi (inf: go to bed) acostarse ♦ vt (fold) doblar hacia dentro ▶ **turn off** vi (from road) desviarse ♦ vt (light, radio etc) apagar; (tap) cerrar; (engine) parar ▶ **turn on** vt (light, radio etc) encender (SP), prender (LAM); (tap) abrir; (engine) poner en marcha ▶ **turn out** vt (light, gas) apagar; (produce) producir ♦ vi (voters) concurrir; **to turn out to be ...** resultar ser ... ▶ **turn over** vi (person) volverse ♦ vt (object) dar la vuelta a; (page) volver ▶ **turn round** vi volverse; (rotate) girar ▶ **turn to** vt fus: **to turn to sb** acudir a algn ▶ **turn up** vi (person) llegar, presentarse; (lost object) aparecer ♦ vt (gen) subir

❏ **turning** n (in road) vuelta
❏ **turning point** n (fig) momento decisivo

turnip ['tə:nɪp] n nabo

turn: **turnout** n concurrencia
❏ **turnover** n (COMM: amount of money) volumen m de ventas; (: of goods) movimiento m ❏ **turnstile** n torniquete m ❏ **turn-up** (BRIT) n (on trousers) vuelta

turquoise ['tə:kwɔɪz] n (stone) turquesa ♦ adj color turquesa

turtle ['tə:tl] n galápago ❏ **turtleneck (sweater)** n jersey m de cuello vuelto

tusk [tʌsk] n colmillo

tutor ['tju:tə?] n profesor(a) m/f
❏ **tutorial** [-'tɔ:rɪəl] n (SCOL) seminario

tuxedo [tʌk'si:dəu] (US) n smóking m, esmoquin m

TV [ti:'vi:] n abbr (= television) tele f

tweed [twi:d] n tweed m

tweezers ['twi:zəz] npl pinzas fpl (de depilar)

twelfth [twelfθ] num duodécimo

twelve [twelv] num doce; **at ~ o'clock** (midday) a mediodía; (midnight) a medianoche

twentieth ['twentɪɪθ] adj vigésimo

twenty ['twentɪ] num veinte

twice [twaɪs] adv dos veces; **~ as much** dos veces más

twig [twɪg] n ramita

twilight ['twaɪlaɪt] n crepúsculo

twin [twɪn] adj, n gemelo/a m/f ♦ vt hermanar ❏ **twin(-bedded) room** n habitación f doble ❏ **twin beds** npl camas fpl gemelas

twinkle ['twɪŋkl] vi centellear; (eyes) brillar

twist [twɪst] n (action) torsión f; (in road, coil) vuelta; (in wire, flex) doblez f; (in story) giro ♦ vt torcer; (weave) trenzar; (roll around) enrollar; (fig) deformar ♦ vi serpentear

twit [twɪt] (inf) n tonto

twitch [twɪtʃ] n (pull) tirón m; (nervous) tic m ♦ vi crisparse

two [tu:] num dos; **to put ~ and ~ together** (fig) atar cabos

type [taɪp] n (category) tipo, género; (model) tipo; (TYP) tipo, letra ♦ vt (letter etc) escribir a máquina ❏ **typewriter** n máquina de escribir

typhoid ['taɪfɔɪd] n tifoidea

typhoon [taɪ'fu:n] n tifón m

typical ['tɪpɪkl] adj típico ❏ **typically** adv típicamente

typing ['taɪpɪŋ] n mecanografía

typist ['taɪpɪst] n mecanógrafo(-a)

tyre ['taɪə?] (US **tire**) n neumático, llanta (LAm) ❏ **tyre pressure** (BRIT) n presión f de los neumáticos

U, u

UFO ['ju:fəu] n abbr (= unidentified flying object) OVNI m

Uganda [ju:'gændə] n Uganda

ugly ['ʌglɪ] adj feo; (dangerous) peligroso

UHT abbr (= UHT milk) leche f UHT, leche f uperizada

UK n abbr = **United Kingdom**

ulcer ['ʌlsə?] n úlcera; (mouth ulcer) llaga

ultimate ['ʌltɪmət] adj último, final; (greatest) máximo ❏ **ultimately** adv (in the end) por último, al final; (fundamentally) a or en fin de cuentas

ultimatum [ʌltɪ'meɪtəm] (pl **ultimatums** or **ultimata**) n ultimátum m

ultrasound ['ʌltrəsaund] n (MED) ultrasonido

ultraviolet ['ʌltrə'vaɪələt] adj ultravioleta

umbrella [ʌm'brelə] n paraguas m inv; (for sun) sombrilla

umpire ['ʌmpaɪə?] n árbitro

UN n abbr (= United Nations) NN. UU.

unable [ʌnˈeɪbl] adj: **to be ~ to do sth** no poder hacer algo

unacceptable [ʌnəkˈsɛptəbl] adj (proposal, behaviour, price) inaceptable; **it's ~ that** no se puede aceptar que

unanimous [juːˈnænɪməs] adj unánime

unarmed [ʌnˈɑːmd] adj (defenceless) inerme; (without weapon) desarmado

unattended [ʌnəˈtɛndɪd] adj desatendido

unattractive [ʌnəˈtræktɪv] adj poco atractivo

unavailable [ʌnəˈveɪləbl] adj (article, room, book) no disponible; (person) ocupado

unavoidable [ʌnəˈvɔɪdəbl] adj inevitable

unaware [ʌnəˈwɛəʳ] adj: **to be ~ of** ignorar □ **unawares** adv: **to catch sb unawares** pillar a algn desprevenido

unbearable [ʌnˈbɛərəbl] adj insoportable

unbeatable [ʌnˈbiːtəbl] adj (team) invencible; (price) inmejorable; (quality) insuperable

unbelievable [ʌnbɪˈliːvəbl] adj increíble

unborn [ʌnˈbɔːn] adj que va a nacer

unbutton [ʌnˈbʌtn] vt desabrochar

uncalled-for [ʌnˈkɔːldfɔːʳ] adj gratuito, inmerecido

uncanny [ʌnˈkænɪ] adj extraño

uncertain [ʌnˈsɜːtn] adj incierto; (indecisive) indeciso □ **uncertainty** n incertidumbre f

unchanged [ʌnˈtʃeɪndʒd] adj igual, sin cambios

uncle [ˈʌŋkl] n tío

unclear [ʌnˈklɪəʳ] adj poco claro; **I'm still ~ about what I'm supposed to do** todavía no tengo muy claro lo que tengo que hacer

uncomfortable [ʌnˈkʌmfətəbl] adj incómodo; (uneasy) inquieto

uncommon [ʌnˈkɒmən] adj poco común, raro

unconditional [ʌnkənˈdɪʃənl] adj incondicional

unconscious [ʌnˈkɒnʃəs] adj sin sentido; (unaware): **to be ~ of** no darse cuenta de ♦ n: **the ~** el inconsciente

uncontrollable [ʌnkənˈtrəʊləbl] adj (child etc) incontrolable; (temper) indomable; (laughter) incontenible

unconventional [ʌnkənˈvɛnʃənl] adj poco convencional

uncover [ʌnˈkʌvəʳ] vt descubrir; (take lid off) destapar

undecided [ʌndɪˈsaɪdɪd] adj (character) indeciso; (question) no resuelto

undeniable [ʌndɪˈnaɪəbl] adj innegable

under [ˈʌndəʳ] prep debajo de; (less than) menos de; (according to) según, de acuerdo con; (sb's leadership) bajo ♦ adv debajo, abajo; **~ there** allí abajo; **~ repair** en reparación □ **undercover** adj clandestino □ **underdone** adj (CULIN) poco hecho □ **underestimate** vt subestimar □ **undergo** (irreg) vt sufrir; (treatment) recibir □ **undergraduate** n estudiante mf □ **underground** n (BRIT: railway) metro; (POL) movimiento clandestino ♦ adj (car park) subterráneo ♦ adv (work) en la clandestinidad □ **undergrowth** n maleza □ **underline** vt subrayar □ **undermine** vt socavar, minar □ **underneath** [ʌndəˈniːθ] adv debajo ♦ prep debajo de, bajo □ **underpants** npl calzoncillos mpl □ **underpass** n (BRIT) n paso subterráneo □ **underprivileged** adj desposeído □ **underscore** vt subrayar □ **undershirt** n (US) n camiseta □ **underskirt** (BRIT) n enaguas fpl

understand [ʌndəˈstænd] vt, vi entender, comprender; (assume) tener entendido ❑ **understandable** adj comprensible ❑ **understanding** adj comprensivo ♦ n comprensión f, entendimiento; (agreement) acuerdo

understatement ['ʌndəsteɪtmənt] n modestia (excesiva); **that's an ~!** ¡eso es decir poco!

understood [ʌndə'stud] pt, pp of **understand** ♦ adj (agreed) acordado; (implied): **it is ~ that** se sobreentiende que

undertake [ʌndə'teɪk] (irreg) vt emprender; **to ~ to do sth** comprometerse a hacer algo

undertaker ['ʌndəteɪkə] n director(a) m/f de pompas fúnebres

undertaking ['ʌndəteɪkɪŋ] n empresa; (promise) promesa

under: **underwater** adv bajo el agua ♦ adj submarino ❑ **underway** adj: **to be underway** (meeting) estar en marcha; (investigation) estar llevándose a cabo ❑ **underwear** n ropa interior ❑ **underwent** vb see **undergo** ❑ **underworld** n (of crime) hampa, inframundo

undesirable [ʌndɪ'zaɪrəbl] adj (person) indeseable; (thing) poco aconsejable

undisputed [ʌndɪ'spjuːtɪd] adj incontestable

undo [ʌn'duː] (irreg) vt (laces) desatar; (button etc) desabrochar; (spoil) deshacer

undone [ʌn'dʌn] pp of **undo** ♦ adj: **to come ~** (clothes) desabrocharse; (parcel) desatarse

undoubtedly [ʌn'dautidlɪ] adv indudablemente, sin duda

undress [ʌn'dres] vi desnudarse

unearth [ʌn'ɜːθ] vt desenterrar

uneasy [ʌn'iːzi] adj intranquil, preocupado; (feeling) desagradable; (peace) inseguro

unemployed [ʌnɪm'plɔɪd] adj parado, sin trabajo ♦ npl: **the ~** los parados

unemployment [ʌnɪm'plɔɪmənt] n paro, desempleo ❑ **unemployment benefit** n (BRIT) subsidio de desempleo or paro

unequal [ʌn'iːkwəl] adj (unfair) desigual; (size, length) distinto

uneven [ʌn'iːvn] adj desigual; (road etc) lleno de baches

unexpected [ʌnɪk'spektɪd] adj inesperado ❑ **unexpectedly** adv inesperadamente

unfair [ʌn'feəʳ] adj: **~ (to sb)** injusto (con algn)

unfaithful [ʌn'feɪθful] adj infiel

unfamiliar [ʌnfə'mɪlɪəʳ] adj extraño, desconocido; **to be ~ with** desconocer

unfashionable [ʌn'fæʃnəbl] adj pasado or fuera de moda

unfasten [ʌn'fɑːsn] vt (knot) desatar; (dress) desabrochar; (open) abrir

unfavourable [ʌn'feɪvərəbl] (US **unfavorable**) adj desfavorable

unfinished [ʌn'fɪnɪʃt] adj inacabado, sin terminar

unfit [ʌn'fɪt] adj bajo de forma; (incompetent): **~ (for)** incapaz (de); **~ for work** no apto para trabajar

unfold [ʌn'fəʊld] vt desdoblar ♦ vi abrirse

unforgettable [ʌnfə'getəbl] adj inolvidable

unfortunate [ʌn'fɔːtʃnət] adj desgraciado; (event, remark) inoportuno ❑ **unfortunately** adv desgraciadamente

unfriendly [ʌn'frendlɪ] adj antipático; (behaviour, remark) hostil, poco amigable

unfurnished [ʌn'fɜːnɪʃt] adj sin amueblar

unhappiness [ʌn'hæpɪnɪs] n tristeza, desdicha

unhappy [ʌn'hæpɪ] adj (sad) triste; (unfortunate) desgraciado; (childhood) infeliz; **~ about/with** (arrangements *etc*) poco contento con, descontento de

unhealthy [ʌnˈhɛlθɪ] *adj* (*place*) malsano; (*person*) enfermizo; (*fig: interest*) morboso

unheard-of [ʌnˈhəːdɒv] *adj* inaudito, sin precedente

unhelpful [ʌnˈhɛlpful] *adj* (*person*) poco servicial; (*advice*) inútil

unhurt [ʌnˈhəːt] *adj* ileso

unidentified [ʌnaɪˈdɛntɪfaɪd] *adj* no identificado, sin identificar; *see also* **UFO**

uniform [ˈjuːnɪfɔːm] *n* uniforme *m* ♦ *adj* uniforme

unify [ˈjuːnɪfaɪ] *vt* unificar, unir

unimportant [ʌnɪmˈpɔːtənt] *adj* sin importancia

uninhabited [ʌnɪnˈhæbɪtɪd] *adj* desierto

unintentional [ʌnɪnˈtɛnʃənəl] *adj* involuntario

union [ˈjuːnjən] *n* unión *f*; (*also:* **trade ~**) sindicato ♦ *cpd* sindical □ **Union Jack** *n* bandera del Reino Unido

unique [juːˈniːk] *adj* único

unisex [ˈjuːnɪsɛks] *adj* unisex

unit [ˈjuːnɪt] *n* unidad *f*; (*section: of furniture etc*) elemento; (*team*) grupo; **kitchen ~** módulo de cocina

unite [juːˈnaɪt] *vt* unir ♦ *vi* unirse □ **united** *adj* unido; (*effort*) conjunto □ **United Kingdom** *n* Reino Unido □ **United Nations (Organization)** *n* Naciones *fpl* Unidas □ **United States (of America)** *n* Estados *mpl* Unidos

unity [ˈjuːnɪtɪ] *n* unidad *f*

universal [juːnɪˈvəːsl] *adj* universal

universe [ˈjuːnɪvəːs] *n* universo

university [juːnɪˈvəːsɪtɪ] *n* universidad *f*

unjust [ʌnˈdʒʌst] *adj* injusto

unkind [ʌnˈkaɪnd] *adj* poco amable; (*behaviour, comment*) cruel

unknown [ʌnˈnəun] *adj* desconocido

unlawful [ʌnˈlɔːful] *adj* ilegal, ilícito

unleaded [ʌnˈlɛdɪd] *adj* (*petrol, fuel*) sin plombo

unleash [ʌnˈliːʃ] *vt* desatar

unless [ʌnˈlɛs] *conj* a menos que; **~ he comes** a menos que venga; **~ otherwise stated** salvo indicación contraria

unlike [ʌnˈlaɪk] *adj* (*not alike*) distinto de or a; (*not like*) poco propio de ♦ *prep* a diferencia de

unlikely [ʌnˈlaɪklɪ] *adj* improbable; (*unexpected*) inverosímil

unlimited [ʌnˈlɪmɪtɪd] *adj* ilimitado

unlisted [ʌnˈlɪstɪd] *adj* (*US*) (*TEL*) que no consta en la guía

unload [ʌnˈləud] *vt* descargar

unlock [ʌnˈlɔk] *vt* abrir (con llave)

unlucky [ʌnˈlʌkɪ] *adj* desgraciado; (*object, number*) que da mala suerte; **to be ~** tener mala suerte

unmarried [ʌnˈmærɪd] *adj* soltero

unmistak(e)able [ʌnmɪsˈteɪkəbl] *adj* inconfundible

unnatural [ʌnˈnætʃrəl] *adj* (*gen*) antinatural; (*manner*) afectado; (*habit*) perverso

unnecessary [ʌnˈnɛsəsərɪ] *adj* innecesario, inútil

UNO [ˈjuːnəu] *n abbr* (= *United Nations Organization*) ONU *f*

unofficial [ʌnəˈfɪʃl] *adj* no oficial; (*news*) sin confirmar

unpack [ʌnˈpæk] *vi* deshacer las maletas ♦ *vt* deshacer

unpaid [ʌnˈpeɪd] *adj* (*bill, debt*) sin pagar, impagado; (*COMM*) pendiente; (*holiday*) sin sueldo; (*work*) sin pago, voluntario

unpleasant [ʌnˈplɛznt] *adj* (*disagreeable*) desagradable; (*person, manner*) antipático

unplug [ʌnˈplʌg] *vt* desenchufar, desconectar

unpopular [ʌnˈpɔpjuləʳ] *adj* impopular, poco popular

unprecedented [ʌnˈprɛsɪdəntɪd] *adj* sin precedentes

unpredictable [ʌnprɪˈdɪktəbl] *adj* imprevisible

unprotected [ˈʌnprəˈtɛktɪd] *adj* (*sex*) sin protección

unqualified [ʌnˈkwɒlɪfaɪd] *adj* sin título, no cualificado; (*success*) total

unravel [ʌnˈrævl] *vt* desenmarañar

unreal [ʌnˈrɪəl] *adj* irreal; (*extraordinary*) increíble

unrealistic [ʌnrɪəˈlɪstɪk] *adj* poco realista

unreasonable [ʌnˈriːznəbl] *adj* irrazonable; (*demand*) excesivo

unrelated [ʌnrɪˈleɪtɪd] *adj* sin relación; (*family*) no emparentado

unreliable [ʌnrɪˈlaɪəbl] *adj* (*person*) informal; (*machine*) poco fiable

unrest [ʌnˈrɛst] *n* inquietud *f*, malestar *m*; (*POL*) disturbios *mpl*

unroll [ʌnˈrəʊl] *vt* desenrollar

unruly [ʌnˈruːlɪ] *adj* indisciplinado

unsafe [ʌnˈseɪf] *adj* peligroso

unsatisfactory [ˈʌnsætɪsˈfæktərɪ] *adj* poco satisfactorio

unscrew [ʌnˈskruː] *vt* destornillar

unsettled [ʌnˈsɛtld] *adj* inquieto, intranquilo; (*weather*) variable

unsettling [ʌnˈsɛtlɪŋ] *adj* perturbador(a), inquietante

unsightly [ʌnˈsaɪtlɪ] *adj* feo

unskilled [ʌnˈskɪld] *adj* (*work*) no especializado; (*worker*) no cualificado

unspoiled [ˈʌnˈspɔɪld], **unspoilt** [ˈʌnˈspɔɪlt] *adj* (*place*) que no ha perdido su belleza natural

unstable [ʌnˈsteɪbl] *adj* inestable

unsteady [ʌnˈstɛdɪ] *adj* inestable

unsuccessful [ʌnsəkˈsɛsful] *adj* (*attempt*) infructuoso; (*writer, proposal*) sin éxito; **to be ~** (*in attempting sth*) no tener éxito, fracasar

unsuitable [ʌnˈsuːtəbl] *adj* inapropiado; (*time*) inoportuno

unsure [ʌnˈʃʊəʳ] *adj* inseguro, poco seguro

untidy [ʌnˈtaɪdɪ] *adj* (*room*) desordenado; (*appearance*) desaliñado

untie [ʌnˈtaɪ] *vt* desatar

until [ənˈtɪl] *prep* hasta ♦ *conj* hasta que; **~ he comes** hasta que venga; **~ now** hasta ahora; **~ then** hasta entonces

untrue [ʌnˈtruː] *adj* (*statement*) falso

unused [ʌnˈjuːzd] *adj* sin usar

unusual [ʌnˈjuːʒʊəl] *adj* insólito, poco común; (*exceptional*) inusitado ❑ **unusually** *adv* (*exceptionally*) excepcionalmente; **he arrived unusually early** llegó más temprano que de costumbre

unveil [ʌnˈveɪl] *vt* (*statue*) descubrir

unwanted [ʌnˈwɒntɪd] *adj* (*clothing*) viejo; (*pregnancy*) no deseado

unwell [ʌnˈwɛl] *adj*: **to be/feel ~** estar indispuesto/sentirse mal

unwilling [ʌnˈwɪlɪŋ] *adj*: **to be ~ to do sth** estar poco dispuesto a hacer algo

unwind [ʌnˈwaɪnd] (*irreg*) *vt* desenvolver ♦ *vi* (*relax*) relajarse

unwise [ʌnˈwaɪz] *adj* imprudente

unwittingly [ʌnˈwɪtɪŋlɪ] *adv* inconscientemente, sin darse cuenta

unwrap [ʌnˈræp] *vt* desenvolver

unzip [ʌnˈzɪp] *vt* abrir la cremallera de

up

KEYWORD

[ʌp] *prep*: **to go/be up sth** subir/estar subido en algo; **he went up the stairs/the hill** subió las escaleras/la colina; **we walked/climbed up the hill** subimos la colina; **they live further up the street** viven más arriba en la calle; **go up that road and turn left** sigue por esa calle y gira a la izquierda

♦ *adv*

1 (*upwards, higher*) más arriba; **up in the mountains** en lo alto (de la montaña); **put it a bit higher up** ponlo un poco más arriba *or* alto; **up there** ahí *or* allí arriba; **up above** en lo alto, por encima, arriba

2: to be up (*out of bed*) estar levantado; (*prices, level*) haber subido

3: up to (*as far as*) hasta; **up to now** hasta ahora *or* la fecha

4: to be up to: it's up to you (*depending on*) depende de ti; **he's not up to it** (*job, task etc*) no es capaz de hacerlo; **his work is not up to the required standard** su trabajo no da la talla; (*inf: be doing*): **what is he up to?** ¿que estará tramando?

♦ *n*: **ups and downs** altibajos *mpl*

up-and-coming [ʌpənd'kʌmɪŋ] *adj* prometedor(a)

upbringing ['ʌpbrɪŋɪŋ] *n* educación *f*

update [ʌp'deɪt] *vt* poner al día

upfront [ʌp'frʌnt] *adj* claro, directo ♦ *adv* a las claras; (*pay*) por adelantado; **to be ~ about sth** admitir algo claramente

upgrade [ʌp'greɪd] *vt* (*house*) modernizar; (*employee*) ascender

upheaval [ʌp'hiːvl] *n* trastornos *mpl*; (*POL*) agitación *f*

uphill [ʌp'hɪl] *adj* cuesta arriba; (*fig: task*) penoso, difícil; **to go ~** ir cuesta arriba

upholstery [ʌp'həʊlstərɪ] *n* tapicería *f*

upmarket [ʌp'mɑːkɪt] *adj* (*product*) de categoría

upon [ə'pɒn] *prep* sobre

upper ['ʌpə*] *adj* superior, de arriba ♦ *n* (*of shoe: also*: **uppers**) empeine *m*
□ **upper-class** *adj* de clase alta

upright ['ʌpraɪt] *adj* derecho; (*vertical*) vertical; (*fig*) honrado

uprising ['ʌpraɪzɪŋ] *n* sublevación *f*

uproar ['ʌprɔː*] *n* escándalo

upset [*n* 'ʌpset, *vb, adj* ʌp'set] *n* (*to plan etc*) revés *m*, contratiempo; (*MED*) trastorno ♦ *vt irreg* (*glass etc*) volcar; (*plan*) alterar; (*person*) molestar, disgustar ♦ *adj* molesto, disgustado; (*stomach*) revuelto

upside-down [ʌpsaɪd'daʊn] *adv* al revés; **to turn a place ~** (*fig*) revolverlo todo

upstairs [ʌp'steəz] *adv* arriba ♦ *adj* (*room*) de arriba ♦ *n* el piso superior

up-to-date ['ʌptə'deɪt] *adj* al día

uptown ['ʌptaʊn] (*US*) *adv* hacia las afueras ♦ *adj* exterior, de las afueras

upward ['ʌpwəd] *adj* ascendente
□ **upward(s)** *adv* hacia arriba; (*more than*): **upward(s) of** más de

uranium [juə'reɪnɪəm] *n* uranio

Uranus [juə'reɪnəs] *n* Urano

urban ['əːbən] *adj* urbano

urge [əːdʒ] *n* (*desire*) deseo ♦ *vt*: **to ~ sb to do sth** animar a algn a hacer algo

urgency ['əːdʒənsɪ] *n* urgencia

urgent ['əːdʒənt] *adj* urgente; (*voice*) perentorio

urinal ['juərɪnl] *n* (*building*) urinario; (*vessel*) orinal *m*

urinate ['juərɪneɪt] *vi* orinar

urine ['juərɪn] *n* orina, orines *mpl*

us [ʌs] *pron* nos; (*after prep*) nosotros(-as); *see also* **me**

US *n abbr* (= *United States*) EE. UU.

USA *n abbr* (= *United States of America*) EE.UU.

use [*n* juːs, *vb* juːz] *n* uso, empleo; (*usefulness*) utilidad *f* ♦ *vt* usar, emplear; **she used to do it** (ella) solía *or* acostumbraba hacerlo; **in ~** en uso; **out of ~** en desuso; **to be of ~** servir; **it's no ~** (*pointless*) es inútil; (*not useful*) no sirve; **to be used to** estar acostumbrado a, acostumbrar ▶ **use up** *vt* (*food*) consumir; (*money*) gastar
□ **used** [juːzd] *adj* (*car*) usado
□ **useful** *adj* útil □ **useless** *adj*

(*unusable*) inservible; (*pointless*) inútil; (*person*) inepto ❑ **user** n usuario(-a) ❑ **user-friendly** adj (*computer*) amistoso

usual ['juːʒuəl] adj normal, corriente; **as ~ como** de costumbre ❑ **usually** adv normalmente

utensil [juː'tensl] n utensilio; **kitchen utensils** batería de cocina

utility [juː'tɪltɪ] n utilidad f; (*public utility*) (empresa de) servicio público

utilize ['juːtɪlaɪz] vt utilizar

utmost ['ʌtməust] adj mayor ♦ n: **to do one's ~** hacer todo lo posible

utter ['ʌtə*] adj total, completo ♦ vt pronunciar, proferir ❑ **utterly** adv completamente, totalmente

U-turn ['juː'tɜːn] n viraje m en redondo

V, v

v. abbr = **verse**; **versus**; (= *volt*) v; (= *vide*) véase

vacancy ['veɪkənsɪ] n (*BRIT: job*) vacante f; (*room*) habitación f libre; **"no vacancies"** "completo"

vacant ['veɪkənt] adj desocupado, libre; (*expression*) distraído

vacate [və'keɪt] vt (*house, room*) desocupar; (*job*) dejar (vacante)

vacation [və'keɪʃən] n vacaciones fpl ❑ **vacationer, vacationist** (*US*) n turista m/f

vaccination [væksɪ'neɪʃən] n vacunación f

vaccine ['væksiːn] n vacuna

vacuum ['vækjuəm] n vacío ❑ **vacuum cleaner** n aspiradora

vagina [və'dʒaɪnə] n vagina

vague [veɪg] adj vago; (*memory*) borroso; (*ambiguous*) impreciso; (*person: absent-minded*) distraído; (: *evasive*): **to be ~** no decir las cosas claramente

(*unusable*) inservible; (*pointless*) inútil;

vain [veɪn] adj (*conceited*) presumido; (*useless*) vano, inútil; **in ~** en vano

Valentine's Day ['væləntaɪnzdeɪ] n día de los enamorados

valid ['vælɪd] adj válido; (*ticket*) valedero; (*law*) vigente

valley ['vælɪ] n valle m

valuable ['væljuəbl] adj (*jewel*) de valor; (*time*) valioso ❑ **valuables** npl objetos mpl de valor

value ['væljuː] n valor m; (*importance*) importancia ♦ vt (*fix price of*) tasar, valorar; (*esteem*) apreciar; **values** npl (*principles*) principios mpl

valve [vælv] n válvula

vampire ['væmpaɪə*] n vampiro

van [væn] n (*AUT*) furgoneta, camioneta

vandal ['vændl] n vándalo(-a) ❑ **vandalism** n vandalismo ❑ **vandalize** vt dañar, destruir

vanilla [və'nɪlə] n vainilla

vanish ['vænɪʃ] vi desaparecer

vanity ['vænɪtɪ] n vanidad f

vapour ['veɪpə*] (*US* **vapor**) n vapor m; (*on breath, window*) vaho

variable ['vɛərɪəbl] adj variable

variant ['vɛərɪənt] n variante f

variation [vɛərɪ'eɪʃən] n variación f

varied ['vɛərɪd] adj variado

variety [və'raɪətɪ] n (*diversity*) diversidad f; (*type*) variedad f

various ['vɛərɪəs] adj (*several: people*) varios(-as); (*reasons*) diversos(-as)

varnish ['vɑːnɪʃ] n barniz m; (*nail varnish*) esmalte m ♦ vt barnizar; (*nails*) pintar (con esmalte)

vary ['vɛərɪ] vt variar; (*change*) cambiar ♦ vi variar

vase [vɑːz] n jarrón m

⚠ Be careful not to translate **vase** by the Spanish word **vaso**.

Vaseline® ['væsɪliːn] n vaselina®

vast [vɑːst] adj enorme

VAT [væt] (*BRIT*) n abbr (= value added tax) IVA m

vault [vɔːlt] n (of roof) bóveda f; (tomb) panteón m; (in bank) cámara acorazada ♦ vt (also: ~ **over**) saltar (por encima de)

VCR n abbr = **video cassette recorder**

VDU n abbr (= visual display unit) UPV f

veal [viːl] n ternera

veer [vɪəʳ] vi (vehicle) virar; (wind) girar

vegan [ˈviːgən] n vegetariano(-a) estricto(-a), vegetaliano(-a)

vegetable [ˈvɛdʒtəbl] n (BOT) vegetal m; (edible plant) legumbre f, hortaliza ♦ adj vegetal

vegetarian [vɛdʒɪˈtɛərɪən] adj, n vegetariano(-a) m/f

vegetation [vɛdʒɪˈteɪʃən] n vegetación f

vehicle [ˈviːɪkl] n vehículo; (fig) medio

veil [veɪl] n velo ♦ vt velar

vein [veɪn] n vena; (of ore etc) veta

Velcro® [ˈvɛlkrəu] n velcro® m

velvet [ˈvɛlvɪt] n terciopelo

vending machine [ˈvɛndɪŋ-] n distribuidor m automático

vendor [ˈvɛndəʳ] n vendedor(a) m/f; **street ~** vendedor(a) m/f callejero(-a)

vengeance [ˈvɛndʒəns] n venganza; **with a ~** (fig) con creces

venison [ˈvɛnɪsn] n carne f de venado

venom [ˈvɛnəm] n veneno; (bitterness) odio

vent [vɛnt] n (in jacket) respiradero; (in wall) rejilla (de ventilación) ♦ vt (fig: feelings) desahogar

ventilation [vɛntɪˈleɪʃən] n ventilación f

venture [ˈvɛntʃəʳ] n empresa ♦ vt (opinion) ofrecer ♦ vi arriesgarse, lanzarse; **business ~** empresa comercial

venue [ˈvɛnjuː] n lugar m

Venus [ˈviːnəs] n Venus m

verb [vəːb] n verbo ❑ **verbal** adj verbal

verdict [ˈvəːdɪkt] n veredicto, fallo; (fig) opinión f, juicio

verge [vəːdʒ] (BRIT) n borde m; "**soft verges**" (AUT) "arcén m no asfaltado"; **to be on the ~ of doing sth** estar a punto de hacer algo

verify [ˈvɛrɪfaɪ] vt comprobar, verificar

versatile [ˈvəːsətaɪl] adj (person) polifacético; (machine, tool etc) versátil

verse [vəːs] n poesía; (stanza) estrofa; (in bible) versículo

version [ˈvəːʃən] n versión f

versus [ˈvəːsəs] prep contra

vertical [ˈvəːtɪkl] adj vertical

very [ˈvɛrɪ] adv muy ♦ adj: **the ~ book which** el mismo libro que; **the ~ last** el último de todos; **at the ~ least** al menos; **~ much** muchísimo

vessel [ˈvɛsl] n (ship) barco; (container) vasija; see **blood**

vest [vɛst] n (BRIT) camiseta; (US: waistcoat) chaleco

vet [vɛt] vt (candidate) investigar ♦ n abbr (BRIT) = **veterinary surgeon**

veteran [ˈvɛtərn] n excombatiente mf, veterano(-a)

veterinary surgeon [ˈvɛtrɪnərɪ-] (US **veterinarian**) n veterinario(-a) m/f

veto [ˈviːtəu] (pl **vetoes**) n veto ♦ vt prohibir, poner el veto a

via [ˈvaɪə] prep por, por medio de

viable [ˈvaɪəbl] adj viable

vibrate [vaɪˈbreɪt] vi vibrar

vibration [vaɪˈbreɪʃən] n vibración f

vicar [ˈvɪkəʳ] n párroco (de la Iglesia Anglicana)

vice [vaɪs] n (evil) vicio; (TECH) torno de banco ❑ **vice-chairman** (irreg) n vicepresidente m

vice versa [ˈvaɪsɪˈvəːsə] adv viceversa

vicinity [vɪˈsɪnɪtɪ] n: **in the ~ (of)** cercano (a)

vicious [ˈvɪʃəs] adj (attack) violento; (words) cruel; (horse, dog) resabio

victim [ˈvɪktɪm] n víctima

victor ['vɪktə] n vencedor(a) m/f

Victorian [vɪk'tɔːrɪən] adj victoriano

victorious [vɪk'tɔːrɪəs] adj vencedor(a)

victory ['vɪktərɪ] n victoria

video ['vɪdɪəu] n vídeo (SP), video (LAm) ❑ **video camera** n videocámara, cámara de vídeo ❑ **video (cassette) recorder** n vídeo (SP), video (LAm) ❑ **video game** n videojuego ❑ **video shop** n videoclub m ❑ **video tape** n cinta de vídeo

vie [vaɪ] vi: **to ~ with sb for sth** competir (con algn por algo)

Vienna [vɪ'enə] n Viena

Vietnam [vjet'næm] n Vietnam m ❑ **Vietnamese** [-nə'miːz] n inv, adj vietnamita m/f

view [vjuː] n vista; (outlook) perspectiva; (opinion) opinión f, criterio ♦ vt (look at) mirar; (fig) considerar; **on ~** (in museum etc) expuesto; **in full ~ (of)** en plena vista (de); **in ~ of the weather/the fact that** en vista del tiempo/del hecho de que; **in my ~** en mi opinión ❑ **viewer** n espectador(a) m/f; (TV) telespectador(a) m/f ❑ **viewpoint** n (attitude) punto de vista; (place) mirador m

vigilant ['vɪdʒɪlənt] adj vigilante

vigorous ['vɪgərəs] adj enérgico, vigoroso

vile [vaɪl] adj vil, infame; (smell) asqueroso; (temper) endemoniado

villa ['vɪlə] n (country house) casa de campo; (suburban house) chalet m

village ['vɪlɪdʒ] n aldea ❑ **villager** n aldeano(-a)

villain ['vɪlən] n (scoundrel) malvado(-a); (in novel) malo; (BRIT: criminal) maleante m

vinaigrette [vɪneɪ'gret] n vinagreta

vine [vaɪn] n vid f

vinegar ['vɪnɪgə] n vinagre m

vineyard ['vɪnjɑːd] n viña, viñedo

vintage ['vɪntɪdʒ] n (year) vendimia, cosecha ♦ cpd de época

vinyl ['vaɪnl] n vinilo

viola [vɪ'əulə] n (MUS) viola

violate ['vaɪəleɪt] vt violar

violation [vaɪə'leɪʃən] n violación f; **in ~ of sth** en violación de algo

violence ['vaɪələns] n violencia

violent ['vaɪələnt] adj violento; (intense) intenso

violet ['vaɪələt] adj violado, violeta ♦ n (plant) violeta

violin [vaɪə'lɪn] n violín m

VIP n abbr (= very important person) VIP m

virgin ['vəːdʒɪn] n virgen f

Virgo ['vəːgəu] n Virgo

virtual ['vəːtjuəl] adj virtual ❑ **virtually** adv prácticamente ❑ **virtual reality** n (COMPUT) mundo or realidad f virtual

virtue ['vəːtjuː] n virtud f; (advantage) ventaja; **by ~ of** en virtud de

virus ['vaɪərəs] n (also COMPUT) virus m

visa ['viːzə] n visado (SP), visa (LAm)

vise [vaɪs] (US) n (TECH) = **vice**

visibility [vɪzɪ'bɪlɪtɪ] n visibilidad f

visible ['vɪzəbl] adj visible

vision ['vɪʒən] n (sight) vista; (foresight, in dream) visión f

visit ['vɪzɪt] n visita ♦ vt (person: US: also: **~ with**) visitar, hacer una visita a; (place) ir a, (ir a) conocer ❑ **visiting hours** npl (in hospital etc) horas fpl de visita ❑ **visitor** n (in museum) visitante mf; (invited to house) visita; (tourist) turista mf ❑ **visitor centre** (US **visitor center**) n centro de información

visual ['vɪzjuəl] adj visual ❑ **visualize** vt imaginarse

vital ['vaɪtl] adj (essential) esencial, imprescindible; (dynamic) dinámico; (organ) vital

vitality [vaɪ'tælɪtɪ] n energía, vitalidad f

vitamin [ˈvɪtəmɪn] n vitamina

vivid [ˈvɪvɪd] adj (account) gráfico; (light) intenso; (imagination, memory) vívo

V-neck [ˈviːnɛk] n cuello de pico

vocabulary [vəʊˈkæbjʊlərɪ] n vocabulario

vocal [ˈvəʊkl] adj vocal; (articulate) elocuente

vocational [vəʊˈkeɪʃənl] adj profesional

vodka [ˈvɒdkə] n vodka m

vogue [vəʊg] n: **in ~** en boga

voice [vɔɪs] n voz f ♦ vt expresar ❑ **voice mail** n fonobuzón m

void [vɔɪd] n vacío; (hole) hueco ♦ adj (invalid) nulo, inválido; (empty): **~ of** carente o desprovisto de

volatile [ˈvɒlətaɪl] adj (situation) inestable; (person) voluble; (liquid) volátil

volcano [vɒlˈkeɪnəʊ] (pl **volcanoes**) n volcán m

volleyball [ˈvɒlɪbɔːl] n vol(e)ibol m

volt [vəʊlt] n voltio ❑ **voltage** n voltaje m

volume [ˈvɒljuːm] n (gen) volumen m; (book) tomo

voluntarily [ˈvɒləntrɪlɪ] adv libremente, voluntariamente

voluntary [ˈvɒləntərɪ] adj voluntario

volunteer [vɒlənˈtɪəˀ] n voluntario(-a) ♦ vt (information) ofrecer ♦ vi ofrecerse (de voluntario); **to ~ to do** ofrecerse a hacer

vomit [ˈvɒmɪt] n vómito ♦ vt, vi vomitar

vote [vəʊt] n voto; (votes cast) votación f; (right to vote) derecho de votar; (franchise) sufragio ♦ vt (chair) elegir; (propose): **to ~ that** proponer que ♦ vi votar, ir a votar; **~ of thanks** voto de gracias ❑ **voter** n votante mf ❑ **voting** n votación f

voucher [ˈvaʊtʃəˀ] n (for meal, petrol) vale m

vow [vaʊ] n voto ♦ vt: **to ~ to do/that** jurar hacer/que

vowel [ˈvaʊəl] n vocal f

voyage [ˈvɔɪɪdʒ] n viaje m

vulgar [ˈvʌlgəˀ] adj (rude) ordinario, grosero; (in bad taste) de mal gusto

vulnerable [ˈvʌlnərəbl] adj vulnerable

vulture [ˈvʌltʃəˀ] n buitre m

W, w

waddle [ˈwɒdl] vi anadear

wade [weɪd] vi: **to ~ through** (water) vadear; (fig: book) leer con dificultad

wafer [ˈweɪfəˀ] n galleta, barquillo

waffle [ˈwɒfl] n (CULIN) gofre m ♦ vi dar el rollo

wag [wæg] vt menear, agitar ♦ vi moverse, menearse

wage [weɪdʒ] n (also: **wages**) sueldo, salario ♦ vt: **to ~ war** hacer la guerra

wag(g)on [ˈwægən] n (horse-drawn) carro; (BRIT RAIL) vagón m

wail [weɪl] n gemido ♦ vi gemir

waist [weɪst] n cintura, talle m ❑ **waistcoat** (BRIT) n chaleco

wait [weɪt] n (interval) pausa ♦ vi esperar; **to lie in ~ for** acechar a; **I can't ~ to** (fig) estoy deseando; **to ~ for** esperar (a) ▶ **wait on** vt fus servir a ❑ **waiter** n camarero ❑ **waiting list** n lista de espera ❑ **waiting room** n sala de espera ❑ **waitress** [ˈweɪtrɪs] n camarera

waive [weɪv] vt suspender

wake [weɪk] (pt **woke** or **waked**, pp **woken** or **waked**) vt (also: **~ up**) despertar ♦ vi (also: **~ up**) despertarse ♦ n (for dead person) vela, velatorio; (NAUT) estela

Wales [weɪlz] n País m de Gales; **the Prince of ~** el príncipe de Gales

walk [wɔːk] n (stroll) paseo; (hike) excursión f a pie, caminata; (gait) paso,

andar m; (in park etc) paseo, alameda
♦ vi andar, caminar; (for pleasure,
exercise) pasear ♦ vt (distance) recorrer
a pie, andar; (dog) pasear; **10 minutes'
~ from here** a 10 minutos de aquí
andando; **people from all walks of life**
gente de todas las esferas ► **walk out**
vi (audience) salir; (workers) declararse
en huelga □ **walker** n (person)
paseante mf, caminante mf □ **walkie-
talkie** ['wɔːkɪ'tɔːkɪ] n walkie-talkie m
□ **walking** n el andar □ **walking
shoes** npl zapatos mpl para andar
□ **walking stick** n bastón m
□ **Walkman®** n Walkman® m
□ **walkway** n paseo

wall [wɔːl] n pared f; (exterior) muro;
(city wall etc) muralla

wallet ['wɔlɪt] n cartera, billetera

wallpaper ['wɔːlpeɪpə'] n papel m
pintado ♦ vt empapelar

walnut ['wɔːlnʌt] n nuez f; (tree) nogal
m

walrus ['wɔːlrəs] (pl ~ or **walruses**) n
morsa

waltz [wɔːlts] n vals m ♦ vi bailar el vals

wand [wɔnd] n (also: **magic ~**) varita
(mágica)

wander ['wɔndə'] vi (person) vagar;
deambular; (thoughts) divagar ♦ vt
recorrer, vagar por

want [wɔnt] vt querer, desear; (need)
necesitar ♦ n: **for ~ of** por falta de
□ **wanted** adj (criminal) buscado;
"wanted" (in advertisements) "se
busca"

war [wɔː'] n guerra; **to make ~ (on)**
declarar la guerra (a)

ward [wɔːd] n (in hospital) sala; (POL)
distrito electoral; (LAW: child: also: **~ of
court**) pupilo(-a)

warden ['wɔːdn] n (BRIT: of institution)
director(a) m/f; (of park, game reserve)
guardián(-ana) m/f; (BRIT: also: **traffic
~**) guardia mf

wardrobe ['wɔːdrəub] n armario,
ropero; (clothes) vestuario

warehouse ['wɛəhaus] n almacén m,
depósito

warfare ['wɔːfɛə'] n guerra

warhead ['wɔːhed] n cabeza armada

warm [wɔːm] adj caliente; (thanks)
efusivo; (clothes etc) abrigado;
(welcome, day) caluroso; **it's ~** hace
calor; **I'm ~** tengo calor ► **warm up** vi
(room) calentarse; (person) entrar en
calor; (athlete) hacer ejercicios de
calentamiento ♦ vt calentar
□ **warmly** adv afectuosamente
□ **warmth** n calor m

warn [wɔːn] vt avisar, advertir
□ **warning** n aviso, advertencia
□ **warning light** n luz f de
advertencia

warrant ['wɔrnt] n autorización f; (LAW:
to arrest) orden f de detención; (: to
search) mandamiento de registro

warranty ['wɔrəntɪ] n garantía

warrior ['wɔrɪə'] n guerrero(-a)

Warsaw ['wɔːsɔː] n Varsovia

warship ['wɔːʃɪp] n buque m or barco
de guerra

wart [wɔːt] n verruga

wartime ['wɔːtaɪm] n: **in ~** en tiempos
de guerra, en la guerra

wary ['wɛərɪ] adj cauteloso

was [wɔz] pt of **be**

wash [wɔʃ] vt lavar ♦ vi lavarse; (sea etc):
to ~ against/over sth llegar hasta/
cubrir algo ♦ n (clothes etc) lavado; (of
ship) estela; **to have a ~** lavarse
► **wash up** vi (BRIT) fregar los platos;
(US) lavarse □ **washbasin** (US) n
lavabo □ **wash cloth** (US) n manopla
□ **washer** n (TECH) arandela
□ **washing** n (dirty) ropa sucia; (clean)
colada □ **washing line** n cuerda de
(colgar) la ropa □ **washing machine**
n lavadora □ **washing powder** (BRIT)
n detergente m (en polvo)

Washington ['wɔʃɪŋtən] n
Washington m

wash: washing-up (BRIT) n fregado,
platos mpl (para fregar) ❏ **washing-
up liquid** (BRIT) n líquido lavavajillas
❏ **washroom** (US) n servicios mpl

wasn't ['wɔznt] = **was not**

wasp [wɔsp] n avispa

waste [weist] n derroche m,
despilfarro; (of time) pérdida; (food)
sobras fpl; (rubbish) basura,
desperdicios mpl ♦ adj (material) de
desecho; (left over) sobrante; (land)
baldío, descampado ♦ vt malgastar,
derrochar; (time) perder; (opportunity)
desperdiciar ❏ **waste ground** (BRIT) n
terreno baldío ❏ **wastepaper
basket** n papelera

watch [wɔtʃ] n (also: **wrist ~**) reloj m;
(MIL: group of guards) centinela m; (act)
vigilancia; (NAUT: spell of duty) guardia
♦ vt (look at) mirar, observar; (: match,
programme) ver; (spy on, guard) vigilar;
(be careful of) cuidarse de, tener
cuidado de ♦ vi ver, mirar; mirar; (keep guard)
montar guardia ► **watch out** vi
cuidarse, tener cuidado ❏ **watchdog**
n perro guardián; (fig) persona u
organismo encargado de asegurarse de
que las empresas actúan dentro de la
legalidad ❏ **watch strap** n pulsera (de
reloj)

water ['wɔːtə'] n agua ♦ vt (plant) regar
♦ vi (eyes) llorar; (mouth) hacerse la
boca agua ► **water down** vt (milk etc)
aguar; (fig: story) dulcificar, diluir
❏ **watercolour** (US **watercolor**) n
acuarela ❏ **watercress** n berro
❏ **waterfall** n cascada, salto de agua
❏ **watering can** n regadera
❏ **watermelon** n sandía
❏ **waterproof** adj impermeable
❏ **water-skiing** n esquí m acuático

watt [wɔt] n vatio

wave [weiv] n (of hand) señal f con la
mano; (on water) ola; (RADIO, in hair)
onda; (fig) oleada ♦ vi agitar la mano;

(flag etc) ondear ♦ vt (handkerchief,
gun) agitar ❏ **wavelength** n longitud
f de onda

waver ['weivə'] vi (voice, love etc)
flaquear; (person) vacilar

wavy ['weivi] adj ondulado

wax [wæks] n cera ♦ vt encerar ♦ vi
(moon) crecer

way [wei] n camino; (distance) trayecto,
recorrido; (direction) dirección f,
sentido; (manner) modo, manera;
(habit) costumbre f; **which ~? — this ~**
¿por dónde?, ¿en qué dirección? —
por aquí; **on the ~** (en route) en (el)
camino; **to be on one's ~** estar en
camino; **to be in the ~** bloquear el
camino; (fig) estorbar; **to go out of
one's ~ to do sth** desvivirse por hacer
algo; **under ~** en marcha; **to lose one's
~** extraviarse; en cierto modo or
sentido; **no ~!** (inf) ¡de eso nada!; **by
the ~ …** a propósito …; **"~ in"** (BRIT)
"entrada"; **"~ out"** (BRIT) "salida"; **the ~
back** el camino de vuelta; **"give ~"** (BRIT
AUT) "ceda el paso"

W.C. n (BRIT) váter m

we [wiː] pl pron nosotros(-as)

weak [wiːk] adj débil, flojo; (tea etc)
claro ❏ **weaken** vi debilitarse; (give
way) ceder ♦ vt debilitar; (person) n
debilidad f; (fault) punto débil; **to
have a weakness for** tener afición or
por

wealth [welθ] n riqueza; (of details)
abundancia ❏ **wealthy** adj rico

weapon ['wepən] n arma; **weapons of
mass destruction** armas de
destrucción masiva

wear [weə'] (pt **wore**, pp **worn**) n (use)
uso; (deterioration through use)
desgaste m ♦ vt (clothes) llevar; (shoes)
calzar; (damage: through use) gastar,
usar ♦ vi (last) durar; (rub through etc)
desgastarse; **evening ~** ropa de
etiqueta; **sportswear/babywear** ropa
de deportes/de niños ► **wear off** vi
(pain etc) pasar, desaparecer ► **wear**

out vt desgastar; *(person, strength)* agotar

weary ['wɪərɪ] adj cansado; *(dispirited)* abatido ♦ vi: **to ~** cansarse

weasel ['wiːzl] n *(ZOOL)* comadreja

weather ['weðəʳ] n tiempo ♦ vt *(storm, crisis)* hacer frente a; **under the ~** *(fig: ill)* indispuesto, pachucho ❑ **weather forecast** n boletín m meteorológico

weave [wiːv] *(pt wove, pp woven)* vt *(cloth)* tejer; *(fig)* entretejer

web [web] n *(of spider)* telaraña; *(on duck's foot)* membrana; *(network)* red f; **the (World Wide) W~** la Red ❑ **web page** n *(página)* web ❑ **website** n espacio Web

Wed. abbr (= Wednesday) miérc

wed [wed] *(pt, pp wedded)* vt casar ♦ vi casarse

we'd [wiːd] = **we had; we would**

wedding ['wedɪŋ] n boda, casamiento; **silver~/golden~ (anniversary)** bodas fpl de plata/de oro ❑ **wedding anniversary** n aniversario de boda ❑ **wedding day** n día m de la boda ❑ **wedding dress** n traje m de novia ❑ **wedding ring** n alianza

wedge [wedʒ] n *(of wood etc)* cuña; *(of cake)* trozo ♦ vt acuñar; *(push)* apretar

Wednesday ['wednzdɪ] n miércoles m inv

wee [wiː] *(Scottish)* adj pequeñito

weed [wiːd] n mala hierba, maleza ♦ vt escardar, desherbar ❑ **weedkiller** n herbicida m

week [wiːk] n semana; **a ~ today/on Friday** de hoy/del viernes en ocho días ❑ **weekday** n día m laborable ❑ **weekend** n fin m de semana ❑ **weekly** adv semanalmente, cada semana ♦ adj semanal ♦ n semanario

weep [wiːp] *(pt, pp wept)* vi, vt llorar

weigh [weɪ] vt, vi pesar; **to ~ anchor** levar anclas ► **weigh up** vt sopesar

weight [weɪt] n peso; *(metal weight)* pesa; **to lose/put on ~** adelgazar/

engordar ❑ **weightlifting** n levantamiento de pesas

weir [wɪəʳ] n presa

weird [wɪəd] adj raro, extraño

welcome ['welkəm] adj bienvenido ♦ n bienvenida ♦ vt dar la bienvenida a; *(be glad of)* alegrarse de; **thank you — you're ~** gracias — de nada

weld [weld] n soldadura ♦ vt soldar

welfare ['welfeəʳ] n bienestar m; *(social aid)* asistencia social ❑ **welfare state** n estado del bienestar

well [wel] n fuente f, pozo ♦ adv bien ♦ adj: **to be ~** estar bien (de salud) ♦ excl ¡vaya!, ¡bueno!; **as ~** también; **as ~ as** además de; **~ done!** ¡bien hecho!; **get ~ soon!** ¡que te mejores pronto!; **to do ~** *(business)* ir bien; *(person)* tener éxito

we'll [wiːl] = **we will; we shall**

well: well-behaved adj bueno ❑ **well-built** adj *(person)* fornido ❑ **well-dressed** adj bien vestido

wellies [inf] ['welɪz] npl *(BRIT)* botas de goma

well: well-known adj *(person)* conocido ❑ **well-off** adj acomodado ❑ **well-paid** [wel'peɪd] adj bien pagado, bien retribuido

Welsh [welʃ] adj galés(-esa) ♦ n *(LING)* galés m ❑ **Welshman** *(irreg)* n galés m ❑ **Welshwoman** *(irreg)* n galesa

went [went] pt of **go**

wept [wept] pt, pp of **weep**

were [wəːʳ] pt of **be**

we're [wɪəʳ] = **we are**

weren't [wəːnt] = **were not**

west [west] n oeste m ♦ adj occidental, del oeste ♦ adv al o hacia el oeste; **the W~** el Oeste, el Occidente ❑ **westbound** ['westbaund] adj *(traffic, carriageway)* con rumbo al oeste ❑ **western** adj occidental ♦ n *(CINEMA)* película del oeste ❑ **West Indian** adj, n antillano(-a) m/f

wet [wɛt] adj (damp) húmedo; (soaked):
~ **through** mojado; (rainy) lluvioso ♦ n
(BRIT: POL) conservador(a) m/f
moderado(-a); **to get ~** mojarse; "~
paint" "recién pintado" □ **wetsuit** n
traje m térmico

we've [wiːv] = **we have**

whack [wæk] vt dar un buen golpe a

whale [weɪl] n (ZOOL) ballena

wharf [wɔːf] (pl **wharves**) n muelle m

what

[wɔt] adj
1 (in direct/indirect questions) qué;
what size is he? ¿qué talla usa?; **what
colour/shape is it?** ¿de qué color/
forma es?
2 (in exclamations): **what a mess!**
¡qué desastre!; **what a fool I am!** ¡qué
tonto soy!
♦ pron
1 (interrogative) qué; **what are you
doing?** ¿qué haces or estás
haciendo?; **what is happening?** ¿qué
pasa or está pasando?; **what is it
called?** ¿cómo se llama?; **what about
me?** ¿y yo qué?; **what about doing
...?** ¿qué tal si hacemos ...?
2 (relative) lo que; **I saw what you
did/was on the table** vi lo que
hiciste/había en la mesa
♦ excl (disbelieving) ¡cómo!; **what, no
coffee!** ¡que no hay café!

whatever [wɔtˈevəʳ] adj: ~ **book you
choose** cualquier libro que elijas
♦ pron: **do ~ is necessary** haga lo que
sea necesario; ~ **happens** pase lo que
pase; **no reason ~** or **whatsoever**
ninguna razón a la que sea; **nothing
~** nada en absoluto

whatsoever [wɔtsəʊˈevəʳ] adj see
whatever

wheat [wiːt] n trigo

wheel [wiːl] n rueda; (AUT: also:
steering ~) volante m; (NAUT) timón m
♦ vt (pram etc) empujar ♦ vi (also: ~
round) dar la vuelta, girar
□ **wheelbarrow** n carretilla
□ **wheelchair** n silla de ruedas
□ **wheel clamp** n (AUT) cepo

wheeze [wiːz] vi resollar

when

[wɛn] adv cuando; **when did it
happen?** ¿cuándo ocurrió?; **I know
when it happened** sé cuándo ocurrió
♦ conj
1 (at, during, after the time that)
cuando; **be careful when you cross
the road** ten cuidado al cruzar la
calle; **that was when I needed you**
fue entonces que te necesité
2 (on, at which): **on the day when I
met him** el día en que le conocí
3 (whereas) cuando

whenever [wɛnˈevəʳ] conj cuando;
(every time that) cada vez que ♦ adv
cuando sea

where [wɛəʳ] adv dónde ♦ conj donde;
this is ~ aquí es donde
□ **whereabouts** adv dónde ♦ n:
nobody knows his whereabouts
nadie conoce su paradero □ **whereas**
conj visto que, mientras □ **whereby**
pron por lo cual □ **wherever** conj
dondequiera que; (interrogative)
dónde

whether [ˈwɛðəʳ] conj si; **I don't know ~
to accept or not** no sé si aceptar o no;
~ **you go or not** vayas o no vayas

which

[wɪtʃ] adj
1 (interrogative: direct, indirect)
qué; **which picture(s) do you want?** ¿qué
cuadro(s) quieres?; **which one?**

¿cuál?

2: in which case en cuyo caso; **we got there at 8 pm, by which time the cinema was full** llegamos allí a las 8, cuando el cine estaba lleno
♦ *pron*
1 (*interrogative*) cúal; **I don't mind which** el/la que sea
2 (*relative: replacing noun*) que; (: *replacing clause*) lo que; (: *after preposition*) (el(la)) que etc el/la cual etc; **the apple which you ate/which is on the table** la manzana que comiste/que está en la mesa; **the chair on which you are sitting** la silla en la que estás sentado; **he said he knew, which is true/I feared** dijo que lo sabía, lo cual *or* lo que es cierto/me temía

whichever [wɪtʃ'evəᵊ] *adj:* **take ~ book you prefer** coja (SP) el libro que prefiera; **~ book you take** cualquier libro que coja

while [waɪl] *n* rato, momento ♦ *conj* mientras; (*although*) aunque; **for a ~** durante algún tiempo

whilst [waɪlst] *conj* = **while**

whim [wɪm] *n* capricho

whine [waɪn] *n* (*of pain*) gemido; (*of engine*) zumbido; (*of siren*) aullido ♦ *vi* gemir; zumbar; (*fig: complain*) gimotear

whip [wɪp] *n* látigo; (*POL: person*) encargado de la disciplina partidaria en el parlamento ♦ *vt* azotar; (*CULIN: beat*) batir; (*move quickly*): **to ~ sth out/off** sacar/quitar algo de un tirón □ **whipped cream** *n* nata *or* crema montada

whirl [wɜːl] *vt* hacer girar, dar vueltas a ♦ *vi* girar, dar vueltas; (*leaves etc*) arremolinarse

whisk [wɪsk] *n* (*CULIN*) batidor *m* ♦ *vt* (*CULIN*) batir; **to ~ sb away** *or* **off** llevar volando a algn

whiskers [ˈwɪskəz] *npl* (*of animal*) bigotes *mpl*; (*of man*) patillas *fpl*

whiskey [ˈwɪskɪ] (*US, Ireland*) *n* = **whisky**

whisky [ˈwɪskɪ] *n* whisky *m*

whisper [ˈwɪspəᵊ] *n* susurro ♦ *vi, vt* susurrar

whistle [ˈwɪsl] *n* (*sound*) silbido; (*object*) silbato ♦ *vi* silbar

white [waɪt] *adj* blanco; (*pale*) pálido ♦ *n* blanco; (*of egg*) clara □ **White House** (*US*) *n* Casa Blanca □ **whitewash** *n* (*paint*) jalbegue *m*, cal *f* ♦ *vt* blanquear

whiting [ˈwaɪtɪŋ] *n inv* (*fish*) pescadilla

Whitsun [ˈwɪtsn] *n* pentecostés *m*

whittle [ˈwɪtl] *vt:* **to ~ away, ~ down** ir reduciendo

whizz [wɪz] *vi:* **to ~ past** *or* **by** pasar a toda velocidad

who

[huː] *pron*
1 (*interrogative*) quién; **who is it?, who's there?** ¿quién es?; **who are you looking for?** ¿a quién buscas?; **I told her who I was** le dije quién era yo
2 (*relative*) que; **the man/woman who spoke to me** el hombre/la mujer que habló conmigo; **those who can swim** los que saben *or* sepan nadar

whoever [huː'evəᵊ] *pron:* **~ finds it** cualquiera *or* quienquiera que lo encuentre; **ask ~ you like** pregunta a quien quieras; **~ he marries** no importa con quién se case

whole [həʊl] *adj* (*entire*) todo, entero; (*not broken*) intacto *n* todo; (*all*): **the ~ of the town** toda la ciudad, la ciudad entera ♦ *n* (*total*) total *m*; (*sum*) conjunto; **on the ~, as a ~** en general □ **wholefood(s)** *n(pl)* alimento(s) *m(pl)* integral(es) □ **wholeheartedly** [həʊlˈhɑːtɪdlɪ] *adv* con entusiasmo

❑ **wholemeal** *adj* integral
❑ **wholesale** *n* venta al por mayor
♦ *adj* al por mayor; *(fig: destruction)*
sistemático ❑ **wholewheat** *adj* =
wholemeal ❑ **wholly** *adv*
totalmente, enteramente

whom

KEYWORD

[huːm] *pron*

1 *(interrogative)*: **whom did you see?**
¿a quién viste?; **to whom did you
give it?** ¿a quién se lo diste?; **tell me
from whom you received it** dígame
de quién lo recibió

2 *(relative)* que; **to whom** a quien(es);
of whom de quien(es), del/de la que
etc; **the man whom I saw/to whom I
wrote** el hombre que vi/a quien
escribí; **the lady about/with whom I
was talking** la señora de (la) que/con
quien *or* (la) que hablaba

whore [hɔː'] *n (inf, pej)* puta

whose

KEYWORD

[huːz] *adj*

1 *(possessive: interrogative)*: **whose
book is this?, whose is this book?**
¿de quién es este libro?; **whose
pencil have you taken?** ¿de quién es
el lápiz que has cogido?; **whose
daughter are you?** ¿de quién eres
hija?

2 *(possessive: relative)* cuyo(-a), *pl*
cuyos(-as); **the man whose son you
rescued** el hombre cuyo hijo
rescataste; **those whose passports I
have** aquellas personas cuyos
pasaportes tengo; **the woman whose
car was stolen** la mujer a quien le
robaron el coche

♦ *pron* de quién; **whose is this?** ¿de

quién es esto?; **I know whose it is** sé
de quién es

why

KEYWORD

[waɪ] *adv* por qué; **why not?** ¿por qué
no?; **why not do it now?** ¿por qué no
lo haces *(or* hacemos *etc)* ahora?

♦ *conj*: **I wonder why he said that** me
pregunto por qué dijo eso; **that's not
why I'm here** no es por eso *(por lo)*
que estoy aquí; **the reason why** la
razón por la que

♦ *excl (expressing surprise, shock,
annoyance)* ¡hombre!, ¡vaya!;
(explaining): **why, it's you!** ¡hombre,
eres tú!; **why, that's impossible** ¡pero
si eso es imposible!

wicked ['wɪkɪd] *adj* malvado, cruel
wicket ['wɪkɪt] *n (CRICKET: stumps)* palos
mpl; *(: grass area)* terreno de juego
wide [waɪd] *adj* ancho; *(area,
knowledge)* vasto, grande; *(choice)*
amplio ♦ *adv*: **to open ~** abrir de par en
par; **to shoot ~** errar el tiro ❑ **widely**
adv (travelled) mucho; *(spaced)* muy; **it
is widely believed/known that ...**
mucha gente piensa/sabe que ...
❑ **widen** *vt* ensanchar; *(experience)*
ampliar ♦ *vi* ensancharse ❑ **wide
open** *adj* abierto de par en par
❑ **widespread** *adj* extendido, general
widow ['wɪdəu] *n* viuda ❑ **widower** *n*
viudo
width [wɪdθ] *n* anchura; *(of cloth)*
ancho
wield [wiːld] *vt (sword)* blandir; *(power)*
ejercer
wife [waɪf] *(pl* **wives)** *n* mujer *f*, esposa
wig [wɪg] *n* peluca
wild [waɪld] *adj (animal)* salvaje; *(plant)*
silvestre; *(person)* furioso, violento;
(idea) descabellado; *(rough: sea)* bravo;
(: land) agreste; *(: weather)* muy

revuelto ❏ **wilderness** ['wɪldənɪs] n desierto ❏ **wildlife** n fauna ❏ **wildly** adv (behave) locamente; (lash out) a diestro y siniestro; (guess) a lo loco; (happy) a más no poder

will

KEYWORD

[wɪl] aux vb

1 (forming future tense): **I will finish it tomorrow** lo terminaré o voy a terminar mañana; **I will have finished it by tomorrow** lo habré terminado para mañana; **will you do it?** — yes I will/no I won't ¿lo harás? — sí/no

2 (in conjectures, predictions): **he will** or **he'll be there by now** ya habrá o debe (de) haber llegado; **that will be the postman** será o debe ser el cartero

3 (in commands, requests, offers): **will you be quiet!** ¿quieres callarte?; **will you help me?** ¿quieres ayudarme?; **will you have a cup of tea?** ¿te apetece un té?; **I won't put up with it!** ¡no lo soporto!

♦ vt (pt, pp willed): **to will sb to do sth** desear que algn haga algo; **he willed himself to go on** con gran fuerza de voluntad, continuó

♦ n voluntad f; (testament) testamento

willing ['wɪlɪŋ] adj (with goodwill) de buena voluntad; (enthusiastic) entusiasta; **he's ~ to do it** está dispuesto a hacerlo ❏ **willingly** adv con mucho gusto

willow ['wɪləʊ] n sauce m

willpower ['wɪlpaʊə[r]] n fuerza de voluntad

wilt [wɪlt] vi marchitarse

win [wɪn] (pt, pp **won**) n victoria, triunfo ♦ vt ganar; (obtain) conseguir, lograr ♦ vi ganar ▶ **win over** vt convencer a

wince [wɪns] vi encogerse

wind¹ [wɪnd] n (MED) gases mpl ♦ vt (take breath away from) dejar sin aliento a

wind² [waɪnd] (pt, pp **wound**) vt enrollar; (wrap) envolver; (clock, toy) dar cuerda a ♦ vi (road, river) serpentear ▶ **wind down** vt (car window) bajar; (fig: production, business) disminuir ▶ **wind up** vt (clock) dar cuerda a; (debate, meeting) concluir, terminar

windfall ['wɪndfɔːl] n golpe m de suerte

winding ['waɪndɪŋ] adj (road) tortuoso; (staircase) de caracol

windmill ['wɪndmɪl] n molino de viento

window ['wɪndəʊ] n ventana; (in car, train) ventanilla; (in shop etc) escaparate m (SP), vidriera (LAm) ❏ **window box** n jardinera de ventana ❏ **window cleaner** n (person) limpiacristales mf inv ❏ **window pane** n cristal m ❏ **window seat** n asiento junto a la ventana ❏ **windowsill** n alféizar m, repisa

windscreen ['wɪndskriːn] (US **windshield**) n parabrisas m inv ❏ **windscreen wiper** (US **windshield wiper**) n limpiaparabrisas m inv

windsurfing ['wɪndsɜːfɪŋ] n windsurf m

windy ['wɪndɪ] adj de mucho viento; **it's ~** hace viento

wine [waɪn] n vino ❏ **wine bar** n enoteca ❏ **wine glass** n copa (para vino) ❏ **wine list** n lista de vinos ❏ **wine tasting** n degustación f de vinos

wing [wɪŋ] n ala; (AUT) aleta ❏ **wing mirror** n (espejo) retrovisor m

wink [wɪŋk] n guiño, pestañeo ♦ vi guiñar, pestañear

winner ['wɪnə[r]] n ganador(a) m/f

winning ['wɪnɪŋ] adj (team) ganador(a); (goal) decisivo; (smile) encantador(a)

winter ['wɪntəʳ] n invierno ♦ vi invernar ❑ **winter sports** npl deportes mpl de invierno ❑ **wintertime** n invierno

wipe [waɪp] n: **to give sth a ~** pasar un trapo sobre algo ♦ vt limpiar; (tape) borrar ▸ **wipe out** vt (debt) liquidar; (memory) borrar; (destroy) destruir ▸ **wipe up** vt limpiar

wire [waɪəʳ] n alambre m; (ELEC) cable m (eléctrico); (TEL) telegrama m ♦ vt (house) poner la instalación eléctrica en; (also: ~ **up**) conectar; (person: telegram) telegrafiar

wiring ['waɪərɪŋ] n instalación f eléctrica

wisdom ['wɪzdəm] n sabiduría, saber m; (good sense) cordura ❑ **wisdom tooth** n muela del juicio

wise [waɪz] adj sabio; (sensible) juicioso

wish [wɪʃ] n deseo ♦ vt querer; **best wishes** (on birthday etc) felicidades fpl; **with best wishes** (in letter) saludos mpl, recuerdos mpl; **to ~ sb goodbye** despedirse de algn; **he wished me well** me deseó mucha suerte; **to ~ to do/sb to do sth** querer hacer/que algn haga algo; **to ~ for** desear

wistful ['wɪstful] adj pensativo

wit [wɪt] n ingenio, gracia; (also: **wits**) inteligencia; (person) chistoso(-a)

witch [wɪtʃ] n bruja

with

KEYWORD

[wɪð, wɪθ] prep

1 (accompanying, in the company of) con (con +mí, tí, sí = conmigo, contigo, consigo); **I was with him** estaba con él; **we stayed with friends** nos quedamos en casa de unos amigos; **I'm (not) with you** (don't understand) (no) te entiendo; **to be with it** (inf: person: up-to-date) estar al tanto; (:

alert) ser despabilado

2 (descriptive, indicating manner etc) con; de; **a room with a view** una habitación con vistas; **the man with the grey hat/blue eyes** el hombre del sombrero gris/de los ojos azules; **red with anger** rojo de ira; **to shake with fear** temblar de miedo; **to fill sth with water** llenar algo de agua

withdraw [wɪθ'drɔː] vt retirar, sacar ♦ vi retirarse; **to ~ money (from the bank)** retirar fondos (del banco) ❑ **withdrawal** n retirada; (of money) reintegro ❑ **withdrawn** pp of **withdraw** ♦ adj (person) reservado, introvertido

withdrew [wɪθ'druː] pt of **withdraw**

wither ['wɪðəʳ] vi marchitarse

withhold [wɪθ'həuld] vt (money) retener; (decision) aplazar; (permission) negar; (information) ocultar

within [wɪð'ɪn] prep dentro de ♦ adv dentro; ~ **reach (of)** al alcance (de); ~ **sight (of)** a la vista (de); ~ **the week** antes de acabar la semana; ~ **a mile (of)** a menos de una milla (de)

without [wɪð'aut] prep sin; **to go ~ sth** pasar sin algo

withstand [wɪθ'stænd] vt resistir a

witness ['wɪtnɪs] n testigo mf ♦ vt (event) presenciar; (document) atestiguar la veracidad de; **to bear ~ to** (fig) ser testimonio de

witty ['wɪtɪ] adj ingenioso

wives [waɪvz] npl of **wife**

wizard ['wɪzəd] n hechicero

wk abbr = **week**

wobble ['wɔbl] vi temblar; (chair) cojear

woe [wəu] n desgracia

woke [wəuk] pt of **wake**

woken ['wəukən] pp of **wake**

wolf [wulf] n lobo

woman ['wumən] (pl **women**) n mujer f

womb [wu:m] n matriz f, útero

women ['wɪmɪn] npl of **woman**

won [wʌn] pt, pp of **win**

wonder ['wʌndə] n maravilla, prodigio; (feeling) asombro ♦ vi: **to ~ whether/why** preguntarse si/por qué; **to ~** at asombrarse de; **to ~ about** pensar sobre or en; **it's no ~ (that)** no es de extrañarse que (+subjun)
□ **wonderful** adj maravilloso

won't [wəunt] = **will not**

wood [wud] n (timber) madera; (forest) bosque m □ **wooden** adj de madera; (fig) inexpresivo □ **woodwind** n (MUS) instrumentos mpl de viento de madera □ **woodwork** n carpintería

wool [wul] n lana; **to pull the ~ over sb's eyes** (fig) engatusar a algn
□ **woollen** (US **woolen**) adj de lana □ **woolly** (US **wooly**) adj lanudo, de lana; (fig: ideas) confuso

word [wə:d] n palabra; (news) noticia; (promise) palabra (de honor) ♦ vt redactar; **in other words** en otras palabras; **to break/keep one's ~** faltar a la palabra/cumplir la promesa; **to have words with sb** reñir con algn □ **wording** n redacción f □ **word processing** n proceso de textos □ **word processor** n procesador m de textos

wore [wɔ:] pt of **wear**

work [wə:k] n trabajo; (job) empleo, trabajo; (ART, LITERATURE) obra ♦ vi trabajar; (mechanism) funcionar, marchar; (medicine) ser eficaz, surtir efecto ♦ vt (shape) trabajar; (stone etc) tallar; (mine etc) explotar; (machine) manejar, hacer funcionar ♦ npl (of clock, machine) mecanismo; **to be out of ~** estar parado, no tener trabajo; **to ~ loose** (part) desprenderse; (knot) aflojarse; **work in** (BRIT: factory) fábrica ► **work out** vi (plans etc) salir bien, funcionar ♦ vt (problem) resolver; (plan) elaborar; **it works out at £100** suma 100 libras □ **worker** n

trabajador(a) m/f, obrero(-a) □ **work experience** n: **I'm going to do my work experience in a factory** voy a hacer las prácticas en una fábrica □ **workforce** n mano de obra □ **working class** n clase f obrera ♦ adj: **working-class** obrero □ **working week** n semana laboral □ **workman** (irreg) n obrero □ **work of art** n obra de arte □ **workout** n (SPORT) sesión f de ejercicios □ **work permit** n permiso de trabajo □ **workplace** n lugar m de trabajo □ **workshop** n taller m □ **work station** n puesto or estación f de trabajo □ **work surface** n encimera □ **worktop** n encimera

world [wə:ld] n mundo ♦ cpd (champion) del mundo; (power, war) mundial; **to think the ~ of sb** (fig) tener un concepto muy alto de algn □ **World Cup** n (FOOTBALL): **the World Cup** el Mundial, los Mundiales □ **world-wide** adj mundial, universal □ **World-Wide Web** n: **the World-Wide Web** el World Wide Web

worm [wə:m] n (also: **earth ~**) lombriz f

worn [wɔ:n] pp of **wear** ♦ adj usado; **worn-out** adj (object) gastado; (person) rendido, agotado

worried ['wʌrɪd] adj preocupado

worry ['wʌrɪ] n preocupación f ♦ vt preocupar, inquietar ♦ vi preocuparse □ **worrying** adj inquietante

worse [wə:s] adj, adv peor ♦ n lo peor; **a change for the ~** un empeoramiento □ **worsen** vt, vi empeorar □ **worse off** adj (financially): **to be worse off** tener menos dinero; (fig): **you'll be worse off this way** estarás peor que nunca

worship ['wə:ʃɪp] n adoración f ♦ vt adorar; **Your W~** (BRIT: to mayor) señor alcalde; (: to judge) señor juez

worst [wə:st] adj, adv peor ♦ n lo peor; **at ~** en lo peor de los casos

worth [wə:θ] n valor m ♦ adj: **to be ~** valer; **it's ~ it** vale or merece la pena; **to be ~ one's while (to do)** merecer la pena (hacer) ❑ **worthless** adj (useless) inútil ❑ **worthwhile** adj (activity) que merece la pena; (cause) loable

worthy ['wə:ði] adj respetable; (motive) honesto; **~ of** digno de

---

would

KEYWORD

[wud] aux vb

1 (conditional tense): **if you asked him he would do it** si se lo pidieras, lo haría; **if you had asked him he would have done it** si se lo hubieras pedido, lo habría or hubiera hecho

2 (in offers, invitations, requests): **would you like a biscuit?** ¿quieres una galleta?; (formal) ¿querría una galleta?; **would you ask him to come in?** ¿quiere hacerle pasar?; **would you open the window please?** ¿quiere or podría abrir la ventana, por favor?

3 (in indirect speech): **I said I would do it** dije que lo haría

4 (emphatic): **it WOULD have to snow today!** ¡tenía que nevar precisamente hoy!

5 (insistence): **she wouldn't behave** no quiso comportarse bien

6 (conjecture): **it would have been midnight** sería medianoche; **it would seem so** parece ser que sí

7 (indicating habit): **he would go there on Mondays** iba allí los lunes

---

wouldn't ['wudnt] = would not

wound[1] [wu:nd] n herida ♦ vt herir

wound[2] [waund] pt, pp of **wind**[2]

wove [wauv] pt of **weave**

woven ['wauvan] pp of **weave**

wrap [ræp] vt (also: **~ up**) envolver; (gift) envolver, abrigar ♦ vi (dress warmly) abrigarse ❑ **wrapper** n (on chocolate) papel m; (BRIT: of book) sobrecubierta ❑ **wrapping** n envoltura, envase m ❑ **wrapping paper** n papel m de envolver; (fancy) papel m de regalo

wreath [ri:θ, pl ri:ðz] n (funeral wreath) corona

wreck [rek] n (ship: destruction) naufragio; (: remains) restos mpl del barco; (pej: person) ruina ♦ vt (car etc) destrozar; (chances) arruinar ❑ **wreckage** n restos mpl; (of building) escombros mpl

wren [ren] n (ZOOL) reyezuelo

wrench [rentʃ] n (TECH) llave f inglesa; (tug) tirón m; (fig) dolor m ♦ vt arrancar; **to ~ sth from sb** arrebatar algo violentamente a algn

wrestle ['resl] vi: **to ~ (with sb)** luchar (con or contra algn) ❑ **wrestler** n luchador(a) m/f (de lucha libre) ❑ **wrestling** n lucha libre

wretched ['retʃid] adj miserable

wriggle ['rɪgl] vi (also: **~ about**) menearse, retorcerse

wring [rɪŋ] (pt, pp **wrung**) vt retorcer; (wet clothes) escurrir; (fig): **to ~ sth out of sb** sacar algo por la fuerza a algn

wrinkle ['rɪŋkl] n arruga ♦ vt arrugar ♦ vi arrugarse

wrist [rɪst] n muñeca

write [raɪt] (pt **wrote**, pp **written**) vt escribir; (cheque) extender ♦ vi escribir ▶ **write down** vt escribir; (note) apuntar ▶ **write off** vt (debt) borrar (como incobrable); (fig) desechar por inútil ▶ **write out** vt escribir ❑ **write-off** n siniestro total ❑ **writer** n escritor(a) m/f

writing ['raɪtɪŋ] n escritura; (hand-writing) letra; (of author) obras fpl; **in ~** por escrito ❑ **writing paper** n papel m de escribir

written ['rɪtn] pp of **write**

wrong [rɒŋ] *adj* (*wicked*) malo; (*unfair*) injusto; (*incorrect*) equivocado, incorrecto; (*not suitable*) inoportuno, inconveniente; (*reverse*) del revés ♦ *adv* equivocadamente ♦ *n* injusticia ♦ *vt* ser injusto con; **you are ~ to do it** haces mal en hacerlo; **you are ~ about that, you've got it ~** en eso estás equivocado; **to be in the ~** no tener razón, tener la culpa; **what's ~?** ¿qué pasa?; **to go ~** (*person*) equivocarse; (*plan*) salir mal; (*machine*) estropearse □ **wrongly** *adv* mal, incorrectamente; (*by mistake*) por error □ **wrong number** *n* (*TEL*): **you've got the wrong number** se ha equivocado de número

wrote [rəut] *pt of* **write**

wrung [rʌŋ] *pt, pp of* **wring**

WWW *n abbr* (= World Wide Web) WWW *m*

X, x

XL *abbr* = **extra large**

Xmas [ˈeksməs] *n abbr* = **Christmas**

X-ray [ˈeksreɪ] *n* radiografía ♦ *vt* radiografiar, sacar radiografías de

xylophone [ˈzaɪləfəun] *n* xilófono

Y, y

yacht [jɒt] *n* yate *m* □ **yachting** *n* (*sport*) balandrismo

yard [jɑːd] *n* patio; (*measure*) yarda □ **yard sale** (*US*) *n* venta de objetos usados (*en el jardín de una casa particular*)

yarn [jɑːn] *n* hilo; (*tale*) cuento, historia

yawn [jɔːn] *n* bostezo ♦ *vi* bostezar

yd. *abbr* (= yard) yda

yeah [jɛə] (*inf*) *adv* sí

year [jɪəʳ] *n* año; **to be 8 years old** tener 8 años; **an eight-~-old child** un niño de ocho años (de edad) □ **yearly** *adj* anual ♦ *adv* anualmente, cada año

yearn [jəːn] *vi*: **to ~ for sth** añorar algo, suspirar por algo

yeast [jiːst] *n* levadura

yell [jel] *n* grito, alarido ♦ *vi* gritar

yellow [ˈjeləu] *adj* amarillo □ **Yellow Pages®** *npl* páginas *fpl* amarillas

yes [jes] *adv* sí ♦ *n* sí *m*; **to say/answer ~** decir/contestar que sí

yesterday [ˈjestədɪ] *adv* ayer ♦ *n* ayer *m*; **~ morning/evening** ayer por la mañana/tarde; **all day ~** todo el día de ayer

yet [jet] *adv* ya; (*negative*) todavía ♦ *conj* sin embargo, a pesar de todo; **it is not finished ~** todavía no está acabado; **the best ~** el/la mejor hasta ahora; **as ~** hasta ahora, todavía

yew [juː] *n* tejo

Yiddish [ˈjɪdɪʃ] *n* yiddish *m*

yield [jiːld] *n* (*AGR*) cosecha; (*COMM*) rendimiento ♦ *vt* ceder; (*results*) producir, dar; (*profit*) rendir ♦ *vi* rendirse, ceder; (*US AUT*) ceder el paso

yob(bo) [ˈjɒb(bəu)] *n* (*BRIT inf*) gamberro

yoga [ˈjəugə] *n* yoga *m*

yog(h)urt [ˈjəugət] *n* = **yog(h)ourt**

yolk [jəuk] *n* yema (de huevo)

you

KEYWORD

[juː] *pron*

1 (*subject: familiar*) tú; (*pl*) vosotros(-as) (*SP*), ustedes (*LAm*); (*polite*) usted; (*pl*) ustedes; **you are very kind** eres/es *etc* muy amable; **you Spanish enjoy your food** a vosotros (*or* ustedes) los españoles os (*or* les) gusta la comida; **you and I will go** iremos tú y yo

2 (*object: direct: familiar*) te; (*pl*) os

(SP), les (LAm); (polite) le; (pl) les; (f) la; (pl) las; **I know you** te/le le conozco **3** (object: indirect: familiar) te; (pl) os (SP), les (LAm); (polite) le; (pl) les; **I gave the letter to you yesterday** te/os etc di la carta ayer **4** (stressed): **I told you to do it** te dije a ti que lo hicieras, es a ti a quien dije que lo hicieras; see also **3, 5** **5** (after prep: NB: con +ti = contigo: familiar) ti; (pl) vosotros(-as) (SP), ustedes (LAm); (: polite) usted; (pl) ustedes; **it's for you** es para ti/ vosotros etc **6** (comparisons: familiar) tú; (pl) vosotros(-as) (SP), ustedes (LAm); (: polite) usted; (pl) ustedes; **she's younger than you** es más joven que tú/vosotros etc **7** (impersonal one): **fresh air does you good** el aire puro (te) hace bien; **you never know** nunca se sabe; **you can't do that!** ¡eso no se hace!

you'd [juːd] = **you had; you would**

you'll [juːl] = **you will; you shall**

young [jʌŋ] adj joven ♦ npl (of animal) cría; (people): **the** — los jóvenes, la juventud ❑ **youngster** n joven mf

your [jɔːʳ] adj tu; (pl) vuestro; (formal) su; see also **my**

you're [juəʳ] = **you are**

yours [jɔːz] pron tuyo (pl), vuestro; (formal) suyo; see also **faithfully; mine[1]; sincerely**

yourself [jɔːˈself] pron tú mismo; (complement) te; (after prep) ti (mismo); (formal) usted mismo; (: complement) se; (: after prep) sí (mismo) ❑ **yourselves** pl pron vosotros

mismos; (after prep) vosotros (mismos); (formal) ustedes (mismos); (: complement) se; (: after prep) sí mismos; see also **oneself**

youth [pl juːðz] n juventud f; (young man) joven m ❑ **youth club** n club m juvenil ❑ **youthful** adj juvenil ❑ **youth hostel** n albergue m de juventud

you've [juːv] = **you have**

Z, z

zeal [ziːl] n celo, entusiasmo

zebra [ˈziːbrə] n cebra ❑ **zebra crossing** (BRIT) n paso de peatones

zero [ˈzɪərəu] n cero

zest [zest] n ánimo, vivacidad f; (of orange) piel f

zigzag [ˈzɪgzæg] n zigzag m ♦ vi zigzaguear, hacer eses

Zimbabwe [zɪmˈbɑːbwɪ] n Zimbabwe m

zinc [zɪŋk] n cinc m, zinc m

zip [zɪp] n (also: ~ fastener, zipper (US)) cremallera (SP), cierre m (LAm), zíper m (MEX, CAm) ♦ vt (also: ~ up) cerrar la cremallera de ❑ **zip code** (US) n código postal ❑ **zipper** (US) n cremallera

zit [zɪt] n grano

zodiac [ˈzəudɪæk] n zodíaco

zone [zəun] n zona

zoo [zuː] n (jardín m) zoo m

zoology [zuˈɔlədʒɪ] n zoología

zoom [zuːm] vi: **to ~ past** pasar zumbando ❑ **zoom lens** n zoom m

zucchini [zuːˈkiːnɪ] (US) n(pl) calabacín(ines) m(pl)

Phrasefinder

Guía del viajero

TOPICS

TEMAS

TOPICS
TEMAS

Hello!	¡Buenos días!
Good evening!	¡Buenas tardes!
Good night!	¡Buenas noches!
Goodbye!	¡Adiós!
What's your name?	¿Cómo se llama usted?
My name is ...	Me llamo ...
This is ...	Le presento a ...
my wife.	*mi mujer.*
my husband.	*mi marido.*
my partner.	*mi pareja.*
Where are you from?	¿De dónde es usted?
I come from ...	Soy de ...
How are you?	¿Cómo está usted?
Fine, thanks.	Bien, gracias.
And you?	¿Y usted?
Do you speak English?	¿Habla usted inglés?
I don't understand Spanish.	No entiendo el español.
Thanks very much!	¡Muchas gracias!

Asking the Way

¿Cómo ir hasta …?

Where is the nearest …?	¿Dónde está el/la … más próximo(-a)?
How do I get there?	¿Cómo voy hasta allí?
How do I get to …?	¿Cómo voy hasta el/la …?
Is it far?	¿Está muy lejos?
How far is it to there?	¿Qué distancia hay hasta allí?
Is this the right way to …?	¿Es éste el camino correcto para ir al/a la/a …?
I'm lost.	Me he perdido.
Can you show me on the map?	¿Me lo puede señalar en el mapa?
Which signs should I follow?	¿Qué indicadores tengo que seguir?
You have to turn round.	Tiene que dar la vuelta.
Go straight on.	Siga todo recto.
Turn left/right.	Tuerza a la izquierda/a la derecha.
Take the second street on the left/right.	Tome la segunda calle a la izquierda/a la derecha.

Car Hire

Alquiler de coches

I want to hire …	Quisiera alquilar …
a car.	*un coche.*
a moped.	*una motocicleta.*
a motorbike.	*una moto.*
A small car, please.	Un coche pequeño, por favor.
An automatic, please.	Un coche con cambio automático, por favor.

GETTING AROUND
TRASLADOS

How much is it for ...?	¿Cuánto cuesta por ...?
one day	*un día*
a week	*una semana*
I'd like to leave the car in ...	Quisiera entregar el coche en ...
Is there a kilometre charge?	¿Hay que pagar kilometraje?
How much is the kilometre charge?	¿Cuánto hay que pagar por kilómetro?
What is included in the price?	¿Qué se incluye en el precio?
I'd like to arrange ...	Quisiera contratar ...
collision damage waiver.	*un seguro con limitación de responsabilidad.*
personal accident insurance.	*un seguro de ocupates.*
I'd like a child seat for a ...-year-old child.	Quisiera un asiento infantil para un niño de ... años.
Please show me the controls.	¿Puede explicarme las funciones de los interruptores?
What do I do if I have an accident/if I break down?	¿Qué debo hacer en caso de accidente/de avería?

Breakdowns | Averías

My car has broken down.	Tengo una avería.
Call the breakdown service, please.	Por favor, llame al servicio de auxilio en carretera.
I'm a member of a rescue service.	Soy socio(-a) de un club del automóvil.
I'm on my own.	Estoy solo(-a).
I have children in the car.	Llevo niños conmigo.

Can you tow me to the next garage, please?	Por favor, remólqueme hasta el taller más próximo.
Where is the next garage?	¿Dónde está el taller más próximo?
... is broken.	... está roto.
The exhaust	*El escape*
The gearbox	*El cambio*
The windscreen	*El parabrisas*
... are not working.	... no funcionan.
The brakes	*Los frenos*
The headlights	*Las luces*
The windscreen wipers	*Los limpiaparabrisas*
The battery is flat.	La batería está descargada.
The car won't start.	El motor no arranca.
The engine is overheating.	El motor se recalienta.
The oil warning light won't go off.	El piloto del aceite no se apaga.
The oil/petrol tank is leaking.	El cárter de aceite/ el depósito de combustible tiene una fuga.
I have a flat tyre.	He tenido un pinchazo.
Can you repair it?	¿Puede repararlo?
When will the car be ready?	¿Cuándo estará listo el coche?
Do you have the parts for ...?	¿Tienen recambios para ...?
The car is still under warranty.	El coche aún tiene garantía.

Parking

Aparcamiento

| Can I park here? | ¿Puedo aparcar aquí? |
| How long can I park here? | ¿Cuánto tiempo puedo dejar aparcado el coche aquí? |

GETTING AROUND
TRASLADOS

Do I need to buy a (car-parking) ticket?	¿Tengo que sacar un ticket de estacionamiento?
Where is the ticket machine?	¿Dónde está el expendedor de tickets de estacionamiento?
The ticket machine isn't working.	El expendedor de tickets de estacionamiento no funciona.
Where do I pay the fine?	¿Dónde puedo pagar la multa?

Petrol Station	**Gasolinera**
Where is the nearest petrol station?	¿Dónde está la gasolinera más próxima?
Fill it up, please.	Lleno, por favor.
30 euros' worth of ..., please.	30 euros de ...
diesel	*diesel.*
(unleaded) economy petrol	*gasolina normal.*
premium unleaded	*súper.*
Pump number ... please.	Número ..., por favor.
Please check ...	Por favor, compruebe ...
the tyre pressure.	*la presión de los neumáticos.*
the oil.	*el aceite.*
the water.	*el agua.*
A token for the car wash, please.	Deme una ficha para el túnel de lavado.

Accident	**Accidentes**
Please call ...	Por favor, llame ...
the police.	*a la policía.*
the emergency doctor.	*al médico de urgencia.*
Here are my insurance details.	Éstos son los datos de mi seguro.

GETTING AROUND
TRASLADOS

Give me your insurance details, please.	Por favor, deme los datos de su seguro.
Can you be a witness for me?	¿Puede ser usted mi testigo?
You were driving too fast.	Usted conducía muy rápido.
It wasn't your right of way.	Usted no tenía preferencia.

Travelling by Car

Viajando en coche

What's the best route to …?	¿Cuál es el mejor camino para ir a …?
Where can I pay the toll?	¿Dónde puedo pagar el peaje?
I'd like a motorway tax sticker …	Quisiera un indicativo de pago de peaje …
for a week.	*para una semana.*
for a month.	*para un mes.*
for a year.	*para un año.*
Do you have a road map of this area?	¿Tiene un mapa de carreteras de esta zona?

Cycling

En bicicleta

Is there a cycle map of this area?	¿Hay mapas de esta zona con carril-bici?
Where is the cycle path to …?	¿Dónde está el carril-bici para ir a …?
How far is it now to …?	¿Cuánto queda para llegar a …?
Can I keep my bike here?	¿Puedo dejar aquí mi bicicleta?
Please lock my bike in a secure place.	Por favor, deje la bicicleta con cadena en un lugar seguro.
My bike has been stolen.	Me han robado la bicicleta.
Where is the nearest bike repair shop?	¿Dónde hay por aquí un taller de bicicletas?

GETTING AROUND
TRASLADOS

The frame is twisted.	El cuadro de la bicicleta se ha torcido.
The brake/gears aren't working.	El freno/el cambio de marchas no funciona.
The chain is broken.	La cadena se ha roto.
I've got a flat tyre.	He tenido un pinchazo.
I need a puncture repair kit.	Necesito una caja de parches.

Train	Ferrocarril
A single to …, please.	Un billete sencillo para …, por favor.
I would like to travel first/second class.	Me gustaría viajar en primera/segunda clase.
Two returns to …, please.	Dos billetes de ida y vuelta para …, por favor.
Is there a reduction …?	¿Hay descuento …?
for students	*para estudiantes*
for pensioners	*para pensionistas*
for children	*para niños*
with this pass	*con este carnet*
I'd like to reserve a seat on the train to … please.	Una reserva para el tren que va a …, por favor.
Non smoking/smoking, please.	No fumadores/fumadores, por favor.
Facing the front, please.	Mirando hacia adelante, por favor.
I want to book a couchette/a berth to …	Quisiera reservar una litera/coche-cama para …
When is the next train to …?	¿Cuándo sale el próximo tren para …?

TRASLADOS

Is there a supplement to pay?	¿Tengo que pagar suplemento?
Do I need to change?	¿Hay que hacer transbordo?
Where do I change?	¿Dónde tengo que hacer transbordo?
Will my connecting train wait?	¿El tren de enlace esperará?
Is this the train for ...?	¿Es éste el tren que va a ...?
Excuse me, that's my seat.	Perdone, éste es mi asiento.
I have a reservation.	Tengo una reserva.
Is this seat free?	¿Está libre este asiento?
Please let me know when we get to ...	¿Por favor, avíseme cuando lleguemos a ...?
Where is the buffet car?	¿Dónde está el coche restaurante?
Where is coach number ...?	¿Cuál es el vagón número ...?

Ferry / Transbordador

Is there a ferry to ...?	¿Sale algún transbordador para ...?
When is the next ferry to ...?	¿Cuándo sale el próximo transbordador para ...?
When is the first/last ferry to ...?	¿Cuándo sale el primer/ último transbordador para ...?
How much is ...?	¿Cuánto cuesta ...?
a single	*el billete sencillo*
a return	*el billete de ida y vuelta*
How much is it for a car/camper with ... people?	¿Cuánto cuesta transportar el coche/coche caravana con ... personas?

Where does the boat leave from?	¿De dónde zarpa el barco?
How long does the crossing take?	¿Cuánto dura la travesía?
Do they serve food on board?	¿Sirven comida en el barco?
Where is ...?	¿Dónde está ...?
the restaurant	*el restaurante*
the bar	*el bar*
the duty-free shop	*la tienda de duty-free*
How do I get to the car deck?	¿Cómo llego a la cubierta donde están los coches?
Where is cabin number ...?	¿Dónde está la cabina número ...?
Do you have anything for seasickness?	¿Tienen algo para el mareo?

Plane — Avión

Where is the luggage for the flight from ...?	¿Dónde está el equipaje procedente de...?
Where can I change some money?	¿Dónde puedo cambiar dinero?
How do I get to ... from here?	¿Cómo se va desde aquí a ...?
Where is ...?	¿Dónde está ...?
the taxi rank	*la parada de taxis*
the bus stop	*la parada del bus*
the information office	*la oficina de información*
I'd like to speak to a representative of British Airways.	Quisiera hablar con un representante de British Airways.
My luggage hasn't arrived.	Mi equipaje no ha llegado.

TRASLADOS

Can you page …?	¿Puede llamar por el altavoz a …?
Where do I check in for the flight to …?	¿Dónde hay que facturar para el vuelo a …?
Which gate for the flight to …?	¿Cuál es la puerta de embarque del vuelo para …?
When is the latest I can check in?	¿Hasta qué hora como máximo se puede facturar?
When does boarding begin?	¿Cuándo es el embarque?
Window/aisle, please.	Ventanilla/pasillo, por favor.
I've lost my boarding pass/ my ticket.	He perdido la tarjeta de embarque/el billete.
I'd like to change/cancel my flight.	Quisiera cambiar la reserva de vuelo/anular la reserva.

Local Public Transport	**Transporte público de cercanías**
How do I get to …?	¿Cómo se llega al/a la/hasta …?
Which number goes to …?	¿Qué línea va hasta …?
Where is the nearest …?	¿Dónde está la próxima …?
bus stop	*parada del bus*
tram stop	*parada de tranvía*
underground station	*estación de metro*
suburban railway station	*estación de cercanías*
Where is the bus station?	¿Dónde está la estación de autobuses?
A ticket, please.	Un billete, por favor.
To …	A …
For … zones.	Para … zonas.
Is there a reduction …?	¿Hay descuento …?
for students	*para estudiantes*

TRASLADOS

for pensioners	*para pensionistas*
for children	*para niños*
for the unemployed	*para desempleados*
with this card	*con este carnet*
Do you have multi-journey tickets/day tickets?	¿Hay tarjetas multiviaje/ billetes para todo un día?
How does the (ticket) machine work?	¿Cómo funciona la máquina (de billetes)?
Do you have a map of the rail network?	¿Tiene un plano de la red de trenes?
Please tell me when to get off.	¿Puede decirme cuándo tengo que bajar?
What is the next stop?	¿Cuál es la próxima parada?
Can I get past, please?	¿Me deja pasar?

Taxi

Taxi

Where can I get a taxi?	¿Dónde puedo coger un taxi?
Call me a taxi, please.	¿Puede llamar a un taxi?
Please order me a taxi for ... o'clock.	Por favor, pídame un taxi para las ...
To the airport/station, please.	Al aeropuerto/a la estación, por favor.
To the ... hotel, please.	Al hotel ..., por favor.
To this address, please.	A esta dirección, por favor.
I'm in a hurry.	Tengo mucha prisa.
How much is it?	¿Cuánto cuesta el trayecto?
I need a receipt.	Necesito un recibo.
I don't have anything smaller.	No tengo moneda más pequeña.
Keep the change.	Quédese con el cambio.
Stop here, please.	Pare aquí, por favor.

ACCOMMODATION
ALOJAMIENTO

Camping

Is there a campsite here?	¿Hay un camping por aquí?
We'd like a site for …	Quisiéramos un lugar para …
a tent.	*una tienda de campaña.*
a camper van.	*un coche caravana.*
a caravan.	*una caravana.*
We'd like to stay one night/ … nights.	Queremos quedarnos una noche/… noches.
How much is it per night?	¿Cuánto es por noche?
Where are …?	¿Dónde están …?
the toilets	*los lavabos*
the showers	*las duchas*
the dustbins	*los contenedores de basura*
Where is …?	¿Dónde está …?
the shop	*la tienda*
the site office	*la oficina de administración*
the restaurant	*el restaurante*
Can we camp here overnight?	¿Podemos acampar aquí esta noche?
Can we park our camper van/caravan here overnight?	¿Podemos aparcar aquí esta noche el coche caravana/la caravana?

Self-Catering
Vivienda para las vacaciones

Where do we get the key for the apartment/house?	¿Dónde nos dan la llave para el piso/la casa?
Which is the key for this door?	¿Qué llave es la de esta puerta?
Do we have to pay extra for electricity/gas?	¿Hay que pagar aparte la luz/el gas?

ACCOMMODATION
ALOJAMIENTO

Where are the fuses?	¿Dónde están los fusibles?
Where is the electricity meter?	¿Dónde está el contador de la luz?
Where is the gas meter?	¿Dónde está el contador del gas?
How does ... work?	¿Cómo funciona ...?
the washing maching	*la lavadora*
the cooker	*la cocina*
the heating	*la calefacción*
the water heater	*el calentador de agua*
Please show us how this works.	¿Puede mostrar cómo funciona, por favor?
Whom do I contact if there are any problems?	¿Con quién debo hablar si hubiera algún problema?
We need ...	Necesitamos ...
a second key.	*otra copia de la llave.*
more sheets.	*más sábanas.*
more crockery.	*más vajilla.*
The gas has run out.	Ya no queda gas.
There is no electricity.	No hay corriente.
Where do we hand in the key when we're leaving?	¿Dónde hay que entregar la llave cuando nos vayamos?
Do we have to clean the apartment/the house before we leave?	¿Hay que limpiar el piso/la casa antes de marcharnos?

Hotel

Hotel

Do you have a ... for tonight?	¿Tienen una ... para esta noche?
single room	*habitación individual*

double room	*habitación doble*
room for ... people	*habitación para ... personas*
with bath	con baño
with shower	con ducha
I want to stay for one night/ ... nights.	Quisiera pasar una noche/ ... noches.
I booked a room in the name of ...	Tengo reservada una habitación a nombre de ...
I'd like another room.	Quisiera otra habitación.
What time is breakfast?	¿Cuándo sirven el desayuno?
Where is breakfast served?	¿Dónde sirven el desayuno?
Can I have breakfast in my room?	¿Podrían traerme el desayuno a la habitación?
Where is ...?	¿Dónde está ...?
the restaurant	*el restaurante*
the bar	*el bar*
the gym	*el gimnasio*
the swimming pool	*la piscina*
Put that in the safe, please.	Por favor, póngalo en la caja fuerte.
I'd like an alarm call for tomorrow morning at ...	Por favor, despiértenme mañana a las ...
I'd like to get these things washed/cleaned.	¿Puede lavarme/limpiarme esto?
Please bring me ...	Por favor, tráigame ...
... doesn't work.	... no funciona.
The key, please.	La llave, por favor.
Room number ...	Número de habitación ...
Are there any messages for me?	¿Hay mensajes para mí?
Please prepare the bill.	Por favor, prepare la cuenta.

SHOPPING
DE COMPRAS

I'm looking for ...	Estoy buscando ...
I'd like ...	Quisiera ...
Do you have ...?	¿Tienen ...?
Can you show me ..., please?	¿Podría mostrarme ...?
Where is the nearest shop which sells ...?	¿Dónde hay por aquí una tienda de ...?
photographic equipment	*fotografía*
shoes	*zapatos*
souvenirs	*recuerdos*
Do you have this ...?	¿Lo tiene ...?
in another size	*en otra talla*
in another colour	*en otro color*
I take size ...	Mi talla es la ...
What shoe size are you?	¿Qué número calza?
I'm a size 5½.	Calzo un cuarenta.
I'll take it.	Me lo quedo.
Do you have anything else?	¿Tienen alguna otra cosa distinta?
That's too expensive.	Es demasiado caro.
I'm just looking.	Sólo estaba mirando.
Do you take ...?	¿Aceptan ...?
credit cards	*tarjetas de crédito*
eurocheques	*eurocheques*

Food Shopping	**Alimentos**
Where is the nearest ...?	¿Dónde hay por aquí cerca ...?
supermarket	*un supermercado*
baker's	*una panadería*
butcher's	*una carnicería*
greengrocer's	*una frutería y verdulería*

SHOPPING
DE COMPRAS

Where can you buy groceries?	¿Dónde se puede comprar comida?
Where is the market?	¿Dónde está el mercado?
When is the market on?	¿Cuándo hay mercado?
a kilo of ...	un kilo de ...
a pound of ...	medio kilo de ...
200 grams of ...	doscientos gramos de ...
... slices of ...	... lonchas de ...
a litre of ...	un litro de ...
a bottle of ...	una botella de ...
a packet of ...	un paquete de ...

Post Office

Correos

Where is the nearest post office?	¿Dónde queda la oficina de Correos más cercana?
When does the post office open?	¿Cuándo abre Correos?
Where can I buy stamps?	¿Dónde puedo comprar sellos?
I'd like ... stamps for postcards/letters to Britain/the United States.	Quisiera ... sellos para postales/cartas a Gran Bretaña/Estados Unidos.
I'd like to post/send ... *this letter.* *this small packet.* *this parcel.*	Quisiera entregar ... *esta carta.* *este pequeño paquete.* *este paquete.*
By airmail/express mail/ registered mail.	Por avión/por correo urgente/ certificado.
I'd like to send a telegram.	Quisiera mandar un telegrama.
Here is the text.	Aquí tiene el texto.

SHOPPING
DE COMPRAS

Is there any mail for me?	¿Tengo correo?
Where is the nearest postbox?	¿Dónde hay un buzón de correos por aquí cerca?

Photos and Videos
Vídeo y fotografía

A colour film/slide film, please.	Un carrete en color/un carrete para diapositivas, por favor.
With twenty-four/thirty-six exposures.	De veinticuatro/treinta y seis fotos.
Can I have a tape for this video camera, please?	Quisiera una cinta para esta cámara.
Can I have batteries for this camera, please?	Quisiera pilas para esta cámara, por favor.
The camera is sticking.	La cámara se atasca.
Can you take the film out, please.	Por favor, saque el carrete.
Can you develop this film, please?	Quisiera revelar este carrete.
I'd like the photos … *matt.* *glossy.* *ten by fifteen centimetres.*	Las fotos las quiero … *en mate.* *en brillo.* *en formato de diez por quince.*
When will the photos be ready?	¿Cuándo puedo pasar a recoger las fotos?
How much do the photos cost?	¿Cuánto cuesta el revelado?
Are you allowed to take photos here?	¿Aquí se pueden sacar fotos?
Could you take a photo of us, please?	¿Podría sacarnos una foto?

LEISURE
OCIO

Sightseeing

Visitas turísticas

Where is the tourist office? ¿Dónde está la oficina de turismo?

Do you have any leaflets about …? ¿Tienen folletos sobre …?

What sights can you visit here? ¿Qué se puede visitar aquí?

Are there any sightseeing tours of the town? ¿Se organizan visitas por la ciudad?

When is … open? ¿Cuándo está abierto(-a) …?
the museum *el museo*
the church *la iglesia*
the castle *el palacio*

How much does it cost to get in? ¿Cuánto cuesta la entrada?

Are there any reductions …? ¿Hay descuento …?
for students *para estudiantes*
for children *para niños*
for pensioners *para pensionistas*
for the unemployed *para desempleados*

Is there a guided tour in English? ¿Hay alguna visita guiada en inglés?

I'd like a catalogue. Quisiera un catálogo.

Can I take photos here? ¿Puedo sacar fotos?

Can I film here? ¿Puedo filmar?

Entertainment

Ocio

What is there to do here? ¿Qué se puede hacer por aquí?

Do you have a list of events? ¿Tiene una guía de ocio?

Where can we ...?	**¿Dónde se puede ...?**
go dancing	*bailar*
hear live music	*escuchar música en directo*
Where is there ...?	**¿Dónde hay ... ?**
a nice bar	*un buen bar*
a good club	*una buena discoteca*
What's on tonight ...?	**¿Qué dan esta noche ...?**
at the cinema	*en el cine*
at the theatre	*en el teatro*
at the opera	*en la ópera*
at the concert hall	*en la sala de conciertos*
Where can I buy tickets for ...?	**¿Dónde puedo comprar entradas para ...?**
the theatre	*el teatro*
the concert	*el concierto*
the opera	*la ópera*
the ballet	*el ballet*
How much is it to get in?	**¿Cuánto cuesta la entrada?**
I'd like a ticket/... tickets for ...	**Quisiera una entrada/... entradas para ...**
Are there any reductions for ...?	**¿Hay descuento para ...?**
children	*niños*
pensioners	*pensionistas*
students	*estudiantes*
the unemployed	*desempleados*

At the Beach | En la playa

Can you swim here/in this lake?	¿Se puede uno bañar aquí/en este lago?
Where is the nearest quiet beach?	¿Dónde hay una playa tranquila por aquí cerca?

OCIO

How deep is the water?	¿Qué profundidad tiene el agua?
What is the water temperature?	¿Qué temperatura tiene el agua?
Are there currents?	¿Hay corrientes?
Is it safe to swim here?	¿Se puede nadar aquí sin peligro?
Is there a lifeguard?	¿Hay socorrista?
Where can you ...?	¿Dónde se puede ... por aquí?
go surfing	*hacer surf*
go waterskiing	*practicar esquí acuático*
go diving	*bucear*
go paragliding	*hacer parapente*
I'd like to hire ...	Quisiera alquilar ...
a beach chair.	*un sillón de playa.*
a deckchair.	*una tumbona.*
a sunshade.	*una sombrilla.*
a surfboard.	*una tabla de surf.*
a jet-ski.	*una moto acuática.*
a rowing boat.	*un bote de remos.*
a pedal boat.	*un patín a pedales.*

Sport / Deporte

Where can we ...?	¿Dónde se puede ...?
play tennis/golf	*jugar a tenis/golf*
go swimming	*ir a nadar*
go riding	*montar a caballo*
go fishing	*ir a pescar*
go rowing	*hacer remo*
How much is it per hour?	¿Cuánto cuesta la hora?
Where can I book a court?	¿Dónde puedo reservar una pista?

LEISURE

OCIO

Where can I hire rackets?	¿Dónde puedo alquilar raquetas de tenis?
Where can I hire a rowing boat/a pedal boat?	¿Dónde puedo alquilar un bote de remos/un patín a pedales?
Do you need a fishing permit?	¿Se necesita un permiso de pesca?
Where will I get a fishing permit?	¿Dónde me pueden dar un permiso de pesca?
Which sporting events can we go to?	¿Qué actividades deportivas se pueden ver por aquí?
I'd like to see ...	Quisiera ver ...
a football match.	*un partido de fútbol.*
a horse race.	*carreras de caballos.*

Skiing

Esquí

Where can I hire skiing equipment?	¿Dónde puedo alquilar un equipo de esquí?
I'd like to hire ...	Quisiera alquilar ...
downhill skis.	*unos esquís (de descenso).*
cross-country skis.	*unos esquís de fondo.*
ski boots.	*unas botas de esquí.*
ski poles.	*unos bastones de esquí.*
Can you tighten my bindings, please?	¿Podría ajustarme la fijación, por favor?
Where can I buy a ski pass?	¿Dónde puedo comprar el forfait?
I'd like a ski pass ...	¿Quisiera un forfait ...
for a day.	*para un día.*

for five days.	*para cinco días.*
for a week.	*para una semana.*
How much is a ski pass?	¿Cuánto cuesta el forfait?
When does the first/last chair-lift leave?	¿Cuándo sale el primer/el último telesilla?
Do you have a map of the ski runs?	¿Tiene un mapa de las pistas?
Where are the beginners' slopes?	¿Dónde están las pistas para principiantes?
How difficult is this slope?	¿Cuál es la dificultad de esta pista?
Is there a ski school?	¿Hay una escuela de esquí?
Where is the nearest mountain rescue service post?	¿Dónde se encuentra la unidad más próxima de servicio de salvamento?
Where is the nearest mountain hut?	¿Dónde se encuentra el refugio más próximo?
What's the weather forecast?	¿Cuál es el pronóstico del tiempo?
What is the snow like?	¿Cómo es el estado de la nieve?
Is there a danger of avalanches?	¿Hay peligro de aludes?

FOOD AND DRINK
COMIDA Y BEBIDA

A table for ... people, please.	Una mesa para ... personas, por favor.
The ... please.	Por favor, ...
menu	*la carta.*
wine list	*la carta de vinos.*
What do you recommend?	¿Qué me recomienda?
Do you have ...?	¿Sirven ...?
any vegetarian dishes	*platos vegetarianos*
children's portions	*raciones para niños*
Does that contain ...?	¿Tiene esto ...?
peanuts	*cacahuetes*
alcohol	*alcohol*
Can you bring (more) ... please?	Por favor, traiga (más) ...
I'll have ...	Para mí ...
The bill, please.	La cuenta, por favor.
All together, please.	Cóbrelo todo junto.
Separate bills, please.	Haga cuentas separadas, por favor.
Keep the change.	Quédese con el cambio.
I didn't order this.	Yo no he pedido esto.
The bill is wrong.	La cuenta está mal.
The food is cold/too salty.	La comida está fría/ demasiado salada.

TELÉFONO

Where can I make a phone call?	¿Dónde puedo hacer una llamada por aquí cerca?
Where is the nearest card phone?	¿Dónde hay un teléfono de tarjetas cerca de aquí?
Where is the nearest coin box?	¿Dónde hay un teléfono de monedas cerca de aquí?
I'd like a twenty-five euro phone card.	Quisiera una tarjeta de teléfono de veinticinco euros.
I'd like some coins for the phone, please.	Necesito monedas para llamar por teléfono.
I'd like to make a reverse charge call.	Quisiera hacer una llamada a cobro revertido.
Hello.	Hola.
This is ...	Soy ...
Who's speaking, please?	¿Con quién hablo?
Can I speak to Mr/Ms ..., please?	¿Puedo hablar con el señor/la señora ...?
Extension ..., please.	Por favor, póngame con el número ...
I'll phone back later.	Volveré a llamar más tarde.
Can you text me your answer?	¿Puede contestame con mensaje de móvil?
Where can I charge my mobile phone?	¿Dónde puedo cargar la batería del móvil?
I need a new battery.	Necesito una batería nueva.
Where can I buy a top-up card?	¿Dónde venden tarjetas para móviles?
I can't get a network.	No hay cobertura.

PRACTICALITIES
DATOS PRÁCTICOS

Passport/Customs | Pasaporte/Aduana

Here is ...
  my passport.
  my identity card.

  my driving licence.
  my green card.
Here are my vehicle documents.
The children are on this passport.
Do I have to pay duty on this?
This is ...
  a present.
  a sample.
This is for my own personal use.
I'm on my way to ...

Aquí tiene ...
  mi pasaporte.
  mi documento de identidad.
  mi permiso de conducir.
  mi carta verde.
Aquí tiene la documentación de mi vehículo.
Los niños están incluidos en este pasaporte.
¿Tengo que declararlo?

Esto es ...
  un regalo.
  una muestra.
Es para consumo propio.

Estoy de paso para ir a ...

At the bank | En el banco

Where can I change money?
Is there a bank/bureau de change here?
When is the bank/bureau de change open?

I'd like ... euros.
I'd like to cash these traveller's cheques/ eurocheques.

¿Dónde puedo cambiar dinero?
¿Hay por aquí un banco/ una casa de cambio?
¿Cuándo está abierto el banco/abierta la casa de cambio?

Quisiera ... euros.
Quisiera cobrar estos cheques de viaje/eurocheques.

DATOS PRÁCTICOS

What's the commission?	¿Cuánto cobran de comisión?
Can I use my credit card to get cash?	¿Puedo sacar dinero en efectivo con mi tarjeta de crédito?
Where is the nearest cash machine?	¿Dónde hay por aquí un cajero automático?
The cash machine swallowed my card.	El cajero automático no me ha devuelto la tarjeta.
Can you give me some change, please.	Deme cambio en monedas, por favor.

Repairs	Reparaciones
Where can I get this repaired?	¿Dónde pueden repararme esto?
Can you repair ...?	¿Puede reparar ...?
these shoes	*estos zapatos*
this watch	*este reloj*
this jacket	*esta chaqueta*
Is it worth repairing?	¿Vale la pena repararlo?
How much will the repairs cost?	¿Cuánto cuesta la reparación?
Where can I have my shoes reheeled?	¿Dónde me pueden poner tacones nuevos?
When will it be ready?	¿Cuándo estará listo?
Can you do it straight away?	¿Puede hacerlo ahora mismo?

Emergency Services	Servicios de urgencia
Help!	¡Socorro!
Fire!	¡Fuego!
Please call ...	Por favor, llame a ...
the emergency doctor.	*un médico de urgencia.*

the fire brigade.	los bomberos.
the police.	la policía.
I need to make an urgent phone call.	Tengo que hacer una llamada urgente.
I need an interpreter.	Necesito un intérprete.
Where is the police station?	¿Dónde está la comisaría?
Where is the nearest hospital?	¿Dónde está el hospital más cercano?
I want to report a theft.	Quisiera denunciar un robo.
.... has been stolen.	Han robado …
There's been an accident.	Ha habido un accidente.
There are … people injured.	Hay … heridos.
My location is …	Estoy en …
I've been …	Me han …
robbed.	robado.
attacked.	atracado.
raped.	violado.
I'd like to phone my embassy.	Quisiera hablar con mi embajada.

Pharmacy	Farmacia
Where is the nearest pharmacy?	¿Dónde hay por aquí una farmacia?
Which pharmacy provides emergency service?	¿Qué farmacia está de guardia?
I'd like something for …	Quisiera algo para …
diarrhoea.	*la diarrea.*
a temperature.	*la fiebre.*
travel sickness.	*el mareo.*
a headache.	*el dolor de cabeza.*
a cold.	*el resfriado.*
I'd like …	Quisiera …
plasters.	*tiritas.*
a bandage.	*un vendaje.*
some paracetamol.	*paracetamol.*
I can't take …	Soy alérgico(-a) a la …
aspirin.	*aspirina.*
penicillin.	*penicilina.*
Is is safe to give to children?	¿Pueden tomarlo los niños?
How should I take it?	¿Cómo tengo que tomarlo?

At the Doctor's	En la consulta médica
I need a doctor.	Necesito que me atienda un médico.
Where is casualty?	¿Dónde está Urgencias?
I have a pain here.	Me duele aquí.
I feel …	Tengo …
hot.	*mucho calor.*
cold.	*frío.*
I feel sick.	Me siento mal.
I feel dizzy.	Tengo mareos.

HEALTH
SALUD

I'm allergic to ...	Tengo alergia a ...
I am ...	Yo ...
pregnant.	*estoy embarazada.*
diabetic.	*soy diabético(-a).*
HIV-positive.	*soy seropositivo(-a).*
I'm on this medication.	Estoy tomando este medicamento.
My blood group is ...	Mi grupo sanguíneo es ...

At the Hospital — En el hospital

Which ward is ... in?	¿En qué unidad está ...?
When are visiting hours?	¿Cuándo son las horas de visita?
I'd like to speak to ...	Quisiera hablar con ...
a doctor.	*un médico.*
a nurse.	*una enfermera.*
When will I be discharged?	¿Cuándo me van a dar de alta?

At the Dentist's — En el dentista

I need a dentist.	Tengo que ir al dentista.
This tooth hurts.	Me duele este diente.
One of my fillings has fallen out.	Se me ha caído un empaste.
I have an abscess.	Tengo un absceso.
I want/don't want an injection for the pain.	Quiero/no quiero que me ponga una inyección para calmar el dolor.
Can you repair my dentures?	¿Me puede reparar la dentadura?
I need a receipt for the insurance.	Necesito un recibo para mi seguro.

Business Travel — Viajes de negocios

I'd like to arrange a meeting with ...	Quisiera concertar hora para una reunión con ...
I have an appointment with Mr/Ms ...	Tengo una cita con el señor/la señora ...
Here is my card.	Aquí tiene mi tarjeta.
I work for ...	Trabajo para ...
How do I get to your office?	¿Cómo se llega a su despacho?
I need an interpreter.	Necesito un intérprete.
Can you copy that for me, please?	Por favor, hágame una copia de eso.
May I use ...?	¿Puedo usar ...?
your phone	*su teléfono*
your computer	*su ordenador*

Disabled Travellers — Minusválidos

Is it possible to visit ... with a wheelchair?	¿La visita a ... es posible también para personas en silla de ruedas?
Where is the wheelchair-accessible entrance?	¿Por dónde se puede entrar con la silla de ruedas?
Is your hotel accessible to wheelchairs?	¿Tiene su hotel acceso para minusválidos?
I need a room ...	Necesito una habitación ...
on the ground floor.	*en la planta baja.*
with wheelchair access.	*con acceso para minusuálidos.*
Do you have a lift for wheelchairs?	¿Tienen ascensor para minusválidos?
Do you have wheelchairs?	¿Tienen sillas de ruedas?
Where is the disabled toilet?	¿Dónde está el lavabo para minusválidos?

TRAVELLERS
VIAJEROS

Can you help me get on/off please?	¿Podría ayudarme a subir/bajar, por favor?
A tyre has burst.	Se ha reventado un neumático.
The battery is flat.	La batería está descargada.
The wheels lock.	Las ruedas se bloquean.

Travelling with children Viajando con niños

Are children allowed in too?	¿Pueden entrar niños?
Is there a reduction for children?	¿Hay descuento para niños?
Do you have children's portions?	¿Sirven raciones para niños?
Do you have ...?	¿Tienen ...?
a high chair	*una sillita*
a cot	*una cama infantil*
a child's seat	*un asiento infantil*
a baby's changing table	*una mesa para cambiar al bebé*
Where can I change the baby?	¿Dónde puedo cambiar al bebé?
Where can I breast-feed the baby?	¿Dónde puedo dar el pecho al niño?
Can you warm this up, please?	¿Puede calentarlo, por favor?
What is there for children to do?	¿Qué pueden hacer aquí los niños?
Is there a child-minding service?	¿Hay aquí un servicio de guardería?
My son/daughter is ill.	Mi hijo/mi hija está enfermo(-a).